ADOLESCENCE

SEVENTH EDITION

ADOLESCENCE

JOHN W. SANTROCK

UNIVERSITY OF TEXAS AT DALLAS

Boston   Burr Ridge, IL   Dubuque, IA   Madison, WI   New York   San Francisco   St. Louis
Bangkok   Bogotá   Caracas   Lisbon   London   Madrid
Mexico City   Milan   New Delhi   Seoul   Singapore   Sydney   Taipei   Toronto

McGraw-Hill

A Division of The **McGraw·Hill** *Companies*

Editorial director: *Jane Vaicunas*
Sponsoring editor: *Mickey Cox*
Developmental editor: *Sharon Greary*
Marketing manager: *Jim Rozsa*
Project manager: *Peggy J. Selle*
Production supervisor: *Sandra Hahn*
Designer: *Lu Ann Schrandt*
Compositor: *GTS Graphics, Inc.*
Typeface: *10/12 Goudy*
Printer: *Quebecor Printing Book Group/Dubuque*

Library of Congress Catalog Number: 96-86263

http://www.mhhe.com

To Tracy and Jennifer, who, as they have matured, have helped me appreciate the marvels of adolescent development.

BRIEF CONTENTS

CONTENTS

S E C T I O N
One
The Nature of Adolescent Development

Introduction

The Science of Adolescent Development

SECTION *Two*
Biological and Cognitive Development

Chapter 3
Biological Processes and Physical Development

Chapter 4
Cognitive Development and Social Cognition

Chapter 5
Information Processing and Intelligence

Contents

S E C T I O N Three
The Contexts of Adolescent Development

Chapter 6
Families

Chapter 7
Peers

Schools

Culture

SECTION Four
Social, Emotional, and Personality Development

Chapter 10
The Self and Identity

Chapter 11
Gender

Section Five
Adolescent Problems, Stress, Health, and Coping

Chapter 15
Adolescent Problems

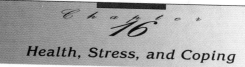

Chapter 16
Health, Stress, and Coping

Contents

LISTS OF FEATURES

CONCEPT TABLES

SOCIOCULTURAL WORLDS OF ADOLESCENCE

CRITICAL THINKING ABOUT ADOLESCENCE

CRITICAL THINKING ABOUT ADOLESCENCE~CONT.

PRACTICAL KNOWLEDGE ABOUT ADOLESCENCE

RESOURCES FOR IMPROVING THE LIVES OF ADOLESCENTS

RESOURCES FOR IMPROVING THE LIVES OF ADOLESCENTS

EXPLORING ADOLESCENT DEVELOPMENT

PREFACE

This book is the seventh edition of *Adolescence*. The seven editions span almost two decades. If anything, the journey of adolescence grows in fascination for me. This is an exciting time to study and write about adolescent development. Scholars around the world are making new discoveries and developing new insights about virtually every domain of adolescent development at a much faster pace than in previous decades. The field of adolescent development is also maturing to the point where the knowledge that is being gained can be applied to adolescents' lives to improve their adaptation, health, and well-being.

When I wrote the first edition of *Adolescence*, I wanted to construct a book that portrays the study of adolescent development in both a scientific *and* an interesting manner. The seventh edition of *Adolescence* continues my effort to both inform and motivate the reader.

SCIENCE AND RESEARCH

Above all else, the seventh edition of *Adolescence* is an extremely up-to-date presentation of research in the three primary domains of development: biological processes, cognitive processes, and socioemotional processes. Research on biological, cognitive, and socioemotional development continues to be the core of the book. This core includes both classic and leading-edge research.

Research Updates

Approximately 30 percent of the references in the seventh edition of *Adolescence* are new. More than 400 come from 1995, 1996, 1997, and in-press sources.

Expert Consultants

The extensive research agenda in many different domains of adolescent development makes it virtually impossible for authors to provide a completely up-to-date rendering of content in all areas. To considerably improve the research content in many areas, the seventh edition of *Adolescence* underwent the most extensive review process of any of the book's seven editions.

For the first time in the seven editions of the book, each individual chapter was reviewed in depth by an expert in the content area of the chapter. The following

truly outstanding experts each served as a research and content advisor for a single chapter in *Adolescence*, seventh edition:

Chapter 1: Introduction
Daniel Offer, University of Michigan
Chapter 2: The Science of Adolescent Development
Glenn Elder, University of North Carolina
Chapter 3: Biological Processes and Physical Development
Elizabeth Susman, Pennsylvania State University
Chapter 4: Cognitive Development and Social Cognition
Daniel Lapsley, Brandon University
Chapter 5: Information Processing and Intelligence
Daniel Keating, Ontario Institute for Studies in Education
Chapter 6: Families
Joseph Allen, University of Virginia
Chapter 7: Peers
Wyndol Furman, University of Denver
Chapter 8: Schools
Allan Wigfield, University of Maryland
Chapter 9: Culture
Nancy Busch-Rossnagel, Fordham University
Chapter 10: The Self and Identity
James Marcia, Simon Fraser University
Chapter 11: Gender
Carol Beale, University of Massachusetts
Chapter 12: Sexuality
P. Lindsay Chase-Lansdale, University of Chicago
Chapter 13: Moral Development, Values, and Religion
James Rest, University of Minnesota
Chapter 14: Achievement, Careers, and Work
Harold Grotevant, University of Minnesota
Chapter 15: Adolescent Problems
Joy Dryfoos, Hastings-on-Hudson, NY
Chapter 16: Health, Stress, and Coping
Nancy Leffert, Search Institute, Minneapolis

In addition, the following individuals recently provided evaluations and feedback to John Santrock's other texts that improved the quality of *Adolescence*, seventh edition:

Steven Ceci *Cornell University*
Daniel Hart *Rutgers University*
Lawrence Walker *University of British Columbia*
Cynthia Graeber *Columbia University*
Diana Baumrind *University of California, Berkeley*
Janet Spence *University of Texas, Austin*
Sandra Graham *UCLA*
Florence Denmark *Pace University*
David Buss *University of Michigan*
James Jones *University of Delaware*
Stanley Gaines *Pomona College*
Richard Brislin *University of Hawaii*
Seth Kalichman *Georgia State University*
Jane Halonen *Alverno College*
Raymond Paloutzian *Westmont College*
James Pennebaker *Southern Methodist University*

These two groups of leading researchers provided invaluable suggestions that are reflected in changes made throughout the seventh edition of *Adolescence*. They have made *Adolescence* a far more accurate, up-to-date portrayal of research on adolescent development in the late 1990s.

Research on Adolescence— Chapter Endpieces

An important new feature in *Adolescence*, seventh edition, is **Research on Adolescent Development**, which appears in the endpiece of each chapter, called "Exploring Adolescent Development." To fully understand the field of adolescent development, students need to explore how the research process works. These endpieces provide students with opportunities to see how scientists who study adolescent development actually conduct research investigations. In the first two chapters, students will learn why research on adolescence is important and how the research journal process works. In each subsequent chapter, students will read a minisimulation of a journal article on one of the chapter's topics.

IMPROVING THE LIVES OF ADOLESCENTS

I hope that when they complete this book, students not only will have acquired a much better understanding of the scientific basis of adolescent development, but also will have increased their wisdom about practical applications to the real lives of adolescents. The seventh edition of *Adolescence* includes extensive information that can be used to improve the lives of adolescents. The increased emphasis on applications appears throughout the book.

Social Policy

A special effort was made to increase the coverage of social policy issues regarding adolescent development. Among the new discussions of social policy are those pertaining to families, peers, schools, sexuality, and the media.

Adolescent Health and Well-Being

This chapter endpiece, the second part of "Exploring Adolescent Development," describes a number of issues in adolescent health and well-being, as well as programs that can be used to intervene in the lives of at-risk adolescents.

Practical Knowledge About Adolescence

This end-of-chapter feature provides descriptions and evaluations of books that will expand students' knowledge about practical applications that can improve the lives of adolescents.

Resources for Improving the Lives of Adolescents

Another unique end-of-chapter feature in *Adolescence*, seventh edition, is the section **Resources for Improving the Lives of Adolescents**. This popular feature was introduced in the sixth edition of the book and has been significantly expanded and modified in this edition. The section lists phone numbers, addresses, brochures, and books that can be used by students and instructors when questions arise about helping adolescents improve their lives.

Culture, Poverty, Ethnicity, and Gender

In this edition the coverage of culture, poverty, ethnicity, and gender was extensively updated. Previous editions of *Adolescence* have been leaders in including up-to-date coverage of these important topics. The current edition is no exception, and many chapters include topics on culture, poverty, ethnicity, and gender not found in other texts on adolescence. Each chapter of *Adolescence* also has a **Sociocultural Worlds of Adolescence** box.

LEARNING SYSTEM

I continue to strive to make this book more student-friendly. I have explored alternative ways of presenting ideas and continue to ask college students of all ages to give me feedback on which strategies are most effective. Covering all of adolescent development's many topics in one book and one course is a challenging task, requiring clear writing and an effective pedagogical system. The learning system in the seventh edition of *Adolescence* includes the following.

Visual Student Preface

Just after the preface, students will come across "To the Student," a visual student preface in which the learning system is visually presented along with information about how to use it effectively.

Beginning of Chapter

The learning system at the beginning of the chapter includes a chapter outline, a preview section, and a high-interest "Images of Adolescence" lead-in to the chapter material.

Within Chapter

Twice in each chapter, concept tables review the main ideas that have been presented so far. Key terms are bold-faced and defined in italics within the text. Visual figures and tables summarize important information. Quotations are sprinkled throughout each chapter to stimulate further thought about topics.

Critical Thinking About Adolescence is a new feature in this edition of *Adolescence*. Twice in each chapter, students will read brief boxes that encourage them to stretch their thinking about an aspect of adolescent development related to the chapter material. In addition, the nature of critical thinking about adolescent development is discussed toward the end of chapter 1. Jane Halonen of Alverno College, a leading expert on critical thinking in teaching psychology, served as the critical-thinking consultant for *Adolescence*, seventh edition. She provided advice about how to include critical thinking in the text and wrote some of the critical-thinking boxes.

End of Chapter

An "Overview" section includes a brief summary of the chapter and encourages students to again read the concept tables for a more detailed review. The "Overview" also includes a new feature—a Cognitive Map—that provides students with a visual organization of the chapter's contents. A listing of page-referenced Key Terms follows. Key Terms are also defined in a glossary at the back of the book.

Student-Friendliness

The text is extremely clear and well organized. Examples of concepts are given at every step of the way. The conversational writing style engages students to think about their own adolescence and the lives of other adolescents. The book also has cartoons, beautiful photographs and artpieces, and many applied features. If students enjoy this book and feel they have considerably more knowledge about both the scientific and the applied worlds of adolescence upon finishing it, then I will have reached my goals for the book's seventh edition.

ANCILLARY MATERIALS

The *Instructor's Course Planner*, the key to this teaching package, was created by Allen H. Keniston and Blaine F. Peden of the University of Wisconsin–Eau Claire. Allen and Blaine are both award-winning teachers and active members of the Council of Teachers of Undergraduate Psychology. This flexible planner provides a variety of useful tools to enhance your teaching efforts, reduce your workload, and increase your enjoyment. For each chapter of the text, the planner provides an outline, an overview, learning objectives, and key terms. These items are also contained in the *Student Study Guide*. The planner also contains lecture suggestions, classroom activities, discussion questions, integrative essay questions, a film list, and a transparency guide. It contains an abundance of handouts and exercises for stimulating classroom discussion and encouraging critical thinking.

The *Test Bank* was constructed by Lynne Blesz Vestal. This comprehensive test bank includes over 1,600 new multiple-choice test questions that are keyed to the text and learning objectives. Each item is designated as factual, conceptual, or applied as defined by the first three levels of Benjamin Bloom's *Taxonomy of Educational Objectives* (1956).

The questions in the *Test Bank* are available on Micro Test III, a powerful but easy-to-use test-generating program by Chariot Software Group. Micro Test is available for Windows and Macintosh. With Micro Test, you can easily select questions from the *Test Bank* and print a test and an answer key. You can customize questions, headings, and instructions, you can add or import questions of your own, and you can print your test in a choice of fonts if your printer supports them.

The *Student Study Guide* was also created by Allen H. Keniston and Blaine F. Peden of the University of Wisconsin–Eau Claire. For each chapter of the text, the student is provided with an outline, an overview, learning objectives, key terms, a guided review, study questions (with answers provided for self-testing), and an integration and application question. The study guide begins with the section "Developing Good Study Habits" to help students study more effectively and efficiently.

The *Human Development Transparency Set*, second edition consists of 141 acetate transparencies. These full-color transparencies, selected by author John Santrock and Janet Simons, include graphics from the text and various outside sources and were expressly designed to provide comprehensive coverage of all major topic areas generally covered in life-span development. A comprehensive annotated guide provides a brief description for each transparency and helpful suggestions for use in the classroom.

A large selection of **Videotapes,** including *Seasons of Life*, is also available to instructors, based upon the number of textbooks ordered by your bookstore.

The *Human Development Interactive Videodisc Set*, produced by Roger Ray of Rollins College, brings life-span development to life with instant access to over 30 brief video segments from the highly acclaimed *Seasons of Life* series. The 2-disc set can be used alone for selecting and sequencing excerpts, or in tandem with a Macintosh computer to add interactive commentary capability, as well as extra video and search options.

The *AIDS Booklet*, fourth edition, by Frank D. Cox of Santa Barbara City College is a brief but comprehensive introduction to acquired immune deficiency syndrome, which is caused by HIV (human immunodeficiency virus) and related viruses.

The *Critical Thinker*, written by Richard Mayer and Fiona Goodchild of the University of California, Santa Barbara, uses excerpts from introductory psychology textbooks to show students how to think critically about psychology. Either this or the AIDS booklet are available at no charge to first-year adopters of our textbook or can be purchased separately.

Annual Editions®

Magazines, newspapers, and journals of the public press provide current, first-rate, relevant educational information. If in your adolescent development course you are interested in exposing your students to a wide range of current, well-balanced, carefully selected articles from some of the most important magazines, newspapers, and journals published today, you may want to consider *Annual Editions: Child Growth and Development*, published by Dushkin/McGraw-Hill. *Annual Editions: Child Growth and Development* is a collection of over 40 articles on topics related to the latest research and thinking in child development.

Taking Sides™

Are you interested in generating classroom discussion and finding a tool to more fully involve your students in their experience of your course? Would you like your students to become more active learners and to develop critical thinking skills? Lastly, are you intrigued by current controversies related to issues in childhood and development? If so, you should examine a new publication from Dushkin/McGraw-Hill, *Taking Sides: Clashing Views on Controversial Issues in Childhood and Society*, edited by Professors Robert L. DelCampo and Diane S. DelCampo of New Mexico State University. *Taking Sides*, a reader that takes a pro/con approach to issues, is designed to introduce students to controversies in childhood and development. The readings, which represent the arguments of leading child behaviorists and social commentators, reflect a variety of viewpoints and have been selected for their liveliness, currency, and substance. There are 17 issues, which are grouped into four parts according to the four developmental phases of childhood: infancy, early childhood, middle childhood, and adolescence. The issues are self-contained and designed to be used independently.

Primis Custom Publishing

Primis Custom Publishing allows you to create original works or tailor existing materials to suit your students' needs. All you need to do is organize chapters from your McGraw-Hill textbook to match your course syllabus. You control the number of chapters, pieces of art and end-of-chapter materials appropriate for your course. You may also include your own materials in the book. With Primis Custom Publishing all the choices are yours. In a few short weeks after consulting with us you can have a professionally printed and bound book delivered to your bookstore. Please contact your local Sales Representative for more information.

ACKNOWLEDGMENTS

The seventh edition of *Adolescence* benefitted from the ideas of a carefully selected group of expert consultants, who were listed at the beginning of the Preface. In addition to those reviewers, I also thank the following individuals for their reviews of previous editions:

Geraldine Brookins   *University of Minnesota*
Christy Buchanan   *Wake Forest University*
William Bukowski   *Concordia University*
James Byrnes   *University of Maryland*
Nancy Galambos   *University of Victoria*
Susan Harter   *University of Denver*
Roger Kobak   *University of Delaware*
Rhoda Unger   *Montclair State College*
Barry Wagner   *Catholic University of America*
Lawrence Walker   *University of British Columbia*
Phyllis Bronstein   *University of Vermont*
Duane Buhrmester   *University of Texas at Dallas*
D. Bruce Carter   *Syracuse University*
Fred Danner   *University of Kentucky*
Sandra Graham   *UCLA*
Algea Harrison   *Oakland University*
Margaret Owen   *Timberlawn Research Foundation*
Michelle Paludi   *Michelle Paludi & Associates*
Robert Siegler   *Carnegie Mellon University*
Dale Shunk   *Purdue University*
Frank Ascione   *Utah State University*
David K. Bernhardt   *Carleton University*
Fredda Blanchard-Fields   *Louisiana State University*
Robert Bornstein   *Miami University*
Deborah Brown   *Friends University*
Stephanie M. Clancy   *Southern Illinois University at Carbondale*
Peggy A. DeCooke   *Northern Illinois University*
R. Daniel DiSalvi   *Kean College*
James A. Doyle   *Roane State Community College*
Richard M. Ehlenz   *Lakewood Community College*
Gene Elliott   *Glassboro State University*
Robert Enright   *University of Wisconsin–Madison*
Douglas Fife   *Plymouth State College*
Martin E. Ford   *Stanford University*
Gregory T. Fouts   *University of Calgary*
Charles Fry   *University of Virginia*
Margaret J. Gill   *Kutztown University*

William Gnagey *Illinois State University*
B. Jo Hailey *University of Southern Mississippi*
Dick E. Hammond *Southwest Texas State University*
Frances Harnick *University of New Mexico, Indian Children's Program, and Lovelace-Bataan Pediatric Clinic*
June V. Irving *Ball State University*
Beverly Jennings *University of Colorado–Denver*
Joline Jones *Worcester State College*
Alfred L. Karlson *University of Massachusetts–Amherst*
Lynn F. Katz *University of Pittsburgh*
Emmett C. Lampkin *Scott Community College*
Royal Louis Lange *Ellsworth Community College*
Neal E. Lipsitz *Boston College*
Nancey G. Lobb *Alvin Community College*
Daniel Lynch *University of Wisconsin–Oshkosh*
Ann McCabe *University of Windsor*
Susan McCammon *East Carolina University*
E. L. McGarry *California State University–Fullerton*

Joseph G. Marrone *Siena College*
John J. Mirich *Metropolitan State College*
John J. Mitchell *University of Alberta*
Joycelyn G. Parish *Kansas State University*
Anne Robertson *University of Wisconsin–Milwaukee*
Tonie E. Santmire *University of Nebraska*
Douglas Sawin *University of Texas*
Vern Tyler *Western Washington University*
Caroyln L. Williams *University of Minnesota*

A final note of thanks goes to my family. Mary Jo Santrock has lived through seven editions of *Adolescence*. I sincerely appreciate her encouragement and support. My daughters—Tracy and Jennifer—have provided me with firsthand experience of watching adolescents develop. Through the years, they have helped me render a treatment of adolescent development that captures its complexity, its subtlety, and its humanity.

$\mathscr{T}$O THE STUDENT

How the Learning System Works

This book contains a number of learning features that will help you master the material more effectively. In this section, each of these features is described and visually presented to help you understand how the learning system in the book works.

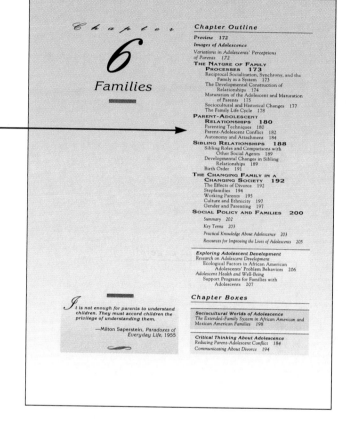

It is not enough for parents to understand children. They must accord children the privilege of understanding them.

—Milton Saperstein, *Paradoxes of Everyday Life,* 1955

Chapter Outline

Each chapter begins with an outline, showing the organization of topics by heading levels. The outline functions as an overview of the chapter's structure.

I come into the fields and spacious palaces of my memory, where are treasures of countless images of things of every manner.

—St. Augustine

IMAGES OF ADOLESCENCE

Reading *Martina*

Barbara Smith is a sixth-grade student at a middle school. Her favorite activity is tennis, so her mother recently bought her a book entitled *Martina,* which is about tennis star Martina Navratilova's life. Barbara finished reading the first eleven pages of the book. She placed it on the table in the hall as she left for tennis practice. Her 8-year-old sister, Nancy, saw Barbara leave the book on the table. She grabbed the book and started to read it. Nancy finished the entire book in 12 minutes. In that 12 minutes, she read several sentences in different chapters as she leafed rapidly through the book. She also studied each of the book's photographs and read some of their captions.

After Barbara returned from tennis practice, she showered, ate, and then read another chapter in *Martina,* which Nancy had returned to its place on the table. She sat quietly for 30 minutes and read the next eighteen pages of the book. A few of the words were difficult, but Barbara got the idea of what Martina's family background was like and how she started to play tennis in her native country of Czechoslovakia. She especially noted how Martina's father spent long hours playing tennis with her and how she dreamed of being a star.

Nancy, Barbara's younger sister, walked by her room just as Barbara finished reading for the evening. Nancy asked, "Did you like the book? I did." Barbara replied, "You are too little to understand it. Little kids can't read this kind of book." Their mother heard them begin to argue and went upstairs to intervene. She asked Nancy what the book was about. Nancy

said, "A tennis player. I can't remember her name, though." Barbara laughed and said, "She doesn't know very much, does she?" The mother reprimanded Barbara for teasing Nancy, then walked out into the hall with Nancy and told her not to worry about what Barbara had said.

The next day, the mother went to Barbara's room while Barbara was at tennis practice and picked up the book about Martina. She sat down and skimmed the book in about an hour, forming a general idea of the book's content. As she read, she made mental notes and developed many concepts about Martina's life both on and off the tennis court.

When we read, we process information and interpret it. So reading serves as a practical example to introduce the topic of information processing in adolescence. To read effectively, adolescents have to perceive and attend to a complex set of visual symbols—words. Note that Barbara and her mother attended more to words and sentences, while Nancy attended more to pictures. Another process in reading is holding the information we process in memory. Note that after about an hour of reading, the mother was able to get the gist of the entire book and hold the book's themes in her memory. But Barbara was able to cover only several chapters of the book in this time frame, and at this point, her memory of what the book was about was much more impoverished than her mother's.

PREVIEW

As adolescents move through their world, they process information—they perceive, attend, remember, think, solve problems, and draw conclusions. Adolescents thirst to know, understand, and create. In this chapter, we will evaluate the role of information processing in adolescent development, the nature of intelligence in adolescence, the extremes of intelligence, and creativity.

Santrock: Adolescence

Images of Adolescence

Following the "Preview" section is an imaginative high-interest piece that focuses on a topic relevant to the chapter's content.

Preview

Opening each chapter is a brief preview of the chapter's main themes is presented to help you think about what lies ahead.

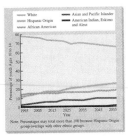

Figure–1.2
Ethnic Minority Population Increases in the United States.
The percentage of African American, Hispanic, and Asian American individuals increased far more from 1980 to 1988 than did the percentage of Whites.

are sociocultural changes more profound than in the increasing ethnic diversity of America's adolescents (Fisher, Jackson & Villarruel, 1997; Halonen & Santrock, 1996) (see figure 1.2).

Twenty percent of all American children and adolescents under the age of 17 in 1989 came from ethnic minority groups—such as African Americans, Hispanics, Native Americans, and Asian Americans. Projections indicate that, by the year 2000, one-third of all American school-age children will fall into this category. This changing demographic tapestry promises not only the richness that diversity produces but also difficult challenges in extending the American dream to individuals of all ethnic and minority groups. Historically, ethnic minorities have found themselves at the bottom of the economic and social order. They have been disproportionately represented among the poor and the inadequately educated (Edelman, 1995). Half of all African American adolescents and one-third of all Hispanic adolescents live in poverty. School dropout rates for minority youth reach the alarming figure of 60 percent in some urban areas. More about the nature of ethnic minority adolescents in the United States appears in Sociocultural Worlds of Adolescence.

Recently, some individuals have voiced dissatisfaction with the use of the term *minority* in the phrase *ethnic minority group*. Such dissatisfaction stems from traditionally associating the term minority with inferiority and deficits. Further, the concept of minority implies that there is a majority. Indeed, it can be argued that there really is no majority in the United States because Whites are actually composed of many different ethnic groups, and Whites are not a majority in the world. When the term *ethnic minority* is used in this text, the use is intentional—not to imply that ethnic minority adolescents should be viewed as inferior or deficient in some way, but to convey the impact that minority status has had on many ethnic minority adolescents. The circumstances of each ethnic group are not solely a function of its own culture. Rather, many ethnic groups have experienced considerable discrimination and prejudice. For example, patterns of alcohol abuse among Native American adolescents cannot be fully understood without considering the exploitation that has accompanied Native Americans' history.

A third, very important dimension of sociocultural contexts that is receiving increased attention is gender. **Gender** *is the sociocultural dimension of being male or female,* while sex refers to the biological dimension of being male or female (Unger & Crawford, 1996). Few aspects of adolescent development are more central to adolescents' identity and to their social relationships than their sex or gender (Paludi, 1995). Society's gender attitudes are changing. But how much? Is there a limit to how much society can determine what is appropriate behavior for male and female adolescents? (Eccles & Wigfield, 1997). A special concern of many feminist writers and scholars is that much of the history of interest in adolescence portrays adolescent development with a "male dominant theme." Just as important themes of this book are to examine cross-cultural issues and the role of ethnicity, an important theme is also to extensively examine gender

18   Santrock: Adolescence

Visual Figures
These include both a description of important content information and photographs that illustrate the content.

Critical Thinking About Adolescence Boxes
These boxes are inserted periodically in each chapter to encourage you to stretch your mind about a topic in that particular section of the chapter.

CRITICAL THINKING ABOUT ADOLESCENCE

Applying Psychology Concepts to Your Own Sexual History

Think about how you learned the "facts of life." Did most of your information come from well-informed sources? Were you able to talk freely and openly with your own parents abut what to expect sexually? Did you acquire some false beliefs through your trial-and-error efforts? As you grew older, did you discover any aspects of your sexual knowledge that had to be revised because it was in error? Based on your experience in learning about sexuality, how do you think sex education should be addressed as a larger health issue in society? How would you develop your psychological argument based on the evidence? By applying psychology's concepts to your own sexual history, you are learning to think critically by creating arguments based on developmental concepts.

The AIDS epidemic has led to an increased awareness of the importance of sex education in adolescence.

most likely to be introduced. The progression is usually from physiological facts to reproductive facts and issues and then to more complicated, value-laden issues.

Sex education programs vary from one school to the next. Many schools have no sex education program at all. Among those that do, a sex education program can range from a well-developed, full-semester course on human sexuality to a 2-week unit on anatomy and physiology. The most common place for adolescents to be given sex education information is in a tenth-grade biology class. Another factor in quality sex education is the teacher. Most instructors in sex education have majored in biology, health education, home economics, or physical education. Few have extensive coursework in human sexuality. While teachers do not need a Ph.D. in human sexuality to be effective sex education instructors,

390   Santrock: Adolescence

Photographs and Legends
Special attention was given to the selection of photographs for *Adolescence*. A number of the photographs were sent in by experts on adolescent development to be included in the text. Legends were carefully written by the author to clarify and elaborate concepts.

Many children and adolescents show an interest in religion, and many religious institutions created by adults (such as this Muslim school in Malaysia) are designed to introduce them to religious beliefs and ensure that they will carry on a religious tradition.

Does this indoctrination work? In many cases it does (Paloutzian, 1996). In general, adults tend to adopt the religious teachings of their upbringing. For instance, individuals who are Catholics by the time they are 25 years of age, and who were raised as Catholics, likely will continue to be Catholics throughout their adult years. If a religious change or reawakening occurs, it is most likely to take place during adolescence.

> *Religion enlightens, terrifies, subdues; it gives faith, inflicts remorse, inspires resolutions, and inflames devotion.*
>
> —Henry Newman, 1853

Religious issues are important to adolescents (Paloutzian & Santrock, 1997). In one recent survey, 95 percent of 13- to 18-year olds said that they believe in God or a universal spirit (Gallup & Bezilla, 1992). Almost three-fourths of adolescents said that they pray, and about one-half indicated that they had attended religious services within the past week. Almost one-half of the youth said that it is very important for a young person to learn religious faith.

Developmental Changes
Adolescence may be an especially important juncture in religious development. Even if children have been indoctrinated into a religion by their parents, because of advances in their cognitive development they might begin to question what their own religious beliefs truly are.

During adolescence, especially late adolescence and the college years, identity development becomes a central focus (Erikson, 1968). Youth want answers to the questions "Who am I? What am I all about as a person? What kind of life do I want to lead?" As part of their search for identity, adolescents begin to grapple in more sophisticated, logical ways with questions like these: "Why am I on this planet? Is there really a God or higher spiritual being, or have I just been believing what my parents and the church imprinted in my mind? What really are my religious views?"

Piaget's (1962) cognitive developmental theory provides a theoretical backdrop for understanding religious development in children and adolescents. For example, in one study, children were asked about their understanding of certain religious pictures and Bible stories (Goldman, 1964). The children's responses fell into three stages closely related to Piaget's theory.

In the first stage (up until 7 or 8 years of age)—*preoperational intuitive religious thought*—children's religious thoughts were unsystematic and fragmented. The

Quotations
Quotations appear in the section opener, twice at the beginning of each chapter, and periodically within each chapter to further stimulate your thinking about the nature of adolescent development.

424   Santrock: Adolescence

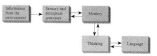

Figure 2.4
A Simple Model of Information Processing.

for their attraction. Tom would be described as rewarding Ann's behavior, and vice versa, for example. No reference would be made to unconscious thoughts, the Oedipus complex, defense mechanisms, and so on.

Behaviorists believe that we should examine only what can be directly observed and measured. At approximately the same time that Freud was interpreting his patients' unconscious minds through early childhood experiences, behaviorists such as Ivan Pavlov and John B. Watson were conducting detailed observations of behavior in controlled laboratory circumstances. Out of the behavioral tradition grew the belief that development is observable behavior, learned through experience with the environment. The two versions of the behavioral approach that are prominent today are the view of B. F. Skinner (1904–1990) and social learning theory.

Skinner's Behaviorism

Behaviorism emphasizes the scientific study of observable behavioral responses and their environmental determinants. In Skinner's behaviorism, the mind, conscious or unconscious, is not needed to explain behavior and development. For him, development is behavior. For example, observations of Sam reveal that his behavior is shy, achievement oriented, and caring. Why is Sam's behavior this way? For Skinner, rewards and punishments in Sam's environment have shaped him into a shy, achievement-oriented, and caring person. Because of interactions with family members, friends, teachers, and others, Sam has *learned* to behave in this fashion.

Since behaviorists believe that development is learned and often changes according to environmental experiences, it follows that rearranging experiences can change development. For behaviorists, shy behavior can be transformed into outgoing behavior; aggressive behavior can be shaped into docile behavior; lethargic, boring behavior can be turned into enthusiastic, interesting behavior.

Social Learning Theory

Some psychologists believe that the behaviorists basically are right when they say development is learned and is

influenced strongly by environmental experiences. However, they believe that Skinner went too far in declaring that cognition is unimportant in understanding development. **Social learning theory** *is the view of psychologists who emphasize behavior, environment, and cognition as the key factors in development.*

The social learning theorists say we are not like mindless robots, responding mechanically to others in our environment. Neither are we like weather vanes, behaving like a Communist in the presence of a Communist or like a John Bircher in the presence of a John Bircher. Rather, we think, reason, imagine, plan, expect, interpret, believe, value, and compare. When others try to control us, our values and beliefs allow us to resist their control.

American psychologists Albert Bandura (1977, 1995, 1997) and Walter Mischel (1995) are the main architects of social learning theory's contemporary version, which was labeled cognitive social learning theory by Mischel (1973). Bandura believes that we learn by observing what others do. Through observational learning (also called modeling or imitation), we cognitively represent the behavior of others and then possibly adopt this behavior ourselves. For example, a boy might observe his father's aggressive outbursts and hostile interchanges with people; when observed with his peers, the young boy might display a style of interaction that is highly aggressive, showing the same behavior as his father. Or a young female might adopt the dominant and sarcastic style of her boss. When observed interacting with one of her subordinates, the young woman says, "I need this work immediately if not sooner; you are so far behind, you think you are ahead!" Social learning theorists believe that we acquire a wide range of such behaviors, thoughts, and feelings through observing others' behavior; these observations form an important part of our development.

Bandura's (1986, 1995, 1997) most recent model of learning and development involves behavior, the person and cognition, and the environment. As shown in figure 2.5, behavior, cognitive and person factors, and environmental influences operate interactively. Behavior can influence cognition, and vice versa; the person's cognitive activities can influence the environment; environmental influences can change the person's thought processes; and so on.

Let's consider how Bandura's model might work in the case of a college student's achievement behavior. As the student diligently studies and gets good grades, her behavior produces positive thoughts about her abilities. As part of her effort to make good grades, she plans and develops a number of strategies to make her studying more efficient. In these ways, her behavior has influenced her thought and her thought has influenced her behavior. At

50   *Santrock: Adolescence*

Key Terms Definitions

Key terms appear in boldface type with their definitions immediately following in italic type. This provides you with a clear understanding of important concepts.

Sociocultural Worlds of Adolescence

This boxed feature highlights various dimensions of the cultural, ethnic, and gender worlds of adolescents. Each chapter has one or more "Sociocultural Worlds" boxes.

SOCIOCULTURAL WORLDS OF ADOLESCENCE

Ethnic Minority Adolescents' Peer Relationships

As ethnic minority children move into adolescence and enter schools with more heterogeneous school populations, they become more aware of their ethnic minority status. Ethnic minority adolescents may have difficulty joining peer groups and clubs in predominantly White schools. Similarly, White adolescents may have peer relations difficulties in predominantly ethnic minority schools. However, schools are only one setting in which peer relations take place; they also occur in the neighborhood and in the community (Jones & Costin, 1997).

Ethnic minority adolescents often have two sets of peer relationships, one at school, the other in the community. Community peers are more likely to be from their own ethnic group in their immediate neighborhood. Sometimes, they go to the same church and participate in activities together, such as Black History Week, Chinese New Year's, or Cinco de Mayo Festival. Because ethnic group adolescents usually have two sets of peers and friends, when researchers ask about their peers and friends, questions should focus on both relationships at school and in the neighborhood and community. Ethnic minority group adolescents who are social isolates at school may be sociometric stars in their segregated neighborhood.

Also, because adolescents are more mobile than children, inquiries should be made about the scope of their social networks.

In one investigation the school and neighborhood friendship patterns of 292 African American and White adolescents who attended an integrated junior high school were studied (DuBois & Hirsch, 1990). Most students reported having an other-ethnic school friend, but only 28 percent of the students saw such a friend frequently outside of school. Reports of an interethnic school friendship that extended to nonschool settings were more common among African American adolescents than White adolescents and among adolescents who lived in an integrated rather than a segregated neighborhood. African American adolescents were more likely than White adolescents to have extensive neighborhood friendship networks, but African American adolescents said they talked with fewer friends during the school day.

Of special interest to investigators is the degree of peer support for an ethnic minority adolescent's achievement orientation. Some researchers argue that peers often dissuade African American adolescents from doing well in school (Murdock & Davis, 1994). However, in one investigation, peer support of achievement was relatively high among Asian American adolescents, moderate among African American and Latino adolescents, and relatively low among Anglo American adolescents (Brown & others, 1990). The low peer support of achievement among Anglo-American adolescents possibly is due to their strong individual, competitive, and social comparison orientation.

Adolescent peer relations take place in a number of settings—at school, in the neighborhood, and in the community, for example. Ethnic minority adolescents often have two sets of peer relationships—one set at school, the other in the community. A special interest is the degree to which peers support an ethnic minority adolescent's achievement orientation.

Chapter 7: Peers   225

CONCEPT TABLE 16.2
Stress and Coping

Concept	Processes/Related Ideas	Characteristics/Description
Stress	What is stress?	Stress is the response of individuals to the circumstances and events, called stressors, that threaten them and tax their coping abilities.
	Factors in stress	Among the most important factors involved in stress are physiological factors, such as the body's response to stress; environmental factors, such as approach/approach, avoidance/avoidance, and approach/avoidance conflicts; personality factors such as the Type A behavior pattern; cognitive factors, such as cognitive appraisal; and sociocultural factors, such as acculturative stress and poverty.
	Resilience	Three sets of characteristics are reflected in the lives of children and adolescents who show resilience amid adversity and disadvantage: (1) cognitive skills and positive responsiveness to others, (2) families marked by warmth, cohesion, and the presence of a caring adult, and (3) the presence of some source of external support.
Coping with Stress	Removal of stress, defense mechanisms, and problem-focused coping	Most adolescents are confronted with more than one stressor. Removing one stressor can be very beneficial. In most cases, problem-focused coping is better than emotion-focused coping and the use of defense mechanisms, especially in coping with stress over the long term.
	Approach and avoidance strategies	Approach strategies are favored over avoidance strategies.
	Positive thinking and self-efficacy	Most of the time, adolescents should think positively and avoid negative thoughts. An optimistic attitude produces a sense of self-efficacy. Positive self-illusions can improve some adolescents' lives, but it is important to guard against unrealistic expectations. A strategy of defensive pessimism helps some adolescents to cope more effectively.
	Support systems	Close, positive attachments to others—especially family and friends—consistently show up as important buffers to stress in adolescents' lives.
	Multiple coping strategies	Adolescents often can and should use more than one coping strategy in dealing with stress.

522   *Santrock: Adolescence*

Concept Tables

Twice in each chapter this feature provides a review of what has been discussed up to that point in the chapter. This effective learning feature helps you to get a handle on material several times a chapter so you don't have to wait until the very end of the chapter, when you would have too much information to digest.

Summary

The overview section consists of two parts:
(1) a brief summary of the chapter's main
contents; and (2) a cognitive map that
provides you with a visual organization of
the chapter's main topics.

$\mathscr{S}$UMMARY

Families continue to play a powerful socializing role in development during the adolescent years. A balanced emphasis on independence, connectedness, and moderate, rather than severe, conflict characterizes the contemporary view of family relationships during adolescence.

We began this chapter by studying the nature of family processes, including reciprocal socialization, synchrony, and the family as a system, the developmental construction of relationships, maturation of the adolescent and maturation of par-

ents, sociocultural and historical changes, and the family life cycle. We also studied parenting techniques and parent-adolescent conflict, autonomy and attachment in adolescence, and sibling relationships, including sibling roles and comparisons with other social agents, developmental changes in sibling relationships, and birth order. We learned about the changing family in a changing society, focusing on the effects of divorce, stepfamilies, working parents, culture and ethnicity, and gender and parenting. And we

examined the nature of social policy and families.

Don't forget that you can obtain an overall summary of the chapter by again studying the two concept tables on pages 190 and 201. Earlier in this chapter we found that adolescents' family and peer worlds are more connected than once was believed. In the next chapter, we explore in greater detail the fascinating world of adolescent peer relations as we continue our coverage of the social contexts of adolescent development.

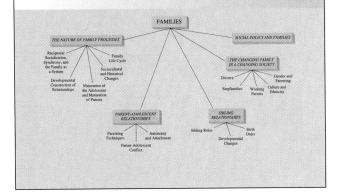

Key Terms

The key terms that were boldfaced in the
chapter are listed at the end of the chapter and
are page-referenced.

$\mathscr{K}$EY TERMS

reciprocal socialization 173	becoming parents and families with children 178	desatellization 185
synchrony 173	family with adolescents 180	resatellization 186
developmental construction views 174	family at midlife 180	second individuation crisis 186
continuity view 174	family in later life 180	secure attachment 187
discontinuity view 175	authoritarian parenting 181	insecure attachment 187
leaving home and becoming a single adult 178	authoritative parenting 181	family structure model of divorce effects 192
launching 178	neglectful parenting 181	multiple-factor model of divorce effects 192
new couple 178	indulgent parenting 181	boundary ambiguity 194
	satellization 185	

$\mathscr{P}$RACTICAL KNOWLEDGE ABOUT ADOLESCENCE

How to Deal with Your Parents
(1991) by Lynn Osterkamp.
New York: Berkley Books.

This book was written for adult children who want to understand and improve their relationships with their parents. Author Lynn Osterkamp is a nationally recognized expert on family conflict and communication. She helps young adults answer such important questions as these:

Why are so many grown-up people still worrying about what their parents think?

Why can't you talk to them the way you talk to other people?

Why do you keep having the same arguments?

How can you stop feeling guilty?

How can you change family gatherings, holidays?

How can you stay out of their relationship and keep them out of yours?

What role would you like for your parents to play in your life today?

How can you make lasting changes?

The book is filled with personal accounts and gives young adults, as well as middle-aged adults, specific strategies for improving communication and resolving conflict with their parents.

Between Parent & Teenager
(1969) by Haim Ginott.
New York: Avon.

Despite the fact that *Between Parent & Teenager* is well past its own adolescence (it was published in 1969), it continues to be one of the most widely read and recommended books for parents who want to communicate more effectively with their teenagers. Author Haim Ginott was a clinical psychologist at Columbia University who died in 1973. Ginott describes a number of commonsense solutions and strategies. For Ginott, parents' greatest challenge in the teenage years is to let go when they want to hold on. Only by letting go can a peaceful and meaningful co-

existence be reached between parents and teenagers, he says. Throughout the book, Ginott connects with parents through catchy phrases such as "Don't collect thorns" (which instructs parents that when they see imperfections in themselves, they often expect perfection on the part of their teenagers) and "Don't step on corns" (which educates parents that adolescents have many imperfections about which they are very sensitive, ranging from zits to dimples). Teenagers don't need parents to remind them of these imperfections.

This book is very entertaining reading and is full of insightful interchanges between parents and teenagers. Ginott's strategies can make the world of parents and adolescents a kinder, gentler world.

Practical Knowledge About Adolescence

Appearing near the end of each chapter, this feature
provides a brief review of books that include practical
information to help adolescents live more effective lives.

$\mathscr{R}$ESOURCES FOR IMPROVING THE LIVES OF ADOLESCENTS

American Anorexia/Bulimia Association
133 Cedar Lane
Teaneck, NJ 07666
201-836-1800

This organization provides information, referrals, and publications related to anorexia nervosa and bulimia.

Building Health Programs for Teenagers (1986)
Children's Defense Fund
25 E Street NW
Washington, DC 20001
202-628-8787

This information provides help in developing health programs for adolescents. A number of excellent ideas about health programs are presented.

Canadian Institute of Child Health/Institut Canadien de la Santé Infantile
885 Meadowlands Drive East, Suite 512
Ottawa, Ontario, K2C 3N2
613-224-4144

The Institute monitors the health of Canadian children, fosters the health and well-being of mothers and infants, promotes a healthy and safe environment to reduce childhood injuries, promotes the physical and socioemotional development of children and encourages individuals and communities to improve the environment for all children and youth.

Comprehensive Adolescent Health Services in the United States (1992)
by Jonathan Klein and others
The Search Institute
Thresher Square West
Suite 210
700 South Third Street
Minneapolis, MN 55415
1-800-888-7828

This document is based on the first national census of adolescent health programs. It reviews more than six hundred existing programs that provide comprehensive or integrated health services to adolescents. Relevant differences between school-based, hospital-based, public health, and other program models are discussed.

Journal of Adolescent Health Care

This journal includes articles about a wide range of health-related and medical issues, including reducing smoking, improving nutrition, health promotion, and physicians' and nurses' roles in reducing health-compromising behaviors of adolescents.

Journal of School Health

This journal covers research and programs that involve school-related dimensions of health, including a number of health education programs.

Kids Help Phone/Jeunesse J'Écoute
2 Bloor Street West, Suite 100, Box 513
Toronto, Ontario M4W 3E2
416-921-7827
800-668-6868

Kids Help Phone is Canada's only bilingual, confidential, 24-hour, toll-free telephone help line for children and teens. Staffed by professionals, the Help Phone provides counseling, educational information and referral services to youth.

The LEARN Program for Weight Control (1988)
by Kelley Brownell
Dallas: American Health

This program can help adolescents change their lifestyle in order to lose weight. Author Kelly Brownell is a highly respected authority on dieting and eating disorders. *LEARN* stands for Lifestyle, Exercise, Attitudes, Relationships, and Nutrition. Brownell weaves his LEARN program through sixteen lessons.

The New Aerobics for Women (1988)
by Kenneth Cooper and Mildred Cooper
New York: Bantam

Older adolescent and college females can benefit from this excellent book on exercise that also includes sound dietary information.

Stop Teenage Addiction to Tobacco
121 Lyman Street, Suite 210
Springfield, MA 01103

This organization's goal is to reduce teenage smoking, especially by controlling tobacco company advertising and better enforcement of laws prohibiting tobacco sales to minors. It publishes a newsletter, *Tobacco and Youth Reporter*.

Resources for Improving the Lives of Adolescents

This intervention tool describes a large
number of resources that can be contacted
to improve the lives of adolescents. Most listings
include both addresses and phone numbers.

Exploring Adolescent Development

This end-of-chapter feature lets you see how the scientists who study adolescents actually conduct their research investigations.

Glossary

Key terms are defined alphabetically in an end-of-book glossary, along with their page references.

Exploring Adolescent Development

To further explore the nature of adolescent development, we will examine a research study on moral reasoning about sexually transmitted diseases and discuss adolescent volunteerism.

RESEARCH ON ADOLESCENT DEVELOPMENT

Moral Reasoning About Sexually Transmitted Diseases

Featured Study

Jadack, R. A., Hyde, J. S., Moore, C. F., & Keller, M. L. (1995). Moral reasoning about sexually transmitted diseases. *Child Development, 66*, 167–177.

The purpose of this study was to investigate moral reasoning related to sexual behavior that could lead to the development of sexually transmitted diseases. Kohlberg's and Gilligan's cognitive developmental theories provided the conceptual framework for the study.

Method

The subjects were 40 college freshmen (mean age = 18.3 years) and 32 college seniors (mean age = 22.3 years). They were presented with hypothetical dilemmas about situations in which sexually transmitted diseases (STDs) could be transmitted. Respondents were asked to explain why they believed that the characters involved in the dilemmas should or should not engage in risky behaviors.

Four moral dilemmas were presented to the students. One dilemma involved a caring relationship in which the protagonist is deciding, before sexual intercourse, whether to tell his partner that he has genital herpes, risking rejection from the partner. Another dilemma involved a casual, noncaring relationship in which the protagonist is deciding whether to tell previous partners about newly diagnosed genital warts.

Results and Discussion

The college students' responses to the moral dilemmas were scored based on Kohlberg's and Gilligan's theories. The college seniors were at a higher stage of reasoning in Kohlberg's theory than were the college freshmen. Typically, the 18-year-olds reasoned at a combined stage 2–stage 3 level, or at a stage 3 level, while the 22-year-olds reasoned at a combined stage 3–stage 4 level, or at a stage 4 level. The 22-year-olds' typical reasoning expected into topics of responsibility and obligation in relationships. Unexpectedly, there were no gender differences in the students' moral reasoning.

ADOLESCENT HEALTH AND WELL-BEING

Volunteerism

Marian Wright Edelman (1992) paints the following portrait to illustrate why we need more volunteers to help children:

- Every morning, 100,000 American children wake up homeless.
- Every 13 seconds, an American child is reported neglected or abused.

- Every 32 seconds, an American baby is born into poverty.
- Every 64 seconds, a baby is born to a teenage mother.
- Every 13 hours, an American preschooler is murdered.

To help safeguard and support our nation's children, we need more people, including adolescents, to volunteer their time and effort. Helping does

not take wealth or power. What it does take is caring, hard work, and persistence.

In many cases, adolescents are willing to help children in need but are never asked to help. Adolescents are nearly four times as likely to volunteer when asked than when they were not asked (Hartkoff & Klopp, 1992).

Adults and adolescents can help children in their communities by donating their time and talent to

434   Santrock: Adolescence

GLOSSARY

A

abnormal behavior Behavior that is maladaptive and harmful. 469

abstract relations Fischer's term for the ability of an adolescent to coordinate two or more abstract ideas; this ability often appears for the first time between 14 and 16 years of age. 121

accommodation This occurs when individuals adjust to new information. 107

acculturation Cultural change that results from continuous, firsthand contact between two distinctive cultural groups. 280, 517

acculturative stress The negative consequences of acculturation. 517

achievement motivation The desire to accomplish something, to reach a standard of excellence, and to expend effort to excel. 440

achievement test This type of test measures what has been learned, or what skills have been mastered. 148

active (niche-picking) genotype-environment interactions The type of interactions that occur when adolescents seek out environments they find compatible and stimulating. 82

addiction Physical dependence on a drug. 471

adolescence The developmental period of transition from childhood to early adulthood; it involves biological, cognitive, and socioemotional changes. 24

adolescent egocentrism The heightened self-consciousness of adolescents, which is reflected in their belief that others are as interested in them as they themselves are and in their sense of personal uniqueness. 122

adolescent generalization gap Adelson's concept of widespread generalizations about adolescents based on information about a limited, highly visible group of adolescents. 13

adoption study A study in which investigators seek to discover whether, in behavior and psychological characteristics, adopted children and adolescents are more like their adoptive parents, who provided a home environment, or their biological parents, who contributed their heredity. Another form of adoption study is to compare adoptive and biological siblings. 80

aerobic exercise Sustained exercise, such as jogging, or swimming, that stimulates heart and lung activity. 510

affectionate love Also called companionate love, this love occurs when an individual desires to have another person near and has a deep, caring affection for that person. 232

AIDS Acquired immune deficiency syndrome, a primarily sexually transmitted disease caused by the HIV virus, which destroys the body's immune system. 386

alternation model This model assumes that it is possible for an individual to know and understand two different cultures. It also assumes that individuals can alter their behavior to fit a particular social context. 280

altruism Unselfish interest in helping another person. 416

amphetamines Called pep pills or uppers, these are widely prescribed stimulants, sometimes in the form of diet pills. 476

anal stage The second Freudian stage of development, occurring between 1½ and 3 years of age, in which the child's greatest pleasure involves the anus or the eliminative functions associated with it. 44

androgens The main class of male sex hormones. 89

androgyny The presence of a high degree of desirable feminine and masculine characteristics in the same individual. 354

anorexia nervosa An eating disorder that involves the relentless pursuit of thinness through starvation. 509

anticonformity This occurs when individuals react counter to a group's expectations and deliberately move away from the actions or beliefs the group advocates. 214

approach/approach conflict This occurs when an individual must choose between two attractive stimuli or circumstances. 515

approach/avoidance conflict This occurs when there is a single stimulus or circumstance, but it has both positive and negative characteristics. 515

approach strategies Coping strategies that include cognitive attempts to understand the stressor and behavioral attempts to cope with the stressor by dealing directly with it or its consequences. 520

aptitude test This type of test predicts an individual's ability to learn a skill, or what the individual can accomplish with training. 148

aptitude-treatment interaction (ATI) This interaction stresses the importance of both the attitudes and the characteristics of the adolescent, such as academic potential or personality traits, and the treatments or experiences, such as the educational techniques, that the adolescent receives. *Aptitude* refers to such characteristics as the academic potential and personality characteristics on which students differ; *treatment* refers to educational techniques, such as structured versus flexible classrooms. 256

assimilation The absorption of ethnic minority groups into the dominant group, which often means the loss of some or virtually all of the behavior and values of the ethnic minority group. 107, 208

attention The concentration and focusing of mental effort. Attention is both selective and shifting. 137

537

Adolescent Health and Well-Being

Closing each chapter, this feature highlights information that will help to improve adolescent health and well-being. Special attention is given to helping at-risk adolescents.

Adolescence

Valen Serov
Woman with Pomegranates

Valen Serov
Woman with Pomegranates

RESOURCES FOR IMPROVING THE LIVES OF ADOLESCENTS

EXPLORING ADOLESCENT DEVELOPMENT

PROLOGUE

Teenagers

Watching the teenagers
in Beaver
using hairspray and
lipstick.
Kissing at ballgames.
Going steady.
And wanting it fast,
wanting it now.
Because all my pretend
had to be hidden.
All my games
secret.
Wanting to be a wide-open child
but too big,
too big.
No more.
Waiting to shave
and wear nylons
and waltz.
Forgetting when
I was last time
a child.
Never knowing
when it
ended.

—Cynthia Rylant
Waiting to Waltz: A Childhood

One

The Nature of Adolescent Development

In no order of things is adolescence the simple time of life.

—Jean Erskine Stewart

Adolescence is a transitional period in the human life span, linking childhood and adulthood. Understanding the meaning of adolescence is important because adolescents are the future of any society. This first section contains two chapters: Chapter 1, "Introduction," and Chapter 2, "The Science of Adolescent Development."

Carl Larsson
In the Hawthorn Hedge, detail

Chapter

1

Introduction

Chapter Boxes

A few years ago, it occurred to me that, when I was a teenager, in the early Depression years, there were no teenagers! Teenagers have sneaked up on us in our own lifetime, and yet it seems they always have been with us. . . . The teenager had not yet been invented, though, and there did not yet exist a special class of beings, bounded in a certain way—not quite children and certainly not adults.

—P. Musgrove, *Youth and Social Order*, 1964

The Youths of Jeffrey Dahmer and Alice Walker

Whatever is formed for long duration arrives slowly to its maturity.

—Samuel Johnson,
The Rambler, 175

PREVIEW

*B*y examining the shape of adolescence, we can understand it better. This book is a window into the nature of adolescents' development—your own and that of every other adolescent of the human species. In this first chapter, you will be introduced to why today is both the best of times and the worst of times for adolescents, the nature of interest in adolescence at different points in history, what today's adolescents are like, the nature of adolescent development, careers in adolescent development, and critical thinking about adolescence.

On page 45 of Jeffrey Dahmer's high school yearbook is a photograph of forty-five honor society students lined up shoulder to shoulder, their hair well combed, their smiles confident. But one senior three rows from the top has no smile, no eyes, no face at all—his image was reduced to a silhouette by an annoyed student editor before the yearbook went to the printer. The silhouette belonged to Jeffrey Dahmer, whose grades ranged from A's to D's. He fell far short of honor society qualifications, but he sneaked into the photo session as if he belonged. The photo session took place just 2 months before he says he killed his first victim, in the spring of 1978, with a barbell.

That was 13 years before he confessed to a horrific string of slayings. In all the years he cried out for attention, the photo session was one of the few times he got caught. By then he had learned to hide behind a mask of normalcy that concealed his contradictory emotions. It was a mask no one pulled down until one night in 1991, when a man in handcuffs dashed out of Dahmer's bizarrely cluttered Milwaukee apartment in a tough Milwaukee neighborhood, called the police, and stammered that Dahmer had tried to kill him. At least seventeen other victims failed to escape from Dahmer's clutches.

Jeffrey Dahmer had a troubled childhood and adolescence. His parents constantly bickered before they divorced. His mother had emotional problems and doted on his younger brother. He felt that his father neglected him, and he had been sexually abused by another boy when he was 8 years old. But the vast majority of people who suffered through a painful childhood and adolescence never go on to commit the grisly crimes that Dahmer committed.

A decade before Dahmer's first murder, Alice Walker, who would later win a Pulitzer Prize for her book *The Color Purple*, spent her days battling racism in Mississippi. She had recently won her first writing fellowship, but rather than use the money to follow her dream of moving to Senegal, Africa, she thrust herself into the heart and heat of the civil rights movement. As a child and an adolescent, Walker knew the brutal effects of poverty and racism. Born in 1944, she was the eighth child of Georgia sharecroppers who earned $300 a year. When Walker was 8, her brother accidentally shot her in the left eye with a BB gun. By the time her parents got her to the hospital a week later (they had no car), she was blind in that eye and it had developed a disfiguring layer of scar tissue. Despite the counts against her as a child and an adolescent, she went on to become an essayist, a poet, an award-winning novelist, a short-story writer, and a social activist. Like her characters (especially the females), she has overcome pain and anger to celebrate the human spirit. Walker writes about people who, as she puts it, "make it, who come out of nothing. People who triumph."

What leads one adolescent, so full of promise, to commit brutal acts of violence and another to turn poverty and trauma into a rich literary harvest? How can we attempt to explain how one adolescent can pick up the pieces of a life shattered by tragedy, such as a loved one's death, whereas another one seems to come unhinged by life's minor hassles? Why is it that some adolescents are whirlwinds—successful in school, involved in a network of friends, and full of energy—while others hang out on the sidelines, mere spectators of life? If you have ever wondered what makes adolescents tick, you have asked yourself the central question we explore in this book.

(Left) Jeffrey Dahmer's senior portrait in high school.

(Right) Alice Walker won the Pulitzer Prize for her book The Color Purple. *Like the characters in her book (especially the women), Walker overcame pain and anger to triumph and celebrate the human spirit.*

© 1986, Washington Post Writers Group. Reprinted with permission.

THE BEST OF TIMES AND THE WORST OF TIMES FOR TODAY'S ADOLESCENTS

It is both the best of times and the worst of times for adolescents. Their world possesses powers and perspectives inconceivable 50 years ago: computers, longer life expectancies, the entire planet accessible through television, satellites, air travel. So much knowledge, though, can be chaotic and dangerous. School curricula have been adapted to teach new topics: AIDS, adolescent suicide, drug and alcohol abuse, incest. The hazards of the adult world—its sometimes fatal temptations—descend upon children and adolescents so early that their ideals may be shattered.

Crack, for example, is far more addictive and deadly than marijuana, the drug of an earlier generation. Strange fragments of violence and sex flash out of the television set and lodge in the minds of youth. The messages are powerful and contradictory. Rock videos suggest orgiastic sex. Public health officials counsel safe sex. Oprah Winfrey conducts seminars on lesbian nuns, exotic drugs, transsexual surgery, serial murders. Television pours a bizarre version of reality into the imaginations of adolescents.

Every stable society transmits values from one generation to the next. That is civilization's work. In today's world, a special concern is the nature of values being communicated to adolescents. Today's parents are raising adolescents in a world far removed from the era of Ozzie and Harriet 30 years ago, when two out of three American families consisted of a father who was the breadwinner, a mother, and the children and adolescents they were raising. Today fewer than one in five families fits that description. Phrases such as *quality time* have found their way into the American vocabulary. Absence is a motif in the lives of many adolescents. It may be an absence of authority and limits, or of emotional commitment (Morrow, 1988).

Growing up has never been easy. In many ways, the developmental tasks of today's adolescents are no different from those of the adolescents of Ozzie and Harriet's world. Adolescence is not a time of rebellion, crisis,

Growing up has never been easy. However, adolescence is not best viewed as a time of rebellion, crisis, pathology, and deviance. A far more accurate vision of adolescence describes it as a time of evaluation, of decision making, of commitment, and of carving out a place in the world. Most of the problems of today's youth are not with the youth themselves. What adolescents need is access to a range of legitimate opportunities and to long-term support from adults who deeply care about them.

pathology, and deviance. A far more accurate vision of adolescence is of a time of evaluation, of decision making, of commitment, of carving out a place in the world. Most of the problems of today's youth are not with the youth themselves. What adolescents need is access to a range of legitimate opportunities and to long-term support from adults who care deeply about them.

Each of us has memories of our adolescence—of relationships with parents, peers, and teachers, and of ourselves. This book is a window to the journey of adolescence. The transition from being a child to being an adult is told in words that I hope stimulate you to think about where you have been, where you are, and where you are going in life. You will see yourself and others as adolescents and be motivated to reflect on how the adolescent years influence who you and others are. This book is about life's rhythm and meaning, about turning mystery into understanding, and about weaving a portrait of one of life's most important developmental periods.

Our historical view of adolescence begins with an overview of how adolescents were perceived by the early Greeks and then turns to perceptions of adolescents during the Middle Ages and the Enlightenment. Next, we examine the lives of adolescents in America's early years, with special emphasis on the time period 1890–1920. Finally, we evaluate the lives of adolescents in the twentieth century and how easy it is to stereotype the adolescents of any historical time frame.

Early History

How were adolescents viewed early in history? What was the nature of adolescence in the early years of America?

The Greeks

In early Greece, both Plato and Aristotle commented about the nature of youth. In *The Republic* (fourth century B.C./1968 translation), Plato described three facets of human development (or, as he called it, the "soul"): desire, spirit, and reason. According to Plato, reason—the highest of the facets—does not develop in childhood, but rather first appears at about the age period we call adolescence today. Plato argued that because reason does not mature in childhood, children's education should focus on sports and music. He also emphasized that the onset of rational thought in adolescence requires a change in the educational curricula: Sports and music should be replaced by science and mathematics.

Plato believed that character, not intellect, should be developed in the early years of childhood. Even though Plato stressed the importance of early experience in the formation of character, he nonetheless pointed out that experiences in later years could modify character. Arguments about the importance of early experience in human development are still prevalent today. Do the first few years of life determine the adolescent's or adult's personality? Are later experiences in adolescence just as important in forming and shaping personality as experiences in the early years? We will return to the early-experience issue later in this chapter.

Aristotle (fourth century B.C./1941 translation) argued that the most important aspect of the age period we now call adolescence is the development of the ability to choose, and that this self-determination becomes the hallmark of maturity. Aristotle believed that, at the onset of adolescence, individuals are unstable and impatient, lacking the self-control to be a mature person. But he felt that by about 21 years of age, most individuals have much better self-control. Aristotle was one of the first to describe specific time periods for stages of human development. He defined three stages: (1) infancy—the first 7 years of life; (2) boyhood—age 7 to puberty; and (3) young manhood—puberty to age 21. Aristotle's view is not unlike some contemporary views, which use labels like *independence*, *identity*, and *career choice* to describe the importance of increased self-determination in adolescence.

The Middle Ages and the Enlightenment

Society's view of adolescence had changed considerably by the Middle Ages, when the child was viewed as a miniature adult. Children and adolescents were believed to have the same interests as adults, and they were treated with the same strict, harsh discipline. In the Middle Ages, neither the adolescent nor the child was given status apart from the adult.

During the eighteenth century, Jean-Jacques Rousseau offered a more enlightened view of adolescence. Rousseau, a French philosopher, did more than any other individual to restore the belief that a child is not the same as an adult. In *Emile* (1762/1962 translation), he argued that treating the child like a miniature adult is potentially harmful. Rousseau believed that, up until the age of 12 or so, children should be free of adult restrictions and allowed to experience their world naturally, rather than have rigid regulations imposed on them.

Rousseau, like Aristotle and Plato, believed that development in childhood and adolescence occurs in a series of stages. Rousseau described four stages of development:

1. *Infancy* (the first 4 to 5 years). The infant is much like an animal, with strong physical needs, and the child is hedonistic (dominated by pleasure and pain).
2. *Savage* (5 to 12 years). During this time, sensory development is most important. Sensory experiences, such as play, sports, and games, should be the focus of education. Like Aristotle, Rousseau argued that reason had not developed by the end of this time period.
3. *Stage 3* (12 to 15 years). Reason and self-consciousness develop during this stage, along with an abundance of physical energy. Curiosity should be encouraged in the education of 12- to 15-year-olds by providing a variety of exploratory activities. According to Rousseau, *Robinson Crusoe* is the best book to read during this stage of human development because it includes insightful ideas about curiosity and exploratory behavior.
4. *Stage 4* (15 to 20 years). The individual begins to mature emotionally during this time period; interest in others replaces selfishness. Virtues and morals also appear at this point in development.

Rousseau, then, helped to restore the belief that development is stratified, or subject to distinct phases.

But his ideas about adolescence were speculative. Other individuals in the nineteenth or twentieth centuries had to bridge the gap between the ideas of philosophers and the empirical approach of scientists.

Adolescence in the Early Years of America

Have adolescents of different eras always had the same interests? Have adolescents always experienced the same kind of academic, work, and family environments as they do today? Today's adolescents spend far more time in school than at work, in structured rather than unstructured environments, and in sessions with their agemates than did their counterparts of the 1800s and early 1900s. Let's look more closely at what adolescence was like during two time periods in the history of America (Kett, 1977).

The Early Republic, 1790–1840. The migration of young people from the farms to urban life began during the time period 1790–1840. School opportunities became a reality, and career choices grew more varied. However, increasing disorderliness and violence characterized the society.

Work apprenticeships took up much of the day for many adolescent boys, with some apprentices beginning as early as the age of 12, others as late as 16 or 17. Some children left home to become servants even at the age of 8 or 9. Many adolescents remained dependent on their families while they engaged in apprentice work experiences.

Approaching the Age of Adolescence, 1840–1900. The most important period within the time frame 1840–1900 was 1880–1900. A gap in economic opportunities developed between lower-class and middle-class adolescents. Middle-class parents were pressed into selecting child-rearing orientations that would ensure the successful placement of their youth in jobs. These child-rearing practices encouraged the adolescent to become passive and conform to societal standards.

To capitalize on the new jobs created by the Industrial Revolution, youth had to stay in school longer and even go on to college. Parents encouraged delay of gratification and self-restraint behaviors because they saw that going to school longer and studying harder meant greater returns for their adolescents in the future.

While college was becoming more of a reality for many youth, it mainly was open to middle-class, but not lower-class, adolescents (Juster & Vinovskis, 1991). Similarly, the youth groups that developed as part of school and church activities were essentially middle-class in nature.

The conformity to adult leadership in most of the youth groups coincided with the general orientation of adolescents at this time in America: Adults know what is right; do what they tell you, and you'll get somewhere someday.

The Twentieth Century

The end of the nineteenth century and the early part of the twentieth century represented an important period in the invention of the concept we now call adolescence. Subsequent changes that adolescents experienced later in the twentieth century also influenced their lives in substantial ways.

The Turn of the Century

Between 1890 and 1920, a number of psychologists, urban reformers, educators, youth workers, and counselors began to mold the concept of adolescence. At this time, young people, especially boys, no longer were viewed as decadent problem causers, but instead were seen as increasingly passive and vulnerable—qualities previously associated only with the adolescent female. When G. Stanley Hall's book on adolescence was published in 1904, as discussed in the next section, it played a major role in restructuring thinking about adolescents. Hall said that while many adolescents appear to be passive, they are experiencing considerable turmoil within.

Educators, counselors, and psychologists began to develop norms of behavior for adolescents. Hall's storm-and-stress concept substantially influenced these norms. As a result, adults attempted to impose conformity and passivity on adolescents in the 1900–1920 period. Examples of this conformity included the encouragement of school spirit, loyalty, and hero worship on athletic teams.

G. Stanley Hall

Historians label G. Stanley Hall (1844–1924) the father of the scientific study of adolescence. Hall's ideas were first published in the two-volume set *Adolescence* in 1904 (see table 1.1).

Hall was strongly influenced by Charles Darwin, the famous evolutionary theorist. Hall applied the scientific and biological dimensions of Darwin's view to the study of adolescent development. Hall believed that all development is controlled by genetically determined physiological factors and that environment plays a minimal role in development, especially during infancy and childhood. He did acknowledge, however, that environment accounts for more change in development in adolescence than in earlier periods. Thus, at least with regard to adolescence, Hall believed—as we do today—that heredity interacts with environmental influences to determine the individual's development.

Like Rousseau, Hall subscribed to a four-stage approach to development: infancy, childhood, youth, and adolescence. According to Hall, adolescence is the period from 12 to 23 years of age and is filled with storm and stress. The **storm-and-stress view** *is Hall's concept that adolescence is a turbulent time charged with conflict and mood swings.* Hall borrowed the label *storm and stress* from the *Sturm und Drang* descriptions of German writers, such as Goethe and Schiller, who wrote

G. Stanley Hall, the father of the scientific study of adolescence. What was the nature of his storm-and-stress view of adolescence?

development. In Hall's view, biological changes in adolescence allow for more complicated social arrangements, such as dating. With regard to education, Hall said that such faculties as civility, scientific thinking, and morality should be intensely taught after the age of 15. However, Hall's developmental vision of education rested mainly on highly speculative theory, rather than specific data. Although Hall believed systematic methods should be used to study adolescents, his research efforts resorted to the creation of rather weak and unconvincing questionnaires.

Even though the quality of his research was suspect, Hall was a giant in the field of adolescence. It was he who began the theorizing, the systematizing, and the questioning that went beyond mere speculating and philosophizing. Indeed, we owe the beginnings of the scientific study of adolescent development to Hall.

Margaret Mead's Sociocultural View of Adolescence

Anthropologist Margaret Mead (1928) studied adolescents on the South Sea island of Samoa. She concluded that the basic nature of adolescents is not biological, as Hall envisioned, but rather sociocultural. She argued that when cultures provide a smooth, gradual transition from childhood to adulthood, which is the way adolescence is handled in Samoa, little storm and stress is associated with the period. Mead's observations of Samoan adolescents revealed that their lives were relatively free of turmoil. Mead concluded that cultures that allow adolescents to observe sexual relations, see babies born, regard death as natural, do important work, engage in sex play, and know clearly

novels full of idealism, commitment to goals, passion, feeling, and revolution. Hall sensed that there was a parallel between the themes of the German authors and the psychological development of adolescents. In Hall's view, adolescents' thoughts, feelings, and actions oscillate between conceit and humility, good and temptation, happiness and sadness. The adolescent might be nasty to a peer one moment, and kind the next moment. At one moment, the adolescent might want to be alone, but seconds later might seek companionship.

Hall's views had implications for the social development and education of adolescents. Hall conceived of development as a biological process that directed social

Anthropologist Margaret Mead (left) with a Samoan adolescent girl. Mead found that adolescence in Samoa was relatively stress-free, although recently her findings have been criticized. Mead's observations and analysis challenged G. Stanley Hall's biological, storm-and-stress view and called attention to the sociocultural basis of adolescence.

tions contributed to the emergence of the concept of adolescence. In the quote that opens this chapter, P. Musgrove comments about the teenager sneaking up on us in our own lifetime. At a point not too long ago in history, the teenager had not yet been invented. The **inventionist view** *states that adolescence is a sociohistorical creation. Especially important in the inventionist view of adolescence are the sociohistorical circumstances at the beginning of the twentieth century, a time when legislation was enacted that ensured the dependency of youth and made their move into the economic sphere more manageable.* We discussed many of these sociohistorical circumstances in our overview of the historical background of adolescence. They included the decline in apprenticeship; increased mechanization during the Industrial Revolution, which also involved upgraded skill requirements of labor and specialized divisions of labor; the separation of work and home; the writings of G. Stanley Hall; urbanization; the appearance of youth groups, such as the YMCA and the Boy Scouts; and age-segregated schools.

Schools, work, and economics are important dimensions of the inventionist view of adolescence (Elder, 1975; Fasick, 1994; Lapsley, Enright, & Serlin, 1985). Some scholars on adolescence argue that the concept of adolescence was invented mainly as a by-product of the motivation to create a system of compulsory public education. In this view, the function of secondary schools is to transmit intellectual skills to youth (Stedman & Smith, 1983). However, other scholars on adolescence argue that the primary purpose of secondary schools is to deploy youth within the economic sphere and to serve as an important cog in the culture's authority structure (Lapsley, Enright, and Serlin, 1985). In this view, the American society "inflicted" the status of adolescence on its youth through child-saving legislation. By developing laws for youth, the adult power structure placed youth in a submissive position that restricted their options, encouraged their dependency, and made their move into the world of work more manageable.

Historians now call the period of 1890–1920 the "age of adolescence" because they believe it was during this time frame that the concept of adolescence was invented. In this period, a great deal of compulsory legislation aimed at youth was enacted. In virtually every state, laws were passed that excluded youth from most employment and required them to attend secondary school. Much of this legislation included extensive enforcement provisions.

Two clear changes resulted from this legislation: decreased youth employment and increased school attendance by youth. From 1910 to 1930, the number of 10- to 15-year-olds who were gainfully employed dropped about 75 percent. In addition, between 1900 and 1930, the number of high school graduates substantially increased (see table 1.2). Approximately 600 percent more individuals graduated from high school in this 30-year time frame.

what their adult roles will be promote a relatively stress-free adolescence. However, in cultures like the United States, in which children are considered very different from adults and where adolescence is not characterized by the aforementioned experiences, adolescence is more likely to be stressful.

More than half a century after Mead's Samoan findings, her work was criticized as biased and error-prone (Freeman, 1983). The current criticism also states that Samoan adolescence is more stressful than Mead observed and that delinquency appears among Samoan adolescents just as it does among Western adolescents. In the current controversy over Mead's findings, some researchers have defended Mead's work (Holmes, 1987).

The Inventionist View

Although adolescence has a biological base, as G. Stanley Hall believed, it also has a sociocultural base, as Margaret Mead believed. Indeed, sociohistorical conditions

TABLE 1.2

Percentage of Growth in High School Graduation, 1870–1940

Year	% Change
1870	
1880	50
1890	83
1900	116
1910	64
1920	112
1930	101
1940	83

Source: Series H598–681, Historical Statistics of the United States.

An analysis of the content of the oldest continuing journal in developmental psychology (*Journal of Genetic Psychology*—earlier called *Pedagogical Seminary*) provided further evidence of history's role in the perception of adolescents (Enright & others, 1987). Four historical periods—the depressions of the 1890s and 1930s, and the two world wars—were evaluated. During the depression periods, scholars wrote about the psychological immaturity of youth and their educational needs. In contrast, during the world wars, scholars did not describe youth as immature, but rather underscored their importance as draftees and factory workers.

Further Changes in the Twentieth Century

In the three decades from 1920 to 1950, adolescents gained a more prominent status in society as they went through a number of complex changes. The lives of adolescents took a turn for the better in the 1920s but moved through difficult times in the 1930s and 1940s. In the 1920s, the Roaring Twenties atmosphere rubbed off on adolescents. Passivity and conformity to adult leadership were replaced by increased autonomy and conformity to peer values. Adults began to model the styles of youth, rather than vice versa. If a new dance came into vogue, the adolescent girl did it first and her mother learned it from her. Prohibition was the law of the time, but many adolescents drank heavily. More permissive attitudes toward the opposite sex developed, and kissing parties were standard fare. Short skirts even led to a campaign by the YWCA against such "abnormal" behavior.

Just when adolescence was getting to be fun, the Great Depression arrived in the 1930s, followed by World War II in the 1940s. Serious economic and political concerns replaced the hedonistic adolescent values of the 1920s. Radical protest groups that were critical of the government increased in number during the 1930s, and World War II exposed adolescents to another serious life-threatening event. Military service provided travel and exposure to other youth from different parts of the United States. This experience promoted a broader perspective on life and a greater sense of independence.

By 1950, the developmental period we refer to as adolescence had come of age—not only did it possess physical and social identity, but legal attention was paid to it as well. Every state had developed special laws for youth between the ages of 16 and 18 or 20. Adolescents in the 1950s have been described as the silent generation. Life was much better for adolescents in the 1950s than it had been in the 1930s and 1940s. The government was paying for many individuals' college educations through the GI Bill, and television was beginning to invade most homes. Getting a college degree, the key to a good job, was on the minds of many adolescents during the 1950s—so were getting married, having a family, and settling down to the life of luxury displayed in television commercials.

While the pursuit of higher education persisted among adolescents in the 1960s, it became painfully apparent that many African American adolescents not only were being denied a college education, but were receiving an inferior secondary education as well. Ethnic conflicts in the form of riots and sit-ins were pervasive, with college-age adolescents among the most vocal participants.

The political protest of adolescents reached a peak in the late 1960s and early 1970s, when millions of adolescents violently reacted to what they saw as immoral American participation in the Vietnam War. As parents watched the 1968 Democratic Convention, they saw not only political speeches in support of candidates but their adolescents fighting with the police, yelling obscenities at adults, and staging sit-ins.

Parents became more concerned in the 1960s about teenage drug use and abuse than in past eras. Sexual permissiveness in the form of premarital sex, cohabitation, and endorsement of previously prohibited sexual conduct also increased.

By the mid 1970s, much of the radical protest of adolescents had abated and was replaced by increased concern for an achievement-oriented, upwardly mobile career to be attained through hard work in high school, college, or a vocational training school. Material interests began to dominate adolescent motives again, while ideological challenges to social institutions seemed to become less central.

Protest in the 1970s also involved the women's movement. The descriptions of adolescents in America in earlier years pertained more to males than to females. The family and career objectives of adolescent females today would barely be recognized by the adolescent females of the 1890s and early 1900s.

For many years, barriers prevented many females and ethnic minority individuals from entering the field of adolescent development. Females and ethnic minority individuals who obtained doctoral degrees were very dedicated and overcame considerable bias. One pioneering female was Leta Hollingworth, who conducted important research on adolescent development, mental retardation, and gifted children (see figure 1.1). Pioneering African American psychologists included Kenneth and Mamie Clark, who conducted research on the self-esteem of African American children (Clark & Clark, 1939). And in 1932, George Sanchez documented cultural bias in intelligence tests for children and adolescents.

We have described some important sociohistorical circumstances experienced by adolescents, and we have evaluated how society viewed adolescents at different points in history. Next we will explore how caution needs to be exercised in generalizing about the adolescents of any era.

Stereotyping Adolescents

It is easy to stereotype a person, groups of people, or classes of people. A **stereotype** *is a broad category that reflects our impressions and beliefs about people. All stereotypes refer to an image of what the typical member of a particular group is like.* We live in a complex world and strive to simplify this complexity. Stereotyping people is one way we do this. We simply assign a label to a group of people—for example, we say that youth are *promiscuous*. Then we have much less to consider when we think about this set of people. Once we assign stereotypes, it is difficult to abandon them, even in the face of contradictory evidence.

Stereotypes about adolescents are plentiful: "They say they want a job, but when they get one, they don't want to work"; "They are all lazy"; "They are all sex fiends"; "They are all into drugs, every last one of them"; "Kids today don't have the moral fiber of my generation"; "The problem with adolescents today is that they all have it too easy"; "They are a bunch of egotistical smart alecks"; and so it goes.

Indeed, during most of the twentieth century, adolescents have been described as abnormal and deviant, rather than normal and nondeviant. Consider Hall's image of storm and stress. Consider also media portrayals of adolescents as rebellious, conflicted, faddish, delinquent, and self-centered—*Rebel Without a Cause* in the late 1950s, and *Easy Rider* in the 1960s, for example. Consider also the current image of adolescents as stressed and disturbed, from *Sixteen Candles* and *The Breakfast Club* in the 1980s to *Boyz N the Hood* in the 1990s.

Such stereotyping of adolescents is so widespread that adolescence researcher Joseph Adelson (1979) called it the **adolescent generalization gap,** *meaning that wide-*

Figure~1.1

Leta Hollingworth.
Women have often been overlooked in the history of psychology. In the field of adolescence, one such overlooked individual is Leta Hollingworth. She was the first individual to use the term gifted to describe youth who scored exceptionally high on intelligence tests (Hollingworth, 1916). She also played an important role in criticizing theories of her time that promoted the idea that males were superior to females (Hollingworth, 1914). For example, she conducted a research study refuting the myth that phases of the menstrual cycle are associated with a decline in performance in females.

spread generalizations about adolescents have developed that are based on information about a limited, often highly visible group of adolescents.

Two studies illustrate the widespread stereotyping of adolescents. In the first study, Daniel Yankelovich (1974) compared the attitudes of adolescents with those of their parents about different values, lifestyles, and codes of personal conduct. There was little or no difference in the attitudes of the adolescents and their parents regarding self-control, hard work, saving money, competition, compromise, legal authority, and private property. There was a substantial difference between the adolescents and their parents with regard to religion (89 percent of the parents said that religion was important to them, compared to only 66 percent of the adolescents). But note that a majority of the adolescents still subscribed to the belief that religion is important.

(a) The Roaring Twenties was a time when adolescents began to behave more permissively. Adults began to model the styles of youth. Adolescent drinking increased dramatically. (b) In the 1940s, many youth served in World War II. Military service exposed many youth to life-threatening circumstances and allowed them to see firsthand the way people in other countries live. (c) In the 1950s, many youth developed a stronger orientation toward education. Television was piped into many homes for the first time. One of the fads of the 1950s, shown here, was seeing how many people could squeeze into a phone booth. (d) In the late 1960s, many youth protested U.S. participation in the Vietnam War. Parents became more concerned about adolescent drug use as well. (e) In the 1970s, 1980s, and 1990s, much of the radical protest of youth quieted down. Today's adolescents are achievement-oriented, more likely to be working at a job, experiencing adult roles earlier, showing more interest in equality of the sexes, and heavily influenced by the media.

Daniel Offer and his colleagues (1988) also documented a stereotypical view of adolescence as highly stressful and disturbed. The self-images of adolescents around the world—in the United States, Australia, Bangladesh, Hungary, Israel, Italy, Japan, Taiwan, Turkey, and West Germany—were sampled. A healthy self-image characterized at least 73 percent of the adolescents studied. They were moving toward adulthood with a healthy integration of previous experiences, self-confidence, and optimism about the future. Although there were some differences in the adolescents, they were happy most of the time, they enjoyed life, they perceived themselves as able to exercise self-control, they valued work and school, they expressed confidence about their

In the study by Daniel Offer and his colleagues (1988), a healthy self-image characterized at least 73 percent of the adolescents studied around the world, including adolescents from Japan and Turkey (inset).

sexual selves, they showed positive feelings toward their families, and they felt they had the capability to cope with life's stresses—not exactly a storm-and-stress portrayal of adolescence.

Beginning with G. Stanley Hall's portrayal of adolescence as a period of storm and stress, for much of this century in the United States and other Western cultures, adolescence has unfortunately been perceived as a problematic period of the human life span that youth, their families, and society had to endure. But as the two research studies just described indicate, a large majority of adolescents are not nearly as disturbed and troubled as the popular stereotype of adolescence suggests. Public attitudes about adolescence emerge from a combination of personal experience and media portrayals, neither of which produces an objective picture of how normal adolescents develop.

Some of the readiness to assume the worst about adolescents likely involves the short memories of adults. Many adults measure their current perceptions of adolescents by memories of their own adolescence. Adults often portray today's adolescents as more troubled, less respectful, more self-centered, more assertive, and more adventurous than they were.

However, in matters of taste and manners, the youth of every generation have seemed radical, unnerving, and different from adults—different in how they look, how they behave, the music they enjoy, their hairstyles, and the clothing they choose. But it is an enormous error to confuse the adolescent's enthusiasm for trying on new identities and enjoying moderate amounts of outrageous behavior with hostility toward parental and societal standards. Acting out and boundary testing are time-honored ways in which adolescents move toward accepting, rather than rejecting, parental values. When my oldest daughter, Tracy, was in her first year of high school, my wife was certain that Tracy was going to waste—she detested Tracy's taste in clothes and hairstyle, didn't like Tracy's friends, didn't care for the boys Tracy was dating, thought she was underachieving in school, and was frightened by some of her escapades. Tracy is now in her early twenties, and observers would be hard-pressed to find vestiges of her earlier so-called immaturity. Tracy's values have become similar to her parents', and her mother no longer worries about Tracy's abilities to become a competent adult.

As mentioned earlier, stereotypes of adolescence are also generated by media portrayals of youth. The media often present sensational and "newsworthy" material, which means that they are far more likely to focus on troubled adolescents than on normal adolescents. Such media coverage conveys the impression that a majority of youth engage in deviant behaviors, when in fact only a minority currently do. As we see next in our consideration of today's adolescents, not only do media messages convey an image of adolescents as highly troubled, but the messages to adolescents from both adults and the media are often ambivalent.

> *In case you're worried about what's going to become of the younger generation, it's going to grow up and start worrying about the younger generation.*
>
> —Roger Allen

TODAY'S ADOLESCENTS

What is the current status of adolescents compared to the status of their counterparts earlier in history? Do adults have idealized images of adolescents, and does society communicate ambivalent messages to adolescents? How complex is adolescent development today? Should our nation's social policy toward adolescence be changed?

The Current Status of Adolescents

Today's adolescents face demands and expectations, as well as risks and temptations, that appear to be more numerous and complex than those adolescents faced only a generation ago (Hamburg, 1993). Nonetheless, contrary to the popular stereotype of adolescents as highly stressed and incompetent, the vast majority of adolescents successfully negotiate the path from childhood to adulthood. By some criteria, today's adolescents are doing better than their counterparts from a decade or two earlier. Today, more American adolescents—especially African American adolescents—complete high school. In the last few years, adolescent accidents and

The Importance of Asking Questions— Exploring Your Own Development as an Adolescent

Asking questions reflects our active curiosity. Children—especially young children—are remarkable for their ability to ask questions. My granddaughter, Jordan, is 3½ years old. *Why* is one of her favorite words, and she asks "Why?" relentlessly. As strong as question-asking is early in our life, many of us ask far fewer questions as adults.

Asking questions can help us engage in critical thinking about adolescent development, including our own development as adolescents. As you go through this course, you might want to ask yourself questions about how you experienced a particular aspect of development. For example, consider your experiences in your family as you were growing up. Questions you could pose to yourself might include these: "How did my parents bring me up? How did the way they reared me influence what I'm like today? How did my relationship with my brothers or sisters affect my development?" Consider also questions like these about your experiences with peers and at school: "Did I have many close friends while I was growing up? How much time did I spend with my peers and friends at various points in childhood and adolescence compared with the time I spent with my parents? What were my schools like? How good were my teachers? How did the schools and teachers affect my achievement orientation today?"

Be curious. Ask questions. Ask your friends or classmates about their experiences as they were growing up and compare them with yours. By asking questions about adolescent development, you are *applying a developmental framework to understanding behavior.*

homicides have declined somewhat, as have drug use, juvenile delinquency, and adolescent pregnancy rates. Most adolescents today have positive self-conceptions and positive relationships with others. As indicated earlier, such contemporary findings do not support a portrayal of adolescence as a highly disturbed, overly stressful time period in the life cycle. Rather, the majority of adolescents find the transition from childhood to adulthood a time of physical, cognitive, and social development that provides considerable challenge, opportunities, and growth.

Yet, while most adolescents experience the transition from childhood to adulthood more positively than is portrayed by many adults and the media, too many adolescents today are not provided with adequate opportunities and support to become competent adults (Noam, 1997; Weissburg & Greenberg, 1997). In many ways, today's adolescents are presented with a less stable environment than that of adolescents a decade or two ago. High divorce rates, high adolescents pregnancy rates, and increased geographic mobility of families contribute to this lack of stability in adolescents' lives. Today's adolescents are exposed to a complex menu of lifestyle options through the media. The rate of adolescent drug use in the United States is the highest for any Western industrialized country. Many of today's adolescents face these temptations, as well as sexual activity, at increasingly younger ages.

The previous discussion underscores an important point about adolescents: They are not a homogeneous group. Most adolescents successfully negotiate the lengthy path to adult maturity, but too large a minority do not. Ethnic, cultural, gender, socioeconomic, age, and lifestyle differences influence the actual life trajectory of each adolescent.

One subgroup of adolescents has been identified as "adultoid"; they perceive themselves as older, engage in higher levels of problem behavior, and are psychologically more immature than their peers (Galambos & Tilton-Weaver, 1996). Adultoids want the privileges of growing up sooner but are less engaged in productive activity than their nonadultoid counterparts.

In sum, different portrayals of adolescents often emerge, depending on the particular group of adolescents being described. As we see next, some of the problems faced by today's adolescents involve idealized images of what adolescents should be and society's ambivalent messages to adolescents.

Shirley Feldman and Glenn Elliott (1990) described how American society seems uncertain about what adolescence should be or should not be. The following examples illustrate how adults' idealized images of adolescents and society's ambivalent messages to adolescents may contribute to adolescents' problems.

- Many adults treasure the independence of youth, yet insist that adolescents do not have the maturity to make autonomous, competent decisions about their lives. Some of the ambiguity in messages about adult status and maturity that society communicates to adolescents appears in the form of laws dictating that they cannot drive until they are 16, vote until they are 18, or drink until age 21. Yet in some states 14-year-olds now have the legal right to choose the parent with whom they want to live after a parental divorce and to override parental wishes about such medical matters as abortion and psychiatric care.

- Society's sexual messages to adolescents are especially ambiguous. Adolescents are somehow supposed to be sexually naive but become sexually knowledgeable. The message to many adolescents is this: "You can experiment with sex and sow your wild oats, but be sure to maintain high standards of maturity and safety." Adolescents must negotiate this formidable task in a society that cannot agree on how much and what kind of explicit sex education adolescents should be given. This same society sanctions alluring messages in the media about the power and attractiveness of sexuality.

- Laws prohibit adolescents from using alcohol, tobacco, or other drugs, and adults decry the high level of drug use by adolescents. Yet many of the very same adults who stereotype and criticize adolescents for their drug use are themselves drug abusers and heavy cigarette smokers.

- Society promotes education and the development of knowledge as essential to success as an adult. Yet adolescents frequently observe the rewards society doles out to individuals who develop their athletic skills and business acumen. As adolescents interact with adults who do not value the process of learning, adolescents may attach more importance to simply attaining a diploma than to the process of getting one.

We have seen that understanding the current status of adolescents requires consideration of their heterogeneity. In addition, many adults have idealized images of adolescents and communicate ambivalent messages to them. To further understand today's adolescents, we turn our attention to the increased recognition of the complexity of adolescent development.

The Complexity of Adolescent Development and Sociocultural Contexts

As researchers more carefully examine the lives of adolescents, they are recognizing that a single developmental model might not accurately characterize all adolescents (Feldman & Elliott, 1990). The most widely described general model of adolescent development states that adolescence is a transition from childhood to adulthood during which individuals explore alternatives and experiment with choices as part of developing an identity. Although this model might accurately fit many White, middle-class adolescents, it is less well suited to adolescents from low-income families, school dropouts, and unemployed adolescents.

For many of these youth, development often is more chaotic and restricted, and social and ethnic barriers too frequently signal the presence of discrimination and prejudice.

Of special importance is the growing interest in the sociocultural contexts of adolescent development. **Contexts** *are the settings in which development occurs, settings influenced by historical, economic, social, and cultural factors.* To sense how important contexts are in understanding adolescent development, consider a researcher who wants to discover whether today's adolescents are more racially tolerant than those of a decade ago. Without reference to the historical, economic, social, and cultural aspects of race relations, adolescents' racial tolerance cannot be fully understood. Each adolescent's development occurs against a cultural backdrop of contexts (McLoyd, 1997 a, b). These contexts or settings include homes, schools, peer groups, churches, cities, neighborhoods, communities, university laboratories, the United States, China, Mexico, Japan, Egypt, and many others, each with meaningful historical, economic, social, and cultural legacies.

Three sociocultural contexts that many adolescent researchers believe merit special attention are culture, ethnicity, and gender. **Culture** *is the behavior patterns, beliefs, and all other products of a particular group of people that are passed on from generation to generation.* The products result from the interaction between groups of people and their environment over many years. A cultural group can be as large as the United States or as small as an African hunter-gatherer group. Whatever its size, the group's culture influences the identity, learning, and social behavior of its members (Booth, Crouter & Landale, 1997; Cole, 1997; Goodnow, 1997; Shweder & others, 1997). For example, the United States is an achievement-oriented culture with a strong work ethic, but recent comparisons of American and Japanese children and youth revealed that the Japanese were better at math, spent more time working on math in school, and spent more time doing homework than Americans did (Stevenson, 1995). **Cross-cultural studies**—*the comparison of a culture with one or more other cultures—provide information about the degree to which adolescent development is similar, or universal, across cultures, or the degree to which it is culture-specific.*

Ethnicity (the word *ethnic* comes from the Greek word for "nation") *is based on cultural heritage, nationality characteristics, race, religion, and language.* Ethnicity is central to the development of an **ethnic identity,** *which is a sense of membership in an ethnic group based upon shared language, religion, customs, values, history, and race.* Each of you is a member of one or more ethnic groups. Your ethnic identity reflects your deliberate decision to identify with an ancestor or ancestral group. If you are of Native American (American Indian) and African slave ancestry, you might choose to align yourself with the traditions and history of Native Americans, although an outsider might believe that your identity is African American. Nowhere

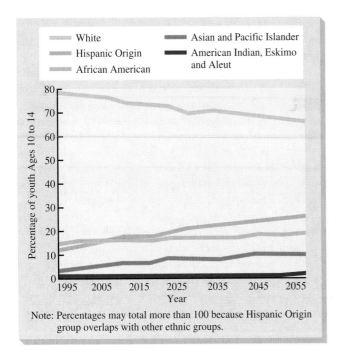

Note: Percentages may total more than 100 because Hispanic Origin group overlaps with other ethnic groups.

Legend:
White
Hispanic Origin
African American
Asian and Pacific Islander
American Indian, Eskimo and Aleut

Y-axis: Percentage of youth Ages 10 to 14
X-axis: Year (1995, 2005, 2015, 2025, 2035, 2045, 2055)

Figure~1.2

Ethnic Minority Population Increases in the United States.
The percentage of African American, Hispanic, and Asian American individuals increased far more from 1980 to 1988 than did the percentage of Whites.

are sociocultural changes more profound than in the increasing ethnic diversity of America's adolescents (Fisher, Jackson & Villarruel, 1997; Halonen & Santrock, 1996) (see figure 1.2).

Twenty percent of all American children and adolescents under the age of 17 in 1989 came from ethnic minority groups—such as African Americans, Hispanics, Native Americans, and Asian Americans. Projections indicate that, by the year 2000, one-third of all American school-age children will fall into this category. This changing demographic tapestry promises not only the richness that diversity produces but also difficult challenges in extending the American dream to individuals of all ethnic and minority groups. Historically, ethnic minorities have found themselves at the bottom of the economic and social order. They have been disproportionately represented among the poor and the inadequately educated (Edelman, 1995). Half of all African American adolescents and one-third of all Hispanic adolescents live in poverty. School dropout rates for minority youth reach the alarming figure of 60 percent in some urban areas. More about the nature of ethnic minority adolescents in the United States appears in Sociocultural Worlds of Adolescence.

Recently, some individuals have voiced dissatisfaction with the use of the term *minority* in the phrase *ethnic minority group*. Such dissatisfaction stems from traditionally associating the term *minority* with inferiority and deficits. Further, the concept of minority implies that there is a majority. Indeed, it can be argued that there really is no majority in the United States because Whites are actually composed of many different ethnic groups, and Whites are not a majority in the world. When the term *ethnic minority* is used in this text, the use is intentional—not to imply that ethnic minority adolescents should be viewed as inferior or deficient in some way, but to convey the impact that minority status has had on many ethnic minority adolescents. The circumstances of each ethnic group are not solely a function of its own culture. Rather, many ethnic groups have experienced considerable discrimination and prejudice. For example, patterns of alcohol abuse among Native American adolescents cannot be fully understood without considering the exploitation that has accompanied Native Americans' history.

A third, very important dimension of sociocultural contexts that is receiving increased attention is gender. **Gender** *is the sociocultural dimension of being male or female,* while *sex* refers to the biological dimension of being male or female (Unger & Crawford, 1996). Few aspects of adolescent development are more central to adolescents' identity and to their social relationships than their sex or gender (Paludi, 1995). Society's gender attitudes are changing. But how much? Is there a limit to how much society can determine what is appropriate behavior for male and female adolescents? (Eccles & Wigfield, 1997). A special concern of many feminist writers and scholars is that much of the history of interest in adolescence portrays adolescent development with a "male dominant theme." Just as important themes of this book are to examine cross-cultural issues and the role of ethnicity, an important theme is also to extensively examine gender

SOCIOCULTURAL WORLDS OF ADOLESCENCE

The Increasing Ethnic Diversity of Adolescents in the United States

Population trends and the United States' inability to prepare ethnic minority adolescents for full participation in American life have produced an imperative for the social institutions that serve ethnic minorities. Schools, colleges, social services, health and mental health agencies, juvenile probation services, and other programs need to become more sensitive to ethnic issues and to provide improved services to ethnic minority and low-income adolescents.

An especially important idea in considering the nature of cultural and ethnic groups is that not only is there ethnic diversity within a culture—the American culture includes Anglo-Americans, African Americans, Latinos, Native Americans, Asian Americans, Italian Americans, Polish Americans, and so on—but there is also diversity within each ethnic group. No cultural characteristic is common to all or nearly all African Americans, or all or nearly all Latinos, and absent in Anglo-Americans, unless it is the experience of being African American or of being Latino and the beliefs that develop from that experience.

African Americans make up the largest easily visible ethnic minority group in the United States. African Americans are distributed throughout the social class structure, although they constitute a larger proportion of low-income individuals than does the majority Anglo-American group. The majority of African American youth stay in school, do not take drugs, do not marry prematurely, and grow up to lead productive lives in spite of social and economic disadvantages.

Latinos also are a diverse group of individuals. Not all Latinos are Catholic, and not all of them have a Mexican heritage. Many of them have cultural ties with South American countries, with Puerto Rico or other Caribbean countries, or with Spain (Garcia & Zea, 1997).

Native Americans also are an extremely diverse and complicated ethnic group, with 511 identifiable tribal units. More than 30 distinct groups are listed under the Asian American designation. And within each of the 511 identifiable Native American tribes and 30 distinct Asian American groups is considerable diversity and individual variation.

America has embraced new ingredients from many cultures, and the cultures often mix their beliefs and identities. Some of the culture of origin is retained, some of it is lost, and some of it is mixed with the American culture. As ethnic minority groups continue to expand at a rapidly increasing rate, an important agenda in the next decade is to give increased attention to the role of culture and ethnicity in understanding adolescent development (Chen, 1997; Scott-Jones, 1997).

The tapestry of American culture has changed dramatically in recent years. Nowhere is the change more noticeable than in the increasing ethnic diversity of America's citizens. Ethnic minority groups—African Americans, Latinos, Native Americans (American Indians), and Asians, for example—will make up approximately one-third of all individuals under the age of 17 in the United States by the year 2000. One of society's challenges is to become more sensitive to ethnicity and to provide improved services to ethnic minority individuals.

Imagining What Your Development as an Adolescent Might Have Been Like in Other Cultural Contexts

Imagine what your development as an adolescent might have been like in a culture that offered few choices compared to the Western world—Communist China during the Cultural Revolution. Young people could not select their job or their mate in rural China. They also were not given the choice of migrating to the city. Imagine also another cultural context, this one in the United States. If you did not grow up in the inner city, imagine what your life as an adolescent would have been like had you grown up there—where most services have moved out, schools are inferior, poverty is extreme, and crime is common. Unfortunately, some of you did grow up in such impoverished circumstances. By examining what your development might have been like in these cultural contexts, you are *engaging in perspective taking and identifying the sociohistorical, cultural factors that influence adolescent development.*

issues. Chapter 9 is devoted exclusively to culture and ethnicity. Chapter 11 is devoted exclusively to gender. Throughout the book, you also will read about issues involving culture, ethnicity, and gender in Sociocultural Worlds of Adolescence boxes and in various chapter discussions. As we will see next, increased recognition of the importance of sociocultural contexts dictates that we carefully examine our society's social policy regarding adolescents' development.

> *We need every human gift and cannot afford to neglect any gift because of artificial barriers of sex or race or class or national origin.*
>
> —**Margaret Mead, *Male and Female* (1949)**

Social Policy and Adolescents' Development

Social policy *is a national government's course of action designed to influence the welfare of its citizens.* A current trend is to conduct adolescent development research that will lead to wise and effective decision making in the area of social policy (Edelman, 1997; Takanishi & DeLeon, 1994). Because more than 20 percent of adolescents are giving birth, because the use and abuse of drugs is widespread among adolescents, and because the specter of AIDS is spreading, the United States needs revised social policy related to adolescents. Figure 1.3 vividly portrays one day in the lives of American youths, suggesting the importance of improved social policy for youth.

Marian Wright Edelman, president of the Children's Defense Fund, has been a tireless advocate of children's rights. Especially troublesome to Edelman (1997) are the indicators of social neglect that place the United States at or near the bottom of industrialized nations in the treatment of children and adolescents. Edelman says that

Psychologist Rhoda Unger (shown talking with college students) urges psychologists to use the word sex only when referring to biological mechanisms (such as sex chromosomes or sexual anatomy) and to use the word gender only when describing the social, cultural, and psychological aspects of being male or female. Like Unger, psychologist Carolyn Sherif noted some of the problems the word sex has brought to the study of gender. Sherif argued that the term sex roles uncritically couples a biological concept (sex) with a sociocultural, psychological concept (gender). Sherif stressed that through this coupling many myths about sex may be smuggled into the concept of sociocultural aspects of male and female roles, causing confusion and possible stereotyping.

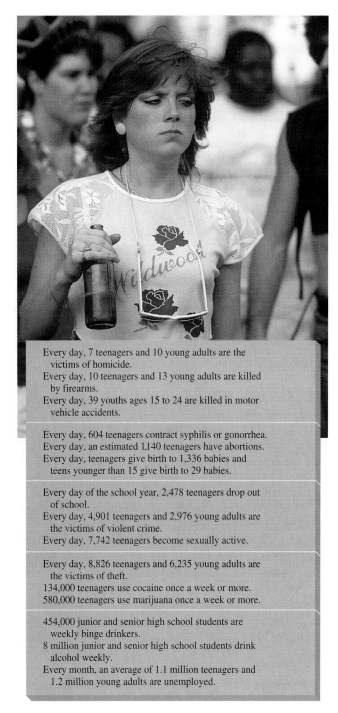

Every day, 7 teenagers and 10 young adults are the victims of homicide.
Every day, 10 teenagers and 13 young adults are killed by firearms.
Every day, 39 youths ages 15 to 24 are killed in motor vehicle accidents.

Every day, 604 teenagers contract syphilis or gonorrhea.
Every day, an estimated 1,140 teenagers have abortions.
Every day, teenagers give birth to 1,336 babies and teens younger than 15 give birth to 29 babies.

Every day of the school year, 2,478 teenagers drop out of school.
Every day, 4,901 teenagers and 2,976 young adults are the victims of violent crime.
Every day, 7,742 teenagers become sexually active.

Every day, 8,826 teenagers and 6,235 young adults are the victims of theft.
134,000 teenagers use cocaine once a week or more.
580,000 teenagers use marijuana once a week or more.

454,000 junior and senior high school students are weekly binge drinkers.
8 million junior and senior high school students drink alcohol weekly.
Every month, an average of 1.1 million teenagers and 1.2 million young adults are unemployed.

Figure~1.3

One Day in the Lives of American Youths.

From Janet Simons, Belva Finlay, and Alice Yang, Adolescent: Young Adult Factbook, *pg 2; Washington, DC: Children's Defense Fund, 1991. Reprinted by permission.*

parenting and nurturing the next generation of children and youth is our society's most important function and that we need to take it more seriously than we have in the past. She points out that we hear a lot from politicians these days about "family values," but that when we examine our nation's policies for families, they don't reflect the politicians' words. Edelman says that we need a better health-care

system for families, safer schools and neighborhoods, better parent education, and improved family support programs.

The shape and scope of social policies related to adolescents are heavily influenced by the U.S. political system, which is based on negotiation and compromise. The values held by individual lawmakers, the nation's economic strengths and weaknesses, and partisan politics all influence the policy agenda and whether the welfare of adolescents will be improved. Developmentalists can play an important role in social policy related to adolescents by helping to develop more positive public support for comprehensive legislation involving the welfare of adolescents, by contributing to and promoting research that will benefit adolescents' welfare, and by providing legislators with information that will influence their support of comprehensive welfare legislation that benefits adolescents.

Who should get the bulk of government dollars for improved well-being? Children? Adolescents? Their parents? The elderly? **Generational inequity** *is the unfair treatment of younger members of an aging society in which older adults pile up advantages by receiving inequitably large allocations of resources, such as Social Security and Medicare.* Generational inequity raises questions about whether the young should have to pay for the old and whether an "advantaged" older population is using up resources that should go to disadvantaged children and adolescents. The argument is that older adults are advantaged because they have publicly provided pensions, health care, food stamps, housing subsidies, tax breaks, and other benefits that younger groups do not have. While the trend of greater services for the elderly has been occurring, the percentage of children and adolescents living in poverty has been rising. Adolescents have especially been underserved by the government.

Bernice Neugarten (1988) says the problem should be viewed not as one of generational inequity, but rather as a major shortcoming of our broader economic and social policies. She believes we should develop a spirit of support for improving the range of options of all people in our society.

Peter Scales (1990) described four social policy recommendations for improving the lives of adolescents. He believes that an effective social policy for the prevention of adolescent problems requires that policymakers make these shifts:

1. From perceiving social problems as separate from each other to perceiving them as interconnected
2. From "throwing money" at crises to investing in broad health promotion, starting early in life and continuing systematically with developmentally appropriate initiatives through late adolescence
3. From expecting immediate program results to anticipating long-term outcomes (which requires a generation of investment—not just a term in office—to determine if programs are working)

4. From viewing policy on adolescents as charity to viewing it as an investment—that is, equating the development of competent adolescents with economic development.

In later chapters, when we discuss such topics as adolescent pregnancy, school dropouts, and substance abuse, social policy implications for reducing such problems will be described.

As the twenty-first century approaches, the well-being of adolescents should be one of America's foremost concerns. The future of our youth is the future of our society. Adolescents who do not reach their full potential, who are destined to make fewer contributions to society than it needs, and who do not take their place as productive adults diminish our society's future.

> *If our American way of life fails the child, it fails us all.*
> —**Pearl Buck, The Child Who Never Grew**

At this point, we have discussed a number of ideas about the history of interest in adolescence and about today's adolescents. A summary of these ideas is presented in concept table 1.1. Next we will turn our attention to a number of issues that confront theorists and researchers as they study adolescent development.

THE NATURE OF DEVELOPMENT

Each of us develops in certain ways like all other individuals, like some other individuals, and like no other individuals. Most of the time, our attention focuses on our individual uniqueness, but researchers who study development are drawn to our shared as well as our unique characteristics. As humans, each of us travels some common paths. Each of us—Leonardo da Vinci, Joan of Arc, George Washington, Martin Luther King, Jr., you, and I—walked at about the age of 1, talked at about the age of 2, engaged in fantasy play as a young child, and became more independent as a youth.

What do we mean when we speak of an individual's development? **Development** *is the pattern of change that begins at conception and continues through the life span. Most development involves growth, although it also includes decay (as in death and dying).* The pattern of movement is complex because it is the product of several processes.

Processes and Periods

Adolescent development is determined by biological, cognitive, and socioemotional processes. Development also is often described in terms of periods.

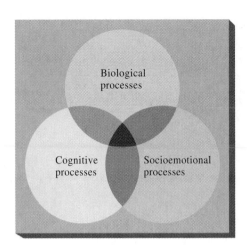

Figure~1.4

Biological, Cognitive, and Socioemotional Processes in Development.
Changes in development are the result of biological, cognitive, and social processes. These processes are interwoven in the development of an individual through the human life span.

Biological, Cognitive, and Socioemotional Processes

Biological processes *involve changes in an individual's physical nature.* Genes inherited from parents, the development of the brain, height and weight gains, motor skills, and the hormonal changes of puberty all reflect the role of biological processes in the adolescent's development. Biological processes and physical development in adolescence are discussed extensively in chapter 3.

Cognitive processes *involve changes in an individual's thought, intelligence, and language.* Memorizing a poem, solving a math problem, and imagining what it would be like to be a movie star all reflect the role of cognitive processes in the adolescent's development. Chapters 4 and 5 discuss cognitive processes in detail.

Socioemotional processes *involve changes in an individual's relationships with other people, in emotions, in personality, and in the role of social contexts in development.* Talking back to parents, an aggressive attack on a peer, the development of assertiveness, an adolescent's joy at the senior prom, and a society's gender-role orientation all reflect the role of socioemotional processes in the adolescent's development. Sections III and IV focus on socioemotional processes and adolescent development.

Biological, cognitive, and socioemotional processes are intricately interwoven. Socioemotional processes shape cognitive processes, cognitive processes advance or restrict socioemotional processes, and biological processes influence cognitive processes. Although the various processes involved in adolescent development are discussed in separate sections of the book, keep in mind that you are studying about the development of an integrated human being who has only one interdependent mind and body (see figure 1.4).

CONCEPT TABLE 1.1
Historical Perspective and Today's Adolescents

Concept	Processes/ Related Ideas	Characteristics/Description
The Best of Times and the Worst of Times for Today's Adolescents	Nature	The world of today's adolescents contains powers and perspectives that were inconceivable 50 years ago. The hazards of the adult world descend on youth early in today's world. Today's parents are raising adolescents in a different world from the one their parents reared them in. A special concern is that adolescents need access to a range of legitimate opportunities and long-term support from adults who deeply care about them.
Historical Perspective	Early history	Plato and Aristotle both proposed views about the nature of adolescence, but in the Middle Ages knowledge about adolescence moved a step backward: Children were seen as miniature adults, not adolescents. Rousseau described a more enlightened view of adolescence. In the eighteenth and most of the nineteenth century, work apprenticeships took up most of the adolescent male's life. Little has been written about adolescent females during this period.
	The twentieth century	Between 1890 and 1920, a cadre of psychologists, urban reformers, and others began to mold the concept of adolescence. G. Stanley Hall, known as the father of the scientific study of adolescence, proposed his storm-and-stress view in the early 1900s. Margaret Mead presented a sociocultural view of adolescence in sharp contrast to Hall's biological view. A number of scholars argue for an inventionist view of adolescence, believing that legislation ensured the dependency of adolescents and made their move into the economic sphere more manageable. Adolescents gained a more prominent status in society from 1920 to 1950. Stereotyping of adolescents of any era is common. Widespread generalizations about adolescents are often based on a limited group of highly visible adolescents—what Adelson called the "adolescent generalization gap."
Today's Adolescents	Current status	Most adolescents today successfully negotiate the path from childhood to adulthood. However, too many of today's adolescents are not provided with adequate opportunities and support. Adolescents are a heterogeneous group—different portraits of adolescents emerge depending on the particular set of adolescents being described. Americans society often has idealized images of what adolescents should be and transmits ambivalent messages to adolescents.
	The complexity of adolescent development and contexts	As researchers carefully examine adolescents' lives, they increasingly recognize the complexity of adolescent development. Because of this complexity, no single developmental model likely fits all adolescents. A special interest today focuses on the contexts of adolescent development, especially the sociocultural contexts of culture, ethnicity, and gender.
	Social policy and adolescents' development	Adolescents are the future of any society. Because too many of today's adolescents are not reaching their full potential, it is important to examine U.S. social policy toward adolescents. Generational inequity is an increasingly debated issue in social policy. Adolescents as an age group have been underserved by the government.

Periods of Development

Development is commonly described in terms of periods. We will consider developmental periods that occur in childhood, adolescence, and adulthood. Approximate age ranges are given for the periods to provide a general idea of when they begin and end.

Childhood. Childhood periods of development include the prenatal period, infancy, early childhood, and middle and late childhood.

The **prenatal period** *is the time from conception to birth*. It is a time of tremendous growth—from a single cell to an organism complete with brain and behavioral capabilities—in approximately 9 months.

Infancy *is the developmental period that extends from birth to 18 or 24 months of age*. Infancy is a time of extreme dependency on adults. Many psychological activities— for example, language, symbolic thought, sensorimotor coordination, social learning, and parent-child relationships—are just beginning.

Early childhood *is the developmental period that extends from the end of infancy to about 5 or 6 years of age; sometimes, the period is called the preschool years*. During this time, young children learn to become more self-sufficient and to care for themselves, develop school readiness (following instructions, identifying letters), and spend many hours in play and with peers. First grade typically marks the end of this period.

Middle and late childhood *is the developmental period that extends from about 6 to 11 years of age; sometimes, the period is called the elementary school years.* Children master the fundamental skills of reading, writing, and arithmetic, and they are formally exposed to the larger world and its culture. Achievement becomes a more central theme of the child's world, and self-control increases.

Adolescence. Our major interest in this book is in the development of adolescents. However, as our developmental timetable suggests, considerable development and experience have occurred before the individual reaches adolescence. No girl or boy enters adolescence as a blank slate with only a genetic blueprint determining thoughts, feelings, and behaviors. Rather, the combination of a genetic blueprint, childhood experiences, and adolescent experiences determines the course of adolescent development. Keep in mind this point about the continuity of development between childhood and adolescence. More about the issue of continuity and discontinuity in development appears shortly.

A definition of adolescence requires consideration of age and also sociohistorical influences. Remember our earlier discussion of the increased interest in the inventionist view of adolescence. With such limitations in mind, **adolescence** *is defined as the developmental period of transition between childhood and adulthood; it involves biological, cognitive, and socioemotional changes.* Although cultural and historical circumstances limit our ability to attribute an exact age range to adolescence, in America and most other cultures today, adolescence begins at approximately 10 to 13 years of age and ends between the ages of 18 and 22 for most individuals. The biological, cognitive, and socioemotional changes of adolescence range from the development of sexual functions to abstract thinking processes to independence.

Developmentalists increasingly describe adolescence in terms of early and late periods. **Early adolescence** *corresponds roughly to the middle school or junior high school years and includes most pubertal change.* **Late adolescence** *refers to approximately the latter half of the second decade of life. Career interests, dating, and identity exploration are often more pronounced in late adolescence than in early adolescence.* Researchers who study adolescents increasingly specify whether their results likely generalize to all adolescents or are more specific to early or late adolescence.

The old view of adolescence was that adolescence is a singular, uniform period of transition resulting in entry to the adult world. In contrast, current approaches in the study of adolescence often examine the precursors and outcomes of a variety of transitions, the constellation of events that define the transitional period, or the timing and sequence of events that take place within a transitional period (Graber, Brooks-Gunn & Peterson, 1996;

Lerner & others, 1996). For instance, puberty and school events are often investigated as key transitions signaling entry into adolescence; completing school or taking one's first full-time job are evaluated as transitional events that determine the exit from adolescence or the entry into adulthood.

Today, developmentalists do not believe that change ends with adolescence (Baltes, Lindenberger & Staudinger, 1997; Lerner, 1997; Santrock, 1997). Remember that development is defined as a lifelong process. Adolescence is part of the life course and, as such, is not an isolated period of development. While adolescence has some unique characteristics, what takes place in adolescence is interconnected with development and experiences in childhood and adulthood.

Adult Development. Do adolescents abruptly enter adulthood? Sociologist Kenneth Keniston (1970) thinks not. Faced with a complex world of work and with highly specialized tasks, many post-teenagers spend an extended period of time in technical institutes, colleges, and postgraduate schools to acquire specialized skills, educational experiences, and professional training. For many, this creates an extended period of economic and personal temporariness. Earnings are often low and sporadic, and established residences may change frequently. Marriage and a family may be shunned. **Youth** *is Keniston's term for the transitional period between adolescence and adulthood that is a time of economic and personal temporariness.* The transition often lasts for 2 to 8 years, although it is not unusual for it to last a decade or longer.

As singer Bob Dylan asked, how many roads do individuals have to go down before they are called adults? Like childhood, and like adolescence, adulthood is not a homogeneous period of development. Developmentalists often describe three periods of adult development: early adulthood, middle adulthood, and late adulthood. **Early adulthood** *usually begins in the late teens or early twenties and lasts through the thirties.* It is a time of establishing personal and economic independence. Career development becomes a more intensified theme than in adolescence. For many young adults, selecting a mate, learning to live with someone in an intimate way, and starting a family take up a great deal of time. The most widely recognized marker of entry into adulthood is the occasion when an individual first takes a more or less permanent, full-time job. This usually happens when individuals finish school—high school for some, college for others, postgraduate training for others (Graber & Brooks-Gunn, in press). However, criteria for determining when an individual has left adolescence and entered adulthood are not clear-cut. Economic independence may be considered a criterion of adulthood, but developing this independence is often a long, drawn-out process rather than an abrupt one. Increasingly, college graduates are returning to live with their parents as they attempt to get their feet on the ground economically. In one study, adolescents often cited taking responsibility for oneself and independent decision making as identifying the onset of adulthood (Scheer & Unger, 1994). And in another recent study, more than 70 percent of college students said that being an adult means accepting responsibility for the consequences of one's actions, deciding on one's own beliefs and values, and establishing a relationship with parents as an equal adult (Arnett, 1995).

In one recent study, individuals averaging 21 years of age said that they reached adult status at about 18 or 19 years of age (Scheer, 1996). In this study, both social status factors (such as financial status and graduation/education) and cognitive factors (such as being responsible and making independent decisions) were cited as involved in reaching adult status. Defining when adolescence ends and adulthood begins is more complex than citing a specific chronological age (Arnett, 1996).

It has been said that adolescence begins in biology and ends in culture. This means that the marker for entry into adolescence is determined by the onset of pubertal maturation and that the marker for entry into adulthood is determined by cultural standards and experiences. As we will discover in chapter 3, defining entry into puberty is not easy either. For boys, is it the first whisker or the first wet dream? For girls, is it the enlargement of breasts or the first period? For boys and girls, is it a spurt in height? We usually can tell when a boy or girl is in puberty, but its actual onset often goes unnoticed.

Our discussion of developmental periods in the human life span continues with a description of the nature of the middle adulthood. **Middle adulthood** *is the developmental period entered at approximately 35 to 45 years of age and exited at some point between approximately 55 and 65 years of age.* This period is especially important in the lives of adolescents because their parents either are about to enter this adult period or are already in it. Middle adulthood is a time of increasing interest in transmitting values to the next generation, enhanced concern about one's body, and increased reflection about the meaning of life. In chapter 6, we will study how the maturation of both adolescents and parents contributes to an understanding of parent-adolescent relationships.

Eventually, the rhythm and meaning of the human life span wend their way to **late adulthood,** *the developmental period that lasts from approximately 60 to 70 years of age until death.* It is a time of adjustment to decreasing strength and health, and to retirement and reduced income. Reviewing one's life and adapting to changing social roles also characterize late adulthood, as do lessened responsibility, increased freedom, and grandparenthood.

> *The first cry of a newborn in Chicago or Zamboango, in Amsterdam or Rangoon, has the same pitch and key, each saying, "I am! I have come through! I belong! I am a member of the human family."* . . . *babies arriving, suckling, growing into youths restless and questioning. Then as grown-ups they seek and hope. They mate, toil, fish, quarrel, sing, fight, pray.*
>
> —**Carl Sandburg, *The Family of Man,* 1955**

The periods of development from conception through adolescence are shown in figure 1.5, along with the processes of development—biological, cognitive, and socioemotional. The interplay of biological, cognitive, and socioemotional processes produces the periods of development.

Developmental Issues

A number of issues are raised in the study of adolescent development. The major issues include these: Is development due more to maturation (nature, heredity) or more to experience (nurture, environment)? Is development more continuous and smooth or more discontinuous and stagelike? Is development due more to early experience or more to later experience?

Maturation and Experience (Nature and Nurture)

We can think of development as produced not only by the interplay of biological, cognitive, and socioemotional processes but also by the interplay of maturation and experience (Zahn-Waxler & others, 1996). **Maturation** *is the orderly sequence of changes dictated by the genetic blueprint we each have.* Just as a sunflower grows in an orderly way—unless defeated by an unfriendly environment—so does a human being grow in an orderly way, according to the maturational view. The range of environments can be vast, but the maturational approach argues that the genetic blueprint produces commonalities in our growth and development. We walk before we talk, speak one word before two words, grow rapidly in infancy and less so in early childhood, experience a rush of sexual hormones in puberty after a lull in childhood, reach the peak of our physical strength in late adolescence and early adulthood and then decline, and so on. The maturationists acknowledge that extreme environments—those that are psychologically barren or hostile—can depress development, but they believe that basic growth tendencies are genetically wired into human beings.

By contrast, other psychologists emphasize the importance of experiences in child development. Experiences run the gamut from individual's biological environment (nutrition, medical care, drugs, and physical accidents) to their social environment (family, peers, schools, community, media, and culture).

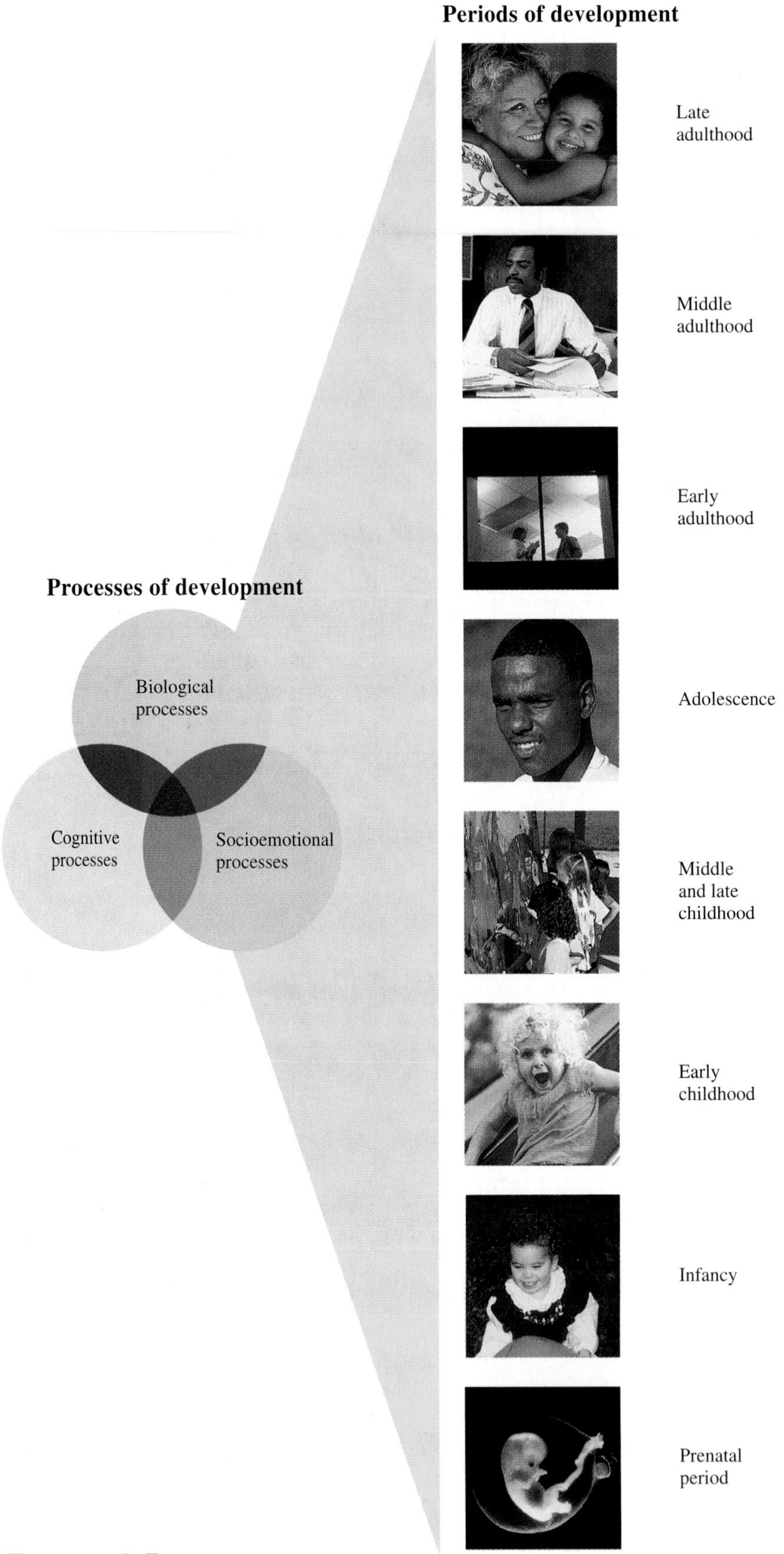

Periods of development

Late
adulthood

Middle
adulthood

Early
adulthood

Adolescence

Middle
and late
childhood

Early
childhood

Infancy

Prenatal
period

Processes of development

Biological
processes

Cognitive
processes

Socioemotional
processes

Figure~1.5

Processes and Periods of Life-Span Development.
The unfolding of the life span's periods of development is influenced by the interplay of biological, cognitive, and socioemotional processes.

The debate about whether development is primarily influenced by maturation or by experience has been a part of psychology since its beginning. This debate is often referred to as the **nature-nurture controversy.** Nature *refers to an organism's biological inheritance*, nurture *to environmental experiences. The "nature" proponents claim biological inheritance is the most important influence on development, the "nurture" proponents that environmental experiences are the most important.*

Ideas about development have been like a pendulum, swinging between nature and nurture. In the 1980s, we witnessed a surge of interest in the biological underpinnings of development, probably because the pendulum previously had swung too far in the direction of thinking that development was exclusively due to environmental experiences. As we entered the 1990s, a heightened interest in sociocultural influences on development emerged, again probably because the pendulum in the 1980s had swung so strongly toward the biological side.

Some adolescent development researchers believe that, historically, too much emphasis has been placed on the biological changes of puberty as determinants of adolescent psychological development (Montemayor & Flannery, 1990). They recognize that biological change is an important dimension of the transition from childhood to adolescence, one that is found in all primate species and in all cultures throughout the world. However, they believe that social contexts (nurture) play important roles in adolescent psychological development as well, roles that until recently have not been given adequate attention.

Continuity and Discontinuity

Think about your development for a moment. Was your growth into the person you are today a gradual growth, like the slow, cumulative

Santrock: Adolescence

growth of a seedling into a giant oak, or did you experience sudden, distinct changes in your growth, like the way a caterpillar changes into a butterfly (see figure 1.6)? For the most part, developmentalists who emphasize experience have described development as a gradual, continuous process; those who emphasize maturation have described development as a series of distinct stages.

Continuity of development *is gradual, cumulative change from conception to death.* A child's first word, while seemingly an abrupt, discontinuous event, is viewed from the continuity perspective as the result of weeks and months of growth and practice. Likewise, puberty, although seemingly an abrupt, discontinuous event, is viewed as a gradual process occurring over several years.

Discontinuity of development *is development through distinct stages in the life span.* According to the discontinuity perspective, each of us passes through a sequence of stages in which change is qualitatively, rather than quantitatively, different. As an oak moves from seedling to giant tree, it becomes *more* oak—its development is continuous. As a caterpillar changes into a butterfly, it does not become more caterpillar; it becomes a *different kind* of organism—its development is discontinuous. For example, at a certain point, a child moves from not being able to think abstractly about the world to being able to do so. At some point, an adult moves from being an individual capable of reproduction to being one who is not. These are qualitative, discontinuous changes in development, not quantitative, continuous changes.

Early and Later Experience

Another important developmental topic is the **early-later experience issue,** *which focuses on the degree to which early experiences (especially early in childhood) or later experiences are the key determinants of development.* That is, if infants or young children experience negative, stressful circumstances in their lives, can those experiences be overcome by later, more positive experiences in adolescence? Or are the early experiences so critical, possibly because they are the infant's first, prototypical experiences, that they cannot be overridden by a later, more enriched environment in childhood or adolescence?

The early-later experience issue has a long history and continues to be hotly debated among developmentalists. Some believe that unless infants experience warm, nurturant caregiving in the first year or so of life, their development will never be optimal (Bowlby, 1989; Sroufe, 1996). Plato was sure that infants who were rocked frequently became better athletes. Nineteenth-century New England ministers told parents in Sunday sermons that the way they handled their infants would determine their children's future character. The emphasis on the importance of early experience rests on the belief that each life is an unbroken trail on which a psychological quality can be traced back to its origin.

Figure~1.6

Continuity and Discontinuity in Development.
Is human development like a seedling gradually growing into a giant oak? Or is it more like a caterpillar suddenly becoming a butterfly?

The early-experience doctrine contrasts with the later-experience view that, rather than achieving statuelike permanence after change in infancy, our development continues to be like the ebb and flow of a river. The later-experience advocates argue that children and adolescents are malleable throughout development and that later sensitive caregiving is just as important as earlier sensitive caregiving. A number of life-span developmentalists, who focus on the entire life span rather than only on child development, stress that too little attention has been given to later experiences in development (Baltes, 1987). They accept that early experiences are important contributors to development, but no more important than later experiences. Jerome Kagan (1992) points out that even children who show the qualities of an inhibited temperament, which is linked to heredity, have the capacity to change their behavior. In his research, almost one-third of a group of children who had an inhibited temperament at 2 years of age were not unusually shy or fearful when they were 4 years of age (Kagan, Snidmar, & Arcus, 1995).

People in Western cultures, especially those steeped in the Freudian belief that the key experiences in development are children's relationships with their parents in the first 5 years of life, have tended to support the idea that early experiences are more important than later experiences (Chan, 1963). In contrast, the majority of people in the world do not share this belief. For example, people in many Asian countries believe that experiences occurring after about 6 to 7 years of age are more important aspects of development than earlier experiences are. This stance stems from the long-standing belief in Eastern cultures that children's reasoning skills begin to develop in important ways in the middle childhood years.

Evaluating the Developmental Issues

As we consider further these three salient developmental issues—nature and nurture, continuity and discontinuity, and early and later experience—it is important to realize that most developmentalists recognize that it is unwise to take an extreme position on these issues. Development is not all nature or all nurture, not all continuity or discontinuity, and not all early experience or all later experience. Nature and nurture, continuity and discontinuity, and early and later experience all affect our development through the human life span. For example, in considering the nature-nurture issue, the key to development is the *interaction* of nature and nurture rather than either factor alone (Loehlin, 1995). An individual's cognitive development, for instance, is the result of heredity-environment interaction, not heredity or environment alone. Much more about the role of heredity-environment interaction appears in chapter 3.

Consider also the behavior of adolescent males and females (Feldman & Elliott, 1990). Nature factors continue to influence differences between adolescent boys and girls in such areas as height, weight, and age at pubertal onset. On the average, girls are shorter and lighter than boys and enter puberty earlier. However, some previously well-established differences between adolescent females and males are diminishing, suggesting an important role for nurture. For example, adolescent females are pursuing careers in math and science in far greater numbers than in the past, and are seeking autonomy in a much stronger fashion. Unfortunately, adolescent females also are increasing their use of drugs and cigarette smoking compared to adolescent females in earlier eras. The shifting patterns of gender similarities and differences underscore the belief that simplistic explanations based only on biological or only on environmental causes are unwise.

Although most developmentalists do not take extreme positions on the developmental issues we have discussed, this consensus has not meant the absence of spirited debate about how strongly development is determined by these factors. Continuing with our example of the behavior of female and male adolescents, are girls less likely to do well in math because of their "feminine" nature or because of society's masculine bias? Consider also adolescents who, as children, experienced poverty, parental neglect, and poor schooling. Could enriched experiences in adolescence overcome the "deficits" they encountered earlier in development? The answers developmentalists give to such questions reflect their stance on the issues of nature and nurture, continuity and discontinuity, and early and later experiences. The answers also influence public policy about adolescents and how each of us lives through the human life span.

CAREERS IN ADOLESCENT DEVELOPMENT

A career in adolescent development is one of the most rewarding vocational opportunities you can pursue. By choosing a career in adolescent development, you will be able to help adolescents reach their potential as productive contributors to society and develop into physically, cognitively, and socially mature individuals. Adults who work professionally with adolescents often feel a sense of pride in their ability to contribute in meaningful ways to the next generation of human beings.

If you decide to pursue a career related to adolescent development, a number of options are available to you. College and university professors teach courses in adolescent development, education, family development, and nursing; counselors, clinical psychologists, pediatricians, psychiatrists, school psychologists, and psychiatric nurses see adolescents with problems and disorders or illnesses; teachers instruct adolescents in secondary schools. In pursuing a career related to development, you can expand your opportunities (and income) considerably by obtaining a graduate degree, although an advanced degree is not absolutely necessary.

Most college professors in development and its related areas of psychology, education, home economics, nursing, and social work have a master's degree and/or doctorate degree that required 2 to 5 years of academic work beyond their undergraduate degree. Becoming a clinical psychologist or counseling psychologist requires 4 to 6 years of graduate work to obtain the necessary Ph.D.; this includes both clinical and research training. School and career counselors pursue a master's or doctorate degree in counseling, often in graduate programs in education departments; these degrees require 2 to 6 years to complete. Becoming a psychiatrist requires 4 years of medical school, plus an internship and a residency in psychiatry; this career path takes 7 to 9 years beyond a bachelor's degree. School psychologists obtain either a master's degree (approximately 2 years) or a D.Ed. degree (approximately 4 to 5 years) in school psychology. School psychologists counsel adolescents and their parents when adolescents have problems in school, often giving psychological tests to assess their personality and intelligence. Psychiatric nursing positions can also be attained with an undergraduate R.N. degree; M.A. and Ph.D. degrees in nursing, which require 2 and 4 to 5 years of graduate training, respectively, are also available.

The field of education plays an especially important role in adolescent development. Departments of education train individuals to teach adolescents in middle and secondary schools and to become school psychologists and guidance counselors. Schools of education also train individuals to become school administrators, college professors, and researchers.

To read further about jobs and careers that involve working with adolescents, turn to table 1.3. The list presented there is not exhaustive but rather is meant to give you an idea of the many opportunities to pursue a rewarding career in adolescent development and its related fields.

CRITICAL THINKING ABOUT ADOLESCENT DEVELOPMENT

What does it mean to think critically about adolescent development? Each of us uses various forms of critical thinking. However, when we learn a new discipline, like adolescent development, we have an opportunity to refine the critical-thinking skills that the discipline emphasizes.

How should your critical-thinking skills change as a result of reading this book and taking this course on adolescent development? You should have more effective critical-thinking skills in ten areas that involve development (see figure 1.7).

As you read this text, you will often be asked to think critically about development. Several times in each chapter you will read boxes called "Critical Thinking About Adolescence." In this chapter, you have already been asked to imagine what your development as an adolescent might have been like if you had grown up in a different culture, which encourages you to engage in perspective taking and identify the sociohistorical and cultural factors that influence adolescent development. And you have been asked to ask yourself questions about your own development as an adolescent, which helps you apply a developmental framework to understanding behavior. In addition to the critical-thinking boxes, you will encounter many other opportunities in the text to enhance your ability to think like a developmentalist and to improve your grasp of the concepts and principles you are learning.

At this point, we have discussed a number of ideas about the nature of development, careers in adolescent development, and critical thinking about adolescent development. A summary of these ideas is presented in concept table 1.2.

TABLE 1.3

Jobs and Careers in Adolescent Development and Related Fields

Jobs/Careers	Degree	Education Required	Nature of Training	Description of Work
Clinical psychologist or counseling psychologist	Ph.D.	5–7 years postundergraduate	Both clinical and research training, including a 1-year internship in a psychiatric hospital or mental health facility	These psychologists diagnose adolescent problems and disorders, administer psychological tests, and conduct psychotherapy sessions. Some work at colleges and universities, where they do some combination of teaching, therapy, and research.
Psychiatrist	M.D.	7–9 years postundergraduate	Four years of medical school plus an internship and residency in psychiatry	Their role is similar to that of clinical psychologists, but psychiatrists can conduct biomedical therapy, such as using drugs to treat adolescent problems. Clinical psychologists cannot prescribe drugs in their attempt to help adolescents.
College/university professor in developmental psychology, education, family processes, clinical or counseling psychology	Ph.D. or M.A.	4–6 years postundergraduate for Ph.D (or D.Ed.); 2 years postundergraduate for M.A.	Take graduate courses, learn how to conduct research, attend and present papers at professional meetings	Professors teach courses in developmental psychology, family development, education, or nursing; conduct research; present papers at professional meetings; write and publish articles and books; and train undergraduates and graduates in these fields.
Middle school and secondary school teacher	Undergraduate degree (minimum)	4 years	A wide range of courses, with a major or concentration in education	These teachers teach one or more subjects; prepare the curriculum; give tests, assign grades, and monitor students' progress; interact with parents and school administrators; attend lectures and workshops involving curriculum planning or help with a special issue; and direct extracurricular programs.
Guidance counselor	Most have M.A.	4 years undergraduate, 2 years of graduate school	Coursework in education and counseling in a school of education; counselor training	Most guidance counselors work with secondary school students, assisting them in educational and career planning. They often give students aptitude tests and evaluate their interests and abilities. They also see students who are having school-related problems, including emotional problems. The counselors refer students to other professionals, such as school psychologists or clinical psychologists, when necessary.
Psychiatric nurse	R.N.	2–5 years	Courses in biological sciences, nursing care; supervised clinical training in psychiatric settings	Psychiatric nurses promote individual's mental health. Some specialize in helping adolescents with mental health problems and work closely with psychiatrists to improve the adolescents' adjustment.
School psychologist	M.A. or Ph.D.	4–6 years of graduate work for Ph.D.; 2 years for M.A.	Includes coursework and supervised training in school settings, usually in a department of educational psychology	School psychologists evaluate and treat a wide range of normal and exceptional adolescents who have school-related problems; work in a school system and see adolescents from a number of schools; administer tests; interview and observe adolescents, and consult with teachers, parents, and school administrators; and design programs to reduce the adolescent's problem behavior.

Apply a Developmental Framework to Understand Behavior

Make Accurate Observations, Descriptions, and Inferences about Adolescent Development

Identify the Sociohistorical, Cultural Contexts that Influence Adolescent Development

Apply Developmental Concepts to Enhance Personal Adaptation

Pursue Alternative Explanations to Understand Adolescent Development Comprehensively

Evaluate the Quality of Conclusions and Strategies Related to Adolescent Development

Engage in Perspective Taking to Better Understand Adolescent Development

Use Knowledge about Adolescent Development to Improve Human Welfare

Demonstrate an Appreciation of Individual Differences in Adolescent Development

Create Arguments Based on Developmental Concepts

Figure~1.7

Critical Thinking About Adolescent Development.

CONCEPT TABLE 1.2

The Nature of Adolescent Development, Developmental Issues, Career Development, and Critical Thinking About Adolescent Development

Concept	Processes/ Related Ideas	Characteristics/Description
The Nature of Development	What is development?	Development is the pattern of movement or change that occurs throughout the life span.
	Biological, cognitive, and socioemotional processes	Development is influenced by an interplay of biological, cognitive, and socioemotional processes.
	Periods of development	Development commonly is divided into the following periods: prenatal, infancy, early childhood, middle and late childhood, adolescence, early adulthood, middle adulthood, and late adulthood. Adolescence is the developmental period of transition between childhood and adulthood; it involves biological, cognitive, and socioemotional changes. In most cultures, adolescence begins at about 10 to 13 years of age and ends at about 18 to 22 years of age. Developmentalists increasingly distinguish between early and late adolescence. *Youth* is Kenniston's term for the transitional period between adolescence and adulthood that is a time of economic and personal temporariness. This period can last 2 to 8 years or longer.
Developmental Issues	Maturation and experience (nature and nurture)	The debate over whether development is due primarily to maturation or to experience is another version of the nature-nurture controversy.
	Continuity and discontinuity	Some developmentalists describe development as continuous (gradual, cumulative change), others describe it as discontinuous (abrupt; sequence of stages).
	Early and later experience	This hotly debated issue focuses on whether early experiences (especially in infancy) are more important in development than later experiences are.
	Evaluating the developmental issues	Most developmentalists recognize that extreme positions on the nature-nurture, continuity-discontinuity, and early/later-experience issues are unwise. Despite this consensus, spirited debate still occurs on these issues.
Careers in Adolescent Development	Their nature	A wide range of opportunities are available to individuals who want to pursue a career related to adolescent development. These opportunities include jobs in college and university teaching, clinical psychology and counseling, schoolteaching and school psychology nursing, and psychiatry.
Critical Thinking About Adolescent Development	Its nature	Critical thinking about adolescent development involves such strategies as applying a developmental framework to understand behavior, making accurate observations and inferences, identifying contextual factors, applying developmental concepts to enhance personal adaptation, pursuing alternative explanations, evaluating the quality of conclusions and strategies, engaging in perspective taking, using knowledge to improve human welfare, demonstrating appreciation of individual differences, and developing arguments based on a developmental framework.

SUMMARY

Adolescents have a special place in any society, for they are the society's future. An important concern is that too many adolescents today will not reach their full potential because they have inadequate support. Far too many adolescents live in poverty, have parents who do not adequately care for them, and go to schools where learning conditions are far from optimal.

We looked at adolescence through a historical lens, studying its early his-tory, important developments in the twentieth century—especially the period 1890–1920—and the stereotyping of adolescents. Our coverage of today's adolescents focused on their current status, complexity and socio-cultural contexts, and social policy. We also evaluated the nature of development, exploring processes (biological, cognitive, and socioemotional) and periods, as well as some important developmental issues (nature/nurture, continuity/discontinuity, and early/later experience). We also read about careers in adolescent development and critical thinking about adolescent development.

Don't forget that you can obtain an overall summary of the chapter by again studying the two concept tables on pages 23 and 32. In the next chapter, we will turn our attention to the field of adolescence as a science.

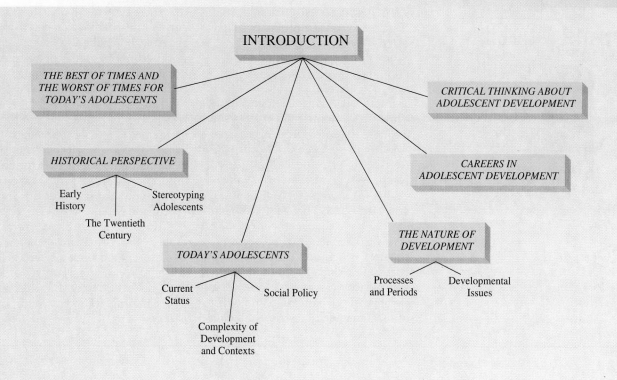

INTRODUCTION

THE BEST OF TIMES AND THE WORST OF TIMES FOR TODAY'S ADOLESCENTS

CRITICAL THINKING ABOUT ADOLESCENT DEVELOPMENT

HISTORICAL PERSPECTIVE

Early History
Stereotyping Adolescents
The Twentieth Century

CAREERS IN ADOLESCENT DEVELOPMENT

TODAY'S ADOLESCENTS

Current Status
Social Policy
Complexity of Development and Contexts

THE NATURE OF DEVELOPMENT

Processes and Periods
Developmental Issues

KEY TERMS

PRACTICAL KNOWLEDGE ABOUT ADOLESCENCE

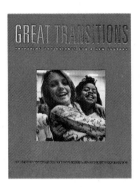

Great Transitions
(1995) by the Carnegie Council on Adolescent Development. New York: Carnegie Corporation.

This recent report by the Carnegie Council on Adolescent Development covers a wide range of topics. Part I focuses on transitions, with a special emphasis on early adolescence. A number of discussions evaluate ways to reduce adolescent risk and enhance opportunities. Part II emphasizes preparing adolescents for the new century. The topics discussed in this section include: reengaging families with their adolescents, educating adolescents for a changing world, promoting adolescent health, strengthening communities with adolescents, and redirecting the pervasive power of the media. This is an excellent resource book for improving the lives of adolescents.

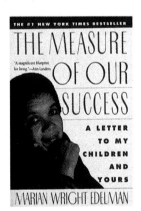

The Measure of Our Success: A Letter to My Children and Yours
(1992) by Marian Wright Edelman. Boston: Beacon Press.

Marian Wright Edelman founded the Children's Defense Fund in 1973 and for more than two decades has been working to advance the health and well-being of America's children, youth, and parents. This slim volume begins with a message to her oldest son, Joshua, 22. There and throughout the book, Edelman conveys the message that parenting and nurturing the next generation is the most important function of a society and that we need to take it more seriously than we have in the past. High on her list of recommended views is the belief that there is no free lunch; don't feel entitled to anything you don't sweat and struggle for. She also warns against working only for money or for power, because they won't save your soul, build a decent family, or help you sleep at night. She also tells her sons, "Remember that your wife is not your mother or your maid." Edelman also admonishes our society for not developing better safety nets for children and youth and not being the caring community that children, youth, and parents need.

Edelman's book stimulates thought about what kind of nation we want to be, what kinds of values mean the most to us, and what we can do to improve the health and well-being of our nation's children, youth, and parents.

You and Your Adolescent

(1990) by Laurence Steinberg and Ann Levine. New York: Harper Perennial.

You and Your Adolescent provides a broad, developmental overview of adolescence, with parental advice mixed in along the way. Author Laurence Steinberg is a professor of psychology at Temple University and a leading researcher in adolescent development.

The book is divided into the preteens (ages 10–13), the teens (ages 14–17), and toward adulthood (ages 18–20).

In Steinberg and Levine's approach, knowing how adolescents develop keeps parents from making a lot of mistakes. This is an excellent book for parents of adolescents. It serves the dual purpose of educating parents about how adolescents develop and giving them valuable parenting strategies for coping with teenagers.

RESOURCES FOR IMPROVING THE LIVES OF ADOLESCENTS

In this first chapter, we list some important agencies and foundations that actively promote improved health and well-being for adolescents. They have a number of books, brochures, working papers, newsletters, and so forth that provide up-to-date information about working and interacting with adolescents more effectively. Contact them to find out what materials on adolescence they have available. In appropriate chapters we will list some specific materials from each of these groups.

Boys Town
Father Flanagan's Boys' Home
Boys Town, NE 68010
800-448-3000

Boys Town has been a resource for abused and neglected boys and girls since 1917. Information about residential homes, hospital care, shelters, family crisis intervention, alternative education, foster care services, and parenting training is available. The hotline number listed above is available free to any parent or adolescent in the United States. Adolescents and parents can call with any problem or serious concern, including physical and sexual abuse, drug abuse, parenting problems, suicide, running away, and school problems. The hotline is staffed by highly trained professionals and includes Spanish-speaking operators. The hotline has a computer database of 50,000 local agencies and services around the country.

Canadian Coalition for the Rights of Children/
Coalition Canadienne Pour les Droits des Enfants
180 Argyle Street, Suite 339
Ottawa, Ontario K2P 1B7
613-788-5085

The Coalition emphasizes the rights of children and youth as outlined by the UN convention on children's rights.

Carnegie Council on Adolescent Development
2400 N Street NW
Washington, DC 20037
202-429-7979

The Carnegie Council on Adolescent Development, headed by David Hamburg, is an operating program of the Carnegie Foundation of New York. Its goal is to improve the health and well-being of adolescents. The council has generated a number of task forces to improve education, reduce adolescent pregnancy, and reduce alcohol and drug use among adolescents.

Children's Defense Fund
25 E Street NW
Washington, DC 20001
202-628-8787

The Children's Defense Fund, headed by Marian Wright Edelman, exists to provide a strong and effective voice for children and adolescents who cannot vote, lobby, or speak for themselves. The Children's Defense Fund is especially interested in the needs of poor, minority, and handicapped children and adolescents. The fund provides information, technical assistance, and support to a network of state and local child and youth advocates.

National Directory of Children and Youth Services (1985)
American Association for Protecting Children
Longmont, CO: Bookmakers Guild
600 pages

This is a comprehensive guide to agencies that deliver services to children and youth. The main section, arranged by state and then by country, provides the names, addresses, phone numbers, and managers of all locatable social services, health and mental health services, and juvenile court/youth agencies in the United States.

National Resource Center for Youth Services
University of Oklahoma College of Continuing Education
202 West 8th Street
Tulsa, OK 74119-1419
918-585-2986

This resource center has available a number of videotapes and publications on adolescents. They also have an annual training conference on working with America's youth that is sponsored by the National Network for youth.

Search Institute
Thresher Square West
700 South Third Street, Suite 210
Minneapolis, MN 55415
612-376-8955

The Search Institute has available a large number of resources for improving the lives of adolescents. In 1995, the Institute began distributing the excellent publications of the Center for Early Adolescence, University of North Carolina, which had just closed. The brochures and books available address school improvement, adolescent literacy, parent education, program planning, and adolescent health, and include resource lists. A free quarterly newsletter is available.

EXPLORING ADOLESCENT DEVELOPMENT

To fully understand the field of adolescent development today, it is important to explore both its research side and its applied side. Thus, each chapter concludes with a section entitled "Exploring Adolescent Development," which has two parts: first, a discussion of some aspect of research on adolescent development, and second, a description of issues and programs involving adolescent health and well-being. The research discussion provides you with an opportunity to see how the scientists who study adolescent development actually conduct research studies. The applied discussion on health and well-being will give you a sense of how professionals who work with adolescents seek solutions to improving the adolescent transition to adulthood.

RESEARCH ON ADOLESCENT DEVELOPMENT

Why Research on Adolescence Is Important

Knowledge in the field of adolescence rests heavily on the development of a broad, competent research base. When I wrote the first edition of *Adolescence* in the late 1970s, only a handful of scholars were studying adolescent development; researchers were studying adults or children, but rarely adolescents. Over the last two decades, and especially the last decade, the research base on adolescence has grown enormously as an increasing number of investigators have become intrigued by issues and questions that involve the developmental period between childhood and adulthood. The growth of research on adolescent development is reflected in the presence of a number of new research journals and the creation of the Society for Research on Adolescence, which consists of an increasing number of scholars from different disciplines devoted to advancing the state of our knowledge about adolescence.

Why were researchers so neglectful of adolescence until recently? For most of the twentieth century, experiences in childhood, especially the early childhood years, were thought to be so critical that later experiences, such as those occurring in adolescence, were believed to have little impact on development. But by the beginning of the 1980s, developmentalists were seriously challenging the early-childhood doctrine, concluding that later experiences were far more important in development than had been commonly believed (Brim & Kagan, 1980). The increase in research interest in adolescence also has resulted from observations that tremendous changes take place between childhood and adulthood (Dornbusch, Petersen, & Hetherington, 1991). Yet another reason for the increase in research involves the recognition that far too many youth today are at risk for not reaching their full potential.

In discussing adolescent development and social policy issues earlier in the chapter, we said that a current trend is an increase in research relevant to social policy. The question of whether adolescent development researchers should conduct research that is relevant to social policy touches on a long-standing issue: Should research be basic or applied? *Basic research*, sometimes called pure research, is the study of issues to obtain knowledge for its own sake rather than for practical applications. Basic research is often conducted to test a theory or to follow up on other research. Rarely is basic research a response to a pressing social problem.

Basic research might or might not eventually be applied to social policy or practical problems. By contrast, *applied research* is the study of issues that have direct practical significance, often with the intent of changing behavior. Thus, social policy research is applied research, not basic research.

A developmentalist who conducts basic research might ask: How does cognitive development change during adolescence? By contrast, a developmentalist who conducts applied research might ask: How can knowledge about changes in adolescent cognitive development be used to educate adolescents more effectively or to help them cope with stress?

Most developmentalists believe that both basic and applied research are important. Although basic research can sometimes produce information that can be applied to improve the well-being of adolescents, it does not guarantee this application. Insisting that research always be relevant is like trying to grow flowers by dealing only with the blossoms and not tending to the roots. Basic research is root research. Without the discovery of basic scientific principles, we would have little knowledge to apply. Today, research on adolescent development includes a wealth of both basic and applied studies.

Improving the Imbalance Between Risk and Opportunity

As we mentioned at the beginning of this chapter, today's world holds experiences for adolescents unlike those encountered by their parents and grandparents. Today's adolescents face greater risks to their health than ever before. Drug and alcohol abuse, depression, violence, pregnancy, sexually transmitted diseases, and school-related problems place far too many of today's adolescents at risk for not reaching their full potential. Estimates suggest that as many as one-fourth of American adolescents are in the high-risk category (Dryfoos, 1995).

Adolescent expert Ruby Takanishi (1993) recently described the importance of improving the opportunity side of the adolescent risk-opportunity equation. Increased clinical and research knowledge suggests a viable approach away from remediation of single problems, such as drug abuse or delinquency or adolescent pregnancy, to the promotion of adolescent health or a cluster of health-enhancing behaviors (Millstein, Petersen, & Nightingale, 1993). This approach recognizes that targeting only one problem behavior, such as drug abuse, may overlook its link to other problems, such as school failure or delinquency.

Because the adolescent interventions of the past have been so targeted, we are only beginning to unravel the clues to the multiple adolescent problems of many at-risk youth. For example, does improving peer resistance skills to combat smoking or other drug abuse also reduce at-risk sexual behavior in adolescents?

A special concern is that just providing information and teaching skills

Ruby Takanishi (right) has worked diligently to improve the adolescent risk-opportunity equation.

to adolescents is not sufficient to improve their health and well-being. Like people at other points in the human life span, adolescents have to be motivated to use information, skills, and services.

Networks of support from families, peers, and caring adults are crucial for improving the lives of at-risk youth. And social policymakers need to target improved economic opportunities for youth and their families.

Each of us who comes in contact with adolescents—as adults, parents, youth workers, professionals, and educators—can help to make a difference in improving their health and well-being. I hope this book and this course improve your knowledge of adolescent development and motivate you to contribute to the health and well-being of today's adolescents.

Georges Seurat
Invitation to the Sideshow, Detail

Chapter

2

The Science of Adolescent Development

ruth is arrived at by the painstaking process of eliminating the untrue.

—Arthur Conan Doyle,
Sherlock Holmes

Chapter Boxes

> *There is nothing quite so practical as a good theory.*
>
> —Kurt Lewin,
> psychologist, 1890–1947

IMAGES OF ADOLESCENCE

The Youths of Erikson and Piaget

PREVIEW

*S*ome individuals have difficulty thinking of adolescent development as being a science in the same way that physics, chemistry, and biology are sciences. Can a discipline that studies pubertal change, parent-adolescent relationships, peer interaction, and adolescent thinking be equated with disciplines that investigate how gravity works and the molecular structure of a compound? Science is defined not by *what* it investigates but by *how* it investigates. Whether you are studying photosynthesis, butterflies, Saturn's moons, or human development, it is the *way* you study that makes the approach scientific or not.

In this chapter, we still study three key ingredients of adolescent development as a science—the scientific method, theories, and methods. You also will learn about some research challenges.

Imagine that you have developed a major theory of adolescent development. What would influence you to construct this theory? A person interested in developing such a theory usually goes through a long university training program that culminates in a doctoral degree. As part of the training, the future theorist is exposed to many ideas about a particular area of development, such as biological, cognitive, or socioemotional development. Another factor that could influence you to develop a particular theory is your life experiences. Two important developmental theorists, whose views are described later in this chapter, are Erik Erikson and Jean Piaget. Let's examine a portion of their lives as they were growing up to discover how their experiences might have contributed to the theories they developed.

Erik Homberger Erikson (1902–1994) was born near Frankfurt, Germany, to Danish parents. Before Erik was born, his parents separated, and his mother left Denmark to live in Germany. At age 3, Erik became ill, and his mother took him to see a pediatrician named Homberger. Young Erik's mother fell in love with the pediatrician, married him, and named Erik after his new stepfather.

Erik attended primary school from the ages of 6 to 10 and then the *gymnasium* (high school) from ages 11 to 18. He studied art and a number of languages rather than science courses, such as biology and chemistry. Erik did not like formal schooling, and this was reflected in his grades. Rather than go to college, at age 18 the adolescent Erikson wandered around Europe, keeping a diary of his experiences. After a year of travel through Europe, he returned to Germany and enrolled in an art school, became dissatisfied, and enrolled in another. Later, he traveled to Florence, Italy. Psychiatrist Robert Coles (1970) described Erikson at this time:

> To the Italians he was not an unfamiliar sight: the young, tall, thin Nordic expatriate with long, blond hair. He wore a corduroy suit and was seen by his family and friends as not odd or "sick" but as a wandering artist who was trying to

come to grips with himself, a not unnatural or unusual struggle. (p. 15)

Jean Piaget (1896–1980) was born in Neuchâtel, Switzerland. Jean's father was an intellectual who taught young Jean to think systematically. Jean's mother was also very bright. His father had an air of detachment from his mother, whom Piaget described as prone to frequent neurotic outbursts.

In his autobiography, Piaget (1952) detailed why he chose to study cognitive development rather than socioemotional or abnormal development:

> I started to forego playing for serious work very early. Indeed, I have always detested any departure from reality, an attitude which I relate to my mother's poor mental health. It was this disturbing factor which at the beginning of my studies in psychology made me keenly interested in psychoanalytic and pathological psychology. Though this interest helped me to achieve independence and to widen my cultural background, I have never since felt any desire to involve myself deeper in that particular direction, always much preferring the study of normalcy and the workings of the intellect to that of the tricks of the unconscious. (p. 238)

At the age of 22, Piaget went to work in the psychology laboratory at the University of Zurich. There he was exposed to the insights of Alfred Binet, who developed the first intelligence test. By the time Piaget was 25, his experience in varied disciplines had helped him to see important links between philosophy, psychology, and biology.

These excerpts from Erikson's and Piaget's lives illustrate how personal experiences might influence a theorist's direction. Erikson's wanderings and search for self contributed to his theory of identity development, and Piaget's intellectual experiences with his parents and schooling contributed to his emphasis on cognitive development.

THEORY AND THE SCIENTIFIC METHOD

According to nineteenth-century French mathematician Henri Poincaré, "Science is built of facts the way a house is built of bricks, but an accumulation of facts is no more science than a pile of bricks is a house." Science *does* depend on the raw material of facts or data, but, as Poincaré indicated, theories of adolescent development are more than just facts. A **theory** *is a coherent set of ideas that help explain data and make predictions.* A theory contains **hypotheses,** *assumptions that can be tested to determine their accuracy.* For example, a theory about adolescent depression explains observations of depressed adolescents and predicts why adolescents get depressed. A theorist might predict that adolescents get depressed because they fail to focus on their strengths and dwell extensively on their weaknesses. This prediction directs observations by telling the theorist to look for exaggerations of weaknesses and underestimations of strengths and skills.

The **scientific method** *is an approach that can be used to discover accurate information about behavior and development that includes the following steps: identify and analyze the problem, collect data, draw conclusions, and revise theories.* For example, suppose researchers decide that they want to help adolescents overcome their depression. They have *identified a problem*, which does not seem to be a difficult task. But as part of this first step, they need to go beyond a general description of the problem by isolating, analyzing, narrowing, and focusing on what they hope to study. What specific strategies do they want to use to reduce adolescents' depression? What aspect of depression do they want to study—its biological, cognitive, or socioemotional components, or some combination of these? Peter Lewinsohn and his colleagues (1990, 1994) believe that the cognitive and behavioral aspects of depression can be improved through a course on coping with depression. One of the course's components involves teaching adolescents or adults to control their negative thoughts. In this first step in the scientific method, the researchers identified and analyzed a problem.

The next step in the scientific method involves *collecting information (data)*. Psychologists observe behavior and draw inferences about thoughts and emotions. For example, in the study of adolescent depression they might observe how effectively adolescents who complete the course on coping with depression monitor their moods and engage in an active lifestyle.

Once psychologists collect data, they use *statistical (mathematical) procedures* to understand the meaning of quantitative data. Psychologists then *draw conclusions*. In the study of adolescent depression, statistics helped the researchers determine whether their observations were due to chance. After psychologists analyze data, they compare their findings with what others have discovered about the same issue or problem.

The final step in the scientific method is *revising theory*. Psychologists have developed a number of theories about why adolescents become depressed and how they can cope with depression (Petersen & others, 1993). Data such as those collected by Lewinsohn and his colleagues force us to evaluate existing theories of depression to determine their accuracy. Over the years, some theories of adolescent development have been discarded and others have been revised. Theories are an integral part of understanding the nature of adolescent development. They will be woven through our discussion of adolescent development in the remainder of the book.

THEORIES OF ADOLESCENT DEVELOPMENT

We will briefly explore four major kinds of theories of adolescent development: psychoanalytic, cognitive, behavioral and social learning, and ecological. The diversity of theories makes understanding adolescent development a challenging undertaking. Just when one theory appears to correctly explain adolescent development, another theory crops up and makes you rethink your earlier conclusion. Remember that adolescent development is complex and multifaceted. Although no single theory has been able to account for all aspects of adolescent development, each theory has contributed an important piece to the puzzle. Although the theories sometimes disagree about certain aspects of adolescent development, much of their information is *complementary* rather than contradictory. Together, the various theories let us see the total landscape of adolescent development in all its richness.

Psychoanalytic Theories

For psychoanalytic theorists, development is primarily unconscious—that is, beyond awareness—and is heavily colored by emotion. Psychoanalytic theorists believe that behavior is merely a surface characteristic. To truly understand development we have to analyze the symbolic meanings of behavior and the deep inner workings of the mind. Psychoanalytic theorists also stress that early experiences with parents extensively shape our development. These characteristics are highlighted in the main psychoanalytic theory, that of Sigmund Freud.

The passions are at once tempters and chastisers. As tempters, they come with garlands of flowers on the brows of youth; as chastisers, they appear with wreaths of snakes on the forehead of deformity. They are angels of light in their delusion; they are fiends of torment in their inflictions.

—**Henry Giles**

Freud's Theory

Freud (1856–1939) developed his ideas about psychoanalytic theory from work with mental patients. A medical doctor who specialized in neurology, he spent most of his years in Vienna, though he moved to London near the end of his career because of the Nazis' anti-Semitism.

Personality Structure. Freud (1917) believed that personality has three structures: the id, the ego, and the superego. The **id** *is the Freudian structure of personality that consists of instincts, which are an individual's reservoir of psychic energy.* In Freud's view, the id is totally unconscious; it has no contact with reality. As children experience the demands and constraints of reality, a new structure of personality emerges—the **ego,** *the Freudian structure of personality that deals with the demands of reality.* The ego is called the "executive branch" of personality because it makes rational decisions. The id and the ego have no morality—they do not take into account whether something is right or wrong. The **superego** *is the Freudian structure of personality that is the moral branch of personality. The superego takes into account whether something is right or wrong.* Think of the superego as what we often refer to as our "conscience." You probably are beginning to sense that both the id and the superego make life rough for the ego. Your ego might say, "I will have sex only occasionally and be sure to take the proper precautions because I don't want a child to interfere with the development of my career." However, your id is saying, "I want to be satisfied; sex is pleasurable." Your superego is at work too: "I feel guilty about having sex."

Remember that Freud considered personality to be like an iceberg. Most of personality exists below our level of awareness, just as the massive part of an iceberg is beneath the surface of the water. Figure 2.1 illustrates this analogy.

Freud believed that adolescents' lives are filled with tension and conflict. To reduce this tension, adolescents keep information locked in their unconscious mind, said Freud. He believed that even trivial behaviors have special significance when the unconscious forces behind them are revealed. A twitch, a doodle, a joke, a smile—each might have an unconscious reason for appearing, according to Freud. For example, 17-year-old Barbara is kissing and hugging Tom. She says, "Oh, *Jeff,* I love you so much." Tom pushes her away and says, "Why did you call me Jeff? I thought you didn't think about him anymore. We need to have a talk!" You probably can remember times when these *Freudian slips* came out in your own behavior.

Defense Mechanisms. The ego resolves conflict between its demands for reality, the wishes of the id, and the constraints of the superego by using **defense mechanisms.** *They are unconscious methods the ego uses to distort reality*

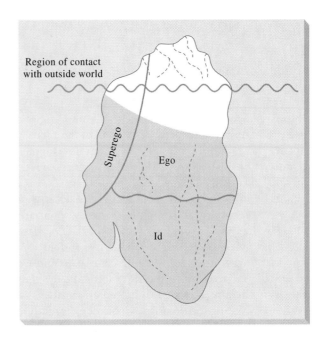

Figure~2.1

Conscious and Unconscious Processes: The Iceberg Analogy. This rather odd-looking diagram illustrates Freud's belief that most of the important personality processes occur below the level of conscious awareness. In examining people's conscious thoughts and their behaviors, we can see some reflections of the ego and the superego. Whereas the ego and superego are partly conscious and partly unconscious, the primitive id is located in the unconscious, totally submerged part of the iceberg.

and protect itself from anxiety. In Freud's view, the conflicting demands of the personality structures produce anxiety. For example, when the ego blocks the id's pleasurable pursuits, we feel anxiety. This diffuse, distressed state develops when the ego senses that the id is going to cause harm to the individual. The anxiety alerts the ego to resolve the conflict by means of defense mechanisms.

Repression *is the most powerful and pervasive defense mechanism, according to Freud. It pushes unacceptable id impulses out of awareness and back into the unconscious mind.* Repression is the foundation from which all other defense mechanisms work; the goal of every defense mechanism is to *repress,* or push, threatening impulses out of awareness. Freud said that our early childhood experiences, many of which he believed are sexually laden, are too threatening and stressful for us to deal with consciously, and that we reduce the anxiety of this conflict through repression.

*They cannot scare me with their empty spaces
Between stars—on stars where no human race is.
I have it in me so much nearer home
To scare myself with my own desert places.*

—Robert Frost

Freud and Schwarzenegger

If Sigmund Freud were alive today, what reactions do you think he might have to the level of violence and sexuality in contemporary action films? Conversely, how do you think Schwarzenegger might have fared in Freud's Victorian Viennese culture? Consideration of these questions sensitizes you to the importance of *identifying the sociohistorical and cultural factors that influence behavior*.

Arnold Schwarzenegger

Victorian Vienna

Sigmund Freud

Both Peter Blos (1989), a British psychoanalyst, and Anna Freud (1966), Sigmund Freud's daughter, believe that defense mechanisms provide considerable insight into adolescent development. Blos states that regression during adolescence is actually not defensive at all, but rather an integral, normal, inevitable, and universal aspect of puberty. The nature of regression may vary from one adolescent to the next. It may involve childhood autonomy, compliance, and cleanliness, or it may involve a sudden return to the passiveness that characterized the adolescent's behavior during childhood.

Anna Freud (1966) developed the idea that defense mechanisms are the key to understanding adolescent adjustment. She believes that the problems of adolescence are not to be unlocked by understanding the id, or instinctual forces, but instead are to be discovered in the existence of "love objects" in the adolescent's past. She argues that the attachment to these love objects, usually parents, is carried forward from the infant years and merely toned down or inhibited during the latency years. During adolescence, these pregenital urges may be reawakened, or, worse, newly acquired genital (adolescent) urges may combine with the urges that developed in early childhood.

Two final points about defense mechanisms are important. First, they are unconscious; adolescents are not aware that they are calling on defense mechanisms to

Anna Freud, Sigmund Freud's daughter, believed that defense mechanisms are an important dimension of the adolescent's development.

protect their ego and reduce anxiety. Second, when used in moderation or on a temporary basis, defense mechanisms are not necessarily unhealthy. For the most part, though, individuals should not let defense mechanisms dominate their behavior and prevent them from facing the demands of reality.

Psychosexual Stages. The **oral stage** *is the first Freudian stage of development, occurring during the first 18 months of life, in which the infant's pleasure centers around the mouth.* Chewing, sucking, and biting are the chief sources of pleasure. These actions reduce tension in the infant.

The **anal stage** *is the second Freudian stage of development, occurring between 1½ and 3 years of age, in which the child's greatest pleasure involves the anus or the eliminative functions associated with it.* In Freud's view, the exercise of anal muscles reduces tension.

The **phallic stage** *is the third Freudian stage of development, which occurs between the ages of 3 and 6; its name comes from the Latin word,* phallus, *which means "penis." During the phallic stage, pleasure focuses on the genitals as the child discovers that self-manipulation is enjoyable.*

In Freud's view, the phallic stage has a special importance in personality development because it is during this period that the Oedipus complex appears. This name comes from Greek mythology, in which Oedipus, the son of the King of Thebes, unwittingly kills his father and marries his mother. The **Oedipus complex,** *in Freudian theory, is the young child's intense desire to replace the parent of the same sex and enjoy the affections of the opposite-sex parent.* Freud's concept of the Oedipus complex has been criticized by some psychoanalysts and writers.

How is the Oedipus complex resolved? At about 5 to 6 years of age, children recognize that their same-sex parent might punish them for their incestuous wishes. To reduce this conflict, the child identifies with the same-sex parent, striving to be like him or her. If the conflict is not resolved, though, the individual may become fixated at the phallic stage.

The **latency stage** *is the fourth Freudian stage of development, which occurs between approximately 6 years of age and puberty; the child represses all interest in sexuality and develops social and intellectual skills.* This activity channels much of the child's energy into emotionally safe areas and helps the child forget the highly stressful conflicts of the phallic stage.

The **genital stage** *is the fifth and final Freudian stage of development, occurring from puberty on. The genital stage is a time of sexual reawakening; the source of sexual pleasure now becomes someone outside of the family.* Freud believed that unresolved conflicts with parents reemerge during adolescence. When these are resolved, the individual is capable of developing a mature love relationship and functioning independently as an adult.

Revisions of Freud's Theory. Freud's theory has undergone significant revisions by a number of psychoanalytic theorists. Many contemporary psychoanalytic theorists place less emphasis on sexual instincts and more emphasis on cultural experiences as determinants of an individual's development. Unconscious thought remains a central theme, but most contemporary psychoanalysts believe that conscious thought makes up more of the iceberg than Freud envisioned. Feminist criticisms of

Karen Horney

Nancy Chodorow

Figure~2.2

Feminist-Based Criticisms of Freud's Theory.
The first feminist-based criticism of Freud's theory was proposed by psychoanalytic theorist Karen Horney (1967). She developed a model of women with positive feminine qualities and self-evaluation. Her critique of Freud's theory included reference to a male-dominant society and culture. Rectification of the male bias in psychoanalytic theory continues today. For example, Nancy Chodorow (1978, 1989) emphasizes that many more women than men define themselves in terms of their relationships and connections to others. Her feminist revision of psychoanalytic theory also stresses the meaningfulness of emotions for women, as well as the belief that many men use the defense mechanism of denial in self-other connections.

Freud's theory have also been made (see figure 2.2). Next, we explore the ideas of an important revisionist of Freud's ideas—Erik Erikson.

Erikson's Theory

Erik Erikson (1902–1994) recognized Freud's contributions but believed that Freud misjudged some important dimensions of human development. For one, Erikson (1968) says we develop in *psychosocial stages*, in contrast to Freud's psychosexual stages. For another, Erikson emphasizes developmental change throughout the human life span, whereas Freud argued that our basic personality is shaped in the first 5 years of life. In Erikson's theory, eight stages of development unfold as we go through the life span. Each stage consists of a unique developmental task that confronts individuals with a crisis that must be faced. For Erikson, this crisis is not a catastrophe but a turning point of increased vulnerability and enhanced potential. The more an individual resolves the crises successfully, the healthier that individual's development will be.

Trust versus mistrust *is Erikson's first psychosocial stage, which is experienced in the first year of life. A sense of trust requires a feeling of physical comfort and a minimal amount of fear and apprehension about the future.* Trust in infancy sets the stage for a lifelong expectation that the world will be a good and pleasant place to live.

Autonomy versus shame and doubt *is Erikson's second stage of development, occurring in late infancy and toddlerhood (ages 1–3). After gaining trust in their caregivers, infants begin to discover that their behavior is their own. They start to assert their sense of independence or autonomy. They realize their will.* If infants are restrained too much or punished too harshly, they are likely to develop a sense of shame and doubt.

Initiative versus guilt *is Erikson's third stage of development, occurring during the preschool years. As preschool children encounter a widening social world, they are challenged more than when they were infants. Active, purposeful behavior is needed to cope with these challenges.* Children are asked to assume responsibility for their bodies, their behavior, their toys, and their pets. Developing a sense of responsibility increases initiative.

Erik Erikson with his wife, Joan, who is an artist. Erikson generated one of the most important developmental theories of the twentieth century.

Uncomfortable guilt feelings may arise, though, in children who are irresponsible and are made to feel too anxious. Erikson has a positive outlook on this stage. He believes that most guilt is quickly compensated for by a sense of accomplishment.

Industry versus inferiority *is Erikson's fourth developmental stage, occurring approximately in the elementary school years. Children's initiative brings them in contact with a wealth of new experiences. As they move into middle and late childhood, they direct their energy toward mastering knowledge and intellectual skills.* At no other time is the child more enthusiastic about learning than at the end of early childhood's period of expansive imagination. The danger in the elementary school years is the development of a sense of inferiority—of feeling incompetent and unproductive. Erikson believes that teachers have a special responsibility for children's development of industry. Teachers should "mildly but firmly coerce children into the adventure of finding out that one can learn to accomplish things which one would never have thought of by oneself" (Erikson, 1968, p. 127).

Identity versus identity confusion *is Erikson's fifth developmental stage, which individuals experience during the adolescent years. At this time individuals are faced with finding out who they are, what they are all about, and where they are going in life.* Adolescents are confronted with many new roles and adult statuses—vocational and romantic, for example. Parents need to allow adolescents to explore many different roles and different paths within

a particular role. If the adolescent explores such roles in a healthy manner and arrives at a positive path to follow in life, then a positive identity will be achieved. If an identity is pushed on the adolescent by parents, if the adolescent does not adequately explore many roles, and if a positive future path is not defined, then identity confusion reigns.

Intimacy versus isolation *is Erikson's sixth developmental stage, which individuals experience during the early adulthood years. At this time, individuals face the developmental task of forming intimate relationships with others.* Erikson describes intimacy as finding oneself yet losing oneself in another. If the young adult forms healthy friendships and an intimate close relationship with another individual, intimacy will be achieved; if not, isolation will result.

Generativity versus stagnation *is Erikson's seventh developmental stage, which individuals experience during middle adulthood. A chief concern is to assist the younger generation in developing and leading useful lives*—this is what Erikson meant by *generativity*. The feeling of having done nothing to help the next generation is *stagnation*.

> *Each of us stands at the heart of the earth pierced through by a ray of sunlight: and suddenly it is evening.*
>
> —Salvatore Quasimodo

Integrity versus despair *is Erikson's eighth and final developmental stage, which individuals experience during late adulthood. In our later years, we look back and evaluate what we have done with our lives.* Through many different routes, the older person may have developed a positive outlook in most or all of the previous developmental stages. If so, the retrospective glances reveal a life well spent, and the person feels a sense of satisfaction—integrity is achieved. If the older adult resolved many of the earlier developmental stages negatively, the retrospective glances likely will yield doubt or gloom—the despair Erikson talks about.

Erikson does not believe that the proper solution to a stage crisis is always completely positive in nature. Some exposure or commitment to the negative end of a person's bipolar conflict is sometimes inevitable—you cannot trust all people under all circumstances and survive, for example. Nonetheless, positive resolutions to stage crises should dominate for optimal development. A summary of Erikson's stages is presented in figure 2.3.

Cognitive Theories

Whereas psychoanalytic theories stress the importance of adolescents' unconscious thoughts, cognitive theories emphasize their conscious thoughts. Two important cognitive theories are Piaget's cognitive development theory and information-processing theory.

Piaget's Theory

The famous Swiss psychologist Jean Piaget (1896–1980) stressed that adolescents actively construct their own cognitive worlds; information is not just poured into their minds from the environment. Piaget emphasized that adolescents adapt their thinking to include new ideas because additional information furthers understanding.

Piaget (1954) also believed that we go through four stages in understanding the world. Each of the stages is age related and consists of distinct ways of thinking. Remember, it is the *different* way of understanding the world that makes one stage more advanced than another; knowing *more* information does not make a child's thinking more advanced in the Piagetian view. This is what Piaget meant when he said a child's cognition is *qualitatively* different in one stage compared with another. What are Piaget's four stages of cognitive development?

The **sensorimotor stage,** *which lasts from birth to about 2 years of age, is the first Piagetian stage. In this stage, infants construct an understanding of the world by coordinating sensory experiences (such as seeing and hearing) with physical, motoric actions—hence the term* sensorimotor. At the beginning of this stage, newborns have little more than reflexive patterns with which to work. At the end

Erikson's stages	Developmental period	Characteristics
Trust versus mistrust	Infancy (first year)	A sense of trust requires a feeling of physical comfort and a minimal amount of fear about the future. Infants' basic needs are met by responsive, sensitive caregivers.
Autonomy versus shame and doubt	Infancy (second year)	After gaining trust in their caregivers, infants start to discover that they have a will of their own. They assert their sense of autonomy, or independence. They realize their will. If infants are restrained too much or punished too harshly, they are likely to develop a sense of shame and doubt.
Initiative versus guilt	Early childhood (preschool years, ages 3–5)	As preschool children encounter a widening social world, they are challenged more and need to develop more purposeful behavior to cope with these challenges. Children are now asked to assume more responsibility. Uncomfortable guilt feelings may arise, though, if the children are irresponsible and are made to feel too anxious.
Industry versus inferiority	Middle and late childhood (elementary school years, 6 years– puberty)	At no other time are children more enthusiastic than at the end of early childhood's period of expansive imagination. As children move into the elementary school years, they direct their energy toward mastering knowledge and intellectual skills. The danger at this stage involves feeling incompetent and unproductive.

Figure~2.3

Erikson's Eight Stages of Human Development.

of the stage, 2-year-olds have complex sensorimotor patterns and are beginning to operate with primitive symbols.

The **preoperational stage,** *which lasts approximately from 2 to 7 years of age, is the second Piagetian stage. In this stage, children begin to represent the world with words, images, and drawings.* Symbolic thought goes beyond simple connections of sensory information and physical action.

However, although preschool children can symbolically represent the world, according to Piaget, they still lack the ability to perform *operations*—in Piagetian terms, the internalized mental actions that allow children to do mentally what they previously did physically.

The **concrete operational stage,** *which lasts from approximately 7 to 11 years of age, is the third Piagetian*

Erikson's stages	Developmental period	Characteristics
Identity versus identity confusion	Adolescence (10–20 years)	Individuals are faced with finding out who they are, what they are all about, and where they are going in life. An important dimension is the exploration of alternative solutions to roles. Career exploration is important. 
Intimacy versus isolation	Early adulthood (20s, 30s)	Individuals face the developmental task of forming intimate relationships with others. Erikson described intimacy as finding oneself yet losing oneself in another person.. 
Generativity versus stagnation	Middle adulthood (40s, 50s)	A chief concern is to assist the younger generation in developing and leading useful lives. 
Integrity versus despair	Late adulthood (60s –)	Individuals look back and evaluate what they have done with their lives. The retrospective glances can either be positive (integrity) or negative (despair). 

Figure~2.3—Continued

In this stage, individuals move beyond the world of actual, concrete experiences and think in abstract and more logical terms. As part of thinking more abstractly, adolescents develop images of ideal circumstances. They might think about what an ideal parent is like and compare their parents with this ideal standard. They begin to entertain possibilities for the future and are fascinated with what they can be. In solving problems, formal operational thinkers are more systematic, developing hypotheses about why something is happening the way it is, then testing these hypotheses in a deductive fashion. Piaget's stages are summarized in table 2.1.

Information Processing

Information processing *is concerned with how individuals process information about their world—how information enters the mind, how it is stored and transformed, and how it is retrieved to perform such complex activities as problem solving and reasoning.* A simple model of cognition is shown in figure 2.4.

Information processing begins when information from the world is detected through sensory and perceptual processes. Then the information is stored, transformed, and retrieved through the processes of memory. Notice in the model that information can flow back and forth between memory and perceptual processes. For example, we are good at remembering the faces we see, yet at the same time our memory of an individual's face may be different from how the individual actually looks. Keep in mind that our information-processing model is a simple one, designed to illustrate the main cognitive processes and their interrelations. Other arrows could be drawn—between memory and language, between thinking and perception, and between language and perception, for example. Also, the boxes in the figure do not represent sharp,

stage. In this stage, children can perform operations. Logical reasoning replaces intuitive thought as long as reasoning can be applied to specific or concrete examples. For instance, concrete operational thinkers cannot imagine the steps necessary to complete an algebraic equation, which is too abstract for thinking at this stage of development.

The **formal operational stage,** *which appears between the ages of 11 and 15, is the fourth and final Piagetian stage.*

Jean Piaget, famous Swiss developmental psychologist, changed forever the way we think about the development of children's and adolescents' minds. Piaget proposed a series of cognitive stages that individuals go through in sequence. He believed that adolescents think in qualitatively different ways about the world than children do.

TABLE 2.1

Piaget's Stages of Cognitive Development

Stage	Description	Age Range
Sensorimotor	An infant progresses from reflexive, instinctual action at birth to the beginning of symbolic thought. The infant constructs an understanding of the world by coordinating sensory experience with physical actions.	Birth to 2 years
Preoperational	The child begins to represent the world with words and images; these words and images reflect increased symbolic thinking and go beyond the connection of sensory information and physical action.	2 to 7 years
Concrete Operational	The child can now reason logically about concrete events and classify objects into different sets.	7 to 11 years
Formal Operational	The adolescent reasons in more abstract and logical ways. Thought is more idealistic.	11 to 15 years

distinct stages in information processing. There is continuity and flow, as well as overlap, between the cognitive processes.

The information-processing approach raises important questions about changes in cognition across the life span. One of these questions is this: Does processing speed increase as children grow older and decrease as adults grow older? Speed of processing is an important aspect of the information-processing approach. Many cognitive tasks are performed under real time pressure. For example, at school we have a limited amount of time to add and subtract and take tests; at work we have deadlines for completing projects. A good deal of evidence indicates that processing speed is slower in younger children than in adolescents, and slower in elderly adults than in young adults, but the causes of these differences have not been determined.

Behavioral and Social Learning Theories

Seventeen-year-old Tom is going steady with 16-year-old Ann. Both have warm, friendly personalities, and they enjoy being together. Psychoanalytic theorists would say that their warm, friendly personalities are derived from long-standing relationships with their parents, especially their early childhood experiences. They also would argue that the reason for their attraction to each other is unconscious; they are unaware of how their biological heritage and early life experiences have been carried forward to influence their personalities in adolescence.

Behaviorists and social learning theorists would observe Tom and Ann and see something quite different. They would examine the adolescents' experiences, especially their most recent ones, to understand the reason

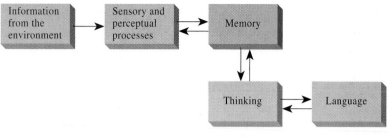

Figure~2.4

A Simple Model of Information Processing.

for their attraction. Tom would be described as rewarding Ann's behavior, and vice versa, for example. No reference would be made to unconscious thoughts, the Oedipus complex, defense mechanisms, and so on.

Behaviorists believe that we should examine only what can be directly observed and measured. At approximately the same time that Freud was interpreting his patients' unconscious minds through early childhood experiences, behaviorists such as Ivan Pavlov and John B. Watson were conducting detailed observations of behavior in controlled laboratory circumstances. Out of the behavioral tradition grew the belief that development is observable behavior, learned through experience with the environment. The two versions of the behavioral approach that are prominent today are the view of B. F. Skinner (1904–1990) and social learning theory.

Skinner's Behaviorism

Behaviorism *emphasizes the scientific study of observable behavioral responses and their environmental determinants.* In Skinner's behaviorism, the mind, conscious or unconscious, is not needed to explain behavior and development. For him, development is behavior. For example, observations of Sam reveal that his behavior is shy, achievement oriented, and caring. Why is Sam's behavior this way? For Skinner, rewards and punishments in Sam's environment have shaped him into a shy, achievement-oriented, and caring person. Because of interactions with family members, friends, teachers, and others, Sam has *learned* to behave in this fashion.

Since behaviorists believe that development is learned and often changes according to environmental experiences, it follows that rearranging experiences can change development. For behaviorists, shy behavior can be transformed into outgoing behavior; aggressive behavior can be shaped into docile behavior; lethargic, boring behavior can be turned into enthusiastic, interesting behavior.

Social Learning Theory

Some psychologists believe that the behaviorists basically are right when they say development is learned and is influenced strongly by environmental experiences. However, they believe that Skinner went too far in declaring that cognition is unimportant in understanding development. **Social learning theory** *is the view of psychologists who emphasize behavior, environment, and cognition as the key factors in development.*

The social learning theorists say we are not like mindless robots, responding mechanically to others in our environment. Neither are we like weather vanes, behaving like a Communist in the presence of a Communist or like a John Bircher in the presence of a John Bircher. Rather, we think, reason, imagine, plan, expect, interpret, believe, value, and compare. When others try to control us, our values and beliefs allow us to resist their control.

American psychologists Albert Bandura (1977, 1995, 1997) and Walter Mischel (1995) are the main architects of social learning theory's contemporary version, which was labeled *cognitive* social learning theory by Mischel (1973). Bandura believes that we learn by observing what others do. Through observational learning (also called modeling or imitation), we cognitively represent the behavior of others and then possibly adopt this behavior ourselves. For example, a boy might observe his father's aggressive outbursts and hostile interchanges with people; when observed with his peers, the young boy might display a style of interaction that is highly aggressive, showing the same behavior as his father. Or a young female might adopt the dominant and sarcastic style of her boss. When observed interacting with one of her subordinates, the young woman says, "I need this work immediately if not sooner; you are so far behind, you think you are ahead!" Social learning theorists believe that we acquire a wide range of such behaviors, thoughts, and feelings through observing others' behavior; these observations form an important part of our development.

Bandura's (1986, 1995, 1997) most recent model of learning and development involves behavior, the person and cognition, and the environment. As shown in figure 2.5, behavior, cognitive and person factors, and environmental influences operate interactively. Behavior can influence cognition, and vice versa; the person's cognitive activities can influence the environment; environmental influences can change the person's thought processes; and so on.

Let's consider how Bandura's model might work in the case of a college student's achievement behavior. As the student diligently studies and gets good grades, her behavior produces positive thoughts about her abilities. As part of her effort to make good grades, she plans and develops a number of strategies to make her studying more efficient. In these ways, her behavior has influenced her thought and her thought has influenced her behavior. At

Albert Bandura, a leading social learning theorist.

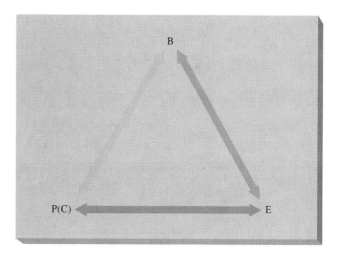

Figure~2.5

Bandura's Model of the Reciprocal Influences of Behavior, Person and Cognitive Factors, and Environment.
P(C) stands for person and cognitive factors, B for behavior, and E for environment. The arrows reflect how relations between these factors are reciprocal rather than unidirectional. Examples of person/cognitive factors include intelligence, skills, and self-control.

the beginning of the semester, her college made a special effort to involve students in a study skills program. She decided to join. Her success, along with that of other students who attended the program, has led the college to expand the program next semester. In these ways, environment influenced behavior, and behavior changed the environment. The expectations of the college administrators that the study skills program would work made it possible in the first place. The program's success has spurred expectations that this type of program could work in other colleges. In these ways, cognition changed the environment, and the environment changed cognition. Expectations are an important variable in Bandura's model.

Like Skinner's behavioral approach, the social learning approach emphasizes the importance of empirical research in studying development. This research focuses on the processes that explain development—the socio-emotional and cognitive factors that influence what we are like as people.

Ecological, Contextual Theories

Two environmental theories that emphasize the importance of ecological, contextual factors in the adolescent's development are (1) Urie Bronfenbrenner's ecological theory and (2) Glenn Elder's contextual life course theory.

Ecological Theory

Urie Bronfenbrenner (1917–) has proposed a strong environmental view of children's development that is receiving increased attention. **Ecological theory** *is Bronfenbrenner's sociocultural view of development. It consists of five environmental systems, ranging from the fine-grained inputs of direct interactions with social agents to the broad-based inputs of culture. The five systems in Bronfenbrenner's ecological theory are the microsystem, mesosystem, exosystem, macrosystem, and chronosystem.* Bronfenbrenner's (1986, 1995; Bronfenbrenner & Morris, 1997) ecological model is shown in figure 2.6.

The **microsystem** *in Bronfenbrenner's ecological theory is the setting in which an individual lives. This context includes the person's family, peers, school, and neighborhood.* It is in the microsystem that most of the direct interactions with social agents take place—with parents, peers, and teachers, for example. The individual

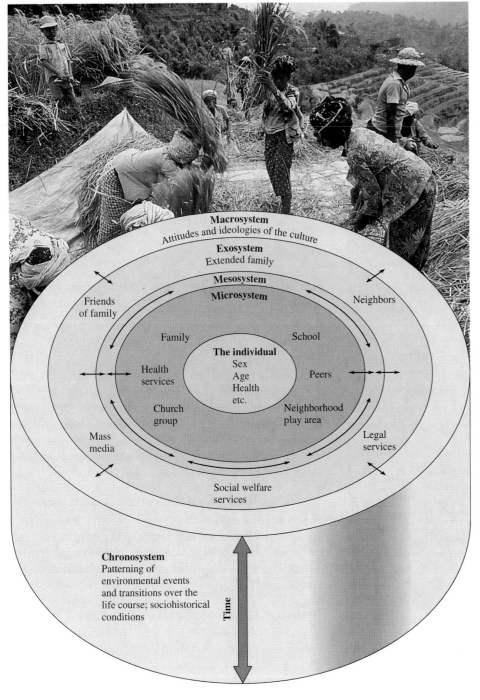

between contexts. Examples are the relation of family experiences to school experiences, school experiences to work experiences, and family experiences to peer experiences. For instance, adolescents whose parents have rejected them may have difficulty developing positive relations with teachers. Developmentalists increasingly believe that it is important to observe behavior in multiple settings—such as family, peer, and school contexts—to obtain a more complete picture of adolescent development.

The **exosystem** *in Bronfenbrenner's ecological theory is involved when experiences in another social setting—in which the individual does not have an active role—influence what the individual experiences in an immediate context.* For example, work experiences may affect a woman's relationship with her husband and their adolescent. The woman might receive a promotion that requires more travel, which might increase marital conflict and change patterns of parent-adolescent interaction. Another example of an exosystem is city government, which is responsible for the quality of parks, recreation centers, and library facilities for children and adolescents.

The **macrosystem** *in Bronfenbrenner's ecological theory involves the culture in which individuals live.* Remember from chapter 1 that *culture* refers to the behavior patterns, beliefs, and all other products of a group of people

Figure~2.6

Bronfenbrenner's Ecological Theory of Development.
Bronfenbrenner's ecological theory consists of five environmental systems: microsystem, mesosystem, exosystem, macrosystem, and chronosystem.

is viewed not as a passive recipient of experiences in these settings, but as someone who helps construct the settings. Bronfenbrenner points out that most of the research on sociocultural influences has focused on microsystems.

The **mesosystem** *in Bronfenbrenner's ecological theory involves relations between microsystems, or connections*

that are passed on from generation to generation. Remember also that *cross-cultural studies*—the comparison of one culture with one or more other cultures—provide information about the generality of adolescent development. To read further about culture's role in adolescent development, turn to Sociocultural Worlds of Adolescence.

Urie Bronfenbrenner developed ecological theory, a perspective that is receiving increased attention. His theory emphasizes the importance of both micro and macro dimensions of the environment in which the adolescent lives.

Glenn Elder has proposed an ecological, contextual view called life course theory. What are some of the key features of life course theory?

The **chronosystem** *in Bronfenbrenner's ecological theory involves the patterning of environmental events and transitions over the life course and sociohistorical circumstances.* For example, in studying the effects of divorce on children, researchers have found that the negative effects often peak in the first year after the divorce and the effects are more negative for sons than for daughters (Hetherington, 1995; Hetherington, Cox, & Cox, 1982). By 2 years after the divorce, family interaction is less chaotic and more stable. With regard to sociocultural circumstances, girls today are much more likely to be encouraged to pursue a career than they were 20 to 30 years ago. In ways such as these, the chronosystem has a powerful impact on adolescents' lives.

It should be pointed out that Bronfenbrenner (1995) recently added biological influences to his theory and now describes it as a bioecological theory. Nonetheless, the ecological, environmental contexts still predominate in Bronfenbrenner's theory.

Life Course Theory

Although Bronfenbrenner's ecological theory strongly emphasizes environmental contexts and includes a chronosystem that involves historical time, it has not had a strong life-span developmental orientation. An environmental, contextual theory that places a stronger emphasis on life-span development is **life course theory,** *Glenn Elder's (1995, 1997, in press) theory that*

the human life span can be best understood by considering lives in their historical time and place, the timing of social roles and life events, the interdependence or connections among lives, and the role of human agency and social constraints in decision making.

Human Lives in Historical Time and Place. Especially in rapidly changing societies, children of different ages are exposed to different historical circumstances. Individuals of different ages may be influenced differently by historical changes. Consider an analysis of the subjects in the Berkeley Longitudinal Study and the impact of the Great Depression on their lives (Elder, 1974, 1979). The older children were born during the early 1920s, the younger children at the decade's end. The older children were too young to leave school and faced a dismal labor market when the economy collapsed in 1929–1933, and they also were too old to be highly dependent on their troubled families. By contrast, the younger children were dependent on their families in the midst of hardship and thus presumably were at a greater risk of impaired development.

Historical influences can also be expressed in different ways in different places. In one study of Depression-era youth, California youth growing up in the San Francisco area managed to escape the limitations of their deprived households by joining the armed forces and using the benefits for higher education (Elder, Modell,

(a)   (b)   (c)

Figure~2.7

Three analogies that have been used to describe the nature of development: *(a)* staircase, *(b)* seedling in a greenhouse, and *(c)* strand of ivy in a forest.

The analogy of a seedling in a greenhouse has been popular for many years in developmental psychology. In this view, the individual is acted upon by the environment (according to Skinner's behavioral perspective) or the individual acts on the world (in Piaget's perspective). This analogy emphasizes the individual as the primary unit of development. Thus, Piaget's theory has characteristics of both the staircase analogy and the seedling-in-a-greenhouse analogy.

The contemporary analogy of a strand of ivy in a forest stresses the many different paths development can take and the importance of contextual factors in that development (Kagan, 1992). In this analogy, development is not as consistently stagelike as the staircase analogy suggests, and the individual is not a solitary scientist as in Piaget's view. An important dimension of the analogy of a strand of ivy in a forest is its emphasis on reciprocal encounters with others and the changing symbolic construction of these relationships. The ecological, contextual theories of Bronfenbrenner and Elder are compatible with this analogy.

Which of these analogies best reflects the way development actually occurs? As with virtually all theories and analogies, each has its adherents, although the ivy analogy has become increasingly popular in recent years. Visual images of the three analogies are shown in figure 2.7.

An Eclectic Theoretical Orientation

An **eclectic theoretical orientation** *does not follow any one theoretical approach, but rather selects and uses whatever is considered the best in each theory.* No single theory described in this chapter is infallible or capable of explaining entirely the rich complexity of adolescent development. Each of the theories has made important contributions to our understanding of adolescent development, but none provides a complete description and explanation.

For these reasons, the four major approaches to adolescent development are presented in this text in an unbiased fashion. As a result, you can view the field of adolescent development as it actually exists—with different theorists drawing different conclusions. Many other theories of adolescent development, not discussed in this chapter, are woven through the discussion of adolescent development in the remainder of the book. For example, chapter 10 examines the humanistic approach, which emphasizes adolescents' development of self, and chapter 14 discusses attribution theory, which emphasizes adolescents' motivation for understanding the causes of their own and others' behavior.

At this point we have discussed a number of ideas about the scientific method and theories of adolescent development. A summary of these ideas is presented in concept table 2.1. Next, we explore the methods adolescent developmentalists use to study adolescents, beginning with the measures they use.

METHODS

Among the methodological decisions that researchers must make when they study adolescent development are which measure or measures to use, which research strategies to adopt, and the time span of the inquiry.

Figure~2.7

Three analogies that have been used to describe the nature of development: (*a*) staircase, (*b*) seedling in a greenhouse, and (*c*) strand of ivy in a forest.

The analogy of a seedling in a greenhouse has been popular for many years in developmental psychology. In this view, the individual is acted upon by the environment (according to Skinner's behavioral perspective) or the individual acts on the world (in Piaget's perspective). This analogy emphasizes the individual as the primary unit of development. Thus, Piaget's theory has characteristics of both the staircase analogy and the seedling-in-a-greenhouse analogy.

The contemporary analogy of a strand of ivy in a forest stresses the many different paths development can take and the importance of contextual factors in that development (Kagan, 1992). In this analogy, development is not as consistently stagelike as the staircase analogy suggests, and the individual is not a solitary scientist as in Piaget's view. An important dimension of the analogy of a strand of ivy in a forest is its emphasis on reciprocal encounters with others and the changing symbolic construction of these relationships. The ecological, contextual theories of Bronfenbrenner and Elder are compatible with this analogy.

Which of these analogies best reflects the way development actually occurs? As with virtually all theories and analogies, each has its adherents, although the ivy analogy has become increasingly popular in recent years. Visual images of the three analogies are shown in figure 2.7.

An Eclectic Theoretical Orientation

An **eclectic theoretical orientation** *does not follow any one theoretical approach, but rather selects and uses whatever is considered the best in each theory.* No single theory described in this chapter is infallible or capable of explaining entirely the rich complexity of adolescent development. Each of the theories has made important contributions to our understanding of adolescent development, but none provides a complete description and explanation.

For these reasons, the four major approaches to adolescent development are presented in this text in an unbiased fashion. As a result, you can view the field of adolescent development as it actually exists—with different theorists drawing different conclusions. Many other theories of adolescent development, not discussed in this chapter, are woven through the discussion of adolescent development in the remainder of the book. For example, chapter 10 examines the humanistic approach, which emphasizes adolescents' development of self, and chapter 14 discusses attribution theory, which emphasizes adolescents' motivation for understanding the causes of their own and others' behavior.

At this point we have discussed a number of ideas about the scientific method and theories of adolescent development. A summary of these ideas is presented in concept table 2.1. Next, we explore the methods adolescent developmentalists use to study adolescents, beginning with the measures they use.

METHODS

Among the methodological decisions that researchers must make when they study adolescent development are which measure or measures to use, which research strategies to adopt, and the time span of the inquiry.

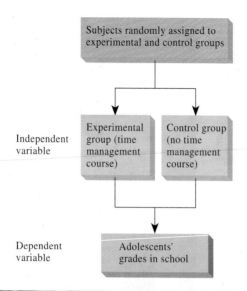

BY BILL HOEST

"That's my dad when he was 10 . . .
He was in some sort of cult."

© 1986; Reprinted courtesy of Bunny Hoest and Parade Magazine.

Figure~2.9

Principles of the Experimental Strategy Applied to the Effects of Time Management Instruction on Adolescents' Grades in School.

Longitudinal Approach

The **longitudinal approach** *is a research strategy in which the same individuals are studied over a period of time, usually several years or more.* In a typical longitudinal study of the same topics discussed under the cross-sectional approach, researchers might structure a test that they administer to children and adolescents when they are 8, 12, and 16 years old. In this example, the same children would be studied over an 8-year time span, allowing investigators to examine patterns of change within each individual child or adolescent. One of the great values of the longitudinal approach is its evaluation of how individual children and adolescents change as they grow up.

Fewer longitudinal than cross-sectional studies are conducted because longitudinal studies are time consuming and costly. A close examination of the longitudinal approach also reveals some additional problems: (1) Because children or adolescents are examined over a long period of time, some of them drop out because they lose interest or move away and cannot be recontacted by the investigator. A fairly common finding is that the remaining adolescents represent a slightly biased sample, in that they tend to be psychologically better or superior to those who have dropped out on almost every dimension the investigator thinks to check out (for example, intelligence, motivation, and cooperativeness). (2) With repeated testing, individual adolescents can become "test-wise," which might increase their ability to perform "better" or "more maturely" the next time the investigator interacts with them.

Cohort Effects

Cohort effects *are effects due to a subject's time of birth or generation but not actually to age.* Today's children and adolescents are living as childhood and adolescence firsts (Louv, 1990). They are the first day-care generation; the first truly multicultural generation; the first generation to grow up in the electronic bubble of an environment defined by computers and new forms of media; the first post-sexual-revolution generation;

the first generation to grow up in new kinds of dispersed, deconcentrated cities, not quite urban, rural, or suburban.

Cohorts can differ in years of education, childrearing practices, health, attitudes toward sex, religious values, and economic status. Cohort effects can powerfully affect the dependent measures in a study ostensibly concerned with age. Researchers have shown that cohort effects are especially important to investigate in the assessment of intelligence (Schaie, 1994). For example, individuals born at different points in time—such as 1920, 1950, and 1980—have had varying opportunities for education, with individuals born earlier having less access.

> *The mark of the historic is the nonchalance with which it picks up an individual and deposits him in a trend, like a house playfully moved in a tornado.*
>
> **—Mary McCarthy**

Florence Denmark (shown here talking with a group of students) has developed a number of guidelines for nonsexist research. Denmark and others believe that psychology needs to be challenged to examine the world in a new way, one that incorporates girls' and women's perspectives.

RESEARCH CHALLENGES

Further challenges in conducting and evaluating research on adolescent development include making sure that subjects are treated in an ethical manner, making sure that every attempt is made to reduce sexism in research, and becoming a wise consumer of information about adolescents.

Ethics

When Pete and Ann, two 19-year-old college students, agreed to participate in an investigation of dating couples, they did not consider that the questionnaire they filled out would get them to think about issues that might lead to conflict in their relationship and possibly end it. One year after this investigation (Rubin & Mitchell, 1976), nine of the ten participants said that they had discussed their answers with their dating partner. In most instances, the discussions strengthened their relationship. But in some cases, the participants used the questionnaire as a springboard to discuss problems or concerns previously hidden. One participant said, "The study definitely played a role in ending my relationship with Larry." In this circumstance, the couple had different views about how long they expected to be together. She anticipated that the relationship would end much sooner than Larry thought. Discussion of their answers to the questions brought the long-term prospects of the relationship out in the open, and eventually Larry found someone who was more interested in marrying him.

At first glance, you would not think that a questionnaire on dating relationships would have any substantial impact on the participants' behavior. But psychologists increasingly recognize that they must

exercise considerable caution to ensure the well-being of the participants in a psychological study. Today, colleges and universities have review boards that evaluate the ethical nature of research conducted at their institutions. Proposed research plans must pass the scrutiny of an ethics research committee before the research can be initiated.

In addition, the American Psychological Association (APA) has developed guidelines for the ethics of its members. The APA code of ethics instructs researchers to protect their subjects from mental and physical harm. The best interests of the subjects need to be kept foremost in the researcher's mind. All subjects, if they are old enough, must give their informed consent to participate in the research study. This requires that subjects know what their participation will entail and any risks that might develop. For example, subjects in an investigation of the effects of divorce on adolescent development should be told beforehand that interview questions might stimulate thought about issues they might not anticipate. The subjects should also be informed that in some instances a discussion of the family's experiences might improve family relationships, while in other instances it might bring up issues that bring the adolescent unwanted stress.

Reducing Sexist Research

Traditional science is presented as being value free and, thus, a valid way of studying mental processes and behavior. However, there is a growing consensus that science in general and psychology in particular are not value free (Paludi, 1995). A special concern is that the vast majority of psychological research has been male oriented and male dominated (Unger & Crawford, 1996). Some

SECTION

Two

Biological and Cognitive Development

I think that what is happening to me is so wonderful and not only what can be seen on my body, but all that is taking place inside. I never discuss myself with anybody; that is why I have to talk to myself about them.

—Anne Frank,
Diary of a Young Girl, 1947

Adolescence is the transition from childhood to adulthood that involves biological, cognitive, and socioemotional development. These strands of development are inter-woven in the adolescent's life. This section focuses on adolescents' biological and cognitive development and consists of three chapters: Chapter 3, "Biological Processes and Physical Development"; Chapter 4, "Cognitive Development and Social Cognition"; and Chapter 5, "Information Processing and Intelligence."

Edgar Degas
Dancer in Her Dressing Room

Chapter

3

Biological Processes and Physical Development

In youth, we clothe ourselves with rainbows and go brave as the zodiac.

—Emerson

Chapter Boxes

Puberty: The time of life when the two sexes begin to first become acquainted.

—Samuel Johnson

PREVIEW

*P*uberty's changes are perplexing to adolescents. Although these changes bring forth doubts, questions, fears, and anxieties, most of us survive them quite well. Our journey through puberty's fascinating moments explores the nature of puberty and its psychological dimensions. But first we will evaluate the contributions of heredity and environment to adolescent development.

I am pretty confused. I wonder whether I am weird or normal. My body is starting to change, but I sure don't look like a lot of my friends. I still look like a kid for the most part. My best friend is only 13, but he looks like he is 16 or 17. I get nervous in the locker room during PE class because when I go to take a shower, I'm afraid somebody is going to make fun of me since I'm not as physically developed as some of the others.

Robert, age 12

I don't like my breasts. They are too small, and they look funny. I'm afraid guys won't like me if they don't get bigger.

Angie, age 13

I can't stand the way I look. I have zits all over my face. My hair is dull and stringy. It never stays in place. My nose is too big. My lips are too small. My legs are too short. I have four warts on my left hand, and people get grossed out by them. So do I. My body is a disaster!

Ann, age 14

I'm short and I can't stand it. My father is 6 feet tall, and here I am only five foot four. I'm 14 already. I look like a kid, and I get teased a lot, especially by other guys. I'm always the last one picked for sides in basketball because I'm so short. Girls don't seem to be interested in me either because most of them are taller than I am.

Jim, age 14

The comments of these four adolescents in the midst of pubertal change underscore the dramatic upheaval in our bodies following the calm, consistent growth of middle and late childhood. Young adolescents develop an acute concern about their bodies. When columnist Bob Greene (1988) dialed a party line called Connections in Chicago to discover what young adolescents were saying to each other, the first things the boys and girls asked for—after first names—were physical descriptions. The idealism of the callers was apparent. Most of the girls described themselves as having long blond hair, being 5 feet, 5 inches tall, and weighing about 110 pounds. Most of the boys said that they had brown hair, lifted weights, were 6 feet tall, and weighed 170 pounds.

HEREDITY AND ENVIRONMENT

Hereditary influences are still important some 10 to 20 years after conception. No matter what the species, there must be some mechanism for transmitting characteristics from one generation to the next. Each adolescent carries a genetic code inherited from his or her parents. The genetic codes of all adolescents are alike in one important way—they all contain the human genetic code. Because of the human genetic code, a fertilized human egg cannot grow into an eel, an egret, or an elephant.

The Nature of Genes

We begin each life as a single cell weighing 1/20 millionth of an ounce! This tiny piece of matter housed our entire genetic code—the information about who we would become. These instructions orchestrated growth from that single cell to an adolescent made of trillions of cells, each containing a perfect replica of the original genetic code. Physically, the hereditary code is carried by biochemical agents called genes and chromosomes. Aside from the obvious physical similarity this code produces among adolescents (such as in anatomy, brain structure, and organs), it also accounts for much of our psychological sameness (or universality).

No one possesses all the characteristics that our genetic structure makes possible. A **genotype** *is a person's genetic heritage, the actual genetic material.* However, not all of this genetic material is apparent in our observed and measurable characteristics. A **phenotype** *is the way an individual's genotype is expressed in observed and measurable characteristics.* Phenotypes include physical traits, such as height, weight, eye color, and skin pigmentation, as well as psychological characteristics, such as intelligence, creativity, personality, and social tendencies. For each genotype, a range of phenotypes can be expressed. Imagine that we could identify all of the genes that would make an adolescent introverted or extraverted. Would measured introversion-extraversion be predictable from knowledge of the specific genes? The answer is no, because even if our genetic model was adequate, introversion-extraversion is a characteristic shaped by experience throughout life. For example, a parent might push an introverted child into social situations and encourage the child to become more gregarious.

Genetic codes predispose adolescents to develop in a particular way, and environments are either responsive or unresponsive to this development (Bouchard, 1995). For example, the genotype of some adolescents may predispose them to be introverted in an environment that promotes a turning inward of personality, yet in an environment that encourages social interaction and outgoingness, these adolescents might become more extraverted. However, the adolescent with this introverted genotype is unlikely to become a strong extravert. The **reaction range** *is the range of possible*

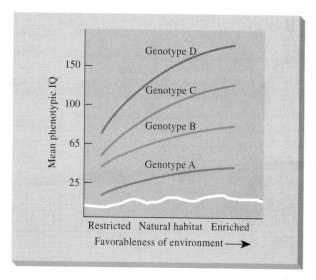

Figure~3.1

Reaction Range.
Although each genotype responds favorably to improved environments, some are more responsive than others to environmental deprivation and enrichment.

phenotypes for each genotype, suggesting the importance of the environment's restrictiveness or enrichment (see figure 3.1).

Sandra Scarr (1984) explains reaction range in the following way: Each of us has a range of potential. For example, an individual might be shorter than average. No matter how well fed the individual is, an individual with "short" genes will never be taller than average. Scarr believes that such characteristics as intelligence and introversion work the same way. That is, there is a range within which the environment can modify intelligence, but intelligence is not completely malleable. Reaction range gives us an estimate of how malleable intelligence is.

Genotypes, in addition to producing many phenotypes, may yield some characteristics that are immune to extensive changes in the environment. These characteristics seem to stay on a particular developmental course regardless of environmental assaults (Waddington, 1957). **Canalization** *is the process by which characteristics take a narrow path or developmental course. Apparently, preservative forces help protect or buffer a person from environmental extremes.* For example, developmental psychologist Jerome Kagan (1984) points to his research on Guatemalan infants who had experienced extreme malnutrition as infants yet showed normal social and cognitive development later in childhood.

Methods

Behavior genetics *is the study of the degree and nature of behavior's hereditary basis.* Behavior geneticists assume that behaviors are jointly determined by the interaction of heredity and environment (Plomin & others, 1997). To study heredity's influence on behavior, behavior geneticists often use either twin studies or adoption studies.

By permission of Johnny Hart and Creators Syndicate, Inc.

In a **twin study,** *the behavioral similarity of identical twins is compared with the behavioral similarity of fraternal twins.* **Identical twins** *(called monozygotic twins) develop from a single fertilized egg that splits into two genetically identical replicas, each of which becomes a person.* **Fraternal twins** *(called dizygotic twins) develop from separate eggs and separate sperm, making them genetically no more similar than ordinary siblings.* Although fraternal twins share the same womb, they are no more alike genetically than are nontwin brothers and sisters, and they may be of different sexes. By comparing groups of identical and fraternal twins, behavior geneticists capitalize on the basic knowledge that identical twins are more similar genetically than are fraternal twins (Silberg & Rutter, 1997). In one twin study, 7,000 pairs of Finnish identical and fraternal twins were compared on the personality traits of extraversion (outgoingness) and neuroticism (psychological instability) (Rose & others, 1988). On both of these personality traits, identical twins were much more similar than fraternal twins were, suggesting the role of heredity in both traits. However, several issues crop up as a result of twin studies. Adults may stress the similarities of identical twins more than those of fraternal twins, and identical twins may perceive themselves as a "set" and play together more than fraternal twins. If so, observed similarities in identical twins could be environmentally influenced.

In an **adoption study,** *investigators seek to discover whether the behavior and psychological characteristics of adopted children are more like those of their adoptive parents, who provided a home environment, or those of their biological parents, who contributed their heredity.* Another form of adoption study is to compare adoptive and biological siblings. In one investigation, the educational levels attained by biological parents were better predictors of adopted children's IQ scores than were the IQs of the children's adopted parents (Scarr & Weinberg, 1983). Because of

These identical twins came from a single fertilized egg that split into two genetic replicas. Identical twins are genetically identical, unlike fraternal twins, who developed from separate fertilized eggs and are not more genetically similar than ordinary siblings.

the genetic relation between the adopted children and their biological parents, the implication is that heredity influences children's IQ scores.

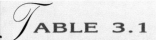

TABLE 3.1

Dimensions and Clusters of Temperament in Chess and Thomas's Research

Temperament Dimension	Description	Temperament Cluster		
		Easy Child	Difficult Child	Slow-to-Warm-Up Child
Rhythmicity	Regularity of eating, sleeping, toileting	Regular	Irregular	
Activity level	Degree of energy movement		High	Low
Approach-withdrawal	Ease of approaching new people and situations	Positive	Negative	Negative
Adaptability	Ease of tolerating change in routine plans	Positive	Negative	Negative
Predominant quality of mood	Degree of positive or negative affect	Positive	Negative	
Intensity of mood expression	Degree of affect when pleased, displeased, happy, sad	Low to moderate	High	Low
Distractibility/attention span/persistence	Ease of being distracted			

Note: This table shows which of the dimensions were critical in spotting a basic cluster of temperament and what the level of responsiveness was for a critical feature. A blank space indicates that the dimension was not strongly related to a basic cluster of temperament.

Temperament

Temperament *is an individual's behavioral style and characteristic way of responding.* Some adolescents' behavioral style is extremely active, others' more tranquil. Some adolescents show a strong curiosity for exploring their environment for great lengths of time; other show less curiosity. Some adolescents respond warmly to people; others are much more shy. All of these behavioral styles represent an adolescent's temperament.

A widely debated issue in temperament research is defining the key dimensions of temperament. Alexander Chess and Stella Thomas (1977) believe that there are three basic types, or clusters, of temperament—easy, difficult, and slow to warm up:

1. An **easy child** *is generally in a positive mood, quickly establishes regular routines, and adapts easily to new experiences.*
2. A **difficult child** *tends to react negatively and fuss a lot, engages in irregular daily routines, and is slow to accept new experiences.*
3. A **slow-to-warm-up child** *has a low activity level, is somewhat negative, shows low adaptability, and displays a low intensity of mood.*

Different dimensions make up these three basic clusters of temperament, as shown in table 3.1. In their longitudinal study, Chess and Thomas found that 40 percent of the children they studied could be classified as "easy," 10 percent as "difficult," and 15 percent as "slow to warm up."

A number of scholars, including Chess and Thomas, conceive of temperament as a stable characteristic of newborns that comes to be shaped and modified by the child's and adolescent's later experiences (Goldsmith, 1988). This raises the question of heredity's role in temperament. Twin and adoption studies conducted to answer this question have found that heredity has a moderate influence on temperament (Plomin, 1993). However, the strength of the influence usually declines as infants become older (Goldsmith & Gottesman, 1981), which supports the belief that temperament becomes more malleable with experience. Alternatively, behavioral indicators of temperament may be more difficult to spot in adolescents.

A difficult temperament or a temperament that reflects a lack of control places the adolescent at risk for problem behavior. In one recent study, a difficult temperament in adolescence was associated with higher levels of depression, drug use, and stressful life events and lower levels of perceived family support (Tubman & Windle, 1995). In another recent longitudinal study, a temperament factor labeled "lack of control" (irritable, distractible), measured by ratings of observed behavior in early childhood (at 3 and 5 years of age), was related to externalized behavior problems (acting out, delinquent behavior) and less-competent behavior as reported by parents and teachers in early adolescence (13 and 15 years of age) (Caspi & others, 1995). Across the same age span, a temperament factor labeled "approach" (friendliness, eagerness to explore new situations) was associated with fewer internalized problems (anxiety, depression) in boys. In a recent extension of this study, undercontrolled and inhibited 3-year-old children grew up to have more problem behaviors at 21 years of age than well-adjusted, reserved, and confident children (Newman & others, 1997).

The **goodness-of-fit model** *states that the adolescent's adaptation is best when there is a congruence, or match, between the adolescent's temperament and the demands of the social environment (for example, the expectations or attitudes of parents, peers, and teachers)* (Galambos & Turner, 1997; Lerner, 1993). A high-strung parent with an adolescent who is difficult and slow to respond to the parent's affection may begin to feel angry or rejected. Parents might withdraw from difficult adolescents, or they might become critical and punish them, which may make the difficult adolescent even more difficult. A more easygoing parent may have a calming effect on a difficult adolescent.

Heredity-Environment Interaction and Development

A common misconception is that behavior geneticists only analyze the effects of heredity on development. Although they believe heredity plays an important role in adolescent development, they also carve up the environment's contribution to heredity-environment interaction.

Passive Genotype-Environment, Evocative Genotype-Environment, and Active Genotype-Environment Interactions

Parents not only provide the genes for the adolescent's biological blueprint for development; they also play important roles in determining the types of environments their offspring will encounter. Behavior geneticist Sandra Scarr (1992) believes that the environments parents select for their children and adolescents depend to some degree on the parents' own genotypes. Behavior geneticists believe that three of the ways heredity and environment interact in this manner are passively, evocatively, and actively. **Passive genotype-environment interactions** *occur when the biological parents, who are genetically related to the child, provide a rearing environment for the child.* For example, the parents may have a genetic predisposition to be intelligent and read skillfully. Because they read well and enjoy reading, they provide their child with books to read, with the likely outcome that their children, given their own, inherited predispositions, will become skilled readers who enjoy reading.

Sandra Scarr has developed a number of important theoretical ideas and conducted a number of research investigations on the roles of heredity and environment in children's and adolescents' development. She believes that the environments parents select for their children and adolescents depend to some degree on the parents' own genotype.

Evocative genotype-environment interactions *occur because a child's genotype elicits certain types of physical and social environments.* For example, active, smiling children receive more social stimulation than passive, quiet children do. Cooperative, attentive adolescents evoke more pleasant and instructional responses from the adults around them than uncooperative, distractible adolescents do.

Active (niche-picking) genotype-environment interactions *occur when children and adolescents seek out environments they find compatible and stimulating.* Niche-picking *refers to finding a niche or setting that is especially suited to one's abilities.* Adolescents select from their surrounding environment some aspect that they respond to, learn about, or ignore. Their active selections of certain environments are related to their particular genotype. Some adolescents, because of their genotype, have the sensorimotor skills to perform well at sports. Others, because of their genotype, may have more ability in music. Adolescents who are athletically inclined are more likely to actively seek out sports environments in which they can perform well, while adolescents who are musically inclined are more likely to spend time in musical environments in which they can successfully perform their skills.

Scarr believes that the relative importance of the three genotype-environment interactions changes as children develop from infancy through adolescence. In infancy, much of the environment that children experience is provided by adults. When those adults are genetically related to the child, the environment they provide is related to their own characteristics and genotypes. Although infants are active in structuring their experiences by actively attending to what is available to them, they cannot seek out and build their own environmental niches as much as older children can. Therefore, passive genotype-environment interactions are more common in the lives of infants and young children than they are for older children and adolescents who can extend their experiences beyond the family's influences and create their environments to a greater degree.

> *The frightening part about heredity and environment is that we parents provide both.*
>
> —Notebook of a Printer

Shared and Nonshared Environmental Influences

Behavior geneticists also believe that another way the environment's role in heredity-environment interactions can be carved up is to consider the experiences that adolescents have in families that are common with other adolescents living in the same home and those that are not common or shared (George, 1996; Manke & Pike, 1997). Behavior geneticist Robert Plomin (1993) believes that common rearing, or shared environment, accounts for little of the variation in adolescents' personalities or interests. In other words, even though two adolescents live under the same roof with the same parents, their personalities are often very different.

Shared environmental influences *are adolescents' common experiences, such as their parents' personalities and intellectual orientation, the family's social class, and the neighborhood in which they live.* By contrast, **nonshared environmental influences** *refer to an adolescent's own unique experiences, both within the family and outside the family, that are not shared with another sibling.*

Parents often do not interact the same with all siblings, and siblings do not all interact the same with their parents (O'Connor, 1994). Siblings often have different peer groups, different friends, and different teachers at school. In one recent study of nonshared environmental influences, the mother, the father, and two adolescent siblings were observed interacting in a problem-solving task (O'Connor & others, 1995). The results confirmed the importance of nonshared environmental influences— on the average, 67 percent of the adolescents' behavior and 65 percent of the parents' behavior could be explained by unique environmental experiences.

Eleanor Maccoby (1992) argues that there are a number of important aspects of family contexts that are shared by all family members. After all, adolescents observe how parents are treating their siblings, and they learn from what they observe as well as what they experience directly. And atmospheres and moods tend to be spread to whoever is present.

Adoption

Recent research suggests that the developmental outcomes of adoption are influenced by both nature and nurture (Ge & others, 1996). Adoption is the social and legal process by which a parent-child relationship is established between a child and a person or persons who are not the child's biological parents. Researchers have found that adopted children and adolescents often show more psychological and school-related problems than nonadopted children (Brodzinsky & others, 1984; Brodzinsky, Lang, & Smith, 1995). Adopted adolescents are referred for psychological treatment two to five times as often as their nonadopted peers (Grotevant & McRoy, 1990).

In one recent large-scale study of 4,682 adopted adolescents and the same number of nonadopted adolescents, adoptees were slightly less well adjusted (Sharma, McGue, & Benson, 1996). However, adoptees actually showed higher levels of prosocial behavior. Also, the later adoption occurred, the more problems the adoptees had. Infant adoptees had the fewest adjustment difficulties; those adopted after they were 10 years of age had the most. This result has policy implications, especially for the thousands of children who are relegated to the foster care system after infancy. Most often, adoptions of older children occur in cases of parental abuse or neglect where parental rights must be involuntarily terminated. This process can be lengthy, and in the absence of other relatives, the children are turned over to the foster care system, where they must wait months or even years to be adopted. In the recent large-scale adoption study by Ann Sharma, Matthew McGue, and Peter Benson (1996), increasingly negative effects occurred if a child was adopted above the age of 2, but the effects were even more deleterious when adoption took place after the age of 10.

Conclusions

In sum, both genes and environment are necessary for an adolescent to even exist. Heredity and environment operate together—or cooperate—to produce an adolescent's intelligence, temperament, height, weight, ability to pitch a baseball, reading talents, and so on (Gottlieb, 1997; Loehlin, 1995). Without genes, there is no adolescent; without environment, there is no adolescent (Scarr & Weinberg, 1980). If an attractive, popular, intelligent girl is elected president of her senior class in high school, should we conclude that her success is due to heredity or to environment? Of course, the answer is

both. Because the environment's influence depends on genetically endowed characteristics, we say the two factors *interact* (Gottlieb, 1997).

GENERAL FEATURES OF PHYSICAL GROWTH

The aspects of adolescents' physical growth that have received the most attention are height and weight, skeletal growth, reproductive functions, and hormonal changes. What are the growth curves like for such bodily characteristics, and what factors influence these growth curves?

Developmental Growth Curves

The developmental growth curves for physical development in general, for the reproductive organs, for the brain and head, and for the lymphoid glands are shown in figure 3.2. Most skeletal and muscular components of growth, such as height and weight, follow the general curve, as do organs like the liver and kidneys. This growth curve changes gradually in the beginning but rises dramatically at about age 12, characterizing what is commonly referred to as the adolescent growth spurt.

However, the growth curve for the reproductive organs changes even more dramatically than the general curve for height and weight. The prepubertal phase of reproductive development is fairly dormant, but the adolescent phase of the curve is even more precipitous than the adolescent phase of the general height and weight curve. Why is there a difference in the growth curves for height and weight as compared to reproductive functions? The answer lies in an analysis of glandular and hormonal

influences. The glands and hormones that control height and weight are not the same ones that regulate reproductive functions. The development of the skeletal and muscular systems, along with that of most organs, is controlled by the pituitary and thyroid glands. On the other hand, the growth of the reproductive organs is regulated by the sex hormones (androgens and estrogens), which show marked increases in activity at the onset of adolescence.

Another growth curve represents the development of the skull, eyes, and ears, which mature sooner than any other parts of the body. At any point during childhood, the head is, in general, more advanced developmentally than any other aspect of the body. And the top parts of the head—the eyes and brain—grow faster than the lower portions, such as the jaw.

Four mechanisms are known to influence growth curves: target-seeking or self-stabilizing factors, maturity gradients, feedback regulation, and body mass (Damon, 1977). Concerning *target-seeking or self-stabilizing factors*, in cases where growth has been stunted by disease or poor nutrition, the individual's growth often catches up with its original path after the negative conditions have been removed. This regulatory force likely has a genetic basis.

Maturity gradients are known to be present in different regions of the body. For example, the head is always more advanced developmentally than the trunk is, and the trunk is always more advanced developmentally than the limbs are.

Feedback regulation involves biological structures adapting to feedback. For example, the secretions of the pituitary gland influence various other glands, such as the thyroid and the sex glands; the pituitary secretions

Figure~3.2

Growth and Maturity of Body Systems as a Percentage of Total Postnatal Growth.

adjust to the levels of hormones in the other glands. When the other glands' secretions reach appropriate levels, the pituitary regulates its output to continue the equilibrium that has developed.

With regard to *body mass*, Rose Frisch and Roger Revelle (1970) argue that the body has built-in sensors that detect when a certain mass is reached. These detectors then trigger the growth spurt that occurs at the onset of puberty. For young girls, a body weight approximating 106 ± 3 pounds triggers menarche (the first menstruation) and the conclusion of the pubertal growth spurt. Body mass predicts the approximate time female adolescents experience menarche in many different cultures.

Brain Growth, Cognitive Development, and Education

Some biologists (Epstein, 1980) and educators (Toepfer, 1979) argue that the brain does not grow in the relatively smooth, continuous fashion illustrated in figure 3.2. These same individuals argue that, just as there is a height, weight, and sexual spurt that characterizes puberty, so, too, there is a spurt in brain growth. Brain growth spurts are said to occur between 2 and 4, 6 and 8, 10 and 12, and 14 and 16 years of age. During these spurts, the brain is believed to increase 5 to 10 percent in size. Since cell formation in the brain is essentially complete at birth, these growth spurts are not due to new cells being formed but to growth within already-formed cells.

The scientists who stress brain growth spurts also believe that these growth spurts affect the brain's synapses, the points of contact between axons (or sending connectors) and dendrites (or receiving connectors). During the growth spurts, the axons and dendrites lengthen.

One biologist, Herman Epstein (1980), proposed a simple hypothesis: When boys and girls move into one of Piaget's cognitive developmental periods, their brains experience an unusual amount of growth as well. How did Epstein measure brain growth? He used two methods: growth of the head, particularly its circumference, which is closely linked to brain size, and evaluation of electrical waves through use of the electroencephalograph (EEG). These brain waves are influenced by cognitive activities like thinking and problem solving.

With regard to head circumference, children appear to experience growth at three points in development: at approximately the onset of Piaget's concrete operational period (6 to 7 years of age), at the onset of formal operational period (about 10 to 12 years of age), and at a second time in the formal operational period (about 14 to 16 years of age). With regard to electrical waves, spurts in electrical activity of the brain coincide with increases in head circumference.

According to Epstein, children experience a spurt of brain growth at three points in development—at 6 to 7, 10 to 12, and 14 to 16 years of age. Epstein argued that such spurts in brain growth have implications for how children and adolescents should be educated. What were Epstein's conclusions, and how have they been criticized?

Do the head circumference and electrical activity data document important changes in Piaget's stages of concrete and formal operational thought? Epstein argued that they do. Not only did Epstein suggest that the brain data indicated underlying changes in Piaget's stages, but he and others (Toepfer, 1979) argued that the brain data have implications for how children and adolescents should be educated. For example, based primarily on the head circumference and brain-wave data, it was publicized that adolescents between the ages of 12 and 14 are likely to be incapable of learning new skills because this age span reflects little or no growth of the brain. It also was emphasized that adolescents can only consolidate earlier learned skills during this time period, so middle and junior high schools should not attempt to teach new learning skills during this age span.

Did the Epstein data warrant such generalizations and implications for the education of adolescents? Quite clearly they did not! The Epstein data described information about the nature of brain growth and included no measures of cognitive or educational skills. Subsequent research revealed that no correlation exists between spurts in head growth and cognitive changes when cognitive skills are actually measured in concert with head growth (McCall & others, 1983). Yet another investigation focused on whether growth spurts in head circumference, as well as other types of growth, such as height and weight, actually correspond to certain developmental growth periods, like 6 to 7 years of age, 10 to 12 years of age, and so forth (Lampl & Emde, 1983). Each boy and girl in the study did show growth spurts, but the growth spurts were not consistently related to developmental time periods.

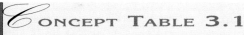

Concept	Processes/ Related Ideas	Characteristics/Description
Heredity	The nature of genes	Each adolescent inherits a genetic code from his or her parents. Physically, the heredity code is carried by biochemical agents called genes and chromosomes. *Genotype* refers to each individual's special configuration of genes. *Phenotype* refers to the individual's observed and measurable characteristics. Introversion-extraversion is moderately influenced by heredity. Genetic transmission is complex, but some principles have been worked out, among them reaction range and canalization.
	Methods	Behavior genetics is the field concerned with the degree and nature of behavior's heredity basis. Among the most important methods developed by behavior geneticists are the twin study and the adoption study.
	Temperament	Temperament is an individual's behavioral style. Chess and Thomas believe that there are three basic temperament clusters: easy, difficult, and slow-to-warm-up. Temperament is influenced strongly by biological factors in infancy but becomes more malleable with experience. In the goodness-of-fit model, an adolescent adapts best when there is a congruence, or match, between the adolescent's temperament and the demands of the social environment.
	Heredity-environment interaction and development	Scarr believes that the environments parents select for their own children and adolescents depend to some degree on the parents' genotypes. Three ways behavior geneticists believe heredity and environment interact in this manner are passively, evocatively, and actively. Plomin argues that it is nonshared environmental experiences that primarily make up the environment's contribution to why one sibling's personality is different from another's. Adopted adolescents have more adjustment problems than nonadopted adolescents. When adoption occurs after the age of 10, it has more negative effects than when it happens in infancy. Without genes, there is no organism; without environment, there is no organism. Because the environment's influence depends on genetically endowed characteristics, we say that the two factors interact.
General Features of Physical Growth	Developmental growth curves	The developmental growth curves include a general growth curve, consisting of most aspects of skeletal and muscular growth; a reproductive curve; a curve for the brain and head; and a curve for lymphoid glands. Some biologists argue that the brain grows in spurts; others disagree. Four mechanisms known to influence growth curves are target-seeking or self-stabilizing factors, maturity gradients, feedback regulation, and body mass.
	Brain growth, cognitive development, and education	There do seem to be some periods of development when brain growth is rapid, although even the consistency of the brain growth spurts have been questioned. The degree to which these brain spurts are closely linked with rapid growth in cognitive skills, such as those associated with the onset of Piagetian stages, has not been documented.

In sum, there do seem to be some periods of development when brain growth is rapid, although even the consistency of the brain growth spurts has been questioned (Harmon, 1984). The degree to which these brain spurts are closely linked with rapid growth in cognitive skills, such as those associated with the onset of Piagetian stages, has not been documented (Overton & Byrnes, 1991).

At this point, we have discussed a number of ideas about heredity and about general features of growth in adolescence. A summary of these ideas is presented in concept table 3.1.

PUBERTY

Comedian Bill Cosby once remarked that the problem with his teenage son was not that he grew, but that he did not know when to stop growing. The adolescent growth spurt takes place in puberty. Our coverage of puberty focuses on physical changes, psychological dimensions, and models of pubertal change.

Physical Changes

To understand puberty's physical changes, we will explore puberty's boundaries and determinants, hormonal changes, and changes in height, weight, and sexual maturation.

From Penguin Dreams and Stranger Things *by Berke Breathed. Copyright © 1985 by The Washington Post Company. By permission of Little, Brown and Company.*

The Boundaries and Determinants of Puberty

Puberty can be distinguished from adolescence. For most of us, puberty has ended long before adolescence is exited, although puberty is the most important marker of the beginning of adolescence. What is puberty? **Puberty** *is a period of rapid physical maturation involving hormonal and bodily changes that occur primarily during early adolescence.*

Imagine a toddler displaying all the features of puberty—a 3-year-old girl with fully developed breasts or a boy just slightly older with a deep male voice. That is what we would see by the year 2250 if the age at which puberty arrives kept getting younger at its present pace. In Norway, **menarche**—*a girl's first menstruation*—occurs at just over 13 years of age, compared to 17 years of age in the 1840s. In the United States—where children mature up to a year earlier than children in European countries—the average age of menarche has been declining an average of about 4 months per decade for the past century (see figure 3.3). Fortunately, however, we are unlikely to see pubescent toddlers, since what has happened in the past century is likely the result of a higher level of nutrition and health. The available information suggests that menarche began to occur earlier at about the time of the Industrial Revolution, a period associated with increased standards of living and advances in medical science (Petersen, 1979).

Genetic factors also are involved in puberty. Puberty is not simply an environmental accident. As indicated earlier, while nutrition, health, and other factors affect puberty's timing and variations in its makeup, the basic genetic program is wired into the nature of the species (Plomin, 1993).

Another key factor in puberty's occurrence is body mass, as was mentioned earlier. Menarche occurs at a relatively consistent weight in girls. A body weight approximating 106 ± 3 pounds can trigger menarche and

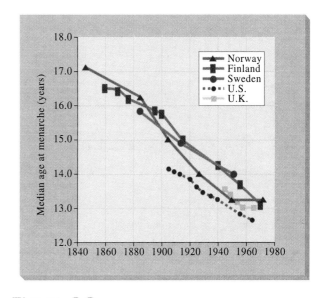

Figure~3.3

Median Ages at Menarche in Selected Northern European Countries and the United States from 1845 to 1969.
Notice the steep decline in the age at which girls experienced menarche in five different countries. Recently the age at which girls experience menarche has been leveling off.

the end of the pubertal growth spurt. For menarche to begin and continue, fat must make up 17 percent of the girl's body weight. Both teenage anorexics whose weight drops dramatically and female athletes in certain sports (such as gymnastics) may become amenorrheic (having an absence or suppression of menstrual discharge).

In summary, puberty's determinants include nutrition, health, heredity, and body mass. So far, our discussion of puberty has emphasized its dramatic changes. Keep in mind, though, that puberty is not a single, sudden event. We know when a young boy or girl is going through puberty, but pinpointing its beginning and its

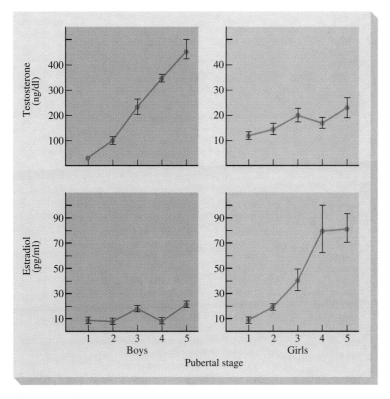

Figure~3.4

Hormone Levels by Sex and Pubertal Stage for Testosterone and Estradiol.
The five stages range from the early beginning of puberty (stage 1) to the most advanced stage of puberty (stage 5).

Two primary classes of hormones are important in pubertal development—androgens and estrogens. **Androgens** *are the main class of male sex hormones.* **Estrogens** *are the main class of female hormones.* Recently, researchers have examined which androgens and which estrogens show the strongest increases during puberty. **Testosterone** *is an androgen that plays an important role in male pubertal development.* Throughout puberty, increasing testosterone levels are associated with a number of physical changes in boys—development of external genitals, increase in height, and voice changes. **Estradiol** *is an estrogen that plays an important role in female pubertal development.* As estradiol level rises, breast development, uterine development, and skeletal changes occur. In one study, testosterone levels increased eighteenfold in boys but only twofold in girls across the pubertal period; estradiol levels increased eightfold in girls but only twofold in boys during puberty (Nottelman & others, 1987) (see figure 3.4). Note that both testosterone and estradiol are present in the hormonal makeup of both boys and girls, but that testosterone dominates in male pubertal development, estradiol in female pubertal development.

The same influx of hormones that puts hair on a male's chest and imparts curvature to a female's breast may contribute to psychological development in adolescence (Dorn & Lucas, 1995). In one study of 108 normal boys and girls ranging in age from 9 to 14, a higher concentration of testosterone was present in boys who rated themselves more socially competent (Nottelman & others, 1987). In another study of 60 normal boys and girls in the same age range, girls with higher estradiol levels expressed more anger and aggression (Inoff-Germain & others, 1988). However, hormonal effects by themselves might account for only a small portion of the variance in adolescent development. For example, in one study, social factors accounted for two to four times as much variance as hormonal factors in young adolescent girls' depression and anger (Brooks-Gunn & Warren, 1989). Also, behavior and moods can affect hormones (Paikoff, Buchanan, & Brooks-Gunn, 1991). Stress, eating patterns, exercise, sexual activity, tension, and depression can activate or suppress various aspects of the hormone system. In sum, the hormone-behavior link is complex.

One additional aspect of the pituitary gland's role in development still needs to be described. Not only does the pituitary gland release gonadotropins that stimulate the testes and ovaries, but through interaction with the hypothalamus the pituitary gland also secretes hormones

end is difficult. Except for menarche, which occurs rather late in puberty, no single marker heralds puberty. For boys, the first whisker or first wet dream are events that could mark its appearance, but both may go unnoticed.

Hormonal Changes

Behind the first whisker in boys and the widening of hips in girls is a flood of **hormones,** *powerful chemical substances secreted by the endocrine glands and carried through the body by the bloodstream.* The endocrine system's role in puberty involves the interaction of the hypothalamus, the pituitary gland, and the gonads (sex glands). The **hypothalamus** *is a structure in the higher portion of the brain that monitors eating, drinking, and sex.* The **pituitary gland** *is an important endocrine gland that controls growth and regulates other glands.* The **gonads** *are the sex glands—the testes in males, the ovaries in females.* How does this hormonal system work? The pituitary sends a signal via *gonadotropins* (hormones that stimulate the testes or ovaries) to the appropriate gland to manufacture the hormone. Then the pituitary gland, through interaction with the hypothalamus, detects when the optimal level of hormones is reached and responds by maintaining gonadotropin secretion.

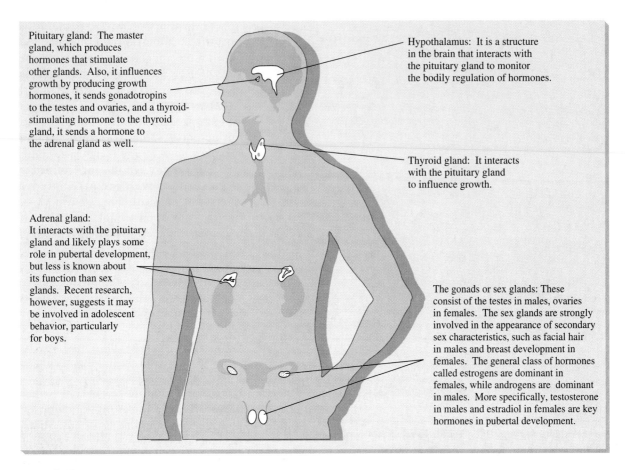

Figure~3.5

The Major Endocrine Glands Involved in Pubertal Change.

that either directly lead to growth and skeletal maturation, or produce such growth effects through interaction with the *thyroid gland,* located in the neck region.

An overview of the location and function of the major endocrine glands is shown in figure 3.5. Now that we have studied the endocrine system's important role in puberty, we turn our attention to the external physical changes that characterize puberty.

Height, Weight, and Sexual Maturation

Among the most noticeable physical changes during puberty are increases in height and weight, and sexual maturation.

Height and Weight   As indicated in figure 3.6, the growth spurt occurs approximately 2 years earlier for girls than for boys. The growth spurt for girls begins at approximately 10½ years of age and lasts for about 2 years. During this time, girls increase in height by about 3½ inches per year. The growth spurt for boys begins at about 12½ years of age and also lasts for about 2 years. Boys usually grow about 4 inches per year during this time frame.

Boys and girls who are shorter or taller than their peers before adolescence are likely to remain so during adolescence. In our society, there is a stigma attached to short boys. At the beginning of the adolescent period, girls tend to be as tall as or taller than boys of their age, but by the end of the middle school years most boys have caught up or, in many cases, even surpassed girls in height. And even though height in the elementary school years is a good predictor of height later in adolescence, there is still room for the individual's height to change in relation to the height of his or her peers. As much as 30 percent of the height of late adolescence is unexplained by height in the elementary school years.

The rate at which adolescents gain weight follows approximately the same developmental timetable as the rate at which they gain height. Marked weight gains coincide with the onset of puberty. During early adolescence, girls tend to outweigh boys, but, just as with height, by about age 14, boys begin to surpass girls.

Sexual Maturation   Think back to the onset of your puberty. Of the striking changes that were taking place in your body, what was the first change that occurred? Researchers have found that male pubertal characteristics

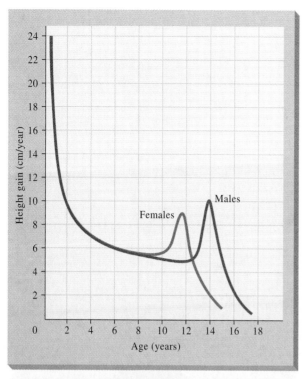

Figure~3.6

Pubertal Growth Spurt.
On the average, the growth spurt that characterizes pubertal change occurs 2 years earlier for girls (age 10½) than for boys (age 12½).

develop in this order: increase in penis and testicle size, appearance of straight pubic hair, minor voice change, first ejaculation (which usually occurs through masturbation or a wet dream), appearance of kinky pubic hair, onset of maximum growth, growth of hair in armpits, more detectable voice changes, and growth of facial hair. Three of the most noticeable areas of sexual maturation in boys are penis elongation, testes development, and growth of facial hair. The normal range and average age of development for these sexual characteristics, along with height spurt, is shown in figure 3.7. Figure 3.8 shows the typical course of male sexual development during puberty.

What is the order of appearance of physical changes in females? First, either the breasts enlarge or pubic hair appears. Later, hair appears in the armpits. As these changes occur, the female grows in height, and her hips become wider than her shoulders. Her first menstruation comes rather late in the pubertal cycle. Initially, her menstrual cycles may be highly irregular. For the first several years, she might not ovulate every menstrual cycle. In some instances, she does not become fertile until 2 years after her period begins. No voice changes comparable to those in pubertal males occur in pubertal females. By the end of puberty, the female's breasts have become more fully rounded. Two of the most noticeable aspects of female pubertal change are pubic hair and breast development. Figure 3.7 shows the normal range and average development of these sexual characteristics and also provides information about menarche and height gain. Figure 3.8 shows the typical course of female sexual development during puberty.

It should be noted that we know less about the sequence of pubertal changes in females than we know about the sequence of such changes in males (Susman, 1995). Pubertal changes in females unfold in a less clear-cut way than they do in males.

Individual Variation in Puberty The pubertal sequence may begin as early as 10 years of age or as late as 13½ for most boys. It may end as early as 13 years or as late as 17 years for most boys. The normal range is wide enough that, given two boys of the same chronological age, one might complete the pubertal sequence before the other one has begun it. For girls, the age range of the first menstrual period is even wider. Menarche is considered within a normal range if it appears between the ages of 9 and 15.

So far, we have primarily been concerned with the physical dimensions of puberty. As we see next, however, the psychological dimensions of puberty also involve some fascinating changes.

Psychological Dimensions

A host of psychological changes accompany an adolescent's pubertal development. Try to remember when you were beginning puberty. Not only did you probably think of yourself differently, but your parents and peers also probably began acting differently toward you. Maybe you were proud of your changing body, even though you were perplexed about what was happening. Perhaps your parents no longer perceived you as someone they could sit in bed with to watch television or as someone who should be kissed goodnight.

There has been far less research on the psychosocial aspects of male pubertal transitions than on those of females, possibly because of the difficulty in defining when the male transitions occur. Wet dreams are one such marker, yet there has been little research on this topic (Susman, 1995).

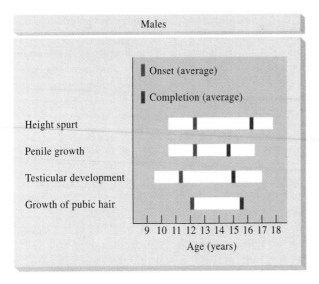

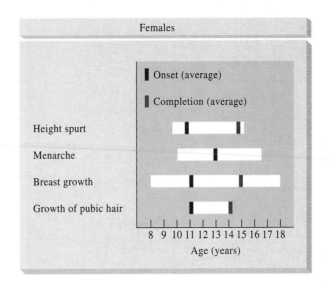

Figure~3.7

Normal Range and Average Development of Sexual Characteristics in Males and Females.

Adapted from "Growing Up" by J. M. Tanner. Copyright © 1973 by Scientific American, Inc. All rights reserved.

Among the intriguing questions posed by developmentalists about puberty's psychological dimensions are the following: What parts of their body image are adolescents most preoccupied with? What are the psychological dimensions of menarche and the menstrual cycle? What are the psychological consequences of early and late maturation? How complex are the issues involved in being on-time or off-time in pubertal development? Are the effects of pubertal timing exaggerated? Let's look further at each of these questions.

Body Image

One psychological aspect of physical change in puberty is certain: Adolescents are preoccupied with their bodies and develop individual images of what their bodies are like. Perhaps you looked in the mirror on a daily and sometimes even hourly basis to see if you could detect anything different about your changing body. Preoccupation with one's body image is strong throughout adolescence, but it is especially acute during puberty, a time when adolescents are more dissatisfied with their bodies than in late adolescence (Wright, 1989).

There are gender differences in adolescents' perceptions of their bodies. In general, girls are less happy with their bodies and have more negative body images, compared to boys, throughout puberty (Brooks-Gunn & Paikoff, 1993; Henderson & Zivian, 1995). Also, as pubertal change proceeds, girls often become more dissatisfied with their bodies, probably because their body fat increases, while boys become more satisfied as they move through puberty, probably because their muscle mass increases (Gross, 1984).

Adolescents show a strong preoccupation with their changing bodies and develop individual images of what their bodies are like. Adolescent boys, as well as adolescent girls, rate body build as one of the most important dimensions of physical attractiveness.

Menarche and the Menstrual Cycle

The onset of puberty and menarche has often been described as a "main event" in most historical accounts of adolescence (Erikson, 1968; Freud, 1958; Hall, 1904). Basically, these views suggest that pubertal changes and events such as menarche produce a different body that

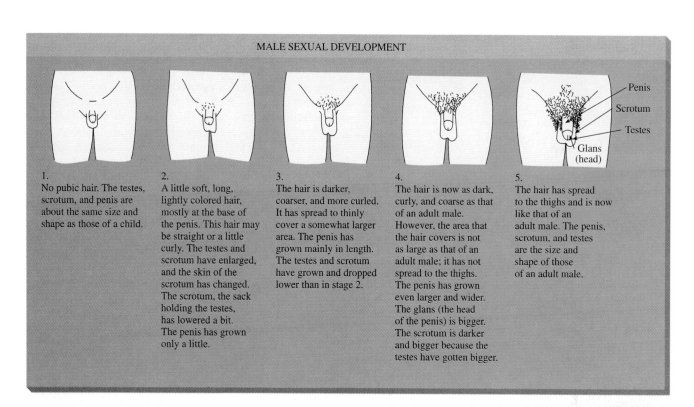

MALE SEXUAL DEVELOPMENT

1.
No pubic hair. The testes, scrotum, and penis are about the same size and shape as those of a child.

2.
A little soft, long, lightly colored hair, mostly at the base of the penis. This hair may be straight or a little curly. The testes and scrotum have enlarged, and the skin of the scrotum has changed. The scrotum, the sack holding the testes, has lowered a bit. The penis has grown only a little.

3.
The hair is darker, coarser, and more curled. It has spread to thinly cover a somewhat larger area. The penis has grown mainly in length. The testes and scrotum have grown and dropped lower than in stage 2.

4.
The hair is now as dark, curly, and coarse as that of an adult male. However, the area that the hair covers is not as large as that of an adult male; it has not spread to the thighs. The penis has grown even larger and wider. The glans (the head of the penis) is bigger. The scrotum is darker and bigger because the testes have gotten bigger.

5.
The hair has spread to the thighs and is now like that of an adult male. The penis, scrotum, and testes are the size and shape of those of an adult male.

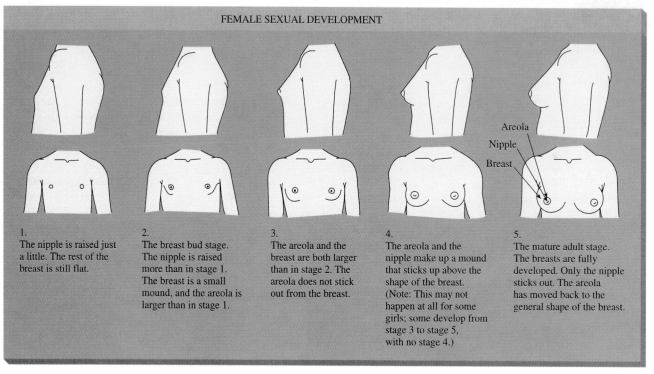

FEMALE SEXUAL DEVELOPMENT

1.
The nipple is raised just a little. The rest of the breast is still flat.

2.
The breast bud stage. The nipple is raised more than in stage 1. The breast is a small mound, and the areola is larger than in stage 1.

3.
The areola and the breast are both larger than in stage 2. The areola does not stick out from the breast.

4.
The areola and the nipple make up a mound that sticks up above the shape of the breast. (Note: This may not happen at all for some girls; some develop from stage 3 to stage 5, with no stage 4.)

5.
The mature adult stage. The breasts are fully developed. Only the nipple sticks out. The areola has moved back to the general shape of the breast.

Figure~3.8

The Five Pubertal Stages of Male and Female Sexual Development.

requires considerable change in self-conception, possibly resulting in an identity crisis. Only recently has there been empirical research directed at understanding the female adolescent's adaptation to menarche and the menstrual cycle (Brooks-Gunn, Graber, & Paikoff, 1994).

In one study of 639 girls, a wide range of reactions to menarche appeared (Brooks-Gunn & Ruble, 1982). However, most of the reactions were quite mild, as girls described their first period as a little upsetting, a little surprising, or a little exciting and positive. In this

Girls' Initiation Rites and Female Circumcision in Primitive Cultures

Africa, especially sub-Saharan Africa, has been the location of many rites of passage for adolescents. Two common themes in female initiation rites are these: (1) a childbirth scenario supposed to guarantee fertility and ease of childbirth, and (2) procedures designed to ensure the achievement of cultural standards of beauty and sexual desirability (Sommer, 1978).

The female's reproductive capabilities and the onset of menstruation are often the central focus of female rites of passage in primitive cultures. In such rites, female circumcision often occurs, which can take one of two forms. The milder form is practiced in twenty countries, mostly in East, West, and Central Africa. All or part of the clitoris, and sometimes the internal vaginal lips, are removed. In the second, more radical type of operation, all of the external genitalia are removed and the outer lips are sewn shut, leaving just a tiny opening, through which urine and menstrual discharge can pass. In Mali, Sudan, and Somalia, the majority of females undergo this radical procedure.

In Africa alone, more than 75 million females are circumcised. Female circumcision is also practiced in some areas of the Middle East and southeastern Asia. One of the main goals of the operation is to ensure that sex is linked with procreation rather than enjoyment. In many cultures, female circumcision is carried out as part of the ceremonial ritual signaling membership in the adult community. An increasing number of African women are trying to eliminate female circumcision. In some countries, their efforts are meeting with some success. For example, in Sudan, a survey of female high school students indicated that, while 96 percent had been circumcised, more than 70 percent strongly recommended that their younger sisters, and young girls in general, should not be circumcised (Taylor, 1985).

study, 120 of the fifth- and sixth-grade girls were telephoned to obtain more personal, detailed information about their experience with menarche. The most frequent theme of the girls' responses was positive—namely, that menarche was an index of their maturity. Other positive reports indicated that the girls could now have children, were experiencing something that made them more like adult women, and now were more like their friends. The most frequent negative aspects of menarche reported by the girls were its hassle (having to carry supplies around) and its messiness. A minority of the girls also indicated that menarche involved physical discomfort, produced behavioral limitations, and created emotional changes.

Questions also were asked about the extent to which the girls communicated with others about the appearance of menarche, the extent to which the girls were prepared for menarche, and how the experience was related to early/late maturation. Virtually all of the girls told their mothers immediately, but most of the girls did not tell anyone else about menarche, with only one in five informing a friend. However, after two or three periods had occurred, most girls had talked with girlfriends about menstruation. Girls not prepared for menarche indicated more negative feelings about menstruation than those who were more prepared for its onset. Girls who matured early had more negative reactions than average- or late-maturing

girls. In summary, menarche initially may be disruptive, especially for unprepared and early-maturing girls, but it typically does not reach the tumultuous, conflicting proportions described by some early theoreticians.

Female reproductive capabilities are often the central focus of female rites of passage to adult status in primitive cultures. More about girls' initiation rites in primitive cultures and concern about female circumcision in these rites is presented in Sociocultural Worlds of Adolescence.

For many girls, menarche occurs on time, but for others is occurs early or late. Next, we examine the effects of early and late maturation on both boys and girls.

Early and Late Maturation

Some of you entered puberty early, others late, and yet others on time. When adolescents mature earlier or later than their peers, might they perceive themselves differently? In the Berkeley Longitudinal Study some years ago, early-maturing boys perceived themselves more positively and had more successful peer relations than did their late-maturing counterparts (Jones, 1965). The findings for early-maturing girls were similar but not as strong as for boys. When the late-maturing boys were studied in their thirties, however, they had developed a stronger sense of identity than had the early-maturing boys (Peskin, 1967).

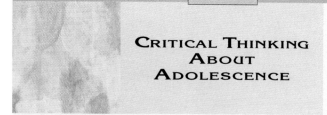

CRITICAL THINKING ABOUT ADOLESCENCE

Blooming Late

Harvey Peskin's (1967) study on late- versus early-maturing boys established that early maturity was negatively related to strength of identity measured around age 30. Can you propose some explanations that might account for the advantage of having been a late-bloomer in adolescence? How many hypotheses or alternative explanations can you generate for this finding?

Late-maturing boys may have had more time to explore a wide variety of options. They may have

focused on career development and achievement that would serve them better in life than their early-maturing counterparts' emphasis on physical status.

These differences have important implications for surviving the sometimes turbulent social aspects of high school. Late bloomers often report feeling harassed by those who are popular and physically well developed in high school. High school reunions later in life can sometimes feel like sweet revenge for the successful late bloomer.

Can you think of other explanations? The speculations that you develop demonstrate your *pursuit of alternative explanations to understand development comprehensively.*

More-recent research, though, confirms that, at least during adolescence, it is advantageous to be an early-maturing rather than a late-maturing boy (Petersen, 1987). Roberta Simmons and Dale Blyth (1987) studied more than 450 individuals for 5 years, beginning in the sixth grade and continuing through the tenth grade, in Milwaukee, Wisconsin. Students were individually interviewed, and achievement test scores and grade point averages were obtained. The presence or absence of menstruation and the relative onset of menses were used to classify girls as early, middle, or late maturers. The peak of growth in height was used to classify boys according to these categories.

In the Milwaukee study, more mixed and complex findings emerged for girls (Simmons & Blyth, 1987). Early-maturing girls had more problems in school, were more independent, and were more popular with boys than late-maturing girls were. The time at which maturation was assessed also was a factor. In the sixth grade, early-maturing girls were more satisfied with their body image than late-maturing girls were, but by the tenth grade, late-maturing girls were more satisfied (see figure 3.9). Why? Because by late adolescence, early-maturing girls are shorter and stockier, while late-maturing girls are taller and thinner. The late-maturing girls in late adolescence have body images that more closely approximate the current American ideal of feminine beauty—tall and thin.

In the last decade an increasing number of researchers have found that early maturation increases girls' vulnerability to a number of problems (Brooks-Gunn & Paikoff, 1993; Stattin & Magnusson, 1990). Early-maturing girls are more likely to smoke, drink, be depressed, have an eating disorder, request earlier

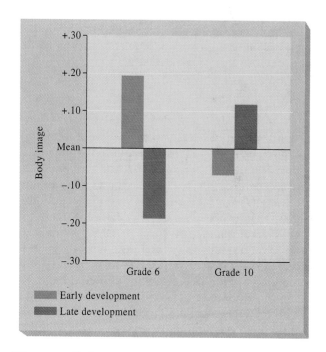

Figure~3.9

Early- and Late-Maturing Adolescent Girls' Perceptions of Body Image in Early and Late Adolescence.

independence from their parents, and have older friends; and their bodies likely elicit responses from males that lead to earlier dating and earlier sexual experiences. In one study, early-maturing girls had lower educational and occupational attainment in adulthood (Stattin & Magnusson, 1990). Apparently as a result of their social and cognitive immaturity, combined with early physical development, early-maturing girls are easily lured into problem behaviors, not recognizing the possible long-term effects on their development (Petersen, 1993).

Complexity of On-Time and Off-Time Pubertal Events in Development

Being on-time or off-time in terms of pubertal events is a complex affair. For example, the dimensions can involve not just biological status and pubertal age, but also chronological age, grade in school, cognitive functioning, and social maturity (Petersen, 1987). Adolescents can be at risk when the demands of a particular social context do not match the adolescents' physical and behavioral characteristics (Lerner, 1987). Dancers whose pubertal status develops on time are one example. In general peer comparisons, on-time dancers should not show adjustment problems. However, they do not have the ideal characteristics for being a dancer, which generally are those associated with late maturity—a thin, lithe body build. The dancers, then, are on time in terms of pubertal development for their peer group in general, but there is an asynchrony to their development in terms of their more focused peer group—dancers.

Are Puberty's Effects Exaggerated?

Some researchers have begun to question whether puberty's effects are as strong as once believed (Montemayor, Adams, & Gulotta, 1990). Have the effects of puberty been exaggerated? Puberty affects some adolescents more strongly than others, and some behaviors more strongly than others. Body image, dating interest, and sexual behavior are quite clearly affected by pubertal change. In one study, early-maturing boys and girls reported more sexual activity and delinquency than did late maturers (Flannery, Rowe, & Gulley, 1993). The recent questioning of puberty's effects, however, suggests that, if we look at overall development and adjustment in the human life span, puberty and its variations have less-dramatic effects for most individuals than is commonly thought. For some young adolescents, the transition through puberty is stormy, but for most it is not. Each period of the human life span has its stresses. Puberty is no different. It imposes new challenges resulting from emerging developmental changes, but the vast majority of adolescents weather these stresses nicely. In addition, there are not only biological influences on adolescent development, but also cognitive and social or environmental influences. As with all periods of human development, these processes work in concert to produce who we are in adolescence. Singling out biological changes as the dominating change in adolescence may not be a wise strategy.

Jeanne Brooks-Gunn has been a pioneer in the study of puberty's role in adolescent development. Her far-ranging research interests include the psychological accompaniments of menarche, adaptive and maladaptive responses to pubertal growth, and adolescent health and well-being.

Although extremely early and late maturation may be risk factors in development, we have seen that the overall effects of early or late maturation are often not great. Not all early maturers will date, smoke, and drink, and not all late maturers will have difficulty in peer relations. In some instances, the effects of school grade are stronger than maturational timing effects are (Petersen & Crockett, 1985). Because the adolescent's social world is organized by grade rather than by pubertal development, this finding is not surprising. However, this does not mean that maturation has no influence on development. Rather, we need to evaluate puberty's effects within the larger framework of interacting biological, cognitive, and socioemotional contexts (Brooks-Gunn, 1992).

Models of Pubertal Change and Behavior

We have just seen that puberty's effects are complex. Given this complexity, it is not surprising that a number of different models have been proposed to explain the linkages between pubertal change and behavior. The possible links include (1) direct hormonal effects, (2) indirect effects via secondary sexual characteristics, (3) connections with social events, and (4) how puberty and social events set adolescents on a particular developmental trajectory (Brooks-Gunn, Graber, & Paikoff, 1994).

Direct Hormonal Effects

The model of direct hormonal effects is the most simplistic model of links between pubertal change and behavior. There has been some support for a link between androgens and aggressive affect in adolescent boys (Susman & others, 1987) but less so for girls (Brooks-Gunn & Warren, 1989). There is less clear-cut evidence linking pubertal hormones with depressive affect than linking them with aggressive behavior and affect. Many developmentalists believe that more complex models than the direct hormonal effects model are needed to explain links between pubertal change and behavior.

Indirect Effects via Secondary Sexual Characteristics

The timing of pubertal development, assessed via changes in hormones and secondary sex characteristics, is a candidate for explaining behavioral and affective changes in early adolescence, especially for girls. For example, early maturation in girls has been associated with depressive affect, whereas late maturation has acted as a buffer against depression (Baydar, Brooks-Gunn, & Warren, 1992).

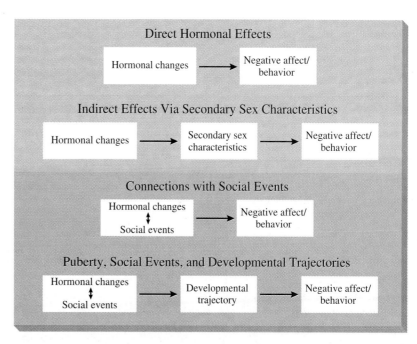

Figure~3.10

Models of Pubertal Change and Behavior.

Connections with Social Events

Another model emphasizes the possibility that social events or contexts contribute to links between pubertal change and behavior. The addition of social factors underscores the fact that biological and psychological development takes place within a social context (Bronfenbrenner, 1995). One study investigated the influence of hormonal functioning, pubertal development (status and timing), and life events on depressive and aggressive affect (Brooks-Gunn & Warren, 1989). Social events (such as life events that occurred at school, at home, and in peer relations) were associated with negative affect to a much greater degree than hormonal changes were. Social events and hormonal change together predicted negative affect better than hormonal change alone did.

Puberty, Social Events, and Developmental Trajectories

Another model suggests that puberty and social events are linked with each other and contribute to negative affect. The assumption is that experiences during puberty set the individual on a trajectory of either high or low levels of affective expression over the course of the adolescent years. In one longitudinal study, initial hormonal changes (in estradiol, for example) were associated with depressive and aggressive affect when initially assessed

and 1 year later (Paikoff, Brooks-Gunn, & Warren, 1991). The linkages remained even when the researchers controlled for such factors as prior affective expression, physical maturation, and physical timing.

Similar linkages have been found in the development of eating behavior problems across the adolescent years. In one study, initial associations among pubertal status, social relationships, and eating problems set the individual on longer-term trajectories, so that girls who had repeated eating problems matured earlier than other girls (Graber & others, 1994). During the early adolescent years, puberty played a key role in determining the particular trajectory that would appear in the late adolescent and young adult years.

Other models of links between pubertal change and behavior have been proposed, but the four models presented here provide a sense of the different explanations that are being developed. A summary of the four models is presented in figure 3.10. To fully document which of these models presents the most accurate portrayal of connections between pubertal change and behavior will require more intensive, longitudinal studies of hormonal systems, social/contextual factors, and behavior.

At this point we have studied a number of ideas about puberty. A summary of these ideas is presented in concept table 3.2.

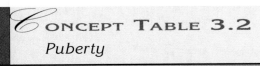

Concept	Processes/ Related Ideas	Characteristics/Description
Physical Changes	Boundaries and determinants	Puberty is a rapid change to physical maturation involving hormonal and bodily changes that occur primarily during early adolescence. Puberty's determinants include nutrition, health, heredity, and body mass.
	Hormonal changes	The endocrine system's influence on puberty involves an interaction of the hypothalamus, the pituitary gland, and the gonads (sex glands). Testosterone, a member of the general class of hormones known as androgens, plays a key role in the pubertal development of males. Estradiol, a member of the general class of hormones known as estrogens, plays a key role in the pubertal development of females. Recent research has documented a link between hormonal levels and the adolescent's behavior. The pituitary gland also stimulates growth, either through the thyroid gland, or more directly, through growth hormones.
	Height, weight, and sexual maturation	The growth spurt for boys occurs about two years later than for girls, with 12 1/2 being the average age of onset for boys and 10 1/2 being the average age of onset for girls. Sexual maturation is a predominant feature of pubertal change and includes a number of changes in physical development, such as penile growth, testicular development, and pubic hair in boys, and pubic hair and breast growth in girls. Individual variation in puberty is extensive, within a normal range that is wide enough that, given two boys of the same chronological age, one may complete the pubertal sequence before the other has begun it.
Psychological Dimensions	Body image	Adolescents show considerable interest in their body image. Young adolescents are more preoccupied and less satisfied with their body image than are late adolescents. Girls have more negative body images throughout puberty than boys do.
	Menarche and the menstrual cycle	Menarche is the girl's first period. Menarche and the menstrual cycle produce a wide range of reactions in girls. Those who are not prepared or who mature early tend to have more negative reactions.
	Early and late maturation	Early maturation favors boys, at least during adolescence. As adults, though, late-maturing boys achieve more successful identities. Researchers are increasingly finding that early-maturing girls are vulnerable to many problems.
	On-time and off-time	Being on-time or being off-time in pubertal development is complex. Adolescents may be at risk when the demands of a particular social context do not match adolescents' physical and behavioral characteristics.
	Are puberty's effects exaggerated?	Recently, some scholars have expressed doubt that puberty's effects on development are as strong as once believed. Adolescent development is influenced by an interaction of biological, cognitive, and social factors, rather than being dominated by biology. While extremely early or late maturation may place an adolescent at risk, the overall effects of early and late maturation are not great. This is not the same as saying that puberty and early or late maturation have no effect on development. They do, but puberty's changes always need to be considered in terms of the larger framework of interacting biological, cognitive, and social factors.
Models of Pubertal Change and Behavior	Their nature	Four models that have been proposed are based on direct hormonal effects; indirect effects via secondary sex characteristics; social events; and puberty, social events, and developmental trajectory.

SUMMARY

It has been said that adolescence begins in biology and ends in culture. Indeed, the biological changes of early adolescence are dramatic and familiar to all of us, although some developmentalists believe these have been given too much attention, to the exclusion of cognitive and socioemotional processes. Puberty brings extensive change to our bodies and modifies how we think about ourselves and how others interact with us.

We began this chapter by studying heredity and the nature of genes, methods, temperament, and heredity-environment interaction. Then we evaluated some general features of physical growth, including developmental growth curves and brain growth, cognitive development, and education. Our extensive coverage of puberty focused on physical changes, psychological dimensions, and models of pubertal change and behavior.

Don't forget that you can obtain an overall summary of the chapter by again studying the two concept tables on pages 87 and 98. In the next chapter, we will turn our attention to some intriguing cognitive changes that occur during adolescence.

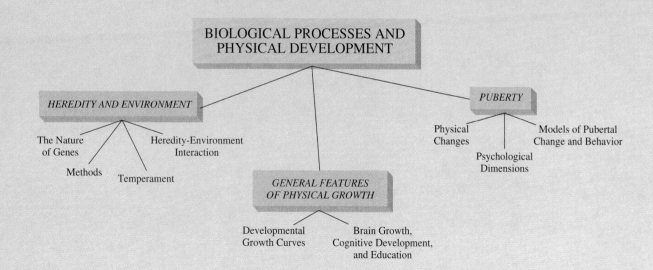

KEY TERMS

genotype 79

phenotype 79

reaction range 79

canalization 79

behavior genetics 79

twin study 80

identical twins 80

fraternal twins 80

adoption study 80

temperament 81

easy child 81

difficult child 81

slow-to-warm-up child 81

goodness-of-fit model 82

passive genotype-environment
    interactions 82

evocative genotype-environment
    interactions 82

active (niche-picking) genotype-
    environment interactions 82

shared environmental influences 83

nonshared environmental
    influences 83

puberty 88

menarche 88

hormones 89

hypothalamus 89

pituitary gland 89

gonads 89

androgens 89

estrogens 89

testosterone 89

estradiol 89

PRACTICAL KNOWLEDGE ABOUT ADOLESCENCE

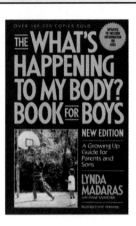

The What's Happening to My Body? Book for Boys
(1991) by Lynda Madaras and D. Saavedra.
New York: Newmarket.

This book is written for parents and focuses on how to help boys cope with pubertal transitions. Among the topics covered are the boy's changing body, growth spurts, reproductive organs, pimples, voice changes, beards, puberty in girls, birth control, and AIDS and other sexually transmitted diseases. Advice is also given about how to communicate with adolescent sons about sexual urges and guilt.

YOU'RE IN CHARGE

A Teenage Girl's Guide to Sex and Her Body

The facts on health, sexuality, hormones, pregnancy, AIDS, and more

Niels H. Lauersen, M.D., Ph.D., and Eileen Stukane
Authors of the bestselling *Listen to Your Body*

You're in Charge
(1993) by Niels Lauersen
and Eileen Stukane.
New York: Fawcett.

This book was written for the teenage girl and tells her about her changing body in plain, nonjudgmental language. Topics include health, sex, hormones, pregnancy, and AIDS. Girls also learn about the ways boys develop, how to cope with stressful sexual encounters, what a girl should know if she thinks she is ready to have sex, myths and realities about a number of sexually transmitted diseases, and the nature of love.

RESOURCES FOR IMPROVING THE LIVES OF ADOLESCENTS

The What's Happening to My Body? Book for Girls
(1987)
by Lynn Madaras
New York: Newmarket

This book tells parents how to help girls through the pubertal transition. Information is included about the changing body, growth spurts, reproductive organs, pimples, and puberty in boys. Advice is given on how to handle sexual urges and guilt.

The Society for Adolescent Medicine
10727 White Oak Avenue
Granada Hills, CA 91344

This organization is a valuable source of information about competent physicians who specialize in treating adolescents. It maintains a list of recommended adolescent specialists across the United States.

EXPLORING ADOLESCENT DEVELOPMENT

To further explore the nature of biological processes and physical development, we will describe a recent research study on biological processes and physical development, and discuss health-care issues related to pubertal timing.

RESEARCH ON ADOLESCENT DEVELOPMENT

The Antecedents of Menarcheal Age

In the "Research on Adolescent Development" sections of Chapters 1 and 2, we described the importance of research in advancing our knowledge about adolescence and the nature of journals that include information about adolescence. Beginning with this chapter and continuing through the remaining chapters, this endpiece will describe an actual research study related to the chapter's content to give you a sense of how the research process works.

In our minisimulation of journal articles, the abstract has been omitted, and in many of the studies the results and discussion sections have been collapsed into one heading. In most journal articles the results and discussion are presented separately. Actual journal articles are also much longer and more detailed than our presentation. Nevertheless, the minisimulations should give you a better feel for how the research process in adolescent development is conducted.

Featured Study

Graber, J. A., Brooks-Gunn, J., & Warren, M. P. (1995). The antecedents of menarcheal age: Heredity, family environment, and stressful life events. *Child Development, 66,* 346–359.

Variations in pubertal development have been linked with several hereditary and environmental antecedents. Researchers recently have evaluated a broad range of environmental stressors and their influence on the development of the reproductive system. The purpose of the present study was to evaluate which of a number of antecedents influence pubertal timing, as indexed by menarche.

Menarche is one of the most studied pubertal events because it not only signals the beginning of reproductive ability but also has psychological significance in the family, peer relations, and society. With regard to genetic influences, variations in age at menarche have been assessed by studying associations between maternal and daughter age at menarche; the results reveal a moderately significant correlation (approximately .30). With regard to environmental influences, physical stressors such as exercise, nutrition, and weight have been associated with pubertal timing. Psychosocial stressors linked with pubertal change have included stressful life events and family factors.

Method

The subjects were 75 premenarcheal, White, middle-class girls 10 to 14 years of age, drawn from a larger longitudinal study of female adolescent development. They completed questionnaires about various aspects of their psychological functioning and development. Physical examinations were conducted at a hospital laboratory in the community.

Girls provided reports of their age at menarche during interviews. Because the subsample of girls in this part of the larger longitudinal study were premenarcheal, their age at menarche was obtained from subsequent assessments. Their breast development was rated on a 5-point scale like the one shown in figure 3.8 of this chapter. Weight, height, and body fat were measured during the hospital lab visit. Maternal age at menarche was used as an index of hereditary transmission, although it does contain environmental contributions. A measure of life events was administered. These are examples of negative life events: breaking up with a boyfriend; parents became separated or divorced. Presence of an adult male was determined based on girls' reports of who lived in their home. Parental approval and warmth, as well as conflict with parents, were assessed with a Family Relations Scale given to the girls. Depressive affect was evaluated by asking the girls to respond to the Depressive Withdrawal Scale, which includes items such as "I am unhappy, sad, or depressed."

Results

Breast development, weight, family relations, and depressive affect predicted age at menarche. More-advanced breast development and heavier weights were associated with younger ages at menarche. Better family relations (such as high warmth and low conflict) and lower depressive affect were linked with later ages of menarche. In this study, body fat, the presence of an adult male in the household, and stressful life events did not predict age at menarche. There was a trend for the mother's age at menarche to be associated with the daughter's age at menarche.

Discussion

The results of this study demonstrate the complexity of the linkages among biological and psychological aspects of development. They also document that the young adolescent's physiological system is responsive to social factors. At this time, the research literature on antecedents of pubertal timing has focused primarily on girls. Whether such factors as depressed affective states influence pubertal timing in boys is not known.

ADOLESCENT HEALTH AND WELL-BEING

Pubertal Timing and Health Care

Early- and late-maturing adolescents usually need a lot of support, especially if they feel that something is wrong with them. Early- and late-maturing adolescents often feel self-conscious about their different developmental status and need to be reassured that it is just a matter of time until their development will become similar to that of their peers. Early-maturing boys are often much less worried and self-conscious about their different developmental status than are other early or late maturers. The concern about early-maturing boys is that they will place too much emphasis on physical and sexual competence and not enough on academic competence, which is also a concern about early-maturing girls.

What can be done to identify off-time maturers who are at risk for problems? Many boys and girls whose development is extremely early or extremely late—such as a boy who has not had a spurt in height by the age of 16 or a girl who has not started her period by the age of 15—are likely to come to the attention of a physician. Girls and boys who are early or late maturers but well within the normal range are less likely to be taken to a physician because of their maturational status. Nonetheless, these girls and boys may have fears and doubts about being normal that they do not raise unless a physician, counselor, or some other health-care provider takes the initiative. A brief discussion outlining the sequence and timing of events and the large individual variations in them might be all that is required to reassure many adolescents who are maturing off-time (Brooks-Gunn, 1988).

Health-care providers might want to discuss the adolescent's off-time development with parents as well as with the adolescent. Information about the peer pressures occurring with off-time development can be beneficial. Early-maturing adolescents are especially vulnerable to adolescent pregnancy and sexually transmitted diseases. In most cases, they have not developed the thinking skills and moral codes to protect themselves from these problems, and they can become easily seduced by older adolescents. Their bodies have literally gotten ahead of their minds. Early-maturing girls can benefit from a discussion of peer pressures to date and to engage in adult-like behavior at early ages.

Late-maturing adolescents often have an especially difficult time developing a positive body image, because most of their peers already began developing much earlier. If pubertal development is extremely late, a physician might recommend hormone injections, once a month for about 3 months. In one study of extended pubertal delay in boys, hormonal treatment worked to increase height, dating interest, and peer relations in several boys, but produced little or no improvement in other boys (Lewis, Money, & Bobrow, 1977).

In sum, most early- and late-maturing boys and girls weather puberty's challenges and stresses competently. For those who do not, discussions with sensitive and knowledgeable health-care providers and parents can improve their coping abilities.

John Singer Sargent
The Brook, detail.

Chapter

4

Cognitive Development and Social Cognition

*T*he thirst to know and understand . . .
these are the goods in life's rich hand.

—Sir William Watson

The thoughts of youth are long, long thoughts.

—Henry Wadsworth Longfellow

The Developing Thoughts of Adolescents

PREVIEW

*I*n this chapter, we explore the fascinating world of adolescents' thoughts. In chapter 2, we briefly examined Piaget's theory of cognitive development. More than any other theory, Piaget's theory has had the most to say about how adolescents think differently than children. We begin by discussing Piaget's ideas about concrete and formal operational thought, then evaluate whether Piaget's ideas adequately explain adolescent cognition, describe Vygotsky's cognitive socialization theory, and finally turn to the intriguing world of adolescents' thoughts about social matters.

When you were a young adolescent, what was your thinking like? Were your thinking skills as good as they are now? Could you solve difficult, abstract problems and reason logically about complex topics? Or did such skills improve in your high school years? Can you come up with any ways your thinking now is better than it was in high school?

Many young adolescents begin to think in more idealistic ways. How idealistic was your thinking when you were in middle school and high school? Did you think more about what is ideal versus what is real as an adolescent or as a child? Has your thinking gotten less idealistic now that you are in college, or do you still think a lot about an ideal world and how you might achieve it?

When we think about thinking, we usually consider it in terms of school subjects like math and English, or solving intellectual problems. But people's thoughts about social circumstances are also important. Psychologists are increasingly studying how adolescents think about social matters.

One of my most vivid memories of the adolescence of my oldest daughter, Tracy, is from when Tracy was 12 years of age.

I had accompanied her and her younger sister, Jennifer (10 at the time), to a tennis tournament. As we walked into a restaurant to have lunch, Tracy bolted for the restroom. Jennifer and I looked at each other, wondering what was wrong. Five minutes later Tracy emerged looking calmer. I asked her what had happened. Her response: "This one hair was out of place and every person in here was looking at me!"

Consider two other adolescents—Margaret and Adam. During a conversation with her girlfriend, 16-year-old Margaret says, "Did you hear about Catherine? She's pregnant. Do you think I would ever let that happen to me? Never." Thirteen-year-old Adam describes himself: "No one understands me, especially my parents. They have no idea of what I am feeling. They have never experienced the pain I'm going through." These experiences of Tracy, Margaret, and Adam represent the emergence of egocentric thought in adolescence. Later in the chapter we will explore adolescent egocentrism in greater detail.

PIAGET'S THEORY AND ADOLESCENT COGNITION

To learn about Piaget's theory of cognitive development, we will discuss its basic nature and processes, then focus on the two stages of thought that Piaget believed primarily characterize the way adolescents think—the concrete operational stage and the formal operational stage.

The Nature of Piaget's Theory and Cognitive Processes

Piaget's theory is the most well known, most widely discussed theory of adolescent cognitive development. Piaget stressed that adolescents are motivated to understand their world because doing so is biologically adaptive. In Piaget's view, adolescents actively construct their own cognitive worlds; information is not just poured into their minds from the environment (van der Veer, 1996). To make sense out of their world, adolescents organize their experiences. They separate important ideas from less important ones. They connect one idea to another. They not only organize their observations and experiences, they also adapt their thinking to include new ideas because additional information furthers understanding. Piaget (1954) believed that adolescents adapt in two ways: through assimilation and accommodation.

> *We are born capable of learning.*
>
> —Jean-Jacques Rousseau

Assimilation *occurs when individuals incorporate new information into existing knowledge.* **Accommodation** *occurs when individuals adjust to new information.* Suppose that a 16-year-old girl wants to learn how to use a computer. Her parents buy her a computer for her birthday. She has never had the opportunity to use one. From her experience and observation, though, she realizes that software discs are inserted in a slot and a switch must be pressed to turn the computer on. Thus far she has incorporated her behavior into a conceptual framework she already had (assimilation). As she strikes several keys, she makes some errors. Soon she realizes that she needs to get someone to help her learn to use the computer efficiently or take a class on using a computer at her high school. These adjustments show her awareness of the need to alter her concept of computer use (accommodation).

Equilibration *is a mechanism in Piaget's theory that explains how children or adolescents shift from one stage of thought to the next. The shift occurs as they experience cognitive conflict or a disequilibrium in trying to understand the world. Eventually, the child or adolescent resolves the conflict and reaches a balance, or equilibrium, of thought.* Piaget believed there is considerable movement between states of cognitive equilibrium and disequilibrium as assimila-

tion and accommodation work in concert to produce cognitive change. For example, if a child believes that the amount of a liquid changes simply because the liquid is poured into a container with a different shape, she might be puzzled by such issues as where the "extra" liquid came from and whether there is actually more liquid to drink. The child will eventually resolve these puzzles as her thought becomes more advanced. In the everyday world, the child is constantly faced with such counterexamples and inconsistencies.

Stages of Cognitive Development

Piaget said that individuals develop through four main cognitive stages: sensorimotor, preoperational, concrete operational, and formal operational. Each of the stages is age related and consists of distinct ways of thinking. It is the *different* way of understanding the world that makes one stage more advanced than the other; knowing *more* information does not make the adolescent's thinking more advanced, in the Piagetian view. This is what Piaget meant when he said that the person's cognition is *qualitatively* different in one stage compared to another. We will briefly redefine the first two stages in Piaget's theory, which were first introduced in chapter 2, and then explain concrete and formal operational thought.

Sensorimotor and Preoperational Thought

The **sensorimotor stage,** *which lasts from birth to about 2 years of age, is the first Piagetian stage. In this stage, infants construct an understanding of the world by coordinating sensory experiences (such as seeing and hearing) with physical, motoric actions—hence the term* sensorimotor. At the beginning of this stage, newborns have little more than reflexive patterns with which to work. By the end of the stage, 2-year-olds have complex sensorimotor patterns and are beginning to operate with primitive symbols.

The **preoperational stage,** *which lasts from about 2 to 7 years of age, is the second Piagetian stage. In this stage, children begin to represent the world with words, images, and drawings.* Symbolic thought goes beyond simple connections of information and action.

Concrete Operational Thought

The **concrete operational stage,** *which lasts from about 7 to 11 years of age, is the third Piagetian stage. In this stage, children can perform operations. Logical reasoning replaces intuitive thought as long as the reasoning can be applied to specific or concrete examples.*

Piaget said that concrete operational thought involves **operations**—*mental actions that allow the individual to do mentally what was done before physically.* And he said that *the concrete operational thinker can engage in mental actions that are reversible.* For example, the concrete operational thinker can mentally reverse liquid from one beaker to another and understand that the volume

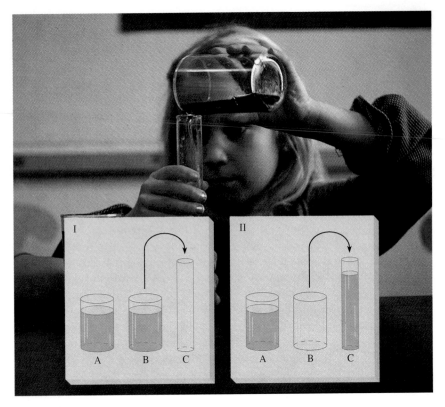

An important aspect of conservation is that children do not conserve all quantities or on all tasks simultaneously. The order of their mastery is this: number, length, liquid quantity, mass, weight, and volume. **Horizontal décalage** *is Piaget's concept that similar abilities do not appear at the same time within a stage of development.* Thus, during the concrete operational stage, conservation of number usually appears first and conservation of volume last. An 8-year-old child might know that a long stick of clay can be rolled into a ball but not understand that the ball and the stick weigh the same. At about 9 years of age, children often recognize that the ball and stick weigh the same, and eventually, at about 11 to 12 years of age, children often understand that the clay's volume is unchanged by rearranging it. Children initially master tasks that are more visible, mastering those not as visually apparent, such as volume, only later.

Classification, *or class inclusion reasoning, is Piaget's concept of concrete operational thought that requires children to systematically organize objects into hierarchies of classes and subclasses.* Figure 4.2 shows an example of the concrete operational child's classification skills involving a family tree of four generations (Furth & Wachs, 1975). This family tree suggests that the grandfather (A) has three children (B, C, and D), each of whom has two children (E through J), and that one of these children (J) has three children (K, L, and M). A child who comprehends this classification system can move up and down a level (vertically), across a level (horizontally), and up and down and across (obliquely) within the system. The concrete operational child understands that person J can at the same time be father, brother, and grandson, for example.

Although concrete operational thought is more advanced than preoperational thought, it has limitations. Logical reasoning replaces intuitive thought as long as the principles can be applied to specific, *concrete* examples. For example, the concrete operational child cannot imagine the steps necessary to complete an algebraic equation, which is too abstract for thinking at this stage of cognitive development. A summary of the characteristics of concrete operational thought is shown in figure 4.3.

Figure~4.1

Piaget's Conservation Task.

The beaker test is a well-known Piagetian test to determine whether the child can think operationally—that is, can mentally reverse actions and show conservation of the substance. *(I)* Two identical beakers are presented to the child. Then the experimenter pours the liquid from B into C, which is taller and thinner than A or B. *(II)* The child is now asked if these beakers (A and C) have the same amount of liquid. The preoperational child says no. When asked to point to the beaker that has more liquid, the preoperational child points to the tall, thin beaker.

is the same even though the beakers differ in height and width. In Piaget's most famous task, a child is presented with two identical beakers, each filled with the same amount of liquid (see figure 4.1). Children are asked if these beakers have the same amount of liquid, and they usually say yes. Then, the liquid from one beaker is poured into a third beaker, which is taller and thinner than the first two (see figure 4.1). Children are then asked if the amount of liquid in the tall, thin beaker is equal to that which remains in one of the original beakers. Concrete operational thinkers answer yes and justify their answers appropriately. Preoperational thinkers (usually children under the age of 7) often answer no and justify their answer in terms of the differing height and width of the beakers. This example reveals the ability of the concrete operational thinker to decenter and coordinate several characteristics (such as height and width), rather than focusing on a single property of an object (such as height).

Conservation *is Piaget's term for an individual's ability to recognize that the length, number, mass, quantity, area, weight, and volume of objects and substances do not change through transformations that alter their appearance.*

Formal Operational Thought

The **formal operational stage** *is Piaget's fourth and final stage of cognitive development, which he believed emerges* from 11 to 15 years of age. Adolescents' developing power of thought opens up new cognitive and social horizons. What are the characteristics of formal operational thought, which Piaget believed develops in adolescence? Most significantly, formal operational thought is more *abstract* than concrete operational thought. Adolescents are no longer limited to actual, concrete experiences as anchors for thought. They can conjure up make-believe situations—events that are purely hypothetical possibilities or strictly abstract propositions—and try to reason logically about them.

The abstract quality of the adolescent's thought at the formal operational level is evident in the adolescent's verbal problem-solving ability. While the concrete operational thinker would need to see the concrete elements A, B, and C to be able to make the logical inference that if A = B and B = C, then A = C, the formal operational thinker can solve this problem merely through verbal presentation.

Another indication of the abstract quality of adolescent thought is an increased tendency to think about thought itself. One adolescent commented, "I began thinking about why I was thinking what I was. Then I began thinking about why I was thinking about why I was thinking about what I was." If this sounds abstract, it is, and it characterizes the adolescent's enhanced focus on thought and its abstract qualities.

Accompanying the abstract nature of formal operational thought in adolescence is thought full of idealism and possibilities. While children frequently think in concrete ways, or in terms of what is real and limited, adolescents begin to engage in extended speculation about

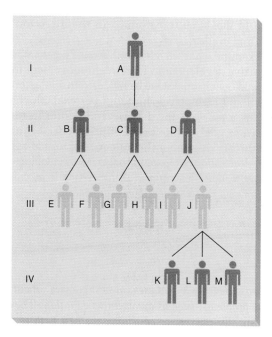

Figure~4.2

Classification: An Important Ability in Concrete Operational Thought.

A family tree of four generations (I to IV): The preoperational child has trouble classifying the members of the four generations; the concrete operational child can classify the members vertically, horizontally, and obliquely (up and down and across).

Can use operations, mentally reversing action; shows conservation skills

Logical reasoning replaces intuitive reasoning, but only in concrete circumstances

Not abstract (can't imagine steps in algebraic equation, for example)

Classification skills—can divide things into sets and subsets and reason about their interrelations

Figure~4.3

Characteristics of Concrete Operational Thought.

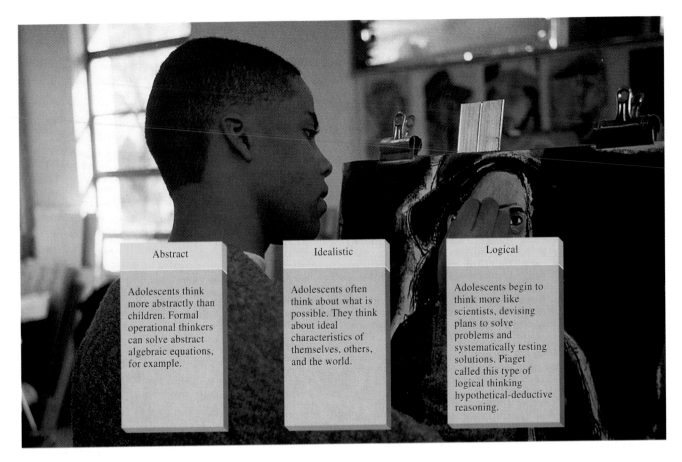

Abstract	Idealistic	Logical
Adolescents think more abstractly than children. Formal operational thinkers can solve abstract algebraic equations, for example.	Adolescents often think about what is possible. They think about ideal characteristics of themselves, others, and the world.	Adolescents begin to think more like scientists, devising plans to solve problems and systematically testing solutions. Piaget called this type of logical thinking hypothetical-deductive reasoning.

Figure~4.5

Characteristics of Formal Operational Thought.
Formal operational thought is abstract, idealistic, and logical.

approximately 15 and 20 years of age. As we see next, many developmentalists believe that there is considerable individual variation in adolescent cognition.

Individual Variation in Adolescent Cognition

Piaget's theory emphasizes universal and consistent patterns of formal operational thought. His theory does not adequately account for the unique, individual differences that characterize the cognitive development of adolescents (Overton & Byrnes, 1991). These individual variations in adolescents' cognitive development have been documented in a number of investigations (Neimark, 1982).

Some individuals in early adolescence are formal operational thinkers; others are not. A review of formal operational thought investigations revealed that only about one of every three eighth-grade students is a formal operational thinker (Strahan, 1983). Some investigators find that formal operational thought increases with age in adolescence; others do not. Many college students and adults do not think in formal operational ways either. For example, investigators have found that from 17 to 67 percent of college students think in formal operational ways (Elkind, 1961; Tomlinson-Keasey, 1972).

Many young adolescents are at the point of consolidating their concrete operational thought, using it more consistently than in childhood. At the same time, many young adolescents are just beginning to think in a formal operational manner. By late adolescence, many adolescents are beginning to consolidate their formal operational thought, using it more consistently. And there often is variation across the content areas of formal operational thought, just as there is in concrete operational thought in childhood. A 14-year-old adolescent might reason at the formal operational level when analyzing algebraic equations but not do so with verbal problem solving or when reasoning about interpersonal relations.

Formal operational thought is more likely to be used in areas in which adolescents have the most experience and knowledge. Children and adolescents gradually build up elaborate knowledge through extensive experience and practice in various sports, games, hobbies, and school subjects, such as math, English, and science. The development of expertise in different domains of life may make possible high-level, developmentally mature-looking thought. In some instances, the sophisticated reasoning of formal operational thought might be responsible. In other instances, however, the thought might be largely due to the accumulation of knowledge that allows more automatic, memory-based processes to function. Some developmentalists wonder if the acquisition of knowledge could account for all cognitive growth. Most, however, argue that *both* cognitive changes in such areas as concrete and formal operational thought *and* the development of expertise through experience are at work in understanding the adolescent's cognitive world. More about knowledge's role in the adolescent's thinking appears in the next chapter.

One proposal argues that Piaget's theory of formal operational thought can be better understood by considering the distinction between "knowing that" and "knowing how" (Byrnes, 1988). "Knowing that" has been called conceptual knowledge or declarative knowledge (Hiebert & LeFevre, 1987). It consists of networks of the core concepts in a given domain, such as biology or physics. "Knowing how" is simply a representation of the steps an individual should follow to solve a problem. It has been referred to as procedural knowledge (Anderson, 1990). For example, in the domain of physics, "knowing that" would consist of understanding the relation between the core concepts of "force" and "mass." In contrast, "knowing how" would consist of understanding how to solve introductory physics test problems using formulas and the like.

The argument by James Byrnes is that Piaget's theory of formal operations can be better understood if it is recast as "knowing that." However, Daniel Keating (1988) argues that Piaget's theory is actually about "knowing how," and that considering his view of formal operations in terms of "knowing that" is a misinterpretation. The lively debate about Piaget's theory of formal operations is likely to continue as experts strive to determine just exactly what Piaget meant by formal operational thought and search for the true nature of adolescent cognitive development.

Formal Operational Thought and Language

As the adolescent's thought becomes more abstract and logical, the use of language also changes. This development includes changes in the use of satire and metaphor, in writing skills, and in conversational skills.

A junior high school student sitting in school makes up satirical labels for his teachers. One he calls "the walking wilt Wilkie and his wilking waste." Another he describes as "the magnificent Manifred and his manifest morbidity." The use of nicknames increases during early adolescence, as does their abstractness—"stilt," "spaz," "nerd," and "marshmallow mouth," for example. These examples reflect the aspect of language known as *satire,* which refers to the use of irony, wit, or derision to expose folly or wickedness. Adolescents use and understand satire more than children do (Demorest & others, 1984). The satire of *Mad* magazine, which relies on double mean-

ing, exaggeration, and parody to highlight absurd circumstances and contradictory happenings, finds a more receptive audience among 13- to 14-year-olds than among 8- to 9-year-olds.

Another aspect of language that comes into use in adolescence is *metaphor,* an implied comparison between two ideas that is conveyed by the abstract meaning contained in the words used. For example, a person's faith and a piece of glass are alike in that they both can be shattered. A runner's performance and a politician's speech are alike in that they both are predictable. Children have a difficult time understanding metaphorical comparisons; adolescents are better able to understand their meaning.

The increased abstractness and logical reasoning of the adolescent's cognition can be witnessed in improved writing ability (Scardamalia, Bereiter, & Goelman, 1982). Organizing ideas is critical to good writing. Logical thinking helps the writer to develop a hierarchical structure, which helps the reader to understand which ideas are general, which are specific, and which are more important than others. Researchers have discovered that children are poor at organizing their ideas prior to writing and have difficulty detecting the salient points in prose passages (Brown & Smiley, 1977). Although adolescents are not yet Pulitzer Prize–winning novelists, they are better than children at recognizing the need for making both general and specific points in their writing. The sentences adolescents string together make more sense than those constructed by children. And adolescents are more likely than children to include an introduction, several paragraphs that represent a body, and concluding remarks when writing an essay.

Most adolescents also are better conversationalists than children are. Adolescents are better at letting individuals take turns in discussions instead of everyone talking at once; they are better at using questions to convey commands ("Why is it so noisy in here?"); they are better at using words like *the* and *a* in ways that enhance understanding ("He is *the* living end!" "He is not just *a* person"); they are better at using polite language in appropriate situations (when a guest comes to the house, for example); and they are better at telling stories that are interesting, jokes that are funny, and lies that convince.

Piaget's Theory and Adolescent Education

Piaget's theory has been widely applied to education, although more extensively with children than with adolescents. Piaget was not an educator and never pretended to be. But he did provide a sound conceptual framework from which to view educational problems. What principles of Piaget's theory of cognitive development can be applied to education? David Elkind (1976) described two. First, the foremost issue in education is *communication.*

In Piaget's theory, the adolescent's mind is not a blank slate. To the contrary, the adolescent has a host of ideas about the physical and natural world. Adolescents come to school with their own ideas about space, time, causality, quantity, and number. Educators need to learn to comprehend what adolescents are saying and to respond to their ideas. Second, adolescents are, by nature, knowing creatures. The best way to nurture this motivation for knowledge is to allow adolescents to spontaneously interact with the environment. Educators need to ensure that they do not dull adolescents' eagerness to know by providing an overly rigid curriculum that disrupts adolescents' rhythm and pace of learning.

Why have applications to adolescent education lagged behind applications to children's education? Adolescents who are formal operational thinkers are at a level similar to that of their teachers and of the authors of textbooks. In Piaget's model, it is no longer necessary to pay attention to qualitative changes in cognition. Also, the structure of education itself changes considerably between elementary and secondary levels. For children, the basic focus of education is the classroom. Children may be involved with, at most, several teachers during the day. In secondary schools, the focus shifts to subject-matter divisions of curriculum. Each teacher sees a student for 45 to 60 minutes a day in connection with one content area (English, history, math, for example). Thus, both teachers and texts may become more focused on the development of curriculum than on the developmental characteristics of students. And when teachers *are* concerned about students' developmental characteristics in adolescence, they pay more attention to social-personality dimensions than to cognitive dimensions.

One main argument that has emerged from the application of Piaget's theory to education is that instruction may too often be at the formal operational level, even though the majority of adolescents are not actually formal operational thinkers. That is, the instruction might be too formal and too abstract. Possibly, it should be less formal and more concrete. Researchers have found that adolescents construct a view of the world on the basis of observations and experiences and that educators should take this into account when developing a curriculum for adolescents (Linn, 1991).

Beyond Formal Operational Thought

Some critics of Piaget's theory argue that specialized thinking about a specific skill represents a higher stage of thought than formal operational thought. Piaget did not believe that this was so. For him, the change to reasoning about a special skill (such as the kind of thinking engaged in by a nuclear physicist or a medical researcher) is no

Many educators and developmentalists believe that science and most other areas of secondary education should follow a hands-on, participatory format rather than a straight lecture format. Many adolescents are not yet full-fledged formal operational thinkers in the hypothetical-deductive sense. Possibly through participatory experiences with science, adolescents can restructure their concrete ways of thinking about the world and logically categorize events and objects in more hypothetical-deductive ways. However, some researchers believe that a supportive context and early attention to the development of reasoning are what are needed to improve adolescents' logical thought.

more than window dressing. According to Piaget, a nuclear physicist may think in ways that an adolescent cannot think, but the adolescent and the nuclear physicist differ only in their familiarity with an academic field of inquiry. They differ in the content of their thought, not in the operations they bring to bear on the content (Piaget, 1970).

Some developmentalists believe that the absolutist nature of adolescent logic and buoyant optimism diminish in early adulthood. According to Gisela Labouvie-Vief (1982), a new integration of thought takes place in early adulthood. She thinks that the adult years produce pragmatic constraints that require an adaptive strategy of less reliance on logical analysis in solving problems. Commitment, specialization, and channeling energy into finding one's niche in complex social and work systems replace the youth's fascination with idealized logic. If we assume that logical thought and buoyant optimism are the criteria for cognitive maturity, we would have to admit that the cognitive activity of adults is too concrete and pragmatic. But from Labouvie-Vief's view, the adult's understanding of reality's constraints reflects maturity, not immaturity.

Adolescents' thoughts are more abstract and idealistic than children's thoughts are. Young adults' thoughts are more pragmatic, specialized, and multiple (less dualistic) than adolescents' thoughts. Older adults may not be as quick with their thoughts as younger adults, but they may have more general knowledge and wisdom. This elderly woman shares the wisdom of her experiences with a classroom of children.

Even Piaget (1967) detected that formal operational thought may have its hazards:

> With the advent of formal intelligence, thinking takes wings and it is not surprising that at first this unexpected power is both used and abused. . . . Each new mental ability starts off by incorporating the world in a process of egocentric assimilation. Adolescent egocentricity is manifested by a belief in the omnipotence of reflection, as though the world should submit itself to idealistic schemes rather than to systems of reality. (pp. 63–64)

Our cognitive abilities are very strong in early adulthood, and they do show adaptation to life's pragmatic concerns. Less clear is whether our logical skills actually decline. Competence as a young adult probably requires doses of both logical thinking skills and pragmatic adaptation to reality. For example, when architects design a building, they logically analyze and plan the structure but understand the cost constraints, environmental concerns, and the time it will take to get the job done effectively.

William Perry (1981) also has charted some important changes in the way young adults think differently than adolescents. He believes that adolescents often view the world in a basic dualistic fashion of polarities—right/wrong, black/white, we/they, or good/bad, for example. As youth mature and move into the adulthood years, they gradually become aware of the diversity of opinion and the multiple perspectives that others hold, which shakes their dualistic perceptions. Their *dualistic thinking* gives way to *multiple thinking*, as they come to understand that authorities may not have all of the answers. They begin to carve out their own territory of individualistic thinking, often believing that everyone is entitled to their own opinion and that one's personal opinion is as good as anyone else's. As these personal opinions become challenged by others, multiple thinking yields to *relative subordinate thinking*, in which an analytical, evaluative approach to knowledge is consciously and actively pursued. Only in the shift to *full relativism* does the adult completely comprehend that truth is relative—that the meaning of an event is related to the context in which that event occurs and is based on the framework that the knower uses to understand that event. In full relativism, the adult recognizes that relativism pervades all aspects of life, not just the academic world. And in full relativism, the adult understands that knowledge is constructed, not given; contextual, not absolute. Perry's ideas, which are oriented toward well-educated, bright individuals, have been widely used by educators and counselors in working with young adults in academic settings.

Another candidate for thought that is more advanced than formal operational thought is wisdom, which, like good wine, may get better with age. What is this thing we call wisdom? **Wisdom** *is expert knowledge about the practical aspects of life*. This practical knowledge involves exceptional insight into human development and life matters, good judgment, and an understanding of how to cope with difficult life problems (Baltes, 1997, in press). Thus, wisdom, more than standard conceptions of intelligence, focuses on life's pragmatic concerns and human conditions. This practical knowledge takes many years to acquire, accumulating through intentional, planned experiences and through incidental experiences. Of course, not all older adults solve practical problems in wise ways. In one recent investigation, only 5 percent of adults' responses to life-planning problems were considered wise, and these wise responses were equally distributed across the early, middle, and late adulthood years (Smith & Baltes, 1990).

What does the possibility that older adults are as wise as or wiser than younger adults mean in terms of the basic issue of intellectual decline in adulthood? Remember that intelligence comes in different forms. In many instances, older adults are not as intelligent as younger adults when speed of processing is involved, and this probably harms their performance on many traditional school-related tasks and standardized intelligence tests. But consideration of general knowledge and something we call wisdom may result in an entirely different interpretation.

Now that we have considered many different ideas about Piaget's theory of adolescent cognition, including the issue of whether there are forms of thought more advanced than formal operational thinking, we turn our attention to evaluating Piagetian contributions and criticisms.

Piagetian Contributions and Criticisms

We have spent considerable time outlining Piaget's theory of cognitive development. Let's briefly summarize some of Piaget's main contributions, and then enumerate criticisms of his theory.

Contributions

We owe Piaget the present field of cognitive development. We owe him a long list of masterful concepts of enduring power and fascination, such as the concepts of object permanence, conservation, assimilation, and

Piaget, shown sitting on a bench, was a genius at observing children. By carefully observing and interviewing children, Piaget constructed his comprehensive theory of children's cognitive development.

accommodation. We also owe Piaget the currently accepted vision of children and adolescents as active, constructive thinkers who, through their commerce with the environment, manufacture their own development (Flavell, 1992).

Piaget was a genius when it came to observing children; his astute observations showed us inventive ways to discover how children, and even infants, act on and adapt to their world. Piaget showed us some important things to look for in cognitive development, including the shift from concrete to formal operational thought. He also showed us how we must make experiences fit our cognitive framework yet simultaneously adapt our cognitive orientation to experience. Piaget also revealed how cognitive change is likely to occur if the situation is structured to allow gradual movement to the next higher level.

Criticisms

Piaget's theory has not gone unchallenged, however. Questions are raised about the following areas: Estimates of the child's and adolescent's competence at different developmental levels; stages; training children to reason at higher levels; and culture and education (Amsel & Renninger, 1997).

Estimates of Competence   Some cognitive abilities emerge earlier than Piaget thought, and their subsequent development is more prolonged than he believed. Conservation of number has been demonstrated in children as young as 3 years of age, although Piaget did not think it came about until 7 years of age. Young children are not as "pre-" this and "pre-" that (precausal, preoperational) as Piaget thought (Flavell, 1992). Some aspects of formal operational thinking that involve abstract reasoning do not consistently emerge in early adolescence as Piaget envisioned. And adults often reason in far more irrational ways than Piaget believed (Siegler, 1996). In sum, recent trends highlight the cognitive competencies of infants and young children, and the cognitive shortcomings of adolescents and adults.

Stages   Piaget conceived of stages as unitary structures of thought, so his theory assumes synchrony in development. That is, various aspects of a stage should emerge at about the same time. But several concrete operational concepts do not appear in synchrony. For example, children do not learn to conserve at the same time as they learn to cross-classify.

Most contemporary developmentalists agree that cognitive development is not as grand-stage-like as Piaget thought. **Neo-Piagetians** *are developmentalists who have elaborated on Piaget's theory; they believe that cognitive development is more specific in many respects than Piaget thought.* Neo-Piagetians don't believe that all of Piaget's ideas should be junked. However, they argue that a more accurate vision of cognitive development involves fewer references to grand stages and more emphasis on the roles of strategies, skills, how fast and automatically children can process information, the task-specific nature of cognition, and the importance of dividing cognitive problems into smaller, more precise steps (Case, 1992).

Neo-Piagetians still believe that cognitive development contains some general properties. They stress that there is a regular, maturation-based increase with age in some aspects of information-processing capacity, such as how fast or efficiently the child or adolescent processes information. As the information-processing capacity increases with age, new and more complex forms of cognition in all content domains are possible because the child or adolescent can now hold in mind and think about more

An outstanding teacher and education in the logic of science and mathematics are important cultural experiences that promote the development of formal operational thought. Schooling and education likely play more important roles in the development of formal operational thought than Piaget envisioned.

things at once. For example, Canadian developmentalist Robbie Case (1985) argues that adolescents have increasingly more available cognitive resources than they did as children because they can process information more automatically, they have more information-processing capacity, and they are more familiar with a range of content knowledge. We will discuss the nature of adolescents' information processing in much greater detail in the next chapter.

Training Children to Reason at a Higher Level   Children who are at one cognitive stage—such as preoperational thought—can be trained to reason at a higher cognitive stage, such as concrete operational thought. This poses a problem for Piaget, who argued that such training works only on a superficial level and is ineffective unless the chid is at a transitional point from one stage to the next.

Culture and Education   Culture and education exert stronger influences on development than Piaget believed (see Sociocultural Worlds of Adolescence). The age at which individuals acquire conservation skills is associated to some extent with the degree to which their culture provides relevant practice. And in many developing countries, formal operational thought is a rare occurrence. As you will learn shortly, there has been a wave of interest in how cognitive development progresses through interaction with skilled adults and peers, and how embeddedness in a culture influences cognitive growth. Such views stand in stark contrast to Piaget's view of the child as a solitary young scientist.

SOCIOCULTURAL WORLDS OF ADOLESCENCE

Culture, Schooling, and Cognitive Development

Consider the following conversation between a researcher and an illiterate Kpelle farmer in the West African country of Liberia (Scribner, 1977):

Researcher: All Kpelle men are rice farmers. Mr. Smith is not a rice farmer. Is he a Kpelle man?

Kpelle Farmer: I don't know the man. I have not laid eyes on the man myself.

Members of the Kpelle culture who had gone through formal schooling were able to answer the researcher in a logical way, unlike the illiterate Kpelle farmer. Piaget may have underestimated the importance of cultural experiences in cognitive development. Many of the activities examined in research on Piaget's cognitive developmental theory, such as conservation, classification, and logical reasoning, have been found to relate to children's, adolescents', and adults' schooling experience (Rogoff, 1993, 1997).

Remembering and classifying lists of unrelated objects are often unusual, rarely practiced activities outside of literate or school-related activities. The categories viewed as most appropriate in literate situations may not be valued in other circumstances. For example, in one investigation of the Kpelle culture, individuals sorted twenty objects into functional groups (a knife with an orange, a potato with a hoe, for example), rather than into the categorical groups the experimenter had in mind (a knife with a hoe, an orange with a potato, for example) (Glick, 1975). When questioned about why they had categorized the objects this way, the Kpelle subjects said that any wise man would know to do things this way. When an exasperated experimenter finally asked, "How would a fool do it? the Kpelle subjects responded with categories of the type that were initially anticipated—piles with food in one, tools in another, and so on.

Individuals who have more schooling, such as older children and people in Western cultures, may excel on cognitive tasks because not only the skills but also the social contexts of testing resemble the activities practiced in school. In contrast with everyday life, where individuals classify and remember things to accomplish a functional goal, in schools and on tests they perform to satisfy an adult's request to do so. Individuals who have gone to school are likely to have more experience engaging in cognitive processes at the request of an adult without having a clear, practical goal.

Researchers have investigated whether special training can improve the conservation skills of children who live in cultures in which the concept of conservation is not widely practiced. For example, in one study, brief training in procedures similar to the standard conservation task improved the performance of rural aboriginal Australian children on the standard beaker conservation task itself (Dasen, Ngini, & Lavalée, 1979). However, even with special training, the rural aboriginal children lagged behind children from the Australian city of Canberra in the acquisition of conservation by approximately 3 years, indicating that the aboriginal culture does not provide practice that is relevant to the conservation concept.

The ability to think in scientific ways—to develop hypotheses, systematically evaluate possible solutions, and deduce a correct answer to a difficult problem—is an important dimension of formal operational thought. A majority of adolescents in the United States do not think in formal operational ways when presented with scientific reasoning problems, but in developing countries, an even smaller portion of adolescents and adults do. In one cross-cultural investigation that included the United States, Germany, Austria, and Italy, only 7 percent of the eighth-grade students reasoned in formal operational ways (Karplus, 1981). In one Italian group, the adolescents did especially well on formal operational tasks. Closer observation revealed that these adolescents had been with the same outstanding teacher for 3 consecutive years, indicating the role that education may play in instilling formal operational thinking. According to observers, in many Third World, developing countries, formal operational thought in the form of scientific thinking is rare. Education in the logic of science and mathematics is an important cultural experience that promotes the development of formal operational thinking. Cultural experiences thus play a much stronger role in formal operational thought than Piaget envisioned (Cole, 1997).

COGNITIVE SOCIALIZATION

Adolescents' cognitive development does not occur in a social vacuum. Lev Vygotsky (1896–1934), a Russian psychologist, recognized this important point more than half a century ago. In Vygotsky's view, differences in adolescents' cognitive performance are often related to identifiable features of the *cognitive environment*. He especially stressed that the cognitive growth of children and adolescents is aided by the guidance of individuals who are skilled in the use of the culture's tools. Vygotsky's emphasis on the importance of social interaction and culture in children's and adolescents' cognitive development contrasts with Piaget's description of the child and adolescent as solitary scientists (Rogoff, 1993, 1997).

One of Vygotsky's most important concepts is the **zone of proximal development (ZPD),** *which refers to the range of tasks that are too difficult for individuals to master alone, but that can be mastered with the guidance and assistance of adults or more skilled adolescents.* Thus, the lower level of the ZPD is the level of problem solving reached by the adolescent working independently. The upper limit is the level of additional responsibility the adolescent can accept with the assistance of an able instructor (see figure 4.6). Vygotsky's emphasis on the ZPD underscored his belief in the importance of social influences on cognitive development. The practical teaching involved in ZPD begins toward the zone's upper limit, where the adolescent is able to reach the goal only through close collaboration with an instructor. With adequate, continuing instruction and practice, the adolescent masters the behavioral sequences necessary to perform the target skill, such as solving an algebraic equation or writing a computer program. As the instruction continues, the performance transfers from the instructor to the adolescent as the teacher gradually reduces the explanations, hints, and demonstrations until the adolescent is able to perform alone. Once the goal is achieved, it may become the foundation for a new ZPD.

To date, Vygotsky's ideas on cognitive socialization have been applied mainly to children's cognitive development. However, some cognitive developmentalists believe that ideas such as Vygotsky's, which emphasize the role of cognitive socialization, have important implications for understanding cognitive growth in adolescence (Keating, 1990). For example, some researchers have found that small-group discourse is related to improved reasoning about complex problems in adolescence (Resnick, 1987). The nature of social activities adolescents experience may play important roles in shaping their thinking.

In the cognitive socialization approach, formal education is but one cultural agent that determines adolescents' cognitive growth (Keating, 1990). Parents, peers,

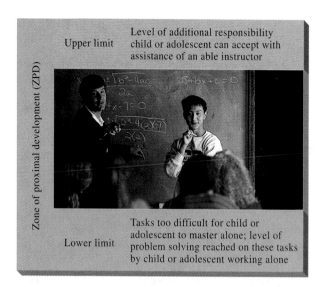

Figure~4.6

Vygotsky's Zone of Proximal Development (ZPD).
Vygotsky's zone of proximal development has a lower limit and an upper limit. Tasks in the ZPD are too difficult for the child or adolescent to perform alone. They require assistance from an adult or a more-skilled youth. As children and adolescents experience the verbal instruction or demonstration, they organize the information in their existing mental structures so they can eventually perform the skill or task alone.

the community, and the technological orientation of the culture are other forces that influence adolescents' thinking. For example, the attitudes toward intellectual competence that adolescents encounter through relationships with their parents and peers affect their motivation for acquiring knowledge. So do the attitudes of teachers and other adults in the community. Media influences, especially through the development of television and the computer, play increasingly important roles in the cognitive socialization of adolescents. For example, does television train adolescents to become passive learners and detract significantly from their intellectual pursuit? We will consider television's role in adolescent development in chapter 9, and in chapter 5 we will examine the computer's role.

The cognitive socialization of adolescents can be improved through the development of more cognitively stimulating environments and additional focus on the role of social factors in cognitive growth (Brown, Metz, & Campione, 1996). Approaches that take into account adolescents' self-confidence, achievement expectations, and sense of purpose are likely to be just as effective as, or even more effective than, more narrow cognitive approaches in shaping adolescents' cognitive growth. For example, a knowledge of physics may be of limited use to inner-city youth with severely limited prospects of employment (Keating, 1990).

CONCEPT TABLE 4.1
Piaget's Theory, Adolescent Cognition, and Cognitive Socialization

Concept	Processes/ Related Ideas	Characteristics/Description
Piaget's Theory and Adolescent Cognition	Nature of Piaget's theory and cognitive processes	Piaget's widely acclaimed theory stresses adaptation, organization, assimilation, accommodation, and equilibration.
	Stages of cognitive development	Piaget said individuals develop through four stages of cognitive development: sensorimotor, preoperational, concrete operational, and formal operational.
	Concrete operational thought	According to Piaget, concrete operational thought occurs between approximately 7 and 11 years of age. It is made up of operations and involves reasoning about objects' properties. Conservation and classification skills are characteristics. It is limited by the inability to reason abstractly about objects.
	Formal operational thought	Abstractness and idealism, as well as hypothetical-deductive reasoning, are highlighted in formal operational thought. Formal operational thought involves the ability to reason about what is possible and hypothetical, as opposed to what is real, and the ability to reflect on one's own thoughts.
	Early and late formal operational thought	Formal operational thought occurs in two phases—an assimilation phase in which reality is overwhelmed (early adolescence) and an accommodation phase in which intellectual balance is restored through a consolidation of formal operational thought (middle years of adolescence).
	Individual variation in adolescent cognition	Individual variation is extensive, and Piaget did not give this adequate attention. Many young adolescents are not formal operational thinkers but rather are consolidating their concrete operational thought.
	Formal operational thought and language	Adolescents develop more sophisticated cognitive strategies for handling words and concepts, prose and writing, and communication.
	Piaget's theory and adolescent education	Piaget's theory has been applied to children's education much more than to adolescents' education. Applications to adolescents' education often follow the belief that instruction is too formal and abstract for adolescents. However, some researchers believe that a supportive context and early attention to reasoning skills promote adolescents' logical thought.
	Beyond formal operational thought	Many life-span developmentalists believe that Piaget was incorrect in assuming that formal operational thought is the highest form of cognition. They argue that more pragmatic, specialized, and multiple (less dualistic) thought takes place in early adulthood and that wisdom may increase throughout the adult years.
Piagetian Contributions and Criticisms	Contributions	Piaget was a genius at observing children. He showed us some important things to look for and mapped out some general cognitive changes.
	Criticisms	Criticisms focus on estimates of children's competence, stages (neo-Piagetians offer more precise views and information-processing explanations of cognitive changes), training children to reason at a higher level, and culture and education.
Cognitive Socialization	Its nature	In Vygotsky's view, differences in adolescents' cognitive performance are often related to identifiable features of the cognitive environment. The cognitive growth of children and adolescents is aided by the guidance of individuals who are skilled in using the tools of the culture. One of Vygotsky's most important concepts is the zone of proximal development. The cognitive socialization approach advocates giving more attention to developing cognitively stimulating environments and to the social factors that influence cognitive growth.

At this point we have studied a numbers of ideas about cognitive developmental theory, Piaget's ideas, and the cognitive socialization of adolescents. A summary of these ideas is presented in concept table 4.1. Our study of the cognitive socialization of adolescents has underscored the important role of culture and stimulating cognitive environments in determining adolescents' cognitive growth. Next, we will examine another aspect of adolescents' social cognitive worlds—their thoughts about social matters.

Santrock: Adolescence

SOCIAL COGNITION

Developmentalists have recently shown a flourish of interest in how children and adolescents reason about social matters. For many years, the study of cognitive development focused primarily on cognition about nonsocial phenomena, such as logic, numbers, words, time, and the like. Now there is a lively interest in how children and adolescents reason about their social world as well (Flavell & Miller, 1997). Our discussion of social cognition focuses on what social cognition is, egocentrism and perspective taking, implicit personality theory, social cognitive monitoring, whether Piaget's theory adequately explains the adolescent's social cognition, and the discussion of social cognition in the remainder of the book.

The Nature of Social Cognition

Social cognition *refers to how individuals conceptualize and reason about their social world—the people they watch and interact with, relationships with those people, the groups in which they participate, and how they reason about themselves and others*. Two main theoretical perspectives have stimulated the development of interest in social cognition—the cognitive developmental view and social information processing.

The Cognitive Developmental View

The cognitive developmental view of social cognition is based primarily on the theories of Jean Piaget (1952) and Lawrence Kohlberg (1976), as well as on the research and thinking of developmental psychologists, such as John Flavell (1992), David Elkind (1976), and Robert Selman (1980). They believe that individuals' social thoughts can be better understood by examining their development.

Kohlberg, in particular, has promoted the role of cognitive developmental theory in understanding different facets of social development. He is known primarily for his contributions to understanding moral development, but he also has expanded Piaget's ideas to account for many social phenomena, not just morality. For example, Kohlberg has applied a cognitive developmental perspective to gender roles, role-taking abilities, peer relations, attachment, and identity.

Like Piaget, Kohlberg believed that biological maturation and environmental experiences interact to produce the individual's stage of thought. Kohlberg said that adolescents attempt to attain intellectual balance or equilibrium. These attempts are influenced by moment-to-moment interactions with people and events in the world. In reaching a new stage of thinking, individuals are able to balance past impressions about the world and themselves with current incoming information. Hence, adolescents who have achieved a stable sense of identity ("I know who I am and where I am going") can handle ostensible threats to their identity ("You aren't working hard enough—you play around too much"). Over a rea-

sonably long period of time, the balance that has been achieved in a particular stage of thought is disrupted because maturing adolescents gain cognitive abilities that enable them to perceive inconsistencies and inadequacies in their thinking. Just as scientists who are confronted with unexplained events and outcomes must reformulate their theories to explain them, so individuals must shift their former ways of thinking to account for new discrepancies. When individuals are able to balance new information with past impressions, they have reached a new stage in thinking.

Hence, children in elementary school may categorize the identities of themselves and others along a limited number of dimensions—even just one or two, such as "He is a boy, and I am a girl." But as they grow into adolescence, children begin to realize that different people are characterized by traits other than just gender. They recognize, for example, that someone's introverted, quiet style of interaction may shape his or her personal identity just as much as or more than his or her "maleness" or "femaleness."

Abstract relations *is developmentalist Kurt Fischer's term for the ability of the adolescent to coordinate two or more abstract ideas; this ability often appears for the first time between 14 and 16 years of age* (Fischer, 1980). For example, at the age of 16, adolescents may be able to coordinate the abstraction of conformity with the abstraction of individualism in thinking about their personality or the personality of others. Consider the adolescent girl who sees herself as a conformist at school, where she dresses in conventional ways and behaves according to school rules, but views herself as an individualist in social relationships, choosing unconventional friends and wearing unusual clothes in their company. By piecing together these abstractions, she likely views herself as being a different kind of person in the two contexts and senses that, in some ways, she is a contradictory person.

Thus, in the cognitive developmental view, adolescence involves considerable change in how individuals think and reason about themselves and others. Later, we will discuss egocentrism and perspective taking in adolescence—two topics that have been important themes of the cognitive developmental view of social cognition. Next, however, we will explore a second view of adolescent cognition—social information processing.

Social Information Processing

Social information processing *emphasizes how individuals use cognitive processes, such as attention, perception, memory, thinking, reasoning, expectancies, and so on, to understand their social world*. Two converging theoretical developments led to the interest in social information processing. First, when personality theorist Walter Mischel (1973) introduced *cognitive social learning theory*, he described a number of cognitive processes that mediate experiences between the social world and the individual's behavior. Mischel spoke of plans, memory, imagery, expectations, and other processes as important contributors to how individuals process information about themselves and their social world.

At the same time, a perspective that was to become the dominant view in cognitive psychology was maturing—the view known as information processing, which, like cognitive social learning theory, was discussed in chapter 2. Some researchers who study social cognition draw heavily from the information-processing perspective as they focus on social memories, social problem solving, social decision making, and so on. Keep in mind, though, that the information-processing perspective is not a developmental perspective, so there is nothing in this view that explains how adolescents process information about themselves and their social world differently than children do. Nonetheless, the information-processing perspective highlights cognitive processes that are central to how individuals understand their social world. Much more about the information-processing perspective appears in chapter 5. Next, we will consider one of the important developmental changes in adolescents' social cognition—egocentrism.

Egocentrism

Adolescent egocentrism *refers to the heightened self-consciousness of adolescents, which is reflected in their belief that others are as interested in them as they themselves are, and in their sense of personal uniqueness.*

David Elkind (1976) believes that adolescent egocentrism can be dissected into two types of social thinking—imaginary audience and personal fable. The **imaginary audience** *refers to the heightened self-consciousness of adolescents that is reflected in their belief that others are as interested in them as they themselves are. The imaginary audience involves attention-getting behavior—the desire to be noticed, visible, and "on stage."* Tracy's comments and behavior, discussed in the Images introduction to the chapter, reflect the imaginary audience. Another adolescent might think that others are as aware of a small spot on his trousers as he is, possibly knowing that he has masturbated. Another adolescent, an eighth-grade girl, walks into her classroom and thinks that all eyes are riveted on her complexion. Adolescents especially sense that they are "on stage" in early adolescence, believing that they are the main actors and all others are the audience.

According to Elkind, the **personal fable** *is the part of adolescent egocentrism involving an adolescent's sense of uniqueness.* The comments of Margaret and Adam, mentioned earlier, reflect the personal fable. Adolescents' sense of personal uniqueness makes them feel that no one can understand how they really feel. For example, an adolescent girl thinks that her mother cannot possibly sense the hurt that she feels because her boyfriend broke up with her. As part of their effort to retain a sense of

Many adolescent girls spend long hours in front of the mirror, depleting cans of hair spray, tubes of lipstick, and jars of cosmetics. How might this behavior be related to changes in adolescent cognitive and physical development?

personal uniqueness, adolescents might craft a story about the self that is filled with fantasy, immersing themselves in a world that is far removed from reality. Personal fables frequently show up in adolescent diaries.

Developmentalists have increasingly studied adolescent egocentrism in recent years. The research interest focuses on what the components of egocentrism really are, the nature of self-other relationships, why egocentric thought emerges in adolescence, and the role of egocentrism in adolescent problems. For example, David Elkind (1985) believes that adolescent egocentrism is brought about by formal operational thought. Others, however, argue that adolescent egocentrism is not entirely a cognitive phenomenon. Rather, they think that the imaginary audience is due both to the ability to think hypothetically (formal operational thought) and the ability to step outside one's self and anticipate the reactions of others in imaginative circumstances (perspective taking) (Lapsley & Murphy, 1985).

Perspective Taking

Perspective taking *is the ability to assume another person's perspective and understand his or her thoughts and feelings.* Robert Selman (1980) proposed a developmental theory of perspective taking that has received considerable attention. He believes perspective taking involves

Adolescent Egocentrism—Does It Ever Go Away?

In my course on adolescence, college students have occasionally commented that they know some people in their twenties who still show the characteristics we have associated with adolescent egocentrism. They want to know if it is maladaptive, when you are in your late teens and twenties, to act as if all eyes are riveted on you, to have a strong desire to be noticed, visible, and "on stage," and to feel like all others are as interested in you as you are.

What do you think? How maladaptive is it for individuals in their late teens and their twenties to show adolescent egocentrism? Isn't it adaptive to show at least some interest in oneself? How can you draw the line between self-interest that is adaptive, protective, and appropriate and self-interest that is maladaptive, selfish, and inappropriate? One good strategy for coming to grips with this issue is to consider the extent to which the egocentrism overwhelms and dominates the individual's life. By evaluating developmental changes in adolescent egocentrism, you are learning to think critically by *applying a developmental framework to understand behavior*.

a series of five stages, ranging from 3 years of age through adolescence (see figure 4.7). These stages begin with the egocentric viewpoint in early childhood and end with in-depth perspective taking in adolescence.

To study adolescents' perspective taking, Selman individually interviews the adolescents, asking them to comment on such dilemmas as the following:

> Holly is an eight-year-old girl who likes to climb trees. She is the best tree climber in the neighborhood. One day while climbing down from a tall tree, she falls . . . but does not hurt herself. Her father sees her fall. He is upset and asks her to promise not to climb trees any more. Holly promises.
>
> Later that day, Holly and her friends meet Shawn. Shawn's kitten is caught in a tree and can't get down. Something has to be done right away or the kitten may fall. Holly is the only one who climbs trees well enough to reach the kitten and get it down, but she remembers her promise to her father. (Selman, 1976, p. 302)

Subsequently, the interviewer asks the adolescents a series of questions about the dilemma, such as these:

> Does Holly know how Shawn feels about the kitten?
> How will Holly's father feel if he finds out she climbed the tree?
> What does Holly think her father will do if he finds out she climbed the tree?
> What would you do in this situation?

By analyzing children's and adolescents' responses to these dilemmas, Selman (1980) concluded that their perspective taking follows the developmental sequence described in figure 4.7.

Selman's research has shown strong support for the sequential nature of perspective taking, although the ages at which children and adolescents reach the perspective-taking stages overlap considerably. In one study, 60 percent of the 10-year-old children were at stage 2 perspective taking; the remaining children were at stages 1 and 3 (Selman & Byrne, 1974). This means that, at the threshold of adolescence, 80 percent are likely to be no higher than stage 2 in social perspective taking. In another study, only 6 of 28 individuals ages 10 to 13 were at stage 3 or higher, with 78 percent of the early adolescents no higher than stage 2 (Byrne, 1973). Stage 3 was not firmly present until about the age of 16. Selman acknowledges considerable overlap in the age ranges he applies to the development of interpersonal understanding—for example, stage 2 (6 years 9 months to 15 years 10 months) and stage 3 (11 years 3 months to 20+ years). It is the attainment of stage 3 perspective taking that some researchers believe accounts for the imaginary audience and personal fable dimensions of adolescent egocentrism (Lapsley, 1993).

Although adolescents' perspective taking can increase their self-understanding, it also can improve their peer group status and the quality of their friendships. For example, in one investigation, the most popular children in the third and eighth grades had competent perspective-taking skills (Kurdek & Krile, 1982). Adolescents who are competent at perspective taking are better at understanding the needs of their companions so that they likely can communicate more effectively with them. And in one study, competence in social perspective coordination was an important influence on adolescent friendship formation following residential relocation (Vernberg & others, 1994).

The relation between the self and another individual is complex. Most major developmental theorists believe that development changes in self-other relationships

---

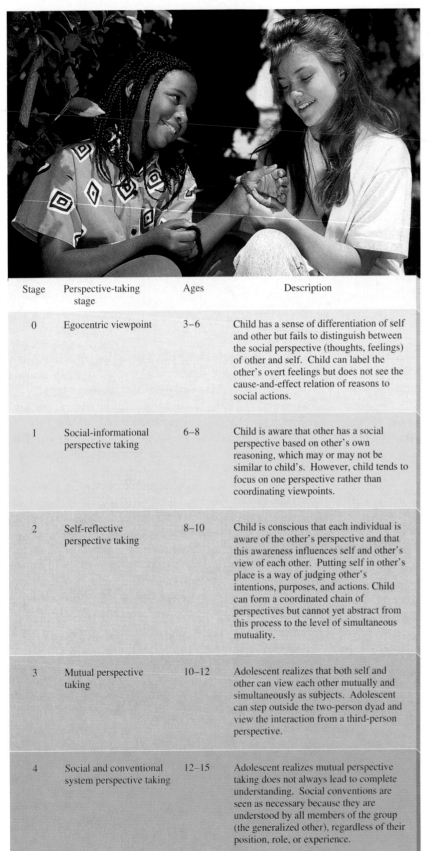

Stage	Perspective-taking stage	Ages	Description
0	Egocentric viewpoint	3–6	Child has a sense of differentiation of self and other but fails to distinguish between the social perspective (thoughts, feelings) of other and self. Child can label the other's overt feelings but does not see the cause-and-effect relation of reasons to social actions.
1	Social-informational perspective taking	6–8	Child is aware that other has a social perspective based on other's own reasoning, which may or may not be similar to child's. However, child tends to focus on one perspective rather than coordinating viewpoints.
2	Self-reflective perspective taking	8–10	Child is conscious that each individual is aware of the other's perspective and that this awareness influences self and other's view of each other. Putting self in other's place is a way of judging other's intentions, purposes, and actions. Child can form a coordinated chain of perspectives but cannot yet abstract from this process to the level of simultaneous mutuality.
3	Mutual perspective taking	10–12	Adolescent realizes that both self and other can view each other mutually and simultaneously as subjects. Adolescent can step outside the two-person dyad and view the interaction from a third-person perspective.
4	Social and conventional system perspective taking	12–15	Adolescent realizes mutual perspective taking does not always lead to complete understanding. Social conventions are seen as necessary because they are understood by all members of the group (the generalized other), regardless of their position, role, or experience.

Figure~4.7

Selman's Stages of Perspective Taking.

are characterized by movement from egocentrism to perspectivism, but the considerable overlap in the age range at which various levels of perspective taking emerge make generalizations about clear-cut stages difficult. Next, we turn our attention to another aspect of social cognition that changes during adolescence—implicit personality theory.

Implicit Personality Theory

Implicit personality theory *is the layperson's conception of personality.* Do adolescents conceptualize an individual's personality differently than children do? Adolescents are more likely to interpret an individual's personality in the way that many personality theorists in psychology do than children are (Barenboim, 1981). Adolescents interpret personality differently than children in three ways. First, when adolescents are given information about another person, they are more likely to consider both previously acquired information and current information, rather than relying only on the concrete information at hand, like children do. Second, adolescents are more likely to detect the situational or contextual variability in personality, rather than thinking that personality is always stable. Third, rather than merely accepting surface traits as a valid description of someone's personality, adolescents are more likely than children to look for deeper, more complex, even hidden causes of personality.

In the following comments obtained in one developmental investigation of how individuals perceive others (Livesley & Bromley, 1973), we can see how the development of an implicit personality theory proceeds:

> Max sits next to me, his eyes are hazel and he is tall. He hasn't got a very big head, he's got a big pointed nose. (p. 213; age seven years, six months)
>
> He smells very much and is very nasty. He has no sense of humor and is very dull. He is always fighting and he is cruel. He does silly things and is very stupid. He has brown hair and cruel eyes. He is sulky and eleven years old and has lots of sisters. I think he is the most horrible boy in

the class. He has a croaky voice and always chews his pencil and picks his teeth and I think he is disgusting. (p. 217; age nine years, eleven months)

Andy is very modest. He is even shyer than I am when near strangers and yet is very talkative with people he knows and likes. He always seems good tempered and I have never seen him in a bad temper. He tends to degrade other people's achievements, and yet never praises his own. He does not seem to voice his opinions to anyone. He easily gets nervous. (p. 221; age fifteen years, eight months)

. . . she is curious about people but naive, and this leads her to ask too many questions so that people become irritated with her and withhold information, although she is not sensitive enough to notice it. (p. 225; young adult)

Social Cognitive Monitoring

As part of their increased awareness of themselves and others, which includes both internal thoughts and external behavior, adolescents monitor their social world more extensively. Consider the circumstance of the following adolescent: Bob, a 16-year-old, feels that he does not know as much as he wants or needs to know about Sally, another 16-year-old. He also wants and needs to know more about Sally's relationship with Brian, a 17-year-old. In his effort to learn about Sally, Bob decides that he wants to know more about the groups that Sally belongs to—her student council friends, the clique she belongs to, and so forth. Bob thinks about what he already knows about all these people and groups, and decides he needs to find out how close he is to his goal of understanding them by taking some appropriate, feedback-producing action. What he discovers by taking that action will determine his social cognitive progress and how difficult his social cognitive task is. Notice that the immediate aim of this feedback-producing action is not to make progress toward the main goal, but to monitor that progress.

Adolescents engage in a number of cognitive monitoring methods on virtually a daily basis. A student might meet someone new and quickly think, "It's going to be hard to really get to know this guy." Another adolescent might check incoming information about an organization (school, club, group of friends) to determine if it is consistent with the adolescent's impressions of the club or the group. Still another adolescent might question someone or paraphrase what that person has just said about her feelings to ensure that he has understood them correctly.

Cognitive developmentalist John Flavell (1979) believes that adolescents' ability to monitor their social cognition effectively may prove to be an important index of their social maturity and competence. Flavell says that, in many real-life situations, the monitoring problem is not to determine how well you understand what a message means, but rather how much you ought to believe it

or do what it says. For example, this aspect of monitoring is especially important in the persuasive appeals to adolescents involving smoking, drinking, engaging in delinquency, having sex, or becoming unthinking followers of this year's flaky cults or movements. Ideas being developed in the area of social cognitive monitoring may someday be parlayed into a method of teaching adolescents to make wise and thoughtful decisions. Next in our discussion of social cognition, we will return to Piaget's theory and consider whether it can explain the many social cognitive changes we have been discussing.

Piaget's Theory and Social Cognitive Change

Can Piaget's theory explain the many social cognitive changes that characterize adolescent development? Some critics of Piaget's approach believe that it cannot (Lapsley, 1993). Formal operational thought is adaptive if the causal structure is known and the deductive rules are correctly followed. Concrete operations are adaptive if the adolescent has a rich and varied social history from which to make the appropriate inductions. What this means is that the kinds of possibilities that concern the typical adolescent—ideological orientation, life plans, social and political commitments, for example—cannot be adequately explained by formal operational thought. The possibilities that spring forth from social life do not require an understanding of perfect logical reasoning in a formal manner, but something else, such as motivation, imagination, desire, and creativity. Rather than formal operational thoughts producing social cognitive change in adolescence, rich and varied social experiences and communication may be sufficient.

Social Cognition in the Remainder of the Text

Interest in social cognition has blossomed, and the approach has infiltrated many aspects of the study of adolescent development. In the next chapter, the topic of social intelligence is examined. In the discussion of families in chapter 6, the emerging cognitive abilities of the adolescent are evaluated in concert with parent-adolescent conflict and parenting strategies. In the description of peer relations in chapter 7, the importance of social knowledge and social information processing in peer relations is highlighted. In the overview of the self and identity in chapter 10, social cognition's role in understanding the self and identity is explored. And in the evaluation of moral development in chapter 13, considerable time is devoted to discussing Kohlberg's theory, which is a prominent aspect of the study of social cognition in adolescence.

At this point, many different aspects of social cognition have been described. A summary of these ideas is presented in concept table 4.2.

EXPLORING ADOLESCENT DEVELOPMENT

To further explore the nature of cognitive development in adolescence, we will examine a research study on the development of the ability to think like a scientist and also evaluate links among cognitive development, risk taking, and health promotion.

RESEARCH ON ADOLESCENT DEVELOPMENT

Thinking Like a Scientist

Featured Study

Kuhn, D., & Brannock, J. (1977). Development of the isolation of variables scheme in experimental and "natural experiment" contexts. *Developmental Psychology, 13,* 9–14.

One way to evaluate advances in thinking is to assess whether individuals have the ability to think the way scientists do when they conceptualize and conduct experiments. Scientific reasoning is often aimed at identifying causal factors. One way to do this is to isolate one of a number of variables as being what causes something to occur. Researchers have been interested in charting when the ability to think scientifically—such as the ability to isolate a key, causal variable—develops. Can children isolate a key causal variable in an experiment? Can young adolescents? Can college students?

Method

The subjects were 20 fourth-graders, 20 fifth-graders, 20 sixth-graders, and 20 college freshmen (both females and males were included at each grade level). Each of the students was given the plant problem (see figure 4.8). The researchers showed the students four plants—two that looked healthy, and two that were clearly in bad shape. A glass of water, either large or small, and a dish containing either dark- or light-colored plant food were adjacent to each plant. A bottle marked "leaf lotion" was also adjacent to two of the plants. The researcher told the students, "I've been raising some plants. I'd like to show them to you and ask what you think. Let's look at this plant first. It seems quite healthy, doesn't it? Every week I give this plant a large glass of water, some of this dark-colored plant food, and a little of the leaf lotion in this bottle. Now I have another plant like this at home that I've just started working on. My plant at home I'm giving a small glass of water each week and some of the light-colored plant food, and I'm not giving it any of the leaf lotion. How do you think my plant at home is going to turn out? How do you know?"

As shown in figure 4.8, the problem was constructed so that one

Figure~4.8

The Plant Problem.

variable (plant food) was operative in influencing the plant's health and the other two variables were ineffective. The students' task, therefore, was to isolate the operative variable and exclude the inoperative ones.

Results and Discussion

Formal operational thought is required to solve the plant problem, and for most individuals this did not appear until adolescence. Only a couple of fourth- and fifth-graders could solve the plant problem. Most of them knew they had to separate the variables, but they still could not distinguish between the operative and the inoperative ones. Not quite half of the sixth-graders but almost all of the college students could isolate the operative variable—plant food. The results document a gradual developmental progression in scientific reasoning, with more-advanced reasoning especially blossoming in adolescence. The results also underscore the presence of individual differences in formal operational thought—several of the fourth- and fifth-graders could solve the plant problem, and several of the college students could not. Researchers today continue to show an interest in studying the development of scientific reasoning in children and adolescents (Amsel, 1995; Fay, 1995).

ADOLESCENT HEALTH AND WELL-BEING

Cognitive Development, Risk Taking, and Health Promotion

The cognitive changes that characterize adolescents have important implications for adolescents' at-risk behavior and health promotion campaigns (Crockett & Petersen, 1993). Some experts argue that adolescents' egocentrism is at the heart of their high levels of risk-taking behavior. The argument is that because adolescents, especially young adolescents, perceive themselves to be invincible, invulnerable, and immune to the laws that apply to others, they often engage in health-compromising, risky ventures (Arnett, 1992; Elkind, 1976). For example, in one recent study, egocentrism was related to reckless sexual behavior in high school students (Arnett, 1995). Others argue that the cognitive dimensions of egocentrism are not the cause of adolescent risk taking (Lapsley, 1993; Millstein, 1993). For example, in one recent study, a pattern of negativity in the family was related to adolescents' risk-taking behaviors (Lefkowitz, Kahlbaugh, & Sigman, 1994).

The increase in hypothetical-deductive reasoning that accompanies formal operational thought should reduce adolescent risk taking and facilitate health promotion efforts. As they mature cognitively, some adolescents are better able to understand health risks, reflect on their behavior, consider the long-term consequences of their actions, and understand symbolic meanings. Unfortunately, their increase in abstract thought and interest in symbolic meaning can make adolescents more susceptible to advertisements that symbolically link health-compromising products such as cigarettes and alcohol with attractiveness, peer acceptance, and adult status.

Consider also the idealism that accompanies formal operational thought and how it might be related to risk taking and health promotion. Adolescents are capable of imagining an ideal world that is free from the ills of the real world. As Piaget (1967) noted, their egocentrism makes it hard for adolescents to recognize the real-world impediments to reaching an ideal state of affairs. It is as if the real world should submit itself to idealistic schemes rather than to systems of reality. The path to their ideal world is not cluttered with afflictions and disasters; it is perceived as a smooth path. Adolescents think, "Afflictions and disasters happen to other people, not me."

Health promotion programs also need to take into account developmental differences in reasoning ability. As a rule, younger adolescents should be presented with more concrete approaches, older adolescents with more abstract, symbolic approaches. However, our coverage of adolescent cognitive development indicated considerable individual variation, so the most effective health promotion strategy may vary even for adolescents of the same age.

In summary, although egocentrism might explain the risk-taking behavior of some adolescents, other reasons also can be involved. The fact that not all adolescents are at the same cognitive developmental stage suggests that multiple approaches to health promotion may be needed—some more concrete, others more symbolic. In the next chapter we will further explore the role of cognition in risk-taking behavior and health promotion by studying the nature of adolescent decision making.

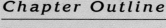

Chapter Outline

Information Processing and Intelligence

Chapter Boxes

*The error of youth is to believe that
intelligence is a substitute for experience, while
the error of age is to believe that experience is a
substitute for intelligence.*

—Slyman Bryson

Reading *Martina*

> *I come into the fields and spacious palaces of my memory, where are treasures of countless images of things of every manner.*
>
> —St. Augustine

PREVIEW

As adolescents move through their world, they process information—they perceive, attend, remember, think, solve problems, and draw conclusions. Adolescents thirst to know, understand, and create. In this chapter, we will evaluate the role of information processing in adolescent development, the nature of intelligence in adolescence, the extremes of intelligence, and creativity.

Barbara Smith is a sixth-grade student at a middle school. Her favorite activity is tennis, so her mother recently bought her a book entitled *Martina*, which is about tennis star Martina Navratilova's life. Barbara finished reading the first eleven pages of the book. She placed it on the table in the hall as she left for tennis practice. Her 8-year-old sister, Nancy, saw Barbara leave the book on the table. She grabbed the book and started to read it. Nancy finished the entire book in 12 minutes. In that 12 minutes, she read several sentences in different chapters as she leafed rapidly through the book. She also studied each of the book's photographs and read some of their captions.

After Barbara returned from tennis practice, she showered, ate, and then read another chapter in *Martina*, which Nancy had returned to its place on the table. She sat quietly for 30 minutes and read the next eighteen pages of the book. A few of the words were difficult, but Barbara got the idea of what Martina's family background was like and how she started to play tennis in her native country of Czechoslovakia. She especially noted how Martina's father spent long hours playing tennis with her and how she dreamed of being a star.

Nancy, Barbara's younger sister, walked by her room just as Barbara finished reading for the evening. Nancy asked, "Did you like the book? I did." Barbara replied, "You are too little to understand it. Shrimps can't read this kind of book." Their mother heard them begin to argue and went upstairs to intervene. She asked Nancy what the book was about. Nancy said, "A tennis player. I can't remember her name, though." Barbara laughed and said, "She doesn't know very much, does she?" The mother reprimanded Barbara for teasing Nancy, then walked out into the hall with Nancy and told her not to worry about what Barbara had said.

The next day, the mother went to Barbara's room while Barbara was at tennis practice and picked up the book about Martina. She sat down and skimmed the book in about an hour, forming a general idea of the book's content. As she read, she made mental notes and developed many concepts about Martina's life both on and off the tennis court.

When we read, we process information and interpret it. So reading serves as a practical example to introduce the topic of information processing in adolescence. To read effectively, adolescents have to perceive and attend to a complex set of visual symbols—words. Note that Barbara and her mother attended more to words and sentences, while Nancy attended more to pictures. Another process in reading is holding the information we process in memory. Note that after about an hour of reading, the mother was able to get the gist of the entire book and hold the book's themes in her memory. But Barbara was able to cover only several chapters of the book in this time frame, and at this point, her memory of what the book was about was much more impoverished than her mother's.

INFORMATION PROCESSING

Information processing is both a framework for thinking about adolescent development and a facet of that development. As a framework, information processing includes certain ideas about how adolescent minds work and the best methods for studying this. As a facet of development, different aspects of information processing change as children make the transition through adolescence to adulthood. For example, changes in attention and memory are essentially changes in the way individuals process information. In the discussion that follows, we will review some basic ideas about the information-processing approach first discussed in chapter 2 and compare the information-processing approach with other cognitive orientations. Then we will examine some basic developmental changes in processing and the nature of attention, memory, and cognitive monitoring in adolescence. Our discussion of information processing continues with an evaluation of its application to adolescent decision making and critical thinking, and concludes with a discussion of the role of computers in adolescents' lives.

The Information-Processing Perspective

As we discussed in chapter 2, information processing is concerned with how individuals analyze the many sources of information in the environment and make sense of these experiences. Information processing includes how information gets into adolescents' minds, how it is stored and transformed, and how it is retrieved to think about and solve problems. The development of the computer promoted this approach—the mind as an information-processing system has been compared to the computer as an information-processing system. The information-processing system raises questions about development, such as How do the ways in which we process information change as we make the transition from childhood to adulthood?

Comparison with Other Perspectives

How does the information-processing perspective differ from the behavioral perspective (chapter 2) and the Piagetian cognitive developmental perspective (chapters 2 and 4)? The behavioral approach focuses on behaviors and the events in the environment that change these behaviors. Traditional principles of behaviorism and learning do little to explain what is going on in the adolescent's mind, although in recent years cognitive social learning theory has emphasized some cognitive processes. Piagetian theory, in contrast, has much to say about the adolescent's mind. For example, Piaget described the adolescent's thoughts as more abstract, idealistic, and logical than the child's. But the Piagetian description is somewhat general—it does not tell us much about how the adolescent reads or solves math problems. It leaves

Information processing includes how information gets into an adolescent's mind, how it is stored and transformed, and how it is retrieved to think about and solve problems.

out some important details about how the adolescent's mind actually works on specific tasks, like solving algebraic equations and writing long essays.

The information-processing perspective tries to correct some of the shortcomings of traditional behaviorism or learning theory and Piagetian cognitive developmental ideas. It describes mental processes and offers details about how these processes work in concrete situations (Klahr & MacWhinney, 1997; Siegler, 1995). Where possible, these descriptions include analyses of all the steps necessary to complete some task, the specific mental processes needed for these steps, and precise estimates of how "hard" or "how long" the mind has to work to execute these steps.

Let's examine how an adolescent's mind might work in processing information about an algebraic equation. An event (S) occurs in the environment. Suppose the event is the appearance of the following algebraic equation on the chalkboard at school: "$2x + 10 = 34$. Solve for x." This event contains information that a person can detect and understand. Success in detecting and making sense of it depends on how completely and efficiently the information is processed. Development can be equated with becoming more skillful and efficient at information processing. Once the processing is complete, the

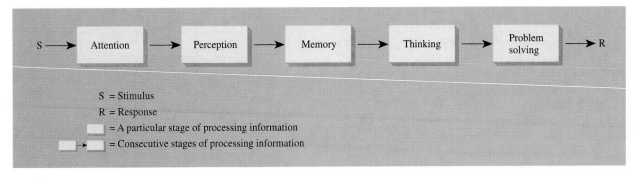

Figure~5.1

Hypothetical Series of Steps Involved in Processing Information to Solve an Algebra Problem.

person produces an observable response (R). In this model, then, cognitive activity refers to the flow of information through the different steps of processing.

Consider how a well-seasoned algebra student engages in cognition. The teacher writes the equation on the board (S). The student looks up and notes that something has been written on the board (*attention*). This "something" is then determined to be a series of numbers, letters, and signs, and—at a higher level of identification—two simple statements: (1) "$2x + 10 = 34$" and (2) "Solve for x" (*perception*). The student must preserve the results of this perceptual analysis over a period of time (*memory*), even if only for the brief interval needed to write the problem on a worksheet.

The student then begins to elaborate on the product of perception and memory (*thinking*). This level of analysis can be described best with an imaginary mental soliloquy (though, of course, the reasoning might take an altogether different track or even a nonverbal form): "Let's see. It's an equation—x is the unknown, and I'm supposed to figure out the value of x. How do I do that?" The final level of analysis (*problem solving*) addresses the question: "How do I do that?" Problem solving then takes the following form: "Okay, $2x + 10 = 34$. First, I have to collect the unknown on one side of the equation and the known values on the other side. To do this, I'll leave the $2x$ where it is—on the left. Then I'll subtract 10 from each side to remove the 10 from the left. This leaves $2x = 24$. Now I have to express the equation as 'x = something,' and it's solved. How do I do this? I know! Divide each side by 2 and that will leave $1x$, or x, on the left side. Now I have $x = 12$. That's the answer!" A summary of the processes used in solving the algebraic equation is presented in figure 5.1.

Figure 5.1 is a necessarily oversimplified representation of information processing that omits a great deal and does not indicate the many routes that the flow of information may take. For example, each hypothetical step (such as perception) may overlap with other steps (for example, memory) or be composed of several substeps. Neither of these features is captured in the diagram, whose

purpose is to focus on the basic elements of information processing. In many instances, information processing is dynamic and simultaneous, and many different models of how this processing takes place have been developed. In chapter 2, another simplified model of information processing was described (figure 2.4) to give a sense of the basic processes involved in adolescent cognition.

Developmental Changes in Information Processing

Three developmental changes in information processing that distinguish adolescents from children are changes in (1) processing speed, (2) processing capacity, and (3) automaticity, each of which we consider in turn.

Processing Speed Many things that children and adolescents do are constrained by how much time is available. A child is told to finish writing a letter in 5 minutes so that the family can leave. A phone message must be written down before the message is forgotten. The teacher gives the adolescent 5 minutes to finish the assigned algebra problems. The speed with which such tasks is completed improves dramatically across the childhood and adolescent years (Stigler, Nusbaum, & Chalip, 1988). The causes of the improvement are not always clear, however. Is a 7-year-old slower to write down a phone message than a 13-year-old because of limitations in the physical act of writing or because of other, more mental limitations, such as the time needed to think of how to spell words correctly or to briefly summarize a message? Do such age differences suggest some maturational, central nervous system differences in maturity? At present, these questions have not been answered.

In one study, processing speed continued to improve in early adolescence (Hale, 1990). Ten-year-olds were approximately 1.8 times slower in processing information than were young adults on such tasks as reaction time, letter matching, mental rotation, and abstract matching. Twelve-year-olds were approximately 1.5 times slower than young adults, but 15-year-olds processed information on the tasks as fast as young adults.

Processing Capacity Information-processing capacity can be viewed as a type of energy needed to perform mental work. The difficulty individuals have in dividing attention when they do two things at once is attributed to limits on capacity. So also is the trouble individuals have in performing complex tasks (such as mentally working a complex geometry problem). Although capacity is thought to be limited at all ages, there is no generally accepted measure of an adolescent's capacity, and thus, findings are ambiguous. For example, it is possible that capacity does not change with age but that children must spend more capacity on lower-level processes (such as identifying stimuli), leaving less capacity for higher-level processes (such as dividing attention or performing complex computations) than adolescents.

Automaticity Some activities are completed with little thought or effort. An able 12-year-old zips through a practice list of multiplication problems with little conscious effort. A 17-year-old adolescent picks up the newspaper and quickly scans the sports section to discover the results of an important basketball game. Both of these examples illustrate relatively automatic information processing. By comparison, imagine a 9-year-old doing long division with three- to five-digit numbers, or an 18-year-old trying to decipher the meaning of a news paragraph in a foreign language studied 4 years earlier and not studied since. These activities require considerable mental processing and effort. For virtually any given task, such as calculating, reading, or writing, adolescents' **automaticity**—*the ability to perform automatically with little or no effort*—is better than children's. Automaticity is clearly linked to speed of processing and processing capacity. As an activity is completed faster, it requires less processing capacity. As processing capacity increases, tasks that were previously considered difficult become easier to complete. Next, we will consider a developmental model of information processing that includes automaticity and processing capacity.

Case's Developmental Information-Processing Model Canadian developmentalist Robbie Case (1985, 1997) proposed an information-processing model that specifies differences in children's and adolescents' cognition. In Case's view, adolescents make considerable gains in a number of cognitive areas: They have increasingly more cognitive resources available to them because of automaticity, increased information-processing capacity, and more familiarity with a range of content knowledge. Because of the reduced load on the cognitive system, adolescents become capable of holding in mind several different dimensions of a topic or problem, whereas children are more likely to focus on only one (Keating, 1990). Next, we consider two cognitive processes involved in adolescents' processing of information—attention and memory.

> *Our life is what our thoughts make it.*
>
> —Marcus Aurelius,
> *Meditations*, 2nd century B.C.

Attention and Memory

Although the bulk of research on information processing has been conducted with children and adults, the information-processing perspective is important in understanding adolescent cognition. As we saw in the example of the adolescent solving an algebraic equation, attention and memory are two important cognitive processes.

Attention

Pay attention is a phrase children and adolescents hear all of the time. Just what is *attention?* **Attention** *is the concentration and focusing of mental effort. Attention also is both selective and shifting.* For example, when adolescents take a test, they must attend to it. This implies that they have the ability to focus their mental effort on certain stimuli (the test questions) while excluding other stimuli, an important aspect of attention called *selectivity.* When selective attention fails adolescents, they have difficulty ignoring information that is irrelevant to their interest or goals. For example, if a television set is blaring while the adolescent is studying, the adolescent may have difficulty concentrating.

Not only is attention selective, but it is also *shiftable.* If a teacher asks students to pay attention to a certain question and they do so, their behavior indicates that they can shift the focus of their mental effort from one stimulus to another. If the telephone rings while the adolescent is studying, the adolescent may shift attention from studying to the telephone. An external stimulus is not necessary to shift attention. At any moment, adolescents can shift their attention from one topic to another, virtually at will. They might think about the last time they went to a play, then think about an upcoming music recital, and so on.

In one investigation, 12-year-olds were markedly better than 8-year-olds and slightly worse than 20-year-olds at allocating their attention in a situation involving two tasks (Manis, Keating, & Morrison, 1980). Adolescents might have more resources available (through increased processing speed, capacity, and automaticity), or they might be more skilled at directing these resources.

Memory

There are few moments when adolescents' lives are not steeped in memory. Memory is at work with each step adolescents take, each thought they think, and each word they utter. **Memory** *is the retention of information over time.* It is central to mental life and to information processing. To successfully learn and reason, adolescents need to hold on to information and to retrieve the information they have tucked away. Two important memory systems are short-term memory and long-term memory. **Short-term memory** *is a limited-capacity memory system in which information is retained for as long as 30 seconds, unless the information is rehearsed, in which case it can be retained longer.* **Long-term memory** *is a relatively permanent memory system that holds huge amounts of information for a long period of time.*

A common way to assess short-term memory is to present a list of items to remember, which is often referred to as a memory span task. If you have taken an IQ test, you probably were asked to remember a string of numbers or words. You simply hear a short list of stimuli—usually digits—presented at a rapid pace (one per second, for example). Then you are asked to repeat the digits back. Using the memory span task, researchers have found that short-term memory increases extensively in early childhood and continues to increase in older children and adolescents, but at a slower pace. For example, in one investigation, memory span increased by 1½ digits between the ages of 7 and 13 (Dempster, 1981). Keep in mind, though, memory span's individual differences, which is why IQ and various aptitude tests are used.

How might short-term memory be used in problem solving? In a series of experiments, Robert Sternberg and his colleagues (1977; Sternberg & Nigro, 1980; Sternberg & Rifkin, 1979) attempted to answer this question by giving third-grade, sixth-grade, ninth-grade, and college students analogies to solve. The main differences occurred between the younger (third and sixth grade) and older (ninth grade and college) students. The older students were more likely to complete the information processing required to solve the analogy task. The children, by contrast, often stopped their processing of information before they had considered all of the necessary steps required to solve the problems. Sternberg believes that incomplete information processing occurred because the children's short-term memory was overloaded. Solving problems such as analogies requires individuals to make continued comparisons between newly encoded information and previously coded information. Sternberg argues that adolescents probably have more storage space in short-term memory, which results in fewer errors on problems like analogies.

In addition to more storage space, are there other reasons adolescents might perform better on memory span tasks and in solving analogies? While many other factors may be involved, information-processing psychologists believe that changes in the speed and efficiency of information processing are important, especially the speed with which information can be identified.

Long-term memory increases substantially in the middle and late childhood years and likely continues to improve during adolescence, although this has not been well documented by researchers. If anything at all is known

In one research study, 12-year-olds were much better than 8-year-olds and only slightly worse than 20-year-olds at allocating their attention in a situation involving two tasks (Manis, Keating, & Morrison, 1980). The adolescents' improved attention may have occurred because they had more processing resources available or because they were more skilled at directing those resources.

about long-term memory, it is that it depends on the learning activities engaged in when learning and remembering information (Pressley & Schneider, 1997; Siegler, 1996). Most learning activities fit under the category of **strategies,** *activities under the learner's conscious control. They sometimes are also called control processes. There are many of these activities, but one of the most important is* organization, *the tendency to group or arrange items into categories.*

> *My thoughts are my company; I can bring them together, select them, detain them, dismiss them.*
> —Walter Savage Landor

Cognitive Monitoring, Decision Making, and Critical Thinking

In many activities it might be quite simple for adolescents to pay attention and memorize as they examine information or attempt to complete a task. They might devote little effort and complete the new task quickly. In contrast, many other activities occur over an extended period of time and require adolescents to mobilize considerable resources. And when adolescents encounter some difficulty or lapse of attention, they must overcome it and get back on track. Three complex cognitive processes are involved in adolescents' ability to control and guide their activities: cognitive monitoring, decision making, and critical thinking.

Reading continues to play a powerful role in adolescents' lives, just as it did when they were children. In the last decade, considerable interest has developed in the process of cognitive monitoring as an important aspect of reading. What do we mean by cognitive monitoring?

Cognitive Monitoring

Cognitive monitoring *is the process of taking stock of what one is currently doing, what will be done next, and how effectively the mental activity is unfolding.* When adolescents engage in an activity like reading, writing, or solving a math problem, they are repeatedly called on to take stock of what they are doing and what they plan to do next. In chapter 4, we saw the importance of social cognitive monitoring in understanding the way adolescents solve social problems. Here we examine the importance of cognitive monitoring in solving problems in the nonsocial aspects of intelligence—reading, writing, math, and so on. For example, when adolescents begin to solve a math problem—especially one that might take a while to finish—they must determine what kind of problem they are working on and a good approach to solving it. And once they undertake a problem solution, thy need to check on whether the solution is working or whether some other approach needs to be taken.

Evidence that children and adolescents need advice to help them monitor their cognitive activities is plentiful (Mayer, 1987). Parents, teachers, and peers can serve as important cognitive-monitoring models and also can interact with adolescents in ways to improve their cognitive monitoring. In one strategy, cognitive monitoring is placed in the hands of peers; that is, instead of adults telling adolescents what to do and checking their performance, this chore is performed by other adolescents.

Instructional programs in reading comprehension (Brown & Palincsar, 1989), writing (Scardamalia, Bereiter, & Steinbach, 1984), and mathematics (Schoenfeld, 1985) have been designed to foster the development of cognitive monitoring. Developmental psychologists Ann Brown and Annemarie Palincsar's program for reading comprehension is an excellent example of a cognitive monitoring instructional program. Students in the program acquire specific knowledge and also learn strategies for monitoring their understanding. **Reciprocal teaching** *is an instructional procedure used by Brown and Palincsar to develop cognitive monitoring; it requires that students take turns in leading a study group in the use of strategies for comprehending and remembering text content.* The instruction involves a small group of students, often working with an adult leader, actively discussing a short text, with the goal of *summarizing* it, asking *questions* to promote understanding, offering *clarifying* statements for difficult or confusing words and ideas, and *predicting* what will come next. The procedure actively involves children and adolescents; it teaches them some techniques for reflecting about their own understanding, and the group interaction is highly motivating and engaging. A flurry of recent research has documented the power of peer collaboration in learning and problem solving (Ayman-Nolley & Church, 1993; Tudge & Winterhoff, 1993).

In addition to cognitive monitoring, two other cognitive activities are especially important in adolescents' everyday cognitive skills—decision making and critical thinking.

Decision Making

Adolescence is a time of increased decision making—about the future, which friends to choose, whether to go to college, which person to date, whether to have sex, whether to buy a car, and so on (Byrnes, 1997; Galotti & Kozberg, 1996). How competent are adolescents at making decisions? In some reviews, older adolescents are described as more competent than younger adolescents, who, in turn, are more competent than children (Keating, 1990). Compared to children, young adolescents are more likely to generate options, to examine a situation from a variety of perspectives, to anticipate the consequences of decisions, and to consider the credibility of sources.

One study documents that older adolescents are better at decision making than younger adolescents are (Lewis, 1981). Eighth-, tenth-, and twelfth-grade students were presented with dilemmas involving the choice of a medical procedure. The oldest students were most likely to spontaneously mention a variety of risks, to recommend consultation with an outside specialist, and to anticipate future consequences. For example, when asked a question about whether to have cosmetic surgery, a twelfth-grader said that different aspects of the situation need to be examined along with its effects on the individual's future, especially relationships with other people. By contrast, an eighth-grader presented a more limited view, commenting on the surgery's effects on getting turned down for a date, the money involved, and being teased by peers.

In sum, older adolescents often make better decisions than do younger adolescents, who, in turn, make

Although driver-training courses can improve adolescents' cognitive and motor skills related to driving, these courses have not been effective in reducing adolescents' high rate of traffic accidents. An important research agenda is to learn more about how adolescents make decisions in practical situations, such as driving.

better decisions than children do. But the decision-making skills of older adolescents are far from perfect, as are those of adults. Indeed, some researchers have recently found that adolescents and adults do not differ in their decision-making skills (Quadrel, Fischoff, & Davis, 1993). For more discussion of these findings that there are no differences in the decision-making skills of adolescents and adults, see the section "Adolescent Health and Well-Being" at the end of the chapter.

The ability to make competent decisions does not guarantee that they will be made in everyday life, where breadth of experience often comes into play (Jacobs & Potenza, 1990; Keating, 1990). For example, driver-training courses improve adolescents' cognitive and motor skills to levels equal to, or sometimes superior to, those of adults. However, driver training has not been effective in reducing adolescents' high rate of traffic accidents (Potvin, Champagne, & Laberge-Nadeau, 1988). An important research agenda is to study the ways adolescents make decisions in practical situations.

Adolescents need more opportunities to practice and discuss realistic decision making (Jones, Rasmussen, & Moffitt, 1997). Many real-world decisions occur in an atmosphere of stress that includes such factors as time constraints and emotional involvement. One strategy for improving adolescent decision making about real-world choices involving such matters as sex, drugs, and daredevil driving is for schools to provide more opportunities for adolescents to engage in role-playing and group problem solving related to such circumstances.

Another strategy is for parents to involve their adolescents in appropriate decision-making activities. In one study of more than 900 young adolescents and a subsample of their parents, adolescents were more likely to participate in family decision making when they perceived

themselves as in control of what happens to them and if they thought that their input would have some bearing on the outcome of the decision-making process (Liprie, 1993).

Critical Thinking

Closely related to making competent decisions is engaging in critical thinking, a current buzzword in education and psychology (Halonen, 1995). Although today's definitions of **critical thinking** vary, they have in common the notions of *grasping the deeper meaning of problems, of keeping an open mind about different approaches and perspectives, and of deciding for oneself what to believe or do.* Another, often implicit assumption is that critical thinking is a very important aspect of everyday reasoning. Adolescents should be encouraged to engage in critical thinking, not just inside the classroom but outside it as well.

Adolescence is an important transitional period in the development of critical thinking (Keating, 1990). Among the cognitive changes that allow improved critical thinking in adolescence are:

- Increased speed, automaticity, and capacity of information processing, which free cognitive resources for other purposes
- More breadth of content knowledge in a variety of domains
- Increased ability to construct new combinations of knowledge
- A greater range and more spontaneous use of strategies or procedures for applying or obtaining knowledge, such as planning, considering alternatives, and cognitive monitoring

Although adolescence is an important period in the development of critical-thinking skills, if a solid basis of fundamental skills (such as literacy and math skills) is not developed during childhood, such critical-thinking skills are unlikely to mature in adolescence. For the subset of adolescents who lack such fundamental skills, potential gains in adolescent thinking are not likely.

Considerable interest has recently developed in teaching critical thinking in schools. Cognitive psychologist Robert J. Sternberg (1985) believes that most school programs that teach critical thinking are flawed. He thinks that schools focus too much on formal reasoning tasks and not enough on the critical-thinking skills needed in everyday life. Among the critical-thinking skills that Sternberg believes adolescents need in everyday life are these: recognizing that problems exist, defining problems more clearly, handling problems with no single right answer or any clear criteria for the point at which the problem is solved (such as selecting a rewarding career), making decisions on issues of personal relevance (such as deciding to have a risky operation), obtaining information, thinking in groups, and developing long-term approaches to long-term problems.

Researchers are increasingly finding that critical-thinking programs are more effective when they are domain-specific rather than domain-general (Resnick, 1987). For example, if the goal is to reduce teenage pregnancy, decision-making skills using teenage pregnancy as the content should be taught. This strategy will be more effective than teaching general logic skills in an effort to reduce teenage pregnancy.

At this time, there is no agreed-upon curriculum of critical thinking that can be taught in a stepwise, developmental fashion to children and adolescents. Many experts in education and psychology, however, believe that the infusion of a critical-thinking approach into all parts of the curriculum would benefit children and adolescents.

In chapter 2, we saw that the computer played an important role in the development of the information-processing perspective. While the information-processing perspective has yet to be widely applied to adolescent education, the computer is rapidly becoming an important aspect of adolescent learning.

Computers and Adolescents

At mid twentieth century, IBM had yet to bring its first computer to market. Now, as we move toward the close of the twentieth century, computers are important influences in adolescents' lives. For some, the computer is a positive tool with the power to transform our schools and revolutionize adolescents' learning. For others, the computer is a menacing force, more likely to undermine than to improve adolescents' education and learning. Let's examine some of computers' possible positive and negative influences.

Positive Influences of Computers on Adolescents

The potential positive influences of computers on adolescents' development include using computers as personal tutors or as multipurpose tools, and the motivational and social effects of computers (Lepper & Gurtner, 1989).

Computer-assisted instruction *involves using computers as tutors to individualize instruction: to present information, to give students practice, to assess students' level of understanding, and to provide additional instruction if needed.* Computer-assisted instruction requires students' active participation, and in giving immediate feedback to students, is patient and nonjudgmental. Over the past two decades, the more than 200 research studies on computer-assisted instruction have generally shown that the effects of computer-assisted instruction are positive. More precisely, the effects are more positive with programs involving tutorials rather than drill and practice, with younger rather than older students, and with lower ability than average or unselected populations (Lepper & Gurtner, 1989).

The computer's second important influence on adolescent development involves the computer's role in experiential learning. Some experts view computers as excellent mediums for open-ended, exploratory, and experiential learning.

Third, computers can function as a multipurpose tool in helping adolescents to achieve academic goals and to become more creative. They are especially helpful in improving adolescents' writing and communication skills. Word-processing programs diminish the drudgery of writing, increasing the probability that adolescents will edit and revise their work. Programs that assist in outlining a paper may help students to organize their thoughts before they write.

Several other themes appear in discussions of computers' positive influence on adolescent development. For one, computer advocates argue that computers make learning more intrinsically motivating (Lepper, 1985). Computer enthusiasts also argue that computers can make learning more fun. In addition, lessons can often be embedded in instructional "games" or puzzles that encourage adolescents' curiosity and sense of challenge. Some computer advocates also argue that increased computer use in schools will lead to increased student cooperation and collaboration, as well as increased intellectual discussion among students. And if computers do increase students' interest, they may free teachers to spend more one-on-one time with students. Finally, computer advocates hope that computers can help to equalize educational opportunity. Since computers allow students to work at their own pace, they might help students who do not normally succeed in schools. Also, because computers are fair and impartial, they should minimize the adverse influences of teacher prejudice and stereotyping.

Some of the most interesting work in the field of computers and education is very distinct from the metaphor of the "artificially intelligent tutor," which dominated the field for some time (Keating, 1996). Instead, one current interest is to find ways for information technology to support extended collaborative discourses on meaningful programs. This emphasis often engages students' interests far more than traditional instruction or computer training programs. One such collaborative learning effort was developed by Marlene Scardamalia, Carl Bereiter, and their colleagues (1989). They call their system "computer-supported intentional learning." Shared responsibility is an important dimension of the system. Students respond to other students' ideas, requests for information, and the like. Teachers can base grades on the helpfulness of such responses. In this computer-based approach, students are given more responsibility for contributing to each other's learning.

Negative Influences of Computers on Adolescents

The potential negative influences of computers on adolescent development include regimentation and dehumanization of the classroom, as well as unwarranted

For three decades, filmmaker Robert Abel made the screen come alive with special effects, influencing the development of such movies as *2001: A Space Odyssey*. Today, Abel is working on creative ways to use computers to educate children and adolescents. His approach blends computers and television. The students, using devices such as a desktop mouse or a touch screen, explore as their curiosity beckons. They can follow a lead from text to photos to music and back again. In an application to art, students see some of Picasso's paintings; then they choose—by clicking with the mouse—various interpretations of the paintings. Abel's combination of computers and television is being tried out in some schools in Los Angeles and should soon be available on a wider basis. Abel's goal is to use the computer/television strategy to turn on students to discover ideas.

"shaping" of the curriculum. Generalizations and limitations of computer-based teaching may also be potential problems (Lepper & Gurtner, 1989).

Skeptics worry that, rather than increased individualization of instruction, computers bring a much greater regimentation and homogenization of classroom learning experiences. While some students may prefer to work autonomously and may learn most effectively when they are allowed to progress on their own, other students may rely on social interaction with and guidance by the teacher for effective learning. And some computer skeptics worry that computers will ultimately increase in-

equality, rather than equality, in educational outcomes. School funding in middle-class neighborhoods is usually better than in low-income areas, and the homes of adolescents in middle-class neighborhoods are more likely to have computers than those in low-income neighborhoods. Thus, an increasing emphasis on computer literacy may be inequitable for children from low-income backgrounds because they have likely had fewer opportunities to use computers. Some critics also worry about the dehumanization of the classroom. They argue that school is a social world as well as a cognitive, learning world. From this perspective, children plugged into computers all day long have little opportunity to engage in social interaction.

A further concern is that computers may inadvertently and inappropriately shape the curriculum. Some subjects, such as mathematics and science, seem to be more easily and successfully adapted to computers than such subjects as art and literature. Consequently, there is concern that computers could eventually shape the curriculum in the direction of science and math.

Yet another concern is the transfer of learning and motivation outside the computer domain. If the instructional effectiveness and motivational appeal of computer-based education depend on the use of impressive technical devices, such as color, animation, and sound effects, how effectively will student learning or motivation transfer to other contexts without these technical supports? Will adolescents provided with the editorial assistance of computers still learn the basic skills needed to progress to more complex forms of creative writing later in their careers? Will adolescents using computers in math gain the proficiency to deal with more complicated math in the future, or will their ability to solve complex conceptual problems in the absence of computers have atrophied? Presently, the answers to these important questions about computers' role in adolescent development are not known.

At this point, we have discussed numerous ideas about information processing, and a summary of these ideas is presented in concept table 5.1. Now we turn our attention to another way of analyzing the adolescent's cognition. We will discover that the study of adolescent intelligence has emphasized individual differences, knowledge, and intelligence tests.

INTELLIGENCE

Robert Sternberg recalls being terrified of taking IQ tests as a child. He says that he literally froze when the time came to take such tests. When he was in the sixth grade, he was sent to take an IQ test with the fifth-graders and still talks about how embarrassing and humiliating the experience was. Sternberg recalls that maybe he was dumb, but he wasn't *that* dumb. He finally overcame his anxieties about IQ tests and performed much better on them. Sternberg then became so fascinated with IQ tests that he devised his own at the age of 13 and began assessing the intellectual abilities of his classmates until the school

Concept	Processes/ Related Ideas	Characteristics/Description
The Information-Processing Perspective	Overview	Information processing is concerned with how individuals analyze the many sources of information in the environment and make sense of these experiences. It includes how information gets into the mind, how it is stored and transformed, and how it is retrieved to think about and solve problems.
	Comparison with other approaches	Traditional principles of behaviorism and learning do little to explain what is going on in the mind. Piaget's cognitive developmental theory provides a general outline of changes in cognition but leaves out some important details about the steps involved in analyzing information. The information-processing perspective tries to correct some of these deficiencies.
	Developmental changes	Adolescents process information faster, have greater processing capacity, and show greater automaticity in processing than children do. According to Case, adolescents have increasingly more cognitive resources available to them because of automaticity, increased capacity, and more familiarity with content knowledge.
Attention and Memory	Attention	Attention is the concentration and focusing of mental effort. Attention is both selective and shifting.
	Memory	Memory is the retention of information over time. It can be divided into short-term memory—information held for up to 30 seconds—and long-term memory—information held indefinitely. Strategies, or control processes, especially organization, improve adolescent memory. Increases in storage space, as well as in speed and efficiency of information processing, are likely involved in the adolescent's superior memory when compared to the child's memory.
Cognitive Monitoring, Decision Making, and Critical Thinking	Cognitive monitoring	Cognitive monitoring is the process of taking stock of what one is doing currently, what will be done next, and how effectively the mental activity is unfolding. Parents, teachers, and peers can be effective sources for improving the adolescent's cognitive monitoring. Reciprocal teaching is an increasingly used instructional strategy.
	Decision making	Adolescence is a time of increased decision making. Older adolescents are more competent at decision making than are younger adolescents, who, in turn, are more competent than children are. The ability to make competent decisions does not guarantee that such decisions will be made in everyday life, where breadth of experience comes into play.
	Critical thinking	Critical thinking involves grasping the deeper meaning of problems, keeping an open mind about different approaches and perspectives, and deciding for oneself what to believe or do. Adolescence is an important transitional period in the development of critical thinking because of such cognitive changes as increased speed, automaticity, and capacity of information processing; more breadth of content knowledge; increased ability to construct new combinations of knowledge; and a greater range and more spontaneous use of strategies.
Computers and Adolescents	Positive effects	Potential positive effects include using computers as personal tutors (computer-assisted instruction) or as multipurpose tools, as well as the motivational and social aspects of computers.
	Negative effects	Potential negative effects include regimentation and dehumanization of the classroom, as well as unwarranted "shaping" of the curriculum. Generalizations and limitations of computer-based teaching may also be a potential problem.

psychologist scolded him. Later in our discussion of intelligence, you will discover that Sternberg recently has developed a provocative theory of intelligence. Our exploration of intelligence focuses on the following questions: What is intelligence? How is intelligence measured? Does intelligence have one or more faces? Can aptitude and achievement tests be distinguished? What are some of the major controversies and issues involving intelligence? What are the extremes of intelligence like?

What Is Intelligence?

Intelligence is a possession that most adolescents value highly, yet it is an abstract concept with few agreed-upon referents. Investigators could agree upon referents for such characteristics as adolescent height, weight, and age, but would be less certain to agree on referents for something like an adolescent's size. Size is a more *abstract* notion than height or weight. An adolescent's size can be estimated only from a set of empirical measures of height and weight. Measuring an adolescent's intelligence is much the same as measuring the adolescent's size, though *much more* abstract; that is, investigators believe that adolescent intelligence exists, but it cannot be measured directly. They cannot peel back an adolescent's scalp and observe the adolescent's intellectual processes in action. The only way to study these intellectual processes is *indirectly*, by evaluating the intelligent acts the adolescent generates. For the most part, psychologists have relied on intelligence tests to provide estimates of adolescents' intelligence.

Throughout much of Western civilization's history, intelligence has been described in terms of knowledge and reasoning (Kail & Pellegrino, 1985). Today, most of us view intelligence in a similar light. In one investigation, individuals were asked to judge which of 250 behaviors were typical of an intelligent individual (Sternberg & others, 1981). Both experts (psychologists researching intelligence) and lay individuals (people of varying backgrounds and education) judged the behaviors similarly. The two groups agreed that intelligence can be divided into two main dimensions. The first is *verbal ability*, reflected in such behaviors as "displays a good vocabulary," "reads with high comprehension," "is knowledgeable about a particular field of knowledge," and "displays curiosity." The second is *problem-solving skills*, reflected in such behaviors as "reasons logically and well," "is able to apply knowledge to problems at hand," and "makes good decisions."

In addition to believing that intelligence involves verbal ability and problem-solving skills, psychologists who study intelligence also emphasize individual differences in intelligence and the assessment of intelligence. **Individual differences** *are the stable, consistent ways adolescents are different from each other*. The study of intelligence has focused extensively on individual differences and their assessment. We can talk about individual differences in the adolescent's personality or any other domain of development, but individual differences in the area of intelligence have received the most attention. For example, an intelligence test indicates whether an adolescent can reason better than most others who have taken the test. **Psychometrics** *is the name psychologists have given to the field that involves the assessment of individual differences*.

> *As many men, as many minds, everyone his own way.*
>
> —Terence

As mentioned earlier, **intelligence** *often is defined as verbal ability and problem-solving skills. In addition, however, intelligence involves the ability to learn from and adapt to the experiences of everyday life*.

Although intelligence can be generally defined, the ways in which intelligence is behaviorally displayed may vary across cultures (Lonner, 1990). For example, in most Western cultures, individuals are considered intelligent if they are both smart (have considerable knowledge and can solve verbal problems) and fast (can process information quickly). However, people in the Buganda culture in Uganda believe that intelligent individuals are wise, slow in thought, and able to say the socially correct thing. Thus, investigators cannot always transport a concept (such as intelligence) from one culture to another and assume its behavioral indicators will be the same. To do so is methodologically unsound, ethnocentric, and often culturally insensitive. As we further discuss the most widely used intelligence tests and the nature of intelligence, you will discover that experts still debate what intelligence is.

Intelligence Tests

Some intelligence tests are administered individually to adolescents, others are given to them in a group setting. First we will consider the individually administered tests.

The Binet and Wechsler Tests

The two individual intelligence tests most widely used with adolescents are the Binet and Wechsler tests.

The Binet Tests   In 1904 the French Ministry of Education asked psychologist Alfred Binet to devise a method that would determine which students did not profit from typical school instruction. School officials wanted to reduce overcrowding by placing those who did not benefit from regular classroom teaching in special schools. Binet and his student Theophile Simon developed an intelligence test to meet this request. The test is referred to as the 1905 Scale and consisted of thirty items, ranging from the ability to touch one's nose or ear when asked to the ability to draw designs from memory and to define abstract concepts.

Binet developed the concept of **mental age (MA)**, *which is an individual's level of mental development relative to others*. Binet reasoned that a mentally retarded child would perform like a normal child of a younger age. He developed norms for intelligence by testing fifty nonretarded children from the ages of 3 to 11. Children suspected of mental retardation were given the test, and their performance was compared with that of children of the same chronological age in the normal sample. Average mental age (MA) scores correspond to chronological age (CA), which is age from birth. A bright child has an MA above CA; a dull child has an MA below CA.

The term **intelligence quotient (IQ)** *was devised in 1912 by William Stern. IQ consists of a child's mental age divided by chronological age and multiplied by 100*:

$$IQ = \frac{MA}{CA} \times 100$$

If mental age is the same as chronological age, then the individual's IQ is 100; if mental age is above chronological age, the IQ is more than 100; if mental age is below chronological age, the IQ is less than 100. Scores noticeably above 100 are considered above average; those noticeably below are considered below average. For example, a 16-year-old with a mental age of 20 would have an IQ of 125, while a 16-year-old with a mental age of 12 would have an IQ of 75.

Over the years, the Binet test has been administered to thousands of children and adults of different ages selected at random from different parts of the United States. Test results have shown that intelligence measured by the Binet approximates a normal distribution (see figure 5.2). A **normal distribution** *is symmetrical, with most test scores falling in the middle of the possible range of scores and few scores appearing toward the extremes of the range.*

The Binet test has been revised many times to incorporate advances in the understanding of intelligence and intelligence testing. The many revisions are called the Stanford-Binet tests (Stanford University is where the revisions were done). Many of the revisions were carried out by Lewis Terman, who applied Stern's IQ concept to the test, developed extensive norms, and provided detailed, clear instructions for each problem on the test.

Intelligence is an abstract concept that has been defined in various ways. The three most commonly agreed-upon aspects of intelligence are the following: (a) verbal ability, as reflected in the verbal skills of these students searching for library books; (b) problem-solving skills, as reflected in the ability of this girl to solve the design problem presented her; and (c) ability to learn from and adapt to experiences of everyday life, as reflected in this handicapped adolescent's adaptation to her inability to walk.

The current Stanford-Binet is given to individuals from the age of 2 through adulthood. It includes a wide variety of items, some requiring verbal responses, others nonverbal responses. For example, items that characterize a 6-year-old's performance on the test include the verbal ability to define at least six words, such as *orange*

The SAT is used widely as a predictor of success in college, but it is only one of many pieces of information that determine whether a college admits a student. High school grades, the quality of the student's high school, letters of recommendation, individual interviews with the student, and special circumstances in the student's life that might have impeded academic ability are taken into account along with the SAT scores.

In recent years, a controversy has developed over whether private coaching can raise a student's SAT scores. The student's verbal and mathematical abilities, which the SAT assesses, have been built over years of experience and instruction. Research shows that private coaching on a short-term basis cannot help raise SAT scores substantially. Researchers have found that, on the average, SAT-preparation courses raise a student's scores only 15 points on the SAT's scale of 200 to 800 points (Kulik, Bangert-Drowns, & Kulik, 1984).

Aptitude Tests and Achievement Tests

Psychologists distinguish between an **aptitude test,** *which predicts an individual's ability to learn a skill or what the individual can accomplish with training,* and an **achievement test,** *which measures what has been learned or what skills have been mastered.* The distinction between these two types of tests is sometimes blurred, however. Both tests assess an individual's current status, both include similar types of questions, and both produce results that usually are highly correlated.

In each of your college classes, you take tests to measure your mastery of the class's content. These tests are achievement tests. If you major in psychology and decide to apply for graduate school, you might take the Graduate Record Exam Subject Test in Psychology. Your scores on this test would be used with other information (such as college grades and interviews) to predict whether you would be successful at graduate work in psychology. The Graduate Record Exam Subject Test in Psychology might contain questions similar to those from various psychology tests in undergraduate school, but this time the test items are being used to predict your performance in graduate school. Thus, the Graduate Record Exam Subject Test in Psychology falls into the category of aptitude test. The test's *purpose,* not its *content,* determines whether it is an aptitude or an achievement test.

The SAT has the ingredients of both an aptitude test and an achievement test. It is an achievement test in the sense that it measures what you have learned in terms of vocabulary, reading comprehension, algebraic skills, and so on; it is an aptitude test in the sense that it is used to predict your performance in college.

Does Intelligence Have a Single Nature?

Is it more appropriate to think of intelligence as an individual's general ability or as a number of specific abilities?

Spearman's Two-Factor Theory and Thurstone's Multiple-Factor Theory

Long before David Wechsler analyzed intelligence in terms of general and specific abilities (giving an individual an overall IQ but also providing information about specific subcomponents of intelligence), Charles Spearman (1927) proposed that intelligence has two factors. **Two-factor theory** *is Spearman's theory that individuals have both general intelligence, which he called g, and a number of specific intelligences, which he called s.* Spearman believed that these two factors accounted for an individual's performance on an intelligence test.

However, some factor approaches abandoned the idea of a general intelligence and searched for specific factors only. **Multiple-factor theory** *is L. L. Thurstone's (1938) theory that intelligence consists of seven primary mental abilities: verbal comprehension, number ability, word fluency, spatial visualization, associative memory, reasoning, and perceptual speed.*

Sternberg's Triarchic Theory

More recently, Robert J. Sternberg (1986, 1997) proposed **triarchic theory,** *a theory that intelligence has three main components: componential intelligence, experiential intelligence, and contextual intelligence.* Consider Ann, who scores high on traditional intelligence tests, such as the Stanford-Binet, and is a star analytical thinker. Consider Todd, who does not have the best test results but has an insightful and creative mind. Consider Art, a street-smart individual who has learned how to deal in practical ways with his world, although his scores on traditional intelligence tests are low.

Sternberg calls Ann's analytical thinking and abstract reasoning *componential intelligence;* it is the closest to what is called intelligence in this chapter and to what commonly is measured by intelligence tests. Sternberg calls Todd's insightful and creative thinking *experiential intelligence* and Art's street-smarts and practical know-how *contextual intelligence.*

In Sternberg's view of componential intelligence, the basic unit in intelligence is a *component,* simply defined as a basic unit of information processing. Sternberg believes that such components include those used to acquire or store information, to retain or retrieve information, to transfer information, to plan, to make decisions, to solve problems, and to carry out problem-solving strategies or translate our thoughts into performance.

The second part of Sternberg's model focuses on experience. According to Sternberg, intelligent individuals have the ability to solve new problems quickly, but they also learn how to solve familiar problems in an automatic, rote way so that their mind is free to handle other problems that require insight and creativity.

The third part of the model involves practical knowledge, such as how to get out of trouble, how to replace a fuse, and how to get along with people. Sternberg (1997) calls this *tacit knowledge*. It includes all of the important information about getting along in the real world that is not taught in school. He believes that tacit knowledge is more important for success in life than explicit, or "book," knowledge.

Gardner's Seven Frames of Mind

Another recent attempt to classify intelligence, the brainchild of developmental psychologist Howard Gardner (1983, 1989), includes seven components, or "frames of mind," as Gardner refers to them. Gardner's classification encompasses a wide diversity of intelligence. For example, consider a 13-year-old boy who springs into motion during a junior high basketball game in a small town. Grabbing a rebound, he quickly dribbles the ball the length of the court, all the while processing the whereabouts of his five opponents and four teammates. He throws the ball to an open teammate who scores on an easy lay-up. Years later the young boy had become a 6-foot-6-inch superstar for the Chicago Bulls—Michael Jordan. Is there intelligence to Jordan's movement and perception of the spatial layout of the basketball court?

Now we turn the clock back 200 years. Another 13-year-old boy is playing a piano at a concert hall in front of a large audience. The young adolescent is Ludwig von Beethoven, whose musical genius was evident at a young age. Did Beethoven have a specific type of intelligence, one we might call musical intelligence?

Jordan and Beethoven are two different types of individuals with different types of abilities. Gardner argues that Jordan's talent reflects his movement intelligence and his ability to analyze the world spatially, and that Beethoven's talent reflects his musical intelligence. Beyond these three forms of intelligence, Gardner argues

that we have four other main forms: verbal intelligence, mathematical intelligence, insightful skills for analyzing ourselves, and insightful skills for analyzing others.

Gardner believes that each of the seven intelligences can be destroyed by brain damage, that each involves unique cognitive skills, and that each shows up in exaggerated fashion both in the gifted and in *idiots savants*, which is French for individuals who are mentally retarded but who have unbelievable skill in a particular domain, such as drawing, music, or computing. For example, an individual may be mentally retarded but be able to respond instantaneously with the correct day of the week (for example, Tuesday or Saturday) when given any date in history (such as June 4, 1926, or December 15, 1746).

Critics of Gardner's approach point out that there are geniuses in many domains other than music. There are outstanding chess players, prizefighters, writers, politicians, physicians, lawyers, preachers, and poets, for example, yet we do not refer to chess intelligence, prizefighter intelligence, and so on. Another criticism of Gardner's theory is that Gardner has never provided evidence for the independence of the seven types of intelligence (Ceci, 1996).

Howard Gardner, here working with a young child, developed the view that intelligence comes in seven different forms: verbal, mathematical, ability to spatially analyze the world, movement skills, insightful skills for analyzing ourselves, insightful skills for analyzing others, and musical skills.

"You're wise, but you lack tree smarts."

Drawing by D. Reilly; © 1988 The New Yorker Magazine, Inc.

Some children and adolescents become extraordinarily gifted, reaching the status of "star." Becoming a "star" takes years of special tutelage with remarkable coaches; extensive support by parents; and day after day, week after week, month after month, and year after year of practice.

cert pianists and sculptors (arts), Olympic swimmers and tennis champions (psychomotor), and research mathematicians and research neurologists (cognitive). They said that the development of their exceptional accomplishments required special environmental support, excellent teaching, and motivational encouragement. Each experienced years of special attention under the tutelage and supervision of a remarkable series of teachers and coaches. All of these stars devoted exceptional amounts of time to practice and training, easily outdistancing the amount of time spent in all other activities combined. Nine-year-old Robert, a violin prodigy, had little time for television, sports, or other activities, for example. He practiced his talent several hours each day after school and spent weekends taking lessons and going to concerts. The stars also received extensive support and encouragement from their parents. Most stars had at least one parent who devoted a considerable part of each day to developing the child's talents. Raising a star requires levels of energy, commitment, sensitivity, and patience that go beyond what most parents

are willing to give. Of course, not all parents want to raise stars, but some who do put unbearable pressure on their children, expecting achievements that far exceed their talents. For every Chris Evert, there are thousands of girls with only mediocre tennis talent whose parents want them to become "another Chris Evert." Such unrealistic expectations always meet with failure and can produce considerable stress in children's lives, and all too often parents push children into activities that bore them rather than excite them (Feldman & Piirto, 1995). The importance of family processes in the development of the gifted was underscored by the finding that the personal adjustment of gifted individuals at midlife was strongly related to the harmony that existed in their family of origin as they were growing up (Tomlinson-Keasey & Little, 1990).

Against All Odds—Disadvantaged Gifted Children and Adolescents

Disadvantaged children and adolescents in the United States come from diverse cultural backgrounds and are often the victims of social discrimination. They live in environments that fail to challenge their creativity and do not provide them with the resources necessary to develop their creativity.

When gifted disadvantaged children and adolescents learn to adapt their behavior to the values and demands of school, they begin to accomplish required tasks successfully, their achievements start to attract teachers' attention, and more opportunities are made available to them. This "snowball" effect has important implications for the adolescent's personal and motivational development (Arroyo & Sternberg, 1993).

Parents in low-income families can help their adolescents develop the self-management skills required to function well in a school setting, but in many instances they do not. For gifted disadvantaged adolescents, teachers and other influential persons in school can compensate for the lack of appropriate direction these adolescents have received at home. Alternative socialization agents can expose gifted disadvantaged adolescents to wide-ranging experiences that influence their emerging view of themselves and their future.

Especially important in the case of gifted disadvantaged adolescents is the development of measures to identify who they are. Traditionally, giftedness has been assessed in one domain—intellectual exceptionality. However, to adequately identify gifted disadvantaged adolescents, it is necessary to widen the assessment procedure to include not only intellectual abilities but also behavior, motivation, and personality attributes. Researchers have found that high-achieving disadvantaged children and adolescents are self-confident, industrious, tough-minded, and individualistic (Comer, 1993). These same characteristics often appear in children and adolescents high in creativity who come from advantaged backgrounds.

Library Association,
ult Services Division
uron Street
L 60611
2433 x 4390

... zation works with public libraries to address
needs. They encourage libraries to hire
for paid employment and to have adolescents
...unteers to help young children.

...n of Science Technology Centers
...ve! Initiative
...mont Avenue NW, Suite 500
...n, DC 20005-3516
...7200

...ation works with science museums throughout
... States to involve adolescents from low-income
...es as exhibition designers and
...cturers.

...Special Olympics/Jeux Olympiques Spéciaux
...ir Avenue West, Suite 209
...Ontario M4V 1M2
...9050

...ympics is the main provider of sport, training, and
... for individuals with mental handicaps. The
...n uses sport to assist persons with a mental
... become all that they can be—physically,
...ocially, emotionally—and to become accepted,
... and productive members of society.

...rs with Canada/Rencontres du Canada
...pé Avenue, P.O. Box 7279
...Ontario K1L 8E3
...1290

...s with Canada gives young Canadians the
... to meet and learn about their country, their
... themselves. It is an education program, open to
... youth. Each week, 130 students come to Ottawa to
...cific theme: arts and culture, science and
..., law, or business and entrepreneurship. During
... students participate in hands-on workshops and
...n themes of their choice with other Canadians
...vinces and territories.

...Association for Gifted Children
...h Street NW, No. 1002
...n, DC 20005
...4268

...association of academicians, educators, and
... The organization's goal is to improve the
... of gifted children. They provide periodic reports
...cation of gifted children and publish the journal
...dren Quarterly.

National Center for Computer Equ
99 Hudson Street
New York, NY 10013
212-925-6635

This organization tries to improve the
in computer education, hoping to provi
access to computer learning. The cente
National Organization of Women (NO

National Center for Fair and Open
342 Broadway
Cambridge, MA 02139
617-864-4810

This center's goal is to reduce prejudice
by eliminating questions with a racial,
bias. It publishes a number of books, in
Standardized Testing Reform Sourcebook.

Odyssey: A Curriculum for Thinki
by M. J. Adams (Coordinator)
Watertown, MA: Mastery Educati

This exceptionally comprehensive pro
improve adolescent decision making in
circumstances. There are about a hund
the teacher's manual describes topics s
reasoning, problem solving, decision m
thinking. There is also a student guide

Teaching Decision Making to Ad
by Ruth Beyth-Marom, Barush Fi
Jacobs, and Lita Furby
The Carnegie Council on Adolesc
2400 N Street NW
Washington, DC 20037
202-429-7979

This working paper provides an overv
programs to teach decision-making sk
authors critically analyze problems wit
and give recommendations for improv
curriculum.

Ꮪ UMMA

Information processing and intelligence are two important dimensions
of adolescent cognition. In the course
of every day of their lives, adolescents
perceive, attend, remember, think,
solve problems, and draw conclusions.

We began this chapter by
discussing information processing,
including ideas about the information-
processing perspective, developmental changes in information processing,
attention and memory, cognitive
monitoring, decision making, critical

thinking, and computers and
cents. Our coverage of inte
focused on what intelligence
whether intelligence has a si
ture, and controversies and
intelligence. We also com
number of perspectives on ad
cognition—Piaget's theory,
sky's theory, learning theor
learning theory, informati
cessing, and psychometric
number of issues. Our discu
the extremes of intelligence

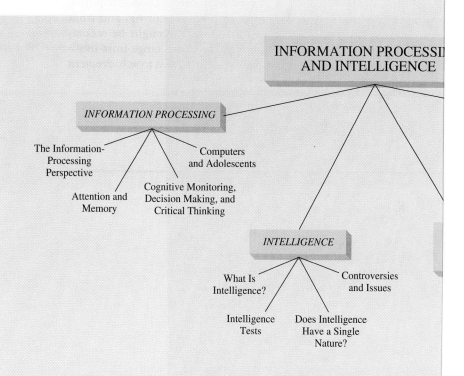

**INFORMATION PROCESSI
AND INTELLIGENCE**

INFORMATION PROCESSING

The Information-
Processing
Perspective

Computers
and Adolescents

Attention and
Memory

Cognitive Monitoring,
Decision Making, and
Critical Thinking

INTELLIGENCE

What Is
Intelligence?

Controversies
and Issues

Intelligence
Tests

Does Intelligence
Have a Single
Nature?

The behaviors of gifted disadvantaged youth are often motivated by the
youth's desire to transform their social and
economic conditions. Because this goal
requires long-range planning and self-
management, giftedness among disadvantaged adolescents needs to be assessed
over time.

Creativity

Most of us would like to be both gifted and
creative. Why was Thomas Edison able
to invent so many things? Was he simply
more intelligent than most people? Did he
spend long hours toiling away in private?
Surprisingly, when Edison was a young boy,
his teacher told him he was too dumb to
learn anything. Other famous people whose
creative genius went unnoticed when they
were young include Walt Disney, who was
fired from a newspaper job because he
did not have any good ideas; Enrico Caruso,
whose music teacher told him that his voice
was terrible; and Winston Churchill, who
failed 1 year of secondary school.

Disney, Edison, Caruso, and
Churchill were intelligent and creative
men; however, experts on creativity believe that intelligence is not the same as
creativity. One common distinction is between **convergent thinking,** *which pro-
duces one correct answer and is characteristic of the kind of
thinking on standardized intelligence tests,* and **divergent
thinking,** *which produces many answers to the same question and is more characteristic of creativity* (Guilford, 1967).
For example, the following is a typical problem on an
intelligence test that requires convergent thinking: "How
many quarters will you get in return for 60 dimes?" The
following question, though, has many possible answers:
"What image comes to mind when you hear the phrase
'sitting alone in a dark room'?" (Barron, 1989). Such responses as "the sound of a violin with no strings" and "patience" are considered creative answers. Conversely,
common answers, such as "a person in a crowd" or "insomnia" are not very creative.

> *The artist finds greater pleasure in painting than in
having completed the picture.*
>
> —Seneca

Creativity *is the ability to think about something in
novel and unusual ways and to come up with unique solutions
to problems.* When creative people, such as artists and

Creative individuals say they have the time and independence in an enjoyable
setting to entertain a wide range of solutions to a particular problem.

scientists, are asked what enables them to solve problems
in novel ways, they say that the ability to find affinities
between seemingly unrelated elements plays a key role.
They also say they have the time and independence in
an enjoyable setting to entertain a wide range of possible solutions to a problem. How strongly is creativity related to intelligence? Although most creative people are
quite intelligent, the reverse is not necessarily true. Many
highly intelligent people (as measured by IQ tests) are
not very creative.

Some experts remain skeptical that we will ever fully
understand the creative process (Baer, 1993). Others
believe that a psychology of creativity is within reach
(Sternberg & Lubat, 1995). Most experts agree, however,
that the concept of creativity as spontaneously bubbling
up from a magical well is a myth. Momentary flashes of
insight, accompanied by images, make up only a small
part of the creative process. At the heart of the creative
process are ability and experience that shape an individual's intentional and sustained effort, often over the
course of a lifetime (Curran, 1997).

At this point, we have discussed a number of ideas
about intelligence and its extremes. A summary of these
ideas is presented in concept table 5.2.

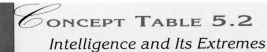

CONCEPT TABLE 5.2

Intelligence and Its Extremes

Concept	Processes/ Related Ideas	Chara...
What Is intelligence?	Its nature	The concept of intelli... indirectly. Intellige... the ability to learn... life. In the study o... individual differenc... intelligence.
Intelligence Tests	The Binet and Wechsler tests	Binet developed the f... He developed the ... the concept of IQ.... number of times. T... tests. The test app... Stanford-Binet, th... intelligence tests.... These tests provid... information about
	Group tests	Group tests are conv... examiner to monit... subject. The SAT ... information to pre...
	Aptitude tests and achievement tests	Aptitude tests predict... individual's future ... individual already ... sometimes blurred
Does Intelligence Have a Single Nature?	Four theories	Psychologists debate... number of specific ... Thurstone's multip... and Gardner's sev... describe the basic ... thinking suggests ... and specific factor
Controversies and Issues in Intelligence	Their nature	Three contemporary ... intelligence is due ... ethnic differences ... use and misuse of
Comparisons of Perspectives on Adolescent Cognition	Nature of differences	We compared six app... the following issue... differences, cogni... child. The approac... learning, cognitive ... psychometrics.
The Extremes of Intelligence and Creativity	Mental retardation	A mentally retarded in... traditional IQ test,... four classifications... moderate retardat... retardation. The tw... cultural-familial.
	Giftedness	A gifted individual has... higher) and superi... how to help gifted ... potential.
	Creativity	Creativity is the abilit... way and to come ...

KEY TERMS

PRACTICAL KNOWLEDGE ABOUT ADOLESCENCE

Frames of Mind
(1983) by Howard Gardner.
New York: Basic Books.

Gardner presents his view of the seven frames of mind, or seven different types of intelligence he believes human beings possess: verbal intelligence, math

intelligence, mover... spatial intelligence ... gence, insightful sk... ourselves, and insig... alyzing others. Gard... ditional views of in... narrow and that tr... gence tests can't tap

Testing & Your Child
(1992) by Virginia E. McCullough.
New York: Plume.

Written for parents, this book describes 150 of the most common educational, psychological, and medical tests. This comprehensive guide ex-

plains who adminis... the tests test for, ... reveal, what prepa... what influences s... follow-up testing ... mended. The tests ... ligence to giftene... to personality.

EXPLORING ADOLESCENT DEVELOPMENT

To further explore adolescent development, we will examine a research study on devel... changes in the speed of information processing and evaluate the nature of adolescent d... making, risk taking, and health.

RESEARCH ON ADOLESCENT DEVELOPMENT

Developmental Changes in the Speed of Processing Information

Featured Study

Hale, S. (1990). A global developmental trend in cognitive processing speed. *Child Development, 61,* 653–663.

One emphasis in the information-processing perspective is that the speed of processing is an important dimension of cognition. Do individuals of different ages process information at the same speed? For example, do young adults process information faster than children do?

Method

Sixteen subjects from each of four age groups (ages 10, 12, 15, and 19) were assessed. All subjects were given subtests (vocabulary, block design) from either the WISC-R (the children/adolescents) or the WAIS-R (the 19-year-olds). There were no significant differences between the four age groups on the subtests. All information-processing stimuli were

presented on a video monitor. The general procedure consisted of presentation of an asterisk in the center of the screen as a fixation point. Subjects were told that when they were ready, they should push the READY button. Upon solving the problem presented on the screen, subjects indicated their selection by pressing one of two other buttons—one to the right, one to the left. If they made an error, they received a 2-second error message on the screen. If their response was correct, an asterisk appeared until the subject began the next trial. A few practice trials preceded each task to ensure that the subjects understood the instructions.

The four tasks consisted of a reaction time task, a letter-matching task, mental rotation task, and an abstract matching task. We will describe the procedure for the first two tasks. On the reaction time task, subjects were instructed to press the left response button if the stimulus was a left arrow (←) and the right response button if it was a right arrow (→). Following four practice trials, subjects

were exposed to 40 experi... als (20 left and 20 right a... the letter-matching task,... were displayed in either ... or lowercase (A, a, D, d,... H, h), presented two at a... jects were told that if th... the same letter, they sh... the right response button;... not the same, they shoul... left button. This procedu... lowed for 80 trials.

Results and Discu...

The 10-year-olds were app... 1.8 times slower than the y... (the 19-year-olds) on all ... 12-year-olds were approxi... times slower than the youn... all tasks, but the 15-... processed information across... young adults. Based on th... appears that early adoles... important time frame for ... ment in the speed of proc... formation across a variet... Exactly why this improvem... in early adolescence ha... been adequately explained

ADOLESCENT HEALTH AND WELL-BEING

Adolescent Decision Making, Risk Taking, and Health

The recent findings that the decision-making skills of adolescents do not differ appreciably from those of adults has important implications for reducing risk taking in adolescence and promoting health (Quadrel, Fischoff,

& Davis, 1993). Unsubstantiated claims about the incompetence of adolescent decision making, especially in older adolescents, can lead to paternalism, in which adults protect adolescents (for instance, by banning "unhealthy" products or publications) from the consequences of their fallible judgments. This widespread attitude threatens to disenfranchise and

stigmatize adolescents. In ... nalistic view, adolescents ... denied the right to govern... tions. Adolescents are view... lems rather than resources.... placed in the flattering pos... ways knowing what is righ...

Perhaps faulty decisio... should not always be blame... lescent problems; the pro...

What is the nature of adolescents' risk-taking?

rest, instead, in society's orientation toward adolescents and its failure to provide adolescents with adequate choices (Keating, 1990; Lightfoot, 1997). For example, a mathematically precocious ninth-grade girl might abandon mathematics, not because of poor decision-making skills but because of a stronger motivation to maintain positive peer relations that would be threatened if she stayed on the math track. The decision of an adolescent in a low-income inner-city area to engage in drug trafficking, even at considerable risk, might not be a consequence of the adolescent's failure to consider all of the relevant information, but might be the outcome of quite sophisticated thinking about risk-benefit ratios in oppressed circumstances that offer limited or nonexistent options. As cognitive developmentalist Daniel Keating (1990) observed, if we dislike adolescents' choices, perhaps we need to provide them with better options from which to choose.

A number of experts on adolescence believe that increased risk taking is due not to maturational factors such as egocentrism but rather to contextual factors such as poverty, poor family and community support of adolescents, and inadequate education (Dryfoos, 1995; Jessor, 1993). Further discussion of these contextual influences on adolescent health and well-being appears in a number of later chapters.

The Contexts of Adolescent Development

M an is a knot, a web, a mesh into which relationships are tied.

—Saint-Exupéry

Adolescent development takes place in social contexts, which provide the setting and socio-historical, cultural backdrop for physical, cognitive, and socio-emotional growth. This third section consists of four chapters: Chapter 6, "Families"; Chapter 7, "Peers"; Chapter 8, "Schools"; and Chapter 9, "Culture."

Chapter

6

Families

It is not enough for parents to understand children. They must accord children the privilege of understanding them.

—Milton Saperstein, *Paradoxes of Everyday Life,* 1955

Chapter Outline

Chapter Boxes

When I was a boy of 14, my father was so ignorant I could hardly stand to have the man around. But when I got to be 21, I was astonished at how much he had learnt in 7 years.

—Mark Twain

PREVIEW

An important contemporary theme of family processes in adolescence is that both autonomy (independence) and attachment (connectedness) to parents are involved in the adolescent's successful adaptation to the world. Historically, the major themes of parent-adolescent relationships were independence and conflict. Today, developmentalists are working to correct past overdramatization of independence, detachment from parents, and high conflict during adolescence. These are being replaced with a balanced emphasis on independence, connectedness, and moderate, rather than severe, conflict in the majority of families. Our extensive tour of family processes in adolescence takes us through the basic nature of family processes, parenting techniques, and parent-adolescent conflict, autonomy and attachment, sibling relationships, the changing family in a changing society, and social policy and families.

IMAGES OF ADOLESCENCE

Variations in Adolescents' Perceptions of Parents

My mother and I depend on each other. However, if something separated us, I think I could still get along O.K. I know that my mother continues to have an important influence on me. Sometimes she gets on my nerves, but I still basically like her, and respect her, a lot. We have our arguments, and I don't always get my way, but she is willing to listen to me.

Amy, age 16

You go from a point at which your parents are responsible for you to a point at which you want a lot more independence. Finally, you are more independent, and you feel like you have to be more responsible for yourself; otherwise you are not going to do very well in this world. It's important for parents to still be there to support you, but at some point, you've got to look in the mirror and say, "I can do it myself."

John, age 18

I don't get along very well with my parents. They try to dictate how I dress, who I date, how much I study, what I do on weekends, and how much time I spend talking on the phone. They are big intruders in my life. Why won't they let me make my own decisions? I'm mature enough to handle these things. When they jump down my throat at every little thing I do, it makes me mad and I say things to them I probably shouldn't. They just don't understand me very well.

Ed, age 17

My father never seems to have any time to spend with me. He is gone a lot on business, and when he comes home, he is either too tired to do anything or plops down and watches TV and doesn't want to be bothered. He thinks I don't work hard enough and don't have values that were as solid as his generation. It is a very distant relationship. I actually spend more time talking to my mom than to him. I guess I should work a little harder in school than I do, but I still don't think he has the right to say such negative things to me. I like my mom a lot better because I think she is a much nicer person.

Tom, age 15

We have our arguments and our differences, and there are moments when I get very angry with my parents, but most of the time they are like heated discussions. I have to say what I think because I don't think they are always right. Most of the time when there is an argument, we can discuss the problem and eventually find a course that we all can live with. Not every time, though, because there are some occasions when things just remain unresolved. Even when we have an unresolved conflict, I still would have to say that I get along pretty good with my parents.

Ann, age 16

The comments of these five adolescents offer a brief glimpse of the diversity that characterizes adolescents' relationships with their parents. Although parent-adolescent relationships vary considerably, researchers are finding that, for the most part, the relationships are both (1) extremely important aspects of adolescent development and (2) more positive than once was believed.

THE NATURE OF FAMILY PROCESSES

Among the important considerations in studying adolescents and their families are reciprocal socialization, synchrony, and the family system; how adolescents construct relationships and how such relationships influence the development of social maturity; sociocultural and historical influences on the family; and the nature of the family life cycle.

Reciprocal Socialization, Synchrony, and the Family as a System

For many years, the socialization of adolescents was viewed as a straightforward, one-way matter of indoctrination. The basic philosophy was that children and adolescents had to be trained to fit into the social world, so their behavior had to be shaped accordingly. However, socialization is much more than molding the child and adolescent into a mature adult. The child and adolescent are not like inanimate blobs of clay that the sculptor forms into a polished statue. **Reciprocal socialization** *is the process by which children and adolescents socialize parents just as parents socialize them.* To get a better feel for how reciprocal socialization works, consider two situations: the first emphasizing the impact of growing up in a single-parent home (parental influences), the second a talented teenage ice skater (adolescent influences). In the first situation, the speaker is 14-year-old Robert:

> I never have seen my father. He never married my mother, and she had to quit school to help support us. Maybe my mother and I are better off that he didn't marry her because he apparently didn't love her . . . but sometimes I get very depressed about not having a father, especially when I see a lot of my friends with their fathers at ball games and such. My father still lives around here, but he has married, and I guess he wants to forget about me and my mother. . . . A lot of times I wish my mother would get married and I could at least have a stepfather to talk with about things and do things with me.

In the second situation, the first speaker is 13-year-old Kathy:

> "Mother, my skating coach says that I have a lot of talent, but it is going to take a lot of lessons and travel to fully develop it." Her mother responds, "Kathy, I just don't know. We will have to talk with your father about it tonight when he gets home from work." That evening, Kathy's father tells his wife, "Look, to do that for Kathy, I will have to get a second job, or you will have to get a job. There is no way we can afford what she wants with what I make."

As developmentalists probe the nature of reciprocal socialization, they are impressed with the importance of synchrony in parent-child and parent-adolescent relationships. **Synchrony** *refers to the carefully coordinated interaction between the parent and the child or adolescent, in which, often unknowingly, they are attuned to each other's behavior.* The turn taking that occurs in parent-adolescent negotiation reflects the reciprocal, synchronous nature of parent-adolescent relationships. The interactions of parents and adolescents in synchronous relationships can be conceptualized as a dance or a dialogue in which successive actions of the partners are closely coordinated. This coordinated dance or dialogue can assume the form of mutual synchrony (each individual's behavior depends on the partner's previous behavior), or it can be reciprocal in a more precise sense: The actions of the partners can be matched, as when one partner imitates the other or there is mutual smiling.

Reciprocal socialization takes place within the social system of a family, which consists of a constellation of subsystems defined by generation, gender, and role. Divisions of labor among family members define particular subsystems, and attachments define others. Each family member is a participant in several subsystems—some dyadic (involving two people), some polyadic (involving more than two people) (Kramer & Lin, 1997; Piotrowski, 1997). The father and adolescent represent one dyadic subsystem, the mother and father another. The mother-father-adolescent represent one polyadic subsystem.

Figure 6.1 shows an organizational scheme that highlights the reciprocal influences of family members and family subsystems (Belsky, 1981). As can be seen by following the arrows in the figure, marital relations, parenting, and adolescent behavior can have both direct and indirect effects on each other. An example of a direct effect is the influence of the parent's behavior on the adolescent. An example of an indirect effect is how the relationship between the spouses mediates the way a parent acts toward the adolescent (Emery & Tuer, 1993). For example, marital conflict might reduce the efficiency of parenting, in which case marital conflict would have an indirect effect on the adolescent's behavior (Wilson & Gottman, 1995).

Interaction between individuals in a family can change, depending on who is present. In one investigation, 44 adolescents were observed either separately with their mother and father (dyadic settings) or in the presence of both parents (triadic setting) (Gjerde, 1986). The presence of the father improved mother-son relationships, but the presence of the mother decreased the quality of father-son relations. This may have occurred because the father takes the strain off the mother by controlling the adolescent or because the mother's presence reduces father-son interaction, which may not be high in many instances. Indeed, in one recent investigation, sons directed more negative behavior toward their mothers than

Figure~6.1

Interaction Between Adolescents and Their Parents: Direct and Indirect Effects.

terminology and also is not always confined to the first 5 years of life, as has been the case in classical psychoanalytic theory. Today's **developmental construction views** *share the belief that as individuals grow up, they acquire modes of relating to others. There are two main variations within this view, one of which emphasizes continuity and stability in relationships throughout the life span and one of which emphasizes discontinuity and change in relationships throughout the life span.*

The Continuity View

In the **continuity view,** *emphasis is on the role that early parent-child relationships play in constructing a basic way of relating to people throughout the life span.* These early parent-child relationships are carried forward to later points in development to influence all subsequent relationships (with peers, with friends, with teachers, and with romantic partners, for example) (Ainsworth, 1979; Bowlby, 1989; Sroufe, 1995; Waters, 1997). In its extreme form, this view states that the basic components of social relationships are laid down and shaped by the security or insecurity of parent-infant attachment relationships in the first year or two of the infant's life. More about the importance of secure attachment in the adolescent's development appears later in the chapter when we discuss autonomy and attachment.

Close relationships with parents also are important in the adolescent's development because these relationships function as models or templates that are carried forward over time to influence the construction of new relationships. Clearly, close relationships do not repeat themselves in an endless fashion over the course of the child's and adolescent's development. And the quality of any relationship depends to some degree on the specific individual with whom the relationship is formed. However, the nature of earlier relationships that are developed over many years often can be detected in later relationships, both with those same individuals and in the formation of relationships with others at a later point in time (Gjerde, Block, & Block, 1991). Thus, the nature of parent-adolescent relationships does not depend only on what happens in the relationship during adolescence.

toward their fathers in dyadic situations (Buhrmester & others, in press). However, in a triadic context of adolescent-mother-father, fathers helped "rescue" mothers by attempting to control the sons' negative behavior.

The Developmental Construction of Relationships

Developmentalists have shown an increased interest in understanding how we construct relationships as we grow up. Psychoanalytic theorists have always been interested in how this process works in families. However, the current explanations of how relationships are constructed is virtually stripped of Freud's psychosexual stage

Relationships with parents over the long course of childhood are carried forward to influence, at least to some degree, the nature of parent-adolescent relationships. And the long course of parent-child relationships also could be expected to influence, again at least to some degree, the fabric of the adolescent's peer relationships, friendships, and dating relationships.

How childhood experiences with parents are carried forward and influence the nature of the adolescent's development is important, but the nature of intergenerational relationships is significant as well. As the life-span perspective has taken on greater acceptance among developmental psychologists, researchers have become interested in the transmission of close relationships across generations (Elder, 1997; Kandel & Wu, 1995).

The middle generation in three generations is especially important in the socialization process. For example, the parents of adolescents can be studied in terms of their relationships with their own parents, when they were children and presently, and in terms of their relationships with their own adolescents, both when the adolescents were children and presently. Life-span theorists point out that the middle-aged parents of adolescents may have to give more help than they receive. Their adolescents probably are reaching the point where they need considerable financial support for education, and their parents, whose generation is living longer than past generations, may also require financial support, as well as more comfort and affection than earlier in the life cycle.

The Discontinuity View

In the **discontinuity view**, *emphasis is on change and growth in relationships over time.* As people grow up, they develop many different types of relationships (with parents, with peers, with teachers, and with romantic partners, for example). Each of these relationships is structurally different. With each new type of relationship, individuals encounter new modes of relating (Buhrmester & Furman, 1987; Furman & Wehner, 1993; Piaget, 1932; Sullivan, 1953; Youniss, 1980). For example, Piaget (1932) argued that parent-child relationships are strikingly different from children's peer relationships. Parent-child relationships, he said, are more likely to consist of parents having unilateral authority over children. By contrast, peer relationships are more likely to consist of participants who relate to each other on a much more equal basis. In parent-child relationships, since parents have greater knowledge and authority, their children often must learn how to conform to rules and regulations laid down by parents. In this view, we use the parental-child mode when relating to authority figures (such as with teachers and experts) and when we act as authority figures (when we become parents, teachers, and experts).

By contrast, relationships with peers have a different structure and require a different mode of relating to others. This more egalitarian mode is later called upon in relationships with romantic partners, friends, and coworkers. Because two peers possess relatively equal knowledge and authority (their relationship is reciprocal and symmetrical), children learn a democratic mode of relating that is based on mutual influence. With peers, children learn to formulate and assert their own opinions, appreciate the perspective of peers, cooperatively negotiate solutions to disagreements, and evolve standards for conduct that are mutually acceptable. Because peer relationships are voluntary (rather than obligatory, as in the family), children and adolescents who fail to become skillful in the symmetrical, mutual, egalitarian, reciprocal mode of relating have difficulty being accepted by peers.

Although the discontinuity view does not deny that prior close relationships (such as with parents) are carried forward to influence later relationships, it does stress that each new type of relationship that children and adolescents encounter (such as with peers, with friends, and with romantic partners) requires the construction of different and even more sophisticated modes of relating to others. Further, in the change/growth version, each period of development uniquely contributes to the construction of relationship knowledge; development across the life span is not solely determined by a sensitive or critical period during infancy.

Maturation of the Adolescent and Maturation of Parents

In the quotation presented at the opening of this chapter, Mark Twain remarked that, when he was 14, his father was so ignorant he could hardly stand to be around him, but when Mark got to be 21, he was astonished at how much his father had learned in those 7 years! Mark Twain's comments suggest that maturation is an important theme of parent-adolescent relationships. Adolescents change as they make the transition from childhood to adulthood, but their parents also undergo change during their adult years (Holmbeck, Paikoff, & Brooks-Gunn, 1995).

Adolescent Changes

Among the changes in the adolescent that can influence parent-adolescent relationships are puberty, expanded logical reasoning, increased idealistic thought, violated expectations, changes in schooling, peers, friendships, dating, and movement toward independence. Several investigations have shown that conflict between parents and adolescents, especially between mothers and sons, is the most stressful during the apex of pubertal growth (Hill & others, 1985; Steinberg, 1988). For example, as shown in figure 6.2, mothers were less satisfied with their sons'

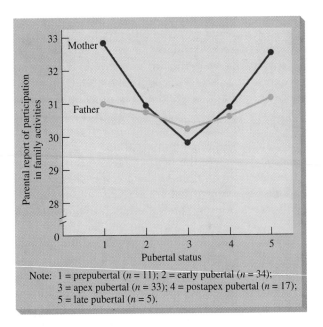

Figure~6.2

Parents' Perception of Their Son's Participation in Family Activities at Five Points in Puberty.

Note: 1 = prepubertal (n = 11); 2 = early pubertal (n = 34); 3 = apex pubertal (n = 33); 4 = postapex pubertal (n = 17); 5 = late pubertal (n = 5).

participation in family activities during the apex of pubertal change (Hill & others, 1985). Observations revealed that the father retains his influence over family decision making throughout the pubertal transition and asserts his authority by requiring the son to be obedient. During pubertal change, mothers and sons interrupt each other more and explain themselves less. Toward the end of pubertal change, sons have grown larger and more powerful. At this time, they are less likely to engage in conflict with their mothers, probably because their mothers defer to them. More about sex differences and similarities in family relations appears later in the chapter. In sum, the adolescent's pubertal status is related to the nature of parent-adolescent relationships.

In terms of cognitive changes, the adolescent can now reason in more logical ways with parents than in childhood. During childhood, parents may be able to get by with saying, "O.K. That is it. We do it my way or else," and the child conforms. But with increased cognitive skills, adolescents no longer are likely to accept such a statement as a reason for conforming to parental dictates. Adolescents want to know, often in fine detail, why they are being disciplined. Even when parents give what seem to be logical reasons for discipline, adolescents' cognitive sophistication may call attention to deficiencies in the reasoning. Such prolonged bouts of discourse with parents are usually uncharacteristic of parent-child relationships but are frequent occurrences in parent-adolescent relationships.

In addition, the adolescent's increasing idealistic thought comes into play in parent-adolescent relationships. Parents are now evaluated vis-á-vis what an ideal parent is like. The very real interactions with parents,

which inevitably involve some negative interchanges and flaws, are placed next to the adolescent's schema of an ideal parent. And, as part of their egocentrism, adolescents' concerns with how others view them are likely to produce overreactions to parents' comments. A mother may comment to her adolescent daughter that she needs a new blouse. The daughter might respond, "What's the matter? You don't think I have good taste? You think I look gross, don't you? Well, you are the one who is gross!" The same comment made to the daughter several years earlier in late childhood probably would have elicited a less intense response.

Another dimension of the adolescent's changing cognitive world related to parent-adolescent relations is the expectations parents and adolescents have for each other (Collins, 1993). The rapid changes of puberty make it difficult to use the individual's past behavior to predict future behavior. For example, preadolescent children are often compliant and easy to manage. As they enter puberty, children begin to question or seek rationales for parental demands (Maccoby, 1984). Parents may perceive this behavior as resistant and oppositional because it departs from the child's usual compliant behavior. Parents often respond to the lack of compliance with increased pressure for compliance. In this situation, expectations that were stabilized during a period of relatively slow developmental change are lagging behind the behavior of the adolescent during the period of rapid pubertal change.

What dimensions of the adolescent's social world contribute to parent-adolescent relationships? Adolescence brings with it new definitions of socially appropriate behavior. In our society, these definitions are associated with changes in schooling arrangements—transitions to middle or junior high school. Adolescents are required to function in a more anonymous, larger environment with multiple and varying teachers. More work is required, and more initiative and responsibility must be shown to adapt successfully. The school is not the only social arena that contributes to parent-adolescent relationships. Adolescents spend more time with peers than when they were children, and they develop more sophisticated friendships than in childhood. Adolescents also begin to push more strongly for independence. In sum, parents are called on to adapt to the changing world of the adolescent's schooling, peer relations, and push for autonomy (Grotevant, 1997).

Parental Changes

Parental changes that contribute to parent-adolescent relationships involve marital satisfaction, economic burdens, career reevaluation and time perspective, and health and body concerns (MacDermid & Crouter, 1995; Silverberg & Steinberg, 1990). Marital dissatisfaction is greater when the offspring is an adolescent than when the offspring is a child or an adult. In addition, parents feel a greater economic burden during the rearing of adolescents. Also during this time, parents may reevaluate their occupational achievement, deciding whether they have met their youthful aspirations of success. They may look to the future and think about how much time they have remaining to accomplish what they want. Adolescents, however, look to the future with unbounded optimism, sensing that they have an unlimited amount of time to accomplish what they desire. Health concerns and an interest in body integrity and sexual attractiveness become prominent themes of adolescents' parents. Even when their body and sexual attractiveness are not deteriorating, many parents of adolescents perceive that they are. By contrast, adolescents have reached or are beginning to reach the peak of their physical attractiveness, strength, and health. Although both adolescents and their parents show a heightened preoccupation with their bodies, adolescents' outcome probably is more positive.

In one recent study of middle-aged parents and their adolescents, the relation between parents' midlife concerns and their adolescents' pubertal development could not be characterized simply as positive, negative, or nil (MacDermid & Crouter, 1995). Parents reported less intense midlife concerns when their adolescents were further along in puberty. Spousal support in midlife emerged as an important factor in helping parents meet the challenges of pubertal changes in their adolescents.

The changes in adolescents' parents just described characterize development in middle adulthood. Most adolescents' parents either are in middle adulthood or are rapidly approaching middle adulthood. However, in the last two decades, the timing of parenthood has undergone some dramatic shifts (Parke & Buriel, 1997). Parenthood is taking place earlier for some, later for others, than in previous decades. First, the number of adolescent pregnancies substantially increased during the 1980s. Second, the number of women who postpone childbearing until their thirties and early forties simultaneously increased. The topic of adolescents as parents is discussed in chapter 12. Here we focus on sociohistorical changes related to postponement of childbearing until the thirties or forties.

There are many contrasts between becoming a parent in adolescence and becoming a parent 15 to 30 years later. Delayed childbearing allows for considerable progress in occupational and educational domains. For both males and females, education usually has been completed, and career development is well established.

The marital relationship varies with the timing of parenthood onset. In one investigation, couples who began childbearing in their early twenties were compared with those who began in their early thirties (Walter, 1986). The late-starting couples had more egalitarian relationships, with men participating in child care and household tasks more often.

Is parent-child interaction different for families in which parents delay having children until their thirties or forties? Investigators have found that older fathers are warmer, communicate better, encourage more achievement, and show less rejection with their children than younger fathers. However, older fathers also are less likely to place demands on children, to enforce rules, and to engage in physical play or sports with their children (MacDonald, 1987). These findings suggest that sociohistorical changes are resulting in different developmental trajectories for many families, trajectories that involve changes in the way marital partners and parents and adolescents interact.

Sociocultural and Historical Changes

Family development does not occur in a social vacuum. Important sociocultural and historical influences affect family processes (Goldscheider, 1997). Family changes may be due to great upheavals in a nation, such as war, famine, or mass immigration (Landale, 1997; Waters, 1997). Or they may be due more to subtle transitions in ways of life. The Great Depression in the early 1930s had some negative effects on families. During its height, the depression produced economic deprivation, adult discontent, depression about living conditions, marital conflict, inconsistent child rearing, and unhealthy lifestyles—heavy drinking, demoralized attitudes, and health disabilities—especially in the father (Elder, 1997). Subtle changes in a culture that have significant influences on the family were described by the famous anthropologist Margaret Mead (1978). The changes focus on the longevity of the elderly and the role of the elderly in the family, the urban and suburban orientation of families and their mobility, television, and a general dissatisfaction and restlessness.

Fifty years ago, the older people who survived were usually hearty and still closely linked to the family, often helping to maintain the family's existence. Today, older people live longer, which means that their middle-aged children are often pressed into a caretaking role for their parents or the elderly parents may be placed in a nursing home. Elderly parents may have lost some of their socializing role in the family during the twentieth century as many of their children moved great distances away.

Many of these family moves are away from farms and small towns to urban and suburban settings. In the small towns and farms, individuals were surrounded by lifelong neighbors, relatives, and friends. Today, neighborhood and extended-family support systems are not nearly as prevalent. Families now move all over the country, often uprooting adolescents from school and peer groups they have known for a considerable length of time. And for many families, this type of move occurs every year or two, as one or both parents are transferred from job to job.

Television also plays a major role in the changing family. Many children who watch television find that parents are too busy working to share this experience with them. Children increasingly experience a world their parents are not a part of. Instead of participating in neighborhood peer groups, children come home after school and plop down in front of the television set. And television allows children and their families to see new ways of life. Lower-class families can look into the family lives of the middle class by simply pushing a button.

Another subtle change in families has been an increase in general dissatisfaction and restlessness. Women have become increasingly dissatisfied with their way of life, which has placed great strain on marriages. With fewer elders and long-term friends close by to help and advise young people during the initial difficult years of marriage and childbearing, marriages begin to fracture at the first signs of disagreement. Divorce has become epidemic in our culture. As women move into the labor market, men simultaneously become restless and look for stimulation outside of family life. The result of such restlessness and the tendency to divorce and remarry has been a hodgepodge of family structures, with far greater numbers of single-parent and step-parent families than ever before in history. Later in the chapter, we discuss such aspects of the changing social world of the adolescent and the family in greater detail.

The Family Life Cycle

As we go through life, we are at different points in the family life cycle. The stages of the family cycle include leaving home and becoming a single adult, the joining of couples through marriage—the new couple, becoming parents and families with children, families with adolescents, families at midlife, and the family in later life. A summary of these stages in the family life cycle is shown in figure 6.3, along with key aspects of emotional processes involved in the transition from one stage to the next, and changes in family status required for developmental change to take place (Carter & McGoldrick, 1989).

Leaving Home and Becoming a Single Adult

Leaving home and becoming a single adult *is the first stage in the family life cycle and involves launching.* **Launching** *is the process in which the youth moves into adulthood and exits his or her family of origin.* Adequate completion of launching requires that the young adult separate from the family of origin without cutting off ties completely or fleeing in a reactive way to find some form of substitute emotional refuge. The launching period is a time for the youth and young adult to formulate personal life goals, to develop an identity, and to become more independent before joining with another person to form a new family. This is a time for young people to sort out emotionally what they will take along from the family of origin, what they will leave behind, and what they will create themselves.

Complete cutoffs from parents rarely or never resolve emotional problems. The shift to adult-to-adult status between parents and children requires a mutually respectful and personal form of relating, in which young adults can appreciate parents as they are, needing neither to make them into what they are not nor to blame them for what they could not be. Neither do young adults need to comply with parental expectations and wishes at their own expense.

The Joining of Families Through Marriage: The New Couple

The **new couple** *is the second stage in the family life cycle, in which two individuals from separate families of origin unite to form a new family system.* This stage involves not only the development of a new marital system, but also a realignment with extended families and friends to include the spouse. Women's changing roles, the increasingly frequent marriage of partners from divergent cultural backgrounds, and the increasing physical distances between family members are placing a much stronger burden on couples to define their relationship for themselves than was true in the past. Marriage is usually described as the union of two individuals, but in reality it is the union of two entire family systems and the development of a new, third system. Some experts on marriage and the family believe that marriage represents such a different phenomenon for women and men that we need to speak of "her" marriage and "his" marriage. In American society, women have anticipated marriage with greater enthusiasm and more positive expectations than men have, although statistically it has not been a very healthy system for them.

Becoming Parents and Families with Children

Becoming parents and families with children *is the third stage in the family life cycle. Entering this stage requires that adults now move up a generation and become caregivers to the younger generation.* Moving through this lengthy stage successfully requires a commitment of time as a parent, understanding the roles of parents, and adapting to developmental changes in children (Santrock, 1998). Problems that emerge when a couple first assumes the parental role are struggles with each other about taking responsibility, as well as refusal or inability to function as competent parents to children.

When people become parents through pregnancy, adoption, or stepparenting, they face disequilibrium and must adapt. Parents want to develop a strong attachment to their infant, but they still want to maintain strong attachments to their spouse and friends, and possibly continue their careers. Parents ask themselves how this new being will change their lives. A baby places new restrictions on partners; no longer will they be able to rush out to a movie on a moment's notice, and money will not be readily available for vacations and other luxuries. Dual-career parents ask, "Will it harm the baby to place her in day care? Will we be able to find responsible baby-sitters?"

Family Life-Cycle Stage	Emotional Process of Transition: Key Principles	Changes in Family Status Required to Proceed Developmentally
1. Leaving home: Single young adults	Accepting emotional and financial responsibility for self	a. Differentiation of self in relation to family of origin b. Development of intimate peer relationships c. Establishment of self in relation to work and financial independence
2. The joining of families through marriage: The new couple	Commitment to new system	a. Formation of marital system b. Realignment of relationships with extended families and friends to include spouse
3. Becoming parents and families with children	Accepting new members into the system	a. Adjusting marital system to make space for child(ren) b. Joining in child-rearing, financial, and household tasks c. Realignment of relationships with extended family to include parenting and grandparenting roles
4. Families with adolescents	Increasing flexibility of family boundaries to include children's independence and grandparents' frailties	a. Shifting of parent-child relationships to permit adolescent to move in and out of system b. Refocus on midlife marital and career issues c. Beginning shift toward joint caring for older generation
5. Midlife families	Accepting a multitude of exits from and entries into the family system	a. Renegotiation of marital system as a dyad b. Development of adult to adult relationships between grown children and their parents c. Realignment of relationships to include in-laws and grandchildren d. Dealing with disabilities and death of parents (grandparents)
6. Families in later life	Accepting the shifting of generational roles	a. Maintaining own and/or couple functioning and interests in face of physiological decline; exploration of new familial and social role options b. Support for a more central role of middle generation c. Dealing with loss of spouse, siblings, and other peers and preparation for own death. Life review and integration.

Figure~6.3

The Stages of the Family Life Cycle.

At some point during the early years of the child's life, parents face the difficult task of juggling their roles as parents and as self-actualizing adults. Until recently in our culture, nurturing our children and having a career were thought to be incompatible. Fortunately, we have come to recognize that the balance between caring and achieving, nurturing and working—although difficult to manage—can be accomplished.

The Family with Adolescents

The **family with adolescents** *represents the fourth stage in the family life cycle. Adolescence is a period of development in which individuals push for autonomy and seek to develop their own identity.* The development of mature autonomy and identity is a lengthy process, transpiring over at least 10 to 15 years. Compliant children become noncompliant adolescents. Parents tend to adopt one of two strategies to handle noncompliance—clamp down and put more pressure on the adolescent to conform to parental values or become more permissive and let the adolescent have extensive freedom. Neither is a wise overall strategy; rather, a more flexible, adaptive approach is best. Later in the chapter we will explore the family worlds of adolescents and their parents in greater detail.

Midlife Families

Family at midlife *is the fifth stage in the family life cycle. It is a time of launching children, playing an important role in linking generations, and adapting to midlife changes in development.* Until about a generation ago, most families were involved in raising their children for much of their adult lives until old age. Because of the lower birth rate and the longer life of most adults, parents now launch their children about 20 years before retirement, which frees many midlife parents to pursue other activities.

> *The generations of living things pass in a short time, and like runners hand on the torch of life.*
>
> —Lucretius, 1st Century B.C.

For the most part, family members maintain considerable contact across generations. Parent-child similarity is most noticeable in religious and political areas, least in gender roles, lifestyle, and work orientation. Gender differences also characterize intergenerational relationships (Nydegger & Mitteness, 1991). In one investigation, mothers and their daughters had much closer relationships during their adult years than did mothers and sons, fathers and daughters, and fathers and sons (Rossi, 1988). Also, in this same investigation, married men were more involved with their wives' kin than with their own. These findings underscore the significance of the woman's role as mother in monitoring access to and feelings toward kin.

The Family in Later Life

The **family in later life** *is the sixth and final stage in the family life cycle. Retirement alters a couple's lifestyle, requiring adaptation. Grandparenting also characterizes many families in this period.* The greatest changes occur in the traditional family, in which the husband works and the wife is a homemaker. The husband may not know what to do with his time, and the wife may feel uneasy having him around the house all of the time. In traditional families, both partners may need to move toward more expressive roles. The husband must adjust from being the good provider to being a helper around the house; the wife must change from being only a good homemaker to being even more loving and understanding. Marital happiness as an older adult is also affected by each partner's ability to deal with personal conflicts, including aging, illness, and eventual death.

PARENT-ADOLESCENT RELATIONSHIPS

We have seen how the expectations of adolescents and their parents often seem violated as adolescents change dramatically during the course of puberty. Many parents see their child changing from a compliant being into someone who is noncompliant, oppositional, and resistant to parental standards. Parents often clamp down tighter and put more pressure on the adolescent to conform to parental standards. Many parents often deal with the young adolescent as if they expect the adolescent to become a mature being within the next 10 to 15 minutes. But the transition from childhood to adulthood is a long journey with many hills and valleys. Adolescents are not going to conform to adult standards immediately. Parents who recognize that adolescents take a long time "to get it right" usually deal more competently and calmly with adolescent transgressions than do parents who demand immediate conformity to parental standards. Yet other parents, rather than placing heavy demands on their adolescents for compliance, do virtually the opposite, letting them do as they please in a very permissive manner.

As we discuss parent-adolescent relationships, we will discover that neither high-intensity demands for compliance nor an unwillingness to monitor and be involved in the adolescent's development is likely to be a wise parenting strategy. Further, we will explore another misperception that parents of adolescents sometimes entertain. Parents may perceive that virtually all conflict with their adolescent is bad. We will discover that a moderate degree of conflict with parents in adolescence is not only inevitable but may also serve a positive developmental function.

Parenting Techniques

Parents want their adolescents to grow into socially mature individuals, and they often feel a great deal of frustration in their role as parents. Psychologists have long searched for parenting ingredients that promote competent social

by Michael Fry

...ONE THING, BEFORE YOU SEND ME UP TO MY ROOM FOR THE REST OF MY LIFE... HAVE YOU READ THOSE STUDIES THAT SAY YOU SHOULD REASON WITH YOUR KIDS INSTEAD OF PUNISHING THEM?

I GUESS SHE HADN'T READ THOSE STUDIES...

development in adolescents. For example, in the 1930s, behaviorist John Watson argued that parents were too affectionate with their charges. Early research focused on a distinction between physical and psychological discipline, or between controlling and permissive parenting. More recently, there has been greater precision in unraveling the dimensions of competent parenting.

Especially widespread is the view of Diana Baumrind (1971, 1991), who believes that parents should be neither punitive nor aloof from their adolescents, but rather should develop rules and be affectionate with them. She emphasizes three types of parenting that are associated with different aspects of the adolescent's social behavior: authoritarian, authoritative, and laissez-faire (permissive). More recently, developmentalists have argued that permissive parenting comes in two forms—neglectful and indulgent.

Authoritarian parenting *is a restrictive, punitive style in which the parent exhorts the adolescent to follow the parent's directions and to respect work and effort. The authoritarian parent places firm limits and controls on the adolescent and allows little verbal exchange. Authoritarian parenting is associated with adolescents' socially incompetent behavior.* For example, an authoritarian parent might say, "You do it my way or else. There will be no discussion!" Adolescents of authoritarian parents often are anxious about social comparison, fail to initiate activity, and have poor communication skills.

In one recent study, the interactive style of families predicted whether they would be successful at solving family problems (Rueter & Conger, 1995). A hostile interactive style was linked with destructive problem solving, while a warm interactive style was associated with effective problem solving.

Authoritative parenting *encourages adolescents to be independent but still places limits and controls on their actions. Extensive verbal give-and-take is allowed, and parents are warm and nurturant toward the adolescent. Authoritative*

parenting is associated with adolescents' socially competent behavior. An authoritative father, for example, might put his arm around the adolescent in a comforting way and say, "You know you should not have done that. Let's talk about how you can handle the situation better next time." The adolescents of authoritative parents are self-reliant and socially responsible.

Authoritative parents also monitor their adolescents' lives. In one recent study, increased parental monitoring was effective in reducing adolescent problem behaviors and improving school performance (Urberg & Wolowicz, 1996).

Permissive parenting comes in two forms: neglectful and indulgent. **Neglectful parenting** *is a style in which the parent is very uninvolved in the adolescent's life. It is associated with adolescents' socially incompetent behavior, especially a lack of self-control.* The neglectful parent cannot answer the questions, "It is 10:00 P.M. Do you know where your adolescent is?" Adolescents have a strong need for their parents to care about them; adolescents whose parents are permissive-indifferent develop the sense that other aspects of the parents' lives are more important than they are. Adolescents whose parents are neglectful are socially incompetent: They show poor self-control and do not handle independence well.

Indulgent parenting *is a style in which parents are highly involved with their adolescents but place few demands or controls on them. Indulgent parenting is associated with adolescents' social incompetence, especially a lack of self-control.* Indulgent parents allow their adolescents to do what they want, and the result is that the adolescents never learn to control their own behavior and always expect to get their way. Some parents deliberately rear their adolescents in this way because they believe that the combination of warm involvement with few restraints will produce a creative, confident adolescent. In one family with indulgent parents, the 14-year-old son moved his parents out of their master bedroom suite and claimed it—along with their expensive stereo system and color television—

Diana Baumrind developed the important concept of authoritative parenting, which is associated with socially competent adolescent behavior. Recently, Baumrind (1991) also found that parents' responsiveness—which includes considerateness and supportiveness—is related to adolescents' social competence.

Conflict with parents increases in early adolescence. Such conflict usually is moderate, an increase that can serve the positive developmental function of promoting independence and identity. Much of the conflict involves the everyday events of family life—keeping a bedroom clean, dressing neatly, getting home by a certain time, and, as shown in the photograph, not talking on the phone forever.

as his. The boy is an excellent tennis player but behaves in the manner of John McEnroe, raving and ranting around the tennis court. He has few friends, is self-indulgent, and has never learned to abide by rules and regulations. Why should he? His parents never made him follow any.

In our discussion of parenting styles, we have talked about parents who vary along the dimensions of acceptance, responsiveness, demand, and control. As shown in figure 6.4, the four parenting styles—authoritarian, authoritative, neglectful, and indulgent—can be described in terms of these dimensions.

In one investigation, Diana Baumrind (1991) analyzed parenting styles and social competence in adolescence. The comprehensive assessment involve observations and interviews with 139 boys and girls 14 years of age and their parents. More than any other factor, the responsiveness (considerateness and supportiveness, for example) of the parents was related to the adolescents' social competence. And when parents had problem behaviors themselves (alcohol problems and marital conflict, for example), adolescents were more likely to have problems and show decreased social competence. Other researchers continue to find support for the belief that authoritarian and permissive parenting are less effective strategies than authoritative parenting (Durbin & others, 1993).

Several caveats about parenting styles are in order. First, the parenting styles do not capture the important theme of reciprocal socialization and synchrony. Keep in mind that adolescents socialize parents, just as parents socialize adolescents. Second, many parents use a combination of techniques rather than a single technique, although one technique may be dominant. Although consistent parenting is usually recommended, the wise parent may sense the importance of being more permissive in certain situations, more authoritarian in others, and yet more authoritative in others.

> *We never know the love of our parents until we have become parents.*
>
> —Henry Ward Beecher

Parent-Adolescent Conflict

Early adolescence is a time when parent-adolescent conflict escalates beyond parent-child conflict (Montemayor, 1982; Weng & Montemayor, 1997). This increase may be due to a number of factors already discussed involving the maturation of the adolescent and the maturation of parents: the biological changes of puberty, cognitive changes involving increased idealism and logical reasoning, social changes focused on independence and identity, violated expectations, and physical, cognitive, and social changes in parents associated with middle adulthood. Parent-adolescent conflict decreases in late adolescence (Laursen & Ferreira, 1994). Although conflict with parents does increase in early adolescence, it does not reach the tumultuous proportions envisioned by G. Stanley Hall at the beginning of the twentieth century (Holmbeck, 1996). Rather, much of the conflict involves the everyday events of family life, such as keeping a bedroom clean, dressing neatly, getting home by a certain time, not talking on the phone forever, and so on. The conflicts rarely involve major dilemmas like drugs and delinquency.

In one recent study of conflict in a number of social relationships, adolescents reported having more disagreements with their mother than with anyone else—followed in order by friends, romantic partners, siblings, fathers, other adults, and peers (Laursen, 1995). In another study of

64 high school sophomores, interviews were conducted in their homes on three randomly selected evenings during a 3-week period (Montemayor, 1982). The adolescents were asked to tell about the events of the previous day, including any conflicts they had with their parents. Conflict was defined as "either you teased your parent or your parent teased you; you and your parent had a difference of opinion; one of you got mad at the other; you and your parent had a quarrel or an argument; or one of you hit the other." During a period of 192 days of tracking the 64 adolescents, an average of 68 arguments with parents was reported. This represents a rate of .35 arguments with parents per day or about one argument every 3 days. The average length of the arguments was 11 minutes. Most conflicts were with mothers, and the majority were between mothers and daughters.

Still, a high degree of conflict characterizes some parent-adolescent relationships. It has been estimated that in about 20 percent of families, parents and adolescents engage in prolonged, intense, repeated, unhealthy conflict (Montemayor, 1982). While this figure represents a minority of adolescents, it indicates that 4 to 5 million American families encounter serious, highly stressful parent-adolescent conflict. And this prolonged, intense conflict is associated with a number of adolescent problems—moving away from home, juvenile delinquency, school dropout rates, pregnancy and early marriage, membership in religious cults, and drug abuse (Brook & others, 1990).

Although in some cases these problems may be caused by intense, prolonged parent-adolescent conflict, in others the problems may have originated before the onset of adolescence. Simply because children are physically much smaller than parents, parents may be able to suppress oppositional behavior. But by adolescence, increased size and strength may result in an indifference to or confrontation with parental dictates. Consider the following circumstance:

| Interviewer | What sort of things does your mother object to your doing when you are out with your friends? |
| Boy | She don't know what I do. |

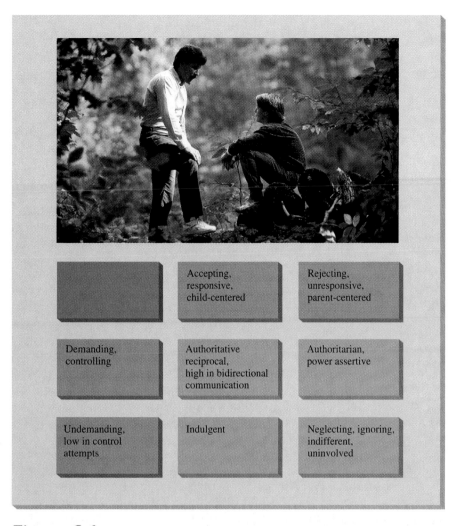

Figure~6.4

A Fourfold Scheme of Parenting Styles.

Interviewer	What about staying out late at night?
Boy	She says, "Be home at eleven o'clock." I'll come home at one.
Interviewer	How about using the family car?
Boy	No. I wrecked mine, and my father wrecked his a month before I wrecked mine, and I can't even get near his. And I got a license and everything. I'm going to hot wire it some night and cut out.
Interviewer	How honest do you feel you can be to your mother about where you've been and what things you have done?
Boy	I tell her where I've been, period.
Interviewer	How about what you've done?

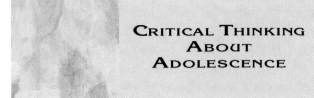

Boy	No. I won't tell her what I've done. If we're going to have a beer bust, I'm not going to tell her. I'll tell her I've been to a show or something.
Interviewer	How about your father?
Boy	I'll tell him where I've been, period.

Judith Smetana (1988, 1993, 1997) believes that parent-adolescent conflict can be better understood by considering the adolescent's changing social cognitive abilities. In her research, she has found that parent-adolescent conflict is related to the different approaches parents and adolescents take when addressing various points of contention. For example, consider an adolescent whose parents are displeased with the way the adolescent dresses. The adolescent often defines the issue as a personal one ("It's my body and I can do what I want to with it"), whereas parents usually define such issues in broader terms ("Look, we are a family and you are part of it. You have a responsibility to us to present yourself in a better fashion"). Many such issues punctuate the lives of parents and adolescents (keeping a room clean, curfew, choice of friends, and so on). As adolescents grow older, they are more likely to see their parents' perspective and look at issues in broader terms.

Autonomy and Attachment

It has been said that there are only two lasting bequests that we can leave our offspring—one is roots, the other wings. These words reflect the importance of attachment and autonomy in the adolescent's successful adaptation to the world. Historically, developmentalists have shown far more interest in autonomy than in attachment during the adolescent period. Recently, however, interest has heightened in attachment's role in healthy adolescent development. Adolescents and their parents live in a coordinated social world, one involving autonomy *and* attachment. In keeping with the historical interest in these processes, we discuss autonomy first.

Autonomy

The increased independence that typifies adolescence is labeled as rebelliousness by some parents, but in many instances the adolescent's push for autonomy has little to do with the adolescent's feelings toward the parents. Psychologically healthy families adjust to adolescents' push for independence by treating the adolescents in more adult ways and including them more in family decision making. Psychologically unhealthy families often remain locked into power-oriented parent control, and parents move even more heavily toward an authoritarian posture in their relationships with their adolescents.

However, it is important to recognize that parental control comes in different forms. In one recent study, adolescent adjustment depended on the type of parental control exerted (Keener & Boykin 1996). Control characterized by psychological manipulation and the imposition of guilt was linked with lower levels of adolescent adjustment; control characterized by parental awareness of the adolescent's activities, efforts to control the adolescent's deviance, and low harshness was associated with better adjustment.

The adolescent's quest for autonomy and sense of responsibility creates puzzlement and conflict for many parents. Parents begin to see their teenagers slipping away from their grasp. Often, the urge is to take stronger control as the adolescent seeks autonomy and personal responsibility. Heated, emotional exchanges may ensue, with either side calling names, making threats, and doing whatever seems necessary to gain control. Parents can become frustrated because they expected their teenager to heed their advice, to want to spend time with the family, and to grow up to do what is right. To be sure, they anticipated that their teenager would have some difficulty adjusting to the changes adolescence brings, but few parents are able to accurately imagine and predict the strength of adolescents' desires to be with their peers and how much they want to show that it is they, not the parents, who are responsible for their success or failure.

The Complexity of Adolescent Autonomy

Defining adolescent autonomy is more complex and elusive than it might seem at first. For most individuals, the term *autonomy* connotes self-direction and independence. But what does it really mean? Is it an internal personality trait that consistently characterizes the adolescent's immunity from parental influence? Is it the ability to make responsible decisions for oneself? Does autonomy imply consistent behavior in all areas of adolescent life, including school, finances, dating, and peer relations? What are the relative contributions of peers and other adults to the development of the adolescent's autonomy?

Adolescent autonomy is *not* a unitary personality dimension that consistently comes out in all behaviors (Hill & Holmbeck, 1986). For example, in one investigation, high school students were asked twenty-five questions about their independence from their families (Psathas, 1957). Four distinct patterns of adolescent autonomy emerged from analyses of the high school students' responses. One dimension was labeled "permissiveness in outside activities" and was represented by such questions as "Do you have to account to parents for the way you spend your money?" A second dimension was called "permissiveness in age-related activities" and was reflected in such questions as "Do your parents help you buy your clothes?" A third independent aspect of adolescent autonomy was referred to as "parental regard for judgment," indicated by responses to items like "In family discussions, do your parents encourage you to give your opinion." And a fourth dimension was characterized as "activities with status implications" and was indexed by parental influence on choice of occupation.

Parental Attitudes

A number of investigators have studied the relation between parental attitudes and adolescent autonomy. In general, authoritarian parenting is associated with low adolescent autonomy (Hill & Steinberg, 1976). Democratic parenting (much like authoritative parenting) is usually associated with increased adolescent autonomy (Kandel & Lesser, 1969), although findings in this regard are less consistent.

Culture, Demographic Factors, and Adolescent Autonomy

Expectations about the appropriate timing of adolescent autonomy often vary across cultures, parents, and adolescents. For example, expectations for early autonomy on the part of adolescents are more prevalent in Whites, single parents, and adolescents themselves than they are in Asian Americans or Latinos, married parents, and parents themselves (Feldman & Rosenthal, 1990).

Developmental Views of Autonomy

Two developmental views of adolescent autonomy have been proposed by David Ausubel and Peter Blos. Ausubel's theory emphasizes the role of parent-child relationships in the adolescent's growth toward maturity. He theorizes that parent-child interactions transform the helpless infant into an independent, self-monitoring individual.

Ausubel (1958) states that, during infancy, parents cater to their children's needs and demands. Later, parents expect children to do things for themselves—for example, use the toilet, pick up their toys, control their tempers, and so forth. As they develop cognitively, children begin to realize that they are not completely autonomous from their parents. This perception creates some conflict for children and may lead to a crisis wherein their self-esteem is threatened. One way children can resolve this conflict is **satellization,** *Ausubel's term for children's relinquishment of their sense of self-power and their acceptance of their dependency on their parents.*

However, Ausubel believes that many parents are not capable of developing or maintaining a satellizing relationship with their children. For satellization to occur, children must perceive that their parents love them unconditionally, and they must be able to entrust their care to their parents' hands. Two parenting styles that do not produce satellization are overvaluation and rejection. Parents who overvaluate continually interact with their children as if the children are in control. For example, some parents live vicariously through their children and hope that their children will accomplish goals they did not, such as becoming a baseball player or a doctor. When parents reject, they view the child as an unwanted part of their existence. The child's needs are served unwillingly and only if necessary. Love and acceptance are absent, or at least are perceived by the child as being absent.

As children approach adolescence, satellization is eventually replaced by **desatellization**—*Ausubel's term for the adolescent process of breaking away and becoming independent from parents.* Total self-rule is not achieved through desatellization. Rather, adolescents move into a preparatory phase wherein their potential separation from parental rule begins to develop. When final desatellization is reached, individuals have secure feelings about themselves and do not demonstrate the need to prove themselves. They show strong exploratory tendencies and focus their energies on tasks and problem solving rather than self-aggrandizement.

Other desatellization mechanisms may occur during adolescence that are unlike the competent form of desatellization just described. In many instances, the

Adolescents make a strong push for independence. As the adolescent pursues autonomy, the wise parent relinquishes control in those areas in which the adolescent makes competent decisions and continues to monitor and guide the adolescent in those areas in which the adolescent is not making mature choices.

other mechanisms may be preliminary steps in the adolescent's attainment of the final stage of desatellization. For example, **resatellization** is *Ausubel's term for a preliminary form of desatellization in which the individual's parents are replaced by other individuals or a group.* Resatellized individuals abdicate their identities to their spouse's identity, or to the identity of a fraternity, sorority, or other social group. As a permanent solution to self/other relationships, resatellization can be detrimental to the adolescent's development. But as a temporary solution, it can provide a testing ground for the development of a more complete, autonomous form of desatellization.

Peter Blos (1962, 1989), borrowing from Margaret Mahler's ideas about the development of independence during early childhood, introduced the concept of individuation to the study of adolescence. Like Mahler, Blos believes that there is a critical sharpening of the boundaries of the adolescent's self as distinct from others, especially parents. The **second individuation crisis** *is Blos's term for adolescents' development of a distinctiveness from their parents, which Blos believes is an attempt to transcend earlier parent-child ties and develop more self-responsibility.* Blos's ideas about individuation are reflected in the following comments of Debbie, a girl in late adolescence:

> Up to a certain age, I believed everything my parents said. Then, in college, I saw all these new ideas, and I said, "Okay, now I'm going to make a new Debbie which has nothing to do with my mother and father. I'm going to start with a clean slate," and what I started to put on it were all new ideas. These ideas were opposite to what my parents believed. But slowly, what's happening is that I'm adding on a lot of the things which they've told me, and I'm taking them as my own, and I'm coming more together with them. (Josselson, 1973, p. 37)

Developmental Transition in Autonomy Involved in Going Away to College Debbie and many other late adolescents experience a transition in the development of autonomy when they leave home and go away to college. The transition from high school to college involves increased autonomy for most individuals. For some, homesickness sets in; for others, sampling the privileges of life without parents hovering around is marvelous. For the growing number of students whose families have been torn by separation and divorce, though, moving away can be especially painful. Adolescents in such families may find themselves in the roles of comforter, confidant, and even caretaker of their parents as well as their siblings. In the words of one college freshman, "I feel responsible for my parents. I guess I shouldn't, but I can't help it. It makes my separation from them, my desire to be free of others' problems, my motivation to pursue my own identity more difficult." For yet others students, the independence of being a college freshman is not always as stressful. According to 18-year-old Brian, "Becoming an adult is kind of hard. I'm having to learn to balance my own checkbook, make my own plane reservations, do my own laundry, and the hardest thing of all is waking up in the morning. I don't have my mother there banging on the door."

In one investigation, the psychological separation and adjustment of 130 college freshmen and 123 college upper-classmen were studied (Lapsley, Rice, & Shadid, 1989). As expected, freshmen showed more psychological dependency on their parents and poorer social and personal adjustment than upperclassmen. Female students also showed more psychological dependency on their parents than male students did. In another recent study, parent-child relationships were less satisfactory prior to the high school-to-college transition (Silver, 1995). And in another recent study, students who went away to college reported feeling closer to their mother, less conflict with parents, and more decision-making control and autonomy than did college students who lived at home (Holmbeck, Durbin, & Kung, 1995).

Adolescent Runaways Why do adolescents run away from their homes? Generally, runaways are very unhappy at home. The reasons many of them leave seem legitimate by almost anyone's standards. When they run away, they usually do not leave a clue to their whereabouts—they just disappear.

Many runaways are from families in which a parent or another adult beats them or sexually exploits them. Their lives may be in danger daily. Their parents may be drug addicts or alcoholics. In some cases, the family may be so poor that the parents are unable to feed and clothe their teenagers adequately. The parents may be so overburdened by their material inadequacies that they fail to give their adolescents the attention and understanding they need. So teenagers hit the streets in search of the emotional and material rewards they are not getting at home.

But runaways are not all from our society's lower class. Teenage lovers, confronted by parental hostility toward their relationship, may decide to run off together and make it on their own. Or the middle-class teenager may decide that he has seen enough of his hypocritical parents—people who try to make him live by one set of moral standards, while they live by a loose, false set of ideals. Another teen may live with parents who constantly bicker. Any of these adolescents may decide that they would be happier away from home.

Running away often is a gradual process, as adolescents begin to spend less time at home and more time on the streets or with a peer group. The parents may be telling them that they really want to see them, to understand them; but runaways often feel that they are not understood at home and that the parents care much more about themselves.

Adolescent runaways are especially susceptible to drug abuse (MacLean & Paradise, 1997). In one investigation, as part of the National Longitudinal Study of Youth Survey, runaway status at ages 14 to 15 was associated with drug abuse and alcohol problems 4 years later at ages 18 to 19 (Windle, 1989). Repeat runaways were more likely to be drug abusers than one-time runaways were. Both one-time and repeat runaways were more likely to be school dropouts when this was assessed 4 years later.

Some provision must be made for runaways' physical and psychological well-being. In recent years, nationwide hotlines and temporary shelters for runaways have been established. However, there are still too few of these shelters, and there is often a noted lack of professional psychological help for the runaways at such shelters.

One exception is the temporary shelter in Dallas, Texas, called Casa de los Amigos (house of friends). At the Casa, there is room for twenty runaways, who are provided with the necessities of life as well as medical and legal assistance. In addition, a professional staff of thirteen includes counselors and case managers, assisted by VISTA volunteers and high school and college interns. Each runaway is assigned a counselor, and daily group discussion sessions expose the youth to one another's feelings. Whenever possible, the counselors explore the possibility of working with the runaways' families to see if all of the family members can learn to help each other in more competent ways than in the past. It is hoped that more centers like Casa de los Amigos will appear in cities in the United States so that runaways will not meet the fates that Sammy and Barbara encountered.

Conclusions In sum, the ability to attain autonomy and gain control over one's behavior in adolescence is acquired through appropriate adult reactions to the adolescent's desire for control. At the onset of adolescence, the average individual does not have the knowledge to make appropriate or mature decisions in all areas of life.

These adolescent girls have run away from home. What is it about family relationships that causes adolescents to run away from home? Are there ways society could better serve runaways?

As the adolescent pushes for autonomy, the wise adult relinquishes control in those areas in which the adolescent can make reasonable decisions and continues to guide the adolescent in areas in which the adolescent's knowledge is more limited. Gradually, adolescents acquire the ability to make mature decisions on their own. The discussion that follows reveals in greater detail how it is erroneous to view the development of autonomy apart from connectedness to parents.

Attachment and Connectedness

Adolescents do not simply move away from parental influence into a decision-making world all their own. As they become more autonomous, it is psychologically healthy for them to be attached to their parents.

Secure and Insecure Attachment Attachment theorists such as British psychiatrist John Bowlby (1989) and American developmental psychologist Mary Ainsworth (1979) argue that secure attachment in infancy is central to the development of social competence. In **secure attachment,** *infants use the caregiver, usually the mother, as a secure base from which to explore the environment. Secure attachment is theorized to be an important foundation for psychological development later in childhood, adolescence, and adulthood. In* **insecure attachment,** *infants either avoid the caregiver or show considerable resistance or ambivalence toward the caregiver. Insecure attachment is theorized to be related to difficulties in relationships and problems in later development.*

In the last decade, developmentalists have begun to explore the role of secure attachment and related concepts, such as connectedness to parents, in adolescent development (Eberly & others, 1997). They believe that attachment to parents in adolescence may facilitate the adolescent's social competence and well-being, as reflected in such characteristics as self-esteem, emotional adjustment, and physical health (Allen & Kuperminc, 1995; Juang & Nyugen, 1997). For example, adolescents who show more satisfaction with help received from parents report more emotional well-being (Burke & Weir, 1979), and adolescents with secure relationships with their parents have higher self-esteem and better emotional well-being (Armsden & Greenberg, 1987). In contrast, emotional detachment from parents is associated with greater feelings of parental rejection and a lower sense of one's own social and romantic attractiveness (Ryan & Lynch, 1989). Thus, attachment to parents during adolescence may serve the adaptive function of providing a secure base from which adolescents can explore and master new environments and a widening social world in a psychologically healthy manner (Allen & Bell, 1995). Secure attachment to parents may buffer adolescents from the anxiety and potential feelings of depression or emotional distress associated with the transition from childhood to adulthood. In one study, when young adolescents had a secure attachment to their parents, they perceived their family as cohesive and reported little social anxiety or feelings of depression (Papini, Roggman, & Anderson, 1990). The importance of both autonomy and relatedness in parent-adolescent relationships was recently documented in a longitudinal study (Allen & Hauser, 1994). Adolescents' ability to establish their autonomy while maintaining a sense of relatedness when interacting with parents at 14 years of age was related to their success in intimate relationships and self-worth in early adulthood.

Secure attachment or connectedness to parents also promotes competent peer relations and positive, close relationships outside of the family. In one investigation in which attachment to parents and peers was assessed, adolescents who were securely attached to parents also were securely attached to peers; those who were insecurely attached to parents also were more likely to be insecurely attached to peers (Armsden & Greenberg, 1984). In another investigation, college students who were securely attached to their parents as young children were more likely to have securely attached relationships with friends, dates, and spouses than were their insecurely attached counterparts (Hazen & Shaver, 1987). And in yet another investigation, older adolescents who had an ambivalent attachment history with their parents reported greater jealousy, conflict, and dependency, along with less satisfaction, in their relationship with their best friend than did their securely attached counterparts (Fisher, 1990). There are times when adolescents reject closeness, connection, and attachment to their parents as they assert their ability to make decisions and to develop an identity. But for the most part, the worlds of parents and peers are coordinated and connected, not uncoordinated and disconnected.

Developmental Transformations   Transformations characterize adolescents' autonomy and connectedness with their families. In one recent study by Reed Larson and his colleagues (1996), 220 White middle-class adolescents from 10 to 18 years of age carried beepers and, when beeped at random times, reported who they were with, what they were doing, and how they were feeling. The amount of time adolescents spent with their families decreased from 35 percent for 10-year-olds to 14 percent for 18-year-olds, suggesting increased autonomy with age. However, increased family connectedness was evident with increased age, with more family conversation about interpersonal issues, especially for girls. As adolescents got older, they were more likely to perceive themselves as leading the interactions. Also, after a decrease in early adolescence, older teenagers reported more favorable affect with others during family interactions.

Conclusions   In sum, the old model of parent-adolescent relationships suggested that, as adolescents mature, they detach themselves from parents and move into a world of autonomy apart from parents. The old model also suggested that parent-adolescent conflict is intense and stressful throughout adolescence. The new model emphasizes that parents serve as important attachment figures, resources, and support systems as adolescents explore a wider, more complex social world. The new model also emphasizes that, in the majority of families, parent-adolescent conflict is moderate rather than severe and that everyday negotiations and minor disputes are normal, serving the positive developmental function of promoting independence and identity (see figure 6.5).

At this point we have discussed a number of ideas about the nature of family processes and parent-adolescent relationships. A summary of these ideas is presented in concept table 6.1. So far in our discussion of families, we have focused on parent-adolescent relationships. But there is another aspect to the family worlds of most adolescents—sibling relationships—which we discuss next.

SIBLING RELATIONSHIPS

Sandra describes to her mother what happened in a conflict with her sister:

> We had just come home from the ball game. I sat down on the sofa next to the light so I could read. Sally (the sister) said, "Get up. I was sitting there first. I just got up for a second to get a drink." I told her I was not

Old model		New model	
Autonomy, detachment from parents; parent and peer worlds are isolated	Intense, stressful conflict throughout adolescence; parent-adolescent relationships are filled with storm and stress on virtually a daily basis	Attachment and autonomy; parents are important support systems and attachment figures; adolescent-parent and adolescent-peer worlds have some important connections	Moderate parent-adolescent conflict common and can serve a positive developmental function; conflict greater in early adolescence, especially during the apex of puberty

Figure~6.5

The Old and New Models of Parent-Adolescent Relationships.

going to get up and that I didn't see her name on the chair. I got mad and started pushing her—her drink spilled all over her. Then she got really mad; she shoved me against the wall, hitting and clawing at me. I managed to grab a handful of hair.

At this point, Sally comes into the room and begins to tell her side of the story. Sandra interrupts, "Mother, you always take her side." Sound familiar? How much does conflict characterize sibling relations? As we examine the roles siblings play in social development, you will discover that conflict is a common dimension of sibling relationships but that siblings also play many other roles in social development.

Sibling Roles and Comparisons with Other Social Agents

More than 80 percent of American adolescents have one or more siblings—that is, brothers and sisters. As anyone who has had a sibling knows, the conflict experienced by Sally and Sandra in their relationship with each other is a common interaction style of siblings. However, conflict is only one of the many dimensions of sibling relations. Adolescent sibling relations include helping, sharing, teaching, fighting, and playing, and adolescent siblings can act as emotional supports, rivals, and communication partners.

In some instances, siblings may be stronger socializing influences on the adolescent than parents are. Someone close in age to the adolescent—such as a sibling—may be able to understand the adolescent's problems and to communicate more effectively than parents can. In dealing with peers, coping with difficult teachers, and discussing taboo subjects (such as sex), siblings may be more influential in socializing adolescents than parents are. Further, in one study, children showed more consistent behavior when interacting with siblings and more varied behavior when interacting with parents (Baskett & Johnson, 1982). In this study, children interacted in much more aggressive ways with their siblings than with their parents. In another study, adolescents reported a higher degree of conflict with their siblings than with anyone else (Buhrmester & Furman, 1990).

Developmental Changes in Sibling Relationships

Although adolescent sibling relations reveal a high level of conflict in comparison to adolescents' relationships

The Nature of Family Processes and Parent-Adolescent Relationships

Concept	Processes/ Related Ideas	Characteristics/Description
The Nature of Family Processes	Reciprocal socialization, synchrony, and the family as a system	The principle of reciprocal socialization states that adolescents socialize parents, just as parents socialize adolescents. Synchrony is an important dimension of reciprocal socialization; it is the carefully coordinated interaction between the parent and the child or adolescent in which each is attuned to each other's behavior. The family is a system of interacting individuals with different subsystems—some dyadic, others polyadic. Belsky's model describes direct and indirect effects of interaction between adolescents and their parents.
	The developmental construction of relationships	The developmental construction views share the belief that as individuals grow up they acquire modes of relating to others. There are two main variations within this view, one that emphasizes continuity and stability in relationships through the life span (called the continuity view) and one that emphasizes discontinuity and change in relationships through the life span (called the discontinuity view).
	Maturation of the adolescent and maturation of parents	The adolescent changes involved include puberty, expanded logical reasoning, increased idealistic and egocentric thought, violated expectations, changes in schooling, peers, friendships, dating, and movement toward independence. Parental changes are associated with midlife—marital dissatisfaction, economic burdens, career reevaluation and time perspective, and health and body concerns.
	Sociocultural and historical changes	Sociocultural and historical changes in families may be due to great upheavals, such as war, or more subtle changes, such as television and the mobility of families.
Parent-Adolescent Relationships	The family life cycle	There are six stages in the family life cycle: leaving home and becoming a single adult; the joining of families through marriage—the new couple; becoming parents and a family with children; the family with adolescents; the midlife family; and the family in later life.
Autonomy and Attachment	Parenting techniques	Authoritarian, authoritative, neglectful, and indulgent are four main parenting categories. Authoritative parenting is associated with adolescents' social competence more than the other styles.
	Parent-adolescent conflict	Conflict with parents increases in early adolescence. Such conflict usually is moderate, an increase that can serve the positive developmental function of promoting autonomy and identity. However, in as many as 20 percent of families, parent-adolescent relationships involve intense conflict.
	Autonomy	Many parents have a difficult time handling the adolescent's push for autonomy. Autonomy is a complex concept with multiple referents. Democratic parenting is associated with adolescent autonomy. Expectations about the appropriate timing of adolescent autonomy often vary across cultures, parents, and adolescents. Two important developmental views of autonomy have been proposed by Ausubel (desatellization) and Blos (individuation). A developmental transition in autonomy occurs when individuals leave home and go away to college. A special concern involves adolescent runaways. The wise parent relinquishes control in areas where the adolescent makes mature decisions and retains more control over areas in which the adolescent's knowledge is more limited.
	Attachment	Adolescents do not simply move away into a world isolated from parents. Attachment to parents increases the probability that the adolescent will be socially competent and explore a widening social world in healthy ways. The social worlds of parents and peers are coordinated and connected. Developmental transformations characterize autonomy and connectedness in adolescence.

with other social agents (parents, peers, teachers, and romantic partners, for example), there is evidence that sibling conflict is actually lower in adolescence than in childhood. In a recent study, the lessened sibling conflict during adolescence was due partly to a dropoff in the amount of time siblings spent playing and talking with each other during adolescence (Buhrmester & Furman, 1990). The decline also reflected a basic transformation in the power structure of sibling relationships that seems to occur in adolescence. In childhood, there is an asymmetry of power, with older siblings frequently playing the role of "boss" or caregiver. This asymmetry of power often produces conflicts when one sibling tries to force the other to comply with his or her demands. As younger siblings grow older and their maturity level "catches up" to older siblings', the power asymmetry decreases. As siblings move through adolescence, most learn how to relate to each other on a more equal footing and, in doing so, come to resolve more of their differences than in childhood. Nonetheless, as we said earlier, sibling conflict in adolescence is still reasonably high.

Birth Order

Birth order has been of special interest to sibling researchers, who want to identify the characteristics associated with being born into a particular slot in a family. Firstborns have been described as more adult oriented, helpful, conforming, anxious, and self-controlled, and less aggressive than their siblings. Parental demands and high standards established for firstborns may result in firstborns realizing higher academic and professional achievements than their siblings. For example, firstborns are overrepresented in *Who's Who* and among Rhodes Scholars. However, some of the same pressures placed on firstborns for high achievement may be the reason firstborns also have more guilt, anxiety, difficulty in coping with stressful situations, and higher admission to guidance clinics.

Birth order also plays a role in siblings' relationships with each other (Vandell, Minnett, & Santrock, 1987). Older siblings invariably take on the dominant role in sibling interaction, and older siblings report feeling more resentful that parents give preferential treatment to younger siblings.

What are later-borns like? Characterizing later-borns is difficult because they can occupy so many different sibling positions. For example, a later-born might be the second-born male in a family of two siblings or a third-born female in a family of four siblings. In two-child families, the profile of the later-born child is related to the sex of his or her sibling. For example, a boy with an older sister is more likely to develop "feminine" interests than a boy with an older brother. Overall, later-borns usually enjoy better relations with peers than firstborns. Last-borns, who are often described as the "baby" in the family even after they have outgrown infancy, run the

More than 80 percent of us have one or more siblings. Any of you who have grown up with siblings know that rivalry is a fact of sibling life, as indicated by these two sisters arguing about the phone. But remember, sibling life is not all rivalry. Adolescent siblings also share special moments of caring and trust.

risk of becoming overly dependent. Middle-borns tend to be more diplomatic, often performing the role of negotiator in times of dispute (Sutton-Smith, 1982).

> *Big sisters are the crab grass in the lawn of life.*
> —Charles Schulz

The popular conception of the only child is of a "spoiled brat" with such undesirable characteristics as dependency, lack of self-control, and self-centered behavior. But research presents a more positive portrayal of the only child, who often is achievement oriented and displays a desirable personality, especially in comparison to later-borns and children from large families (Thomas, Coffman, & Kipp, 1993).

So far our consideration of birth-order effects suggest that birth order might be a strong predictor of adolescent behavior. However, an increasing number of family researchers believe that birth order has been overdramatized and overemphasized. The critics argue that, when all of the factors that influence adolescent behavior are considered, birth order itself shows limited ability to predict adolescent behavior. Consider just sibling relationships alone. They vary not only in birth order, but also in number of siblings, age of siblings, age spacing of siblings, and sex of siblings.

Consider also the temperament of siblings. Researchers have found that siblings' temperamental traits (such as "easy" and "difficult"), as well as differential treatment of siblings by parents, influence how siblings get along (Brody, Stoneman, & Burke, 1987). Siblings with "easy" temperaments who are treated in relatively equal ways by parents tend to get along with each other the best, whereas siblings with "difficult" temperaments, or siblings whose parents gave one sibling preferential treatment, get along the worst.

Beyond temperament and differential treatment of siblings by parents, think about some of the other important factors in adolescents' lives that influence their behavior beyond birth order. They include heredity, models of competency or incompetency that parents present to adolescents on a daily basis, peer influences, school influences, socioeconomic factors, sociohistorical factors, cultural variations, and so on. When someone says first-borns are always like this, but last-borns are always like that, you now know that they are making overly simplistic statements that do not adequately take into account the complexity of influences on an adolescent's behavior. Keep in mind, though, that, although birth order itself may not be a good predictor of adolescent behavior, sibling relationships and interaction are important dimensions of family processes in adolescence.

We have discussed many aspects of adolescents and their families, but much more remains. Especially important is the nature of the changing family in a changing society.

THE CHANGING FAMILY IN A CHANGING SOCIETY

More adolescents are growing up in a greater variety of family structures than ever before in history (Dreman, 1997; Hernandez, 1997). Many mothers spend the greater part of their day away from their children. More than one of every two mothers with a child under the age of 5, and more than two of every three with a child from 6 to 17 years of age, is in the labor force. And the increasing number of children and adolescents who are growing up in a single-parent families is staggering. One estimate indicates that 25 percent of the children born between 1910 and 1960 lived in a single-parent family at some time in their childhood or adolescence. However, at least 50 percent of the children born in the 1980s will spend part of their childhood or adolescence in a single-parent family. Further, about 11 percent of all American households now are made up of stepparent families. What are the effects of divorce, of remarriage, and of working parents on adolescents? What role do culture and ethnicity play in parenting? What is the nature of gender and parenting?

The Effects of Divorce

What models of how divorce affects adolescents have developmentalists constructed? What are some of the key factors in understanding how divorce influences adolescent development?

Models of Divorce Effects

Two main models have been proposed to explain how divorce affects children's and adolescents' development: the family structure model and the multiple-factor model. The **family structure model of divorce effects** *states that any differences in adolescents are due to family structure variations, such as the father's absence in one set of the families.* However, family structure (such as father-present versus father-absent) is only one of many factors that influence the adolescent's development and adjustment in single-parent families. Even when researchers compare the development of adolescents in more precise family structures (such as divorced versus widowed), there are many factors other than family structure that need to be examined to explain the adolescent's development. As we see next, a second model of the effects of divorce on adolescent development goes beyond the overly simplistic family structure father-absence model.

The **multiple-factor model of divorce effects** *takes into account the complexity of the divorce context and examines a number of influences on the adolescent's development, including not only family structure, but also the strengths and weaknesses of the adolescent prior to the divorce, the nature of the events surrounding the divorce itself, the type of custody involved and visitation patterns, socioeconomic status, and postdivorce family functioning.* Researchers are finding that the availability and use of support systems (relatives, friends, housekeepers), an ongoing positive relationship between the custodial parent and the ex-spouse, authoritative parenting, financial resources, and the adolescent's competencies at the time of the divorce are important factors in how successfully the adolescent adapts to the divorce of parents (Hetherington & Stanley-Hagan, 1995). Thus, just as the family structure factor of birth order by itself is not a good predictor of adolescent development, neither is the family structure factor of father absence. In both circumstances—birth order and father absence—there are many other factors that always have to be taken into consideration when explaining the adolescent's development is at issue. Let's further examine what some of those complex factors are for adolescents who experience the divorce of their parents.

Age and Developmental Changes

The age of the child or adolescent at the time of the divorce needs to be considered. Young children's responses to divorce are mediated by their limited cognitive and social competencies, their dependency on parents, and possibly inferior day care.

The cognitive immaturity that creates considerable anxiety for children who are young at the time of their parents' divorce may benefit the children over time. Ten years after the divorce of their parents, adolescents had few memories of their own earlier fears and suffering or their parents' conflict (Wallerstein, Corbin, & Lewis, 1988). Nonetheless, approximately one-third of these children continued to express anger about not being able to grow up in an intact, never-divorced family. Those who were adolescents at the time of their parents' divorce were more likely to remember the conflict and stress surrounding the divorce some 10 years later, in their early adult years. They, too, expressed disappointment at not being able to grow up in an intact family and wondered if their life would not have been better if they had been able to do so.

Recent evaluations of children and adolescents 6 years after the divorce of their parents by developmental psychologist E. Mavis Hetherington (1995) found that living in a nonremarried mother-custody home had long-term negative effects on boys, with deleterious outcomes appearing consistently from kindergarten to adolescence. No negative effects on preadolescent girls were found. However, at the onset of adolescence, early-maturing girls from divorced families engaged in frequent conflict with their mothers, behaved in noncompliant ways, had lower self-esteem, and experienced more problems in heterosexual relationships.

Conflict

Many separations and divorces are highly emotional affairs that immerse the adolescent in conflict. Conflict is a critical aspect of family functioning that often outweighs the influence of family structure on the adolescent's development. For example, adolescents in divorced families low in conflict function better than adolescents in intact, never-divorced families high in conflict (Black & Pedro-Carroll, 1993). Although the escape from conflict that divorce provides may be a positive benefit for adolescents, in the year immediately following the divorce, the conflict does not decline but increases. At this time, adolescents—especially boys—in divorced families show more adjustment problems than adolescents in intact families with both parents present. During the first year after the divorce, the quality of parenting the adolescent experiences is often poor; parents seem to be preoccupied with their own needs and adjustment—experiencing anger, depression, confusion, and emotional instability—which inhibits their ability to respond sensitively to the adolescent's needs. During the second year after the divorce, parents are more effective in their child-rearing duties, especially with daughters (Hetherington, Cox, & Cox, 1982).

E. Mavis Hetherington has conducted a number of important research studies on the effects of divorce on children's and adolescents' development. In a recent longitudinal study, Hetherington found that at the onset of adolescence early-maturing girls from divorced families engage in frequent conflict with their mothers, behave in noncompliant ways, have low self-esteem, and experience problems in heterosexual relationships.

Sex of the Child and the Nature of Custody

The sex of the child or adolescent and the sex of the custodial parent are important considerations in evaluating the effects of divorce on children and adolescents. One research study directly compared 6- to 11-year-old children living in father-custody and mother-custody families (Santrock & Warshak, 1986). On a number of measures, including videotaped observations of parent-child interaction, children living with the same-sex parent were more socially competent—happier, more independent, higher in self-esteem, and more mature—than children living with the opposite-sex parent. Most studies have found support for the same-sex parent-child custodial arrangement (Lee & others, 1994), but in one study adolescents were better adjusted in mother-custody or joint-custody families than in father-custody families (Buchanan, Maccoby, & Dornbusch, 1992). In this study the best predictors of positive adolescent outcomes were the closeness of the adolescent to the custodial parent and the custodial parent's monitoring of the adolescent.

Income and Economic Stress

An increasing number of studies reveal that income is a significant factor in the adjustment of parents and adolescents in divorced families (Kalil, 1994). For mothers with custody of their children and adolescents, income usually drops in a dramatic fashion following divorce, whereas postdivorce income for fathers with custody does not (Santrock & Warshak, 1986). Today, women

Communicating About Divorce

If parents decide to obtain a divorce, how should they communicate with their adolescent about the divorce? For one thing, they should explain the separation as soon as daily activities in the home make it obvious that one parent is leaving. If possible, both parents should be present when the adolescent is told about the separation. Adolescents also should be told that anytime they want to talk with someone about the separation, they should come to the parents. It is healthy for adolescents to get their pent-up emotions out in the open in discussions with their parents and to learn that their parents are willing to listen to their feelings and fears. Can you think of other strategies divorcing parents can use to effectively communicate with their adolescents? By thinking about ways to communicate with adolescents about divorce, you are learning to think critically by *using knowledge about development to improve human welfare*.

are far less likely to receive alimony, or spousal support, than in the past. Even when alimony or child-support payments are awarded to a woman, they are poorly enforced.

Conclusions

In sum, large numbers of children and adolescents are growing up in divorced families. Most children and adolescents initially experience considerable stress when their parents divorce, and they are at risk for developing problem behaviors. However, divorce can also remove children and adolescents from conflicted marriages. Many children and adolescents emerge from divorce as competent individuals. In recent years, developmentalists have moved away from the view that single-parent families are atypical or pathological, focusing more on the diversity of children's and adolescents' responses to divorce and the factors that facilitate or disrupt the development and adjustment of children and adolescents in these family circumstances (Hetherington & Stanley-Hagan, 1995).

Stepfamilies

The number of remarriages involving children and adolescents has grown steadily in recent years, although the rate of increase in both divorce and stepfamilies slowed in the 1980s. Stepfather families, in which a woman has custody of children from a previous marriage, make up 70 percent of stepfamilies. Stepmother families make up almost 20 percent of stepfamilies, and a small minority are blended with both partners bringing children from a previous marriage. A substantial percentage of stepfamilies produce children of their own.

Like divorce, remarriage has also become commonplace in American society. The United States has the highest remarriage rate in the world, and Americans tend to remarry soon after divorce. Younger women remarry more quickly than older women, and childless women, divorced prior to the age of 25, have higher remarriage rates than women with children. The more money a divorced male has, the more likely he is to remarry, but for women the opposite is true. Remarriage satisfaction, similar to satisfaction in first marriages, appears to decrease over time. In fact, few differences have been found, regarding the factors that predict marital satisfaction, between first marriages and remarriage (Coleman & Ganong, 1990).

Just like couples who are first married, remarried individuals often have unrealistic expectations about their stepfamily. Thus, an important adjustment for remarried persons is to develop realistic expectations. Money and the complexities of family structure in the remarried family often contribute to marital conflict.

Many variations in remarriage have the potential for what is called **boundary ambiguity**—*the uncertainty in stepfamilies about who is in or out of the family and who is performing or responsible for certain tasks in the family system.* The uncertainty of boundaries likely increases stress for the family system and the probability of behavior problems in children.

Research on stepfamilies has lagged behind research on divorced families, but a number of investigators have turned their attention to this increasingly common family structure (Hetherington, 1995; Jodl & Dalton, 1996). Following remarriage of their parents, children of all ages show a resurgence of behavior problems (Freeman, 1993). Younger children seem to eventually form an attachment to a step-parent and accept the stepparenting role. However, the developmental tasks facing adolescents make them especially vulnerable to the entrance of a stepparent. At the time they are searching for an identity and exploring sexual and other close relationships outside the family, a nonbiological parent may increase the stress associated with these important tasks. In one study, entrance of a stepfather when children were 9 years

was esp
coping v
have al:
joblessn
developi

Cultu

Culture:
such as \
extent t(
and how
1995). A
enting (
parentin
most co
one that
& Rohn
majority
a "truth"
namely, t
velopme
least som

Eth
ican fam
liance or
educatio
extended
nority gr
ple, more
five or m
children i
cousins, a
ican chil

As \
single-pai
American
comparis
parent ho
time, mon
prompt th
adolescen
educated
White An
cents are
than Whit
Although
youth, poc
supportive

Som
nic minori
communit
messages, |
ence than
can also pi
ment. Anc
minority fa

old or older was associated with more problems than when the stepfather family was formed earlier (Hetherington, 1993).

Following the remarriage of the custodial parent, an emotional upheaval usually occurs in girls, and problems in boys often intensify. Over time, boys seem to improve more than girls in stepfather families. Sons who frequently are involved in conflicted or coercive relations with their custodial mothers probably have much to gain from living with a warm, supportive stepfather. In contrast, daughters who have a close relationship with their custodial mothers and considerable independence frequently find a stepfather both disruptive and constraining.

Adolescents' relationships with their biological parents are more positive than with their stepparents, regardless of whether a stepmother or stepfather family is involved. However, stepfathers are often distant and disengaged from their stepchildren. As a rule, the more complex the stepfamily, the more difficult the adolescent's adjustment. Families in which both parents bring children from a previous marriage have the highest level of behavioral problems.

In the recent investigation by E. Mavis Hetherington (1993, 1995), both parenting techniques and the school environment were associated with whether children coped effectively both with living in a divorced family and a stepfamily. From the first grade on, an authoritative environment (an organized, predictable environment with clearly defined standards, and a responsive, nurturant environment) was linked with greater achievement and fewer problems in children than three other environments—authoritarian (coercive, power assertive, punitive, more criticism than praise, little responsiveness to individual children's needs, and low nurturance), permissive (low structure, disorganized, and high warmth), and chaotic/neglecting (disorganized, in-effective, erratic though usually harsh control, unstructured, low expectations, and hostile relationships). In divorced families, when only one parent was authoritative, or when neither parent was authoritative, an authoritative school improved the child's adjustment. A chaotic/neglectful school environment had the most adverse effects on children, which were most marked when there was no authoritative parent in the home.

Now that we have considered the changing social worlds of adolescents when their parents divorce and remarry, we turn our attention to another aspect of the changing family worlds of adolescents—the situation when both parents work.

Working Parents

Interest in the effects of parental work on the development of children and adolescents has increased in recent years. Our examination of parental work focuses on the following issues: the role of working mothers in adolescents' development, the adjustment of latchkey adolescents, the effects of relocation on adolescent development, and the influence of unemployment on adolescents' lives.

Working Mothers

Most of the research on parental work has focused on young children. Little attention has been given to early adolescence, even though it is during this period that many mothers return to full-time work, in part due to presumed independence of their young adolescents. In one recent study, 10- to 13-year olds carried electronic pagers for 1 week and completed self-report forms in response to random signals sent to them every other hour (Richards & Duckett, 1994). The most striking aspect of the study was the absence of significant differences associated with maternal employment. There were few differences in the quantity and quality of time associated with maternal employment. Other researchers have arrived at similar conclusions (Lerner, Jacobson, & del Gaudio, 1992). As one of the leading authorities on maternal employment, Lois Hoffman (1989), stated, maternal employment is a fact of modern life. It is not an aberrant aspect of it, but a response to other social changes that meets the needs not met by the previous family ideal of a full-time mother and homemaker. Not only does it meet the parents' needs, but in many ways, it may be a pattern better suited to socializing children for the adult roles they will occupy. This is especially true for daughters, but it is true for sons, too. The broader range of emotions and skills that each parent presents is more consistent with this adult role. Just as the father shares the breadwinning role and the child-rearing role with the mother, so the son, too, will be more likely to share these roles. The rigid gender-role stereotyping perpetuated by the divisions of labor in the traditional family is not appropriate for the demands children of both sexes will have made on them as adults. The needs of the growing child require the mother to loosen her hold on the child, and this task may be easier for the working woman whose job is an additional source of identity and self-esteem.

Gender differences have sometimes been associated with parental work patterns. In some studies, no gender differences are found, but in others, maternal employment has greater benefits for adolescent daughters than for sons (Law, 1992), and in yet others, adolescent sons benefit academically and emotionally when they identify with the work patterns of their fathers more than with those of their mothers (Orthner, Giddings, & Quinn, 1987).

In one recent study, Nancy Galambos and her colleagues (1995) studied the effects of parents' work overload on their relationships with their adolescent and on the adolescent's development. They found some evidence for the impact of work overload, but the effects differed for mothers and fathers. The mother's warmth and acceptance shown toward the adolescent helped to reduce the negative impact of her work overload on the adolescent's development. The key factor for fathers was parent-adolescent conflict—when it was lower, the negative impact of the father's work overload on the adolescent's development was reduced. Also, when both parents were stressed, parent-adolescent conflict was highest.

Latch

While th...
ated with...
of adolesc...
ther scruti...
adolescen...
time they...
or 7:00 P....
lescents l...
home, tak...
home whi...
adolescen...
during eac...
during the...

Tho...
than 1,50...
slight maj...
experienc...
fast, hurr...
How do la...
and struct...
its and pare...
children...
trouble—...
dalizing. T...
dicated ju...
Maryland,...
vestigatior...
Angeles an...
11 hours a...
abused alc...
terparts wh...
or after sch...
cent expert...
lect Commi...
the lack of a...
in the after-...
lems. Lipsit...
because it...
for Early Ad...
director, ex...
clinical hel...

Althou...
to problem...
latchkey ado...
riences of all...
to give speci...
lescents' live...
latchkey ex...
and authorit...
more effectiv...
resisting peer...
berg, 1986)....
at developme...
that research...
analyses of ac...

Leon Spillaert
Girls with White Stockings
© 1997 Estate of Leon Spillaert/Licensed by VAGA, New York, NY

196

was especially difficult for children whose parents were coping with changes in their work status. Other researchers have also recently found that economic downturn and joblessness can have negative effects on the adolescent's development (Gomel, Tinsley, & Clark, 1995; Lord, 1995).

Culture and Ethnicity

Cultures vary on a number of issues involving families, such as what the father's role in the family should be, the extent to which support systems are available to families, and how children should be disciplined (Harkness & Super, 1995). Although there are cross-cultural variations in parenting (Whiting & Edwards, 1988), in one study of parenting behavior in 186 cultures around the world, the most common pattern was a warm and controlling style, one that was neither permissive nor restrictive (Rohner & Rohner, 1981). The investigators commented that the majority of cultures have discovered, over many centuries, a "truth" that only recently emerged in the Western world—namely, that children's and adolescents' healthy social development is most effectively promoted by love and at least some moderate parental control.

Ethnic minority families differ from White American families in their size, structure and composition, reliance on kinship networks, and level of income and education (Chen & Yu, 1997; Hughes, 1997). Large and extended families are more common among ethnic minority groups than among White Americans. For example, more than 30 percent of Latino families consist of five or more individuals. African American and Latino children interact more with grandparents, aunts, uncles, cousins, and more distant relatives than do White American children.

As we saw earlier in our discussion of divorce, single-parent families are more common among African Americans and Latinos than among White Americans. In comparison with two-parent households, single-parent households often have more-limited resources of time, money, and energy. This shortage of resources may prompt them to encourage early autonomy among their adolescents. Also, ethnic minority parents are less well educated and engage in less joint decision making than White American parents. And ethnic minority adolescents are more likely to come from low-income families than White American adolescents are (McLoyd, 1997a). Although impoverished families often raise competent youth, poor parents may have a diminished capacity for supportive and involved parenting (McLoyd, 1990).

Some aspects of home life can help to protect ethnic minority youth from social patterns of injustice. The community and family can filter out destructive racist messages, parents can provide alternate frames of reference than those presented by the majority, and parents can also provide competent role models and encouragement. And the extended-family system in many ethnic minority families provides an important buffer to stress.

The extended-family system in African American and Mexican families is addressed in Sociocultural Worlds of Adolescence.

Gender and Parenting

What is the mother's role in the family? The father's role? How can mothers and fathers become cooperative, effective partners in parenting?

The Mother's Role

What do you think of when you hear the word *motherhood*? If you are like most people, you associate motherhood with a number of positive qualities, such as being warm, selfless, dutiful, and tolerant (Matlin, 1993). And while most women expect that motherhood will be happy and fulfilling, the reality is that motherhood has been accorded relatively low prestige in our society. When stacked up against money, power, and achievement, motherhood unfortunately doesn't fare too well and mothers rarely receive the appreciation they warrant. When children and adolescents don't succeed or they develop problems, our society has had a tendency to attribute the lack of success or the development of problems to a single source—mothers. One of psychology's most important lessons is that behavior is multiply determined. So it is with adolescent development—when development goes awry, mothers are not the single cause of the problems even though our society stereotypes them in this way.

The reality of motherhood in the 1990s is that while fathers have increased their child-rearing responsibilities somewhat, the main responsibility for children and adolescents still falls on the mother's shoulders (Brooks & Bronstein, 1996). In one recent study, adolescents said that their mothers were more involved in parenting then fathers in both the ninth and twelfth grades (Sputa & Paulson, 1995). Mothers do far more family work than fathers do—two to three times more (Thompson & Walker, 1989). A few "exceptional" men do as much family work as their wives; in one study the figure was 10 percent of the men (Berk, 1985). Not only do women do more family work than men, the family work most women do is unrelenting, repetitive, and routine, often involving cleaning, cooking, child care, shopping, laundry, and straightening up. The family work most men do is infrequent, irregular, and nonroutine, often involving household repairs, taking out the garbage, and yard work. Women report that they often have to do several tasks at once, which helps to explain why they find domestic work less relaxing and more stressful than men do.

Because family work is intertwined with love and embedded in family relations, it has complex and contradictory meanings. Most women feel that family tasks are mindless but essential. They usually enjoy tending to the needs of their loved ones and keeping the family going, even if they do not find the activities themselves enjoyable and fulfilling. Family work is both positive and

The Extended-Family System in African American and Mexican American Families

The African American cultural tradition of an extended-family household—in which one or several grandparents, uncles, aunts, siblings, or cousins either live together or provide support—has helped many African American parents cope with adverse social conditions, such as economic impoverishment (McAdoo, 1996; Taylor, 1997). The extended-family tradition can be traced to the African heritage of many African Americans, in which a newly married couple does not move away from relatives. Instead, the extended family assists its members with basic family functions. Researchers have found that the extended African American family helps to reduce the stress of poverty and single parenting through emotional support, the sharing of income and economic responsibility, and surrogate parenting (Wilson, 1989). The presence of grandmothers in the households of many African American adolescents and their infants has been an important support system both for the mothers and their infants (Stevens, 1984). In one recent study of African American families, mothers whose interactions with their own mothers were characterized by an open, flexible, and autonomous style were able to provide similarly appropriate parenting to their young children (Wakschlag, Chase-Lansdale, & Brooks-Gunn, 1996). In two investigations by Ronald Taylor (1994, 1996), kinship support in African American families was positively associated with the adolescent's self-reliance and negatively associated with problem behaviors. Also, in Taylor's most recent study (Taylor, 1996), kinship support was positively related to adolescents' grades in school.

Active and involved extended-family support systems also help parents of other ethnic groups cope with poverty and its related stress (Lomnitz, 1997). A basic value in Mexico is represented by the saying "As long as our family stays together, we are strong." Mexican children are brought up to stay close to their families, often playing with siblings rather than with schoolmates or neighborhood children, as American children usually do. Unlike the father in many American families, the Mexican father is the undisputed authority on all family matters and is usually obeyed without question. The mother is revered as the primary source of affection and care. This emphasis on family attachment leads the Mexican to say, "I will achieve mainly because of my family, and for my family, rather than myself." By contrast, the self-reliant American would say, "I will achieve mainly because of my ability and initiative and for myself rather than for my family." Unlike most Americans, families in Mexico tend to stretch out in a network of relatives that often runs to scores of individuals.

Both cultures—Mexican and American—have undergone considerable change in recent decades. Whether Mexican adolescents will gradually take on the characteristics of American adolescents, or whether American adolescents will shift closer to Mexican adolescents, is difficult to predict. The cultures of both countries will probably move to a new order more in keeping with future demands, retaining some common features of the old while establishing new priorities and values.

A 14-year-old adolescent, his 6-year-old sister, and their grandmother. The African American cultural tradition of an extended family household has helped many African American parents cope with adverse social conditions.

The family reunion of the Limon family in Austin, Texas. Mexican American children often grow up in families with a network of relatives that runs into scores of individuals.

What do you think the father's role in adolescent development should be? What role did your father play in your development?

negative for women. They are unsupervised and rarely criticized, they plan and control their own work, and they have only their own standards to meet. However, women's family work is often worrisome, tiresome, menial, repetitive, isolating, unfinished, inescapable, and often unappreciated. It is not surprising that men report that they are most satisfied with their marriage than women do.

In sum, the role of the mother brings with it benefits as well as limitations (Villani, 1997). Although motherhood is not enough to fill most women's entire lives, for most mothers, it is one of the most meaningful experiences in their lives (Hoffnung, 1984).

The Father's Role

The father's role has undergone major changes (Lamb, 1997; Mintz, 1997; Parke, 1995; Polina & Overby, 1996). During the colonial period in America, fathers were primarily responsible for moral teaching. Fathers provided guidance and values, especially through religion. With the Industrial Revolution, the father's role changed; he gained the responsibility as the breadwinner, a role that continued through the Great Depression. By the end of World War II, another role for fathers emerged, that of a gender-role model. Although being a breadwinner and moral guardian continued to be important father roles, attention shifted to his role as a male, especially for sons. Then, in the 1970s, the current interest in the father as an active, nurturant, caregiving parent emerged. Rather than being responsible only for the

discipline and control of older children and for providing the family's economic base, the father now is being evaluated in terms of his active, nurturant involvement with his children.

How actively involved are today's fathers with their children? Fathers in two-parent families typically spend about one-fourth to one-third as much time with young children as do mothers, although in the past decade fathers have slightly increased their participation (Biller, 1993). Having a father at home is no guarantee of meaningful paternal involvement with the child or adolescent. While some fathers are exceptionally committed parents, other fathers are virtual strangers to their children and youth even though they reside in the same household (Burton & Synder, 1997).

> *It is clear that most American children suffer too . . . little father.*
>
> —Gloria Steinem

Adolescents' social development can significantly benefit from interaction with a caring, accessible, and dependable father who fosters a sense of trust and confidence (Way, 1997). In one investigation, Frank Furstenberg and Kathleen Harris (1992) documented how nurturant fathering can overcome children's difficult life circumstances. In low-income African American families, children who reported close attachments and feelings of identification with their fathers during adolescence were twice as likely as young adults to have found a stable job or to have entered college, and were 75 percent less likely to have become unwed parents, 80 percent less likely to have been in jail, and 50 percent less likely to have developed depression. Unfortunately, however, only 10 percent of the economically disadvantaged children they studied experienced a stable, close relationship with their father during childhood and adolescence. In two other studies, college females and males reported better personal and social adjustment when they had grown up in a home with a nurturant, involved father rather than a negligent or rejecting father (Fish & Biller, 1973; Reuter & Biller, 1973). And in another recent study, fathers characterized by positive affect had adolescents who were less likely to be depressed (Duckett & Richards, 1996).

Partners in Parenting

Parents' cooperation, mutual respect, balanced communication, and attunement to each other's needs help the adolescent to develop positive attitudes toward both males and females (Biller, 1993). It is much easier for working parents to cope with changing family circumstances when the father and the mother equitably share child-rearing responsibilities. Mothers feel less stress and have more positive attitudes toward their husbands when their husbands are supportive partners. Researchers have found

that egalitarian marital relationships have positive effects on adolescent development, fostering their trust and encouraging communication (Yang & others, 1996).

SOCIAL POLICY AND FAMILIES

We have seen in this chapter that parents play very important roles in adolescent development. Although adolescents are moving toward independence, they are still connected with their families, which are far more important to them than is commonly believed. We know that competent adolescent development is most likely to happen when adolescents have parents who do the following (Small, 1990):

- Show them warmth and respect
- Demonstrate sustained interest in their lives
- Recognize and adapt to their changing cognitive and socioemotional development
- Communicate expectations for high standards of conduct and achievement
- Display authoritative, constructive ways of dealing with problems and conflict

However, compared to families with young children, families with adolescents have been neglected in community programs and public policies. The Carnegie Council on Adolescent Development (1995) recently identified some key opportunities for improving social policy regarding families with adolescents. These are some of the council's recommendations:

- School, cultural arts, religious, and youth organizations, and health-care agencies, should examine the extent to which they involve parents in activities with adolescents and should develop ways to engage parents and adolescents in activities they both enjoy.

- Professionals such as teachers, psychologists, nurses, physicians, youth specialists, and others who have contact with adolescents need to not only work with the individual adolescent but increase the time they spend interacting with the adolescent's family.
- Employers should extend to the parents of young adolescents the workplace policies now reserved only for the parents of young children. These policies include flexible work schedules, job sharing, telecommuting, and part-time work with benefits. This change in work/family policy would free parents to spend more time with their teenagers.
- Community institutions such as businesses, schools, and youth organizations should become more involved in providing after-school programs. After-school programs for elementary school children are increasing, but such programs for adolescents are rare. More high-quality, community-based programs for adolescents are needed in the after-school, weekend, and vacation time periods.
- Congress should consider extending the child-care tax credit to cover children in the early-adolescent time frame, about 10 to 14 years of age. Although such an extension raises complex issues, the value of such a policy change is clear: Families would benefit from placing their young adolescents in high-quality after-school programs.

At this point, we have discussed a number of ideas about sibling relationships, the changing family in a changing society, and social policy and families. A summary of these ideas is presented in concept table 6.2. In the next chapter we study the role of peers in adolescent development.

CONCEPT TABLE 6.2

Sibling Relationships, the Changing Family in a Changing Society, and Social Policy

Concept	Processes/ Related Ideas	Characteristics/Description
Sibling Relationships	Sibling roles and comparisons with other social agents	Sibling relationships often involve more conflict than relationships with other individuals. However, adolescents also share many positive moments with siblings through emotional support and social communication.
	Developmental changes	Although sibling conflict in adolescence is reasonably high, it is, nonetheless, often lower than in childhood.
	Birth order	Birth order has been of special interest, and differences between firstborns and later-borns have been reported. The only child often shows greater competence than the stereotype of the spoiled only child suggests. However, an increasing number of family researchers believe that the effects of birth order have been overdramatized and that other factors are more important in predicting the adolescent's behavior.
The Changing Family in a Changing Society	Divorce	Two main models of divorce effects have been proposed: the family structure model and the multiple-factor model. The family structure model is overly simplistic. The contemporary multiple-factor model takes into account the complexity of the divorce context, including conflict and postdivorce family functioning. Among the important factors in understanding the effects of divorce on adolescents are age and developmental changes, conflict, sex of the child, the nature of custody, and income.
	Stepfamilies	Just as divorce produces disequilibrium and stress for adolescents, so does remarriage. Over time, boys seem to improve more than girls in stepfather families. Adolescence is an especially difficult time for adjustment to the entrance of a stepparent. Children's relationships with biological parents are consistently better than with stepparents, and children's adjustment is adversely affected the more complex the stepfamily becomes. An authoritative environment at home and at school help children adjust to living in a divorced or stepparent family.
	Working parents	Overall, the mother's working outside the home does not have an adverse effect on the adolescent's development. Latchkey experiences do not have a uniformly negative influence on adolescent development. Parental monitoring and participation in structured activities with competent supervision are important influences on latchkey adolescents' adjustment. Relocation may have a more adverse effect on adolescents than children, but research on this issue is sparse. Unemployment of parents has a detrimental effect on adolescent development.
	Culture and ethnicity	Authoritative parenting is the most common child-rearing pattern around the world. Ethnic minority families differ from White American families in their size, structure, and composition, their reliance on kinship networks, and their levels of income and education.
	Gender and parenting	Most people associate motherhood with a number of positive images, but the reality is that motherhood is accorded a relatively low status in our society. Over time, the father's role in the child's and adolescent's development has evolved from moral teacher to breadwinner to gender-role model to nurturant caregiver. Fathers are much less involved in child rearing than mothers are. Father-mother cooperation and mutual respect help the adolescent to develop positive attitudes toward both males and females.
Social Policy and Families	Recommendations	Families with adolescents have been neglected in social policy. A number of recommendations were made to help parents provide more support for their adolescents.

Summary

Families continue to play a powerful socializing role in development during the adolescent years. A balanced emphasis on independence, connectedness, and moderate, rather than severe, conflict characterizes the contemporary view of family relationships during adolescence.

We began this chapter by studying the nature of family processes, including reciprocal socialization, synchrony, and the family as a system, the developmental construction of relationships, maturation of the adolescent and maturation of parents, sociocultural and historical changes, and the family life cycle. We also studied parenting techniques and parent-adolescent conflict, autonomy and attachment in adolescence, and sibling relationships, including sibling roles and comparisons with other social agents, developmental changes in sibling relationships, and birth order. We learned about the changing family in a changing society, focusing on the effects of divorce, stepfamilies, working parents, culture and ethnicity, and gender and parenting. And we examined the nature of social policy and families.

Don't forget that you can obtain an overall summary of the chapter by again studying the two concept tables on pages 190 and 201. Earlier in this chapter we found that adolescents' family and peer worlds are more connected than once was believed. In the next chapter, we explore in greater detail the fascinating world of adolescent peer relations as we continue our coverage of the social contexts of adolescent development.

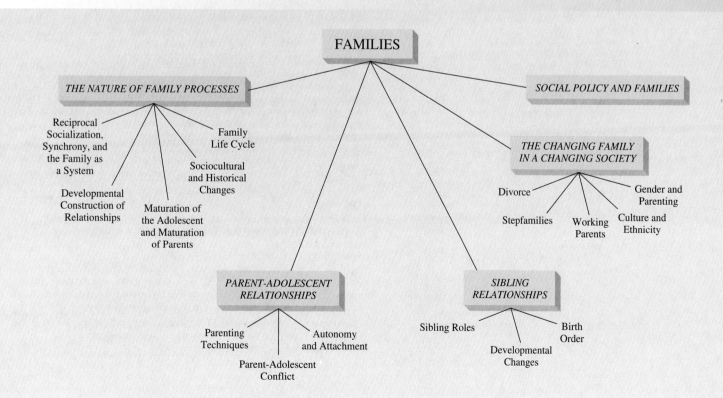

PRACTICAL KNOWLEDGE ABOUT ADOLESCENCE

How to Deal with Your Parents

(1991) by Lynn Osterkamp.
New York: Berkley Books.

This book was written for adult children who want to understand and improve their relationships with their parents. Author Lynn Osterkamp is a nationally recognized expert on family conflict and communication. She helps young adults answer such important questions as these:

Why are so many grown-up people still worrying about what their parents think?

Why can't you talk to them the way you talk to other people?

Why do you keep having the same arguments?

How can you stop feeling guilty?

How can you change family gatherings, holidays?

How can you stay out of their relationship and keep them out of yours?

What role would you like for your parents to play in your life today?

How can you make lasting changes?

The book is filled with personal accounts and gives young adults, as well as middle-aged adults, specific strategies for improving communication and resolving conflict with their parents.

Between Parent & Teenager

(1969) by Haim Ginott.
New York: Avon.

Despite the fact that *Between Parent & Teenager* is well past its own adolescence (it was published in 1969), it continues to be one of the most widely read and recommended books for parents who want to communicate more effectively with their teenagers. Author Haim Ginott was a clinical psychologist at Columbia University who died in 1973. Ginott describes a number of commonsense solutions and strategies. For Ginott, parents' greatest challenge in the teenage years is to let go when they want to hold on. Only by letting go can a peaceful and meaningful co-existence be reached between parents and teenagers, he says. Throughout the book, Ginott connects with parents through catchy phrases such as "Don't collect thorns" (which instructs parents that when they see imperfections in themselves, they often expect perfection on the part of their teenagers) and "Don't step on corns" (which educates parents that adolescents have many imperfections about which they are very sensitive, ranging from zits to dimples). Teenagers don't need parents to remind them of these imperfections.

This book is very entertaining reading and is full of insightful interchanges between parents and teenagers. Ginott's strategies can make the world of parents and adolescents a kinder, gentler world.

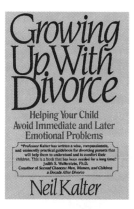

Growing Up with Divorce

(1990) by Neil Kalter.
New York: Free Press.

Growing Up With Divorce is written for divorced parents and provides them with information to help their children and youth avoid emotional problems. Neil Kalter is a highly respected child clinical psychologist who is director of the Center for the Child and Family at the University of Michigan. Kalter offers practical strategies for parents to help their children and adolescents cope with the anxiety, anger, and confusion that can appear immediately after the separation or divorce or may develop after a number of years. Separate problems and concerns of children and adolescents of different ages and sexes at each stage of divorce are portrayed. Divorce expert Robert Weiss praised the book and said that parents in any divorced circumstance can benefit from the book, and well-known authority on divorce Judith Wallerstein advises divorced parents that Kalter's book is a treasure of valuable advise for comforting their children and adolescents.

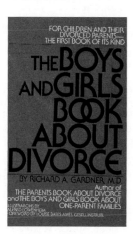

The Boys and Girls Book About Divorce

(1983) by Richard Gardner.
Northvale, NJ: Jason Aronson.

The Boys and Girls Book About Divorce is written for older children and adolescents to help them cope with their parents' separation and divorce. Author Richard Gardner is a highly respected child psychiatrist who is on the faculty of Columbia University College of Physicians and Surgeons. Most of what Gardner tells youth comes from his therapy experiences with divorced families. He talks directly to adolescents about their feelings after the divorce, who is and is not to blame for the divorce, parents' love for their children, how to handle their angry feelings, and their fear of being left alone and abandoned. Then he tells adolescents how to get along better with their divorced mother and father, as well as how to deal with many other challenging and emotional circumstances the adolescents are likely to face.

The Boys and Girls Book About Divorce is an excellent book and is more appropriate for children and adolescents 10 to 12 years of age or older.

Raising Black Children

(1992) by James P. Comer and Alvin E. Poussaint.
New York: Plume.

Raising Black Children is written by two of the most highly respected experts on African American children and youth—James Comer and Alvin Poussaint, professors of psychiatry at Yale and Harvard, respectively. Comer and Poussaint argue that African American parents face additional difficulties in raising emotionally healthy African American children and youth because of race and income problems. Comer and Poussaint's guide contains almost a thousand child-rearing questions they have repeatedly heard from African American parents across the income spectrum. The issues on which they give advice to parents include how to improve the African American child's self-esteem and identity, how to confront racism, how to teach their children and adolescents to handle anger, conflict, and frustration, and how to deal with the mainstream culture and retain an African American identity. This is an excellent book for African American parents that includes wise suggestions that are not in most child-rearing books (almost all others are written for White parents and do not deal with special problems faced by ethnic minority parents or parents from low-income backgrounds).

Santrock: Adolescence

Big Brothers/Big Sisters of America
17 South 17th Street, Suite 1200
Philadelphia, PA 19103
215-567-2748

Single mothers and single fathers who are having problems with a son or daughter may want to get a responsible adult to spend at least one afternoon every other week with the son or daughter. Big Brothers and Big Sisters are available to talk with the adolescent about problems and engage in enjoyable activities with the youth. The national organization will help you get in contact with the local Big Brothers/Big Sisters branch.

Big Brothers and Sisters of Canada/Grands Frères et Grandes Soeurs du Canada
5230 South Service Road
Burlington, Ontario L7L 5K2
905-639-0461

The mission of Big Brothers and Sisters is to foster and stimulate the development of relationships between adult volunteers and children.

Fatherhood Project
c/o Bank Street College of Education
610 West 12th Street
New York, NY 10025
212-222-6700

This project functions as a national clearinghouse that provides information on father-participation programs; its goal is to increase the nurturant role of fathers in children's and adolescents' development.

***Living with 10- to 15-Year-Olds: A Parent Education Curriculum* (1992)**
Center for Early Adolescence
University of North Carolina
D-2 Carr Mill Town Center
Carrboro, NC 27510
919-966-1148

This parent-education curriculum is appropriate for use by schools, community groups, religious groups, and other organizations that provide families with guidance. In-depth information about the following topics is provided:

- Understanding early adolescence
- Communicating with young adolescents
- Risk-taking behavior and young adolescents
- Talking about sexuality

Phone Friend

This program is designed for children and adolescents whose parents are not home in the after-school hours. Phone Friend connects adolescents with an adult they can talk with in the after-school hours if problems arise. Phone Friend has more than four hundred chapters in the United States.

Missing Children's Network Canada/Le Réseau Enfants
Retour Canada
231 Saint-Jacques Street West, Suite 406
Montréal, Quebec N2Y 1M6
514-843-4333

The Network's mission is to assist in the search for missing children and to educate the public to prevent more children from becoming victims of aggression and exploitation.

Runaway Hotline
Nationwide: 800-392-3352
In Texas: 800-231-6946

This is a toll-free, 24-hour-a-day hotline for children or adolescents who are separated from parents or guardians for whatever reason. It allows children and adolescents anywhere in the United States to find shelter, food, medical help, and counseling in the area from which the individual is calling.

Stepfamily Association of America
602 East Joppa Road
Baltimore, MD 21204
410-823-7570

This organization provides a support network for step-parents, remarried parents, and their children. It has local chapters across the United States and published materials on stepfamilies.

***Who to Call: The Parent's Source Book* (1992)**
by Daniel Starer
New York: William Morrow

This extensive resource guide provides a wide array of phone numbers and contacts for parents. Among the topics covered are adolescence, education, addiction, sports, special-needs children and youth, camps, and dozens of diseases.

Youth in Single-Parent Families
by Peter Bensen and Eugene Roehlkepartain
Minneapolis: Search Institute.

This report includes recommendations for strategies that can strengthen one-parent families.

EXPLORING ADOLESCENT DEVELOPMENT

To further explore adolescent development, we will examine a research study on ecological factors in the development of African American adolescents and evaluate support programs for families with adolescents.

RESEARCH ON ADOLESCENT DEVELOPMENT

Ecological Factors in African American Adolescents' Problem Behaviors

Featured Study

Mason, C. A., Cauce, A. R., Gonzales, N., Hiraga, Y., & Grove, K. (1994). An ecological model of externalizing behaviors in African-American adolescents: No family is an island. *Journal of Research on Adolescence, 4,* 639–655.

In this study, a two-step ecological model was used to predict externalizing behavior among African American seventh- and eighth-graders. It was predicted that the exosystem (in Bronfenbrenner's terms, the environmental contexts that adolescents do not themselves participate in but that nonetheless can influence their development) variables of parental work environment and parental social support would have an impact on the adolescent's development by influencing the microsystem (Bronfenbrenner's term for contexts in which the adolescent directly interacts with other social agents) variables of parental warmth, parental use of restrictive control, and conflict within the family.

Method

The subjects were 144 seventh- and eighth-grade African American girls and boys, as well as at least one parent or parental figure of each child. Both the adolescent and one or both parents were interviewed and filled out questionnaires. The parent measures included (1) the Job Autonomy Scale, which measures the degree of autonomy experienced at work—a sample item is "Can you do your job your own way?"; (2) the Social Support Questionnaire, which assesses the social support parents receive; (3) the Child Rearing Practices Report, which measures warmth and restrictive control; and (4) a conflict scale, which taps parent-adolescent conflict. Both the parent(s) and the adolescent filled out the Neighborhood Environment Scale, which assesses the level of neighborhood crime and problem behavior. Items include such areas as gang activity and vandalism. The parents also were given the Child Behavior Checklist, which assesses their perception of the adolescent's externalized problem behaviors, such as acting-out behavior, delinquency, and other undercontrolled behav-iors. The adolescents were given the Behavioral Competence Subscale of the widely used Self-Perception Profile for Adolescents.

Results and Discussion

The study provided support for the two-step ecological model: Work environment and social network ecosystem factors influenced the parents' perceptions of the family microsystem, which in turn affected adolescent problem behavior. These are examples of the pathways that occurred: (1) a two-step pathway from feeling overcontrolled as a worker to reporting overcontrol as a parent or having an undercontrolled adolescent, and (2) a two-step pathway beginning with dissatisfaction (at work or with one's social network), filtering through family conflict, and culminating with the adolescent's externalized problem behaviors. Parent and adolescent reports of the neighborhood environment were not related to microsystem factors, but they did directly affect adolescent development—the worse the neighborhood, the more externalized behavior problems the adolescent showed.

Support Programs for Families with Adolescents

Controversy swirls about how to help parents more effectively rear their adolescents. The Family Support Act was passed in 1988, linking family welfare payments to job training or work obligations and strengthening child-support enforcement strategies, so that families would ultimately become economically independent.

Family policies can be divided into those that help parents in their "breadwinning" roles and those that concentrate on their nurturing and caregiving roles. Breadwinning family policy supports the family as a viable economic unit, usually by ensuring a specified minimal level of income. Nurturing and caregiving family policy focuses on the inner life of the family by promoting positive family functioning and the development and well-being of individual family members.

The family policies of the United States are overwhelmingly treatment oriented; only those families and individuals who already have problems are eligible. Few preventive programs are available on a widespread basis. For example, families on the verge of having their youth placed in foster care are eligible, and often required, to have counseling; families in which problems are brewing, but not yet full-blown, usually can't qualify for public services. Most experts on family policy believe more attention should be given to preventing family problems.

Preventive programs for families with adolescents need to be more comprehensive in the services and information they provide, establish more opportunities for parents to receive support from other parents, and be maintained over a longer period of time. Too few prevention programs have been targeted for improving the family management of ethnic minority parents (Small, 1990).

One program that bears further attention is the Children's Aid Society in New York City (Simons, Finlay, & Yang, 1991). The Children's Aid Society has three youth development centers that serve Harlem's mostly African American and Latino communities. The adolescents are mainly from single-parent households supported by some form of public assistance. They usually get their medical care from emergency rooms because they do not have health insurance.

In fifteen 2-hour discussions, family life and sex-education courses cover pregnancy prevention, gender roles, social roles, and intimacy for adolescents. The adolescents' parents also participate in a course about how to talk to adolescents about sex and how to prevent child abuse. Adolescents also participate in a sports program that emphasizes discipline and self-control. A theater program of weekly workshops with actors and actresses from Harlem's National Black Theater is also part of the Children's Aid Society program. The workshops address motivation and appropriate self-expression by examining such questions as "How do you express anger?" and "How can you ask a question in class?" Career awareness and job preparation classes are available through the Job Club.

Funding for the program comes from the New York State Department of Social Services, foundations, corporations, and individuals. The cost per person is about $1,750, and the program serves more than three hundred adolescents and one hundred parents.

Chapter 7

Peers

*A man's growth is seen in the successive
choirs of his friends.*

—Ralph Waldo Emerson, 1841

IMAGES OF ADOLESCENCE

Adolescents and Their Peers

PREVIEW

When you think back to your adolescent years, many of your most enjoyable moments were spent with peers—on the telephone, at school activities, in the neighborhood, on dates, at dances, or just fooling around. The nature of peer relationships undergoes important changes during adolescence. In childhood, the focus of peer relations is often on being liked by classmates and being included in playground games or lunchroom conversations. Being overlooked or, worse yet, being disliked and rejected by classmates, can have damaging effects on children's psychological development that are sometimes carried forward to adolescence. Beginning in early adolescence, teenagers typically prefer to have a smaller number of friendships that are more intense and intimate than those of younger children. Cliques, or crowds, usually take on more important roles in adolescence, as adolescents begin to "hang out" together. A special concern involves increased social policy initiatives involving peers and youth organizations. At some point in adolescence, individuals usually become interested in dating and romantic relationships. In this chapter, we will examine such fascinating aspects of the society of peers, a society that involves peer relations, friendships, peer groups, and dating.

Peer relations play powerful roles in the lives of adolescents. Consider the circumstances of the following adolescents:

- Angela, age 13, has just moved to a new city with her parents. As she walks into her new middle school for the first time, she says to herself, "What are they going to think about me? Are they going to like me? Am I going to fit in here? How should I act?"

- Robert, age 14, has been best friends with Michael, also 14, for 2 years now. They live near each other, attend the same middle school, play basketball together after school, take most of their classes together, and share some secrets.

- Al, age 16, is a member of a clique at his high school known as the "bad riders." He drives his motorcycle to school, wears a black leather jacket and jeans every day, smokes, drinks, and hangs out with his motorcycle buddies. He and his friends describe their group as the "baddest" in town. "Don't nobody want to mess with us," Al proudly says.

- Louise, age 15, is a loner. She is shy and has always felt uncomfortable in social situations. She does reasonably well in her classes, but she wishes she had more friends and were included more in activities and groups.

These are but a few examples of how much importance adolescents attach to peer relations, friendships, and being part of the group. Think back to your own adolescence for a moment—to the time when you were in middle or junior high school. How important was it for you to be liked by your peers? to be included in the clique you thought was the best? Who were your best friends? How important were they to you? Did you have one or two best friends throughout adolescence, or did you change friends from time to time? Did your parents ever try to get you to change who you hung out with? Did your friends or members of your clique ever cause you to get into trouble? How similar were you to your friends? Were you about the same age? Did you share the same interests? As you aged from a young adolescent in middle school to an older adolescent in high school, did your peer relations, friendships, and cliques change? Thinking for a few moments about these questions pertaining to your own adolescence should provide a context for better understanding the worlds of adolescent peers that we are about to discuss.

THE NATURE OF PEER RELATIONS

What are the peer group's functions? How extensively do adolescents conform to their peers? What is the nature of peer popularity, neglect, and rejection? What is the role of social knowledge and social information processing in peer relations? What strategies do developmentalists use to improve the social skills of adolescents who are having difficulty in peer relations? We consider each of these questions in turn.

Peer Group Functions

To many adolescents, how they are seen by peers is the most important aspect of their lives. Some adolescents will go along with anything, just to be included as a member of the group. To them, being excluded means stress, frustration, and sadness. Contrast Bob, who has no close friends, with Steve, who has three close buddies he pals around with all of the time. Sally was turned down by the club at school that she was working for 6 months to get into, in contrast to Sandra, who is a member of the club and who frequently is told by her peers how "super" her personality is.

Some friends of mine have a 13-year-old daughter. Last year, she had a number of girlfriends—she spent a lot of time on the phone talking with them, and they frequently visited each other's homes. Then her family moved, and this 13-year-old girl had to attend a school with a lower socioeconomic mix of students than at her previous school. Many of the girls at the new school feel that my friend's daughter is "too good" for them, and because of this she is having difficulty making friends this year. One of her most frequent complaints is, "I don't have any friends. . . . None of the kids at school ever call me. And none of them ever ask me over to their houses. What can I do?"

Peers *are children or adolescents who are of about the same age or maturity level.* Same-age peer interaction serves a unique role in U.S. culture (Hartup, 1983). Age grading would occur even if schools were not age graded and adolescents were left alone to determine the composition of their own societies. After all, one can learn to be a good fighter only among age-mates: The bigger guys will kill you, and the little ones are no challenge. One of the most important functions of the peer group is to provide a source of information about the world outside the family. From the peer group, adolescents receive feedback about their abilities. Adolescents learn whether what they do is better than, as good as, or worse than what other adolescents do. Learning this at home is difficult because siblings are usually older or younger.

Children spend an increasing amount of time in peer interaction during middle and late childhood and adolescence. In one investigation, children interacted with peers 10 percent of their day at age 2, 20 percent at

age 4, and more than 40 percent between the ages of 7 and 11 (Barker & Wright, 1951). In a typical school day, there were 299 episodes with peers per day. By adolescence, peer relations occupy large chunks of an individual's life. In one investigation, over the course of one weekend, young adolescent boys and girls spent more than twice as much time with peers as with parents (Condry, Simon, & Bronfenbrenner, 1968).

What do adolescents do when they are with their peers? In one study, sixth-graders were asked what they do when they are with their friends (Medrich & others, 1982). Team sports accounted for 45 percent of boys' activities but only 26 percent of girls'. General play, going places, and socializing were common listings for both sexes. Most peer interactions occur outside the home (although close to home), occur more often in private than public places, and occur more between children of the same sex than of the opposite sex.

Are peers necessary for development? When peer monkeys who have been reared together are separated from one another, they become depressed and less advanced socially (Suomi, Harlow, & Domek, 1970). The human development literature contains a classic example of the importance of peers in social development. Anna Freud (Freud & Dann, 1951) studied six children from different families who banded together after their parents were killed in World War II. Intensive peer attachment was observed; the children were a tightly knit group, dependent on one another and aloof with outsiders. Even though deprived of parental care, they became neither delinquent nor psychotic.

Good peer relations may be necessary for normal social development in adolescence. Social isolation, or the inability to "plug in" to a social network, is linked with many different forms of problems and disorders, ranging from delinquency and problem drinking to depression (Hops & others, 1997; Kupersmidt & Coie, 1990). In one recent study of adolescents, positive peer relationships were associated with positive social adjustment (Ryan & Patrick, 1996). Peer relations in childhood and adolescence are also related to later development. In one study, poor peer relations in childhood were associated with dropping out of school and delinquency in late adolescence (Roff, Sells, & Golden, 1972). In another study, harmonious peer relations during adolescence were linked with positive mental health at midlife (Hightower, 1990).

As you might have detected from our discussion of peer relations thus far, peer influences can be both positive and negative (Rubin, Bukowski & Parker, 1997). Both Jean Piaget (1932) and Harry Stack Sullivan (1953) were influential theorists who stressed that it is through peer interaction that children and adolescents learn the symmetrical reciprocity mode of relationships discussed in chapter 6. Children explore the principles of fairness and justice by working through disagreements with peers. They also learn to be keen observers of peers' interests

Parent-Peer Linkages in Your Adolescence

Think back to your middle school/junior high and high school years. What was your relationship with your parents like? Were you securely attached or insecurely attached to them? How do you think your relationship with your parents affected your friendship and peer re-lations in adolescence? Later in the chapter we will discuss dating and romantic relationships. As a preview to that material, consider this question: Do you think that observing your parents' marital lives and interacting with your parents while you were growing up have influenced your dating and romantic relationships? If so, how? By exploring links between your experiences with your parents and your adolescent dating experiences, you are learning to think critically by *creating arguments based on developmental concepts*.

and perspectives in order to smoothly integrate themselves into ongoing peer activities. In addition, Sullivan argued that adolescents learn to be skilled and sensitive partners in intimate relationships by forging close friendships with selected peers. These intimacy skills are carried forward to help form the foundation of later dating and marital relationships, according to Sullivan.

By contrast, some theorists have emphasized the negative influences of peers on children's and adolescents' development. Being rejected or overlooked by peers leads some adolescents to feel lonely or hostile. Further, such rejection and neglect by peers are related to an individual's subsequent mental health and criminal problems. Some theorists have also described the adolescent peer culture as a corrupt influence that undermines parental values and control. Further, peers can introduce adolescents to alcohol, drugs, delinquency, and other forms of behavior that adults view as maladaptive.

Family-Peer Linkages

For many years, parents and peers were thought of as disparate, if not oppositional, forces in the adolescent's development. Adolescents do show a strong motivation to be with their peers and become independent. However, it is incorrect to assume that movement toward peer involvement and autonomy are unrelated to parent-adolescent relationships. Recent studies have provided persuasive evidence that adolescents live in a connected world with parents and peers, not a disconnected one (Ladd & Sieur, 1995; Mounts, 1997; Smith & Crockett, 1997).

What are some of the ways the worlds of parents and peers are connected? Parents' choices of neighborhoods, churches, schools, and their own friends influence the pool from which their adolescents select possible friends (Cooper & Ayers-Lopez, 1985). For example, parents can choose to live in a neighborhood with playgrounds, parks, and youth organizations or in a neighborhood where houses are far apart, few adolescents live, and youth organizations are not well developed.

Parents may model or coach their adolescents in ways of relating to peers. In one study, parents acknowledged that they recommended specific strategies to their adolescents to help them develop more positive peer relations (Rubin & Sloman, 1984). For example, parents discussed with their adolescents ways that disputes could be mediated and how to become less shy. They also encouraged them to be tolerant and to resist peer pressure. And in one study, young adolescents talked more frequently about peer-related problems with their mothers than with their fathers (Gauze, 1994).

In addition, as we discussed in chapter 6, an increasing number of researchers have found that secure attachment to parents is related to the adolescent's positive peer relations. In one study, adolescents who were securely attached to parents were also securely attached to their peers; adolescents who were insecurely attached to their parents were likewise insecurely attached to their peers (Armsden & Greenberg, 1984). And in another study, older adolescents who had an ambivalent attachment history with their parents reported less satisfaction in their relationship with their best friend than did their securely attached counterparts (Fisher, 1990).

As can be seen, there is much more connectedness between the family and peer worlds of adolescents than once was believed. Throughout adolescence, the worlds of parents and peers work in coordinated ways to influence the adolescent's development.

Peer Conformity

Conformity comes in many forms and affects many aspects of adolescents' lives. Do adolescents take up jogging because everyone else is doing it? Do adolescents let their hair grow long one year and cut it short the next because of fashion? Do adolescents take cocaine if pressured by others, or do they resist the pressure? **Conformity** *occurs when individuals adopt the attitudes or behavior of others because of real or imagined pressure from them.* The pressure to conform to peers becomes very strong during the adolescent years. Consider the comments of Kevin, an eighth grader:

> I feel a lot of pressure from my friends to smoke and steal and things like that. My parents do not allow me to smoke, but my best friends are really pushing me to do it. They call me a pansy and a momma's boy if I don't. I really don't like the idea of smoking, but my good friend Steve told me in front of some of our friends, "Kevin, you are an idiot and a chicken wrapped up in one little body." I couldn't stand it any more, so I smoked with them. I was coughing and humped over, but I still said, "This is really fun—yeah, I like it." I felt like I was part of the group.

Also, think about the statement by 14-year-old Andrea:

> Peer pressure is extremely influential in my life. I have never had very many friends, and I spend quite a bit of time alone. The friends I have are older. . . . The closest friend I have had is a lot like me in that we are both sad and depressed a lot. I began to act even more depressed than before when I was with her. I would call her up and try to act even more depressed than I was because that is what I thought she liked. In that relationship, I felt pressure to be like her.

Each of you, individually, walkest with the tread of a fox, but collectively ye are geese.

—Solon, Ancient Greece

Conformity to peer pressure in adolescence can be positive or negative. Teenagers engage in all sorts of negative conformity behavior—use seedy language, steal, vandalize, and make fun of parents and teachers. However, a great deal of peer conformity is not negative and consists of the desire to be involved in the peer world, such as dressing like friends and wanting to spend huge chunks of time with members of a clique. Such circumstances may involve prosocial activities as well, as when clubs raise money for worthy causes.

In a study focused on negative, neutral, and positive aspects of peer conformity, Thomas Berndt (1979) studied 273 third-grade through twelfth-grade students. Hypothetical dilemmas that were presented to the students required the students to make choices about conformity with friends on prosocial and antisocial behavior and about conformity with parents on neutral and prosocial behaviors. For example, one prosocial item questioned whether students relied on their parents' advice in such situations as deciding about helping at the library or instructing another child to swim. An antisocial question asked a boy what he would do if one of his peers wanted him to help steal some candy. A neutral question asked a girl if she would follow peer suggestions to engage in an activity she wasn't interested in—such as going to a movie she did not want to see.

Some interesting developmental patterns were found in this investigation. In the third grade, parent and peer influences often directly contradicted each other. Since parent conformity is much greater for third-grade children, children of this age are probably still closely tied to and dependent on their parents. However, by the sixth grade, parent and peer influences were found to be no longer in direct opposition. Peer conformity had increased, but parent and peer influences were operating in different situations—parents had more impact in some situations, while peers had more clout in others.

By the ninth grade, parent and peer influences were once again in strong opposition to each other, probably because the conformity of adolescents to the social behavior of peers is much stronger at this grade level than at any other. At this time, adolescent adoption of anti-social standards endorsed by the peer group inevitably leads to conflict between adolescents and parents. Researchers have also found that the adolescent's attempt to gain independence meets with more parental opposition around the ninth grade than at any other time (Douvan & Adelson, 1966).

A stereotypical view of parent-child relationships suggests that parent-peer opposition continues into the late high school and college-age years. But Berndt (1979) found that adolescent conformity to antisocial, peer-endorsed behavior decreases in the late high school years, and agreement between parents and peers begins to increase in some areas. In addition, by the eleventh and twelfth grades, students show signs of developing a decision-making style more independent of peer and parental influence. Figure 7.1 summarizes the peer

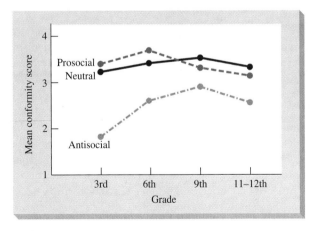

Figure~7.1

Mean Scores for Peer Conformity on Different Types of Behavior.
Higher scores indicate greater conformity: The neutral point is 3.5. Notice that the most dramatic changes occurred for conformity to antisocial peer standards, which peaked in the ninth grade.

Most adolescents conform to the mainstream standards of their peers. However, the rebellious or anticonformist adolescent reacts counter to the mainstream peer group's expectations, deliberately moving away from the actions or beliefs this group advocates.

conformity to antisocial, neutral, and prosocial standards found in Berndt's (1979) study. One study revealed support for Berndt's findings that susceptibility to peer pressure increases in early adolescence (Leventhal, 1994).

While most adolescents conform to peer pressure and societal standards, some adolescents are nonconformist or anticonformist. **Nonconformity** *occurs when individuals know what people around them expect but do not use those expectations to guide their behavior.* Nonconformists are independent, as when a high school student chooses to not be a member of a clique. **Anticonformity** *occurs when individuals react counter to a group's expectations and deliberately move away from the actions or beliefs the group advocates.* Two contemporary versions of anticonformist teenagers are "skinheads" and "punks."

In sum, peer pressure is a pervasive theme of adolescents' lives. Its power can be observed in almost every dimension of adolescents' behavior—their choice of dress, music, language, values, leisure activities, and so on. Parents, teachers, and other adults can help adolescents to deal with peer pressure (Clasen & Brown, 1987). Adolescents need many opportunities to talk with both peers and adults about their social worlds and the pressures involved. The developmental changes of adolescence often bring forth a sense of insecurity. Young adolescents may be especially vulnerable because of this insecurity and the many developmental changes taking place in their lives. To counter this stress, young adolescents need to experience opportunities for success, both in and out of school, that increase their sense of being in control. Adolescents can learn that their social world is reciprocally controlled. Others may try to control them, but they can exert personal control over their actions and influence others in turn. Next, in our discussion of peer popularity, neglect, and rejection, we discuss further the powerful role that peer relations plays in adolescent development.

Teenagers are people who express a burning desire to be different by dressing exactly alike.

—**Anonymous**

Peer Statuses

Every adolescent wants to be popular—you probably thought about popularity a lot when you were in junior and senior high school. Teenagers commonly think, "What can I do to have all of the kids at school like me?" "How can I be popular with both girls and guys?" "What's wrong with me? There must be something wrong, or I would be more popular." Sometimes, adolescents go to great lengths to be popular; and in some cases, parents go to even greater lengths to try to insulate their adolescents from rejection and to increase the likelihood that they will be popular. Students show off and cut up because it gets attention and makes their peers laugh. Parents set up elaborate parties, buy cars and clothes for their teens, and drive adolescents and their friends all over in the hope that their sons or daughters will be popular.

Popular children *are frequently nominated as a best friend and rarely are disliked by their peers.* Researchers have discovered that popular children and adolescents give out reinforcements, listen carefully, maintain open lines of communication with peers, are happy, act like themselves, show enthusiasm and concern for others, and are self-confident without being conceited (Hartup, 1983). In one study, popular youth were more likely than unpopular youth to communicate clearly with their peers, elicit their peers' attention, and maintain conversation with peers (Kennedy, 1990).

Certain physical and cultural factors also affect adolescents' popularity. Adolescents who are physically attractive are more popular than those who are not (Kennedy, 1990) and, contrary to what some believe, brighter adolescents are more popular than less intelligent ones. Adolescents growing up in middle-class surroundings tend to be more popular than those growing up in lower-class surroundings, presumably in part because they are more in control of establishing standards for popularity (Hollingshead, 1975). But remember that findings such as these reflect group averages—there are many physically attractive teenagers who are unpopular, and some physically unattractive ones who are very well liked. Sociologist James Coleman (1980) points out that, for adolescents in the average range, there is little or no relation between physical attractiveness and popularity. It is only in the extremes (very attractive and very unattractive) that a link between popularity and attractiveness holds.

Developmentalists distinguish three types of children who have a different status than popular children: Those who are (1) neglected, (2) rejected, or (3) controversial (Wentzel & Asher, 1995). **Neglected children** are infrequently nominated as a best friend but are not disliked by their peers. **Rejected children** are infrequently nominated as someone's best friend and are actively disliked by their peers. **Controversial children** are frequently nominated both as someone's best friend and as being disliked.

Rejected children and adolescents often have more serious adjustment problems later in life than those who are neglected (Dishion & Spracklen, 1996). For example, in one study, 112 fifth-grade boys were evaluated over a period of 7 years until the end of high school (Kupersmidt & Coie, 1990). The key factor in predicting whether rejected children would engage in delinquent behavior or drop out of school later during adolescence was their aggression toward peers in elementary school.

Not all rejected children and adolescents are aggressive. Although aggression and its related characteristics of impulsiveness and disruptiveness underlie rejection about half the time, approximately 10 to 20 percent of rejected children and adolescents are shy (Cillessen & others, 1992).

How can neglected children and adolescents be trained to interact more effectively with their peers? The goal of training programs with neglected children and adolescents is often to help them attract attention from their peers in positive ways and to hold their attention by asking questions, by listening in a warm and friendly way, and by saying things about themselves that relate to the peers' interests. They also are taught to enter groups more effectively.

The goal of training programs with rejected children and adolescents is often to help them listen to peers and "hear what they say" instead of trying to dominate peer interactions. Rejected children and adolescents are trained to join peers without trying to change what is taking place in the peer group.

One issue that has been raised about improving the peer relations of rejected children and adolescents is whether the focus should be on improving their prosocial skills (better empathy, careful listening, improved communication skills, and so on) or on reducing their aggressive, disruptive behavior and improving their self-control (Coie & Koeppl, 1990). In one study, socially rejected young adolescents were coached on the importance of showing behaviors that would improve their chance of being liked by others (Murphy & Schneider, 1994). The intervention was successful in improving the friendships of the socially rejected youth.

Improving the prosocial skills of rejected adolescents, though, does not automatically eliminate their aggressive or disruptive behavior. Aggression often leads to reinforcement because peers give in to aggressive youths' demands. Thus, in addition to teaching better prosocial skills to rejected adolescents, direct steps must also be taken to eliminate their aggressive actions. Further, acquiring positive status with peers may take time to achieve because it is hard for peers to change their opinions if adolescents frequently engage in aggressive conduct (Coie & Dodge, 1997).

The controversial peer status had not been studied until recently. In one study, girls who had controversial peer status in the fourth grade were more likely to become adolescent mothers than were girls of other peer statuses (Underwood, Kupersmidt, & Coie, 1996). Also, aggressive girls had more children than nonaggressive girls did.

Next, we will turn our attention to the role of social cognition in understanding peer relations. Part of this discussion further considers ideas about reducing the aggression of children and adolescents in their peer encounters.

Social Cognition

Recall from our discussion of intelligence in chapter 5 that a distinction can be made between knowledge and process. In studying cognitive aspects of peer relations, the same distinction can be made. Learning about the social knowledge adolescents bring with them to peer relations is important, as is studying how adolescents process information during peer interaction.

As children move into adolescence, they acquire more social knowledge, and there is considerable individual variation in how much one adolescent knows about what it takes to make friends, to get peers to like him or her, and so forth. For example, does the adolescent know that giving out reinforcements will increase the likelihood that he or she will be popular? That is, does Mary consciously know that, by telling Barbara such things as "I really like that sweater you have on today" and "Gosh, you sure are popular with the guys," she will enhance the likelihood Barbara will want her to be her friend? Does the adolescent know that, when others perceive that he or she is similar to them, he or

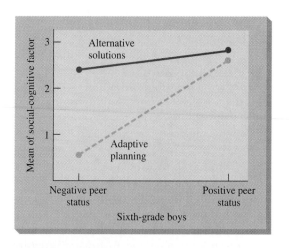

Figure~7.2

Generation of Alternative Solutions and Adaptive Planning by Negative- and Positive-Peer-Status Boys.
Notice that negative-peer-status boys were less likely to generate alternative solutions and plan ahead than were their positive-peer-status counterparts.

she will be liked better by the others? Does the adolescent know that friendship involves sharing intimate conversations and that a friendship likely is improved when the adolescent shares private, confidential information with another adolescent? To what extent does the adolescent know that comforting and listening skills will improve friendship relations? To what extent does the adolescent know what it takes to become a leader? Think back to your adolescent years. How sophisticated were you in knowing about such social matters? Were you aware of the role of nice statements and perceived similarity in determining popularity and friendship? While you may not have been aware of these factors, those of you who were popular and maintained close friendships likely were competent at using these strategies.

From a social cognitive perspective, children and adolescents may have difficulty in peer relations because they lack appropriate social cognitive skills (Dodge,

1993). One investigation explored the possibility that social cognitive skill deficits characterize children who have peer-related difficulties (Asarnow & Callan, 1985). Boys with and without peer adjustment difficulties were identified, and then a number of social cognitive processes or skills were assessed. These included the boys' ability to generate alternative solutions to hypothetical problems, to evaluate these solutions in terms of their effectiveness, to describe self-statements, and to rate the likelihood of self-statements. It was found that boys without peer adjustment problems generated more alternative solutions, proposed more assertive and mature solutions, gave less intense aggressive solutions, showed more adaptive planning, and evaluated physically aggressive responses less positively than the boys with peer adjustment problems. For example, as shown in figure 7.2, negative-peer-status sixth-grade boys were not as likely to generate alternative solutions and were much less likely to adaptively plan ahead than their positive-peer-status counterparts.

In one recent study of sixth- and seventh-graders, knowledge of both appropriate and inappropriate strategies for making friends was related positively to prosocial behavior and peer acceptance and negatively to antisocial behavior (Wentzel & Erdley, 1993). The appropriate and inappropriate strategies generated by students are listed in table 7.1.

Now let's examine how social information processing might be involved in peer relations. For example, consider the situation when a peer accidentally trips and knocks a boy's soft drink out of his hand. The boy misinterprets the encounter as hostile, which leads him to retaliate aggressively against the peer. Through repeated encounters of this kind, peers come to perceive the boy as having a habit of acting inappropriately. Kenneth Dodge (1983) argues that children go through five steps in processing information about their social world: decoding of social cues, interpretation, response search, selecting an optimal response, and enactment. Dodge has found that aggressive boys are more likely to perceive another child's actions as hostile when the peer's intention is ambiguous. And when aggressive boys search for cues to determine a peer's intention, they respond more rapidly, less efficiently, and less reflectively than nonaggressive children. These are among the social cognitive factors believed to be involved in children's and adolescents' conflicts with each other.

Conglomerate Strategies for Improving Social Skills

Conglomerate strategies, *also referred to as coaching, involve the use of a combination of techniques, rather than a single approach, to improve adolescents' social skills.* A conglomerate strategy might consist of demonstration or modeling of appropriate social skills, discussion, and reasoning about the social skills, as well as the use of

TABLE 7.1

Appropriate and Inappropriate Strategies for Making Friends at School

Category	Examples
Strategies Appropriate for Making Friends	
Initiate interaction	Learn about friend: ask for their name, age, favorite activities. Prosocial overtures: introduce self, start a conversation, invite them to do things.
Be nice	Be nice, kind, considerate.
Prosocial behavior	Honesty and trustworthiness: tell the truth, keep promises. Be generous, sharing, cooperative.
Respect for self and others	Respect others, have good manners: be polite, courteous, listen to what others say. Have a positive attitude and personality: be open to others, be friendly, be funny. Be yourself. Enhance your own reputation: be clean, dress neatly, be on best behavior.
Provide social support	Be supportive: help, give advice, show you care. Engage in activities together: study or play, sit next to one another, be in same group. Enhance others: compliment them.
Strategies Inappropriate for Making Friends	
Pscyhological aggression	Show disrespect, bad manners: be prejudiced, inconsiderate, use others, curse, be rude. Be exclusive, uncooperative: don't invite them to do things, ignore them, isolate them, don't share or help them. Hurt their reputation or feelings: gossip, spread rumors, embarrass them, criticize them.
Negative self-presentation	Be self-centered: be snobby, conceited, jealous, show off, care only about yourself. Be mean, have bad attitude or affect: be mean, cruel, hostile, a grouch, angry all the time. Hurt own reputation: be a slob, act stupid, throw temper tantrums, start trouble, be a sissy.
Antisocial behavior	Physical aggression: fight, trip, spit, cause physical harm. Verbal aggression or control: yell at others, pick on them, make fun of them, call them names, be bossy. Dishonesty, disloyalty: tell lies, steal, cheat, tell secrets, break promises. Break school rules: skip school, drink alcohol, use drugs.

reinforcement for their enactment in actual social situations. In one coaching study, students with few friends were selected and trained in ways to have fun with peers (Oden & Asher, 1975). The "unpopular" students were encouraged to participate fully, to show interest in others, to cooperate, and to maintain communication. A control group of students (who also had few friends) was directed in peer experiences but was not coached specifically in terms of improved peer strategies. Subsequent assessment revealed that the coaching was effective, with the coached group members showing more sociability when observed in peer relationships than their noncoached counterparts.

Other recent efforts to teach social skills also have used conglomerate strategies (Merrell & Gimpel, 1997; Repinski & Leffert, 1994). In one study, middle school adolescents were instructed in ways to improve their self-control, stress management, and social problem solving (Weissberg & Caplan, 1989). For example, as problem situations arose, teachers modeled and students practiced six sequential steps: (1) stop, calm down, and think before you act; (2) go over the problem and state how you feel; (3) set a positive goal; (4) think of lots of solutions; (5) plan ahead for the consequences; (6) go ahead and try the best plan. The 240 adolescents who participated in the program improved their ability to devise cooperative solutions to problem situations, and their teachers reported that the students showed improved social relations in the classroom following the program. In another study, boys and girls in a low-income area of New Jersey were given instruction in social decision making, self-control, and group awareness (Clabby & Elias, 1988). When compared with boys and girls who did not receive the training, the program participants were more sensitive to the feelings of others, more mindful of the consequences of their actions, and better able to analyze problem situations and act appropriately.

Social skills training programs have generally been more successful with children 10 years of age or younger than with adolescents (Malik & Furman, 1993). Peer reputations become more fixed as cliques and peer groups become more salient in adolescence. Even if adolescents develop new skills and engage in appropriate interactions, their peers might not change their evaluation of them. In such instances, intervention that changes such perceptions is needed.

One such intervention strategy involves cooperative group training. In this approach, children or adolescents work toward a common goal that holds promise for changing reputations. Most cooperative group programs have been conducted in academic settings, but other contexts might be used. For example, participation in cooperative games and sports increases sharing and feelings of happiness. And some Nintendo and video games require cooperative efforts by the players.

The world of peers is one of varying acquaintances: For hours every day, adolescents interact with some adolescents they barely know and with others that they know well. It is to the latter type—friends—that we now turn.

FRIENDSHIP

The important role of friendships in adolescent development is exemplified in the following description by a 13-year-old girl:

> My best friend is nice. She's honest, and I can trust her. I can tell her my innermost secrets and know that nobody else will find out about them. I have other friends, too, but she is my best friend. We consider each other's feelings and don't want to hurt each other. We help each other out when we have problems. We make up funny names for people and laugh ourselves silly. We make lists of which boys are the sexiest and which are the ugliest, which are the biggest jerks, and so on. Some of these things we share with other friends; some we don't.

Its Importance

Adolescents' friendships serve six functions (Gottman & Parker, 1987) (see figure 7.3).

1. *Companionship.* Friendship provides adolescents with a familiar partner, someone who is willing to spend time with them and join in collaborative activities.

2. *Stimulation.* Friendship provides adolescents with interesting information, excitement, and amusement.

3. *Physical support.* Friendship provides time, resources, and assistance.

4. *Ego support.* Friendship provides the expectation of support, encouragement, and feedback that helps adolescents to maintain an impression of themselves as competent, attractive, and worthwhile individuals.

5. *Social comparison.* Friendship provides information about where adolescents stand vis-à-vis others and whether adolescents are doing okay.

6. *Intimacy/affection.* Friendship provides adolescents with a warm, close, trusting relationship with another individual, a relationship that involves self-disclosure.

Companionship

Stimulation

Physical support

Ego support

Social comparison

Intimacy/affection

Figure~7.3

The Functions of Friendships.

Sullivan's Ideas

Harry Stack Sullivan (1953) was the most influential theorist to discuss the importance of adolescent friendships. He argued that there is a dramatic increase in the psychological importance and intimacy of close friends during early adolescence. In contrast to other psychoanalytic theorists' narrow emphasis on the importance of parent-child relationships, Sullivan contended that friends also play important roles in shaping children's and adolescents' well-being and development. In terms of well-being, he argued that all people have a number of basic social needs, including the need for tenderness (secure attachment), playful companionship, social acceptance, intimacy, and sexual relations. Whether or not these needs are fulfilled largely determines our emotional well-being. For example, if the need for playful companionship goes unmet, then we become bored and depressed; if the need for social acceptance is not met, we suffer a lowered sense of self-worth. Developmentally, friends become increasingly depended upon to satisfy these needs during adolescence, and thus the ups-and-downs of experiences with friends increasingly shape adolescents' state of well-being. In particular, Sullivan believed that the need for intimacy intensifies during early adolescence, motivating teenagers to seek out close friends. He felt that, if adolescents failed to forge such close friendships, they would experience painful feelings of loneliness coupled with a reduced sense of self-worth.

Research findings support many of Sullivan's ideas. For example, adolescents report more often disclosing intimate and personal information to their friends than do younger children (Buhrmester & Furman, 1987). Adolescents also say they depend more on friends than parents to satisfy needs for companionship, reassurance of worth, and intimacy (Furman & Buhrmester, in press). In one study, daily interviews with 13- to 16-year-old adolescents over a 5-day period were conducted to find out how much time they spent engaged in meaningful interactions with friends and parents (Buhrmester & Carbery, 1992). Adolescents spent an average of 103 minutes per day in meaningful interactions with friends compared to just 28 minutes per day with parents. In addition, the quality of friendship is more strongly linked to feelings of well-being during adolescence than during childhood. Teenagers with superficial friendships, or no close friendships at all, report feeling lonelier and more depressed, and they have a lower sense of self-esteem than teenagers with intimate friendships (Buhrmester, 1990; Yin, Buhrmester, & Hibbard, 1996). And in another study, friendship in early adolescence was a significant predictor of self-worth in early adulthood (Bagwell, Newcomb, & Bukowski, 1994).

The increased closeness and importance of friendship challenges adolescents to master evermore sophisticated social competencies. Viewed from the developmental constructionist perspective described in chapter 6, adolescent friendship represents a new mode of relating to others that is best described as a *symmetrical intimate mode*. During childhood, being a good friend involves being a good playmate: Children must know how to play cooperatively and must be skilled at smoothly entering ongoing games on the playground. By contrast, the greater intimacy of adolescent friendships demands that teenagers learn a number of close relationship competencies, including knowing how to self-disclose appropriately, being able to provide emotional support to friends, and managing disagreements in ways that do not undermine the intimacy of the friendship. These competencies require more sophisticated skills in perspective taking, empathy, and social problem solving than were involved in childhood playmate competencies.

In addition to the role they play in the socialization of social competence, friendship relationships are often important sources of support (Berndt, 1996). Sullivan described how adolescent friends support one another's sense of personal worth. When close friends disclose

their mutual insecurities and fears about themselves, they discover that they are not "abnormal" and that they have nothing to be ashamed of. Friends also act as important confidants that help adolescents work through upsetting problems (such as difficulties with parents or the breakup of romance) by providing both emotional support and informational advice. Friends can also protect "at risk" adolescents from victimization by peers (Bukowski, Sippola, & Boivin, 1995). In addition, friends can become active partners in building a sense of identity. During countless hours of conversation, friends act as sounding boards as teenagers explore issues ranging from future plans to stances on religious and moral issues.

Intimacy and Similarity

In the context of friendship, *intimacy* has been defined in different ways. For example, it has been defined broadly to include everything in a relationship that makes the relationship seem close or intense. In most research studies, though, **intimacy in friendship** is *defined narrowly as self-disclosure or sharing of private thoughts*. Private or personal knowledge about a friend also has been used as an index of intimacy (Selman, 1980; Sullivan, 1953).

> *Each friend represents a world in us, a world possibly not born until they arrive, and it only by this meeting that a new world is born.*
>
> —Anaïs Nin

The most consistent finding in the last two decades of research on adolescent friendships is that intimacy is an important feature of friendship (Berndt & Perry, 1990; Bukowski, Newcomb, & Hoza, 1987). When young adolescents are asked what they want from a friend or how they can tell someone is their best friend, they frequently say that a best friend will share problems with them, understand them, and listen when they talk about their own thoughts or feelings. When young children talk about their friendships, comments about intimate self-disclosure or mutual understanding are rare. In one investigation, friendship intimacy was more prominent in 13- to 16-year-olds than in 10- to 13-year-olds (Buhrmester, 1989).

Are the friendships of adolescent girls more intimate than the friendships of adolescent boys? When asked to describe their best friends, girls refer to intimate conversations and faithfulness more than boys do. For example, girls are more likely to describe their best friend as "sensitive just like me" or "trustworthy just like me" (Duck, 1975). The assumption behind this gender difference is that girls are more oriented toward interpersonal relationships. Boys may discourage one another from openly disclosing their problems, as part of their masculine, competitive nature (Maccoby, 1995). Boys make themselves vulnerable to being called "wimps" if

One of the most important aspects of friendship is being able to share private thoughts.

they can't handle their own problems and insecurities. However, in one recent study, sex differences in initial self-disclosure were not found for African American adolescents (Jones, Costin, & Ricard, 1994).

In one recent study of adolescent peer networks, the most robust finding was that female students were more integrated into school social networks than males were (Urberg & others, 1995). Girls were also more likely than boys to have a best friend and to be a clique member.

Adolescents also regard loyalty or faithfulness as more critical in friendships than children do (Rotenberg, 1993). When talking about their best friend, adolescents frequently refer to the friend's willingness to stand up for them when around other people. Typical comments are: "Bob will stick up for me in a fight," "Sally won't talk about me behind my back," or "Jennifer wouldn't leave me for somebody else." In these descriptions, adolescents underscore the obligations of a friend in the larger peer group.

In one recent study of adolescent peer networks in the sixth grade through the twelfth grade, adolescents were more selective in naming friends (Urberg & others, 1995). In the twelfth grade, they made and received fewer friendship choices and had fewer mutual friends. This increased selectivity might be due to increased social cognitive skills that allow older adolescents to make more accurate inferences about who likes them.

Another predominant characteristic of friendship is that, throughout the childhood and adolescent years,

friends are generally similar—in terms of age, sex, ethnicity, and many other factors (Luo, Fang, & Aro, 1995). Friends often have similar attitudes toward school, similar educational aspirations, and closely aligned achievement orientations. Friends like the same music, wear the same kind of clothes, and prefer the same leisure activities (Berndt, 1982). If friends have different attitudes about school, one of them may want to play basketball or go shopping rather than do homework. If one friend insists on completing homework while the other insists on playing basketball, the conflict may weaken the friendship, and the two may drift apart.

Mixed-Age Friendships

Although most adolescents develop friendships with individuals who are close to their own age, some adolescents become best friends with younger or older individuals. A common fear, especially among parents, is that adolescents who have older friends will be encouraged to engage in delinquent behavior or early sexual behavior. Researchers have found that adolescents who interact with older youths do engage in these behaviors more frequently, but it is not known whether the older youths guide younger adolescents toward deviant behavior or whether the younger adolescents were already prone to deviant behavior before they developed the friendship with the older youths (Billy, Rodgers, & Udry, 1984).

In a longitudinal study of eighth-grade girls, early-maturing girls developed friendships with girls who were

CONCEPT TABLE 7.1

Peers and Friends

Concept	Processes/ Related Ideas	Characteristics/Description
Peers	Peer group functions	The nature of peer relationships undergoes important changes during adolescence. Peers are individuals who are about the same age or maturity level. Peers provide a means of social comparison and a source of information about the world outside the family. Good peer relations may be necessary for normal social development in adolescence. The inability to "plug in" to a social network in childhood or adolescence is associated with a number of problems and disturbances. Thus, peer influences can be both positive and negative. Both Piaget and Sullivan stressed that peer relations provide the context for learning the symmetrical reciprocity mode of relationships.
	Family-peer linkages	Recent studies have provided persuasive evidence that adolescents live in a connected world with parents and peers, not a disconnected one.
	Peer conformity	Conformity occurs when individuals adopt the attitudes or behavior of others because of real or imagined pressure from the others. Conformity to antisocial peer standards peaks around the eighth to ninth grades, then lessens by the twelfth grade. A distinction is made between nonconformists and anticonformists.
	Peer statuses	Popular children are frequently nominated as a best friend and rarely are disliked by their peers. Neglected children are infrequently nominated as a best friend but are not disliked by their peers. Rejected children are infrequently nominated as a best friend and are actively disliked by peers. Controversial children are frequently nominated both as someone's best friend and as being disliked. Rejected children are at risk for a number of problems.
	Social cognition	Social knowledge and social information-processing skills are associated with improved peer relations.
	Conglomerate strategies for improving social skills	Conglomerate strategies, also referred to as coaching, involve the use of a combination of techniques, rather than a single approach, to improve adolescents' social skills.
Friendship	Its importance	Adolescents' friendships serve six functions: companionship, stimulation, physical support, ego support, social comparison, and intimacy/affection.
	Sullivan's ideas	Harry Stack Sullivan was the most influential theorist to discuss the importance of adolescent friendships. He argued that there is a dramatic increase in the psychological importance and intimacy of close friends during early adolescence. Research findings support many of Sullivan's ideas.
	Intimacy and similarity	These are two of the most common characteristics of friendships. Intimacy in friendship is defined narrowly as self-disclosure or sharing of private thoughts. Similarity—in terms of age, sex, ethnicity, and many other factors—is also important to a friendship.
	Mixed-age friendships	Adolescents who become close friends with older individuals engage in more deviant behaviors than adolescents whose best friends are the same age. Early-maturing girls are more likely than their later-maturing counterparts to have older friends, who may encourage deviant behavior.

chronologically older but biologically similar to them (Magnusson, 1988). Because of their associations with older friends, the early-maturing girls were more likely than their peers to engage in a number of deviant behaviors, such as being truant from school, getting drunk, and stealing. Also, as adults (26 years of age), the early-maturing girls were more likely to have had a child and were less likely to be vocationally and educationally oriented than their later-maturing counterparts. Thus, parents do seem to have reason to be concerned when their adolescents become close friends with individuals who are considerably older than they are.

At this point, we have discussed many ideas about the nature of peer relations and friendships. A summary of these ideas is presented in concept table 7.1. Next, we consider another aspect of the adolescent's social world—groups.

ADOLESCENT GROUPS

During your adolescent years, you probably were a member of both formal and informal groups. Examples of formal groups include the basketball team or drill team, the Girl Scouts or Boy Scouts, the student council, and

so on. A more informal group could be a group of peers, such as a clique. Our study of adolescent groups focuses on the functions of groups and how groups are formed, differences between children groups and adolescent groups, cultural variations, cliques, and youth organizations.

Group Function and Formation

Why does an adolescent join a study group? A church? An athletic team? A clique? Groups satisfy adolescents' personal needs, reward them, provide information, raise their self-esteem, and give them an identity. Adolescents might join a group because they think that group membership will be enjoyable and exciting and satisfy their need for affiliation and companionship. They might join a group because they will have the opportunity to receive rewards, either material or psychological. For example, an adolescent may reap prestige and recognition from membership on the school's student council. Groups also are an important source of information. As adolescents sit in a study group, they learn effective study strategies and valuable information about how to take tests. The groups in which adolescents are members—their family, their school, a club, a team—often make them feel good, raise their self-esteem, and provide them with an identity.

Any group to which adolescents belong has two things in common with all other groups: norms and roles. **Norms** *are rules that apply to all members of a group.* An honor society, for example, might require all members to have a 3.5 grade point average. A school might require its male students to have hair that does not go below the collar of their shirt. A football team might require its members to work on weight lifting in the off-season. **Roles** *are certain positions in a group that are governed by rules and expectations. Roles define how adolescents should behave in those positions.* In a family, parents have certain roles, siblings have other roles, and grandparents have still other roles. On a basketball team, many different roles must be filled: center, forward, guard, rebounder, defensive specialist, and so on.

In a classic study designed to learn more about how adolescent groups are formed, social psychologist Muzafer Sherif and his colleagues (1961) brought together a group of 11-year-old boys at a summer camp called Robbers Cave in Oklahoma. The boys were divided into two groups. In-groupness was promoted by creating competition between the groups of boys. In the first week, one group hardly knew the other group existed. One group become known as the Rattlers (a tough and cussing group whose shirts were emblazoned with a snake insignia) and the other as the Eagles.

Near the end of the first week, each group learned of the other's existence. It took little time for "we-they" talk to surface: "They had better not be on our ball field." "Did you see the way one of them was sneaking around?" Sherif, who disguised himself as a janitor so he could unobtrusively observe the Rattlers and Eagles, then set

up competition between the groups in the form of baseball, touch football, and tug-of-war. Counselors juggled and judged events so that the teams were close. Each team perceived the other to be unfair. Raids, burning the other group's flag, and fights resulted. Ethnocentric out-group derogation was observed when the Rattlers and Eagles held their noses in the air as they passed each other. Rattlers described all Rattlers as brave, tough, and friendly and called all Eagles sneaky and smart alecks. The Eagles reciprocated by labeling the Rattlers cry-babies.

After in-groupness and competition transformed the Rattlers and Eagles into opposing "armies," Sherif devised ways to reduce hatred between the groups. He tried noncompetitive contact, but that did not work. Positive relations between the Rattlers and Eagles were attained only when both groups were required to work cooperatively to solve a problem. Three superordinate goals that required the efforts of both groups were (1) working together to repair the only water supply to the camp, (2) pooling their money to rent a movie, and (3) cooperating to pull the camp truck out of a ditch. All of these dilemmas were created by Sherif.

In addition to recruiting boys for camp to explore the nature of group formation, Sherif has also simply gone out to street corners and hangouts in towns and cities to find out what adolescent groups are like. In one such effort (Sherif & Sherif, 1964), the observers went to a town and began to infiltrate student gathering places. They got to know the adolescent boys and become their confidants by doing such things as buying them a new basketball when their old ball got a hole in it. After the observers gained the adolescents' acceptance, they began to record information about the conversations and activities of the youth. The strategy was to spend several hours with them and then write down what had transpired.

What do adolescent boys do when they get together regularly on their own volition? The Sherifs found that, in each group of adolescents they studied, much time was spent just "hanging around" together, talking and joking. In addition, many of the groups spent a great deal of time participating in, discussing, or attending athletic events and games. The only exceptions were groups from lower-class neighborhoods.

Cars occupied the minds of many of the group members. Whether they owned cars or not, the adolescent boys discussed, compared, and admired cars. Those who did not own cars knew what kinds they wanted. The boys also discussed the problem of having access to a car so they could go somewhere or take a girl out. The adolescents who did have cars spent tremendous amounts of time in and around cars with their buddies. On numerous occasions, the adolescent boys just drove around, looking to see what was going on around town or wanting to be seen by others.

Discussions about girls frequently infiltrated the adolescent boys' conversations. As part of this talk, they

focused extensively on sexual activities. They planned, reminisced, and compared notes on girls. Particularly in the middle- and upper-income adolescent groups, looking for opportunities to be with girls and making sure they had dates for the weekend were important group activities.

Much time in every group was spent reflecting on past events and planning for games, parties, and so forth. Thus, despite the fact that the boys just "hung around" a lot, there were times when they constructively discussed how they were going to deal or cope with various events.

Adults were depicted in the adolescents' conversations as a way to obtain needed resources (such as cars, money, and athletic equipment); as figures whose authorization was needed; as obstacles to be overcome; and, occasionally, in terms of obligation.

Although the particular activities of the adolescent boys differed from group to group, the general nature of the activities of all the groups was remarkably similar. All the groups were preoccupied with the pleasure of one another's company, the problems of having places to meet with peers apart from adults, relationships with adult authorities, relationships with the opposite sex, and appurtenances of being an adult male (including a car).

Also, in every group the Sherifs studied, the members engaged in some form of deviant behavior not sanctioned by adults. The most common behavior of this type involved alcoholic beverages. In one of the highest socioeconomic groups, the boys regularly drank, sometimes engaged in illicit sexual activities, and set up a boy-girl swimming party at a motel by forging the registration. The party included not only illegal drinking but the destruction of property as well. The boys paid for the property destruction themselves without ever telling their parents what had happened.

Children Groups and Adolescent Groups

Children groups differ from adolescent groups in several important ways. The members of children groups often are friends or neighborhood acquaintances, and the groups usually are not as formalized as many adolescent groups. During the adolescent years, groups tend to include a broader array of members; in other words, adolescents other than friends or neighborhood acquaintances often are members of adolescent groups. Try to recall the student council, honor society, or football team at your junior high school. If you were a member of any of these organizations, you probably remember that they were made up of many individuals you had not met before and that they were a more heterogeneous group than your childhood peer groups. Rules and regulations were probably well defined, and captains or leaders were formally elected or appointed in the adolescent groups.

A well-known observational study by Dexter Dunphy (1963) indicates that opposite-sex participation in groups increases during adolescence. In late childhood, boys and girls participate in small, same-sex groups. As they move into the early adolescent years, the same-sex groups begin to interact with each other. Gradually, the leaders and high-status members form further groups based on mixed-sex relationships. Eventually, the newly created mixed-sex groups replace the same-sex groups. The mixed-sex groups interact with each other in large crowd activities, too—at dances and athletic events, for example. In late adolescence, the crowd begins to dissolve as couples develop more serious relationships and make long-range plans that may include engagement and marriage. A summary of Dunphy's ideas is presented in figure 7.4.

Ethnic and Cultural Variations

Whether adolescents grow up as part of the peer culture in a ghetto or in a middle-class suburban area influences the nature of the groups to which they belong. For example, in a comparison of middle-class and lower-class adolescent groups, lower-class adolescents displayed more aggression toward the low-status members of the group but showed less aggression toward the president of the class or group than their middle-class counterparts (Maas, 1954).

In many schools, peer groups are strongly segregated according to social class and ethnicity. In schools with large numbers of middle- and lower-class students, middle-class students often assume the leadership roles in formal organizations, such as student council, the honor society, fraternity-sorority groups, and so on. Athletic teams are one type of adolescent group in which African American adolescents and adolescents from low-income families have been able to gain parity or even surpass adolescents from middle- and upper-income families in achieving status.

Ethnic minority adolescents, especially immigrants, may rely on peer groups more than White adolescents (Spencer & Dornbusch, 1990). This is especially true when ethnic minority adolescents' parents have not been very successful in their careers. The desire to be accepted by the peer group is especially strong among refugee adolescents, whose greatest threat is not the stress of belonging to two cultures but the stress of belonging to none (Lee, 1988).

For many ethnic minority youth, especially immigrants, peers from their own ethnic group provide a crucial sense of brotherhood or sisterhood within the majority culture. Peer groups may form to oppose those of the majority group and to provide adaptive supports that reduce feelings of isolation. More about the peer groups of ethnic minority adolescents appears in Sociocultural Worlds of Adolescence.

So far, we have considered adolescents' peer relations in different socioeconomic and ethnic minority groups. Are there also some cultures in which the peer group plays a different role than in the United States? In some cultures, children are placed in peer groups for much greater lengths of time at an earlier

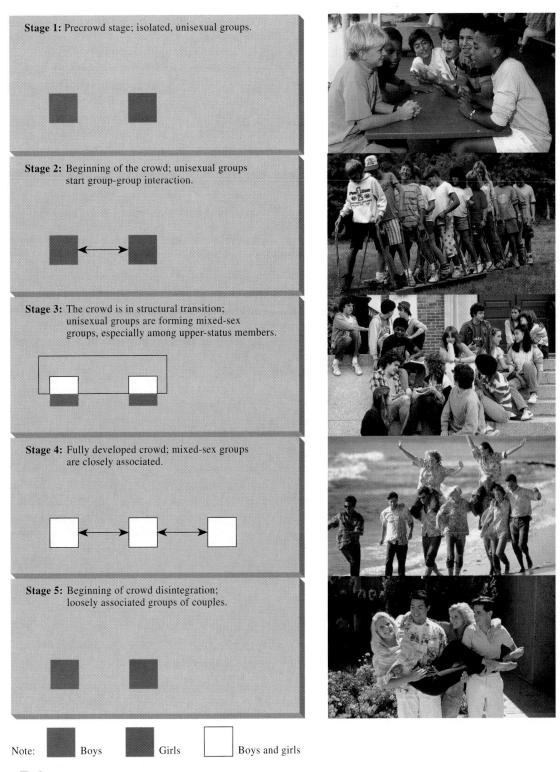

Stage 1: Precrowd stage; isolated, unisexual groups.

Stage 2: Beginning of the crowd; unisexual groups start group-group interaction.

Stage 3: The crowd is in structural transition; unisexual groups are forming mixed-sex groups, especially among upper-status members.

Stage 4: Fully developed crowd; mixed-sex groups are closely associated.

Stage 5: Beginning of crowd disintegration; loosely associated groups of couples.

Note: ⬛ Boys   ⬛ Girls   ⬜ Boys and girls

Figure~7.4

Dunphy's Progression of Peer Group Relations in Adolescence.

age than they are in the United States. For example, in the Murian culture of eastern India, both male and female children live in a dormitory from the age of 6 until they get married (Barnouw, 1975). The dormitory is a religious haven where members are devoted to work and spiritual harmony. Children work for their parents, and the parents arrange the children's marriages. When the children wed, they must leave the dormitory.

Adolescent cliques have been mentioned on several occasions in this chapter. For example, in the discussion of Dunphy's work, the importance of heterosexual

SOCIOCULTURAL WORLDS OF ADOLESCENCE

Ethnic Minority Adolescents' Peer Relationships

As ethnic minority children move into adolescence and enter schools with more heterogeneous school populations, they become more aware of their ethnic minority status. Ethnic minority adolescents may have difficulty joining peer groups and clubs in predominantly White schools. Similarly, White adolescents may have peer relations difficulties in predominantly ethnic minority schools. However, schools are only one setting in which peer relations take place; they also occur in the neighborhood and in the community (Jones & Costin, 1997).

Ethnic minority adolescents often have two sets of peer relationships, one at school, the other in the community. Community peers are more likely to be from their own ethnic group in their immediate neighborhood. Sometimes, they go to the same church and participate in activities together, such as Black History Week, Chinese New Year's, or Cinco de Mayo Festival. Because ethnic group adolescents usually have two sets of peers and friends, when researchers ask about their peers and friends, questions should focus on both relationships at school and in the neighborhood and community. Ethnic minority group adolescents who are social isolates at school may be sociometric stars in their segregated neighborhood.

Also, because adolescents are more mobile than children, inquiries should be made about the scope of their social networks.

In one investigation the school and neighborhood friendship patterns of 292 African American and White adolescents who attended an integrated junior high school were studied (DuBois & Hirsch, 1990). Most students reported having an other-ethnic school friend, but only 28 percent of the students saw such a friend frequently outside of school. Reports of an interethnic school friendship that extended to nonschool settings were more common among African American adolescents than White adolescents and among adolescents who lived in an integrated rather than a segregated neighborhood. African American adolescents were more likely than White adolescents to have extensive neighborhood friendship networks, but African American adolescents said they talked with fewer friends during the school day.

Of special interest to investigators is the degree of peer support for an ethnic minority adolescent's achievement orientation. Some researchers argue that peers often dissuade African American adolescents from doing well in school (Murdock & Davis, 1994). However, in one investigation, peer support of achievement was relatively high among Asian American adolescents, moderate among African American and Latino adolescents, and relatively low among Anglo American adolescents (Brown & others, 1990). The low peer support of achievement among Anglo-American adolescents possibly is due to their strong individual, competitive, and social comparison orientation.

Adolescent peer relations take place in a number of settings—at school, in the neighborhood, and in the community, for example. Ethnic minority adolescents often have two sets of peer relationships—one at school, the other in the community. A special interest is the degree to which peers support an ethnic minority adolescent's achievement orientation.

relationships in the evolution of adolescent cliques was noted. Let's now examine adolescent cliques in more detail.

Cliques

Most peer group relations in adolescence can be categorized in one of three ways: individual friendships, the crowd, and cliques. The **crowd** *is the largest, most loosely defined, and least personal unit of the adolescent peer society. Crowd members often meet because of their mutual interest in an activity.* For example, crowds get together at large parties or intermingle at school dances. **Cliques** *are smaller in size, involve more intimacy among members, and are more cohesive than crowds. However, they usually are larger in size and involve less intimacy than friendships.* In contrast to crowds, the members of both friendships and cliques come together because of mutual attraction.

Allegiance to cliques, clubs, organizations, and teams exerts powerful control over the lives of many adolescents. Group identity often overrides personal identity. The leader of a group may place a member in a position of considerable moral conflict, asking in effect, "What's more important, our code or your parents?" or "Are you looking out for yourself, or for the members of the group?" Labels like *brother* and *sister* sometimes are adopted and used in group members' conversations with one another. These labels symbolize the intensity of the bond between the members and suggest the high status of membership in the group.

One of the most widely quoted studies of adolescent cliques and crowds is that of James Coleman (1961). Students in ten different high schools were asked to identify the leading crowds in their schools. They also were asked to name the students who were the most outstanding in athletics, popularity, and different school activities. Regardless of the school sampled, the leading crowds were likely to be composed of male athletes and popular girls. Much less power in the leading crowd was attributed to the bright student.

Think about your high school years—what were the cliques, and which one were you in? While the names of the cliques change, we could go to almost any high school in the United States and find three to six well-defined cliques or crowds.

Cliques have been portrayed as playing a pivotal role in the adolescent's maintenance of self-esteem and development of a sense of identity (Coleman, 1961; Erikson, 1968; Tapper, 1996). Several theoretical perspectives suggest how clique membership might be linked with the adolescent's self-esteem. In an extension of Erikson's identity development theory, virtually all 13- to 17-year-olds regard clique membership as salient, and self-esteem is higher among clique members than nonmembers (at least those satisfied with the crowd). The peer group is a "way station" between relinquishing childhood dependence on parents and adult self-definition, achievement, and autonomy. Group affiliation and acceptance by the clique is important in keeping the adolescent's self-concept positive during this long transition period. Social comparison theory also has implications for understanding clique attachment and self-esteem. It implies that, while group members as a whole may have higher self-esteem than nonmembers, there are differences among group members according to the position of their clique in the peer group status hierarchy. This argument is based on the belief that individuals often compare their own attributes with those of significant others to evaluate the adequacy of their ideas or characteristics.

In one study, Bradford Brown and Jane Lohr (1987) examined the self-esteem of 221 seventh- through twelfth-graders. The adolescents were either associated with one of the five major school cliques or were relatively unknown by classmates and not associated with any school clique. Cliques included the following: jocks (athletically oriented), populars (well-known students who lead social activities), normals (middle-of-the-road students who make up the masses), druggies/toughs (known for illicit drug use or other delinquent activities), and nobodies (low in social skills or intellectual abilities). The self-esteem of the jocks and the populars was highest, while that of the nobodies was lowest. But one group of adolescents not in a clique had self-esteem equivalent to the jocks and the populars. This group was the independents, who indicated that clique membership was not important to them. Keep in mind that these data are correlational—self-esteem could increase an adolescent's probability of becoming a clique member just as clique membership could increase the adolescent's self-esteem.

In Bradford Brown's most recent research on cliques, the following conclusions were reached (Brown, Dolcini, & Leventhal, 1995; Brown, Mory, & Kinney, 1994):

1. *The influence of cliques is not entirely negative.* Cliques emerge in adolescence to provide youth with provisional identities they can adopt, at least temporarily, on their way to a more integrated identity later in development. In Brown's research with 1,000 midwestern middle school and high school students, peer pressure was strongest regarding getting good grades, finishing high school, and spending time with friends. The students reported little pressure to engage in drinking, drug use, sexual intercourse, and other potentially health-compromising behaviors.

2. *The influence of cliques is not uniform for all adolescents.* Cliques vary not only in terms of dress, grooming styles, musical tastes, and hangouts at school, but also in terms of more-consequential activities such as effort in school or deviant behavior (Youniss, McLellan, & Strouse, 1994). Thus, whether cliques are "friend" or "foe" depends largely on the particular crowd with which the adolescent is associated. Furthermore,

in Brown's research, one-third of the student body floated among several crowds; some students—isolates—were totally detached from cliques.

3. *Developmental changes occur in cliques.* In Brown's research, barriers against moving from one clique or crowd to another were much stronger in the ninth grade than in the twelfth grade. It was easier for high school seniors than for freshman to shift affiliations among crowds or forge friendships across crowd lines.

Clique membership is also associated with drug use and sexual behavior. In one recent study, five adolescent cliques were identified: jocks (athletes), brains (students who enjoy academics), burnouts (adolescents who get into trouble), populars (social, student leaders), nonconformists (adolescents who go against the norm), as well as a none/average group (Prinstein, Fetter, & La Green, 1996). Burnouts and nonconformists were the most likely to smoke cigarettes, drink alcohol, and use marijuana; brains were the least likely. Jocks were the most sexually active clique.

> *I didn't belong as a kid, and that always bothered me. If only I'd known that one day my differentness would be an asset, then my early life would have been much easier.*
>
> —Bette Midler

Youth Organizations

Youth organizations can have an important influence on the adolescent's development (Snider & Miller, 1993). More than four hundred national youth organizations currently operate in the United States (Erickson, in press). The organizations include career groups, such as Junior Achievement; groups aimed at building character, such as Girl Scouts and Boy Scouts; political groups, such as Young Republicans and Young Democrats; and ethnic groups, such as Indian Youth of America (Price & others, 1990). They serve approximately 30 million young people each year. The largest youth organization is 4-H, with nearly 5 million participants. The smallest are AS-PIRA, a Latino youth organization that provides intensive educational enrichment programs for about 13,000 adolescents each year, and WAVE, a dropout-prevention program that serves about 8,000 adolescents each year.

Adolescents who join such groups are more likely to participate in community activities in adulthood and have higher self-esteem, are better educated, and come from families with higher incomes than their counterparts who do not participate in youth groups (Erickson, 1982). Participation in youth groups can help adolescents practice the interpersonal and organizational skills that are important for success in adult roles.

To increase the participation of low-income and ethnic minority adolescents in youth groups, Girls Clubs and

These adolescents are participating in Girls Club and Boys Club activities. This type of organization can have an important influence on adolescents' lives. Adolescents who participate in youth organizations on a regular basis participate more in community activities as adults and have higher self-esteem than their counterparts who do not.

Boys Clubs are being established in locations where young adolescents are at high risk for dropping out of school, becoming delinquents, and developing substance-abuse problems. The locations are fifteen housing projects in different American cities. The club programs are designed to provide individual, small-group, and drop-in supportive services that enhance educational and personal development. Preliminary results suggest that the Boys and Girls Clubs help to reduce vandalism, drug abuse, and delinquency (Boys and Girls Clubs of America, 1989).

SOCIAL POLICY, PEERS, AND YOUTH ORGANIZATIONS

Two important areas can be targeted for improvements in social policy and adolescent development: (1) increased use of peers in tutoring and counseling, and (2) expansion and improvement of youth organizations.

Peer Tutoring and Counseling

We need to increase the number of effective peer-mediated programs that promote health and education (Carnegie Council on Adolescent Development, 1995). Peers are powerful influences on adolescents, for better or for worse. The social policy challenge is to increase positive peer influences on adolescents. Programs led by respected peers can provide adolescents with the attention and advice they need to cope with ongoing problems (Moorhead & Hayward, 1997).

Because peers have high credibility during adolescence, they can reach some adolescents who would otherwise fall through the cracks. When teachers and other professionals provide competent training and supervision, peer-led education and health interventions can be effective.

Peer-led programs on smoking can substantially reduce the onset of smoking in adolescence (Hamburg, 1990). In these programs, older peer leaders who have successfully resisted the lure of addictive substances can serve as models for younger adolescents and children. Peer leaders can teach younger adolescents social skills that will help them resist peer pressure to take drugs or engage in sex. Older peers can teach academic skills to younger peers.

One-to-one tutoring can benefit adolescents who are having difficulty in school. This is true not only when the tutor is a teacher or other professional; it also is true when the tutor is a trained, supervised peer, especially an older peer. There is also substantial evidence that peer tutoring benefits not only the student being tutored but the tutor as well. A well-functioning program of students as auxiliary teachers frees teachers to use their professional skills more fully than would otherwise be possible.

Youth Organizations

The Carnegie Council report *A Matter of Time: Risk and Opportunity in the Nonschool Hours* (1992) focused attention on how youth-oriented organizations can play an urgently needed and expanded role in helping adolescents lead more competent lives. The report noted that promising programs already exist, but they reach too few adolescents, especially those who are in the greatest need of support and guidance. When asked what they want from such organizations, adolescents say they want secure and stable relationships with caring peers and adults, safe and attractive places to relax and be with their friends, and opportunities to develop life skills, contribute to their communities, and feel competent. Good youth programs provide precisely what adolescents say they want.

To expand the number of good youth programs, innovative partnerships can support such programs with financial and other resources. For example, several federal agencies give organizations funds directed toward decreasing such problems as youth violence and substance abuse.

So far in our discussion of peers in adolescence, we have discussed the nature of peer relations, friendships, group behavior, and social policy. But one aspect of peer relations remains to be discussed—dating.

DATING AND ROMANTIC RELATIONSHIPS

While many adolescent boys and girls have social interchanges through formal and informal peer groups, it is through dating that more serious contacts between the sexes occur (Feiring, 1995). Many agonizing moments are spent by young male adolescents worrying about whether they should call a certain girl and ask her out: "Will she turn me down?" "What if she says yes, what do I say next?" "How am I going to get her to the dance? I don't want my mother to take us!" "I want to kiss her, but what if she pushes me away?" "How can I get to be alone with her?" And, on the other side of the coin: "What if no one asks me to the dance?" "What do I do if he tries to kiss me?" Or, "I really don't want to go with him. Maybe I should wait two more days and see if Bill will call me." Think about your junior high, high school, and early college years. You probably spent a lot of time thinking about how you were going to get a particular girl or boy to go out with you. And many of your weekend evenings were probably spent on dates, or on envying others who had dates. Some of you went steady, perhaps even during junior high school; others of you may have been engaged to be married by the end of high school.

Romantic experiences during adolescence are believed to play an important role in the development of identity and intimacy (Erikson, 1968). Dating in adolescence likely helps to shape the course of subsequent romantic relationships and marriages in adulthood. The increasing problems of teenage pregnancy, date rape, and sexually transmitted diseases suggest that early romance is an important dimension of development (Furman & Wehner, 1993).

In one study, adolescents involved in romantic relationships reported less social isolation and loneliness than did their counterparts who were not involved in romantic relationships (Connolly & Johnson, 1993). In this study, boys involved in romantic relationships were more popular with their peers than those who were not in a romantic relationship.

Adolescent Dating

Our further exploration of adolescent dating focuses on its functions, age at onset and frequency of dating, male and female dating patterns and scripts, and what attracts adolescents to each other.

Functions of Dating

Dating is a relatively recent phenomenon. It wasn't until the 1920s that dating as we know it became a reality, and even then, its primary role was for the purpose of selecting and winning a mate. Prior to this period, mate selection was the sole purpose of dating, and "dates" were carefully monitored by parents, who completely controlled the nature of any heterosexual companionship. Often, parents bargained with each other about the merits of their adolescents as potential marriage partners and even chose mates for their children. In recent times, of course, adolescents have gained much more control over the dating process and who they go out with. Furthermore, dating has evolved into something more than just courtship for marriage.

Dating today can serve at least eight functions (Paul & White, 1990):

1. Dating can be a form of recreation. Adolescents who date seem to have fun and see dating as a source of enjoyment and recreation.

2. Dating is a source of status and achievement. Part of the social comparison process in adolescence involves evaluating the status of the people one dates: are they the best looking, the most popular, and so forth.

3. Dating is part of the socialization process in adolescence: It helps the adolescent to learn how to get along with others and assists in learning manners and sociable behavior.

4. Dating involves learning about intimacy and serves as an opportunity to establish a unique, meaningful relationship with a person of the opposite sex.

5. Dating can be a context for sexual experimentation and exploration.

6. Dating can provide companionship through interaction and shared activities in an opposite-sex relationship.

7. Dating experiences contribute to identity formation and development; dating helps adolescents to clarify their identity and to separate from their families of origin.

8. Dating can be a means of mate sorting and selection, thereby retaining its original courtship function.

One investigation studied developmental changes in the functions of dating (Roscoe, Dian, & Brooks, 1987). Early (sixth-grade), middle (eleventh-grade), and late (college) adolescents were asked their reasons for dating and their concerns in selecting a dating partner. Early and middle adolescents had an egocentric and immediate gratification orientation toward dating functions (recreation was the most important function, followed by intimacy and status). In contrast, late adolescents placed more emphasis on reciprocity in dating relationships (intimacy was the most important function, followed by companionship, socialization, and recreation). Also, early adolescent concerns in selecting a dating partner stressed status seeking and dependence on others' approval of themselves. In contrast, late adolescents stressed more independence and future orientation in their dating concerns. In sum, the early and middle adolescents were primarily self-focused in their dating relationships, while late adolescents focused more on the reciprocal aspects of dating relationships and on what dating is supposed to be like.

The sociocultural context exerts a powerful influence on adolescent dating patterns and on mate selection (Xiaohe & Whyte, 1990). Values and religious beliefs of people in various cultures often dictate the age at which dating begins, how much freedom in dating is allowed, whether dates must be chaperoned by adults or parents, and the roles of males and females in dating. For example, Latino and Asian American cultures have more conservative standards regarding adolescent dating than the Anglo-American culture. Dating may be a source of cultural conflict for many immigrants and their families who have come from cultures in which dating begins at a late age, little freedom in dating is allowed, dates are chaperoned, and adolescent girls' dating is especially restricted.

Age of Onset and Frequency of Dating

Most girls in the United States begin dating at the age of 14, while most boys begin sometime between the ages of 14 and 15 (Sorenson, 1973). Most adolescents have their first date sometime between the ages of 12 and 16. Fewer than 10 percent have a first date before the age of 10, and by the age of 16, more than 90 percent have had at least one date. More than 50 percent of the tenth-, eleventh-, and twelfth-graders in one study averaged one or more dates per week (Dickinson, 1975). About 15 percent of these high school students dated less than once per month, and about three out of every four students had "gone with" someone at least once. A special concern is early dating and "going with" someone, which in one recent study were associated with adolescent pregnancy and problems at home and school (Degirmencioglu, Saltz, & Ager, 1995; Downey & Bonica, 1997).

In one recent study of 15-year-olds' romantic relationships, although most subjects said that they had had a girlfriend or boyfriend in the past 3 years, most were not currently dating (Feiring, 1996). Most of the 15-year-olds had had short-term dating relationships, averaging 4 months. Less than 10 percent had had a dating relationship that lasted for a year or longer. Although the length of their dating relationships was relatively brief, contact was very frequent. The adolescents reported seeing each other in person and talking on the phone almost daily. Dating occurred more in a group than in a couples-alone context. What did adolescents say they did when they were on a date? The most frequent dating activities were going to a movie, dinner, hanging out at a mall or school, parties, and visiting each others' homes. In another recent study, the average length of a dating relationship for tenth-graders was 5 to 6 months, increasing to more than 8 months for twelfth-graders (Dowdy & Kliewer, 1996). In this study, dating-related conflict between adolescents and parents was less frequent for twelfth-graders than for tenth-graders.

Dating, then, is an important aspect of adolescents' social relationships (Feiring, 1997). Adolescents who do not date very much may feel left out of the mainstream in their high school and community. Clinical and counseling psychologists have developed a number of social skills training programs for individuals who have problems getting a date or who have difficulty during the course of a dating relationship.

Male and Female Dating Scripts

Do male and female adolescents bring different motivations to the dating experience? In one recent study they

In the early twentieth century, dating served mainly as a courtship for marriage. What are the functions of dating today?

did (Feiring, 1996). Fifteen-year-old girls were more likely to describe romance in terms of interpersonal qualities, boys in terms of physical attraction. For young adolescents, the affiliative qualities of companionship, intimacy, and support were frequently mentioned as positive dimensions of romantic relationships, but love and security were not. Also, the young adolescents described physical attraction more in terms of being cute, pretty, or handsome than in terms of sexuality (such as being a good kisser). Possibly the failure to discuss sexual interests was due to the adolescents' discomfort in talking about such personal feelings with an unfamiliar adult.

Dating scripts *are the cognitive models that adolescents and adults use to guide and evaluate dating interactions.* In one recent study, first dates were highly scripted along gender lines (Rose & Frieze, 1993). Males followed a proactive dating script, females a reactive one. The male's script involved initiating the date (asking for and planning it), controlling the public domain (driving and opening doors), and initiating sexual interaction (making physical contact, making out, and kissing). The female's script focused on the private domain (concern about appearance, enjoying the date), participating in the structure of the date provided by the male (being picked up, having doors opened), and responding to his sexual gestures. These gender differences give males more power in the initial stage of a relationship.

What Attracts Adolescents to Each Other?

Does just being around another adolescent increase the likelihood a relationship will develop? Do birds of a feather flock together—that is, are adolescents likely to associate with those who are similar to them? How important is the attractiveness of the other adolescent?

As we have already seen, adolescents' friends are much more like them than unlike them; so are adolescents' dates. Adolescents' dates are likely to share similar attitudes, behavior, and characteristics—clothes, intelligence, personality, political attitudes, ethnic background, values, religious attitudes, lifestyle, physical attractiveness, and so on. In some limited cases and on some isolated characteristics, opposites attract; for example, an introvert may wish to be with an extravert, a blond may prefer a brunette, a short adolescent may prefer a tall adolescent, an adolescent from a low-income background may be attracted to an adolescent with money. But overall, adolescents desire to date others with characteristics similar to theirs.

Consensual validation *explains why adolescents are attracted to others who are similar to themselves. Adolescents' own attitudes and behavior are supported, or validated, when someone else's attitudes and behaviors are similar to theirs.* Also, dissimilar others are unlike the adolescent and therefore unknown; thus, the adolescent may be able to gain control over similar others, whose attitudes and behavior the adolescent can predict. Similarity also implies that adolescents enjoy interacting with the other individual in mutually satisfying activities, many of which require a partner with similarly disposed behavior and attitudes.

A characteristic of close relationships that deserves special mention is physical attractiveness. How important is physical attractiveness in determining whether an adolescent will like or love someone? In one experiment, college students assumed that a computer had determined their date on the basis of similar interests, but the dates actually were randomly assigned (Walster & others, 1966). The students' social skills, physical appearance, intelligence, and personality were measured. Then a dance was set up for the matched partners. At intermission, the partners were asked in private to indicate the most positive aspects of their date that contributed to his or her attractiveness. The overwhelming determinant of attractiveness was looks, not other factors such as personality or intelligence. Other research has documented the importance of physical attraction in close relationships. For example, physically attractive individuals have more dates, are more popular with their peers, have more positive encounters with teachers, and report more success in obtaining a marital partner (Simpson, Campbell, & Berscheid, 1986).

Why do adolescents want to be associated with attractive others? As with similarity, being around physically attractive individuals is rewarding. They validate that the adolescent, too, is attractive. As part of the rewarding experience, the adolescent's self-image is enhanced. Looking at attractive individuals is also aesthetically pleasing. The adolescent assumes that, if others are physically attractive, they will have other desirable traits that interest the adolescent.

But not every adolescent can date Rob Lowe or Madonna. How do adolescents deal with this in their

At some point in their junior or senior high school years, a number of adolescents "go steady" or "go with" each other. Going steady is more serious in high school than in middle school. The longer a couple goes steady, the more likely they are to consider marriage.

dating relationships? While beautiful girls and handsome boys seem to have an advantage, adolescents ultimately tend to seek out someone at their own level of attractiveness. The **matching hypothesis** states that, *although individuals may prefer a more attractive person in the abstract, they end up choosing someone who is close to their level of attractiveness.*

Evaluating Your Adolescent Dating Experiences

Think back to your middle school/junior high and high school years. How much time did you spend thinking about dating? What were your dating experiences like? What would you do over again the same way? What would you do differently? What characteristics did you seek in the people you wanted to date? Were you too idealistic? What advice would you give to today's adolescents about dating and romantic relationships? By evaluating your own dating experiences in adolescence, you are learning to think critically by *applying a developmental framework to understand behavior.*

Several additional points help clarify the role of physical beauty and attraction in our close relationships. Much of the research has focused on initial or short-term encounters; attraction over the course of months and years often is not evaluated. As relationships endure, physical attraction probably assumes less importance. Rocky Dennis, as portrayed in the movie *Mask,* is a case in point. Rocky's peers and even his mother initially wanted to avoid Rocky, whose face was severely distorted, but over the course of his childhood and adolescent years, the avoidance turned into attraction and love as people got to know him.

Our criteria for beauty may vary from one culture to another and from one point in history to another, so, although attempts are being made to quantify beauty and to arrive at the ultimate criteria for such things as a beautiful female face, beauty is relative. In the 1940s and 1950s in the United States, a Marilyn Monroe body build (a well-rounded, shapely appearance) and face was the cultural ideal for women. In the 1970s, some women aspired to look like Twiggy and other virtually anorexic females. In the 1990s, the desire for thinness has not ended, but what is culturally beautiful is no longer pleasingly plump or anorexic but, rather, a tall stature with moderate curves. The current image of attractiveness also includes the toning of one's body through physical exercise and healthy eating habits. As we will see next, though, there is more to close relationships than physical attraction.

Romantic Love and Its Construction

Romantic love *is also called passionate love or eros; it has strong sexual and infatuation components, and it often predominates in the early part of a love relationship.* The fires of passion burn hot in romantic love. It is the type of love Juliet had in mind when she cried, "O Romeo, Romeo, wherefore art thou Romeo?" It is the type of love portrayed in new songs that hit the charts virtually every week. Romantic love also sells millions of books for such writers as Danielle Steel. Well-known love researcher Ellen Berscheid (1988) says that we mean romantic love when we say we are "in love" with someone. She believes that it is romantic love we need to understand if we are to learn what love is all about.

Romantic love characterizes most adolescent love, and romantic love is also extremely important among college students. In one investigation, unattached college males and females were asked to identify their closest relationship (Berscheid, Snyder, & Omoto, 1989). More than half named a romantic partner, rather than a parent, sibling, or friend.

Romantic love includes a complex intermingling of emotions—fear, anger, sexual desire, joy, and jealousy, for example. Note that not all of these emotions are positive. In one investigation, romantic lovers were more likely to be the cause of a person's depression than were friends (Berscheid & Fei, 1977).

Berscheid (1988; Berscheid, Snyder, & Omoto, 1989) believes that the topic of sexual desire is vastly neglected in the study of romantic love. When asked what romantic love truly is, she concluded, "It's about 90 percent sexual desire." Berscheid said that this still is an inadequate answer but that "to discuss romantic love without also prominently mentioning the role sexual arousal and desire plays in it is very much like printing a recipe for tiger soup that leaves out the main ingredient."

Another type of love is **affectionate love,** *also called companionate love, which occurs when individuals desire to have another person near and have a deep, caring affection for that person.* There is a strong belief that affectionate love is more characteristic of adult love than adolescent love and that the early stages of love have more romantic ingredients than the later stages.

Love is a canvas furnished by nature and embroidered by imagination.

—Voltaire

Similarity, physical attractiveness, and sexuality are important ingredients of dating relationships. So is intimacy, which is discussed in greater detail in chapter 10. But to fully understand dating relationships in adolescence, we need to know how experiences with family members and peers contribute to the way adolescents construct their dating relationships, as first discussed in chapter 6 with regard to the developmental construction view of relationships.

In the continuity version of the developmental construction view, relationships with parents are carried forward to influence the construction of other relationships, such as dating. Thus, adolescents' relationships with opposite-sex parents, as well as same-sex parents, contribute to adolescents' dating. For example, the adolescent male whose mother has been nurturant but not smothering probably feels that relationships with females will be rewarding. By contrast, the adolescent male whose mother has been cold and unloving toward him likely feels that relationships with females will be unrewarding.

Adolescents' observations of their parents' marital relationship also contribute to their own construction of dating relationships. Consider an adolescent girl from a divorced family who grew up watching her parents fight on many occasions. Her dating relationships may take one of two turns: She may immerse herself in dating relationships to insulate herself from the stress she has experienced, or she may become aloof and untrusting with males and not wish to become involved heavily in dating relationships. Even when she does date considerably, she may find it difficult to develop a trusting relationship with males because she has seen promises broken by her parents.

According to Peter Blos (1962, 1989), at the beginning of adolescence, boys and girls try to separate themselves from the opposite-sex parent as a love object. As adolescents separate themselves, they often are self-centered. Blos believes that this narcissism gives adolescents a sense of strength. Especially in early adolescence, this narcissistic self-orientation is likely to produce self-serving, highly idealized, and superficial dating relationships.

There has been little empirical investigation of how parents and friends influence the manner in which adolescents construct dating relationships. Mavis Hetherington (1972, 1977) found that divorce was associated with a stronger heterosexual orientation of adolescent daughters than was the death of a parent or living in an intact family. Further, the daughters of divorced parents had a more negative opinion of males than did the girls from other family structures. And girls from divorced and widowed families were more likely to marry images of their fathers than were girls from intact families. Hetherington believes that females from intact families likely have had a greater opportunity to work through relationships with their fathers and therefore are more psychologically free to date and marry someone different than their fathers. Parents also are more likely to be involved or interested in their daughters' dating patterns and relationships than their sons'. For example, in one investigation, college females were much more likely than their male counterparts to say that their parents tried to influence who they dated during adolescence (Knox & Wilson, 1981). They also indicated that it was not unusual for their parents to try to interfere with their dating choices and relationships.

So far we have been discussing the continuity version of the developmental construction view. By contrast, in the discontinuity version of the developmental construction view, early adolescent friendships provide the opportunity to learn modes of relating that are carried over into romantic relationships (Furman & Wehner, 1993; Sullivan, 1953). Sullivan believed that it is through intimate friendships that adolescents learn a mature form of love he referred to as "collaboration." Sullivan felt that it was this collaborative orientation, coupled with sensitivity to the needs of the friend, that forms the basis of satisfying dating and marital relationships. He also pointed out that dating and romantic relationships give rise to new interpersonal issues that youths had not encountered in prior relationships with parents and friends. Not only must teenagers learn tactics for asking partners for dates (and gracefully turning down requests), but they must also learn to integrate sexual desires with psychological intimacy desires. These tactics and integration are not easy tasks and it is not unusual for them to give rise to powerful feelings of frustration, guilt, and insecurity.

In addition to past relationships with parents and friends influencing an adolescent's dating relationships, family members and peers can directly influence dating experiences. For example, sibling relationships influence adolescent dating. In one investigation, siblings were important resources for dating (O'Brien, 1990). In this study, adolescents said that they got more support for dating from siblings than from their mothers. In late adolescence, siblings were viewed as more important advisors and confidants than mothers when concerns about dating were involved. Sometimes, adolescents use siblings to their advantage when dealing with parents. In one study, younger siblings pointed to how their older siblings were given dating privileges that they had been denied (Place, 1975). In this investigation, an adolescent would sometimes side with a sibling when the sibling was having an argument with parents in the hope that the sibling would reciprocate when the adolescent needed dating privileges the parents were denying.

Peer relations are also involved in adolescent dating. In Dunphy's research, discussed earlier in the chapter, all large peer crowds in adolescence were heterosexual, and males in these crowds were consistently older than females (Dunphy, 1963). In this research, group leaders also played an important role. Both the leaders of large crowds and smaller cliques were highly involved with the opposite sex. Leaders dated more frequently, were more

Concept	Processes/ Related Ideas	Characteristics/Description
Adolescent Groups	Functions of groups	Groups satisfy adolescents' personal needs, reward them, provide information, raise their self-esteem, and give them an identity.
	Group formation	Norms are rules that apply to all members of a group. Roles are rules and expectations that govern certain positions in the group. Sherif's classic study documented how adolescents behave in group settings; superordinate tasks reduced adolescents' intergroup hostility.
	Children groups and adolescent groups	Children groups are less formal, less heterogeneous, and less heterosexual than adolescent groups. Dunphy found that adolescent group development moves through five stages.
	Ethnic and cultural variations	More aggression is directed at low-status members in lower-class groups. In many schools, peer groups are segregated according to ethnic group and social class. However, peer relations take place in diverse settings. Ethnic minority adolescents often have two sets of peers—one at school, one in the community. A special concern is peer support for the ethnic minority adolescent's achievement orientation. Ethnic minority adolescents, especially immigrants, may turn to the peer group more than White adolescents. In some cultures, children are placed in peer groups for greater lengths of time and at a much earlier age than in the United States.
	Cliques	Cliques are in between friendships and crowds in size and intimacy. Almost every secondary school has three to six well-defined cliques. Membership in certain cliques—jock and populars, for example—is associated with increased self-esteem. Independents also have high self-esteem.
	Youth organizations	Youth organizations can have an important influence on the adolescent's development. More than four hundred national youth organizations currently exist in the United States. To increase participation of low-income and ethnic minority adolescents in youth organizations, and improve the education and personal development of youth, Boys and Girls Clubs are being established in a number of cities.
Social Policy, Peers, and Youth Organizations	Peer tutoring and counseling	We need to increase the number of effective peer-mediated programs that promote adolescent health and education.
	Youth organizations	Youth-oriented organizations can play an urgently needed and expanded role in helping adolescents lead more competent lives.
Dating and Romantic Relationships	Adolescent dating	Dating can be a form of recreation, be a source of social status and achievement, be a part of the socialization process, involve learning about intimacy, provide a context for sexual experimentation, provide companionship, contribute to identity development, and be a means of mate sorting and selection. Most adolescents date regularly, with girls beginning, on the average, at age 14 and boys between the ages of 14 and 15. Females often show a stronger interest in interpersonal relationships in dating, whereas males show a stronger interest in physical attraction. Male dating scripts are proactive, females' are reactive. Similarity and physical attraction are important reasons adolescents want to date someone. The matching hypothesis and consensual validation are involved in understanding dating attraction.
	Romantic love and its construction	Romantic love, also called passionate love, involves sexuality and passion more than affectionate love. Romantic love is especially prominent in adolescents and college students. Affectionate love is more prominent in middle and late adulthood and is more likely to characterize the later stages of love. The developmental construction view emphasizes how relationships with parents, siblings, and peers influence how adolescents construct their romantic relationships. Dunphy's study found that group leaders play an important role in dating.

likely to go steady, and achieved these dating patterns earlier than nonleaders in the cliques. Leaders also were ascribed the task of maintaining a certain level of heterosexual involvement in the group. Peer leaders functioned as dating confidants and advisors, even putting partners together in the case of "slow learners."

At this point, we have discussed a number of ideas about the nature of adolescent groups and dating, and a summary of these ideas is presented in concept table 7.2. One setting in which peer relations take place is school. In the next chapter, we study the role of schools in adolescent development.

SUMMARY

We began this chapter by discussing the nature of peer relations, including peer group functions, family-peer linkages, peer conformity, peer popularity, neglect, and rejection, social knowledge and social information processing, and conglomerate strategies for improving adolescents' social skills. Our coverage of friendships focused on the importance of friendship, Sullivan's ideas on friendship, intimacy, and similarity in friendship, and mixed-age friendships. In our study of adolescent groups we read about group function and formation, children groups and adolescent groups, ethnic and cultural variations, cliques, and youth organizations. We studied about social policy, including information on peer tutoring and counseling, as well as youth organizations. We also learned about dating and romantic relationships, including the functions of dating, age of onset and frequency of dating, going steady, male and female dating patterns and scripts, what attracts adolescents to each other, romantic love, and the developmental construction of romantic relationships.

Don't forget that you can obtain an overall summary of the chapter by again studying the two concept tables on pages 221 and 234. In the next chapter, we will continue our exploration of the social contexts of adolescent development by focusing on schools.

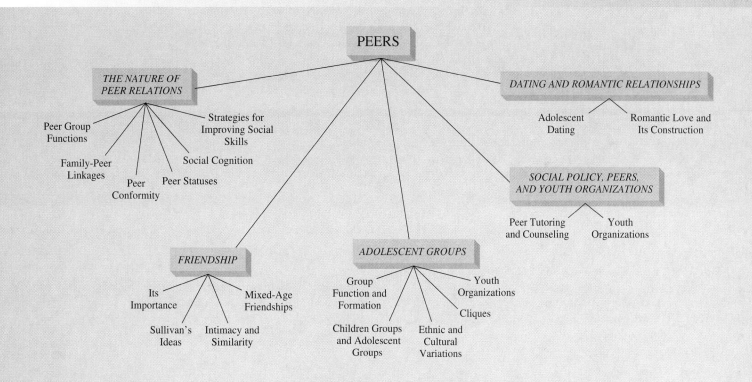

PRACTICAL KNOWLEDGE ABOUT ADOLESCENCE

Shyness
(1987) by Philip Zimbardo.
Reading, MA: Addison-Wesley.

Shyness gives advice about how to overcome shyness and be more gregarious. Author Philip Zimbardo is a highly respected social psychologist at Stanford University. He explores why people become shy and the roles that parents, teachers, peers, friends, and culture play in creating shy individuals. Zimbardo describes several behavior modification strategies for overcoming shyness and spells out fifteen steps to becoming more confident in social situations. Although the book is oriented mainly toward adults, the recommendations can be easily adapted for children and adolescents.

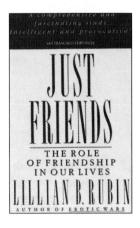

Just Friends
(1985) by Lillian Rubin.
New York: HarperCollins.

Just Friends explores the nature of friendship and intimacy. Rubin analyzes the valued yet fragile bond of friendship between males, between females and males, between best friends, and in couples. Rubin believes that friends are central players throughout our development. Written mainly for adults, the ideas can be easily adapted to adolescent friendships.

Boys and Girls Clubs of America
771 First Avenue
New York, NY 10017
212-351-5900

The Boys and Girls Clubs of America is a national, nonprofit youth organization that provides support services to almost 1,500 Boys and Girls Club facilities. The goal of the organization is to promote the health and social, vocational, and moral development of boys and girls from the ages of 6 to 18.

Boys and Girls Clubs of Canada/Clubs des Garçons et Filles du Canada
7030 Woodbine Avenue, Suite 703
Markham, Ontario L3R 6G2
416-477-7272

Boys and Girls Clubs, with families and other adults, offer children and youth opportunities to develop skills, knowledge, and values to become fulfilled individuals.

Directory of American Youth Organizations (1983)
Judith Erickson
Communications & Public Service
Boys Town, NE 68010
402-498-1111

A classified directory of 250 national, adult-sponsored organizations that enroll children and adolescents. National addresses, phone numbers for contact persons, and brief notes about the organizations are included.

Life-Skills Training: Preventive Interventions for Young Adolescents (1990)
by Beatrix Hamburg
Carnegie Council on Adolescent Development
2400 N Street NW
Washington, DC 20037
202-429-7979

This overview focuses on crucial skills for improving adolescent education and health. Among the emphases are programs that involve

- Nonviolent conflict resolution
- Friendship formation
- Peer resistance
- Assertiveness
- Renegotiation of relationships with adults

National Peer Helpers Association
818-240-2926

This association has publications and information on peer programs across the United States.

Youth-Reaching-Youth Project
202-783-7949

The Youth-Reaching-Youth Project offers a model peer program that involves young people and students in preventing and reducing alcohol use among high-risk youth.

EXPLORING ADOLESCENT DEVELOPMENT

To further explore the nature of adolescent development, we will examine a research study on the academic lives of neglected, rejected, popular, and controversial adolescents, as well as discuss the Midnight Basketball League, an attempt to improve the well-being of adolescents in high-poverty areas.

RESEARCH ON ADOLESCENT DEVELOPMENT

The Academic Lives of Adolescents with Different Peer Statuses

Featured Study

Wentzel, K. R. & Asher, S. R. (1995). The academic lives of neglected, rejected, popular, and controversial children. *Child Development, 66,* 754–763.

The purpose of this study was to examine the academic characteristics of adolescents with varying peer statuses—rejected adolescents, neglected adolescents, controversial adolescents, and popular adolescents. Another goal was to learn about the academic orientations of behavioral subgroups of rejected adolescents. Neglected adolescents and controversial adolescents have especially been understudied.

Method

The subjects were 423 sixth- and seventh-grade girls and boys (11–13 years of age) in a predominantly working-class midwestern community.

Participating classrooms (21) were chosen by the school principals to represent a wide range of student ability. Sociometric status was determined from best-friend nominations and peer acceptance ratings. Peer assessment items were used to identify aggressive and submissive subgroups of rejected adolescents. Students were asked to nominate classmates who "start fights" and "are easy to push around." Students were also asked to nominate classmates who were "good students"— that is, those who perform well academically. School motivation was assessed by using both teacher reports and student reports. Students completed Satisfaction with School and Commitment to Classwork scales. Teachers responded to such questions as "How often does this student work independently?" and "How often does this student act impulsively, without thinking?" to evaluate self-regulated learning. Teachers also responded to the following question for each of their students: "How much would you like to have this student in your class again next year?" Teachers also rated their students in regard to their prosocial and compliant behavior.

Results and Discussion

Neglected adolescents had positive academic profiles. When compared with an average-status student, neglected adolescents reported higher levels of motivation and were described by teachers as self-regulated learners, as more prosocial and compliant, and as being better liked by teachers. Aggressive-rejected but not submissive-rejected adolescents had problematic academic profiles. A note of caution is needed. This was a correlational study, so causal conclusions cannot be drawn regarding peer status and academic behavior. Research that systematically explores causal mechanisms between social and academic functioning are needed to understand more fully the role of peer relations in adolescents' academic lives.

The Midnight Basketball League

The dark side of peer relations is nowhere more present than in the increasing number of youth gangs. Beginning in 1990, the Chicago Housing Authority began offering young gang members an alternative to crime—the Midnight Basketball League (MBL) (Simons, Finlay, & Yang, 1991). Most crimes were being committed between 10 P.M. and 2 A.M. by males in their late teens and early twenties. The MBL offers these males a positive diversion during the time they are most likely to get into trouble. There are eight teams in the housing projects and 160 players in all. The year-round program provides top-quality basketball shoes, uniforms, championship rings, all-star games, and awards banquets.

Attitude is considered more important than ability, so most teams consist of one or two stars and eight or nine enthusiastic, mediocre-to-poor players. Different gang factions are represented on each team.

Basketball, however, is only one component of the MBL. To stay in the league, players must follow rules that prohibit fighting, unsportsmanlike behavior, profanity, drugs, alcohol, radios, and tape players. If they break the rules, they don't play basketball. Practices are mandatory and so are

Players in a recent Midnight Basketball League in Chicago. Gil Walker, MBL Commissioner, is the first person on the left in the front row.

workshops after each game. During the workshops, youth are encouraged to seek drug-abuse counseling, vocational counseling and training, life skills advising, basic health care, adult education and GED services, and various social services. The program is funded by the Chicago Housing Authority and private donations.

In a recent year, not one of the MBL players had been in trouble, and 54 of the 160 participants registered for adult education classes once the season had ended. The program has been replicated in Hartford, Connecticut, Louisville, Kentucky, Washington, D.C., and many other cities. For more information about the MBL, contact Gil Walker, MBL Commissioner, Chicago Housing Authority, 534 East 37th Street, Chicago, IL 60653, 312-791-4768.

Chapter

8

Schools

The world rests on the breath of the children in the schoolhouse.

—The Talmud

The whole art of teaching is only the art of awakening the natural curiosity of young minds.

—Anatole France, 1881

PREVIEW

*I*n youth we learn. An important context for that learning is school. We often think of school as the place where academic learning dominates. But schools are much more than academic classrooms where students think, reason, and memorize. The school is also an important social arena for adolescents, where friends, cliques, and crowds take on powerful meanings. In this chapter, we will explore the following questions: What is the nature of schools for adolescents? What transitions take place in adolescents' schooling? How do school size, classroom characteristics, teacher characteristics, and peer relations at school influence adolescent development? Have schools done a better job of educating middle-class White students than of educating low-income minority students? What should be the social policy initiatives for educating adolescents? What is the best way to educate adolescents with a disability?

From No More "What If" Questions to Authors' Week

Some schools for adolescents are ineffective, others effective, as revealed in the following excerpts (Lipsitz, 1984):

> A teacher in a social studies class squelches several imaginative questions, exclaiming, "You're always asking 'what if' questions. Stop asking 'what if.' " When a visitor asks who will become president if the president-elect dies before the electoral college meets, the teacher explodes, "You're as bad as they are! That's another 'what if' question!"
>
> A teacher drills students for a seemingly endless amount of time on prime numbers. After the lesson, not one student can say why it is important to learn prime numbers.
>
> A visitor asks a teacher if hers is an eighth-grade class. "It's called eighth grade," the teacher answers harshly, "but we know it's really kindergarten, right class?"
>
> In a predominantly Latino school, only the one adult hired as a bilingual teacher speaks Spanish.
>
> In a biracial school, the principal and the guidance counselor cite test scores with pride. They are asked if the difference between the test scores of African American and white students is narrowing: "Oh, that's an interesting question!" says the guidance counselor with surprise. The principal agrees. It has never been asked by or of them before.

The preceding vignettes are from middle schools where life seems to be difficult and unhappy for students. By contrast, consider the following circumstances in effective middle schools (Lipsitz, 1984):

> Everything is peaceful. There are open cubbies instead of locked lockers. There is no theft. Students walk quietly in the corridors. "Why?" they are asked. "So as not to disturb the media center," they answer, which is self-evident to them, but not the visitor. . . . When asked, "Do you like this school?" [They] answer, "No, we don't like it. We love it!"
>
> When asked how the school feels, one student answered, "It feels smart. We're smart. Look at our test scores."

Comments from one of the parents of a student at the school are revealing: "My child would have been a dropout. In elementary school, his teacher said to me, 'That child isn't going to give you anything but heartaches.' He had perfect attendance here. He didn't want to miss a day. Summer vacation was too long and boring. He got here and someone cared for him."

The humane environment that encourages teachers' growth is translated by the teachers into a humane environment that encourages students' growth. The school feels cold when one first enters. It has the institutional feeling of any large school building with metal lockers and impersonal halls. Then one opens the door to a team area, and it is filled with energy, movement, productivity, doing. There is a lot of informal relating among students and between students and teachers. Visible from one vantage point are students working on written projects, putting the last touches on posters, watching a film, and working independently from reading kits. . . . Most know what they are doing, can say why it is important, and go back to work immediately after being interrupted.

Authors' Week is a special activity built into the school's curriculum that entices students to consider themselves in relation to the rich variety of making and doing in peoples' lives. Based on student interest, availability, and diversity, authors are invited to discuss their craft. Students sign up to meet with individual authors. They must have read one individual book by the author. Students prepare questions for their sessions with the authors. Sometimes, an author stays several days to work with a group of students on his or her manuscript.

THE NATURE OF ADOLESCENTS' SCHOOLING

Today, virtually all American adolescents under the age of 16 and most 16- to 17-year-olds are in school. More than half of all youth continue their education after graduating from high school by attending technical schools, colleges, or universities. Schools for adolescents are vast and varied settings with many functions and diverse makeups.

Functions of Adolescents' Schools

During the twentieth century, U.S. schools have assumed a more prominent role in the lives of adolescents. From 1890 to 1920, virtually every state developed laws that excluded youth from work and required them to attend school. In this time frame, the number of high school graduates increased by 600 percent. By making secondary education compulsory, the adult power structure placed adolescents in a submissive position and made their move into the adult world of work more manageable. In the nineteenth century, high schools were mainly for the elite, with the educational emphasis on classical, liberal arts courses. By the 1920s, educators perceived that the secondary school curriculum needed to be changed. Schools for the masses, it was thought, should not just involve intellectual training but training for work and citizenship. The curriculum of secondary schools became more comprehensive and grew to include general education, college preparatory, and vocational education courses. As the twentieth century unfolded, secondary schools continued to expand their orientation, adding courses in music, art, health, physical education, and other topics. By the middle of the twentieth century, schools had moved further toward preparing students for comprehensive roles in life (Conant, 1959). Today, secondary schools have retained their comprehensive orientation, designed to train adolescents intellectually but vocationally and socially as well.

Although school attendance has consistently increased for more than 150 years, the distress over alienated and rebellious youth brought up the issue of whether secondary schools actually benefit adolescents. In the 1970s, three independent panels agreed that high schools contributed to adolescent alienation and actually impeded the transition to adulthood (Brown, 1973; Coleman & others, 1974; Martin, 1976). The argument is that high schools segregate adolescents into "teenage warehouses," isolating them in their own self-contained world with their own values away from adult society. The prestigious panels stressed that adolescents should be given educational alternatives to the comprehensive high school, such as on-the-job community work, to increase their exposure to adult roles and to decrease their isolation from

adults. Partially in response to these reports, a number of states lowered the age at which adolescents could leave school from 16 to 14.

Now, in the last two decades of the twentieth century, the back-to-basics movement has gained momentum. The **back-to-basics movement** *stresses that the function of schools should be the rigorous training of intellectual skills through such subjects as English, mathematics, and science.* Back-to-basics advocates point to the excessive fluff in secondary school curricula, with too many alternative subjects that do not give students a basic education in intellectual subjects. They also believe that schools should be in the business of imparting knowledge to adolescents and should not be concerned about adolescents' social and emotional lives. Critics of the fluff in schools also sometimes argue that the school day should be longer and that the school year should be extended into the summer months. Back-to-basics advocates want students to have more homework, more tests, and more discipline. They usually believe that adolescents should be behind their desks and not roaming around the room, while teachers should be at the head of the classroom, drilling knowledge into adolescents' minds.

Much of the current back-to-basics emphasis is a reaction against the trend toward open education in the 1970s. The open-education approach, which was based on the British educational system, allowed adolescents to learn and develop at their own pace within a highly structured classroom. However, too many school systems that implemented open education in the United States thought it meant tearing down classroom walls and letting adolescents do whatever they wanted. Incorrect application of open education in American schools resulted in a strong backlash against it.

Adolescent educators Arthur Powell, Eleanor Farrar, and David Cohen (1985) conducted an in-depth examination of fifteen diverse high schools across the United States by interviewing students, teachers, and school personnel, as well as by observing and interpreting what was happening in the schools. The metaphor of the "shopping mall" high school emerged as the authors tried to make sense of the data they had collected.

Variety, choice, and neutrality are important dimensions of the "shopping mall" high school. Variety appears in the wide range of courses offered (in one school, 480 courses in the curriculum!), with something for apparently every student. Variety usually stimulates choice. Choice is often cited as a positive aspect of curricula, but the choice often rests in the hands of students, who, in too many instances, make choices based on ignorance rather than information. The investigators found that the diversity of individuals, multiple values, and wide range of course offerings combined to produce neutrality. Because they try to accommodate the needs of different student populations, high schools may become neutral institutions that take few stands on the products and services they offer. The shopping mall is an intriguing metaphor for America's high schools and provides insight into some general characteristics that have emerged.

Should the main and perhaps only major goal of schooling for adolescents be the development of an intellectually mature individual? Or should schools also focus on the adolescent's maturity in social and emotional development? Should schools be comprehensive and provide a multifaceted curriculum that includes many electives and alternative subjects to a basic core? These provocative questions continue to be heatedly debated in educational and community circles (Short & Talley, 1997; Tirozzi & Uro, 1997).

> *In the first place God made idiots. That was for practice. Then he made school boards.*
>
> —Mark Twain

The debate about the function of schools produces shifts of emphases, much like a swinging pendulum, moving toward basic skills at one point in time, toward options, frills, or comprehensive training for life at another, and so on back and forth (Cross, 1984). What we should strive for, though, is not a swinging pendulum but something like a spiral staircase; that is, we should continually be developing more sophisticated ways of fulfilling the varied and changing functions of schools.

So far in our discussion of the function of schools, we have been examining the nature of U.S. secondary schools. The nature of secondary schools around the world is the focus of Sociocultural Worlds of Adolescence.

Do Schools Make a Difference?

Schools have a great deal of influence on children and adolescents. By the time students graduate from high school, they have accumulated more than 10,000 hours in the classroom. School influences are more powerful today than in past generations because more individuals are in school longer. For example, in 1900, 11.4 percent of 14- to 17-year-olds were in school. Today, 94 percent of this age group are in school.

Children and adolescents spend many years in schools as members of a small society in which there are tasks to be accomplished; people to be socialized and to be socialized by; and rules that define and limit behavior, feelings, and attitudes. The experiences children and adolescents have in this society are likely to have a strong influence in such areas as identity development, belief in one's competence, images of life and career possibilities, social relationships, standards of right and wrong, and conceptions of how a social system beyond the family functions.

Schools' influence on children and adolescents has been evaluated from two points of view: (1) Is there a difference between the cognitive performances of those who have gone to school and those who have not? (2) Can schools override the negative effects of poverty? Concerning the first question, schooled children and adolescents usually outperform their unschooled counterparts on a variety of cognitive tasks (Cole & Cole, 1993). However, investigators do not yet have a complete picture of how schooling affects adolescent social development. Research on the second question, regarding poverty, has been controversial. The disagreement is rooted in the work of sociologists James Coleman and Christopher Jencks (Coleman & others, 1966; Jencks & others, 1972). In such investigations, characteristics of schools were compared with family and economic factors as predictors of school achievement and success. Both Coleman and Jencks argue that the evidence supports their belief that schools have little impact on the cognitive development of poverty-stricken students.

Critics fault Coleman and Jencks on a variety of issues, including the methods they used for collecting their data. One of the most serious criticisms leveled at them is that their analysis is too global, that it was conducted at the level of the school as a whole rather than at the more fine-grained level of everyday happenings in classrooms. In their studies of achievement in school and after, dissenters have compared the effectiveness of schools and classrooms and arrived at the exact opposite conclusion from Coleman and Jencks (Rutter & others, 1979). These researchers identify an important idea that is carried through the remainder of this chapter—namely, that academic and social patterns are intricately interwoven. Schools that produced high achievement in lower-income students were identified not only by particular types of curriculum and time involved in teaching, but by many features of the climate of the school, such as the nature of the teachers' expectations and the patterns of interaction between teachers and students. In other words, various aspects of the school as a social system contributed to the achievement of students in the school.

Additional research on whether schools make a difference in a student's achievement suggests that this question cannot be appropriately addressed without considering the extensive variation in schooling. Schools vary even in similar neighborhoods serving similar populations. And they may differ on such dimensions as whether they are integrated or segregated, coed or single sex, parochial or secular, rural or urban, and large or small. Schools are also different in terms of their social climates, educational ideologies, and concepts of what constitutes the best way to promote the adolescent's development.

Schools' Changing Social Developmental Contexts

The social context differs at the preschool, elementary, and secondary level. The preschool setting is a protected environment, whose boundary is the classroom. In this limited social setting, preschool children interact with one or two teachers, almost always female, who are powerful figures in the young child's life. The

SOCIOCULTURAL WORLDS OF ADOLESCENCE

Cross-Cultural Comparisons of Secondary Schools

Secondary schools in different countries share a number of similar features, but differ on others (Cameron & others, 1983; George, 1987; Thomas, 1988). Here, we examine the similarities and differences in secondary schools in six countries: Australia, Brazil, Germany, Japan, Russia, and the United States.

Most countries mandate that children begin school at 6 to 7 years of age and stay in school until they are 14 to 17 years of age. Brazil requires students to go to school only until they are 14 years of age, while Russia mandates that students stay in school until they are 17. Germany, Japan, Australia, and the United States require school attendance until ages 15 to 16.

Most secondary schools around the world are divided into two or more levels, such as middle school (or junior high school) and high school. However, Germany's schools are divided according to three educational ability tracks: (1) The main school provides a basic level of education, (2) the middle school gives students a more advanced education, and (3) the academic school prepares students for entrance to a university. German schools, like most European schools, offer a classical education, which includes courses in Latin and Greek.

Japanese secondary schools have an entrance exam, but secondary schools in the other five countries do not. Only Australia and Germany have comprehensive exit exams.

The United States is the only country in the world in which sports are an integral part of the public school system. Only a few private schools in other countries have their own sports teams, sports facilities, and highly organized sports events.

The nature of the curriculum is often similar in secondary schools in different countries, although there are some differences in content and philosophy. For example, at least until recently, the secondary schools in Russia have emphasized the preparation

of students for work. The "labor education program," which is part of the secondary school curriculum, includes vocational training and on-the-job experience. The idea is to instill in youth a love for manual work and a positive attitude about industrial and work organizations. Russian students who are especially gifted—academically, artistically, or athletically—attend special schools where the students are encouraged to develop their talents and are trained to be the very best in their vocation. With the breakup of the Soviet Union, it will be interesting to follow what changes in education take place in Russia.

In Brazil, students are required to take Portuguese (the native language) and four foreign languages (Latin, French, English, and Spanish). Brazil requires these languages because of the country's international character and emphasis on trade and commerce. Seventh-grade students in Australia take courses in sheep husbandry and weaving, two areas of economic and cultural interest in the country. In Japan, students take a number of Western courses in addition to their basic Japanese courses; these courses include Western literature and languages (in addition to Japanese literature and language), Western physical education (in addition to Japanese martial arts classes), and Western sculpture and handicrafts (in addition to Japanese calligraphy). The Japanese school year is also much longer than that of other countries (225 days, versus 180 days in the United States, for example).

The juku or "cramming school," is available to Japanese adolescents in the summertime and after school. It provides coaching to help them improve their grades and their entrance exam scores for high schools and universities. The Japanese practice of requiring an entrance exam for high school is a rarity among the nations of the world.

(a)

(b)

The transition from elementary school to middle or junior high school can be stressful. (a) Boys and girls in the last year of elementary school are in the "top-dog" position as the biggest, most powerful students in the school. However, (b) boys and girls in the first year of middle or junior high school are in the "bottom-dog" position as the smallest, least powerful students in the school.

support from teachers. Friendship patterns also influenced the students' adjustment. Students who reported more contact with their friends and higher-quality friendships had more positive perceptions of themselves and of their junior high school than their low-friendship counterparts.

Two recent studies further highlight the factors that mediate school transition during early adolescence. In the first study, when parents were attuned to their young adolescents' developmental needs and supported their autonomy in decision-making situations, the young adolescents showed better adjustment and higher self-esteem across the transition from elementary school to junior high school (Eccles, Lord, & Buchanan, 1996). In the second study, support from parents and friends was associated with better adjustment of young adolescents following the school transition of both sixth- and ninth-graders (Costin & Jones, 1994).

What Makes a Successful Middle School?

Joan Lipsitz (1984) searched the nation for the best middle schools. Extensive contacts and observations were made. Based on the recommendations of education experts and observations in schools in different parts of the United States, four middle schools were chosen for their outstanding ability to educate young adolescents. The most striking feature of these middle schools was their willingness and ability to adapt all school practices to the individual differences in physical, cognitive, and social development of their students. The schools took seriously the knowledge investigators have developed about young adolescents. This seriousness was reflected in decisions about different aspects of school life. For example, one middle school fought to keep its schedule of mini-courses on Friday so that every student could be with friends and pursue personal interests. Two other middle schools expended considerable energy on a complex

(a)

(b)

The transition from elementary school to middle or junior high school can be stressful. (a) Boys and girls in the last year of elementary school are in the "top-dog" position as the biggest, most powerful students in the school. However, (b) boys and girls in the first year of middle or junior high school are in the "bottom-dog" position as the smallest, least powerful students in the school.

support from teachers. Friendship patterns also influenced the students' adjustment. Students who reported more contact with their friends and higher-quality friendships had more positive perceptions of themselves and of their junior high school than their low-friendship counterparts.

Two recent studies further highlight the factors that mediate school transition during early adolescence. In the first study, when parents were attuned to their young adolescents' developmental needs and supported their autonomy in decision-making situations, the young adolescents showed better adjustment and higher self-esteem across the transition from elementary school to junior high school (Eccles, Lord, & Buchanan, 1996). In the second study, support from parents and friends was associated with better adjustment of young adolescents following the school transition of both sixth- and ninth-graders (Costin & Jones, 1994).

What Makes a Successful Middle School?

Joan Lipsitz (1984) searched the nation for the best middle schools. Extensive contacts and observations were made. Based on the recommendations of education experts and observations in schools in different parts of the United States, four middle schools were chosen for their outstanding ability to educate young adolescents. The most striking feature of these middle schools was their willingness and ability to adapt all school practices to the individual differences in physical, cognitive, and social development of their students. The schools took seriously the knowledge investigators have developed about young adolescents. This seriousness was reflected in decisions about different aspects of school life. For example, one middle school fought to keep its schedule of mini-courses on Friday so that every student could be with friends and pursue personal interests. Two other middle schools expended considerable energy on a complex

SOCIOCULTURAL WORLDS OF ADOLESCENCE

Cross-Cultural Comparisons of Secondary Schools

Secondary schools in different countries share a number of similar features, but differ on others (Cameron & others, 1983; George, 1987; Thomas, 1988). Here, we examine the similarities and differences in secondary schools in six countries: Australia, Brazil, Germany, Japan, Russia, and the United States.

Most countries mandate that children begin school at 6 to 7 years of age and stay in school until they are 14 to 17 years of age. Brazil requires students to go to school only until they are 14 years of age, while Russia mandates that students stay in school until they are 17. Germany, Japan, Australia, and the United States require school attendance until ages 15 to 16.

Most secondary schools around the world are divided into two or more levels, such as middle school (or junior high school) and high school. However, Germany's schools are divided according to three educational ability tracks: (1) The main school provides a basic level of education, (2) the middle school gives students a more advanced education, and (3) the academic school prepares students for entrance to a university. German schools, like most European schools, offer a classical education, which includes courses in Latin and Greek.

Japanese secondary schools have an entrance exam, but secondary schools in the other five countries do not. Only Australia and Germany have comprehensive exit exams.

The United States is the only country in the world in which sports are an integral part of the public school system. Only a few private schools in other countries have their own sports teams, sports facilities, and highly organized sports events.

The nature of the curriculum is often similar in secondary schools in different countries, although there are some differences in content and philosophy. For example, at least until recently, the secondary schools in Russia have emphasized the preparation of students for work. The "labor education program," which is part of the secondary school curriculum, includes vocational training and on-the-job experience. The idea is to instill in youth a love for manual work and a positive attitude about industrial and work organizations. Russian students who are especially gifted—academically, artistically, or athletically—attend special schools where the students are encouraged to develop their talents and are trained to be the very best in their vocation. With the breakup of the Soviet Union, it will be interesting to follow what changes in education take place in Russia.

In Brazil, students are required to take Portuguese (the native language) and four foreign languages (Latin, French, English, and Spanish). Brazil requires these languages because of the country's international character and emphasis on trade and commerce. Seventh-grade students in Australia take courses in sheep husbandry and weaving, two areas of economic and cultural interest in the country. In Japan, students take a number of Western courses in addition to their basic Japanese courses; these courses include Western literature and languages (in addition to Japanese literature and language), Western physical education (in addition to Japanese martial arts classes), and Western sculpture and handicrafts (in addition to Japanese calligraphy). The Japanese school year is also much longer than that of other countries (225 days, versus 180 days in the United States, for example).

The juku or "cramming school," is available to Japanese adolescents in the summertime and after school. It provides coaching to help them improve their grades and their entrance exam scores for high schools and universities. The Japanese practice of requiring an entrance exam for high school is a rarity among the nations of the world.

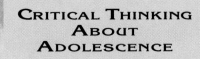

CRITICAL THINKING
ABOUT
ADOLESCENCE

Evaluating Your Own Middle or Junior High School

What was your own middle or junior high school like? How did it measure up to Lipsitz's criteria for effective schools for young adolescents? Did the school characteristically take individual differences into account? Did the administrators and teachers adequately address the unique needs of young adolescents as separate from those of children and older adolescents? Was socioemotional development emphasized as much as cognitive development? By evaluating your own middle school or junior high school, you are learning to think critically by *applying a developmental framework to understand behavior.*

school organization so that small groups of students worked with small groups of teachers who could vary the tone and pace of the school day, depending on students' needs. Another middle school developed an advisory scheme so that each student had daily contact with an adult who was willing to listen, explain, comfort, and prod the adolescent. Such school policies reflect thoughtfulness and personal concern about individuals whose developmental needs are compelling. Another aspect observed was that, early in their existence—the first year in three of the schools and the second year in the fourth school—these effective middle schools emphasized the importance of creating an environment that was positive for the adolescent's social and emotional development. This goal was established not only because such environments contribute to academic excellence but also because social and emotional development are intrinsically valued as important in themselves in adolescents' schooling.

Recognizing that the vast majority of middle schools do not approach the excellent schools described by Joan Lipsitz (1984), in 1989 the Carnegie Council on Adolescent Development issued an extremely negative evaluation of U.S. middle schools. In the report—*Turning Points: Preparing American Youth for the Twenty-First Century*—the conclusion was reached that most young adolescents attend massive, impersonal schools; learn from seemingly irrelevant curricula; trust few adults in school; and lack access to health care and counseling. The Carnegie report recommends:

- Developing smaller "communities" or "houses" to lessen the impersonal nature of large middle schools
- Lowering student-to-counselor ratios from several hundred-to-1 to 10-to-1
- Involving parents and community leaders in schools
- Developing curriculum that produces students who are literate, understand the sciences, and have a sense of health, ethics, and citizenship

Joan Lipsitz (shown here talking with young adolescents) has been an important spokesperson for the needs of adolescents. Former director of the Center for Early Adolescence at the University of North Carolina, she wrote the widely acclaimed book, *Successful Schools for Young Adolescents.*

- Having teachers team-teach in more flexibly designed curriculum blocks that integrate several disciplines, instead of presenting students with disconnected, rigidly separated 50-minute segments
- Boosting students' health and fitness with more in-school programs and helping students who need public health care to get it

Through its Middle Grade School State Policy Initiative, the Carnegie Foundation of New York is implementing the *Turning Points* recommendations in nearly 100 schools and 15 states nationwide. A national evaluation of this initiative is currently under way. Data from

(a)

(b)

(a) The transition from high school to college has a number of parallels with the transition from elementary school to middle or junior high school, including the "top-dog" phenomenon. (b) An especially important aspect of the transition to college is reduced interaction with parents.

the state of Illinois already show that in 42 schools participating in at least 1 year of the study since 1991, enactment of the *Turning Points* recommendations is associated with significant improvements in students' reading, math, and language arts achievement. In 31 schools with several years of data, the same pattern of positive results has been found *within* schools over time. That is, as schools continue to implement the *Turning Points* recommendations, students' achievement continues to improve (Carnegie Council on Adolescent Development, 1995).

> *What does education often do? It makes a straight-cut ditch of a free, meandering brook.*
>
> —Henry David Thoreau

Transition from High School to College

Just as the transition from elementary school to middle or junior high school involves change and possible stress, so does the transition from high school to college. In many ways, the two transitions involve parallel changes. Going from a senior in high school to a freshman in college replays the "top-dog" phenomenon of going from the oldest and most powerful group of students to the

youngest and least powerful group of students. For many of you, the transition from high school to college was not too long ago. You may vividly remember the feeling of your first days, weeks, and months on campus. You were called a freshman. Dictionary definitions of *freshmen* describe them not only as being in the first year of high school or college but as being novices or beginners. *Senior* not only designates the fourth year of high school or college, but also implies being above others in decision-making power. The transition from high school to college involves a move to a larger, more impersonal school structure, interaction with peers from more diverse geographical and sometimes more diverse ethnic backgrounds, and increased focus on achievement and performance, and their assessment.

But as with the transition from elementary school to middle or junior high school, the transition from high school to college can have positive aspects. Students are more likely to feel grown up, have more subjects from which to select, have more time to spend with peers, have more opportunities to explore different lifestyles and values, enjoy greater independence from parental monitoring, and may be more challenged intellectually by academic work.

In one recent study, the transition from high school to college or full-time work was characterized as a time of growth rather than hardship (Aseltine & Gore, 1993). During this transition, the individuals showed lower

		Students %	Parents %
College representatives at "College Nights"	Relevant	62	65
	Accurate	73	68
High school counselors	Relevant	57	49
	Accurate	70	62
Comparative guides	Relevant	53	50
	Accurate	65	59
College publications	Relevant	32	34
	Accurate	59	49

Figure~8.2

Evaluation of Major Sources of College Information by College-Bound High School Seniors and Their Parents (percentage agreeing).

levels of depression and delinquency than when they were in the last 2 years of high school. The improvement was related to better relationships with their parents.

For many individuals, a major change from high school to college is reduced contact with parents. One investigation revealed that going away to college might not only benefit the individual's independence but also improve relationships with parents (Sullivan & Sullivan, 1980). Two groups of parents and their sons were studied. One group of sons left home to board at college; the other group remained home and commuted daily to college. The students were evaluated both before they had completed high school and after they were in college. Those who boarded at college were more affectionate toward their parents, communicated better with them, and were more independent from them than their counterparts who remained at home and attended college. In another recent study, preestablished affective relationships were related to college adjustment (Takahashi & Majima, 1994). Peer-oriented students adjusted better to the high school/college transition than family-dominant students did.

The large number of individuals who go directly to college after completing high school delay formal entry into the adult world of work. You may remember from chapter 1 the description of *youth*, a post-high-school age period involving a sense of economic and personal "temporariness" (Kenniston, 1970). For many individuals, going to college postpones career or marriage/family decisions. The major shift to college attendance occurred in the post–World War II years, as the GI Bill opened up a college education for many individuals. Since the 1960s, college attendance has steadily increased.

Students often go to college expecting something special. As one high school student said, "My main concern is that, without a college education, I won't have much chance in today's world. I want a better life, which to me, means going to college." While high school students usu-

ally approach college with high expectations, their transition from high school to college may be less than ideal. In a study of undergraduate education in the United States, the Carnegie Foundation for the Advancement of Teaching pointed out the disturbing discontinuity between public high schools and institutions of higher learning (Boyer, 1986). Almost half of the prospective college students surveyed said that trying to select a college is confusing because there is no sound basis for making a decision. Many high school seniors choose a college almost blindfolded. Once enrolled, they may not be satisfied with their choice and may transfer or drop out, sometimes for the wrong reasons. The transition from high school to college needs to become smoother. As a first step, public schools should take far more responsibility for assisting students in the transition from high schools to college. Public high schools could learn considerably from the best private schools, which have always taken this transition seriously, according to the Carnegie Foundation report. Colleges also need to provide more helpful guidance to prospective students, going beyond glossy brochures and becoming more personalized in their interaction with high school students. Figure 8.2 suggests that college representatives, high school counselors, comparative guides, and college publications have a long way to go.

Today's college freshmen appear to be experiencing more stress and depression than in the past, according to a UCLA survey of more than 300,000 freshmen at more than 500 colleges and universities (Astin & others, 1997). In 1987, 16 percent of college freshmen said they frequently felt overwhelmed; in 1996 that figure had risen to almost 30 percent. Fear of failing in a success-oriented world is frequently given as a reason for stress and depression among college students. The pressure to succeed in college, get an outstanding job, and make lots of money is pervasive, according to many of the students.

High School Dropouts and Noncollege Youth

Dropping out of high school has been viewed as a serious educational and societal problem for many decades. By leaving high school before graduating, many dropouts have educational deficiencies that severely curtail their economic and social well-being throughout their adult lives. In this section, we study the scope of the problem, the causes of dropping out, and ways to reduce dropout rates.

High School Dropout Rates

Over the past 40 years, the proportion of adolescents who have not finished high school to those who have has decreased considerably. In 1940, more than 60 percent of 25- to 29-year-olds had not completed high school. Today, this figure is approximately 15 percent.

Despite the overall decline in high school dropout rates, the higher dropout rate of ethnic minority students and low-income students, especially in large cities, remains a major concern. Although the dropout rates of most ethnic minority students have been declining, the rates remain substantially above those of White students. Thirty-five percent of 20- to 21-year-old Latinos, 18 percent of 20- to 21-year-old African Americans, and 14 percent of 20- to 21-year-old White Americans have dropped out of school. Dropout rates are extremely high for Native Americans: fewer than 10 percent graduate from high school. In some inner-city areas, the dropout rate for ethnic minority students is especially high, reaching more than 50 percent in Chicago, for example (Hahn, 1987). Latino dropout rates have declined little, if at all, in the past decade. Although the dropout rate of African Americans has declined considerably in recent years, it still remains above that of White students (see figure 8.3).

Might school personnel overestimate the ability of parents to assume responsibility for keeping their youth in school? In one recent 4-year longitudinal study, 100 at-risk Mexican American adolescents were assessed from 15 to 19 years of age (Romo & Falbo, 1995). Schools significantly overestimated the resources of most of the youths' parents, many of whom could not speak English. Many of the Mexican American parents thought that school personnel were the education experts and that therefore the educators should know how to motivate students to come to school, adequately perform schoolwork, and graduate from high school.

The Causes of Dropping Out

Students drop out of school for school-related, economic, family-related, peer-related, and personal reasons. School-related problems are consistently associated with dropping out of school (Ianni & Orr, 1996; McDougall, Schonert-Reichl, & Hymel, 1996). In one investigation, almost 50 percent of the dropouts cited school-

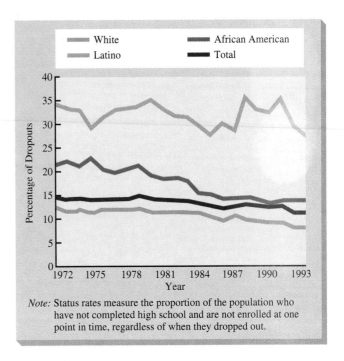

Note: Status rates measure the proportion of the population who have not completed high school and are not enrolled at one point in time, regardless of when they dropped out.

Figure~8.3

High School Dropout Rates.

related reasons for leaving school, such as not liking school, being suspended, or being expelled (Rumberger, 1983). Twenty percent of the dropouts (but 40 percent of the Latino students) cited economic reasons for dropping out. Many of these students quit school and go to work to help support their families. Socioeconomic status is the main factor in family background that is strongly related to dropping out of school: Students from low-income families are more likely to drop out than those from middle-income families. Many school dropouts have friends who also are school dropouts. Approximately one-third of the girls who drop out of school do so for personal reasons, such as pregnancy or marriage. However, overall, males are more likely than females to drop out.

Most research on dropouts has focused on high school students. One recent study focused on middle school dropouts (Rumberger, 1995). The observed differences in dropout rates among ethnic groups were related to differences in family background—especially socioeconomic status. Lack of parental academic support, low parental supervision, and low parental educational expectations for their adolescents were also related to dropping out of middle school.

Many of the factors just mentioned were related to dropping out of school in one large-scale investigation called *The High School and Beyond Study*, in which 30,000 high school sophomores were followed through graduation (Goertz, Ekstrom, & Rock, 1991). High school dropouts were more likely to come from low-income families, be in vocational programs, be males, be an ethnic minority (but not Asian American), and be in an urban school district (compared to rural or suburban). In addition, high school dropouts had lower grades in school (especially in reading), more disciplinary problems, lower rates of homework completion, lower self-esteem, lower educational expectations, and a more externalized sense of control. In one recent longitudinal study, high school dropouts had less language stimulation early in their development, compared to students who graduated from high school in a normal time frame (Cohen, 1994). And in another recent longitudinal study, very high, cumulative, early family stress had an impact on about one-half of the adolescents who subsequently dropped out of school (Jacobs, Garnier, & Weisner, 1996). In this same study, children at risk for dropping of school who subsequently showed resilience and did not drop out of school had a more positive relational system within the family.

These adolescents participate in the "I Have a Dream" Program, a comprehensive, long-term dropout prevention program that has been very successful.

Reducing the Dropout Rate and Improving the Lives of Noncollege Youth

The dropout rate can be reduced and the lives of noncollege youth improved by strengthening the schools and by bridging the gap between school and work (William T. Grant Foundation Commission on Work, Family, and Citizenship, 1988).

Part of the solution lies within schools. Students may work hard through twelve grades of school, attain adequate records, learn basic academic skills, graduate in good standing, and still experience problems in getting started in a productive career. Others may drop out of school because they see little benefit from the type of education they are getting. Although no complete cure-all, strengthening schools is an important dimension of reducing dropout rates. While the education reform movements of the 1980s have encouraged schools to set higher standards for students and teachers, most of the focus has been on college-bound students. But reform movements should not penalize students who will not go to college. One way non-college-bound youth are being helped is through chapter 1 of the Education Consolidation and Improvement Act, which provides extra services for low-achieving students. States and communities need to establish clear goals for school completion, youth employment, parental involvement, and youth community service. For example, it should be the goal of every state to reduce the dropout rate to 10 percent or less by the year 2000.

One innovative program is the I Have a Dream (IHAD) Program, a comprehensive, long-term dropout prevention program administered by the National "I Have a Dream" Foundation in New York. Local IHAD projects around the country "adopt" entire grades (usually the third or fourth) from public elementary schools, or corresponding age-cohorts from public housing developments. These children—"Dreamers"—are then provided with a program of academic, social, cultural, and recreational activities throughout their elementary, middle school, and high school years. An important part of this program is that it is personal rather than institutional: IHAD sponsors and staff develop close long-term relationships with the children. When participants complete high school, IHAD provides the tuition assistance necessary for them to attend a state or local college or vocational school.

The IHAD Program was created in 1981, when philanthropist Eugene Lang made an impromptu offer of college tuition to a class of graduating sixth-graders at P.S. 121 in East Harlem. Statistically, 75 percent of the students should have dropped out of school; instead, 90 percent graduated and 60 percent went on to college. Since the National IHAD Foundation was created in 1986, it has grown to number over 150 Projects in 57 cities and 28 states, serving some 12,000 children.

Community institutions, especially schools, need to break down the barriers between work and school. Many youth step off the education ladder long before reaching the level of a professional career, often with nowhere to step next, left to their own devices to search for work. These youth need more assistance than they are now receiving. Among the approaches worth considering are these:

- Monitored work experiences, such as through cooperative education, apprenticeships, internships, preemployment training, and youth-operated enterprises
- Community and neighborhood services, including voluntary service and youth-guided services

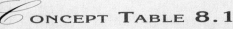

CONCEPT TABLE 8.1

The Nature of Schooling and Transitions in Schooling

Concept	Processes/Related Ideas	Characteristics/Description
The Nature of Adolescents' Schooling	Functions of schools	In the nineteenth century, secondary schools were for the elite. By the 1920s, they had changed, becoming more comprehensive and training adolescents for work and citizenship, as well as training intellect. The comprehensive high school remains today, but the functions of secondary schools continue to be debated. Supporters of the back-to-basics movement maintain that the function of schools should be intellectual development; others argue for more comprehensive functions, including social and vocational development.
	Do schools make a difference?	Some sociologists have argued that schools have little impact on adolescents' development, but when researchers have conducted more precise, observational studies of what goes on in schools and classrooms, the effects of schooling become more apparent.
	Schools' changing social developmental contexts	The social context differs at the preschool, elementary school, and secondary school levels, increasing in scope and complexity for adolescents.
Transitions in Schooling	Transition to middle or junior high school	The emergence of junior high schools in the 1920s and 1930s was justified on the basis of physical, cognitive, and social changes that characterize early adolescence, as well as on the need for more schools in response to the growing student population. Middle schools have become more popular in recent years and coincide with earlier pubertal development. The transition to middle or junior high school coincides with many social, familial, and individual changes in the adolescent's life. The transition involves moving from the "top-dog" to the "bottom-dog" position.
	What makes a successful middle school?	Successful schools for young adolescents take individual differences in development seriously, show a deep concern for what is known about early adolescence, and emphasize social and emotional development as much as intellectual development. In 1989, the Carnegie Corporation recommended a major redesign of middle schools.
	Transition from high school to college	In a number of ways, the transition from high school to college parallels the transition from elementary to middle or junior high school, including the "top-dog" phenomenon. An especially important transition for most adolescents is reduced interaction with parents. A special problem today is the discontinuity between public high schools and colleges.
	High school dropouts and noncollege youth	Dropping out of high school has been a serious problem for decades. Many dropouts have educational deficiencies that curtail their economic and social well-being for much of their adult lives. Some progress has been made in that dropout rates for most ethnic minority groups have declined in recent decades, although dropout rates for inner-city, low-income minorities are still precariously high. Dropping out of school is associated with demographic, family-related, peer-related, school-related, economic, and personal factors. The dropout rate could be reduced and the lives of noncollege youth improved by strengthening the schools and by bridging the gap between school and work.

The Exceptional Student in the Regular Classroom 6/e by Gearheart/Weishahn, © 1996. Adapted by permission of Prentice-Hall, Inc., Upper Saddle River, NJ.

- Redirected vocational education, the principal thrust of which should not be preparation for specific jobs but acquisition of basic skills needed in a wide range of work
- Guarantees of continuing education, employment, or training, especially in conjunction with mentoring programs
- Career information and counseling to expose youth to job opportunities and career options as well as to successful role models

- School volunteer programs, not only for tutoring but to provide access to adult friends and mentors

At this point, we have discussed a number of ideas about the nature of adolescent schooling and transitions in schooling. A summary of these ideas is presented in concept table 8.1. Next, we describe some dimensions of schools and classrooms, and characteristics of teachers and peers, that influence adolescent development.

SCHOOLS, CLASSROOMS, TEACHERS, PEERS, AND PARENTS

Schools and classrooms vary along many dimensions, including size of school or class and school or class atmosphere, with some schools and classes being highly structured, others more unstructured. Adolescents' lives in school also involve thousands of hours of interactions with teachers and peers. A special concern is parent involvement in the adolescent's schooling.

Size, Structure, and Climate of Schools

What size were the schools you went to as an adolescent? Do you think they were too big? too small? Let's explore the effects of school size, as well as classroom size, on adolescent development.

School Size and Classroom Size

A number of factors led to the increased size of secondary schools in the United States: increasing urban enrollments, decreasing budgets, and an educational rationale of increased academic stimulation in consolidated institutions. But is bigger really better? No systematic relation between school size and academic achievement has been found, but more prosocial and possibly less antisocial behavior occur in small schools (Rutter & others, 1979). Large schools, especially those with more than 500 to 600 students, might not provide a personalized climate that allows for an effective system of social control. Students may feel alienated and not take responsibility for their conduct. This might be especially true for unsuccessful students who do not identify with their school and who become members of oppositional peer groups. The responsiveness of the school can mediate the impact of school size on adolescent behavior. For example, in one investigation, low-responsive schools (which offered few rewards for desirable behavior) had higher crime rates than high-responsive schools (McPartland & McDill, 1976). Although school responsiveness may mediate adolescent conduct, small schools may be more flexible and responsive than larger schools.

Besides the belief that smaller schools provide adolescents with a better education, there also is a belief that smaller classes are better than larger classes. Traditional schools in the Untied States have 30 to 35 students per classroom. Analysis of a large number of investigations revealed that, as class size increases, achievement decreases (Glass & Smith, 1978). The researchers concluded that a pupil who would score at about the 63rd percentile on a national test when taught individually would score at about the 37th percentile when taught in a class of 40 students per classroom. They also concluded that being taught in a class of 20 students versus a class of 40 students is an advantage of about 10 percentile points on national achievement tests in the subject. These researchers also found that the greatest gains in achievement occurred among students who were taught in classes of 15 students or less. In classes of 20 to 40 students, class size had a less dramatic influence on students' achievement. Although this research has been criticized on methodological grounds, other researchers have reanalyzed the data using different techniques and arrived at the same conclusions (Hedges & Stock, 1983).

Unfortunately, to maximize each adolescent's learning potential, classes would have to be so small that few schools could afford to staff and house them (Klein, 1985). While class sizes of 15 students or less are not feasible for all subjects, one alternative is to allocate a larger portion of resources to those grade levels or subjects that seem the most critical. For example, some schools are beginning to reduce class size in core academic subjects, such as mathematics, English, and science, while having higher class sizes in elective subjects.

Classroom Structure and Climate

The most widely debated issue in classroom structure and climate focuses on open versus traditional classrooms. The open versus traditional concept is multidimensional. Open classrooms, or open schools, have characteristics such as the following:

- Free choice of activities by students
- Space flexibility
- Varied, enriched learning materials
- Emphasis on individual and small-group instruction
- A teacher who is more a facilitator than a director of learning
- Students who learn to assume responsibility for their learning
- Multi-age groupings of children
- Team-teaching
- Classrooms without walls in which the physical arrangement of the school is more open

Overall, researchers have found that open classrooms are associated with lower language achievement but improved attitudes toward school (Giaconia & Hedges, 1982).

Beyond the overall effects of open versus traditional classrooms, it is important to evaluate how specific dimensions of open classrooms are related to specific dimensions of the adolescent's development. In this regard, researchers have found that individualized instruction (adjusting rate, methods, materials, small-group methods) and role of the adolescent (the degree of activity in learning) are associated with positive effects on the adolescent's self-concept (Giaconia & Hedges, 1982).

Person-Environment Fit and Aptitude-Treatment Interaction

Some of the negative psychological changes associated with adolescent development might result from a mismatch between the needs of developing adolescents and the opportunities afforded them by the schools they attend. Adolescent expert Jacqueline Eccles and her colleagues (Eccles & others, 1993) described ways in which developmentally appropriate school environments can be created that match up better with adolescents' needs. Their recommendations are based on a large-scale study of 1,500 young adolescents in middle-income communities in Michigan. These adolescents were studied as they made the change from the sixth grade in an elementary school to the seventh grade in a junior high school.

Both the early adolescents and their teachers reported less opportunity for adolescent participation in classroom decision making in the seventh grade than in the sixth grade. By contrast, the students wanted to participate more in classroom decision making in the seventh grade than in the sixth grade. According to Eccles and her colleagues, such findings represent a person-environment mismatch that harms adolescent development.

As we have just seen, the characteristics and motivation of the adolescent need to be considered in determining what form of education is developmentally appropriate for them. In education, this match is usually referred to as **aptitude-treatment interaction (ATI)**, *which stresses the importance of both adolescents' characteristics and motivation and the treatments or experiences they receive in schools. Aptitude refers to such characteristics as the academic potential and personality characteristics on which students differ; treatment refers to educational techniques, such as structured versus flexible classrooms.*

Researchers have found that adolescents' achievement level (aptitude) interacts with classroom structure (treatment) to produce the best learning (Cronbach & Snow, 1977). For example, students who are highly achievement oriented usually do well in a flexible classroom and enjoy it; low-achievement-oriented students usually fare worse and dislike such flexibility. The reverse often appears in structured classrooms.

Teachers, Peers, and Parents

Adolescents' development is influenced by teachers and peers at school. In addition, an increasingly important issue is parent involvement in schooling.

Interactions with Teachers

Virtually everyone's life is affected in one way or another by teachers. You probably were influenced by teachers as you grew up. One day you may have, or perhaps you already have, children and adolescents whose lives will be guided by many different teachers. You likely can remember several of your teachers vividly. Perhaps one never smiled,

"You'll find 'Teaching Methods That Never Fail' under fiction."

Reprinted by permission of Ford Button.

another required you to memorize everything in sight, and yet another always appeared vibrant and encouraged question asking. Psychologists and educators have tried to compile a profile of a good teacher's personality traits, but the complexity of personality, education, learning, and individuals makes this a difficult task. Nonetheless, some teacher traits are associated with positive student outcomes more than others—enthusiasm, ability to plan, poise, adaptability, warmth, flexibility, and awareness of individual differences, for example. And in one study, positive teacher expectations were linked with higher student achievement (Jussim & Eccles, 1993).

Erik Erikson (1968) believes that good teachers produce a sense of industry, rather than inferiority, in their students. Good teachers are trusted and respected by the community and know how to alternate work and play, study and games, says Erikson. They know how to recognize special efforts and to encourage special abilities. They also know how to create a setting in which adolescents feel good about themselves and know how to handle those adolescents to whom school is not important. In Erikson's (1968) own words, adolescents should be "mildly but firmly coerced into the adventure of finding out that one can learn to accomplish things which one would never have thought of by oneself."

Other recommendations for successful teaching with young adolescents have been offered by adolescent educator Stephanie Feeney (1980). She believes that meaningful learning takes place when the developmental characteristics of the age group are understood, when trust has been established, and when adolescents feel free to explore, to experiment, and to make mistakes.

The variability and change that characterizes young adolescents make them a difficult age group to instruct. The student who leans on the teacher one day for help may be strutting around independently the next day. Teachers who work successfully with young adolescents probably have vivid memories of their own adolescence and likely have mastered the developmental tasks of those years. Able to recall their youthful vulnerability, they understand and respect their students' sensitivity to criticism, desire for group acceptance, and feelings of being acutely conspicuous. Successful teachers of adolescents are secure in their own identity and comfortable with their sexuality. Possessing clear values, they use power and authority wisely and are sensitive to their students' feelings. Young adolescents respond best to teachers who exercise natural authority—based on greater age, experience, and widom—rather than arbitrary authority or abdication of authority by being pals with the adolescent. Young adolescents need teachers who are fair and consistent, who set reasonable limits, and who realize that adolescents need someone to push against while testing those limits.

In the study of adolescents and schooling by Jacquelynne Eccles and her colleagues (1993), some characteristics of the teachers in the seventh grade have implications for the quality of adolescent education. Seventh-grade teachers had less confidence in their teaching efficacy than their sixth-grade counterparts did. Also, students who moved from high-efficacy teachers in the sixth grade to low-efficacy teachers in the seventh grade had lower expectations for themselves and said school was more difficult at the end of the seventh grade than did adolescents who experienced no change in teacher efficacy or who moved from low-efficacy to high-efficacy teachers.

Student-teacher relationships began to deteriorate after the transition to junior high school. Also, students who moved from elementary school teachers they perceived to be supportive to junior high school teachers they perceived to be unsupportive showed a decline in the value they attached to an important school subject—math. Low-achieving students were especially at risk when they moved to less facilitative classroom environments after the junior high transition.

Interactions with Peers

The peer group is an important source of status, friendship, and belonging in the school setting. The peer group also is a learning community in which social roles and standards related to work and achievement are formed. At school, adolescents are with each other for at least six hours per day. The school also provides the locus for many of the adolescent's activities after school and on weekends.

James Coleman (1961) conducted a classic investigation of the association patterns of students. He found that social structures vary from school to school. In some schools, the association patterns of students are very intense, while in others, they are more casual. In small schools,

more students are members of various cliques than in large schools, where simple pair relationships occur more frequently. There are even differences in group structures among the large schools. In one suburban school that Coleman studied, the social structure was far more complete and fully developed than in another. Probably because of greater community solidarity, middle-class status, and greater parental interest in the schooling process, many more community functions were carried out in and after school in the first school. Clustering social activities around a school helps to strengthen the social system of the students.

Coleman (1961) analyzed the peer associations of boys and girls separately in small schools. Boys achieved status within their schools in a variety of ways. In some schools, the "all-around boy"—athlete, ladies' man, and, to some extent, scholar—achieved status, while in other schools, being either an athlete or a scholar was enough to assure high status. However, recall from our discussion of cliques in chapter 7 that, in most schools, being an intellect does not qualify a student for high status in the peer society.

The association patterns of the girls varied considerably in small schools as well. Elmtown had the largest number of girl cliques, the largest percentage of girls in cliques, and the smallest average clique size. Marketville was the opposite in each of these respects. In Marketville and Maple Grove, middle-class girls from well-educated families formed cliques that dominated social activities, school activities, and adolescent attention. Teachers perceived these cliques as being in control of the student body and clique members as the girls most encouraged by the adults in the community.

Athletic achievement played an important role in the status systems of boys in all ten schools Coleman (1961) studied. Why are athletics so important in the status systems of American high schools? Adolescents identify strongly with their schools and communities. The identification, in part at least, is due to the fact that the school and the community of adolescents are virtually synonymous. They compete as a school against other schools in athletic contests. So the heroes of the system—those with high status—are the boys who win for the school and the community of adolescents. When they win, the entire school and the entire community of adolescents feel better about themselves.

Because boys have had greater opportunity to participate in interscholastic athletics than girls have, they have been more likely to attain high-status positions in schools. However, in the 1970s, the federal government took a major step toward reducing this form of discrimination against female adolescents. Title IX of the 1972 Educational Amendments Act prohibits any educational program from receiving federal funds if sex discrimination is practiced. So far, this act has not produced parity for girls and boys in interscholastic athletics, but girls have made greater strides than ever before in participating in interscholastic events.

In the last two decades, female adolescents have made enormous strides in their participation in interscholastic events.

While research on male athletic participation has produced consistent findings of its high status in schools, research on female athletic participation has produced mixed findings. In one investigation, the type of sport females participated in was studied to determine its relation to status in the school (Kane, 1988). One hundred and twenty-one male students were asked to indicate which female athlete they would like to date—one identified with gender-inappropriate sports (such as basketball) or one identified with gender-appropriate sports (like tennis). As predicted, females associated with gender-appropriate sports were accorded more status than females associated with gender-inappropriate sports.

Since the passage of Title IX, female enrollments in previously male-dominated fields, such as engineering, law, and business, have more than doubled, and reams have been written about sexism in the language, policies, and practices of education. More about gender roles in schools appears later in chapter 11, "Gender," and in Sociocultural Worlds of Adolescence.

Parents and Schools

It is commonly believed that parent involvement is important in the child's schooling but that parents play a much smaller role in the adolescent's schooling. Increasingly, though, researchers are finding that parents can be key factors in schooling at all grade levels (Connors & Epstein, 1995; Ryan & others, 1995). However, parents are not as involved in their adolescents' schooling as they or the schools would like (Comer, 1988). Even though parental involvement is minimal in elementary school, it is even less in secondary school (Eccles & Harold, 1993).

Joyce Epstein (1990) has provided a framework for understanding how parental involvement in adolescents' schooling can be improved. First, *families have a basic obligation to provide for the safety and health of their adolescents*. Many parents are not knowledgeable about the normal age-appropriate changes that characterize adolescents. School-family programs can help to educate parents about the normal course of adolescent development. Schools also can offer programs about health issues in adolescence, including sexually transmitted diseases, depression, drugs, delinquency, and eating disorders. Schools also can help parents find safe places for their adolescents to spend time away from home. Schools are community buildings that could be used as program sites by youth organizations and social service agencies.

Second, *schools have a basic obligation to communicate with families about school programs and the individual progress of their adolescents*. Teachers and parents rarely get to know each other in the secondary school years. Programs are needed to facilitate more direct and personalized parent-teacher communication. Parents also need to receive better information about curricular choices that may be related to eventual career choices. This is especially important with regard to females and ethnic minority students enrolling in science and math courses.

Third, *parents' involvement at school needs to be increased*. Parents and other family members may be able to assist teachers in the classroom in a variety of ways, such as tutoring, teaching special skills, and providing clerical or supervisory assistance. Such involvement is especially important in inner-city schools.

Fourth, *parent involvement in the adolescent's learning activities at home needs to be encouraged*. Secondary schools often raise a concern about parents' expertise and ability in helping their adolescents with homework. Given this concern, schools could provide parents with supplementary educational training so that parents can be more helpful and confident in their ability. "Family Math" and "Family Computers" are examples of programs that have been developed by some secondary schools to increase parent involvement in adolescent learning.

Fifth, *parents need to be increasingly involved in decision making at school*. Parent-teacher associations are the most common way for parents to be involved in school decision making. In some school districts, school improvement teams consisting of school staff and parents have been formed to address specific concerns.

Sixth, *collaboration and exchange with community organizations need to be encouraged*. Agencies and businesses can join with schools to improve adolescents' educational experiences. Business personnel can especially provide insights into careers and the world of work. Some schools have formed partnerships with businesses, which provide some financial backing for special projects.

William H. Johnson
Girl in Green Dress

The boy on the left is a tutor in the Valued Youth Program, which takes at-risk middle and high school students and gives them the responsibility of tutoring elementary school children.

The Valued Youth Program

In twenty-nine secondary schools across the country, there is a program that takes middle and high school students who are in at-risk situations and gives them the responsibility of tutoring elementary school children (Simons, Finlay, & Yang, 1991). The hope is that the tutoring experience will improve the young adolescents' feelings about themselves and school. The belief also is that students often learn their subject matter better if they have to teach it to others.

During one class period a day for 4 days a week, students in the Valued Youth Program (VYP), developed by the Intercultural Development Research Association, walk, or ride a bus, with a teacher to a nearby elementary school. Each tutor works with three children on subjects such as mathematics or reading and stays with them for the entire school year. On the fifth day of the week, the tutors work with their teacher at their own school, discussing tutoring skills, reflecting on how the week has gone, and brushing up on their own literacy skills. For their work, the tutors receive course credit and minimum-wage pay.

One of the VYP tutors reported, "Tutoring makes me want to come to school because I have to come and teach the younger kids." He also said that he doesn't miss many days of school because when he does miss school the children always ask him where he has been and tell him that they missed him. He says that he really likes the kids he teaches and that if he had not been a tutor he probably would have dropped out of school by now.

In a recent analysis, fewer than 1 percent of the Valued Youth Program tutors had dropped out of school, compared with a 14 percent national dropout rate (Intercultural Development Research Association, 1996). New sites have recently brought the Valued Youth Program to 76 schools in 16 cities.

Exploring Adolescent Development

To further explore the nature of adolescent development, we will examine a research study on cooperative learning and discuss a peer tutoring project for at-risk middle and secondary school students.

Research on Adolescent Development

Cooperative Learning

Featured Study

Stevens, R. J., & Slavin, R. E. (1995). The cooperative elementary school: Effects on students' achievement, attitudes, and social relations. *American Educational Research Journal, 32,* 321–351.

Cooperative learning methods have been studied for more than two decades and have been increasingly used in elementary and secondary schools. Most applications of cooperative learning have been implemented teacher by teacher, usually one subject at a time, and few studies have covered more than one semester. Could cooperative learning be used on a broad scale in many subjects and over extended time frames to basically change the organization of schools and classrooms? This was one of the main questions addressed in this study.

The components of the cooperative learning model were these: using cooperative learning across a variety of content areas, full-scale inclusion of academically disabled students in regular classrooms, teachers' using peer coaching, teachers' planning cooperatively, and parent involvement in the school.

Method

The subjects were 1,012 second- to sixth-grade students in a suburban Maryland school district. Twenty-one classes in the two treatment schools were matched with 24 classes in the three comparison schools on the basis of achievement test scores in a number of areas. The schools were located in predominantly working-class neighborhoods. Slightly fewer than 10 percent of the students were learning disabled.

Each component of the cooperative learning program was gradually phased in during the first year. Prior to implementation of the component, faculty were given training on its use. During the school year, members of the research staff observed classes, met with teachers, and observed steering committee meetings to facilitate the implementation of the cooperative learning program.

Assessment of the program's results was conducted over a 2-year period. In the spring of the first and second years of the study, teachers administered the California Achievement Test. Both pre- and posttest, students' attitudes toward, and their perceived ability in, various school subjects were evaluated, and students' social relations also were assessed by asking the students to list the names of their friends in the class.

Results

After the first year of the program's implementation, students in the cooperative schools had higher achievement in reading vocabulary than did the students in the regular schools. After the second year, students in the cooperative schools had higher achievement in reading vocabulary, reading comprehension, language expression, and math computation than did their regular-classroom counterparts. After 2 years, academically disabled students in the cooperative schools had higher achievement in a wide variety of academic subjects than did their peers in the regular schools. The social relations of students in the cooperative schools also were better.

Discussion

Because the experimental cooperative learning program had so many components, it is difficult to determine which component(s) made the program a success. Nonetheless, the results support the belief that cooperative learning can be applied across many subject domains. Future research should disentangle which of these components give cooperative learning an advantage.

Should There Be Separate Schools for Girls and for Boys?

Should girls and boys learn together or in single-sex schools? Single-sex schools have become an endangered species. They are illegal in the public sector and have declined in the private sector. Originally 100 percent of Catholic schools were single-sex, but today almost 60 percent are coeducational.

Even as single-sex schools fight to survive, recent research has offered a stunning message: Schools without boys appear to be good for girls (Hollinger, 1993). Although some critics point to flaws in the research methods, the evidence is persuasive. Girls in single-sex schools have higher self-esteem, are more interested in nontraditional subjects such as math and science, and are less likely to stereotype jobs and careers than are their coeducational counterparts.

In all-girl schools, girls have more appropriate role models and mentors—females. Girls are more likely to be educational players, rather than educational spectators, in single-sex schools. One science teacher commented that she used to teach in a coed school and had to be constantly vigilant because the boys were so verbally aggressive, demanding attention. The teacher had to establish a personal relationship with the girls before they would talk or take intellectual risks in the classroom. Another teacher mentioned that when a classroom is all female, girls speak out, but when boys are in the class, girls stop asking questions (Sadker & Sadker, 1994).

What about single-sex schools for boys? Do they show the same benefits as single-sex schools for girls? The jury is still out on this issue, with mixed research findings and mixed commentary from teachers (Hollinger, 1993). Amid the contradictory findings is one positive benefit of all-male schools: boys in these schools value and enjoy nontraditional topics such as literature and art more than their coeducational counterparts do (Foon, 1988). However, there also is a negative side to all-male schools: the most clearly disturbing forms of sexism occur in all-male schools. In some all-male schools, classroom discussions have been observed to degenerate into discussions of girls as sex objects.

So what should we do? Promoters of coeducation argue that boys and girls learning together is a more realistic system and the best preparation for a democratic society. Advocates for girls' schools say that girls do not get a fair chance in coed schools

and that the research evidence is now very strong in documenting this. One of the leading researchers on single-sex schools, Valerie Lee (1994), concluded that much depends on the particular school. In her research, there was a wide range of quality and equality in single-sex schools. Some girls' schools looked like throwbacks to nineteenth-century finishing schools to prepare little ladies, while others paid serious attention to gender and encouraged assertiveness and question asking. Lee does not come down on one side or the other on the issue of single-sex schools versus coeducation, but she does argue that the good single-sex girls' schools—those that increase girls' self-esteem and encourage their intellectual curiosity—should not be allowed to become extinct.

What are some of the potential advantages and disadvantages of single-sex schools for girls?

259

SOCIOCULTURAL WORLDS OF ADOLESCENCE

Should There Be Separate Schools for Girls and for Boys?

Should girls and boys learn together or in single-sex schools? Single-sex schools have become an endangered species. They are illegal in the public sector and have declined in the private sector. Originally 100 percent of Catholic schools were single-sex, but today almost 60 percent are coeducational.

Even as single-sex schools fight to survive, recent research has offered a stunning message: Schools without boys appear to be good for girls (Hollinger, 1993). Although some critics point to flaws in the research methods, the evidence is persuasive. Girls in single-sex schools have higher self-esteem, are more interested in nontraditional subjects such as math and science, and are less likely to stereotype jobs and careers than are their coeducational counterparts.

In all-girl schools, girls have more appropriate role models and mentors—females. Girls are more likely to be educational players, rather than educational spectators, in single-sex schools. One science teacher commented that she used to teach in a coed school and had to be constantly vigilant because the boys were so verbally aggressive, demanding attention. The teacher had to establish a personal relationship with the girls before they would talk or take intellectual risks in the classroom. Another teacher mentioned that when a classroom is all female, girls speak out, but when boys are in the class, girls stop asking questions (Sadker & Sadker, 1994).

What about single-sex schools for boys? Do they show the same benefits as single-sex schools for girls? The jury is still out on this issue, with mixed research findings and mixed commentary from teachers (Hollinger, 1993). Amid the contradictory findings is one positive benefit of all-male schools: boys in these schools value and enjoy nontraditional topics such as literature and art more than their coeducational counterparts do (Foon, 1988). However, there also is a negative side to all-male schools: the most clearly disturbing forms of sexism occur in all-male schools. In some all-male schools, classroom discussions have been observed to degenerate into discussions of girls as sex objects.

So what should we do? Promoters of coeducation argue that boys and girls learning together is a more realistic system and the best preparation for a democratic society. Advocates for girls' schools say that girls do not get a fair chance in coed schools and that the research evidence is now very strong in documenting this. One of the leading researchers on single-sex schools, Valerie Lee (1994), concluded that much depends on the particular school. In her research, there was a wide range of quality and equality in single-sex schools. Some girls' schools looked like throwbacks to nineteenth-century finishing schools to prepare little ladies, while others paid serious attention to gender and encouraged assertiveness and question asking. Lee does not come down on one side or the other on the issue of single-sex schools versus coeducation, but she does argue that the good single-sex girls' schools—those that increase girls' self-esteem and encourage their intellectual curiosity—should not be allowed to become extinct.

What are some of the potential advantages and disadvantages of single-sex schools for girls?

Chapter 8: Schools

In summary, the collaborative relationship between parents and schools has usually decreased as children move into the adolescent years. Yet parent involvement might be just as important in the adolescent's schooling as in the child's schooling. For example, in one recent study, a program designed to increase parents' involvement in the education of their middle school students had positive effects on the students' school performance (Epstein & Dunbar, 1995). It is to be hoped that the future will bring much greater family/school/community collaboration in the adolescent years (Eccles & Harold, 1993).

SOCIAL CLASS AND ETHNICITY IN SCHOOLS

Sometimes, the major function of schools has appeared to be to train adolescents to contribute to a middle-class society. Politicians who vote on school funding have been from middle-class or elite backgrounds, school board members have often been from middle-class backgrounds, and principals and teachers also have had middle-class upbringing. Critics argue that schools have not done a good job of educating lower-class and ethnic minority children to overcome the barriers that block the enhancement of their position (Shade, Kelly & Oberg, 1997).

Social Class

In *Dark Ghetto*, Kenneth Clark (1965), the only African American to become president of the American Psychological Association, described the ways lower- and middle-class adolescents are treated differently in school. Clark observed that teachers in middle-class schools spent more time teaching students and evaluated students' work more than twice as much as teachers in low-income schools. Clark also observed that teachers in low-income schools made three times as many negative comments to students as did teachers in middle-class schools, who made more positive than negative comments to students. The following observations vividly describe a school in a large, urban slum area:

> It is 2 P.M., beginning of the sixth-period class, and Warren Benson, a young teacher, looks around the room. Eight students are present out of thirty. "Where is everybody?" he demands. "They don't like your class," a girl volunteers. Three girls saunter in. Cora, who is playing a cassette recorder, bumps over to her desk in time with the music. She lowers the volume. "Don't mark us down late," she shouts. "We was right here, you mother f_____."
> . . . Here you find students from poverty homes, students who can't read, students with drug problems, students wanting to drop out.

Teachers have lower expectations for adolescents from low-income families than for adolescents from middle-class families (Entwistle, 1990). A teacher who knows that an adolescent comes from a low-income family may spend less time trying to help the adolescent solve a problem and may anticipate that the adolescent will get into trouble. Teachers may perceive that low-income parents are not interested in helping the adolescent, so they may make fewer efforts to communicate with them.

Teachers from low-income backgrounds often have different attitudes toward students from low-income backgrounds than teachers from middle-income backgrounds. Possibly because they have experienced inequities themselves, teachers from low-income backgrounds may be more empathetic to the difficulties faced by adolescents from similar backgrounds. In one study, when asked to rate the most common characteristics of their students from low-income backgrounds, middle-class teachers checked "lazy," "rebellious," and "fun-loving"; teachers from low-income backgrounds checked "happy," "cooperative," "energetic," and "ambitious" (Gottlieb, 1966). Teachers from a low-income background perceive students from a similar background as behaving in adaptive ways, whereas teachers from a middle-class background perceive the same behaviors as falling short of middle-class standards.

Ethnicity

Adolescents from lower-class backgrounds are not the only students who have difficulties in school; so do adolescents from various ethnic backgrounds (Fenzel & Magaletta, 1993; Tharp, 1989). Martin Luther King once said, "I have a dream—that my four little children will one day live in a nation where they will not be judged by the color of their skin but by the content of their character." Like adolescents from low-income backgrounds, adolescents from different ethnic minority groups also have difficulty in schools. In most American schools, African Americans, Latinos, Native Americans, and Asian Americans are minorities. Many teachers have been ignorant of the different cultural attitudes, values, and behaviors that non-Anglo adolescents have learned in their communities (Chavkin, 1993). The social and academic development of ethnic minority students depends on the teacher's expectations; the teacher's experience in working with adolescents from diverse cultural backgrounds; the curriculum; the presence of role models in schools for ethnic minority students; the quality of the relations between school personnel and parents from different ethnic, economic, and educational backgrounds; and the relations between the school and the community. Our further discussion of ethnicity and schools focuses on the school experiences of different ethnic groups, teacher expectations, the family's role, desegregation and busing, cooperative learning and the jigsaw classroom, and the cultural subordination and exploitation of ethnic minority groups.

The School Experiences of Different Ethnic Groups

School segregation is still a factor in the education of African American and Latino adolescents (Simons, Finlay, & Yang, 1991). Almost one-third of African American and Latino students attend schools in which 90 percent or more of the students are from ethnic minority groups. In the last two decades, the proportion of Latino adolescents in predominantly minority schools has increased, while the proportion of African American adolescents in this type of schooling has decreased somewhat.

The school experiences of adolescents from different ethnic groups vary considerably. African American and Latino students are much less likely than White or Asian students to be enrolled in academic, college preparatory programs, and much more likely to be enrolled in remedial and special education programs. African American adolescents are twice as likely as adolescents from other ethnic groups to be enrolled in educable mentally retarded programs. Asian American adolescents are the least likely of any ethnic group to be in any special education program for students with disabilities. Asian American students are much more likely than any other ethnic group to be taking advanced math and science courses in high school. Almost one-fourth of all Asian American students take advanced placement calculus, compared with less than 3 percent of all other students, and Asian American students are three times as likely as any other ethnic group to take advanced placement chemistry or physics. African Americans are twice as likely as Latinos, Native Americans, or Whites to be suspended from school or corporally punished.

Catherine Cooper and her colleagues (1995) recently explored the experiences of Latino and African American junior high, high school, and college students who participate in university programs designed to link students' contexts of families, peers, school, college, and work. They commented on how academic outreach programs help to bridge the gaps across their contexts. Many of the students saw their schools and neighborhoods as contexts where people expected them to fail, become pregnant and leave school, or engage in delinquent activities. The outreach programs provided students with academic expectations and moral goals to do "something good for your people," such as working in their communities and encouraging their siblings to attend college.

In this research, two patterns stood out. First, students felt that *gatekeeping* was occurring when students and counselors discouraged them from taking classes required for university admission or attempted to enroll them in noncollege tracks. Second, students also described *brokering* across these barriers when families, teachers, program staff, siblings, and friends provided a refuge from such experiences and spoke up for them at school.

In the context of such experiences, the adolescents developed a sense of their future by drawing on positive and negative role models and reflecting on their own role in helping themselves and causing themselves difficulties. They mentioned family and academically involved friends, the dropping out and arrests of peers and friends, and their own negative experiences as strengthening their determination to study hard and prove the gatekeepers wrong.

Dr. Henry Gaskins began an after-school tutorial program for ethnic minority students in 1983 in Washington, D.C. For 4 hours every weeknight and all day Saturday, 80 students receive one-on-one assistance from Gaskins and his wife, two adult volunteers, and academically talented peers. Those who can afford it contribute five dollars to cover the cost of school supplies. In addition to tutoring in specific subjects, Gaskins's home-based academy helps students to set personal goals and to commit to a desire to succeed. Many of his students come from families in which the parents are high school dropouts and either cannot or are not motivated to help their adolescents achieve in school. In addition, the academy prepares students to qualify for scholarships and college entrance exams. Gaskins was recently awarded the President's Volunteer Action Award at the White House.

In a 20-year follow-up of African American teenage mothers who gave birth in the late 1960s in Baltimore, a number of factors predicted whether their offspring would complete high school or go on to college (Brooks-Gunn, Guo, & Furstenberg, 1993). The more years their father was present, high maternal educational aspirations in the child's first year of life, being prepared for school, and not repeating a grade during elementary school were predictors of completing high school. Few years on welfare, high preschool cognitive ability, attendance in preschool, and no grade failure in elementary school predicted whether the African American female students would go on to college.

Teacher Expectations

Do teachers have lower academic expectations for minority group adolescents? The evidence indicates that teachers look for and reward achievement-oriented behavior in White students more often than in African American students (Hudley, 1997; Scott-Jones, 1993). When teachers praise African American students for their academic performance, the praise is often qualified: "This is a good paper. It is better than yesterday's." Also teachers criticize gifted African American students more than gifted White students, possibly because they do not expect intellectual competence in Black students (Baron, Tom, & Cooper, 1985).

The following comments of Imani Perry (1988), a 15-year-old African American student, underscore the problems many ethnic minority adolescents face in school:

> Black and Hispanic students have less chance of building strong relationships with teachers because their appearance and behavior may be considered offensive to middle-class White teachers. These students show signs of what White teachers, and some teachers of color, consider disrespect, and they do not get the nurturing relationships that develop respect and dedication. They are considered less intelligent, as can be seen in the proportion of Blacks and Hispanics in lower-level as opposed to upper-level classes. There is less of a teacher-student contact with "underachievers" because they are guided into peer tutoring programs. . . . The sad part of the situation is that many students believe that this type of teaching is what academic learning is all about. They have not had the opportunity to experience alternative ways of teaching and learning. From my experience in public school, it appears that many minority students will never be recognized as capable of analytical and critical thinking.

Family Influences

Parents' attitudes and behavior can either improve or detract from ethnic minority adolescents' school performance. In one investigation that controlled for social class, authoritarian and permissive parenting were both associated with poor grades, while authoritative parenting was associated with better grades (Dornbusch & others, 1987). However, more than parenting styles is involved in understanding ethnic minority adolescents' school performance, because many Asian American adolescents' parents follow an authoritarian parenting style, yet many Asian American adolescents, especially Japanese and Chinese American, often excel in school. A special concern is the large number of African American and Latino adolescents who grow up in single-parent families. For example, half of African American adolescents are likely to remain with a single parent through the end of adolescence, in contrast to only 15 percent of White American adolescents (McLoyd, in press). Among ethnic minorities, about 70 percent of African American and Latino adolescents raised by single mothers are poor (Ford Foundation, 1984). Poor school performance among many ethnic minority youth is related to this pattern of single-parenting and poverty (Dornbusch & others, 1985).

Desegregation and Busing

One of the largest efforts to study ethnicity in school has focused on desegregation and busing. Desegregation attempts to improve the proportions of ethnic minority and White student populations in schools. Efforts to improve this ratio have often involved busing students, usually minority group students, from their home neighborhood to more distant schools. The underlying belief is that bringing different groups together will reduce stereotyped attitudes and improve intergroup relations. But busing tells us nothing about what goes on inside the school once students get there. Minority group adolescents bused to a predominantly white school are often resegregated in the classroom through seating patterns, ability grouping, and tracking systems. Overall, the findings pertaining to desegregation through busing have shown dismal results (Minuchin & Shapiro, 1983).

Improvements in interethnic relations among adolescents in schools depend on what happens after students arrive at the school. In one comprehensive national investigation of factors that contribute to positive interethnic relations, more than 5,000 fifth-grade students and more than 400 tenth-grade students were evaluated (Forehand, Ragosta, & Rock, 1976). Multiethnic curricula, projects focused on ethnic issues, mixed work groups, and supportive teachers and principals led to improved interethnic relations. Next, we examine a strategy to improve interethnic relations in classrooms.

Cooperative Learning and the Jigsaw Classroom

Cooperative learning *involves joint participation by all members of a group in achieving a learning goal. Each member contributes to the learning process.* The strategy of emphasizing cooperation rather than competition in learning has been widely promoted in recent years in American classrooms. A number of researchers have found that cooperative learning is associated with enhanced student outcomes, including increases in self-esteem, better academic performance, friendships among classmates, and improved interethnic perceptions (Aronson, 1986; Slavin, 1989).

When the schools of Austin, Texas, were desegregated through extensive busing, the outcome was increased ethnic tension among African Americans, Mexican Americans, and Anglos, producing violence in the schools. The superintendent consulted with Eliot Aronson, a prominent social psychologist, who was a professor at the University of Texas at Austin at the time. Aronson thought it was more important to prevent ethnic tension than to control it. This led him to observe a number of school classrooms in Austin. What he saw was fierce competition between individuals of unequal status.

Aronson stressed that the reward structure of the classrooms needed to be changed from a setting of unequal competition to one of cooperation among equals, without making curriculum changes. To accomplish this, Aronson developed a form of cooperative learning he called the "jigsaw classroom." How does the jigsaw classroom work? Consider a class of thirty students,

A Latino father at his daughter's high school graduation. Parents play an important role in the education of ethnic minority adolescents. Many African American and Latino adolescents grow up in low-income, single-parent families and do not receive the support this Latino girl has been given.

some Anglo, some African American, some Latino. The lesson to be learned focuses on Joseph Pulitzer's life. The class might be broken up into five groups of six students each, with the groups being as equal as possible in ethnic composition and academic achievement level. The lesson about Pulitzer's life could be divided into six parts, with one part given to each member of the six-person group. The parts might be paragraphs from Pulitzer's biography, such as how the Pulitzer family came to the United States, his childhood, his early work, and so on. The components are like the parts of a jigsaw puzzle. They have to be put together to form the complete puzzle.

Each student in the group is given an allotted time to study. Then the group meets, and each member tries to teach a part to the group. After an hour or so, each member is tested on the entire life of Pulitzer, with each member receiving an individual rather than a group score. Each student, therefore, must learn the entire lesson. Learning depends on the cooperation and effort of other members. Aronson believes that this type of learning increases students' interdependence through cooperatively reaching a common goal.

Cooperative learning is an important addition to learning strategies, but esteemed social psychologist Roger Brown (1986) offers a caveat. According to Brown, academic achievement is as much, or more, an individual "sport" as a team "sport." *Individuals*, not *groups*, graduate from high school, enter college, and take jobs. A parent with an advantaged adolescent in a cooperative learning classroom thus may react with increased ethnic

hostility when the adolescent brings home a lower grade than is typical. The adolescent may tell his father, "The teacher is getting us to teach each other. In my group, we have this kid named Carlos, who can barely speak English." While cooperative learning is an important strategy for reducing interethnic hostility, caution needs to be exercised in its use because of the unequal status of the participants and achievement's individual orientation.

The Subordination and Exploitation of Ethnic Minority Adolescents in Education

American anthropologist John Ogbu (1989) proposed the controversial view that ethnic minority youth are placed in a position of subordination and exploitation in the American educational system. He believes that ethnic minority adolescents, especially African Americans and Latinos, have inferior educational opportunities, are exposed to teachers and administrators who have low academic expectations for them, and encounter negative stereotypes about ethnic minority groups. Ogbu states that ethnic minority opposition to the middle-class White educational system stems from a lack of trust because of years of discrimination and oppression. Says Ogbu, it makes little sense to do well academically if occupational opportunities are often closed to ethnic minority youth and young adults.

Completing high school, or even college, does not always bring the same job opportunities for many ethnic minority youth as for White youth (Entwistle, 1990). In terms of earnings and employment rates, African American high school graduates do not do as well as their White counterparts. In one study, the more aware African American adolescents were of discrimination, the less important they perceived academic achievement to be and the less engaged they were in their schoolwork (Taylor & others, 1994). Many Latino youth also gave up on school because they did not perceive rewards for remaining in school (that is, they did not perceive adequate job opportunities to justify remaining in school).

SOCIAL POLICY AND THE EDUCATION OF ADOLESCENTS

In *Turning Points*, the Carnegie Council on Adolescent Development (1989) issued a set of eight principles for transforming adolescents' education. These principles can form the core of social policy initiatives for improving the education of adolescents, especially young adolescents. The eight principles are these:

- *Create communities for learning.* Many American middle and high schools are large, impersonal institutions. Teachers have few opportunities to develop the stable relationships with students that are essential to teaching them effectively. Unacceptably large schools should be brought to a human scale by creating "schools-within-schools," or "houses" within the school, and then dividing these subunits into smaller "teams" of teachers and students. Such smaller groupings can enable each student to receive increased individual attention in a supportive context.
- *Teach a core of common knowledge.* An important task for educators is to identify the most important principles and concepts within each academic discipline and concentrate their efforts on integrating these ideas into a connected, interdisciplinary curriculum. Depth and quality of information should be emphasized rather than coverage of a large quantity of information. *Turning Points* also considers community service to be an integral part of the curriculum. Community service can stimulate adolescents to think critically about real-world problems.
- *Provide an opportunity for all students to succeed.* A troubling dimension of schools is the inequitable distribution of opportunities to learn among youth. Educators can do a great deal more to teach students of diverse abilities. One strategy is to expand cooperative learning. Researchers have found that cooperative learning in mixed-ability learning groups helps high achievers deepen their understanding of material by explaining it to lower achievers, who in turn benefit by receiving help as needed from their peers. Cooperative learning can also help students to become acquainted with classmates from different ethnic and cultural backgrounds.

- *Strengthen teachers and principals.* States and school districts need to give teachers and principals more authority in transforming their schools. The teachers and principals know more about what will effectively work in their schools than do administrators and government officials, who are often far removed from the classrooms. The creation of governance committees composed of teachers, principals, support staff, parents, and community representatives can make schools more effective.
- *Prepare teachers for the middle grades.* Most teachers in middle schools are not specifically educated to teach young adolescents. Teacher education programs need to develop curricula that train middle school teachers to work with the special needs of young adolescents.
- *Improve academic performance through better health and fitness.* Schools for adolescents do not often have the support of health and social service agencies to address adolescents' physical and mental health needs. Developmentally appropriate health facilities, based in or near schools, need to be established.
- *Engage families in the education of adolescents.* Despite the clearly documented positive effects of parental involvement in education, parental involvement of all types declines considerably in adolescence, often to the point where it is nonexistent. An important social policy recommendation is to involve parents in decision making in significant ways, especially in low-income and ethnic minority neighborhoods. Parents who are involved in planning the school's work feel useful, develop confidence in their relations with the school staff, and are more likely to attend school functions, which signals to their adolescents that education is important.
- *Connect schools with communities.* "Full-service schools" should be considered in many locations. They represent a variety of school-based efforts to assist students and their families. These efforts include comprehensive youth-service programs, community schools, and family resource centers. Strengthening the academic environment in conjunction with supporting students and the basic needs of their families is the common core of all such efforts.

ADOLESCENTS WITH A DISABILITY

Adolescents with a disability can be especially sensitive about their differentness and how it is perceived by others. Life is not always fair for adolescents with a disability. Adjusting to school and peers is often difficult for them.

TABLE 8.1

Estimates of the Percentage and Number of Adolescents with a Disability in the United States

Disability	% of Population	Number of Children, Ages 5 to 18
Visual impairment (includes blindness)	0.1	55,000
Hearing impairment (includes deafness)	0.5–0.7	275,000–385,000
Speech handicap	3.0–4.0	1,650,000–2,200,000
Orthopedic and health impairments	0.5	275,000
Emotional disorder	2.0–3.0	1,100,000–1,650,000
Mental retardation	2.0–3.0	1,100,000–1,650,000
Learning disabilities	2.0–3.0	1,100,000–1,650,000
Multiple handicaps	0.5–0.7	275,000–385,000
Total	*10.6–15.0*	*5,830,000–8,250,000*

Reprinted with the permission of Simon & Schuster from the Macmillan College text *The Exceptional Student in the Regular Classroom*, 5/E by Bill R. Gearheart, Mel W. Weishahn, and Carol J. Gearheart. Copyright © 1992 by Macmillan Publishing Company.

Scope and Education

An estimated 10 to 15 percent of the U.S. population of children between the ages of 5 and 18 are classified as children with a disability. Table 8.1 shows the percentages of children with a disability in different areas—ranging from 3 to 4 percent of children having a speech disability to 0.1 percent having a visual impairment.

Public Law 94-142 *is the federal government's mandate to provide a free and appropriate education for all children and adolescents. A key provision of the bill is to develop an individualized education program for children and adolescents with special needs.* Individualized educational plans should meet with the approval of the children's parents, counselors, educational authorities, and, when feasible, the children themselves.

Many adolescents with a disability are taught in the regular classroom today. This used to be called mainstreaming, but today the term *mainstreaming* is being replaced with the term **inclusion,** *which refers to educating children and adolescents in their natural environment, such as typical elementary and secondary school classrooms* (Siegel, 1997). More than a decade ago it was considered appropriate to educate children with a disability outside the regular classroom. The trend today, though, is to fully include all such students in the regular classroom.

Usually some of the education of students with a disability takes place in a resource room in addition to the regular classroom. The resource room is an instructional classroom for students with a disability and the professionals who work with them. The resource professional has training in working with children with a disability.

Eighteen-year-old Chandra "Peaches" Allen was born without arms. Despite this handicap, she has learned to write, eat, type, paint, and draw with her feet. She can even put on earrings. She is well-known for her artistic skills. She has won three grand-prize awards for her art in various shows. She is getting ready to enter college and plans to pursue a career in art and physical therapy. Chandra Allen's accomplishments reflect remarkable adaptation and coping. She is an excellent example of how handicapped adolescents can conquer a disability and pursue meaningful goals.

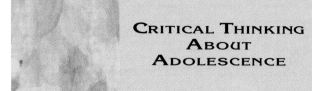

Learning Disabilities

Paula doesn't like kindergarten and can't seem to remember the names of her teacher or classmates. Bobby's third-grade teacher complains that his spelling is awful and that he is always reversing letters. Thirteen-year-old Tim hates to read. He says it is too hard for him and the words just don't make any sense to him. Each of these children has a learning disability. Children and adolescents with **learning disabilities** *(1) are of normal or above-normal intelligence, (2) have difficulties in several academic areas but usually do not show deficits in others, and (3) are not suffering from some other conditions or disorders that could explain their learning problems.* The breadth of definitions of learning disabilities has generated controversy about just what learning disabilities are.

The global concept of learning disabilities includes problems in listening, thinking, memory, reading, writing, spelling, and math (Spear-Swerling & Sternberg, 1994). Attention deficits involving an inability to sit still, pay attention, and concentrate are also classified as learning disabilities. Estimates of the percentage of children with a learning disability in the United States are as broad as the definition, ranging from 1 to 30 percent. The U.S. Department of Education puts the number of identified children with a learning disability between the ages of 3 and 21 at approximately 2 million.

Improvement to the lives of adolescents with a learning disability will come from (1) recognizing the complex, multifaceted nature of learning disabilities (biological, cognitive, and socioemotional dimensions need to be considered) and (2) becoming more precise in our analysis of the learning environments in which these adolescents participate. The following discussion of a subtype of learning disability—attention-deficit hyperactivity disorder—illustrates this complexity and preciseness.

Attention-Deficit Hyperactivity Disorder

Matthew has messy handwriting, and he has trouble attending to the teacher's instructions. Matthew is almost always in motion. He can't sit still for more than a few minutes at a time. His mother describes him as very fidgety. Matthew has **attention-deficit hyperactivity disorder,** *the technical term for what is commonly called hyperactivity. This disorder is characterized by a short attention span, distractibility, and high levels of physical activity.* Children and adolescents with this disorder do not pay attention and have difficulty concentrating on what they are doing. Estimates of the percentage of children with attention-deficit hyperactivity disorder vary from less than 1 percent to 5 percent. Although young children or even infants show characteristics of this disorder, the vast majority of hyperactive children are identified in the first three grades of elementary school when teachers recognize that they have great difficulty paying attention, sitting still, and concentrating on their schoolwork.

What makes Jimmy so impulsive, Sandy so distractible, and Harvey so excitable? Possible causes include heredity, prenatal damage, diet, family dynamics, and the physical environment. As we saw in chapter 3, the influence of heredity on temperament is increasingly considered; activity level is one aspect of temperament that differentiates one child from another very early in development. Approximately four times as many boys as girls are hyperactive. This sex difference may be due to differences in the brains of boys and girls determined by genes on the Y chromosome. Prenatal hazards may also produce hyperactive behavior. Excessive drinking by women during pregnancy is associated with poor attention and concentration by their offspring at 4 years of age, for example (Streissguth & others, 1984). With regard to diet, severe vitamin deficiencies can lead to attentional problems. Vitamin B deficiencies are of special concern. Caffeine and sugar may also contribute to attentional problems.

A wide range of psychotherapies and drug therapy has been used to improve the lives of hyperactive children (Rapport, 1997). For unknown reasons, some drugs that stimulate the brains and behaviors of adults have a quieting effect on the brains and behaviors of children. The drugs most widely prescribed for hyperactive children are amphetamines, especially Ritalin. Amphetamines work effectively for some hyperactive children, but not all. As many as 20 percent of hyperactive children treated with Ritalin do not respond to it. Even when Ritalin works, it

CONCEPT TABLE 8.2

Schools, Classrooms, Teachers, Peers, and Parents, Social Class and Ethnicity, and Adolescents with a Disability

Concept	Processes/Related Ideas	Characteristics/Description
Schools, Classrooms, Teachers, Peers, and Parents	Size, structure, and climate	Smaller is usually better when school size and classroom size are at issue. Large schools, especially those with more than 500 to 600 students, may not provide a personalized climate that allows for an effective system of social control. Most class sizes are 30 to 35 students, but class sizes of 15 students or fewer benefit student learning.
		The open-classroom concept is multidimensional. Specific dimensions of open and traditional classrooms need to be considered, as well as specific outcomes.
	Person-environment fit and aptitude-treatment interaction Teachers, peers, and parents	Some of the negative psychological changes associated with adolescent development may result from a mismatch between the needs of developing adolescents and the opportunities afforded by the schools they attend. Closely related to concerns about person-environment fit is aptitude-treatment interaction.
		Teacher characteristics involve many different dimensions, and compiling a profile of a competent teacher of adolescents is difficult. At school, adolescents are with each other for at least 6 hours a day, and the school is a setting for many after-school and weekend peer activities. Parental involvement usually decreases as the child moves into adolescence. Epstein argues that greater collaboration between families, schools, and communities would improve the adolescent's development.
Social Class and Ethnicity	Social class	Secondary schools have had a strong middle-class bias. Teachers have lower expectations for students from low-income backgrounds, although teachers from these backgrounds see these students' behavior as more adaptive than teachers from middle-class backgrounds.
	Ethnicity	The school experiences of different ethnic groups vary considerably. Improvements in interethnic relations among adolescents in schools depend on what happens at school after adolescents arrive. Multiethnic curricula, projects focused on interethnic issues, supportive teachers and administrators, and cooperative learning benefit students from ethnic minority backgrounds. John Ogbu proposed the controversial view that ethnic minority youth are placed in a position of subordination and exploitation in the American educational system.
Social Policy and the Education of Adolescents	Recommendations	Recommendations include creating communities for learning, teaching a core of common knowledge, providing an opportunity for all students to succeed, strengthening teachers and principals, preparing teachers for the middle grades, improving academic performance through better health and fitness, engaging families in the education of adolescents, and connecting schools with communities.
Adolescents with a Disability	Scope and education	An estimated 10 to 15 percent of U.S. children 5 to 18 years of age are classified as having a disability. Public Law 94-182 mandates a free and appropriate education for all children. A key provision for children with special needs is an individualized education program. The term *inclusion,* which refers to educating children in their natural environment, is replacing the term *mainstreaming.*
	Learning disabilities	Adolescents with a learning disability have normal or above-normal intelligence, have difficulties in some areas but not others, and do not suffer from some other disorder that could explain their learning problems. Learning disabilities are complex.
	Attention-deficit hyperactivity disorder	This is the technical term for what is commonly called "hyperactivity." This disorder is characterized by a short attention span, distractibility, and high levels of physical activity.

is also important to consider the social world of the hyperactive child. The teacher is especially important in this social world, helping to monitor the child's academic and social behavior to determine whether the drug works and whether the prescribed dosage is correct.

Attention-deficit hyperactivity disorder has received far less attention in adolescents than in children (Faigel & others, 1995). In many individuals this disorder does not disappear at puberty, and it can play a critical role in the academic and social lives of adolescents. Estimates suggest that attention-deficit hyperactivity disorder decreases in only about one-third of adolescents (Fischer & others, 1990).

At this point we have discussed a number of ideas about schools, classrooms, teachers, peers, and parents, social class and ethnicity, and adolescents with a disability. A summary of these ideas is presented in concept table 8.2. In the next chapter we turn to a discussion of the role of culture in adolescent development.

SUMMARY

There is a growing consensus that the way most schools function today does not meet the basic needs of adolescents. In this chapter, we described a number of ways that the education of adolescents could be significantly improved.

We began this chapter by describing the nature of adolescents' schooling, including the functions of adolescents' schools, whether schools make a difference, and schools' changing social developmental contexts. Then, we discussed transitions in schooling—the transition to middle or junior high school, what makes a successful middle school, the transition from high school to college, and high school dropouts and noncollege youth. Our coverage of schools and classrooms, teachers and peers, and parents and schools focused on school and classroom size, classroom structure and climate, person-environment fit and aptitude-treatment interaction, interaction with teachers, interaction with peers, and ways to improve family/school/community collaboration. We studied about social policy and the education of adolescents. We also described adolescents with a disability, including their numbers and education, learning disabilities, and attention-deficit hyperactivity disorder.

Don't forget that you can obtain an overall summary of the chapter by again reading the two concept tables on pages 254 and 267. In this chapter we discussed the nature of schools in different cultures and the role of ethnicity in schooling. In the next chapter, we provide an even more in-depth discussion of the roles of culture and ethnicity in adolescent development.

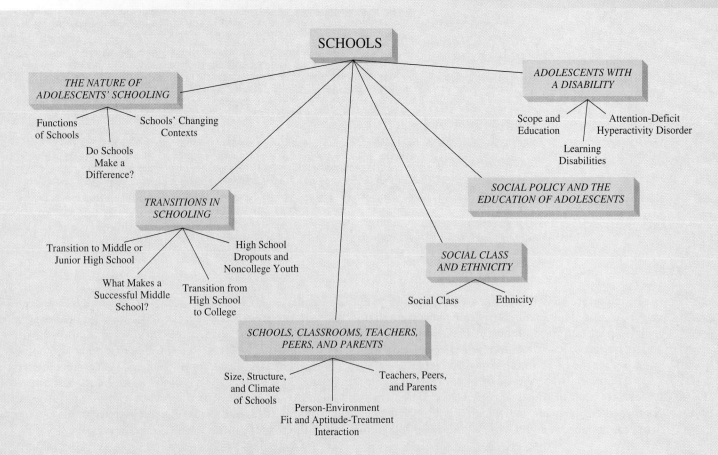

𝒫RACTICAL KNOWLEDGE ABOUT ADOLESCENCE

Smart Schools, Smart Kids

(1992) by Edward B. Fiske.
New York: Touchstone.

This book takes the reader on a tour of dozens of pioneering schools in the United States and describes how successful programs work, problems they have encountered, and the results they have achieved. Fiske says that too many of America's schools are put together on the outdated nineteenth-century factory model of schools. He addresses how to develop learning communities, how to incorporate new technologies into classrooms, and how to go beyond testing. The book also tackles the learning crisis in children's education, providing many vivid examples of the tragedies of poor schools and the victories of competent schools.

Successful Schools for Young Adolescents

(1984) by Joan Lipsitz.
New Brunswick, NJ:
Transaction Books.

This book is a classic resource for people involved in middle school education. The book establishes a set of criteria for evaluating middle school effectiveness. Emphasis is placed on understanding adolescent development, school effectiveness research, and public policy. In-depth case studies of four successful middle schools that foster healthy social development and learning are described.

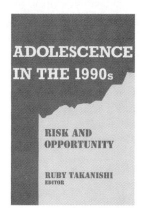

Adolescence in the 1990s.

(1993) edited by Ruby Takanishi.
New York: Teachers College
Press.

A number of experts on adolescence address the risk and opportunity for adolescents in today's world. Many chapters focus on improving the quality of schooling for adolescents. Among the topics covered are changing views of adolescence in contemporary society, school and community programs, parent-school involvement, improving the school-to-work transition, a comparison of adolescence and schooling in the United States and Germany, and adolescence and the mass media. An annotated bibliography of selected publications on the adolescent years is also included. This is an up-to-date, authoritative treatment of issues involved in risk and opportunity for adolescents, especially those at risk for problems.

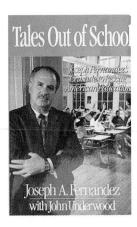

Tales Out of School

(1993) by Joseph A. Fernandez. Boston: Little, Brown.

Author Joseph Fernandez was head of the Dade County School System in Florida and currently heads the New York City School System. The book describes his crusade to improve America's schools. His book is a call to arms on behalf of America's children. Fernandez tells how we can restore order and how we can achieve academic excellence in schools. The changes he recommends include more school-based management, in which principals, teachers, and parents collaborate in decision-making about schools; and satellite schools that are located in the workplace. This is a provocative book that provides a number of revolutionary ideas about revamping our nation's schools.

RESOURCES FOR IMPROVING THE LIVES OF ADOLESCENTS

Adolescent Literacy: What Works and Why (1993)
By Judith Davidson and David Koppenhaver
Center for Early Adolescence
University of North Carolina
D-2 Carr Mill Town Center
Carrboro, NC 27510
919-966-1148

This book presents a self-assessment and planning process that can help improve a middle school by taking a comprehensive look at the school's literacy policies and practices. A number of up-to-date resources are provided.

Association for Children and Adults with Learning Disabilities (ACLD)
4156 Library Road
Pittsburgh, PA 15234
412-341-1515

This organization provides free information and referrals to anyone, it publishes a newsletter, *ACLD Newsbriefs*, and distributes brochures and books related to learning disabilities.

Before It's Too Late: Dropout Prevention in the Middle Grades (1988)
By Gayle Dorman and Anne Wheelock
Center for Early Adolescence
University of North Carolina
D-2 Carr Mill Town Center
Carrboro, NC 27510
919-966-1148

This report explores how the middle school is a key time in preventing school dropout. A comprehensive middle school dropout prevention program is outlined along with a timetable for implementation.

Canadian Association for School Health (CASH)/L'Association Canadienne Pour la Santé en Milieu Scolaire
2835 Country Woods Drive
Surrey, British Columbia V4A 9P9

CASH promotes the use of a comprehensive school health approach, a practical and adaptable framework for promoting the health of children and youth.

Children with Attention Deficit Disorder (CHADD)
1859 Pine Island Road, Suite 185
Plantation, FL 33322
305-384-6869

This organization consists of nearly sixty chapters devoted to supplying parents, teachers, and concerned professionals with information and support. CHADD publishes a newsletter and provides information about how to start a self-help group focused on attention deficit disorder.

Children's Aid Society
105 East 22nd Street
New York, NY 10010
212-460-4917

This organization collaborates with the New York City school system to get community organizations to provide school-based programs for students and their families, including after-school tutoring.

City Lights School
724 Ninth Street NW, Suite 420
Washington, DC 20001
202-347-5010

City Lights is a school for troubled youth in Washington, DC. About one hundred 14- to 21-year-olds are enrolled in the school, which features remedial education, GED and college preparation, psychological services, vocational counseling and job placement, and substance-abuse prevention and treatment. The typical student is a disadvantaged foster child years behind and suffering severe emotional problems. The educational component relies on self-paced computer-assisted education that teaches academic as well as practical living skills. It costs $10,000 a year to educate one adolescent at City Lights School; it would cost $50,000 to keep the same adolescent in jail.

City Youth Constitutional Rights Foundation
601 South Kingsley Drive
Los Angeles, CA 90005
213-487-5590

This foundation sponsors the service learning program called City Youth, LA: Education and Community Action. The program provides teachers with training and materials to help their students identify community problems. The program also promotes respect for ethnic diversity.

Council for Exceptional Children (CEC)
1920 Association Drive
Reston, VA 22091
703-620-3660

The CEC maintains an information center on the education of handicapped children and adolescents and publishes materials on a wide variety of topics.

Families and Schools in a Pluralistic Society (1993)
Edited by Nancy Feyl Chavkin
Albany: State University of New York Press

This book portrays the nature of education for different ethnic minority groups. A number of leading scholars contributed insightful knowledge about ways to better educate ethnic minority adolescents.

Human Biology Middle Grades Life Science Curriculum
Department of Biological Sciences
Building 80–2160
Stanford University
Stanford, CA 94305
415-723-1509

This curriculum, developed and tested by Stanford University scientists in collaboration with middle school teachers across the United States, combines the study of ecology, evolution, and genetics; physiology; human development; society and culture; and health and safety. The curriculum not only provides excellent science instruction but also promotes healthy adolescent behavior.

National Dropout Prevention Center
205 Martin Street
Clemson University
Clemson, SC 29634
803-656-2599

The center operates as a clearinghouse for information about dropout prevention and at-risk youth and publishes the *National Dropout Prevention Newsletter*.

School-Based Youth Services Program
New Jersey Department of Human Services
222 South Warren Street
Trenton, NJ 08625-0700
609-292-1617

This program operates in 37 sites in or near schools. The sites are open during and after school, on weekends, and all summer. They offer a core set of services, all of which require parental consent. Services include primary and preventive health/care, individual and family counseling, drug- and alcohol-abuse counseling, recreation, and summer and part-time job development.

Turning Points (1989)
Carnegie Council on Adolescent Development
2400 N Street NW
Washington, DC 20037-1153
202-429-7979

This comprehensive report concludes that the education most of the nation's young adolescents are receiving is seriously inadequate. The report includes a number of recommendations for meeting the educational needs of young adolescents.

ℰXPLORING ADOLESCENT DEVELOPMENT

To further explore the nature of adolescent development, we will examine a research study on cooperative learning and discuss a peer tutoring project for at-risk middle and secondary school students.

ℛESEARCH ON ADOLESCENT DEVELOPMENT

Cooperative Learning

Featured Study

Stevens, R. J., & Slavin, R. E. (1995). The cooperative elementary school: Effects on students' achievement, attitudes, and social relations. *American Educational Research Journal, 32*, 321–351.

Cooperative learning methods have been studied for more than two decades and have been increasingly used in elementary and secondary schools. Most applications of cooperative learning have been implemented teacher by teacher, usually one subject at a time, and few studies have covered more than one semester. Could cooperative learning be used on a broad scale in many subjects and over extended time frames to basically change the organization of schools and classrooms? This was one of the main questions addressed in this study.

The components of the cooperative learning model were these: using cooperative learning across a variety of content areas, full-scale inclusion of academically disabled students in regular classrooms, teachers' using peer coaching, teachers' planning cooperatively, and parent involvement in the school.

Method

The subjects were 1,012 second- to sixth-grade students in a suburban Maryland school district. Twenty-one classes in the two treatment schools were matched with 24 classes in the three comparison schools on the basis of achievement test scores in a number of areas. The schools were located in predominantly working-class neighborhoods. Slightly fewer than 10 percent of the students were learning disabled.

Each component of the cooperative learning program was gradually phased in during the first year. Prior to implementation of the component, faculty were given training on its use. During the school year, members of the research staff observed classes, met with teachers, and observed steering committee meetings to facilitate the implementation of the cooperative learning program.

Assessment of the program's results was conducted over a 2-year period. In the spring of the first and second years of the study, teachers administered the California Achievement Test. Both pre- and posttest, students' attitudes toward, and their perceived ability in, various school subjects were evaluated, and students' social relations also were assessed by asking the students to list the names of their friends in the class.

Results

After the first year of the program's implementation, students in the cooperative schools had higher achievement in reading vocabulary than did the students in the regular schools. After the second year, students in the cooperative schools had higher achievement in reading vocabulary, reading comprehension, language expression, and math computation than did their regular-classroom counterparts. After 2 years, academically disabled students in the cooperative schools had higher achievement in a wide variety of academic subjects than did their peers in the regular schools. The social relations of students in the cooperative schools also were better.

Discussion

Because the experimental cooperative learning program had so many components, it is difficult to determine which component(s) made the program a success. Nonetheless, the results support the belief that cooperative learning can be applied across many subject domains. Future research should disentangle which of these components give cooperative learning an advantage.

Chapter

9

Culture

O ur most basic common link is that we all inhabit this planet. We all breathe the same air. We all cherish our children's future.

—John F. Kennedy, address, American University, 1963

Chapter Outline

Chapter Boxes

Consider the flowers of a garden: though differing in kind, color, form and shape, yet, inasmuch as they are refreshed by the waters of one spring, revived by the breath of one wind, invigorated by the rays of one sun, this diversity increases their charm, and adds unto their beauty. . . How unpleasing to the eye if all the flowers and plants, the leaves and blossoms, the fruits, the branches and the trees of that garden were all of the same shape and colour! Diversity of hues, form and shape, enriches and adorns the garden.

—Abud'l-Baha

PREVIEW

Although we on planet Earth have much in common wherever and however we live, we also vary according to our cultural and ethnic backgrounds. The socio-cultural worlds of adolescents are described throughout this text. Because culture and ethnicity are such pervasive dimensions of adolescent development, we devote most of this chapter to the study of cultural and ethnic factors that influence the development of adolescents. We also will explore how television and other media influence adolescent development.

Dating Problems of a 16-Year-Old Japanese American Girl and School Problems of a 17-Year-Old Chinese American Boy

Sonya, a 16-year-old Japanese girl was upset over her family's reaction to her White American boyfriend. Her parents refused to meet him and more than once threatened to disown her. Her older brothers also reacted angrily to Sonya's dating a White American, warning that they were going to beat him up. Her parents were also disturbed that Sonya's grades, above average in middle school, were beginning to drop.

Generational issues contributed to the conflict between Sonya and her family (Nagata, 1989). Her parents had experienced strong sanctions against dating Whites when they were growing up and were legally prevented from marrying anyone but a Japanese. As Sonya's older brothers were growing up, they valued ethnic pride and solidarity. The brothers saw her dating a White as "selling out" her own ethnic group. Sonya's and her family members' cultural values obviously differ.

Michael, a 17-year-old Chinese American high school student, was referred to an outpatient adolescent crisis center by the school counselor for depression and suicidal tendencies (Huang & Ying, 1989). Michael was failing several subjects and was repeatedly absent or late for school. Michael's parents were successful professionals who told the therapist that there was nothing wrong with them or with Michael's younger brother and sister, so what, they wondered, was wrong with Michael! What was wrong was that the parents expected all of their children to become doctors. They were frustrated and angered by Michael's school failures, especially since he was the firstborn son, who in Chinese families is expected to achieve the highest standards of all siblings.

The therapist underscored the importance of the parents' putting less pressure for achievement on Michael and gradually introduced more realistic expectations for Michael (who was not interested in becoming a doctor and did not have the necessary academic record anyway). The therapist supported Michael's desire not to become a doctor and empathized with the pressure he had experienced from his parents. As Michael's school attendance improved, his parents noted his improved attitude toward school and supported a continuation of therapy. Michael's case illustrates how expectations that Asian American youth will be "whiz kids" can become destructive.

Sonya's and Michael's circumstances underscore the importance of culture in understanding adolescent development. The cultural heritage of the families had a strong influence on the conflict Sonya and Michael experienced in their families and on their behavior outside of the family—in Sonya's case, dating; in Michael's case, school. Of course, a family's cultural background does not always produce conflict between adolescents and other family members, but the two cases described here reveal the importance of understanding a family's cultural values, especially those of ethnic minority families.

CULTURE AND ADOLESCENCE

What is culture, and why is it relevant to the study of adolescence? What is the importance of cross-cultural comparisons? How does change take place within and across cultures? What are rites of passage?

What Is Culture?

In chapter 1, **culture** *is defined as the behavior, patterns, beliefs, and all other products of a particular group of people that are passed on from generation to generation.* The products result from the interaction between groups of people and their environment over many years. For example, in the "Images of Adolescence" section at the beginning of this chapter, we read about how the cultural values of Sonya's parents and brothers conflicted with her dating interests. We also read how the Chinese American cultural tradition of Michael's parents led to Michael's school-related problems.

Culture is a broad concept—it includes many components and can be analyzed in many ways. We already have analyzed the effects of three important cultural settings on adolescent development—the family, peers, and school. Later in this chapter, we will examine how much time adolescents spend in these and other settings.

Cross-cultural expert Richard Brislin (1993) recently described a number of features of culture, including these:

- Culture is made up of ideals, values, and assumptions about life that guide people's behaviors.
- Culture is made by people.
- Culture is transmitted from generation to generation, with the responsibility for transmission resting on the shoulders of parents, teachers, and community leaders.
- Culture's influence often becomes noticed the most in well-meaning clashes between people from very different cultural backgrounds.
- Despite compromises, cultural values still remain.
- When their cultural values are violated or when their cultural expectations are ignored, people react emotionally.
- It is not unusual for people to accept a cultural value at one point in their life and reject it at another point. For example, rebellious adolescents and young adults may accept a culture's values and expectations after having children of their own.

Two additional important dimensions of culture in adolescents' lives are social class and ethnicity. **Social class,** *also called socioeconomic status or SES, refers to a grouping of people with similar occupational, educational, and economic characteristics.* In this chapter, for example, we evaluate what it is like for an adolescent to grow up in poverty. As we saw in chapter 1, **ethnicity** *is based on cultural heritage, nationality characteristics, race, religion, and language.* Nowhere

are sociocultural changes more profound than in the increasing ethnic diversity of America's adolescents. In this chapter, we study African American adolescents, Latino adolescents, Asian American adolescents, and Native American adolescents, and the sociocultural issues involved in their development. This chapter concludes with an overview of how an important dimension of culture—television and other media—affects adolescent development.

The Relevance of Culture to the Study of Adolescence

If the study of adolescence is to be a relevant discipline in the twenty-first century, increased attention will have to be focused on culture and ethnicity (Greenfield & Suzuki, 1997; Matsumoto, 1997). The future will bring extensive contact between people from varied cultural and ethnic backgrounds. Schools and neighborhoods can no longer be the fortresses of one privileged group whose agenda is the exclusion of those with a different skin color or different customs. Immigrants, refugees, and ethnic minority individuals increasingly refuse to become part of a homogeneous melting pot, instead requesting that schools, employers, and governments honor many of their cultural customs. Adult refugees and immigrants might find more opportunities and better-paying jobs here, but their children and adolescents might learn attitudes in school that challenge traditional authority patterns at home (Brislin, 1993).

For the most part, the study of adolescents has, so far, been ethnocentric, emphasizing American values, especially middle-class, White, male values. Cross-cultural psychologists point out that many of the assumptions about contemporary ideas in fields like adolescence were developed in Western cultures (Triandis, 1994). One example of **ethnocentrism**—*the tendency to favor one's own group over other groups*—is the American emphasis on the individual or self. Many Eastern countries, such as Japan, China, and India, are group oriented. So is the Mexican culture. The pendulum may have swung too far in the individualistic direction in many Western cultures.

People in all cultures have a tendency to (Brewer & Campbell, 1976):

- Believe that what happens in their culture is "natural" and "correct" and that what happens in other cultures is "unnatural" and "incorrect"
- Perceive their cultural customs as universally valid; that is, what is good for us is good for everyone
- Behave in ways that favor their cultural group
- Feel proud of their cultural group
- Feel hostile toward other cultural groups

In fact, many cultures define being human by reference to their own cultural group. The ancient Greeks distinguished between those who spoke Greek and those whose language was incomprehensible and sounded like

Culture has a powerful impact on people's lives. In Xinjian, China, a woman prepares for horseback courtship. Her suitor must chase her, kiss her, and evade her riding crop—all on the gallop. A new marriage law took effect in China in 1981. The law sets a minimum age for marriage—22 years for males, 20 years for females. Late marriage and late childbirth are critical aspects of China's effort to control population growth.

"barber" (a repetitive chatter), so they called them *barbarians*. The ancient Chinese labeled themselves "the central kingdom." In many languages, the word for *human* is the same as the name of the tribe. The implication is that people from other cultures are not perceived as fully human (Triandis, 1994).

Global interdependence is no longer a matter of belief or choice. It is an inescapable reality. Adolescents are not just citizens of the United States or Canada. They are citizens of the world, a world that through advances in technology and transportation has become increasingly interactive. By understanding the behavior and values of cultures around the world, we may be able to interact more effectively with each other and make this planet a more hospitable, peaceful place to live (Cushner & Brislin, 1997).

Cross-Cultural Comparisons

Early in this century, overgeneralizations about the universal aspects of adolescents were made based on data and experience in a single culture—the middle-class culture of the United States (Havighurst, 1976). For example, it was believed that adolescents everywhere went through a period of "storm and stress" characterized by self-doubt and conflict. However, as we saw in chapter 1, when Margaret Mead visited the island of Samoa, she found that the adolescents of the Samoan culture were not experiencing much stress.

As we also discovered in chapter 1, **cross-cultural studies** *involve the comparison of a culture with one or more other cultures, which provides information about the degree to which adolescent development is similar, or universal, across cultures, or the degree to which it is culture-specific.* The study of adolescence has emerged in the context of Western industrialized society, with the practical needs and social norms of this culture dominating thinking about adolescents. Consequently, the development of adolescents in Western cultures has evolved as the norm for all adolescents of the human species, regardless of economic and cultural circumstances. This narrow viewpoint can produce erroneous conclusions about the nature of adolescents. To develop a more global, cosmopolitan perspective on adolescents, we will consider adolescents' achievement behavior and sexuality in different cultures, as well as rites of passage.

Cross-cultural studies involve the comparison of a culture with one or more other cultures. Shown here is a 14-year-old !Kung girl who has added flowers to her beadwork during the brief rainy season in the Kalahari desert in Botswana, Africa. Delinquency and violence occur much less frequently in the peaceful !Kung culture than in most other cultures around the world.

Achievement

The United States is an achievement-oriented culture, and U.S. adolescents are more achievement oriented than the adolescents in many other countries. Many American parents socialize their adolescents to be achievement oriented and independent. In one investigation of 104 societies, parents in industrialized countries like the United States placed a higher value on socializing adolescents for achievement and independence than did parents in nonindustrialized countries like Kenya, who placed a higher value on obedience and responsibility (Bacon, Child, & Barry, 1963).

Anglo-American adolescents are more achievement oriented than Mexican and Mexican American adolescents are. For example, in one study, Anglo-American adolescents were more competitive and less cooperative than their Mexican and Mexican American counterparts (Kagan & Madsen, 1972). In this study, Anglo-Americans were more likely to discount the gains of other students when they could not reach the goals themselves. In other investigations, Anglo-American youth were more individual centered, while Mexican youth were more family centered (Holtzmann, 1982).

Some developmentalists believe that the American culture is too achievement oriented for rearing mentally healthy adolescents (Elkind, 1981).

Although Anglo-American adolescents are more achievement oriented than adolescents in many other cultures, they are not as achievement oriented as many Japanese, Chinese, and Asian American adolescents. For example, as a group, Asian American adolescents demonstrate exceptional achievement patterns (Stevenson, 1995). Asian American adolescents exceed the national average for high school and college graduates. Eighty-six percent of Asian Americans, compared to 64 percent of White Americans, are in some higher-education program 2 years after high school graduation. Clearly, education and achievement are highly valued by many Asian American youth. More about Asian American youth appears later in this chapter and in chapter 14, where we discuss achievement.

Sexuality

Culture also plays a prominent role in adolescent sexuality. Some cultures consider adolescent sexual activity normal; others forbid it. Consider the Ines Beag and

HUNTER-GATHERERS, NORTH AMERICA, LATE 20TH CENTURY

© 1994 by Sidney Harris.

Mangaian cultures: Ines Beag is a small island off the coast of Ireland. Its inhabitants are among the most sexually repressed in the world. They know nothing about French kissing or hand stimulation of the penis. Sex education does not exist. They believe that, after marriage, nature will take its course. The men think that intercourse is bad for their health. Individuals in this culture detest nudity. Only babies are allowed to bathe nude, and adults wash only the parts of their body that extend beyond their clothing. Premarital sex is out of the question. After marriage, sexual partners keep their underwear on during intercourse! It is not difficult to understand why females in the Ines Beag culture rarely, if ever, achieve orgasm (Messinger, 1971).

By contrast, consider the Mangaian culture in the South Pacific. Boys learn about masturbation as early as age 6 or 7. At age 13, boys undergo a ritual that introduces them to manhood in which a long incision is made in the penis. The individual who conducts the ritual instructs the boy in sexual strategies, such as how to help his partner achieve orgasm before he does. Two weeks after the incision ceremony, the 13-year-old boy has intercourse with an experienced woman. She helps him to hold back his ejaculation so she can achieve orgasm with him. Soon after, the boy searches for girls to further his sexual experience, or they seek him, knowing that he now is a "man." By the end of adolescence, Mangaians have sex virtually every night.

American adolescents experience a culture more liberal than that of the Ines Beag but one that does not come close to matching the liberal sexual behavior of the Mangaians. The cultural diversity in the sexual behavior of adolescents is testimony to the power of environmental experiences in determining sexuality. As we move up in the animal kingdom, experience seems to take on more power as a determinant of sexuality. Although human beings cannot mate in midair like bees or display their plumage as magnificently as peacocks, adolescents can talk about sex with one another, read about it in magazines, and watch it on television and at the movies.

Models of Cultural Change

The models that have been used to understand the process of change that occurs in transitions within and between cultures are (1) assimilation, (2) acculturation, (3) alternation, (4) multiculturalism, and (5) fusion (LaFromboise, Coleman, & Gerton, 1993). **Assimilation** *occurs when individuals relinquish their cultural identity and move into the larger society.* The nondominant group might be absorbed into an established "mainstream," or many groups might merge to form a new society (often called a "melting pot"). Individuals often suffer from a sense of alienation and isolation until they have been accepted into, and perceive their acceptance in, the new culture.

Acculturation *is cultural change that results from continuous, firsthand contact between two distinctive cultural groups.* In contrast to assimilation (which emphasizes that people will eventually become full members of the majority group's culture and lose their identification with their culture of origin), the acculturation model stresses that people can become competent participants in the majority culture while still being identified as a member of a minority culture (Hurtado, 1997).

The **alternation model** *assumes that it is possible for an individual to know and understand two different cultures. It also assumes that individuals can alter their behavior to fit a particular social context.* The alternation model differs from the assimilation and acculturation models in the following way: In the alternation model, it is possible to maintain a positive relationship with both cultures (LaFromboise, Coleman, & Gerton, 1993).

The **multicultural model** *promotes a pluralistic approach to understanding two or more cultures. This model argues that people can maintain their distinct identities while working with others from different cultures to meet common national or economic needs.* Cross-cultural psychologist John Berry (1990) believes that a multicultural society encourages all groups to (a) maintain and/or develop their

group identity, (b) develop other-group acceptance and tolerance, (c) engage in intergroup contact and sharing, and (d) learn each other's language. In the multicultural model, people can maintain a positive identity as members of their culture of origin while simultaneously developing a positive identity with another culture. Berry argues that there are four choices people can make in a situation requiring adaptation in plural societies: (1) assimilate, (2) integrate, (3) separate, or (4) become marginalized. We have already defined assimilation. Let's explore what integration, separation, and marginalization mean.

Integration *involves the maintenance of cultural integrity as well as movement to become an integral part of the larger culture.* In this type of cultural arrangement, a number of cultural groups cooperate within a larger social system ("a mosaic"). **Separation** *is self-imposed withdrawal from the larger culture.* However, if imposed by the larger society, separation becomes *segregation*. People might maintain their traditional way of life because they desire an independent existence (as in "separatist" movements), or the dominant culture might exercise its power to exclude the other culture (as in slavery and apartheid). **Marginalization** *is the process in which groups lose cultural and psychological contact with both their traditional culture and the larger, dominant culture.* Marginalization often involves feelings of alienation and a loss of identity. According to Berry, separation and marginalization are the least adaptive responses, assimilation and integration the most adaptive.

The **fusion model** *reflects the assumptions behind the melting pot theory, which implies that cultures sharing economic, political, or geographic boundaries will fuse together until they are distinguishable and form a new culture.* Each culture brings to the melting pot various strengths and weaknesses that take on new forms through interaction of cultures as equal partners. The fusion model differs from the assimilation and acculturation models in that no cultural superiority is assumed in the fusion model (Phinney & Devitch-Navarro, 1997).

Depending on the situation and person, any of these models might explain people's experiences as they acquire competency in a new culture. For example, consider an African American family that has moved from the rural South to live in a city. One member of the family might assimilate into the dominant Anglo culture, another might follow the path of acculturation, a third member might choose to actively alternate between the two cultures, and yet a fourth member might choose to live in a context in which the two cultures exist side by side as described in the multicultural or fusion models. Teresa LaFromboise and her colleagues (1993) argue that the more people are able to maintain active and effective relationships through alternation between the cultures, the less difficulty they will have in acquiring and maintaining competency in both cultures.

Rites of Passage

Rites of passage *are ceremonies or rituals that mark an individual's transition from one status to another, especially into adulthood.* Some societies have elaborate rites of passage that signal the adolescent's transition to adulthood; others do not. In many primitive cultures, rites of passage are the avenue through which adolescents gain access to sacred adult practices, knowledge, and sexuality (Sommer, 1978). These rites often involve dramatic practices intended to facilitate the adolescent's separation from the immediate family, especially the mother. The transformation usually is characterized by some form of ritual death and rebirth, or by means of contact with the spiritual world. Bonds are forged between the adolescent and the adult instructors through shared rituals, hazards, and secrets to allow the adolescent to enter the adult world. This kind of ritual provides a forceful and discontinuous entry into the adult world at a time when the adolescent is perceived to be ready for the change.

Africa, especially sub-Saharan Africa, has been the location of many rites of passage for adolescents. Under the influence of Western culture, many of the rites are disappearing today, although some vestiges remain. In locations where formal education is not readily available, rites of passage are still prevalent.

Americans do not have formal rites of passage that mark the transition from adolescence to adulthood. Some religious and social groups, however, have initiation ceremonies that indicate an advance in maturity—the Jewish bar mitzvah, the Catholic confirmation, and social debuts, for example.

School graduation ceremonies come the closest to being culturewide rites of passage in the United States. The high school graduation ceremony has become nearly universal for middle-class adolescents and increasing numbers of adolescents from low-income backgrounds (Fasick, 1988). Nonetheless, high school graduation does not result in universal changes—many high school graduates continue to live with their parents, to be economically dependent on them, and to be undecided about career and lifestyle matters. Another rite of passage for increasing numbers of American adolescents is sexual intercourse (Halonen & Santrock, 1996). By the end of adolescence, more than 70 percent of American adolescents have had sexual intercourse.

The absence in America of clear-cut rites of passage makes the attainment of adult status ambiguous. Many individuals are unsure whether they have reached adult status or not. In Texas, the age for beginning employment is 15, but many younger adolescents and even children are employed, especially Mexican immigrants. The age for driving is 16, but when emergency need is demonstrated, a driver's license can be obtained at age 15. Some parents might not allow their son or daughter to obtain a driver's license even at age

These Congolese Kota boys painted their faces as part of a rite of passage to adulthood. What kinds of rites of passage do American adolescents have?

16, believing that 16-year-olds are too young for this responsibility. The age for voting is 18, and the age for drinking recently has been raised to 21. Exactly when adolescents become adults in America has not been clearly delineated as it has in some primitive cultures, where rites of passage are universal.

Now that we have gained a more global perspective on adolescence, let's turn our attention to American adolescents and examine the social contexts in which they spend time. Then, we will study the nature of social class and ethnicity, two cultural dimensions that are important in understanding American adolescents, as well as adolescents in other cultures.

THE SETTINGS IN WHICH ADOLESCENTS SPEND THEIR TIME

What do adolescents do during a typical week? Of course, the answer to this question to some extent depends on adolescents' culture. Adolescents in a small hunter-gatherer culture in Africa spend much of their time in very different ways than American adolescents do. Kikuyu adolescents in central Kenya spend two-thirds of their waking hours in chores and family maintenance tasks (Munroe & others, 1983). Girls in rural India spend a similar two-thirds of their time in maintenance

Santrock: Adolescence

The Apache Indians of the American Southwest celebrate a girl's entrance into puberty with a four-day ritual that includes special dress, day long activities, and solemn spiritual ceremonies.

This young Jewish boy is shown at his bar mitzvah, a Jewish initiation ceremony that takes place when the boy reaches the age of 13. The bar mitzvah gives the boy adult status in the Jewish religion.

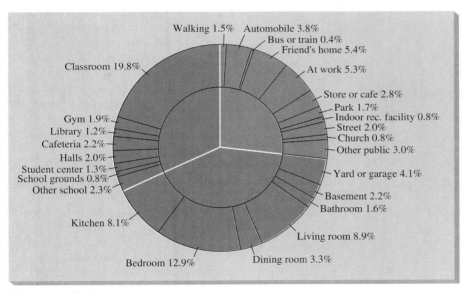

Figure~9.1

Where Adolescents Spend Their Time.
This graph shows the percentage of self-reports in each location. In this and the figures that follow, one percentage point is equivalent to approximately 1 hour per week spent in the given location or activity.

influence what women and men they will become (Larson & Richards, 1989).

Developmental researchers Mihaly Csikszentmihalyi and Reed Larson (1984) have extensively studied how much time adolescents spend in different settings, what adolescents spend their time doing, and the people with whom adolescents spend their time. They use the **experience sampling method** *in which participants carry electronic pagers, usually for a week, and provide reports on their activities when signaled by the pagers at random times.* Remember that the community chosen to be studied does not perfectly mirror adolescents everywhere.

In one study, a heterogeneous sample of 75 ninth- through twelfth-graders, approximately half boys and half girls, and approximately half from a lower-middle-class and half from an upper-middle-class background, in urban and suburban areas near Chicago were beeped 40 to 50 randomly chosen times (Csikszentmihalyi & Larson, 1984). The paths of the adolescents' lives passed through three main social contexts—home, school, and public settings, such as parks, buses, supermarkets, and friends' homes (see figure 9.1).

tasks, including 1½ hours fetching water, while boys spend two-thirds of their time in leisure (Saraswathi & Dutta, 1988). Contemporary Japanese adolescents spend well over half of their waking hours doing schoolwork. How adolescents spend their waking hours provides insight into the nature of their developmental experiences in a culture and the circumstances that

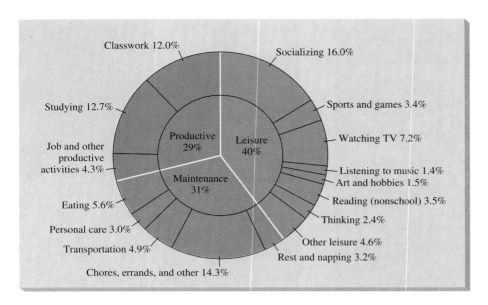

Figure~9.2

What Adolescents Spend Their Time Doing.

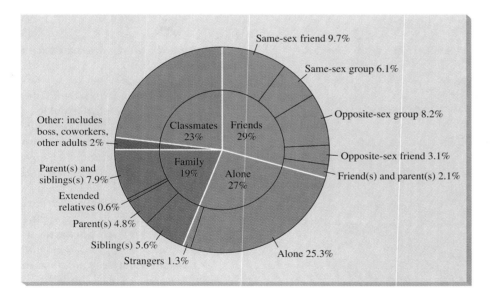

Figure~9.3

People with Whom Adolescents Spend Their Time.

Chicago adolescents is considerably less than the time spent studying by adolescents in some other technologically advanced cultures, such as Japan. In the Chicago sample, combined school and study time added up to 11 hours less per week than for Japanese adolescents. And Japanese adolescents spend 69 more days in school each year than American adolescents. With regard to work, 41 percent of the Chicago adolescents were employed and worked an average of 18 hours per week.

The main leisure activity of the Chicago adolescents was socializing, which took up about one-sixth of their waking hours. They also spent about three times as much time talking with friends and peers as they did talking with parents and adults. And 13 percent of their talking occurred via the phone! The Chicago adolescents spent far more time socializing and talking than did their counterparts in Japan, Germany, and Russia. The Chicago adolescents also spent some of their leisure time watching television, engaging in sports, playing games, pursuing hobbies, reading, and listening to music.

What percentage of time do adolescents spend with different people? As shown in figure 9.3, the Chicago adolescents were not usually in the company of an adult. They were with their family for one-fifth of their waking hours, but only a portion of this time was spent with parents. A full 50 percent of the week's waking hours were spent with peers, partly in the classroom, partly outside of class with friends. One-fourth of their day was spent in solitude.

In a study with younger adolescents, Reed Larson and his colleagues beeped 401 fifth- through ninth-grade students in the Chicago area to determine how they were spending their time (Larson & Kleiber, 1990; Larson & Richards, 1989). For the youngest participants, play, television viewing, and other home- and family-centered activities filled a major portion of their waking hours. However, a different pattern of time use characterized the older subjects, who were in early adolescence. Talking,

What were the adolescents doing when they were beeped? As indicated in figure 9.2, they spent 29 percent of their time in productive activities, mainly involving schoolwork. They spent an additional 31 percent in maintenance activities like eating, resting, bathing, and dressing. They spent the remainder of their time in other activities, such as talking, engaging in sports, and reading, which can be classified primarily as leisure. By far, the largest amount of time spent in a single activity was studying, which took up 13 percent of the adolescents' waking hours. However, the time spent studying by the

listening to music, and other solitary and friend-centered activities became more common in early adolescence. Participation in sports also declined in early adolescence.

In another recent study involving the use of the "beeper" methodology, Reed Larson and Marsye Richards (1994) had mothers, fathers, and adolescents carry electronic pagers for a week and record their activities and emotions when beeped at random times. The result was a portrait of the hour-by-hour emotional realities lived by families with adolescents. Differences between the fast-paced daily realities lived by each family member created considerable potential for misunderstanding and conflict. Because family members were often attending to different priorities, needs, and stressors, their realities were often out of sync. Even when they wanted to share leisure activity, their interests were at odds. One father said that his wife likes to shop, his daughter likes to play video games, and he likes to stay home. Although the main theme of this work was the hazards of contemporary life, some families with adolescents were buoyant and their lives were coordinated.

SOCIAL CLASS AND POVERTY

Many subcultures exist within countries. For example, the values and attitudes of adolescents growing up in an urban ghetto or rural Appalachia may differ from those of adolescents growing up in a wealthy suburb. In this section, we will study the nature of social class and poverty.

The Nature of Social Class

Earlier in this chapter, social class (also called socioeconomic status or SES) was defined as the grouping of people with similar occupational, educational, and economic characteristics. Social class, or social stratification as it also is sometimes called, carries with it certain inequities. Generally, members of a society have (1) occupations that vary in prestige, and some individuals have more access than others to higher-status occupations; (2) different levels of educational attainment, and some individuals have more access than others to better education; (3) different economic resources; and (4) different levels of power to influence a community's institutions. These differences in the ability to control resources and to participate in society's rewards produce unequal opportunities for adolescents.

The number of visibly different social classes depends on the community's size and complexity. In most investigators' descriptions of social classes, two to five categories are included. In a five-class structure, upper, upper-middle, lower-middle, upper-lower, and lower-lower classes are delineated. In a two-class structure, lower and middle classes are delineated. Sometimes the lower class is described as working-class, blue-collar, or low-income; sometimes the middle class is described as managerial-class, white-collar, or middle-income. Examples of lower-class occupations are factory worker, manual laborer,

welfare recipient, and maintenance worker; examples of middle-class occupations are salesperson, manager, and professional (doctor, lawyer, teacher, accountant, and so on).

Socioeconomic Variations in Families, Schools, and Neighborhoods

The families, schools, and neighborhoods of adolescents have socioeconomic characteristics. Some adolescents have parents who have a great deal of money, and who work in prestigious occupations. These adolescents live in attractive houses and neighborhoods, and attend schools where the mix of students is primarily from middle- and upper-class backgrounds. Other adolescents have parents who do not have very much money and who work in less prestigious occupations. These adolescents do not live in very attractive houses and neighborhoods, and they attend schools where the mix of students is mainly from lower-class backgrounds. Such variations in neighborhood settings can influence adolescents' adjustment (Coulton & Korbin, 1995; Leffert & Blyth, 1996; Sampson & Earls, 1995). In one recent study, neighborhood crime and isolation were linked with low self-esteem and psychological distress in adolescents (Roberts, Jacobson, & Taylor, 1996).

In America and most Western cultures, social class differences in child rearing exist (Hoff-Ginsberg & Tardif, 1995). Working-class, low-income parents often place a high value on external characteristics, such as obedience and neatness, whereas middle-class parents often place a high value on internal characteristics, such as self-control and delay of gratification. There also are social class differences in parenting behaviors. Middle-class parents are more likely to explain something, use verbal praise, accompany their discipline with reasoning, and ask their children and adolescents questions. By contrast, parents from low-income, working-class households are more likely to discipline children and adolescents with physical punishment and criticize them (Heath, 1983).

Social class differences in families also are involved in an important aspect of the adolescent's intellectual orientation. Most school tasks require students to use and process language. As part of developing language skills, students must learn to read efficiently, write effectively, and give competent oral reports. Although variation exists within a social class, middle-class students make use of verbal skills, especially reading, more than students from low-income backgrounds (also called working-class students). As shown in figure 9.4, in one investigation, working-class adolescents read less and watched television more than did middle-class adolescents (Erlick & Starry, 1973). Although television involves some verbal activity, it is primarily a visual medium, suggesting that working-class adolescents prefer a visual medium to a verbal medium.

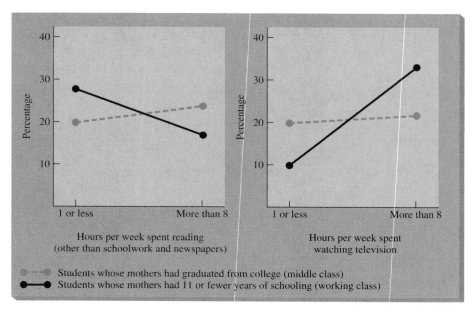

Figure~9.4

The Reading and Television Habits of High School Students from Working-Class Families.

Like their parents, children and adolescents from low-income backgrounds are at high risk for experiencing mental health problems (McLoyd, 1993, 1997a). Social maladaptation and psychological problems, such as depression, low self-confidence, peer conflict, and juvenile delinquency, are more prevalent among poor adolescents than among economically advantaged adolescents (Gibbs & Huang, 1989). Although psychological problems are more prevalent among adolescents from low-income backgrounds, these adolescents vary considerably in intellectual and psychological functioning. For example, a sizable portion of adolescents from low-income backgrounds perform well in school; some perform better than many middle-class students. When adolescents from low-income backgrounds are achieving well in school, it is not unusual to find a parent or parents making special sacrifices to provide the necessary living conditions and support that contribute to school success.

In one study, although positive times occurred in the lives of ethnically diverse young adolescents growing up in poverty, many of their negative experiences were worse than those of their middle-class counterparts (Richards & others, 1994). These adversities involved (1) physical punishment and lack of structure at home, (2) violence in the neighborhood, and (3) domestic violence in their buildings.

Schools in low-income neighborhoods often have fewer resources than schools in high-income neighborhoods do. The schools in the low-income areas also are likely to have more students with lower achievement test scores, lower rates of graduation, and smaller percentages of students going to college (Garbarino & Asp, 1981).

For example, in one profile, 80 percent of urban disadvantaged students scored in the bottom half of standardized tests for reading and math (*The Research Bulletin*, 1991). In some instances, however, federal aid to schools has provided a context for enhanced learning in low-income areas. The school personnel in schools in lower-class neighborhoods often are different than in middle-class settings. Younger, less experienced teachers often are the ones who end up with jobs in schools in lower-class neighborhoods, while older, more experienced teachers are more often found in schools in middle-class neighborhoods.

Poverty

In a report on the state of America's children and adolescents, the Children Defense Fund (1992) described what life is like for all too many youth. When sixth-graders in a poverty-stricken area of St. Louis were asked to describe a perfect day, one boy said he would erase the world, then he would sit and think. Asked if he wouldn't rather go outside and play, the boy responded, "Are you kidding, out there?"

The world is a dangerous and unwelcoming place for too many of America's youth, especially those whose families, neighborhoods, and schools are low-income (Edelman, 1997). Some adolescents are resilient and cope with the challenges of poverty without any major setbacks, but too many struggle unsuccessfully. Each child of poverty who reaches adulthood unhealthy, unskilled, or alienated keeps our nation from being as competent and productive as it can be (Children's Defense Fund, 1992).

The Nature of Poverty

Poverty is defined by economic hardship, and its most common marker is the federal poverty threshold (Huston, McLoyd, & Coll, 1994). The poverty threshold was originally based on the estimated cost of food (a basic diet) multiplied by 3. This federal poverty marker is adjusted annually for family size and inflation. Although the federal poverty index has been criticized (it is not adjusted for geographic region or noncash benefits, such as food stamps, for example), it is widely used in both research and policy. Other indices of economic hardship that are used in some studies include parent unemployment, unstable work history, income loss, and low socioeconomic status.

Measuring poverty in a valid way is difficult because it is a conglomerate of conditions. Poor children and their

Adolescents from the lowest strata of working-class families are of special concern. Economic poverty makes it very difficult for adolescents to succeed in school and life.

families are often exposed to poor health conditions, inadequate housing and homelessness, environmental toxins, and violent or unsupportive neighborhoods. Unlike income loss or unemployment due to job loss, poverty is not a homogeneous variable or distinct event. Also, unemployment, unstable work history, and income loss do not always push families into poverty.

Thus, despite the simplicity of the federal poverty index (estimated cost of food multiplied by 3), poverty is not a homogeneous, static circumstance. Rather, poverty varies along several dimensions, including its pervasiveness and duration, as well as its ecological context. Some adolescents have lived in chronic poverty that has lasted all of their lives, while others experience poverty for a shorter time. Also, poverty effects can vary by ecological context. The stark visibility of poor, urban ghettos and their proximity to major research universities probably accounts for the fact that most childhood poverty studies involve urban children, despite the fact that poverty is as high or higher in rural areas, especially among African American and Mexican American children (Huston, McLoyd, & Coll, 1994). For example, adolescents living in rural poverty are more likely to grow up in two-parent rather than one-parent families than are adolescents living in urban poverty. In one recent study, the damaging effects of poverty were visible in rural families (Brody & others, 1994). In this study of rural two-parent African American families, lack of financial resources led to greater depression and less optimism in mothers and fathers, which in turn were linked with conflict and lack of co-parenting support. Another recent study in the rural Midwest revealed that economic stress was linked with coercive family relations and developmental problems in young adolescents (Conger & others, 1994).

Let's further consider some of the psychological ramifications of living in poverty. First, the poor are often powerless. In occupations, they rarely are the decision makers. Rules are handed down to them in an authoritarian manner. Second, the poor are often vulnerable to disaster. They are not likely to be given notice when they are laid off from work and usually do not have financial resources to fall back on when problems arise. Third, their range of alternatives is often restricted. Only a limited number of jobs are open to them. Even when alternatives are available, the poor might not know about them or be prepared to make a wise decision, because of inadequate education and inability to read well. Fourth, being poor means having less prestige. This lack of prestige is transmitted to children early in their lives. The child in poverty observes that many other children wear nicer clothes and live in more attractive houses.

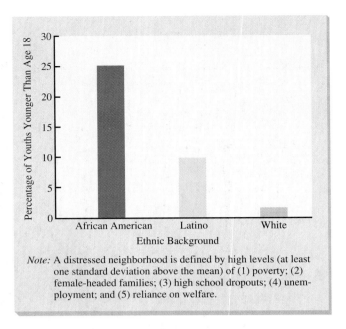

Note: A distressed neighborhood is defined by high levels (at least one standard deviation above the mean) of (1) poverty; (2) female-headed families; (3) high school dropouts; (4) unemployment; and (5) reliance on welfare.

Figure~9.5

Living in distressed neighborhoods.

The Scope of Poverty

In a recent year (1993), almost 22 percent of the nation's children lived in poverty (U.S. Bureau of the Census, 1994), a percentage about twice that of other industrialized nations. For example, Canada's child poverty rate is about 9 percent and Sweden's is about 2 percent (Danziger & Danziger, 1993).

Poverty in the United States is demarcated along ethnic lines. In 1993, 47 percent of African American children and 40 percent of Latino children lived in poverty (U.S. Bureau of the Census, 1994). Ethnic minority youth are also more likely than Anglo-American youth to experience persistent poverty and live in isolated poor urban neighborhoods where social supports are minimal and threats to positive development are abundant (Jarrett, 1995) (see figure 9.5).

Why is poverty among American youth so high? Three reasons are apparent (Huston, McLoyd, & Coll, 1994): (1) Economic changes have eliminated many blue-collar jobs that paid reasonably well, (2) the percentage of youth living in single-parent families headed by the mother has increased, and (3) government benefits were reduced during the 1970s and 1980s.

When poverty is persistent and long-standing, it can have especially damaging effects on children. In one study, the longer children lived in families with income below the poverty line, the lower was the quality of their home environments (Garrett, Ng'andu, and Ferron, 1994). Also in this study, improvements in family income had their strongest effects on the home environments of chronically poor children. In another study, children in families experiencing both persistent and occasional poverty had lower IQs and more internalized behavior problems than never-poor children, but persistent poverty had a much stronger negative effect on these outcomes than occasional poverty did (Duncan, Brooks-Gunn, & Klebanov, 1994).

Searching for Factors That Mediate the Effects of Poverty on Adolescent Development

What processes mediate the adverse influences of poverty on adolescent development? A major criticism of much research on the relation of social structure (such as social class and poverty) to cognitive and socioemotional development has been its failure to move beyond sociodemographic variables and investigate the process variables that mediate these linkages (Huston, 1995; Huston, McLoyd, & Coll, 1994).

Some researchers are beginning to remedy this problem. For example, in one study, reanalysis of data from a classic sociodemographic study of juvenile delinquency (Glueck & Glueck, 1950) revealed that erratic, threatening, and harsh discipline, low levels of maternal supervision, and weak parent-son emotional attachment mediated the effects of poverty on delinquent behavior (Sampson & Laub, 1994). In one study by Vonnie McLoyd and her colleagues (1994), unemployment among single-parent African American mothers negatively affected adolescents' socioemotional functioning by increasing maternal depression and, in turn, increasing punishment of the adolescent. In another recent study, a negative home environment (such as inadequate provision of appropriate play, lack of maternal involvement with the child) at 30 months of age was linked with low academic achievement in the sixth grade (Susman & Adam, 1995).

A special concern is the high percentage of single mothers in poverty, more than one-third of whom are in poverty, compared to only 10 percent of single fathers. McLoyd (1990, 1993) concludes that because poor, single mothers are more distressed than their middle-class counterparts are, they often show low support, nurturance, and involvement with their children. Among the reasons for the high poverty rate of single mothers are women's low pay, infrequent awarding of alimony payments, and poorly enforced child support by fathers. The term **feminization of poverty** *refers to the fact that far more women than men live in poverty. Women's low income, divorce, and the resolution of divorce cases by the judicial system, which leaves women with less money than they and their children need to adequately function, are the likely causes of the feminization of poverty.*

A downward trajectory is not inevitable for youth living in poverty (Carnegie Council on Adolescent Development, 1995). One potential positive path for such youth is to become involved with a caring mentor. The Quantum Opportunities Program, funded by the Ford

Foundation, was a 4-year, year-around mentoring effort. The students were entering the ninth grade at a high school with high rates of poverty, were minorities, and came from families that received public assistance. Each day for 4 years, mentors provided sustained support, guidance, and concrete assistance to their students.

The Quantum program required students to participate in (1) academic-related activities outside school hours, including reading, writing, math, science, and social studies, peer tutoring, and computer skills training; (2) community service projects, including tutoring elementary school students, cleaning up the neighborhood, and volunteering in hospitals, nursing homes, and libraries; and (3) cultural enrichment and personal development activities, including life skills training, and college and job planning. In exchange for their commitment to the program, students were offered financial incentives that encouraged participation, completion, and long-range planning. A stipend of $1.33 was given to students for each hour they participated in these activities. For every 100 hours of education, service, or development activities, students received a bonus of $100. The average cost per participant was $10,600 for the 4 years, which is one-half the cost of 1 year in prison.

An evaluation of the Quantum project compared the mentored students with a nonmentored control group. Sixty-three percent of the mentored students graduated from high school but only 42 percent of the control group did; 42 percent of the mentored students are currently enrolled in college but only 16 percent of the control group are. Further, control-group students were twice as likely as the mentored students to receive food stamps or welfare, and they had more arrests. Such programs clearly have the potential to overcome the intergenerational transmission of poverty and its negative outcomes.

At this point, we have discussed a number of ideas about culture, cross-cultural comparisons, the settings in which adolescents spend time, and social class and poverty. A summary of these ideas is presented in concept table 9.1. Next, we turn our attention to another important aspect of culture—ethnicity.

ETHNICITY

Adolescents live in a world that has been made smaller and more interactive by dramatic improvements in travel and communication. Adolescents also live in a world that is far more diverse in its ethnic makeup than it was in past decades. Ninety-three languages are spoken in Los Angeles alone! With these changes have come conflicts and concerns about what the future will bring.

- In 1992, riots broke out in Los Angeles after African American Rodney King was beaten by White police and the police were acquitted of any wrongdoing by a jury. The beating and the trial brought racial animosities to the surface.

- In 1993, in what had formerly been Yugoslavia, adolescents experienced the renewal of ancient animosities as Serbs and Croats pummeled and killed each other. Even UN intervention and boycotts can't stem the underlying ethnic hatred and killing.
- In Germany, an increasing number of youth join the neo-Nazi movement. Some German-born citizens want an ethnic cleansing of their country; non-German-born immigrants are being beaten and killed.
- In Miami, Florida, English is a problem for half of the population. That is a sharp increase from the 30 percent 10 years ago who said they had problems communicating in English and reflects the influx of Hispanic and Creole-speaking Haitian immigrants.
- In the Middle East, Jews and Arabs live in separate communities and loathe each other. Territorial disputes and threats of war are virtually daily occurrences.
- In 1994, South Africa held its first elections open to Black candidates. Nelson Mandela won handily over his White opponent, Frederik Willem de Klerk. However, he took on the presidential responsibilities of a country in which a history of apartheid and oppression has made Blacks into second-class citizens. The White ruling class has only grudgingly given up ground. Racially motivated riots and killings continue to occur.

As mentioned earlier in the chapter, *ethnicity* refers to the cultural heritage, national characteristics, race, religion, and language of individuals. As evidenced by the waves of ethnic animosity around the world today, we need to better understand ethnicity.

Domains and Issues

What is the nature of ethnicity, social class, differences, and diversity? Is adolescence a special juncture in the development of ethnic minority adolescents? How do prejudice, discrimination, and bias affect adolescents? What is the nature of value conflicts, assimilation, and pluralism?

Ethnicity, Social Class, Differences, and Diversity

Much of the research on ethnic minority adolescents has failed to tease apart the influences of ethnicity and social class. Ethnicity and social class can interact in ways that exaggerate the influence of ethnicity because ethnic minority individuals are overrepresented in the lower socioeconomic levels of American society (Spencer & Dornbusch, 1990). Consequently, too often researchers have given ethnic explanations of adolescent development that were largely based on socioeconomic status rather than ethnicity. For example, decades of research on group differences in self-esteem failed to consider the

Culture, Social Class, and Poverty

Concept	Processes/ Related Ideas	Characteristics/Description
Culture and Adolescence	The nature of culture	Culture refers to the behavior, patterns, beliefs, and all other products of a particular group of people that are passed on from generation to generation.
	The relevance of culture	If the study of adolescence is to be a relevant discipline in the twenty-first century, increased attention will need to focus on culture and ethnicity.
	Cross-cultural comparisons	Cross-cultural studies involve the comparison of a culture with one or more other cultures, which provides information about the degree to which adolescent development is universal or culture-specific. The study of adolescence emerged in the context of Western industrialized society.
	Models of cultural change	The models that have been used to understand the cultural changes that occur in transitions within and between cultures include (1) assimilation, (2) acculturation, (3) alternation, (4) multiculturalism, and (5) fusion. The multicultural model promotes a pluralistic approach to understanding two or more cultures. There are four choices people can make in a situation requiring adaptation in plural societies: (1) assimilate, (2) integrate, (3) separate, or (4) marginalize.
	Rites of passage	Rites of passage are ceremonies that mark an individual's transition from one status to another, especially into adulthood. In primitive cultures, rites of passage are often well-defined, but in contemporary America, they are not.
The Settings in Which Adolescents Spend Their Time	Their nature	Using the experience sampling method, which involves beeping adolescents on electronic pagers, researchers found that adolescents spent 29 percent of their time in productive activities, 31 percent in maintenance activities such as eating and resting, and the remainder of their time primarily in leisure. The single activity in which the largest amount of time was spent was studying.
Social Class and Poverty	The nature of social class	Social class, also called socioeconomic status or SES, is the grouping of people with similar occupational, educational, and economic characteristics. Social class often carries with it certain inequities.
	Socioeconomic variations in families, schools, and neighborhoods.	The families, schools, and neighborhoods of adolescents have socioeconomic characteristics that are related to the adolescent's development. Parents from low-income families are more likely to value external characteristics and to use physical punishment and criticism than are their middle-class counterparts.
	Poverty	Poverty is defined by economic hardship, and its most common marker is the federal poverty threshold (based on the estimated cost of food, multiplied by 3). Measuring poverty is difficult because it involves many conditions, including how pervasive and long-lasting it is, as well as ecological contexts (such as rural or urban). The subculture of the poor is characterized not only by economic hardship, but also by social and psychological handicaps. When poverty is persistent and long-standing, it can have especially devastating effects on development. Too much of the research on poverty has been limited to sociodemographic variables and has not sought to discover the factors that mediate the effects of poverty on children's development.

socioeconomic status of African American and White American children and adolescents (Hare & Castenell, 1985). When the self-esteem of African American adolescents from low-income backgrounds is compared with that of White American adolescents from middle-class backgrounds, the differences are often large but not informative because of the confounding of ethnicity and social class (Scott-Jones, 1995).

While some ethnic minority youth are from middle-class backgrounds, economic advantage does not entirely enable them to escape their ethnic minority status. Middle-class ethnic minority youth still encounter much of the prejudice, discrimination, and bias associated with being

a member of an ethnic minority group. Often characterized as a "model minority" because of their strong achievement orientation and family cohesiveness, Japanese Americans still experience stress associated with ethnic minority status (Sue, 1990). Although middle-class ethnic minority adolescents have more resources available to counter the destructive influences of prejudice and discrimination, they still cannot completely avoid the pervasive influences of negative stereotypes about ethnic minority groups.

Not all ethnic minority families are poor, but poverty contributes to the stressful life experiences of many ethnic minority adolescents. Vonnie McLoyd (1990)

Some of today's adolescents live in contexts with extensive conflict, such as (*a*) the renewal of ancient animosities between Serbs and Croats in what was Yugoslavia, (*b*) neo-Nazi movement in Germany, (*c*) the Middle East, where Jews and Arabs engage in hostile encounters, and (*d*) Los Angeles, where riots broke out following the beating of Rodney King by police.

concluded that ethnic minority youth experience a disproportionate share of the adverse effects of poverty and unemployment in America today. Thus, many ethnic minority adolescents experience a double disadvantage: (1) prejudice, discrimination, and bias because of their ethnic minority status, and (2) the stressful effects of poverty.

Historical, economic, and social experiences produce legitimate differences between various ethnic minority groups, and between ethnic minority groups and the majority White group (Halonen & Santrock, 1996). Individuals living in a particular ethnic or cultural group adapt to the values, attitudes, and stresses of that culture. Their behavior, while possibly different from our own, is, nonetheless, often functional for them. Recognizing and respecting these differences is an important aspect of getting along with others in a diverse, multicultural world. Adolescents, as well as each of us, need to take the perspective of individuals from ethnic and cultural groups that are different than ours and think, "If I were

in their shoes, what kind of experiences might I have had?" "How would I feel if I were a member of their ethnic or cultural group?" "How would I think and behave if I had grown up in their world?" Such perspective taking often increases our empathy and understanding of individuals from ethnic and cultural groups different from ours.

Unfortunately, the emphasis often placed by society and science on the differences between ethnic minority groups and the White majority has been damaging to ethnic minority individuals. Ethnicity has defined who will enjoy the privileges of citizenship and to what degree and in what ways (Jones, 1994). An individual's ethnic background has determined whether the individual will be alienated, oppressed, or disadvantaged.

The current emphasis on differences between ethnic groups underscores the strengths of various ethnic minority groups and is long overdue. For example, the extended-family support system that characterizes many ethnic minority groups is now recognized as an important factor in coping. And researchers are finding that African

American males are better than Anglo males at nonverbal cues, multilingual/multicultural expression, improvised problem solving, and using body language in communication (Evans & Whitfield, 1988).

For too long, the ways ethnic minority groups differed from Whites were conceptualized as *deficits* or inferior characteristics on the part of the ethnic minority group. Indeed, research on ethnic minority groups often focused only on a group's negative, stressful aspects. For example, research on African American adolescent females invariably examined such topics as poverty, unwed motherhood, and dropping out of school. These topics continue to be important research areas of adolescent development, but research on the positive aspects of African American adolescent females in a pluralistic society is also much needed and sorely neglected. The self-esteem, achievement, motivation, and self-control of adolescents from different ethnic minority groups deserve considerable study.

Another important dimension of ethnic minority adolescents is their diversity, a point made in chapter 1 but that deserves a second mention. Ethnic minority groups are not homogeneous; they have different social, historical, and economic backgrounds (Stevenson, 1995). For example, Mexican, Cuban, and Puerto Rican immigrants are Latinos but they had different reasons for migrating, came from varying socioeconomic backgrounds in their native countries, and experience different rates and types of employment in the United States (Ramirez, 1989). The U.S. federal government now recognizes the existence of 511 *different* Native American tribes, each having a unique ancestral background with differing values and characteristics. Asian Americans include the Chinese, Japanese, Philippinos, Koreans, and Southeast Asians, each group having distinct ancestries and languages. The diversity of Asian Americans is reflected in their educational attainment: Some achieve a high level of education, while many others have no education whatsoever. For example, 90 percent of Korean American males graduate from high school, but only 71 percent of Vietnamese American males do.

Sometimes, well-meaning individuals fail to recognize the diversity within an ethnic group (Sue, 1990). For example, a sixth-grade teacher went to a human relations workshop and was exposed to the necessity of incorporating more ethnicity into her instructional planning. She had two Mexican American adolescents in her class, and she asked them to be prepared to demonstrate to the class on the following Monday how they danced at home. The teacher expected both of them to perform Mexican folk dances, reflecting their ethnic heritage. The first boy got up in front of the class and began dancing in a typical American fashion. The teacher said, "No, I want you to dance like you and your family do at home, like you do when you have Mexican American celebrations." The boy informed the teacher that his family did not dance that way. The second boy demonstrated a Mexican folk dance to the class. The first boy was highly assimilated into the American culture and did not know how to dance Mexican folk dances. The second boy was less assimilated and came from a Mexican American family that had retained more of its Mexican heritage.

This example illustrates the diversity and individual differences that exist within any ethnic minority group. Failure to recognize diversity and individual variations results in the stereotyping of an ethnic minority group. Next, we will study how adolescence is a special juncture in an ethnic minority individual's development.

Adolescence: A Special Juncture for Ethnic Minority Individuals

For ethnic minority individuals, adolescence is often a special juncture in their development (Spencer & Dornbusch, 1990). Although children are aware of some ethnic and cultural differences, most ethnic minority individuals first consciously confront their ethnicity in adolescence. In contrast to children, adolescents have the ability to interpret ethnic and cultural information, to reflect on the past, and to speculate about the future. As they cognitively mature, ethnic minority adolescents become acutely aware of how the majority White culture evaluates their ethnic group (Comer, 1993). As one researcher commented, the young African American child may learn that Black is beautiful but conclude as an adolescent that White is powerful (Semaj, 1985).

Ethnic minority youths' awareness of negative appraisals, conflicting values, and restricted occupational opportunities can influence their life choices and plans for the future (Spencer & Dornbusch, 1990). As one ethnic minority youth stated, "The future seems shut off, closed. Why dream? You can't reach your dreams. Why set goals? At least if you don't set any goals, you don't fail."

For many ethnic minority youth, a special concern is the lack of successful ethnic minority role models (Blash & Unger, 1992). The problem is especially acute for inner-city ethnic minority youth. Because of the lack of adult ethnic minority role models, some ethnic minority youth may conform to middle-class White values and identify with successful White role models. However, for many ethnic minority adolescents, their ethnicity and skin color limit their acceptance by the White culture. Thus, they face a difficult task: negotiating two values systems—that of their own ethnic group and that of the White society. Some adolescents reject the mainstream, forgoing the rewards controlled by White Americans; others adopt the values and standards of the majority White culture; and still others take the difficult path of biculturality.

The nature of identity development in ethnic minority adolescents is discussed further in chapter 10, "The Self and Identity." Next, we will examine the prejudice, discrimination, and bias experienced by many ethnic minority adolescents.

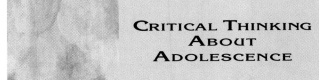

CRITICAL THINKING ABOUT ADOLESCENCE

Reconstructing Prejudice

No matter how well-intentioned adolescents are, their life circumstances have probably given them some prejudices. If they don't maintain particular prejudices toward people with different cultural and ethnic backgrounds, there might be other kinds of people who bring out prejudices in them. For example, prejudices can be developed about people who have certain religious beliefs or political convictions, people who are unattractive or too attractive, people with unpopular occupations (police officers, lawyers), people with a disability, and people from bordering towns.

Psychologist William James once observed that one function of education is to rearrange prejudices. How could adolescents' education rearrange prejudices like the ones we have listed? Consider prejudice toward ethnic minority groups, the main focus of our discussion of prejudice in this chapter. One strategy might be to adopt the jigsaw classroom concept involving cooperative learning, which was discussed in chapter 8. What other strategies might work? By thinking about ways to reduce prejudice on the part of adolescents, you are learning to think critically by *evaluating the quality of conclusions about adolescent development.*

Margaret Beale Spencer, shown here talking with adolescents, believes that adolescence is a critical juncture in the identity development of ethnic minority individuals. Most ethnic minority individuals consciously confront their ethnicity for the first time in adolescence.

Prejudice, Discrimination, and Bias

Prejudice *is an unjustified negative attitude toward an individual because of the individual's membership in a group.* The group toward which the prejudice is directed can be made up of people of a particular ethnic group, sex, age, religion, or other detectable difference. Our concern here is prejudice against ethnic minority groups.

In a recent Gallup poll, Americans stated that they believe that the United States is ethnically tolerant and that overt racism is basically unacceptable (*Asian Week*, 1990). However, many ethnic minority individuals continue to experience persistent forms of prejudice, discrimination, and bias (Sue, 1990). Ethnic minority adolescents are taught in schools that often have a middle-class, White bias and in classroom contexts that are not adapted to ethnic minority adolescents' learning styles. They are assessed by tests that are often culturally biased and are evaluated by teachers whose appreciation of their abilities may be hindered by negative stereotypes about ethnic minorities (Spencer & Dornbusch, 1990). Discrimination and prejudice continue to be present in the media, interpersonal interactions, and daily conversations. Crimes, strangeness, poverty, mistakes, and deterioration are often mistakenly attributed to ethnic minority individuals or foreigners (van Dijk, 1987).

As Asian American researcher Stanley Sue (1990) points out, people frequently have opposing views about discrimination and prejudice. On one side are individuals who value and praise the significant strides made in civil rights in recent years, pointing to affirmative action programs as proof of these civil rights advances. On the other side are individuals who criticize American institutions, such as education, because they believe that many forms of discrimination and prejudice still characterize these institutions.

Stanley Sue, shown lecturing to Asian Americans, has been an important advocate of increased research on ethnic minority issues in psychology. Sue has conducted extensive research on the role of ethnicity in understanding abnormal behavior and psychotherapy. He also has provided considerable insight into ethnic minority issues.

Progress has been made in ethnic minority relations, but discrimination and prejudice still exist, and equality has not been achieved. Much remains to be accomplished (Halonen & Santrock, 1996).

In the end, antiblack, antifemale, and all forms of discrimination are equivalent to the same thing—antihumanism.

—**Shirley Chisholm,**
Unbought and Unbossed (1970)

Value Conflicts, Assimilation, and Pluralism

Stanley Sue (1990) believes that value conflicts are often involved when individuals respond to ethnic issues. These value conflicts have been a source of considerable controversy. According to Sue, without properly identifying the assumptions and effects of the conflicting values, it is difficult to resolve ethnic minority issues.

Let's examine a value conflict that Sue describes—assimilation versus pluralism—and see how it might influence an individual's responses to an ethnic minority issue: One faculty member commented that he was glad that his psychology department was interested in teaching students about ethnic and cultural issues. He felt that, by becoming aware of the cultures of different groups, students would improve their understanding of their own and other cultures. However, another faculty member disagreed. She felt that students' knowledge of ethnic minority issues and different cultures was a relevant concern, but she argued that the department's scarce resources should not be devoted to ethnic and cultural issues. She also believed that if too much attention was given to ethnic and cultural issues, it might actually increase the

segregation of students and even cause friction among ethnic and cultural groups. She commented that we all live in this society and therefore must all learn the same skills to succeed. In Sue's (1990) perspective, a value conflict involving assimilation and pluralism underlies these opposing views about whether a psychology department should devote any, or increased, funds to teaching students about ethnicity and culture.

As we indicated earlier, **assimilation** *refers to the absorption of ethnic minority groups into the dominant group, which often means the loss of some or virtually all of the behavior and values of the ethnic minority group.* Individuals who adopt an assimilation stance usually advocate that ethnic minority groups should become more American. By contrast, **pluralism** *is the coexistence of distinct ethnic and cultural groups in the same society.* Individuals who adopt a pluralistic stance usually advocate that cultural differences should be maintained and appreciated (Camino, 1995).

For many years, an assimilation approach was thought to be the best course for American society because the mainstream was believed to be superior in many ways. Even though many individuals today reject the notion that the mainstream culture is intrinsically superior to ethnic minority cultures, the assimilation approach is currently resurfacing with a more complex face. Advocates of the assimilation approach now often use practical and functional arguments rather than intrinsic superiority arguments to buttress their point of view. For example, assimilation advocates stress that educational programs for immigrant children (Mexican, Chinese, and so on) should stress the learning of English as early as possible, rather than bilingual education. Their argument is that spending time on any language other than English may be a handicap, especially since a second language is not functional in the classroom. By contrast, the advocates of pluralism argue that an English-only approach reasserts the mainstream-is-right-and-best belief. Thus, responses to the ethnic minority issue of bilingual education involve a clash of fundamental values. As Sue asks, how can one argue against the development of functional skills and to some degree the support of Americanization? Similarly, how can one doubt that pluralism, diversity, and respect for different cultures is valid? Sue believes that the one-sidedness of the issue is the main problem. Advocates of assimilation often overlook the fact that a consensus might be lacking on what constitutes functional skills or that a particular context might alter what skills are useful. For example, with an increasing immigrant population, the ability to speak Spanish or Japanese might be an asset, as is the ability to interact with and collaborate with diverse ethnic groups.

Sue believes that one way to resolve value conflicts about sociocultural issues is to conceptualize or redefine them in innovative ways. For example, in the assimilation/pluralism conflict, rather than deal with the assumption that assimilation is necessary for the development of functional skills, one strategy is to focus on the fluctuating criteria of what skills are considered functional or the possibility that developing functional skills does not prevent the existence of pluralism. For instance, the classroom instructor might use multicultural examples when teaching social studies, while also discussing culturally universal (etic) and culturally specific (emic) approaches to American and other cultures.

> *I* am here and you will know that I am the best and will hear me. The color of my skin or the kink of my hair or the spread of my mouth has nothing to do with what you are listening to.
>
> —Leontyne Price

Ethnic Minority Adolescents

Now that we have considered a number of ideas about ethnic minority adolescents in general, we turn our attention to specific ethnic minority groups in America, beginning with African American adolescents.

African American Adolescents

African American adolescents make up the largest easily visible ethnic minority group in the United States. African American adolescents are distributed throughout the social class structure, although they constitute a larger proportion of poor and lower-class individuals than does the majority White group (McLoyd, 1993, 1997a). No cultural characteristic is common to all or nearly all African Americans and absent in Whites, unless it is the experience of being African American and the ideology that develops from that experience (Havighurst, 1987).

The majority of African American youth stay in school, do not take drugs, do not prematurely get married and become parents, are employed and eager to work, are not involved in crime, and grow up to lead productive lives in spite of social and economic disadvantage. While much of the writing and research about African American adolescents has focused on low-income youth from families mainly residing in inner cities, the majority of African American youth do not reside in the ghettos of inner cities. At the heart of the new model of studying African American youth is recognition of the growing diversity in African American communities in the United States (Burton & Allison, 1995; McHale, 1995).

TABLE 9.1

Some Characteristics of African American Adolescents

An African American male teenager between the ages of 15 and 19 is nine times more likely than his White peer to be a homicide victim.

An African American female teenager is more than twice as likely as her White peer to have a baby.

An African American teenager is more than twice as likely as a White teenager to be enrolled in a remedial math class.

An African American high school graduate is only half as likely as a White graduate to receive a bachelor's degree 4 years after high school.

One African American teenager in every two lives with only one parent.

One African American teenager in every three lives with a parent who did not graduate from high school.

One African American teenager in every three lives with an unemployed parent.

From Janet Simons, Belva Finlay, and Alice Yang, *The Adolescent & Young Adult Fact Book,* page 4; Washington, DC: Children's Defense Fund, 1991. Reprinted by permission.

Prejudice against African Americans in some occupations still persists, but the proportion of African American males and females in middle-class occupations has been increasing since 1940. A substantial and increasing proportion of African American adolescents are growing up in middle-class families and share middle-class values and attitudes with White middle-class adolescents. Nonetheless, large numbers of African American adolescents still live in poverty-enshrouded ghettos. Table 9.1 illustrates some of the characteristics of African American adolescents.

In one investigation of African Americans, a mixture of factors was related to the problems of adolescents in the inner city (Wilson, 1987). Increased social isolation in concentrated areas of poverty and little interaction with the mainstream society were related to the difficulties experienced by inner-city African American youth. Unattractive jobs and a lack of community standards to reinforce work increased the likelihood that inner-city African American youth would turn to either underground illegal activity, idleness, or both.

In the inner city, African American youth are increasingly unlikely to find legitimate employment, to some extent because of the lack of even low-paying jobs (Spencer & Dornbusch, 1990). The exodus of middle-income African Americans from the cities to the suburbs has removed leadership, reduced the tax base, decreased the educated political constituency, and diminished the support of churches and other organizations.

In many ethnic minority communities, religious institutions play an important role. Many African Americans report that their religious beliefs help them to get along with others and to accept the realities of the American occupational system (Spencer & Dornbusch, 1990). In one research study of successful African American students, a strong religious faith was common (Lee, 1985). In this study, regular church attendance characterized the lives of the successful African American students, many of whom mentioned Jesus Christ, Martin Luther King, and deacons as important influences in their lives. For many African American families, the church has served as an important resource and support system, not only in spiritual matters, but in the development of a social network as well.

As mentioned earlier, there is a high percentage of single-parent African American families, many of whom are in low-income categories. These family circumstances tax the coping ability of single parents and can have negative effects on children and adolescents (Wilson, Cook & Arrington, 1997). However, a characteristic of many African American families that helps to offset the high percentage of single-parent households is the extended-family household—in which one or several grandparents, uncles, aunts, siblings, or cousins either live together or provide support. The extended-family system has helped many African American parents to cope with adverse social conditions and economic impoverishment. The African American extended family can be traced to the African heritage of many African Americans; in many African cultures, a newly married couple does not move away from relatives. Instead, the extended family assists its members with basic family functions. Researchers have found that the extended family helps to reduce the stress of poverty and single-parenting through emotional support, sharing of income and economic responsibility, and surrogate parenting (McAdoo, 1996). The presence of grandmothers in the households of many African American adolescents and their infants has also been an important support system for the teenage mother and the infant (Stevens, 1984).

Latino Adolescents

The number of Latinos in the United States has increased 30 percent since 1980 to 19 million. Latinos now account for almost 8 percent of the U.S. population. Most trace their roots to Mexico (63 percent), Puerto Rico (12 percent), and Cuba (5 percent), the rest to Central and South American countries and the Caribbean. By the year 2000, their numbers are expected to swell to 30 million, 15 percent of the U.S. population. And roughly one-third of all

TABLE 9.2

Some Characteristics of Latino Adolescents

A Latino teenager is twice as likely as a White teenager to have no health insurance.

Sixteen- and 17-year-old Latina girls are four times more likely than their White peers to be behind in school.

Male Latino 18- and 19-year-olds are five times more likely than their White peers to be behind in school.

Latino 18- and 19-year-olds are more than twice as likely as their White peers to be school dropouts.

One Latino teenager in every two lives with a parent who did not graduate from high school.

One Latino teenager in every four lives with an unemployed parent.

From Janet Simons, Belva Finlay, and Alice Yang, *The Adolescent & Young Adult Fact Book,* page 5; Washington, DC: Children's Defense Fund, 1991. Reprinted by permission.

Latinos in the United States marry non-Latinos, promising a day when Latino culture will be more intertwined with other cultures here.

By far the largest group of Latino adolescents consists of those who identify themselves as having a Mexican origin, although many of them were born in the United States (Domino, 1992). Their largest concentration is in the U.S. Southwest. They represent more than 50 percent of the student population in the schools of San Antonio and close to that percentage in the schools of Los Angeles. Mexican Americans have a variety of lifestyles and come from a range of socioeconomic statuses—from affluent professional and managerial status to migrant farm worker and welfare recipient in big-city barrios. Even though they come from families with diverse backgrounds, Latino adolescents have one of the lowest educational levels of any ethnic minority group in the United States. Social support from parents and school personnel may be especially helpful in developing stronger academic achievement in Latino youth (Field, 1991). Table 9.2 portrays some characteristics of Latino adolescents.

Many Latino adolescents have developed a new political consciousness and pride in their cultural heritage. Some have fused strong cultural links to Mexican and Indian cultures with the economic limitations and restricted opportunities in the barrio. **Chicano** *is the name politically conscious Mexican American adolescents give themselves to reflect the combination of their Spanish-Mexican-Indian heritage and Anglo influences.*

The tapestry of American society is rapidly changing with an increasing number of ethnic minority youth. What issues are involved in the development of African American, Latino, Asian American, and Native American youth in America?

Like for African American adolescents, the church and family play important roles in Latino adolescents' lives. Many, but not all, Latino families are Catholic. And a basic value in Mexico is represented by saying, "As long as our family stays together, we are strong." Mexican children are brought up to stay close to their family, a tradition continued by Mexican Americans. Unlike the father in many Anglo-American families, the Mexican father is the undisputed authority on all family matters and is usually obeyed without question. The mother is revered as the primary source of affection and care. This emphasis on family attachment leads the Mexican to say, "I will achieve mainly because of my family, and for my family, rather than myself." By contrast, the self-reliant American would say, "I will achieve mainly because of my ability and initiative, and for myself, rather than for my family." Unlike most American families, Mexican families tend to stretch out in a network of relatives that often runs to scores of individuals. Mexican American families also tend to be large and have a strong extended-family orientation.

Asian American Adolescents

Asian American adolescents are the fastest-growing segment of the American adolescent population, and they, too, show considerable diversity. In the 1970s census, only three Asian American groups were prominent—Japanese, Chinese, and Philippino. But in the last two decades, there has been rapid growth in three other groups—Koreans, Pacific Islanders (Guam and Samoa), and Vietnamese (Huang, 1989).

Adolescents of Japanese or Chinese origin can be found in virtually every large city. While their grasp of the English language is usually good, they have been raised in a subculture in which family loyalty and family influence are powerful. This has tended to maintain their separate subcultures. The Japanese American adolescents are somewhat more integrated into the Anglo lifestyle than are the Chinese American adolescents. However, both groups have been very successful in school. They tend to take considerable advantage of educational opportunities.

SOCIOCULTURAL WORLDS OF ADOLESCENCE

Canada

Canada is a vast and diverse country with a population of approximately 27 million people. Although Canada shares a number of similarities with the United States, there are some important differences (Siegel & Wiener, 1993). Canada comprises a mixture of cultures that are loosely organized along the lines of economic power. The Canadian cultures include these:

- Native peoples, or First Nations, who were Canada's original inhabitants
- Descendants of French settlers who came to Canada during the seventeenth and eighteenth centuries
- Descendants of British settlers who came to Canada during and after the seventeenth century, or from the United States after the American Revolution in the latter part of the eighteenth century

The late nineteenth century brought three more waves of immigrants:

- From Asia, mainly China, immigrants came to the west coast of Canada in the latter part of the nineteenth and early twentieth centuries.

- From various European countries, immigrants came to central Canada and the prairie provinces during the early twentieth century and following World War II.
- From countries in economic and political turmoil (in Latin America, the Caribbean, Asia, Africa, the Indian subcontinent, the former Soviet Union, and the Middle East), immigrants have come to many different parts of Canada.

Canada has two official languages—English and French. Primarily French-speaking individuals reside mainly in Quebec; primarily English-speaking individuals reside mainly in other Canadian provinces. In addition to its English- and French-speaking populations, Canada has a large multicultural community. In three large Canadian cities—Toronto, Montreal, and Vancouver—more than 50 percent of the children and adolescents come from homes in which neither English nor French is the native language (Siegel & Wiener, 1993).

Native American Adolescents

Approximately 100,000 Native American (American Indian) adolescents are scattered across many tribal groups in about twenty states. About 90 percent are enrolled in school. About 15,000 are in boarding schools, many of which are maintained by the federal government's Bureau of Indian Affairs. Another 45,000 are in public schools on or near Indian reservations. In these schools, Native American adolescents make up more than 50 percent of the students. The remaining 30,000 are in public schools where they are an ethnic minority. A growing proportion of Native American adolescents have moved to large cities.

Native American adolescents have experienced an inordinate amount of discrimination. While virtually any minority group experiences some discrimination in being a member of a larger, majority-group culture, in the early years of the United States, Native Americans were the victims of terrible physical abuse and punishment. Injustices that these 800,000 individuals experienced are reflected in their having the lowest standard of living,

the highest teenage-pregnancy rate, the highest suicide rate, and the highest school dropout rate of any ethnic group in the United States (Clarke, 1997; LaFromboise & Low, 1989).

America: A Nation of Many Cultures

America has been and continues to be a great receiver of ethnic groups. It has embraced new ingredients from many cultures. The cultures often collide and cross-pollinate, mixing their ideologies and identities. Some of the culture of origin is retained, some of it lost, some of it mixed with the American culture. One after another, immigrants have come to America and been exposed to new channels of awareness and, in turn, exposed Americans to new channels of awareness. African American, Latino, Asian American, Native American, and other cultural heritages mix with the mainstream, receiving a new content and giving a new content. The ethnicity of Canadian youth is discussed in Sociocultural Worlds of Adolescence.

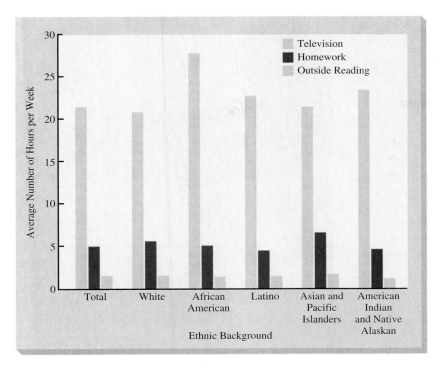

Figure~9.6

Weekly After-School Activities of Eighth-Graders.

TELEVISION AND OTHER MEDIA

Few developments in society over the last 30 years have had a greater impact on adolescents than television (Huston & Wright, 1997). The persuasion capabilities of television are staggering. As they have grown up, many of today's adolescents have spent more time in front of the television set than with their parents or in the classroom. Radio, records, rock music, and music video are other media that are especially important influences in the lives of many adolescents.

Functions and Use of Media

The functions of media for adolescents include these (Arnett, 1994):

1. *Entertainment.* Adolescents, like adults, often use media simply for entertainment and an enjoyable diversion from everyday concerns.

2. *Information.* Adolescents use media to obtain information, especially about topics that their parents may have been reluctant to discuss in the home, such as sexuality.

3. *Sensation.* Adolescents tend to be higher in sensation seeking than adults are; certain media provide intense and novel stimulation that appeals to adolescents.

4. *Coping.* Adolescents use media to relieve anxiety and unhappiness. Two of the most frequently endorsed coping responses of adolescents are "listen to music" and "watch TV."

5. *Gender-role modeling.* Media present models of female and male gender roles; these media images of females and males can influence adolescents' gender attitudes and behavior.

6. *Youth culture identification.* Media use gives many adolescents a sense of being connected to a larger peer network and culture, which is united by the kinds of values and interests conveyed through adolescent-oriented media.

If the amount of time spent in an activity is any indication of its importance, then there is no doubt that the mass media play important roles in adolescents' lives (Fine, Mortimer, & Roberts, 1990). Adolescents spend a third or more of their waking hours with some form of mass media, either as a primary focus or as a background for other activities. Estimates of adolescent television viewing range from 2 to 4 hours per day, with considerable variation around the averages: Some adolescents watch little or no television; others view as much as 8 hours a day. Television viewing often peaks in late childhood and then begins to decline at some point in early adolescence in response to competing media and the demands of school and social activities (Huston & Alvarez, 1990). Figure 9.6 shows the extensive amount of time young adolescents spend watching television compared to doing housework and reading.

As television viewing declines, the use of music media—radio, records and tapes, and music video—increases 4 to 6 hours per day by the middle of adolescence (Fine, Mortimer, & Roberts, 1990; Larson, Kubey, & Colletti, 1989). As adolescents get older, movie attendance increases—more than 50 percent of 12- to 17-year-olds report at least monthly attendance. In recent years, viewing of videocassettes has become a common adolescent activity, with adolescent involvement at 5 to 10 hours per week (Wartella & others, 1990).

Adolescents also use the print media more than children do. Newspaper reading often begins at about 11 to 12 years of age and gradually increases until 60 to 80 percent of late adolescents report at least some newspaper reading. In similar fashion, magazine and book reading gradually increase during adolescence. Approximately one-third of high school juniors and seniors say that they read magazines daily, while 20 percent say that they read nonschool books daily, reports that are substantiated by the sales of teen-oriented books and magazines. However, comic book reading declines steeply between the ages of 10 and 18.

Large, individual differences characterize all forms of adolescent media use. In addition to the age differences just described, gender, ethnicity, socioeconomic status, and intelligence are all related to which media are used, to what extent, and for what purposes. For example, female adolescents watch more television and listen to more music than male adolescents do; African American adolescents view television and listen to more music than White American adolescents do, with African American females showing the most frequent viewing and listening (Greenberg, 1988). Brighter adolescents and adolescents from middle-class families are more likely to read the newspaper and news magazines, and also are more likely to watch television news, than are less intelligent adolescents and adolescents from low-income backgrounds (Chafee & Yang, 1990).

Television

The messages of television are powerful. What are television's functions? How extensively does television affect adolescents? What is MTV's role in adolescents' lives?

Television's Functions

Television has been called a lot of things, not all of them good. Depending on one's point of view, it is a "window to the world," the "one-eyed monster," or the "boob tube." Scores on national achievement tests in reading and mathematics, while showing a small improvement recently, have generally been lower than in the past decades—and television has been attacked as one of the reasons. Television may take adolescents away from the printed media and books. One study found that children who read books and the printed media watched television less than those who did not (Huston, Siegle, & Bremer, 1983). It is argued that television trains individuals to become passive learners. Rarely, if ever, does television require active responses from the observer. Heavy television use may produce not only a passive learner, but a passive lifestyle. In one investigation of 406 adolescent males, those who watched little television were more physically fit and physically active than those who watched a lot (Tucker, 1987).

Television also can deceive. It can teach adolescents that problems are easily resolved and that everything turns out all right in the end. For example, it takes only about 30 to 60 minutes for detectives to sort through a complex array of clues and discover the killer—and they always find the killer. Violence is pictured as a way of life in many shows, and police are shown to use violence and break moral codes in their fight against evildoers. And the lasting results of violence are rarely brought home to the viewer. An individual who is injured in a TV

The Cosby Show was an excellent example of how television can present positive models for ethnic minority children and adolescents.

show suffers for only a few seconds. In real life, the individual might take months or even years to recover, or perhaps does not recover at all.

A special concern is how ethnic minority groups are portrayed on television. Ethnic minorities have historically been underrepresented and misrepresented on television (Schiff & Truglio, 1995; Williams & Cox, 1995). Ethnic minority characters—whether African American, Asian, Latino, or Native American—have often been presented as less dignified and less positive than White characters (Condry, 1989). One investigation examined television character portrayals of ethnic minorities from 4:00 to 6:00 P.M. and 7:00 to 11:00 P.M., which are heavy adolescent viewing times (Williams & Condry, 1989). The percentage of White characters far exceeded the actual percentage of Whites in the United States; the percentages of African American, Asian American, and Latino characters fell short of the population statistics. Latino characters were especially underrepresented—only 0.6 percent of the characters were Latino, while Latinos comprise 8 percent of the U.S. population. Ethnic minorities held lower-status jobs and were more likely than Whites to be cast as criminals or victims.

But there are some positive aspects to television's influence on adolescents (Clifford, Gunter, & McAleer, 1995). For one thing, television presents adolescents with a world that is different from the one in which they live. This means that, through television, adolescents are exposed to a wider variety of views and knowledge than when they are informed only by their parents, teachers, and peers. Before television's advent, adolescents' identification models came in the form of parents, relatives, older siblings, neighborhood peers, famous individuals heard about in conversation or on the radio and read about in newspapers or magazines, and the film stars seen in movies. In the past, many of the identification figures came from family or peers whose attitudes, clothing styles, and occupational objectives were relatively homogeneous. The imagery and pervasiveness of television have exposed children and adolescents to hundreds of different neighborhoods, cultures, clothing fashions, career possibilities, and patterns of intimate relationships.

Television and Violence

How strongly does televised violence influence a person's behavior? In one longitudinal investigation, the amount of violence viewed on television at age 8 was significantly related to the seriousness of criminal acts performed as an adult (Huesmann, 1986). In another investigation, long-term exposure to television violence was significantly related to the likelihood of aggression in 1,565 12- to 17-year-old boys (Belson, 1978). Boys who watched the most aggression on television were the most likely to commit a violent crime, swear, be aggressive in sports, threaten violence toward another boy, write graffiti, or break windows.

These investigations are *correlational,* so we cannot conclude from them that television violence causes individuals to be more aggressive, only that watching television violence is *associated with* aggressive behavior. In one experiment, children were randomly assigned to one of two groups: One group watched shows taken directly from violent Saturday morning cartoon offerings on 11 different days; the second group watched cartoon shows with all of the violence removed (Steur, Applefield, & Smith, 1971). The children then were observed during play. The children who saw the TV cartoon violence kicked, choked, and pushed their playmates more than the children who watched nonviolent TV cartoon shows did. Because the children were assigned randomly to the two conditions (TV cartoons with violence versus TV cartoons with no violence), we can conclude that exposure to TV violence *caused* the increased aggression in this study.

In a review of more than three decades of research on television violence, several conclusions were reached (Comstock & Paik, 1991). First, televised violence can affect adolescents' behavior by influencing their cognitive scripts. For example, frequent viewing of police drama can shape viewer conceptions of how to respond when approached by a real police officer. Second, susceptibility to a given message varies considerably, depending on the viewer's interests, needs, and concerns. Third, various message characteristics affect individual interpretations of the televised violence, such as whether the violence is rewarded or punished, whether the violence is presented within the range of social norms, and whether the violence is familiar or useful to the viewer.

Some critics have argued that the effects of television violence are not large and do not warrant the conclusion that television violence causes aggressive behavior (McQuire, 1986). However, others have concluded that TV violence can induce aggressive or antisocial behavior in children and adolescents (Roberts, 1993; Strasburger, 1995). Of course, television is not the *only* cause of aggression. There is no *single* cause of any social behavior. Aggression, like all other social behaviors, is multiply determined.

Television and Sex

Adolescents like to watch television programs with sexual content. In one recent study, the four TV programs preferred most by adolescents were the ones with the highest percentage of interactions containing sexual messages (Ward, 1994). Watching television sex can influence some adolescents' behavior. In one study, college students who frequently watched soap operas (with their heavy dose of sexual themes) gave higher estimates of the number of real-life love affairs, out-of-wedlock children, and divorces than did their infrequently viewing counterparts (Buerkel-Rothfuss & Mayes, 1981). High school and college students who attributed great sexual proficiency and satisfaction to television characters reported less satisfaction with their own first experience with intercourse than did students not making such attributions (Baran, 1976). And in another study, adolescents who were frequent viewers of television had more difficulty separating the world of television from real life (Truglio, 1990).

These studies, along with a number of others, lead to the conclusion that television teaches children and adolescents about sex (Bence, 1989, 1991). Over the past decade, sexual content on television has increased and become more explicit. The consistent sexual messages adolescents learn from television's content are that sexual behaviors usually occur between unmarried couples, that contraception is rarely discussed, and that the negative consequences of sexuality (such as an unwanted pregnancy and sexually transmitted diseases) are rarely shown (Greenberg & others, 1986).

A special concern about adolescents and television sex is that while parents and teachers often feel comfortable discussing occupational and educational choices, independence, and consumer behavior with adolescents, they usually don't feel comfortable discussing sex with them (Roberts, 1993). The resulting absence of competing information (peers do talk about sex but often perpetuate ignorance) intensifies television's role in imparting information about sex. Nonetheless, as with television aggression, whether television sex influences the behavior of adolescents depends on a number of factors, including the adolescent's needs, interests, concerns, and maturity.

The Media and Music

Anyone who has been around adolescents very long knows that many of them spend huge amounts of time listening to music on the radio, playing CDs or tapes of their favorite music, or watching music videos on television. Approximately two-thirds of all records and tapes are purchased by the 10- to 24-year-old age group. And one-third of the nation's 8,200 radio stations aim their broadcast rock music at adolescent listeners.

Music tastes become more specific and differentiated from the beginning to the end of adolescence (Christenson & Roberts, 1991). In early adolescence, individuals often prefer middle-of-the road, top 40 rock music. By high school, however, adolescents frequently identify with much narrower music types, such as heavy metal, new wave, rap, and so on. Boys prefer "harder" forms of rock, girls softer, more romantic forms of "pop."

Music meets a number of personal and social needs for adolescents. The most important personal needs are mood control and silence filling. Somewhat surprisingly, relatively few adolescents say that popular music lyrics are very important to them. Few use music "to learn about the world," although African American adolescents are more likely than their White counterparts to say popular music fulfills this function for them.

Popular music's social functions range from providing a party atmosphere to expressing rebellion against authority. However, the latter function is not as common as popular stereotypes suggest.

The music adolescents enjoy on records, tapes, radio, and television is an important dimension of their culture. Rock music does not seem to be a passing fad, having been around now for more than 35 years. Recently, it has had its share of controversy. Starting in 1983, MTV (the first music video television channel) and music videos in general were targets of debate in the media. About a year later, rock music lyrics were attacked by the Parents Music Resource Center (PMRC). This group charged in a congressional hearing that rock music lyrics were dangerously shaping the minds of adolescents in the areas of sexual morality, violence, drugs, and satanism. The national Parent Teacher Association agreed. And Tipper Gore (1987), a PMRC founder, voiced her views about the dangers of rock music lyrics in a book.

"Beavis and Butt-head" is the most popular MTV program. What kind of models do these characters provide for adolescents? They torture animals, harass girls, and sniff paint thinner. They like to burn things. And they emit an insidious laugh, "Huh-huh, huh-huh, huh-huh." They were initially created by a beginner animator for a festival of "sick and twisted" cartoons, but quickly gained fame—their own nightly MTV program, T-shirts, dolls, a book, a comic book, a movie, CDs (including one with Cher), and a Christmas special. What age group are Beavis and Butt-head most likely to appeal to? Why? Are some adolescents more likely than others to be attracted to them?

Associations have been found between a preference for heavy metal music and reckless or antisocial behavior. For example, researchers have found that heavy metal music is more popular among antisocial youth than among the general population (Wass, Miller, & Redditt, 1991). In one study, male fans of heavy metal music were more likely to engage in reckless driving and casual sex and to use drugs than were males who were not fans of heavy metal music (Arnett, 1991). In this same study, female heavy metal fans were more likely to engage in unprotected sex, marijuana use, shoplifting, and vandalism than were females who were not fans of heavy metal. In yet another study, heavy metal music was more popular among adolescents who used drugs than among those who did not (King, 1988). However, these studies are correlational in nature, so we cannot conclude that the music causes problem behaviors in adolescents—it is only related to the problem behaviors. That is, young people with particular views are attracted to a particular kind of music, such as punk. At the same time, it may be these particular young people who pay attention to, comprehend, and are vulnerable to the lyrics' influence.

One of the most frightening claims made by detractors of heavy metal music is that the music causes adolescents to attempt or commit suicide. This was exemplified in highly publicized cases in which parents charged that songs by Judas Priest and Ozzy Osbourne were related to their adolescents' suicides. However, no research data link depression or suicide to heavy metal or rap music (Ballard & Coates, in press).

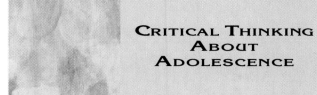

How Sexist Is MTV?

MTV is very popular with adolescents, yet, as we have indicated, its programming sometimes is sexist. Construct a rating scale that assesses sexism. Then with rating scale and pen in hand, watch one evening's fare of MTV (2 hours is enough—try 1 hour of music videos and 1 hour of "Beavis and Butt-head") and evaluate it according to your scale. One strategy for developing your rating scale would be to concretely describe some sexist behaviors (like degrading comments about females, provocative sexist lyrics, and so on) and use these behaviors as categories for your ratings. Try to come up with five to ten behavioral categories that reflect sexism, then, each time you observe one of the behaviors, place a checkmark in its column. After 2 hours of observing, total the number of checkmarks in each of the columns and overall. Evaluate your findings—does MTV contain sexist fare? How much?

By developing a rating scale to measure sexism and observing the incidence of sexism on MTV, you are learning to think critically by *making accurate observations, descriptions, and inferences about adolescent development.*

Motivation, experience, and knowledge are factors in the interpretation of lyrics. In one investigation, preadolescents and adolescents often missed sexual themes in lyrics (Prinsky & Rosenbaum, 1987). Adult organizations such as the PMRC interpret rock music lyrics in terms of sex, violence, drugs, and satanism more than adolescents themselves do. In this investigation, it was found that, in contrast to these adult groups, adolescents interpreted their favorite songs in terms of love, friendship, growing up, life's struggles, having fun, cars, religion, and other topics in teenage life.

Social Policy and the Media

Adolescents are exposed to an expanding array of media that carry messages that shape adolescents' judgments and behavior. The following social policy initiatives were recommended by the Carnegie Council on Adolescent Development (1995):

- *Encourage socially responsible programming.* There is good evidence of a link between media violence and adolescent aggression. The media also shape many other dimensions of adolescents' development—gender, ethnic, and occupational roles, as well as standards of beauty, family life, and sexuality. Writers, producers, and media executives need to recognize how powerful their messages are to adolescents and work with experts on adolescent development to provide more positive images to youth.
- *Support public efforts to make the media more adolescent friendly.* Essentially, the American media regulate themselves in regard to their influence on adolescents. All other Western nations have stronger regulations than the United States to foster appropriate educational programming.
- *Encourage media literacy programs as part of school curricula, youth and community organizations, and family life.* Many adolescents do not have the knowledge and skills to critically analyze media messages. Media literacy programs should focus not only on television, but also on newspapers, magazines, radio, videos, music, and electronic games.
- *Increase media presentations of health promotions.* Community-wide campaigns using public service announcements in the media have been successful in reducing smoking and increasing physical fitness in adolescents. Use of the media to promote adolescent health and well-being should be increased.
- *Expand opportunities for adolescents' views to appear in the media.* The media should increase the number of adolescent voices in their presentations by featuring editorial opinions, news stories, and videos authored by adolescents. Some schools have shown that this strategy of media inclusion of adolescents can be an effective dimension of education.

One organization that is trying to do something about the media's impact on adolescents is Mediascope, which is developing an ethics curriculum on violence to be used in courses that train the thousands of film students who hope to become moviemakers. Mediascope is also monitoring the entire television industry to assess such issues as the gratuitous use of violence.

At this point we have discussed a number of ideas about ethnicity and television and the media. A summary of these ideas is presented in concept table 9.2.

CONCEPT TABLE 9.2

Ethnicity, Television, and the Media

Concept	Processes/ Related Ideas	Characteristics/Description
Ethnicity	Domains and issues	Much of the research on ethnic minority adolescents has not teased apart the influences of social class and ethnicity. Historical, economic, and social experiences produce legitimate differences between many ethnic minority groups, and between ethnic minority groups and the White majority. Too often differences have been interpreted as deficits in ethnic minority groups. Diversity is another important characteristic of ethnic minority groups—failure to recognize this diversity results in stereotyping. Adolescence is often a special juncture in the development of ethnic minority individuals. Many ethnic minority adolescents continue to experience prejudice, discrimination, and bias. Value conflicts are often involved when individuals respond to ethnic issues. One prominent value conflict involves assimilation versus pluralism.
	Ethnic minority adolescents	African Americans make up the largest visible ethnic minority group. The church and extended family have helped many African Americans cope with stressful circumstances. Latino adolescents trace their roots to many countries, including Mexico, Puerto Rico, Cuba, and Central America. Asian Americans are also a diverse group of individuals—and the fastest growing segment of the U.S. population. Native American—also called American Indian—adolescents have faced painful discrimination and have high dropout rates from school.
	America: A nation of many cultures	America has been and continues to be a great receiver of ethnic groups. The cultures mix their ideologies and their identities. Adolescents in Canada are exposed to some cultural dimensions similar to those of their counterparts in the United States. Although Canada is a cultural mosaic, its main ethnic ties are British and French.
Television and Other Media	Functions and use of media	The functions of media for adolescents include entertainment, information, sensation, coping, gender-role modeling, and youth culture identification. Adolescents spend a third or more of their waking hours with some form of mass media. Estimates of television viewing range from 2 to 4 hours a day. Television viewing often declines in adolescence, when the use of music media increases. Adolescents also use the print media more than children do. Large individual differences characterize all forms of adolescent media use.
	Television	Television's functions include providing information and entertainment and portraying a world beyond the family, peers, and school. However, television may train adolescents to become passive learners and adopt a passive lifestyle. Special concerns include the way ethnic minorities are portrayed on television, as well as the way sex and aggression are shown.
	The media and music	Adolescents are heavy consumers of CDs, tapes, and rock music. Music tastes are more general at the beginning of adolescence; by high school, they are more specific and differentiated. Music meets a number of personal and social needs of the adolescents.
	Social policy and the media	Recommended social policy initiatives include encouraging socially responsible programming, supporting public efforts to make the media more adolescent friendly, encouraging media literacy programs, increasing media presentations of health promotions, and expanding opportunities for adolescent voices to appear in the media.

SUMMARY

Culture and ethnicity are pervasive dimensions of adolescent development. Adolescents live in a world that has been made smaller and more interactive by dramatic improvements in communication and travel. They also live in a world that is far more diverse in its ethnic makeup than it was in past decades.

We began this chapter by discussing what culture is and its relevance to the study of adolescence, which included information about cross-cultural comparisons and rites of passage. Next we studied the settings in which adolescents spend their time; then we

studied social class, including its nature, socioeconomic variations in families, schools, and neighborhoods, and poverty. We also spent considerable time reading about ethnicity, including ethnicity, social class, differences, and diversity; adolescence as a special juncture in the development of ethnic minority individuals; prejudice, discrimination, and bias; value conflicts, assimilation, and pluralism; African American adolescents; Latino adolescents; Asian American adolescents; Native American adolescents; and the United States and Canada. Our coverage of television and other

media focused on the functions and use of media, television, the media and the music, and social policy.

Don't forget that you can obtain an overall summary of the chapter by again reading the two concept tables on pages 290 and 304. This concludes our discussion of culture and ethnicity, and this is the final chapter in Section III of the book, "The Contexts of Adolescent Development." In Section IV, we will turn our attention to the social, emotional, and personality development of adolescents, first by studying the self and identity in chapter 10.

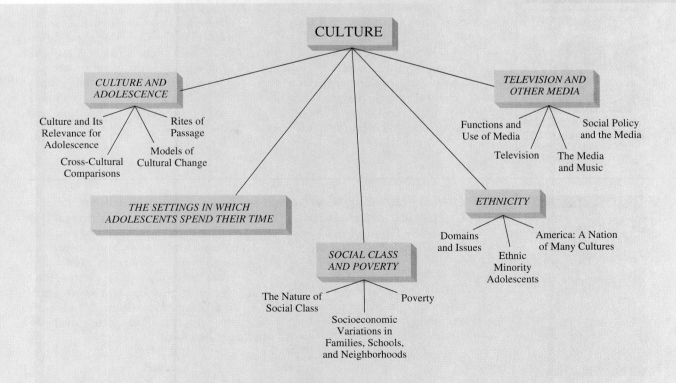

𝒫RACTICAL KNOWLEDGE ABOUT ADOLESCENCE

The Adolescent & Young Adult Fact Book

(1993) by Janet Simons, Belva Finlay, and Alice Yang. Washington, DC: Children's Defense Fund.

This book is filled with valuable charts that describe the roles that poverty and ethnicity play in adolescent development. Many of the charts display information separately for African American, Latino, and Asian adolescents. Special attention is given to prevention and intervention programs that work with adolescents from low-income and ethnic minority backgrounds. Topics discussed include families, health, substance abuse, crime, victimization, education, employment, sexual activity, and pregnancy.

Children of Color

(1989) by Jewelle Taylor Gibbs and Larke Nahme Huang and Associates.
San Francisco: Jossey-Bass.

This book provides a detailed examination of ethnic minority child and adolescent development, along with helpful recommendations for psychological interventions with children and adolescents from ethnic minority groups who are having problems. African American, Chinese, Latino, Japanese, and Native American children and adolescents are discussed. Intervention strategies that are sensitive to cultural expectations, linguistic differences, and family structures of youth from different ethnic groups are presented. Throughout the book, numerous case studies show how interventions can be successful with ethnic minority children and adolescents.

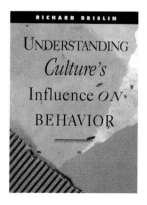

Understanding Culture's Influence on Behavior

(1993) by Richard Brislin.
Fort Worth, TX: Harcourt Brace.

This is an excellent book on culture's role in behavior and development. Especially good are the discussions of culture's influence on how we are socialized, formal educational experiences, interacting with people from different cultures, culture and gender, and culture and health. Author Brislin also makes some intriguing predictions about the future, including the effects of extensive intercultural contact and the importance of culture in studying behavior.

Advocates for Youth Media Project
3733 Motor Avenue, Suite 204
Los Angeles, CA 90034
310-559-5700

This project promotes responsible portrayals of sexuality in the entertainment media. The project members work with media professionals by sponsoring informational events and offering free consultation services to writers, producers, and other media personnel.

Canadian Ethnocultural Council/Conseil Ethnoculturel du Canada
251 Laurier Avenue West, Suite 110
Ottawa, Ontario K1P 5J6
613-230-3867

CEC's objective is to secure equality of opportunity, of rights, and of dignity for ethnocultural minorities and all other Canadians.

El Puente
Luis Garden-Acosta
211 South Fourth Street
Brooklyn, NY 11211
718-387-0404

This is the community program for high-risk Latino youth in Brooklyn, New York, that we described in Adolescent Health and Well-Being. To learn more about El Puente's programs, contact Mr. Garden-Acosta.

Fédération de la Jeunesse Canadienne Française
325 Dalhousie, Suite 440
Ottawa, Ontario K1N 7G2
613-562-4624

The Fédération represents Francophone youth living in areas where they are the language minority. It represents its membership with other organizations and at all levels of government. It promotes the development of Acadian and Francophone youth and the protection of language rights and freedoms. Projects include implementing community radio, bursaries and study programs.

Healthy Communities, Healthy Youth
by Dale Blyth and Eugene Roehlkepartain
Minneapolis: Search Institute

This report highlights the impact of community mental health on vulnerable youth and proposes strategies for parents, educators, and others who are working to strengthen their communities.

How to Save the Children (1992)
by Amy Hatkoff and Karen Klopp
New York: Simon & Schuster

This is an excellent guide to volunteerism in America. It provides a number of avenues you can pursue if you are concerned about our nation's children and youth.

Popular Music in Early Adolescence (1990)
by Peter Cristenson and Donald Roberts
Washington, DC: Carnegie Council on Adolescent Development
2400 N Street NW
Washington, DC 20037
202-429-7979

This working paper provides a detailed overview of the role of popular music in the development of young adolescents. Policy and research recommendations are made.

Quantum Opportunity Program
1415 North Broad Street
Philadelphia, PA 19122
215-236-4500

This is a year-round youth development program funded by the Ford Foundation. It has demonstrated that intervening in the lives of 13-year-old African Americans from poverty backgrounds can significantly improve their prospects.

So You Want to Make a Difference: Advocacy Is the Key
202-234-8494

This is a citizen's guide to taking action that is available through the Office of Management and Budget. This guide informs you of ways you can become an advocate for the needs of children and adolescents.

Strategies for Enhancing Adolescents' Health Through Music Media (1990)
by June Flora
Washington, DC: Carnegie Council on Adolescent Development
2440 N Street NW
Washington, DC 20037
202-429-7979

This commentary describes a number of strategies to enhance the health behavior of adolescents and their families.

UNICEF Canada
443 Mount Pleasant Road
Toronto, Ontario M4S 2L8
416-482-4444

UNICEF Canada's aim is to involve Canadians in meeting the needs of children and youth around the world. It raises funds to help ensure the survival, growth, and long-term development of the world's underserved children. UNICEF Canada's Jeunesse UNICEF Youth Club, Campus Ambassador clubs, and school and community-based education/advocacy/fund raising programs are opportunities for Canadian youth to explore and take action on global development issues.

Within Our Reach: Breaking the Cycle of Disadvantage (1988)
by Lisbeth Schoor
New York: Doubleday

This excellent book discusses the interventions that work with disadvantaged children and youth.

EXPLORING ADOLESCENT DEVELOPMENT

To further explore the nature of adolescent development, we will examine a research study on educational risk and resilience in African American youth, and we will also describe El Puente, a program designed to improve the health and well-being of adolescents located in a predominantly low-income Latino area of Brooklyn, New York.

RESEARCH ON ADOLESCENT DEVELOPMENT

Educational Risk and Resilience in African American Youth

Featured Study

Connell, J. P., Spencer, M. B., & Aber, J. L. (1994). Educational risk and resilience in African-American youth: Context, self, action, and outcomes in school. *Child Development, 65,* 493–506.

The educational problems of poor, African American, inner-city youth have been well documented. Most of this research focuses on differences between these youth and White middle-class youth. Much less attention has been given to variation and diversity within this group. Yet analysis of within-group variation is necessary if we are to understand why some youth fail, some survive, and others even thrive in high-risk contexts. In this study, the goal was to test a human motivation model that focuses on context, self, and action as predictors of risk and resilient outcomes in African American youth.

Method

Three independent samples (urban areas in Atlanta, New York City, and upstate New York) of 10- to 16-year-old African American boys and girls were studied. Census data involving such information as socioeconomic factors, crowding, and joblessness were used to determine the risk status of neighborhood contexts. The main index of family economic status was obtained from school records regarding eligibility for free or reduced school lunch programs. Educational outcomes were assessed using an identification system that involved such factors as presence in school, the number of core courses being taken, grade point average, national achievement test scores, and degree of risk for school departure. Questionnaires were given to the adolescents in their school classrooms to assess the following: parental involvement; the adolescent's perception of her or his competence (perceived ability to produce effort to develop and con-

trol academic outcomes); and an action component involving engagement versus disaffection, measured by items tapping emotional engagement in school (such as happy, bored) and behavioral engagement (paying attention, doing schoolwork, putting forth effort, and turning in work on time).

Results and Discussion

Parental involvement predicted the perceived competence of the African American youth, which in turn predicted the youths' reports of their engagement in school. Engagement then predicted school performance and adjustment. Youth who showed more disaffected patterns of behavior and emotion in school had less support from their parents than those who reported more engaged patterns of behavior. The results of this study confirm that competent family involvement should be an important target for interventions in the lives of at-risk African American youth.

El Puente

El Puente ("the bridge") was opened in New York City in 1983 because of community dissatisfaction with the health, education, and social services youth were receiving (Simons, Finlay, & Yang, 1991). El Puente emphasizes five areas of youth development: health, education, achievement, personal growth, and social growth.

El Puente is located in a former Roman Catholic church on the south side of Williamsburg in Brooklyn, a neighborhood made up primarily of low-income Latino families, many of which are far below the poverty line. Sixty-five percent of the residents receive some form of public assistance. The neighborhood has the highest school dropout rate for Latinos in New York City and the highest felony rate for adolescents in Brooklyn.

When the youths, aged 12 through 21, first enroll in El Puente, they meet with counselors and develop a 4-month plan that includes the programs they are interested in joining. At the end of 4 months, youth and staff develop a plan for continued participation. Twenty-six bilingual classes are offered in such subjects as the fine arts, theater, photography, and dance. In addition, a medical and fitness center, GED night school, and mental health and social services centers are also a part of El Puente.

These adolescents participate in the programs of El Puente, located in a predominantly low-income Latino neighborhood in Brooklyn, New York. The El Puente program stresses five areas of youth development: health, education, achievement, personal growth, and social growth.

El Puente is funded through state, city, and private organizations and serves about three hundred youth. The program has been replicated in Chelsea and Holyoke, Massachusetts, and two other sites in New York are being developed.

Social, Emotional, and Personality Development

H e who would learn to fly one day must learn to stand and walk and climb and dance: one cannot fly into flying.

—Friedrich Nietzsche,
Thus Spake Zarathustra,
1883

So far, we have studied the biological, cognitive, and social contexts of adolescent development. In this section, we will examine the adolescent's social, emotional, and personality development. Section IV consists of five chapters: Chapter 10, "The Self and Identity"; Chapter 11, "Gender"; Chapter 12, "Sexuality"; Chapter 13, "Moral Development, Values, and Religion"; and Chapter 14, "Achievement, Careers, and Work."

Pablo Picasso
Young Boy with Dog, detail

Chapter

10

The Self and Identity

"Who are you?" said the Caterpillar. Alice replied, rather shyly, "I—I hardly know, Sir, just at present—at least I know who I was when I got up this morning, but I must have changed several times since then."

—Lewis Carroll,
Alice in Wonderland, 1865

Chapter Outline

Chapter Boxes

IMAGES OF ADOLESCENCE

A 15-Year-Old Girl's Self-Description

How do adolescents describe themselves? How would you have described yourself when you were 15 years old? What features would you have emphasized? The following is a self-portrait of one 15-year-old girl:
What am I like as a person? Complicated! I'm sensitive, friendly, outgoing, popular, and tolerant, though I can also be shy, self-conscious, and even obnoxious. Obnoxious! I'd *like* to be friendly and tolerant all of the time. That's the kind of person I *want* to be, and I'm disappointed when I'm not. I'm responsible, even studious now and then, but on the other hand, I'm a goof-off, too, because if you're too studious, you won't be popular. I don't usually do that well at school. I'm a pretty cheerful person, especially with my friends, where I can even get rowdy. At home I'm more likely to be anxious around my parents. They expect me to get all A's. It's not fair! I worry about how I probably *should* get better grades. But I'd be mortified in the eyes of my friends. So I'm usually pretty stressed-out at home, or sarcastic, since my parents are always on my case. But I really don't understand how I can switch so fast. I mean, how can I be cheerful one minute, anxious the next, and then be sarcastic? Which one is the *real* me? Sometimes, I feel phony, especially around boys. Say I think some guy might be interested in asking me out. I try to act different, like Madonna. I'll be flirtatious and fun-loving. And then everybody, I mean *everybody* else is looking at me like they think I'm totally weird. Then I get self-conscious and embarrassed and become radically introverted, and I don't know who I really am! Am I just trying to impress them or what? But I don't really care what they think anyway. I don't *want* to care, that is. I just want to know what my close friends think. I can be my true self with my close friends. I can't be my real self with my parents. They don't understand me. What do *they* know about what it's like to be a teenager? They still treat me like I'm still a kid. At least at school people treat you more like you're an adult. That gets confusing, though. I mean, which am I, a kid or an adult? It's scary, too, because I don't have any idea what I want to be when I grow up. I mean, I have lots of *ideas*. My friend Sheryl and I talk about whether we'll be stewardesses, or teachers, or nurses, veterinarians, maybe mothers, or actresses. I know I *don't* want to be a waitress or a secretary. But how do you decide all of this? I really don't know. I mean, I think about it a lot, but I can't resolve it. There are days when I wish I could just become immune to myself. (Harter, 1990b, pp. 352–353)

PREVIEW

*T*he 15-year-old girl's self-description that you just read exemplifies the increased introspective nature of self-portrayal in adolescence and the adolescent's complex search for identity. This chapter is about the self and about the search for identity in adolescence.

THE SELF

Adolescents carry with them a sense of who they are and what makes them different from everyone else. They cling to this identity and develop a sense that this identity is becoming more stable. Consider one adolescent male's self-description: "I am male, bright, an athlete, a political liberal, an extravert, and a compassionate individual." He takes comfort in his uniqueness: "No one else is quite like me. I am 5 feet 11 inches tall and weigh 160 pounds. I live in a suburb and plan to attend the state university. I want to be a sports journalist. I am an expert at building canoes. When I am not going to school and studying, I write short stories about sports figures, which I hope to publish someday." Real or imagined, an adolescent's developing sense of self and uniqueness is a motivating force in life. Our exploration of the self begins with information about adolescents' self-understanding and then turns to their self-esteem and self-concept.

Self-Understanding

Adolescents' self-understanding becomes more introspective, but it is not completely interiorized. Rather, self-understanding is a social-cognitive construction. Adolescents' developing cognitive capacities interact with their sociocultural experiences to influence self-understanding. The questions about self-understanding that we will examine include these: What is self-understanding? What are some important dimensions of adolescents' self-understanding? How integrated is adolescents' self-understanding?

What is Self-Understanding?

Self-understanding *is the adolescent's cognitive representation of the self, the substance and content of the adolescent's self-conceptions.* For example, a 12-year-old boy understands that he is a student, a boy, a football player, a family member, a video game lover, and a rock music fan. A 14-year-old girl understands that she is a cheerleader, a student council member, and a movie fan. An adolescent's self-understanding is based, in part, on the various roles and membership categories that define who adolescents are (Harter, 1990a). Though not the whole of personal identity, self-understanding provides identity's rational underpinnings.

Three facets of self-understanding are (a) personal memories, (b) representations, and (c) theories about the self (Garcia, Hart, & Johnson-Ray, in press). *Personal memories* are autobiographical episodes that are especially important in individuals' thoughts about themselves. These might include memories of a fight with one's parents, a day spent with a friend, a teacher saying how good your work is, and so on.

Representations of the self include the generalized ascriptions individuals make about their selves. For example, individuals have representations of their actual selves (such as "I am big, smart, and socially awkward"), ideal selves ("I want to be a teacher and be respected by the community"), and past selves ("I used to be very shy").

Theories about the self enable individuals to identify which characteristics of the self are relevant, arrange these characteristics in hierarchical order of importance, and make claims about how these characteristics are related to each other. Theories about the self provide an individual with a sense of identity and a source of orientation to the world.

Dimensions of Adolescents' Self-Understanding

The development of self-understanding in adolescence is complex and involves a number of aspects of the self (Harter, 1997). Let's examine how the adolescent's self-understanding differs from the child's.

Abstract and Idealistic   Remember from our discussion of Piaget's theory of cognitive development in chapters 2 and 4 that many adolescents begin to think in more *abstract* and *idealistic* ways. When asked to describe themselves, adolescents are more likely than children to use abstract and idealistic labels. Consider 14-year-old Laurie's abstract description of herself: "I am a human being. I am indecisive. I don't know who I am." Also consider her idealistic description of herself: "I am a naturally sensitive person who really cares about people's feelings. I think I'm pretty good-looking." Not all adolescents describe themselves in idealistic ways, but most adolescents distinguish between the real self and the ideal self.

Differentiated   Adolescents' self-understanding becomes increasingly *differentiated*. Adolescents are more likely than children to describe themselves with contextual or situational variations. For example, 15-year-old Amy describes herself with one set of characteristics in relation to her family and another set of characteristics in relation to her peers and friends. Yet another set of characteristics appears in her self-description regarding her romantic relationship. In sum, adolescents are more likely than children to understand that one possesses different selves, depending on one's role or particular context.

Contradictions Within the Self   After adolescence ushers in the need to differentiate the self into multiple roles in different relational contexts, this naturally leads to potential contradictions between these differentiated selves. In one study, Susan Harter (1986) asked

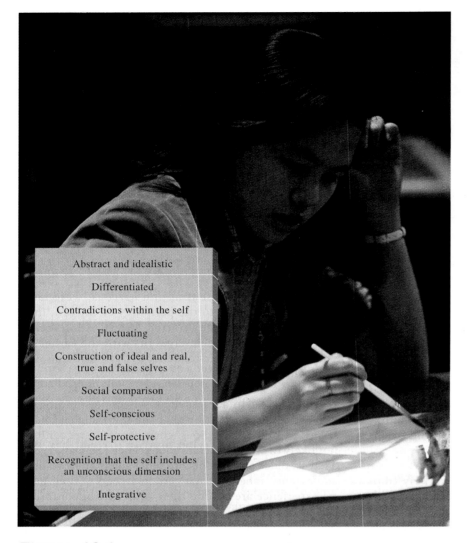

| Abstract and idealistic |
| Differentiated |
| Contradictions within the self |
| Fluctuating |
| Construction of ideal and real, true and false selves |
| Social comparison |
| Self-conscious |
| Self-protective |
| Recognition that the self includes an unconscious dimension |
| Integrative |

Figure~10.1

Characteristics of Adolescents' Self-Understanding.

result in heightened self-awareness and consciousness. This heightened self-focus leads to consideration of the self and the many changes that are occurring in it, which can produce doubt about who the self is and which facets of the self are "real" (Hart, 1996).

James Marcia (1996) believes that changes in the self in adolescence can best be understood by dividing them into early ("deconstruction"), middle ("reconstruction"), and late ("consolidation") phases. That is, the adolescent initially is confronted by contradictory self-descriptions, followed by attempts to resolve contradictions, and subsequently develops a more integrated self-theory (identity).

At this point, we have discussed a number of characteristics of adolescents' self-understanding. A summary of these characteristics is presented in figure 10.1. Remember from the introduction of the self, that self-conception involves not only self-understanding but also self-esteem and self-concept. That is, not only do adolescents try to define and describe attributes of the self (self-understanding), but they also evaluate these attributes (self-esteem and self-concept).

Self-Esteem and Self-Concept

What are self-esteem and self-concept? How are they measured? Are some domains more salient to the adolescent's self-esteem than others are? How do relationships with parents and peers influence adolescents' self-esteem? What are the consequences of adolescents' low self-esteem? How can adolescents' self-esteem be increased?

detect inconsistencies across their various roles (with parents, friends, and romantic partners, for example) but are much more troubled by these contradictions than younger (11- to 12-year-old) and older (17- to 18-year-old) adolescents are (Damon & Hart, 1988).

> *The living self has one purpose only: to come into its own fullness of being, as a tree comes into full blossom, or a bird into spring beauty, or a tiger into lustre.*
>
> **—D. H. Lawrence**

Conclusions As we have seen, the development of self-understanding in adolescence is complex and involves a number of aspects of the self. Rapid changes that occur in the transition from childhood to adolescence

What Are Self-Esteem and Self-Concept?

Self-esteem *is the global evaluative dimension of the self. Self-esteem is also referred to as self-worth or self-image.* For example, an adolescent might perceive that she is not merely a person, but a *good* person. Of course, not all adolescents have an overall positive image of themselves. **Self-concept** *refers to domain-specific evaluations of the self.* Adolescents can make self-evaluations in many domains of their lives—academic, athletic, appearance, and so on. In sum, self-esteem refers to global self-evaluations, self-concept to more domain-specific evaluations.

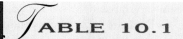

TABLE 10.1

Behavioral Indicators of Self-Esteem

Positive Indicators	Negative Indicators
1. Gives others directives or commands	1. Puts down others by teasing, name-calling, or gossiping
2. Uses voice quality appropriate for situation	2. Uses gestures that are dramatic or out of context
3. Expresses opinions	3. Engages in inappropriate touching or avoids physical contact
4. Sits with others during social activities	4. Gives excuses for failures
5. Works cooperatively in a group	5. Glances around to monitor others
6. Faces others when speaking or being spoken to	6. Brags excessively about achievements, skills, appearance
7. Maintains eye contact during conversation	7. Verbally puts self down; self-deprecation
8. Initiates friendly contact with others	8. Speaks too loudly, abruptly, or in a dogmatic tone
9. Maintains comfortable space between self and others	9. Does not express views or opinions, especially when asked
10. Little hesitation in speech, speaks fluently	10. Assumes a submissive stance

From R. C. Savin-Williams and D. H. Demo, "Conceiving or Misconceiving the Self: Issues in Adolescent Self-Esteem" in *Journal of Early Adolescence*, 3:121–140. Copyright © H.E.L.P. Books, Inc. Reprinted by permission of Sage Publications.

> *It is difficult to make people miserable when they feel worthy of themselves.*
>
> —**Abraham Lincoln**

Investigators have not always made clear distinctions between self-esteem and self-concept, sometimes using the terms interchangeably or not precisely defining them. As you read the remaining discussion of self-esteem and self-concept, the distinction between self-esteem as global self-evaluation and self-concept as domain-specific self-evaluation should help you to keep the terms straight.

Measuring Self-Esteem and Self-Concept

Measuring self-esteem and self-concept hasn't always been easy, especially in assessments of adolescents (Wylie, 1969). For many years measures were designed primarily for children or for adults, with little attention given to adolescents. Susan Harter (1989b) developed a separate measure for adolescents: the Self-Perception Profile for Adolescents. It taps eight domains—scholastic competence, athletic competence, social acceptance, physical appearance, behavioral conduct, close friendship, romantic appeal, and job competence—plus global self-worth. The adolescent measure has three skill domains not present in her child measure—job competence, romantic appeal, and close friendship.

Some assessment experts argue that a combination of several methods should be used in measuring self-esteem. In addition to self-reporting, rating of an adolescent's self-esteem by others and observations of the adolescent's behavior in various settings could provide a more complete and more accurate self-esteem picture. Peers, teachers, parents, and even others who do not know the adolescent can be asked to rate the adolescent's self-esteem. Adolescents' facial expressions and the extent to which they congratulate or condemn themselves are also good indicators of how they view themselves. For example, adolescents who rarely smile or rarely act happy are revealing something about their self-esteem. One investigation that used behavioral observations in the assessment of self-esteem shows some of the positive as well as negative behaviors that can provide clues to the adolescent's self-esteem (see table 10.1) (Savin-Williams & Demo, 1983). By using a variety of methods (such as self-report and behavioral observations) and obtaining information from various sources (such as the adolescent, parents, friends, and teachers), investigators probably can construct a more accurate picture of the adolescent's self-esteem.

Are Some Domains More Salient Than Others to Adolescents' Self-Esteem?

Physical appearance is an especially powerful contributor to self-esteem in adolescence. For example, in Harter's (1989a) research, physical appearance consistently correlates the most strongly with global self-esteem, followed by peer social acceptance. Harter also has found that the strong association between perceived appearance and general self-worth is not confined to adolescence but holds across the life span, from early childhood through middle age. And in one recent study, adolescents' self-concepts regarding their physical attractiveness were the strongest predictor of their overall self-esteem (Lord & Eccles, 1994).

Parental and Peer Influences on Self-Esteem

Two important sources of social support that contribute to adolescents' self-esteem are relationships with parents and peers. In the most extensive investigation of parent-child relationships and self-esteem, a measure of self-esteem was given to boys, and the boys and their mothers were interviewed about their family relationships (Coopersmith, 1967). Based on these assessments, the following parenting attributes were associated with boys' high self-esteem:

- Expression of affection
- Concern about the boys' problems
- Harmony in the home
- Participation in joint family activities
- Availability to give competent, organized help to the boys when they needed it
- Setting clear and fair rules
- Abiding by these rules
- Allowing the boys freedom within well-prescribed limits

Remember that because these findings are correlational, researchers cannot say that these parenting attributes *cause* children's high self-esteem. Such factors as expression of affection and allowing children freedom within well-prescribed limits probably are important determinants of children's self-esteem, but researchers still must say that *they are related to* rather than *they cause* children's self-esteem, based on the available research data that are correlational.

Peer judgments gain increasing importance among older children and adolescents. In one investigation, peer support contributed more strongly to the self-esteem of young adolescents than to that of children, although parenting support was an important factor in self-esteem for both children and young adolescents (Harter, 1987). In this study, peer support was a more important factor than parenting support for late adolescents. Two types of peer support were studied: classmate support and close-friend support. Classmate support contributed more strongly to adolescents' self-esteem at all ages than close-friend support. Given that, in most instances, close friends provide considerable support, it may be that their regard is not perceived as enhancing; rather, the adolescent may need to turn to somewhat more objective sources of support to validate his or her self-esteem.

Consequences of Low Self-Esteem

For most adolescents, low self-esteem results in only temporary emotional discomfort (Damon, 1991). But in some adolescents, low self-esteem can translate into other problems (DuBois, Felner, & Brand, 1997; Zimmerman, Copeland, & Shope, 1997). Low self-esteem has been implicated in depression, suicide, anorexia nervosa, delinquency, and other adjustment problems (Fenzel, 1994; Harter & Marold, 1992). The seriousness of the problem depends not only on the nature of the adolescent's low self-esteem but on other conditions as well. When low self-esteem is compounded by difficult school transitions or family life, or by other stressful events, the adolescent's problems can intensify.

Increasing Adolescents' Self-Esteem

Four ways adolescents' self-esteem can be improved are through (1) identifying the causes of low esteem and the domains of competence important to the self, (2) emotional support and social approval, (3) achievement, and (4) coping (see figure 10.2).

Identifying adolescents' sources of self-esteem—that is, competence in domains important to the self—is critical to improving self-esteem. Self-esteem theorist and researcher Susan Harter (1990b) points out that the self-esteem enhancement programs of the 1960s, in which self-esteem itself was the target and individuals were encouraged to simply feel good about themselves, were ineffective. Rather, Harter believes that intervention must occur at the level of the *causes* of self-esteem if the individual's self-esteem is to improve significantly.

Adolescents have the highest self-esteem when they perform competently in domains important to the self. Therefore, adolescents should be encouraged to identify and value their areas of competence.

Emotional support and social approval in the form of confirmation from others also powerfully influence adolescents' self-esteem (Harter, 1990b). Some youth with low self-esteem come from conflicted families or conditions in which they experienced abuse or neglect—situations in which support is unavailable. In some cases, alternative sources of support can be implemented, either informally through the encouragement of a teacher, a coach, or another significant adult, or more formally, through programs such as Big Brothers and Big Sisters. While peer approval becomes increasingly important during adolescence, both adult and peer support are important influences on the adolescent's self-esteem. In one recent study, both parental and peer support were related to the adolescent's general self-worth (Robinson, 1995).

Achievement also can improve adolescents' self-esteem (Bednar, Wells, & Peterson, 1995). For example, the straightforward teaching of real skills to adolescents often results in increased achievement and, thus, in enhanced self-esteem. Adolescents develop higher self-esteem because they know what tasks are important for achieving goals, and they have experienced

Figure~10.2

Four Main Ways to Improve Self-Esteem.

Identifying the causes of low self-esteem and which domains of competence are important to the self
Emotional support and social approval
Achievement
Coping

performing them or similar behaviors. The emphasis on the importance of achievement in improving self-esteem has much in common with Bandura's cognitive social learning concept of *self-efficacy*, which refers to individuals' beliefs that they can master a situation and produce positive outcomes.

Self-esteem also is often increased when adolescents face a problem and try to cope with it rather than avoid it (Lazarus, 1991). If coping rather than avoidance prevails, adolescents often face problems realistically, honestly, and nondefensively. This produces favorable self-evaluative thoughts, which lead to the self-generated approval that raises self-esteem. The converse is true of low self-esteem. Unfavorable self-evaluations trigger denial, deception, and avoidance in an attempt to disavow that which has already been glimpsed as true. This process leads to self-generated disapproval as a form of feedback to the self about personal adequacy.

At this point, we have discussed a number of ideas about the self in adolescence, including information about self-understanding and self-esteem. A summary of these ideas is presented in concept table 10.1. Next, we turn our attention to an important concept related to the self: identity.

IDENTITY

By far the most comprehensive and provocative theory of identity development has been told by Erik Erikson. Some experts on adolescence consider Erikson's ideas to be the single most influential theory of adolescent development. Erikson's theory was introduced in chapter 2. Here that introduction is expanded, beginning with a reanalysis of his ideas on identity. Then we examine some contemporary thoughts on identity, the four statuses of identity, developmental changes, family influences on identity, cultural and ethnic aspects of identity, gender and identity development, and identity and intimacy.

Erikson's Ideas on Identity

Who am I? What am I all about? What am I going to do with my life? What is different about me? How can I make

CONCEPT TABLE 10.1

The Self

Concept	Processes/ Related Ideas	Characteristics/Description
Self-Understanding	What is self-understanding?	Self-understanding is the adolescent's cognitive representation of the self, the substance and content of the adolescent's self-conceptions. Self-understanding provides the rational underpinnings of personal identity.
	Dimensions of self-understanding	Dimensions of self-understanding include: abstract and idealistic; differentiated; contradictions within the self; fluctuating; real and ideal, true and false selves; social comparison; self-conscious; self-protective; unconscious; and self-integrative.
Self-Esteem and Self-Concept	What are self-esteem and self-concept?	Self-esteem is the global evaluative dimension of the self. Self-esteem also is referred to as self-worth or self-image. Self-concept refers to domain-specific evaluations of the self.
	Measuring self-esteem and self-concept	For too long, little attention was given to developing measures specifically for adolescents. One adolescent-specific measure is Harter's Self-Perception Profile for Adolescents. Some assessment experts believe that several methods should be used to measure self-esteem, including observations of the adolescent's behavior.
	Are some domains more salient than others to the adolescent's self-esteem?	Perceived physical appearance is an especially strong contributor to global self-esteem. Peer acceptance follows physical appearance in contributing to global self-esteem in adolescence.
	Parental and peer influences	In Coopersmith's study, children's self-esteem was associated with such parenting attributes as parental affection and allowing children freedom within well-prescribed limits. These associations are correlational. Peer judgments gain increasing importance among older children and adolescents. In one study of the contribution of peer support to adolescent self-esteem, classmate support was more powerful than close-friend support.
	Consequences of low self-esteem	For most adolescents, low self-esteem results in only temporary emotional discomfort. But for others, low self-esteem can translate into other problems such as depression, suicide, anorexia nervosa, and delinquency.
	Increasing adolescents' self-esteem	Four ways to increase adolescents' self-esteem are through (1) identifying the causes of low self-esteem and which domains of competence are important to the self; (2) emotional support and social approval; (3) achievement; and (4) coping.

it on my own? Not usually considered during childhood, these questions surface as common, virtually universal, concerns during adolescence. Adolescents clamor for solutions to these questions that revolve around the concept of identity, and it was Erik Erikson (1950, 1968) who first understood how central such questions are to understanding adolescent development. That today identity is believed to be a key concept in adolescent development is a result of Erikson's masterful thinking and analysis.

Revisiting Erikson's Views on Identity and the Human Life Span

Identity versus identity confusion is Erikson's fifth developmental stage, which individuals experience during the adolescent years. At this time, adolescents examine who they are, what they are all about, and where they are going in life. Adolescents are confronted with many new roles, such as vocational and romantic roles. **Psychosocial moratorium** is Erikson's term for the gap between childhood security and adult autonomy that adolescents experience as part of their identity exploration. As adolescents explore and search their culture's identity files, they often experiment with different roles. Youths who successfully cope with these conflicting identities emerge with a new sense of self that is both refreshing and acceptable. Adolescents who do not successfully resolve this identity crisis suffer what Erikson calls identity confusion. The confusion takes one of two courses: Individuals withdraw, isolating themselves from peers and family, or they immerse themselves in the world of peers and lose their identity in the crowd.

Mahatma Gandhi was the spiritual leader of India in the middle of the twentieth century. What factors does Erikson believe contributed to Gandhi's identity development? In his Pulitzer Prize–winning novel on Mahatma Gandhi's life, Erikson describes the personality formation of Gandhi during his youth:

> Straight and yet not stiff; shy and yet not withdrawn; intelligent and yet not bookish; willful and yet not stubborn; sensual and yet not soft . . . We must try to reflect on the relation of such a youth to his father because the Mahatma places service to the father and the crushing guilt of failing in such service in the center of his adolescent turbulence. Some historians and political scientists seem to find it easy to interpret this account in psychoanalytic terms; I do not. For the question is not how a particular version of the Oedipal complex "causes" a man to be both great and neurotic in a particular way, but rather how such a young person . . . manages the complexes which constrict other men. (Erikson, 1969, p. 113)

Erikson's ideas about adolescent identity development reveal rich insights into adolescents' thoughts and feelings. Reading one or more of his original writings is worthwhile. A good starting point is *Identity: Youth and Crisis* (1968). Other works that portray identity development are *Young Man Luther* (1962) and *Gandhi's Truth* (1969)—the latter won a Pulitzer Prize.

Personality and Role Experimentation

Two core ingredients in Erikson's theory of identity development are personality and role experimentation. As indicated earlier, Erikson believes that adolescents face an overwhelming number of choices and at some point during youth enter a period of psychological moratorium. During this moratorium, they try out different roles and personalities before they reach a stable sense of self. They may be argumentative one moment, cooperative the next moment. They may dress neatly one day, sloppily the next day. They may like a particular friend one week, despise the friend the next week. This personality experimentation is a deliberate effort on the part of adolescents to find out where they fit in the world.

As they gradually come to realize that they will be responsible for themselves and their own lives, adolescents search for what those lives are going to be. Many parents and other adults, accustomed to having children go along with what they say, may be bewildered or incensed by the wisecracks, the rebelliousness, and the rapid mood changes that accompany adolescence. It is important for these adults to give adolescents the time and the opportunities to explore different roles and personalities. In turn, most adolescents eventually discard undesirable roles.

There are literally hundreds of roles for adolescents to try out, and probably just as many ways to pursue each role. Erikson believes that, by late adolescence, vocational roles are central to identity development, especially in a highly technological society like the United States. Youth who have been well trained to enter a workforce that offers the potential of reasonably high self-esteem will experience the least stress during the development of identity. Some youth have rejected jobs offering good pay and traditionally high social status, choosing instead to work in situations that allow them to be more genuinely helpful to their fellow humans, such as in the Peace Corps, in mental health clinics, or in schools for children from low-income backgrounds. Some youth prefer unemployment to the prospect of working at a job they feel they would be unable to perform well or at which they would feel useless. To Erikson, this attitude reflects the desire to achieve a meaningful identity through being true to oneself, rather than burying one's identity in that of the larger society.

> *Explore thyself. Herein are demanded the eye and the nerve.*
>
> **—Henry David Thoreau**

The Complexity of Erikson's Theory

The development of an integrated sense of identity is a long, complex, and difficult task. American adolescents are expected to master many different roles. It is the rare, perhaps nonexistent, adolescent who does not have serious doubts about handling at least some of these roles competently. In Erikson's view, identity is complex, involving at least seven dimensions (Bourne, 1978):

1. *Genetic.* Erikson describes identity development as a developmental product or outcome that incorporates the individual's experiences over the first five stages of development. Identity development reflects the way the adolescent has resolved prior stages, such as trust versus mistrust, autonomy versus doubt, initiative versus guilt, and industry versus inferiority.

2. *Adaptive.* The adolescent's identity development can be viewed as an adaptive accomplishment or

Exploring Your Identity Development

Now that you have read about various aspects of identity development, this is a good time to explore your own identity development. How can you gain insight into your personal self or identity? One way is to list adjectives that describe you. You also could ask people who know you well, such as several family members and/or friends, to give you some feedback about how they honestly would describe you. How well does their perception match your self-perception? Consider also your interests, attitudes, and hobbies. How did you develop your personal characteristics and interests? Try to trace their origins. Tracing the development of aspects of yourself can help you gain insight into your own identity formation. By exploring your identity development, you are learning to think critically by *applying developmental concepts to enhance personal adaptation.*

achievement. Identity is the adaptation of adolescents' special skills, capacities, and strengths to the society in which they live.

3. *Structural.* Identity confusion is a breakdown in time perspective, initiative, and ability to coordinate present behavior toward future goals. This kind of breakdown implies a structural deficit.

4. *Dynamic.* Erikson believes that identity formation begins where the usefulness of identification ends. It arises from childhood identifications with adults but absorbs them in new configurations, which, in turn, are dependent on society's roles for youth.

5. *Subjective or experiential.* Erikson believes that the individual senses either an inner feeling of cohesiveness or a lack of assuredness.

6. *Psychosocial reciprocity.* Erikson emphasizes the mutual relationship of adolescents with their social world and community. Identity development is not just an intrapsychic self-representation but involves relationships with people, community, and society.

7. Existential status. Erikson thinks that adolescents seek the meaning to their life as well as the meaning of life in general, much like an existential philosopher.

Some Contemporary Thoughts on Identity

Contemproary views of identity development suggest several important considerations. First, identity development is a lengthy process, in many instances a more gradual, less cataclysmic transition than Erikson's term *crisis* implies (Baumeister, 1991). Second, as just indicated, identity development is extraordinarily complex (Marcia, 1989). Identity formation neither begins nor ends with adolescence. It begins with the appearance of attachment, the development of a sense of self, and the emergence of independence in infancy, and reaches its final phase with a life review and integration in old age. What is important about identity development in adolescence, especially late adolescence, is that, for the first time, physical development, cognitive development, and social development advance to the point at which the individual can sort through and synthesize childhood identities and identifications to construct a viable path toward adult maturity. Resolution of the identity issue at adolescence does not mean that identity will be stable through the remainder of life. An individual who develops a healthy identity is flexible and adaptive, open to changes in society, in relationships, and in careers (Adams, Gulotta, & Montemayor, 1992). This openness assures numerous reorganizations of identity's contents throughout the identity-achieved individual's life.

Identity formation does not happen neatly, and it usually does not happen cataclysmically. At the bare minimum, it involves commitment to a vocational direction, an ideological stance, and a sexual orientation. Synthesizing the identity components can be a long and drawn-out process, with many negations and affirmations of various roles and faces. Identity development gets done in bits and pieces. Decisions are not made once and for all, but have to be made again and again. And the decisions might seem trivial at the time: whom to date, whether or not to break up, whether or not to have intercourse, whether or not to take drugs, whether or not to go to college or finish high school and get a job, which major, whether to study or to play, whether or not to be politically active, and so on. Over the years of adolescence, the decisions begin to form a core of what the individual is all about as a human being—what is called his or her identity.

The Four Statuses of Identity

Eriksonian researcher James Marcia (1966, 1980, 1989, 1991, 1994) believes that Erikson's theory of identity development contains four statuses of identity, or ways of resolving the identity crisis: identity diffusion, identity foreclosure, identity moratorium, and identity achievement. The extent of an adolescent's crisis and commitment are used to classify the individual according to one of the four identity statuses. **Crisis** *is defined as a period of identity development during which the adolescent is choosing among meaningful alternatives.* Most researchers use the term *exploration* rather than *crisis*, although, in the spirit of Marcia's formulation, the term *crisis* is used

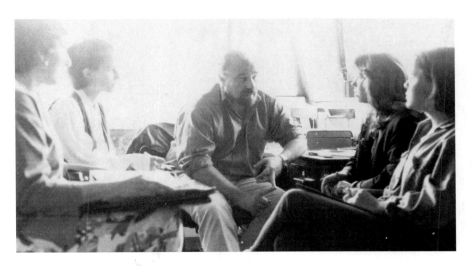

James Marcia, shown talking with college students, developed the concept of identity status. Over three decades, Marcia has greatly advanced our understanding of identity development.

here. **Commitment** *is a part of identity development in which adolescents show a personal investment in what they are going to do.*

Identity diffusion *is Marcia's term for the state adolescents are in when they have not yet experienced a crisis (that is, they have not yet explored meaningful alternatives) or made any commitments.* Not only are they undecided about occupational and ideological choices, they are also likely to show little interest in such matters. **Identity foreclosure** *is Marcia's term for the state adolescents are in when they have made a commitment but have not experienced a crisis.* This occurs most often when parents hand down commitments to their adolescents, usually in an authoritarian way. In these circumstances, adolescents have not had adequate opportunities to explore different approaches, ideologies, and vocations on their own. **Identity moratorium** *is*

Marcia's term for the state of adolescents who are in the midst of a crisis, but whose commitments either are absent or are only vaguely defined. **Identity achievement** *is Marcia's term for an adolescent's having undergone a crisis and having made a commitment.* Marcia's four statuses of identity development are summarized in figure 10.3.

The identity status approach has been sharply criticized by some researchers and theoreticians (Blasi, 1988; Cote & Levine, 1988; Lapsley & Power, 1988). They believe that the identity status approach distorts and trivializes Erikson's notions of crisis and commitment. For example, concerning crisis, Erikson emphasized youth's questioning the perceptions and expectations of one's culture and developing an autonomous position with regard to one's society. In the identity status approach, these complex questions are dealt with by simply evaluating whether a youth has thought about certain issues and has considered alternatives. Erikson's idea of commitment loses the meaning of investing oneself in certain lifelong projects and is interpreted simply as having made a firm decision or not. Others still believe that the identity status approach is a valuable contribution to understanding identity (Archer, 1989; Marica, 1991; Waterman, 1989).

Developmental Changes

In Marcia's terms, young adolescents are primarily in the identity statuses of diffusion, foreclosure, or moratorium. At least three aspects of the young adolescent's development are important in identity formation (Marcia, 1987, 1996): Young adolescents must be confident that they have parental support, must have an established sense of industry, and must be able to adopt a self-reflective stance toward the future.

Some researchers believe the most important identity changes take place in youth rather than earlier in adolescence. For example, Alan Waterman (1985, 1989, 1992) has found that from the years preceding high school through the last few years of college, there is an increase in the number of individuals who are identity achieved, along with a decrease in those who are identity diffused. College upperclassmen are more likely to be identity achieved than college freshmen or high school students are. Many young adolescents are identity diffused. These developmental changes are especially true for vocational choice. For religious beliefs and political ideology, fewer college students have reached the identity-achieved status, with a substantial number characterized

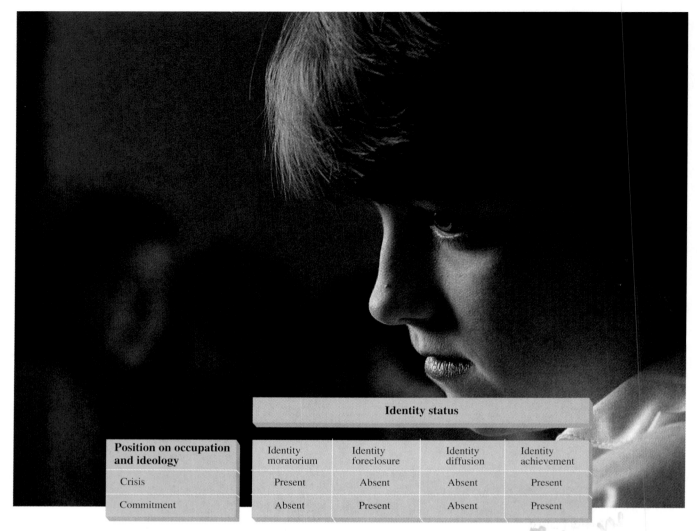

Figure~10.3

Marcia's Four Statuses of Identity.

Position on occupation and ideology	Identity status			
	Identity moratorium	Identity foreclosure	Identity diffusion	Identity achievement
Crisis	Present	Absent	Absent	Present
Commitment	Absent	Present	Absent	Present

by foreclosure and diffusion. Thus, the timing of identity may depend on the particular life area involved, and many college students are still wrestling with ideological commitments (Arehart & Smith, 1990; Harter, 1990b).

> *The thoughts of youth are long, long thoughts.*
> —Henry Wadsworth Longfellow, 1858

Many identity status researchers believe that a common pattern of individuals who develop positive identities is to follow what are called "MAMA" cycles of moratorium–achievement–moratorium–achievement (Archer, 1989). These cycles may be repeated throughout life (Francis, Fraser, & Marcia, 1989). Personal, family, and societal changes are inevitable, and as they occur, the flexibility and skill required to explore new

alternatives and develop new commitments are likely to enhance an individual's coping skills. Regarding commitment, Marcia (1996) believes that the first identity is just that—it is not, and should not be expected to be, the final product.

Family Influences on Identity

Parents are important figures in the adolescent's development of identity. In studies that relate identity development to parenting styles, democratic parents, who encourage adolescents to participate in family decision making, foster identity achievement. Autocratic parents, who control the adolescent's behavior without giving the adolescent an opportunity to express opinions, encourage identity foreclosure. Permissive parents, who provide little guidance to adolescents and allow them to make their own decisions, promote identity diffusion (Enright & others, 1980).

"Do you have any idea who I am?"

Drawing by Koren; © 1988 The New Yorker Magazine, Inc.

In addition to studies on parenting styles, researchers have also examined the role of individuality and connectedness in the development of identity. Developmentalist Catherine Cooper and her colleagues (Carlson, Cooper, & Hsu, 1990; Cooper & Grotevant, 1989; Grotevant & Cooper, 1985, in press) believe that the presence of a family atmosphere that promotes both individuality and connectedness are important in the adolescent's identity development. **Individuality** *consists of two dimensions: self-assertion, the ability to have and communcate a point of view; and separateness, the use of communication patterns to express how one is different from others.* **Connectedness** *also consists of two dimensions: mutuality, sensitivity to and respect for others' views; and permeability, openness to others' views.* In general, Cooper's research findings reveal that identity formation is enhanced by family relationships that are both individuated, which encourages adolescents to develop their own point of view, and connected, which provides a secure base from which to explore the widening social worlds of adolescence. However, when connectedness is strong and individuation weak, adolescents often have an identity foreclosure status; by contrast, when connectedness is weak, adolescents often reveal an identity confusion status (Archer & Waterman, 1994).

Stuart Hauser and his colleagues (Hauser & Bowlds, 1990; Hauser & others, 1984) also have illuminated family processes that promote the adolescent's identity development. They have found that parents who use *enabling* behaviors (such as explaining, accepting, and giving empathy) facilitate the adolescent's identity development more than do parents who use *constraining* behaviors (such as

judging and devaluing). In sum, family interaction styles that give the adolescent the right to question and to be different, within a context of support and mutuality, foster healthy patterns of identity development (Harter, 1990b).

Cultural and Ethnic Aspects of Identity

Erikson was especially sensitive to the role of culture in identity development. He pointed out that, throughout the world, ethnic minority groups have struggled to maintain their cultural identities while blending into the dominant culture (Erikson, 1968). Erikson said that this struggle for an inclusive identity, or identity within the larger culture, has been the driving force in the founding of churches, empires, and revolutions throughout history.

For ethnic minority individuals, adolescence is often a special juncture in their development (Bat-Chava & others, 1997; Kurtz, Cantu, & Phinney, 1996; Spencer & Dornbusch, 1990). Although children are aware of some ethnic and cultural differences, most ethnic minority individuals consciously confront their ethnicity for the first time in adolescence. In contrast to children, adolescents have the ability to interpret ethnic and cultural information, to reflect on the past, and to speculate about the future (Wong, 1997). As they cognitively mature, ethnic minority adolescents become acutely aware of the evaluations of their ethnic group by the majority White culture (Comer, 1993). As one researcher commented, the young African American might learn as a child that Black is beautiful but conclude as an adolescent that White is powerful (Semaj, 1985).

Ethnic minority youths' awareness of negative appraisals, conflicting values, and restricted occupational opportunities can influence their life choices and plans for the future (Spencer & Dornbusch, 1990). As one ethnic minority youth stated, "The future seems shut off, closed. Why dream? You can't reach your dreams. Why set goals? At least if you don't set any goals, you don't fail."

Many ethnic minority youth lack successful ethnic minority role models with whom to identify (Blash & Unger, 1992). The problem is especially acute for inner-city ethnic minority youth. Because of the lack of adult ethnic minority role models, some ethnic minority youth might conform to middle-class White values and identify with successful White role models. However, for many adolescents, their ethnicity and skin color limit their acceptance by the White culture. Thus, many ethnic minority adolescents have the difficult task of negotiating two

SOCIOCULTURAL WORLDS OF ADOLESCENCE

The Development of Identity in Native American Children and Youth

Substandard living conditions, poverty, and chronic unemployment place many Native American youths at risk for school failure and poor health, which can contribute to problems in developing a positive identity (LaFromboise & Low, 1989). A special concern is the negative image of Native Americans that has been perpetuated for centuries in the majority White American culture. To consider further the development of identity in Native American youth, we will examine the experiences of a 12-year-old Hopi Indian boy.

The Hopi Indians are a quiet, thoughtful people who go to great lengths not to offend anyone. In a pueblo north of Albuquerque, a 12-year-old boy speaks: "I've been living in Albuquerque for a year. The Anglos I've met, they're different. I don't know why. In school, I drew a picture of my father's horse. One of the other kids wouldn't believe that it was ours. He said, 'You don't really own that horse.' I said, 'It's a horse my father rides, and I feed it every morning.' He said, 'How come?' I said, 'My uncle and my father are good riders, and I'm pretty good.' He said, 'I can ride a horse better than you, and I'd rather be a pilot.' I told him I never thought of being a pilot."

The Hopi boy continues, "Anglo kids, they won't let you get away with anything. Tell them something, and fast as lightning and loud as thunder, they'll say, 'I'm better than you, so there!' My father says it's always been like that."

The Native American adolescent is not really angry or envious of the White adolescent. Maybe he is in awe of his future power, maybe he fears it, and the White adolescent can't keep from wondering somehow that he has missed out on something and may end up "losing" (Coles, 1986).

The following words of another American Indian vividly capture some important ingredients of a Hopi adolescent's interest in a peaceful identity:

Rivers flow.   A small pebble
The sea sings.   On a giant shore;
Oceans roar.   Who am I
Tides rise.   To ask who I am?
Who am I?   Isn't it enough to be?

The Native American adolescent's quest for identity involves a cultural meshing of tribal customs and the technological, educational demands of modern society.

value systems—that of their own ethnic group and that of the White society. Some adolescents reject the mainstream, foregoing the rewards controlled by White Americans; others adopt the values and standards of the majority White culture; and yet others take the difficult path of biculturalism (Hiraga & others, 1993).

In one investigation, ethnic identity exploration was higher among ethnic minority than among White American college students (Phinney & Alipuria, 1990). In this same investigation, ethnic minority college students who had thought about and resolved issues involving their ethnicity had higher self-esteem than did their ethnic minority counterparts who had not. In another investigation, the ethnic identity development of Asian American, African American, Latino, and White American tenth-grade students in Los Angeles was studied

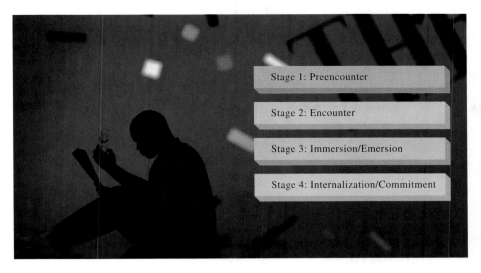

Figure~10.4

Four Stages of Ethnic Minority Identity Development.

(Phinney, 1989). Adolescents from each of the three ethnic minority groups faced a similar need to deal with their ethnic-group identification in a predominantly White American culture. In some instances, the adolescents from the three ethnic minority groups perceived different issues to be important in their resolution of ethnic identity. For Asian American adolescents, pressures to achieve academically and concerns about quotas that make it difficult to get into good colleges were salient issues. Many African American adolescent females discussed their realization that White American standards of beauty (especially hair and skin color) did not apply to them; African American adolescent males were concerned with possible job discrimination and the need to distinguish themselves from a negative societal image of African American male adolescents. For Latino adolescents, prejudice was a recurrent theme, as was the conflict in values between their Latino culture heritage and the majority culture. To read further about identity development in ethnic minority youth, turn to Sociocultural Worlds of Adolescence.

The contexts in which ethnic minority youth live influence their identity development (Stanton-Salazar & Dornbusch, in press). Many ethnic minority youth in the United States live in low-income urban settings where support for developing a positive identity is absent. Many of these youth live in pockets of poverty, are exposed to drugs, gangs, and criminal activities, and interact with other youth and adults who have dropped out of school and/or are unemployed. In such settings, effective organizations and programs for youth can make important contributions to developing a positive identity.

Shirely Heath and Milbrey McLaughlin (1993) studied sixty youth organizations that involved 24,000 adolescents over a period of 5 years. They found that these organizations were especially good at building a sense of ethnic pride in inner-city ethnic youth. Heath and McLaughlin believe that many inner-city youth have too much time on their hands, too little to do, and too few places to go. Inner-city youth want to participate in organizations that nurture them and respond positively to their needs and interests. Organizations that perceive youth as fearful, vulnerable, and lonely but also frame them as capable, worthy, and eager to have a healthy and productive life contribute in positive ways to the identity development of ethnic minority youth.

African American psychologists Janet Helms (1990, 1995) and William Cross (1972), as well as Asian American psychologists Derald Wing Sue and David Sue (1972), believe that a number of stages are involved in the development of an ethnic identity, whether for minorities or for Whites (Halonen & Santrock, 1996). Helms amended Cross's model of minority identity development to include four stages (see figure 10.4):

Stage 1: Preencounter. In this first stage, ethnic minority individuals prefer dominant cultural values to those of their own culture. Their role models, lifestyles, and value systems are adopted from the dominant group, while the physical and/or cultural characteristics that single them out as ethnic minority individuals are a source of pain and stress. For example, African Americans might perceive their own physical features as undesirable and their African cultural values and ways a handicap to success in American society.

Stage 2: Encounter. Although moving to the encounter stage is usually a gradual process, reaching this stage can occur because of an event that makes individuals realize that they will never be members of mainstream White America. A monumental event, such as the assassination of Martin Luther King, Jr., or more personal "identity-shattering" events can serve as triggers. In the encounter stage, ethnic minority individuals begin to break through their denial. For example, Latinos who feel ashamed of their cultural upbringing might have conversations with Latinos who are proud of their cultural heritage. Ethnic minority individuals become aware during the encounter stage that not all cultural values of the dominant group are beneficial to them. Conflicting attitudes about the self, minority group culture, and the dominant culture are characteristic of the encounter stage. Ethnic minority individuals want to identify with the minority group but do not know how to develop this identity. The recognition that an identity must be developed and not found leads to the third stage.

Stage 3: Immersion/Emersion. At the beginning of this stage—immersion—ethnic minority individuals completely endorse minority views and reject the dominant society. Individuals become strongly motivated to eliminate the oppression of their ethnic minority group. Movement into this stage likely occurs because (1) individuals begin to resolve some conflicts from the previous stage and develop a better understanding of such societal forces as racism, oppression, and discrimination; and (2) individuals begin to ask themselves, "Why should I feel ashamed of who I am?" The answer at this point often elicits both guilt and anger—the guilt of "selling out" in the past, which is perceived as contributing to the ethnic minority group's oppression, and anger at having been oppressed and "brainwashed" by the dominant group.

In the second phase of this stage—emersion—individuals experience feelings of discontent and discomfort with their rigid views of the immersion phase and develop notions of greater individual autonomy. Emersion allows them to vent the anger that characterized the beginning of this stage, through rap groups, explorations of their own culture, discussions of racial/ethnic issues, and so on. Education and opportunities to expel hostile feelings allow individuals to level off emotionally so that they can think more clearly and adaptively. They no longer find it necessary to reject everything from the dominant culture and accept everything from their own culture. They now have the autonomy to reflect on the strengths and weaknesses of their culture, and to decide which parts of the culture will become a part of their identity.

Stage 4: Internalization/Commitment. The main theme of this stage of ethnic minority identity development is that individuals experience a sense of fulfillment regarding the integration of their personal and cultural identities. They have resolved the conflicts and discomforts of the

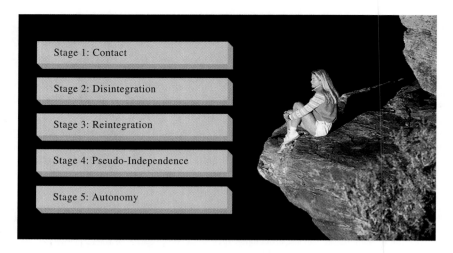

Figure~10.5

Five Stages of White Ethnic Identity Development.

immersion/emersion stage and attained greater self-control and flexibility. They also more objectively examine the cultural values of other ethnic minority individuals and groups, as well as those of the dominant group. At this stage, individuals want to eliminate all forms of oppression. The commitment in this stage refers to the behavioral enactment of the newly realized identity. Individuals take actions—whether large, such as engaging in large-scale political or social activism, or small, such as performing everyday activities that are consistent with their ethnic identity—to eliminate oppression.

Helms (1990) also proposed a model of White ethnic identity, in which White individuals move from a stage of naiveté about racial issues to a sophisticated stage of biculturalism or racial transcendence. Helms's theory assumes that consciousness of ethnic identity in both minority and majority individuals increases understanding of success or failure in cross-ethnic interactions. Helms's five stages of White ethnic identity development are these (see figure 10.5):

Stage 1: Contact. White individuals are oblivious to ethnic/racial/cultural issues. They rarely think of themselves in ethnic or racial terms.

Stage 2: Disintegration. White individuals become aware of the social implications of race and ethnicity on a personal level, caught between the privileges of the White culture and the humane desire to treat ethnic minority individuals fairly.

Stage 3: Reintegration. White persons idealize anything associated with the White culture and denigrate anything associated with ethnic minority cultures. Anger is most common at this stage.

Stage 4: Pseudo-Independence. White individuals develop an understanding of the privileges of "Whiteness" and recognize a personal responsibility to combat racism.

Stage 5: Autonomy. White individuals develop a multicultural or transcendent world view. At this stage, individuals have adopted a positive, nonracist "White identity," feeling a kinship with people regardless of their race and seeking to abolish the oppression of ethnic minority groups.

Although the identity development models include distinct stages, the boundaries between the stages are not always abrupt and clearly defined. In many instances, one stage blends into the next. Also, not all individuals experience the entire range of these stages in their lifetime. Some individuals are born and raised in a family functioning at stage 4 in the White identity development model and may never experience the earlier stages.

Gender and Identity Development

In Erikson's (1968) classic presentation of identity development, the division of labor between the sexes was reflected in his assertion that males' aspirations were mainly oriented toward career and ideological commitments, while females' were centered around marriage and childbearing. In the 1960s and 1970s researchers found support for Erikson's assertion about gender differences in identity. For example, vocational concerns were more central to the identity of males, and affiliative concerns were more important in the identity of females (La Voie, 1976). However, in the last decade, as females have developed stronger vocational interests, these gender differences are disappearing (Madison & Foster-Clark, 1996; Waterman, 1985).

Some investigators believe that females and males go through Erikson's stages in different order. One view is that for males, identity formation precedes the stage of intimacy, while for females, intimacy precedes identity (Douvan & Adelson, 1966). These ideas are consistent with the belief that relationships and emotional bonds are more important concerns of females, while autonomy and achievement are more important concerns of males (Gilligan, 1990). In one study, the development of a clear sense of self by adolescent girls was related to their concerns about care and response in relationships (Rogers, 1987). In another investigation, a strong sense of self in college women was associated with their ability to solve problems of care in relationships while staying connected with both self and others (Skoe & Marcia, 1988). Indeed, conceptualization and measurement of identity development in females should include interpersonal content (Patterson, Sochting, & Marcia, 1992).

The task of identity exploration might be more complex for females than for males, in that females might try to establish identities in more domains than males do. In today's world, the options for females have increased and thus can at times be confusing and conflicting, especially for females who hope to successfully integrate family and career roles (Archer, 1994; Josselson, 1994; Streitmatter, 1993).

Identity and Intimacy

As we go through our adolescence, youth, and early adulthood, most of us are motivated to successfully juggle the development of identity and intimacy. We now examine the development of intimacy in adolescence and then study the nature of loneliness.

Intimacy

Erikson (1968) believes that intimacy should come after individuals are well on their way to establishing a stable and successful individual identity. Intimacy is another life crisis in Erikson's scheme—if intimacy is not developed in early adulthood, the individual may be left with what Erikson calls isolation. **Intimacy versus isolation** *is Erikson's sixth developmental stage, which individuals experience during early adulthood. At this time, individuals face the task of forming intimate relationships with others.* Erikson describes intimacy as finding oneself, yet losing oneself in another. If young adults form healthy friendships and an intimate relationship with another individual, intimacy will be achieved; if not, isolation will result.

In one recent study of unmarried college students 18 to 23 years of age, a strong sense of self, expressed through identity achievement and an instrumental orientation, was an important factor in forming intimate connections, for both males and females (Madison & Foster-Clark, 1996). However, insecurity and a defensive posture in relationships were expressed differently in males' and females' relationships, with males displaying greater superficiality and females more dependency.

An inability to develop meaningful relationships with others can harm an individual's personality. It may lead individuals to repudiate, ignore, or attack those who frustrate them. Such circumstances account for the shallow, almost pathetic attempts of youth to merge themselves with a leader. Many youths want to be apprentices or disciples of leaders and adults who will shelter them from the harm of the "out-group" world. If this fails, and Erikson believes that it must, sooner or later the individuals retreat to search themselves to discover where they went wrong. This introspection sometimes leads to painful depression and isolation and can contribute to a mistrust of others and restrict the youths' willingness to act on their own initiative.

Adolescents and young adults show different styles of intimate interaction. Jacob Orlofsky (1976) developed one classification with five styles: intimate, preintimate, stereotyped, pseudointimate, and isolated (Orlofsky, Marcia, & Lesser, 1973). In the **intimate style,** *the individual forms and maintains one or more deep and long-lasting love relationships.* In the **preintimate style,** *the individual shows* mixed emotions about commitment, an ambivalence reflected in the strategy of offering love without obligations or long-lasting bonds. In the **stereotyped style,** *the individual has superficial relationships that tend to be dominated by friendship ties with same-sex rather than opposite-sex individuals.* In the **pseudointimate style,** *the individual maintains a long-lasting sexual attachment with little or no depth or closeness.* In the **isolated style,** *the individual withdraws from social encounters and has little or no attachment to same- or opposite-sexed individuals.* Occasionally, the isolate shows signs of developing close interpersonal relationships, but usually the interactions are stressful. In one investigation, intimate and preintimate individuals were more sensitive to their partners' needs and were more open in their friendships than individuals in the other three intimacy statuses were (Orlofsky, Marcia, & Lesser, 1973).

A desirable goal is to develop a mature identity and have positive, close relationships with others. Kathleen White and her colleagues (1987) developed a model of relationship maturity that includes this goal at its highest level. Individuals are described as moving through three levels of relationship maturity: self-focused, role-focused, and individuated-connected.

The **self-focused level** *is the first level of relationship maturity, at which one's perspective of another or a relationship is concerned only with how it affects oneself.* The individual's own wishes and plans overshadow those of others, and the individual shows little concern for others. Intimate communication skills are in the early developing, experimental stages. In terms of sexuality, there is little understanding of mutuality or consideration of another's sexual needs.

The **role-focused level** *is the second or intermediate level of relationship maturity, at which perceiving others as individuals in their own right begins to develop. However, at this level, the perspective is stereotypical and emphasizes social acceptability.* Individuals at this level know that acknowledging and respecting another is part of being a good friend or a romantic partner. Yet commitment to an individual, rather than the romantic partner role itself, is not articulated. Generalizations about the importance of communication in relationships abound, but underlying this talk is a shallow understanding of commitment.

The **individuated-connected level** *is the highest level of relationship maturity, at which there is evidence of self-understanding, as well as consideration of others' motivations and anticipation of their needs. Concern and caring involve emotional support and individualized expression of interest.* Commitment is made to specific individuals with whom a relationship is shared. At this level, individuals understand the personal time and investment needed to make a relationship work. In White's view, the individuated-connected level is not likely to be reached until adulthood. She believes that most individuals making the transition from adolescence to adulthood are either self-focused or role-focused in their relationship maturity.

Loneliness

We often think of older adults as the loneliest individuals, but surveys have found that the highest levels of loneliness often appear during late adolescence and youth (Cutrona, 1982). Some adolescents feel lonely because they have strong needs for intimacy but have not yet developed the social skills or relationship maturity to satisfy these needs. They might feel isolated and sense that they do not have anyone they can turn to for intimacy. In one recent study, teenage loneliness appeared to be part of a depressive complex for girls while signaling poor scholastic functioning for boys (Koenig & Faigeles, 1995). Society's contemporary emphasis on self-fulfillment and achievement, the importance attached to commitment in relationships, and the decline in stable, close relationships are among the reasons feelings of loneliness are common today.

Loneliness is associated with an individual's sex, attachment history, self-esteem, and social skills. A lack of time spent with females, on the part of both males and females, is associated with loneliness. Lonely adolescents are not adequately integrated into the peer system and might not have close friends (Hicks & Connolly, 1995). Also, individuals who are lonely often have a poor relationship with their parents. Early experiences of rejection and loss (as when a parent dies) can cause a lasting effect of feeling alone. Lonely individuals often have low self-esteem and tend to blame themselves more than they deserve for their inadequacies. Lonely individuals also are often deficient in social skills. For example, they show inappropriate self-disclosure, self-attention at the expense of attention to a partner, or an inability to develop comfortable intimacy.

The social transition to college is a time when loneliness may develop, as individuals leave behind the familiar world of hometown and family. Many college freshmen feel anxious about meeting new people and developing a new social life. As one student commented:

> My first year here at the university has been pretty lonely. I wasn't lonely at all in high school. I lived in a fairly small town—I knew everyone and everyone knew me. I was a member of several clubs and played on the basketball team. It's not that way at the university. It is a big place, and I've felt like a stranger on so many occasions. I'm starting to get used to my life here, and the last few months I've been making myself meet people and get to know them, but it has not been easy.

As reflected in the comments of this freshman, individuals usually cannot bring their popularity and social standing from high school into the college environment. There might be a dozen high school basketball stars, National Merit scholars, and former student council presidents on a single dormitory floor. Especially if students attend college away from home, they face the task of forming completely new social relationships.

In one investigation conducted 2 weeks after the school year began, 75 percent of the 354 college freshmen said that they had felt lonely at least part of the time since arriving on campus (Cutrona, 1982). More than 40 percent said that their loneliness was moderate to severe in intensity. Students who were the most optimistic and had the highest self-esteem were more likely to overcome their loneliness by the end of the freshmen year. Loneliness is not reserved only for college freshmen, though. It is not uncommon to find a number of upperclassmen who are also lonely.

Researchers have developed measures of loneliness. Individuals are asked to respond to statements such as these:

"I don't feel in tune with the people around me."

"I can't find companionship when I want it."

Individuals who consistently respond that they never or rarely feel in tune with people around them and rarely or never can find companionship when they want it are likely to fall into the category of moderately or intensely lonely.

According to Robert Weiss (1973), loneliness is virtually always a response to the absence of some particular type of relationship. Weiss distinguished two forms of loneliness—*emotional isolation* and *social isolation*—which correspond to the absence of different types of social provisions. **Emotional isolation** *is a type of loneliness that arises when a person lacks an intimate attachment relationship; single, divorced, and widowed adults often experience this type of loneliness.* In contrast, **social isolation** *is a type of loneliness that occurs when a person lacks a sense of integrated involvement. Being deprived of participation in a group or community involving companionship, shared interests, organized activities, and meaningful roles causes a person to feel alienated, bored, and uneasy.* Recently relocated married couples often experience social isolation and long for involvement with friends and community.

It is common for adolescents to experience both types of loneliness. Being left out of clique and crowd activities can give rise to painful feelings of social isolation. Not having an intimate dating or romantic partner can give rise to the loneliness of emotional isolation.

Individuals can reduce their loneliness by either changing their social relations or changing their social needs and desires (Peplau & Perlman, 1982). Probably the most direct and satisfying choice is to improve their social relations by forming new relationships, by using their existing social network more competently, or by creating "surrogate" relationships with pets, television personalities, and the like. The second way to reduce loneliness is to reduce one's desire for social contact. Over the short run, individuals can accomplish this by selecting activities they can enjoy alone rather than those that require another's company. Over the long run, though, effort should be made to form new relationships. A third coping strategy that some individuals unfortunately adopt involves distracting themselves form their painful feelings of loneliness by consuming alcohol or other drugs to "drown their sorrows" or by becoming a workaholic. Some of the negative health consequences of loneliness may be the product of such maladaptive coping strategies. If you perceive yourself to be a lonely individual, you might consider contacting the counseling center at your college for advice on ways to reduce your loneliness and to improve your social skills in relationships.

At this point, we have discussed a number of ideas about identity. A summary of these ideas is presented in concept table 10.2.

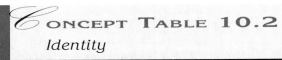

Concept	Processes/ Related Ideas	Characteristics/Description
Erikson's Ideas on Identity	Their nature	Identity versus identity confusion is the fifth stage in Erikson's theory, which individuals experience in adolescence. As adolescents are confronted with new roles, they enter a psychosocial moratorium. Two core ingredients of Erikson's ideas on identity are personality and role experimentation. In technological societies like the United States, the vocational role is especially important. Identity development is a lengthy process, in many cases more gradual than Erikson envisioned. Identity development is also extraordinarily complex and proceeds in bits and pieces.
The Four Statuses of Identity and Developmental Changes	The four statuses	Marcia proposed four identity statuses—identity diffusion, identity foreclosure, identity moratorium, and identity achievement —that are based on crisis (exploration) and commitment.
	Developmental changes	Some experts believe that the main identity changes take place in youth rather than earlier in adolescence. Individuals often follow "moratorium–achievement–moratorium–achievement" cycles throughout the adult years.
Family, Cultural, Ethnic, and Gender Aspects of Identity	Family influences	Parents are important figures in adolescents' identity development. Researchers have found that democratic parenting, individuality and connectedness, and enabling behaviors facilitate identity development.
	Cultural and ethnic factors	Erikson is especially sensitive to the role of culture in development, underscoring how, throughout the world, ethnic minority groups have struggled to maintain their cultural identities while blending into the majority culture. Adolescence is often a special juncture in the identity development of ethnic minority individuals, because for the first time they consciously confront their ethnic identity. Helms proposed a model of ethnic minority identity development and also a model for White individuals.
	Gender	According to Erikson's theory, there are sex differences in identity development, with adolescent males having a stronger vocational identity, adolescent females a stronger social identity in terms of marriage and family roles. Some researchers have found that sex differences in identity development are disappearing, but others argue that relationships and emotional bonds are more central to the identity development of females than to that of males.
Identity and Intimacy	Intimacy	Intimacy versus isolation is Erikson's sixth stage of development, which individuals experience during early adulthood. Orlofsky described five styles of intimate interaction. White proposed a model of relationship maturity.
	Loneliness	Surveys often find that the highest levels of loneliness occur during late adolescence and youth. The social transition to college is a time when loneliness may develop. Weiss distinguished between two types of loneliness: emotional isolation and social isolation.

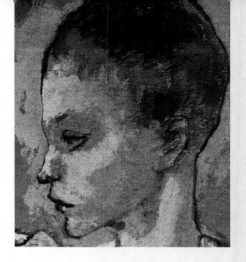

This chapter on the self and identity has been about how adolescents perceive themselves, evaluate themselves, feel about themselves, and explore who they are.

We began the chapter by examining a 15-year-old girl's complex self-description and then studied three important aspects of the self—self-understanding, self-esteem, and self-concept. In reading about self-understanding, we learned what self-understanding is and the dimensions of self-understanding in adolescence. In reading about self-esteem and self-concept, we learned what they are, how they can be measured, whether some dimensions of self-esteem are more salient than others in adolescence, parental and peer influences on self-esteem, the consequences of low self-esteem, and how to increase adolescents self-esteem. Our exploration of identity focused on Erikson's ideas on identity, some contemporary thoughts on identity, the four statuses of identity, developmental changes, family influences on identity, cultural and ethnic aspects of identity, gender and identity development, and identity and intimacy.

Don't forget that you can obtain an overall summary of the chapter by again studying the two concept tables on pages 322 and 334. Although we studied gender development only briefly in this chapter—examining gender's role in identity development—in the next chapter we extensively evaluate the role of gender in adolescent development.

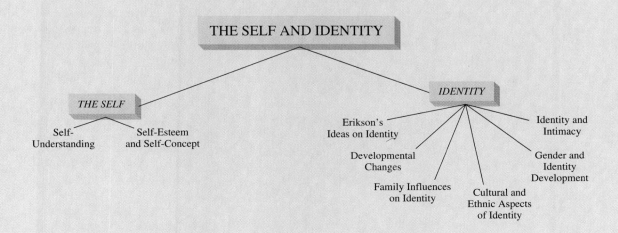

THE SELF AND IDENTITY

THE SELF

Self-Understanding

Self-Esteem and Self-Concept

IDENTITY

Erikson's Ideas on Identity

Developmental Changes

Family Influences on Identity

Cultural and Ethnic Aspects of Identity

Identity and Intimacy

Gender and Identity Development

PRACTICAL KNOWLEDGE ABOUT ADOLESCENCE

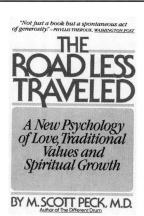

"Not just a book but a spontaneous act of generosity." –PHYLLIS THEROUX, WASHINGTON POST

THE ROAD LESS TRAVELED

A New Psychology of Love, Traditional Values and Spiritual Growth

BY M. SCOTT PECK, M.D.
Author of The Different Drum

The Road Less Traveled
(1978) by M. Scott Peck.
New York: Simon & Schuster.

The Road Less Traveled presents a spiritual and emotionally based approach to self-fulfillment. Peck begins by stating that life is difficult and that we all suffer pain and disappointment. He believes we should face up to life's difficulties and not be lazy. Indeed, Peck equates laziness with the original sin, going on to say that people's tendency to avoid problems and emotional suffering is the root of mental disorders. Peck also believes that people are thirsting for integrity in their lives. They are not happy with a country that has "In God we trust" as one of its main emblems and at the same time still leads the world's arms race. They also can't tolerate being just Sunday-morning Christians, he says. To achieve integrity, Peck believes, people need to move spirituality into all phases of their lives.

Peck speaks of four important tools to use in life's journey: delaying gratification, accepting responsibility, dedication to the truth, and balancing. After a thorough analysis of each, Peck explores the will to use them, which he calls love. Then, he probes further and analyzes the relation of growth and religion, which leads him to examine the final step of "the road less traveled": grace. By "grace," Peck means the whole range of human activities that support the human spirit. Grace operates at the interface between persons and God and at the frontier between unconscious and conscious thought, in Peck's view.

The Road Less Traveled has been an immensely popular book, on the *New York Times* bestseller list for more than a year. Peck has developed a cultlike following, especially among young people. The book's enthusiasts say that Peck recognized some important voids in people's lives, especially the need for an integrated, spiritually based existence. Some critics say that Peck's ideas are not new and that his thoughts are occasionally fuzzy, especially when he arrives at the meeting point between God and persons, and unconscious and conscious selves.

DAVID D. BURNS, M.D.
Author of the bestselling FEELING GOOD

INTIMATE CONNECTIONS

THE CLINICALLY
PROVEN PROGRAM
FOR MAKING
CLOSE FRIENDS AND
FINDING A LOVING
PARTNER

Intimate Connections

(1985) by David D. Burns.
New York: William Morrow.

Intimate Connections presents a program for overcoming loneliness. Author David Burns believes loneliness is a state of mind primarily caused by the faulty assumption that a loving partner is needed *before* a person can feel happy and secure. Burns says the first step in breaking free from the loneliness pattern is learning to like and love yourself. He also makes a distinction between two types of loneliness: (1) sit-uational loneliness, which lasts only for a brief time, and (2) chronic loneliness, which persists and results from problems that have plagued people for a long time, even years.

Burns says that, to overcome chronic loneliness, individuals have to change their patterns of perception that created the loneliness and continue to perpetuate it. The author explains how to make social connections and how to get close to others. Checklists, worksheets, daily mood logs, and a number of self-assessments appear throughout the book.

RESOURCES FOR IMPROVING THE LIVES OF ADOLESCENTS

Adolescent Identity Formation (1992)
by Gerald Adams, Thomas Gulotta, and Raymond
Montemayor (Eds.)
Newbury Park, CA: Sage

This book provides an up-to-date portrayal of a number of aspects of identity development in adolescence. It includes chapters on a feminist's approach to identity, ethnic identity, and the role of identity in adolescent problems.

Gandhi (1969)
by Erik Erikson
New York: Norton

This Pulitzer Prize–winning novel by Erik Erikson, who developed the concept of identity as a central aspect of adolescent development, analyzes the life of Mahatma Gandhi, the spiritual leader of India in the middle of the twentieth century. Erikson reveals how Gandhi's adolescence played a pivotal role in his personality formation.

Scorpions (1988)
By W. D. Myers
New York: HarperCollins

This winner of a Newbery Award (presented for the most distinguished contribution to American literature for children and adolescents) has as its central character an adolescent who is undergoing an identity crisis. The character, Jamal, struggles with identity confusion, which propels him into the Scorpion gang. The book also includes insightful portrayals of experiences that relate to Erikson's stage of industry and inferiority.

Self-Esteem: The Puzzle of Low Self-Regard (1991)
by Roy Baumeister (Ed.)
New York: Plenum

An excellent book on low self-esteem and how it can be raised. Includes a chapter by Susan Harter on causes and consequences of low self-esteem in children and adolescents.

Students Commission/TG *Magazine*/
Teen Generation Inc.
202 Cleveland Street
Toronto, Ontario M4S 2W6
416-487-3204

The Commission is a voice for youth, publishing the ideas, work, and opinions of youth in a variety of media. It trains youth in communication and in leadership and teamwork skills, and hosts an annual national youth conference. *TG Magazine* is produced by high school students on co-op placement.

Exploring Adolescent Development

To further explore the nature of adolescent development, we will examine a research study on perceived support and its relation to adolescents' self-worth, and we will discuss the nature of education, work, and identity development.

Research on Adolescent Development

Perceived Support and Adolescents' Self-Worth

Featured Study

Robinson, N. S., (1995). Evaluating the nature of perceived support and its relation to perceived self-worth in adolescents. *Journal of Research on Adolescence, 5,* 253–280.

The purpose of this study was to better understand the link between adolescents' perceptions of global self-worth and their perceptions of different types of support—approval, emotional support, and instrumental aid. It was hypothesized that positive regard or approval from others—especially approval from peers, because they represent such an important reference group for adolescents—would be related most strongly to self-worth.

Method

The subjects were 370 seventh- and eighth-grade students from two middle schools and 189 ninth- to twelfth-graders from one high school. Both females and males were studied, and the schools served primarily Anglo-American middle-class adolescents.

The main measures included the Perceived Social Support Scale and the Self-Perception Profile. A revised version of Harter's Social Support Scale for Children was administered. Separate subscales tap emotional support (such as "perceptions of how much people in their lives care about their feelings" or "listen to them when they are upset"), approval (such as the extent to which people "praise them or say nice things about them," "are really proud of them," or "like most of the things they do"), and instrumental aid (such as the level of assistance or aid provided along the lines of "helping them do the things they cannot do themselves" or "teaching them about the things they want to know"). Adolescents were asked the extent to which each of the three types of support was being provided by five sources: mother, father, best friend, classmates, and teacher. For high school students, a sixth source was added: a person in whom they were romantically interested. Modified versions of Harter's Self-Perception Profile were given to the adolescents, a shortened version of the Self-Perception Profile for Children was given to the middle school students,

and a shortened version of the Self-Perception Profile for Adolescents was given to the high school students. These measures assess students' perceptions of their competence in four domains (academic, social, physical appearance, and behavior/conduct) and their perceptions of global self-worth. The items on the global self-worth scale (the only part of this measure that is of interest in this study) ask to what extent individuals are happy or pleased with themselves, like the way they are carrying out their lives, like who they are, and think that the way they do things is fine.

Results and Discussion

Perceptions of approval from others, especially a peer reference group such as classmates, were more strongly related to general self-worth than were perceptions of emotional support or instrumental aid. Females consistently reported higher levels of approval, emotional support, and instrumental aid from their best friends than did males. Parental support and peer support were acknowledged as important throughout adolescence.

Explorations in Education, Work, and Identity Development

Susan Harter (1990b) addressed the importance of developing programs for youth that promote the *active* and *realistic* exploration of broad identity goals, such as educational and occupational choices. Such programs may take the form of on-the-job experiences, as occurs in the Boston Compact Youth Incentive Program, which provides students with well-paying summer jobs if they maintain a good record of school attendance and performance. Another program strengthens the link between high school activities and the world of work and provides opportunities for exploring alternatives (Lang & Rivera, 1987). This program emphasizes adolescents' choice of areas they are both interested and competent in, letting them choose educational opportunities that further their development in these domains. This strategy is consistent with Harter's conclusion that the highest levels of self-esteem are found in individuals who are performing competently in domains that are important to the self.

One strategy is to encourage society to recognize the positive benefits of competence in many different domains, not just academic competence. Another strategy is to acknowledge that education is the primary means for achieving success, and to provide individuals with poor academic skills and low self-esteem better support and more individualized attention. The inspiration of Latino

Shown here is a scene from the movie *Stand and Deliver*, in which Latino high school teacher Jaime Escalante (played by James Olmos, in the center with a cap) spent many evenings and weekends tutoring Latino students in math in addition to effectively teaching the students math in the classroom. Escalante's commitment and motivation were transferred to the students, many of whom obtained college scholarships and passed advanced placement tests in calculus.

high school teacher Jaime Escalante, documented in the movie *Stand and Deliver*, reflects this latter strategy. Escalante was a California high school teacher who spent many evenings and weekends tutoring Latino students in math, in addition to effectively teaching the students math in the classroom. Escalante's commitment and motivation were transferred to the Latino high school students, many of whom obtained college scholarships and passed advanced placement tests in calculus. Insisting that high school and college athletes maintain

a respectable grade point average is a policy that endorses the importance of academic achievement and competence in other domains, as is the requirement that students maintain respectable grades to participate in jobs programs.

Daniel Garber
Tanis, 1915, detail

Chapter

11

Gender

It is fatal to be man or woman pure and simple; one must be woman-manly or man-womanly.

—Virginia Woolf

Chapter Outline

Chapter Boxes

*As the man beholds
the woman
As the woman sees
the man,
Curiously they note
each other,
As each other they only can.*

—Bryan Procter,
The Sexes

Tomorrow's Gender Worlds of Today's Adolescents

Controversy swirls around today's females and males. Females increasingly struggle to gain influence and change the worlds of business, politics, and relationships with males. The changes are far from complete, but social reformers hope that a generation from now the struggles of the last decades of the twentieth century will have generated more freedom, influence, and flexibility for females. Possibly in the next generation, when today's adolescents become tomorrow's adults, such issues as equal pay, child care, abortion, rape, and dosmetic violence will no longer be discussed as "women's issues" but, rather, as economic issues, family issues, and ethical issues—reflecting the equal concern of females *and* males. Possibly one of today's adolescent females will become the head of a large corporation several decades from now and the appointment will not make headlines by virtue of her gender. Half the presidential candidates may be women and nobody will notice.

What would it take for today's adolescent females to get from here to there? The choices are not simple ones. When Barbara Bush went to Wellesley College to celebrate motherhood and wifely virtues, she stimulated a national debate among the young on what it means to be a successful woman. The debate was further fueled by TV anchorwoman Connie Chung's announcement that she would abandon the fast track at CBS in a final drive to become a mother at age 44. At the same time, male role models are also in flux. Wall Street star Peter Lynch, the head of Fidelity Investment's leading mutual fund, resigned to have more time with his family and to pursue humanitarian projects (Gibbs, 1990). In 1993, both Chung and Lynch returned to work.

When asked to sketch their futures, many of today's youth say they want good careers, good marriages, and two or three children, but they don't want their children to be raised by strangers (Spade & Reese, 1991). Idealistic? Maybe. Some will reach these goals; some will make other choices as they move from adolescence into adulthood, and then through the adult years. Some of today's adolescents will choose to remain single as they move into adulthood and pursue their career goals; others will become married but not have children; and yet others will balance the demands of family and work. In a word, not all of today's females have the same goals; neither do all of today's males. What is important is to develop a society free of barriers and discrimination, one that allows females and males to freely choose, to meet their expectations, and to realize their potential.

PREVIEW

*T*his chapter is about gender, about adolescents' worlds as females and males. Among the questions we will explore are these: What is gender? What are the biological, social, and cognitive influences on gender? Are there many gender differences, or are most of what we consider to be differences actually stereotypes? How can gender roles be classified? Is there an intensification of gender in adolescence? Are there windows of gender opportunity? What are some women's and men's issues involved in understanding gender and adolescence?

WHAT IS GENDER?

Nowhere in adolescents' social development have more sweeping changes occurred in recent years than in the area of gender. What exactly is meant by *gender*? Whereas the term *sex* refers to the biological dimension of being male or females, **gender** *refers to the sociocultural dimension of being male or female*. Few aspects of adolescents' development are more central to their identity and to their social relationships than gender. One aspect of gender bears special mention: A **gender role** *is a set of expectations that prescribes how females or males should think, act, and feel*. For example, should males be more assertive than females, and should females be more sensitive than males to others' feelings?

BIOLOGICAL, SOCIAL, AND COGNITIVE INFLUENCES ON GENDER

How strong is biology's influence on gender? How extensively do children's and adolescents' experiences shape their gender development? How do cognitive factors influence gender development? We will explore the answers to each of these questions.

Biological Influences

In our examination of biological influences on gender behavior in adolescence, we will first discuss pubertal change, especially its role in increasing sexual interest, and second we will examine Freud's and Erikson's ideas about anatomy and destiny.

Pubertal Change and Sexuality

Biology's influence on gender behavior involves pubertal change. Pubertal change contributes to an increased incorporation of sexuality into the gender attitudes and behavior of adolescents. As their bodies are flooded with hormones, many girls desire to be the very best female possible, and many boys strive to be the very best male possible. The increased incorporation of sexuality into gender behavior means that adolescent girls often display increased stereotypical female behavior and adolescent boys often display increased stereotypical male behavior. In many cases, adolescent girls and boys show these behaviors even more intensely when they interact with opposite-sex peers, especially with individuals they would like to date. Thus, female adolescents might behave in an affectionate, sensitive, charming, and soft-spoken manner, and male adolescents might behave in an assertive, cocky, cynical, and forceful way, because they perceive that such behaviors enhance their sexuality and attractiveness.

There have been few attempts to relate puberty's sexual changes to gender behavior. Researchers have found that sexual behavior is related to hormonal changes in puberty, at least for boys. For example, in one study, adolescent sex researcher Robert Udry (1990) found that rising androgen levels were related to boys' increased sexual activity. For adolescent girls, androgen levels and sexual activity were associated, but girls' sexual activity was more strongly influenced by the type of friends they had than by their hormone levels. In the same study, Udry investigated whether hormone increases in puberty were related to gender behaviors, such as being affectionate, charming, assertive, and cynical, but found no significant associations.

While puberty's biological changes set the stage for increased incorporation of sexuality into gender behavior, how sexuality becomes a part of gender is determined by such social influences as cultural standards for sex and peer group norms for dating (Brooks-Gunn & Reiter, 1990). One explanation for increased differences in gender behavior was the increased socialization to conform to traditional masculine and feminine roles. However, puberty plays a role in gender intensification because it is a signaling to socializing others—such as parents, peers, and teachers—that the adolescent is beginning to approach adulthood and, therefore, should begin to act in ways that resemble the stereotypical female or male adult.

In sum, gender intensification in adolescence likely includes not only increased social pressures to conform to traditional masculine and feminine roles but also pubertal changes that introduce sexuality into gender behavior. Masculinity and femininity are renegotiated during adolescence, and much of this renegotiation involves sexuality. Further discussion of gender intensification appears later in the chapter.

Freud and Erikson—Anatomy Is Destiny

Both Sigmund Freud and Erik Erikson argued that an individual's genitals influence his or her gender behavior and, therefore, that anatomy is destiny. One of Freud's basic assumptions was that human behavior and history are directly related to reproductive processes. From this assumption arose his belief that gender and sexual behavior are essentially unlearned and instinctual. Erikson (1968) extended Freud's argument, claiming that the psychological differences between males and females stem from their anatomical differences. Erikson argued that, because of genital structure, males are more intrusive and aggressive, females more inclusive and passive. Critics of the anatomy-is-destiny view believe that experience is not given enough credit. The critics say that females and males are more free to choose their gender roles than Freud and Erikson allow. In response to the critics, Erikson modified his view, saying that females in today's world are transcending their biological heritage and correcting society's overemphasis on male intrusiveness.

Social Influences

In American culture, adults discriminate between the sexes shortly after the infant's birth. The "pink and blue" treatment may be applied to boys and girls before they even leave the hospital. Soon afterward, differences in hairstyles, clothes, and toys become obvious. Adults and peers reward these differences throughout development. And boys and girls learn gender roles through imitation or observational learning by watching what other people say and do. In recent years, the idea that parents are the critical socialization agents in gender-role development has come under fire (Huston & Alvarez, 1990). Parents are only one of the sources through which the individual learns gender roles. Culture, schools, peers, the media, and other family members are others. Yet, especially in the early years of development, parents may be the most important influences on gender development.

Parental Influences

Parents, by action and example, influence their children's and adolescents' gender development. During the transition from childhood to adolescence, parents allow boys more independence than girls, and concern about girls' sexual vulnerability may cause parents to monitor their behavior more closely and ensure that they are chaperoned. Families with young adolescent daughters indicate that they experience more intense conflict about sex, choice of friends, and curfews than do families with young adolescent sons (Papini & Sebby, 1988). When parents place severe restrictions on their adolescent sons, it is disruptive to their sons' development (Baumrind, 1991).

Parents often have different expectations for their adolescent sons and daughters, especially in such academic areas as math and science. For example, many parents believe that math is more important for their sons' futures than for their daughters', and their beliefs influence the value adolescents place on math achievement (Eccles, 1987). More about gender and achievement appears later in this chapter.

Social learning theory has been especially important in understanding social influences on gender. The **social learning theory of gender** *emphasizes that children's and adolescents' gender development occurs through observation and imitation of gender behavior, and through rewards and punishments they experience for gender-appropriate and -inappropriate behavior.* By observing parents and other adults, as well as peers, at home, at school, in the neighborhood, and in the media, adolescents are exposed to a myriad of models who display masculine and feminine behavior. And parents often use rewards and punishments to teach their daughters to be feminine ("Karen, that dress you are wearing makes you look so pretty.") and their sons to be masculine ("Bobby, you were so aggressive in that game. Way to go!").

One major change in the gender-role models adolescents have been exposed to in recent years is the increasing number of working mothers. Most adolescents today have a mother who is employed at least part-time. Although maternal employment is not specific to adolescence, it does influence gender-role development, and its influence likely depends on the age of the child or adolescent involved. Young adolescents may be especially attuned to understanding adult roles, so their mothers' role choices may be important influences on their concepts and attitudes about women's roles (Huston & Alvarez, 1990). Adolescents with working mothers have less-stereotyped concepts of female roles (and sometimes male roles as well) than do adolescents whose mothers are full-time homemakers. They also have more positive attitudes about nontraditional roles for women. Daughters of employed mothers have higher educational and occupational aspirations than do daughters of homemakers (Hoffman, 1989). Thus, working mothers often serve as models who combine traditional feminine home roles with less traditional activities away from home.

> *Children need models rather than critics.*
> —Joseph Joubert

Peers

Parents provide the earliest discrimination of gender behavior, but before long, peers join in the societal process of responding to and modeling masculine and feminine behavior. In middle and late childhood, children show a clear preference for being with and liking same-sex peers (Maccoby, 1996). After extensive observations of elementary school playgrounds, two researchers characterized the play settings as "gender school," pointing out that boys teach one another the required masculine behavior and reinforce it, and that girls also teach one another the required feminine behavior and reinforce it (Luria & Herzog, 1985).

In earlier chapters, we learned that adolescents spend increasing amounts of time with peers. In adolescence, peer approval or disapproval is a powerful influence on gender attitudes and behavior. Peers can socialize gender behavior partly by accepting or rejecting others on the basis of their gender-related attributes. Deviance from sex-typed norms often leads to low peer acceptance, but within a broad range of normal behavior it is not clear that conformity to sex-typed personality attributes is a good predictor of peer acceptance (Huston & Alvarez, 1990).

School and Teacher Influences

In certain ways, both girls and boys might receive an education that is not fair (Sadker & Sadker, 1994). For example:

- Girls' learning problems are not identified as often as boys' are.
- Boys are given the lion's share of attention in schools.

As reflected in this tug-of-war battle between boys and girls, the playground in elementary school is like going to "gender school." Elementary school children show a clear preference for being with and liking same-sex peers. Eleanor Maccoby (at right) has studied children's gender development for many years. She believes peers play especially strong roles in socializing each other about gender roles. How does the gender socializing role of peers possibly change when puberty takes place?

- Girls start school testing higher than boys in every academic subject, yet they graduate from high school scoring lower than boys do on the SAT exam.
- Pressure to achieve is more likely to be heaped on boys than on girls.

Consider the following research study (Sadker & Sadker, 1986). Observers were trained to collect data in more than 100 fourth-, sixth-, and eighth-grade classrooms. At all three grade levels, male students were involved in more interactions with teachers than female students were, and male students were given more attention than their female counterparts were. Male students were also given more remediation, more criticism, and more praise than female students. Further, girls with strong math abilities are given lower-quality instruction than their male counterparts are (Eccles, 1993).

Myra Sadker and David Sadker (1994), who have been studying gender discrimination in schools for more than two decades, believe that many educators are unaware of the subtle ways in which gender infiltrates the school's environment. Their hope is that sexism can be eradicated in the nation's schools.

A special concern is that most middle and junior high schools consist of independent, masculine learning environments, which appear better suited to the learning style of the average adolescent boy than to that of the average adolescent girl (Huston & Alvarez, 1990). Compared to elementary schools, middle and junior high schools provide a more impersonal environment, which meshes better with the autonomous orientation of male adolescents than with the relationship, connectedness orientation of female adolescents.

There is concern about gender equity not only in secondary schools, but in colleges and universities as well (Paludi, 1995). In some colleges, male students dominate class discussions. In one study, numerous hours of videotape supplied by twenty-four professors at Harvard University were analyzed (Krupnick, 1985). Males usually dominated the class discussion, especially in classes in which the instructor and the majority of the students were male. At one state university, female and male students participated virtually equally in class discussion (Crawford & MacLeod, 1990). Reports from all-female institutions (such as Smith and Wellesley) suggest that females there are often assertive in the classroom (Matlin, 1993).

Females interested in the sciences hear the message that they don't fit in this area not only from society but also sometimes from professors themselves. Another group of females who are vulnerable to the "don't fit in" message are women of color. In one study, female and male Latino students who were enrolled at two Ivy League colleges were interviewed (Ethier & Deaux, 1990). Some of the Latina students especially felt uncomfortable, tense, and aware of being different at the predominantly

Anglo institutions. Other Latina students perceived little discomfort or prejudicial treatment, reflecting individual variations in these ethnic minority females.

Mass-Media Influences

As already described, adolescents encounter male and female roles in their everyday interactions with parents, peers, and teachers. The messages about gender roles carried by the mass media also are important influences on adolescents' gender development (Huston & Alvarez), 1990).

Television directed at adolescents might be the most extreme in its portrayal of the sexes, especially of teenage girls (Beal, 1994). In one study, teenage girls were shown as primarily concerned with dating, shopping, and their appearance (Campbell, 1988). They were rarely depicted as interested in school or career plans. Attractive girls were often portrayed as "airheads" and intelligent girls as unattractive.

Another highly stereotyped form of programming specifically targeted toward teenage viewers is rock music videos. What adolescents see on MTV and rock music videos is highly stereotyped and slanted toward a male audience (for example, the "Beavis and Butt-head" and "Wayne and Garth" shows). Females are twice as likely to be dressed provocatively in music videos as in prime-time programming, and aggressive acts are often perpetrated by females in music videos—for example, in one scene a woman pushes a man to the ground, holds him down, and kisses him (Sherman & Dominick, 1986). MTV has been described as a teenage boy's "dreamworld," filled with beautiful, aroused women who outnumber men, who seek out and even assault men to have sex, and who always mean yes even when they say no (Jhally, 1990).

Early adolescence may be a period of heightened sensitivity to television messages about gender roles. Young adolescents increasingly view programs designed for adults that include messages about gender-appropriate behavior, especially in heterosexual relationships. Cognitively, adolescents engage in more idealistic thoughts than children do, and television certainly has its share of idealized characters with whom adolescents can identify and imitate—highly appealing models who are young, glamorous, and successful.

The world of television is highly gender-stereotyped and conveys clear messages about the relative power and importance of women and men (Huston & Alvarez, 1990). Males are overrepresented, and females are underrepresented. On virtually every type of program, males outnumber females by approximately two or three to one (Williams & others, 1986). Men and women usually engage in sex-typed occupational and family roles. In the 1970s, female characters appeared more often than males in the contexts of the home, romance, and physical appearance, males more frequently than females in the

A special concern is that, because they are more impersonal and encourage independence more than elementary schools do, most middle and junior high schools are better suited to the learning styles of males.

contexts of work, cars, and sports. By the mid 1980s, when females were portrayed outside the home, their roles were almost as likely to be nontraditional (for example, police officer or attorney) as traditional (for example, secretary or nurse). Men continued to be shown almost entirely in traditional male occupations. In one analysis, women were shown as sexual objects (that is, in scanty clothing or engaged in sexually provocative behavior) in 35 percent of the commercial television programs in 1985 (Williams & others, 1986). Such portrayals are even more frequent on music videos. Male characters are portrayed more often than female characters as aggressive, dominant, competent, autonomous, and active, while female characters are more often portrayed as passive.

Researchers have studied how early adolescent television viewing influences gender attitudes and behavior (Morgan, 1982, 1987). The researchers adopt the assumption that television carries sexist messages and that

Females are often portrayed in sexually provocative ways on MTV and in rock videos.

the more the adolescent is exposed, the greater the number of stereotyped messages the adolescent likely receives. In one investigation of eighth-grade boys and girls, heavy television viewing predicted an increased tendency to endorse traditional gender-role divisions of labor with respect to household chores (Morgan, 1987).

If television can communicate sexist messages and influence adolescents' gender behavior, might nonstereotyped gender messages on television reduce sexist behavior? One major effort to reduce gender stereotyping was the television series "Freestyle" (Johnston, Etteman, & Davidson, 1980). The series was designed to counteract career stereotypes in 9- to 12-year-olds. After watching "Freestyle," both girls and boys were more open to nontraditional career possibilities. The benefits of "Freestyle" were greatest for students who viewed the TV series in the classroom and who participated in discussion groups about the show led by their teacher. Classroom discussion was especially helpful in altering boys' beliefs, which were initially more stereotyped than girls'.

However, in one study with young adolescents 12 to 13 years of age, the strategy of nonstereotyped television programming backfired (Durkin & Hutchins, 1984). The young adolescents watched sketches about people who held nontraditional jobs, such as a male secretary, a male nurse, and a female plumber. After viewing the series, the adolescents still held traditional views about careers, and in some cases they were even more disapproving of the alternative careers than they had been before watching the TV series. Thus, once stereotypes are strongly in place, it is difficult to modify them.

Cognitive Influences

So far, we have discussed a number of biological and social influences on adolescents' gender behavior. Cognitive theories stress that adolescents actively construct their gender world. In this section, we look at two cognitive theories: the cognitive developmental theory of gender and gender schema theory.

Cognitive Developmental Theory

According to the **cognitive developmental theory of gender,** *children's gender-typing occurs after they have developed a concept of gender. Once they begin to consistently conceive of themselves as male or female, children often organize their world on the basis of gender.* Based on Piaget's theory and initially proposed by developmentalist Lawrence Kohlberg (1966), the cognitive developmental theory of gender proceeds in the following fashion: A young girl decides, "I am a girl. I want to do girl things; therefore, the opportunity to do girl things is rewarding." Having acquired the ability to categorize, children strive toward consistency in using categories and in their behavior.

Kohlberg's cognitive developmental theory emphasizes that the main changes in gender development occur in childhood. By the concrete operational stage (the third stage in Piaget's theory, entered at 6 to 7 years of age), children understand gender constancy—that a male is still a male regardless of whether he wears pants or a skirt, or whether his hair is short or long, for example (Tavris & Wade, 1984).

Childhood decides.

—Jean-Paul Sartre

Are there any cognitive developmental changes in adolescence that might influence gender behavior? The abstract, idealized, logical characteristics of formal operational thought mean that adolescents now have the cognitive capacity to analyze their self and decide what they want their gender identity to be. Adolescence is the developmental period when individuals begin to focus increased attention on vocational and lifestyle choices. With their increased cognitive skills, adolescents become more aware of the gender-based nature of vocational and lifestyle behavior. As adolescents pursue an identity— "Who am I, what am I all about, and where am I going in life?"—gender roles are one area in which they have choices to make. Recall the discussion of gender and identity in the last chapter. As females have developed stronger vocational interests, sex differences (adolescent males explore and make commitments to a vocational role more than adolescent females) are now turning into similarities. However, as adolescent females pursue an identity, they often show a greater interest in relationships and emotional bonds than adolescent males do. In sum, both the changes ushered in by formal operational thought and the increased interest in identity concerns lead adolescents to examine and redefine their gender attitudes and behavior.

Gender Schema Theory

A **schema** *is a cognitive structure, a network of associations that organizes and guides an individual's perceptions. A* **gender schema** *organizes the world in terms of female and male.* **Gender schema theory** *states that an individual's attention and behavior are guided by an internal motivation to conform to gender-based sociocultural standards and stereotypes.* Gender schema theory suggests that "gender typing" occurs when individuals are ready to encode and organize information along the lines of what is considered appropriate or typical for males and females in society. Gender schema theory emphasizes the active construction of gender but also accepts that societies determine which schemas are important and the associations involved (Ruble & Martin, 1997). In most cultures, these definitions involve a sprawling network of gender-linked associations, which encompass not only features directly related to female and male persons—such as anatomy, reproductive function, division of labor, and personality attributes—but also features more remotely or metaphorically related to sex, such as an abstract shape's angularity or roundness and the periodicity of the moon. No other dichotomy of life's experiences seems to have as many features linked to it as does the distinction between being male and being female (Paludi, 1995).

As a real-life example of gender schema's influence on adolescents, consider a 17-year-old high school student deciding which hobby to try from among the many available possibilities. The student could ask about how expensive each possibility is, whether it can be done in cold weather, whether or not it can be done during the school week, whether it will interfere with studying, and so on. But the adolescent also is likely to look at the hobby through the lens of gender and ask: "What sex is the hobby? What sex am I? Do they match? If they do, I will consider the hobby further. If not, I will reject it." This student consciously may not be aware of his or her gender schema's influence on the decision of which hobby to pursue. Indeed, in many of our everyday encounters, we consciously are not aware of how gender schemas affect our behavior.

GENDER STEREOTYPES, SIMILARITIES, AND DIFFERENCES

How pervasive is gender stereotyping? What are the real differences between boys and girls?

Gender Stereotyping

Gender stereotypes *are broad categories that reflect our impressions and beliefs about females and males.* All stereotypes, whether they are based on gender, ethnicity, or other groupings, refer to an image of what the typical member of a particular social category is like. The world is extremely complex. Every day we are confronted with thousands of different stimuli. The use of stereotypes is one way we simplify this complexity. If we simply assign a label (such as the quality of softness) to someone, we then have much less to consider when we think about the individual. However, once labels are assigned they are remarkably difficult to abandon, even in the face of contradictory evidence.

Many stereotypes are so general they are ambiguous. Consider the stereotypes for "masculine" and "feminine." Diverse behaviors can be called on to support each stereotype, such as scoring a touchdown or growing facial hair for "masculine" and playing with dolls or wearing lipstick for "feminine." The stereotype may be modified in the face of cultural change. At one point in history, muscular development may be thought of as masculine; at another point, masculinity might be associated with a more lithe, slender physique. The behaviors popularly agreed upon as reflecting a stereotype can also fluctuate according to socioeconomic circumstances. For example, lower socioeconomic groups might be more likely than higher socioeconomic groups to include "rough and tough" as part of a masculine stereotype.

> *If you are going to generalize about women, you will find yourself up to here in exceptions.*
>
> —Dolores Hitchens,
> *In a House Unknown* (1973)

Even though the behaviors that are supposed to fit the stereotype often do not, the label itself can have significant consequences for the individual. Labeling a male "feminine" and a female "masculine" can produce significant social reactions to the individuals in terms of status and acceptance in groups, for example.

How widespread is feminine and masculine stereotyping? According to a far-ranging study of college students in thirty countries, stereotyping of females and males is pervasive (Williams & Best, 1982). Males were widely believed to be dominant, independent, aggressive, achievement oriented, and enduring, while females were widely believed to be nurturant, affiliative, less esteemed, and more helpful in times of distress.

In a more recent investigation, women and men who lived in more highly developed countries perceived themselves as more similar than did women and men who lived in less-developed countries (Williams & Best, 1989). In the more highly developed countries, women were more likely to attend college and be gainfully employed. Thus, as sexual equality increases, male and female stereotypes, as well as actual behavioral differences, may diminish. In this investigation, women were more likely to perceive similarity between the sexes than men were (Williams & Best, 1989). And the sexes were perceived more similarly in Christian than in Muslim societies.

Stereotypes often are negative and sometimes involve prejudice and discrimination. **Sexism** *is prejudice and discrimination against an individual because of her or his sex.* A person who says that women cannot be competent lawyers is expressing sexism; so is a person who says that men cannot be competent nursery school teachers. Prejudice and discrimination against women have a long history, and they continue. Consider a true story about Ann Hopkins, one of only a few female accountants employed by the very large firm Price Waterhouse (Fiske & others, 1991). Hopkins had performed admirably in her work at Price Waterhouse. She had more billable hours than any of her 87 male co-workers and had brought in $25 million in new business for the firm. However, when a partnership in the firm opened up, Hopkins was not chosen. The executives at Price Waterhouse said that she had weak interpersonal skills, needed a "charm school" course, and was too "macho." Hopkins filed a lawsuit against Price Waterhouse. After a lengthy trial, the U.S. Supreme Court ruled in Hopkins's favor, stating that gender-based stereotyping played a significant role in her being denied a partnership in the firm.

Sexism can be obvious, as when a chemistry professor tells a female premed student that women belong in the home (Matlin, 1993). Sexism can also be more subtle, as when the word *girl* is used to refer to a mature woman. In one recent analysis, an attempt was made to distinguish between old-fashioned and modern sexism (Swim & others, 1995). *Old-fashioned sexism* is characterized by endorsement of traditional gender roles, differential treatment for men and women, and a stereotype that females are less competent than males. Like modern racism, *modern sexism* is characterized by the denial that there is still discrimination, antagonism toward women's demands, and lack of support for policies designed to help women (for example, in education and work). Table 11.1 shows the types of items that were developed to measure old-fashioned and modern sexism.

Gender Similarities and Differences

There is a growing consensus in gender research that differences between the sexes have often been exaggerated (Hyde & Plant, 1995). Remember our discussion of reducing sexist research in psychology in chapter 2. It is not unusual to find statements such as the following: "While only 32 percent of females were found to . . . , fully 37 percent of the males were. . . ." This difference of 5 percent likely is a very small difference, and may or may not even be statistically significant or capable of being replicated in a separate study (Denmark & Paludi, 1993). And generalizations that claim that males outperform females, such as "males outperform females in math," do not mean that all males outperform all females. Rather, such a statement means, in the case

"So according to the stereotype, you can put two and two together, but I can read the handwriting on the wall."

of our example, that the average math achievement scores for males at certain ages are higher than the average math achievement scores for females at those ages. The math achievement scores of females and males overlap considerably, so that while an *average* difference might favor males, many females have higher math achievement than many males. Further, there is a tendency to think of differences between females and males as biologically based. Remember that when differences occur, they might be socioculturally based.

> *There is more difference within the sexes than between them.*
>
> —Ivy Compton-Burnett

Let's now examine some of the differences between the sexes, keeping in mind that (a) the differences are averages—not all females versus all males; (b) even when differences are reported, there is considerable overlap between the sexes; and (c) the differences may be due primarily to biological factors, sociocultural factors, or both (Caplan & Caplan, 1994). First, we examine physical and biological differences, and then we turn to cognitive and social differences.

Physical/Biological

From conception on, females are less likely than males to die, and females are less likely than males to develop physical or mental disorders. Estrogen strengthens the immune system, making females more resistant to infection, for example. Female hormones also signal the liver to produce more "good" cholesterol, which makes their blood vessels more elastic than males'. Testosterone

TABLE 11.1

Types of Items Developed to Measure Old-Fashioned and Modern Sexism

Old-Fashioned Sexism

Women are generally not as smart as men.

I would not be as comfortable having a woman for a boss as I would be having a man for a boss.

It is more important to encourage boys than to encourage girls to participate in athletics.

Women are not as capable as men of thinking logically.

When both parents are employed and their child gets sick at school, the school should call the mother rather than the father.

Modern Sexism

Discrimination against women is no longer a problem in the United States.

Women rarely miss out on good jobs because of sexist discrimination.

It is rare to see women treated in a sexist manner on television.

On the average, people in our society treat husbands and wives equally.

Society has reached the point where women and men have equal opportunities for achievement.

It is not easy to understand why women's groups are still concerned about societal limitations on women's opportunities.

It is not easy to understand the anger of women's groups in America.

Over the past few years, the government and news media have been showing more concern about the treatment of women than is warranted by women's actual experiences.

Note: Endorsement of the above items reflects old-fashioned sexism and modern sexism, respectively. The wording of the items has been changed from the original research for ease of understanding.

From Janet K. Swim, et al., "Sexism and Racism: Old-Fashioned and Modern Prejudices" in *Journal of Personality and Social Psychology,* 68:212. Copyright © 1995 by the American Psychological Association. Some data adapted from McConahay's Modern Racism Scale, 1986. Reprinted with permission.

triggers the production of low-density lipoprotein, which clogs blood vessels. Males have twice the risk of coronary disease as females. Higher levels of stress hormones cause faster clotting in males, but also higher blood pressure than in females. Adult females have about twice the body fat of their male counterparts, most of it concentrated around breasts and hips. In males, fat is more likely to go to the abdomen. On the average, males grow to be 10 percent taller than females. Male hormones promote the growth of long bones; female hormones stop such growth at puberty.

Similarity was the rule rather than the exception in a recent study of metabolic activity in the brains of females and males (Gur & others, 1995). The exceptions involved areas of the brain that involve emotional expression and physical expression (which are more active in females). Overall, though, there are many physical differences between females and males. Are there as many cognitive differences?

Cognitive

According to a classic review of gender differences in 1974, Eleanor Maccoby and Carol Jacklin (1974) concluded that males have better math skills and better visuospatial ability (the kind of skills an architect needs to design a building's angles and dimensions), while females have better verbal abilities. More recently, Maccoby (1987) revised her conclusion about several gender dimensions. She said that the accumulation of research evidence now suggests that differences in verbal ability between females and males have virtually disappeared, but that the math and visuospatial differences still exist. Another recent analysis also found that the spatial difference favors males (Voyer, Voyer, & Bryden, 1995).

Some experts in the gender area, such as Janet Shibley Hyde (1993), believe that the cognitive differences between females and males have been exaggerated. For example, Hyde argues that there is considerable overlap in the distributions of females' and males' scores on math and visuospatial tasks. Figure 11.1 shows that although males outperform females on visuospatial tasks, their scores overlap substantially with females' scores. Thus, while the *average* difference favors males, many females have higher scores on visuospatial tasks than most males do.

Figure~11.1

Mathematics Performance of Males and Females.
Notice that, although an average male's mathematics performance is higher than an average female's, the overlap between the sexes is substantial. Not all males have better mathematics performance than all females—the substantial overlap indicates that, although the average score of males is higher, many females outperform many males on such tasks.

Socioemotional

Most males are more active and aggressive than most females (Fabes, Knight, & Higgins, 1995; Maccoby & Jacklin, 1974). The consistent difference in aggression often appears in children's development as early as 2 years of age.

Females and males also differ in their social connectedness. Boys often define themselves apart from their caregivers and peers, while girls emphasize their social ties. As adults, females often become more caring, supporting, and empathic, while males become more independent, self-reliant, and unexpressive.

Unless you've been isolated on a mountaintop away from people, television, magazines, and newspapers, you probably know the master stereotype about gender and emotion: She is emotional, he is not. This stereotype is a powerful and pervasive image in our culture (Shields, 1991).

Is this stereotype confirmed when researchers study the nature of emotional experiences in females and males? Researchers have found that females and males are often more alike in the way they experience emotion than the master stereotype would lead us to believe. Females and males often use the same facial expressions, adopt the same language, and describe their emotional experiences similarly when they keep diaries about their life experiences. Thus, the master stereotype that females are emotional and males are not is simply that—a stereotype. Given the complexity and vast territory of emotion, we should not be surprised that this stereotype is not supported when actual emotional experiences are examined. For many emotional experiences, researchers do not find differences between females and males—both sexes are equally likely to feel love, jealousy, anxiety in new social situations, anger when they are insulted, grief when close relationships end, and embarrassment when they make mistakes in public (Tavris & Wade, 1984).

For some areas of achievement, gender differences are so large they can best be described as nonoverlapping. For example, no major league baseball players are female, and 96 percent of all registered nurses are female. In contrast, many measures of achievement-related behaviors do not reveal gender differences. For example, girls show just as much persistence at tasks. The question of whether males and females differ in their expectations for success at various achievement tasks is not yet settled.

Gender Controversy

Not all psychologists agree that differences between females and males are rare or small. Alice Eagly (1995) stated that such a belief arose from a feminist commitment to similarity between the sexes as a route to political equality, and from piecemeal and inadequate interpretations of relevant empirical research. Many feminists express a fear that differences between females

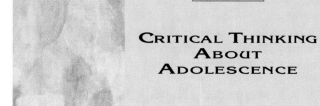

and males will be interpreted as deficiencies in females and as biologically based, which could promote the old stereotypes that women are inferior to men (Unger & Crawford, 1992). According to Eagly, contemporary psychology has produced a large body of research that reveals that behavior is sex differentiated to varying extents.

Evolutionary psychologist David Buss (1995) argues that men and women differ psychologically in those domains in which they have faced different adaptive problems across their evolutionary history. In all other domains, predicts Buss, the sexes will be found to be psychologically similar. He cites males' superiority in the cognitive domain of spatial rotation. This ability is essential for hunting, in which the trajectory of a projectile must anticipate the trajectory of a prey animal as each moves through space and time. Buss also cites a sex difference in casual sex, with men engaging in this behavior more than women do. In one study, men said that ideally they would like to have more than eighteen sex partners in their lifetime, whereas women stated that ideally they would like to have only four or five (Buss & Schmitt, 1993). In another study, 75 percent of the men but none of the women approached by an attractive stranger of the opposite sex consented to a request for sex (Clark & Hatfield, 1989). Such sex differences, says Buss, are exactly the type predicted by evolutionary psychology.

In sum, controversy swirls about the issue of whether sex differences are rare and small or common and large (Maracek, 1995), evidence that negotiating the science and politics of gender is not an easy task.

Gender in Context

When thinking about gender similarities and differences, keep in mind that the context in which females and males are thinking, feeling, and behaving should be taken into account. To see how context affects gender, let's further explore gender in relation to helping behavior and emotion.

Males are more likely to help in contexts in which a perceived danger is present and they feel competent to help (Eagly & Crowley, 1986). For example, males are more likely than females to help a person who is stranded by the roadside with a flat tire; automobile problems are an area about which many males feel a sense of competence. By contrast, when the context involves volunteering time to help a child with a personal problem, females are more likely to help than males are, because there is little danger present and females feel more competent at nurturing. In many cultures, girls show more caregiving behavior than boys do (Blakemore, 1993). However, in the few cultures where they both care for younger siblings on a regular basis, girls and boys are similar in their tendencies to nurture (Whiting, 1989).

Context is also relevant to gender differences in the display of emotions (Anderson & Leaper, 1996; Shields, 1991). Consider anger. Males are more likely to show anger toward strangers, especially other males, when they feel that they have been challenged. Males also are more likely than females to turn their anger into aggressive action (Tavris & Wade, 1984). Differences between males and females in the display of emotion occur most often in the contexts that highlight social roles and relationships. For example, females are more likely than males to discuss emotion in terms of interpersonal relationships (Saarni, 1988) and to express fear and sadness, especially when communicating with their friends and family.

At this point we have discussed a number of ideas about what gender is; biological, social, and cognitive influences on gender; and gender stereotyping, similarities, and differences. A summary of these ideas is presented in concept table 11.1.

ONCEPT TABLE 11.1

The Nature of Gender, Biological, Social, and Cognitive Influences, and Gender Stereotypes, Similarities, and Differences

Concept	Processes/ Related Ideas	Characteristics/Description
What Is Gender?	Its nature	Gender refers to the social dimension of being male or female. A gender role is a set of expectations that prescribes how females or males should think, act, and feel.
Biological, Social, and Cognitive Influences on Gender	Biological influences	Because of pubertal change, sexuality plays a more important role in adolescents' general development than it does in children's development. Puberty's effects are socially mediated. Freud's and Erikson's ideas promote the idea that anatomy is destiny. Today's developmentalists are all interactionists when biological and environmental influences on gender are at issue.
	Social influences	Both identification theory and social learning theory emphasize the adoption of parents' gender characteristics. Peers are especially adept at rewarding gender-appropriate behavior. There is still concern about gender inequity in education. A special concern is that middle schools are better suited for males because these schools have an impersonal environment that promotes independence. Despite improvements, TV still portrays males as more competent than females. The idealized characters on television may especially appeal to adolescents' idealized thoughts.
	Cognitive influences	Both cognitive developmental and gender schema theories emphasize the role of cognition in gender development.
Gender Stereotypes, Similarities, and Differences	Stereotypes	Gender stereotypes are widespread around the world, especially emphasizing the male's power and the female's nurturance.
	Similarities and differences	A number of physical and biological differences exist between females and males. Some experts, such as Hyde, argue that cognitive differences between males and females have been exaggerated. In terms of socioemotional development, males are more aggressive and active than females, while females emphasize social ties more than males do.
	Gender controversy	Currently, there is controversy over the issue of how similar or different females and males are in a number of areas.
	Gender in context	Context is an important dimension in understanding gender.

GENDER-ROLE CLASSIFICATION

How were gender roles classified in the past? What is androgyny? Is a strong masculine orientation related to problem behaviors in adolescent males? What is gender-role transcendence?

The Past

Not too long ago, it was accepted that boys should grow up to be masculine and that girls should grow up to be feminine, that boys are made of frogs and snails and puppy dogs' tails, and that girls are made of sugar and spice and all that's nice. Today, diversity characterizes gender roles and the feedback individuals receive from their culture. A girl's mother might promote femininity, the girl might be close friends with a tomboy, and the girl's teachers at school might encourage her assertiveness.

In the past, the well-adjusted male was expected to be independent, aggressive, and power oriented. The well-adjusted female was expected to be dependent, nurturant, and uninterested in power. Further, masculine characteristics were considered to be healthy and good by society; female characteristics were considered to be undesirable. A classic study in the early 1970s summarized the traits and behaviors that college students believed were characteristic of males and those they believed were characteristic of females (Broverman & others, 1972). The traits clustered into two groups that were labeled "instrumental" and "expressive." The instrumental traits paralleled the male's purposeful, competent entry into the outside world to gain goods for his family; the expressive traits paralleled the female's responsibility to be warm and emotional in the home. Such stereotypes harm females more than males because the characteristics assigned to males are more valued than those assigned to females. Such beliefs and stereotypes have led to the negative treatment of females because of their sex (sexism). Females receive less attention in schools, are less visible in leading roles on television, are rarely depicted as competent, dominant characters in children's books, are paid less than males even when they have more education, and are underrepresented in decision-making roles throughout our society, from corporate executive suites to Congress.

Androgyny

In the 1970s, as both males and females became dissatisfied with the burdens imposed by their strictly stereotyped roles, alternatives to "masculinity" and "femininity" were explored. Instead of thinking of masculinity and femininity as a continuum, with more of one meaning less of the other, it was proposed that individuals could show both expressive *and* instrumental traits. This thinking led to the development of the concept of **androgyny,** *the presence of a high degree of desirable masculine and feminine characteristics in the same individual* (Bem, 1977; Spence & Helmreich, 1978). The androgynous individual might be a male who is assertive (masculine) and nurturant (feminine), or a female who is dominant (masculine) and sensitive to others' feelings (feminine).

Measures have been developed to assess androgyny. One of the most widely used gender measures, the Bem Sex-Role Inventory, was constructed by a leading early proponent of androgyny, Sandra Bem. To see what the items on Bem's measure are like, see table 11.2. Based on their responses to the items in the Bem sex-role inventory, individuals are classified as having one of four gender-role orientations: masculine, feminine, androgynous, or undifferentiated (see figure 11.2). The androgynous individual is simply a female or a male who has a high degree of both feminine (expressive) and masculine (instrumental) traits. No new characteristics are used to describe the androgynous individual. A feminine individual is high on feminine (expressive) traits and low on masculine (instrumental) traits; a masculine individual shows the reverse of these traits. An undifferentiated person is not high on feminine or masculine traits.

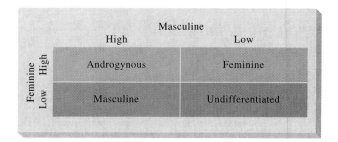

Figure~11.2

Gender-Role Classification.

Androgynous individuals are described as more flexible and more mentally healthy than either masculine or feminine individuals. Individuals who are undifferentiated are the least competent. To some degree, though, the context influences which gender role is most adaptive. In close relationships, a feminine or androgynous gender role may be more desirable because of the expressive nature of close relationships. However, a masculine or androgynous gender role may be more desirable in academic and work settings because of the instrumental nature of these settings. And the culture in which individuals live also plays an important role in determining what is adaptive. On the one hand, increasing numbers of children in the United States and other modernized countries such as Sweden are being raised to behave in androgynous ways. On the other hand, traditional gender roles continue to dominate the cultures of many countries around the world. Sociocultural Worlds of Adolescence discusses traditional gender roles in Egypt and China.

Can and should androgyny be taught to children and adolescents in school? In one investigation, tenth-through twelfth-grade students from three high schools in British Columbia were given a twenty-unit course in gender roles (Kahn & Richardson, 1983). Students analyzed the history and modern development of male and female gender roles and evaluated the function of traditionally accepted stereotypes of females and males. The course centered on student discussion, supplemented by films, videotapes, and guest speakers. The materials included exercises to heighten students' awareness of their attitudes and beliefs, role reversal of typical gender-role behavior, role-playing of difficult work and family conflict circumstances, and assertiveness training for direct, honest communication.

A total of 59 students participated in the gender-role course. To determine whether the course changed the adolescents' gender-role orientation, these students were compared to fifty-nine students from the same schools who did not take the gender-role course. Prior to the start of the course, all students were given the Bem Sex-Role Inventory. No differences between the two groups were found at that time. After the students completed the course, they and the control group were given the Attitudes Toward Women Scale (Spence & Helmreich, 1972). In

Santrock: Adolescence

TABLE 11.2

The Bem Sex-Role Inventory: Are You Androgynous?

The following items are from the Bem Sex-Role Inventory. To find out whether you score as androgynous, first rate yourself on each item, on a scale from 1 (never or almost never true) to 7 (always or almost always true).

1. self-reliant	16. strong personality	31. makes decisions easily	46. aggressive
2. yielding	17. loyal	32. compassionate	47. gullible
3. helpful	18. unpredictable	33. sincere	48. inefficient
4. defends own beliefs	19. forceful	34. self-sufficient	49. acts as a leader
5. cheerful	20. feminine	35. eager to soothe hurt feelings	50. childlike
6. moody	21. reliable	36. conceited	51. adaptable
7. independent	22. analytical	37. dominant	52. individualistic
8. shy	23. sympathetic	38. soft-spoken	53. does not use harsh language
9. conscientious	24. jealous	39. likable	54. unsystematic
10. athletic	25. has leadership abilities	40. masculine	55. competitive
11. affectionate	26. sensitive to the needs of others	41. warm	56. loves children
12. theatrical	27. truthful	42. solemn	57. tactful
13. assertive	28. willing to take risks	43. willing to take a stand	58. ambitious
14. flatterable	29. understanding	44. tender	59. gentle
15. happy	30. secretive	45. friendly	60. conventional

(a) Add up your ratings for items 1, 4, 7, 10, 13, 16, 19, 22, 25, 28, 31, 34, 37, 40, 43, 46, 49, 55, and 58. Divide the total by 20. That is your masculinity score.

(b) Add up your ratings for items 2, 5, 8, 11, 14, 17, 20, 23, 26, 29, 32, 35, 38, 41, 44, 47, 50, 53, 56, and 59. Divide the total by 20. That is your femininity score.

(c) If your masculinity score is above 4.9 (the approximate median for the masculinity scale) and your femininity score is above 4.9 (the approximate femininity median) then you would be classified as androgynous on Bem's scale.

From Janet S. Hyde, *Half the Human Experience: The Psychology of Women,* 3d ed. Copyright © 1985 D. C. Heath and Company, Lexington, KY. Reprinted by permission.

two of the schools, students who took the gender-role course had more-liberal attitudes about the female's role in society than students who did not take the course. In these schools, the students were primarily girls who chose to take the course as an elective. In the third school, students who took the gender-role course actually had more conservative attitudes toward the female's role in society than those who did not take the course. The gender-role class in the third school was required and was made up almost equally of males and females.

Another attempt to produce a more androgynous gender-role orientation in students also met with mixed results (Guttentag & Bray, 1976). The curriculum lasted for 1 year and was implemented in the kindergarten, fifth, and ninth grades. It involved books, discussion materials, and classroom exercises. The program was most successful with the fifth-graders and least successful with the ninth-graders, who displayed a boomerang effect of developing a more rigid gender-role orientation. The program's success varied from class to class, being most effective when the teacher produced sympathetic reaction in the peer group. However, some classes ridiculed and rejected the curriculum.

Ethical concerns are raised when the program involves teaching children and adolescents to depart from socially approved behavior patterns, especially when there is no evidence of extreme sex typing in the groups to whom the interventions are applied. The advocates of androgyny programs believe that traditional sex typing is psychologically harmful for all children and adolescents and that it has prevented many girls and women from experiencing equal opportunity. While some people believe that androgyny is more adaptive than either a traditional masculine or a traditional feminine pattern, ignoring the imbalance within our culture that values masculinity more than femininity is impossible.

Traditional Masculinity and Problem Behaviors in Adolescent Males

In our discussion of masculinity so far, we have discussed how the masculine role has been accorded a prominent status in the United States, as well as in most other cultures.

Gender Roles in Egypt and China

In recent decades, roles assumed by males and females in the United States have become increasingly similar—that is, androgynous. In many countries, though, gender roles have remained more gender-specific. For example, in Egypt the division of labor between Egyptian males and females is dramatic: Egyptian males are socialized to work in the public sphere, females in the private world of home and child rearing. The Islamic religion dictates that the man's duty is to provide for his family, the woman's duty to care for her family and household (Dickersheid & others, 1988). Any deviations from this traditional gender-role orientation are severely disapproved of.

Egypt is not the only country in which males and females are socialized to behave, think, and feel in strongly gender-specific ways. Kenya and Nepal are two other cultures in which children are brought up under very strict gender-specific guidelines (Munroe, Himmin, & Munroe, 1984). In the People's Republic of China, the female's status has historically been lower than the male's. The teachings of the fifth-century B.C. Chinese philosopher Confucius were used to reinforce the concept of the female as an inferior being. Beginning with the 1949 revolution in China, women began to achieve more economic freedom and more-equal status in marital relationships. However, even with the sanctions of a socialist government, the old patriarchal traditions of male supremacy in China have not been completely uprooted. Chinese women still make considerably less money than Chinese men in comparable positions, and in rural China a tradition of male supremacy still governs many women's lives.

Thus, although females in China have made considerable strides, complete equality remains a distant objective. And in many cultures, such as Egypt and other countries where the Muslim religion predominates, gender-specific behavior is pronounced, and females are not given access to high-status positions.

In Egypt near the Aswan Dam, women are returning from the Nile River, where they have filled their water jugs. How might gender-role socialization for girls in Egypt compare to that in the United States?

In China, females and males are usually socialized to behave, feel, and think differently. The old patriarchal traditions of male supremacy have not been completely uprooted. Chinese women still make considerably less money than Chinese men, and, in rural China (such as here in the Lixian village of Sichuan), male supremacy still governs many women's lives.

Gender Roles and the Future

In the last two decades, there has been considerable change in gender roles in the United States. How much change have you personally experienced? What changes do you think will occur in gender roles in the twenty-first century? Or do you believe that gender roles will stay about the way they are now?

There is a practical side to considering these questions. How will you attempt to raise your children, in terms of gender roles? Will gender neutrality be your goal? Will you encourage more traditional distinctions? Evaluating gender roles and the future encourages you to think critically by *applying developmental concepts to enhance personal adaptation.*

However, might there be a negative side to traditional masculinity, especially in adolescence? An increasing number of gender theorists and researchers believe there is.

Joseph Pleck and his colleagues (Pleck, 1983; Pleck, Sonnenstein, & Ku, in press) believe that what defines traditional masculinity in many Western societies includes engaging in certain behaviors that, although officially socially disapproved, validate masculinity. That is, in the male adolescent culture, male adolescents perceive that they are more masculine, and that others will perceive them as more masculine, if they engage in premarital sex, drink alcohol and take drugs, and participate in delinquent activities.

In one investigation, the gender-role orientation and problem behaviors of 1,680 15- to 19-year-old males were assessed (Pleck, Sonnenstein, & Ku, in press). In this study—referred to as the National Survey of Adolescent Males—there was strong evidence that problem behaviors in adolescent males are associated with their attitudes toward masculinity. The adolescent males who reported traditional beliefs about masculinity (for example, endorsing such items as "A young man should be tough, even if he's not big"; "It is essential for a guy to get respect from others"; and "Men are always ready for sex") also were likely to say that they had school difficulties, engaged in alcohol and drug use, participated in delinquent activities, and were sexually active.

In another recent investigation by Joseph Pleck and his colleagues (1994), the roles of risk and protective influences in adolescent males' problem behaviors were studied. Risk factors for problems included low parental education, being the son of a teenage mother, living in a mother-headed household or a nonmaternal family (father only, foster family, grandparents, alone), lenient family rules, and infrequent church attendance. Protective factors included strict family rules and frequent church attendance.

The idea that male problem behaviors have something to do with "masculinity" has recently gotten the attention of policymakers. Louis Sullivan (1991), former U.S. Department of Health and Human Services secretary, called for action to address a generation whose manhood is measured by the caliber of gun he carries or the number of children he fathers. In a similar vein, Virginia Governor Douglas Wilder (1991) urged policymakers to get across the message that, contrary to what many of today's youths think, making babies is no act of manhood. Addressing and challenging traditional beliefs about masculinity in adolescent males may have the positive outcome of helping reduce their problem behaviors.

Gender-Role Transcendence

Although the concept of androgyny was an improvement over exclusive notions of femininity and masculinity, it has turned out to be less of a panacea than many of its early proponents envisioned (Paludi, 1995). Some theorists, such as Pleck (1983), believe that the idea of androgyny should be replaced with **gender-role transcendence,** *the belief that, when an individual's competence is at issue, it should not be conceptualized on the basis of masculinity, femininity, or androgyny, but rather on a person basis.* Thus, rather than merging gender roles or stereotyping people as "masculine" or "feminine," Pleck believes we should begin to think about people as people. However, both the concepts of androgyny and gender-role transcendence draw attention away from women's unique needs and the power imbalance between women and men in most cultures (Hare-Muston & Maracek, 1988).

> To be meek, patient, tactful, modest, honorable, brave, is not to be either manly or womanly; it is to be humane.
>
> —Jane Harrison

DEVELOPMENTAL CHANGES AND JUNCTURES

What changes take place during early adolescence that might affect gender roles? Is early adolescence a critical juncture in female development?

Early Adolescence and Gender Intensification

As females and males experience many physical and social changes during early adolescence, they have to come to terms with new definitions of their gender roles (Belansky & Clements, 1992; Huston & Alvarez, 1990). During early adolescence, individuals develop the adult, physical aspects of their sex. Some theorists and researchers have proposed that, with the onset of puberty, girls and boys experience an intensification in gender-related expectations. The **gender intensification hypothesis** *states that psychological and behavioral differences between boys and girls become greater during early adolescence because of increased socialization pressures to conform to traditional masculine and feminine gender roles* (Hill & Lynch, 1983; Lynch, 1991). Puberty's role in gender intensification might involve a signaling to socializing others—parents, peers, and teachers, for example—that the adolescent is beginning to approach adulthood and, therefore, should begin to act more in ways that resemble the stereotypical female or male adult. In one study, sex differences in gender-role attitudes increased across the early adolescent years. Gender-role attitudes were measured by the Attitudes toward Women Scale (Galambos & others, 1985), which assesses the extent to which adolescents approve of gender-based division of roles. For example, the adolescent is asked such questions as whether girls should have the same freedom as boys. Other researchers also have reported evidence of gender intensification in early adolescence (Hill & Lynch, 1983). However, not every female and male shows gender intensification during puberty, and the family context recently has been found to influence how strongly gender intensification occurs (Crouter, Manke, & McHale, 1995).

Is Early Adolescence a Critical Juncture for Females?

Carol Gilligan has conducted extensive interviews with girls from 6 to 18 years of age (Gilligan, 1992; Gilligan, Brown, & Rogers, 1990). She and her colleagues have reported that girls consistently reveal detailed knowledge about human relationships that is based on listening and watching what happens between people. According to Gilligan, girls can sensitively pick up different rhythms in relationships and often are able to follow the pathways of feelings. Gilligan believes that girls experience life differently than boys do; in Gilligan's words, girls have a "different voice."

Gilligan also states that girls come to a critical juncture in their development when they reach adolescence. Gilligan says that, in early adolescence, (usually around 11 to 12 years of age), girls become aware that their intense interest in intimacy is not prized by the male-dominated culture, even though society values women as caring and altruistic. The dilemma, says Gilligan, is that girls are presented with a choice that makes them appear either selfish (if they become independent and self-sufficient) or selfless (if they remain responsive to others). Gilligan states that, as young adolescent girls experience this dilemma, they increasingly "silence" their "different voice." They become less confident and more tentative in offering their opinions, which often persists into adulthood. Some researchers believe that this self-doubt and ambivalence too often translates into depression and eating disorders among adolescent girls.

The gender intensification hypothesis states that psychological and behavioral differences between boys and girls become greater during early adolescence because of increased socialization pressures to conform to traditional masculine and feminine gender roles. Puberty's role in gender intensification may involve a signaling to socializing others—parents, peers, and teachers, for example—that the adolescent is beginning to approach adulthood and, therefore, should begin to act in ways that resemble the stereotypical female or male adult.

Carol Gilligan (right, in maroon dress) with some of the females she has interviewed about their relationships with others. According to Gilligan, girls experience life differently than boys do; in Gilligan's words, girls have a "different voice." She believes that relationships color every aspect of a female's life. Girls use conversation to expand and understand relationships, and they see people as mutually dependent. Gilligan believes that adolescence is a special juncture in the development of females because it is during this time that girls become aware that their intense interest in intimacy is not prized by the male-dominated culture, even though society values women as caring and altruistic. The dilemma is that girls are presented with a choice that makes them look either selfish or selfless. Gilligan believes that, as adolescent girls experience this dilemma, they increasingly silence their distinctive voice. She thinks that society needs to acknowledge the authenticity and importance of females' distinctive relationship voices.

Contextual variations influence whether adolescent girls silence their "voice." In one recent study, Susan Harter and her colleagues (1996) found evidence for a refinement of Gilligan's position, in that feminine girls reported lower levels of voice in public contexts (at school with teachers and classmates) but not in more private interpersonal relationships (with close friends and parents). However, androgynous girls reported a strong voice in all contexts. Harter and her colleagues also found that adolescent girls who buy into societal messages that females should be seen and not heard are at most risk in their development. The greatest liabilities occurred for females who not only lacked a "voice" but who emphasized the importance of appearance. In focusing on their outer selves, these girls face formidable challenges in meeting the punishing cultural standards of attractiveness.

Some critics argue that Gilligan and her colleagues overemphasize differences in gender. One of those critics is developmentalist Eleanor Maccoby, who says that Gilligan exaggerates the differences between males and females in intimacy and connectedness. Other critics fault Gilligan's research strategy, which rarely includes a comparison group of boys or statistical analysis. Instead, Gilligan conducts extensive interviews with girls and then provides excerpts from the girls' narratives to buttress her ideas. Other critics fear that Gilligan's findings reinforce stereotypes—females as nurturing and sacrificing, for example—that might undermine females' struggle for equality. These critics say that Gilligan's "different voice" perhaps should be called "the voice of the victim." What we should be stressing, say these critics, is more opportunities for females to reach higher levels of achievement and self-determination.

In reply, revisionists such as Gilligan say that their work provides a way to liberate females and transform a society that has far too long discriminated against females. They also say that if females' approach to life is acknowledged as authentic, women will no longer have to act like men. The revisionists argue that females' sensitivity in relationships is a special gift in our culture. Influenced by Gilligan's and other feminists' thinking, some schools are beginning to incorporate the feminine voice into their curriculum. For example, at the Emma Willard School in Troy, New York, the entire curriculum has been revamped to emphasize cooperation rather than competition, and to encourage girls to analyze and express ideas from their own perspective rather than responding in stereotyped or conformist ways.

Whether you believe the connectionist arguments of Gilligan or the achievement/self-determination arguments of her critics, there is increasing evidence that adolescence is a critical juncture in the psychological development of females. In a national survey conducted by the American Association of University Women, girls revealed a significantly greater drop in self-esteem during adolescence than boys did. And in another recent study, the self-esteem of girls declined during adolescence (Rosner & Rierdan, 1994). At ages 8 and 9, 60 percent of the girls were confident and assertive and felt positive about themselves, compared to 67 percent of the boys. However, over the next 8 years, the girls' self-esteem fell 31 percentage points—only 29 percent of high school girls felt positive about themselves. Across the same age range, boys' self-worth dropped 21 points—leaving 46 percent of the high school boys with high self-esteem, which makes for a gender gap of 17 percentage points.

WOMEN'S AND MEN'S ISSUES

Feminist scholars are developing new perspectives that focus on girls' and women's experiences and development. What are these women's issues? And what men's issues are relevant to adolescent development?

Women's Issues

Many feminist scholars believe that, historically, psychology has portrayed human behavior with a "male dominant theme" (Jordan, 1997; Paludi, 1995). They also believe that sexism is still rampant in society. As a leading feminist scholar, Jean Baker Miller (1986), wrote in *Toward a New Psychology of Women*,

> In the last decade it has become clearer that if women are trying to define and create a full personhood, we are engaged in a huge undertaking. We see that this attempt means building a new way of living which encompasses all realms of life, from global economic, social and political levels to the most intimate personal relationships. (p. xi)

Feminist scholars are putting greater emphasis on women's life experiences and development, including girls and women as authorities about their own experiences, or, as Harvard psychologist Carol Gilligan (1992) advocates, listening to women's voices.

> *We need every human gift and cannot afford to neglect any gift because of artificial barriers of sex or race or class or national origin.*
>
> —Margaret Mead, *Male and Female* (1949)

Miller (1986) has been an important voice in stimulating the examination of psychological issues from a female perspective. She believes that the study of women's psychological development opens up paths to a better understanding of all psychological development, male or female. She also concludes that, when researchers examine what women have been doing in life, they find that a large part of it is active participation in the development of others. In Miller's view, women often try to interact with others in ways that foster the others' development along many dimensions—emotionally, intellectually, and socially.

Many feminist thinkers believe that it is important for women not only to maintain their competency in relationships but to be self-motivated too. Miller believes that, through increased self-determination and already developed relationship skills, many women will gain greater power in the American culture. As feminist scholar Harriet Lerner (1989) concludes in her book *The Dance of Intimacy*, it is important for women to bring to their relationships nothing less than a strong, assertive, independent, and authentic self. She believes that competent relationships are those in which the separate "I-ness" of both persons can be appreciated and enhanced while staying emotionally connected to each other.

Not only is a distinct female voice an important dimension of the feminist perspective on gender, but so is the effort to reduce and eventually end prejudice and discrimination against females (Paludi, 1995; Winstead, Derlega, & Rose, 1997). Although females have broken through many male bastions in the past several decades, feminists argue that much work is left to be done. Feminists today believe that too many people passively accept traditional gender roles and believe that discrimination no longer exists in politics, work, the family, and education. They encourage individuals to question these assumptions, and especially strive to get females to evaluate the gender circumstances of their lives. For example, if you are a female, you may remember situations in which you were discriminated against because of your sex. If derogatory comments are made to you because you are a female, you may ask yourself why you have allowed these comments to go unchallenged or why they made you so angry. Feminists hope that, if you are a male, you will become more conscious of gender issues, of female and male roles, and of fairness and sensitivity in interactions and relationships between females and males.

Men's Issues

The male of the species—what is he really like? What does he really want? As a result of the women's movement and its attack on society's male bias and discrimination against women, men have developed their own movement (Levant, 1995; Pollack, 1995). The men's movement has not been as political or as activist as the women's movement. Rather, it has been more an emotional, spiritual movement that reasserts the importance of masculinity and urges men to resist women's efforts to turn them into "soft" males. Or it has been a psychological movement that recognizes men's need to be less violent and more nurturant but still retain much of their masculine identity. Many of the men's movement disciples argue that society's changing gender arena has led many men to question what being a man really means.

Herbert Goldberg (1976, 1980) became a central figure in the early development of the men's movement in the 1970s and early 1980s, mainly as a result of his writings about men's rights in *The Hazards of Being Male* and *The New Male*. Goldberg argues that a critical difference between men and women creates a precipitous gulf between them. That difference: Women can sense and articulate their feelings and problems; men, because of their masculine conditioning, can't. The result is an armor of masculinity that is defensive and powerful in maintaining self-destructive patterns. Goldberg says that most men have been effective work machines and performers but most else in their lives suffers. Men live about 8 years less than women on the average, have higher hospitalization rates, and show more behavioral problems. In a word, Goldberg believes millions of men are killing themselves by striving to be "true" men, a heavy price to pay for masculine "privilege" and power.

Once a year, the giant wooden phallus made during one of Robert Bly's male retreats is raised and used as a centerpiece for a naming ceremony at the Mendocino Men's Conference in California.

How can men solve their dilemma and live more physically and psychologically healthy lives? Goldberg argues that men need to get in touch with their emotions and their bodies. They can't do this by just piggy-backing on the changes that are occurring in women's attitudes, he says. Rather, men need to develop their own realization of what is critical for their survival and well-being. Goldberg especially encourages men to

- Recognize the suicidal "success" syndrome and avoid it
- Understand that occasional impotence is nothing serious
- Become aware of their real needs and desires and get in touch with their own bodies
- Elude the binds of masculine role-playing
- Relate to liberated women as their equal rather than serving as their guilty servant or hostile enemy
- Develop male friendships

Goldberg's messages to men that they need to become more attuned to their inner self and emotional makeup and work on developing more positive close relationships are important ones. Other gender specialists echo Goldberg's belief that males need to improve the quality of their close relationships (Bergman, 1995; Levant & Pollack, 1995).

Gender researcher Joseph Pleck (1995) believes that a major problem in the male's life is the American culture's emphasis on his need to prove his masculinity. Why do so many males feel they have to prove their masculinity? Pleck gives two main reasons: (1) because they have been socialized to believe that their masculinity is something they have to prove, or (2) because it is in the male's essential makeup that his masculinity can never be fully established like a female's can.

One author who helped to usher in a renewed interest in the men's movement in the 1990s is Robert Bly, a poet, storyteller, translator, and best-selling author who is a disciple of Carl Jung's ideas. In *Iron John*, Bly says we live in a society that hasn't had fathers around since the Industrial Revolution. With no viable rituals for introducing young boys to manhood, today's men are left confused. Bly thinks that too many of today's males are "soft," having bonded with their mothers because their fathers were unavailable. These "soft" males know how to follow instead of lead, how to be vulnerable, and how to go with the flow, says Bly. He believes that they don't know what it's like to have a deep masculine identity. Iron John, a hairy mythological creature, has a deep masculine identity. He is spontaneous and sexual, an action taker, a boundary definer, and an earth preserver. He has untamed impulses and thoughtful self-discipline.

Bly not only writes poetry and books. He and his associates conduct 5-week-long gatherings and weekend workshops for men. At these gatherings, the participants try to capture what it is like to be a true man by engaging in such rituals as drum beating and naming ceremonies.

Many critics do not like Bly's strong insistence on the separateness of the sexes. Only masculine men and feminine women populate Bly's world. Feminist critics deplore Bly's approach, saying it is a regression to the old macho model of masculinity. Not everyone applauds Bly's belief that men can learn to become true men by going off into the woods to beat drums, dance around the fire, and bare their souls.

What is the future of the women's and men's movements? Perhaps at some point they can work together toward an "androgynous" or "gender-role transcendent" movement that allows females and males to express themselves as human beings, thus freeing themselves from the constraints and rigidity of traditional gender roles.

At this point we have discussed a number of ideas about gender-role classification, developmental changes and junctures, and women's and men's issues. A summary of these ideas is presented in concept table 11.2.

ONCEPT TABLE 11.2

Gender-Role Classification, Developmental Changes and Junctures, and Women's and Men's Issues

Concept	Processes/ Related Ideas	Characteristics/Description
Gender-Role Classification	The past	In the past, a well-adjusted male was supposed to show instrumental traits, a well-adjusted female expressive traits. Masculine traits were more valued by society. Sexism was widespread.
	Androgyny	In the 1970s, alternatives to traditional masculinity and femininity were explored. It was proposed that individuals could show both expressive and instrumental traits. This thinking led to the development of the concept of androgyny, the presence of desirable masculine and feminine traits in one individual. Gender-role measures often categorize individuals as masculine, feminine, androgynous, or undifferentiated. Most androgynous individuals are flexible and mentally healthy, although the particular context and the individual's culture also determine the adaptiveness of a gender-role orientation.
	Traditional masculinity and problem behaviors in adolescent males	What defines traditional masculinity in many Western societies includes engaging in certain behaviors, that, while officially disapproved of, validate masculinity. Researchers have found that problem behaviors in adolescent males—school problems, drug use, and delinquency—are associated with their traditional beliefs in masculinity.
	Gender-role transcendence	One alternative to androgyny is gender-role transcendence, but, like androgyny, it draws attention away from the imbalance of power between males and females.
Developmental Changes and Junctures	Early adolescence and gender intensification	The gender intensification hypothesis states that psychological and behavioral differences between boys and girls become greater during early adolescence because of increased socialization pressures to conform to traditional gender roles.
	Is early adolescence a critical juncture for females?	Gilligan believes that girls come to a critical juncture in their development during early adolescence: They become aware that their intense interest in intimacy is not prized by the male-dominated society. Some critics, though, argue that Gilligan exaggerates gender differences in intimacy and connectedness. Some critics also argue that what we should be stressing is more opportunities for females to reach higher levels of achievement and self-determination.
Women's and Men's Issues	Women's issues	Feminist scholars are developing new perspectives that focus on girls' and women's experiences and development. Emphases include both connectedness and self-determination as contributors to women's well-being. The feminist perspective stresses the importance of reducing and eventually ending prejudice and discrimination against females.
	Men's issues	As a result of the women's movement, men have developed their own movement. Herb Goldberg has been a central figure in the men's movement. A special concern is the self-destructive behavior patterns of males that involve low interest in the inner self and a lack of connectedness to others.

SUMMARY

This chapter has been about gender, our social worlds as females and males. Nowhere in social development has there been more sweeping changes and more controversial issues than in gender. Few aspects of life are more central to our identity and social relationships than gender.

We began this chapter by contemplating what tomorrow's gender worlds of today's adolescents will be like. Then we examined what gender is, gender controversy, gender in context, and biological, social, and cognitive influences on gender. We also studied gender stereotypes, similarities, and differences. Our coverage of gender-role classification focused on the past, androgyny, traditional masculinity and problem behaviors in adolescent males, and gender-role transcendence. We read about developmental changes and junctures, as well as women's and men's issues.

Don't forget that you can obtain an overall summary of the chapter by again reading the two concept tables on pages 353 and 362. Adolescents' worlds as female and male include not only gender, but also sexuality, which we discuss in the next chapter.

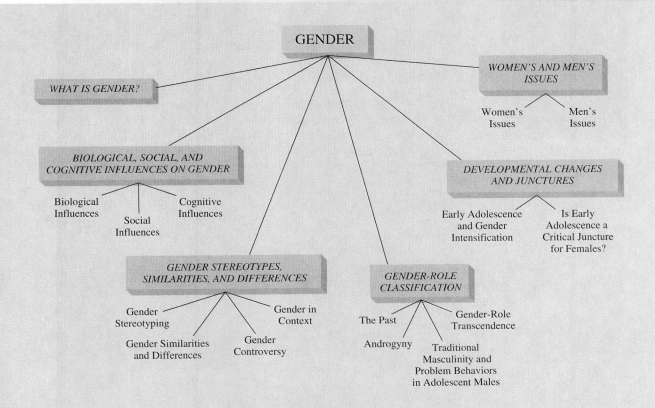

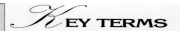

KEY TERMS

gender 343
gender role 343
social learning theory of gender 344
cognitive developmental theory of
    gender 347

schema 348
gender schema 348
gender schema theory 348
gender stereotypes 348
sexism 349

androgyny 354
gender-role transcendence 357
gender intensification
    hypothesis 358

PRACTICAL KNOWLEDGE ABOUT ADOLESCENCE

The Mismeasure of Woman
(1992) by Carol Tavris.
New York: Simon & Schuster

Tavris believes that no matter how hard women try, they can't measure up. They are criticized for being too female or not female enough, but they are always judged and mismeasured by how well they fit into a male world. *The Mismeasure of Woman* contains a thorough review of research studies that document how females are ignored, misrepresented, or even harmed by the still male-dominated health professions, which base their standards of normalcy on male anatomy, physiology, and psychology.

This is an excellent book on gender stereotyping, similarities and differences between the sexes, and how females should be measured by their own standards, not males'. It is well-documented and captivating in presenting a witty portrayal of women's issues and dilemmas, and what can be done about them.

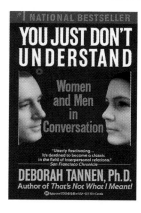

You Just Don't Understand
(1990) by Deborah Tannen.
New York: Ballantine.

The subtitle of this book is "Women and Men in Conversation." This is a book about how women and men communicate—or, all too often, miscommunicate—with each other. *You Just Don't Understand* reached the status of being number one on bestseller lists. Tannen shows that friction between women and men in conversation often develops because boys and girls were brought up in two virtually distinct cultures. As we indicated in the text, Tannen believes that the two gender cultures are distinguished by rapport talk (women) and report talk (men).

Tannen's book has especially connected with many females, who after reading it want their husband or boyfriend to read it. The book is well written, well researched, and entertaining. Tannen has a keen sense for pinpointing ways in which talk gets us into trouble as females and males.

The New Male

(1980) by Herb Goldberg.
New York: Signet.

This book is subtitled "From Macho to Sensitive but Still Male." Goldberg's purpose in writing *The New Male* was to explore what the world of the traditional male has been like in the past, including his relationship with females; what the male's world is like in today's era of changing gender roles; and what the future could hold for males if they examine, reshape, and expand their gender role behavior and self-awareness. Goldberg argues that the way the traditional male role has been defined has made it virtually impossible for males to explore their inner self, examine their feelings, and show sensitivity toward others.

Goldberg does tell males not to let the new feminist female walk all over them, but his message of challenging males to explore their inner self, get in touch with their feelings, and pay more attention to developing meaningful relationships is hardly antifeminist. Engaging in these activities, says Goldberg, does not mean being less of a male. Rather, doing so makes males more complete, caring human beings. And that is an important message.

RESOURCES FOR IMPROVING THE LIVES OF ADOLESCENTS

A New Psychology of Men (1995)
by Ronald Levant and William Pollack
New York: Basic Books

This edited volume includes chapters by leading authorities in men's issues and gender roles related to the male's development. The contributors detail how some male problems are unfortunate by-products of the current way males are socialized.

Girl Guides of Canada/Guides du Canada
50 Merton Street
Toronto, Ontario M4S 1A3
416-487-5281

The aim of the Girl Guides is to help girls and young women become responsible citizens, able to give leadership and service to the community, whether local, national, or global.

The Psychology of Women (1993)
by Margaret Matlin
Fort Worth, TX: Harcourt Brace

This very up-to-date text on the psychology of women contains several excellent chapters on gender development in children and adolescents.

YMCA of the USA
101 North Wacker Drive
Chicago, IL 60606

The YMCA provides a number of programs for teenage boys. A number of personal health and sports programs are available.

YWCA of Canada
80 Gerrard Street East
Toronto, Ontario M5B 1E6
416-593-9886

The YWCA of Canada supports women and girls seeking physical, intellectual, social, and spiritual help for themselves, their families and their communities.

YWCA of the USA
726 Broadway
New York, NY 10003

The YWCA promotes health, sports participation, and fitness for women and girls. Its programs include instruction in health, teen pregnancy prevention, family life education, self-esteem enhancement, parenting, and nutrition.

*E*XPLORING ADOLESCENT DEVELOPMENT

To further explore adolescent development, we will examine a research study on the family context of gender intensification in early adolescence and discuss the gender worlds of adjustment in adolescence.

*R*ESEARCH ON ADOLESCENT DEVELOPMENT

Family Context and Gender Intensification

Featured Study

Crouter, A. C., Manke, B. A., & McHale, S. M. ((1995). The family context of gender intensification in early adolescence. *Child Development, 66,* 317–329.

Researchers have noted that during early adolescence an increasing divergence between boys and girls occurs in several areas of development, such as gender-role attitudes and math. The explanation for this increasing divergence has usually been that during adolescence there is increased socialization pressure to conform to traditional masculine and feminine roles. In this study, it was hypothesized that gender-differential socialization would increase early in adolescence, but that the family context would mediate gender intensification in early adolescence. More specifically, it was predicted that gender intensification would be strongest in families in which (a) parents maintained a traditional division of labor, and (b) there was an opposite-sex younger sibling in the family.

Method

The study was longitudinal in nature, focusing on 144 young adolescents who were 9 to 11 years of age when initially assessed (152 adolescents were initially assessed at time 1; 144 of them remained in the study at the second assessment 1 year later). The families were intact (stepfamilies and divorced families were not included). Fathers were employed full-time; mothers' work hours varied.

At both assessments, the families participated in two types of data collection: home interviews and a series of telephone interviews. The following measures were included: (1) Background characteristics, such as parents' educational levels, work hours, and incomes, obtained during home interviews. (2) Adolescents' participation in household tasks. In telephone interviews, adolescents reported whether they had performed each of twelve household tasks, such as making beds, cleaning, and doing outdoor work. (3) Parent-child joint activities, based on an interview with the adolescent that focused on the extent to which the parent and adolescent shared activities, such as going to religious services, watching television, or playing a video game. (4) Parental monitoring, based on a set of questions asked parents and adolescents about such areas as where and with whom the adolescent spent time that day. (5) Parental division of labor, based on husbands' and wives' reports of their involvement in each of eleven household tasks, such as cooking and gardening.

Results and Discussion

Based on longitudinal analyses of adolescents' participation in "feminine" and "masculine" household chores, adolescents' involvement in dyadic activities with mothers and fathers, and parental monitoring, gender intensification was apparent for some activities but not for others. When gender intensification was apparent, it usually emerged in some family contexts but not others. Only dyadic parent-adolescent involvement was characterized by an overall pattern of gender intensification in which girls became increasingly involved with their mothers and boys with their fathers; this pattern was strongest in families in which the adolescent had a younger, opposite-sex sibling. Results of this study underscore the important point made earlier in this chapter: Gender is a key context for understanding adolescent development.

ADOLESCENT HEALTH AND WELL-BEING

Gender Worlds of Adjustment

In many areas of life, what were once considered weaknesses of females are now considered strengths (Tavris, 1992). In our society, autonomy, which generally refers to being self-sufficient, independent, and pursuing one's own goals, has been considered an indication of healthy adjustment. In the early years of the women's movement, many feminists stressed that females should be more independent—that is, more "like males." Now many females are arguing that the pursuit of autonomy is a trap and a delusion, and that females should value their natural relatedness and nurturance as healthier signs of adjustment.

Suppose an adolescent comes to a counselor for relationship problems and that the adolescent is caught in an unhealthy and unfulfilling relationship. Think for a moment about whether the gender of the adolescent might influence the counselor's treatment choice. Traditional theories and therapies would characterize the adolescent as dependent, submissive, and not able to separate or individuate properly. The traditional counselor or therapist might also encourage the adolescent to separate, get out of the relationship, develop self-sufficiency, take care of himself/herself, be less dependent, and find fulfillment elsewhere or develop other pursuits.

If the adolescent is female, she might find these traditional recommendations threatening and ominous. If her sense of identity is based on her relationship, she might not know how to disconnect in the ways just outlined. If the adolescent is male, he might have arrived at the counselor's office embarrassed and downcast because he needs "help," feels he is not strong, and senses that he does not have control over his emotions. He also might feel bad for allowing relationships to play such an important role in his life.

Females may be especially confused about such contexts, getting caught up in society's double bind. Fortunately, some counselors and therapists are changing the way they relate to females who have a relationship problem. They begin by affirming and validating the importance of connectedness, relationships, attachment, and caring, regardless of whether the individual is a female or a male. They believe that individuals should not perceive themselves as bad because the relationship is so important to them.

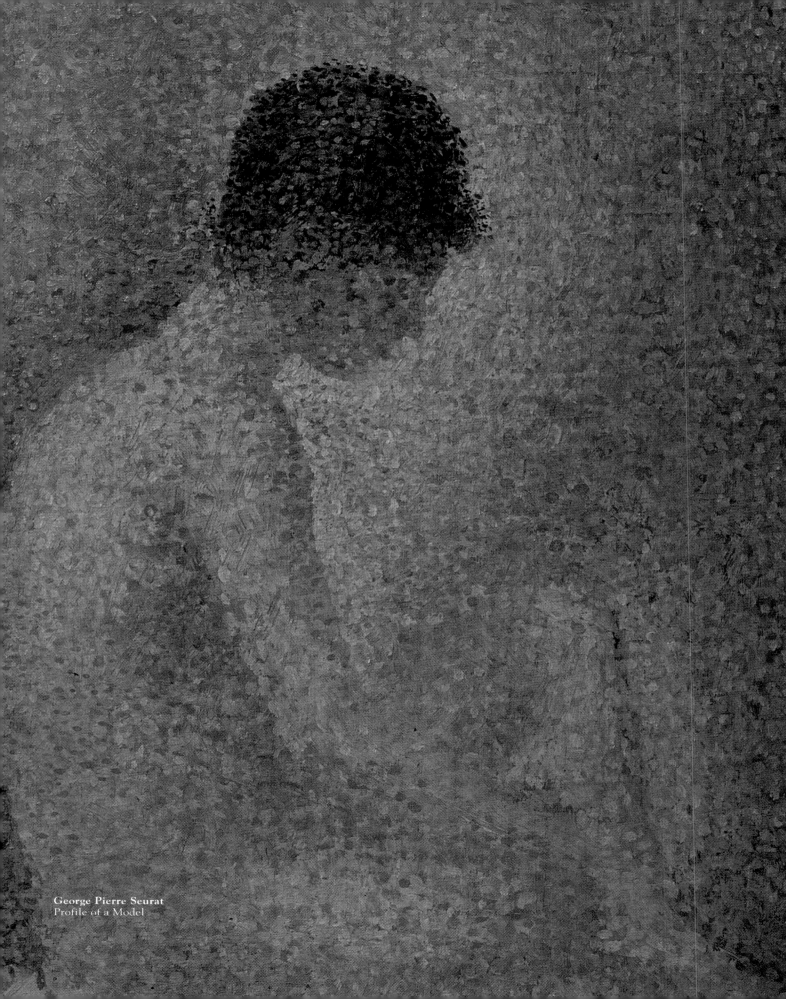

George Pierre Seurat
Profile of a Model

Chapter
12
Sexuality

If we listen to boys and girls at the very moment they seem most pimply, awkward, and disagreeable, we can penetrate a mystery most of us once felt heavily within us, and have now forgotten. This mystery is the very process of creation of man and woman.

—Colin Mcinnes,
The World of Children

Chapter Outline

Chapter Boxes

> *We are born twice over; the first time for existence, the second for life; Once as human beings and later as men or as women.*
>
> —Jean-Jacques Rousseau

PREVIEW

During adolescence, the lives of males and females become wrapped in sexuality. In chapter 3, we studied the biological basis of sexual maturation, including the timing of these changes and the hormones involved. Here, we focus on the sexual attitudes and experiences of adolescents. Adolescence is a time of sexual exploration and experimentation, of sexual fantasies and sexual realities, of incorporating sexuality into one's identity. Adolescents have an almost insatiable curiosity about sexuality's mysteries. They think about whether they are sexually attractive, whether they will grow more, whether anyone will love them, and whether it is normal to have sex. The majority of adolescents manage eventually to develop a mature sexual identity, but for most there are periods of vulnerability and confusion along life's sexual journey. In this chapter, the coverage of adolescent sexuality includes discussions of sexual attitudes and behavior, adolescent pregnancy, sexually transmitted diseases, sexual knowledge and sex education, forcible sexual behavior, and sexual well-being and social policy.

IMAGES OF ADOLESCENCE

The Mysteries and Curiosities of Adolescent Sexuality

I am 16 years old, and I really like this one girl. She wants to be a virgin until she marries. We went out last night, and she let me go pretty far, but not all the way. I know she really likes me, too, but she always stops me when things start getting hot and heavy. It is getting hard for me to handle. She doesn't know it, but I'm a virgin, too. I feel I am ready to have sex. I have to admit I think about having sex with other girls, too. Maybe I should be dating other girls.

Frank C.

I'm 14 years old. I have a lot of sexy thoughts. Sometimes, just before I drift off to sleep at night, I think about this hunk who is 16 years old and plays on the football team. He is so gorgeous, and I can feel him holding me in his arms and kissing and hugging me. When I'm walking down the hall between classes at school, I sometimes start daydreaming about guys I have met and wonder what it would be like to have sex with them. Last year I had this crush on the men's track coach. I'm on the girls' track team, so I saw him a lot during the year. He hardly knew I thought about him the way I did, although I tried to flirt with him several times.

Amy S.

Is it weird to be a 17-year-old guy and still be a virgin? Sometimes, I feel like the only 17-year-old male on the planet who has not had sex. I feel like I am missing out on something great, or at least that's what I hear. I'm pretty religious, and I sometimes feel guilty when I think about sex. The thought runs through my mind that maybe it is best to wait until I'm married or at least until I have a long-term relationship that matters a lot to me.

Tom B.

I'm 15 years old, and I had sex for the first time recently. I had all of these expectations about how great it was going to be. He didn't have much experience either. We were both pretty scared about the whole thing. It was all over in a hurry. My first thought was, "Is that all there is?" It was a very disappointing experience.

Claire T.

Adolescent sexuality is filled with curiosity, confusion, and at times, vulnerability.

SEXUAL ATTITUDES AND BEHAVIOR

Gathering information about sexual attitudes and behavior is not always a straightforward affair. Consider how you would respond if someone asked you, "How often do you have intercourse?" or "How many different sexual partners have you had?" The people most likely to respond to sexual surveys are those with liberal sexual attitudes who engage in liberal sexual behaviors. Thus, research is limited by the reluctance of individuals to candidly answer questions about extremely personal matters and by researchers' inability to get any answer, candid or otherwise, from individuals who simply refuse to talk to strangers about sex (Halonen & Santrock, 1996). In addition, when asked about their sexual activity, do individuals respond truthfully or with socially desirable answers? For example, might a ninth-grade boy report that he has had sexual intercourse even if he has not because he is afraid someone will find out that he is sexually inexperienced? With these cautions in mind, we will now examine heterosexual attitudes and behavior, homosexual attitudes and behavior, self-stimulation, and contraception.

Heterosexual Attitudes and Behavior

What is the progression of adolescent sexual behaviors? How extensively have heterosexual attitudes and behaviors changed in the twentieth century? What sexual scripts do adolescents follow? Are some adolescents more vulnerable to irresponsible sexual behavior than others? We examine each of these questions.

The Progression of Adolescent Sexual Behaviors

Adolescents engage in a rather consistent progression of sexual behaviors (DeLamater & MacCorquodale, 1979). Necking usually comes first, followed by petting. Next comes intercourse, or, in some cases, oral sex, which has increased substantially in adolescence in recent years. In an investigation of tenth- through twelfth-graders, 25 percent of the males and 15 percent of the females who reported not having had intercourse reported having had oral sex (Newcomer & Udry, 1985). In one study of the progression of sexual behaviors, 18- to 23-year-olds were asked to remember whether they had engaged in various sexual behaviors and, if they had, to state the age at which they had experienced each of them (DeLamater & MacCorquodale, 1979). As shown in table 12.1, necking and petting occurred earlier than genital contact or sexual intercourse. Oral sex occurred last. Notice that male adolescents engaged in various sexual behaviors approximately 6 months to a year earlier than female adolescents. The gradual progression shown in table 12.1 might be more representative of

TABLE 12.1

The Age at First Experience for Various Sexual Behaviors

	Approximate Age at First Experience	
	Males	Females
Necking	14.0	15.0
French kissing	15.0	16.0
Breast fondling	16.0	16.5
Male/female genitals	17.0	17.5
Female/male genitals	17.0	17.5
Intercourse	17.5	18.0
Male oral/female genitals	18.0	18.5
Female oral/male genitals	18.0	18.5

From DeLamater, John and Patricia MacCorquodale, *Premarital Sexuality: Attitudes, Relationships, Behavior.* © 1979. (Madison: The University of Wisconsin Press.) Reprinted by permission of The University of Wisconsin Press.

White Americans than of African Americans. In one study, African American adolescents were more likely to move toward intercourse at an earlier age and to spend less time in necking, petting, and genital contact before engaging in sexual intercourse (Smith & Udry, 1985).

> *How is it that, in the human body, reproduction is the only function to be performed by an organ of which an individual carries only one half so that he has to spend an enormous amount of time and energy to find another half?*
>
> —François Jacob,
> *The Possible and the Actual*

Adolescent Heterosexual Behavior—Trends and Incidence

Had you been a college student in 1940, you probably would have had a very different attitude toward many aspects of sexuality than you do today, especially if you are female. A review of college students' sexual practices and attitudes from 1900 to 1980 reveals two important trends (Darling, Kallen, & VanDusen, 1984) (see figure 12.1): First, the percentage of young people reporting intercourse has dramatically increased, and, second, the proportion of females reporting sexual intercourse has increased more rapidly than that of males, although

TABLE 12.2

Percentage of Young People Sexually Active at Specific Ages

Age	Females	Males
15	5.4%	16.6%
16	12.6	28.7
17	27.1	47.9
18	44.0	64.0
19	62.9	77.6
20	73.6	83.0

Reprinted with permission from *Risking the Future: Adolescent Sexuality, Pregnancy, and Childbearing.* Copyright 1987 by the National Academy of Sciences. Courtesy of the National Academy Press, Washington, DC.

Figure~12.1

Percentage of College Women and College Men Who Reported Having Sexual Intercourse.
A summary of data from studies conducted from 1900 to 1980.

the initial base for males was greater. Prior to 1970, about twice as many college males as college females reported that they had engaged in sexual intercourse, but since 1970 the proportion of males and females has become about equal. These changes suggest major shifts in the standards governing sexual behavior—that is, movement away from a double standard in which it was more acceptable for males than females to have intercourse.

More American adolescents are sexually active, and their sexual activity increased during the 1980s (Michael & others, 1994; Miller, Christopherson, & King, 1993). Trends in adolescents' sexual activity in the 1980s were examined in two studies: one focused on females, the other on males. From 1982 to 1988, the proportion of adolescent girls 15 to 19 years of age who had sexual intercourse increased from 47 percent to 53 percent (Forrest & Singh, 1990). Most of the change is due to an increase among

White and nonpoor adolescents. In a 1988 survey, 58 percent of the adolescent girls reported having had two or more sexual partners. In a survey of male adolescent sexual activity, comparisons were made between 1979 and 1988 (Sonenstein, Pleck, & Ku, 1989). Two-thirds of the 17- to 19-year-old males reported being sexually active in 1979, a figure that increased to three-fourths in 1988. In a recent national study (the National Youth Risk Behavior Survey), 54 percent of the adolescents in grades 9 through 12 said they had had sexual intercourse (Centers for Disease Control, 1992). In this study, 39 percent of the adolescents reported having had sexual intercourse in the past 3 months. Also in this study, 54 percent of high school students reported having had two or more sex partners in their lifetime. Nineteen percent reported having had four or more partners.

Other studies have documented that adolescent males are more likely to report having had sexual intercourse and being sexually active than adolescent females are (Hayes, 1987). As indicated in table 12.2, 44 percent of 18-year-old females and 64 percent of 18-year-old males said that they were sexually active. While the gap is closing, males still report that they are sexually active at an earlier age than females. Although, as indicated earlier, sexual activity among White adolescents increased in the 1980s, African American adolescents are still more sexually active than White adolescents (Hayes, 1987). As shown in table 12.3, at every point in adolescence African American adolescents are more likely to have had sexual intercourse than White or Latino adolescents are. Notice also that Latina girls are the least likely to be sexually active in adolescence.

Regarding younger adolescents, surveys indicate that 5 to 17 percent of girls 15 years and younger have

TABLE 12.3

Percentage of Teenagers Who Have Had Sexual Intercourse, by Age, Sex, and Ethnicity

Sex and Ethnicity	Percentage Who Were Sexually Active, by Age		
	15	17	19
Females			
Total	5%	44%	74%
White	5	42	72
African American	10	59	85
Latino	4	40	70
Males			
Total	17%	64%	83%
White	12	60	81
African American	42	86	94
Latino	19	67	84

Source: National Longitudinal Survey of Youth Center for Human Resource Research, Ohio State University, 1983.

had sexual intercourse. Among boys the same age, the range is 16 percent to 38 percent (National Research Council, 1987; Ostrov & others, 1985). At age 13, boys also show earlier experience with sexual intercourse than girls do—12 percent versus 5 percent (Dreyer, 1982). The pressure on male adolescents in American society to have sexual intercourse is reflected in these figures, even though male adolescents enter puberty, on the average, 2 years later than female adolescents. In one recent study, adolescent males said that boys do expect sex from girls (Crump & others, 1996). They also said that the typical adolescent male does not force sex, but does put pressure on females to have sex. And in a recent national survey, adolescents 12 to 18 years of age said that the following are "often a reason" teenagers have sex (Kaiser Family Foundation, 1996):

- A boy or girl is pressuring them (61 percent of girls, 23 percent of boys)
- They think they are ready (59 percent of boys, 51 percent of girls)
- They want to be loved (45 percent of girls, 28 percent of boys)
- They don't want people to tease them for being a virgin (43 percent of boys, 38 percent of girls)

In some areas of the United States, the percentages of sexually active young adolescents even may be greater. In an inner-city area of Baltimore, 81 percent of

the males at age 14 said that they already had engaged in sexual intercourse. Other surveys in inner-city, low-income areas also reveal a high incidence of early sexual intercourse (Clark, Zabin, & Hardy, 1984).

In summary, approximately half of all adolescents today have had sexual intercourse by the age of 18, although the percentage varies by sex, ethnicity, and context. Male, African American, and inner-city adolescents report the highest percentages of sexual intercourse. While sexual intercourse can be a meaningful experience for older, more mature adolescents, many adolescents are not prepared to handle sexual experiences, especially in early adolescence. In one recent study, the earlier in adolescence boys and girls engaged in sexual intercourse, the more likely they were to show adjustment problems (Bingham & Crockett, 1996).

Adolescent Female and Male Sexual Scripts

As adolescents explore their sexual identities, they engage in sexual scrips. A **sexual script** is a stereotyped pattern of role prescriptions for how individuals should sexually behave. Females and males have been socialized to follow different sexual scripts. Differences in female and male sexual scripting can cause problems and confusions for adolescents as they work out their sexual identities. Female adolescents learn to link sexual intercourse with love (Michael & others, 1994). They often rationalize their sexual behavior by telling themselves that they were swept away by love. A number of investigators have revealed that adolescent females, more than adolescent males, report being in love as the main reason for being sexually active (Cassell, 1984). Far more females than males have intercourse with partners they love and would like to marry. Other reasons for having sexual intercourse include giving in to male pressure, gambling that sex is a way to get a boyfriend, curiosity, and sexual desire unrelated to loving and caring. Adolescent males might be aware that their female counterparts have been socialized into a love ethic. They also might know the pressure that many girls feel to have a boyfriend. This classic male line shows how males understand female thinking about sex and love: "If you really loved me, you would have sex with me." The female adolescent who says "If you really loved me, you would not put so much pressure on me" shows insight into male sexual motivation.

Some experts on adolescent sexuality, though, believe that we are moving toward a new norm suggesting that sexual intercourse is acceptable, but mainly within the boundary of a loving and affectionate relationship (Dreyer, 1982). As part of this new norm, promiscuity, exploitation, and unprotected sexual intercourse are more often perceived as unacceptable by adolescents. One variation of the new norm is that intercourse is acceptable in a nonlove relationship, but physical or emotional exploitation of the partner is not (Cassell, 1984). The new norm suggests that the double standard that once existed does not operate as it did. That is, physical and emotional exploitation of adolescent females by males is not as prevalent today as in prior decades.

Other experts on adolescent sexuality are not so sure that the new norm has arrived (Gordon & Gilgun, 1987). They argue that remnants of the double standard, unfortunately, still flourish. In most investigations, about twice as many boys as girls report positive feelings about sexual intercourse. Females are more likely to report guilt, fear, and hurt. Adolescent males feel considerable pressure from their peers to have experienced sexual intercourse and to be sexually active (Michael & others, 1994). I remember vividly the raunchy conversations that filled our basketball locker room in junior high school. By the end of the ninth grade, I was sure that I was the only virgin on the fifteen-member team, but of course there was no way I let my teammates know that. As one young adolescent recently remarked, "Look, I feel a lot of pressure from my buddies to go for the score." Further evidence for the male's physical and emotional exploitation of the female was found in a survey of 432 adolescents 14 to 18 years old (Goodchilds & Zellman, 1984). Both males and females accepted the right of the male adolescent to be sexually aggressive, but let the female set the limits for the male's

sexual overtures. Another attitude related to the double standard was the belief that females should not plan ahead to have sexual intercourse but should instead be swept up in the passion of the moment, not taking contraceptive precautions. Unfortunately, while we have chipped away at some parts of the sexual double standard, other aspects appear to remain.

Vulnerable Adolescents and Sexuality

Vulnerable adolescents are most likely to show irresponsible sexual behavior (Gordon & Gilgun, 1987). Adolescents who feel inadequate, who do not have adequate opportunities for education and work, and who feel the need to prove something to themselves through sex are at risk for irresponsible sexual behavior. It is not a coincidence that minority group and low-income adolescents use contraceptives less frequently and have higher pregnancy rates than do White, middle-income adolescents. Minority group and low-income adolescents have less access to information and to services. Their irresponsible behavior and lack of social support can lead to pregnancy, sexually transmitted diseases, and psychological stress (Scott-Jones & White, 1990).

Adolescents who do not plan to go to college are less likely to postpone having sex than those who do plan to go (Miller & Simon, 1974). Drinking, drug abuse, and truancy also are associated with sexual activity (Rosenbaum & Kandel, 1990). Some investigators consider these behaviors to be part of a general pattern of deviance during adolescence (Jessor & Jessor, 1975). Adolescents who depend heavily on their peers and are less involved with their families are more likely to be sexually involved, with male adolescents' dependence on male peers being a strong factor in predicting their sexual activity (Jessor & others, 1983). Also, in one study, having a mother who began childbearing early and living in a low-income family were related to adolescent girls' having intercourse at an early age (Crockett & Bingham, 1994). And in another study, the younger sisters of childbearing adolescents had more permissive sexual attitudes and were more likely to have already had sex than the younger sisters of nonchildbearing adolescents (East, 1994). Further, in another study, adolescent girls who were sexually active reported less frequent and less supportive communication with parents than did those who were not sexually active (Furman, Wehner, & Underwood, 1994).

Negative self-conceptions also can be associated with sexual activity. Some sexually active adolescents may be motivated to have sex because of feelings of low self-worth. Some girls are socialized to believe that sex is one of the few things that can make them feel good about themselves. However, using sex in this way results in exploitation and increased, rather than decreased, feelings of inadequacy. More information about adolescents

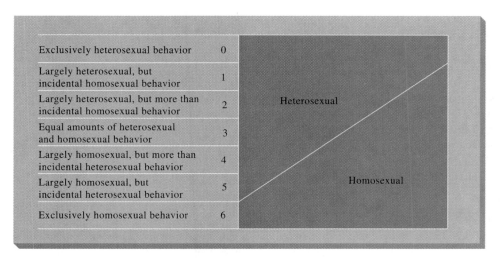

Exclusively heterosexual behavior	0
Largely heterosexual, but incidental homosexual behavior	1
Largely heterosexual, but more than incidental homosexual behavior	2
Equal amounts of heterosexual and homosexual behavior	3
Largely homosexual, but more than incidental heterosexual behavior	4
Largely homosexual, but incidental heterosexual behavior	5
Exclusively homosexual behavior	6

Figure~12.2

The Continuum of Sexual Orientation.
The continuum of sexual orientation ranges from exclusive heterosexuality, which Kinsey and associates (1948) rated as 0, to exclusive homosexuality (a rating of 6). People who are about equally attracted to both sexes (ratings 2 to 4) are bisexual.

who are vulnerable to behaving in sexually irresponsible ways appears later in the chapter in the discussion of contraceptive use and pregnancy.

Homosexual Attitudes and Behavior

Most individuals think that heterosexual behavior and homosexual behavior are distinct patterns that can be easily defined. In fact, however, preference for a sexual partner of the same or opposite sex is not always a fixed decision, made once in life and adhered to forever. For example, it is not unusual for an individual, especially a male, to engage in homosexual experimentation in adolescence, but not engage in homosexual behavior as an adult. And some individuals engage in heterosexual behavior during adolescence, then turn to homosexual behavior as adults.

Until the end of the nineteenth century, it was generally believed that people were either heterosexual or homosexual. Today, it is more acceptable to view sexual orientation as a continuum from exclusive heterosexuality to exclusive homosexuality. Pioneering this view were Alfred Kinsey and his associates (1948), who described sexual orientation as a continuum on a six-point scale, with 0 signifying exclusive heterosexuality and 6 indicating exclusive homosexuality (see figure 12.2). Some individuals are **bisexual**, *being sexually attracted to people of both sexes.* In Kinsey's research, approximately 1 percent of individuals reported being bisexual (1.2 percent of males and 0.7 percent of females) and between 2 to 5 percent of individuals reported being homosexual (4.7 percent of males and 1.8 percent of females). In a recent national survey, only 2.3 percent of males said they

have had same-sex experience and only 1.1 percent said they are exclusively gay (Alan Guttmacher Institute, 1993). And in another recent national study, the percentage of individuals who reported being active homosexuals was much lower (2.7 percent of males and 1.3 percent of females) than the ofttimes reported, rumored 10 percent (Michael & others, 1994).

Individuals who have negative attitudes toward homosexuals also are likely to favor severe controls for AIDS, such as excluding AIDS carriers from the workplace and schools. Having irrational negative feelings against homosexuals is called *homophobia.* In its more extreme forms, homophobia can result in ridicule, beatings, or even murder; more typically it is associated with avoidance of homosexuals, faulty beliefs about the homosexual lifestyle (such as believing the falsehood that most child molesters are homosexuals), and subtle or overt discrimination in housing, employment, and other areas of life.

Although the development of gay or lesbian identity has been widely studied in adults, few researchers have investigated the gay or lesbian identity (often referred to as the coming-out process) in adolescents. In one study of gay male adolescents, coming out was conceptualized in three stages: sensitization; awareness with confusion, denial, guilt, and shame; and acceptance (Newman & Muzzonigro, 1993). The majority of the gay adolescents said they felt different from other boys as children. The average age at having their first crush on another boy was 12.7 years, and the average age at realizing they were gay was 12.5 years. Most of the boys said they felt confused when they first became aware that they were gay. About half of the boys said they initially tried to deny their identity as a gay. Parents who had strong traditional family values (belief in the importance of religion, emphasis on marriage and having children) were less accepting of their gay sons than were parents who had weaker traditional family values.

In a recent comprehensive survey of adolescent sexual orientation in almost 35,000 junior and senior high school students in Minnesota, 4.5 percent reported predominantly homosexual attractions (Remafedi & others, in press). Homosexual identities, attractions, and behaviors increased with age. More than 6 percent of the 18-year-olds said they had predominantly homosexual attractions. How many of these youths later become gay is not known, although it is widely accepted that many adolescents who engage in homosexual behavior in adolescence do not continue the practice into adulthood.

Reactions to homosexual self-recognition range from relief and happiness ("Now I understand and I feel better") to anxiety, depression, and suicidal thoughts ("I can't let anybody know; I've got to kill myself"). Gay adolescents often develop a number of defenses against self-recognition and labeling. The defenses include these (Savin-Williams & Rodriguez, 1993):

"I guess I was drunk."

"It was just a phase I was going through."

"I've heard that all guys do it once."

"I just love her and not all girls."

"I was lonely."

"I was just curious."

Such defenses might be temporary, or they might be lifelong. They might have some positive outcomes (such as redirecting sexual energies into successful academic pursuits) or destructive outcomes (such as marrying a person whom one does not find erotically or emotionally attractive).

One of the harmful aspects of the stigmatization of homosexuality is the self-devaluation engaged in by gay individuals (Patterson, 1995; Savin-Williams & Rodriguez, 1993). One common form of self-devaluation is called *passing*, the process of hiding one's real social identity. Passing strategies include giving out information that hides one's homosexual identity or avoiding one's true sexual identity. Passing behaviors include lying to others and saying, "I'm straight and attracted to opposite-sex individuals." Such defenses against self-recognition are heavily entrenched in our society. Without adequate support, and with fear of stigmatization, many gay and lesbian youth return to the closet and then reemerge at a safer time later, often in college. A special concern is the lack of support gay adolescents receive from parents, teachers, and counselors (Davis & Stewart, 1997; Gruskin, 1994).

Earlier, when we discussed the continuum of sexual orientation, we mentioned a bisexual orientation, in which the individual shows both heterosexual and homosexual interests. It is not unusual for some adolescents to experiment with bisexual behavior and for gay youth to experience bisexual interests early in their sexual development.

In one recent study of gay and bisexual youth, same-sex sexual behavior corresponded to the timing of maturation (that is, early maturers began to have same-sex sexual encounters earlier than later maturers did), but sexual behavior with members of the opposite sex did not (Savin-Williams, 1995). For these gay and bisexual youths,

then, initiation of sex with same-sex partners was closely synchronized with biological cues, but sexual behavior with opposite-sex partners began, instead, according to a social clock.

Why are some individuals homosexual and others heterosexual? Speculation about this question has been extensive, but no firm answers are available. Homosexual and heterosexual males and females have similar physiological responses during sexual arousal and seem to be aroused by the same types of tactile stimulation. Investigators find no differences between homosexuals and heterosexuals for a wide range of attitudes, behaviors, and adjustments (Bell, Weinberg, & Mammersmith, 1981; Savin-Williams, 1995). Both the American Psychiatric Association and the American Psychological Association recognized that homosexuality is not a form of mental illness and discontinued classification of homosexuality as a disorder in the 1970s.

Recently researchers have explored the possible biological basis of homosexuality. In this regard, we will evaluate hormone, brain, and twin studies regarding homosexual orientation. The results of hormone studies have been inconsistent. Indeed, if male homosexuals are given male sexual hormones (androgens), their sexual orientation does not change; their sexual desire merely increases. A very early critical period might influence sexual orientation. In the second to fifth months after conception, exposure of the fetus to hormone levels characteristic of females might cause the individual (female or male) to become attracted to males (Ellis & Ames, 1987). If this critical-period hypothesis turns out to be correct, it would explain why clinicians have found that sexual orientation is difficult, if not impossible, to modify (Meyer-Bahlburg and others, 1995).

With regard to anatomical structures, neuroscientist Simon LeVay (1991) found that an area of the hypothalamus that governs sexual behavior is twice as large (about the size of a grain of sand) in heterosexual men as in homosexual men. The area is about the same size in homosexual men as in heterosexual women. Critics of LeVay's work point out that many of the homosexuals in the study had AIDS and their brains could have been altered by the disease.

One study investigated homosexual orientation in pairs of twins (Whitman, Diamond, & Martin, 1993). The researchers began with a group of homosexuals, each of whom had a twin sibling, and investigated the sexual orientation of the siblings. The siblings who were a monozygotic twin of a homosexual came from the same fertilized egg as the homosexual and thus were genetically identical to the homosexual. Of these, almost two-thirds had a homosexual orientation. The siblings who were a dizygotic twin of a homosexual came from a different fertilized egg than the homosexual and thus were genetically no more similar to the homosexual than a nontwin sibling would be. Of these, less than one-third had a homosexual orientation. The authors interpret their results as supporting a biological interpretation of homosexuality. However, not all of the monozygotic twins had a homosexual orientation, so clearly environmental factors were involved in at least those cases.

An individual's sexual orientation—heterosexual or homosexual—is most likely determined by a combination of genetic, hormonal, cognitive, and environmental factors (Strickland, 1995). Most experts on homosexuality believe that no one factor alone causes homosexuality and that the relative weight of each factor may vary from one individual to the next. In effect, no one knows exactly what causes an individual to be homosexual. Scientists have a clearer picture of what does not cause homosexuality. For example, children raised by gay or lesbian parents or couples are no more likely to be homosexual than are children raised by heterosexual parents. There also is no evidence that male homosexuality is caused by a dominant mother or a weak father, or that female homosexuality is caused by girls' choosing male role models.

Self-Stimulation

As indicated earlier, a heterosexual continuum of necking, petting, and intercourse or oral sex characterizes many adolescents' sexual experiences. Substantial numbers of adolescents, though, have sexual experience outside of this heterosexual continuum through masturbation or same-sex behavior. Most boys have an ejaculation for the first time at about 12 to 13 years of age. Masturbation, genital contact with a same-sex or other-sex partner, or a wet dream during sleep are common circumstances for ejaculation.

Masturbation is the most frequent sexual outlet for many adolescents. In one investigation, masturbation was commonplace among adolescents (Haas, 1979). More than two-thirds of the boys and one-half of the girls masturbated once a week or more. Adolescents today do not feel as guilty about masturbation as they once did, although they still may feel embarrassed or defensive about it (Sorensen, 1973). In past eras, masturbation was denounced as causing everything from warts to insanity. Today, as few as 15 percent of adolescents attach any stigma to masturbation (Hyde, 1985).

In one study, the masturbation practices of female and male college students were studied (Leitenberg, Detzer, & Srebnik, 1993). Almost twice as many males as females said they had masturbated (81 percent versus 45 percent), and the males who masturbated did so three times more frequently during early adolescence and early adulthood than did the females who masturbated during the same age periods. No association was found between engaging in masturbation during preadolescence and/or early adolescence and sexual adjustment in adulthood.

Contraceptive Use

The following conversation between an adolescent boy and girl reveals a communication pattern that happens far too often (Gordon, 1987):

Susan:	Come in.
Skip:	I'm sorry I'm late, Susan. I had to go to the U store and the library and run around and, you know, all kinds of things and I'm sorry . . .
Susan:	Yeah, well I'm glad you came. I called because I want to talk to you.
Skip:	Yeah. How was your day today?
Susan:	Oh, all right. Did you get much studying done?
Skip:	No, I was running around and uh, you know, just thinking, sitting around.
Susan:	Yeah, I've been thinking a lot also. I really want to talk with you about last night. (pause)
Skip:	Are you sorry or anything?
Susan:	No, I'm not sorry—I'm just really worried.
Skip:	(surprise) About what?
Susan:	You know I'm not using any birth control.
Skip:	(shock) You're not using any birth control? (pause) No, I didn't know you weren't using any birth control. How was I supposed to . . . How could you do that?
Susan:	My mother always told me the man would take care of it.
Skip:	The man can take care of it, but I *wasn't* taking care of it, obviously. It's the woman's responsibility to take care of it—you know that. All women use the pill nowadays.
Susan:	Not all women use the pill, and why is it my responsibility if we're both involved? Besides, we never really talked about it, and when was I supposed to bring it up, in the middle of . . . I didn't know you were planning to go to bed.
Skip:	I didn't plan it. Aw, come on, Susan. You don't plan things like that—they just happen.
Susan:	We both must have been thinking about it . . . Why didn't we say anything? Aren't we supposed to trust each other?
Skip:	Sure we trust each other. Aw, come on, it's not that. It's just not the kind of thing you talk about. Susan, could you

see me going up to you and saying, "Susan are you using any . . . " I can't say that. I can't say it.

Susan: Skip, I'm really scared. I could be pregnant. What are we going to do? (looking at each other scared and questioningly)

Adolescents are increasing their use of contraceptives. The level of contraceptive use at first intercourse for 15- to 19-year-old adolescents increased substantially between 1982 and 1988, rising from 48 percent to 65 percent (Forrest & Singh, 1990). Condom use among 15- to 19-year-old boys increased from 21 percent in 1979 to 58 percent in 1988 (Sonenstein, Pleck, & Ku, 1989). And in one recent study, 70 percent of adolescents who had initiated sexual activity reported using a condom at last intercourse (Barone & others, 1994). The threat of AIDS and other sexually transmitted diseases is apparently responsible for adolescents' increased use of contraceptives.

Although adolescent contraceptive use is increasing, many adolescents still do not use contraceptives, or they use them inconsistently; and when all ages of adolescents are considered, a majority of females do not use contraception at first intercourse (Johnson & Green, 1993). As shown in figure 12.3, 70 percent of adolescent females under the age of 15 did not use any contraceptive method at first intercourse, while 53 percent of 18- to 19-year-old females did not. Older adolescents were more likely to rely on the pill or the diaphragm; younger adolescents were more likely to use a condom or withdrawal. Also, in one recent study, adolescent females reported changing their behavior in the direction of safer sex practices more than did adolescent males (Rimberg & Lewis, 1994).

What factors are related to contraceptive use? Being from a low-income family is one of the best predictors of adolescents' nonuse of contraceptives. Younger adolescents are less likely to use contraceptives than older adolescents (Hofferth, 1990). Not being involved in a steady, committed dating relationship is also associated with a lack of contraceptive use (Chilman, 1979). In addition, adolescents with poor coping skills, lack of a future orientation, high anxiety, poor social adjustment, and a negative attitude toward contraceptives

	Age at First Intercourse		
	Under 15	**15–17**	**18–19**
No contraceptive method	70%	57%	53%
Pill	14	21	31
Condom	44	44	38
Rhythm	5	4	7
Withdrawal	30	25	15
Diaphragm	0	1	2

Figure~12.3

Contraceptive Use by Adolescent Females.
The percentage of adolescent females who used a contraceptive method at first intercourse, and method used, by age.

are not as likely to use contraceptives. Further, degree of personal concern about AIDS and the perception that a partner would appreciate condom use are associated with more consistent use of condoms by male adolescents (Pleck, Sonenstein, & Ku, 1991). Condom use is inhibited by concerns about embarrassment and reduced sexual pleasure. Also, in one recent study, adolescent females indicated that past contraceptive risk-taking experiences that did not lead to negative consequences were related to greater contraceptive risk taking in the future and to perceptions of less risk of pregnancy (Jacobs, 1994). Educational efforts that include information about AIDS and pregnancy prevention may promote more consistent use of condoms by adolescent males.

While American adolescents' use of contraceptives increased in the 1980s, adolescents in Canada, Great Britain, France, Sweden, and the Netherlands are still more likely to use contraceptives than are adolescents in the United States (Forrest, 1990). U.S. adolescents are especially less likely to use effective contraceptives like the pill than their counterparts in other countries. Next, we will study one of the outcomes of failure to use contraceptives or to abstain from sexual intercourse—adolescent pregnancy.

ADOLESCENT PREGNANCY

Angela is 15 years old and pregnant. She reflects, "I'm three months pregnant. This could ruin my whole life. I've made all of these plans for the future, and now they are down the drain. I don't have anybody to talk with about my problem. I can't talk to my parents. There is no way they can understand." Pregnant adolescents were once virtually invisible and unmentionable. But yesterday's secret has become today's national dilemma. Our exploration of adolescent pregnancy focuses on its incidence and nature, its consequences, cognitive factors that may be involved, adolescents as parents, and ways adolescent pregnancy rates can be reduced.

Incidence and Nature of Adolescent Pregnancy

They are from different ethnic groups and from different places, but their circumstances have the same stressfulness. Each year more than 500,000 American teenagers become pregnant, and more than 70 percent of them are unmarried (Child Trends, 1996). They represent a flaw in America's social fabric. Like Angela, far too many become pregnant in their early or middle adolescent years. More than 200,000 females in the United States have a child before their eighteenth birthday. As one 17-year-old Los Angeles mother of a 1-year-old son said, "We are children having children." The only bright spot in adolescent pregnancy statistics is that small declines in the teenage birth rate began to appear in 1992 and 1993; the rate rose by one-fourth between 1986 and 1991.

Adolescents are increasing their use of contraceptives, although large numbers of sexually active adolescents still do not use contraceptives, especially at first intercourse.

Despite the rise in the teenage birth rate in the late 1980s, the rate is lower now than it was in the 1950s and 1960s. What is different now, though, is the steady rise in births to unmarried teenagers (see figure 12.4). Dramatic changes have swept through the American culture in the last three decades, changes that involve sexual attitudes and social morals. As we saw in figure 12.4, adolescents gave birth at a higher rate in 1950 than they do today, but that was a time of early marriage. The overwhelming majority of births to adolescent mothers in the 1950s occurred within a marriage and mainly involved females 17 years of age and older. Two to three decades ago, if an unwed adolescent girl became pregnant, her parents often had her swiftly married in a "shotgun wedding." If marriage was impractical, the girl would discreetly disappear, the child would be put up for adoption, and the predicament would never be discussed again. Abortion was not a real option for most adolescent females until 1973, when the Supreme Court ruled that it could not be outlawed.

In today's world, if the adolescent girl does not choose to have an abortion (almost 40 percent do), she usually keeps the baby and raises it without the traditional involvements of marriage. With the stigma of illegitimacy now being less severe, adolescent girls are less likely to

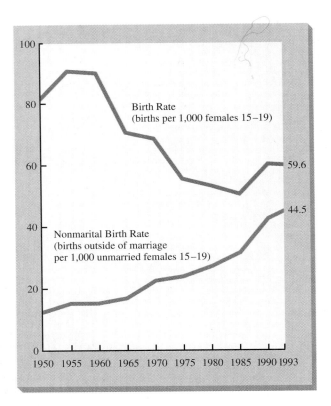

Figure~12.4

Trends in the teenage birth rate and the nonmarital teenage birth rate, 1950–1993.

give up their babies for adoption. Fewer than 5 percent do, compared with approximately 35 percent in the early 1960s. But even though there is now less stigma associated with being an unmarried mother, the lives of most pregnant adolescent females are anything but rosy.

The adolescent pregnancy rate in the United States is much higher than in other industrialized countries. It is more than twice as high as the rates in England, France, and Canada, almost three times as high as the rate in Sweden, and seven times as high as the rate in the Netherlands (Child Trends, 1996; Jones & others, 1985; Kenney, 1987). Though American adolescents are no more sexually active than their counterparts in these other countries, they are many times more likely to become pregnant.

Consequences of Adolescent Pregnancy

The consequences of America's high adolescent pregnancy rate are cause for great concern. Adolescent pregnancy creates health risks for both the offspring and the mother. Infants born to adolescent mothers are more likely to have low birth weights—a prominent factor in infant mortality—as well as neurological problems and childhood illness (Dryfoos, 1990). Adolescent mothers often drop out of school, fail to gain employment, and become dependent on welfare. Although many adolescent mothers resume their education later in life, they generally do not catch up

with women who postpone childbearing. In the National Longitudinal Survey of Work Experience of Youth, it was found that only half of the 20- to 26-year-old women who first gave birth at age 17 had completed high school by their twenties (the percentage was even lower for those who gave birth at a younger age) (see figure 12.5) (Mott & Marsiglio, 1985). By contrast, among young females who waited until age 20 to have a baby, more than 90 percent had obtained a high school education (Kenney, 1987). Among the younger adolescent mothers, almost half had obtained a general equivalency diploma (GED), which does not often open up good employment opportunities.

These educational deficits have negative consequences for the young females themselves and for their children (Kenney, 1987). Adolescent parents are more likely than those who delay childbearing to have low-paying, low-status jobs, or to be unemployed. The mean family income of White females who give birth before age 17 is approximately half that of families in which the mother delays birth until her middle or late twenties.

Cognitive Factors in Adolescent Pregnancy

With their developing idealism and ability to think in more abstract and hypothetical ways, young adolescents may get caught up in a mental world far removed from reality, one that may involve a belief that things cannot

Santrock: Adolescence

Age at first birth	Total %	High school completion by 1983, diploma %	GED %
15	45	24	21
16	49	28	21
17	53	38	15
18	62	52	10
19	77	68	9
Under 20	90	86	4

Figure~12.5

High School Completion by Young Women Who Have Borne Children.
Percentage distribution of women, ages 20 to 26 in 1983, by type of high school completion, according to age at birth of first child.

or will not happen to them and that they are omnipotent and indestructible. These cognitive changes have intriguing implications for adolescents' sex education (Lipsitz, 1980). Having information about contraceptives is not enough—what seems to predict whether or not adolescents will use contraceptives is their acceptance of themselves and their sexuality. This acceptance requires not only emotional maturity but cognitive maturity.

Most discussions of adolescent pregnancy and its prevention assume that adolescents have the ability to anticipate consequences, to weigh the probable outcome of behavior, and to project into the future what will happen if they engage in certain acts, such as sexual intercourse. That is, prevention is based on the belief that adolescents have the cognitive ability to approach problem solving in a planned, organized, and analytical manner. However, many adolescents are just beginning to develop these capacities, and others have not developed them at all.

The personal fable described in chapter 4 may be associated with adolescent pregnancy. The young adolescent might say, "Hey, it won't happen to me." If adolescents are locked into this personal fable, they might not respond well to a course on sex education that preaches prevention. A developmental perspective on cognition suggests what can be taught in sex education courses for young adolescents.

Late adolescents (18 to 19 years of age) are to some degree realistic and future oriented about sexual experiences, just as they are about careers and marriage. Middle adolescents (15 to 17 years of age) often romanticize sexuality. But young adolescents (10 to 15 years of age) seem to experience sex in a depersonalized way that is filled with anxiety and denial. This depersonalized orientation toward sex is not likely to lead to preventive behavior.

Consider the outcome if the following are combined: early adolescent cognition, the personal fable, anxiety about sex, gender-role definitions about what is masculine and what is feminine, the sexual themes of music, the sexual overtones of magazines and television, and a societal standard that says that sex is appropriate for adults but promiscuous for adolescents. That is, society tells

adolescents that sex is fun, harmless, adult, and forbidden. The combination of early physical maturation, risk-taking behavior, egocentrism, the inability to think futuristically, and an ambivalent, contradictory culture makes sex difficult for adolescents to handle. Add to this the growing need for adolescents to develop a commitment, especially in a career. Yet youth, especially low-income, minority group youth, face high unemployment rates, which can turn them away from the future and intensively toward the present. Piece together information about early adolescent development, America's sexual ambivalence, and adolescents' vulnerability to economic forces and the result is social dynamite.

Adolescents as Parents

Children of adolescent parents face problems even before they are born. Only one of every five pregnant adolescent girls receives any prenatal care at all during the important first 3 months of pregnancy. Pregnant adolescents are more likely to have anemia and complications related to prematurity than are mothers aged 20 to 24. The problems of adolescent pregnancy double the normal risk of delivering a low-birth-weight baby (one that weighs under 5.5 pounds), a category that places that infant at risk for physical and mental deficits (Dryfoos, 1990).

Infants who escape the medical hazards of having an adolescent mother might not escape the psychological and social perils (Brooks-Gunn & Chase-Lansdale, 1995; Luster & others, 1995). Children born to adolescent mothers do not do as well on intelligence tests and have more behavioral problems than do those born to mothers in their twenties (Silver, 1988). Adolescent mothers have less desirable child-rearing practices and less realistic expectations for their infants' development than do older mothers (Osofsky, 1990). Said one 18-year-old adolescent mother, "Not long after he was born, I began to resent him. I wouldn't play with him the first year. He didn't talk until he was two—he would just grunt. I'm sure some of his slow development is my fault. Now I want to make up for it and try to give him extra attention, but he still is behind his age." Other adolescent mothers might get excited about having "this little adorable thing" and anticipate that their world with their child will be marvelous. But as the infant demands more and more of their attention and they have to take care of the infant instead of going out on dates, their positive expectations turn sour.

So far, we have talked exclusively about adolescent mothers. Although some adolescent fathers are involved with their children, the majority are not. In one study, only one-fourth of adolescent mothers with a 3-year-old child said the father had a close relationship with her and the child (Leadbetter, Way, & Raden, 1994). Another study showed that in the last two decades there was a dramatic decline in father involvement with the children of adolescent mothers (Leadbetter, 1994).

Adolescent fathers have lower incomes, less education, and more children than do men who delay having children until their twenties. One reason for these difficulties is that the adolescent father compounds his problem of getting his girlfriend pregnant by dropping out of school (Resnick, Wattenberg, & Brewer, 1992). As soon as he leaves school, the adolescent father moves directly into a low-paying job. Adolescent fathers are saying to themselves, "You need to be a good father. The least you can do is get a job and provide some support."

Many young fathers have little idea of what a father is supposed to do. They may love their baby but not know how to behave. American society has given them few guidelines and few supports. Programs designed to help adolescent fathers are still relatively rare, but they are increasing. Terry, who is now 21, has a 17-month-old child and is himself the child of adolescent parents. After receiving support from the Teenage Pregnancy and Parenting Project in San Francisco, he is now a counselor there. He reports, "My father was a parent when he was an adolescent. So was my grandfather. I know it will stop with my son" (Stengel, 1985).

Reducing Adolescent Pregnancy

Serious, extensive efforts are needed to help pregnant adolescents and young mothers enhance their educational and occupational opportunities (Rupert & Rubovits, 1997). Adolescent mothers also need extensive help in obtaining competent day care and in planning for the future (Klaw & Saunders, 1994). John Conger (1988) offered the following four recommendations for attacking the high rate of adolescent pregnancy: (1) sex education and family planning, (2) access to contraceptive methods, (3) the life options approach, and (4) broad community involvement and support, each of which we consider in turn.

We badly need age-appropriate family-life education for America's adolescents, including sex education that begins in childhood and continues through adolescence (Gardon, 1997). Although it is still a controversial issue, sex education in the schools is favored by a large majority of parents. Much more about sex education is discussed later in this chapter.

In addition to age-appropriate family-life and sex education, sexually active adolescents need access to contraceptive methods. These needs often can be handled through adolescent clinics that provide comprehensive, high-quality health services. At four of the nation's oldest adolescent clinics, in St. Paul, Minnesota, the overall annual rate of first-time pregnancies has dropped from 80 per 1,000 to 29 per 1,000 (Schorr, 1989). These clinics offer everything from immunizations to sports physicals to treatment for sexually transmitted diseases. Significantly, they also advise adolescents on contraception and dispense prescriptions for birth control (provided parents have agreed beforehand to allow their adolescents to visit the clinic). An important aspect of the clinics is the presence of individuals trained to understand the special needs and confusions of the adolescent age group.

Better sex education, family planning, and access to contraceptive methods alone will not remedy the adolescent pregnancy crisis, especially for high-risk adolescents. Adolescents have to become *motivated* to reduce their pregnancy risk. This motivation will come only when adolescents look to the future and see that they have an opportunity to become self-sufficient and successful. Adolescents need opportunities to improve their academic and career-related skills, job opportunities, life-planning consultation, and extensive mental health services.

Finally, for adolescent pregnancy prevention to ultimately succeed, we need broad community involvement and support (Duckett, 1997). This support is a major reason for the success of pregnancy prevention efforts in other developed nations where rates of adolescent pregnancy, abortion, and childbearing are much lower than in America despite similar levels of sexual activity. In Holland, as well as other European countries such as Sweden, sex does not carry the mystery and conflict it does in American society. Holland does not have a mandated sex education program, but adolescents can obtain contraceptive counseling at government-sponsored clinics for a small fee. The Dutch media also have played an important role in educating the public about sex through frequent broadcasts focused on birth control, abortion, and related matters. Dutch adolescents do not consider having sex without contraception.

So far, we have discussed four ways to reduce adolescent pregnancy: sex education and family planning, access to contraceptive methods, life options, and broad community involvement and support. A fifth, very important consideration, especially for young adolescents, is abstention. Abstention is increasingly being included as a theme in sex education classes.

At this point we have examined many aspects of sexual attitudes and behavior, as well as adolescent pregnancy. A summary of these ideas is presented in concept table 12.1.

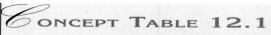

CONCEPT TABLE 12.1

Sexual Attitudes and Behaviors, and Adolescent Pregnancy

Concept	Processes/ Related Ideas	Characteristics/Description
Sexual Attitudes and Behavior	Heterosexual attitudes and behavior	Adolescents engage in a rather consistent progression of sexual behaviors—necking, petting, intercourse, and in some cases, oral sex. The number of adolescents reporting having had intercourse has significantly increased in the twentieth century, and the proportion of females engaging in intercourse has increased more rapidly than that of males. National data indicate that approximately half of all adolescents today have had sexual intercourse by the age of 18, although the percentage varies by sex, ethnicity, and context. Male, African American, and inner-city adolescents report the highest incidence of sexual activity. As adolescents develop their sexual identity, they follow certain sexual scripts, which are different for females and males.
	Homosexual attitudes and behavior	About 4 percent of males and 3 percent of females choose to be exclusively homosexual. Today, it is widely accepted that sexual orientation should be viewed as a continuum from exclusive heterosexuality to exclusive homosexuality. An individual's sexual orientation—whether heterosexual or homosexual—is likely caused by a mix of genetic, hormonal, cognitive, and environmental factors.
	Self-stimulation	Self-stimulation is part of the sexual orientation of virtually all adolescents and one of their most frequent sexual outlets.
	Contraceptive use	Adolescents are increasing their use of contraceptives, but large numbers still do not use contraception; a majority of adolescent females do not use contraception at first intercourse. Younger adolescents and adolescents from low-income backgrounds are less likely to use contraceptives than their older counterparts from middle-class backgrounds.
Adolescent Pregnancy	Incidence and nature of adolescent pregnancy	More than 1 million American adolescents become pregnant each year. Eight of ten adolescent pregnancies are unintended. The only bright spot in adolescent pregnancy statistics is that the adolescent pregnancy rate is leveling off or possibly even declining. America's adolescent pregnancy rate is the highest in the Western world. Dramatic changes have swept through the American culture in the last three decades regarding adolescent sexuality and pregnancy.
	Consequences of adolescent pregnancy	Adolescent pregnancy increases health risks for both the mother and the offspring. Adolescent mothers often drop out of school, fail to gain employment, and become dependent on welfare.
	Cognitive factors in adolescent pregnancy	The personal fable of adolescents may make pregnancy prevention difficult.
	Adolescents as parents	The infants of adolescent parents are at risk both medically and psychologically. Adolescent mothers are less effective in rearing their children than are older mothers. Many adolescent fathers do not have a close relationship with their baby and the adolescent mother.
	Reducing adolescent pregnancy	Reductions in adolescent pregnancy require sex education and family planning, access to contraceptive methods, the life options approach, broad community involvement and support, and abstention.

SEXUALLY TRANSMITTED DISEASES

Tammy, age 15, just finished listening to an expert lecture in her health class. We overhear her talking to one of her girlfriends as she walks down the school corridor: "That was a disgusting lecture. I can't believe all the diseases you can get by having sex. I think she was probably trying to scare us. She spent a lot of time talking about AIDS, which I have heard that normal people do not get. Right? I've heard that only homosexuals and drug addicts get AIDS. And I've also heard that gonorrhea and most other sexual diseases can be cured, so what is the big deal if you get something like that?" Tammy's view of sexually transmitted diseases (formerly called venereal disease or VD)—that they always happen to someone else, that they can be easily cured without any harm done, that they are too disgusting for a nice young person to hear about, let alone get—is common among adolescents. Tammy's view is wrong. Adolescents who are having sex run the risk of getting sexually transmitted diseases.

Sexually transmitted diseases (STDs) *are diseases that are contracted primarily through sexual contact. This contact is not limited to vaginal intercourse but includes oral-genital and anal-genital contact as well. STDs are an increasing health problem.*

Types

Among the main STDs adolescents can get are bacterial infections (such as gonorrhea and syphilis), chlamydia, and two STDs caused by viruses—genital herpes and AIDS (acquired immune deficiency syndrome).

Gonorrhea

Gonorrhea *is a sexually transmitted disease that is commonly called the "drip" or the "clap." It is reported to be one of the most common STDs in the United States and is caused by a bacterium from the gonococcus family, which thrives in the moist mucous membranes lining the mouth, throat, vagina, cervix, urethra, and anal tract.* The bacterium is spread by contact between the infected moist membranes of one individual and the membranes of another. Thus, virtually all forms of sexual contact can spread the gonococcus, although transfer does not necessarily occur with every contact. Males have a 10 percent chance of becoming infected with each exposure to gonococcus. Females have more than a 40 percent chance of infection with each exposure because of the large surface area of the vaginal mucous membrane.

Symptoms of gonorrhea appear in males from 3 days to a month after contact. The symptoms include discharge from the penis, burning during urination, blood in the urine, aching pain or pressure in the genitals, and swollen and tender lymph glands in the groin. Unfortunately, 80 percent of infected females show no symptoms in the early stages of the disease, although pelvic inflammation is common at this early point. Untreated, the disease causes infection in the reproductive area and pelvic region within 2 months. Scarring of the fallopian tubes and infertility may result. Gonorrhea can be successfully treated in its early stages with penicillin or other antibiotics. Despite reporting laws, many gonorrhea cases go unreported. The incidence of reported gonorrhea cases in 1990 was 690,000, down from 1 million in 1975 but still well above the number of reported cases in other industrialized countries (Alan Guttmacher Institute, 1993).

Syphilis

Syphilis *is a sexually transmitted disease caused by the bacterium* Treponema pallidum, *a member of the spirochete family.* The spirochete needs a warm, moist environment to survive, and it is transmitted by penile-vaginal, oral-genital, or anal contact. It can also be transmitted from a pregnant woman to her fetus after the fourth month of pregnancy. If the mother is treated before this time with penicillin, the syphilis will not be transmitted to the fetus.

Syphilis occurs in four stages: primary, secondary, latent, and tertiary. In the primary stage, a sore or chancre appears at the site of the infection. The sore heals after 4 to 6 weeks, giving the impression that the problem has gone away, but, untreated, it moves into the secondary stage. Several symptoms occur at this stage, including a rash, fever, sore throat, headache, swollen glands, joint pain, poor appetite, and hair loss. Treatment with penicillin can be successful if begun at this stage or earlier.

Without treatment, symptoms of the secondary stage go away after 6 weeks, and the disease enters a latent stage. The spirochetes spread throughout the body, and, in 50 to 70 percent of those affected, remain there for years in the same stage. After the first 2 years, the disease can no longer be transmitted through sexual contact but can still be passed from a pregnant woman to her fetus. For 30 to 50 percent of those who reach the latent stage, a final, tertiary stage follows. In this advanced stage, syphilis can cause paralysis, insanity, or even death. In 1988, 103,000 cases of syphilis were reported to the Public Health Service, and in many areas of the United States syphilis is on the rise.

Chlamydia

Chlamydia, *the most common of all sexually transmitted diseases, is named for* Chlamydia trachomitis, *an organism that spreads by sexual contact and infects the genital organs of both sexes.* Although fewer individuals have heard of chlamydia than have heard of gonorrhea and syphilis, its incidence is much higher (Morris, Warren, & Aral, 1993). About 4 million Americans are infected with chlamydia each year. In fact, about 10 percent of all college students have chlamydia. This STD is highly

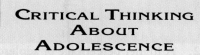

infectious, and women run a 70 percent risk of contracting it in a single sexual encounter. The male risk is estimated at between 25 and 50 percent.

Males with chlamydia often get treatment because of noticeable symptoms in the genital region; however, females are asymptomatic. Therefore, many females go untreated and the chlamydia spreads to the upper reproductive tract where it can cause pelvis inflammatory disease (PID). The resultant scarring of tissue in the fallopian tubes can result in infertility or in ectopic pregnancies (tubal pregnancies), or a pregnancy in which the fertilized egg is implanted outside the uterus. One-quarter of females who have PID become infertile; multiple cases of PID increase the rate of infertility to half. Some researchers suggest that chlamydia is the number one preventable cause of female infertility.

We now turn to two STDs that are caused by viruses—herpes genitalis and acquired immune deficiency syndrome (AIDS). Neither of these STDs is curable.

Genital Herpes

Genital herpes *is a sexually transmitted disease caused by a large family of viruses with many different strains. These strains produce other, nonsexually transmitted diseases such as chicken pox and mononucleosis. Herpes simplex, an STD, has two variations.* Type I is characterized by cold sores and fever blisters. Type II includes painful sores on the lower body—genitals, thighs, and buttocks. Type I infections can be transmitted to the lower body, and Type II infections can be transmitted to the mouth through oral-genital contact. Approximately 75 percent of individuals exposed to an infected partner will develop herpes.

Three to 5 days after contact, itching and tingling can occur, followed by an eruption of sores and blisters. The attacks can last up to 3 weeks and may recur in a few weeks or a few years. The blisters and sores in subsequent attacks are usually milder, but while the virus is dormant in the body, it can travel to the brain and other parts of the nervous system. The transmission through the nervous system is rare, but it can cause such disorders as encephalitis and blindness. Herpes infections can also be transmitted from a pregnant woman to her offspring at birth, leading to brain damage or even death for the infant. A cesarean section can prevent infection, which occurs as the baby moves through the birth canal. Females with herpes are also eight times more likely to develop cervical cancer than are unaffected females (*Harvard Medical School Newsletter*, 1981). As many as 100 million Americans are infected with Type I herpes and 9 million with Type II. Approximately 600,000 new cases of Type II herpes appeared annually in the United States during the 1980s.

Although drugs such as acyclovir can be used to alleviate symptoms, there is no known cure for herpes. Therefore, people infected with herpes often experience severe emotional distress in addition to the considerable physical discomfort. The virus can be transmitted through

curany tailored and include incentives to participate. Outreach workers who are familiar and respected might be able to break through the barriers of fear and mistrust

nonlatex condoms and foams, making infected individuals reluctant about sex, angry about the unpredictability of their lives, and fearful that they won't be able to cope with the pain of the next attack. For these reasons, support groups for victims of herpes have been established.

There are some differences in AIDS cases in adolescents, compared to AIDS cases in adults:

1. A higher percentage of adolescent AIDS cases are acquired by heterosexual transmission.

Chapter

13

Moral Development, Values, and Religion

*I*t is one of the beautiful compensations of this life that no one can sincerely try to help another without helping himself.

—Charles Dudley Warner, 1873

Chapter Boxes

> *Without civic morality,*
> *communities perish; without*
> *personal morality, their*
> *survival has no value.*
>
> —Bertrand Russell

IMAGES OF ADOLESCENCE

The Morals of a High School Newspaper

Fred, a senior in high school, wanted to publish a mimeographed newspaper for students so that he could express many of his opinions. He wanted to speak out against some of the school's rules, like the rule forbidding boys to have long hair.

Before Fred started his newspaper, he asked his principal for permission. The principal said that it would be all right if, before every publication, Fred would turn over all his articles for the principal's approval. Fred agreed and turned in several articles for approval. The principal approved all of them, and Fred published two issues of the paper in the next two weeks.

But the principal had not expected that Fred's newspaper would receive so much attention. Students were so excited about the paper that they began to organize protests against the hair regulation and the other school rules. Angry parents objected to Fred's opinions. They phoned the principal, telling him that the newspaper was unpatriotic and should not be published. As a result of the rising excitement, the principal ordered Fred to stop

publishing. He gave as a reason that Fred's activities were disruptive to the operation of the school. (Rest, 1986, p. 194)

The preceding story about Fred and his newspaper raises a number of questions related to adolescents' moral development:

Should the principal have stopped the newspaper?

When the welfare of the school is threatened, does the principal have the right to give orders to students?

Does the principal have the freedom of speech to say no in this case?

When the principal stopped the newspaper, was he preventing full discussion of an important problem?

Is Fred actually being loyal to his school and patriotic to his country?

What effect would stopping the newspaper have on the students' education in critical thinking and judgments?

Was Fred in any way violating the rights of others in publishing his own opinions?

PREVIEW

$\mathcal{T}$he story and the questions that followed in the "Images of Adolescence" section are a common method of investigating adolescents' moral judgments. The strategy is to find out how adolescents think about moral dilemmas. Among the questions we will attempt to answer in this chapter are these: What is moral development? What is the nature of adolescents' moral thoughts, moral behavior, moral feelings, and altruism? Should adolescents be morally educated, and if so, what should that education be like? What is the nature of adolescents' values, and what role does religion play in their lives?

What moral dilemmas might crop up for adolescents who are responsible for the school newspaper?

What Is Moral Development?

Moral development is one of the oldest topics of interest to those who are curious about human nature. Today, most people have strong opinions about acceptable and unacceptable behavior, ethical and unethical behavior, and ways in which acceptable and ethical behaviors are to be fostered in adolescents.

Moral development *concerns rules and values about what people should do in their interactions with other people.* In studying these rules and values, developmentalists examine three domains:

First, how do adolescents *reason* or *think* about rules for ethical conduct? For example, an adolescent can be presented with a story in which someone has a conflict about whether or not to cheat in a particular situation, such as taking an exam in school. The adolescent is asked to decide what is appropriate for the character to do and why. This was the strategy used in the "Images of Adolescence" section regarding Fred's newspaper. The focus is placed on the reasoning adolescents use to justify their moral decisions.

Second, how do adolescents actually *behave* in moral circumstances? For example, with regard to cheating, the emphasis is on observing adolescents' cheating and the environmental circumstances that produced and maintain the cheating. Adolescents might be observed through a one-way mirror as they are taking an exam. The observer might note whether they take out "cheat" notes, look at another students' answers, and so on.

Third, how do adolescents *feel* about moral matters? In the example of cheating, do the adolescents feel enough guilt to resist temptation? If adolescents do cheat, do feelings of guilt after the transgression keep them from cheating the next time they face temptation? The remainder of this discussion of moral development focuses on these three facets—thought, behavior, and feelings. Keep in mind that although we have separated moral development into three components—thought, behavior, and feelings—the components often are interrelated. For example, if the focus is on the individual's behavior, it is still important to evaluate the person's intentions (moral thought). And emotions accompany moral reasoning and can distort moral reasoning.

It is important to note that moral development involves both *interpersonal dimensions* (involving others' rights and well-being) and *intrapersonal dimensions* (involving a person's basic values and sense of self) (Walker, 1996; Walker & Hennig, in press). The interpersonal dimension of moral development regulates people's social interactions and arbitrates conflicts. The intrapersonal dimension regulates a person's activities when she or he is not engaged in social interaction. In sum, moral development is a multifaceted concept.

Moral Thought

How do adolescents think about standards of right and wrong? Piaget had some thoughts about this question. So did Lawrence Kohlberg.

Piaget's Ideas and Cognitive Disequilibrium Theory

Interest in how children and adolescents think about moral issues was stimulated by Piaget (1932), who extensively observed and interviewed children from the ages of 4 to 12. Piaget watched children play marbles to learn how they used and thought about the game's rules. He also asked children questions about ethical issues—theft, lies, punishment, and justice, for example. Piaget concluded that children think in two distinct ways about morality, depending on their developmental maturity. **Heteronomous morality** *is the first stage of moral development in Piaget's theory, occurring at 4 to 7 years of age. Justice and rules are conceived of as unchangeable properties of the world, removed from the control of people.* **Autonomous morality,** *the second stage of moral development in Piaget's theory, is displayed by older children (about 10 years of age and older). The child becomes aware that rules and laws are created by people, and that, in judging an action, one should consider the actor's intentions as well as the consequences.* Children 7 to 10 years of age are in a transition between the two stages, evidencing some features of both.

A heteronomous thinker judges the rightness or goodness of behavior by considering the consequences of the behavior, not the intentions of the actor. For example, the heteronomous thinker says that breaking twelve cups accidentally is worse than breaking one cup intentionally while trying to steal a cookie. For the moral autonomist, the reverse is true. The actor's intentions assume paramount importance. The heteronomous thinker also believes that rules are unchangeable and are handed down by all-powerful authorities. When Piaget suggested to a group of young children that new rules be introduced into the game of marbles, they resisted. By contrast, older children—moral autonomists—accept change and recognize that rules are merely convenient, social agreed-upon conventions, subject to change by consensus.

The heteronomous thinker also believes in **immanent justice,** *Piaget's concept that, if a rule is broken, punishment will be meted out immediately.* The young child somehow believes that the violation is connected automatically to the punishment. Thus, young children often look around worriedly after committing a transgression, expecting inevitable punishment. Immanent justice also implies that if something unfortunate happens to someone, it must be because the person had transgressed earlier. Older children, who are moral autonomists, recognize that punishment is socially mediated and occurs only if a relevant person witnesses the wrongdoing and that, even then, punishment is not inevitable.

Story subject	Grade		
	7	9	12
	Percentage		
Alcohol	2	0	5
Civil rights	0	6	7
Drugs	7	10	5
Interpersonal relations	38	24	35
Physical safety	22	8	3
Sexual relations	2	20	10
Smoking	7	2	0
Stealing	9	2	0
Working	2	2	15
Other	11	26	20

Figure~13.1

Actual Moral Dilemmas Generated by Adolescents.

importance in the monks' moral views, and their concerns about prevention of suffering and the role of compassion are not captured by Kohlberg's theory. More about cultural variations in adolescents' moral thought appears in Sociocultural Worlds of Adolescence. In sum, although Kohlberg's approach does capture much of the moral reasoning voiced in various cultures around the world, as we have just seen, there are some important moral concepts in particular cultures that his approach misses or misconstrues (Walker, 1996).

Gender and the Care Perspective

In chapter 12, we discussed Carol Gilligan's view that relationships and connections to others are critical aspects of female development. Gilligan (1982, 1992) also has criticized Kohlberg's theory of moral development. She believes that his theory does not adequately reflect relationships and concern for others. The **justice perspective** *is a moral perspective that focuses on the rights of the individual; individuals stand alone and independently make moral decisions. Kohlberg's theory is a justice perspective.* By contrast, the **care perspective** *is a moral perspective that views people in terms of their connectedness with others and emphasizes interpersonal communication, relationships with others, and concern for others. Gilligan's theory is a care perspective.* According to Gilligan, Kohlberg greatly underplayed the care perspective in moral de-

This 14-year-old boy in Nepal is thought to be the sixth holiest Buddhist in the world. In one study of twenty adolescent male Buddhist monks in Nepal, the issue of justice, a basic theme in Kohlberg's theory, was not a central focus in the monks' moral views. Also, the monks' concerns about prevention of suffering and the importance of compassion are not captured in Kohlberg's theory.

Cross-Cultural Comparisons of Moral Development

Cultural meaning systems vary around the world, and these systems shape children's morality (Miller, 1995). Consider a comparison of American and Indian Hindu Brahman children (Shweder, Mahapatra, & Miller, 1987). Like people in many other non-Western societies, Indians view moral rules as part of the natural world order. This means that Indians do not distinguish between physical, moral, and social regulation, as Americans do. For example, in India, violations of food taboos and marital restrictions can be just as serious as acts intended to cause harm to others. In India, social rules are seen as inevitable, much like the law of gravity.

As shown in figure 13.A, there is some, but not much, overlap in the moral concerns of children in Indian and American cultures. For Americans accustomed to viewing morality as a freely chosen social contract, Indian beliefs pose a different world view, one that is not easy to reconcile with such treasured ideas as the autonomy of an individualized conscience.

The interviews conducted by Richard Shweder and his colleagues (1987) with Indian and American children revealed sharp cultural differences in what people judge to be right and wrong. For example, Indian and American children disagree about eating beef. On the other hand, there are areas of overlap between the two cultures. For example, both think that breaking promises and ignoring beggars is wrong.

According to moral development theorist and researcher William Damon (1988), where culturally specific practices take on profound moral and religious significance, as in India, the moral development of children focuses extensively on their adherence to custom and convention. In contrast, Western moral doctrine tends to elevate abstract principles, such as justice and welfare, to a higher moral status than customs or conventions. As in India, socialization practices in many Third World countries actively instill in children a great respect for their culture's traditional codes and practices.

Another recent research investigation by Joan Miller and David Bersoff (in press) documented how the majority of Asian Indian children, adolescents, and adults give priority to interpersonal needs in moral conflict situations, whereas the majority of Americans give priority to an individual's justice. Americans were more likely than Indians to downplay the importance of caring in conflict situations, which is likely an outgrowth of the stronger emphasis on an individual's rights in America.

Disagreement: Brahman children think it is right;
American children think it is wrong.

—Hitting an errant child with a cane
—Eating with one's hands
—Father opening a son's letter

Disagreement: Brahman children think it is wrong;
American children think it is right.

—Addressing one's father by his first name
—Eating beef
—Cutting one's hair and eating chicken after father's death

Agreement: Brahman and American children think it is wrong.

—Ignoring a beggar
—Destroying another's picture
—Kicking a harmless animal
—Stealing flowers

Agreement: Brahman and American children think it is right.

—Men holding hands

Figure~13.A

Agreements/Disagreements Between American and Indian Hindu Brahman Children About Right and Wrong.

velopment. She believes that this may have happened because he was a male, because most of his research was with males rather than females, and because he used male responses as a model for his theory.

In extensive interviews with girls from 6 to 18 years of age, Gilligan and her colleagues found that girls consistently interpret moral dilemmas in terms of human relationships and base these interpretations on listening and watching other people (Gilligan, 1990; Gilligan, Brown, & Rogers, 1990). According to Gilligan, girls have the ability to sensitively pick up different rhythms in relationships and often are able to follow the pathways of feelings. Gilligan believes that girls reach a critical juncture in their development when they reach adolescence. Usually around 11 to 12 years of age, girls become aware that their intense interest in intimacy is not prized by the male-dominated culture, even though society values women as caring and altruistic. The dilemma is that girls are presented with a choice that makes them look either selfish or selfless. Gilligan believes that, as adolescent girls experience this dilemma, they increasingly silence their "distinctive voice."

Researchers have found support for Gilligan's claim that females' and males' moral reasoning often centers around different concerns and issues (Galotti, Kozberg, & Farmer, 1990; Garmon, Basinger, & Gibbs, 1995; Skoe & Gooden, 1993). However, one of Gilligan's initial claims—that traditional Kohlbergian measures of moral development are biased against females—has been extensively disputed. For example, most research studies using the Kohlberg stories and scoring system do not find sex differences (Walker, 1984, 1991). Thus, the strongest support for Gilligan's claims comes from studies that focus on items and scoring systems pertaining to close relationships, pathways of feelings, sensitive listening, and the rhythm of interpersonal behavior (Galotti, Kozberg, & Farmer, 1990).

While females often articulate a care perspective and males a justice perspective, the gender difference is not absolute, and the two orientations are not mutually exclusive (Lyons, 1990). For example, in one study, 53 of 80 females and males showed either a care or a justice perspective, but 27 subjects used both orientations, with neither predominating (Gilligan & Attanucci, 1988).

Moral Reasoning and Social Conventional Reasoning

Some researchers have questioned whether reasoning about moral matters is distinct from reasoning about social matters (Turiel, 1978; Ward, 1991). **Social conventional reasoning** *refers to thoughts about social consensus and convention, as opposed to moral reasoning that stresses ethical issues.* Advocates of the social conventional reasoning approach argue that conventional rules are created to control behavioral irregularities (Enright, Lapsley, & Olson, 1984; Lapsley, 1993; Lapsley, Enright,

& Serlin, 1986). In this way, the actions of individuals can be controlled and the existing social system maintained. Conventional rules are arbitrary. For example, not eating food with one's fingers is a social conventional rule, as is raising one's hand before talking in class.

By contrast, moral rules are not arbitrary. Also, moral rules are not created by social consensus, but rather are obligatory, widely applicable, and somewhat impersonal (Turiel, 1978). Thus, rules pertaining to lying, stealing, cheating, and physically harming another person are moral rules because violation of these rules affronts ethical standards that exist apart from social consensus and convention. In sum, moral judgments are structured as concepts of justice, whereas social conventional judgments are structured as concepts of social organization (Lapsley, Enright, & Serlin, 1986).

So far, we have discussed a number of ideas about the nature of moral thought. One of the criticisms of Kohlberg's cognitive theory of moral development is that he did not give adequate attention to moral behavior. Next, we examine the nature of moral behavior.

MORAL BEHAVIOR

What are the basic processes that behaviorists and social learning theorists believe are responsible for adolescents' moral behavior? How do cognitive social learning theorists view adolescents' moral development?

Basic Processes

Social learning theory emphasizes the moral behavior of adolescents. The familiar processes of reinforcement, punishment, and imitation have been invoked to explain how and why adolescents learn certain moral behaviors and why their behaviors differ from one another. The general conclusions to be drawn are the same as for other domains of social behavior. When adolescents are reinforced for behavior that is consistent with laws and social conventions, they are likely to repeat that behavior. When models who behave "morally" are provided, adolescents are likely to adopt their behavior. And when adolescents are punished for immoral or unacceptable behavior, those behaviors can be eliminated, but at the expense of sanctioning punishment by its very use and of causing emotional side effects for the adolescent.

To these general conclusions can be added several qualifiers. The effectiveness of reinforcement and punishment depends on how consistently they are administered and the schedule that is adopted. The effectiveness of modeling depends on the characteristics of the model (such as power, warmth, uniqueness, and so on) and the presence of cognitive processes, such as symbolic codes and imagery, to enhance retention of the modeled behavior.

What kind of adult moral models are adolescents being exposed to in American society? Do such models usually do what they say? Adolescents are especially tuned in to adult hypocrisy, and evidence indicates that they are right to believe that many adults display a double standard, their moral actions not always corresponding to their moral thoughts. A poll of 24,000 adults sampled views on a wide variety of moral issues. Detailed scenarios of everyday moral problems were developed to test moral decision making. Consider the example of whether the adult would knowingly buy a stolen color television set. More than 20 percent said that they would, even though 87 percent said that this act is probably morally wrong. And approximately 31 percent of the adults said that they would be more likely to buy the stolen television if they knew they would not get caught. While moral thought is an important dimension of moral development, these data glaringly underscore that what people believe about right and wrong does not always correspond with how they will act in moral situations.

In addition to emphasizing the role of environmental determinants and the gap between moral thought and moral action, social learning theorists also emphasize that moral behavior is situationally dependent. That is, they say that adolescents are not likely to display consistent moral behavior in diverse social settings. In a classic investigation of moral behavior—one of the most extensive ever conducted—Hugh Hartshorne and Mark May (1928–1930) observed the moral responses of 11,000 children and adolescents who were given the opportunity to lie, cheat, and steal in a variety of circumstances—at home, at school, at social events, and in athletics. A completely honest or a completely dishonest child or adolescent was difficult to find. Situation-specific moral behavior was the rule. Adolescents were more likely to cheat when their friends pressured them to do so and when the chance of being caught was slim. Other analyses suggest that some adolescents are more likely to lie, cheat, and steal than others, indicating more consistency of moral behavior in some adolescents than in others (Burton, 1984).

Cognitive Social Learning Theory of Moral Development

The **cognitive social learning theory of moral development** *emphasizes a distinction between adolescents' moral competence—the ability to produce moral behaviors—and moral performance—those behaviors in specific situations* (Mischel & Mischel, 1975). Competence, or acquisition, depends primarily on cognitive-sensory processes; it is the outgrowth of these processes. Competencies include what adolescents are capable of doing, what they know, their skills, their awareness of moral rules and regulations, and their cognitive ability to construct behaviors. Adolescents' moral performance, or behavior, however, is determined by their motivation and the rewards and incentives to act in a specific moral way. Albert Bandura (1991) also believes that moral development is best understood by considering a combination of social and cognitive factors, especially those involving self-control.

One reason that social learning theorists have been critical of Kohlberg's view is that, as mentioned earlier, they believe that he placed too little emphasis on moral behavior and the situational determinants of morality. However, while Kohlberg argued that moral judgment is an important determinant of moral behavior, he, like the Mischels, stressed that the individual's interpretation of both the moral and the factual aspects of a situation leads him or her to a moral decision (Kohlberg & Candee, 1979). For example, Kohlberg mentioned that "extramoral" factors, like the desire to avoid embarrassment, may cause individuals to avoid doing what they believe to be morally right. In sum, both the Mischels and Kohlberg believe that moral action is influenced by a complex of factors. Overall, the findings are mixed with regard to the association of moral thought and behavior (Arnold, 1989), although one investigation with college students found that individuals with both highly principled moral reasoning and high ego strength were less likely to cheat in a resistance-to-temptation situation than were their low-principled and low-ego-strength counterparts (Hess, Lonky, & Roodin, 1985).

At this point, we have discussed a number of ideas about the nature of moral development, moral thought, and moral behavior. A summary of these ideas is presented in concept table 13.1. As we see next, there is a reemergence of interest in the emotional aspects of moral development.

MORAL FEELINGS

Among the ideas formulated about the development of moral feelings are the concepts developed by psychoanalytic theorists, the role of child-rearing techniques, the nature of empathy, and the role of emotions in moral development.

Psychoanalytic Theory

As discussed in chapter 2, Sigmund Freud's psychoanalytic theory describes the *superego* as one of the three main structures of personality (the id and the ego being the other two). In Freud's classical psychoanalytic theory, an individual's superego—the moral branch of personality—develops in early childhood when the child resolves the Oedipus conflict and identifies with the same-sex parent. According to Freud, one reason why children resolve the Oedipus conflict is to alleviate the fear of losing their parents' love and of being punished for their unacceptable sexual wishes toward the opposite-sex parent. To reduce anxiety, avoid punishment, and maintain parental affection, children form a superego by identifying with the same-sex parent. In Freud's view, through this identification, children internalize the parents' standards of right and wrong that reflect societal prohibitions. Also, children turn inward the hostility that was previously aimed at the same-sex parent. This inwardly directed hostility is then experienced self-punitively (and

Concept	Processes/ Related Ideas	Characteristics/Description
What Is Moral Development?	Its nature	Moral development concerns rules and conventions about what people should do in their interactions with others. The three main domains of moral development are thought, behavior, and feelings.
Moral Thought	Piaget's ideas and cognitive disequilibrium theory	Piaget argued that, from four to seven years of age, children are in the stage of heteronomous morality, and from about the age of 10 on, are in the stage of autonomous morality. Formal operational thought may undergird changes in the moral reasoning of adolescents. Cognitive disequilibrium theory states that adolescence is an important period in moral development, especially as individuals move from the relatively homogeneous grade school to the more heterogeneous high school and college environments, where they are faced with contradictions between the moral concepts they have accepted and experiences outside their family and neighborhood. Older adolescents often come to understand that their set of beliefs is but one of many and that there is considerable debate about what is right and what is wrong.
	Kohlberg's ideas on moral development	Kohlberg developed a provocative theory of the development of moral reasoning. He argued that moral development consists of three levels—preconventional, conventional, and postconventional—and six stages (two at each level). Increased internalization characterizes movement to levels 2 and 3. Kohlberg's longitudinal data show a relation of the stages to age, although the highest two stages, especially stage 6, rarely appear. Influences on the Kohlberg stages include cognitive development, modeling, cognitive conflict, peer relations, and role-taking opportunities.
	Kohlberg's critics	Criticisms involve an overemphasis on moral thought and an underemphasis on moral behavior, the quality of the research, inadequate consideration of culture's role in moral development, and underestimation of the care perspective in moral development. Gilligan believes that Kohlberg's theory reflects a justice perspective (individual); she advocates a stronger care perspective (views people in terms of their connectedness with others and emphasizes interpersonal communication). Gilligan also believes that adolescence is a critical juncture in the development of a moral voice for females. Researchers have found support for Gilligan's claim that females' and males' moral reasoning often centers around different concerns, although sex differences in Kohlberg's stages have not been consistently found. Studies that focus more extensively on items pertaining to close relationships and that use scoring systems that emphasize connectedness support Gilligan's claims.
	Moral reasoning and social conventional reasoning	Social conventional reasoning refers to thoughts about social consensus and convention, as opposed to moral reasoning, which stresses ethical issues.
Moral Behavior	Reinforcement, punishment, imitation, and situation-specific moral behavior	Behaviorists and social learning theorists argue that adolescents' moral behavior is determined by the processes of reinforcement, punishment, and imitation. Situational variability in moral behavior is stressed.
	Cognitive social learning theory of moral development	The cognitive social learning theory of moral development emphasizes a distinction between moral competence (the ability to produce moral behaviors) and moral performance (those behaviors in specific situations). In general, social learning theorists are critical of Kohlberg's theory, believing that he placed too little emphasis on moral behavior and its situational variability.

unconsciously) as guilt. In the psychoanalytic account of moral development, self-punitiveness of guilt keeps children, and later on, adolescents from committing transgressions. That is, children and adolescents conform to societal standards to avoid guilt.

In Freud's view, the superego consists of two main components—the ego ideal and the conscience—which promote children and adolescents' development of moral feelings. The **ego ideal** *is the component of the superego that involves ideal standards approved by parents*, whereas the **conscience** *is the component of the superego that involves behaviors not approved of by parents*. An individual's ego-ideal rewards the individual by conveying a sense of pride and personal value when the individual acts according to moral standards. The conscience punishes the individual for acting immorally by making the individual feel guilty and worthless. In this way, self-control replaces parental control.

What role do parents play in their adolescent's moral development?

> *What is moral is what you feel good after and what is immoral is what you feel bad after.*
>
> **—Ernest Hemingway**

Erik Erikson (1970) argued that there are three stages of moral development: specific moral learning in childhood, ideological concerns in adolescence, and ethical consolidation in adulthood. According to Erikson, during adolescence, individuals search for an identity. If adolescents become disillusioned with the moral and religious beliefs they acquired during childhood, they are likely to lose, at least temporarily, their sense of purpose and feel that their lives are empty. This may lead to adolescents' search for an ideology that will give some purpose to their life. For the ideology to be acceptable, it must both fit the evidence and mesh with adolescents' logical reasoning abilities. If others share this ideology, a sense of community is felt. For Erikson, ideology surfaces as the guardian of identity during adolescence because it provides a sense of purpose, assists in tying the present to the future, and contributes meaning to the behavior (Hoffman, 1980).

Child-Rearing Techniques and Moral Development

Both Piaget and Kohlberg held that parents do not provide any unique or essential inputs to children's moral development. However, they did believe that parents are responsible for providing general role-taking opportunities and cognitive conflict. Nonetheless, Piaget and Kohlberg did not see parents as playing the primary role in moral development, reserving that role for peers (Walker, 1996).

In Freud's psychoanalytic theory, the aspects of child rearing that encourage moral development are practices that instill the fears of punishment and of losing parental love. Developmentalists who have studied child-rearing techniques and moral development have focused on parents' discipline. These discipline techniques include love withdrawal, power assertion, and induction (Hoffman, 1970). Love withdrawal comes closest to the psychoanalytic emphasis on fear of losing parental love. **Love withdrawal** *is a discipline technique in which a parent removes attention or love from the child*, as when the parent refuses to talk to the child or states a dislike for the child. For example, the parent might say, "I'm going to leave you if you do that again," or "I don't like you when you do that." **Power assertion** *is a discipline technique in which a parent attempts to gain control over the child or the child's resources*. Examples include spanking, threatening, or removing privileges. **Induction** *is the discipline technique in which a parent uses reason and explanation of the consequences for others of the child's actions*. Examples of induction include, "Don't hit him. He was only trying to help," and "Why are you yelling at her? She didn't mean to trip you."

Moral development theorist and researcher Martin Hoffman (1970) believes that any discipline produces arousal on the child's part. Love withdrawal and power assertion are likely to evoke a very high level of arousal, with love withdrawal generating considerable anxiety and power assertion considerable hostility. Induction is more likely to produce a moderate level of arousal in adolescents, a level that permits them to attend to the cognitive rationales parents offer. When a parent uses power assertion and love withdrawal, the adolescent may be so aroused that, even if the parent gives accompanying explanations about the consequences for others of the adolescent's actions, the adolescent might not attend to them. Power assertion presents parents as weak models of self-control—as individuals who cannot control their feelings. Accordingly, adolescents may imitate this model of poor self-control when they face stressful circumstances. The use of induction, however, focuses the adolescent's attention on the action's consequences for others, not on the adolescent's own shortcomings. For these reasons, Hoffman (1988) believes that parents should use induction to encourage adolescents' moral development. In research on parenting techniques, induction is more positively related to moral development than is love withdrawal or power assertion, although the findings vary according to developmental level and socioeconomic status. Induction works better with elementary-school-aged children than with preschool children (Brody & Shaffer, 1982) and better with middle-class than with lower-class children (Hoffman, 1970). Older children and adolescents are probably better able to understand the reasons given to them and are better at perspective taking. Some theorists believe that the internalization of society's moral standards is more likely among middle-class than among lower-class individuals because internalization is more rewarding in the middle-class culture (Kohn, 1977).

In sum, a number of developmentalists believe that family processes play a more important role in moral development than Kohlberg did. They argue that inductive discipline contributes to moral motivation and that parental values influence children's and adolescents' developing moral thoughts (Boyes & Allen, 1993; Walker, 1993).

Empathy

Positive feelings, such as empathy, contribute to adolescents' moral development. Feeling **empathy** *means reacting to another's feelings with an emotional response that is similar to the other's response.* Although empathy is experienced as an emotional state, it often has a cognitive component—the ability to discern another's inner psychological states, or what we have previously called *perspective taking.*

At about 10 to 12 years of age, individuals develop an empathy for people who live in unfortunate circumstances (Damon, 1988). Children's concerns are no longer limited to the feelings of particular persons in situations they directly observe. Instead, 10- to 12-year-olds expand their concerns to the general problems of people in unfortunate circumstances—the poor, the handicapped, and the socially outcast, for example. This newfound sensitivity may lead older children to behave altruistically, and later may give a humanitarian flavor to adolescents' development of ideological and political views.

Although every adolescent may be capable of responding with empathy, not all do. Adolescents' empathic behavior varies considerably. For example, in older children and adolescents, empathic dysfunctions can contribute to antisocial behavior. Some delinquents convicted of violent crimes show a lack of feeling for their victims' distress. A 13-year-old boy convicted of violently mugging a number of elderly people, when asked about the pain he had caused one blind woman, said, "What do I care? I'm not her" (Damon, 1988). In one recent study, parental empathy was associated with adolescent empathy (Marshall & others, 1994).

The Contemporary Perspective on the Role of Emotions in Moral Development

We have seen that classical psychoanalytic theory emphasizes the power of unconscious guilt in moral development but that other theories, such as that of Damon, emphasize the role of empathy. Today, many developmentalists believe that both positive feelings, such as empathy, sympathy, admiration, and self-esteem, and negative feelings, such as anger, outrage, shame, and guilt, contribute to adolescents' moral development (Damon, 1988; Eisenberg, 1997). When strongly experienced, these emotions influence adolescents to act in accord with standards of right and wrong. Such emotions as empathy, shame, guilt, and anxiety over other people's violations of standards are present early in development and undergo developmental change throughout childhood and adolescence. These emotions provide a natural base for adolescents' acquisition of moral values, both orienting adolescents toward moral events and motivating them to pay close attention to such events. However, moral emotions do not operate in a vacuum to build adolescents' moral awareness, and they are not sufficient in themselves to generate moral responsivity. They do not give the "substance" of moral regulation—the rules, values, and standards of behavior that adolescents need to understand and act on. Moral emotions are inextricably interwoven with the cognitive and social aspects of adolescents' development.

In a recent study of fifth-, eighth-, and eleventh-graders, parents were the individuals most likely to evoke guilt (Williams & Bybee, 1994). With development, guilt evoked by members of the extended family and siblings was less prevalent, but guilt engendered by girlfriends or boyfriends was more frequent. At the higher grade levels, the percentage of students reporting guilt over aggressive, externalizing behavior declined, whereas those mentioning guilt over internal thoughts and inconsiderateness increased. Males were more likely to report guilt over externalizing behaviors, whereas females reported more guilt over violating norms of compassion and trust.

The web of feeling, cognition, and social behavior is also experienced in altruism—the aspect of adolescents' moral development we discuss next.

ALTRUISM

Altruism *is an unselfish interest in helping another person.* While adolescents have often been described as egocentric and selfish, adolescent acts of altruism are, nevertheless, plentiful—the hardworking adolescent who places a one-dollar bill in the church offering plate each week; the adolescent-sponsored car washes, bake sales, and concerts organized to make money to feed the hungry and help children who are mentally retarded; and the adolescent who takes in and cares for a wounded cat. How do psychologists account for such altruistic acts?

Reciprocity and exchange are involved in altruism (Brown, 1986). Reciprocity is found throughout the human world. Not only is it the highest moral principle in Christianity, but it is also present in every widely practiced religion in the world—Judaism, Hinduism, Buddhism, and Islam. Reciprocity encourages adolescents to do unto others as they would have others do unto them. In one recent study, adolescents showed more helping behavior around the house when mothers were involved with and spent time helping the adolescent (Eberly & Montemayor, 1996).

Not all adolescent altruism is motivated by reciprocity and exchange, but self-other interactions and relationships help us to understand altruism's nature (Eisenberg & others, 1995). The circumstances most likely to involve altruism by adolescents are empathetic or sympathetic emotion for an individual in need or a close relationship between the benefactor and the recipient (Clark & others, 1987). Altruism occurs more often in adolescence than in childhood, although examples of caring for others and comforting someone in distress occur even during the preschool years (Eisenberg, 1991).

> *But you cannot give to people what they are incapable of receiving.*
>
> —Agatha Christie, *Funerals Are Fatal* (1953)

Forgiveness *is an aspect of altruism that occurs when the injured person releases the injurer from possible behavioral retaliation.* In one investigation, individuals from the fourth grade through college and adulthood were asked questions about forgiveness (Enright, Santos, & Al-Mabuk, 1989). The adolescents were especially swayed by peer pressure in their willingness to forgive others. Consider one 12-year-old girl's response to Kohlberg's dilemma of Heinz and the druggist:

> *Interviewer:* "Suppose all of Heinz's friends come to see him and say, 'Please be more mature about this. We want you to be friends with the druggist.' Would it help him to forgive the druggist? Why/why not?"
>
> *Girl:* "Probably, because Heinz would think they wanted him to. They would influence him."

In response to the same question, a 15-year-old girl said, "Yes, it would be his friends showing him the outside view. They would help him." The adolescent forgiveness theme that emerged was that the injured party often fails to see the best course of action. Outside aid, especially from friends, helps the harmed person to clarify the problem and then forgive.

Emerson once said, "The meaning of good and bad, better, and worse, is simply helping or hurting." By developing adolescents' capacity for empathy and altruism, America can become a nation of *good* people who *help* rather than hurt.

MORAL EDUCATION

The moral education of adolescents has become a widely discussed topic. Many parents worry that their adolescents are growing up without traditional values. Teachers complain that many of their students are unethical. Among the questions about moral education we examine are these: What is the hidden curriculum? What is the nature of direct moral education versus indirect moral education? What is values clarification? What is cognitive moral education? How should we foster adolescents' moral growth?

The Hidden Curriculum

The **hidden curriculum** *is the pervasive moral atmosphere of a school.* This atmosphere includes school and classroom rules, attitudes toward academics and extracurricular activities, the moral orientation of teachers and school administrators, and text materials. More than half a century ago, educator John Dewey (1933) recognized that, whether or not they offer specific programs in moral education, schools provide moral education through the hidden curriculum. Schools, like families, are settings for moral development. Teachers serve as models of ethical or unethical behavior. Classroom rules and peer relations at school transmit attitudes about cheating, lying, stealing, and consideration of others. The school administration, through its rules and regulations, represents a value system to students.

Direct and Indirect Moral Education

Approaches to moral education can be classified as either direct or indirect (Benninga, 1988). **Direct moral education** *involves either emphasizing values or character traits during specified time slots or integrating these values or traits throughout the curriculum.* **Indirect moral education** *involves encouraging adolescents to define their own and others' moral values and helping them to define the moral perspectives that support those values.*

Direct Moral Education (Character Education)

In the direct moral education approach, instruction in specified moral concepts can take the form of example and definition, class discussions and role-playing, or rewarding students for proper behavior. The use of McGuffey Readers during the early part of the twentieth century exemplifies the direct approach. The stories and poems in the readers taught moral behavior and character in addition to academics.

In indirect moral education, children and adolescents are encouraged to define their own and others' values and are helped to define the moral perspectives that support those values. The most widely adopted indirect moral education approaches are values clarification and cognitive moral education.

Many of the current character education approaches advocate the development of a "basic moral literacy" to prevent youth from engaging in immoral behavior and doing harm to others and themselves. Many of the character education interventions are at the level of the elementary school. Recent books that advocate this character education approach include *The Book of Virtues* (Bennett, 1993), *Educating for Character* (Lickona, 1991), *Reclaiming Our Schools* (Wynne & Ryan, 1993), and *Greater Expectations* (Damon, 1995).

The political campaigns of many office-seekers now emphasize "the moral crisis," "the breakdown of family values," "America's moral decline," "moral illiteracy," "the values crisis," and so on. Movements include the Character Education Partnership, the Character Education Network, the Aspen Declaration on Character Education, and the publicity campaign "Character Counts."

William Bennett (1986), former U.S. secretary of education, wrote:

> If college is really interested in teaching its students a clear lesson in moral responsibility, it should tell the truth about drugs in a straightforward way. This summer, our college presidents should send every student a letter saying they will not tolerate drugs on campus—period. The letter should then spell out precisely what the college's policy will be toward students who use drugs. Being simple and straightforward about moral responsibility is not the same as being simplistic and unsophisticated.

Bennett also believes that every elementary and secondary school should have a discipline code, making it clear to adolescents and parents what the school expects of them. Then the school should enforce the code.

Indirect Moral Education

The most widely adopted indirect approaches to moral education are values clarification and cognitive moral education.

Values Clarification   Values clarification *is an indirect moral education approach that focuses on helping students to clarify what their lives are for and what is worth working for.* In values clarification, students are asked questions or presented with dilemmas and expected to respond, either individually or in small groups. The intent is to help students to define their own values and to become aware of others' values.

In the following values clarification example, students are asked to select from among ten people the six who will be admitted to a fallout shelter during World War III (Benninga, 1988): A fallout shelter under your administration in a remote Montana highland contains only enough space, air, food, and water for six people for three months, but ten people wish to be admitted. The ten have agreed by radio contact that, for the survival of the human race, you must decide which six of them shall be saved. You have exactly 30 minutes to make up your mind before Washington goes up in smoke. These are your choices:

1. A 16-year-old girl of questionable IQ, a high school dropout, pregnant.
2. A policeman with a gun (which cannot be taken from him), thrown off the force recently for brutality.
3. A clergyman, 75.
4. A woman physician, 36, known to be a confirmed racist.
5. A male violinist, 46, who served seven years for pushing narcotics.
6. A 20-year-old Black militant, no special skills.
7. A former prostitute, female, 39.
8. An architect, a male homosexual.
9. A 26-year-old law student.
10. The law student's 25-year-old wife who spent the last nine months in a mental hospital, still heavily sedated. They refuse to be separated.

In this exercise, no answers are considered right or wrong. The clarification of values is left up to the individual student. Advocates of the values clarification approach argue that it is value-free. Critics argue that because of its controversial content, it offends community standards, and they also say that because of its relativistic nature, values clarification undermines accepted values and fails to stress truth and what is right behavior (Oser, 1986).

Cognitive Moral Education Like values clarification, cognitive moral education also challenges direct moral instruction. **Cognitive moral education** *is an indirect moral education approach that emphasizes that adolescents adopt such values as democracy and justice as their moral reasoning is developed.* In this approach, students' moral standards are allowed to develop through their attention to environmental settings and exercises that encourage more advanced moral thinking. Thus, in contrast to values clarification, cognitive moral education is not value-free. Such values as democracy and justice are emphasized. The advocates of cognitive moral education argue that, when moral standards are imposed—as in the direct moral education approach—adolescents can never completely integrate and fully understand moral principles, and that only through participation and discussion can adolescents learn to apply the rules and principles of cooperation, trust, community, and self-reliance.

Lawrence Kohlberg's theory of moral development has extensively influenced the cognitive moral education approach. Contrary to what some critics say, Kohlberg's theory is neither completely relativistic nor completely morally neutral. Higher-level moral thinking is clearly preferred to lower-level moral thinking. And Kohlberg's theory stresses that higher-level thinking can be stimulated through focused discussion of dilemmas. Also, in the 1980s, Kohlberg (1986) revised his

views on moral education by placing more emphasis on the school's moral atmosphere, not unlike John Dewey did many years ago.

Damon's Comprehensive Approach to Moral Education

Developmentalist William Damon (1988, 1995) believes that moral education should follow what is known about the nature of children's and adolescents' moral development. From scientific studies and his own observations of moral development in children and adolescents, Damon believes that the six principles explained below should serve as the foundation for the development of moral education programs:

1. Adolescents experience classic moral issues facing humans everywhere—issues of fairness, honesty, responsibility, kindness, and obedience, for example—simply by participating in social relationships. Thus, adolescents' moral awareness develops within their normal social experiences. Their moral awareness may need to be guided, informed, and enhanced, but it does not need to be imposed directly in a punitive, authoritarian manner.
2. Adolescents' moral awareness is shaped and supported by natural emotional reactions to observations and events. Such emotional reactions as empathy support moral compassion and altruism. Emotions like shame, guilt, and fear support obedience and rule adoption. Children's and adolescents' attachment feelings for parents provide an affective foundation for developing respect for authority.
3. Interactions with parents, teachers, and other adults introduce children and adolescents to important social standards and rules. These interactions produce knowledge and respect for the social order, including its principles of organization and legitimate authority. Authoritative adult-adolescent (parent-adolescent or teacher-adolescent) relationships, in which extensive verbal give-and-take and nonpunitive adult control that justifies demands are present, yield the most positive results for adolescents' moral judgment and behavior.
4. Peer relations introduce children and adolescents to the norms of direct reciprocity and to the standards of sharing, cooperation, and fairness. Through peer relations, children and adolescents learn about mutuality, equality, and perspective taking, which promote the development of altruism.
5. Broad variations in social experiences can produce substantial differences in moral reasoning among children and adolescents. One

such variation is the different roles and expectations that girls and boys experience, especially in traditional social environments. As discussed earlier in the chapter, Carol Gilligan (1982, 1992) believes that the moral development of girls is often oriented more toward relationships and that the moral development of boys is often oriented more toward justice and the individual. There is reason to believe that such orientations can be socially transformed as cultures change. According to Damon, there should be an increased emphasis on both boys and girls learning the principles of care *and* justice.

6. Moral development in schools is determined by the same cognitive and social processes that apply to moral development in other settings. This means that adolescents acquire moral values by actively participating in adult-adolescent and peer relationships that support, enhance, and guide their natural moral tendencies. According to Damon, adolescents' morality is not enhanced by lessons or lectures in which adolescents are passive recipients of information or, even worse, captive and recalcitrant audiences. Further, the quality of social interaction in a school setting communicates a moral message that is more enduring than direct, declarative statements and lectures by teachers. To receive a competent moral education in a democratic society, adolescents need to experience egalitarian interactions that reflect democratic values— among them equality, fairness, and responsibility.

Damon (1988, 1995) believes that, for teachers and parents to contribute positively to an adolescent's moral development, they need to practice *respectful engagement* with the adolescent. Adolescents need guidance, but, for the guidance to register, adolescents need to be productively engaged, and their own initiatives and reactions must be respected.

Damon recognizes that parents alone, or schools alone, are not completely responsible for adolescents' moral development. Adolescents' moral education occurs both in and out of school through adolescents' interactions with parents, peers, and teachers, and through their experiences with society's standards. These interactions are not value-free, and although there is some disagreement about exactly what should be communicated to adolescents in the course of moral education, there is more agreement than is commonly acknowledged. Some fundamental values are shared widely enough to be transmitted without hesitation to adolescents. For example, no one wants adolescents to follow a path of dishonesty, drug abuse, or cruel

antisocial behavior, and all of us want adolescents to endorse justice, abide by legitimate authority, consider the needs of others, and be responsible citizens in a democratic society.

Damon's approach contrasts with the permissive approach, which assumes that children's and adolescents' moral growth is enhanced when they are left alone. It also stands in contrast to the indoctrinational approach of direct moral education, which states that children and adolescents can learn moral values by passively listening to the demands of authority figures. Damon's ideas have much in common with cognitive moral education, but they go beyond the traditional view of cognitive moral education, which focuses almost exclusively on the role of schools, peers, and cognition in moral development. Damon's view is more comprehensive because it recognizes the importance of emotions, parent-adolescent relations, and culture in moral development, and integrates these with the influence of schools, peers, and cognition in a meaningful way.

Critics of Damon's approach say that he gives too much credit to emotions in explaining moral development and not enough to cognition, and that he does not adequately integrate the emotional and cognitive dimensions of moral development. Critics also point out that his views are more relevant to young children's emerging morality than to the adolescent's moral development and its domains of ideology, cognitive transformations in trying to understand society, and idealistic interpretations of cooperation (Rest, 1996). Nonetheless, Damon (1988, 1995) has made important contributions to our understanding of moral education, especially through his emphasis on emotions and parental roles.

Rest's Four-Component Model

James Rest (1995) believes that moral development builds upon four basic processes: moral sensitivity, moral judgment, moral motivation, and moral character.

Moral sensitivity *involves interpreting situations and being aware of how our actions affect other people.* It involves being aware of the different possible lines of action and how each line of action could affect the parties concerned, including oneself. Moral sensitivity consists of imaginatively constructing possible scenarios (often from limited cues and partial information), envisioning consequent chains of events in the real world, and empathy and role-taking skills. Moral sensitivity is needed to become aware that there is a moral issue in a situation.

Moral judgment *involves making decisions about which actions are right and which are wrong.* Once the person is aware that these various lines of action are possible, the question becomes, Which line of action has greater moral justification? This is the process emphasized by Piaget and Kohlberg. Even at an early age people have intuitions about what is fair and moral and make moral judgments

Component	Education
Moral sensitivity	Sensitivity approaches
Moral judgment	Cognitive moral education
Moral motivation	Communitarian approach
Moral character	Character education

Figure~13.2

Rest's Components of Moral Development and Their Application to Education.

about even the most complex human activities. The psychologist's job is to understand how these intuitions arise and determine what governs their application to real-world events.

Moral motivation *involves prioritizing moral values over other personal values.* People have many values, including those related to careers, affectionate relationships, aesthetic preferences, institutional loyalties, hedonistic pleasures, excitement, and so on. Why place a higher priority on moral values than on these other values? The behavior of the most evil people the world has ever known, such as Hitler and Stalin, can be explained in terms of the low priority they gave to moral values and need not be explained as due to deficiencies in moral sensitivity and moral judgment. Further, people like Hitler and Stalin probably rated high on the next component of moral development.

Moral character *involves having the strength of your convictions, persisting, and overcoming distractions and obstacles.* An individual might have all of the first three components (might be sensitive to moral issues, have good judgment, and give high priority to moral values), but if the person does not have moral character, he or she might wilt under pressure or fatigue, fail to follow through, or become distracted or discouraged, and fail to produce moral behavior. Moral character presupposes that the person has set goals and that achieving those goals involves the strength and skills to act in accord with those goals. The individual with moral character does not act impulsively and has considerable self-discipline.

Rest's four-component model is useful in comparing different approaches to moral education (see figure 13.2):

1. The dilemma discussion approach, promoted in Kohlberg's earlier writings, emphasizes moral judgment. This cognitive moral education approach is still widely used with individuals in college or professional schools; it assumes that students are already advanced in basic socialization (by virtue of having made it through

so much schooling). Here the main social concern is to prepare professionals to make decisions that will be morally right.

2. The character education approach emphasizes the fourth component—moral character—and the development of self-discipline consistent with living in civilized society. Children, especially those prone to juvenile delinquency, are special targets of character education. The main social concern in character education is to eliminate the destructive behavior of youth (such as violence, drugs, and adolescent pregnancy).

3. Sensitivity approaches—such as sensitivity training for improved face-to-face communication, sensitivity to cultural diversity, sensitivity to sexual harassment, and sensitivity to physical and psychological abuse—emphasize the first component: moral sensitivity. The sensitivity approaches are aimed at individuals of all ages.

4. The communitarian approach suggests that students, usually middle school and secondary school students, should be involved in community service. The main social concern is to strengthen ties to social units larger than just the family. By emphasizing the importance of rootedness in the community, this approach is aimed at the third component of moral development—moral motivation.

At various times in our discussion of moral development there have been references to adolescents' moral values. Let's examine these now.

VALUES, RELIGION, AND CULTS

What are adolescents' values like today? How powerful is religion in adolescents' lives? Why do some adolescents run away to join cults? We consider each of these questions in turn.

Values

Adolescents carry with them a set of values that influences their thoughts, feelings, and actions (Flanagan, 1997). What were your values when you were an adolescent? Are the values of today's adolescents changing?

Over the past two decades, adolescents have shown an increased concern for personal well-being and a decreased concern for the well-being of others, especially for the disadvantaged (Astin, Green, & Korn, 1987; Astin & others, 1997). As shown in figure 13.3, today's college freshmen are more strongly motivated to be well off financially and less motivated to develop a meaningful philosophy of life than were their counterparts of 20 or even 10 years ago. Student commitment to becoming very well off financially as a "very important" reason for

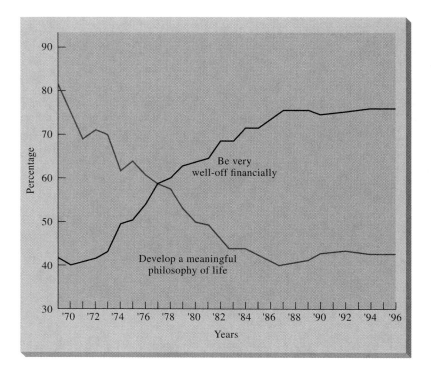

Figure~13.3

Changing Freshman Life Goals, 1970–1996.
The percentages indicated are in response to the question of identifying a life goal as "essential" or "very important." There has been a significant reversal in freshman life goals in the last two decades, with a far greater percentage of today's college freshmen stating that a "very important" life goal is to be well off financially, and far fewer stating that developing a meaningful philosophy of life is a "very important" life goal.

attending college reached a record high in the 1996 survey (73 percent), declining only slightly to 74.1 percent in 1994, compared to 50 percent in 1971.

However, two aspects of values that increased during the 1960s continue to characterize many of today's youth: self-fulfillment and self-expression (Conger, 1981, 1988). As part of their motivation for self-fulfillment, many adolescents show great interest in their physical health and well-being. Greater self-fulfillment and self-expression can be laudable goals, but if they become the only goals, self-destruction, loneliness, or alienation can result. Young people also need to develop a corresponding sense of commitment to others' welfare. Encouraging adolescents to have a strong commitment to others, in concert with an interest in self-fulfillment, is an important task for America at the close of the twentieth century.

Some signs indicate that today's adolescents are shifting toward a stronger interest in the welfare of society. For example, between 1986 and 1996, there was an increase in the percentage of freshmen who said that they were strongly interested in participating in community action programs (24 percent in 1996 compared to 18 percent in 1986) and in helping to promote racial understanding (35 percent in 1996 compared to 27 percent

in 1986). In one recent study, adolescents' participation in community service stimulated them to reflect on society's political organization and moral order (Yates, 1995). More adolescents are showing an active interest in the problems of homelessness, child abuse, hunger, and poverty (Conger, 1988). The percentage of adolescents who believe that it is desirable to work for a social service organization rose from 11 percent in 1980 to 17 percent in 1989 (Johnston, Bachman, & O'Malley, 1990). Whether these small increments in concern for the community and society will continue to increase in the remainder of the 1990s is difficult to predict.

> *Without civic morality communities perish; without personal morality their survival has no value.*
>
> —**Bertrand Russell**

Three major aspects of adolescent community service have been studied (Yates & Youniss, 1997, in press): (1) *The characteristics and motivations of participants in comparison to nonparticipants.* For example, in one study undergraduates who participated in off-campus

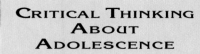

CRITICAL THINKING ABOUT ADOLESCENCE

Values Billboards

Over the last two decades or so, Americans have adopted a popular form of dress that provides an opportunity for interpreting the values that individuals hold: decorated T-shirts. By observing and interpreting the wardrobes of adolescents, you might be able to determine what musical groups and sports teams are their favorites, what colleges they aspire to attend, and a host of other information. In addition, these data can

imply values. For example, if you encounter an adolescent with a T-shirt that proclaims recent participation in a bowling tournament, you can reasonably infer that the adolescent values competition.

Carefully observe the next ten adolescents with decorated T-shirts that you encounter. What do you observe about the preferences they are displaying? What can you infer about the wearer's values from the identities they promote? How confident are you about your interpretations? By observing and interpreting the decorated clothes of adolescents, you are learning to think critically by *making accurate observations, descriptions, and inferences about adolescent development.*

There are some signs that today's adolescents are shifting toward a stronger interest in the welfare of society, as evidenced by the volunteer work these adolescents are doing on Earth Day.

volunteer work of a charitable or helping nature showed greater personal competence (in grades, mastery motivation, and engagement in goal-related activities) than those who did not participate in this type of work (Serow, Ciechalski, & Daye, 1990). (2) *The effects of service participation.* For example, in one study researchers measured adolescents' level of alienation before and after involvement in service activities (Calabrese & Schumer, 1986). They found that the adolescents showed less alienation after participating in the service activities. (3) *The process of service participation.* In this type of study, researchers seek to explain what occurs during the course of the service experience to affect the participants (Eyler & Giles, 1997). Process-oriented studies portray experience as a sequence of changes and describe service as a process of adjusting to a new social context and role. There are few process-oriented studies of community service. In one recent study, the majority of essays written by high school students after serving in a soup kitchen included evaluations of societal stereotypes and inequity, as well as the student's role in bringing about change (Yates & Youniss, in press). The evaluations occurred at three levels: (1) articulating stereotypes, (2) comparing one's situation with that of others, and (3) reflecting on justice and responsibility.

Religion

Many children and adolescents show an interest in religion, and religious institutions created by adults are designed to introduce certain beliefs to them and ensure that they will carry on a religious tradition. For example, societies have invented Sunday schools, parochial education, tribal transmission of religious traditions, and parental teaching of children at home.

Many children and adolescents show an interest in religion, and many religious institutions created by adults (such as this Muslim school in Malaysia) are designed to introduce them to religious beliefs and ensure that they will carry on a religious tradition.

Does this indoctrination work? In many cases it does (Paloutzian, 1996). In general, adults tend to adopt the religious teachings of their upbringing. For instance, individuals who are Catholics by the time they are 25 years of age, and who were raised as Catholics, likely will continue to be Catholics throughout their adult years. If a religious change or reawakening occurs, it is most likely to take place during adolescence.

> *Religion enlightens, terrifies, subdues; it gives faith, inflicts remorse, inspires resolutions, and inflames devotion.*
>
> **—Henry Newman, 1853**

Religious issues are important to adolescents (Paloutzian & Santrock, 1997). In one recent survey, 95 percent of 13- to 18-year olds said that they believe in God or a universal spirit (Gallup & Bezilla, 1992). Almost three-fourths of adolescents said that they pray, and about one-half indicated that they had attended religious services within the past week. Almost one-half of the youth said that it is very important for a young person to learn religious faith.

Developmental Changes

Adolescence may be an especially important juncture in religious development. Even if children have been indoctrinated into a religion by their parents, because of advances in their cognitive development they might begin to question what their own religious beliefs truly are.

During adolescence, especially late adolescence and the college years, identity development becomes a central focus (Erikson, 1968). Youth want answers to the questions "Who am I? What am I all about as a person? What kind of life do I want to lead?" As part of their search for identity, adolescents begin to grapple in more sophisticated, logical ways with questions like these: "Why am I on this planet? Is there really a God or higher spiritual being, or have I just been believing what my parents and the church imprinted in my mind? What really are my religious views?"

Piaget's (1962) cognitive developmental theory provides a theoretical backdrop for understanding religious development in children and adolescents. For example, in one study, children were asked about their understanding of certain religious pictures and Bible stories (Goldman, 1964). The children's responses fell into three stages closely related to Piaget's theory.

In the first stage (up until 7 or 8 years of age)—*preoperational intuitive religious thought*—children's religious thoughts were unsystematic and fragmented. The

How do religious thought and behavior change as children and adolescents develop? How are children's and adolescents' religious conceptions influenced by their cognitive development?

children often either did not fully understand the material in the stories or did not consider all of the evidence. For example, one child's response to the question "Why was Moses afraid to look at God?" (Exodus 3:6) was "Because God had a funny face!"

In the second stage (occurring from 7 or 8 to 13 or 14 years of age)—*concrete operational religious thought*—children focused on particular details of pictures and stories. For example, when asked why Moses was afraid to look at God, one child said, "Because it was a ball of fire. He thought he might burn him." Another child responded, "It was a bright light and to look at it might blind him."

In the third stage (age 14 through the remainder of adolescence)—*formal operational religious thought*—adolescents revealed a more abstract, hypothetical religious understanding. For example, one adolescent said that Moses was afraid to look at God because "God is holy and the world is sinful." Another youth responded, "The awesomeness and almightiness of God would make Moses feel like a worm in comparison."

Other researchers have found similar developmental changes in children and adolescents. For example, in one study, at about 17 or 18 years of age adolescents increasingly commented about freedom, meaning, and hope—abstract concepts—when making religious judgments (Oser & Gmunder, 1991).

Religiousness and Sexuality in Adolescence

One area of religion's influence on adolescent development involves sexual activity (McLaughlin & others, 1997). Although variability and change in church teachings make it difficult to characterize religious doctrines simply, most churches discourage premarital sex. Thus, the degree of adolescents' participation in religious organizations may be more important than religious affiliation as a determinant of premarital sexual attitudes and behavior. Adolescents who attend religious services frequently may hear messages about abstaining from sex. Involvement of adolescents in religious organizations also enhances the probability that they will become friends with adolescents who have restrictive attitudes toward premarital sex. In one study, adolescents who attended church frequently and valued religion in their lives were less experienced sexually and had less permissive attitudes toward premarital sex than their counterparts who attended church infrequently and said that religion did not play a strong role in their lives (Thornton & Camburn, 1989). However, while religious involvement is associated with a lower incidence of sexual activity among adolescents, adolescents who are religiously involved and sexually active are less likely to use medical methods of contraception (especially the pill) than their sexually active counterparts with low religious involvement.

The Hare Krishna is one of several religious cults that have attracted the attention of youth.

Why do some adolescents leave home and become members of a cult? Some experts believe that the failures of organized religion and the church, as well as a weakening of family life, are causes (Spilka, 1991). What kind of youth are most vulnerable to the appeal of cults? Six characteristics have been identified (Swope, 1980):

1. *Idealistic.* Due to the teachings and example of family, religious leaders, peers, educators, and others, there has developed within young people a desire to help others, to improve society, and often to know God better. The cults manipulate this idealism, convincing members that only within their specialized groups can such inclinations be actualized.

2. *Innocent.* Because relationships with religious leaders in the past have been wholesome, the potential recruit naively believes that all who claim to speak in the name of God are sincere and trustworthy. Elmer Gantry and Jim Jones notwithstanding, the trappings of religion are a powerful lure here.

3. *Inquisitive.* On college and high school campuses around the country, intelligent young people, looking for interesting groups to join, are approached by enthusiastic, "together" recruiters who invite them to meetings where, they are told, they will meet other fine young people. It sounds exciting. Discussion, they are assured, will focus on ecology, world problems, religion, ethics, education—anything in which the recruit has shown some interest.

4. *Independent.* Many young people are recruited into cults when they are away from home— independent for the first time. Parents of such students are not always aware of how their children spend evenings and weekends, and often do not learn that they have left college until several weeks or months after they drop out. Backpackers are particular targets for cult recruiters. These young people are often lonely and susceptible to invitations for free meals and fellowship.

5. *Identity-seeking.* Young adults in every generation experience identity crises as they seek to determine their strengths and weaknesses, value systems, goals, and religious and social beliefs.

6. *Insecure.* Inquisitive young people—looking for new experiences, seeking to clarify their own identities, away from the influence of family, friends, and mentors—develop uneasy feelings of insecurity. Lacking trusted counselors to whom they can turn when upset or disturbed, they are especially vulnerable to smiling, friendly people who show great interest in them and manipulate them through what one cult calls "love bombing."

At this point, we have discussed a number of ideas about moral feelings, altruism, moral education, values, religion, and cults. A summary of these ideas is presented in concept table 13.2.

CONCEPT TABLE 13.2
Moral Feelings, Altruism, Moral Education, and Values, Religion, and Cults

Concept	Processes/Related Ideas	Characteristics/Description
Moral Feelings	Psychoanalytic theory	The superego—the moral branch—is one of the three main personality structures in Freud's theory. The superego has two main parts: ego ideal and conscience. Erikson believes that ideological concerns are a key dimension of moral development in adolescence.
	Child-rearing techniques	The focus in on parental discipline styles—love withdrawal, induction, and power assertion. Induction has been the most effective in promoting moral development.
	Empathy	At the beginning of adolescence, individuals often start showing more empathy for people in unfortunate circumstances.
	Contemporary perspective	Both positive feelings (such as empathy) and negative feelings (such as guilt) contribute to adolescents' moral development. Moral emotions are interwoven with the cognitive and social dimensions of moral development.
Altruism	Its nature	Altruism is an unselfish interest in helping someone else. Although adolescents have been described as selfish, they do engage in altruism. Adolescents are especially swayed by peer pressure to forgive others.
Moral Education	The hidden curriculum	This refers to the pervasive moral atmosphere of a school.
	Direct and indirect moral education	Direct moral education involves emphasizing either values or character traits. Indirect moral education involves encouraging adolescents to define their own and others' values while helping them define their moral perspective. The two main approaches to indirect moral education are values clarification and cognitive moral education.
	Damon's comprehensive approach	Damon believes that moral education should accord with what we know about moral development and should involve active participation by the adolescent.
	Rest's four-component model	Rest argues that moral development can best be understood by considering four components of morality—sensitivity, judgment, motivation, and character.
Values, Religion, and Cults	Values	Over the last two decades, adolescents have shown an increased concern for personal well-being and a decreased concern for the welfare of others. Recently, adolescents have shown a slight increase in concern for community and societal issues. Three main aspects of adolescent community service have been studied: characteristics and motivations of participants; effects of service participation; and the process of service participation.
	Religion	Many children and adolescents show an interest in religion, and religious institutions are designed to introduce them to religious beliefs. Adolescence may be a special juncture in religious development for many individuals. Piaget's theory provides a cognitive background for understanding religious development. Linkages between religiousness and sexuality occur in adolescence. Fowler proposed a life-span theory of religious development.
	Cults	Cult membership in the United States is extensive. It may appeal to adolescents because of weaknesses in organized religion and families.

*S*UMMARY

One of adolescence's most important tasks is learning right from wrong. To accomplish this task, adolescents need to *think* and *feel* morally, and *act* accordingly.

We began this chapter by reflecting on the morals of a high school newspaper and then evaluated what moral development is. Our coverage of moral thought focused on Piaget's ideas and cognitive disequilibrium theory, Kohlberg's theory, Kohlberg's critics, especially Gilligan, as well as moral reasoning and social conventional reasoning. Our study of moral behavior covered reinforcement, punishment, imitation, and situational variations, and the cognitive social learning theory of moral development. We also read about moral feelings, including psychoanalytic theory, child-rearing techniques, empathy, and the contemporary perspective on the role of emotions in moral development. We learned about altruism, and we studied moral education, including the hidden curriculum, direct and indirect moral education, Damon's comprehensive moral education approach, and Rest's four-component model. We examined the influence of values, religion, and cults in adolescents' lives.

Remember that you can obtain an overall summary of this chapter by again studying the two concept tables on pages 414 and 429. In this chapter, we learned that, in the last decade, adolescents had a strong motivation to be financially well off. With this value in mind, in the next chapter we will turn our attention to the nature of achievement, careers, and work in adolescent development.

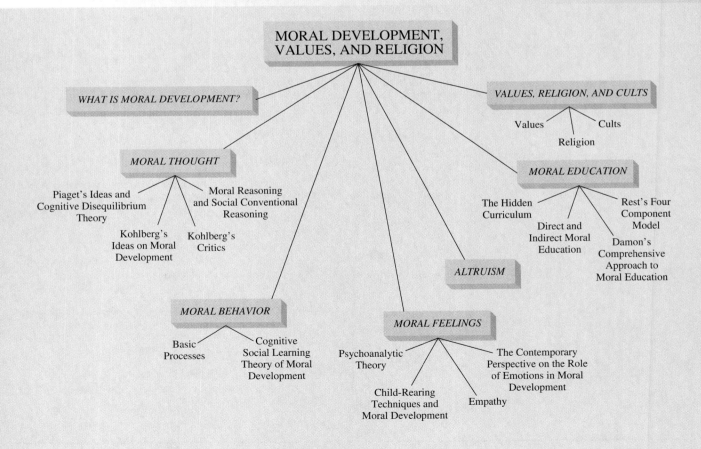

PRACTICAL KNOWLEDGE ABOUT ADOLESCENCE

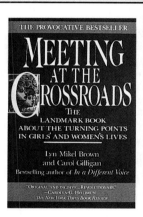

Meeting at the Crossroads

(1992) by Lyn Mikel Brown and Carol Gilligan. Cambridge, MA: Harvard University Press.

This recent book provides a vivid portrayal of how adolescent girls are often ignored and misunderstood as they make their passage through adolescence. Brown and Gilligan developed a listener's guide, a method of following the pathways of girls' thoughts and feelings. Girls' voices at many different points in adolescence are revealed, and recommendations for how to listen more sensitively to their needs are given.

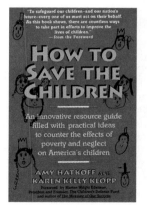

How to Save the Children

(1992) by Amy Hatkoff and Karen Klopp. New York: Simon & Schuster.

This is an innovative resource guide filled with practical ideas about how volunteerism can help to counter the effects of poverty and neglect on America's children. *How to Save the Children* has more than two hundred specific suggestions for things you or an adolescent can do to help children. The book is a clearinghouse of ideas, addresses, and phone numbers for individuals who want to become involved in volunteering their time and talents. A forward by Marian Wright Edelman, president of the Children's Defense Fund, tells how important volunteering is to improving the health and well-being of our nation's children.

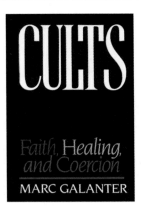

Cults

(1989) by Marc Galanter. New York: Oxford University Press.

This is an A-to-Z book about cults. Covering everything from the mass weddings of Sun Myung Moon's Unification Church to the mass suicide at Jonestown, Galanter explains how charismatic cults indoctrinate their members. *Cults* is a probing psychological journey into the lives and minds of cult members. The dangers of cults for adolescents are clearly presented.

RESOURCES FOR IMPROVING THE LIVES OF ADOLESCENTS

Canadian 4-H Council, Canadian 4-H Foundation/ Conseil des 4-H du Canada, Fondation des 4-H du Canada
1690 Woodward Drive, Suite 208
Ottawa, Ontario K2C 3R8
613-723-4444

4-H in Canada began in 1913 as a community-based organization dedicated to the growth and development of rural youth. Today's program reaches both farm and nonfarm rural youth and focuses on technical skill development related to agriculture as well as on personal development of life skills, such as citizenship, leadership, responsibility, and independence.

Congress of National Black Churches, Inc./Project Spirit
1225 Eye Street NW, Suite 750
Washington, DC 20005-3914
202-371-1091

This organization seeks to generate support for the spiritual, economic, and social needs of African Americans. *Spirit* stands for Strength, Perseverance, Imagination, Responsibility, Integrity, and Talent, and Project Spirit seeks to instill these qualities in 12- to 16-year-old African Americans. Among the project's goals are to provide after-school activities, support academic achievement, and teach practical life skills. Project Spirit currently operates in 65 churches in seven states and in the District of Columbia.

Curriculum for Social Justice
by Gretchen Buchenholz
212-831-1322

This curriculum helps youth to become advocates for children and to increase awareness of homelessness and poverty. For a copy of the curriculum, call the phone number listed above.

Four-One-One
7304 Beverly Street
Annandale, VA 22003
703-354-6270

This is a clearinghouse for information on community and national volunteer organizations. The organization provides references and other information about how to start and manage successful volunteer programs. It maintains a library of 3,000 volumes and sponsors, one of which is Super Volunteers, which encourages youth to become involved as volunteers.

National 4-H Council
7100 Connecticut Avenue
Chevy Chase, MD 20815
301-962-2820

This private, nonprofit organization has as its central mission the provision of opportunities for youth.

National Helpers Network, Inc.
245 Fifth Avenue, Suite 1705
New York, NY 10016-8728
212-679-7461

This network developed the Early Adolescent Helper Program, an approach to service learning. The program has the dual goal of raising adolescents' self-esteem and improving communities through adolescent service participation. Among the services adolescents provide are those involving environmental concerns, neighborhood improvement, and tutoring. Students also participate in weekly seminars that encourage them to reflect on their active involvement in the community.

Religious Index One: Periodicals
ATLA
5600 South Woodlawn Avenue
Chicago, IL 60637

This is a subject index to literature on religion. It indexes 328 journal titles, 16,000 articles, and 15,000 book reviews. Information about adolescents includes parent-adolescent relations, church work with youth, drugs and youth, puberty, the YMCA, the YWCA, and youth movements.

Starserve
701 Santa Monica Boulevard, Suite 220
Santa Monica, CA 90401
800-888-8232

This organization has sent a kit of materials to every school in the United States to encourage teachers to motivate students to become involved in community service. For further information, call the toll-free number listed above.

Youth Action Network/Réseau Action Jeunesse
100 Adelaide Street West, Suite 906
Toronto, Ontario M5H 1S3
416-368-2277

Youth Action Network is dedicated to inspiring and facilitating youth education and involvement with environmental and social issues. It provides youth with contacts, information, resources, and inspiration. Current projects include the Resource Action Centre, Youth Action Workshops, and Youth Action Canada.

$\mathcal{E}$XPLORING ADOLESCENT DEVELOPMENT

To further explore the nature of adolescent development, we will examine a research study on moral reasoning about sexually transmitted diseases and discuss adolescent volunteerism.

$\mathcal{R}$ESEARCH ON ADOLESCENT DEVELOPMENT

Moral Reasoning About Sexually Transmitted Diseases

Featured Study

Jadack, R. A., Hyde, J. S., Moore, C. F., & Keller, M. L. (1995). Moral reasoning about sexually transmitted diseases. *Child Development, 66,* 167–177.

The purpose of this study was to investigate moral reasoning related to sexual behavior that could lead to the development of sexually transmitted diseases. Kohlberg's and Gilligan's cognitive developmental theories provided the conceptual framework for the study.

Method

The subjects were 40 college freshmen (mean age = 18.3 years) and 32 col-

lege seniors (mean age = 22.3 years). They were presented with hypothetical dilemmas about situations in which sexually transmitted diseases (STDs) could be transmitted. Respondents were asked to explain why they believed that the characters involved in the dilemmas should or should not engage in risky behaviors.

Four moral dilemmas were presented to the students. One dilemma involved a caring relationship in which the protagonist is deciding, before sexual intercourse, whether to tell his partner that he has genital herpes, risking rejection from the partner. Another dilemma involved a casual, noncaring relationship in which the protagonist is deciding whether to tell previous partners about newly diagnosed genital warts.

Results and Discussion

The college students' responses to the moral dilemmas were scored based on Kohlberg's and Gilligan's theories. The college seniors were at a higher stage of reasoning in Kohlberg's theory than were the college freshmen. Typically, the 18-year-olds reasoned at a combined stage 2–stage 3 level, or at a stage 3 level, while the 22-year-olds reasoned at a combined stage 3–stage 4 level, or at a stage 4 level. The 22-year-olds' typical reasoning extended into topics of responsibility and obligation in relationships. Unexpectedly, there were no gender differences in the students' moral reasoning.

$\mathcal{A}$DOLESCENT HEALTH AND WELL-BEING

Volunteerism

Marian Wright Edelman (1992) paints the following portrait to illustrate why we need more volunteers to help children:

- Every morning, 100,000 American children wake up homeless.
- Every 13 seconds, an American child is reported neglected or abused.

- Every 32 seconds, an American baby is born into poverty.
- Every 64 seconds, a baby is born to a teenage mother.
- Every 13 hours, an American preschooler is murdered.

To help safeguard and support our nation's children, we need more people, including adolescents, to volunteer their time and effort. Helping does

not take wealth or power. What it does take is caring, hard work, and persistence.

In many cases, adolescents are willing to help children in need but are never asked to help. Adolescents are nearly four times as likely to volunteer when asked than when they were not asked (Hatkoff & Klopp, 1992).

Adults and adolescents can help children in their communities by donating their time and talent to effective child-serving programs. Even the smallest contributions can make a difference (Hatkoff & Klopp, 1992). In a program called Common Cents of New York, community members "harvest" the pennies in their neighborhoods. In just 1 month, students at Dalton Middle School in New York City collected $29,000 in pennies and change, which they donated to programs for homeless children.

Adolescents can help by taking an active role in community affairs. They can express their views at public forums, churches, and town meetings. Many community boards, public officials, and city agencies have youth advisory councils where adolescents' views on pending issues can be heard. And in one recent study, the volunteer experiences of adolescents in a summer work camp stimulated them to rethink their political attitudes associated with service (Switzer & Dew, 1995).

Many cities also have youth corps volunteer programs in which students spend a year doing community service and in return receive special training, a weekly stipend, and money toward a college education. Most schools and communities have information about youth corps, and the National Association of Service and Conservation Corps is a clearinghouse for youth corps programs (202-331-9647).

Many schools also have community service programs. In such programs, adolescents can become involved in a host of projects, including mentoring, tutoring, working in a soup kitchen, or helping children at a shelter. If the adolescent's school doesn't have a community service program, then the adolescent can start one. Youth Service America (202-783-8855) is a good source of information for adolescents who want to start a community service program.

Required community service has increased in high schools. In a recent survey, 15 percent of the nation's largest school districts had this requirement in 1995 (National and Community Service Coalition, 1995). Several national organizations and education groups, such as the National Service-Learning Cooperative/Clearinghouse, were established to promote the integration of service into school and university curricula. And several large corporations, such as IBM and the Prudential Insurance Company, have sponsored community service programs for youth (Yates, 1996).

However, even though required community service has increased in secondary schools, most adolescents do not participate in such helping behavior. In one recent study of more than 40,000 students in grades 6 through 12, more than 50 percent said they had not spent time helping people who are poor, hungry, sick, or unable to care for themselves; almost two-thirds said they spend zero hours in volunteer work to help other people (Benson, 1993).

In a recent study conducted with a sample of adolescents in Camden, New Jersey, one of the poorest cities in the United States, a number of African American and Latino American adolescents were nominated by community leaders for having demonstrated unusual commitments to caring for others or serving the community (Hart & Fegley, 1995). Even in the face of trying circumstances, these adolescents had a strong caring orientation.

Shown here are individuals working in the National Helpers Network. In this program, adolescents help their community by donating their time and individual talent.

Louis Feuchter
The Red Dress

Chapter
14
Achievement, Careers, and Work

Whatever you can do, or dream you can, begin it. Boldness has genius, power, and magic in it.

—Johann Wolfgang von Goethe

. . . to lift artificial weights from all shoulders; to clear the paths of laudable pursuit; to afford all an unfettered start, and a fair chance in the race of life.

—Abraham Lincoln,
First annual message to Congress

PREVIEW

American adolescents live in an achievement-oriented world with standards that tell them success is important. The standards suggest that success requires a competitive spirit, a motivation to do well, and the wherewithal to cope with adversity and persist until obstacles are overcome. In the "Images of Adolescence" section, you will read about the importance of achievement in the lives of two Asian American adolescents. In this chapter we will examine the achievement orientation of adolescents from many different backgrounds. This chapter is about achievement, careers, and work.

Kim-Chi and Thuy

Kim-Chi Trinh was only 9 years old in Vietnam when her father used his savings to buy passage for her on a fishing boat. It was a costly and risky sacrifice for the family, who placed Kim-Chi on the small boat, among strangers, in the hope that she eventually would reach the United States, where she would get a good education and enjoy a better life.

Kim made it to the United States and coped with a succession of three foster families. When she graduated from high school in San Diego in 1988, she had a straight-A average and a number of college scholarship offers. When asked why she excels in school, Kim-Chi says that she has to do well because she owes it to her parents, who are still in Vietnam.

Kim-Chi is one of a wave of bright, highly motivated Asians who are immigrating to America. Asian Americans are the fastest-growing ethnic minority group in the United States—two out of five immigrants are now Asian. Although Asian Americans make up only 2.4 percent of the U.S. population, they constitute 17 percent of the undergraduates at Harvard, 18 percent at MIT, 27 percent at the University of California at Berkeley, and a staggering 35 percent at the University of California at Irvine (Butterfield, 1990).

Not all Asian American youth do this well, however. Poorly educated Vietnamese, Cambodian, and Hmong refugee youth are especially at risk for school-related problems. Many refugee children's histories are replete with losses and trauma. Thuy, a 12-year-old Vietnamese girl, has been in the United States for 2 years and resides with her father in a small apartment with a cousin's family of five in the inner city of a West Coast metropolitan area (Huang, 1989). While trying to escape from Saigon, the family became separated, and the wife and two younger children remained in Vietnam. Thuy's father has had an especially difficult time adjusting to the United States, struggling with English classes and being unable to maintain several jobs as a waiter. When Thuy received a letter from her mother saying that her 5-year-old brother had died, Thuy's schoolwork began to deteriorate, and she showed marked signs of depression—lack of energy, loss of appetite, withdrawal from peer relations, and a general feeling of hopelessness. At the insistence of the school, she and her father went to the child and adolescent unit of a community mental health center. It took the therapist a long time to establish credibility with Thuy and her father, but eventually they began to trust the therapist as a good listener who had competent advice about how to handle different experiences in the new country. The therapist also contacted Thuy's teacher, who said that Thuy had been involved in several interethnic skirmishes at school. With the assistance of the mental health clinic, the school initiated interethnic student panels to address cultural differences and discuss reasons for ethnic hostility. Thuy was selected to participate in these panels. Her father became involved in the community mutual assistance association, and Thuy's academic performance began to improve.

ACHIEVEMENT

Some developmentalists worry that the United States is rapidly becoming a nation of hurried, wired people who are raising their youth to become the same way—too uptight about success and failure, and far too worried about how personal accomplishments compare with those of others (Elkind, 1981). Others worry that our achievement expectations for youth have been too too low (Honig, 1996). In this section, we will focus on the importance of adolescence in achievement. We also will discuss motivation, achievement motivation, attribution theory and intrinsic-extrinsic motivation, mastery-oriented versus helpless-oriented achievement patterns, and achievement in ethnic minority adolescents.

The Importance of Adolescence in Achievement

Adolescence is a critical juncture in achievement (Henderson & Dweck, 1990). New social and academic pressures force adolescents toward different roles, roles that often involve more responsibility. Achievement becomes a more serious business in adolescence, and adolescents begin to sense that the game of life is now being played for real (Yoon & others, 1996). They even may begin to perceive current successes and failures as predictors of future outcomes in the adult world. And as demands on adolescents intensify, different areas of their lives may come into conflict. Adolescents' social interests may cut into the time they need to pursue academic matters, or ambitions in one area may undermine the attainment of goals in another, as when academic achievement leads to social disapproval.

Whether or not adolescents effectively adapt to these new academic and social pressures is determined, in part, by psychological, motivational, and contextual factors (Eccles, Wigfield & Schiefele, 1997). Indeed, adolescents' achievement is due to much more than their intellectual ability. Students who are less bright than others often show an adaptive motivational pattern—persistent at tasks and confident about their ability to solve problems, for example—and turn out to be high achievers. In contrast, some of the brightest students show maladaptive achievement patterns—give up easily and do not have confidence in their academic skills, for example—and turn out to be low achievers. We now examine what we mean by *motivation*, which plays an important role in adolescents' achievement.

Motivation

Motivation is *why* individuals behave the way they do. Why is an adolescent hungry? Why is another adolescent studying so hard? Two important dimensions of the "whys" of behavior are activation and direction. First, when adolescents are motivated, they do something. Their behavior is activated or energized. If adolescents are

Adolescence is a critical juncture in achievement. New social and academic pressures force adolescents toward different roles, roles that often involve more responsibility. Whether or not an adolescent effectively adapts to these new academic and social pressures is determined, in part, by psychological and motivational factors.

hungry, they might go to the refrigerator for a snack. If they are motivated to get a good grade on a test, they might study hard. Second, when adolescents are motivated, their behavior also is directed. Why does an adolescent behave one way when there are several options available? For example, if a father reprimands his son for failing to clean up his room before going out, one adolescent might ignore the reprimand, another adolescent might hurry to clean up the room before departing, and a third adolescent might start a verbal argument. Motivation thus focuses on how adolescents direct their behavior or, put another way, the specific behaviors adolescents select in certain situations but not others. To summarize, **motivation** *is why individuals behave, think, and feel the way they do, with special consideration of the activation and direction of their behavior.*

Achievement Motivation

Think about yourself and your friends for a moment. Are you more achievement oriented than they are or less so? If researchers asked you and your friends to tell stories about achievement-related themes, could they actually determine which of you is more achievement oriented?

Some adolescents are highly motivated to succeed and spend a lot of energy striving to excel; others are not as motivated to succeed and do not work as hard to achieve.

Figure~14.1

Type of Stimulus Used to Assess Achievement Motivation. By asking individuals to tell a story about ambiguous stimuli like this picture, David McClelland assessed the nature of an individual's achievement motivation.

These two types of adolescents vary in their **achievement motivation,** *the desire to accomplish something, to reach a standard of excellence, and to expend effort to excel.* Borrowing from Henry Murray's (1938) theory and measurement of personality, psychologist David McClelland (1955) assessed achievement motivation by showing individuals ambiguous pictures that are likely to stimulate achievement-related responses (see figure 14.1). Individuals were asked to tell a story about the picture, and their comments were scored according to how strongly the story reflected achievement. Researchers found that individuals whose stories reflected high achievement motivation had a stronger hope for success than fear of failure, were moderate rather than low- or high-risk takers, and persisted with effort when tasks became difficult (Atkinson & Raynor, 1974). Early research also indicated that independence training by parents promoted achievement, but more recent research reveals that parents need to set high standards for achievement, model achievement-oriented behavior, and reward adolescents for their achievement, if their adolescents are to be achievement oriented (Huston-Stein & Higgens-Trenk, 1978). In one recent study, a combination of parenting style (demandingness and responsiveness) and involvement was related to positive adolescent achievement outcomes (Paulson, 1994). And in another recent study, middle school students had the highest grades when their parents, teachers, and school were authoritative (Paulson, Marchant, & Rothlisberg, 1995).

A concept related to achievement motivation was developed by Matina Horner (1972), who pointed out that much of the research on achievement motivation was based on male experiences. She found that females' achievement-related responses were different from those of males. She theorized that females do not express the same achievement imagery as males because of **fear of success,** *individuals' worry that they will be socially rejected if they are successful.* Some years later, fear of success, originally believed to be confined to females, also was found to be present in males. Females still worried about social rejection, but males worried that all of their achieving would end up being for an unsatisfying goal (Williams, 1987).

Today, fear of success is a much-debated concept. It has not been able to explain why there are so few females in Congress or so few female orchestra conductors. Nonetheless, many females still report a conflict between traditional femininity and competitive achievement. The final explanation is likely to involve an interaction between achievement motivation and the gender-role socialization practices discussed in chapter 11. For example, African American females, who are less likely than White American females to have been traditionally socialized, have lower fear of success (Weston & Mednick, 1970).

Attribution Theory and Intrinsic-Extrinsic Motivation

Shakespeare once wrote, "Find out the cause of this effect, or rather say, the cause of this defect, for the effect defective comes by cause." Attribution theorists have taken Shakespeare's comment to heart. They argue that individuals want to know the causes of people's behavior because the knowledge promotes more effective coping with life's circumstances. **Attribution theory** *states that individuals are motivated to discover the underlying causes of behavior as part of the effort to make sense out of the behavior.* In a way, attribution theorists say, adolescents are like intuitive scientists, seeking the cause behind what happens.

The reasons individuals behave the way they do can be classified in a number of ways, but one basic distinction stands out above all others—the distinction between internal causes, such as the actor's personality traits or motives, and external causes, which are environmental, situational factors such as rewards or task difficulty (Heider, 1958). If adolescents do not do well on a test, do they attribute it to the teacher's plotting against them and making the test too difficult (external cause) or to their not studying hard enough (internal cause)? The answer to such a question influences how adolescents feel about themselves. If adolescents believe that their performance is the teacher's fault, they will not feel as bad as when they do not spend enough time studying.

An extremely important aspect of internal causes for achievement is *effort.* Unlike many causes of success, effort is under adolescents' control and amenable to change.

Santrock: Adolescence

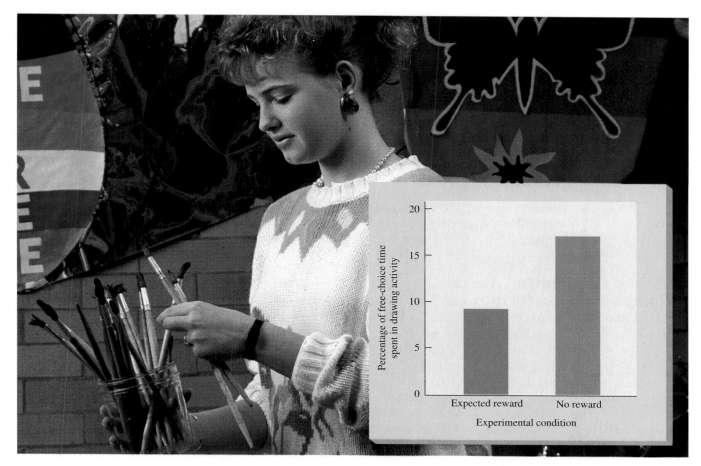

Figure~14.2

Intrinsic Motivation and Drawing Activity.
Of students with an initial high interest in art, those who had received no mention of a reward spent more time in art activity than did students who expected a reward for their participation (Lepper, Greene, & Nisbett, 1973).

The importance of effort in achievement is recognized by most children and adolescents. In one study, third- to sixth-grade students felt that effort was the most effective strategy for good school performance (Skinner, Wellborn, & Connell, 1990).

Closely related to the concept of internal and external causes of behavior is the concept of intrinsic and extrinsic motivation. Adolescents' achievement motivation—whether in school, at work, or in sports—can be divided into two main types: **intrinsic motivation,** *the internal desire to be competent and to do something for its own sake;* and **extrinsic motivation,** *the desire to accomplish something in order to obtain external rewards or avoid external punishments.* If you work hard in college because a personal standard is important to you, intrinsic motivation is involved. But if you work hard in college because you know it will bring you a higher-paying job when you graduate, extrinsic motivation is at work.

A frequent concern is whether to offer a reward to adolescents if they achieve (extrinsic motivation), or whether to let their internal, self-determined motivation

operate (intrinsic motivation). If an adolescent is not producing competent work, seems bored, or has a negative attitude, incentives may help to improve motivation. However, external rewards sometimes get in the way of achievement motivation. Educational psychologist Adele Gottfried (1990) has shown that intrinsic motivation is related to higher school achievement and lower academic anxiety in fourth- through eighth-grade students. And in one investigation, students with a strong interest in art spent more time drawing when they expected no reward than did their counterparts who knew that they would be rewarded. (Lepper, Greene, & Nisbett, 1973) (see figure 14.2).

> *The reward of a thing well done is to have done it.*
> —**Ralph Waldo Emerson,**
> ***Essays,* Second Series, 1844**

In many instances, an adolescent's achievement is motivated by *both* internal and external factors. Some of the most achievement-oriented adolescents are those who have a high personal standard for achievement (internal) as well as a strong sense of competitiveness and a desire to do better than others (external). In one investigation, low-achieving math students who engaged in individual goal setting (internal) and were given comparative information about their peers' achievement (external) worked more math problems and got more of them correct than did their counterparts who experienced either condition alone (Schunk, 1983). Other research suggests that social comparison by itself, though, is not a wise strategy (Ames & Ames, 1989). The argument is that social comparison puts the individual in an ego-involved, threatened, self-focused state rather than a task-involved, effortful, strategy-focused state (Nicholls, 1984).

Mastery Orientation Versus Helpless and Performance Orientations

Closely related to an emphasis on intrinsic motivation, attributions of internal causes of behavior, and the importance of effort in achievement is a mastery orientation. Valanne Henderson and Carol Dweck (1990) have found that adolescents show two distinct responses to difficult or challenging circumstances. Adolescents with a **helpless orientation** *seem trapped by the experience of difficulty and attribute their difficulty to a lack of ability.* They frequently say things like, "I'm not very good at this," even though they may have earlier demonstrated their ability through numerous successes. And once they view their behavior as failure, they often feel anxious about the situation, and their performance worsens even further. Adolescents with a **mastery orientation** *are task oriented. Instead of focusing on their ability, they are concerned about their learning strategies and the process of achievement rather than outcomes.* Mastery-oriented adolescents often instruct themselves to pay attention, to think carefully, and to remember strategies that have worked for them in previous situations. They frequently report feeling challenged and excited by difficult tasks, rather than being threatened by them. In one recent study, task-focused policies and practices in middle school environments were linked with positive motivational shifts in early adolescence (Anderman, Maehr, & Midgley, 1996).

Another issue in motivation involves whether to adopt a mastery or a performance orientation. We already have described what a mastery orientation is like. A **performance orientation** *involves being concerned with the achievement outcome. Winning is what matters and happiness is thought to result from winning.*

What sustains mastery-oriented individuals is the sense of efficacy and satisfaction they feel from effectively dealing with the world in which they live. By contrast, what sustains performance-oriented individuals is winning.

Although skills often are involved in winning, performance-oriented individuals do not always view themselves as necessarily having skills. Rather, they see themselves as using tactics, such as undermining others, to get what they want.

Does all of this mean that mastery-oriented individuals do not like to win and that performance-oriented individuals are not motivated to experience the sense of efficacy that comes from being able to take credit for one's success? No. A matter of emphasis or degree is involved, though. For mastery-oriented individuals, winning isn't everything, and for performance-oriented individuals, skill development and a sense of efficacy take a back seat to winning.

In summary, a number of psychological and motivational factors influence an adolescent's achievement. Especially important in the adolescent's ability to adapt to new academic and social pressures are achievement motivation, internal attributions of effort, intrinsic motivation, and a mastery achievement orientation. Next, we examine the role of ethnicity in adolescents' achievement.

Achievement in Ethnic Minority Adolescents

The diversity that exists among ethnic minority adolescents, a concept discussed in chapters 1 and 9, also is evident in their achievement (Fletcher, 1995; Swanson, 1995). For example, the "Images of Adolescence" section that opened this chapter indicated that although many Asian American adolescents have a very strong achievement motivation, some do not. Later in this section we will return to a discussion of achievement by Asian American adolescents.

Another important point in examining the achievement of ethnic minority adolescents involves differences. Too often, the achievements of ethnic minority group adolescents—especially African American, Latino, and Native American—have been interpreted as "deficits" by middle-class White standards. Rather than perceiving individuals as *culturally different*, many conclusions unfortunately portray the cultural distinctiveness of African Americans, Latinos, and Native Americans as deficient in some way (Jones, 1994).

As also indicated in chapter 9, the socioeconomic status of ethnic minority adolescents has not been adequately studied in most investigations. In many instances, when ethnicity *and* social class are investigated in the same study, social class is a much better predictor of achievement than ethnicity is. Middle-class adolescents fare better than their lower-class counterparts in a variety of achievement situations—expectations for success, achievement aspirations, and recognition of the importance of effort, for example (Gibbs, 1989).

Educational psychologist Sandra Graham (1986, 1990) conducted a number of investigations that revealed not only stronger social class than ethnic differences in

UCLA psychologist Sandra Graham is shown here talking with adolescent boys about motivation. She has conducted important research showing that middle-class African-American children—like their White counterparts—have high achievement expectations and understand that their failure is often due to lack of effort rather than to lack of luck.

Harold Stevenson and his colleagues have found that Asian schools embrace many of the ideals Americans have for their own schools, but are more successful in implementing them in interesting and productive ways that make learning more enjoyable for children and adolescents.

achievement, but also the importance of studying ethnic minority group motivation in the context of general motivational theory. Her inquiries focused on the causes that African American children and adolescents give for their achievement orientation—why they succeed or fail, for example. She was struck by how consistently middle-class African American children and adolescents do not fit the stereotype of either deviant or special populations. They, like their middle-class White American counterparts, have high achievement expectations and understand that failure is often due to lack of effort rather than to luck.

The indisputable fact is that too many ethnic minority group individuals are faced with educational, career, and social barriers (Jones, 1994). Individuals from ethnic minority groups have benefited from the Civil Rights Act of 1964, but much more progress is needed. We do not have all of the answers to the problems of poverty and racial prejudice in America, but as the Reverend Jesse Jackson commented, hopefully we have begun to ask some of the right questions. As discussed in Sociocultural Worlds of Adolescence, some of the right questions are beginning to be asked and answered with regard to African American and Latino students enrolled in math and science courses.

Cross-Cultural Comparisons

At the same time that researchers are concerned about the low achievement of African American, Latino, and Native American adolescents, they are intrigued by the high achievement of Japanese, Chinese, and Asian American adolescents (Evans, 1992). To explore the reasons

underlying such high achievement, Harold Stevenson and his colleagues (Stevenson, 1992, 1995; Stevenson & others, 1990) conducted extensive investigations of children's and adolescents' achievement in the United States, China, and Japan for almost two decades.

The stimulation for this research comes from the poor performance of American students on tests of mathematics and science in comparison to students in other countries. For example, in one cross-national study of math achievement, American eighth- and twelfth-grade students were below the national average in problem solving, geometry, algebra, calculus, and other areas of math (McKnight & others, 1987). In contrast, Japanese eighth-graders had the highest average scores of children from twenty countries, and, in the twelfth grade, Japanese students were second only to Chinese students in Hong Kong. In a recent cross-national comparison of the math and science achievement of 9- to 13-year-olds, Korean and Taiwanese students placed first and second, respectively (Educational Testing Service, 1992). In this cross-national study, 9- to 13-year-old students in the United States finished 13th (out of 15) in science and 15th (out of 16) in math achievement.

These conclusions were reached by Stevenson and his colleagues after completing five different cross-national studies of children and adolescents in the United States,

SOCIOCULTURAL WORLDS OF ADOLESCENCE

Modifying the Math Study Strategies of African American College Students

In 1986, African Americans and Latinos were awarded just eight of the more than six hundred doctoral degrees in math in the United States. At every level—high school, college, and graduate school—comparatively smaller percentages of African American and Latino students enroll in math and science courses. The rate of enrollment, especially for African American students, declined in the 1980s. With more than one-fourth of America's college-age population African American or Latino in 1995, increasing the number of African Americans and Latinos in math and science is critical.

Motivated to discover why the enrollment rate of African Americans and Latinos is so low, University of California–Berkeley mathematician Philip Treisman extensively compared 20 African American and 20 Chinese college students who were enrolled in freshman calculus. At Berkeley, as at many American universities, Asian American students often have the highest rate of success in math. Treisman observed the students in the library, their dormitory rooms, and even their homes. He interviewed their families. The differences between the African American and the Chinese students were not due to motivation, income, family support, or academic preparation. Even African American students who came with the best test scores and other positive predictors tended to do poorly in math, for example. The most striking observation was that the African American students were virtually isolated in their study of math. Eighteen of the twenty African American students always studied alone—the two who studied together eventually dropped out to marry each other. Many erected a wall between their intellectual and social lives. Treisman found that, for many graduates of inner-city and predominantly ethnic minority high schools, the self-reliance that may have helped them get into a top college—by buffering them from the distractions at their secondary schools—became their downfall at

Berkeley. The students had no way to check out their understanding of math or science, no way to check out what Berkeley as an institution required of them.

Within 4 weeks after arriving at Berkeley, thirteen of the twenty Chinese students found study mates, and several others were still searching. The study groups came together after the students had done extensive individual work. Group study was a final, but very important, step. Studying together, the students picked up solutions they had missed. If no student had solved a problem, members of the group recognized its difficulty and thus avoided self-criticism. In these groups, students tested their perceptions of what professors expected, what the university expected, and how many hours they should be studying. They shared tips for handling the bureaucratic maze and for lining up financial aid and housing. They chatted about how to deal with the White community.

Based on his experiences with the African American and Chinese students, Treisman developed a math workshop with three overriding principles: (1) Help ethnic minority students excel, not just avoid failure; (2) emphasize collaborative learning and small-group teaching methods; and (3) require faculty sponsorship. The accomplishments of the math workshop over 7 years of operations include these: Fifty-five percent of the workshop's 231 African American students (compared with 21 percent of the 234 African American students not in the workshop) have earned a grade of B– or better in first-year calculus. African American students in the workshop have consistently scored a full grade higher than nonworkshop African American students. Among African American workshop participants who entered Berkeley in 1978 or 1979, 44 percent graduated in math-based majors, while only 10 percent of the nonworkshop African American students did.

Freshman mathematics and science courses too often have been the burial ground for the aspirations of African American and Latino students who have entered college with the goal of majoring in some area of math or science. Programs such as Philip Treisman's reveal how the underachievement of African American and Latino students can be turned into accomplishment (Charles A. Dana Foundation Report, 1988).

China, Taiwan, and Japan. In these studies, Asian children and adolescents consistently outperformed their U.S. counterparts in math. And the longer they were in school, the wider the gap between the Asian and the American students' math scores became—the lowest differential was

in the first grade, the highest was in the eleventh grade.

To learn more about the reasons for these large cross-cultural differences, the researchers spent hundreds of hours observing in classrooms; interviewing teachers, students, and mothers; and giving questionnaires to fathers. They found that American parents were very satisfied with their children's achievement and education but that the parents' standards were low in comparison to Asian parents'. Also, American parents emphasize that their children's math achievement is determined more by innate ability, whereas Asian parents believe their children's math achievement is due more to effort and training.

In 1990, former president George Bush and the nation's governors adopted a well-publicized goal: to change American education in ways that will help students to lead the world in math achievement by the year 2000. Stevenson (1995) says that is unlikely to happen because American standards and expectations for students' math achievement are too low by international standards.

Even though Asian students do well in math achievement, might there be a dark underside of too much stress and tension in the students and their schools? Stevenson (1995) has not found that to be the case. He asked eleventh-grade students in Japan and the United States how often in the past month they had experienced feelings of stress, depression, aggression, and other problems, such as not being able to sleep well. They also asked the students about how often they felt nervous when they took tests. On all of these characteristics, the Japanese students expressed less distress and fewer problems than the American students did. Such findings do not support the Western stereotype that Asian students are tense, wired individuals driven by relentless pressures for academic excellence. However, the findings should be interpreted cautiously because Asians tend not to disclose personal information, especially of a stressful nature.

Critics of cross-national studies say that such comparisons are flawed because the percentage of adolescents who go to school, and the curricula, vary within each country. Even in the face of such criticism, there is a growing consensus based on different research teams that American adolescents' achievement is very low, that American educators' and parents' expectations for students' math achievement are too low, and that American schools are long overdue for an extensive overhaul.

As mentioned at the beginning of this section, many Asian American adolescents do not fit the "whiz-kid, superachiever" image; instead, they are struggling just to learn English. The whiz-kid image fits many of the adolescents of Asian immigrant families who arrived in the United States in the late 1960s and early 1970s. Many of these immigrants came from Hong Kong, South Korea, India, and the Philippines. The image also fits many of the more than 100,000 Indochinese (primarily Vietnamese) immigrants who arrived in the United States after the Vietnam War in 1975. Both groups included mostly middle- to upper-income professional people who were reasonably well educated and who passed along a strong interest in education and a strong work

ethic to their children and adolescents. For thousands of other Asian Americans, including a high percentage of the 600,000 Indochinese refugees who fled Vietnam, Laos, and Cambodia in the late 1970s, the problems are legion. Many in this wave of refugees lived in poor surroundings in their homelands. They came to the United States with few skills and little education. They speak little English and have a difficult time finding a decent job. They often share housing with relatives. Adjusting to school is difficult for their children and adolescents. Some drop out. Some are attracted to gangs and drugs. Better school systems use a range of culturally focused academic programs and social services to help these children and adolescents adapt more effectively to life in America.

At this point, we have discussed a number of ideas about adolescents' achievement. A summary of these ideas is presented in concept table 14.1. Achievement serves as a foundation for adolescents' career development, the topic we turn to next.

CAREER DEVELOPMENT

What are the future occupations of today's adolescents? What theories have been developed to direct our understanding of adolescents' career choices? What roles do exploration, decision making, and planning play in career development? How do sociocultural factors affect career development?

Tomorrow's Jobs for Today's Adolescents

For almost half a century the United States Bureau of Labor Statistics has published the *Occupational Outlook Handbook*, a valuable source for career information. The following information comes from the 1996–1997 edition (the handbook is revised every 2 years). The current long-term shift from goods-producing to service-producing employment will continue. By the year 2000, nearly four out of every five jobs will be in industries that provide services, such as banking, insurance, health care, education, data processing, and management consulting. Continued expansion of the service-producing sector generates a vision of a workforce dominated by cashiers, retail sales workers, and waiters. In addition to the creation of millions of clerical, sales, and service jobs, the service sector will also be adding jobs for engineers, accountants, lawyers, nurses, and many other managerial, professional, and technical workers. In fact, the fastest growing careers will be those that require the most educational preparation.

The range of employment growth in various careers will be diverse. As indicated in figure 14.3, the greatest growth in jobs will be for technicians and related support occupations. Workers in this group provide technical assistance to engineers, scientists, and other

Concept	Processes/ Related Ideas	Characteristics/Description
The Importance of Adolescence in Achievement	Its nature	Adolescence is a critical juncture in achievement. Social and academic pressures force adolescents to cope with achievement in new ways. Whether or not adolescents effectively adapt to these new social and academic pressures is determined, in part, by psychological and motivational factors.
Motivation and Achievement Motivation	Motivation	Motivation focuses on *why* individuals behave, think, and feel the way they do, with special consideration of the activation and direction of their behavior.
	Achievement motivation	Achievement motivation is the desire to accomplish something, to reach a standard of excellence, and to expend effort to excel. McClelland studied variations of achievement motivation by getting individuals to tell stories involving achievement-related themes. Horner developed the concept of fear of success, which is individuals' worry that they will be socially rejected if they are successful.
Attribution Theory, Intrinsic-Extrinsic Motivation, and Mastery Orientation Versus Helpless and Performance Orientations	Attribution theory	Attribution theory states that individuals are motivated to discover the underlying causes of behavior as part of the effort to make sense out of the behavior. One basic distinction in the causes of behavior is between internal causes and external causes. An extremely important aspect of internal causes for achievement is effort.
	Intrinsic-extrinsic motivation	Intrinsic motivation is the internal desire to be competent and to do something for its own sake. Extrinsic motivation is influenced by external rewards and punishments. Adolescents' intrinsic motivation is related to higher school achievement and lower academic anxiety, although in many instances, achievement is influenced by both internal and external factors.
	Mastery orientation versus helpless and performance orientations	Individuals with a mastery orientation are task oriented. Instead of focusing on their ability, they are concerned about their learning strategies and the process of achievement rather than outcomes. In contrast, individuals with a helpless orientation seem trapped by the experience of difficulty and attribute their difficulty to a lack of ability. Individuals with a performance orientation are concerned with achievement outcomes rather than achievement processes; winning is what matters to them, and they believe that happiness is a result of winning. Experts recommend a mastery orientation rather than a helpless or performance orientation in achievement contexts.
Achievement in Ethnic Minority Adolescents and Cross-Cultural Comparisons	Ethnicity	A special concern is the achievement of adolescents from various ethnic groups. Too often, ethnic differences are interpreted as "deficits" by middle-class White standards. When ethnicity and social class are considered in the same study, social class is often a much better predictor of achievement than ethnicity. Middle-class adolescents fare better than their lower-class counterparts in a variety of achievement situations.
	Cross-cultural comparisons	Psychologists have shown a special interest in the high achievement levels of Asians and Asian American adolescents. Japanese schools and parents place a much stronger emphasis on education and achievement, especially math achievement, than their American counterparts. However, the diversity that exists among ethnic minority adolescents also is evident in their achievement.

Occupational group	Percent change in employment, 1990–2005
Total, all occupations	20 37
Technicians and related support occupations	32
Professional specialty occupations	29
Service occupations	27
Executive, administrative, and managerial occupations	24
Marketing and sales occupations	21
Transportation and material moving occupations	20
Construction trades and extractive occupations	16
Mechanics, installers, and repairers	13
Administrative support occupations, including clerical	8
Handlers, equipment cleaners, helpers, and laborers	5
Agriculture, forestry, fishing, and related occupations	−4
Production occupations	

Figure~14.3

How Employment Change Will Vary Widely by Broad Occupational Group.

professional workers as well as operate and program technical equipment. This group also includes the fastest growing occupation—paralegals. Professional specialty occupations are expected to grow 24 percent from 1988 to 2000. Much of this growth is a result of rising demand for engineers, computer specialists, lawyers, health diagnosing and treating occupations, and preschool, elementary, and secondary school teachers. The greatest decrease in jobs will be in agriculture, forestry, fishing, and related occupations.

Theories of Career Development

Three main theories describe the manner in which adolescents make choices about career development: Ginzberg's developmental theory, Super's self-concept theory, and Holland's personality type theory.

Ginzberg's Developmental Theory

Developmental career choice theory *is Eli Ginzberg's theory that children and adolescents go through three career-choice stages: fantasy, tentative, and realistic* (Ginzberg, 1972; Ginzberg & others, 1951). When asked what they want to be when they grow up, young children may answer "a doctor," "a superhero," "a teacher," "a movie star," "a sports star," or any number of other occupations. In

childhood, the future seems to hold almost unlimited opportunities. Ginzberg argues that, until about the age of 11, children are in the *fantasy stage* of career choice. From the ages of 11 to 17, adolescents are in the *tentative stage* of career development, a transition from the fantasy stage of childhood to the realistic decision making of young adulthood. Ginzberg believes that adolescents progress from evaluating their interests (11 to 12 years of age) to evaluating their capacities (13 to 14 years of age) to evaluating their values (15 to 16 years of age). Thinking shifts from less subjective to more realistic career choices at around 17 to 18 years of age. Ginzberg calls the period from 17 to 18 years of age through the early twenties the *realistic stage* of career choice. During this time, the individual extensively explores available careers, then focuses on a particular career, and finally selects a specific job within the career (such as family practitioner or orthopedic surgeon, within the career of doctor).

Critics have attacked Ginzberg's theory on a number of grounds. For one, the initial data were collected from middle-class youth, who probably had more career options open to them. And, as with other developmental theories (such as Piaget's), the time frames are too rigid. Moreover, Ginzberg's theory does not take into account individual differences—some adolescents make mature decisions about careers (and stick with them) at much earlier ages than specified by Ginzberg. Not all children engage in career fantasies, either. In a revision of his theory, Ginzberg (1972) conceded that lower-class individuals do not have as many options available as middle-class individuals do. Ginzberg's general point—that at some point during late adolescence or early adulthood more realistic career choices are made—probably is correct.

Super's Self-Concept Theory

Career self-concept theory *is Donald Super's theory that individuals' self-concept plays a central role in their career choice. Super believes that it is during adolescence that individuals first construct a career self-concept* (Super, 1967, 1976). He emphasizes that career development consists of five different phases. First, at about 14 to 18 years of age, adolescents develop ideas about work that mesh with their already existing global self-concept—this phase is called *crystallization*. Between 18 and 22 years of age, they narrow their career choices and initiate behavior that enables them to enter some type of career—this phase is called *specification*. Between 21 and 24 years of age, young adults complete their education or training and enter the world of work—this phase is called *implementation*. The decision on a specific, appropriate career is made between 25 and 35 years of age—this phase is called *stabilization*. Finally, after the age of 35, individuals seek to advance their careers and to reach higher-status positions—this phase is called *consolidation*. The age ranges should be thought of as approximate rather than rigid. Super believes that career exploration in adolescence is a key ingredient of adolescents' career self-concept. He constructed the Career Development Inventory to assist counselors in promoting adolescents' career exploration.

Holland's Personality Type Theory

Personality type theory *is John Holland's theory that an effort should be made to match an individual's career choice with his or her personality* (Holland, 1973, 1987). According to Holland, once individuals find a career that fits their personality, they are more likely to enjoy that particular career and to stay in a job for a longer period of time than individuals who work at jobs not suited to their personality. Holland believes that six basic personality types need to be considered when matching the individual's psychological makeup to a career (see figure 14.4):

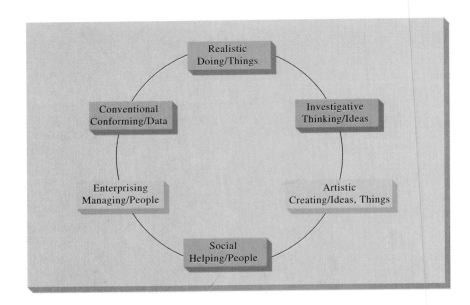

Figure~14.4

Holland's Model of Personality Types and Career Choices.

1. *Realistic.* These individuals are physically strong, deal in practical ways with problems, and have very little social know-how. They are best oriented toward practical careers, such as labor, farming, truck driving, and construction.

2. *Intellectual.* These individuals are conceptually and theoretically oriented. They are thinkers rather than doers. They often avoid interpersonal relations and are best suited to careers in math and science.

3. *Social.* These individuals often have good verbal skills and interpersonal relations. They are likely to be best equipped to enter "people" professions, such as teaching, social work, counseling, and the like.

4. *Conventional.* These individuals show a distaste for unstructured activities. They are best suited for jobs as subordinates, such as bank tellers, secretaries, and file clerks.

5. *Enterprising.* These individuals energize their verbal abilities toward leading others, dominating individuals, and selling people on issues or products. They are best counseled to enter careers such as sales, politics, and management.

6. *Artistic.* These individuals prefer to interact with their world through artistic expression, avoiding conventional and interpersonal situations in many instances. These youth should be oriented toward such careers as art and writing.

If all individuals fell conveniently into Holland's personality types, career counselors would have an easy job. But individuals are more varied and complex than Holland's theory suggests. Even Holland (1987) now admits that most individuals are not pure types. Still, the basic idea of matching the abilities and attitudes of individuals to particular careers is an important contribution to the career field (Vondracek, 1991). Holland's personality types are incorporated into the Strong-Campbell Vocational Interest Inventory, a widely used measure in career guidance.

Criticism of Career Choice Theories

Career development theories have been criticized on a number of fronts. Some critics argue that they are too simple. Others stress that there is little data to support them. Also, theories such as Holland's assume that interests and abilities are fixed during adolescence and early adulthood; critics emphasize that individuals can continue to change and develop as they grow older (Mortimer & Lorence, 1979). Further, career choice is influenced by many factors other than personality; such factors include individual preferences, the influences of parents, peers, and teachers, and sociocultural dimensions.

Cognitive Factors

Exploration, decision making, and planning play important roles in adolescents' career choices. In countries where equal employment opportunities have emerged—such as the United States, Canada, Great Britain, and France—exploration of various career paths is critical in adolescents' career development. Adolescents often approach career exploration and decision making with considerable ambiguity, uncertainty, and stress. Many of

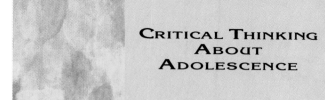

the career decisions made by youth involve floundering and unplanned changes. Many adolescents do not adequately explore careers on their own and also receive little direction from guidance counselors at their schools. On the average, high school students spend less than 3 hours per year with guidance counselors, and in some schools the average is even less (National Assessment of Educational Progress, 1976). In many schools, students not only do not know what information to seek about careers, they do not know how to seek it.

One of the important aspects of planning in career development is awareness of the educational requirements for a particular career. In one investigation, a sample of 6,029 high school seniors from fifty-seven different school districts in Texas was studied (Grotevant & Durrett, 1980). Students lacked accurate information about two aspects of careers: (1) the educational requirements of careers they desired and (2) the vocational interests predominantly associated with their career choices.

Career development is related to identity development in adolescence. Career decidedness and planning are positively related to identity achievement, whereas career planning and decidedness are negatively related to identity moratorium and identity diffusion statuses (Wallace-Broscious, Serafica, & Osipow, 1994). Adolescents farther along in the process of identity formation are better able to articulate their occupational choices and their next steps in obtaining short-term and long-term goals (Raskin, 1985). By contrast, adolescents in the moratorium and diffusion statuses of identity are more likely to struggle with making occupational plans and decisions.

Sociocultural Influences

Not every individual born into the world can grow up to become a nuclear physicist or a doctor—there is a genetic limitation that keeps some adolescents from performing at the high intellectual levels necessary to enter such careers. Similarly, there are genetic limitations that restrict some adolescents from becoming professional football players or professional golfers. But there usually are many careers available to each of us, careers that provide a reasonable match with our abilities. Our sociocultural experiences exert strong influences on career choices from among the wide range available. Among the important sociocultural factors that influence career development are social class, parents and peers, schools, and gender.

Social Class

The channels of upward mobility open to lower-class youth are largely educational in nature. The school hierarchy from grade school through high school, as well as through college and graduate school, is programmed to orient individuals toward some type of career. Less than 100 years ago, it was believed that only 8 years of education were necessary for vocational competence, and anything beyond that qualified the individual for advanced placement in higher-status occupations. By the middle of the twentieth century, the high school diploma had already lost ground as a ticket to career success. College rapidly became a prerequisite for entering a higher-status occupation. Employers reason that an individual with a college degree is a better risk than a high school graduate or a high school dropout.

Parents and Peers

Parents and peers also are strong influences on adolescents' career choices. Although some experts argue that American parents have achievement expectations that are too low, David Elkind (1981) believes that today's parents are pressuring their adolescents to achieve too much, too soon. In some cases, though, adolescents are not challenged enough by their parents. Consider the 25-year-old female

"Your son has made a career choice, Mildred. He's going to win the lottery and travel a lot."

© 1986; Reprinted courtesy of Bunny Hoest and Parade Magazine.

Parents play an important role in the adolescent's achievement. It is important for parents to neither pressure the adolescent too much nor challenge the adolescent too little.

who vividly describes the details of her adolescence that later prevented her from seeking a competent career. From early in adolescence, both of her parents encouraged her to finish high school, but at the same time they emphasized that she needed to get a job to help them pay the family's bills. She was never told that she could not go to college, but both parents encouraged her to find someone to marry who could support her financially. This very bright girl is now divorced and feels intellectually cheated by her parents, who socialized her in the direction of marriage and away from a college education.

From an early age, children see and hear about what jobs their parents have. In some cases, parents even take their children to work with them on jobs. Recently, when we were building our house, the bricklayer brought his two sons to help with the work. They were only 14 years old, yet they were already engaging in apprenticeship work with their father.

Unfortunately, many parents want to live vicariously through their son's or daughter's career achievements. The mother who did not get into medical school and the father who did not make it as a professional athlete may pressure their youth to achieve a career status beyond the youth's talents.

Many factors influence parents' role in adolescents' career development (Young, 1994). For one, mothers who work regularly outside the home and show effort and pride in their work probably have strong influences on their adolescents' career choices. A reasonable conclusion is that when both parents work and enjoy their work, adolescents learn work values from both parents.

Anna Roe (1956) argued that parent-child relationships play an important role in occupation selection. For example, she said that individuals who have warm and accepting parents are likely to choose careers that include work with people, such as sales positions and public relations jobs. By contrast, she stated, individuals

who have rejecting or neglectful parents are more likely to choose careers that do not require a good "personality" or strong social skills, such as accounting and engineering. Critics argue that Roe's ideas are speculative, might not hold in today's world, and are too simple (Grotevant, 1996).

Peers also can influence adolescents' career development. In one investigation, when adolescents had friends and parents with high career standards, they were more likely to seek higher-status careers, even if they came from low-income families (Simpson, 1962).

School Influences

Schools, teachers, and counselors can exert a powerful influence on adolescents' career development. School is the primary setting where individuals first encounter the world of work. School provides an atmosphere for continuing self-development in relation to achievement and work. And school is the only institution in society that is presently capable of providing the delivery systems necessary for career education—instruction, guidance, placement, and community connections.

A national survey revealed the nature of career information available to adolescents (Chapman & Katz, 1983). The most common single resource was the *Occupational Outlook Handbook* (OOH), with 92 percent of the schools having one or more copies. The second major source was the *Dictionary of Occupational Titles* (DOT), with 82 percent having this book available for students. Fewer than 30 percent had no established committee to review career information resources. When students talked to counselors, it was more often about high school courses than about career guidance.

School counseling has been criticized heavily, both inside and outside the educational establishment. Insiders complain about the large number of students per school counselor and the weight of noncounseling administrative

duties. Outsiders complain that school counseling is ineffective, biased, and a waste of money. Short of a new profession, several options are possible (William T. Grant Foundation Commission, 1988). First, twice the number of counselors are needed to meet all student's needs. Second, there could be a redefinition of teachers' roles, accompanied by retraining and reduction in teaching loads, so that classroom teachers could assume a stronger role in handling the counseling needs of adolescents. The professional counselor's role in this plan would be to train and assist teachers in their counseling and to provide direct counseling in situations the teacher could not handle. Third, the whole idea of school counselors would be abandoned, and counselors would be located elsewhere—in neighborhood social service centers or labor offices, for example. (Germany forbids teachers to give career counseling, reserving this task for officials in well-developed networks of labor offices.)

The College Board Commission on Precollege Guidance and Counseling (1986) recommends other alternatives. It believes that local school districts should develop broad-based planning that actively involves the home, school, and community. Advocating better-trained counselors, the commission supports stronger partnerships between home and school to increase two-way communication about student progress and better collaboration among schools, community agencies, colleges, businesses, and other community resources.

Gender

Because many females have been socialized to adopt nurturing roles rather than career or achieving roles, they traditionally have not planned seriously for careers, have not explored career options extensively, and have restricted their career choices to careers that are gender-stereotyped (Jozefowicz, Barber, & Mollasis, 1994). The motivation for work is the same for both sexes. However, females and males make different choices because of their socialization experiences and the ways that social forces structure the opportunities available to them.

As growing numbers of females pursue careers, they are faced with questions involving career and family: Should they delay marriage and childbearing and establish their career first? Or should they combine their career, marriage, and childbearing in their twenties? Some females in the last decade have embraced the domestic patterns of an earlier historical period. They have married, borne children, and committed themselves to full-time mothering. These "traditional" females have worked outside the home only intermittently, if at all, and have subordinated the work role to the family role.

Many other females, though, have veered from this time-honored path. They have postponed motherhood. They have developed committed, permanent ties to the workplace that resemble the pattern once reserved only for males. When they have had children, they have strived to combine a career and motherhood. While there have always been "career" females, today their numbers are growing at an unprecedented rate.

> *The test for whether or not you can hold a job should not be the arrangement of your chromosomes.*
> —Bella Abzug, *Bella!* (1972)

As already mentioned, parents play an important role in their son's and daughters' career development. In one recent study, 1,500 mothers and their young adolescent sons and daughters were studied to determine the role of maternal expectations, advice, and provision of opportunities in their sons' and daughters' occupational aspirations (Eccles & others, 1991; Harold & Eccles, 1990). Mothers were more likely to encourage their sons to consider the military, to expect their sons to go into the military right after high school, and to discuss the education needed for, and likely income of, different jobs with sons. Expecting marriage right after high school and discussing the problems of combining work and family were topics more common to mother-daughter interactions. Also, mothers were more worried that their daughters would not have a happy marriage, and they were more likely to want their sons to have a job that would support a family.

Further information in this study indicated that mothers worked more with boys on a computer; they also provided boys with more computers, software, and programs. The mothers also bought more math or science books and games for boys, and more often enrolled boys in computer classes. Boys were provided more sports opportunities, while girls were given more opportunities in music, art, and dance. Mothers said that boys have more talent in math and are better suited for careers involving math, while they believed that girls have more talent in English and are better suited for careers related to English. In sum, there were differences in the kinds of advice and opportunities provided and in the expectations, aspirations, and ability assessments held by mothers for their sons and daughters.

Were the maternal advice, provision of opportunities, expectations, and ability assessments associated with adolescents' occupational aspirations in this study? Yes, they were. Mothers tended to provide more math or science books to daughters who aspired to male-typed occupations (nontraditional girls) than to daughters who aspired to female-typed jobs (traditional girls). Mothers talked more about the importance of looking good to their daughters who aspired to more female-typed occupations than to their daughters who aspired to male-typed jobs. They also expected daughters who aspired to more female-typed occupations to be more likely to get married right after high school than their nontraditional counterparts. Further, several of the mothers' and adolescent daughters' family/work-role values were related. For example, mothers' belief that it was better if the man was the breadwinner and the woman took care of the family was related to their adolescent daughters' identical belief. Mothers' belief that working mothers can establish just as warm and secure a relationship with their children as nonworking mothers was related to their adolescent daughters' belief that it is okay for mothers to have full-time careers. Nontraditional girls were more likely to endorse the belief that women are better wives and mothers if they have paid jobs.

In sum, this research study documented that parental socialization practices in the form of provision of opportunities, expectations, and beliefs are important sources of adolescent females' and males' occupational aspirations

(Harold & Eccles, 1990). Also, in one recent study, one of the best predictors of adolescent girls' continuing participation in mathematics and science was teacher support (MacLean & others, 1994).

Some of the brightest and most gifted females do not have achievement and career aspirations that match their talents. One investigation found that high-achieving females had much lower expectations for success than did high-achieving males (Stipek & Hoffman, 1980). In the gifted research program at Johns Hopkins University, many mathematically precocious females did select scientific and medical careers, although only 46 percent aspired to a full-time career, compared to 98 percent of the males (Fox, Brody, & Tobin, 1979).

To help talented females redirect their life paths, some high schools are using programs developed by colleges and universities. Project CHOICE (Creating Her Options In Career Education) was designed by Case Western University to detect barriers in reaching one's potential. Gifted eleventh-grade females received individualized counseling that included interviews with female role models, referral to appropriate occupational groups, and information about career workshops. A program at the University of Nebraska was successful in encouraging talented female high school students to pursue more prestigious careers (Kerr, 1983). This was accomplished through individual counseling and participation in a "Perfect Future Day," in which girls shared their career fantasies and discussed barriers that might impede their fulfilling their fantasies. Internal and external constraints were evaluated, gender-role stereotypes were discouraged, and high aspirations were applauded. While these programs have short-term success in redirecting the career paths of high-ability females, in some instances, the effects fade over time—6 months or more, for example. Improving the career alternatives for all female youth, not just those of high ability, however, should be a priority.

Ethnic Minority Adolescents

What is the nature of theory and research on career development in ethnic minority youth? What intervention strategies have been tried to improve their career development?

Theory and Research. African Americans, Asian Americans, Latinos, and Native Americans are four distinct subgroups of the American culture. Yet they share a history of exclusion from mainstream American society. This exclusion has occurred in history books, the educational system, the social class structure, and the labor force (Osipow & Littlejohn, 1995).

The goals of many ethnic groups recently have changed, so that instead of valuing a melting pot that emphasizes similarities and minimizes differences, they have come to value pluralism. The emphasis on pluralism involves an increasing reluctance to surrender one's roots, language, and culture. In some cases pluralism might be incompatible with standard work practices and schedules. For example, standard working hours make it difficult for members of some religious groups to engage in required daily prayer schedules or observe religious holidays.

There is little theory or research on the career development of ethnic minority adolescents. Yet almost every index of social and economic adjustment suggests that the career development of many ethnic groups— African Americans, Latinos, and so on—needs urgent attention (Brown, 1995; Arbona, 1995).

Intervention.   Given the low rates of high school completion for Native Americans, Latinos, and African Americans, some intervention in the lives of these ethnic minority youth is needed (Betz & Fitzgerald, 1995). One suggestion is to provide more-specialized career counseling for ethnic minority groups (Bowman, 1995). For example, group counseling might be more comfortable and less threatening to some ethnic minority groups, such as African Americans.

Math and science awareness interventions also are needed. One such intervention is a career-linking program that has been effectively used with inner-city middle school students (Fouad, 1995). The intervention combined printed career information, speakers and role models, field trips, and integration of career awareness into the curriculum. The intervention increased students' knowledge of careers, and the students performed better in math and science than a control group of students who did not get the career intervention experience. Two years after the intervention, the students also had chosen more difficult math courses than the control group students.

To intervene effectively in the career development of ethnic minority youth, counselors need to increase their knowledge of communication styles, values regarding the importance of the family, the impact of language fluency, and achievement expectations in various ethnic minority groups. Counselors need to be aware of and respect the cultural values of ethnic minority youth, but such values need to be discussed within the context of the realities of the educational and occupational world (Leong, 1995). For example, assertiveness training might be called for when Asian youth are following a cultural tradition of nonassertiveness. The counselor can emphasize to these youth that they can choose when and where to follow the more assertive style.

In our discussion of careers, we have studied how adolescents choose the occupation they will work in as adults. Next, we consider another important aspect of their work worlds—their work as adolescents.

WORK

One of the greatest changes in adolescents' lives in recent years has been the increased number of adolescents who work in some part-time capacity and still attend school on a regular basis. Our discussion of adolescents and work includes information about the sociohistorical context of adolescent work, the advantages and disadvantages of part-time work, bridging the gap from school to work, and an added chance for adolescents in the world of work.

Sociohistorical Context of Adolescent Work

Over the past century, the percentage of youth who work full-time as opposed to those who are in school has decreased dramatically. In the late 1800s, fewer than one of every twenty high school age adolescents were in school. Today more than nine of every ten adolescents receive high school diplomas. In the nineteenth century, many adolescents learned a trade from their father or some other adult member of the community.

Even though prolonged education has kept many contemporary youth from holding full-time jobs, it has not prevented them from working on a part-time basis while going to school (Mortimer, 1991). Most high school seniors have had some work experience. In a national survey of 17,000 high school seniors, three of four reported some job income during the average school week (Bachman, 1982). For 41 percent of the males and 30 percent of the females, this income exceeded $50 a week. The typical part-time job for high school seniors involves 16 to 20 hours of work per week, although 10 percent work 30 hours a week or more.

In 1940, only one of twenty-five tenth-grade males attended school and simultaneously worked part-time. In the 1970s, the number increased to more than one of every four. And, in the 1980s, as just indicated, three of four combined school and part-time work. Adolescents also are working longer hours now than in the past. For example, the number of 14- to 15-year-olds who work more than 14 hours per week has increased substantially in the last three decades. A similar picture emerges for 16-year-olds. In 1960, 44 percent of 16-year-old males who attended school worked more than 14 hours a week, but by the 1980s the figure had increased to more than 60 percent.

What kinds of jobs are adolescents working at today? About 17 percent who work do so in restaurants, such as McDonald's and Burger King, waiting on customers and cleaning up. Other adolescents work in retail stores as cashiers or salespeople (about 20 percent), in offices as clerical assistants (about 10 percent), or as unskilled laborers (about 10 percent). In one recent study, boys reported higher self-esteem and well-being when they perceived that their jobs were providing skills that would be useful to them in the future (Mortimer & others, 1992).

What are the effects of working and going to school on adolescents' grades and integration into school activities?

Do male and female adolescents take the same types of jobs, and are they paid equally? Some jobs (such as busboy, gardener, manual laborer, newspaper carrier) are held almost exclusively by male adolescents, while other jobs (such as baby-sitter, maid) are held almost exclusively by female adolescents. Male adolescents work longer hours and are paid more per hour than female adolescents (Helson, Elliot, & Leigh, 1989).

Advantages and Disadvantages of Part-Time Work in Adolescence

Does the increase in work have benefits for adolescents? In some cases, yes; in others, no. Ellen Greenberger and Laurence Steinberg (1981, 1986) examined the work experiences of students in four California high schools. Their findings disproved some common myths. For example, generally it is assumed that adolescents get extensive on-the-job training when they are hired for work. The reality is that they got little training at all. Also, it is assumed that youths—through work experiences—learn to get along better with adults. However, adolescents reported that they rarely felt close to the adults with whom they worked. The work experiences of the adolescents did help them to understand how the business world works, how to get and how to keep a job, and how to manage money. Working also helped adolescents to learn to budget their time, to take pride in their accomplishments, and to evaluate their goals. But working adolescents often have to give up sports, social affairs with peers, and sometimes sleep. And they have to balance the demands of work, school, family, and peers.

Greenberger and Steinberg asked students about their grade point averages, school attendance, satisfaction from school, and the number of hours spent studying and participating in extracurricular activities since they began working. They found that the working adolescents had lower grade point averages than nonworking adolescents. More than one of four students

reported that their grades dropped when they began working; only one of nine said that their grades improved. But it was not just working that affected adolescents' grades—more important was *how long* they worked. Tenth-graders who worked more than 14 hours a week suffered a drop in grades. Eleventh-graders worked up to 20 hours a week before their grades dropped. When adolescents spend more than 20 hours per week working, there is little time to study for tests and to complete homework assignments.

In addition to work's affecting grades, working adolescents felt less involved in school, were absent more, and said that they did not enjoy school as much as their nonworking counterparts did. Adolescents who worked also spent less time with their families—but just as much time with their peers—as their nonworking counterparts. Adolescents who worked long hours also were more frequent users of alcohol and marijuana.

More-recent research confirms the link between part-time work during adolescence and problem behaviors. In one recent large-scale study, the role of part-time work in the adjustment of more than 70,000 high school seniors was investigated (Bachman & Schulenberg, 1993). Consistent with other research, part-time work in high school was associated with a number of problem behaviors: insufficient sleep, not eating breakfast, not exercising, not having enough leisure time, and using drugs. For the most part, the results occurred even when students worked 1 to 5 hours per week, but they became more pronounced after 20 hours of work per week. And in another recent study, taking on a job for more than 20 hours per week was associated with increasing disengagement from school, increased delinquency and drug use, increased autonomy from parents, and diminished self-reliance (Steinberg, Fegley, & Dornbusch, 1993). In sum, the overwhelming evidence is that working part-time while going to high school is associated with a number of problem behaviors when the work consumes 20 or more hours of the adolescent's week (Hansen, 1996).

Some states have responded to these findings by limiting the number of hours adolescents can work while they are attending secondary school. In 1986, in Pinellas County, Florida, a new law placed a cap on the previously unregulated hours that adolescents could work while school is in session. The allowable limit was set at 30 hours, which—based on research evidence—is still too high.

The Transition from School to Work

In some cases, the media have exaggerated the degree of adolescent unemployment. For example, based on data collected by the U.S. Department of Labor, nine of ten adolescents are either in school, working at a job, or both. Only 5 percent are out of school, without a job, and looking for full-time employment. Most adolescents who are unemployed are not unemployed for long. Only 10 percent are without a job for 6 months or longer. Most unemployed adolescents are school dropouts.

Certain segments of the adolescent population, however, are more likely than others to be unemployed. For example, a disproportionate percentage of unemployed adolescents are African American. As indicated in table 14.1, the unemployment situation is especially acute for African American and Latino youth between the ages of 16 and 19. The job situation, however, has improved somewhat for African American adolescents: In 1969, 44 percent of African American 16- to 19-year-olds were unemployed; today, that figure is approximately 32 percent.

How can adolescents be helped to bridge the gap between school and work? For adolescents bound for higher education and a professional degree, the educational system provides ladders from school to career. Most youth, though, step off the educational ladder before reaching the level of a professional career. Often, they are on their own in their search for work. Recommendations for bridging the gap from school to work were described briefly in chapter 8, on schools, but are expanded on here (William T. Grant Foundation Commission, 1988):

1. Monitored work experiences, including cooperative education, internships, apprenticeships, preemployment training, and youth-operated enterprises, should be implemented. These experiences provide opportunities for youth to gain work experience, to be exposed to adult supervisors and models in the workplace, and to relate their academic training to the workplace.

2. Community and neighborhood services, including individual voluntary service and youth-guided services, should be expanded. Youth need experiences not only as workers but as citizens. Service programs not only expose youth to the adult world, but provide them with a sense of the obligations of citizenship in building a more caring and competent society.

3. Vocational education should be redirected. With few exceptions, today's vocational education does not prepare youth adequately for specific jobs. However, its hands-on methods can provide students with valuable and effective ways of acquiring skills they will need to be successful in a number of jobs. One promising approach is the

TABLE 14.1

Unemployment Rates of Youth: 1988 (Percentage Unemployed)

Years of Age	Total	White	African American	Latino
Total, 16–24:				
16–19	15.3%	13.1%	32.4%	21.9%
20–24	8.7	7.1	19.6	9.8
Nonstudents:				
16–19	16.6%	14.2%	33.6%	21.3%
20–24	9.2	7.4	20.2	10.1
Students:				
16–19	13.9%	11.9%	30.9%	23.2%
20–24	6.3	5.4	15.3	7.6

Source: Bureau of Labor Statistics, *Employment and Earnings*, Vol. 36, No. 1 (USGPO, Washington, DC), January 1989, pp. 162–168.

career academy, which originated in Philadelphia and recently was replicated extensively in California (Glover & Marshall, 1993). At the end of the ninth grade, students at risk for failure are identified and invited to volunteer for a program based on a school-within-a-school format. The students and teachers remain together for 3 years. Students spend the tenth grade catching up on academic course work; computers and field trips are integrated into the curriculum. In the eleventh grade, every student has a mentor from industry who introduces the student to his or her workplace and joins the student for recreational activities at least once a month. By the end of the eleventh grade, the student obtains a summer job with one of the business partners. Students who stay in the program are promised a job when they graduate from high school.

4. Incentives need to be introduced. Low motivation and low expectations for success in the workplace often restrict adolescents' educational achievement. Recent efforts to guarantee postsecondary and continuing education and to provide guaranteed employment, and guaranteed work-related training for students who do well show promise of encouraging adolescents to work harder and be more successful in school.

5. Career information and counseling need to be improved. A variety of information and counseling approaches can be implemented to

expose adolescents to job opportunities and career options. These services can be offered both in school and in community settings. They include setting up career information centers, developing the capacity of parents as career educators, and expanding the work of community-based organizations.

6. More school volunteers should be used. Tutoring is the most common form of school volunteer activity. However, adults are needed even more generally—as friends, as mentors for opening up career opportunities, and for assisting youth in mastering the dilemmas of living in a stressful time.

Improving education, elevating skill levels, and providing "hands-on" experience will help adolescents to bridge the gap between school and work. We need to address the needs of youth if we are to retain the confidence of youth who have been brought up to believe in the promise of the American Dream.

Nineteen-year-old Hanne Madsen of Nordborg, Denmark, is a third-year computer science student at a technical school. She earns $7.42 an hour as an apprentice at Danfoss, a heating and refrigeration manufacturer that is Denmark's largest employer. In Denmark, 50 percent of high school graduates serve apprenticeships, compared to only 3 percent in the United States. In Denmark, vocational students continue to take liberal arts courses and can get back into the college track if they wish.

> *The deepest hunger in humans is the desire to be appreciated.*
>
> **—William James**

An Added Chance

For most youth over the age of 18 who lack a high school diploma, more traditional schooling is probably not the solution. The following recommendations by the William T. Grant Foundation Commission (1988) describe an expanded array of opportunities for youth who are out of school and out of work:

1. Intensive academic skills training should be implemented in all employment training programs where they are not currently offered. The *Job Corps* is an intensive intervention that has been extensively evaluated and fine-tuned. Though it is not for everyone, evaluations have indicated that the Job Corps increases earnings,

enables its graduates to be employed longer, and gives society a net return of $1.46 for every tax dollar invested.

2. *State and local youth corps* currently operate in fourteen states and twelve cities. They incorporate various dimensions of the Job Corps experience (Hamilton, 1991). Other states and communities operate summer programs. An evaluation of the California Conservation Corps indicated that the work of the corps provided a positive economic return.

3. *Nonresidential preemployment training* is accomplished by a number of national organizations that specialize in preemployment training and basic skills remediation. Their efforts deserve further encouragement and support.

CONCEPT TABLE 14.2
Career Development and Work

Concept	Processes/Related Ideas	Characteristics/Description
Career Development	Tomorrow's jobs for today's adolescents	The long-term shift from goods-producing to service-producing employment will continue. The fastest-growing careers will be those that require the most education.
	Theories of career development	Three prominent theories are Ginzberg's developmental theory, Super's vocational self-concept theory, and Holland's personality type theory. Criticisms of each of the theories have been made.
	Cognitive factors	Exploration, decision making, and planning are important cognitive dimensions of career development.
	Sociocultural influences	Among the important sociocultural factors that influence adolescent career development are social class, parents and peers, schools, gender, and ethnicity.
Work	Sociohistorical context	Adolescents are not as likely to hold full-time jobs today as their counterparts of the nineteenth century were. The number of adolescents who work part-time, though, has increased dramatically.
	Advantages and disadvantages of part-time work	Advantages include learning how the business world works, how to get and keep a job, how to manage money, how to budget time, how to take pride in accomplishments, and how to evaluate goals. Disadvantages include giving up sports, social affairs with peers, and sometimes sleep, as well as balancing the demands of school, family, peers, and work. Grades, identification with the school, and school participation might decline when adolescents work long hours.
	The transition from school to work	Rates of adolescent unemployment are sometimes exaggerated, but some adolescents—especially ethnic minority adolescents from low-income backgrounds—face major unemployment problems. To bridge the gap between school and work, we need to put in place a number of changes, including better monitoring of adolescents' work experiences and better career counseling.
	An added chance	For youth over 18 who lack a high school diploma, we need to improve their academic skills training, improve the coordination of agencies that serve them, and take a number of other steps as well.

4. The *Job Training Partnership Act*'s potential for serving at-risk youth has not been adequately realized. Only 5 percent of eligible youth are currently being served.

5. The *Armed Forces* also can be used more effectively. Although only 9 percent of all recruits lack a high school diploma, the proportion is likely to increase dramatically with the changing youth demographics. The armed forces should expand programs to upgrade the academic and work skills of its members.

6. To obtain maximum effectiveness for added-chance programs, coordination among agencies that serve youth needs to be improved.

The implementation of the National Youth Service could help improve the transitions from high school to work and to college or postsecondary training. It also could strengthen added-chances programs for youth and be used to strengthen schools. Service to others can build unity among youth from diverse backgrounds while providing valuable learning experiences for the volunteers (Glover & Marshall, 1993).

At this point, we have discussed many aspects of careers and work. A summary of these ideas is presented in concept table 14.2.

SUMMARY

American adolescents grow up in an achievement-oriented world. Some critics believe it is too achievement oriented, yet others believe American adolescents', parents', and schools' expectations for achievement are too low. A special concern is the forgotten half, about 20 million noncollege youth.

We began this chapter by considering the importance of achievement in the lives of two Asian American adolescents and then focused on the importance of adolescence in achievement, the nature of motivation, achievement motivation, attribution theory and intrinsic-extrinsic motivation, mastery versus helpless orientation, achievement in ethnic minority adolescents, and cross-cultural comparisons. Then we studied career development, evaluating tomorrow's jobs for today's adolescents, theories of career development (Ginzberg's, Super's, and Holland's), exploration, decision making, and planning, and the sociocultural influences of social class, parents and peers, schools, and gender, and gifted female adolescents. Our coverage of work included the sociohistorical context of adolescent work, advantages and disadvantages of part-time work in adolescence, the transition from school to work, and added-chance programs.

Remember that you can obtain an overall summary of this chapter by again studying the two concept tables on pages 446 and 457. At various points in this book we have discussed problems and disorders in adolescence. For example, in this chapter we explored the high unemployment rate of inner-city, ethnic minority youth. Next we turn to Section V, "Adolescent Problems, Stress, Health, and Coping," starting with chapter 15, "Adolescent Problems."

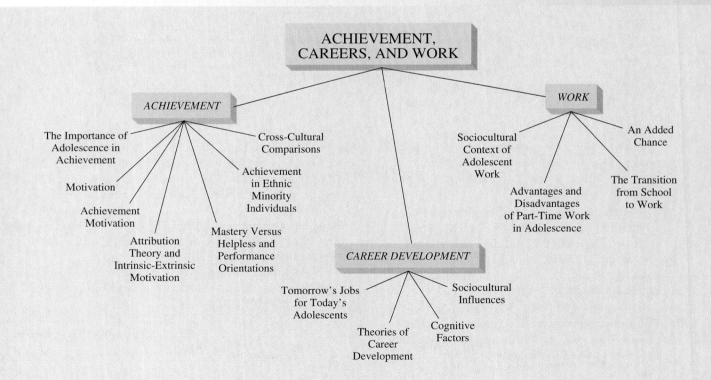

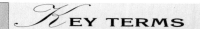

KEY TERMS

PRACTICAL KNOWLEDGE ABOUT ADOLESCENCE

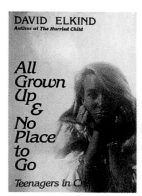

All Grown Up & No Place to Go: Teenagers in Crisis
(1984) by David Elkind.
Reading, MA: Addison-Wesley.

Elkind believes that raising teenagers in today's world is more difficult than ever. He argues that teenagers are expected to confront adult challenges too early in their development. By being pressured into adult roles too soon, today's youth are all grown up with no place to go, hence the title of the book. Elkind believes that the main reason teenagers are pressed into adult roles too early is that parents are more committed to their own self-fulfillment than to their adolescents'. These parents of the "me" generation are often too quick to accept their teenagers' outward sophistication as a sign of emotional maturity. Teens' emotional needs are also neglected by a school system that is up-to-date in computer gadgetry but is bankrupt in responding to adolescents' emotional needs and individual differences, says Elkind. He also believes that the media exploit adolescents by appealing to their vulnerability to peer pressure.

Greetings from High School
(1991) by Marian Salzman and Teresa Reisgies.
Princeton, NJ: Peterson's Guides.

This is a book by, for, and about adolescents. It has a number of helpful suggestions about such topics as choosing the right high school, teacher-student relations, making the most of a guidance counselor, summer jobs and volunteer opportunities, choosing the right college, and exploring career options.

What Color Is Your Parachute?

(1997) by Richard Bolles. Berkeley, CA: Ten Speed Press.

What Color Is Your Parachute? is an extremely popular book on job hunting. Author Richard Bolles is an Episcopal priest who changed from pastoral counseling to career counseling. *What Color Is Your Parachute?* was first published in 1970. Since 1975, an annual edition has appeared. This book has become the career seeker's bible. Bolles tries to answer concerns about the job-hunting process and refers readers to many sources that provide valuable information. Unlike many self-help books on job hunting, *What Color Is Your Parachute?* does not necessarily assume that you are a recent college graduate seeking your first job. He also spends considerable time discussing job-hunting for people who seek to change careers. Bolles describes many myths about job hunting and successfully combats them.

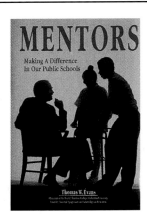

Mentors

(1992) by Thomas Evans. Princeton, NJ: Peterson's Guides.

This book describes the enriching experiences of dozens of motivated individuals—from eye-to-the-future executives to conscientious parents—whose passion for education, especially the education of poor children, has carried them to the classroom and beyond. Author Evans describes how to make a difference in a child's life. The difference consists of becoming involved as a mentor for a child and developing a role as a tutor for students in a one-on-one situation. Evans gives explicit instructions on how to become an effective mentor of a child. Mentoring has helped many children and adolescents become more competent, and Evans' book is an excellent overview of the topic.

Center for Youth Development and Policy Research
Academy for Educational Development
1255 23rd Street NW, Suite 400
Washington, DC 20037
202-884-800

This center explores different avenues to expand opportunities for youth work through postsecondary educational institutions and employers.

The Encyclopedia of Careers and Vocational Guidance
(1981) (5th ed.)
by William Hopke (Ed.)
Chicago: J. G. Ferguson

This is a cross-referenced, two-volume encyclopedia using job titles and classifications of the *Dictionary of Occupational Titles*. It can benefit students, counselors, and teachers who want to learn about career development and vocational choice.

Generation 2000/Génération 2000
347 Bay Street, Suite 800
Toronto, Ontario M5H 2R3
416-777-2590

Generation 2000 inspires youth to understand and appreciate Canadian issues and diversity while striving toward positive cooperative action in their communities and on a national level. The largest program, a national tour of Canadian high schools, takes about eight teams of five throughout the country. Following a theatrical presentation to raise awareness of social, economic, and other national issues, workshops explore issues that affect the local community. Participants are encouraged to take responsibility and act on these issues. By sharing ideas, information, and resources with others across Canada, students achieve positive, cooperative action on local and national issues.

Jobs Corps
Employment Training Administration
200 Constitution Ave., NW
Washington, DC 20210
202-535-0550

This national, federally funded training program provides education, vocational training, and work experience for disadvantaged youth 16 to 21 years of age.

Junior Achievement of Canada/Jeunes
Entreprises du Canada
1 Westside Drive
Toronto, Ontario M9C 1B2
416-622-4602

The mission of Junior Achievement is to provide practical business education and experience to Canadian youth. It achieves this by bringing business, education, and youth together for their mutual benefit.

National Youth Employment Coalition
1501 Broadway, Room 111
New York, NY 10036
212-840-1801

This organization promotes youth employment.

Peterson's Summer Opportunities
for Kids and Teenagers

Published annually by Peterson's Guides; available at most bookstores. This guide provides a wealth of opportunities that adolescents can choose from when deciding how to spend their summer.

Through Mentors
202-393-0512

Mentors are recruited from corporations, government agencies, universities, and professional firms. Their goal is to provide every youth in the District of Columbia with a mentor through high school. To learn how to become involved in a mentoring program or to start such a program, call the number listed above. Also, the National One-to-One Partnership Kit guides businesses in establishing mentoring programs (call 202-338-3844).

What Kids Need to Succeed
by Peter Benson, Judy Galbraith, and Pamela
Espeland
Minneapolis: Search Institute

This easy-to-read book presents commonsense ideas for parents, educators, and youth workers that can help youth succeed.

Zillions
Consumer Reports for Kids
Subscription Department
P.O. Box 51777
Boulder, CO 80321-1777
800-786-8001

This junior version of *Consumer Reports* teaches children and adolescents 8 to 14 years of age how to handle money and be an informed consumer. It is published bimonthly.

Exploring Adolescent Development

To further explore the nature of adolescent development, we will examine a research study on the motivation and math achievement of high school students in different cultures, and we will discuss the development of more experience-based educational options for adolescents.

Research on Adolescent Development

Motivation and Math Achievement of Adolescents in Different Cultures

Featured Study

Chen, C., & Stevenson, H. W. (1995). Motivation and mathematics achievement: A comparative study of Asian-American, Caucasian-American, and East Asian high school students. *Child Development, 66,* 1215–1234.

This study examined the motivation and math achievement of Asian American, White American, and East Asian students. Although Asian Americans constitute only a small percentage of American students, they are a large percentage of those who are the most successful in their academic work. Their remarkable achievements inevitably lead to questions about how they manage to be so successful. Factors that have been proposed as being responsible for their academic success include selective immigration and genetic factors, the role of family and peers, and the importance of academic success for upward mobility. In the present study, it was assumed that culture enters into students' academic achievement through the social contexts of family, school, and peers.

Method

The subjects were 304 Asian American, 1,958 White American, 1,475 Chinese (Taiwanese), and 1,120 Japanese eleventh-graders (mean age = 17.6 years). Students were given a curriculum-based mathematics test and a questionnaire that included basic demographic information about the family, reasons for studying hard, beliefs about the importance of effort in achievement, attitudes toward mathematics, daily use of time, beliefs about peer norms, and self-reports of psychological well-being.

Results and Discussion

Mathematics scores of the Asian American students were higher than those of the White American students but lower than those of the Chinese and Japanese students. Factors associated with the achievement of Asian American and East Asian students included having parents and peers who have high academic standards, believing that the road to success is through effort, having positive attitudes about achievement, studying diligently, and facing less interference with their schoolwork from jobs and informal peer interactions. Contrary to the popular belief that Asian American students' high achievement necessarily takes a psychological toll, these students did not report a greater frequency of maladjustive symptoms than White American students did. The findings of this study support a cultural-motivational theory of academic achievement. Beliefs and attitudes that lead to a high level of motivation and achievement-related behaviors reflect a cultural heritage that emphasizes education and the ability of people to benefit intellectually from the diligent application of effort.

$\mathscr{A}$DOLESCENT HEALTH AND WELL-BEING

Toward More Options

The William T. Grant Foundation Commission (1988) endorsed a mixture of abstract and practical learning opportunities and a combination of conceptual study with concrete applications and practical problem solving. They urged that a new look should be taken at cooperative education, work-study, apprenticeships, internships, service-learning, community service, youth-operated enterprises, on-the-job training, and mentorship. They became convinced that these experience-based educational opportunities can benefit adolescents.

Education does not take place just in a traditional school. It also can take place in the workplace, the media, museums and cultural institutions, public and nonprofit agencies, youth agencies and community services, field studies and workshops, and community-based organizations in the inner city. Trigonometry learned in the school's machine shop or in the workplace complements learning in the classroom. Botany can be learned in a horticultural laboratory, at a field station, or, perhaps better yet, in both locations.

The commission also agreed with educator John Goodlad (1984) that appropriately conceived vocational-technical education, combining hands-on work experience with mastery of academic conceptual ideas, deserves far more attention than it currently enjoys among educators and policymakers. The type of individual who wants to learn how to apply geometry before and while learning the theorems, or to overhaul a carburetor and valves before and while learning the theories of combustion and energy conversion, is often turned off by an educational system that almost uniformly insists that classroom-taught abstract ideas and theories must precede application.

Educational methods and work experiences need to be better linked. The responsibility of schools is not solely to prepare students for college or work, and cooperative work strategies, experiential learning, and instruction that requires thinking skills instead of rote memorization better prepare adolescents for the complex workplace they will soon have to enter.

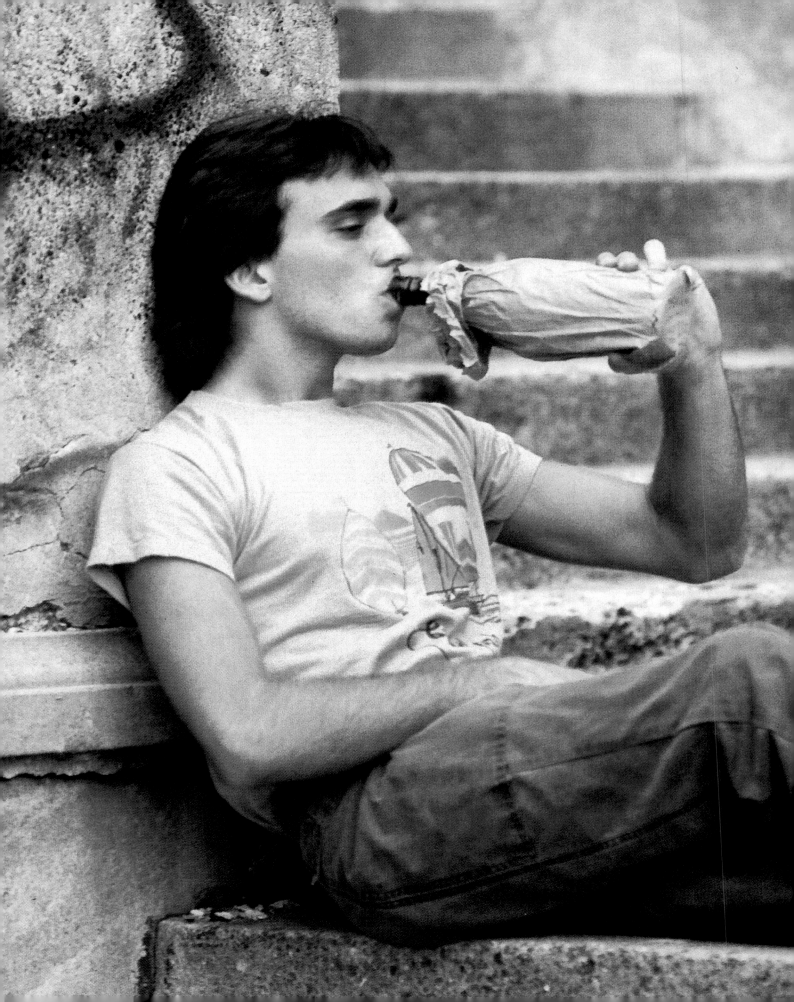

Adolescent Problems, Stress, Health, and Coping

There is no easy path leading out of life, and few are the easy ones that lie within it.

—Walter Savage Landor,
Imaginary Conversations,
1824

Modern life is stressful and leaves its psychological scars on too many adolescents, who, unable to cope effectively, never reach their human potential. The need is not only to find better treatments for adolescents with problems, but to find ways to encourage adolescents to adopt healthier lifestyles, which can prevent problems from occurring in the first place. This section consists of two chapters: Chapter 15, "Adolescent Problems" and Chapter 16, "Health, Stress, and Coping."

Will Barnet
The Silent Seasons—Spring, detail
©1997 Will Barnet/Licensed by VAGA, New York, NY

Chapter

15

Adolescent Problems

*hey cannot scare me with their empty
spaces
Between stars—on stars where no human
race is.
I have it in me so much nearer home
To scare myself with my own desert
places.*

—Robert Frost, 1936

We are all mad at some time or another.

—Battista Mantuanus,
Ecologues, 1500

PREVIEW

Annie and Arnie in the "Images of Adolescence" section have serious problems. Their alcohol dependency and delinquency are but two of the many problems and disorders that can emerge in adolescents' journey to maturity. Throughout this book, we have focused on normal adolescent development, though there have been many examples of adolescents with problems. In this chapter, we will look more closely at some of the major problems that adolescents can develop. To begin, though, we will discuss the nature of abnormality.

Annie and Arnie

Some mornings, Annie, a 15-year-old cheerleader, was too drunk to go to school. Other days, she would stop for a couple of beers or a screwdriver on the way to school. She was tall and blonde and good-looking, and no one who sold her liquor, even at 8:00 A.M., questioned her age. She got her money from baby-sitting and what her mother gave her to buy lunch. Finally, Annie was kicked off the cheerleading squad for missing practice so often. Soon she and several of her peers were drinking almost every morning. Sometimes, they skipped school and went to the woods to drink. Annie's whole life began to revolve around her drinking. It went on for 2 years, and, during the last summer, anytime she saw anybody she was drunk. After a while, her parents began to detect Annie's problem. But even when they punished her, she did not stop drinking. Finally, Annie started dating a boy she really liked and who would not put up with her drinking. She agreed to go to Alcoholics Anonymous and has just successfully completed treatment. She has stopped drinking for 4 consecutive months now, and continued abstinence is the goal.

Arnie is 13 years old. He has a history of committing thefts and physical assaults. The first theft occurred when Arnie was 8—he stole a cassette player from an electronics store. The first physical assault took place a year later, when he shoved his 7-year-old brother up against the wall, bloodied his face, and then threatened to kill him with a butcher knife. Recently, the thefts and physical assaults have increased. In the last week, he stole a television set and struck his mother repeatedly and threatened to kill her. He also broke some neighborhood streetlights and threatened youths with a wrench and a hammer. Arnie's father left home when Arnie was 3 years old. Until the father left, his parents argued extensively, and his father often beat up his mother. Arnie's mother indicates that, when Arnie was younger, she was able to control him, but in the last several years she has not been able to enforce any sanctions on his antisocial behavior. Arnie's volatility and dangerous behavior have resulted in the recommendation that he be placed in a group home with other juvenile delinquents.

THE NATURE OF ABNORMALITY

What is abnormal behavior, and what causes it? What are the characteristics of adolescent disorders?

What Is Abnormal Behavior?

Defining what is normal and what is abnormal is not a simple task. Among other complications, what is abnormal may vary from one culture to another, and from time to time in the same culture. Early in this century in the United States, masturbation was thought to cause everything from warts to insanity; today, there is a much more accepting attitude toward masturbation, and it is not considered abnormal.

Does being atypical mean that an individual is abnormal? Madonna is atypical but is not considered abnormal because she is an outstanding singer and music video performer. Steffi Graf also is not abnormal even though she became a top tennis professional at a young age. And while Troy Aikman is a masterful quarterback, that atypicality does not make him abnormal. If being atypical does not make an individual abnormal, what does? **Abnormal behavior** *is behavior that is maladaptive and harmful.* Such behavior fails to promote the well-being, growth, and fulfillment of the adolescent and, ultimately, others. Maladaptive behavior takes many forms—committing suicide; experiencing depression; having bizarre, irrational beliefs; assaulting others; and becoming addicted to drugs, for example. These abnormal behaviors interfere with adolescents' ability to function effectively in the world and can harm others.

What Causes Abnormal Behavior?

Causes of adolescents' abnormal, maladaptive, or harmful behavior include biological, psychological, and sociocultural factors.

The Biological Approach

Proponents of the biological approach believe that abnormal behavior is due to a physical malfunction of the body, that if an adolescent behaves uncontrollably, is out of touch with reality, or is severely depressed, biological factors are the culprits. Today, scientists and researchers who adopt the biological approach often focus on brain processes and genetic factors as the causes of abnormal behavior.

The **medical model,** *also called the disease model, was the forerunner of the biological approach. The medical model states that abnormality is a disease or illness precipitated by internal bodily causes.* From this perspective, abnormalities are called mental *illnesses,* and the individuals are *patients* in *hospitals* and are treated by *doctors.*

The Psychological and Sociocultural Approaches

Although the biological approach provides an important perspective for understanding abnormal behavior, many psychologists believe that it underestimates the importance of psychological and sociocultural factors in abnormal behavior. Emotional turmoil, inappropriate learning, distorted thoughts, and inadequate relationships, rather than brain processes or genes, are of interest in the psychological and sociocultural approaches.

Advocates of the psychological and sociocultural approaches also criticize the medical model because they believe that it encourages labeling of mental disturbances. When adolescents are labeled "mentally ill," they may begin to perceive themselves as sick and, thus, not assume responsibility for coping with their problems (Szasz, 1977).

Most experts on abnormal behavior agree that many psychological disorders are universal, appearing in most cultures. However, the frequency and intensity of abnormal behavior often vary across cultures. Variations in disorders are related to social, economic, technological, religious, and other cultural factors (Costin & Draguns, 1989).

An Interactionist Approach

The normality or abnormality of adolescent behavior cannot be determined without considering the complexity of adolescents and the multiple influences on behavior. Neither the biological nor the psychological and sociocultural approaches independently capture this complexity. Adolescents' abnormal behavior is influenced by biological factors (brain processes and heredity, for example), by psychological factors (emotional turmoil and distorted thoughts, for example), and by social factors (inadequate relationships, for example). These factors interact to produce adolescents' abnormal behavior.

Characteristics of Adolescent Disorders

The spectrum of adolescent disorders is wide. The disorders vary in their severity and in terms of the adolescent's developmental level, sex, and social class. Some adolescent disorders are short-lived; others may persist over many years. One 13-year-old adolescent might show a pattern of acting-out behavior that is disruptive to his classroom. As a 14-year-old, he might be assertive and aggressive, but no longer disruptive. Another 13-year-old might show a similar pattern of acting-out behavior. At age 16, she might have been arrested for numerous juvenile offenses and still be a disruptive influence in the classroom.

Some disorders are more likely to appear at one developmental level than at another. For example, fears are more common in early childhood, many school-related problems surface for the first time in middle and late childhood, and drug-related problems become more common in adolescence (Achenbach & Edelbrock, 1981). In one study, depression, truancy, and drug abuse were more common among older adolescents, while arguing, fighting, and being too loud were more common among younger adolescents (Edelbrock, 1989).

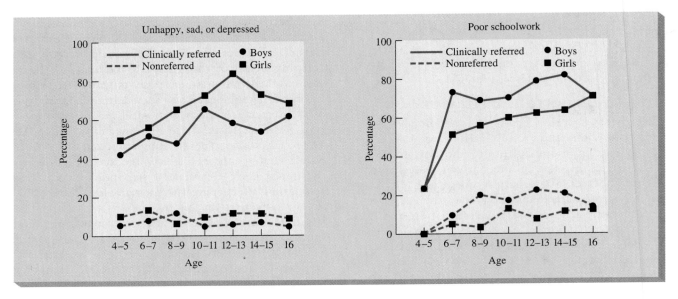

Figure~15.1

The Two Items Most Likely to Differentiate Between Clinically Referred and Clinically Nonreferred Children and Adolescents.

In the large-scale investigation by Thomas Achenbach and Craig Edelbrock (1981), adolescents from a lower-class background were more likely to have problems than those from a middle-class background. Most of the problems reported for adolescents from a lower-class background were undercontrolled, externalizing behaviors—destroying others' things and fighting, for example. These behaviors also were more characteristic of boys than girls. The problems of middle-class adolescents and girls were more likely to be overcontrolled and internalizing—anxiety or depression, for example.

The behavioral problems most likely to cause adolescents to be referred to a clinic for mental health treatment were feelings of unhappiness, sadness, or depression, and poor school performance (see figure 15.1). Difficulties in school achievement, whether secondary to other kinds of disturbances or primary problems in themselves, account for many referrals of adolescents.

In another investigation, Achenbach and his colleagues (1991) studied the problems and competencies of 2,600 children and adolescents 4 to 16 years old assessed at intake into mental health services and 2,600 demographically matched nonreferred children and adolescents. Lower-socioeconomic-status children and adolescents had more problems and fewer competencies than did their higher-socioeconomic-status counterparts. Children and adolescents had more problems when they had fewer related adults in their homes, had biological parents who were unmarried in their homes, had parents who were separated or divorced, lived in families who received public assistance, and lived in households in which family members had received mental health services. Children and adolescents who had more externalized problems came from families in which parents were unmarried, separated, or divorced, as well as from families receiving public assistance. Now that we have considered some general characteristics of adolescent problems, let's turn our attention to some specific problems beginning with drug abuse.

DRUGS AND ALCOHOL

Why do adolescents take drugs? How pervasive is adolescent drug use in the United States? What are the nature and effects of various drugs taken by adolescents? What factors contribute to adolescent drug use? These are among the questions we now evaluate.

Why Do Adolescents Take Drugs?

When Sigmund Freud experimented with cocaine, he was searching for possible medical uses for the substance, among them a use in eye surgery. He soon found that the drug produced an ecstatic feeling and wrote to his fiancée to inform her of how just a small dose provided lofty, wonderful sensations. Over time, Freud stopped taking cocaine, though, because it became apparent that some individuals experienced bad effects from the drug, and several died from overdoses.

Since the beginning of history, humans have searched for substances that would sustain and protect them and also act on the nervous system to produce pleasurable sensations. Individuals are attracted to drugs because drugs help them to adapt to an ever-changing environment. Smoking, drinking, and taking drugs reduce tension and frustration, relieve boredom and fatigue, and in some cases help adolescents to escape the harsh realities of their world. Drugs provide pleasure by giving inner peace, joy, relaxation, kaleidoscopic perceptions, surges of exhilaration, or prolonged heightened sensation. They may help some adolescents to get along better in their world. For example, amphetamines may help the adolescent to stay awake to study for an exam. Drugs also satisfy adolescents' curiosity—some adolescents take drugs because they are intrigued by sensational accounts of drugs in the media, while others may listen to a popular song and wonder if the drugs described can provide them with unique, profound experiences. Drugs are taken for social reasons also, allowing adolescents to feel more comfortable and to enjoy the company of others.

But the use of drugs for personal gratification and temporary adaptation carries a very high price tag: drug dependence, personal and social disorganization, and a predisposition to serious and sometimes fatal diseases (Gullotta, Adams, & Montemayor, 1995). Thus, what is intended as adaptive behavior is maladaptive in the long run. For example, prolonged cigarette smoking, in which the active drug is nicotine, is one of the most serious yet preventable health problems. Smoking has been described by some experts as "suicide in slow motion."

As adolescents continue to take a drug, the drug produces **tolerance,** *which means that a greater amount of the drug is needed to produce the same effect.* The first time adolescents take 5 milligrams of Valium, a very relaxed feeling results, but after a person takes the pill every day for 6 months, 10 milligrams may be needed to achieve the same effect.

Addiction *is the body's physical dependence on a drug.* When an addicted adolescent's body is not supplied with an adequate dose of the addictive drug, the adolescent is said to go into withdrawal. **Withdrawal** *is undesirable intense pain and craving for an addictive drug.* **Psychological dependence** *is a psychological need to take a drug, as when adolescents take drugs to help them cope with problems and stresses in their lives.* In both physical addiction and psychological dependence, the drug plays a powerful role in adolescents' lives. Let's now look at trends in overall drug use by adolescents in the United States.

Trends in Overall Drug Use

The 1960s and 1970s were a time of marked increases in the use of illicit drugs. During the social and political unrest of those years, many youth turned to marijuana, stimulants, and hallucinogens. Increases in adolescent alcohol consumption during this period also were noted (Robinson & Greene, 1988). More precise data about drug use by adolescents have been collected in recent years.

Each year since 1975, Lloyd Johnston, Gerald Bachman, and Patrick O'Malley, working at the Institute of Social Research at the University of Michigan, have carefully monitored drug use by America's high school seniors in a wide range of public and private high schools. They also sample younger adolescents' and college students' drug use from time to time.

The use of drugs among U.S. secondary school students rose again in 1996, continuing a trend that began in 1991 among eighth-grade students and in 1992 among tenth- and twelfth-grade students (Johnston, O'Malley, & Bachman, 1996). The proportion of eighth-graders taking any illicit drug in the last 12 months has more than doubled from 1991 figures (from 11 percent to 24 percent). Since 1992 the proportion of adolescents using any illicit drugs in the prior 12 months has nearly doubled among tenth-graders (from 20 to 38 percent) and risen by about half among twelfth-graders (from 27 to 40 percent).

In 1996, marijuana use, in particular, continued the strong resurgence that began in the early 1990s, with increased use at all three grade levels. Among eighth-graders, annual prevalence (the proportion reporting use in the 12 months prior to the survey) tripled from 6 percent in 1991 to 18 percent in 1995. Among tenth-graders, annual prevalence more than doubled from the low point in 1992 of 15 percent to 34 percent in 1996; among twelfth-graders, annual prevalence increased by nearly two-thirds, from the low point of 22 percent in 1992 to 36 percent in 1996.

Johnston, O'Malley and Bachman (1996) concluded that drugs have been perceived recently as being less dangerous, and that such a perception is usually accompanied by an increase in use. An overview of trends in the percentage of high school seniors who reported having taken various drugs in the last 30 days is presented in table 15.1.

The United States has the highest rate of drug use among the world's industrialized nations. Also, the University of Michigan survey likely underestimates the percentage of adolescents who take drugs, because it does not include high school dropouts, who have a higher rate of drug use than do students who are still in high school.

A special concern emerged in the 1992–1996 University of Michigan surveys. Eighth-graders, most of whom were 13 to 14 years old, increased their use of a number of drugs—marijuana, cocaine, LSD, stimulants, and inhalants. These young adolescents probably did not have the opportunity to learn about the harmfulness of drugs through the media as earlier cohorts did.

In the 1993–1996 surveys, Johnston, Bachman, and O'Malley found that perceived danger and peer norms are critical to reducing drug use in adolescence. They have found no evidence that reduced availability accounts for increases or decreases in adolescent drug use. Let's now examine in greater detail a number of drugs that adolescents take.

TABLE 15.1

Percentage of High School Seniors Who Used Particular Drugs in the Last 30 Days

	Class of 1978	Class of 1979	Class of 1980	Class of 1981	Class of 1982	Class of 1983	Class of 1984	Class of 1985
Approximate Number of Students	17,800	15,500	15,900	17,500	17,700	16,300	15,900	16,000
Marijuana/Hashish	37.1	36.5	33.7	31.6	28.5	27.0	25.2	25.7
Inhalants	—	3.2	2.7	2.5	2.5	2.5	2.6	3.0
Hallucinogens	—	5.3	4.4	4.5	4.1	3.5	3.2	3.8
Cocaine	3.9	5.7	5.2	5.8	5.0	4.9	5.8	6.7
Heroin	0.3	0.2	0.2	0.2	0.2	0.2	0.3	0.3
Stimulants	8.7	9.9	12.1	15.8	10.7	8.9	8.3	6.8
Sedatives	4.2	4.4	4.8	4.6	3.4	3.0	2.3	2.4
Tranquilizers	3.4	3.7	3.1	2.7	2.4	2.5	2.1	2.1
Alcohol	72.1	71.8	72.0	70.7	69.7	69.4	67.2	65.9
Cigarettes	36.7	34.4	30.5	29.4	30.0	30.3	29.3	30.1

Source: Johnston, L. D., O'Malley, P. M., & Bachman, J. G. (1996, December 19). *The rise in drug use in teens continues in 1996.* Ann Arbor, MI: Institute of Social Research, Table 4.

Alcohol

To learn more about the role of alcohol in adolescents' lives, we examine how alcohol influences behavior, the use and abuse of alcohol by adolescents, and risk factors in adolescents' alcohol abuse.

Effects of Alcohol on Adolescents' Behavior

Alcohol is an extremely potent drug. It acts on the body primarily as a depressant and slows down the brain's activities. However, in low doses, alcohol can be a stimulant. If used in sufficient quantities, it will damage or even kill biological tissues, including muscle and brain cells. The mental and behavioral effects of alcohol include reduced inhibition and impaired judgment. Initially, adolescents feel more talkative and more confident when they use alcohol. However, skilled performances, such as driving, become impaired, and as more alcohol is ingested, intellectual functioning, behavioral control, and judgment become less efficient. Eventually, the drinker becomes drowsy and falls asleep. With extreme intoxication, the drinker may lapse into a coma. Each of these behavioral effects varies according to how the adolescent's body metabolizes alcohol, the individual's body weight, the amount of alcohol ingested, and whether previous drinking has led to tolerance.

Alcohol is the most widely used drug by U.S. adolescents. It has produced many enjoyable moments and many sad ones as well. Alcoholism is the third leading killer in the United States. Each year, approximately 25,000 individuals are killed, and 1.5 million injured, by drunk drivers. In 65 percent of the aggressive male acts against females, the offender has been under the influence of alcohol (Goodman & others, 1986). In numerous instances of drunk driving and assaults on females, the offenders have been adolescents. More than 13 million individuals are classified as alcoholics, many of whom established their drinking habits during adolescence.

> *Alcohol is a good preservative for everything but brains.*
>
> —Mary Pettibone Poole,
> *A Glass Eye at a Keyhole*, 1938

Adolescent Alcohol Use and Abuse

How extensive is alcohol use by adolescents? Actually, alcohol use by high school seniors has gradually declined—monthly prevalence has declined from 72 percent in 1980 to 51 percent in 1996, for example. The prevalence of drinking five or more drinks in a row—called binge drinking—during the prior 2-week interval fell from 41 percent in 1981 to 31 percent in 1996. Figure 15.2 shows the

Class of 1986	Class of 1987	Class of 1988	Class of 1989	Class of 1990	Class of 1991	Class of 1992	Class of 1993	Class of 1994	Class of 1995	Class of 1996
15,200	16,300	16,300	16,700	15,200	15,000	15,800	16,300	15,400	15,400	14,300
23.4	21.0	18.0	16.7	14.0	13.8	11.9	15.5	19.0	21.2	21.9
3.2	3.5	3.0	2.7	2.9	2.6	2.5	2.8	2.7	3.2	2.5
3.5	2.8	2.3	2.9	2.3	2.2	2.1	2.7	3.1	4.4	3.5
6.2	4.3	3.4	2.8	1.9	1.4	1.3	1.3	1.5	1.8	2.0
0.2	0.2	0.2	0.3	0.2	0.2	0.3	.2	.3	.6	.5
5.5	5.2	4.6	4.2	3.7	3.2	2.8	3.7	4.0	4.0	4.1
2.2	1.7	1.4	1.6	1.4	1.5	1.2	1.3	1.8	2.3	2.1
2.1	2.0	1.5	1.3	1.2	1.4	1.0	1.2	1.4	1.8	2.0
65.3	66.4	63.9	60.0	57.1	54.0	51.3	51.0	50.1	51.3	50.8
29.6	29.4	28.7	28.6	29.4	28.3	27.8	29.9	31.2	33.5	34.0

trends in the percentage of students in different grades who report having been drunk in the past year and in the past 30 days. There has been much less change in binge drinking among college students. In 1994, 40 percent of college students reported that they engaged in binge drinking, about the same percentage as in 1980 (Johnston, O'Malley, & Bachman). There remains a substantial sex difference in the percentages of college students who engage in binge drinking—31 percent for females versus 52 percent for males in 1994.

Risk Factors in Adolescents' Alcohol Abuse

Among the risk factors in adolescents' abuse of alcohol are heredity, family influences, certain aspects of peer relations, ethnicity, and personality characteristics. There is increasing evidence of a genetic predisposition to alcoholism, although it is important to remember that both genetic and environmental factors are involved (Moos, Finney, & Cronkite, 1990).

Adolescent alcohol use is related to parent and peer relations. Adolescents who drink heavily often come from unhappy homes in which there is a great deal of tension, have parents who give them little nurturance, are insecurely attached to their parents, have parents who use poor family management practices (low monitoring, unclear expectations, few rewards for positive behavior), and

have parents who sanction alcohol use (Barnes, Farrell, & Banerjee, 1995; Peterson & others, 1994). The peer group is especially important in adolescent alcohol abuse (Dielman & others, 1992). In one study, exposure to peer use and misuse of alcohol, along with susceptibility to peer pressure, were strong predictors of adolescent alcohol abuse (Dielman, Shope, & Butchart). Whether adolescents have older, same-age, or younger peers as friends is also related to alcohol and drug abuse in adolescence. In one study, adolescents who took drugs were more likely to have older friends than were their counterparts who did not take drugs (Blyth, Durant, & Moosbrugger, 1985).

Ethnicity also is related to alcohol abuse among adolescents. Alcohol abuse is especially problematic for Native American youth (Gfellner & Hundleby, 1994). In one national survey, Native American adolescents had a 42 percent problem-drinking rate, compared to 34 percent for Anglo-American adolescents (Donovan & Jessor, 1978). In one recent study of Native American adolescents, stress, having experienced physical abuse, and having a parent who uses alcohol and/or drugs on a weekly basis were related to the use and abuse of alcohol by the adolescents (Huston, Hoberman, & Nugent, 1994). And in another recent study, serious problem drinking was predictive of depressive symptoms in Native American adolescent girls and antisocial behavior in Native American adolescent boys (Mitchell & others, 1996).

	Last year		Last 30 days	
	1992	1996	1992	1996
8th	18	20	8	10
10th	37	40	18	21
12th	50	52	30	31

Figure~15.2

Trends in the Percentage of Eighth-, Tenth-, and Twelfth-Graders Who Have Been Drunk in the Last Year and in the Last 30 Days.

average family incomes, African American and Latino adolescents have higher abstention rates and lower rates of alcohol abuse than White adolescents do (Bettes & others, 1990). In one recent study, the same parenting factors (support, monitoring, and parent-adolescent communication) were related to fewer adolescent alcohol problems for both African American and White adolescents (Barnes, Farrell, & Banerjee, 1994). Also in this study, religion served as a protective factor against alcohol abuse for African American adolescents, while White adolescents were more susceptible to peer drinking influences.

Is there a personality profile that also might provide information about adolescents at risk for alcohol abuse? Alcohol researcher Robert Cloninger (1991) found that three traits present as early as 10 years of age are associated with alcoholism at the age of 28: (1) easily bored, needing constant activity and challenge; (2) driven to avoid negative consequences of actions; and (3) craving immediate external reward for effort. Cloninger advises parents who notice these traits in their children and young adolescents to ensure that their children have a structured, challenging environment and to provide them with considerable support.

A strong family support system is clearly an important preventive strategy in reducing alcohol abuse by adolescents. Are there others? Would raising the minimum drinking age have an effect? In one investigation, raising the minimum drinking age did lower the frequency of automobile crashes involving adolescents, but raising the drinking age alone did not reduce alcohol abuse (Wagennar, 1983). Another effort to reduce alcohol abuse involved a school-based program in which adolescents discussed alcohol-related issues with peers (Wodarski & Hoffman, 1984). At a 1-year follow-up, students in the intervention schools reported less alcohol abuse and had discouraged each other's drinking more often than had students in other schools who had not been involved in the peer discussion of alcohol-related issues. Efforts to help the adolescent with a drinking problem vary enormously. Therapy may include working with other family members, peer-group discussion sessions, and specific

There is no single, concise answer to the problem of alcohol abuse in Native American youth. It is a complex problem that involves cultural, historical, educational, and economic circumstances. Proposed solutions include education and prevention programs that involve the tribal community, programs that include both parents and youth, and economic development programs (Johnson, Swartz, & Martin, 1995).

Although African American and Latino families include more single-parent households and have lower

behavioral techniques. Unfortunately, there has been little interest in identifying different types of adolescent alcohol abusers and then attempting to match treatment programs to the particular problems of the adolescent drinker. Most efforts simply assume that adolescents with drinking problems are a homogeneous group, and do not take into account the varying developmental patterns and social histories of different adolescents. Some adolescents with drinking problems may be helped more through family therapy, others through peer counseling, and yet others through intensive behavioral strategies, depending on the type of drinking problem and the social agents who have the most influence on the adolescent (Maguin, Zucker, & Fitzgerald, 1995).

Other Drugs

What are the patterns of adolescent use for other drugs, such as hallucinogens, stimulants, and depressants?

Hallucinogens

Hallucinogens *are drugs that modify an individual's perceptual experiences and produce hallucinations. Hallucinogens are called psychedelic (mind-altering) drugs.* First, we discuss LSD, which has powerful hallucinogenic properties, and then marijuana, a milder hallucinogen.

LSD LSD, *lysergic acid diethylamide, is a hallucinogen that, even in low doses, produces striking perceptual changes.* Objects glow and change shape. Colors becomes kaleidoscopic. Fabulous images unfold as users close their eyes. Sometimes the images are pleasurable, sometimes unpleasant or frightening. In one drug trip, an LSD user might experience a cascade of beautiful colors and wonderful scenes; in another drug trip, the images might be frightening and grotesque. LSD's effects on the body may include dizziness, nausea, and tremors. Emotional and cognitive effects may include rapid mood swings or impaired attention and memory. LSD's popularity in the 1960s and early 1970s was followed by a reduction in use by the mid 1970s as its unpredictable effects became well publicized. However, use of LSD by high school seniors has increased in the 1990s. Also, there has been an upward drift in LSD use by college students. Annual use by college students rose from 3.4 percent in 1989 to 5.2 percent in 1994 (Johnston, O'Malley, & Bachman, 1995). The concerns about "bad trips" from LSD were the concerns of an earlier generation. Today, the negative effects of LSD are little publicized, which may account for its increased use among college students.

Marijuana Marijuana, *a milder hallucinogen than LSD, comes from the hemp plant* Cannabis sativa, *which originated in Central Asia but is now grown in most parts of the world.* Marijuana is made of the hemp plant's dry leaves; its dried resin is known as hashish. The active ingredient in marijuana is THC, which stands for the chemical delta-9-tetrahydrocannabinol. This ingredient does not resemble the chemicals of other psychedelic drugs. Because marijuana is metabolized slowly, its effects may be present over the course of several days.

The physical effects of marijuana include increases in pulse rate and blood pressure, reddening of the eyes, coughing, and dryness of the mouth. Psychological effects include a mixture of excitatory, depressive, and hallucinatory characteristics, making the drug difficult to classify. The drug can produce spontaneous and unrelated ideas; perceptions of time and place can be distorted; verbal behavior may increase or cease to occur at all; and sensitivity to sounds and colors might increase. Marijuana also can impair attention and memory, which suggests that smoking marijuana is not conducive to optimal school performance. When marijuana is used daily in heavy amounts, it also can impair the human reproductive system and may be involved in some birth defects. Marijuana use by adolescents decreased in the 1980s—for example, in 1979, 37 percent smoked marijuana at least once a month, but by 1996 that figure had dropped to 22 percent (Johnston, O'Malley, & Bachman, 1995). However, the 1996 figure of 22 percent represents a significant increase in marijuana use from 12 percent in 1992.

Marijuana continues to be a controversial drug in the legal realm. In 1968, under California law, possession of marijuana for personal use was a felony carrying a penalty of 1 to 10 years of prison on first offense and up to life imprisonment on the third offense. That situation changed dramatically in 1976 when a new California law reduced the possession of an ounce or less of marijuana to a misdemeanor with a maximum fine of $100. Laws for marijuana vary from one state to another, and groups such as the National Organization for the Reform of Marijuana Laws (NORML) continue to push for more lenient legal penalties.

Stimulants

Stimulants *are drugs that increase the activity of the central nervous system.* The most widely used stimulants are caffeine, nicotine, amphetamines, and cocaine. Stimulants increase heart rate, breathing, and temperature but decrease appetite. Stimulants increase energy, decrease feelings of fatigue, and lift mood and self-confidence. After the effects wear off, though, the user often becomes tired, irritable, and depressed, and may experience headaches. Stimulants can be physically addictive.

Cigarette smoking (in which the active drug is nicotine) is one of the most serious yet preventable health problems. Smoking is likely to begin in grades 7 through 9, although sizable portions of youth are still establishing regular smoking habits during high school and college. Since the national surveys by Johnston, Bachman, and O'Malley began in 1975, cigarettes have been the substance most frequently used on a daily basis by high

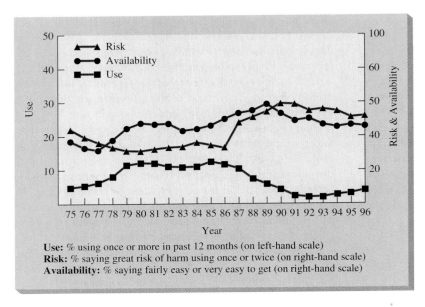

Figure~15.3

Cocaine and High School Seniors.
Trends in perceived availability, perceived risk of trying, and prevalence of use in past year for high school seniors.

Legend in figure:
- ▲ Risk
- ● Availability
- ■ Use

Use: % using once or more in past 12 months (on left-hand scale)
Risk: % saying great risk of harm using once or twice (on right-hand scale)
Availability: % saying fairly easy or very easy to get (on right-hand scale)

Axis labels: Use (left), Risk & Availability (right), Year (bottom). Years: 75 76 77 78 79 80 81 82 83 84 85 86 87 88 89 90 91 92 93 94 95 96

"I'll tell you one thing. As soon as I'm thirteen I'm gonna stop!"

Reprinted by permission: Tribune Media Services.

school seniors. While adolescents' use of cigarettes dropped between 1976 and 1981 (from 38.8 percent to 29.4 percent, for use in the last 30 days), it has recently increased (to 34 percent in 1996) (Johnston, O'Malley, & Bachman, 1996). Almost one-third of high school seniors still do not feel that great risk is associated with smoking. Much more about smoking appears in the next chapter, where methods of preventing adolescent smoking are described.

Amphetamines *are widely prescribed stimulants, sometimes appearing in the form of diet pills. They are called "pep pills" and "uppers."* Amphetamine use among high school seniors, college students, and adults has decreased

significantly. Use of amphetamines in the last 30 days by high school seniors declined from 10.7 percent in 1982 to 4.1 percent in 1996 (Johnston, O'Malley, & Bachman, 1996). However, use of over-the-counter stay-awake pills, which usually contain caffeine as their active ingredient, has sharply increased. Two other classes of stimulants—"look-alikes" and over-the-counter diet pills—declined in use in recent years. Still, 40 percent of females have tried diet pills by the end of their senior year in high school, and 10 percent have tried them within the last month.

Cocaine *is a stimulant that comes from the coca plant, native to Bolivia and Peru.* For many years, Bolivians and Peruvians chewed on the plant to increase their stamina. Today, cocaine is either snorted or injected in the form of crystals or powder. The effect is a rush of euphoric feelings, which eventually wear off, followed by depressive feelings, lethargy, insomnia, and irritability. Cocaine can have a number of damaging effects on the body, resulting in heart attacks, strokes, or brain seizures. In the case of University of Maryland basketball star Len Bias, it meant death following cardiac arrest.

How many adolescents use cocaine? Use of cocaine by high school seniors dropped from a peak of 6.7 percent in 1985 to 2.0 percent in 1996 (use at some time in the last 30 days) (Johnston, O'Malley, & Bachman, 1996). Cocaine use by college students has declined considerably—from a peak of 7.9 percent in 1982 to 1.0 percent in 1994 (use in last 30 days). A growing percentage of high school students are reaching the conclusion that cocaine use entails considerable, unpredictable risk. Still, the percentage of adolescents and young adults who have used cocaine is precariously high. About one of every thirteen high school seniors has tried cocaine at least once. The trends in perceived availability, perceived risk of trying, and prevalence of use in the past year by high school seniors are shown in figure 15.3. As can be seen, cocaine use by high school seniors in 1996 dropped to a level similar to that in 1975.

A troublesome part of the cocaine story rests in the dangerous shift in how it is administered, due in large part to the advent of crack cocaine—an inexpensive, purified, smokable form of the drug. Crack use is especially heavy among non-college-bound youth in urban settings. In the late 1980s and early 1990s, adolescents' use of crack declined (from 4.1 percent in 1986 to 1.5 percent in 1993—for use in the last year). However, in 1995–1996, an increase in adolescents' use of crack occurred—to 2.1 percent (Johnston, Bachman, & O'Malley, 1996).

Depressants

Depressants *are drugs that slow down the central nervous system, bodily functions, and behavior.* Medically, depressants have been used to reduce anxiety and to induce sleep. Among the most widely used depressants are alcohol, which we discussed earlier, barbiturates, and tranquilizers. Though used less frequently, the opiates are especially dangerous depressants.

Barbiturates, *such as Nembutal and Seconal, are depressant drugs that induce sleep or reduce anxiety.* **Tranquilizers,** *such as Valium and Xanax, are depressant drugs that reduce anxiety and induce relaxation.* They can produce symptoms of withdrawal when an individual stops taking them. Since the initial surveys, begun in 1975, of drug use by high school seniors, use of depressants has decreased. For example, use of barbiturates at least every 30 days in 1975 was 4.7 percent; in 1996, it was only 2.1 percent. Over the same time period, tranquilizer use also decreased, from 4.1 percent to 2.0 percent, for 30-day prevalence.

Opiates, *which consist of opium and its derivatives, depress the activity of the central nervous system. They are commonly known as narcotics.* Many drugs have been produced from the opium poppy, among them morphine and heroin (which is converted to morphine when it enters the brain). For several hours after taking an opiate, an individual feels euphoria, pain relief, and an increased appetite for food and sex; however, the opiates are among the most physically addictive drugs. The body soon craves more heroin and experiences very painful withdrawal unless more is taken. Recently, another hazardous consequence of opiate addiction has surfaced. Most heroin addicts inject the drug intravenously. When addicts share their needles with others, blood from the needles can be passed on. When this blood comes from an individual with AIDS, the virus can be spread from one user to another. Heroin is widely perceived by adolescents as having a greater risk of harm for the user. Its low use reflects this perception. Thirty-day use by high school seniors was 0.4 percent in 1975 and 0.5 percent in 1996.

At this point, we have discussed a number of depressants, stimulants, and hallucinogens. Their medical uses, duration of effects, overdose symptoms, health risks, physical addiction risk, and psychological dependence risk are summarized in figure 15.4.

The Roles of Development, Parents, Peers, and Schools in Adolescent Drug Abuse

Earlier, we discussed the factors that place adolescents at risk for alcohol abuse. Researchers also have examined the factors that are related to drug use in adolescence, especially the roles of development, parents, peers, and schools (Petraitis, Flay, & Miller, 1995).

Most adolescents become drug users at some point in their development, whether their use is limited to alcohol, caffeine, and cigarettes, or extended to marijuana, cocaine, and hard drugs. A special concern involves adolescents using drugs as a way of coping with stress, which can interfere with the development of competent coping skills and responsible decision making. Researchers have found that drug use in childhood or early adolescence has more detrimental long-term effects on the development of responsible, competent behavior than drug use that occurs in late adolescence (Newcomb & Bentler, 1989). When they use drugs to cope with stress, young adolescents often enter adult roles of marriage and work prematurely without adequate socioemotional growth and experience greater failure in adult roles.

How early are adolescents beginning drug use? National samples of eighth- and ninth-grade students were included in the Institute for Social Research survey of drug use for the first time in 1991 (Johnston, O'Malley, & Bachman, 1992). Early on in the increase in drug use in the United States (late 1960s, early 1970s), drug use was much higher among college students than among high school students, who in turn had much higher rates of drug use than did middle or junior high school students. However, today the rates for college and high school students are similar, and the rates for young adolescents are not as different from those for older adolescents as might be anticipated.

Drinking in the past year was reported by 47 percent of the eighth-graders, 65 percent of the tenth-graders, and 73 percent of the twelfth-graders. Twenty percent of the eighth-graders said they had engaged in binge drinking. Cigarette smoking had already been tried by 50 percent of the eighth-graders, with 21 percent of them (average age of 13) smoking in the past 30 days. Relatively few students had initiated cocaine use by the eighth grade (4.5 percent use ever) or the tenth grade (6.5 percent ever). An age differentiation also appeared for marijuana use, which tends to be one of the first illegal drugs tried by adolescents. Of the eighth-graders, 23 percent reported using marijuana in the prior year, compared with 40 percent of the tenth-graders and 45 percent of the high school seniors. Inhalant drugs, such as glues, aerosols, and butane, are rather commonly used by young adolescents—12 percent of eighth-graders reported use of inhalant drugs in the prior year, for example, while only 10 percent of the tenth- and 8 percent of the twelfth-graders reported such use (Johnston, O'Malley, & Bachman, 1996).

Parents, peers, and social support play important roles in preventing adolescent drug abuse. A developmental model of adolescent drug abuse has been proposed by Judith Brook and her colleagues (1990). They believe that the initial step in adolescent drug abuse is laid down in the childhood years, when children fail to receive nurturance from their parents and grow up in conflict-ridden families. These children fail to internalize their parents' personality, attitudes, and behavior, and later carry this absence of parental ties into adolescence.

	Medical uses	Duration of effects	Short-term effects
Depressants			
Alcohol	Pain relief	3–6 hours	Relaxation, depresses brain activity, slows behavior, reduces inhibitions
Barbiturates	Sleeping pill	1–16 hours	Relaxation, induces sleep
Tranquilizers	Anxiety reduction	4–8 hours	Relaxation, slows behavior
Opiates (narcotics)	Pain relief	3–6 hours	Euphoric feelings, drowsiness, nausea
Stimulants			
Amphetamines	Weight control	2–4 hours	Increases alertness, excitability; decreases fatigue, irritabilily
Cocaine	Local anesthetic	1–2 hours	Increases alertness, excitability, euphoric feelings; decreases fatigue, irritabilty
Hallucinogens			
LSD	None	1–12 hours	Strong hallucinations, distorted time perception
Marijuana	Treatment of the eye disorder glaucoma	2–4 hours	Euphoric feelings, relaxation, mild hallucinations, time distortion, attention and memory impairment

One glass of wine equals one can of beer in alcoholic content.

Cocaine is extracted from coca plants.

Cannabis paraphernalia, drug equipment or gadgets, is usually sold in "head shops" for use in smoking marijuana.

Figure~15.4

Psychoactive Drugs: Their Use, Effects, and Addictive Characteristics.

Overdose	Health risks	Risk of physical addiction	Risk of psychological dependence
Disorientation, loss of consciousness, even death at high blood-alcohol levels	Accidents, brain damage, liver disease, heart disease, ulcers, birth defects	Moderate	Moderate
Breathing difficulty, coma, possible death	Accidents, coma, possible death	High	High
Breathing difficulty, coma, possible death	Accidents, coma, possible death	Low	Low–moderate
Convulsions, coma, possible death	Accidents, infectious diseases such as AIDS	Very high	Very high
Extreme irritability, feelings of persecution, convulsions	Insomnia, hypertension, malnutrition, possible death	Moderate	High
Extreme irritability, feelings of persecution, convulsions cardiac arrest, possible death	Insomnia, hypertension, malnutrition, possible death	Moderate–high	High
Severe mental disturbance, loss of contact with reality	Accidents	None	Very low
Fatigue, disoriented behavior	Accidents, respiratory disease	None	Low–moderate

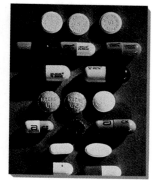

Tranquilizers are used for reducing anxiety and inducing depression.

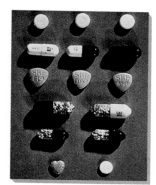

Amphetamines are stimulants used to increase alertness and energy.

Shown here is a private, illegal laboratory for manufacturing LSD.

"Just tell me where you kids get the idea to take so many drugs."

© 1990 by Sidney Harris.

Adolescent characteristics, such as lack of a conventional orientation and inability to control emotions, are then expressed in affiliations with peers who take drugs, which, in turn, leads to drug use. In recent studies, Brook and her colleagues have found support for their model.

Positive relationships with parents and others are important in reducing adolescents' drug use (Myers, Wagner, & Brown, 1997). In one study, social support (which consisted of good relationships with parents, siblings, adults, and peers) during adolescence substantially reduced drug abuse (Newcomb & Bentler, 1988). In another study, adolescents were most likely to take drugs when both their parents took drugs (such as tranquilizers, amphetamines, alcohol, or nicotine) and their peers took drugs (Kandel, 1974).

In a review of the role that schools can play in the prevention of drug abuse, Joy Dryfoos (1990) concluded that a consensus is beginning to be reached.

1. Early intervention in schools is believed to be more effective than later intervention. This intervention works best when implemented before the onset of drug use. Middle school is often mentioned as an excellent time for the inclusion of drug-abuse programs in schools.

2. Nonetheless, school-based drug-abuse prevention requires a kindergarten-through-twelfth-grade approach, with age-appropriate components available. When school prevention programs are provided, the students need follow-up and continuous attention. Counseling about drug abuse should be available throughout the school years.

3. Teacher training is an important element in school-based programs. The best-designed drug-abuse curriculum is ineffective in the hands of an inadequately prepared teacher. School systems need to provide time and resources for in-service training and supervision.

4. Social skills training, especially focused on coping skills and resistance to peer pressure, is the most promising of the new wave of school-based curricula. However, the effectiveness of these social skills training programs over the long term and whether or not they are as effective with high-risk youth as with others are not known.

5. Peer-led programs are often more effective than teacher-led or counselor-led programs, especially when older students (senior high) are the leaders and role models for younger students (junior high and middle school).

6. Most of the school-based programs have been general programs directed at all students, rather than specific programs targeted at high-risk adolescents. More programs aimed at the high-risk group are needed.

7. The most effective school-based programs are often part of community-wide prevention efforts that involve parents, peers, role models, media, police, courts, businesses, youth-serving agencies, as well as schools.

The basic philosophy of community-wide programs is that a number of different programs have to be in place. The Midwestern Prevention Program, developed by Mary Ann Pentz and her colleagues (Pentz, 1993; Rohrbach & others, 1995), implemented a community-wide health-promotion campaign that used local media, community education, and parent programs in concert with a substance-abuse curriculum in the schools. Evaluations of the program after 18 months and after 4 years revealed significantly lower rates of alcohol and marijuana use by adolescents in the program than by their counterparts in other areas of the city where the program was not in operation.

At this point, we have discussed a number of ideas about the nature of abnormality and about drugs and alcohol. A summary of these ideas is presented in concept table 15.1. Next, we consider another pervasive problem in adolescence—juvenile delinquency.

JUVENILE DELINQUENCY

Thirteen-year-old Arnie, in the "Images of Adolescence" section that opened this chapter, has a history of thefts and physical assaults. Arnie is a juvenile delinquent. What is a juvenile delinquent? What are the antecedents of delinquency? What types of interventions have been used to prevent or reduce delinquency?

What Is Juvenile Delinquency?

The term **juvenile delinquency** *refers to a broad range of behaviors, from socially unacceptable behavior (such as acting out in school) to status offenses (such as running away) to criminal acts (such as burglary). For legal purposes, a distinction*

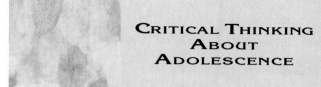

Developing a Drug-Abuse Program for Adolescents

Drug abuse is a major problem for adolescents in the United States. We have covered many different topics about drug abuse, including the nature of addiction, as well as the roles of development, parents, peers, and schools in drug abuse. Imagine that you have just been appointed the head of the President's Commission on Adolescent Drug Abuse. What would be the first program you would try to put in place? What would its components be? Would schools be a major locus of the intervention? Would the media play a key role in the program? By considering what program you would try to put in place first if you were the head of the President's Commission on Adolescent Drug Abuse, you are learning to think critically by *using knowledge about development to improve human welfare*.

CONCEPT TABLE 15.1
The Nature of Abnormality, and Drugs and Alcohol

Concept	Processes/Related Ideas	Characteristics/Description
The Nature of Abnormality	What is abnormal behavior?	Abnormal behavior is behavior that is maladaptive and harmful.
	What causes abnormal behavior?	Biological, psychological, and environmental/sociocultural factors have been proposed as causes. Many psychologists have criticized the medical model and its emphasis on disorders as diseases.
	Characteristics of adolescent disorders	The spectrum of adolescent disorders is wide, varying in severity and in terms of adolescents' developmental level, sex, and social class. Middle-class and female adolescents have more internalized problems, while their low-income, male counterparts have more externalized problems.
Drugs and Alcohol	Why do adolescents take drugs?	Drugs have been used since the beginning of human existence for pleasure, utility, curiosity, and social reasons. Understanding drugs requires knowledge of addiction and psychological dependence.
	Trends in overall drug use	The 1960s and 1970s were times of marked increase in the use of illicit drugs. Drug use began to decline in the 1980s but has increased in the 1990s. The United States has the highest rate of drug use of any industrialized country.
	Alcohol	Alcohol is primarily a depressant and is the drug most widely used by youth. Alcohol abuse is a major problem in adolescence. Risk factors for adolescent alcohol abuse include heredity, negative family and peer influences, ethnicity, and personality characteristics.
	Other drugs	Other drugs that can be harmful to adolescents are hallucinogens (such as LSD and marijuana, which have seen increased use by adolescents recently), stimulants (such as nicotine, amphetamines, and cocaine), and depressants (such as barbiturates, tranquilizers, and alcohol).
	The roles of development, parents, peers, and schools in adolescent drug abuse	Drug use in childhood or early adolescence has more detrimental long-term effects than when its onset occurs in late adolescence. Parents, peers, and social support play important roles in preventing adolescent drug abuse. Considerable interest has developed in the role of schools in preventing adolescent drug abuse. Early intervention, a kindergarten through twelfth-grade approach, teacher training, social skills training, peer-led programs, programs aimed at high-risk groups, and community-wide prevention efforts are important components of successful school-based programs.

TABLE 15.2

Percentage of 10- to 17-Year-Olds Arrested, by Type of Offense, in 1986		
	Percentage of 10- to 14-Year Olds	Percentage of 15- to 17-Year-Olds
Total Arrests	*2.9%*	*10.9%*
Serious Crimes	*1.3%*	*3.6%*
Larceny/theft	0.8	2.0
Burglary	0.3	0.8
Motor vehicle theft	—	0.4
Aggravated assault	—	0.3
Robbery	—	0.2
Other Arrests	*1.6%*	*7.3%*
Liquor law violations	—	1.1
Vandalism	0.2	0.5
Disorderly conduct	0.1	0.5
Other assaults	0.2	0.5
Drug abuse	—	0.5
Runaways	0.3	0.7

From *Adolescents at Risk: Prevalence and Prevention* by Joy G. Dryfoos. Copyright © 1991 by Joy G. Dryfoos. Used by permission of Oxford University Press, Inc.

is made between index offenses and status offenses. **Index offenses** *are criminal acts, whether they are committed by juveniles or adults. They include such acts as robbery, aggravated assault, rape, and homicide.* **Status offenses,** *such as running away, truancy, underage drinking, sexual promiscuity, and uncontrollability, are less serious acts. They are performed by youth under a specified age, which classifies them as juvenile offenses.* States often differ in the age used to classify an individual as a juvenile or an adult. Approximately three-fourths of the states have established age 18 as a maximum for defining juveniles. Two states use age 19 as the cutoff, seven states use age 17, and four states use age 16. Thus, running away from home at age 17 may be an offense in some states but not others.

In addition to the legal classifications of index offenses and status offenses, many of the behaviors considered delinquent are included in widely used classifications of abnormal behavior. **Conduct disorder** *is the psychiatric diagnostic category used when multiple behaviors occur over a 6-month period. These behaviors include truancy, running away, fire setting, cruelty to animals, breaking and entering, excessive fighting, and others. When three or more of these behaviors co-occur before the age of 15 and the child or adolescent is considered unmanageable or out of control, the clinical diagnosis is conduct disorder.*

In sum, most children or adolescents at one time or another act out or do things that are destructive or troublesome for themselves or others. If these behaviors occur often in childhood or early adolescence, psychiatrists diagnose them as conduct disorders. If these behaviors result in illegal acts by juveniles, society labels them as *delinquents*.

How many juvenile delinquents or children and adolescents with conduct disorder are there? Figures are somewhat sketchy and depend on the criteria used. The most concrete figures are legally defined, but many adolescents who engage in delinquent behavior are never arrested. Table 15.2 was compiled from the *Unified Crime Reports*, which gather data on all arrests in the United States every year according to type of crime and age (Flanagan & Jamieson, 1988). As indicated in the table, about 3 percent of 10- to 14-year-olds and 11 percent of 15- to 17-year-olds were arrested in 1986 for an offense. Based on self-reported patterns of behavior, a large number of adolescents—as many as 20 percent—are at risk for committing offenses that could result in arrests. Overall, the prevalence of delinquency has probably not changed much in the last decade (Dryfoos, 1990).

What Are the Antecedents of Delinquency?

Predictors of delinquency include identity (negative identity), self-control (low degree), age (early initiation), sex

Antecedent	Association with delinquency	Description
Identity	Negative identity	Erikson believes delinquency occurs because the adolescent fails to resolve a role identity.
Self-control	Low degree	Some children and adolescents fail to acquire the essential controls that others have acquired during the process of growing up.
Age	Early initiation	Early appearance of antisocial behavior is associated with serious offenses later in adolescence. However, not every child who acts out becomes a delinquent.
Sex	Males	Boys engage in more antisocial behavior than girls do, although girls are more likely to run away. Boys engage in more violent acts.
Expectations for education and school grades	Low expectations and low grades	Adolescents who become delinquents often have low educational expectations and low grades. Their verbal abilities are often weak.
Parental influences	Monitoring (low), support (low), discipline (ineffective)	Delinquents often come from families in which parents rarely monitor their adolescents, provide them with little support, and ineffectively discipline them.
Peer influences	Heavy influence, low resistance	Having delinquent peers greatly increases the risk of becoming delinquent.
Socioeconomic status	Low	Serious offenses are committed more frequently by lower-class males.
Neighborhood quality	Urban, high crime, high mobility	Communities often breed crime. Living in a high-crime area, which also is characterized by poverty and dense living conditions, increases the probability that a child will become a delinquent. These communities often have grossly inadequate schools.

Figure~15.5

The Antecedents of Juvenile Delinquency.

Adapted from Adolescents at Risk: Prevalence and Prevention *by Joy G. Dryfoos. Copyright © 1990 by Joy G. Dryfoos. Reprinted by permission of Oxford University Press, Inc.*

(male), expectations for education (low expectations, little commitment), school grades (low achievement in early grades), peer influence (heavy influence, low resistance), socioeconomic status (low), parental role (lack of monitoring, low support, and ineffective discipline), and neighborhood quality (urban, high crime, high mobility). A summary of these antecedents of delinquency is presented in figure 15.5. We will now examine several of these antecedents in greater detail: identity, self-control, family processes, and social class/community.

Identity

According to Erik Erikson's (1968) theory of development, adolescence is the stage when the crisis of identity versus identity diffusion should be resolved. Not surprisingly, Erikson's ideas about delinquency are linked to adolescents' ability to positively resolve this crisis. Erikson believes that the biological changes of puberty initiate concomitant changes in the social expectations placed on adolescents by family, peers, and schools. These biological and social changes allow for two kinds of integration to occur in adolescents' personality: (1) the establishment of a sense of consistency in life and (2) the resolution of role identity, a sort of joining of adolescents' motivation, values, abilities, and styles with the role demands placed on adolescents.

Erikson believes that delinquency is characterized more by a failure of adolescents to achieve the second kind of integration, involving the role aspects of identity. He comments that adolescents whose infant, childhood, or adolescent experiences have somehow restricted them from acceptable social roles or made them feel that they cannot measure up to the demands placed on them may choose a negative course of identity development. Some of these adolescents may take on the role of the delinquent, enmeshing themselves in the most negative currents of the youth culture available to them. Thus, for Erikson, delinquency is an attempt to establish an identity, although it is a negative one.

Self-Control

Juvenile delinquency also can be described as the failure to develop sufficient behavioral self-control. Some children fail to develop the essential controls that others have acquired during the process of growing up. Most youths have learned the difference between acceptable and unacceptable behavior, but juvenile delinquents have not. They may fail to distinguish between acceptable and unacceptable behavior, or they may have learned this distinction but failed to develop adequate control in using the distinction to guide their behavior. An understanding of delinquency thus requires study of different aspects of the development of self-control—for example, delay of gratification and self-imposed standards of conduct. Failure to delay gratification is related to cheating and to a general lack of social responsibility often revealed in delinquent behavior (Mischel & Gilligan, 1964).

Delinquents also may have developed inadequate standards of conduct. Adolescents about to commit an antisocial act must invoke self-critical thoughts to inhibit the tendency to commit the illegal action. These self-critical standards are strongly influenced by adolescents' models. Thus, adolescents whose parents, teachers, and peers exhibit self-critical standards usually develop the self-control needed to refrain from an illegal or antisocial act. Other adolescents, however, may be exposed to models who praise antisocial acts. For example, adolescents whose peer models praise or engage in antisocial deeds may follow their example, especially if family models of high conduct are lacking.

In one recent study, support for the belief that self-control plays an important role in delinquency was found (Feldman & Weinberger, 1994). Effective parenting in childhood (use of consistent, child-centered, and nonaversive strategies) was associated with boys' acquisition of self-regulatory skills. In turn, having these skills as internal attributes was related to lower rates of delinquency in adolescence.

The expected consequences of negative actions also influence the adolescents' decision to engage in or refrain from delinquent behavior. When youth expect some sort of reward for delinquent behavior, they are more likely to perform the antisocial act than if they expect punishment. The expected rewards can take many different forms—the acquisition of stolen goods, for example, or high status in the gang or in the neighborhood peer groups.

Whether or not adolescents engage in juvenile delinquency may also be affected by the competence they have achieved in different aspects of life. Consider youth who do well in academic subjects at school, who actively participate in socially desirable clubs, or who develop athletic skills. These youth are likely to develop a positive view of themselves and receive reinforcement from others for prosocial behavior. Most delinquents, however, have achieved few ego-enhancing competencies. Antisocial behavior is one way they can demonstrate self-competence and receive reinforcement from the delinquent subculture (Kazdin, 1995).

Family Processes

Although there has been a long history of interest in defining the family factors that contribute to delinquency (Glueck & Glueck, 1950; McCord, McCord, & Gudeman, 1960; Rutter, 1971), the most recent focus has been on the nature of family support and family management practices (Lytton, 1995). Disruptions or omissions in the parents' applications of family support and management practices are consistently linked with antisocial behavior by children and adolescents (Moran, Chang, & Pettit, 1994). These family support and management practices include monitoring adolescents' whereabouts, using effective discipline for antisocial behavior, calling on effective problem-solving skills, and supporting the development of prosocial skills.

The parents of delinquents are less skilled in discouraging antisocial behavior than are the parents of nondelinquents. Parental monitoring of adolescents is especially important in whether adolescents become delinquents

(DeVet, Brodsky, & Ialongo, 1997). In one investigation, parental monitoring of adolescents' whereabouts was the most important family factor in predicting delinquency (Patterson & Stouthamer-Loeber, 1984). "It's 10 P.M., do you know where your children are?" seems to be an important question for parents to answer affirmatively. Family discord and inconsistent and inappropriate discipline also are associated with delinquency.

An important question is whether family experiences cause delinquency, are the consequences of delinquency, or are merely associated or correlated with delinquency. The associations may simply reflect some third factor, such as genetic influences; may be the result of the disturbing effect of the child's behavior on the family; or may indicate that family stress can produce delinquency through some environmental effect. In a review of research on the family-delinquency link, Michael Rutter and Norman Garmezy (1983) concluded that family influences do have some kind of environmental influence on delinquency. The research by Gerald Patterson and his colleagues (Patterson, DeBaryshe, & Ramsey, 1989) documents that inadequate parental supervision, involving poor monitoring of adolescents, and inconsistent, inappropriate discipline are key family factors in determining delinquency.

Social Class/Community

Although juvenile delinquency is less exclusively a lower-class problem than it was in the past, some characteristics of the lower-class culture are likely to promote delinquency. The norms of many lower-class peer groups and gangs are antisocial, or counterproductive to the goals and norms of society at large (McCord, 1990). Getting into and staying out of trouble in some instances becomes a prominent feature of the lives of some adolescents from lower-class backgrounds. Status in the peer group may be gauged by how often the adolescent can engage in antisocial conduct yet manage to stay out of jail. Since lower-class adolescents have less opportunity to develop skills that are socially desirable, they may sense that they can gain attention and status by performing antisocial actions. Being "tough" and "masculine" are high-status traits for lower-class boys, and these traits are often gauged by adolescents' success in performing delinquent acts and getting away with them.

The nature of a community can contribute to delinquency (Tolan, Guerra, & Kendall, 1995). A community with a high crime rate allows adolescents to observe many models who engage in criminal activities and might be rewarded for their criminal accomplishments. Such communities often are characterized by poverty, unemployment, and feelings of alienation from the middle class. The quality of schools, funding for education, and organized neighborhood activities are other community factors that may be related to delinquency. Are there caring adults in the schools and neighborhood who can

A current special concern in low-income areas is escalating gang violence.

convince adolescents with delinquent tendencies that education is the best route to success? When family support becomes inadequate, then such community supports take on added importance in preventing delinquency.

Even if adolescents grow up in high-crime communities, their peer relations can influence whether or not they become delinquent (Dishion, Andrews, & Crosby, 1995). In one investigation of 500 delinquents and 500 nondelinquents in Boston, a much higher percentage of the delinquents had regular associations with delinquent peers (Glueck & Glueck, 1950).

A recent, special concern in low-income areas is escalating gang violence, which is being waged on a level more lethal than ever before. Knives and clubs have been replaced by hand grenades and automatic weapons, frequently purchased with money made from selling drugs. The lure of gang membership is powerful, especially for children and adolescents who are disconnected from family, school, work, and the community. Children as young as 9 to 10 years of age cling to the fringes of neighborhood gangs, eager to prove themselves worthy of membership by the age of 12. Once children are members of a gang, it is difficult to get them to leave. Recommendations for preventing gang violence include identifying disconnected children in elementary schools and initiating counseling with the children and their families. More about life in gangs and an effort in Detroit that has made a difference in reducing gang participation appear in Sociocultural Worlds of Adolescence.

Violence and Youth

An increasing concern is the high rate of violence displayed by adolescents. According to the United States Department of Education (1993), 16 percent of seniors reported that they had been threatened with a weapon at school; 7 percent said they had been injured with a weapon. One of every five high school students routinely carries a firearm, knife, or club. Many teachers say they have been verbally abused, physically threatened, or actually attacked by students. And homicide remains the leading cause of death among African Americans, regardless of gender or age.

In one recent study of high school students, aggressive and violent behavior was related to binge drinking and sexual activity in males, to any alcohol use and use of illegal drugs in White females, and to sexual activity in African American females (Valois & others, 1995). In the same study, the strongest predictors for carrying a weapon were alcohol use and sexual activity.

According to Ervin Staub (1996, in press), the conditions and experiences that create youth violence are the opposite of those that generate caring, helping, and altruism. They frustrate, or fail to fulfill, adolescents' basic needs for security, a positive identity that includes a sense of effectiveness, positive connections to other people, and comprehension of reality. The origins of aggression in socialization and experience include neglect, rejection, harsh treatment, and lack of nurturance (Dodge, 1993). Such practices create a need for

SOCIOCULTURAL WORLDS OF ADOLESCENCE

Frog and Dolores

He goes by the name of Frog. He is the cocky prince of the barrio in East Los Angeles. He has street smarts. Frog happily smiles as he talks about raking in $200 a week selling crack cocaine. He proudly details his newly acquired membership in a violent street gang, the Crips. Frog brags about using his drug money to rent a convertible on weekends, even though at less than 5 feet in height, he can barely see over the dashboard. Frog is 13 years old.

With the advent of crack, juvenile arrests in New York City tripled from 1983 to 1987 and almost quadrupled in the same time frame in Washington, D.C. Adults who founded the crack trade recognized early on that young adolescents do not run the risk of mandatory jail sentences that courts hand out to adults. Being a lookout is the entry-level position for 9- and 10-year-olds. They can make as much as $100 a day warning dealers that police are in the area. The next step up the ladder is as a runner, a job that can pay as much as $300 a day. A runner transports drugs to the dealers on the street from makeshift factories where cocaine powder is cooked into rock-hard crack. And, at the next level, older adolescents can reach the status of dealer. In a hot market like New York City, they can make over $1,000 a day.

The escalating drug-related gang violence is difficult to contain or reduce. Police crackdowns across the country seem to have had a minimal impact. In a recent weekend-long raid of drug-dealing gangs in Los Angeles, police arrested 1,453 individuals, including 315 adolescents. Half had to be released for lack of evidence. The Los Angeles County juvenile facilities are designed to house 1,317, but today they overflow with more than 2,000 adolescents.

Counselors, school officials, and community workers report that turning around the lives of children and adolescents involved in drug-related gang violence is extremely difficult. When impoverished children can make $100 a day, it is hard to wean them away from gangs. Federal budgets for training and employment programs, which provide crucial assistance to disadvantaged youth, have been reduced dramatically.

However, in Detroit, Michigan, Dolores Bennett has made a difference. For 25 years, she has worked long hours trying to find things to keep children from low-income families busy. Her activities have led to the creation of neighborhood sports teams, regular fairs and picnics, and an informal job-referral service for the children and youth in the neighborhood. She also holds many casual get-togethers for the youth in her small, tidy, yellow frame house. The youth talk openly and freely about their problems and their hopes, knowing that Dolores will listen. Dolores says that she has found being a volunteer to be priceless. On the mantel in her living room are hundreds of pictures of children and adolescents with whom she has worked. She points out that most of them did not have someone in their homes who would listen to them and give them love. America needs more Dolores Bennetts.

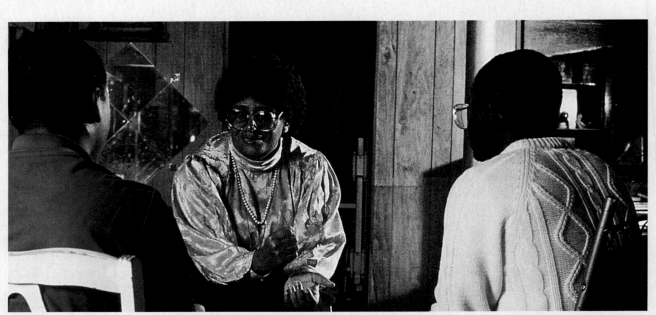

Dolores Bennett, volunteer in a low-income area of Detroit, Michigan, talks with and listens to two of her "children."

self-defense. Permissiveness in the form of a lack of rules or lack of their enforcement contributes to aggression. Modeling of aggression—by parents, in the neighborhood, and on television—increases aggression. Aggression is reinforced when members of coercive families use force to exert influence or to stop others' undesired actions. Prejudice and discrimination against ethnic minority youth also is a factor in violence (Staub & Rosenthal, 1994). And the strongest predictor of violence is poverty (Hill & others, 1994).

Gangs are a major source of violence. Youth who encounter the socialization factors just mentioned often turn to and associate with other less socially and educationally successful youth. Gangs can satisfy their unfulfilled basic needs, such as needs for a positive identity, connection to peers, and feelings of effectiveness and control. However, gangs also often promote power, violence toward out-groups, and violent action. Violence in gangs often revolves around issues of territory, honor, and drugs (Crowley & others, 1997).

Intervening with children before they develop ingrained antisocial behaviors is an important dimension of reducing violence in youth. Slogan campaigns and scare tactics do not work. In one successful intervention, Positive Adolescents Choices Training (PACT), African American 12- to 15-year-olds learn to manage their anger and resolve conflicts peacefully (Hammond, 1993). Through the use of culturally sensitive videotapes, students learn to give and receive feedback, control their anger, and negotiate and compromise. The videotapes show peer role models demonstrating these skills, along with adult role models who encourage the participants to practice the techniques. Over the past 3 years, students in the program have spent less time in juvenile court for violence-related offenses than have nonparticipants in a control group. The program students also have shown a drop in violence-related school suspensions and have improved their social and conflict-resolution skills.

The Safe Schools Act can help to foster programs such as PACT. Under the bill, schools can receive grants up to $3 million a year over 2 years to develop their own violence prevention programs. The initiatives could include comprehensive school safety strategies, coordination with community programs and agencies, and improved security to keep weapons out of the schools. To ensure that programs focus on prevention more than on enforcement, the grants allow only 33 percent of the funds to be used for metal detectors and security guards.

Interventions can reduce or prevent youth violence (Carnegie Council on Adolescent Development, 1995; Goldstein & Conoley, 1997). Effective prevention factors include developmentally appropriate schools, supportive families, and youth and community organizations. One promising specific strategy for preventing youth violence is the teaching of conflict management as part of health education in elementary and middle schools. To build resources for such programs, the Carnegie

Foundation is supporting a national network of violence prevention practitioners. Let's now examine prevention and intervention further.

Prevention and Intervention

Brief descriptions of the varied attempts to reduce delinquency would fill a large book. These attempts include forms of individual and group psychotherapy, family therapy, behavior modification, recreation, vocational training, alternative schools, survival camping and wilderness canoeing, incarceration and probation, Big Brothers and Big Sisters, community organizations, and Bible reading (Gold & Petronio, 1980). However, surprisingly little is known about what actually does help to reduce delinquency, and in many instances prevention and intervention have not been successful (Rabkin, 1987).

Although few successful models of delinquency prevention and intervention have been identified, many experts on delinquency agree that the following points deserve closer examination as prevention and intervention possibilities (Dryfoos, 1990):

1. Programs should be broader than just focusing on delinquency. For example, it is virtually impossible to improve delinquency prevention without considering the quality of education available to high-risk youth.

2. Programs should have multiple components because no one component has been found to be the "magic bullet" that decreases delinquency.

3. Programs should begin early in the child's development to prevent learning and conduct problems.

4. Schools play an important role. Schools with strong governance, fair discipline policies, student participation in decision making, and high investment in school outcomes by both students and staff have a better chance of curbing delinquency.

5. Efforts should often be directed at institutional rather than individual change. Especially important is upgrading the quality of education for disadvantaged children.

6. While point 5 is accurate, researchers have found that intensive individual attention and personalized planning also are important factors in working with children at high risk for becoming delinquent.

7. Program benefits often "wash out" after the program stops. Thus, maintenance programs and continued effort are usually necessary.

In her review of delinquency prevention, Joy Dryfoos (1990) also outlined what has *not* worked in preventing delinquency. Ineffective attempts include preventive casework, group counseling, pharmacological interventions (except for extremely violent behavior), work experience, vocational education, "scaring straight" efforts, and the juvenile justice system. Current school practices that are ineffective in reducing delinquency include suspension, detention, expulsion, security guards, and corporal punishment.

So far, we have discussed a number of ideas about juvenile delinquency as well as substance abuse by adolescents. Next, we consider two additional problems in adolescence—depression and suicide.

DEPRESSION AND SUICIDE

As mentioned earlier in the chapter, one of the most frequent characteristics of adolescents referred for psychological treatment is sadness or depression, especially among girls. In this section, we discuss the nature of adolescent depression and adolescent suicide.

Depression

Increasingly, in the study of adolescent depression, distinctions are made between depressed mood, depressive syndromes, and clinical depression (Petersen & others, 1993). The term **depressed mood** *refers to periods of sadness or unhappy mood that can last for a brief or an extended period of time. They might occur as a result of the loss of a significant relationship or failure on an important task.* **Depressive syndromes** *refers to a cluster of behaviors and emotions that include both anxiety and depression; symptoms include feeling lonely, crying, fear of doing bad things, feeling the need to be perfect, feeling unloved, feeling worthless, nervous, guilty, or sad, and worrying.* **Clinical depression** *involves being diagnosed as experiencing major depressive disorder (MDD) or dysthymic disorder.*

Major depressive disorder *is present when the adolescent has experienced five or more of the following symptoms for at least a 2-week period at a level that differs from previous functioning: (a) depressed mood or irritable most of the day, (b) decreased interest in pleasurable activities, (c) changes in weight or failure to make necessary weight gains in adolescence, (d) sleep problems, (e) psychomotor agitation or retardation, (f) fatigue or loss of energy, (g) feelings of worthlessness or abnormal amounts of guilt, (h) reduced concentration and decision-making ability, and (i) repeated suicidal ideation, attempts, or plans of suicide.*

Dysthymic disorder *occurs when adolescents have a period of at least 1 year in which they have shown depressed or irritable mood every day without more than 2 symptom-free months. Further, dysthymic disorder requires the presence of at least two of the following symptoms: (a) eating problems, (b) sleeping problems, (c) lack of energy, (d) low self-esteem, (e) reduced concentration or decision-making ability, and (f) feelings of hopelessness.*

How many adolescents have depressed mood, depressive syndromes, and clinical depression? Although

Depression is more likely to occur in adolescence than in childhood and more likely to characterize female adolescents than male adolescents.

no nationally representative epidemiological study of adolescent depression has been conducted, an increasing number of studies focus on adolescent depression and allow estimates to be made. With regard to depressed mood, 25 to 40 percent of adolescent girls report having been in a depressed mood in the previous 6 months; the figure for boys is 15 to 20 percent (Achenbach & others, 1991). An estimated 5 percent of adolescents have a depressive syndrome (Achenbach & others, 1991). The figures for clinical depression have an extremely wide range, but nonclinical samples reveal an average of 7 percent of adolescents with clinical depression; clinical samples are naturally much higher, averaging 42 percent of adolescents (Petersen & others, 1993).

Adolescent girls consistently show higher rates of depressive disorders and mood problems than do adolescent boys (Culbertson, 1997; Leadbeater, Blatt, & Quinlan, 1995). Among the reasons given for the sex difference are these: Females tend to ruminate on their depressed mood and amplify it, while males tend to distract themselves from the mood; girls' self-images, especially their body image, are often more negative than for boys during adolescence; and society is biased against females (Nolen-Hoeksema & Girgus, 1994).

Why does depression occur in adolescence? As with other disorders, biogenetic and socioenvironmental causes have been proposed (Hayward, Killen, & Taylor, 1994). Some psychologists believe that understanding adolescent depression requires information about experiences in both adolescence and childhood. For example, John Bowlby (1989) believes that insecure mother-infant attachment, a lack of love and affection in child rearing, or the actual loss of a parent in childhood creates a negative cognitive set. This schema built up during early experiences can cause children to interpret later losses as yet other failures to produce enduring close, positive relationships. From Bowlby's developmental construction view, early experiences, especially those involving loss, produce a cognitive schema that is carried forward to influence the way later experiences are interpreted. When these new experiences involve further loss, the loss serves as the immediate precipitant of depression.

In a longitudinal study of nonclinical children, the relationship between parent-child interaction during preschool and depression symptoms of the child at age 18 was examined (Gjerde & Block, 1990). The findings were significant only for the mother-daughter dyad. When mothers combined authoritarian control with nurturance in early childhood, at age 18, their daughters were more likely to show depression. In this "double-bind" circumstance, the daughters were prevented from moving beyond the mother-daughter dyad toward an independent and autonomous engagement with the wider world. While girls often find it more difficult to break ties with their mothers than boys do, a maternal orientation of combined authoritarian control and nurturance is likely to interfere even further with transformation of the mother-daughter relationship from one of high dependency on the mother to one that permits the daughter's indivuation and psychological separation.

Another cognitive view stresses that individuals become depressed because, early in their development, they acquire a cognitive schema characterized by self-devaluation and lack of confidence about the future (Beck, 1976). These habitual negative thoughts magnify and expand depressed adolescents' negative experiences. Depressed adolescents, then, may blame themselves far more than is warranted. In one study of female college students, depressed females consistently evaluated their performance more negatively than was warranted (Clark & Nelson, 1990).

Another factor thought to be important in understanding adolescent depression is **learned helplessness,** *which occurs when individuals are exposed to averse stimulation, such as prolonged stress or pain, over which they have no control. This experience fosters a sense of hopelessness and a general belief that nothing can be done to improve the situation.* In other words, depressed adolescents may be apathetic because they cannot reinstate the rewards they previously experienced. For example, an adolescent girl may not be able to make her boyfriend come back to her. Martin Seligman (1989), who originally proposed the concept of learned helplessness, has speculated that depression is so common among adolescents and young adults today because of widespread hopelessness,

brought about by an increased emphasis on self, independence, and individualism and a decreased emphasis on connectedness to others, family, and religion.

Follow-up studies of depressed adolescents indicate that the symptoms of depression experienced in adolescence predict similar problems in adulthood (Garber & others, 1988). This means that adolescent depression needs to be taken seriously. It does not just automatically go away. Rather, adolescents who are diagnosed as having depression are more likely to experience the problem on a continuing basis in adulthood than are adolescents not diagnosed as having depression. In one recent longitudinal study, transient problems in adolescence were related to situation specific factors (such as negative peer events), whereas chronic problems were defined by individual characteristics, such as internalizing behaviors (Brooks-Gunn & Graber, 1995).

Other family factors are involved in adolescent depression. Having a depressed parent is a major risk factor for depression in childhood, and this experience can carry through into adolescence. Parents who are emotionally unavailable, immersed in marital conflict, and have economic problems often set the stage for the emergence of depression in their adolescent children (Marmorstein & Shiner, 1996; Sheeber & others, 1996).

Poor peer relationships also are associated with adolescent depression. Not having a close relationship with a best friend, having less contact with friends, and peer rejection increase depressive tendencies in adolescents (Vernberg, 1990).

The experience of difficult changes or challenges is associated with depressive symptoms in adolescence (Compas & Grant, 1993). Parental divorce increases depressive symptoms in adolescents. Also, when adolescents go through puberty at the same time as they move from elementary school to middle or junior high school, they report being depressed more than do adolescents who go through puberty after the school transition (Petersen, Sarigiani, & Kennedy, 1991).

> *I was much too far out all my life*
> *And not waving but drowning*
>
> —**Stevie Smith, 1957, Not Waving but Drowning**

Suicide

Suicide occurs rarely in childhood and early adolescence, but beginning at about age 15 the suicide rate increases dramatically. Between the ages of 15 and 19, White American males have a rate of 18 suicides per 100,000; between the ages of 20 and 24, they have a rate of 28 suicides per 100,000. Suicide rates for African American adolescents and female adolescents are lower, with the rate for African American female adolescents the lowest. Suicide accounts for about 12 percent of the mortality in the

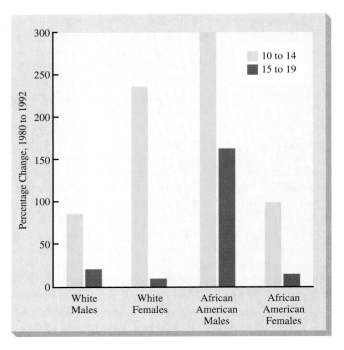

Figure~15.6

The rate of suicide is rising among White and African American adolescents.

are also often involved in suicide attempts, as reflected in a long history of family instability and unhappiness or a lack of supportive friendships (Rubenstein & others, 1989). In an investigation of suicide in gifted women, previous suicide attempts, anxiety, conspicuous instability in work and relationships, depression, or alcoholism were present in the women's lives (Tomlinson-Keasey, Warren, & Elliott, 1986). These factors are similar to those found to predict suicide in gifted men (Shneidman, 1971).

Genetic factors also may be involved in suicide. The closer an individual's genetic relation to someone who has committed suicide, the more likely that the individual will also commit suicide (Wender & others, 1986).

What is the psychological profile of the suicidal adolescent like? Suicidal adolescents often have depressive symptoms (Hammen, 1992). Although not all depressed adolescents are suicidal, depression is the most frequently cited factor associated with adolescent suicide (Pfeffer, 1986). A sense of hopelessness, low-self-esteem, and high self-blame are also associated with adolescent suicide (Shagle & Barber, 1994).

Table 15.3 provides valuable information about the early warning signs of suicide among adolescents. In addition, table 15.4 explains what to do and what not to do when you suspect an adolescent is contemplating suicide.

adolescent and young adult age group. The suicide rate has tripled since the 1950s. And, as shown in figure 15.6, the greatest percentage of increase in suicide has occurred in early adolescence.

While males are about three times more likely to commit suicide than females, females are more likely to attempt suicide. The explanation for this is that males use more lethal methods when attempting suicide, such as shooting, while females use more passive methods, such as sleeping pills.

Estimates indicate that six to ten suicide attempts occur for every suicide in the general population. For adolescents, the figure is as high as fifty attempts for every life taken. As many as two of every three college students have thought about suicide on at least one occasion. In one study, such thoughts began to surface in a serious vein at about 9 years of age and increased thereafter (Bolger & others, 1989).

Why do adolescents attempt suicide? Although there is no simple answer to this important question, it is helpful to think about suicide in terms of immediate (proximal) and earlier (distal) experiences (Maris, Silverman, & Canetto, 1997). Immediate, highly stressful circumstances, such as the loss of a boyfriend or girlfriend, failing in class at school, or an unwanted pregnancy, can trigger a suicide attempt. In addition, drugs have been more involved in suicide attempts in recent years than in the past (Reinherz & others, 1994). Earlier experiences

THE INTERRELATION OF PROBLEMS AND DISORDERS IN ADOLESCENCE, AND PROGRAMS FOR REDUCING PROBLEMS

This and other chapters have described the major problems adolescents are at risk for developing. In many instances, adolescents have more than one problem. In this section, we examine the interrelation of problems and disorders in adolescence and then explore some important ideas for reducing adolescent problems.

The Interrelation of Problems and Disorders in Adolescence

Very-high-risk youth *have multiple problem behaviors and make up as much as 10 percent of the adolescent population* (Dryfoos,1990). *This group includes adolescents who have been arrested or have committed serious offenses, have dropped out of school or are behind their grade level, are heavy users of drugs, drink heavily, regularly use cigarettes and marijuana, and are sexually active but do not use contraception. Many, but not all, of these highest-risk youth "do it all."*

High-risk youth *include as much as another 15 percent of adolescents. They participate in many of the same*

TABLE 15.3

The Early Warning Signs of Suicide in Adolescents

1. The adolescent makes suicide threats, such as: "I wish I was dead"; "My family would be better off without me"; "I don't have anything to live for."

2. A prior suicide attempt, no matter how minor. Four out of five people who commit suicide have made at least one previous attempt.

3. Preoccupation with death in music, art, and personal writing.

4. Loss of a family member, pet or boyfriend/girlfriend through death, abandonment, breakup.

5. Family disruptions, such as unemployment, serious illness, relocation, divorce.

6. Disturbances in sleeping and eating habits, and in personal hygiene.

7. Declining grades and lack of interest in school or activities that previously were important.

8. Dramatic changes in behavior patterns, such as a very gregarious adolescent's becoming very shy and withdrawn.

9. Pervasive sense of gloom, helplessness, and hopelessness.

10. Withdrawal from family members and friends; feelings of alienation from significant others.

11. Giving away prized possessions and otherwise getting affairs in order.

12. Series of accidents or impulsive, risk-taking behaviors; drug or alcohol abuse; disregard for personal safety; taking dangerous dares. (With regard to drug or alcohol abuse, there has been a dramatic increase in recent years in the number of adolescent suicides committed while the adolescent is under the influence of alcohol or drugs.

Reprinted from *Living with 10- to 15-Year-Olds: A Parent Education Curriculum* by Gayle Dorman. Copyright by the Center for Early Adolescence, Carrboro, NC, 1982, rev. ed. 1992. Used with permission.

behaviors as very-high-risk youth but with slightly lower frequency and less deleterious consequences. They commit less serious delinquent offenses; are heavy users of alcohol, cigarettes, and marijuana; often engage in unprotected intercourse; and are frequently behind in school. This group of high-risk youth are often engaged in two to three problem behaviors.

Researchers are increasingly finding that problem behaviors in adolescence are interrelated. An overview of the interrelation of adolescent problem behaviors suggests the following (Dryfoos, 1990):

1. Delinquency is related to early sexual activity, early pregnancy, substance abuse, and dropping out of school.

2. Early initiation of smoking and drinking is associated with later, heavier use of cigarettes and alcohol, as well as the use of marijuana and other illicit drugs.

3. Heavy substance abuse is related to early sexual activity, lower grades, dropping out, and delinquency.

4. Early initiation of sexual activity is associated with the use of cigarettes, alcohol, marijuana, and other illicit drugs; lower grades; dropping out of school; and delinquency.

5. Early childbearing is related to early sexual activity, heavy drug use, low academic achievement, dropping out of school, and delinquency.

6. School failure leads to dropping out of school. Lower grades are associated with substance abuse and early childbearing. Truancy and misbehavior in school are associated with substance abuse, dropping out of school, and delinquency.

Common Components of Programs That Successfully Prevent or Reduce Adolescent Problems

Joy Dryfoos (1990) analyzed the programs that have been successful in preventing or reducing adolescent problems and outlined eleven common program components. Of these eleven components, the first two—the importance of providing individual attention to high-risk adolescents and the need to develop broad, community-wide interventions—had the widest applications. This finding supports the idea that successful programs meet the needs of high-risk adolescents at the personal level within the context of broader changes in the environment. Dryfoos's eleven program components are these:

1. *Intensive Individualized Attention.* In a number of different successful programs, a high-risk adolescent is attached to a responsible adult who gives the adolescent attention and deals with the adolescent's specific needs. In a successful substance-abuse program, a student assistance counselor was available full-time for individual counseling and referral for treatment. In a successful delinquency program, a family worker gave extensive care to a predelinquent and the family to help them to make the changes needed in their lives to avoid repeated delinquent acts.

2. *Community-Wide Multiagency Collaborative Approaches.* The basic philosophy of community-wide programs is that a number of different programs and services have to be in place (Phillips, 1997). One successful substance-abuse program implemented a community-wide health promotion

TABLE 15.4

What to Do and What Not to Do When You Suspect an Adolescent Is Likely to Attempt Suicide

What to Do

1. Ask direct, straightforward questions in a calm manner: "Are you thinking about hurting yourself?"

2. Assess the seriousness of the suicidal intent by asking questions about feelings, important relationships, who else the person has talked with, and the amount of thought given to the means to be used. If a gun, pills, rope, or other means have been obtained and a precise plan developed, the situation is clearly dangerous. Stay with the person until some type of help arrives.

3. Be a good listener and be very supportive without being falsely reassuring.

4. Try to persuade the adolescent to obtain professional help and assist him or her in getting this help.

What Not to Do

1. Do not ignore the warning signs.

2. Do not refuse to talk about suicide if an adolescent approaches you about the topic.

3. Do not react with horror, disapproval, or repulsion.

4. Do not give false reassurances by saying things like, "Everything is going to be okay." Also do not give out simple answers or platitudes like, "You have everything to be thankful for."

5. Do not abandon the adolescent after the crisis has gone by or after professional help has commenced.

Reprinted from *Living with 10- to 15-Year-Olds: A Parent Education Curriculum* by Gayle Dorman. Copyright by the Center for Early Adolescence, Carrboro, NC, 1982, rev. ed. 1992. Used with permission.

campaign that used local media and community education in concert with a substance-abuse curriculum in the schools. In a successful delinquency program, a neighborhood development approach involved local residents in neighborhood councils, who worked with the schools, police, courts, gang leaders, and the media.

3. *Early Identification and Intervention.* Reaching adolescents and their families before adolescents develop problems, or at the beginning of their problems, is a successful strategy. One preschool program serves as an excellent model for the prevention of delinquency, pregnancy, substance abuse, and dropping out of school. Operated by the High Scope Foundation in Ypsilanti, Michigan, the Perry Preschool has a long-term, positive impact on its students (Berrueta-Clement & others, 1986). This enrichment program, directed by David Weikart, services disadvantaged Black American children. They attend a high-quality, 2-year preschool program and receive weekly home visits from program personnel. Based on official police records, by age 19, individuals who had attended Perry Preschool were less likely to have been arrested and reported fewer adult offenses than a control group. The Perry Preschool students also were less likely to drop out of school, and teachers rated their social behavior as more competent than that of a control group who did not receive the enriched preschool experience.

4. *Locus in the Schools.* Many of the successful programs were located in the schools. This is not surprising, because the acquisition of basic skills is the bottom line for most high-risk children and adolescents (Dryfoos, in press). Programs in which the school principal was one of the key elements were especially effective. In some instances, the principal was an important factor in school reorganization, in the development of school teams for delinquency and substance-abuse prevention, in facilitating school-based clinics, and as a liaison with student assistance counselors.

5. *Administration of School Programs by Agencies Outside of Schools.* In each problem area of adolescence, agencies or organizations outside of the schools often had the main responsibility for implementing programs in the schools. In one strategy, university-based researchers (such as James Comer at Yale and Cheryl Perry at Minnesota) obtained grants to develop a school-based program. In another strategy, nonprofit youth services and research organizations (such

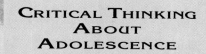
Why Is a Course of Risk Taking in Adolescence Likely to Have More Serious Consequences Today Than in the Past?

The world is a dangerous place for too many of America's teenagers, especially those from low-income families, neighborhoods, and schools. Many adolescents are resilient and cope with the challenges of adolescence without too many setbacks, but other adolescents struggle unsuccessfully to find jobs, are written off as losses by their schools, become pregnant before they are ready to become parents, or risk their health through drug abuse. Adolescents in virtually every era have been risk takers, testing limits and making shortsighted judgments. But why are the consequences of choosing a course of risk taking possibly more serious today than they have ever been? By evaluating the consequences of pursuing a course of risk taking today, you are learning to think critically by *identifying the sociocultural and historical contexts of development*.

as Public/Private Ventures or the Academy for Educational Development) implemented demonstration projects in schools or communities with support from foundations or government agencies. And in yet another strategy, local health or youth service agencies collaborated with schools and obtained money from foundations or a state health agency.

6. *Location of Programs Outside of Schools.* Not every successful program is located within a school. Some programs may be more effective if they are community-based rather than school-based. Some youth are "turned off" by school, and they may be better served by programs in community centers, churches, businesses, or youth service centers. Some of these programs may be beneficial to very-high-risk youth, such as homeless and runaway adolescents, especially in providing them with overnight shelter.

7. *Arrangements for Training.* Many of the successful programs hire special staff members, who require training to develop a program. In many cases, they are asked to use a certain strategy (such as behavior modification) or a new curriculum (such as life skills training). School-based programs often involve the implementation of new concepts, such as cooperative learning. Many of the model programs have teams, made up of support personnel (social worker, psychologist, counselor), the school principal, parents (in some instances), and occasionally students. These teams also need training to carry out the plan of the program.

8. *Social Skills Training.* A number of successful programs use social skills training as part of their strategy. Social skills training often involves teaching youth about their own risky behavior, providing them with the skills to cope with high-risk situations and to resist negative peer influence, and helping them to make healthy decisions about their futures. Role-playing, rehearsal, peer instruction, and media analysis are examples of social skills training techniques. However, few of the social skills training programs have demonstrated success with very-high-risk youth.

9. *Use of Peers in Intervention.* Successful program developers are aware of the importance of peers in adolescent development. The most successful programs use older peers—either as classroom instructors in social skills training, or as tutors and mentors—to influence or help younger peers. In some programs, the peer tutors are paid. Students who are selected to act as peer mentors often gain the most from the experience.

10. *Use of Parents in Interventions.* Many programs report less success in involving parents than they would like. However, a number of successful programs have demonstrated that parents can play an important role in intervention. Two approaches that have produced positive results involve (1) home visits that provide parent education and support, and (2) use of parents as classroom aides. Parents have also been recruited as members of school teams and advisory committees.

CONCEPT TABLE 15.2
Juvenile Delinquency, Depression, Suicide, the Interrelation of Problems and Disorders, and Programs for Reducing Problems

Concept	Processes/ Related Ideas	Characteristics/Description
Juvenile Delinquency	What is juvenile delinquency?	The term *juvenile delinquency* refers to a broad range of behaviors, from socially unacceptable behavior to status offenses. For legal purposes, a distinction is made between index offenses and status offenses. Conduct disorder is a psychiatric category often used to describe delinquent-type behaviors. Self-reported patterns suggest that about 20 percent of adolescents engage in delinquent behaviors.
	Antecedents	Predictors of delinquency include a negative identity, low self-control, early initiation of delinquency, weak educational orientation, heavy peer influence, low parental monitoring, ineffective discipline, and living in an urban, high-crime area.
	Violence and youth	The high rate of violence among youth is an increasing concern.
	Prevention and intervention	Successful programs focus not on delinquency alone but rather on multiple problems. They begin early and often involve schools.
Depression and Suicide	Depression	Increasingly, distinctions are being made between depressed mood, depressed syndromes, and clinical depression (major depression and dysthymia). Female adolescents are more likely to have mood and depressive disorders than their male counterparts are. Biological and socioemotional causes have been proposed.
	Suicide	The suicide rate has tripled since the 1950s. White males are most likely to commit suicide, African American females the least likely. As with depression, both proximal and distal factors are often involved in suicide.
The Interrelation of Problems, and Programs for Reducing Problems	The interrelation of problems	Very-high-risk youth have multiple problem behaviors and make up as many as 10 percent of adolescents. The four main problems that prevent adolescents from reaching their potential are drug abuse, delinquency, pregnancy, and school-related problems. High-risk youth make up as many as 15 percent of adolescents and often have 2 or 3 of the above problems; very-high-risk-youth tend to "do it all" and engage in all of the problems.
	Common components of successful programs	Of the eleven common components of successful prevention and intervention programs, the two that have the widest application are (1) providing individual attention and (2) broad, community-wide intervention. A third important component is early intervention before adolescence begins.

11. *Involvement of the World of Work.* Successful programs often use innovative approaches to introduce career planning, expose youth to work experiences, and prepare them to enter the labor force. Successful programs have a variety of work-related components, such as a combination of life-planning curricula with school remediation and summer job placement, creation of opportunities for volunteer community service, and payment to high-risk youth to become tutors for younger children.

At this point, we have discussed a number of ideas about juvenile delinquency, depression, and suicide, the interrelation of problems and disorders, and programs for reducing problems. A summary of these ideas is presented in concept table 15.2.

©1997 Will Barnett/Licensed by VAGA,
New York, NY

SUMMARY

Too many adolescents are left with the scars of psychological problems that do not allow them to reach their full potential. Although the majority of adolescents do not have problems or disorders, it has been estimated that approximately 25 percent of adolescents are at risk for serious problems.

We began this chapter by describing the alcohol and delinquency encounters of Annie and Arnie, then evaluated the nature of abnormality, including what abnormal behavior is, what causes it, and characteristics of adolescent disorders. Our extensive coverage of drugs and alcohol focused on why adolescents take drugs, trends in overall drug use, alcohol, hallucinogens, stimulants, depressants, and the roles of development, parents, peers, and schools in adolescent drug abuse. Next, we studied juvenile delinquency, examining what juvenile delinquency is, the antecedents of delinquency, violence and youth, and prevention and intervention. We also learned about depression and suicide, as well as the interrelation of problems and disorders in adolescence and the common components of programs that successfully prevent or reduce adolescent problems.

Don't forget that you can obtain an overall summary of the chapter by again reading the two concept tables on pages 481 and 494. The stress of modern life contributes to adolescent problems and disorders. In the next chapter, we will turn to the nature of stress, health, and coping in adolescence.

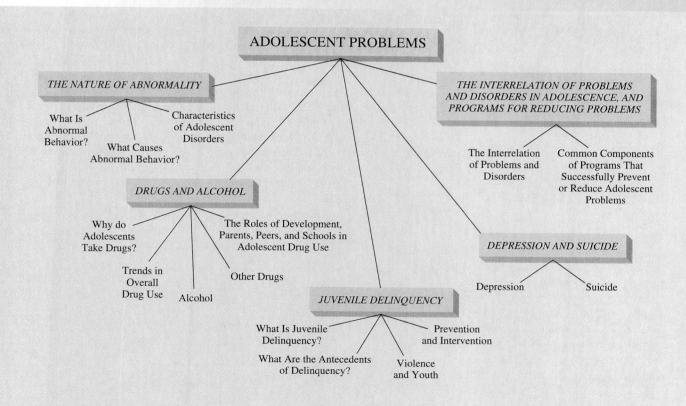

PRACTICAL KNOWLEDGE ABOUT ADOLESCENCE

Adolescents at Risk
(1990) by Joy Dryfoos. New York: Oxford University Press.

This is an excellent book on adolescent problems. Dryfoos describes four main problems that keep adolescents from reaching their potential: drug problems, delinquency, pregnancy, and school-related problems. She provides helpful sketches of programs that are successful in treating these problems. She argues that many at-risk adolescents have more than one problem and that treatment needs to take this interrelatedness of problems into account. School and community programs are especially highlighted.

The Making of a Drug-Free America
(1992) by Mathea Falco. New York: Times Books.

The author makes the point that the way Americans think about illegal drugs contrasts dramatically with the way they think about many legal addictive drugs. The millions of Americans who abuse alcohol, tobacco, and prescription drugs like Valium are thought to need help, not punishment. Author Falco argues that early prevention efforts have often failed because they rely too heavily on scare tactics and moral exhortations, which results in a loss of credibility with youth. She describes programs that are tailored to children's and adolescents' interests and concerns.

Building Assets in Youth
Search Institute
700 South Third Street, Suite 210
Minneapolis, MN 55415
800-888-7828

This recently produced video is based on research with 600 communities. Its positive approach to working with youth focuses on supporting youth, reducing at-risk behavior, and developing community commitment to youth. A leader's guide gives complete scripts and handouts for discussion with parents, youth, and other groups. (12 minutes long, $24.95)

**Canadian Centre on Substance Abuse/
Centre Canadien de Lutte Contre l'Alcoolisme
et les Toxicomanies**
112 Kent Street, Suite 480
Ottawa, Ontario K1P 5P2
613-235-4048

The Centre provides leadership and national focus to substance abuse activity in Canada through policy, research, public information exchange, and coordinator services.

**Canadian Guidance and Counseling
Foundation/Fondation Canadienne d'Orientation
et de Consultation**
411 Roosevelt Avenue, Suite 202
Ottawa, Ontario K2A 3X9
613-729-6164

The Foundation supports research and development projects, establishes partnerships to improve counseling and guidance services, prepares and publishes relevant information and provides continuing professional development of guidance and counseling practitioners.

Depression in Adolescence (1992)
by Anne Petersen, Bruce Compas, and
Jeanne Brooks-Gunn
Carnegie Council on Adolescent Development
2400 N Street NW
Washington, DC 20037
202-429-7979

This working paper commissioned by the Carnegie Council on Adolescent Development provides an excellent overview of adolescent depression, including risk and protective factors, the role of gender, and approaches to treatment and prevention.

Do It Now Foundation
P.O. Box 27568
Tempe, AZ 85285
520-491-0393

This organization provides information about alcohol and drug-related problems. Strategies for drug education are available.

Juvenile Justice and Delinquency Prevention
National Criminal Justice Reference Service
Box 6000
Rockville, MD 20850
800-638-8736

This agency serves as a national clearinghouse for information on delinquency. The program answers questions, makes referrals, and distributes a number of publications.

National Adolescent Suicide Hotline
800-621-4000

This hotline can be used 24 hours a day by teenagers contemplating suicide, as well as by their parents.

National Clearinghouse for Alcohol Information
P.O. Box 2345
1776 Each Jefferson Street
Rockville, MD 20852
301-468-2600

This clearinghouse provides information about a wide variety of issues related to drinking problems, including adolescent drinking.

School Challenge Campaign
800-541-8787

Parents, school officials, and organizations can obtain free information on how to establish an antidrug program in local communities or schools. The program is sponsored by the Department of Education.

Students Against Drunk Driving (SADD)
P.O. Box 800
Marlborough, MA 01752

SADD has more than 16,000 chapters. The organization's goal is to educate adolescents about the dangers of drinking and driving. SADD publishes a newsletter and guidelines for starting new groups.

**Target—Helping Students Cope with Alcohol
and Drugs**
P.O. Box 20626
11724 Plaza Circle
Kansas City, MO 64195
800-366-6667

Target provides information about drug abuse by adolescents and publishes a monthly newsletter for high schools, as well as brochures.

Violence Prevention for Young Adolescents (1991)
by Renee Wilson-Brewer, Stu Cohen, Lydia
O'Donnell, and Irene Goodman
Carnegie Council on Adolescent Development
2400 N Street NW
Washington, DC 20037
202-429-7979

This paper provides an overview of violence prevention programs. Eleven different programs are outlined, including several designed to curb gang violence.

Youth Suicide National Center
204 East 2nd Avenue, Suite 203
San Mateo, CA 94401
415-347-3961

This is a national clearinghouse that develops and distributes educational materials on suicide and reviews current youth suicide prevention and support programs. Publications include *Suicide in Youth and What You Can Do About It* and *Helping Your Child Choose Life: A Parent's Guide to Youth Suicide*.

To further explore the nature of adolescent development, we will examine a research study on predicting serious delinquency and substance abuse in aggressive boys, and we will discuss some guidelines for seeking therapy when an adolescent shows problem behaviors.

*R*ESEARCH ON ADOLESCENT DEVELOPMENT

Predicting Serious Delinquency and Substance Use Among Aggressive Boys

Featured Study

O'Donnell, J., Hawkins, J. D., & Abbott, R. D. (1995). Predicting serious delinquency and substance use among aggressive boys. *Journal of Consulting and Clinical Psychology, 63,* 529–537.

Early aggressive behavior places boys at increased risk for a variety of later problem behaviors, including delinquency and drug abuse. However, not all boys who show aggressive behavior in childhood continue to engage in problem behaviors in adolescence. The purpose of this study was to identify the factors in aggressive boys' lives that would decrease or increase their likelihood of engaging in serious delinquency and substance abuse in early adolescence.

Method

Teachers identified a sample of 52 aggressive 10- and 11-year-old boys. The ten-item aggression scale filled out by teachers included such items as "Argues a lot," "Cruelty, bullying or meanness to others," "Physical attacks on people," and "Gets in many fights." A number of sociodemographic variables and behavioral characteristics of individuals and families that have

been linked to later problem behaviors were measured. These included the degree of early aggressive behavior, ethnicity, socioeconomic status, mobility, and family composition.

Factors predicted to inhibit adolescent problem behavior were assessed by measures given to the child, parents, and teacher when the boys were 12 to 13 years of age. These scales measured skills for prosocial development (presence/absence of social skills, such as talking too much, interrupting, thinking about the consequences of actions, and problem-solving skills), family bonding and management practices (attachment to mother and father, family interaction, and proactive family management practices), school bonding and achievement (commitment to school, attachment to school, educational expectations, grades, and teacher support), norms against substance use (child's perception of risks associated with substance use and the accepta-bility of substance use by peers), and interaction with antisocial others (extent of involvement in the child's antisocial peer network and interaction with adults involved in health-compromising behaviors, such as excessive drinking), and antisocial behavior.

The outcome measures were problem behavior scales given to the students when they were 13 to 14 years of

age. Specific criteria were developed to measure serious delinquent behavior (such as whether in the past year they had committed delinquent acts such as taking things worth more than $50, had been arrested by the police, and had bought, held, or sold stolen goods) and substance use (such as whether in the past month they had engaged in such behaviors as smoking cigarettes, drinking alcohol, and using marijuana).

Results and Discussion

If boys were characterized by the following when they were 12 to 13 years of age, they were less likely to show serious delinquent behavior and engage in substance abuse when they were 13 to 14 years of age:

- Prosocial involvement
- Positive school and achievement patterns
- Positive family experiences
- Awareness of the risks associated with drug abuse
- Low involvement with peers and adults engaged in health-compromising behaviors

The results of this study suggest that to be effective, preventive interventions aimed at aggressive boys should be designed to target multiple contexts, including individuals, peers, schools, and families.

Some Guidelines for Seeking Therapy When an Adolescent Shows Problem Behaviors

Determining whether an adolescent needs professional help when she or he engages in problem behaviors is not an easy task. Adolescents, by nature, tend to have mercurial moods and engage in behaviors that are distasteful to adults and run counter to their values. In many cases, though, such behaviors are only part of the adolescent's search for identity, are very normal, and do not require professional help. Too often when an adolescent first shows a problem behavior, such as drinking or stealing, parents panic and fear that their adolescent is going to turn into a drug addict or a hardened criminal. Such fears usually are not warranted—virtually every adolescent drinks alcohol at some point in the transition from childhood to adulthood, and likewise, virtually every adolescent engages in at least one or more acts of juvenile delinquency. By overreacting to such initial occurrences of adolescent problem behaviors, parents can exacerbate their relationship with the adolescent and thereby contribute to increased parent-adolescent conflict.

What are the circumstances under which parents should seek professional help for their adolescent's problems? Laurence Steinberg and Ann Levine (1990) developed five guidelines for determining when to get professional help if an adolescent is showing problem behaviors:

- If the adolescent is showing severe problem behaviors, such as depression, anorexia nervosa, drug addiction, repeated delinquent acts, or serious school-related problems, parents should not try to treat these problems alone and probably should seek professional help for the adolescent.

- If the adolescent has a problem, but the parents do not know what the problem is, they may want to seek professional help for the adolescent. An example is an adolescent who is socially withdrawn and doesn't have many friends, which could be due to extreme shyness, depression, stress at school, drug involvement, or any of a number of other reasons. If parents do not know what the adolescent's problem is, how can they help the adolescent? Professionals can often make specific diagnoses and provide recommendations for helping the adolescent.

- If parents have tried to solve the adolescent's problem but have not been successful and the problem continues to disrupt the adolescent's life, then parents may wish to seek professional help for the adolescent. Frequent truancy, chronic running away, or repeated, hostile opposition to authority are examples of such problems.

- If parents realize they are part of the adolescent's problem, they may wish to seek professional help for the family. Constant, intense, bitter fighting that disrupts the everyday living of the family is a good example. Rarely is one individual the single cause of extensive family dissension. A therapist can objectively analyze the family's problems and help the family members to see why they are fighting so much to find ways to reduce the fighting.

- When the family is under extensive stress (from the death of a family member or a divorce, for example) and the adolescent is not coping well (for example, becomes depressed or drinks a lot), professional help may be needed.

George Pierre Seurat
Bathers At Asnieres, detail

Chapter

16

Health, Stress, and Coping

Look to your health and if you have it value it next to a good conscience; for health is a blessing we mortals are capable of.

—Izaak Walton,
The Compleat Angler, 1653

PREVIEW

*S*tress, obesity, and exercise—the themes of Alan's, Sarah's, and Brian's comments, respectively, in the "Images of Adolescence" section—are issues in the burgeoning interest in adolescents' stress and health. We will begin this chapter by exploring the nature of health and adolescent development.

IMAGES OF ADOLESCENCE

Alan's Stress, Sarah's Obesity, and Brian's Exercise

I never thought it would be so hard to grow up. I feel a lot of pressure. My parents put a lot of pressure on me. They say they don't, but they do. I'm afraid to bring home a B on my report card. They want me to be perfect. I feel anxious every day about achieving. I want to be able to get into one of the top colleges, but I don't know if it's worth all of this anxiety and nervous feelings I have inside of me. I don't want to feel this way. Sometimes, my heart starts pounding really fast when I get nervous, and I'm not always able to settle myself down. I remember when I was in elementary school I was a lot happier. I didn't seem to care as much about what other people thought, and I was more fun to be around. The competition for grades wasn't as tough then. In the last several years, I've noticed how much more intense the push for good grades is. I wish someone could help me cope better with all of these pressures.

Alan, age 16

Food is a major problem in my life. Let's face it—I'm fat. Fat and ugly. I don't like myself, and I know other people don't like me either. I'm only 5 feet 4 inches tall and I weigh 166 pounds. I hate being fat, but I can't seem to lose weight. In the last year, I haven't grown in height, but I have gained 20 pounds. Some girls think they are fat but they really aren't.

I heard this one girl talking yesterday about how fat she was. No way. She is about 5 feet tall and probably doesn't weigh over 100 pounds. She should be in my body. It seems like the fatter I get, the more I want to eat. I hear about all of these diets, but from what I know, none of them work in the long run. I've thought about going on one hundreds of times, especially right after I've pigged out. But I just get up the next day and start pigging out again. I'm a hopeless case.

Sarah, age 15

A lot of kids in my class are in pitiful physical shape. They never exercise, except in gym class, and even then a lot of them hardly ever break a sweat. During lunch hour, I see some of the same loafers hanging out and smoking a bunch of cigarettes. Don't they know what they are doing to their bodies? All I can say is that I'm glad I'm not like them. I'm on the basketball team, and during the season, the coach runs us until we are exhausted. In the summer, I still play basketball and do a lot of swimming. Just last month, I started lifting weights. I don't know what I would do without exercise. I couldn't stand to be out of shape.

Brian, age 14

HEALTH AND ADOLESCENT DEVELOPMENT

How have views of health changed through history? What role does adolescence play in forming positive health behaviors? What are the main causes of death in adolescence? How does adolescent health vary by age, socioeconomic status, ethnicity, and sex?

Health Conceptions Through History

Oriental physicians around 2600 B.C., and later Greek physicians around 500 B.C., recognized that good habits are essential for good health. Instead of blaming magic or the gods for illness, they realized that human beings are capable of exercising some control over their health. The physician's role was as a guide, assisting the patient in restoring a natural and emotional balance.

As we approach the twenty-first century, once again we recognize the power of lifestyles and psychological states in promoting health. **Health psychology** *is a multidimensional approach to health that emphasizes psychological factors, lifestyle, and the nature of the health-care delivery system.* In 1978, to underscore the increasing interest in psychology's role in health, a new division of the American Psychological Association, called health psychology, was formed. **Behavioral medicine** *is a field closely related to health psychology; it attempts to combine medical and behavioral knowledge to reduce illness and to promote health.* The interests of health psychologists and behavioral medicine researchers are broad: They include examination of why children, adolescents, and adults do or do not comply with medical advice, how effective media campaigns are in reducing adolescent smoking, psychological factors in losing weight, the role of exercise in reducing stress, and access to health care.

The Role of Adolescence in Developing Positive Health Behaviors

Many of the factors linked to poor health habits and early death in the adult years begin during adolescence. Some behaviors also warrant considerable concern because of their potential for harm during adolescence, such as the use of drugs and the neurological damage they can cause, as well as the potentially deadly combination of drugs and driving (Millstein, Petersen, & Nightingale, 1993).

The U.S. Public Health Services (1991) set up health goals for the year 2000. The goals for adolescents included significantly reducing their risk in the areas of nutrition, physical activity and fitness, substance abuse, sexual behavior, violence, unintentional injury, oral health, and mental health.

Leading Causes of Death in Adolescence

Medical improvements have increased the life expectancy of today's adolescents compared to their counterparts who lived earlier in the twentieth century. Still, life-threatening factors continue to exist in adolescents' lives.

The three leading causes of death in adolescence are accidents, suicide, and homicide (Takanishi, 1993). More than half of all deaths in adolescents ages 10 to 19 are due to accidents, and most of those involve motor vehicles, especially for older adolescents. Risky driving habits, such as speeding, tailgating, and driving under the influence of alcohol or other drugs, may be more important causes of these accidents than is lack of driving experience. In about 50 percent of the motor vehicle fatalities involving an adolescent, the driver has a blood alcohol level of 0.10 percent, twice the level needed to be "under the influence" in some states. A high rate of intoxication is also often present in adolescents who die as pedestrians or while using recreational vehicles.

Suicide accounts for 6 percent of the deaths in the 10-to-14 age group, a rate of 1.3 per 100,000 population; in the 15-to-19 age group, suicide accounts for 12 percent of deaths, or 9 per 100,000 population. As reported in chapter 15, since the 1950s the adolescent suicide rate has tripled.

Homicide is yet another leading cause of death in adolescence. During 1988, 5,771 youths between the ages of 15 and 24 died in homicides. Homicide is especially high among African American male adolescents; they are three times more likely to be killed by guns than by natural causes (Simons, Finlay, & Yang, 1991). Let's further examine some sociodemographic factors in adolescent death.

Age, Socioeconomic Status, Ethnicity, and Sex

The mortality rate for adolescents in a recent year was 31 per 100,000 population between the ages of 12 and 14, 66 per 100,000 between the ages of 15 and 17, and 102 per 100,000 between the ages of 18 and 19.

Between the early part of adolescence (ages 10 to 14) and the late part of adolescence (ages 15 to 19), adolescent mortality rates more than triple as causes of mortality change, with a shift toward more violent causes of death (Millstein, Petersen, & Nightingale, 1993). Youth who live in impoverished, high-density metropolitan areas are especially likely to be victims in homicides. Marked ethnic differences emerge in a number of areas of adolescent mortality. African American adolescent males are especially likely to be involved in homicides, while White American adolescent males are much more likely to commit suicide. In late adolescence, homicide is the leading cause of death for African American males. Male adolescents die at a rate more than twice that of their female peers, primarily because of their involvement in motor vehicle accidents. Now that we have considered the leading causes of death in adolescence, we will turn our attention to the nature of health and illness in adolescence.

HEALTH AND ILLNESS

Even though America has become a health-conscious nation and we are aware of the importance of nutrition and exercise in our lives, many of us still smoke, eat junk food, have extra flab hanging around our middle, and spend too much of our lives as couch potatoes. This description fits too many adolescents as well as adults.

Adolescents often reach a level of health, strength, and energy they never will match during the remainder of their lives. They also have a sense of uniqueness and invulnerability that leads them to think that illness and disorder will not enter their lives. And they possess a time perspective that envisions the future as having few or no boundaries. Adolescents believe that they will live forever and recoup any lost health or modify any bad habits they might develop. Given this combination of physical and cognitive factors, is it any wonder that so many adolescents have poor health habits?

Cognitive Factors in Adolescents' Health Behavior

Among the cognitive factors in adolescents' health behavior are concepts of health behavior, beliefs about health, health knowledge, and decision making.

Concepts of Health Behavior

Concepts of health and illness develop in concert with Piaget's stages of cognitive development (Burbach & Peterson, 1986). Young children perceive health and illness in simplistic terms, describing vague feelings and depending on others to determine when they are ill. As children get older, they develop a concept of health and begin to understand that health has multiple causes. In early adolescence, some individuals still do not recognize the multiple causes of health, and relatively concrete thinking about illness predominates. By late adolescence, many individuals have become formal operational thinkers and view health in more hypothetical and abstract ways. They are now more likely to describe health in terms of psychological, emotional, and social components, and to consider their personal behavior important for their health (Millstein, 1991).

Beliefs About Health

Adolescents' health beliefs include beliefs about vulnerability and behavior (Millstein, Petersen, & Nightingale, 1993). Adolescents, as well as adults, underestimate their vulnerability to harm (Kamler & others, 1987). While they usually recognize that behaviors such as substance abuse and unprotected sexual intercourse are potential health hazards, they often underestimate the potentially negative consequences of these behaviors. They also anticipate, sometimes incorrectly, that the risks associated with certain behaviors will decrease as they get older.

Health Knowledge

Adolescents generally are poorly informed about health issues and have significant misperceptions about health (Centers for Disease Control, 1988). Younger adolescents have less factual knowledge about a variety of health topics, including sexually transmitted diseases and drug abuse, than older adolescents do.

Decision Making

In chapter 5, we discussed how young adolescents are better at decision making than children but are worse at decision making than older adolescents. The decision-making skills of older adolescents and adults, however, are far from perfect. And the ability to make decisions does not guarantee that such decisions will be made in everyday life, where breadth of experience comes into play (Keating, 1990). For example, driver-training courses improve adolescents' cognitive and motor skills to levels equal to, or sometimes superior to, those of adults. However, driver training has not been effective in reducing adolescents' high rate of traffic accidents (Potvin, Champagne, & Laberge-Nadeau, 1988). Thus, an important research agenda is to study the way adolescents make decisions in practical health situations (Crockett & Petersen, 1993).

Sociocultural Factors in Adolescents' Health Behavior

Sociocultural factors influence health through their roles in setting cultural norms about health, through social relationships that provide emotional support, and through the encouragement of healthy or unhealthy behaviors.

Cultural and Ethnic Variations

In considering the health of ethnic minority group adolescents, it is important to recognize that there are large within-group differences in living conditions and lifestyles and that these differences are influenced by social class, status as an immigrant, social skills, language skills, occupational opportunities, and social resources, such as the availability of meaningful social support networks. At present, there is little research information about the role of ethnicity in adolescents' health beliefs and behavior. However, researchers do know what some of the important health issues are for various ethnic minority adolescents and adults (Earls, 1993). To learn about some of these issues, turn to Sociocultural Worlds of Adolescence.

Poverty is related to poor health in adolescents. In the National Health Interview Study (1991), 7 percent of the adolescents living in poverty were in only fair or poor health, compared to 2 percent of adolescents in

The Health Status of Ethnic Minority Adolescents

Felipe Castro and Delia Magana (1988) developed a course in health promotion for ethnic minority children, adolescents, and adults, which they teach at UCLA. A summary of some of the issues they discuss follows.

For African Americans, historical issues of prejudice and racial segregation are important considerations. The chronic stress of discrimination and poverty continue to negatively affect the health of many African Americans. Personal and support systems are viable ways to improve the health of African Americans. Their extended-family network may be especially helpful in coping with stress (Boyd-Franklin, 1989; McAdoo, 1993).

For many Latinos, some of the same stressors mentioned for African Americans are associated with migration to the United States by Puerto Ricans, Mexicans, and Latin Americans. Language is likely a barrier for unacculturated Latinos in doctor-patient communications. In addition, there is increasing evidence that diabetes occurs at an above-average rate in Latinos (Gardner & others, 1984), making this disease a major health problem that parallels the above-average rate of high blood pressure among African Americans.

For Asian Americans, it is important to consider their broad diversity in national backgrounds and lifestyles. They range from highly acculturated Japanese Americans, who may be better educated than many Anglo-Americans and have excellent access to health care, to the many Indochinese refugees, who have few economic resources and poor health status.

Cultural barriers to adequate health care include the aforementioned financial resources and language skills. In addition, members of ethnic minority groups are often unfamiliar with how the medical system operates, confused about the need to see numerous people, and uncertain about why they have to wait so long for service (Snowden & Cheung, 1990).

Other barriers may be specific to certain cultures, reflecting different ideas regarding what causes disease and how disease should be treated. For example, Chinese Americans have access to folk healers in every Chinatown in the United States. Depending on their degree of acculturation to Western society, a Chinese American might go to a folk healer first, or to a Western doctor first, but invariably consults a folk healer for follow-up care. Chinese medicines are usually used for home care. These include ginseng tea for many ailments, boiled centipede soup for cancer, and eucalyptus oil for dizziness resulting from hypertension.

Native Americans view Western medicine as a source of crisis intervention, a quick fix for broken legs or other symptoms. They do not view Western medicine as a source for treatment of the causes of disease or for preventive intervention. For example, they are unlikely to attend a seminar on the prevention of alcohol abuse. They also are reluctant to become involved in care that requires a long hospitalization or that necessitates surgery.

Both Navajo Indians and Mexican Americans rely on family members to make decisions about treatment choices. Doctors who expect such patients to decide on the spot whether or not to undergo treatment will likely embarrass the patient or force the patient to give an answer that may lead to canceled appointments if the family members veto the decision.

Mexican Americans also believe that some illnesses are due to natural causes, while others are due to supernatural causes. Depending on their level of acculturation, they may be disappointed and confused by doctors who do not show an awareness of how to treat diseases with supposed supernatural origins.

Health-care professionals can increase their effectiveness with culturally diverse populations by improving their knowledge of what patients bring to the health-care setting in the way of attitudes, beliefs, and folk health practices. Such information should be integrated into the Western-prescribed treatment rather than ignored at the risk of alienating the patient.

---

nonpoor households. In another study, 9 percent of the 10- to 18-year-olds below the poverty line, compared to 6 percent of those above it, had a chronic condition that resulted in some loss of ability to conduct the normal activities of adolescence (Newacheck, 1989).

What are some of the mechanisms that can produce poor health in adolescents who live in poverty conditions?

They include income, family environment, schools and community groups, and psychological factors (Klerman, 1993).

Having insufficient income to meet basic needs can make particular behaviors difficult—seeking medical care, for example. Low income often causes families to live in inner-city ghettos where there are few role models who engage in health-enhancing behaviors. Poor adolescents are often less connected to sources that might advocate or model positive behaviors or urge the avoidance of negative ones. These sources include families, schools, and community organizations. Poor adolescents seem to be strongly influenced by peers who engage in health-compromising behaviors, possibly because of inadequate emotional support from the family. Adolescents may be likely to practice health-promoting behaviors if they believe they have the power to influence their future. Alienation or a sense of powerlessness or hopelessness is not likely to lead to health promotion. In a national study of eighth-graders, perception of personal control over one's life was highest among those from the highest social class status and lowest among those from the lowest social class status (Hafner & others, 1990). The poor adolescents were more likely than their more affluent counterparts to believe that goals can be reached through luck rather than planning or effort.

Family and Peers

The family is an important aspect of social support for adolescents' health. Positive health behaviors are best achieved when adolescents develop a sense of autonomy within a supportive family context (Melby, 1995). In addition to providing social support, parents and older siblings are important models for children's and adolescents' health (Elliott, 1993).

Peers and friends also play important roles in adolescents' health behavior (Millstein, 1993). A number of research studies have documented the association between unhealthy behaviors in adolescents and their friends, but the association might not be causal. For example, adolescents might choose friends who support their negative health behaviors. A special concern in adolescents' health behaviors is peer pressure. Adolescents who have a limited capacity to resist dares often engage in risk-taking behaviors at the urging of their peers.

Health Services

While adolescents have a greater number of acute health conditions than adults do, they use private physician services at a lower rate than any other age group does (Edelman, 1995). And adolescents often underutilize other health-care systems as well (Millstein, 1988). Health services are especially unlikely to meet the health needs of younger adolescents, ethnic minority adolescents, and adolescents living in poverty. Among the chief barriers to better health services for adolescents are cost, poor organization, and availability of health services, as well as confidentiality of care. Also, few health-care providers receive any special training for working with adolescents. Many say that they feel unprepared to provide services such as contraceptive counseling and accurate evaluation of what constitutes abnormal behavior in adolescence (Irwin, 1993). Health-care

providers may transmit to their patients their discomfort in discussing such topics as sexuality, which may lead to adolescents' unwillingness to discuss sensitive issues with them.

Now that we have considered some important aspects of health and illness—cognitive factors, sociocultural factors, and health services—we turn our attention to some specific health problems in adolescence as part of our discussion on promoting health.

PROMOTING HEALTH

Adolescents' health profile can be improved by reducing the incidence of certain health-impairing lifestyles, such as smoking and overeating, and by engaging in health-improving lifestyles that include good nutrition and exercise.

Reducing Cigarette Smoking

Smoking begins primarily during childhood and adolescence. One recent study found that once young adolescents began to smoke cigarettes, the addictive properties of nicotine made it extremely difficult for them to stop smoking (Melby & Vargas, 1996). Adolescent smoking peaked in the mid 1970s, then began to decline through 1980. However, cigarette smoking rose again in 1996 for American youth (Johnston, O'Malley, & Bachman, 1996). This is the fourth year in a row of increase for eighth- and tenth-graders, the third year for twelfth-graders.

Among both eighth- and tenth-graders, the proportion who reported smoking in the 30 days prior to the survey has increased by one-third since 1991. Twenty-one percent of the eighth-graders and 30 percent of the tenth-graders now report such use. Since 1992, the smoking rate has risen by more than one-fifth among high school seniors, with 34 percent now saying they have smoked within the last 30 days.

Peer disapproval of cigarette smoking has dropped over the last several years, and the percentage of adolescents who see smoking as dangerous has been declining since 1993. Among eighth-graders, only one-half think there is great risk to smoking a pack or more a day.

Cigarettes are readily available to these underage youth. Of the eighth-graders, most of whom are 13 to 14 years of age, three-fourths said that they can get cigarettes fairly easily if they want them. By the tenth grade, more than 90 percent say they can buy cigarettes easily.

In another study, smoking initiation rates increased rapidly after 10 years of age and peaked at 13 to 14 years of age (Escobedo & others, 1993). Students who began smoking at 12 years of age or younger were more likely to be regular and heavy smokers than were students who began at older ages. Students who had participated in interscholastic sports were less likely to be regular and heavy smokers than were their counterparts who were not sports participants. In another recent study, adolescents

THE FAR SIDE By GARY LARSON

The real reason dinosaurs became extinct

whose parents smoked were more likely to be smokers themselves than were adolescents whose parents did not smoke (Kandel & Wu, 1995). Maternal smoking was more strongly related to smoking by young adolescents (especially girls) than paternal smoking was.

Traditional school health programs have often succeeded in educating adolescents about the long-term health consequences of smoking but have had little effect on adolescent smoking behavior. That is, adolescent smokers know as much about the health risks of smoking as do nonadolescent smokers, but this knowledge has had little impact on reducing their smoking behavior (Miller & Slap, 1989). The need for effective intervention has prompted investigators to focus on those factors that place young adolescents at high risk for future smoking, especially social pressures from peers, family members, and the media.

A number of research teams have developed strategies for interrupting behavioral patterns that lead to smoking (Bruess & Richardson, 1992; Perry, Kelder, & Komro, 1993). In one investigation, high school students were recruited to help seventh-grade students resist peer pressure to smoke (McAlister & others, 1980). The high school students encouraged the younger adolescents to resist the influence of high-powered ads suggesting that liberated women smoke by saying, "She is not really liberated if she is hooked on tobacco." The students also engaged in role-playing exercises called "chicken." In these situations, the high school students called the younger adolescents "chicken" for not trying a cigarette. The seventh-graders practiced resistance to the peer pressure by saying, "I'd be a real chicken if I smoked just to impress you." Following several sessions, the students in the smoking prevention group were 50 percent less likely to begin smoking compared to a group of seventh-grade students in a neighboring junior high school, even though the parents of both groups of students had the same smoking rate.

One comprehensive health approach that includes an attempt to curb cigarette smoking by adolescents was developed by clinical psychologist Cheryl Perry and her colleagues (1988). Three programs were developed based on peer group norms, healthy role models, and social skills training. Elected peer leaders were trained as instructors. In seventh grade, adolescents were offered "Keep It Clean," a six-session course emphasizing the negative effects of smoking. In eighth grade, students were involved in "Health Olympics," an approach that included exchanging greeting cards on smoking and health with peers in other countries. In ninth grade, students participated in "Shifting Gears," which included six sessions focused on social skills. In the social skills program, students critiqued media messages and created their own positive health videotapes. At the same time as the school intervention, a community-wide smoking cessation program, as well as a diet and health awareness campaign, were initiated. After 5 years, students who were involved in the smoking and health program were much less likely to smoke cigarettes, use marijuana, or drink alcohol than their counterparts who were not involved in the program.

The tobacco industry does prey on adolescents' motivation to feel grown up by including in their advertisements "cool" people who smoke—successful young women smoking Virginia Slims cigarettes, handsome Marlboro men in rich surroundings with beautiful women at their sides, for example. The advertisements encourage adolescents to associate cigarette smoking with a successful, active lifestyle. Legislators are working on the introduction of more stringent laws to further regulate the tobacco industry, since smoking is the only industry in America that will have killed 3 million of its best customers between 1964 and the year 2000, according to the U.S. Department of Health and Human Services.

Nutrition

The recommended range of energy intake for adolescents takes into account the different needs of adolescents, their growth rate, and their level of exercise. Males have higher energy needs than females. Older adolescent girls also have slightly lower energy needs than younger adolescent girls. Some adolescents' bodies burn energy faster than others. **Basal metabolism rate (BMR)** *is the minimum amount of energy an individual uses in a resting state.* As shown in figure 16.1, BMR gradually declines from the beginning of adolescence through the end of adolescence.

Concern is often expressed over adolescents' tendency to eat between meals. However, the choice of foods is much more important than the time or place of eating. Fresh vegetables and fruits as well as whole-grain products are needed to complement the foods high in energy value and protein that adolescents commonly choose.

A special concern in American culture is the amount of fat in our diet. Many of today's adolescents virtually live on fast-food meals, which contributes to the increased fat levels in their diet. More fast-food meals are high in protein, especially meat and dairy products. But the average American adolescent does not have to worry about getting enough protein. What should be of concern is the vast number of adolescents who consume large quantities of fast foods that are not only high in protein but

high in fat. The American Heart Association recommends that the daily limit for calories from fat should be approximately 30 percent. Compare this amount with the percentage shown in figure 16.2. Clearly, many fast-food meals contribute to excess fat intake by adolescents.

Eating Disorders

A tall, slender, 16-year-old girl goes into the locker room of a fitness center, throws her towel across the bench, and looks squarely in the mirror. She yells, "You fat pig. You are nothing but a fat pig." America is a nation obsessed with food, spending extraordinary amounts of time thinking about, eating, and avoiding food. Eating disorders are complex, involving genetic inheritance, physiological factors, cognitive factors, and environmental experiences. In one study, girls who in early adolescence felt most negatively about their bodies were more likely to develop eating problems 2 years later (Attie & Brooks-Gunn, 1989). In one recent study, adolescent girls who had positive relationships with both parents tended to have healthier eating patterns (Swarr & Richards, 1996). And in another recent study, girls who were both physically involved with their boyfriends and in pubertal transition were the most likely to be dieting or engaging in disordered eating patterns (Cauffman, 1994). The three most prominent eating disorders are obesity, anorexia nervosa, and bulimia.

Obesity

Adolescent obesity involves genetic inheritance, physiological mechanisms, cognitive factors, and environmental influences. Some adolescents may have inherited a tendency to be overweight. Only 10 percent of children who do not have obese parents become obese themselves, whereas about 40 percent of children who have one obese parent become obese, and about 70 percent of children who have two obese parents become obese. The extent

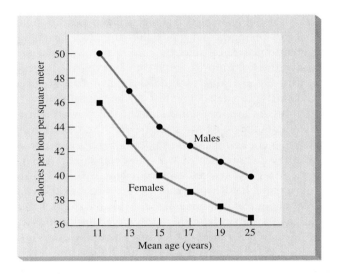

Figure~16.1

Basal Metabolic Rates (BMR) for Adolescent Females and Males.

Selected meal	Calories	Percent of calories from fat
Burger King Whopper, fries, vanilla shake	1,250	43
Big Mac, fries, chocolate shake	1,100	41
McDonald's Quarter-Pounder with cheese	418	52
Pizza Hut 10-inch pizza with sausage, mushrooms, pepperoni, and green pepper	1,035	35
Arby's roast beef plate (roast beef sandwich, two potato patties, and coleslaw), chocolate shake	1,200	30
Kentucky Fried Chicken dinner (three pieces chicken, mashed potatoes and gravy, coleslaw, roll)	830	50
Arthur Treacher's fish and chips (two pieces breaded, fried fish, french fries, cola drink)	900	42
Typical restaurant "diet plate" (hamburger patty, cottage cheese, etc.)	638	63

Figure~16.2

Fat and Calorie Intake of Selected Fast-Food Meals.

to which this is due to genes or experiences with parents cannot be determined in research with humans, but animals can be bread to have a propensity for fatness.

Another factor in the weight of adolescents is **set point,** *the weight maintained when no effort is made to gain or lose weight.* Set point is influenced by adolescents' basal metabolism rate, discussed earlier. Researchers have discovered that individuals with a slow metabolism are most likely to gain weight (Brownell & Stein, 1989). And, as indicated in figure 16.2, BMR drops sharply from the beginning to the end of adolescence. During the adult years, BMR continues to decline, but at a much slower rate than in adolescence. To some extent, a declining BMR helps to explain why there are more fat older adolescents than fat younger adolescents. Scientists are working on drugs that they hope will be able to raise the BMR of overweight adolescents, although, as we will see shortly, something else is able to raise metabolism rate and burn calories.

Adolescents' insulin levels also are important factors in eating behavior and obesity. American health psychology researcher Judith Rodin (1984) argues that what adolescents eat influences their insulin levels. When adolescents eat complex carbohydrates, such as cereals, bread, and pasta, insulin levels go up but fall off gradually. When adolescents consume simple sugars, such as candy bars and Cokes, insulin levels rise and then fall, often sharply—producing the sugar low with which many of us are all too familiar.

Glucose levels in the blood also are affected by these complex carbohydrates and simple sugars, and in similar ways. The consequence is that adolescents are more likely to eat within the next several hours after eating simple sugars than they are after eating complex carbohydrates. And the food adolescents eat at one meal influences how much they will eat at the next meal. So consumption of doughnuts and candy bars, in addition to providing only minimal nutritional value, sets up an ongoing sequence of what and how much adolescents crave the next time they eat.

Rodin also believes that exercise is an important part of weight loss and weight maintenance for adolescents. She points out that no matter what an adolescent's genetic background, aerobic exercise increases metabolic rate, which helps to burn calories. Exercise not only burns up calories but continues to raise metabolic rate for several hours *after* the exercise. Exercise actually lowers the body's set point for weight, making it much easier to maintain a lower weight (Bennett & Gurin, 1982).

Many obese adolescents feel that everything would be great in their lives if only they could lose weight. As one adolescent commented, "Losing weight would make my parents happy, my peers at school would like me, and I could concentrate on other things." A typical example is Debby, who at age 17 had been obese since she was 12. She came from a middle-class family and her parents pressured her to lose weight, repeatedly sending her to reducing centers and to physicians. One summer, Debby was sent to a diet camp, where she went from 200 to 150 pounds. On returning home, she was terribly disappointed when her parents pressured her to lose more. With increased tension and parental preoccupation with her weight, she gave up all efforts at dieting, and her weight rose rapidly. Debby isolated herself and continued her preoccupation with food. Later, clinical help was sought and, fortunately, Debby was able to work through her hostility toward her parents and understand her self-destructive behavior. Eventually, she gained a sense of self-control and became willing to reduce for herself and not for her parents or her peers.

Medical personnel and psychologists have become increasingly concerned with the health hazards associated with obesity. Eating patterns established in childhood and adolescence are highly associated with obesity in adulthood—80 percent of obese adolescents become obese adults. Obesity is estimated to characterize 25 percent of today's American adolescents. As we see next, a less common condition has received considerable attention in recent years.

Anorexia Nervosa and Bulimia

Fifteen-year-old Jane gradually eliminated foods from her diet to the point where she subsisted by eating *only* applesauce and eggnog. She spent hours observing her own body, wrapping her fingers around her waist to see if it was getting any thinner. She fantasized about becoming a beautiful fashion model and wearing designer bathing suits. But even when she reached 85 pounds, Jane still felt fat. She continued to lose weight, eventually emaciating herself. She was hospitalized and treated for **anorexia nervosa,** *an eating disorder that involves the relentless pursuit of thinness through starvation.* Eventually, anorexia nervosa can lead to death, as it did for popular singer Karen Carpenter.

Anorexia nervosa primarily afflicts females during adolescence and the early adulthood years; only about 5 percent of anorexics are males. Most adolescents with this disorder are White and come from well-educated, middle- and upper-income families. Although anorexics avoid eating, they have an intense interest in food. They cook for others, they talk about food, and they insist on watching others eat. Anorexics have a distorted body image, perceiving that they will become attractive only when they become skeletal in appearance. As self-starvation continues and the fat content of the body drops to a bare minimum, menstruation usually stops. Behavior is often hyperactive.

Numerous causes of anorexia have been proposed, including societal, psychological, and physiological factors (Fisher & others, 1995). The societal factor most often held responsible is the current fashion image of thinness. Psychological factors include motivation for attention,

Anorexia nervosa has become a prominent problem in adolescent females.

bulimic goes on an eating binge and then purges by self-induced vomiting or by using a laxative. Sometimes, the binges alternate with fasting, at other times with normal eating. Like anorexia nervosa, bulimia is primarily a female disorder. Bulimia has become prevalent among college women. Some estimates indicate that as many as one in two college women binge and purge at least some of the time. However, other estimates reveal that true bulimics—those who binge and purge on a regular basis—make up less than 2 percent of the college female population (Stunkard, 1987). Another survey of 1,500 high school and university students found that 4 percent of the high school students and 5 percent of the university students were bulimic (Howatt & Saxton, 1988). Anorexics can control their eating; bulimics cannot. Depression is a common characteristic of bulimics. Bulimia can produce gastric and chemical imbalances in the body. Many of the causes proposed for anorexia nervosa also are offered for bulimia (Garner & Garfinkel, 1997).

Now that we have considered the dangers of smoking, the nature of nutrition, and eating problems in adolescence, we turn our attention to one of the most important factors in helping adolescents to keep from gaining too much weight or in losing weight and maintaining the weight loss—exercise. As we learned earlier, exercise not only burns calories, but it continues to raise the basal metabolism rate for several hours *after* the exercise.

Exercise

A special interest in recent years involves **aerobic exercise**, *sustained exercise—jogging, swimming, or cycling, for example—that stimulates heart and lung activity*. Studies of the effects of exercise on health have focused on the role of exercise in preventing heart disease. Most health experts recommend that we should try to raise our heart rate to 60 percent of our maximum rate. Maximum heart rate is calculated as 220 minus your age, so if you are 20, you should aim for an exercise heart rate of 120 (220 − 20 = 200 × 0.60 = 120). Some health experts recommend that, regardless of other risk factors (smoking, high blood pressure, being overweight, heredity), if we exercise enough to burn more than 2,000 calories per week, we can cut our risk of heart attack by an impressive two-thirds (Sherwood, Light, & Blumenthal, 1989). Burning up 2,000 calories a week through exercise requires a lot of effort, however, far more than most of us are willing to expend. Burning 300 calories a day through exercise would require one of the following: swimming or running for about 25 minutes, walking for 45 minutes at about 4 miles an hour, or participating in aerobic dancing for 30 minutes.

Many of our patterns of health are long-standing. Our experiences as children and adolescents contribute to our health practices as adults. Are today's children and adolescents getting enough exercise? In a national assessment comparing 6- to 17-year-olds' physical fitness in 1980

desire for individuality, denial of sexuality, and a way of coping with overcontrolling parents. Anorexics sometimes have families that place high demands for achievement on them. Unable to meet their parents' high standards, they feel unable to control their own lives. By limiting their food intake, anorexics gain some sense of self-control. Physiological causes involve the hypothalamus, which becomes abnormal in a number of ways when an adolescent becomes anorexic. But the bottom line is that, at this time, the exact causes of anorexia nervosa are uncertain.

Bulimia *is an eating disorder in which the individual consistently follows a binge-and-purge eating pattern.* The

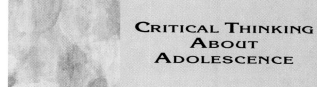

How Can We Get Adolescents to Develop a Healthy Diet and to Exercise?

Promoting healthy diet and exercise remains one of the most challenging goals regarding adolescents. The negative influences on adolescent eating and physical activity are stronger and more numerous than the positive ones. The post powerful and pervasive negative influences are from television, the food industry, peers, and family. And because automobiles are now used so extensively, adolescents tend to exercise little. Effective programs that promote healthy eating and physical activity create social and physical environments that make it easier to follow a healthy diet and exercise regularly. What can we do to make it easier for adolescents to eat healthy foods and exercise more? What roles could be played by the media, schools, and parents? By considering how we can get adolescents to develop a healthy diet and exercise, you are learning to think critically by *applying developmental concepts to enhance personal adaptation*.

---

and 1989, ratings of "satisfactory" on the entire test, which included sprints, sit-ups, push-ups, and long jumps, dropped from 43 percent in 1980 to 32 percent in 1989.

> *We look instead of play. We ride instead of walk.*
> —John F. Kennedy, Presidential Address, 1961

Some health experts blame television for the poor physical condition of American adolescents. In one investigation, adolescents who watched little television were much more physically fit than were their heavy-television-viewing counterparts (Tucker, 1987). The more adolescents watch television, the more they are likely to be overweight. No one is quite sure whether this is because they spend their leisure time in front of a television set, because they eat a lot of junk food they see advertised on television, or because less physically fit youth find physical activity less reinforcing than watching television.

The family plays an important role in children's and adolescents' exercise program. A wise strategy is for families to take up vigorous physical activities that parents and children can enjoy together. Running, swimming, cycling, and hiking especially are recommended. However, in encouraging children and adolescents to exercise more, parents should not encourage them beyond their physical limits or expose them to intense competitive pressures that take the fun out of sports and exercise. For example, long-distance running may be too strenuous for young children and can result in bone injuries. Recently, the number of children participating in strenuous events such as marathons and triathalons has increased. Doctors are beginning to see injuries in children that previously they only saw in adults, such as stress fractures and tendinitis. If left to their own devices, how many 8-year-old children would want to prepare for a marathon?

Some of the blame for the poor physical condition of U.S. children and adolescents falls on U.S. schools, many of which fail to provide physical education class on a daily basis. One extensive investigation of behavior in physical education classes at four different schools revealed how little vigorous exercise takes place in these classes (Parcel & others, 1987). Boys and girls moved through space only 50 percent of the time they were in the classes, and they moved continuously an average of only 2.2 minutes. In sum, not only does the adolescent's school week include inadequate physical education classes, but the majority of adolescents do not exercise vigorously even when they are in physical education classes. Further, while we hear a lot about the exercise revolution among adults, most children and adolescents report that their parents are poor role models when it comes to vigorous physical exercise (Feist & Brannon, 1989).

Does it make a difference if children and adolescents are pushed to exercise more vigorously in school? One investigation provided an affirmative answer to this question (Tuckman & Hinkle, 1988). One hundred fifty-four boys and girls were randomly assigned to either three 30-minute running programs per week or to regular attendance in physical education classes. Although the results sometimes varied by sex, for the most part those in the running program had increased cardiovascular health and showed increased creativity. For example, the running-program boys had less body fat, and the running-program girls had more creative involvement in their classrooms.

An exciting possibility is that physical exercise might provide a buffer to adolescents' stress. In one investigation of 364 females in grades 7 through 11 in Los Angeles, the negative impact of stressful events on health declined as exercise levels increased, suggesting that

---

An increasing number of educators and developmentalists believe that daily exercise is an important aspect of adolescents' lives. One way to ensure that adolescents get adequate exercise is to increase participation in physical education classes throughout all grades of secondary schools. Once in these classes, adolescents require encouragement from instructors to exercise vigorously.

- Health promotion, including behavior modification and health education; stronger programs for dealing with adolescents' smoking, alcohol and drug abuse, nutrition, physical fitness, and mental health
- Satisfaction of the health needs of special populations, such as a better understanding of health prevention in African American and Latino populations

At this point, we have discussed a number of ideas about health psychology and behavioral medicine, the causes of death in adolescence, health and illness, and promoting health. A summary of these ideas is presented in concept table 16.1. Next, we consider another important factor in adolescents' health—stress and how to cope with it.

exercise can be a valuable resource for combating adolescents' life stresses (Brown & Siegel, 1988). In another investigation, adolescents who exercised regularly coped more effectively with stress and had more positive identities than did adolescents who engaged in little exercise (Grimes & Mattimore, 1989).

In the fourth century B.C., Aristotle commented that the quality of life is determined by its activities. In today's world, we know that exercise is one of the principal activities that improves the quality of life, both adolescents' and adults'.

Toward Healthier Adolescent Lives

Adolescents' health involves far more than trips to a doctor when sick and treatments for disease. Researchers are becoming increasingly aware that adolescents' behavior determines whether they will develop a serious illness or whether they will be healthy (Minkler, 1989). Health psychologists and behavioral medicine specialists believe that the next major step in improving the general health of American adolescents will be primarily behavioral, not medical.

What should be America's health goals for adolescents? A number of recommendations are being made for the year 2000. Among them are the following objectives of the federal government and the Society for Public Health Education (Breslow, 1990):

- The development of preventive services targeting unintended pregnancy and such diseases as cancer, heart disease, and AIDS

STRESS

Stress is a sign of the times. No one really knows whether today's adolescents experience more stress than their predecessors did, but it does seem that their stressors have increased. Among the stress-related questions we examine are these: What is stress? What is the body's response to stress? What environmental factors are involved in stress? Do personality factors influence stress? How do cognitive factors influence stress? How do sociocultural factors influence stress?

What Is Stress?

Stress is not easy to define. Initially, the term *stress* was loosely borrowed from physics. Humans, it was thought, are in some ways similar to physical objects, such as metals, that resist moderate outside forces but lose their resiliency at some point of greater pressure. But unlike metal, adolescents can think and reason and experience a myriad of social circumstances that make defining stress more complex in psychology than in physics (Hobfoll, 1989). In adolescents, is stress the threats and challenges the environment places on them, as when we say, "Sally's world is so stressful, it is overwhelming her"? Is stress adolescents' responses to such threats and challenges, as when we say, "Bob is not coping well with the problems in his life; he is experiencing a lot of stress and his body is falling apart"? Because debate continues on whether stress is the threatening events in adolescents' worlds or their responses to those events, a broad definition of stress is best:

Health and Adolescent Development, Health and Illness, and Promoting Health

Concept	Processes/ Related Ideas	Characteristics/Description
Health and Adolescent Development	Health conceptions through history	Today, we recognize the power of lifestyle and psychological states in adolescent health. Health psychology and behavioral medicine are two important approaches.
	The role of adolescence in developing positive health behaviors	Many of the factors linked with poor health habits and early death in the adult years begin in adolescence.
	Leading causes of death in adolescence	The three leading causes of death in adolescents are accidents, suicide, and homicide.
	Age, socioeconomic status, ethnicity, and sex	These factors affect the mortality rate for adolescents—male adolescents die at a rate twice that of their female counterparts, for example.
Health and Illness	Cognitive factors	Cognitive factors in adolescents' health include concepts of health behavior, beliefs about health, health knowledge, and decision making.
	Sociocultural factors	These influence health through their roles in setting cultural norms about health, social relationships that provide support, and encouragement of healthy or unhealthy behaviors.
	Health services	Adolescents use health services less than any other age group, even though they have a number of acute health conditions. There are many barriers to providing better services for adolescents, and these need to be examined.
Promoting Health	Reducing cigarette smoking	Cigarette smoking is common in adolescence. Current prevention efforts focus on helping adolescents cope with social pressures from family, peers, and the media.
	Nutrition	Understanding nutrition in adolescence involves understanding recommended energy intake, basal metabolism rate, and fat in the diet.
	Eating disorders	Three prominent eating disorders in adolescence are obesity, anorexia nervosa, and bulimia. Societal, psychological, and physiological factors have been proposed as causes of these eating disorders.
	Exercise	Experts agree that adolescents are not getting enough exercise. Television and schools have been criticized for contributing to these poor exercise habits. An exciting possibility is that exercise can serve as a buffer against stress.
	Toward healthier adolescent lives	Recommendations for the year 2000 include preventive services, health promotion, and targeting special adolescent populations such as African American and Latino adolescents.

Stress is the response of individuals to the circumstances and events, called stressors, that threaten them and tax their coping abilities.

Factors in Stress

As with other aspects of adolescents' lives, adolescents' stress is determined not by a single factor but, rather, by multiple factors. Among the most important factors that determine whether adolescents will experience stress are physical factors (such as the body's response to stress), environmental factors (such as overload, conflict, and frustration, as well as life events and daily hassles), personality factors (such as the impatience and anger involved in the Type A behavior pattern), cognitive factors (such as cognitive appraisal), sociocultural factors (such as acculturative stress and poverty), and adolescents' coping strategies (such as removing stress, reducing defense mechanisms, increasing problem-focused coping,

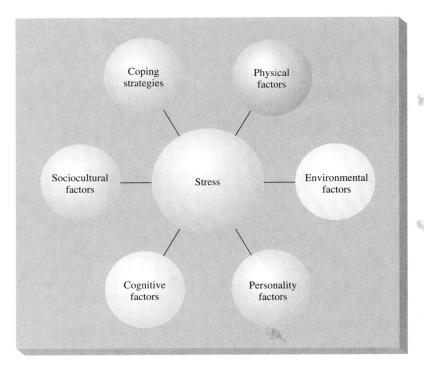

Figure~16.3

Factors Involved in Adolescents' Stress.
Among the most important factors involved in understanding adolescents'
stress are physical factors (the body's response to stress), environmental
factors, personality factors, cognitive factors, sociocultural factors, and
coping strategies.

developing positive thinking and self-efficacy, enlisting
the help of support systems, and using multiple coping
strategies). A summary of these factors involved in
stress is presented in figure 16.3.

The Body's Response to Stress

According to the Austrian-born founder of stress research, the late Hans Selye (1974, 1983), stress simply
is the wear and tear in the body due to the demands
placed on it. Any number of environmental events or
stimuli produce the same stress response in the body.
Selye observed patients with different problems: the
death of someone close, loss of income, arrest for em-
bezzlement. Regardless of which problem the patient
had, similar symptoms appeared: loss of appetite, muscular weakness, and decreased interest in the world.

The **general adaptation syndrome (GAS)** *is Selye's
concept that describes the common effects on the body
when demands are placed on it. The GAS consists of three
stages: alarm, resistance, and exhaustion.* First, in the *alarm
stage,* the individual enters a temporary state of shock,
a time when resistance to stress is below normal. The
individual detects the presence of stress and tries to eliminate it. Muscle tone is lost, temperature decreases,
and blood pressure drops. Then, a rebound called

countershock occurs, in which resistance to
stress begins to pick up; the adrenal cortex
enlarges, and hormone release increases.
The alarm stage is short. Not much later,
the individual moves into the *resistance
stage,* during which resistance to stress is
intensified, and an all-out effort is made to
combat stress. In the resistance stage, the
individual's body is flooded with stress hormones; blood pressure, heart rate, temperature, and respiration all increase. If the
all-out effort to combat stress fails and stress
persists, the individual moves into the *exhaustion stage,* at which time wear and
tear on the body increases, the person
may collapse in a state of exhaustion, and
vulnerability to disease increases. Figure
16.4 provides an illustration of Selye's general adaptation syndrome.

Not all stress is bad, though. **Eustress**
*is Selye's concept that describes the positive
features of stress.* Competing in an athletic event, writing an essay, or pursuing
someone who is attractive requires the body
to expend energy. Selye does not say that
we should avoid these fulfilling experiences
in life, but he does emphasize that we should
minimize the wear and tear on our bodies.

One of the main criticisms of Selye's
view is that human beings do not always
react to stress in the uniform way he proposed. There is
much more to understanding stress in humans than knowing their physical reactions to it. We also need to know
about their personality, their physical makeup, their
perceptions, and the context in which the stressor occurred.

Environmental Factors

Many factors, big and small, can produce stress in adolescents' lives. In some instances, extreme events, such
as war, an automobile accident, or the death of a friend,
produce stress. In others, the everyday pounding of
being overloaded with school and work, of being frustrated in unhappy family circumstances, or of living in
poverty produce stress. What makes some situations stressful and others less stressful for adolescents?

Overload, Conflict, and Frustration Sometimes, circumstances become so intense that adolescents no longer
can cope. Adolescents are known for their interest in
listening to loud music, but when noise remains at a
high level—such as a loud siren—for a prolonged period
of time the individual's adaptability becomes over-
loaded at some point. This overload can occur with work,
too. An adolescent may say, "There are not enough hours
in the day to do all I have to do."

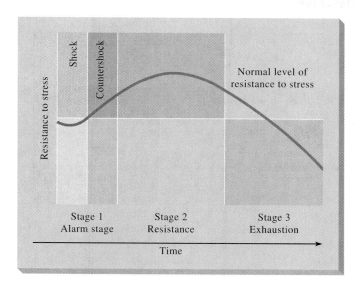

Figure~16.4

Selye's General Adaptation Syndrome.
The general adaptation syndrome (GAS) describes an individual's general response to stress. In the first stage (alarm), the body enters a temporary state of shock, a time when resistance to stress is below normal. Then a rebound called "countershock" occurs, in which resistance to stress begins to pick up. Not much later, the individual moves into the second state (resistance), during which resistance to stress is intensified in an all-out effort to combat stress. If the effort fails and stress persists, the individual moves into the third and final stage (exhaustion), when wear and tear on the body worsens, the person may collapse in a state of exhaustion, and vulnerability to disease increases.

From Hans Selye, The Stress of Life, 2d ed. Copyright © 1978 McGraw-Hill, Inc., New York, NY. Reproduced by permission of McGraw-Hill, Inc.

The buzzword for overload in today's world is **burnout,** *a hopeless, helpless feeling brought on by relentless work-related stress.* Burnout leaves its sufferers in a state of physical and emotional exhaustion. On a number of campuses, college burnout is the most common reason students leave school before earning their degrees, reaching a rate of 25 percent at some schools. Dropping out of college for a semester or two used to be considered a sign of weakness. Now sometimes called "stopping out" because the student fully intends to return, it may be encouraged for some students who are feeling overwhelmed by stress. Before recommending "stopping out," though, most counselors suggest examining ways the overload could be reduced and possible coping strategies that would allow the student to remain in school. The simple strategy of taking a reduced class load or a better-balanced load sometimes works, for example. Most college counseling services have professionals who can effectively work with students to alleviate the sense of being over-loaded and overwhelmed by life.

Stimuli not only overload adolescents—they can also be a source of conflict. Conflict occurs when adolescents must decide between two or more incompatible stimuli. Three major types of conflict are approach/approach, avoidance/avoidance, and approach/avoidance. The **approach/approach conflict** *is when the individual must choose between two attractive stimuli or circumstances.* Should an adolescent go out with the tall, thin, good-looking person or with the rich, more stockily built person? Should the adolescent decide to take a summer job as a lifeguard or as a salesperson? The approach/approach conflict is the least stressful of the three types of conflict because either choice leads to a positive result.

The **avoidance/avoidance conflict** *is when the individual must choose between two unattractive stimuli or circumstances.* Adolescents want to avoid both, but they must choose one. Will the adolescent go to the dentist to have a bad tooth pulled or endure the toothache? Is the adolescent going to go through the stress of an oral presentation in class or not show up and get a zero? Obviously, these conflicts are more stressful than having the luxury of choosing between two approach circumstances. In many instances, adolescents delay their decision about an avoidance/avoidance conflict until the last possible moment.

The **approach/avoidance conflict** *involves a single stimulus or circumstance that has both positive and negative characteristics.* For example, an adolescent may really like a particular individual and even be thinking about getting married. The possibility of steady love and affection is attractive, but, on the other hand, marriage at this time might hinder college and a career. The adolescent looks at a menu and faces a dilemma—the double chocolate delight would be sumptuous, but is it worth the extra pound of weight? The adolescent's world is full of approach/avoidance conflicts, and they can be very stressful. In these circumstances, adolescents often vacillate before deciding. As the adolescent approaches decision time, avoidance tendencies usually dominate.

Frustration is another circumstance that produces stress for adolescents. **Frustration** *refers to any situation in which the individual cannot reach a desired goal.* If adolescents want something and cannot have it, they feel frustrated. Adolescents' worlds are full of frustrations that build up to make their lives stressful—not having enough money to buy a car, not getting a good job, not getting an A average, being late for school because of traffic, and not being able to get a date with a particular person. Failures and losses are especially frustrating—for example, not getting grades that are high enough to get into the desired college, or the death of someone the adolescent is close to. Sometimes the frustrations adolescents experience are major life events—as in the divorce of their parents or the suicide of a friend. Others are an accumulation of daily hassles.

Life Events and Daily Hassles Adolescents can experience a spectrum of stresses, ranging from ordinary to severe (Kostelecky, 1997). At the ordinary end are experiences that occur in most adolescents' lives and for which there are reasonably well-defined coping patterns.

Type Z Behavior

Drawing by D. Reilly; © 1987 The New Yorker Magazine, Inc.

For example, most parents are aware that siblings are jealous of one another and that, when one sibling does well at something, the other sibling(s) will be jealous. They know how jealousy works and know ways to help adolescents cope with it. More severe stress occurs when children or adolescents become separated from their parents. Healthy coping patterns for this stressful experience are not spelled out well. Some adolescents are well cared for, others are ignored, when there is a separation caused by divorce, death, illness, or foster placement. Even more severe are the experiences of adolescents who have lived for years in situations of neglect or abuse. Victims of incest also experience severe stress, with few coping guidelines.

In many instances, more than one stress occurs at a time in adolescents' lives. Researchers have found that, when several stresses are combined, the effects may be compounded (Rutter & Garmezy, 1983). For example, in one investigation, British psychiatrist Michael Rutter (1979) found that boys and girls who were under two chronic life stresses were four times as likely to eventually need psychological services as were those who had to cope with only one chronic stress. A similar multiplier effect was found for boys and girls who experienced more than one short-term strain at a time.

Recently, psychologists have emphasized that life's daily experiences as well as life's major events may be the culprits in stress. Enduring a tense family and living in poverty do not show up on scales of major life events in adolescents' development, yet the everyday pounding adolescents experience in these living conditions can add up to a highly stressful life and, eventually, psychological disturbance or illness (Compas & Wagner, 1991). In one study, 16- to 18-year-old adolescents who experienced the most daily hassles had the most negative self-images (Tolan, Miller, & Thomas, 1988).

Personality Factors—Type A Behavior Pattern

Are aspects of adolescents' personalities associated with adolescents' stress and health? In recent years, researchers have focused the most attention in this area on the **Type A behavior pattern,** *a cluster of characteristics—excessively competitive, hard-driven, impatient, irritable, and hostile—thought to be related to coronary problems.* Most research on the Type A behavior pattern has been conducted with adults. Recently, researchers have examined the different components of Type A behavior to determine a more precise link with coronary risk. People who are hostile or consistently turn anger inward are more likely to develop heart disease (Williams, 1989). Hostile, angry individuals have been labeled "hot reactors," meaning that they have intense physiological reactions to stress—their hearts race, their breathing hurries, and their muscles tense up, which could lead to heart disease. Behavioral medicine researcher Redford Williams believes that everyone has the ability to control anger and to develop more trust in others, which he thinks will reduce the risk for heart disease.

Researchers recently have examined the Type A behavior pattern in children and adolescents and found that Type A children and adolescents have more illnesses, cardiovascular symptoms, muscle tension, and sleep disturbances (Murray & others, 1988). Some researchers have found that Type A children and adolescents are more likely to have Type A parents; this association is strongest for fathers and sons (Weidner & others, 1988). In one investigation, when Type A parents were observed interacting with their sons and daughters, the parents often criticized their offsprings' failures and compared their performances to those of others (Eagleston & others, 1986). Such stressful family circumstances may set the tone for ineffective ways of coping with stress and a tendency to develop cardiovascular symptoms.

As in research on adults, when studying children and adolescents it is important to determine which components of the Type A behavior pattern are associated more strongly than others with coronary-prone behavior and low levels of competence. In one study of 990 adolescents, the components of the Type A behavior pattern that were associated with a low level of competent functioning (low self-esteem, low achievement standard, and external locus of control) were being impatient and aggressively competitive (Keltikangas-Järvinen & Raikkonen, 1990). Another important question about the Type A behavior pattern in children and adolescents involves its stability over the childhood and adolescent years. In one study, the most stable component of the Type A behavior pattern over time was the impatience-aggression component (Keltikangas-Järvinen, 1990). Nonetheless, researchers still have not documented whether Type A children or adolescents grow up to become Type A adults and have more coronary problems as adults.

Cognitive Factors

Most of us think of stress as environmental events that place demands on our lives, such as losing one's notes from a class, being yelled at by a friend, failing a test, or being in a car wreck. While there are some common ways that adolescents and adults experience stress, not everyone perceives the same events as stressful. For example, one adolescent might perceive an upcoming interview for college admission as threatening, while another adolescent might perceive it as challenging. One adolescent might perceive a D grade on a paper as threatening, while another adolescent might perceive the same grade as challenging. To some degree, then, what is stressful for adolescents depends on how they cognitively appraise and interpret events. This view has been most clearly presented by stress researcher Richard Lazarus (1993). **Cognitive appraisal** *is Lazarus' term for individuals' interpretation of events in their lives as harmful, threatening, or challenging, and their determination of whether they have the resources to effectively cope with the event.*

In Lazarus' view, events are appraised in two steps: primary appraisal and secondary appraisal. In **primary appraisal,** *adolescents interpret whether an event involves harm or loss that has already occurred, a threat of some future danger, or a challenge to be overcome. Harm* is adolescents' appraisal of the damage the event has already inflicted. For example, if an adolescent skipped school yesterday and missed an exam, the harm has already been done. *Threat* is adolescents' appraisal of potential future damage an event may bring. For example, missing the exam may lower the teacher's opinion of the adolescent and increase the probability that the adolescent will get a low grade in the course at the end of the semester. *Challenge* is adolescents' appraisal of the potential to overcome the adverse circumstances of an event and ultimately profit from the event. For example, the adolescent who skipped school and missed the exam may develop a commitment to never get into that situation again and thus become a better student.

After adolescents cognitively appraise an event for its harm, threat, or challenge, Lazarus says, they subsequently engage in secondary appraisal. In **secondary appraisal,** *adolescents evaluate their resources and determine how effectively they can be used to cope with the event.* This appraisal is called *secondary* because it comes after primary appraisal and depends on the degree to which the event has been appraised as harmful, threatening, or challenging. Coping involves a wide range of potential strategies, skills, and abilities for effectively managing stressful events. For example, if the adolescent who missed the exam learns that the teacher will give a makeup exam 2 days later, the adolescent might not experience much stress. However, if the teacher says that the adolescent has to write a lengthy term paper for missing the test, the adolescent may cognitively appraise the situation and determine that this additional requirement places considerable demands on his or her time and wonder whether this requirement can be met. In this case, the adolescent's secondary appraisal indicates a more stressful situation than simply having to take a makeup test several days later (Sears & others, 1994).

Lazarus believes that adolescents' experience of stress is a balance of primary and secondary appraisal. When harm and threat are high, and challenge and resources are low, stress is likely to be high; when harm and threat are low, and challenge and resources are high, stress is more likely to be moderate or low.

Sociocultural Factors

Among the sociocultural factors involved in stress are acculturative stress and socioeconomic status, each of which we consider in turn.

Acculturative Stress **Acculturation** *refers to cultural change that results from continuous, firsthand contact between two distinctive cultural groups.* **Acculturative stress** *is the negative consequence of acculturation.* Members of ethnic minority groups have historically encountered hostility, prejudice, and lack of effective support during crises, which contributes to alienation, social isolation, and heightened stress (Al-Issa & Tousignant, 1997). As upwardly mobile ethnic minority families have attempted to penetrate all-White neighborhoods, interracial tensions often mount. Similarly, racial tensions and hostility often emerge among the various ethnic minorities as they each struggle for limited housing and employment opportunities, seeking a fair share of a limited market. Clashes become inevitable as Latino family markets spring up in African American urban neighborhoods, as Vietnamese extended families displace Puerto Rican apartment dwellers, and as the increasing enrollment of Asian students on college campuses is perceived as a threat to affirmative action policies by other non-White ethnic minority students.

While race relations in the United States have historically been conceptualized as Black/White, this is no longer the only combination of racial animosity. As the numbers of Latinos and Asians have increased dramatically, and as Native Americans have crossed the boundaries of their reservations, the visibility of these groups has brought them into contact not only with the mainstream White society, but with one another as well. Depending on the circumstances, this contact has sometimes been harmonious, sometimes antagonistic.

Although the dominant White society has tried on many occasions to enslave or dispossess entire populations,

Confronted with overt or covert attempts at segregation, many ethnic minority groups have developed their own communities and social structures, which include (a) African American churches, one of which is attended by this church youth group; (b) Latino kin systems, as reflected in this large extended family gathering, and (c) Native American "bands" and tribal associations, as reflected in this Native American celebration.

these ethnic minority groups have survived and flourished. In the face of severe stress and oppression, they have shown remarkable resilience and adaptation. Confronted with overt or covert attempts at segregation, they have developed their own communities and social structures, including African American churches, Vietnamese mutual assistance associations, Chinese American family associations, Japanese-language schools, Indian "bands" and tribal associations, and Latino kin systems, at the same time as they learn to negotiate with the dominant White culture in America. They essentially have mastered two cultures and have developed impressive competencies and coping strategies for adapting to life in America. The resilience and adaptation of ethnic minority groups can teach us much about coping and survival in the face of overwhelming adversity.

Socioeconomic Status Poverty imposes considerable stress on adolescents and their families. Chronic life conditions, such as inadequate housing, dangerous neighborhoods, burdensome responsibilities, and economic uncertainties are potent stressors in the lives of the poor. The incidence of poverty is especially pronounced among ethnic minority adolescents and their families. For example, African American women heading families face a risk of poverty that is more than ten times that of White men heading families. Puerto Rican female family heads face a poverty rate that is almost fifteen times that found among White male family heads. Many individuals who become poor during their lives remain poor for 1 or 2 years. However, African Americans and female family heads are at risk for experiencing persistent poverty. The average poor African American child experiences poverty for almost 20 years.

Poverty is related to threatening and uncontrollable events in adolescents' lives. For example, poor females are more likely to experience crime and violence than middle-class females are (Belle, 1990). Poverty also undermines sources of social support that play a role in buffering the effects of stress.

Resilience

Even when children and adolescents are faced with adverse conditions, such as poverty, are there characteristics that help to buffer them and make them resilient to developmental outcomes? Some children and adolescents do triumph over life's adversities (Markstrom & Tryon, 1997; Masten & Hubbard, 1995). Norman Garmezy (1993) has studied resilience amid adversity and disadvantage for a number of years. He concludes that three factors often appear to help children and adolescents become resilient to stress: (1) cognitive skills (attention, reflectiveness) and positive responsiveness to others; (2) families, including those in poverty, marked by warmth, cohesion, and some caring adult such as a grandparent who takes responsibility in the absence of responsive parents or in the presence of intense marital discord; and (3) the presence of some source of external support, as when a strong maternal substitute in the form of a teacher, a neighbor, parents of peers, or even an institutional structure such as a caring agency or a church is available. These three factors characterized the developmental course of resilient individuals in a longitudinal study (Werner, 1989).

Garmezy (1993) described a setting in a Harlem neighborhood of New York City to illustrate resilience: In the foyer of the walkup apartment building is a large frame on a wall in the entranceway. It displays the photographs of children who live in the apartment building, with a written request that if anyone sees any of the children endangered on the street, they bring them back to the apartment house. Garmezy commented that this is an excellent example of adult competence and concern for the safety and well-being of children.

COPING WITH STRESS

If you think back to the first 2 weeks of this class, you may remember students who used to sit near you who do not come to class anymore. Every semester, several students stop showing up for classes, often after the first exam. They never talk to the instructor about their performance in the class, and they do not go through the proper procedures for dropping the class. The result of their immediate stress avoidance is having to face the delayed stressful circumstance of getting an F on their record at the end of the semester. Students also sometimes strike out in anger when faced with stress. One student who flunked one of my classes came to my office and delivered a few choice epithets after he received his grade. The next day, he returned to apologize, saying that he deserved the F and that he also had failed two other classes. The behaviors of these two types of students—those who avoid stress and those who discharge anger—are two often ineffective ways of coping with stress. What are the best strategies for coping with stress?

Removal of Stress, Defense Mechanisms, and Problem-Focused Coping

Stress is so abundant in American society that adolescents are often confronted with more than one stressor at the same time. A college student might be taking an extra course load, not have enough money to eat regularly, and be having problems in a relationship. As mentioned earlier in the chapter, researchers have found that, when several stressors are simultaneously experienced, the effects can be compounded (Rutter & Garmezy, 1983). For example, as we noted earlier, in one investigation individuals who were under two chronic life stressors were four times more likely to eventually need psychological services as those who only had to cope with one chronic stressor (Rutter, 1979). Thus, the student with school, financial, and relationship stressors would likely benefit from removal of one of the stressors, such as dropping one class and taking a normal course load.

Richard Lazarus (1993) believes that coping takes one of two forms. **Problem-focused coping** *is Lazarus' term for the cognitive strategy used in coping with stress by individuals who face their troubles and try to solve them.* For example, if you are having trouble with a class, you might go to the study skills center at your college or university and enter a training program to learn how to study more effectively. You have faced your problem and attempted to do something about it.

Emotion-focused coping *is Lazarus' term for coping with stress in which individuals respond to stress in an emotional manner, especially using defensive appraisal.* Emotion-focused coping involves using defense mechanisms, as discussed in chapter 2. In emotion-focused coping, adolescents might avoid something, rationalize what has happened to them, deny that it is occurring, or laugh it off. Adolescents who use emotion-focused coping might avoid going to school, saying that school does not matter, deny that they are having a problem, and laugh and joke about it with their friends. In one investigation, depressed individuals used more avoidant coping strategies than nondepressed individuals did (Ebata & Moos, 1989).

There are times when emotion-focused coping is adaptive (Peterson & Ding, 1995). For example, denial is one of the main protective psychological mechanisms that enables adolescents to cope with the flood of feelings that occur when the reality of death or dying becomes too great. In other circumstances, emotion-focused coping is not adaptive. Adolescents who deny that they are not doing well in school, when in reality they are flunking two classes, are not responding adaptively. Neither are adolescents who deny that the person they were dating does not love them anymore, when in reality that person is going steady with someone else. However, denial can be used to avoid the destructive impact of shock by postponing the time when adolescents have to deal with stress. Over the long term, though, adolescents should use problem-focused rather than emotion-focused coping (Blanchard-Fields & Robinson, 1987; Ebata, 1991).

Approach and Avoidance Coping Strategies

Coping strategies can also be categorized as approach to avoidance. **Approach strategies** *include cognitive attempts to understand the stressor and behavioral attempts to cope with the stressor by dealing directly with it or its consequences.* **Avoidance strategies** *include cognitive attempts to deny or minimize the stressor and behavioral attempts to withdraw from or avoid the stressor.* In one recent study, adolescents who used approach strategies to cope with stress were older, more active, appraised the focal stressor as controllable and as a challenge, and had more ongoing social resources (Ebata & Moos, 1994). Adolescents who used more avoidance strategies were easily distressed, had more chronic stressors, and had experienced more negative life events in the previous year. In general, approach strategies are associated with better adjustment in adolescence than are avoidance strategies.

> *I am not afraid of storms because I am learning how to sail my ship.*
>
> —Louisa May Alcott

Positive Thinking and Self-Efficacy

"Don't worry, be happy" go the words of the popular tune by Bobby McFerrin, "Cause when you worry, your face will frown, and that will bring everybody down." Is McFerrin's cheerful optimism a good coping strategy for adolescents? Most of the time, adolescents *do* want to avoid negative thinking when handling stress. A positive mood improves adolescents' ability to process information more efficiently, makes them more altruistic, and gives them higher self-esteem. An optimistic attitude is superior to a pessimistic one in most instances, producing a sense that adolescents are controlling their environment, or what cognitive social learning theorist Albert Bandura (1986, 1994) calls *self-efficacy*. A negative mood increases adolescents' chances of getting angry, feeling guilty, and magnifying their mistakes. Several months before 17-year-old Michael Chang became the youngest male to win the French Open Tennis Championships, sport psychologist Jim Loehr (1989) pieced together videotaped segments of the most outstanding points Chang had played during the past year. Chang periodically watched the videotape, always seeing himself winning and in a positive mood and never seeing himself making mistakes.

For a number of years, seeing reality as accurately as possible was described as the best path to health for

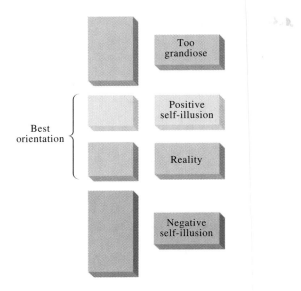

Figure~16.5

Reality and Self-Illusion.
In Baumeister's model of self-illusion, the best-adjusted individuals often have self-illusions that are slightly above average. Having too grandiose an opinion of yourself or thinking negatively about yourself can have negative consequences. For some individuals, seeing things too accurately can be depressing. Overall, in most contexts, a reality orientation or a slightly above average self-illusion may be most effective.

adolescents. Recently, though, researchers have found increasing evidence that maintaining some positive illusions about oneself and the world is healthy. Happy adolescents often have high opinions of themselves, give self-serving explanations for events, and have exaggerated beliefs about their ability to control the world around them (Snyder, 1988).

Illusions, whether positive or negative, are related to adolescents' self-esteem. Adolescents might have thoughts about themselves that are too grandiose or too negative, and both have negative consequences. Rather, the ideal overall orientation might be an optimal margin of illusion in which adolescents see themselves as slightly more positive than they actually are (see figure 16.5). For some adolescents, seeing things too accurately can lead to depression. Seeing one's suffering as meaningless and random does not help adolescents to cope and move forward, even if the suffering *is* random and meaningless. An absence of positive illusions may also thwart adolescents from undertaking the risky and ambitious projects that yield the greatest rewards (Baumeister, 1989).

In some cases, though, a strategy of defensive pessimism actually may work best in handling stress. By imagining negative outcomes, adolescents prepare themselves for forthcoming stressful circumstances (Norem & Cantor, 1986). For example, an honors student may be worried that she will flunk the next test. For her, thoughts of failure might not be paralyzing but

instead might motivate her to do everything necessary to ensure that she will do well on the test. By imagining potential problems, she may develop relevant strategies for dealing with or preventing negative outcomes. Positive *and* negative thinking, then, are involved in coping with stress.

At this point, we have found that such factors as removing stress, reducing the use of defense mechanisms, increasing problem-focused coping, thinking positively, and following a self-efficacy strategy can help adolescents to cope with stress. As we see next, psychologists increasingly believe that support systems are also extremely valuable in helping adolescents to cope with stress.

Support Systems

Adolescents' physical and social worlds are more crowded, polluted, noisy, and achievement-oriented than those of their counterparts who lived a century ago. In such a world, support systems are often needed to buffer stress. Close, positive attachments to others—especially to family and friends—consistently show up as important buffers to stress in adolescents' lives (Seiffge-Krenke, 1995; Youniss & Smollar, 1985). In one study, adolescents coped with stress better when they had a close affective relationship with their mothers (Wagner, Cohen, & Brook, 1991). In another study, peers were the most likely source of overall support for adolescents, followed by mothers (O'Brien, 1990). In this study, peers provided more support than siblings did in all categories and more than both parents in all areas except financial support, future/career planning, and personal values. Siblings provided more support for dating than mothers did. Patterns of support seeking were generally similar across gender, but when differences did exist, female adolescents were more likely than their male counterparts to go to peers and mothers for support. In future/career planning, lifestyle, dating support, and personal values, male adolescents were as likely to seek support from fathers as from mothers.

Multiple Coping Strategies

As we have seen, there are many different ways for adolescents to cope effectively—and ineffectively—with stress. An important point about effective coping strategies is that adolescents can often use more than one to help them deal with stress (Wolchick & Sandler, 1997). For example, the advice to an adolescent who is experiencing a great deal of stress might include the following: Develop a more positive attitude, reduce your anger, make sure you have one or two friends in whom you can confide, quit smoking, lose weight, exercise several times a week, use problem-focused coping strategies, and develop more positive images of yourself. One of these alone may not be able to turn the tide against stress, but a combination of them may be effective.

At this point, we have discussed a number of ideas about stress and coping. A summary of these ideas is presented in concept table 16.2.

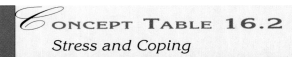
Concept	Processes/ Related Ideas	Characteristics/Description
Stress	What is stress?	Stress is the response of individuals to the circumstances and events, called stressors, that threaten them and tax their coping abilities.
	Factors in stress	Among the most important factors involved in stress are physiological factors, such as the body's response to stress; environmental factors, such as approach/approach, avoidance/avoidance, and approach/avoidance conflicts; personality factors such as the Type A behavior pattern; cognitive factors, such as cognitive appraisal; and sociocultural factors, such as acculturative stress and poverty.
	Resilience	Three sets of characteristics are reflected in the lives of children and adolescents who show resilience amid adversity and disadvantage: (1) cognitive skills and positive responsiveness to others, (2) families marked by warmth, cohesion, and the presence of a caring adult, and (3) the presence of some source of external support.
Coping with Stress	Removal of stress, defense mechanisms, and problem-focused coping	Most adolescents are confronted with more than one stressor. Removing one stressor can be very beneficial. In most cases, problem-focused coping is better than emotion-focused coping and the use of defense mechanisms, especially in coping with stress over the long term.
	Approach and avoidance strategies	Approach strategies are favored over avoidance strategies.
	Positive thinking and self-efficacy	Most of the time, adolescents should think positively and avoid negative thoughts. An optimistic attitude produces a sense of self-efficacy. Positive self-illusions can improve some adolescents' lives, but it is important to guard against unrealistic expectations. A strategy of defensive pessimism helps some adolescents to cope more effectively.
	Support systems	Close, positive attachments to others—especially to family and friends—consistently show up as important buffers to stress in adolescents' lives.
	Multiple coping strategies	Adolescents often can and should use more than one coping strategy in dealing with stress.

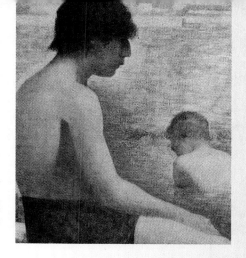

SUMMARY

Adolescence, especially early adolescence, is a time when a number of health-compromising behaviors either occur for the first time or intensify. Adolescence is a critical juncture for the development of positive health behaviors.

We began this chapter by considering Alan's stress, Sarah's obesity, and Brian's exercise. Then we evaluated health and adolescent development, including health conceptions through history, the role of adolescence in developing positive health behaviors, leading causes of death in adolescence, and age, socioeconomic status, ethnicity, and sex. Our coverage of health and illness focused on cognitive factors, sociocultural factors, and health services. We also read about promoting health, studying the dangers of cigarette smoking, nutrition, eating disorders, exercise, and moving toward healthier lives. Then, we studied stress, including what stress is, the body's response to stress, environmental factors, personality factors (Type A behavior pattern), cognitive factors, sociocultural factors, and resilience. We also learned about coping with stress, exploring such topics as removal of stress, defense mechanisms, and problem-focusing coping; approach and avoidance strategies; positive thinking and self-efficacy; support systems; and multiple coping strategies.

Don't forget that you can obtain an overall summary of the chapter by again reading the two concept tables on pages 513 and 522. This concludes the sixteenth and final chapter of the book. However, one final part of the book remains. The Epilogue reviews some of the main issues and themes of adolescent development we have studied and provides a montage of thoughts to stimulate your thinking about what adolescent development is all about.

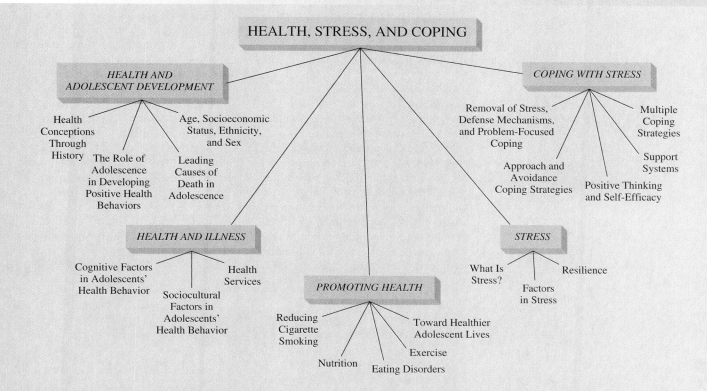

KEY TERMS

PRACTICAL KNOWLEDGE ABOUT ADOLESCENCE

Kid Fitness
(1992) by Kenneth Cooper.
New York: Bantam Books.

Author Kenneth Cooper developed the concept of aerobic fitness. In this book he adapts to children and adolescents his ideas that have helped millions of adults become more physically fit. Cooper describes a total program of diet and exercise designed to improve children's and adolescents' physical fitness and foster healthy eating habits. Customized programs are presented for children and adolescents of all fitness levels, from the physically unfit to the average youth to the athletically gifted. The book includes a comprehensive checklist of tests to help gauge the adolescent's level of physical fitness. Standard fitness levels for children and adolescents from 5 to 16+ are provided. This is an excellent book for improving adolescents' physical fitness and eating habits.

The New Fit or Fat (revised ed.)
(1991) by Covert Bailey.
Boston: Houghton Mifflin.

The New Fit or Fat describes ways to become healthy by developing better diet and exercise routines. Author Covert Bailey has a master of science degree in nutritional biochemistry from MIT and heads the Bailey Fit-or-Fat Center in Oregon. Bailey argues that the basic problem for overweight people is not losing weight, which fat adolescents and adults do periodically, but gaining weight, which fat people do more easily than do those with a different body chemistry. He explores ways the body stores fat and analyzes why crash diets don't work. He explains the relation between fat metabolism and weight, concluding that the ultimate cure for obesity is aerobic exercise coupled with a sensible low-fat diet.

This book originally was published in 1977 as Fit or Fat. The 1991 edition is greatly expanded with new information on fitness lifestyles and recent scientific advances. A new chapter also answers readers' most frequently asked questions about Bailey's views on diet and exercise. This book offers solid, no-nonsense advice on how to lose weight and become more physically fit.

American Anorexia/Bulimia Association
133 Cedar Lane
Teaneck, NJ 07666
201-836-1800

This organization provides information, referrals, and publications related to anorexia nervosa and bulimia.

Building Health Programs for Teenagers (1986)
Children's Defense Fund
25 E Street NW
Washington, DC 20001
202-628-8787

This information provides help in developing health programs for adolescents. A number of excellent ideas about health programs are presented.

Canadian Institute of Child Health/Institut Canadien de la Santé Infantile
885 Meadowlands Drive East, Suite 512
Ottawa, Ontario, K2C 3N2
613-224-4144

The Institute monitors the health of Canadian children, fosters the health and well-being of mothers and infants, promotes a healthy and safe environment to reduce childhood injuries, promotes the physical and socioemotional development of children and encourages individuals and communities to improve the environment for all children and youth.

Comprehensive Adolescent Health Services in the United States (1992)
by Jonathan Klein and others
The Search Institute
Thresher Square West
Suite 210
700 South Third Street
Minneapolis, MN 55415
1-800-888-7828

This document is based on the first national census of adolescent health programs. It reviews more than six hundred existing programs that provide comprehensive or integrated health services to adolescents. Relevant differences between school-based, hospital-based, public health, and other program models are discussed.

Journal of Adolescent Health Care

This journal includes articles about a wide range of health-related and medical issues, including reducing smoking, improving nutrition, health promotion, and physicians' and nurses' roles in reducing health-compromising behaviors of adolescents.

Journal of School Health

This journal covers research and programs that involve school-related dimensions of health, including a number of health education programs.

Kids Help Phone/Jeunesse J'Écoute
2 Bloor Street West, Suite 100, Box 513
Toronto, Ontario M4W 3E2
416-921-7827
800-668-6868

Kids Help Phone is Canada's only bilingual, confidential, 24-hour, toll-free telephone help line for children and teens. Staffed by professionals, the Help Phone provides counseling, educational information and referral services to youth.

The LEARN Program for Weight Control (1988)
by Kelley Brownell
Dallas: American Health

This program can help adolescents change their lifestyle in order to lose weight. Author Kelly Brownell is a highly respected authority on dieting and eating disorders. *LEARN* stands for Lifestyle, Exercise, Attitudes, Relationships, and Nutrition. Brownell weaves his LEARN program through sixteen lessons.

The New Aerobics for Women (1988)
by Kenneth Cooper and Mildred Cooper
New York: Bantam

Older adolescent and college females can benefit from this excellent book on exercise that also includes sound dietary information.

Stop Teenage Addiction to Tobacco
121 Lyman Street, Suite 210
Springfield, MA 01103

This organization's goal is to reduce teenage smoking, especially by controlling tobacco company advertising and better enforcement of laws prohibiting tobacco sales to minors. It publishes a newsletter, *Tobacco and Youth Reporter*.

EXPLORING ADOLESCENT DEVELOPMENT

To further explore the nature of adolescent development, we will examine a research study that involved an intervention program to improve adolescent adjustment, and we will discuss the nature of health promotion for adolescents.

RESEARCH ON ADOLESCENT DEVELOPMENT

Improving Adolescent Adjustment

Featured Study

Caplan, M., Weissberg, R. P., Grober, J. S., Sivo, P. J., Grady, K., & Jacoby, C. (1992). Social competence promotion with inner-city and suburban young adolescents: Effects on social adjustment and alcohol use. *Journal of Consulting and Clinical Psychology, 60,* 56–63.

This study focused on the impact of a school-based intervention program focused on skills, social adjustment, and substance abuse in young adolescents. The intervention emphasized the broad-based promotion of competence.

Method

The subjects were 282 sixth- and seventh-graders from an inner-city middle school and a suburban middle school. The Positive Youth Develop-ment Program is a highly structured 121-page, 20-session curriculum de-signed to promote adolescent com-petence. Specifically, the curriculum focuses on six main units: stress management, self-esteem, social prob-lem solving, substance and health information, assertiveness, and social networks. Teaching techniques in-clude discussion, videotapes, diaries, small-group role playing, work sheets, and homework assignments. The cur-riculum was presented in six program classes during two 50-minute class pe-riods per week over a 15-week period. Master's-level health educators co-taught the program with classroom teachers. The health educators and classroom teachers were trained by the program developers through a series of six 2-hour workshops, as well as weekly on-site consultation. Nine control-group classes received regular academic instruction in science, which included a series of lessons pertaining to the physical effects of drug use.

Students and teachers filled out surveys and rating scales before and after the intervention program time frame. The pre- and postassessments consisted of measures to assess (a) cop-ing skills, (b) social and emotional adjustment, and (c) self-reported intentions and use of alcohol and drugs.

Results and Discussion

The intervention program was suc-cessful in improving the students' skills in handling interpersonal prob-lems and coping with anxiety. Teacher ratings revealed improve-ments in the intervention group's constructive conflict resolution with peers, impulse control, and popu-larity. And the intervention was suc-cessful in preventing excessive alcohol use. In general, the inter-vention program was beneficial for both the inner-city and the subur-ban adolescents.

Promoting the Health of Young Adolescents

Early adolescence is a time when many health-compromising behaviors—drug abuse, unprotected sex, poor dietary habits, and lack of exercise, for example—either occur for the first time or intensify. As children move through puberty and often develop a feeling that they should be able to engage in adultlike behaviors, they essentially ask, "How should I use my body?" According to David Hamburg and his colleagues (1993), any responsible education must answer that basic question with a substantial life science curriculum that provides adolescents with accurate information about their own bodies, including what the consequences are for engaging in health-compromising behaviors.

Most adolescent health experts believe that a life science education program should be an important part of the curriculum in all middle schools (Hamburg, 1990; Kolbe, Collins, & Cortese, 1997). This education would consist of providing adolescents with a better understanding of adolescent development, including puberty (its biological and social ramifications), the reproductive system, sexual behavior, sexually transmitted diseases, nutrition, diet, and exercise. In addition, young adolescents should have readily accessible health services, nutritious food in the cafeteria, a smoke-free and physically safe environment, and appropriate physical fitness activities for all students.

Many adolescent health experts also believe that life skills training should be part of the life science curriculum (Hamburg, 1990; Hamburg & others, 1993). Life skills training programs teach young adolescents how to make informed, deliberate, and constructive decisions that will reduce their health-compromising behaviors. Life skills training programs also can improve the interpersonal skills of young adolescents, helping them relate better with others and solve interpersonal problems more effectively.

In the past decade, one new school-based model for enhancing the life opportunities of adolescents is the full-service school, which encompasses school-based primary health clinics, youth service programs, and other innovative services to improve access to health and social services. These programs have in common the use of school facilities for delivering services through partnerships with community agencies, a shared vision of youth development, and financial support from sources outside of school systems, especially states and foundations. Organizing a full-service school requires careful planning to involve school personnel, community agencies, parents, and students. Evaluation of the full-service school's effectiveness is still scattered, although some recent results are encouraging with regard to adolescents' health and mental health care, dropout rates, substance abuse, pregnancy prevention, and improved attendance (Dryfoos, 1995).

It is also important to remember that health promotion in adolescence should not be solely the responsibility of schools. Adolescent health can benefit from the cooperation and integration of a number of societal institutions: the family, schools, the health-care system, the media, and community organizations (Hamburg & others, 1993).

Vermeer
Head of Young Girl

EPILOGUE

Adolescents: The Future of Society

In the end the power behind development is life.

—Erik Erikson

As the twenty-first century approaches, the well-being of adolescents is one of our most important concerns. We all cherish the future of adolescents, for they are the future of any society. Adolescents who do not reach their full potential, who are destined to make fewer contributions to society than society needs, and who do not take their place as productive adults diminish that society's future. In this epilogue, we will revisit a number of important themes and issues in adolescent development and then present a montage of thoughts that convey the beauty, power, and complexity of adolescents' development.

Our journey through adolescence has been long and complex, and you have read about many facets of adolescents' lives. This is a good time to stand back and ask yourself what you have learned. What theories, studies, and ideas struck you as more important than others? What did you learn about your own development as an adolescent? Did anything you learned stimulate you to rethink how adolescents develop? how you developed into the person you are today?

THEMES AND ISSUES IN ADOLESCENT DEVELOPMENT

As we look back across the chapters of *Adolescence*, some common themes and issues emerge. Let's explore what some of the most important themes and issues are.

The Storm-and-Stress View of Adolescence Has Been Overdramatized

Growing up has never been easy. However, adolescence is not best viewed as a time of rebellion, crisis, pathology, and deviance. A far more accurate vision of adolescence describes it as a time of evaluation, of decision making, of commitment, and of carving out a place in the world. Most problems of today's youth are not with the youth themselves. What adolescents need is access to a range of legitimate opportunities and long-term support from adults who deeply care about them.

In matters of taste and manners, the youth of every generation have seemed radical, unnerving, and different from adults—different in how they look, how they behave, the music they enjoy, their hairstyles, and the clothing they choose. But it is an enormous error to confuse the adolescent's enthusiasm for trying on new identities and enjoying moderate amounts of outrageous behavior with hostility toward parental and societal standards. Acting out and boundary testing are time-honored ways in which adolescents move toward accepting, rather than rejecting, parental values.

Although adolescence has been portrayed too negatively for too long, many adolescents today are at risk for not reaching their full potential. They do experience far too much storm and stress. This discussion underscores an important point about adolescents: They are not a homogeneous group. Different portrayals of adolescence emerge, depending on the particular group of adolescents being described.

We Need to Dramatically Reduce the Number of Adolescents at Risk for Not Reaching Their Potential

Although we emphasized that the majority of adolescents navigate the long journey of adolescence successfully, far too many adolescents in America are not reaching their potential because they are not being adequately reared by caregivers, not being adequately instructed in school, and not being adequately supported by society. Adolescents who do not reach their full potential and do not grow up to make competent contributions to their world invariably have not been given adequate individual attention and support as they were growing up. Adolescents need parents who love them; monitor their development; are sensitive to their needs; have a sound understanding of their own, as well as their adolescents', development; and help to steer them away from health-compromising behaviors.

We also need schools that place a greater emphasis on a curriculum that is developmentally appropriate and pays closer attention to adolescent health and well-being. This needs to be accomplished at all levels of education, but especially in the middle school and junior high school years. And we need to give more attention to our nation's social policy, especially in terms of ways to break the poverty cycle that enshrouds more than 25 percent of adolescents in the United States. Our nation's political values need to reflect greater concern for the inadequate conditions in which far too many adolescents live. To reduce the number of adolescents at risk for not reaching their full potential, community-wide agency cooperation and integration, as well as early prevention or early intervention, need to be given special attention.

Adolescent Development Is Embedded in Sociocultural, Historical Contexts

Throughout this book we have emphasized the importance of considering the contexts in which the adolescent develops. *Context* refers to the setting in which development occurs, a setting that is influenced by historical, economic, social, and cultural factors. These contexts or settings include homes, schools, peers groups, churches, neighborhoods, communities, cities, the United States, Canada, Russia, France, Japan, Egypt, and many others—each with meaningful historical, economic, social, and cultural legacies.

In the twentieth century alone in the United States, successive waves of adolescents have witnessed dramatic historical changes, including two world wars and their violence, the Great Depression and its economic woes, the advent of television and computers, increased levels of education, and altered gender roles. And as new generations appear, they increasingly have had an ethnic minority heritage.

Global interdependence is no longer a matter of belief or preference. It is an inescapable reality. By increasing our knowledge of the behavior, values, and nature of adolescent development in cultures around the world, we can learn about the universal aspects of adolescent development, cultural variations in their development, and how to interact with adolescents more effectively to make this planet a more hospitable, peaceful place to live.

Understanding our own culture better also can improve adolescents' lives. There is a special sense of urgency in addressing the nature of ethnicity and how it affects adolescent development because of the dramatic changes in the ethnic composition of America's population. The Asian, Latino, and African American populations are expected to increase at a much faster pace than the Anglo-American population in the foreseeable future. At a point early in the twenty-first century, one-third of the population in the United States will be members of ethnic minority groups.

To help adolescents of any ethnic heritage reach their full potential, we need to do the following:

- Recognize the diversity within every cultural and ethnic group. Not recognizing this diversity leads to unfortunate, harmful stereotyping.

- Understand that there are legitimate differences among cultural and ethnic groups. Recognizing and accepting these differences are important dimensions of getting along with others in a diverse, multicultural world. For too long, differences between ethnic minority individuals and Anglo-Americans were characterized as deficits on the part of ethnic minority individuals.
- Recognize and accept similarities among cultural and ethnic groups when differences have been incorrectly assumed. Through much of its history, America has had a White, middle-class bias. The search for legitimate similarities among White Americans and ethnic minority Americans is important because incorrectly assumed differences involve stereotyping and can lead to prejudice.
- Reduce discrimination and prejudice. Discrimination and prejudice continue to haunt too many adolescent lives—in interpersonal relations, in the media, and in daily conversations. Crimes, strangeness, poverty, mistakes, and deterioration too often are attributed to ethnic minority individuals without full consideration of the circumstances.
- Consider different sides of sensitive cultural and ethnic issues. We need to see things from different points of view and encourage adolescents to do likewise. If we don't seek alternative explanations and interpretations of problems and issues, our conclusions, and those of adolescents, may be based solely on expectations, prejudices, stereotypes, and personal experiences.

The Family Plays an Important Role in Adolescent Development

At a point not too long ago, we heard rumblings about the decreasing influence of the family in adolescents' lives and how the family as we had come to know it was breaking down. Although the structure of many families has changed as a result of increasing numbers of divorced, working-mother, and stepparent families, the family is still a powerful socializing influence on adolescent development. Regardless of the type of culture and family structure in which adolescents grow up, they benefit enormously when one or both parents are highly involved in their upbringing, provide them with warmth and nurturance, help them to develop self-control, and provide them with an environment that promotes their health and well-being.

Competent parents are knowledgeable about the nature of adolescent development, effectively monitor their adolescent's life, and adapt their behavior as the adolescent grows and matures.

A special concern is that too many of America's adolescents grow up in low-income families and suffer the stressful and burdensome perils of poverty. In a number of places in *Adolescence* we called attention to programs that will benefit adolescents who live in low-income settings. These programs currently are improving the lives of thousands of adolescents but need to be expanded to help far more adolescents than currently are being served by them.

For those of you who will become parents someday, or are already parents, I underscore how important it is for each of you to take seriously the rearing of your children and adolescents. Remember that good parenting takes an incredible amount of time—so if you become a parent, you should be willing to commit yourself, day after day, week after week, month after month, and year after year, to providing your children and adolescents with a warm, supportive, safe, and stimulating environment that will make them feel secure and allow them to reach their full potential as human beings. This is true for fathers as well as mothers. Although there has been an increase in the amount of time fathers spend with their adolescents, far too many fathers still do not develop adequate relationships with their adolescent daughters and sons.

Adolescents Deserve a Better Education

The importance of education in adolescence development was highlighted throughout *Adolescence*. There is a widespread agreement that something needs to be done about our nation's schools. We need schools that place a stronger emphasis on education that is developmentally appropriate. This needs to be accomplished at all levels of education, but especially in the middle school and junior high school grades.

The information and thinking society of the twenty-first century will not be content with products of education who have been trained to merely take in and recycle information handed out by teachers and other authority figures. Today's adolescents, who will become tomorrow's adults, need to experience an education that teaches them to think for themselves and to generate new information. This transformation is occurring in some, but not nearly enough, schools.

Schools and classrooms for adolescents also need to be smaller, place more emphasis on health and well-being, involve parents and community leaders, provide better counseling services, and be more sensitive to individual variations in adolescent development. In short, our nation's secondary schools need a major overhaul if we are to truly be sensitive to how adolescents develop.

Adolescents Deserve to Live and Develop in a More Equitable Gender World

Another important dimension of adolescents' lives that needs to be addressed in helping them reach their full potential is gender. Throughout *Adolescence* we emphasized how the world of adolescents and adults has not been a very fair gender world. Not only have ethnic minority adolescents grown up in a world that has confronted them with bias and discrimination, so have adolescent girls.

An important goal of this book has been to extensively evaluate the gender worlds of adolescents and to promote gender equity in adolescent development. I (your author) have two daughters who are now in their mid twenties. As Tracy and Jennifer were growing up, there were many instances when I felt they experienced bias and discrimination because they were females—in school, in athletics, and in many other contexts of their lives. My wife and I wanted them to have the opportunities to reach their full potential and not be limited by a gender-biased society and authority figures. Our hope was that they would not only develop strengths in traditional feminine domains, such as relationship skills, but also acquire a sense of self-assertiveness, a traditionally masculine domain, that would serve them well in their quest to become competent persons. I hope that all adolescents have this opportunity, and that Tracy's and Jennifer's adolescents will have fewer gender barriers to break through than they did.

Knowledge About Adolescent Development Has Benefited from a Diversity of Theories and an Extensive Research Enterprise

A number of theories have made important contributions to our understanding of adolescent development. From the social theories of Erikson and Bronfenbrenner to the cognitive theory of Piaget, each has contributed an important piece of the developmental puzzle. However, no single theory is capable of predicting, explaining, and organizing the rich, complex, multifaceted landscape of the adolescent's developmental journey. The inability of a single theory to explain all of adolescent development should not be viewed as a shortcoming of the theory. Any theory that attempts to explain all of adolescent development is too general. The field of adolescent development has been moved forward by theories that are precise and zero in on key aspects of one or two dimensions of adolescents' lives rather than by theories that try to do everything.

Knowledge about adolescent development has also benefited from a research effort that has greatly expanded over the last two decades. The science of adolescent development is rapidly becoming a highly sophisticated field in which collecting evidence about adolescent development is based on well-defined rules, exemplary practices, mathematical procedures for handling the evidence, and drawing inferences from what has been found.

Adolescents Benefit from Both Basic and Applied Research

Across the sixteen chapters of *Adolescence*, we have discussed both basic research and applied research. Basic research, sometimes called pure research, is the study of issues to obtain knowledge for its own sake rather than for practical application. By contrast, applied research is the study of issues that have direct practical significance, often with the intent of changing human behavior. Social policy research is applied research, not basic research.

A developmentalist who conducts basic research might ask: How is the cognitive development of adolescents different from that of children? By contrast, a developmentalist who conducts applied research might ask: How can knowledge about adolescents' and children's cognitive development be used to educate them more effectively or help them cope more effectively with stress?

Most developmentalists believe that both basic and applied research contributes to improving adolescents' lives. Although basic research sometimes produces information that can be applied to improve the well-being of adolescents, it does not guarantee this application. But insisting that research always be relevant is like trying to grow flowers by focusing only on the blossoms and not tending to the roots.

Adolescent Development Is Influenced by an Interaction of Heredity and Environment

Both heredity and environment are necessary for adolescents to even exist. Heredity and environment operate together—or cooperate—to produce an adolescent's height and weight, ability to shoot a basketball, intelligence, reading skills, temperament, and all other dimensions of the adolescent's development.

In chapter 1, we discussed the nature-nurture controversy, the debate about whether development is primarily influenced by heredity and maturation (nature) or by environment and experience (nurture). The debate shows no signs of subsiding, but for now virtually all developmentalists are interactionists, accepting that adolescent development is determined by both heredity and environment. Behavior geneticists continue to specify more precisely the nature of heredity-environment interaction through concepts such as those of passive, evocative, and active genotype/environment interactions and shared and nonshared environmental influences.

Adolescent Development Involves Both Continuity and Discontinuity

Some developmentalists emphasize the continuity of development, the view that development involves gradual, cumulative change from conception to death. Others stress the discontinuity of development, the view that development consists of distinct stages in the life span.

Development involves both continuity and discontinuity. For example, although Piaget's stages reflect discontinuity, in the sense that adolescents change from being concrete to formal operational thinkers, researchers have found that children's and adolescents' intelligence shows more continuity than once was believed. Who is right? Probably both. As Piaget envisioned, most concrete operational children do not think hypothetically and don't solve problems in a scientific manner. In this aspect, development is stagelike, as Piaget proposed. However, as information-processing psychologists believe, adolescents' thinking is not as stagelike as Piaget believed.

Adolescent Development Is Determined by Both Early and Later Experiences

Adolescents' development is determined by both early and later experiences. However, developmentalists still debate how strong the contributions of each type of experience are. The early-experience advocates argue that early experiences, especially in infancy, are more important than later experiences are. They believe, for example, that warm, nurturant, sensitive parenting in the first year of life is necessary for optimal later development, even in adolescence or adulthood. Later experiences in childhood and adolescence are not as important in shaping the individual's developmental path, they say.

By contrast, other developmentalists stress that later experiences are just as important as early experiences in adolescent development. That is, warm, nurturant, sensitive parenting is just as important in the elementary school years and adolescence in shaping development as it is in infancy. People in Western cultures are stronger advocates of early experience, those in Eastern cultures of later experiences. The debate continues.

Adolescent Development Is Determined by an Interaction of Biological, Cognitive, and Socioemotional Processes

Biological processes involve changes in the adolescent's physical nature, such as genes inherited from parents and the hormonal changes of puberty. Cognitive processes involve changes in the adolescent's thought and intelligence, such as memorizing a poem or solving a math problem. Socioemotional processes involve changes in the adolescent's relationships with other people, emotions, and personality, such as the intimate conversation of two friends, an adolescent girl's sadness and depression, and a shy, introverted adolescent boy.

In many parts of the book, you read about how biological, cognitive, and socioemotional processes are intricately interwoven. For example, biology plays a role in adolescents' temperament, especially influencing how shy or gregarious they are. Inadequate parenting and schooling can harm the adolescent's intelligence. Cognitive changes substantially alter how adolescents think about their parents and peers. Both theory and research focused on adolescent development are becoming more integrated and less compartmentalized as links across different domains are sought.

Adolescent Development Involves Both Commonalities with Other Adolescents and Individual Variation

Most every adolescent develops like all other adolescents, in certain ways. Most every adolescent is reared by one or more adult caregivers who have more power than the adolescent does; most every adolescent engages in peer relations, goes to school, and becomes more independent and searches for an identity.

But adolescents are not always like collections of geese; they are unique, each adolescent writing an individual history. One adolescent may grow up in the well-manicured lawns of suburbia, another in the ghetto confines of an inner city. One adolescent may be tall, another short. One adolescent may be a genius, another mentally retarded. One adolescent may have been abused as a child, another lavished with love. And one adolescent may be highly motivated to learn, another could care less.

Adolescent Development Is Determined by Internal/External and Self/Other Influences

Controversy still surrounds whether adolescents are architects of their own development (internal, self-determined) or whether their development primarily is orchestrated by the external forces of others. However, most experts on adolescence recognize that development is not entirely external and other-determined and, likewise, not entirely internal and self-generated. Trying to tease apart internal/external and self/other influences is extraordinarily difficult because the adolescent is always embedded in a social context with others. To be certain, adolescents are not helplessly buffeted about by their environment. Adolescents bring certain developmental capacities to any situation and act on the situation. At the same time, however, they interact with others who offer their own versions of the world, which adolescents sometimes learn from and adopt for themselves. At times, adolescents are like solitary scientists, crafting their own books of dreams and reality as Piaget envisioned; at other times, they are socially intertwined with skilled teachers and peers, as Vygotsky conceived.

America, especially male America, has had a history of underscoring the importance of self-determination and individualism. Recently, however, females have challenged the status of self-determination as a more important human value than being connected to others and competent at relationships. And as psychologists have become more interested in cultures around the world, they have begun to recognize that many cultures, especially Eastern cultures, promote values that emphasize concern for others, interdependence, and harmonious relationships. It is important for us to raise a nation of adolescents who not only value a separate "I," uniqueness, and self-determination, but who also value connectedness with others, concern for others, and harmony in relationships.

Adolescents' Behavior Is Multiply Determined

An important aspect of thinking about the behavior of any adolescent is that the adolescent's behavior is multiply determined. When we think about what causes an adolescent's behavior, we often lean toward explaining it in terms of a single cause. Consider a 12-year-old adolescent boy named Bobby. His teachers say that he is having trouble in school because he is from a father-absent home. The implication is that not having a father present in the home causes Bobby's poor academic performance. Not having a father may be one factor in Bobby's poor performance in school, but many others also influence his behavior. These factors include his genetic heritage and a host of environmental and sociocultural experiences, both in the past and in the present. On closer inspection of Bobby's circumstances, we learn that not only has his father been absent all of Bobby's life, but that his extended-family support system also has been weak. We also learn that he lives in a low-income area with little community support for recreation, libraries, and families. The school system in which Bobby is enrolled has a poor record of helping low-achieving adolescents and has little interest in developing programs for adolescents from disadvantaged circumstances. We could find other reasons that help explain Bobby's poor school achievement, but these examples illustrate the importance of going beyond accepting a single cause as the reason for an adolescent's behavior. As with each of us, Bobby's behavior is multiply determined.

Adolescents Will Benefit from an Interdisciplinary Approach to Their Development

Some of you taking this class on adolescence are being taught by a developmental psychologist, others by someone who specializes in human development or family relationships, others by an educational psychologist or professor in an education department, others by a nurse or pediatrician, and yet others by professors from different disciplines. The field of adolescent development has become more interdisciplinary. Our knowledge about adolescents, and how to improve adolescents' lives, has benefited, and will continue to benefit, from the contributions of scholars and professionals in a number of disciplines, including developmental psychology, education and educational psychology, pediatrics and nursing, clinical psychology, counseling, and psychiatry, sociology, anthropology, and law. The collaboration between developmental psychologists and pediatricians, nurses, and psychiatrists is one example of this interdisciplinary cooperation; the emerging area of how development influences adolescents' health reflects this cross-disciplinary trend.

THE JOURNEY OF ADOLESCENCE

We have come to the end of this book. I hope you can now look back and say that you learned a lot about adolescents, not only other adolescents but yourself as an adolescent and how your adolescent years contributed to who you are today. The insightful words of philosopher Søren Kierkegaard capture the importance of looking backward to understand ourselves: "Life is lived forward, but understood backwards." I also hope that those of you who become the parents of adolescents or work with adolescents in some capacity—whether as teacher, counselor, or community leader—feel that you now have a better grasp of what adolescence is all about. I leave you with the following montage of thoughts and images that convey the power, complexity, and beauty of adolescence in the human life span:

In no order of things is adolescence the time of simple life. Adolescents feel like they can last forever, think they know everything, and are quite sure about it. They clothe themselves with rainbows and go brave as the zodiac, flashing from one end of the world to the other both in mind and body. In many ways, today's adolescents are privileged, wielding unprecedented economic power. At the same time, they move through a seemingly endless preparation for life. They try on one face after another, seeking to find a face of their own. In their most pimply and awkward moments, they become acquainted with sex. They play furiously at "adult games" but are confined to a society of their own peers. They want their parents to understand them and hope that their parents will accord them the privilege of understanding them. Their generation of young people is the fragile cable by which the best and the worst of their parents' generation is transmitted to the present. In the end, there are only two lasting gifts parents can leave youth— one is roots, the other is wings.

John W. Santrock

GLOSSARY

abnormal behavior   Behavior that is maladaptive and harmful.   469

abstract relations   Fischer's term for the ability of an adolescent to coordinate two or more abstract ideas; this ability often appears for the first time between 14 and 16 years of age.   121

accommodation   This occurs when individuals adjust to new information.   107

acculturation   Cultural change that results from continuous, firsthand contact between two distinctive cultural groups.   280, 517

acculturative stress   The negative consequences of acculturation.   517

achievement motivation   The desire to accomplish something, to reach a standard of excellence, and to expend effort to excel.   440

achievement test   This type of test measures what has been learned, or what skills have been mastered.   148

active (niche-picking) genotype-environment interactions   The type of interactions that occur when adolescents seek out environments they find compatible and stimulating.   82

addiction   Physical dependence on a drug.   471

adolescence   The developmental period of transition from childhood to early adulthood; it involves biological, cognitive, and socioemotional changes.   24

adolescent egocentrism   The heightened self-consciousness of adolescents, which is reflected in their belief that others are as interested in them as they themselves are and in their sense of personal uniqueness.   122

adolescent generalization gap   Adelson's concept of widespread generalizations about adolescents based on information about a limited, highly visible group of adolescents.   13

adoption study   A study in which investigators seek to discover whether, in behavior and psychological characteristics, adopted children and adolescents are more like their adoptive parents, who provided a home environment, or their biological parents, who contributed their heredity. Another form of adoption study is to compare adoptive and biological siblings.   80

aerobic exercise   Sustained exercise, such as jogging, or swimming, that stimulates heart and lung activity.   510

affectionate love   Also called companionate love, this love occurs when an individual desires to have another person near and has a deep, caring affection for that person.   232

AIDS   Acquired immune deficiency syndrome, a primarily sexually transmitted disease caused by the HIV virus, which destroys the body's immune system.   386

alternation model   This model assumes that it is possible for an individual to know and understand two different cultures. It also assumes that individuals can alter their behavior to fit a particular social context.   280

altruism   Unselfish interest in helping another person.   416

amphetamines   Called pep pills or uppers, these are widely prescribed stimulants, sometimes in the form of diet pills.   476

anal stage   The second Freudian stage of development, occurring between 1½ and 3 years of age, in which the child's greatest pleasure involves the anus or the eliminative functions associated with it.   44

androgens   The main class of male sex hormones.   89

androgyny   The presence of a high degree of desirable feminine and masculine characteristics in the same individual.   354

anorexia nervosa   An eating disorder that involves the relentless pursuit of thinness through starvation.   509

anticonformity   This occurs when individuals react counter to a group's expectations and deliberately move away from the actions or beliefs the group advocates.   214

approach/approach conflict   This occurs when an individual must choose between two attractive stimuli or circumstances.   515

approach/avoidance conflict   This occurs when there is a single stimulus or circumstance, but it has both positive and negative characteristics.   515

approach strategies   Coping strategies that include cognitive attempts to understand the stressor and behavioral attempts to cope with the stressor by dealing directly with it or its consequences.   520

aptitude test   This type of test predicts an individual's ability to learn a skill, or what the individual can accomplish with training.   148

aptitude-treatment interaction (ATI)   This interaction stresses the importance of both the attitudes and the characteristics of the adolescent, such as academic potential or personality traits, and the treatments or experiences, such as the educational techniques, that the adolescent receives. *Aptitude* refers to such characteristics as the academic potential and personality characteristics on which students differ; *treatment* refers to educational techniques, such as structured versus flexible classrooms.   256

assimilation   The absorption of ethnic minority groups into the dominant group, which often means the loss of some or virtually all of the behavior and values of the ethnic minority group.   107, 208

attention   The concentration and focusing of mental effort. Attention is both selective and shifting.   137

attention-deficit hyperactivity disorder A disorder characterized by a short attention span, distractibility, and high levels of physical activity. Also called hyperactivity. 266

attribution theory The theory that individuals are motivated to discover the underlying causes of behavior as part of the effort to make sense out of behavior. 440

authoritarian parenting This is a restrictive, punitive style in which the parent exhorts the adolescent to follow the parent's directions and to respect work and effort. Firm limits and controls are placed on the adolescent, and little verbal exchange is allowed. This style is associated with adolescents' socially incompetent behavior. 181

authoritative parenting This style encourages adolescents to be independent but still places limits and controls on their actions. Extensive verbal give-and-take is allowed, and parents are warm and nurturant toward the adolescent. This style is associated with adolescents' socially competent behavior. 181

automaticity The ability to perform automatically with little or no effort. 137

autonomous morality The second stage of moral development in Piaget's theory, displayed by older children (about 10 years of age and older). The child becomes aware that rules and laws are created by people and that, in judging an action, one should consider the actor's intentions as well as the consequences. 405

autonomy versus shame and doubt Erikson's second stage of development, occurring in late infancy and toddlerhood (1–3 years). 45

avoidance/avoidance conflict This occurs when an individual must make a choice between two unattractive stimuli, both of which he or she wants to avoid. 515

avoidance strategies Coping strategies that include cognitive attempts to deny or minimize the stressor and behavioral attempts to withdraw from or avoid the stressor. 520

back-to-basics movement This philosophy stresses that the function of schools should be the rigorous training of intellectual skills through such subjects as English, mathematics, and science. 243

barbiturates Depressant drugs that induce sleep or reduce anxiety; examples are Nembutal and Seconal. 477

basal metabolism rate (BMR) The minimum amount of energy an individual uses in a resting state is the BMR. 507

becoming parents and families with children The third stage in the family life cycle, in which adults now move up a generation and become caregivers to the younger generation. 178

behavior genetics The study of the degree and nature of behavior's hereditary basis. 79

behavioral medicine This field is closely related to health psychology in that it attempts to combine medical and behavioral knowledge to reduce illness and promote health. 503

behaviorism The developmental theory that emphasizes the scientific study of observable behavioral responses and their environmental determinants. 50

biological processes Changes in an individual's physical nature. 22

bisexual A person who is attracted to people of both sexes. 375

boundary ambiguity The uncertainty in stepfamilies about who is in or out of the family and who is performing or responsible for certain tasks in the family system. 194

bulimia In this eating disorder, the individual consistently follows a binge-and-purge eating pattern. 510

burnout A hopeless, helpless feeling brought on by relentless work-related stress. 515

canalization The process by which characteristics take a narrow path or developmental course. Apparently, preservative forces help protect a person from environmental extremes. 79

care perspective The moral perspective of Carol Gilligan, that views people in terms of their connectedness with others and emphasizes interpersonal communication, relationships with others, and concern for others. 410

career self-concept theory Super's theory that individuals' self-concepts play a central role in their career choices and that in adolescence individuals first construct their career self-concept. 447

case study This is an in-depth look at an individual; it is used mainly by clinical psychologists when the unique aspects of a person's life cannot be duplicated, for either practical or ethical reasons. 58

Chicano The name politically conscious Mexican American adolescents give themselves, reflecting the combination of their Spanish-Mexican-Indian heritage and Anglo influence. 296

chlamydia The most common of all sexually transmitted diseases, named for *Chlamydia trachomitis*, an organism that spreads by sexual contact and infects the genital organs of both sexes. 384

chronosystem In Bronfenbrenner's ecological theory, the patterning of environmental events and transitions over the life course and sociohistorical circumstances. 53

classification Piaget's concept of concrete operational thought, the stage in which children become able to systematically organize objects into hierarchies of classes and subclasses. Also called class inclusion reasoning. 108

clinical depression This involves being diagnosed as experiencing major depressive disorder or dysthymic disorder. 488

cliques These units are smaller, involve more intimacy, and are more cohesive than crowds. They are, however, larger and involve less intimacy than friendships. 226

cocaine A stimulant that comes from the coca plant, which is native to Bolivia and Peru. 476

cognitive appraisal   Using this term, Lazarus describes individuals' interpretations of events in their lives as harmful, threatening, or challenging and their determination of whether they have the resources to cope effectively with the event.   517

cognitive developmental theory of gender   In this view, children's gender-typing occurs after they have developed a concept of gender. Once they begin to consistently conceive themselves as male or female, children often organize their world on the basis of gender.   347

cognitive disequilibrium theory   Hoffman's theory that adolescence is an important period in moral development, in which, because of broader experiences associated with the move to high school or college, individuals recognize that their set of beliefs is but one of many and that there is considerable debate about what is right and wrong.   406

cognitive monitoring   The process of taking stock of what one is currently doing, what will be done next, and how effectively the mental activity is unfolding.   139

cognitive moral education   An indirect moral education approach that emphasizes that individuals adopt such values as democracy and justice as their moral reasoning is developed.   419

cognitive processes   Changes in an individual's thought, intelligence, and language.   22

cognitive social learning theory of moral development   The theory that distinguishes between *moral competence*—the ability to produce moral behaviors—and *moral performance*—those behaviors in specific situations.   413

cohort effects   Effects due to an individual's time of birth or generation but not actually to age.   64

commitment   The part of identity development in which adolescents show a personal investment in what they are going to do.   325

community rights versus individual rights   The fifth stage in Kohlberg's theory of moral development. Individuals understand that values and laws are relative and that standards vary from one person to another.   407

computer-assisted instruction   A teaching strategy that involves using computers as tutors to individualize instruction: to present information, to give students practice, to assess students' level of understanding, and to provide additional information if needed.   141

concrete operational stage   The third Piagetian developmental stage, which lasts from 7 to 11 years of age. Children can perform operations, and logical reasoning replaces intuitive thought as long as reasoning can be applied to specific or concrete examples.   47, 107

conduct disorder   The psychiatric diagnostic category for the occurrence of multiple delinquent activities over a 6-month period. These behaviors include truancy, running away, fire setting, cruelty to animals, breaking and entering, and excessive fighting.   482

conformity   This occurs when individuals adopt the attitudes or behaviors of others because of real or imagined pressure from them.   213

conglomerate strategies   These strategies, also referred to as coaching, involve the use of a combination of techniques to improve adolescents' social skills.   216

connectedness   An important element in adolescent identity development. It consists of two dimensions: mutuality, sensitivity to and respect for others' views; and permeability, openness to others' views.   327

conscience   The component of the superego that involves behaviors disapproved of by parents.   415

consensual validation   This explains why adolescents are attracted to others who are similar to themselves. The adolescent's own attitudes and behavior are supported when someone else's attitudes and behavior are similar to theirs.   231

conservation   Piaget's term for an individual's ability to recognize that the length, number, mass, quantity, area, weight, and volume of objects do not change through transformations that alter their appearance.   108

contexts   Settings in which development occurs. These settings are influenced by historical, economic, social, and cultural factors.   17

continuity of development   Gradual, cumulative change from conception to death.   27

continuity view   A developmental view that emphasizes the role of early parent-child relationships in constructing a basic way of relating to people throughout the life span.   174

controversial children   Children who are frequently nominated both as a best friend and as being disliked.   215

conventional reasoning   The second, or intermediate, level in Kohlberg's theory of moral development. Internalization is intermediate. Individuals abide by certain standards (internal), but they are the standards of others (external), such as parents or the laws of society.   407

convergent thinking   Thinking that produces only one correct answer and is characteristic of the type of thinking elicited by standardized intelligence tests.   161

cooperative learning   Joint participation by all members of a group in achieving a learning goal. Each member contributes to the learning process.   262

correlation coefficient   A number based on statistical analysis, used to describe the degree of association between two variables.   61

correlational strategy   The goal in this strategy is to describe the strength of the relation between two or more events or characteristics.   61

creativity   The ability to think about something in a novel and unusual way and to come up with unique solutions to problems.   161

crisis   A period of identity development during which the adolescent is choosing among meaningful alternatives.   325

critical thinking A style of thinking that involves grasping the deeper meaning of problems, keeping an open mind about different approaches and perspectives, and deciding for oneself what to do or believe. 140

cross-cultural studies Studies that compare a culture with one or more other cultures. Such studies provide information about the degree to which adolescent development is similar, or universal, across cultures or about the degree to which it is culture-specific. 17, 278

cross-sectional approach A research strategy in which individuals of different ages are compared all at one time. 63

crowd The largest, most loosely defined, and least personal unit of adolescent peer society. Crowds often meet because of their mutual interest in an activity. 226

cultural-familial retardation A mental deficit in which no evidence of organic brain damage can be found; IQs range from 50 to 70. Psychologists suspect that such mental deficits result from the normal variation that distributes people along the range of intelligence scores above 50, combined with growing up in a below-average intellectual environment. 157

culture The behavior, patterns, beliefs, and all other products of a particular group of people that are passed on from generation to generation. 17, 277

culture-fair tests Intelligence tests that attempt to not be culturally biased. 154

date, or acquaintance, rape Coercive sexual activity directed at someone with whom the perpetrator is at least casually acquainted. 392

dating scripts The cognitive models that adolescents and adults use to guide and evaluate dating interactions. 230

defense mechanisms The psychoanalytic term for unconscious methods used by the ego to distort reality in order to protect itself from anxiety. 42

dependent variable The factor that is measured in an experiment; it may change because of the manipulation of the independent variable. 63

depressants Drugs that slow the central nervous system, bodily functions, and behavior. 477

depressed mood Periods of sadness or unhappy mood that can last for a brief or an extended period of time. They may occur as a result of the loss of a significant relationship or failure on an important task. 488

depressive syndromes A cluster of behaviors and emotions that includes feeling lonely, crying, fear of doing bad things, feeling the need to be perfect, feeling unloved, feeling worthless, nervous, guilty, or sad, and worrying. 488

desatellization Ausubel's term for the adolescent process of breaking away and becoming independent from parents. 185

development The pattern of change that begins at conception and continues through the life cycle. Most development involves growth, although it also includes decay (as in death and dying). 22

developmental career choice theory Ginzberg's theory that children and adolescents go through three career-choice stages: fantasy, tentative, and realistic. 447

developmental construction views Views sharing the belief that as individuals grow up, they acquire modes of relating to others. There are two main variations of this view. One emphasizes continuity and stability in relationships throughout the life span; the other emphasizes discontinuity and changes in relationships throughout the life span. 174

difficult child A temperament category that involves reacting negatively, fussing a lot, engaging in irregular daily routines, and being slow to accept new experiences. 81

direct moral education Education that involves either emphasizing values or character traits during specified time slots or integrating those values or traits throughout the curriculum. 417

discontinuity of development Development progressing through distinct stages in the life span. 27

discontinuity view A developmental view that emphasizes change and growth in relationships over time. 175

divergent thinking Thinking that produces many different answers to one question and is more characteristic of creativity than of traditional intelligence. 161

dysthymic disorder This occurs when adolescents have a period of at least 1 year in which they have shown depressed or irritable mood every day without more than 2 symptom-free months. Further, dysthymic disorder requires the presence of at least two of the following symptoms: eating problems; sleeping problems; lack of energy; low self-esteem; reduced concentration or decision-making ability; and feelings of hopelessness. 488

early adolescence The developmental period that corresponds roughly to the middle school or junior high school years and includes most pubertal change. 24

early adulthood The developmental period that usually begins in the late teens or early twenties and lasts through the thirties. 24

early childhood The developmental period that extends from the end of infancy to about 5 or 6 years of age; sometimes called the preschool years. 23

early formal operational thought In this portion of Piaget's stage of formal operational thought, adolescents' increased ability to think in hypothetical ways produces unconstrained thought with unlimited possibilities. In this early period, formal operational thought submerges reality, and there is an excess of assimilation as the world is perceived too subjectively and idealistically. 111

early-later experience issue This issue focuses on the degree to which early experiences (especially early in childhood) or later experiences are the key determinants of development. 27

easy child A temperament category that involves being in a positive mood, quickly establishing routines, and adapting easily to new experiences. 81

eclectic theoretical orientation An orientation in which one does not follow any single theoretical approach, but instead selects and uses whatever is best in each theory. 56

ecological theory Bronfenbrenner's sociocultural view of development, involving five environmental systems—microsystem, mesosystem, eosystem, macrosystem, and chronosystem. These emphasize the role of social contexts in development. 51

ego The Freudian structure of personality that deals with the demands of reality. 42

ego ideal The component of the superego that involves ideal standards approved by parents. 415

emic approach In this approach, the goal is to describe behavior in one culture or ethnic group in terms that are meaningful and important to the people in that group, without regard to other cultures or ethnic groups. 59

emotion-focused coping Lazarus's term for the coping strategy in which individuals respond to stress in an emotional manner, especially using defensive appraisal. 519

emotional isolation A type of loneliness that arises when a person lacks an intimate attachment relationship; single, divorced, and widowed adults often experience this type of loneliness. 333

empathy Reacting to another's feelings with an emotional response that is similar to the other's response. 416

equilibration A mechanism in Piaget's theory that explains how children and adolescents shift from one stage of thought to the next. The shift occurs as they experience cognitive conflict or a disequilibrium in trying to understand the world. Eventually, they resolve the conflict and reach an equilibrium of thought. 107

estradiol An estrogen that plays an important role in female pubertal development. 89

estrogens The main class of female sex hormones. 89

ethnic gloss Using an ethnic label, such as *African American, Latino, Asian American,* or *Native American,* in a superficial way that makes an ethnic group seem more homogeneous than it actually is. 60

ethnic identity A sense of membership based upon the language, religions, customs, values, history, and race of an ethnic group. 17

ethnicity A dimension of culture based on cultural heritage, nationality, race, religion, and language. 17, 277

ethnocentrism A tendency to favor one's group over other groups. 277

etic approach The goal in this approach is to describe behaviors so that generalizations can be made across cultures. 59

eustress This is Selye's concept of the positive features of stress. 514

evocative genotype-environment interactions The type of interactions that occur when the adolescent's genotype elicits certain types of physical and social environments. 82

exosystem In Bronfenbrenner's ecological theory, this is involved when experiences in a system in which the individual does not have an active role influence what the individual experiences in the immediate context. 52

experience sampling method A research method in which participants carry electronic pagers, usually for a week, and provide reports on their activities when signaled by the pagers at random times. 283

experimental strategy This strategy allows investigators to precisely determine behavior's causes by performing an experiment in a precisely regulated setting in which one or more of the factors believed to influence the behavior being studied are manipulated and all others are held constant. 61

extrinsic motivation The desire to accomplish something in order to obtain external rewards or avoid external punishments. 441

family at midlife The fifth stage in the family life cycle. It is a time of launching children, playing an important role in linking generations, and adapting to midlife changes in development. 180

family in later life The sixth and final stage in the family life cycle. Retirement alters a couple's lifestyle, requiring adaptation. Grandparenting also characterizes many families in this period. 180

family structure model of divorce effects This model states that when adolescents from different family structures are compared, any differences in the adolescents are due to family structure variations. 192

family with adolescents The fourth stage in the family life cycle. Adolescence is a period of development in which individuals push for autonomy and seek to develop their own identities. 180

fear of success This occurs when individuals worry that they will be socially rejected if they are successful. 440

feminization of poverty The fact that far more women than men live in poverty. Women's low income, divorce, and the resolution of divorce cases by the judicial system, which leaves women with less money than they and their children need to adequately function, are the likely causes. 288

forgiveness This is an aspect of altruism that occurs when an injured person releases the injured from possible behavioral retaliation. 417

formal operational stage The fourth and final Piagetian developmental stage, which appears between the ages of 11 and 15. Individuals move beyond the world of concrete experiences and think in abstract and more logical terms. 48, 109

fraternal twins Twins who develop from separate eggs and separate sperm, making them genetically no more similar than nontwin siblings. Also called dizygotic twins. 80

frustration Any situation in which an individual cannot reach a desired goal. 515

fusion model This model reflects the assumptions behind the melting pot theory, which implies that cultures sharing economic, political, or geographic boundaries will fuse together until they are indistinguishable and form a new culture. 281

gender The sociocultural dimension of being male or female. 18, 343

gender intensification hypothesis This hypothesis states that psychological and behavioral differences between boys and girls become greater during early adolescence because of increased socialization pressures to conform to masculine and feminine gender roles. 358

gender role A set of expectations that prescribes how females and males should think, act, and feel. 343

gender-role transcendence The belief that, when an individual's competence is at issue, it should be conceptualized not on the basis of masculinity, femininity, or androgyny but, rather, on a person basis. 357

gender schema A cognitive structure that organizes the world in terms of male and female. 348

gender schema theory According to this theory, an individual's attention and behavior are guided by an internal motivation to conform to gender-based sociocultural standards and stereotypes. 348

gender stereotypes Broad categories that reflect our impressions and beliefs about females and males. 348

general adaptation syndrome (GAS) Selye's three-stage model of the common effects on the body when demands are placed on it. The stages are alarm, resistance, and exhaustion. 514

generational inequity The unfair treatment of younger members of an aging society in which older adults pile up advantages by receiving inequitably large allocations of resources, such as Social Security and Medicare. 21

generativity versus stagnation Erikson's seventh developmental stage, occurring during middle adulthood. A chief concern is to assist the younger generation in developing and leading useful lives—this is what Erikson meant by generativity. 46

genital herpes A sexually transmitted disease caused by a large family of viruses of different strains. These strains produce other, nonsexually transmitted diseases such as chicken pox and mononucleosis. Herpes simplex, an STD, has two variations. 385

genital stage The fifth and final Freudian stage of development, occurring from puberty on. This stage is one of sexual reawakening; the source of sexual pleasure now becomes someone outside of the family. 44

genotype A person's genetic heritage; the actual genetic material. 79

gifted Having above-average intelligence, usually an IQ of 120 or higher, and a superior talent for something. 158

gonads The sex glands—the testes in males and the ovaries in females. 89

gonorrhea Reported to be one of the most common STDs in the United States, this sexually transmitted disease is caused by a bacterium called *gonococcus*, which thrives in the moist mucous membranes lining the mouth, throat, vagina, cervix, urethra, and anal tract. This disease is commonly called the "drip" or the "clap." 384

goodness-of-fit model According to this model, an adolescent adapts best when there is a congruence, or match, between the adolescent's temperament and the demands of the social environment (such as the expectations and attitudes of parents, peers, and teachers). 82

hallucinogens Drugs that alter an individual's perceptual experiences and produce hallucinations; also called psychedelic or mind-altering drugs. 475

health psychology A multidimensional approach to health that emphasizes psychological factors, lifestyle, and the nature of the health-care delivery system. 503

helpless orientation Children with a helpless orientation seem trapped by the experience of difficulty and attribute their difficulty to a lack of ability. 442

heteronomous morality The first stage of moral development in Piaget's theory, occurring at 4 to 7 years of age. Justice and rules are conceived of as unchangeable properties of the world, removed from the control of people. 405

hidden curriculum The pervasive moral atmosphere that characterizes schools. 417

high-risk youth Youth who engage in the same behaviors as very-high-risk youth but with slightly lower frequency and less deleterious consequences. They commit less-serious delinquent offenses, are heavy users of alcohol, cigarettes, and marijuana, often engage in unprotected sexual intercourse, and are frequently behind in school. These constitute about 15 percent of the adolescent population. 490

horizontal décalage Piaget's concept that similar abilities do not appear at the same time within a stage of development. 108

hormones Powerful chemical substances secreted by the endocrine glands and carried through the body by the bloodstream. 89

hypothalamus A structure in the higher portion of the brain that monitors eating, drinking, and sex. 89

hypotheses Assumptions that can be tested to determine their accuracy. 41

hypothetical-deductive reasoning Piaget's term for adolescents' ability, in the stage of formal operational thought, to develop hypotheses, or best guesses, about ways to solve problems, such as algebraic equations. They then systematically deduce, or conclude, the best path to follow in solving the problem. 110

id The Freudian structure of personality that consists of instincts, which are an individual's reservoir of psychic energy. 42

identical twins Twins who develop from a single fertilized egg, which splits into two genetically identical replicas, each of which becomes a person. Also called monozygotic twins. 80

identity achievement Marcia's term for an adolescent's having undergone a crisis and made a commitment. 325

identity diffusion Marcia's term for the state adolescents are in when they have not yet experienced a crisis or made any commitments. 325

identity foreclosure Marcia's term for the state adolescents are in when they have made a commitment but have not experienced a crisis. 325

identity moratorium Marcia's term for the state of adolescents who are in the midst of a crisis, but whose commitments either are absent or are only vaguely defined. 325

identity versus identity confusion Erikson's fifth developmental stage, which individuals experience during the adolescent years. At this time, individuals are faced with finding out who they are, what they are all about, and where they are going in life. 46, 322

idiographic needs Needs that are important to the individual, not to the group. 67

imaginary audience According to Elkind, the imaginary audience involves attention-getting behavior—the desire to be noticed, visible, and "on stage." 122

immanent justice Piaget's concept that if a rule is broken, punishment will be meted out immediately. 405

implicit personality theory The layperson's conception of personality. 124

inclusion Educating children in their natural environment, such as typical elementary and secondary school classrooms. 265

independent variable The manipulated, influential, experimental factor in an experiment. 62

index offenses Whether they are committed by juveniles or adults, these are criminal acts, such as robbery, rape, and homicide. 482

indirect moral education An educational approach that encourages adolescents to define their own and others' values and helps define the moral perspectives that support those values. 417

individual differences The stable, consistent ways in which adolescents are different from each other. 144

individualism and purpose The second stage in Kohlberg's theory of moral development. Moral thinking is based on rewards and self-interest. 407

individuality An important element in adolescent identity development. It consists of two dimensions: self-assertion, the ability to have and communicate a point of view; and separateness, the use of communication patterns to express how one is different from others. 327

individuated-connected level The highest level of relationship maturity, at which there is evidence of an understanding of oneself, as well as consideration of others' motivations and anticipation of their needs. Concern and caring involve emotional support and individualized expression of interest. 332

induction A discipline technique in which a parent uses reason and explanation of the consequences for others of a child's actions. 415

indulgent parenting A style in which parents are highly involved with their adolescents but place few demands or controls on them. This is associated with adolescents' social incompetence, especially a lack of self-control. 181

industry versus inferiority Erikson's fourth developmental stage, occurring approximately in the elementary school years. Children's initiative brings them into contact with a wealth of new experiences. As they move into middle and late childhood, they direct their energy toward mastering knowledge and intellectual skills. 46

infancy The developmental period that extends from birth to 18 or 24 months. 23

information processing A model of cognition concerned with how individuals process information about their world—how information enters the mind, how it is stored and transformed, and how it is retrieved to perform such complex activities as problem solving and reasoning. 48

initiative versus guilt Erikson's third stage of development, occurring during the preschool years. As preschool children encounter a widening social world, they are challenged more than when they were infants. Active, purposeful behavior is needed to cope with these challenges. 45

insecure attachment In this attachment pattern, infants either avoid the caregiver or show considerable resistance or ambivalence toward the caregiver. This pattern is theorized to be related to difficulties in relationships and problems in later development. 187

integration The maintenance of cultural integrity while becoming an integral part of the larger culture. 281

integrity versus despair Erikson's eighth and final developmental stage, occurring in late adulthood. In our later years, we look back and evaluate what we have done with our lives, and experience a sense of either integrity or despair. 46

intelligence Often defined as verbal ability and problem-solving skills, intelligence also involves the ability to learn from and adapt to the experiences of everyday life. 144

intelligence quotient (IQ) Devised in 1912 by William Stern, IQ consists of a child's mental age divided by chronological age and multiplied by 100. 144

internalization The developmental change from behavior that is externally controlled to behavior that is controlled by internal standards and principles. 406

interpersonal norms The third stage in Kohlberg's theory of moral development. Individuals value trust, caring, and loyalty to others as the basis of moral judgments. 407

intimacy in friendship In most research, this is defined narrowly as self-disclosure or sharing of private thoughts. 219

intimacy versus isolation Erikson's sixth developmental stage, which individuals experience during the early adulthood years. At this time, individuals face the developmental task of forming intimate relationships with others. 46, 331

intimate style The individual forms and maintains one or more deep and long-lasting love relationships. 331

intrinsic motivation The internal desire to be competent and to do something for its own sake. 441

inventionist view The view that adolescence is a sociohistorical creation. Especially important in this view are the sociohistorical circumstances at the beginning of the twentieth century, a time when legislation was enacted that ensured the dependency of youth and made their move into the economic sphere more manageable. 11

isolated style The individual withdraws from social encounters and has little or no attachment to same- or opposite-sex individuals. 332

J

justice perspective A moral perspective that focuses on the rights of the individual; individuals independently make moral decisions. 410

juvenile delinquency A broad range of child and adolescent behaviors, including socially unacceptable behavior, status offenses, and criminal acts. 480

L

laboratory This is a controlled setting in which many of the complex factors of the "real world" are removed. 58

late adolescence Approximately the latter half of the second decade of life. Career interests, dating, and identity exploration are often more pronounced in late adolescence than in early adolescence. 24

late adulthood The developmental period that lasts from about 60 to 70 years of age until death. 25

late formal operational thought This period involves a restoration of intellectual balance. Adolescents now test the products of their reasoning against experience, and a consolidation of formal operational thought takes place. An intellectual balance is restored as the adolescent accommodates to the cognitive upheaval that has occurred. 111

latency stage The fourth Freudian stage of development, which occurs between approximately 6 years of age and puberty; the child represses all interest in sexuality and develops social and intellectual skills. 44

launching The process in which the youth moves into adulthood and exits his or her family of origin. 178

learned helplessness A sense of hopelessness and futility that develops in individuals when they have been exposed to averse stimulation, such as prolonged stress or pain, over which they have no control. 489

learning disabilities Individuals with learning disabilities have normal intelligence and academic difficulties in several areas, but they are not suffering from an overt condition or disorder that would explain their learning problems. 266

leaving home and becoming a single adult This is the first stage in the family life cycle and involves launching. 178

life course theory Glenn Elder's theory that human development can be best understood by considering lives in their historical time and place, the timing of social roles and life events, the interdependence or connections among lives, and the role of human agency and social constraints in decision making. 53

life-history records Records that present information about a lifetime chronology of events and activities; they often involve a combination of data records on education, work, family, and residence. 60

long-term memory A relatively permanent memory system that holds huge amounts of information for a long period of time. 138

longitudinal approach A research strategy in which the same individuals are studied over a period of time, usually several years or more. 64

love withdrawal A discipline technique in which a parent removes attention or love from a child. 415

LSD Lysergic acid diethylamide, a hallucinogen that, even in low doses, produces striking perceptual changes. 475

M

macrosystem In Bronfenbrenner's ecological theory, the system of culture in which an individual lives. 52

major depressive disorder This is present when the adolescent has experienced five or more of the following symptoms for at least a 2-week period at a level that differs from previous functioning: depressed mood or irritable most of the day; decreased interest in pleasurable activities; changes in weight or failure to make necessary weight gains in adolescence; sleep problems; psychomotor agitation or retardation; fatigue or loss of energy; feelings of worthlessness or abnormal amounts of guilt; reduced concentration and decision-making ability; and repeated suicidal ideation, suicide attempts, or plans of suicide. 488

marginalization The process in which groups are put out of cultural and psychological contact with both their traditional culture and the larger, dominant culture. 281

marijuana Originally from central Asia but now grown in most parts of the world, this mild hallucinogen comes from the hemp plant *Cannabis sativa*. 475

mastery orientation Children with a mastery orientation are task oriented. Instead of focusing on their ability, they are concerned about their learning strategies and the process of achievement rather than outcomes. 442

matching hypothesis This states that, although individuals may prefer a more attractive person in the abstract, they end up choosing someone who is close to their level of attractiveness. 231

maturation The orderly sequence of changes dictated by a genetic blueprint. 25

medical model Also called the disease model, this model was the forerunner of the biological approach. It states that abnormality is a disease or an illness precipitated by internal bodily causes. 469

memory The retention of information over time. 137

menarche A girl's first menstruation. 88

mental age (MA) According to Binet, this is an individual's level of mental development in relation to that of others. 144

mental retardation A condition of limited mental ability in which an individual has a low IQ, usually below 70 on a traditional test of intelligence, has difficulty adapting to everyday life, and has onset of these conditions during the so-called developmental period (by the age of 18). 157

mesosystem In Bronfenbrenner's ecological theory, the system of relations among microsystems, or connections between contexts. Examples are the relation of family experiences to school experiences, school experiences to work experiences, and family experiences to peer experiences. 52

microsystem In Bronfenbrenner's ecological theory, this system is the setting in which an individual lives. This context includes the person's family, peers, school, and neighborhood. The most direct interactions with social agents occur in the microsystem. 51

middle adulthood The developmental period that is entered at about 35 to 45 years and exited at about 55 to 65 years of age. 25

middle and late childhood The developmental period that extends from about 6 to 11 years of age; sometimes called the elementary school years. 24

moral character Having the strength of your convictions, persisting, and overcoming distractions and obstacles. 421

moral development Rules and values about what people should do in their interactions with other people. 405

moral judgment Making decisions about which actions are right and which are wrong. 420

moral motivation Prioritizing moral values over other personal values. 421

moral sensitivity Interpreting situations and being aware of how our actions affect other people. 420

motivation What impels individuals to behave, think, and feel the way they do, especially regarding the activation and direction of their behavior. 439

multicultural model This model promotes a pluralistic approach to understanding two or more cultures. It argues that people can maintain their distinctive identities while working with others from different cultures to meet common national or economic needs. 280

multiple-factor model of divorce effects This model takes into account the complexity of the divorce context and examines a number of influences on the adolescent's development, including such factors as type of custody, socioeconomic status, postdivorce family functioning, and strengths and weaknesses of the adolescent prior to the divorce. 192

multiple-factor theory Thurstone's theory that intelligence consists of seven primary mental abilities: verbal comprehension, number ability, word fluency, spatial visualization, associative memory, reasoning, and perceptual speed. 148

naturalistic observation A method in which scientists observe behavior in real-world settings and make no effort to manipulate or control the situation. 58

nature-nurture controversy *Nature* refers to an organism's biological inheritance, *nurture* to environmental experiences. "Nature" proponents claim that biological inheritance is the most important influence on development; nurture proponents claim that environmental experiences are the most important. 26

neglected children Children who are infrequently nominated as a best friend but are not disliked by their peers. 215

neglectful parenting A style in which the parent is very uninvolved in the adolescent's life. It is associated with adolescents' social incompetence, especially a lack of self-control. 181

neo-Piagetians Developmentalists who have elaborated on Piaget's theory; they believe that cognitive development is more specific than Piaget thought. 117

new couple The second stage in the family life cycle, in which two individuals from separate families of origin unite to form a new family system. 178

nomothetic research Research that is conducted at the group level, in which individual variation is not a major focus. 67

nonconformity This occurs when individuals know what people around them expect but do not use those expectations to guide their behavior. 214

nonshared environmental influences The adolescent's own unique experiences, both within a family and outside the family, that are not shared by another sibling. 83

normal distribution   A symmetrical pattern of scores in which most test scores fall in the middle of the possible range of scores and few scores appear toward either of the extremes of the range.   145

norms   Rules that apply to all members of a group.   222

Oedipus complex   In Freudian theory, the young child's intense desire to replace the parent of the same sex and enjoy the affections of the opposite-sex parent.   44

operations   Mental actions that allow an individual to do mentally what was done before physically. A concrete operational thinker can reverse actions mentally.   107

opiates   Opium and its derivatives, drugs that depress the activity of the central nervous system; commonly known as narcotics.   477

oral stage   The first Freudian stage of development, occurring during the first 18 months of life, in which the infant's pleasure centers around the mouth.   44

organic retardation   A form of mental retardation involving some physical damage and caused by a genetic disorder or brain damage.   157

passive genotype-environment interactions   Interactions that occur when parents who are genetically related to the child provide a rearing environment for the child.   82

peers   Children or adolescents who are of about the same age or maturity level.   211

performance orientation   Individuals with a performance orientation are concerned with achievement outcomes rather than achievement processes; winning is what matters to them, and they believe that happiness is a result of winning.   442

personal fable   According to Elkind, this is the part of adolescent egocentrism that involves an adolescent's sense of uniqueness.   122

personality type theory   Holland believes that an effort should be made to match an individual's career choice with his or her personality.   448

perspective taking   The ability to assume another person's perspective and understand his or her thoughts and feelings.   122

phallic stage   The third Freudian stage of development, which occurs between the ages of 3 and 6; its name comes from the Latin word *phallus*, which means "penis." During this stage, the child's pleasure focuses on the genitals, and the child discovers that self-manipulation is enjoyable.   44

phenotype   The way an individual's genotype is expressed in observed and measurable characteristics.   79

pituitary gland   An important endocrine gland that controls growth and regulates other glands.   89

pluralism   The coexistence of distinct ethnic and cultural groups in the same society.   294

popular children   Children who are frequently nominated as a best friend and are rarely disliked by their peers.   214

possible self   What individuals might become, what they would like to become, and what they are afraid of becoming.   316

postconventional reasoning   The highest level in Kohlberg's theory of moral development. Morality is completely internalized.   407

power assertion   A discipline technique in which a parent attempts to gain control over a child or a child's resources.   415

preconventional reasoning   The lowest level in Kohlberg's theory of moral development. The individual shows no internalization of moral values— moral reasoning is controlled by external rewards and punishment.   407

preintimate style   The individual shows mixed emotions about commitment, an ambivalence reflected in the strategy of offering love without obligations.   331

prejudice   An unjustified negative attitude toward an individual because of her or his membership in a group.   293

prenatal period   The time from conception to birth.   23

preoperational stage   The second Piagetian developmental stage, which lasts from about 2 to 7 years of age. Children begin to represent the world with words, images, and drawings.   107

primary appraisal   In this state, adolescents interpret whether an event involves harm or loss that has already occurred, a threat of future danger, or a challenge to be overcome.   517

problem-focused coping   Lazarus's term for the cognitive coping strategy used by individuals who face their troubles and try to solve them.   519

pseudointimate style   The individual maintains a long-lasting sexual attachment with little or no depth or closeness.   332

psychological dependence   A psychological need to take a drug, as when adolescents take a drug to help them cope with stress or problems.   471

psychometrics   The field that involves the assessment of individual differences.   144

psychosocial moratorium   Erikson's term for the gap between childhood security and adult autonomy that adolescents experience as part of their identity exploration.   322

puberty   A period of rapid physical maturation involving hormonal and bodily changes that occur primarily in early adolescence.   88

Public Law 94-142   The federal government's mandate to provide a free and appropriate education for all children and adolescents. A key provision of this bill is to develop an individualized education program for children and adolescents with special needs.   265

punishment and obedience orientation   The first stage in Kohlberg's theory of moral development. Moral thinking is based on punishment.   407

questionnaire   This is similar to a highly structured interview except that respondents read the questions and mark their answers on paper, rather than respond verbally to an interviewer.   58

random assignment This occurs when researchers assign subjects to experimental and control conditions by chance, thus reducing the likelihood that the results of the experiment will be due to preexisting differences in the two groups. 62

rape Forcible sexual intercourse with a person who does not consent to it. 392

reaction range The range of phenotypes for each genotype, suggesting the importance of the environment's restrictiveness or enrichment. 79

reciprocal socialization The process by which children and adolescents socialize parents, just as parents socialize them. 173

reciprocal teaching An instructional procedure developed by Brown and Palincsar to develop cognitive monitoring; it requires that students take turns in leading the study group in the use of strategies for comprehending and remembering text content. 139

rejected children Children who are infrequently nominated as a best friend and are actively disliked by their peers. 215

repression The most powerful and pervasive defense mechanism. It pushes unacceptable id impulses out of awareness and back into the unconscious mind. 42

resatellization Ausubel's term for a preliminary form of desatellization in which the individual's parents are replaced by other individuals or a group. 186

rites of passage Ceremonies or rituals that mark an individual's transition from one status to another, especially into adulthood. 281

role-focused level The second or intermediate level of relationship maturity, at which perceiving others as individuals in their own right begins to develop. However, at this level the perspective is stereotypical and emphasizes social acceptability. 332

roles Certain positions in a group that are governed by rules and expectations. Roles define how adolescents should behave in those positions. 222

romantic love Also called passionate love or eros, this love has strong sexual and infatuation components, and it often predominates in the early part of a love relationship. 232

satellization Ausubel's term for children's relinquishment of their sense of self-power and their acceptance of their dependency on their parents. 185

schema A cognitive structure or network of associations that organizes and guides an individual's perception. 348

scientific method An approach that can be used to discover accurate information about behavior and development that includes the following steps: identify and analyze the problem, collect data, draw conclusions, and revise theories. 41

second individuation crisis Blos's term for adolescents' development of a distinctiveness from their parents, which Blos believes is an attempt to transcend earlier parent-child ties and develop more self-responsibility. 186

secondary appraisal In this state, adolescents evaluate their resources and determine how effectively they can be used to cope with an event. 517

secure attachment In this attachment pattern, infants use their primary caregiver, usually the mother, as a secure base from which to explore the environment. Secure attachment is theorized to be an important foundation for psychological development later in childhood, adolescence, and adulthood. 187

self-concept Domain-specific evaluations of the self. 318

self-esteem The global evaluative dimension of the self. Self-esteem is also referred to as self-worth or self-image. 318

self-focused level The first level of relationship maturity, at which one's perspective of another or of a relationship is concerned only with how it affects oneself. 332

self-understanding The adolescent's cognitive representation of the self, the substance and content of the adolescent's self-conceptions. 315

sensorimotor stage The first of Piaget's developmental stages, in which infants construct an understanding of the world by coordinating sensory experiences with motoric actions—hence, the name *sensorimotor*. This stage lasts from birth to about 2 years of age. 47, 107

separation Self-imposed withdrawal from the larger culture. 281

set point The weight maintained when no effort is made to gain or lose weight. 509

sexism Prejudice and discrimination against an individual because of her or his sex. 349

sexual script A stereotyped pattern of role prescriptions for how individuals should behave sexually. Females and males have been socialized to follow different sexual scripts. 373

sexually transmitted diseases (STDs) Diseases that are contracted primarily through sexual contact. This contact is not limited to vaginal intercourse but includes oral-genital contact and anal-genital contact as well. 384

shared environmental influences Adolescents' common environmental experiences that are shared with their siblings, such as their parents' personalities and intellectual orientation, the family's social class, and the neighborhood in which they live. 83

short-term memory A limited-capacity memory system in which information is retained for as long as 30 seconds, unless the information is rehearsed, in which case it can be retained longer. 138

slow-to-warm-up child A temperament category that involves having a low activity level, being somewhat negative, showing low adaptability, and displaying a low intensity of mood. 81

social class Also called socioeconomic status or SES, this refers to a grouping of people with similar occupational, educational, and economic characteristics. 277

social cognition How individuals conceptualize and reason about their social world—the people they watch and interact with, relationships with those people, the groups in which they participate, and how they reason about themselves and others. 121

social conventional reasoning Thoughts about social consensus and convention, as opposed to moral reasoning that stresses ethical issues. 412

social information processing How individuals use cognitive processes, such as attention, perception, memory, thinking, reasoning, expectancies, and so on, to understand their social world. 121

social isolation A type of loneliness that occurs when a person lacks a sense of integrated involvement. Being deprived of participation in a group or community involving companionship, shared interests, organized activities, and meaningful roles causes a person to feel alienated, bored, and uneasy. 333

social learning theory The view of psychologists who emphasize a combination of behavior, environment, and cognition as the key factors in development. 50

social learning theory of gender This theory emphasizes that children's and adolescents' gender development occurs through observation and imitation of gender behavior, and through rewards and punishments they experience for gender-appropriate and -inappropriate behavior. 344

social policy A national government's course of action designed to influence the welfare of its citizens. 19

social systems morality The fourth stage in Kohlberg's theory of moral development. Moral judgments are based on understanding the social order, law, justice, and duty. 407

socioemotional processes Changes in an individual's relationships with other people, emotions, personality, and social contexts. 22

standardized tests Tests that require an individual to answer a series of written or oral questions. These tests have two distinct features: First, psychologists usually total an individual's score to yield a single score, or set of scores, that reflects something about the individual. Second, psychologists compare the individual's score with the scores of a large group of persons to determine how the individual responded relative to others. 59

status offenses Performed by youths under a specified age, these are juvenile offenses that are not as serious as index offenses. These offenses may include such acts as drinking under age, truancy, and sexual promiscuity. 482

stereotype A broad category that reflects our impressions and beliefs about people. All stereotypes refer to an image of what the typical member of a particular group is like. 13

stereotyped style The individual has superficial relationships that tend to be dominated by friendship ties with same-sex rather than opposite-sex individuals. 332

stimulants Drugs that increase the activity of the central nervous system. 475

storm-and-stress view G. Stanley Hall's concept that adolescence is a turbulent time charged with conflict and mood swings. 9

strategies Activities that are under the learner's conscious control. They may also be called control processes, and there are many of them. One of the most important is organization, which is the tendency to group items into categories. 138

stress Stressors are circumstances and events that threaten or tax an individual's coping ability. Stress is the response to stressors. 513

superego The Freudian structure of personality that is the moral branch. This branch takes into account whether something is right or wrong. 42

synchrony The carefully coordinated interaction between the parent and the child or adolescent in which, often unknowingly, they are attuned to each other's behavior. 173

syphilis A sexually transmitted disease caused by the bacterium *Treponema pallidum*, a spirochete. 384

temperament An individual's behavioral style and characteristic way of responding. 81

testosterone An androgen that plays an important role in male pubertal development. 89

theory A coherent set of ideas that help explain data and make predictions. 41

tolerance A physical state in which a greater amount of a drug is needed to produce the same effect as had earlier been produced by a smaller amount of the drug. 471

top-dog phenomenon The circumstance of moving from the top position (in elementary school, the oldest, biggest, and most powerful students) to the lowest position (in middle or junior high school, the youngest, smallest, and least powerful students). 246

tranquilizers Depressant drugs that reduce anxiety and induce relaxation; examples are Valium and Xanax. 477

triarchic theory Sternberg's theory that intelligence has three main components: componential intelligence, experiential intelligence, and contextual intelligence. 148

trust versus mistrust Erikson's first psychosocial stage, which is experienced in the first year of life. A sense of trust requires a feeling of physical comfort and a minimal amount of fear and apprehension about the future. 45

twin study A study in which the behavioral similarity of identical twins is compared with the behavioral similarity of fraternal twins. 80

two-factor theory Spearman's theory that individuals have both general intelligence, which he called g, and a number of specific intelligences, which he called s, both of which account for performance on an intelligence test. 148

Type A behavior pattern   An individual with this cluster of characteristics is excessively competitive, hard-driven, impatient, irritable, and hostile. This pattern is thought to be related to coronary problems. 516

U

universal ethical principles   The sixth and highest stage in Kohlberg's theory of moral development. Individuals develop a moral standard based on universal human rights.   407

V

values clarification   An indirect moral education approach that focuses on helping students clarify what their lives are for and what is worth working for.   418

very-high-risk youth   Youth who have multiple problem behaviors; these constitute up to 10 percent of the adolescent population. This group includes adolescents who have been arrested or have committed serious offenses, have dropped out of school or are behind their grade level, use drugs heavily, drink heavily, regularly smoke cigarettes and marijuana, and are sexually active but do not use contraception. Many of these youth "do it all." 490

W

wisdom   According to Baltes, this is expert knowledge about the practical aspects of life.   116

withdrawal   Undesirable intense pain and craving for an addictive drug. 471

Y

youth   Kenniston's term for the transitional period between adolescence and adulthood that is a time of economic and personal temporariness.   24

Z

zone of proximal development (ZPD)   In Vygotsky's theory, the range of tasks that are too difficult for an individual to master alone but that can be mastered with the guidance of adults or more highly skilled adolescents.   119

EFERENCES

A

Achenbach, T. M., & Edelbrock, C. S. (1981). Behavioral problems and competencies reported by parents of normal and disturbed children aged four through sixteen. *Monographs of the Society for Research in Child Development, 46* (1, Serial No. 188).

Achenbach, T. M., Howell, C. T., Quay, H. C., & Conners, C. K. (1991). National survey of problems and competencies among four- to sixteen-year-olds. *Monographs of the Society for Research in Child Development,* Serial No. 225 (Vol. 56, No. 3).

Adelson, J. (1979, January). Adolescence and the generalization gap. *Psychology Today,* pp. 33–37.

Ainsworth, M. D. S. (1979). Infant-mother attachment. *American Psychologist, 34,* 932–937.

Alan Guttmacher Institute. (1993). *National survey of the American male's sexual habits.* Unpublished data. New York: Author.

Al-Issa, I., & Tousignant, M. (1997). *Ethnicity, immigration, and psychopathology.* New York: Plenum.

Allen, J. P., & Bell, K. L. (1995, March). *Attachment and communication with parents and peers in adolescence.* Paper presented at the meeting of the Society for Research in Child Development, Indianapolis.

Allen, J. P., & Hauser, S. T. (1994, February). *Adolescent-family interactions as predictors of qualities of parental, peer, and romantic relationships at age 25.* Paper presented at the meeting of the Society for Research on Adolescence, San Diego.

Allen, J. P., & Kuperminc, G. P. (1995, March). *Adolescent attachment, social competence, and problematic behavior.* Paper presented at the meeting of the Society for Research in Child Development, Indianapolis.

Allison, K. W. (1993). Adolescents living in "nonfamily" and alternative settings. In R. M. Lerner (Ed.), *Early adolescence.* Hillsdale, NJ: Erlbaum.

American Association of University Women. (1993). *Hostile hallways.* Washington, DC: Author.

American College Health Association. (1989, May). *Survey of AIDS on American college and university campuses.* Washington, DC: American College Health Association.

Ames, C., & Ames, R. (Eds.). (1989). *Research on motivation in education. Goals and cognitions.* (Vol. 3). San Diego: Academic Press.

Amsel, E. (1995, March). *The development of causal attributions in two physics domains.* Paper presented at the meeting of the Society for Research in Child Development, Indianapolis.

Amsel, E., & Renninger, K. A. (1997). *Change and development.* Mahwah, NJ: Erlbaum.

Anastasi, A. (1988). *Psychological testing* (6th ed.). New York: Macmillan.

Anderman, E. M., Maehr, M. L., & Midgley, C. (1996). *Declining motivation after the transition to middle school: Schools can make a difference.* Unpublished manuscript, University of Kentucky, Lexington.

Anderson, J. R. (1990). *Cognitive psychology and its implications* (3rd ed.). New York: W. H. Freeman.

Anderson, K. J., & Leaper, C. (1996, March). *The social construction of emotion and gender between friends.* Paper presented at the meeting of the Society for Research on Adolescence, Boston.

Andre, T., Frevert, R. L., & Schuchmann, D. (1989). From whom have college students learned what about sex? *Youth and Society, 20,* 241–268.

Arbona, C. (1995). Theory and research on racial and ethnic minorities: Hispanic minorities. In F. T. L. Leong (Ed.), *Career development and vocational behavior of racial and ethnic minorities.* Hillsdale, NJ: Erlbaum.

Archer, S. L. (1989). The status of identity: Reflections on the need for intervention. *Journal of Adolescence, 12,* 345–359.

Archer, S. L. (Ed.) (1994). *Intervention for adolescent identity development.* Newbury Park, CA: Sage.

Archer, S. L., & Waterman, A. S. (1994). Adolescent identity development: Contextual perspectives. In C. B. Fisher & R. M. Lerner (Eds.), *Applied developmental psychology.* New York: McGraw-Hill.

Arehart, D. M., & Smith, P. H. (1990). Identity in adolescence: Influences on dysfunction and psychosocial task issues. *Journal of Youth and Adolescence, 19,* 63–72.

Argyle, M., & Beit-Hallahmi, B. (1985). *The social psychology of religion.* London: Routledge & Kegan Paul.

Aristotle. (1941). *Rhetorica* (W. R. Roberts, Trans.). In R. McKeon (Ed.), *The basic works of Aristotle.* New York: Random House.

Armsden, G., & Greenberg, M. T. (1984). *The inventory of parent and peer attachment: Individual differences and their relationship to psychological well-being in adolescence.* Unpublished manuscript, University of Washington.

Armsden, G., & Greenberg, M. T. (1987). The inventory of parent and peer attachment: Individual differences and their relationship to psychological well-being in adolescence. *Journal of Youth and Adolescence, 16,* 427–454.

Arnett, J. (1992). Reckless behavior in adolescence: A developmental perspective. *Developmental Review, 12,* 339–373.

Arnett, J. (1995, March). *Developmental contributors to adolescent reckless behavior.* Paper presented at the meeting of the Society for Research in Child Development, Indianapolis.

Arnett, J. (1996, March). *Subjective conceptions of adult status.* Paper presented at the meeting of the Society for Research on Adolescence, Boston.

Arnett, J. D. (1991). Heavy metal music and reckless behavior among adolescents. *Journal of Youth and Adolescence, 20,* 573–592.

Arnett, J. D. (1995, March). *Are college students adults?* Paper presented at the meeting of the Society for Research in Child Development, Indianapolis.

Arnold, M. L. (1989, April). *Moral cognition and conduct: A quantitative review of the literature.* Paper presented at the Society for Research in Child Development meeting, Kansas City.

Aronson, E. (1986, August). *Teaching students things they think they know all about: The case of prejudice and desegregation*. Paper presented at the meeting of the American Psychological Association, Washington, DC.

Arroyo, C. G., & Sternberg, R. J. (1993). *Against all odds: A view of the gifted disadvantaged*. Manuscript, Department of Psychology, Yale University, New Haven, CT.

Asarnow, J. R., & Callan, J. W. (1985). Boys with peer adjustment problems: Social cognitive processes. *Journal of Consulting and Clinical Psychology, 53*, 80–87.

Aseltine, R. H., & Gore, S. (1993). Mental health and social adaptation following the transition from high school. *Journal of Research on Adolescence, 3*, 247–270.

Asian Week. (1990, June 29). Poll finds racial tension decreasing. p. 4.

Astin, A. W., Green, K. C., & Korn, W. S. (1987). *The American freshman: Twenty-year trends*. Los Angeles: UCLA Higher Education Research Institute.

Astin, A. W., Korn, W. S., Sax, L. J., & Mahoney, K. M. (1994). *The American freshman: National norms for fall 1994*. Los Angeles: UCLA, Higher Education Research Institute.

Astin, A. W., Parrott, S. A., Korn, W. S., & Sax, L. J. (1997). *The American freshman: Thirty year trends*. Los Angeles, CA: Higher Education Research Institute, UCLA.

Atkinson, J. W., & Raynor, I. O. (1974). *Motivation and achievement*. Washington, DC: V. H. Winston & Sons.

Attie, I., & Brooks-Gunn, J. (1989). Development of eating problems in adolescent girls: A longitudinal study. *Developmental Psychology, 25*, 70–79.

Ausubel, D. P. (1958). *Theory and problems of child development*. New York: Grune & Stratton.

Ayman-Nolley, S., & Church, R. B. (1993, March). *Social and cognitive mechanisms of learning through interaction with peers*. Paper presented at the biennial meeting of the Society for Research in Child Development, New Orleans.

Azuma, H. (1997, April). *The development of close relationships in Japan and the United States*. Paper presented at the meeting of the Society for Research in Child Development, Washington, DC.

Bachhuber, T. (1992). 13 ways to pass along real information to students. *Journal of Career Planning and Employment, 27*, 67–70.

Bachman, J. G. (1982, June 28). *The American high school student: A profile based on national survey data*. Paper presented at the conference entitled "The American High School Today and Tomorrow," Berkeley, CA.

Bachman, J. G. (1991). Dropouts, school. In R. M. Lerner, A. C. Petersen, & J. Brooks-Gunn (Eds.), *Encyclopedia of adolescence* (Vol. 1). New York: Garland.

Bachman, J. G., & Schulenberg, J. (1993). How part-time work intensity relates to drug use, problem behavior, time use, and satisfaction among high school seniors: Are these consequences or just correlates? *Developmental Psychology, 29*, 220–235.

Bacon, M. K., Child, I. L., & Barry, H. (1963). A cross-cultural study of correlates of crime. *Journal of Abnormal and Social Psychology, 66*, 291–300.

Baer, J. (1993). *Creativity and divergent thinking*. Hillsdale, NJ: Erlbaum.

Bagwell, C. L., Newcomb, A. F., & Bukowski, W. M. (1994, February). *Early adolescent friendship as a predictor of adult adjustment: A twelve year follow-up investigation*. Paper presented at the biennial meeting of the Society for Research on Adolescence, San Diego.

Ballard, M. E., & Coates, S. (in press). The immediate effects of homicidal, suicidal and non-violent heavy metal and rap songs on the moods of college students. *Journal of Youth and Adolescence*.

Baltes, P. B. (1987). Theoretical propositions of life-span developmental psychology: On the dynamics between growth and decline. *Developmental Psychology, 23*, 611–626.

Baltes, P. B. (1993). The aging mind: Potential and limits. *Gerontologist, 33*, 580–594.

Baltes, P. B. (1997, February). Interview. *APA Monitor, 28*, pp. 1, 9.

Baltes, P. B., Lindenberger, U., & Staudinger, U. M. (1997). Life-span theory in developmental psychology. In R. M. Lerner (Ed), *Handbook of child psychology* (5th Ed., Vol. 1). New York: Wiley.

Baltes, P. B. (in press). On the incomplete architecture of human ontogeny. *American Psychologist*.

Bancroft, J. (1990). The impact of sociocultural influences on adolescent sexual development: Further considerations. In J. Bancroft & J. M. Reinisch (Eds.), *Adolescence and puberty*. New York: Oxford University Press.

Bandura, A. (1965). Influence of models' reinforcement contingencies on the acquisition of imitative responses. *Journal of Personality and Social Psychology, 1*, 589–595.

Bandura, A. (1977). *Social learning theory*. Englewood Cliffs, NJ: Prentice Hall.

Bandura, A. (1986). *Social foundations of thought and action: A social cognitive theory*. Englewood Cliffs, NJ: Prentice Hall.

Bandura, A. (1991). Social cognitive theory of moral thought and action. In W. M. Kurtines & J. L. Gewirtz (Eds.), *Handbook of moral behavior and development* (Vol. 1). Hillsdale, NJ: Erlbaum.

Bandura, A. (1994). Social cognitive theory of mass communication. In J. Bryant & D. Zillman (Eds.), *Media effects*. Hillsdale, NJ: Erlbaum.

Bandura, A. (1995). (Ed.). *Self-efficacy in changing societies*. New York: Cambridge University Press.

Bandura, A. (1997). *Self-efficacy: The exercise of self-control*. New York: W. H. Freeman.

Banks, E. C. (1993, March). *Moral education curriculum in a multicultural context: The Malaysian primary curriculum*. Paper presented at the biennial meeting of the Society for Research in Child Development, New Orleans.

Baran, S. J. (1976). How TV and film portrayals affect sexual satisfaction in college and adolescent sexual image. *Journal of Broadcasting, 20*, 61–88.

Barenboim, C. (1981). The development of person perception in childhood and adolescence: From behavioral comparisons to psychological constructs to psychological comparisons. *Child Development, 52*, 129–144.

Barker, R., & Wright, H. F. (1951). *One boy's day*. New York: Harper.

Barnes, G. M., Farrell, M. P., & Banerjee, S. (1994). Family influences on alcohol abuse and other problem behaviors among Black and White adolescents in a general population sample. *Journal of Research on Adolescence, 4*, 183–202.

Barnes, G. M., Farrell, M. P., & Banerjee, S. (1995). Family influences on alcohol abuse and other problem behaviors among Black and White Americans. In G. M. Boyd, J. Howard, & R. A. Zucker (Eds.), *Alcohol problems among adolescents*. Hillsdale, NJ: Erlbaum.

Barnouw, V. (1975). *An introduction to anthropology. Vol 2: Ethnology.* Homewood, IL: Dorsey Press.

Baron, R., Tom, D., & Cooper, H. (1985). Social class, race, and teacher expectations. In J. Dusek & G. Joseph (Eds.), *Teacher expectancies.* Hillsdale, NJ: Erlbaum.

Barone, C., Ayers, T. S., Ickovics, J., Weissberg, R. P., & Katz, S. (1994, February). *High-risk sexual behavior among urban adolescents: An analysis of sociodemographic factors.* Paper presented at the meeting of the Society for Research on Adolescence, San Diego.

Barron, F. (1989, April). The birth of a notion: Exercises to tap your creative potential. *Omni,* pp. 112–119.

Barth, R. P. (1989). *Reducing the risk: Building skills to prevent pregnancy.* Student workbook, EDRS Price document (abstract).

Baskett, L. M., & Johnston, S. M. (1982). The young child's interaction with parents versus siblings. *Child Development, 53,* 643–650.

Bat-Chava, Y., Allen, L., Aber, J. L., & Seidman, E. (1997, April). *Racial and ethnic identity and the contexts of development.* Paper presented at the meeting of the Society for Research in child Development, Washington, DC.

Baumeister, R. F. (1989). *Masochism and the self.* Hillsdale, NJ: Erlbaum.

Baumeister, R. F. (1991). Identity crisis. In R. M. Lerner, A. C. Petersen, & J. Brooks-Gunn (Eds.), *Encyclopedia of adolescence* (Vol. 1). New York: Garland.

Baumrind, D. (1971). Current patterns of parental authority. *Developmental Psychology Monographs, 4*(1, Pt. 2).

Baumrind, D. (1991). Effective parenting during the early adolescent transition. In P. A. Cowan & E. M. Hetherington (Eds.), *Advances in family research* (Vol. 2). Hillsdale, NJ: Erlbaum.

Baydar, N., Brooks-Gunn, J., & Warren, M. P. (1992). *Changes in depressive symptoms in adolescent girls over four years: The effects of pubertal maturation and life events.* Unpublished manuscript, Department of Psychology, Columbia University, New York City.

Beal, C. R. (1994). *Boys and girls: The development of gender roles.* New York: McGraw-Hill.

Beck, A. (1976). *Cognitive therapy and the emotional disorders.* New York: International Universities Press.

Bednar, R. L., Wells, M. G., & Peterson, S. R. (1995). *Self-esteem* (2nd ed.). Washington, DC: American Psychological Association.

Belansky, E. S., & Clements, P. (1992, March). *Adolescence: A crossroads for gender-role transcendence or gender-role intensification.* Paper presented at the meeting of the Society for Research on Adolescence, Washington, DC.

Bell, A. P., Weinberg, M. S., & Mammersmith, S. K. (1981). *Sexual preference: Its development in men and women.* New York: Simon & Schuster.

Bell, K. L. (1995, March). *Attachment and flexibility at self-presentation during the transition to adulthood.* Paper presented at the meeting of the Society for Research in Child Development, Indianapolis.

Belle, D. (1990). Poverty and women's mental health. *American Psychologist, 45,* 385–389.

Belsky, J. (1981). Early human experience: A family perspective. *Developmental Psychology, 17,* 3–23.

Belson, W. (1978). *Television violence and the adolescent boy.* London: Saxon House.

Bem, S. L. (1977). On the utility of alternative procedures for assessing psychological androgyny. *Journal of Consulting and Clinical Psychology, 45,* 196–205.

Bem, S. L. (1981). Gender schema theory: A cognitive account of sex-typing. *Psychological Review, 88,* 354–364.

Bence, P. (1989, April). *Adolescent dating behavior and TV soaps: Guided by "The Guiding Light"?* Paper presented at the biennial meeting of the Society for Research in Child Development, Kansas City.

Bence, P. (1991). Television, adolescents and development. In R. M. Lerner, A. C. Petersen, & J. Brooks-Gunn (Eds.), *Encyclopedia of adolescence* (Vol. 2). New York: Garland.

Bennett, W. (1993). *The book of virtues.* New York: Simon & Schuster.

Bennett, W. I., & Gurin, J. (1982). *The dieter's dilemma: Eating less and weighing more.* New York: Basic Books.

Bennett, W. J. (1986). *First lessons: A report on elementary education in America.* Washington, DC: U.S. Government Printing Office.

Benninga, J. S. (1988, February). An emerging synthesis in moral education. *Phi Delta Kappan,* pp. 415–418.

Benson, P. (1993). *The troubled journey: A portrait of 6th–12th grade youth.* Minneapolis: Search Institute.

Bergman, S. J. (1995). Men's psychological development: A relational perspective. In R. F. Levant & W. S. Pollack (Eds.), *A new psychology of men.* New York: Basic.

Berk, S. F. (1985). *The gender factory: The apportionment of work in American households.* New York: Plenum.

Bernard, H. S. (1981). Identity formation in late adolescence: A review of some empirical findings. *Adolescence, 16,* 349–358.

Berndt, T. J. (1979). Developmental changes in conformity to peers and parents. *Developmental Psychology, 15,* 608–616.

Berndt, T. J. (1982). The features and effects of friendship in early adolescence. *Child Development, 53,* 1447–1460.

Berndt, T. J. (1996). Transitions in friendship and friends' influence. In J. A. Graber, J. Brooks-Gunn, & A. C. Petersen (Eds.), *Transitions through adolescence.* Mahwah, NJ: Erlbaum.

Berndt, T. J., & Perry, T. B. (1990). Distinctive features and effects of early adolescent friendships. In R. Montemayor (Ed.), *Advances in adolescent research.* Greenwich, CT: JAI Press.

Berrueta-Clement, J., Schweinhart, L., Barnett, W., & Weikart, D. (1986). The effects of early educational intervention on crime and delinquency in adolescence and early adulthood. In J. Burchard & S. Burchard (Eds.), *Prevention of delinquent behavior.* Newbury Park, CA: Sage.

Berry, J. W. (1971). Ecological and cultural factors in spatial perceptual development. *Canadian Journal of Behavioral Science, 3,* 324–336.

Berry, J. W. (1983). Textured contexts: Systems and situations in cross-cultural psychology. In S. H. Irvine & J. W. Berry (Eds.), *Human assessment and cultural factors.* New York: Plenum.

Berry, J. W. (1990). Psychology of acculturation: Understanding individuals moving between cultures. In R. W. Brislin (Eds.), *Applied cross-cultural psychology.* Newbury Park, CA: Sage.

Berscheid, E. (1988). Some comments on love's anatomy: Or, whatever happened to old-fashioned lust? In R. J. Sternberg & M. L. Barnes (Eds.), *Anatomy of love.* New Haven, CT: Yale University Press.

Berscheid, E., & Fei, J. (1977). Sexual jealousy and romantic love. In G. Clinton & G. Smith (Eds.), *Sexual jealousy.* Englewood Cliffs, NJ: Prentice Hall.

Berscheid, E., Snyder, M., & Omoto, A. M. (1989). Issues in studying close relationships. In C. Hendrick (Ed.), *Close relationships.* Newbury Park, CA: Sage.

Bettes, B. A., Dusenbury, L., Kerner, J., James-Ortiz, S., & Botvin, G. J. (1990). Ethnicity and psychosocial factors in alcohol and tobacco use in adolescence. *Child Development, 61,* 557–565.

Betz, N. E., & Fitzgerald, L. F. (1995). Career assessment and intervention with racial and ethnic minorities. In F. T. L. Leong (Ed.), *Career development and vocational behavior of racial and ethnic minorities.* Hillsdale, NJ: Erlbaum.

Biller, H. B. (1993). *Fathers and families: Paternal factors in child development.* Westport, CT: Auburn House.

Billy, J. O. G., Rodgers, J. L., & Udry, J. R. (1984). Adolescent sexual behavior and friendship choice. *Social Forces, 62,* 653–678.

Bilodeau, A., Forget, G., & Tetreault, J. (1992, March). *Preventing teenage pregnancy: A pilot project in two low-income communities of eastern Montreal.* Paper presented at the meeting of the Society for Research on Adolescence, Washington, DC.

Bingham, C. R., & Crockett, L. J. (1996). Longitudinal adjustment patterns of boys and girls experiencing early, middle, and late sexual intercourse. *Developmental Psychology, 32,* 647–658.

Black, A. E., & Pedro-Carroll, J. L. (1993, March). *The long-term effects of interpersonal conflict and parental divorce among late adolescents.* Paper presented at the biennial meeting of the Society for Research in Child Development, New Orleans.

Black, K. A., & McCartney, K. (1995, March). *Associations between adolescent attachment to parents and peer interactions.* Paper presented at the meeting of the Society for Research in Child Development, Indianapolis.

Blain, M. D., Thompson, J. M., & Whiffen, V. E. (1993). Attachment and perceived social support in late adolescence. *Journal of Adolescent Research, 8,* 226–241.

Blakemore, J. E. O. (1993, March). *Preschool children's interest in babies: Observations in naturally occurring situations.* Paper presented at the biennial meeting of the Society for Research in Child Development, New Orleans.

Blanchard-Fields, F., & Robinson, S. (1987, April). *Controllability and adaptive coping from adolescence through older adulthood.* Paper presented at the biennial meeting of the Society for Research in Child Development, Baltimore.

Blash, R., & Unger, D. G. (1992, March). *Cultural factors and the self-esteem and aspirations of African-American adolescent males.* Paper presented at the meeting of the Society for Research on Adolescence, Washington, DC.

Blasi, A. (1988). Identity and the development of the self. In D. Lapsley & F. C. Power (Eds.), *Self, ego, and identity: Integrative approaches.* New York: Springer-Verlag.

Bloom, B. S. (Ed.). (1985). *Developing talent in young people.* New York: Ballantine.

Blos, P. (1962). *On adolescence.* New York: Free Press.

Blos, P. (1989). The inner world of the adolescent. In A. H. Esman (Ed.), *International annals of adolescent psychiatry* (Vol. 1). Chicago: University of Chicago Press.

Blyth, D. A., Durant, D., & Moosbrugger, L. (1985, April). *Perceived intimacy in the social relationships of drug- and nondrug-using adolescents.* Paper presented at the meeting of the Society for Research in Child Development, Toronto.

Bolger, N., Downey, G., Walker, E., & Steininger, P. (1989). The onset of suicidal ideation in childhood and adolescence. *Journal of Youth and Adolescence, 18,* 175–190.

Booth, A., Crouter, A. C., & Landale, N. (1997). *Immigration and the family.* Mahwah, NJ: Erlbaum.

Bouchard, T. J. (1995, August). *Heritability of intelligence.* Paper presented at the meeting of the American Psychological Association, New York City.

Bourne, E. (1978). The state of research on ego identity: A review and appraisal (Part 1). *Journal of Youth and Adolescence, 7,* 223–251.

Bowlby, J. (1989). *Secure attachment.* New York: Basic Books.

Bowman, S. L. (1995). Career intervention strategies and assessment issues for African Americans. In F. T. L. Leong (Ed.), *Career development and vocational behavior of racial and ethnic minorities.* Hillsdale, NJ: Erlbaum.

Boyd-Franklin, N. (1989). *Black families in therapy: A multisystems approach.* New York: Guilford.

Boyer, E. L. (1986, December). Transition from school to college. *Phi Delta Kappan,* pp. 283–287.

Boyes, M. C., & Allen, S. G. (1993). Styles of parent-child interaction and moral reasoning in adolescence. *Merrill-Palmer Quarterly, 39,* 551–570.

Boyes, M. C., Giordano, R., & Galperyn, K. (1993, March). *Moral orientation and interpretive contexts of moral deliberation.* Paper presented at the biennial meeting of the Society for Research in Child Development, New Orleans.

Boys and Girls Clubs of America (1989, May 12). *Boys and Girls Clubs in public housing projects: Interim report.* Minneapolis: Boys and Girls Clubs of America.

Bray, J. H., & Berger, S. H. (1994, February). *Longitudinal impact of parenting on adolescent adjustment in stepfamilies.* Paper presented at the meeting of the Society for Research on Adolescence, San Diego.

Breslow, L. (1990). The future of public health: Prospects in the United States for the 1990s. In *Annual Review of Public Health* (Vol. 11). Palo Alto, CA: Annual Reviews.

Brewer, M. B., & Campbell, D. T. (1976). *Ethnocentrism and intergroup attitudes.* New York: Wiley.

Brim, O. G., & Kagan, J. (1980). Constancy and change: A view of the issues. In O. G. Brim & J. Kagan (Eds.), *Constancy and change in human development.* Cambridge, MA: Harvard University Press.

Brislin, R. (1993). *Understanding culture's influence on behavior.* Fort Worth, TX: Harcourt Brace.

Brislin, R. W. (1990). Applied cross-cultural psychology: An introduction. In R. W. Brislin (Ed.). (1993). *Applied cross-cultural psychology.* Newbury Park, CA: Sage.

Brock, L. J., & Jennings, G. H. (1993). What daughters in their 30s wish their mothers had told them. *Family Relations, 42,* 61–65.

Brody, G. H., & Shaffer, D. R. (1982). Contributions of parents and peers to children's moral socialization. *Developmental Review, 2,* 31–75.

Brody, G. H., Stoneman, Z., & Burke, M. (1987). Child temperaments, maternal differential behavior and sibling relationships. *Developmental Psychology, 23,* 354–362.

Brodzinsky, D. M., Lang, R., & Smith, D. W. (1995). Parenting adopted children. In M. H. Bornstein (Ed.), *Handbook of parenting* (Vol. 3). Hillsdale, NJ: Erlbaum.

Brodzinsky, D. M., Schechter, D. E., Braff, A. M., & Singer, L. M. (1984). Psychological and academic adjustment in adopted children. *Journal of Consulting and Clinical Psychology, 52,* 582–590.

Bronfenbrenner, U. (1986). Ecology of the family as a context for human development: Research perspectives. *Developmental Psychology, 22,* 723–742.

Bronfenbrenner, U. (1995). The bioecological model from a life course perspective. In P. Moen, G. H. Elder, & K. Luscher (Eds.), *Examining lives in context.* Washington, DC: American Psychological Association.

Bronfenbrenner, U. (1995, March). *The role research has played in Head Start.* Paper presented at the meeting of the Society for Research in Child Development, Indianapolis.

Bronfenbrenner, U., & Morris, P. A. (1997). The ecology of developmental processes. In R. M. Lerner (Ed.), *Handbook of child psychology* (5th Ed., Vol. 1). New York: Wiley.

Brook, J. S., Brook, D. W., Gordon, A. S., Whiteman, M., & Cohen, P. (1990). The psychological etiology of adolescent drug use: A family interactional approach. *Genetic Psychology Monographs, 116,* no. 2.

Brooks, T., & Bronstein, P. (1996, March). *Cross-cultural comparison of mothers' and fathers' behaviors toward girls and boys.* Paper presented at the meeting of the Society for Research on Adolescence, Boston.

Brooks-Gunn, J. (1988). Antecedents and consequences of variations in girls' maturational timing. In M. D. Levine & E. R. McAnarney (Eds.), *Early adolescent transitions.* Lexington, MA: Lexington Books.

Brooks-Gunn, J. (1992, March). *Revisiting theories of "storm and stress": The role of biology.* Paper presented at the meeting of the Society for Research on Adolescence, Washington, DC.

Brooks-Gunn, J., & Chase-Landsdale, P. L. (1995). Adolescent parenthood. In M. H. Bornstein (Ed.), *Children and parenting* (Vol. 3). Hillsdale, NJ: Erlbaum.

Brooks-Gunn, J., Duncan, G., Glebanov, P. K., & Sealand, N. (1993). Do neighborhoods influence child and adolescent development? *American Journal of Sociology, 99,* 353–395.

Brooks-Gunn, J., & Graber, J. A. (1995, March). *Depressive affect versus positive adjustment: Patterns of resilience in adolescent girls.* Paper presented at the meeting of the Society for Research in Child Development, Indianapolis.

Brooks-Gunn, J., Graber, J. A., & Paikoff, R. L. (1994). Studying links between hormones and negative affect: Models and measures. *Journal of Research on Adolescence, 4,* 469–486.

Brooks-Gunn, J., Guo, G., & Furstenberg, F. F. (1993). Who drops out of and who continues beyond high school? A 20-year follow-up of Black urban youth. *Journal of Research on Adolescence, 3,* 271–294.

Brooks-Gunn, J., & Paikoff, R. (1993). "Sex is a gamble, kissing is a game": Adolescent sexuality, contraception, and sexuality. In S. P. Millstein, A. C. Petersen, & E. O. Nightingale, (Eds.), *Promoting the health behavior of adolescents.* New York: Oxford University Press.

Brooks-Gunn, J., & Paikoff, R. (in press). Sexuality and developmental transitions during adolescence. In J. Schulenberg, J. Maggs, & K. Hurrelmann (Eds.), *Health risks and developmental transitions during adolescence.* New York: Cambridge University Press.

Brooks-Gunn, J., & Ruble, D. N. (1982). The development of menstrual-related beliefs and behaviors during early adolescence. *Child Development, 53,* 1567–1577.

Brooks-Gunn, J., & Warren, M. P. (1989). The psychological significance of secondary sexual characteristics in 9- to 11-year-old girls. *Child Development, 59,* 161–169.

Broughton, J. (1983). The cognitive developmental theory of adolescent self and identity. In B. Lee & G. Noam (Eds.), *Developmental approaches to self.* New York: Plenum.

Broverman, I., Vogel, S., Broverman, D., Clarkson, F., & Rosenkranz, P. (1972). Sex-role stereotypes: A current appraisal. *Journal of Social Issues, 28,* 59–78.

Brown, A. C., & Orthner, D. K. (1990). Relocation and personal well-being among early adolescents. *Journal of Early Adolescence, 10,* 366–381.

Brown, A. L., & Palincsar, A. M. (1989). Guided, cooperative learning and individual knowledge acquisition. In L. B. Resnick (Ed.), *Knowing and learning: Essays in honor of Robert Glaser.* Hillsdale, NJ: Erlbaum.

Brown, A. L., & Smiley, S. S. (1977). Rating the importance of structural units of prose passages: A problem of metacognitive development. *Child Development, 48,* 1–8.

Brown, A. L., Bransford, J. D., Ferrara, R. A., & Campione, J. C. (1983). Learning, remembering, and understanding. In P. H. Mussen (Ed.), *Handbook of child psychology* (4th ed., Vol. 3). New York: Wiley.

Brown, A. L., Metz, K. E., & Campione, J. C. (1996). Social interaction and individual understanding in a community of learners: The influence of Piaget and Vygotsky. In A. Tryphon & J. Voneche (Eds.), *Piaget-Vygotsky.* Mahwah, NJ: Erlbaum.

Brown, B. B., Dolcini, M. M., & Leventhal, A. (1995, March). *The emergence of peer crowds: Friend or foe to adolescent health?* Paper presented at the meeting of the Society for Research on Child Development, Indianapolis.

Brown, B. B., & Huang, B. H. (1995). Examining parenting practices in different peer contexts: Implications for adolescent trajectories. In L. J. Crockett & A. C. Crouter (Eds.), *Pathways through adolescence.* Hillsdale, NJ: Erlbaum.

Brown, B. B., & Lohr, M. J. (1987). Peer-group affiliation and adolescent self-esteem: An integration of ego-identity and symbolic-interaction theories. *Journal of Personality and Social Psychology, 52,* 47–55.

Brown, B. B., Mory, M., & Kinney, D. A. (1994). Casting adolescent crowds in relational perspective: Caricature, channel, and context. In R. Montemayor, G. R. Adams, & T. P. Gullotta (Eds.), *Advances in adolescent development: Vol. 6. Personal relationships during adolescence.* Newbury Park, CA: Sage.

Brown, B. B., Steinberg, L., Mounts, N., & Philipp, M. (1990, March). *The comparative influence of peers and parents on high school achievement: Ethnic differences.* Paper presented at the meeting of the Society for Research in Adolescence, Atlanta.

Brown, F. (1973). *The reform of secondary education: Report of the national commission on the reform of secondary education.* New York: McGraw-Hill.

Brown, J. D., & Siegel, J. D. (1988). Exercise as a buffer of life stress: A prospective study of adolescent health. *Health Psychology, 7,* 341–353.

Brown, M. T. (1995). The career development of African Americans: Theoretical and empirical issues. In F. T. L. Leong (Ed.), *Career development and vocational behavior of racial and ethnic minorities.* Hillsdale, NJ: Erlbaum.

Brown, R. (1986). *Social psychology* (2nd ed.). New York: Macmillan.

Browne, M. W. (1994, October 16). What is intelligence, and who has it? *New York Times Book Review,* pp. 2–3, 41–42.

Brownell, K. D., & Stein, L. J. (1989). Metabolic and behavioral effects of weight loss and regain: A review of the animal and human literature. In A. J. Stunkard & A. Baum (Eds.), *Perspectives on behavioral medicine*. Hillsdale, NJ: Erlbaum.

Bruess, C. E., & Richardson, G. E. (1992). *Decisions for health* (3rd ed.). Dubuque, IA: Brown & Benchmark.

Buchanan, C. M., Maccoby, E. E., & Dornbusch, S. M. (1992). Adolescents and their families after divorce: Three residential arrangements compared. *Journal of Research on Adolescence, 2,* 261–291.

Buerkel-Rothfuss, D., & Mayes, S. (1981). Soap opera viewing: The cultivation effect. *Journal of Communication, 31,* 108–115.

Buhrmester, D. (1989). *Changes in friendship, interpersonal competence, and social adaptation during early adolescence*. Unpublished manuscript, Department of Psychology, UCLA, Los Angeles.

Buhrmester, D., & Carbery, J. (1992, March). *Daily patterns of self-disclosure and adolescent adjustment*. Paper presented at the biennial meeting of the Society for Research on Adolescence, Washington, DC.

Buhrmester, D., & Furman, W. (1987). The development of companionship and intimacy. *Child Development, 58,* 1101–1113.

Buhrmester, D., & Furman, W. (1990). Perceptions of sibling relationships during middle childhood and adolescence. *Child Development, 61,* 1387–1398.

Buhrmester, D., Camparo, L., Christensen, A., Gonzalez, L. S., & Hinshaw, S. P. (in press). Mothers and fathers interacting in dyads and triads with normal and hyperactive sons. *Developmental Psychology*.

Bukowski, W. M., Newcomb, A. F., & Hoza, B. (1987). Friendship conceptions among early adolescents: A longitudinal study of stability and change. *Journal of Early Adolescence, 7,* 143–152.

Bukowski, W. M., Sippola, L. K., & Boivin, M. (1995, March). *Friendship protects "at risk" children from victimization by peers*. Paper presented at the meeting of the Society for Research in Child Development, Indianapolis.

Burbach, D. J., & Peterson, L. (1986). Children's concept of physical illness. *Health Psychology, 5,* 307–325.

Burbules, N. C., & Linn, M. C. (1988). Response to contradiction: Scientific reasoning during adolescence. *Journal of Educational Psychology, 80,* 67–75.

Burdyshaw, C., & Fowler, M. (1986). *Family life education through teen theatre*. EDRS Price Report.

Burke, R. J., & Weir, T. (1979). Helping responses of parents and peer and adolescent well-being. *Journal of Psychology, 102,* 49–62.

Burton, L., & Allison, K. W. (1995). Social context and adolescence: Alternative perspectives on developmental pathways for African-American teens. In L. J. Crockett & A. C. Crouter (Eds.), *Pathways through adolescence*. Hillsdale, NJ: Erlbaum.

Burton, L. M., & Synder, A. R. (1997). The invisible man revisited. In A. Booth & A. C. Crouter (Eds.), *Men in families*. Mahwah, NJ: Erlbaum.

Burton, R. V. (1984). A paradox in theories and research in moral development. In W. W. Kurtines & J. L. Gewirtz (Eds.), *Morality, moral behavior, and moral development*. New York: Wiley.

Buss, D. M. (1995). Psychological sex differences: Origins through sexual selection. *American Psychologist, 50,* 164–168.

Buss, D. M., & Schmitt, D. P. (1993). Sexual strategies theory: An evolutionary perspective on human mating. *Psychological Review, 100,* 204–232.

Butterfield, F. (1990, January). Why they excel. *Parade Magazine*, pp. 4–6.

Byrne, D. (1973). *The development of role-taking in adolescence*. Unpublished doctoral dissertation, Harvard University Graduate School of Education.

Byrnes, J. P. (1988a). Formal operations: A systematic reformulation. *Developmental Review, 8,* 66–87.

Byrnes, J. P. (1988b). What's left is closer to right. *Developmental Review, 8,* 385–392.

Byrnes, J. P. (1997). *The nature and development of decision making*. Mahwah, NJ: Erlbaum.

Calabrese, R. L., & Schumer, H. (1986). The effects of service activities on adolescent alienation. *Adolescence, 21,* 675–687.

Cameron, J., Cowan, L., Holmes, B., Hurst, P., & McLean, M. (Eds.). (1983). *International handbook of educational systems*. New York: Wiley.

Camino, L. A. (1995). Understanding intolerance and multiculturalism: A challenge for practitioners, but also for researchers. *Journal of Adolescent Research*.

Campbell, C. Y. (1988, August 24). Group raps depiction of teenagers. *Boston Globe*, p. 44.

Campbell, D. T., & LeVine, R. A. (1968). Ethnocentrism and intergroup relations. In R. Abelson & others (Eds.), *Theories and cognitive consistency: A sourcebook*. Chicago: Rand McNally.

Campbell, F. A., & Ramey, C. T. (1994). Effects of early intervention on intellectual and academic achievement: A follow-up study of children from low-income families. *Child Development, 65,* 684–698.

Caplan, M., Weissberg, R. P., Grober, J. S., Sivo, P. J., Grady, K., & Jacoby, C. (1992). Social competence promotion with inner-city and suburban young adolescents: Effects on social adjustment and alcohol use. *Journal of Consulting and Clinical Psychology, 60,* 56–63.

Carlson, C., Cooper, C., & Hsu, J. (1990, March). *Predicting school achievement in early adolescence: The role of family process*. Paper presented at the meeting of the Society for Research in Adolescence, Atlanta.

Carnegie Council on Adolescent Development. (1989). *Turning points: Preparing American youth for the twenty-first century*. New York: Carnegie Foundation.

Carnegie Council on Adolescent Development. (1992). *A matter of time: Risk and opportunity in the nonschool hours*. Washington, DC: Author.

Carnegie Council on Adolescent Development. (1995). *Great transitions*. New York: Carnegie Foundation.

Carter, B., & McGoldrick, M. (1989). Overview: The changing family life cycle—a framework for family therapy. In B. Carter & M. McGoldrick (Eds.), *The changing family life cycle* (2nd ed.). Boston: Allyn & Bacon.

Case, R. (1985). *Intellectual development: Birth to adulthood*. New York: Academic Press.

Case, R. (1992). *The mind's staircase*. Hillsdale, NJ: Erlbaum.

Case, R. (Ed.). (1992). *The mind's staircase*. Hillsdale, NJ: Erlbaum.

Case, R. (1997). The development of conceptual structures. In D. Kuhn & R. S. Siegler (Eds.), *Handbook of child psychology* (5th Ed., Vol. 2). New York: Wiley.

Caspi, A., Henry, B., McGee, R. O., Moffitt, T. E., & Silva, P. A. (1995). Temperamental origins of child and adolescent behavior problems: From age three to age fifteen. *Child Development, 66,* 55–68.

Cassell, C. (1984). *Swept away: Why women fear their own sexuality*. New York: Simon & Schuster.

Castro, F. G., & Magana, D. (1988). A course in health promotion in ethnic minority populations. In P. A. Bronstein & K. Quina (Eds.), *Teaching a psychology of people*. Washington, DC: American Psychological Association.

Cauffman, B. E., (1994, February). *The effects of puberty, dating, and sexual involvement on dieting and disordered eating in young adolescent girls*. Paper presented at the meeting of the Society for Research on Adolescence, San Diego.

CDC National AIDS Clearinghouse. (1993). *Update: Acquired immunodeficiency syndrome—United States, 1992*. Rockville, MD: Author.

Ceci, S. (1990). *On intelligence . . . more or less: A bioecological treatise*. Englewood Cliffs, NJ: Prentice Hall.

Ceci, S. (1996). Unpublished review of *Child Development* (8th ed.) by J. W. Santrock. Dubuque, IA: Brown & Benchmark.

Ceci, S. J. & Barnett, S. M. (1997, April). *Convergence or divergence in intelligence?* Paper presented at the meeting of the Society for Research in Child Development, Washington, DC.

Centers for Disease Control. (1988). HIV-related beliefs, knowledge, and behaviors among high school students. *Morbidity and Mortality Weekly Reports, 37*, 717–721.

Centers for Disease Control. (1992, January). *The CDC survey of adolescent sexual activity*. Atlanta: Author.

Chafee, S. H., & Yang, S. M. (1990). Communication and political socialization. In O. Ichilov (Ed.), *Political socialization, citizen education, and democracy*. New York: Columbia University Press.

Chan, W. S. (1963). *A source book in Chinese philosophy*. Princeton, NJ: Princeton Books.

Chapman, W., & Katz, M. R. (1983). Career information systems in secondary schools: A survey and assessment. *Vocational Guidance Quarterly, 31*, 165–177.

Charles A. Dana Foundation Report. (1988, Spring). *Dana award winner's innovations in educating minority students in math and science attract nationwide attention*. New York: Charles A. Dana Foundation, pp. 1–5.

Chase-Lansdale, P. S., & Brooks-Gunn, J. (1994). Correlates of adolescent pregnancy. In C. B. Fisher & R. M. Lerner (Eds.), *Applied developmental psychology*. New York: McGraw-Hill.

Chavkin, N. F. (1993). Introduction: Families and schools. In N. F. Chavkin (Ed.), *Families and schools in pluralistic society*. Albany: State University of New York Press.

Chavkin, N. F., & Williams, D. W. (1993). Minority parents and the elementary school: Attitudes and practices. In N. F. Chavkin (Ed.), *Families and schools in a pluralistic society*. Albany: State University of New York Press.

Chen, C., & Stevenson, H. W. (1995). Motivation and mathematics achievement: A comparative study of Asian-American, Caucasian-American, and East Asian high school students. *Child Development, 66*, 1215–1234.

Chen, C. (1997, April). *Acculturation of values and attitude: A study of Chinese early and late adolescents*. Paper presented at the meeting of the Society for Research in Child Development, Washington, DC.

Chen, L. A., & Yu, P. P. H. (1997, April). *Parental ethnic socialization in Chinese American families*. Paper presented at the meeting of the Society for Research in Child Development, Washington, DC.

Chess, S., & Thomas, A. (1977). Temperamental individuality from childhood to adolescence. *Journal of Child Psychiatry, 16*, 218–226.

Child Trends. (1996). *Facts at a glance*. Washington, DC: Child Trends.

Children's Defense Fund. (1992). *The state of America's children, 1992*. Washington, DC: Author.

Chilman, C. (1979). *Adolescent sexuality in a changing American society: Social and psychological perspectives*. Washington, DC: Public Health Service, National Institute of Mental Health.

Christenson, P. W., & Roberts, D. F. (1991, August). *Music media in adolescent health promotion: Problems and prospects*. Paper presented at the meeting of the American Psychological Association, San Francisco.

Cillessen, A. H. N., Van Ijzendoorn, H. W., Van Lieshout, C. F. M., & Hartup, W. W. (1992). Heterogeneity among peer-rejected boys: Subtypes and stabilities. *Child Development, 63*, 893–905.

Clabby, J. G., & Elias, M. J. (1988). Improving social problem-solving and awareness. *William T. Grant Foundation Annual Report*, p. 18.

Clark, D. A., & Beck, A. T. (1989). Cognitive theory and therapy of anxiety and depression. In P. C. Kendall & D. Watson (Eds.), *Anxiety and depression*. San Diego: Academic Press.

Clark, K. (1965). *Dark ghetto*. New York: Harper.

Clark, K. B., & Clark, M. P. (1939). The development of the self and the emergence of racial identification in Negro preschool children. *Journal of Social Psychology, 10*, 591–599.

Clark, M. S., Powell, M. C., Ovellette, R., & Milberg, S. (1987). Recipient's mood, relationship type, and helping. *Journal of Personality and Social Psychology, 43*, 94–103.

Clark, R. D., & Hatfield, E. (1989). Gender differences in receptivity to sexual offers. *Journal of Psychology and Human Sexuality, 2*, 39–55.

Clark, S. D., Zabin, L. S., & Hardy, J. B. (1984). Sex, contraception, and parenthood: Experience and attitudes among urban black young men. *Family Planning Perspectives, 16*, 77–82.

Clark, V. F., & Nelson, W. M. (1990). Negative expectations and self-evaluations in dysphoria. *Journal of Youth and Adolescence, 19*, 57–62.

Clasen, D. R., & Brown, B. B. (1987). Understanding peer pressure in the middle school. *Middle School Journal, 19*, 21–23.

Clausen, J. A. (1993). *American lives*. New York: Free Press.

Clifford, B. R., Gunter, B., & McAleer, J. L. (1995). *Television and children*. Hillsdale, NJ: Erlbaum.

Cloninger, C. R. (1991, January). *Personality traits and alcoholic predisposition*. Paper presented at the conference of the National Institute on Drug Abuse, University of California at Los Angeles.

Cochran, S. D., & Mays, V. M. (1990). Sex, lies, and HIV. *New England Journal of Medicine, 322*(11) 774–775.

Cohen, S. E. (1994, February). *High school dropouts*. Paper presented at the meeting of the Society for Research on Adolescence, San Diego.

Coie, J. D., & Koeppl, G. K. (1990). Adapting intervention to the problems of aggressive and disruptive rejected children. In S. R. Asher & J. D. Coie (Eds.), *Peer rejection in childhood*. New York: Cambridge University Press.

Coie, J. D., & Dodge, K. A. (1997). Aggression and antisocial behavior. In N. Eisenberg (Ed.), *Handbook of child psychology* (5th Ed., Vol. 3). New York: Wiley.

Colby, A., Kohlberg, L., Gibbs, J., & Lieberman, M. (1983). A longitudinal study of moral judgment. *Monographs of the Society for Research in Child Development, 48* (21, Serial No. 201).

Cole, M. (1997). *Cultural psychology*. Cambridge, MA: Harvard U. Press.

Cole, M., & Cole, S. R. (1993). *The development of children* (2nd ed.). New York: Scientific American.

Coleman, J. S. (1961). *The adolescent society*. New York: Free Press.

Coleman, J. S. (1980). The peer group. In J. Adelson (Ed.), *Handbook of adolescent psychology*. New York: Wiley.

Coleman, J. S. (1995, March). *Adolescent sexual knowledge: Implications for health and health risks*. Paper presented at the meeting of the Society for Research in Child Development, Indianapolis.

Coleman, J. S., Campbell, E. Q., Hobson, C. J., McPartland, J., Mood, A. M., Weinfield, F. D., & York, R. L. (1966). *Equality of educational opportunity*. Washington, DC: U.S. Government Printing Office.

Coleman, J. S., et al. (1974). *Youth: Transition to adulthood*. Report of the Panel on Youth of the President's Science Advisory Committee. Chicago: University of Chicago Press.

Coleman, M., & Ganong, L. H. (1990). Remarriage and stepfamily research in the 1980s: Increased interest in an old form. *Journal of Marriage and the Family, 52*, 925–939.

Coles, R. (1970). *Erik H. Erikson: The growth of his work*. Boston: Little, Brown.

Coles, R. (1986). *The political life of children*. Boston: Little, Brown.

Coll, C. T. G., Erkut, S., Alarcon, O., Garcia, H. A. V., & Tropp, L. (1995, March). *Puerto Rican adolescents and families: Lessons in construct and instrument development*. Paper presented at the meeting of the Society for Research in Child Development, Indianapolis.

Coll, C. T. G., Meyer, E. C., & Brillion, L. (1995). Ethnic and minority parenting. In M. H. Bornstein (Ed.), *Children and parenting* (Vol. 2). Hillsdale, NJ: Erlbaum.

College Board Commission on Precollege Guidance and Counseling. (1986). *Keeping the options open*. New York: College Entrance Examination Board.

Collins, W. A. (1993, March). *Parental behavior during adolescence: Individual and relationship significance*. Paper presented at the biennial meeting of the Society for Research in Child Development, New Orleans.

Comer, J. P. (1988). Educating poor minority children. *Scientific American, 259*, 42–46.

Comer, J. P. (1993). *African-American parents and child development: An agenda for school success*. Paper presented at the biennial meeting of the Society for Research on Child Development, New Orleans.

Compas, B. E., & Grant, K. E. (1993, March). *Stress and adolescent depressive symptoms: Underlying mechanisms and processes*. Paper presented at the biennial meeting of the Society for Research in Child Development, New Orleans.

Compas, B. E., & Wagner, B. M. (1991). Psychosocial stress during adolescence: Intrapersonal and interpersonal processes. In M. E. Colten, & S. Gore (Eds.), *Adolescent stress: Causes and consequences*. Hawthorne, NY: Aldine de Gruyter.

Comstock, G., & Paik, H. (1991). *Television and the American child*. San Diego: Academic Press.

Conant, J. B. (1959). *The American high school today*. New York: McGraw-Hill.

Condry, J. C. (1989). *The psychology of television*. Hillsdale, NJ: Erlbaum.

Condry, J. C., Simon, M. L., & Bronfenbrenner, U. (1968). *Characteristics of peer- and adult-oriented children*. Unpublished manuscript, Cornell University, Ithaca, NY.

Conger, J. J. (1981). Freedom and commitment: Families, youth, and social change. *American Psychologist, 36*, 1475–1484.

Conger, J. J. (1988). Hostages to the future: Youth, values, and the public interest. *American Psychologist, 43*, 291–300.

Conger, R. D. (1994, February). *Family risks and resilience for adolescent alcohol abuse*. Paper presented at the meeting of the Society for Research on Adolescence, San Diego.

Conger, R. D., Ge, X., Elder, G. H., Lorenz, F. O., & Simons, R. L. (1994). Economic stress, coercive family process, and developmental problems of adolescents. *Child Development, 65*, 541–561.

Connell, J. P., Spencer, M. B., & Aber, J. L. (1994). Educational risk and resilience in African-American youth: Context, self, action, and outcomes in school. *Child Development, 65*, 493–506.

Connolly, J. A., & Johnson, A. M. (1993, March). *The psychosocial context of romantic relationships in adolescence*. Paper presented at the biennial meeting of the Society for Research in Child Development, New Orleans.

Connors, L. J., & Epstein, J. L. (1995). Parent and school partnerships. In M. H. Bornstein (Ed.), *Children and parenting* (Vol. 4). Hillsdale, NJ: Erlbaum.

Cooper, C. R. (1995, April). *Multiple worlds, multiple selves: Cultural perspectives on contexts in childhood and adolescence*. Paper presented at the meeting of the Society for Research in Child Development, Indianapolis.

Cooper, C. R. (1995, March). *Multiple selves, multiple worlds: Cultural perspectives on individuality and connectedness in adolescent development*. Paper presented at the meeting of the Society for Research in Child Development, Indianapolis.

Cooper, C. R., & Ayers-Lopez, S. (1985). Family and peer systems in early adolescence: New models of the role of relationships in development. *Journal of Early Adolescence, 5*, 9–22.

Cooper, C. R., & Grotevant, H. D. (1989, April). *Individuality and connectedness in the family and adolescents' self and relational competence*. Paper presented at the meeting of the Society for Research in Child Development, Kansas City.

Coopersmith, S. (1967). *The antecedents of self-esteem*. San Francisco: W. H. Freeman.

Costin, F., & Draguns, J. G. (1989). *Abnormal psychology: Patterns, issues, interventions*. New York: Wiley.

Costin, S. E., & Jones, (1994, February). *The stress-protective role of parent and friend support for 6th and 9th graders following a school transition*. Paper presented at the meeting of the Society for Research on Adolescence, San Diego.

Cote, J. E., & Levine, C. (1988). On critiquing the identity status paradigm: A rejoinder to Waterman. *Developmental Review, 8*, 209–218.

Coulton, C. J., & Korbin, J. E. (1995, March). *How do measures of community organization differ in African-American and European-American neighborhoods?* Paper presented at the meeting of the Society for Research in Child Development, Indianapolis.

Cowan, P. (1978). *Piaget with feeling*. New York: Holt, Rinehart & Winston.

Crawford, M., & MacLeod, M. (1990). Gender in the college classroom: An assessment of the "chilly climate" for women. *Sex Roles, 23*, 101–122.

Crockett, L. J., & Bingham, C. R. (1994, February). *Family influences on girls' sexual experience and pregnancy risk*. Paper presented at the meeting of the Society for Research on Adolescence, San Diego.

Crockett, L. J., & Petersen, A. C. (1993). Adolescent development: Health risks and opportunities for health promotion. In S. G. Millstein, A. C. Petersen, & E. O. Nightingale (Eds.), *Promoting the health of adolescents*. New York: Oxford University Press.

Cronbach, L. J., & Snow, R. E. (1977). *Aptitudes and instructional methods*. New York: Irvington.

Cross, K. P. (1984, November). The rising tide of school reform reports. *Phi Delta Kappan*, pp. 167–172.

Cross, W. E. (1972). The Negro-to-Black conversion experience. *Black World, 20*, 13–27.

Crouter, A. C., Manke, B. A., & McHale, S. M. (1995). The family context of gender intensification in early adolescence. *Child Development, 66*, 317–329.

Crouter, & N. Landale (Eds.), *Immigration and the family*. Mahwah, NJ: Erlbaum.

Crowley, C. L., Lavery, B., Siegel, A., & Cousins, J. H. (1997, April). *Moving beyond labels: Approaching gang involvement through behavior*. Paper presented at the meeting of the Society for Research in Child Development, Washington, DC.

Crump, A. D., Haynie, D., Aarons, S., & Adair, E. (1996, March). *African American teenagers' norms, expectations, and motivations regarding sex, contraception, and pregnancy*. Paper presented at the meeting of the Society for Research on Adolescence, Boston.

Csikszentmihalyi, M., & Larson, R. (1984). *Being adolescent*. New York: Basic Books.

Culbertson, F. M. (1997). Depression and gender. *American Psychologist, 52*, 25–31.

Curran, J. M. (1997, April). *Creativity across the life-span: Taking a new perspective*. Paper presented at the meeting of the Society for Research in Child Development, Washington, DC.

Cushner, K., & Brislin, R. W. (Eds.) (1997). *Improving cultural interactions*. Thousand Oaks, CA: Sage.

Cutrona, C. E. (1982). Transition to college: Loneliness and the process of social adjustment. In L. A. Peplau & D. Perlman (Eds.), *Loneliness: A sourcebook of current theory, research, and therapy*. New York: Wiley.

Damon, A. (1977). *Human biology and ecology*. New York: W. W. Norton.

Damon, W. (1988). *The moral child*. New York: Free Press.

Damon, W. (1995). *Greater expectations*. New York: Free Press.

Damon, W., & Hart, D. (1988). *Self-understanding in childhood and adolescence*. New York: Cambridge University Press.

Dannhausen-Brun, C. A., Shalowitz, M. U., & Berry, C. A. (1997, April). *Challenging the assumptions: Teen moms and public policy*. Paper presented at the meeting of the Society for Research in Child Development, Washington, DC.

Danzinger, S., & Danzinger, S. (1993). Child poverty and public policy: Toward a comprehensive antipoverty agenda. *Daedalus: America's Childhood, 122*, 57–84.

Darling, C. A., Kallen, D. J., & VanDusen, J. E. (1984). Sex in transition, 1900–1984. *Journal of Youth and Adolescence, 13*, 385–399.

Dasen, P. R., Ngini, L., & Laval/aa/ee, M. (1979). Cross-cultural training studies of concrete operations. In L. H. Eckenberger, W. J. Lonner, & Y. H. Poortinga (Eds.), *Cross-cultural contributions to psychology*. Boston: Allyn & Bacon.

Davis, L., & Stewart, R. (1997, July). *Building capacity for working with lesbian, gay, bisexual, and transgender youth*. Paper presented at the conference on Working with America's Youth, Pittsburgh, PA.

Degirmencioglu, S. M., Saltz, E., & Ager, J. W. (1995, March). *Early dating and "going steady": A retrospective and prospective look*. Paper presented at the meeting of the Society for Research in Child Development, Indianapolis.

DeLamater, J., & MacCorquodale, P. (1979). *Premarital sexuality*. Madison: University of Wisconsin Press.

Demorest, A., Meyer, C., Phelps, E., Gardner, H., & Winner, E. (1984). Words speak louder than actions: Understanding deliberately false remarks. *Child Development, 55*, 1527–1534.

Dempster, F. N. (1981). Memory span: Sources of individual and developmental differences. *Psychological Bulletin, 89*, 63–100.

Denmark, F. L., & Paludi, M. A. (Eds.). (1993). *Handbook on the psychology of women*. Westport, CT: Greenwood Press.

Denmark, F. L., Russo, N. F., Frieze, I. H., Sechzur, J. (1988). Guidelines for avoiding sexism in psychological research: A report of the ad hoc committee on nonsexist research. *American Psychologist, 43*, 582–585.

Denner, J. (1994, February). *The development of dieting and bulimic behavior*. Paper presented at the meeting of the Society for Research on Adolescence, San Diego.

Dewey, J. (1933). *How we think: A restatement of the relation of reflective thinking to the educative process*. Lexington, MA: D. C. Heath.

DeVet, K. A., Brodsky, A. E., & Ialongo, N. S. (1997, April). *Parent monitoring in dangerous neighborhoods*. Paper presented at the meeting of the Society for Research in Child Development, Washington, DC.

Dickerscheid, J. D., Schwarz, P. M., Noir, S., & El-Taliawy, T. (1988). Gender concept development of preschool-aged children in the United States and Egypt. *Sex Roles, 18*, 669–677.

Dickinson, G. E. (1975). Dating behavior of black and white adolescents before and after desegregation. *Journal of Marriage and the Family, 37*, 602–608.

Dielman, T. E., Schulenberg, J., Leech, S., & Shope, J. T. (1992, March). *Reduction of susceptibility to peer pressure and alcohol use/misuse through a school-based prevention program*. Paper presented at the meeting of the Society for Research on Adolescence, Washington, DC.

Dielman, T. E., Shope, J. T., & Butchart, A. T. (1990, March). *Peer, family, and intrapersonal predictors of adolescent alcohol use and misuse*. Paper presented at the meeting of the Society for Research in Adolescence, Atlanta.

Dishion, T. J., Andrews, D. W., & Crosby, L. (1995). Antisocial boys and their friends in early adolescence: Relationship characteristics, quality, and interactional process. *Child Development, 66*, 139–151.

Dishion, T. J., & Spracklen, K. M. (1996, March). *Childhood peer rejection in the development of adolescent substance abuse*. Paper presented at the meeting of the Society for Research on Adolescence, Boston.

Dodge, K. A. (1983). Behavioral antecedents of peer social status. *Child Development, 54*, 1386–1399.

Dodge, K. A. (1993). Social cognitive mechanisms in the development of conduct disorder and depression. *Annual Review of Psychology, 44*, 559–584.

Dodge, K. A. (1993, March). *Social information processing and peer rejection factors in the development of behavior problems in children*. Paper presented at the biennial meeting of the Society for Research in Child Development, New Orleans.

Domino, G. (1992). Acculturation of Hispanics. In S. B. Knouse, P. Rosenfeld, & A. Culbertson (Eds.), *Hispanics in the workplace*. Newbury Park, CA: Sage.

Donovan, J. E., & Jessor, R. (1978). Adolescent problem drinking: Psychosocial correlates in a national sample study. *Journal of Studies on Alcohol, 39*, 1506–1524.

Dorn, L. D., & Lucas, F. L. (1995, March). *Do hormone-behavior relations vary depending upon the endocrine and psychological status of the adolescent.* Paper presented at the meeting of the Society for Research in Child Development, Indianapolis.

Dornbusch, S. M., Carlsmith, J. M., Bushwall, S. J., Ritter, P. I., Leidman, P. H., Hastorf, A. H., & Gross, R. T. (1985). Single parents, extended households, and the control of adolescents. *Child Development, 56*, 326–341.

Dornbusch, S. M., Petersen, A. C., & Hetherington, E. M. (1991). Projecting the future of research on adolescence. *Journal of Research on Adolescence, 1*, 7–17.

Dornbusch, S. M., Ritter, P. L., Leiderman, P. H., Roberts, D. F., & Fraleigh, M. J. (1987). The relation of parenting style to adolescent school performance. *Child Development, 58*, 1244–1257.

Douvan, E., & Adelson, J. (1966). *The adolescent experience*. New York: Wiley.

Dowdy, B. B., & Kliewer, W. (1996, March). *Dating, parent-adolescent conflict, and autonomy.* Paper presented at the meeting of the Society for Research on Adolescence, Boston.

Downey, G., & Coyne, J. C. (1990). Children of depressed parents: An integrative review. *Psychological Bulletin, 108*, 50–76.

Downey, G., & Bonica, C. A. (1997, April). *Characteristics of early adolescent dating relationships.* Paper presented at the meeting of the Society for Research in Child Development, Washington, D.C.

Dreman, S. (1997). *The families of the 21st century*. Mahwah, NJ: Erlbaum.

Dreyer, P. H. (1982). Sexuality during adolescence. In B. B. Wolman (Ed.), *Handbook of developmental psychology*. Englewood Cliffs, NJ: Prentice Hall.

Dreyer, P. H., Jennings, T., Johnson, L., & Evans, D. (1994, February). *Culture and personality in urban schools: Identity status, self-concept, and locus of control among high school students in monolingual and bilingual homes.* Paper presented at the meeting of the Society for Research on Adolescence, San Diego.

Dryfoos, J. G. (1990). *Adolescents at risk: Prevalence and prevention*. New York: Oxford University Press.

Dryfoos, J. G. (1995). Full service schools: Revolution or fad? *Journal of Research on Adolescence, 5*, 147–172.

Dryfoos, J. G. (in press). School as a place for health, mental health, and social service centers. *Teachers College Record*.

DuBois, D. L., & Hirsch, B. J. (1990). School and neighborhood friendship patterns of blacks and whites in early adolescence. *Child Development, 61*, 524–536.

DuBois, D. L., Felner, R. D., & Brand, S. (1997, April). *Self-esteem profiles and adjustment in early adolescence: A two-year longitudinal study.* Paper presented at the meeting of the Society for Research in Child Development, Washington, DC.

Duck, S. W. (1975). Personality similarity and friendship choices by adolescents. *European Journal of Social Psychology, 5*, 351–365.

Duckett, E., & Richards, M. H. (1996, March). *Fathers' time in child care and the father-child relationship.* Paper presented at the meeting of the Society for Research on Adolescence, Boston.

Duckett, R. H. (1997, July). *Strengthening families/building communities.* Paper presented at the conference on Working with America's Youth, Pittsburgh, PA.

Duncan, G. J., Brooks-Gunn, J., & Klebanov, P. K. (1994). Economic deprivation and early childhood development. *Child Development, 65*, 296–318.

Dunphy, D. C. (1963). The social structure of urban adolescent peer groups. *Society, 26*, 230–246.

Durbin, D. L., Darling, N., Steinberg, L., & Brown, B. B. (1993). Parenting style and peer group membership among European-American adolescents. *Journal of Research on Early Adolescence, 3*, 87–100.

Durkin, K., & Hutchins, G. (1984). Challenging traditional sex role stereotypes via career education broadcasts: The reactions of young secondary school pupils. *Journal of Educational Television, 10*, 25–33.

Eagleston, J. R., Kirmil-Gray, K., Thoresen, C. E., Widenfield, S. A., Bracke, P., Helft, L., & Arnow, B. (1986). Physical health correlates of Type-A behavior in children and adolescents. *Journal of Behavioral Medicine, 9*, 341–362.

Eagly, A. H. (1995). The science and politics of comparing men and women. *American Psychologist, 50*, 145–158.

Eagly, A. H., & Crowley, M. (1986). Gender and helping behavior: A meta-analytic review of the social psychological literature. *Psychological Bulletin, 100*, 283–308.

Earls, F. (1993). Health promotion for minority adolescents: Cultural considerations. In S. G. Millstein, A. C. Petersen, & E. O. Nightingale (Eds.), *Promoting the health of adolescents*. New York: Oxford University Press.

East, P. L. (1994, February). *The younger sisters of childbearing adolescents: Their sexual and childbearing attitudes, expectations, and behaviors.* Paper presented at the meeting of the Society for Research on Adolescence, San Diego.

Ebata, A. T. (1991). Stress and coping in adolescence. In R. M. Lerner, A. C. Petersen, & J. Brooks-Gunn (Eds.), *Encyclopedia of adolescence* (Vol. 2). New York: Garland.

Ebata, A. T., & Moos, R. H. (1994). Personal, situational, and contextual correlates of coping in adolescence. *Journal of Research in Adolescence, 4*, 99–125.

Eberly, M. B., & Montemayor, R. (1996, March). *Adolescent prosocial behavior toward mothers and fathers: A reflection of parent-adolescent relationships.* Paper presented at the meeting of the Society for Research on Adolescence, Boston.

Eberly, M. B., Hascall, S. A., Andrews, H., & Marshall, P. M. (1997, April). *Contributions of attachment quality and adolescent prosocial behavior to perceptions of parental influence: A longitudinal study.* Paper presented at the meeting of the Society for Research in Child Development, Washington, DC.

Eccles, J. (1987). Gender roles and achievement patterns: An expectancy value perspective. In J. M. Reinisch, L. A. Rosenblum, & S. A. Sanders (Eds.), *Masculinity/femininity*. New York: Oxford University Press.

Eccles, J. S. (1993, March). *Psychological and social barriers to women's participation in mathematics and science.* Paper presented at the biennial meeting of the American Educational Research Association, Atlanta.

Eccles, J. S., & Buchanan, C. M. (1992, March). *Hormones and behavior at early adolescence: A theoretical overview.* Paper presented at the meeting of the Society for Research on Adolescence, Washington, DC.

Eccles, J. S., & Harold, R. D. (1993). Parent-school involvement during the adolescent years. In R. Takanishi (Ed.), *Adolescence in the 1990s*. New York: Columbia University Press.

Eccles, J. S., Jacobs, J., Harold, R., Yoon, K., Aberbach, A., & Dolan, C. F. (1991, August). *Expectancy effects are alive and well on the home front: Influences on, and consequences of, parents' beliefs regarding their daughters' and sons' abilities and interests*. Paper presented at the meeting of the American Psychological Association, San Francisco.

Eccles, J. S., Lord, S., & Buchanan, C. M. (1996). School transitions in early adolescence: What are we doing to our young people? In J. A. Graber, J. Brooks-Gunn, & A. C. Petersen (Eds.), *Transitions in adolescence*. Mahwah, NJ: Erlbaum.

Eccles, J. S., Midgley, C., Wigfield, A., Buchanan, C. M., Reuman, D., Flanagan, C., & Mac Iver, D. (1993). Development during adolescence: The impact of stage-environment fit on young adolescents' experiences in schools and families. *American Psychologist, 48*, 90–101.

Eccles, J. S., & Wigfield, A. L. (1997, April). *Gendered values and attitudes: Developmental, historical, and cultural changes*. Paper presented at the meeting of the Society for Research in Child Development, Washington, DC.

Eccles, J. S., Wigfield, A., & Schiefele, U. (1997). Motivation to succeed. In N. Eisenberg (Ed), *Handbook of child psychology* (5th Ed., Vol. 3). New York: Wiley.

Edelbrock, C. S. (1989, April). *Self-reported internalizing and externalizing problems in a community sample of adolescents*. Paper presented at the meeting of the Society for Research in Child Development, Kansas City.

Edelman, M. W. (1992). Foreword. In A. Hatkoff & K. Klopp, *How to save the children*. New York: Simon & Schuster.

Edelman, M. W. (1996). *The state of America's children*. Washington, DC: Children's Defense Fund.

Edelman, M. W. (1997, April). *Children, families and social policy*. Paper presented at the meeting of the Society for Research in Child Development, Washington, DC.

Educational Testing Service. (1992, February). *Cross-national comparisons of 9–13 year olds' science and math achievement*. Princeton, NJ: Educational Testing Service.

Eisenberg, N. (1991). Prosocial development in adolescence. In R. M. Lerner, A. C. Petersen, & J. Brooks-Gunn (Eds.), *Encyclopedia of adolescence* (Vol. 2). New York: Garland.

Eisenberg, N., & Murphy, B. (1995). Parenting and children's moral development. In M. H. Bornstein (Ed.), *Children and parenting* (Vol. 4). Hillsdale, NJ: Erlbaum.

Eisenberg, N., Carolo, G., Murphy, B., & Van Court, P. (1995). Prosocial development in late adolescence: A longitudinal study. *Child Development, 66*, 1179–1197.

Eisenberg, N., & Fabes, R. A. (1997). Prosocial development. In N. Eisenberg (Ed.), *Handbook of child psychology* (5th Ed., Vol. 3). New York: Wiley.

Elder, G. H. (1974). *Children of the Great Depression*. Chicago: University of Chicago Press.

Elder, G. H. (1975). Adolescence in the life cycle. In S. E. Dragastin & G. H. Elder (Eds.), *Adolescence in the life cycle: Psychological change and social context*. New York: Wiley.

Elder, G. H. (1979). Historical change in life patterns and personality. In P. B. Baltes & O. G. Brim (Eds.), *Life-span development and behavior* (Vol. 2). New York: Academic Press.

Elder, G. H. (1995). The life course paradigm: Social change and individual development. In P. Moen, G. H. Elder, & K. Luscher (Eds.), *Examining lives in context*. Washington, DC: American Psychological Association.

Elder, G. H. (in press). Human lives in changing societies: Life course and developmental insights. In R. B. Cairns & E. J. Costello (Eds.), *Developmental science*. New York: Cambridge University Press.

Elder, G. H., Modell, J., & Parke, R. D. (Eds.). (1993). *Children in time and place: Developmental and historical insights*. New York: Cambridge University Press.

Elder, G. H., Shanahan, M. J., & Clipp, E. C. (1994). When war comes to men's lives: Life course patterns in family, work, and health. *Psychology and Aging, 9*, 5–16.

Elder, G. H. (1997, April). *The life course as developmental theory*. Paper presented at the meeting of the Society for Research in Child Development, Washington, DC.

Elkind, D. (1961). Quantity conceptions in junior and senior high school students. *Child Development, 32*, 551–560.

Elkind, D. (1976). *Child development and education: A Piagetian perspective*. New York: Oxford University Press.

Elkind, D. (1981). *The hurried child*. Reading, MA: Addison-Wesley.

Elkind, D. (1985). Reply to D. Lapsley and M. Murphy's *Developmental Review* paper. *Developmental Review, 5*, 218–226.

Elliott, D. S. (1993). Health-enhancing and health-compromising lifestyles. In S. G. Millstein, A. C. Petersen, & E. O. Nightingale (Eds.), *Promoting the health of adolescents*. New York: Oxford University Press.

Ellis, L., & Ames, M. A. (1987). Neurohormonal functioning and sexual orientation: A theory of homosexuality-heterosexuality. *Psychological Bulletin, 101*, 233–258.

Emery, R. E., & Tuer, M. (1993). Parenting and the marital relationship. In T. Luster & L. Okagaki (Eds.), *Parenting: An ecological perspective*. Hillsdale, NJ: Erlbaum.

Enright, R. D., Lapsley, D., & Olson, L. (1984). Moral judgment and the social cognitive development research program. In S. Modgil & C. Modgil (Eds.), *Lawrence Kohlberg: Consensus and controversy*. Slough, England: NFER Press.

Enright, R. D., Lapsley, D. K., Dricas, A. S., & Fehr, L. A. (1980). Parental influence on the development of adolescent autonomy and identity. *Journal of Youth and Adolescence, 9*, 529–546.

Enright, R. D., Levy, V. M., Harris, D., & Lapsley, D. K. (1987). Do economic conditions influence how theorists view adolescents? *Journal of Youth and Adolescence, 16*, 541–559.

Enright, R. D., Santos, M. J. D., & Al-Mabuk, R. (1989). The adolescent as forgiver. *Journal of Adolescence, 12*, 95–110.

Entwistle, D. R. (1990). Schools and the adolescent. In S. S. Feldman & G. R. Elliott (Eds.), *At the threshold: The developing adolescent*. Cambridge, MA: Harvard University Press.

Epstein, H. T. (1980). EEG developmental stages. *Developmental Psychobiology, 13*, 629–631.

Epstein, J. L. (1990). School and family connections: Theory, research, and implications for integrating sociologies of education and family. In D. G. Unger & M. B. Sussman (Eds.), *Families in community settings: Interdisciplinary responses*. New York: Haworth Press.

Epstein, J. L. (1992). School and family partnerships. *Encyclopedia of educational research* (6th ed.). New York: Macmillan.

Epstein, J. L., & Dunbar, S. L. (1995). Effects on students of an interdisciplinary program linking social studies, art, and family volunteers in the middle grades. *Journal of Early Adolescence, 15,* 114–144.

Erickson, J. B. (1982). *A profile of community youth organization members, 1980.* Boys Town, NE: Boys Town Center for the Study of Youth Development.

Erickson, J. B. (in press). *Directory of American youth organizations* (2nd rev. ed.). Boys Town, NE: Boys Town, Communications and Public Services Division.

Erikson, E. H. (1950). *Childhood and society.* New York: W. W. Norton.

Erikson, E. H. (1962). *Young man Luther.* New York: W. W. Norton.

Erikson, E. H. (1968). *Identity: Youth and crisis.* New York: W. W. Norton.

Erikson, E. H. (1969). *Gandhi's truth.* New York: W. W. Norton.

Erikson, E. H. (1970). Reflections on the dissent of contemporary youth. *International Journal of Psychoanalysis, 51,* 11–22.

Erlick, A. C., & Starry, A. R. (1973, June). *Sources of information for career decisions.* Report of Poll No. 98, Purdue Opinion Panel.

Escobedo, L. G., Marcus, S. E., Holtzman, D., & Giovino, G. A. (1993). Sports participation, age at smoking initiation, and risk of smoking among U.S. high school students. *Journal of the American Medical Association, 269,* 1391–1395.

Ethier, K., & Deaux, K. (1990). Hispanics in ivy: Assessing identity and perceived threat. *Sex Roles, 20,* 59–70.

Evans, B. J., & Whitfield, J. R. (Eds.). (1988). *Black males in the United States: An annotated bibliography from 1967 to 1987.* Washington, DC: American Psychological Association.

Evans, I. M., Cicchelli, T., Cohen, M., & Shapiro, N. (1995). *Staying in school.* Baltimore: Paul Brookes.

Evans, M. E. (1992, March). *Achievement and achievement-related beliefs in Asian and Western contexts: Cultural and gender differences.* Paper presented at the meeting of the Society for Research on Adolescence, Washington, DC.

Eyler, J., & Giles, D. (1997). The importance of program quality in service-learning. In A. S. Waterman (Ed.), *Service-learning.* Mahwah, NJ: Erlbaum.

Fabes, R. A., Knight, G. P., & Higgins, D. A. (1995, March). *Gender differences in aggression: A meta-analytic reexamination of time and age effects.* Paper presented at the meeting of the Society for Research in Child Development, Indianapolis.

Faigel, H. C., Sznajderman, S., Tishy, O., Turel, M., & Pinus, U. (1995). Attention deficit disorder during adolescence: A review. *Journal of Adolescent Health, 16,* 174–184.

Falbo, T., & Poston, D. L. (1993). The academic, personality, and physical outcomes of only children in China. *Child Development, 64,* 18–35.

Falbo, T. L., & Romo, H. D. (1994, February). *Hispanic parents and public education: The gap between cultures.* Paper presented at the meeting of the Society for Research on Adolescence, San Diego.

Farley, J. E. (1990). *Sociology.* Englewood Cliffs, NJ: Prentice Hall.

Fasick, F. A. (1994). On the "invention" of adolescence. *Journal of Early Adolescence, 14,* 6–23.

Fay, A. L. (1995, March). *Factors affecting the content and structure of children's science explanations.* Paper presented at the meeting of the Society for Research in Child Development, Indianapolis.

Feeney, S. (1980). *Schools for young adolescents: Adapting the early childhood model.* Carrboro, NC: Center for Early Adolescence.

Feiring, C. (1995, March). *The development of romance from 15 to 18 years.* Paper presented at the meeting of the Society for Research in Child Development, Indianapolis.

Feiring, C. (1996). Concepts of romance in 15-year-old adolescents. *Journal of Research on Adolescence, 6,* 181–200.

Feiring, C. (1997, April). *Gender identity and the development of adolescent romance.* Paper presented at the meeting of the Society for Research in Child Development, Washington, DC.

Feist, J., & Brannon, L. (1989). *An introduction to behavior and health.* Belmont, CA: Wadsworth.

Feldman, D. H., & Piirto, J. (1995). Parenting talented children. In M. H. Bornstein (Ed.), *Handbook of parenting.* Hillsdale, NJ: Erlbaum.

Feldman, S. S., & Elliott, G. R. (1990). Progress and promise of research on normal adolescent development. In S. S. Feldman & G. Elliott (Eds.). *At the threshold: The developing adolescent.* Cambridge, MA: Harvard University Press.

Feldman, S. S., & Rosenthal, D. A. (1990). The acculturation of autonomy expectations in Chinese high schoolers residing in two Western nations. *International Journal of Psychology, 25,* 259–281.

Feldman, S. S., & Weinberger, D. A. (1994). Self-restraint as a mediator of family influences on boys' delinquent behavior: A longitudinal study. *Child Development, 65,* 195–211.

Fenzel, L. M. (1994, February). *A prospective study of the effects of chronic strains on early adolescent self-worth and school adjustment.* Paper presented at the meeting of the Society for Research on Adolescence, San Diego.

Fenzel, L. M., Blyth, D. A., & Simmons, R. G. (1991). School transitions, secondary. In R. M. Lerner, A. C. Petersen, & J. Brooks-Gunn (Eds.), *Encyclopedia of adolescence* (Vol. 2). New York: Garland.

Fenzel, L. M., & Magaletta, P. R. (1993, March). *Predicting intrinsic motivation of Black early adolescents: The roles of school strain, academic competence, and self-esteem.* Paper presented at the biennial meeting of the Society for Research in Child Development, New Orleans.

Field, L. D. (1991, April). *The role of social support in Hispanic adolescents' academic achievement.* Paper presented at the biennial meeting of the Society for Research in Child Development, San Francisco.

Figueira-McDonough, J. (1992). Community structure and female delinquency rates. *Youth and Society, 24,* 3–30.

Fine, G. A., Mortimer, J. T., & Roberts, D. F. (1990). Leisure, work, and the mass media. In S. S. Feldman & G. R. Elliott (Eds.), *At the threshold: The developing adolescent.* Cambridge, MA: Harvard University Press.

Firpo-Triplett, R. (1997, July). *Is it flirting or sexual harassment?* Paper presented at the conference onWorking with America's Youth, Pittsburgh, PA.

Fischer, K. W. (1980). A theory of cognitive development: The control and construction of hierarchies of skills. *Psychological Review, 87,* 477–531.

Fischer, K. W., & Lazerson, A. (1984). *Human development.* San Francisco: W. H. Freeman.

Fischer, M., Barkley, R. A., Edelbrock, C. S., & Smallish, L. (1990). The adolescent outcome of hyperactive children diagnosed by research criteria: II. Academic, attentional, and neuropsychological status. *Journal of Consulting and Clinical Psychology, 58,* 580–588.

Fish, K. D., & Biller, H. B. (1973). Perceived childhood paternal relationships and college females' personal adjustment. *Adolescence, 8,* 415–420.

Fisher, C. B., Jackson, J. F., & Villarruel, F. A. (1997). The study of African-American and Latin-American children and youth. In R. M. Lerner (Ed.), *Handbook of child psychology* (5th Ed., Vol. 1). New York: Wiley.

Fisher, D. (1990, March). *Effects of attachment on adolescents' friendships.* Paper presented at the meeting of the Society for Research in Adolescence, Atlanta.

Fisher, M., Golden, N. H., Katzman, D. K., Kreipe, R. E., Rees, J., Schebendach, J., Sigman, G., Ammerman, S., & Hoberman, H. M. (1995). Eating disorders in adolescents: A background paper. *Journal of Adolescent Health, 16,* 420–437.

Fisher, T. D. (1987). Family communication and the sexual behavior and attitudes of college students. *Journal of Youth and Adolescence, 16,* 481–495.

Fiske, S. T., Bersoff, D. N., Borgida, E., Deaux, K., & Heilman, M. E. (1991). Social science research on trial: Use of sex stereotyping research in *Price Waterhouse v. Hopkins. American Psychologist, 23,* 399–427.

Flanagan, A. S. (1996, March). *Romantic behavior of sexually victimized and nonvictimized women.* Paper presented at the meeting of the Society for Research on Adolescence, Boston.

Flanagan, C. A., & Eccles, J. S. (1993). Changes in parents' work status and adolescents' adjustment at school. *Child Development, 64,* 246–257.

Flanagan, C. (1997, April). *Youth, family values, and civil society.* Paper presented at the meeting of the Society for Research in Child Development, Washington, DC.

Flannery, D. J., Rowe, D. C., & Gulley, B. L. (1993). Impact of pubertal status, timing, and age on adolescent sexual experience and delinquency. *Journal of Adolescent Research, 8,* 21–40.

Flavell, J. H. (1979). Metacognition and cognitive monitoring: A new area of psychological inquiry. *American Psychologist, 34,* 906–911.

Flavell, J. H. (1992). Cognitive development: Past, present, and future. *Developmental Psychology, 28,* 998–1005.

Flavell, J. H., Miller, P. A., & Miller, S. A. (1993). *Cognitive development* (3rd ed.). Englewood Cliffs, NJ: Prentice Hall.

Flavell, J. H., & Miller, P. H. (1997). Social cognition. In D. Kuhn & R. S. Siegel (Eds.), *Handbook of child psychology* (5th Ed., Vol. 3). New York: Wiley.

Fletcher, A. (1995, March). *Parental and peer influences on academic achievement in African-American girls.* Paper presented at the meeting of the Society for Research in Child Development, Indianapolis.

Foon, A. (1988). The relationship between school type and adolescent self-esteem, attribution styles, and affiliation needs: Implications for educational outcome. *British Journal of Educational Psychology, 58,* 44–54.

Forehand, G., Ragosta, J., & Rock, D. (1976). *Conditions and processes of effective school desegregation.* Princeton, NJ: Educational Testing Service.

Forrest, J. D. (1990). Cultural influences on adolescents' reproductive behavior. In J. Bancroft & J. M. Reinisch (Eds.), *Adolescence and puberty.* New York: Oxford University Press.

Forrest, J. D., & Singh, S. (1990). The sexual and reproductive behavior of American women, 1982–1988. *Family Planning Perspectives, 22,* 206–214.

Fouad, N. A. (1995). Career behavior of Hispanics: Assessment and career intervention. In F. T. L. Leong (Ed.), *Career development and vocational behavior of racial and ethnic minorities.* Hillsdale, NJ: Erlbaum.

Fowler, J. W. (1981). *Stages of faith: The psychology of human development and the quest for faith.* New York: HarperCollins.

Fox, L. H., Brody, L., & Tobin, D. (1979). *Women and mathematics.* Baltimore: Johns Hopkins University, Intellectually Gifted Study Group.

Francis, J., Fraser, G., & Marcia, J. E. (1989). *Cognitive and experimental factors in moratorium-achievement (MAMA) cycles.* Unpublished manuscript, Department of Psychology, Simon Fraser University, Burnaby, British Columbia.

Fraser, K. (1994, February). *Ethnic differences in adolescents' possible selves: The role of ethnic identity in shaping self-concept.* Paper presented at the meeting of the Society for Research on Adolescence, San Diego.

Fraser, S. (Ed.). (1995). *The bell curve wars: Race, intelligence, and the future of America.* New York: Basic Books.

Freeman, D. (1983). *Margaret Mead and Samoa.* Cambridge, MA: Harvard University Press.

Freeman, H. S. (1993, March). *Parental control of adolescents through family transitions.* Paper presented at the biennial meeting of the Society for Research in Child Development, New Orleans.

Freud, A. (1958). *The ego and the mechanisms of defense.* New York: International Universities Press.

Freud, A. (1966). Instinctual anxiety during puberty. In *The writings of Anna Freud: The ego and the mechanisms of defense.* New York: International Universities Press.

Freud, A., & Dann, S. (1951). Instinctual anxiety during puberty. In A. Freud, *The ego and its mechanisms of defense.* New York: International Universities Press.

Freud, S. (1917). *A general introduction to psychoanalysis.* New York: Washington Square Press.

Friedman, H. S., Tucker, J. S., Schwartz, J. E., Tomlinson-Keasey, C., Martin, L. R., Wingard, D. L., & Criqui, M. H. (1995). Psychosocial and behavioral predictors of longevity: The aging and death of the "Termites." *American Psychologist, 50,* 69–78.

Frisch, R. E. (1991). Puberty and body fat. In R. M. Lerner, A. C. Petersen, & J. Brooks-Gunn (Eds.), *Encyclopedia of adolescence.* New York: Garland.

Frisch, R. E., & Revelle, R. (1970). Height and weight at menarche and a hypothesis of critical body weights and adolescent events. *Science, 169,* 397–399.

Furman, W., & Wehner, E. A. (1993, March). *Adolescent romantic relationships: A developmental perspective.* Paper presented at the biennial meeting of the Society for Research in Child Development, New Orleans.

Furman, W., Wehner, E. A., & Underwood, S. (1994, February). *Sexual behavior, sexual communication, and relationships.* Paper presented at the meeting of the Society for Research on Adolescence, San Diego.

Furstenberg, F. F., Brooks-Gunn, J., & Chase-Lansdale, L. (1989). Teenage pregnancy and childbearing. *American Psychologist, 44,* 313–320.

Furstenberg, F. F., Jr., & Harris, K. T. (1992). When fathers matter/why fathers matter: The impact of paternal involvement on the offspring of adolescent mothers. In R. Lerman and T. Ooms (Eds.), *Young unwed fathers.* Philadelphia: Temple University Press.

Furth, H. G., & Wachs, H. (1975). *Thinking goes to school.* New York: Oxford University Press.

G

Galambos, N. L., & Maggs, J. L. (1991). Out-of-school care of young adolescents and self-reported behavior. *Developmental Psychology, 27,* 644–655.

Galambos, N. L., Petersen, A. C., Richards, M., & Gitleson, I. B. (1985). The Attitudes toward Women Scale for Adolescents (AWSA): A study of reliability and validity. *Sex Roles, 13,* 343–356.

Galambos, N. L., & Sears, H. A. (1995, March). *Depressive symptoms in adolescents: Examining family matters.* Paper presented at the meeting of the Society for Research in Child Development, Indianapolis.

Galambos, N. L., Sears, H. A., Almeida, D. M., & Kolaric, G. C. (1995). Parents' work overload and problem behavior in young adolescents. *Journal of Research on Adolescence, 5,* 201–224.

Galambos, N. L., & Tilton-Weaver, L. (1996, March). *The adultoid adolescent: Too much, too soon.* Paper presented at the meeting of the Society for Research on Adolescence, Boston.

Galambos, N. L., & Turner, P. K. (1997, April). *Shaping parent-adolescent relations: Examining the goodness-of-fit in parent and adolescent temperaments.* Paper presented at the meeting of the Society for Research in Child Development, Washington, DC.

Galanter, M. (1989). *Cults: Faith, healing, and coercion.* New York: Oxford University Press.

Galloti, K. M., & Kozberg, S. F. (1996). Adolescents' experience of a life-framing decision. *Journal of Youth and Adolescence, 25,* 3–16.

Gallup, G., & Poling, D. (1980). *The search for America's faith.* New York: Abington.

Gallup, G. W., & Bezilla, R. (1992). *The religious life of young Americans.* Princeton, NJ: Gallup Institute.

Galotti, K. M., Kozberg, S. F., & Farmer, M. C. (1990, March). *Gender and developmental differences in adolescents' conceptions of moral reasoning.* Paper presented at the meeting of the Society for Research in Adolescence, Atlanta.

Garbarino, J., & Asp, C. E. (1981). *Successful schools and competent students.* Lexington, MA: Lexington Books.

Garber, J., Kriss, M. R., Koch, M., & Lindholm, L. (1988). Recurrent depression in adolescents: A follow-up study. *Journal of the American Academy of Child and Adolescent Psychiatry, 27,* 49–54.

Garcia, J. G., & Zea, M. C. (1997). *Psychological interventions and research with Latino populations.* Needham Heights, MA: Allyn & Bacon.

Garcia, L., Hart, D., & Johnson-Ray, R. (in press). What do children and adolescents think about themselves? A developmental account of self-concept development. In S. Hala (Ed.), *The development of social cognition.* London: University College of London.

Gardner, H. (1983). *Frames of mind.* New York: Basic Books.

Gardner, H. (1989). Beyond a modular view of mind. In W. Damon (Ed.), *Child development today and tomorrow.* San Francisco: Jossey-Bass.

Gardner, L. I., Stern, M. P., Haffner, S. M., Gaskill, S. P., Hazuda, H. P., Relethford, J. H., & Eifter, C. W. (1984). Prevalence of diabetes in Mexican Americans: Relationships to percent of gene pool derived from native American sources. *Diabetes, 33,* 86–92.

Gardon, F. E. (1997, July). *The challenge of sexuality education in underserved and low income communities.* Paper presented at the conference on Working with America's Youth, Pittsburgh, PA.

Garmezy, N. (1993). Children in poverty: Resilience despite risk. *Psychiatry, 56,* 127–136.

Garmon, L., Basinger, K. S., & Gibbs, J. C. (1995, March). *Gender differences in the expression of moral judgment.* Paper presented at the meeting of the Society for Research in Child Development, Indianapolis.

Garner, D. M., & Garfinkel, P. E. (1997). *Handbook of treatment for eating disorders.* New York: Plenum.

Garrett, P., Ng'andu, N., & Ferron, J. (1994). Poverty experiences of young children and the quality of their home environments. *Child Development, 65,* 331–345.

Gauze, C. M. (1994, February). *Talking to Mom about friendship: What do mothers know?* Paper presented at the meeting of the Society for Research on Adolescence, San Diego.

Ge, X., Conger, R. D., Cadoret, R. J., Neiderhiser, M. M., Yates, W., Troughton, E., & Stewart, M. A. (1996). The developmental interface between nature and nurture: A mutual influence model of child antisocial behavior and parent behaviors. *Developmental Psychology, 32,* 574–590.

George, C. M. (1996, March). *Gene-environment interactions: Testing the bioecological model during adolescence.* Paper presented at the meeting of the Society for Research on Adolescence, Boston.

George, R. (1987). *Youth policies and programs in selected countries.* Washington, DC: William T. Grant Foundation.

Gfellner, B. M., & Hundleby, J. D. (1994, February). *Patterns of drug use and social activities among Native American and White adolescents.* Paper presented at the Society for Research on Adolescence, San Diego.

Giaconia, R. M., & Hedges, L. V. (1982). Identifying features of effective open education. *Review of Educational Research, 52,* 579–602.

Gibbs, J. T. (1989). Black American adolescents. In J. T. Gibbs & L. N. Huang (Eds.), *Children of color.* San Francisco: Jossey-Bass.

Gibbs, J. T., & Huang, L. N. (1989). A conceptual framework for assessing and treating minority youth. In J. T. Gibbs & L. N. Huang (Eds.), *Children of color.* San Francisco: Jossey-Bass.

Gibbs, N. (1990, Fall). The dreams of youth. *Time* (Special Issue), pp. 10–14.

Gilligan, C. (1982). *In a different voice.* Cambridge, MA: Harvard University Press.

Gilligan, C. (1990). Teaching Shakespeare's sister. In C. Gilligan, N. Lyons, and T. Hanmer (Eds.), *Making connections: The relational worlds of adolescent girls at Emma Willard School.* Cambridge: Harvard University Press.

Gilligan, C. (1992, May). *Joining the resistance: Girls' development in adolescence.* Paper presented at the symposium on development and vulnerability in close relationships, Montreal, Quebec.

Gilligan, C., & Attanucci, J. (1988). Two moral orientations. In C. Gilligan, J. V. Ward, J. M. Taylor, & B. Bardige (Eds.), *Mapping the moral domain.* Cambridge, MA: Harvard University Press.

Gilligan, C., Brown, L. M., & Rogers, A. G. (1990). Psyche embedded: A place for body, relationships, and culture in personality theory. In A. I. Rabin, R. A. Zuker, R. A. Emmons, & S. Frank (Eds.), *Studying persons and lives.* New York: Springer.

Ginzberg, E. (1972). Toward a theory of occupational choice: A restatement. *Vocational Guidance Quarterly, 20,* 169–176.

Ginzberg, E., Ginzberg, S. W., Axelrad, S., & Herman, J. L. (1951). *Occupational choice*. New York: Columbia University.

Gjerde, P. F. (1986). The interpersonal structure of family interaction settings: Parent-adolescents relations in dyads and triads. *Developmental Psychology, 22*, 297–304.

Gjerde, P. F., & Block, J. (1990, March). *The preschool context of 18-year-olds with depressive symptoms: A prospective study*. Paper presented at the meeting of the Society for Research in Adolescence, Atlanta.

Gjerde, P. F., Block, J., & Block, J. H. (1991). The preschool family context of 18-year-olds with depressive symptoms: A prospective study. *Journal of Research on Adolescence, 1*, 63–92.

Glass, G. V., & Smith, M. L. (1978, September). *Meta-analysis of research on the relationship of class size and achievement*. San Francisco: Far West Educational Laboratory.

Glassman, M. J. (1997, April). *Moral action in the context of social activity*. Paper presented at the meeting of the Society for Research in Child Development, Washington, DC.

Glick, J. (1975). Cognitive development in cross-cultural perspective. In F. Horowitz (Ed.), *Review of child development research* (Vol. 4). Chicago: University of Chicago Press.

Glover, R. W., & Marshall, R. (1993). Improving the school-to-work transition of American adolescents. In R. Takanishi (Ed.), *Adolescence in the 1990s*. New York: Teachers College Record.

Glueck, S., & Glueck, E. (1950). *Unraveling juvenile delinquency*. New York: Commonwealth Fund.

Glueck, S., & Glueck, E. (1950). *Unraveling juvenile delinquency*. Cambridge, MA: Harvard University Press.

Goertz, M. E., Ekstrom, R. B., & Rock, D. (1991). Dropouts, high school: Issues of race and sex. In R. M. Lerner, A. C. Petersen, & J. Brooks-Gunn (Eds.), *Encyclopedia of adolescence* (Vol. 1). New York: Garland.

Gold, M., & Petronio, R. J. (1980). Delinquent behavior in adolescence. In J. Adelson (Ed.), *Handbook of adolescent psychology*. New York: Wiley.

Goldberg, H. (1976). *The hazards of being male*. New York: Signet.

Goldberg, H. (1980). *The new male*. New York: Signet.

Goldman, R. (1964). *Religious thinking from childhood to adolescence*. London: Routledge & Kegan Paul.

Goldscheider, F. C. (1997). Family relationships and life course strategies for the 21st century. In S. Dreman (Ed.), *The family on the threshold of the 21st century*. Mahwah, NJ: Erlbaum.

Goldsmith, H. H. (1988, August). *Does early temperament predict late development?* Paper presented at the meeting of the American Psychological Association, Atlanta.

Goldsmith, H. H., & Gottesman, I. I. (1981). Origins of variation in behavioral style: A longitudinal study of temperament in young twins. *Child Development, 52*, 91–103.

Goldstein, A. P., & Conoley, J. C. (1997). *School violence intervention*. New York: Guilford.

Gomel, J. N., Tinsley, B. J., & Clark, K. (1995, March). *Family stress and coping during times of economic hardship: A multi-ethnic perspective*. Paper presented at the meeting of the Society for Research in Child Development, Indianapolis.

Goodchilds, J. D., & Zellman, G. L. (1984). Sexual signalling and sexual aggression in adolescent relationships. In N. M. Malamuth & E. D. Donnerstein (Eds.), *Pornography and sexual aggression*. New York: Academic Press.

Goodlad, J. A. (1984). *A place called school*. New York: McGraw-Hill.

Goodman, R. A., Mercy, J. A., Loya, F., Rosenberg, M. L., Smith, J. C., Allen, N. H., Vargas, L., & Kolts, R. (1986). Alcohol use and interpersonal violence: Alcohol detected in homicide victims. *American Journal of Public Health, 76*, 144–149.

Goodnow, J. J. (1995, March). *Incorporating "culture" into accounts of development*. Paper presented at the meeting of the Society for Research in Child Development, Indianapolis.

Goodnow, J. J. (1997, April). *What do cultural perspectives add to analyses of socialization on interactions within the family*. Paper presented at the meeting of the Society for Research in Child Development, Washington, DC.

Gordon, K. A. (1987). *Great expectations: Unprotected intercourse scenario*. Princeton, NJ: Princeton University, McCosh Health Center.

Gordon, S., & Gilgun, J. F. (1987). Adolescent sexuality. In V. B. Van Hasselt & M. Hersen (Eds.), *Handbook of adolescent psychology*. New York: Pergamon.

Gore, T. (1987). *Raising PG kids in an X-rated society*. Nashville, TN: Abingdon Press.

Gottfried, A. (1990). Academic intrinsic motivation on young elementary school children. *Journal of Educational Psychology, 82*, 525–538.

Gottlieb, D. (1966). Teaching and students: The views of Negro and white teachers. *Sociology of Education, 37*, 345–353.

Gottlieb, G. (1997). *Synthesizing nature-nurture*. Mahwah, NJ: Erlbaum.

Gottman, J. M., & Parker, J. G. (Eds.). (1987). *Conversations with friends*. New York: Cambridge University Press.

Graber, J. A., & Brooks-Gunn, J. (1996). Transitions and turning points: Navigating the passage from childhood to adolescence. *Developmental Psychology, 32*, 768–776.

Graber, J. A., & Brooks-Gunn, J. (in press). Expectations for and precursors of leaving home in young women. In J. A. Graber and J. S. Dubas (Eds.), *Leaving home*. San Francisco: Jossey-Bass.

Graber, J. A., Brooks-Gunn, J., & Petersen, A. C. (1996). Adolescent transitions in context. In J. A. Graber, J. Brooks-Gunn, & A. C. Petersen (Eds.), *Transitions through adolescence: Interpersonal domains and contexts*. Mahwah, NJ: Erlbaum.

Graber, J. A., Brooks-Gunn, J., & Warren, M. P. (1995). The antecedents of menarcheal age: Heredity, family environment, and stressful life events. *Child Development, 66*, 346–359.

Graber, J. A., Brooks-Gunn, J., Paikoff, R. L., & Warren, M. P. (1994). Prediction of eating problems: An 8-year study of adolescent girls. *Developmental Psychology, 30*, 823–834.

Graham, S. (1986, August). *Can attribution theory tell us something about motivation in blacks?* Paper presented at the meeting of the American Psychological Association, Washington, DC.

Graham, S. (1990). Motivation in Afro-Americans. In G. L. Berry & J. K. Asamen (Eds.), *Black students: Psychosocial issues and academic achievement*. Newbury Park, CA: Sage.

Gray, W. M., & Hudson, L. M. (1984). Formal operations and the imaginary audience. *Developmental Psychology, 20*, 619–627.

Greenberg, B. S. (1988). *Mass media and adolescents: A review of research reported from 1980–1987*. Manuscript prepared for the Carnegie Council on Adolescent Development.

Santrock: Adolescence

Greenberg, B. S., Stanley, C., Siemicki, M., Heeter, C., Soderman, A., & Linsangan, R. (1986). *Sex content on soaps and prime-time television series most viewed by adolescents.* Project CAST Report /ns/2. East Lansing: Michigan State Department of Telecommunication.

Greenberger, E., & Steinberg, L. (1981). *Project for the study of adolescent work: Final report.* Report prepared for the National Institute of Education, U.S. Department of Education, Washington, DC.

Greenberger, E., & Steinberg, L. (1986). *When teenagers work: The psychological social costs of adolescent employment.* New York: Basic Books.

Greene, B. (1988, May). The children's hour. *Esquire Magazine,* pp. 47–49.

Greenfield, P. M., & Suzuki, L. K. (1997). Culture and human development. In I.E. Sigel & K. A. Renninger (Eds.), *Handbook of child psychology* (5th Ed., Vol. 4). New York: Wiley.

Grimes, B., & Mattimore, K. (1989, April). *The effects of stress and exercise on identity formation in adolescence.* Paper presented at the biennial meeting of the Society for Research in Child Development, Kansas City.

Gross, R. T. (1984). Patterns of maturation: Their effects on behavior and development. In M. D. Levine & P. Satz (Eds.), *Middle childhood: Development and dysfunction.* Baltimore: University Park Press.

Grotevant, H. D.(1996). Unpublished review of *Adolescence* (7th ed.) by J. W. Santrock. Dubuque, IA: Brown & Benchmark.

Grotevant, H. D. (1997). Adolescent development in family contexts. In N. Eisenberg (Ed.), *Handbook of child psychology* (5th Ed. Vol. 3). New York: Wiley.

Grotevant, H. D., & Cooper, C. R. (1985). Patterns of interaction in family relationships and the development of identity exploration in adolescence. *Child Development, 56,* 415–428.

Grotevant, H. D., & Cooper, C. R. (in press). Individuality and connectedness in adolescent development: Review and prospects for research on identity, relationships, and context. In E. Skoe & A. von der Lippe (Eds.), *Personality development in adolescence: A cross-national and life-span perspective.* London: Routledge.

Grotevant, H. D., & Durrett, M. E. (1980). Occupational knowledge and career development in adolescence. *Journal of Vocational Behavior, 17,* 171–182.

Grotevant, H. D., & McRoy, R. G. (1990). Adopted adolescents in residential treatment: The role of the family. In D. M. Brodzinsky & M. D. Schechter (Eds.), *The psychology of adoption.* New York: Oxford University Press.

Gruskin, E. (1994, February). *A review of research on self-identified gay, lesbian, and bisexual youth from 1970–1993.* Paper presented at the meeting of the Society for Research on Adolescence, San Diego.

Guilford, J. P. (1967). *The structure of intellect.* New York: McGraw-Hill.

Gullotta, T. P., G. R. Adams, & R. Montemayor (Eds.). (1995). *Substance misuse in adolescence.* Newbury Park, CA: Sage.

Gur, R. C., Mozley, L. H., Mozley, P. D., Resnick, S. M., Karp, J. S., Alavi, A., Arnold, S. E., & Gur, R. E. (1995). Sex differences in regional cerebral glucose metabolism during a resting state. *Science, 267,* 528–531.

Guttentag, M., & Bray, H. (1976). *Undoing sex stereotypes: Research and resources for educators.* New York: McGraw-Hill.

Haas, A. (1979). *Teenage sexuality: A survey of teenage sexual behavior.* New York: Macmillan.

Hafner, A., Ingels, S., Schnieder, B., & Stevenson, D. (1990). *A profile of the American eighth grader: NELS: 88. Student descriptive summary.* Washington, DC: U.S. Government Printing Office.

Hahn, A. (1987, December). Reaching out to America's dropouts: What to do? *Phi Delta Kappan,* pp. 256–263.

Haidt, J. D. (1997, April). *Cultural and class variations in the domain of morality and the morality of conventions.* Paper presented at the meeting of the Society for Research in Child Development, Washington, DC.

Hale, S. (1990). A global developmental trend in cognitive processing speed. *Child Development, 61,* 653–663.

Hall, G. S. (1904). *Adolescence* (Vols. 1 & 2). Englewood Cliffs, NJ: Prentice Hall.

Halonen, J. (1995). Demystifying critical thinking. *Teaching of Psychology, 22,* 75–81.

Halonen, J. S., & Santrock, J. W. (1996). *Psychology: The contexts of behavior* (2nd ed.). Dubuque, IA: Brown & Benchmark.

Hamburg, B. A. (1990). *Life skills training: Preventive interventions for adolescents.* Washington, DC: Carnegie Council on Adolescent Development.

Hamburg, B. A. (1990). *Life skills training: Preventive interventions for young adolescents.* Washington, DC: Carnegie Council on Adolescent Development.

Hamburg, D. A. (1993). The opportunities of early adolescence. In R. Takanishi (Ed.), *Adolescence in the 1990s.* New York: Teachers College Press.

Hamburg, D. A., Millstein, S. G., Mortimer, A. M., Nightingale, E. O., & Petersen, A. C. (1993). Adolescent health promotion in the twenty-first century: Current frontiers and future directions. In S. G. Millstein, A. C. Petersen, & E. O. Nightingale (Eds.), *Promoting the health of adolescents.* New York: Oxford University Press.

Hammen, C. (1992). Cognitive, life stress, and interpersonal approaches to a developmental psychopathology model of depression. *Development and Psychopathology, 4,* 189–206.

Hammond, W. R. (1993, August). Participant in open forum with the APA Commission on Youth and Violence, meeting of the American Psychological Association, Washington, DC.

Hansen, D. (1996, March). *Adolescent employment and psychosocial outcomes: A comparison of two employment contexts.* Paper presented at the meeting of the Society for Research on Adolescence, Boston.

Hare, B. R., & Castenell, L. A. (1985). No place to run, no place to hide: Comparative status and future prospects of Black boys. In M. B. Spencer, G. K. Brookins, & W. R. Allen (Eds.), *Beginnings: The social and affective development of Black children.* Hillsdale, NJ: Erlbaum.

Hare-Muston, R., & Marecek, J. (1988). The meaning of difference: Gender theory, postmodernism, and psychology. *American Psychologist, 43,* 455–464.

Harkness, S., & Super, C. M. (1995). Culture and parenting. In M. H. Bornstein (Ed.), *Children and parenting* (Vol. 2). Hillsdale, NJ: Erlbaum.

Harmon, D. S. (1984). Brain growth theory and educational psychology. *Psychological Reports, 55,* 59–66.

Harold, R. D., & Eccles, J. S. (1990, March). *Maternal expectations, advice, and provision of opportunities: Their relationships to boys' and girls' occupational aspirations.* Paper presented at the meeting of the Society for Research in Adolescence, Atlanta.

Hart, D. (1996). Unpublished review of *Child Development* (8th ed.) by J. W. Santrock. Dubuque, IA: Brown & Benchmark.

Hart, D., & Fegley, S. (1995). Prosocial behavior and caring in adolescence: Relations to self-understanding and social judgment. *Child Development, 66,* 1346–1359.

Hart, D., Field, N., Garfinkle, J., & Singer, J. (in press). Representations of self and other: A semantic space model. *Journal of Personality.*

Harter, S. (1986). Processes underlying the construction, maintenance, and enhancement of the self-concept of children. In J. Suls & A. Greenwald (Eds.), *Psychological perspective on the self* (Vol. 3). Hillsdale, NJ: Erlbaum.

Harter, S. (1987). The determinants and mediational role of global self-worth in children. In N. Eisenberg (Ed.), *Contemporary issues in developmental psychology.* New York: Wiley.

Harter, S. (1989a). Causes, correlates, and the functional role of global self-worth: A life-span perspective. In J. Kolligian & R. Sternberg (Eds.), *Perceptions of competence and incompetence across the life-span.* New Haven, CT: Yale University Press.

Harter, S. (1989b). *Self-perception profile for adolescents.* Denver: University of Denver, Department of Psychology.

Harter, S. (1990a). Processes underlying adolescent self-concept formation. In R. Montemayor, G. R. Adams, & T. P. Gullotta (Eds.), *From childhood to adolescence: A transitional period?* Newbury Park, CA: Sage.

Harter, S. (1990b). Self and identity development. In S. S. Feldman & G. R. Elliott (Eds.), *At the threshold: The developing adolescent.* Cambridge, MA: Harvard University Press.

Harter, S. (1997). The development of self-representations. In N. Eisenberg (Ed.), *Handbook of child psychology* (5th Ed., Vol. 3). New York: Wiley.

Harter, S., & Lee, L. (1989). *Manifestations of true and false selves in adolescence.* Paper presented at the meeting of the Society for Research in Child Development, Kansas City.

Harter, S., & Marold, D. B. (1992). Psychosocial risk factors contributing to adolescent suicide ideation. In G. Noam & S. Borst (Eds.), *Child and adolescent suicide.* San Francisco: Jossey-Bass.

Harter, S., & Monsour, A. (1992). Developmental analysis of conflict caused by opposing attributes in the adolescent self-portrait. *Developmental Psychology, 28,* 251–260.

Harter, S., Marold, D. B., Whitesell, N. R., & Cobbs, G. (in press). A model of the effects of perceived parent and peer support on adolescent false self behavior. *Child Development.*

Harter, S., Waters, P., & Whitesell, N. (1996, March). *False self behavior and lack of voice among adolescent males and females.* Paper presented at the meeting of the Society for Research on Adolescence, Boston.

Hartshorne, H., & May, M. S. (1928–1930). *Moral studies in the nature of character: Studies in deceit* (Vol. 1); *Studies in self-control* (Vol. 2); *Studies in the organization of character* (Vol. 3). New York: Macmillan.

Hartup, W. W. (1983). Peer relations. In P. H. Mussen (Ed.), *Handbook of child psychology* (4th ed., Vol. 4). New York: Wiley.

Harvard Medical Newsletter. (1981). Cambridge, MA: Harvard Medical School, Department of Continuing Education.

Hatkoff, A., & Klopp, K. (1992). *How to save the children.* New York: Simon & Schuster.

Hauser, S. T., & Bowlds, M. K. (1990). Stress, coping, and adaptation. In S. S. Feldman & G. R. Elliott (Eds.), *At the threshold: The developing adolescent.* Cambridge, MA: Harvard University Press.

Hauser, S. T., Powers, S. I., Noam, G. G., Jacobson, A. M., Weisse, B., & Follansbee, D. J. (1984). Familial contexts of adolescent ego development. *Child Development, 55,* 195–213.

Havighurst, R. J. (1976). A cross-cultural view. In J. F. Adams (Ed.), *Understanding adolescence.* Boston: Allyn & Bacon.

Havighurst, R. J. (1987). Adolescent culture and subculture. In V. B. Van Hasselt & M. Hersen (Eds.), *Handbook of adolescent psychology.* New York: Pergamon.

Hawkins, J. A., & Berndt, T. J. (1985, April). *Adjustment following the transition to junior high school.* Paper presented at the biennial meeting of the Society for Research in Child Development, Toronto.

Hayes, C. (Ed.). (1987). *Risking the future: Adolescent sexuality, pregnancy, and childbearing* (Vol. 1). Washington, DC: National Academy Press.

Haynie, D., & McLellan, J. (1992, March). *Continuity in parent and peer relationships.* Paper presented at the meeting of the Society for Research on Adolescence, Washington, DC.

Hayward, C., Killen, J., & Taylor, C. B. (1994, February). *Puberty and the onset of depressive, eating disorder, and panic symptoms in girls.* Paper presented at the meeting of the Society for Research on Adolescence, San Diego.

Hazen, C., & Shaver, P. (1987). Romantic love conceptualized as an attachment process. *Journal of Personality and Social Psychology, 51,* 511–524.

Heath, S. B. (1983). *Ways with words.* Cambridge, England: Cambridge University Press.

Heath, S. B., & McLaughlin, M. W. (Eds.). (1993). *Identity and inner-city youth.* New York: Teachers College Press.

Hechinger, J. (1992). *Fateful choices.* New York: Hill & Wang.

Hedges, L. V., & Stock, W. (1983, Spring). The effects of class size: An examination of rival hypotheses. *American Educational Research Journal,* pp. 63–85.

Heider, F. (1958). *The psychology of interpersonal relations.* New York: Wiley.

Helms, J. E. (1990, August). *Black and White racial identity theory and professional interracial collaboration.* Paper presented at the meeting of the American Psychological Association, Boston.

Helms, J. E. (1995). An update of Helms' white and people of color racial identity models. In J. G. Ponterotto, J. M. Casas, L. A. Suzuk, & C. M. Alexander (Eds.), *Handbook of multicultural counseling.* Newbury Park, CA: Sage.

Helson, R., Elliot, T., & Leigh, J. (1989). Adolescent antecedents of women's work patterns. In D. Stern & D. Eichorn (Eds.), *Adolescence and work.* Hillsdale, NJ: Erlbaum.

Henderson, K. A., & Zivian, M. T. (1995, March). "The development of gender differences in adolescent body image." Paper presented at the meeting of the Society for Research in Child Development, Indianapolis.

Henderson, V. L., & Dweck, C. S. (1990). Motivation and achievement. In S. S. Feldman & G. R. Elliott (Eds.), *At the threshold: The developing adolescent.* Cambridge, MA: Harvard University Press.

Hernandez, D. J. (1997). Child development and the social demography of childhood. *Child Development, 68,* 149–169.

Hernstein, R. J., & Murray, C. (1994). *The bell curve: Intelligence and class structure in modern life.* New York: Free Press.

Hess, L., Lonky, E., & Roodin, P. A. (1985, April). *The relationship of moral reasoning and ego strength to cheating behavior*. Paper presented at the meeting of the Society for Research in Child Development, Toronto.

Hetherington, E. M. (1972). Effects of father-absence on personality development in adolescent daughters. *Developmental Psychology, 7*, 313–326.

Hetherington, E. M. (1977). *My heart belongs to daddy: A study of the remarriages of daughters of divorcees and widows*. Unpublished manuscript, University of Virginia.

Hetherington, E. M. (1993, March). *An overview of the Virginia longitudinal study of divorce and remarriage with a focus on early adolescence*. Paper presented at the biennial meeting of the Society for Research in Child Development, New Orleans.

Hetherington, E. M. (1995, March). *The changing American family and the well-being of children*. Paper presented at the meeting of the Society for Research in Child Development, Indianapolis.

Hetherington, E. M., Cox, M., & Cox, R. (1982). Effects of divorce on children and parents. In M. E. Lamb (Ed.), *Nontraditional families*. Hillsdale, NJ: Erlbaum.

Hetherington, E. M., & Stanley-Hagan, M. M. (1995). Parenting in divorced and remarried families. In M. H. Bornstein (Ed.), *Children and parenting* (Vol. 4). Hillsdale, NJ: Erlbaum.

Hicks, R., & Connolly, J. A. (1995, March). *Peer relations and loneliness in adolescence: The interactive effects of social self-concept, close friends, and peer networks*. Paper presented at the meeting of the Society for Research in Child Development, Indianapolis.

Hiebert, J., & LeFevre, P. (Eds.). (1987). *Conceptual and procedural knowledge: The case of mathematics*. Hillsdale, NJ: Erlbaum.

Hightower, E. (1990). Adolescent interpersonal and familial percursors of positive mental health at midlife. *Journal of Youth and Adolescence, 19*, 257–275.

Hill, H. S., Soriano, F. I., Chen, A., & LaFromboise, T. (1994). Sociocultural factors in the etiology and prevention of violence among ethnic minority youth. In L. Eron, J. H. Gentry, & P. Schlegel (Eds.), *Reason to hope*. Washington, DC: American Psychological Association.

Hill, J. P., & Holmbeck, G. N. (1986). Attachment and autonomy during adolescence. *Annals of Child Development, 3*, 145–189.

Hill, J. P., & Lynch, M. E. (1983). The intensification of gender-related role expectations during early adolescence. In J. Brooks-Gunn & A. C. Petersen (Eds.), *Girls at puberty: Biological and psychosocial perspectives*. New York: Plenum.

Hill, J. P., & Steinberg, L. D. (1976, April 26–30). *The development of autonomy in adolescence*. Paper presented at the Symposium on Research on Youth Problems, Fundacion Orbegoza Eizaquirre, Madrid, Spain.

Hill, J. P., Holmbeck, G. N., Marlow, L., Green, T. M., & Lynch, M. E. (1985). Pubertal status and parent-child relations in families of seventh-grade boys. *Journal of Early Adolescence, 5*, 31–44.

Hiraga, Y., Cauce, A. M., Mason, C., & Ordonez, N. (1993, March). *Ethnic identity and the social adjustment of biracial youth*. Paper presented at the biennial meeting of the Society for Research in Child Development, New Orleans.

Hirsch, B. J., & Rapkin, B. D. (1987). The transition to junior high school: A longitudinal study of self-esteem, psychological symptomatology, school life, and social support. *Child Development, 58*, 1235–1243.

Hobfoll, S. E. (1989). Conservation of resources: A new attempt at conceptualizing stress. *American Psychologist, 44*, 513–524.

Hoff-Ginsberg, E., & Tardif, T. (1995). Socioeconomic status and parenting. In M. H. Bornstein (Ed.), *Children and parenting* (Vol. 2). Hillsdale, NJ: Erlbaum.

Hofferth, S. L. (1990). Trends in adolescent sexual activity, contraception, and pregnancy in the United States. In J. Bancroft & J. M. Reinisch (Eds.), *Adolescence and puberty*. New York: Oxford University Press.

Hoffman, L. W. (1989). Effects of maternal employment in the two-parent family. *American Psychologist, 44*, 283–292.

Hoffman, L. W. (1996). Progress and problems in the study of adolescence. *Developmental Psychology, 32*, 777–780.

Hoffman, M. L. (1970). Moral development. In P. H. Mussen (Ed.), *Manual of child psychology* (3rd ed., Vol. 2). New York: Wiley.

Hoffman, M. L. (1980). Moral development in adolescence. In J. Adelson (Ed.), *Handbook of adolescent psychology*. New York: Wiley.

Hoffman, M. L. (1988). Moral development. In M. H. Bornstein & M. E. Lamb (Eds.), *Developmental psychology: An advanced textbook* (2nd ed.). Hillsdale, NJ: Erlbaum.

Hoffnung, M. (1984). Motherhood: Contemporary conflict for women. In J. Freeman (Ed.), *Women: A feminist perspective* (3rd ed.). Palo Alto, CA: Mayfield.

Hofstede, G. (1980). *Culture's consequences*. Newbury Park, CA: Sage.

Holland, J. L. (1973). *Making vocational choices: A theory of careers*. Englewood Cliffs, NJ: Prentice Hall.

Holland, J. L. (1987). Current status of Holland's theory of careers: Another perspective. *Career Development Quarterly, 36*, 24–30.

Hollinger, D. (Ed.). (1993). *Single-sex schooling: Perspectives from practice and research*. Washington, DC: U.S. Department of Education, Office of Educational Research and Improvement.

Hollingshead, A. B. (1975). *Elmtown's youth and Elmtown revisited*. New York: Wiley.

Hollingworth, L. S. (1914). *Functional periodicity: An experimental study of the mental and motor abilities of women during menstruation*. New York: Teachers College, Columbia University.

Hollingworth, L. S. (1916). Sex differences in mental tests. *Psychological Bulletin, 13*, 377–383.

Holmbeck, G. N. (1996). A model of family relational transformations during the transition to adolescence: Parent-adolescent conflict and adaptation. In J. A. Graber, J. Brooks-Gunn, & A. C. Petersen (Eds.), *Transitions in adolescence*. Mahwah, NJ: Erlbaum.

Holmbeck, G. N., Durbin, D., & Kung, E. (1995, March). *Attachment, autonomy, and adjustment before and after leaving home: Sullivan and Sullivan revisited*. Paper presented at the meeting of the Society for Research in Child Development, Indianapolis.

Holmbeck, G. N., Paikoff, R. L., & Brooks-Gunn, J. (1995). Parenting adolescents. In M. H. Bornstein (Ed.), *Children and parenting* (Vol. 1). Hillsdale, NJ: Erlbaum.

Holmes, L. D. (1987). *Quest for the real Samoa: The Mead-Freeman controversy and beyond*. South Hadley, MA: Bergin & Garvey.

Holtzmann, W. (1982). Cross-cultural comparisons of personality development in Mexico and the United States. In D. Wagner & H. W. Stevenson (Eds.), *Cultural perspectives on child development*. San Francisco: W. H. Freeman.

Honig, A. (1996). Review of *Child Development*. (8th ed.). Dubuque, IA: Brown & Benchmark.

Hops, H., Davis, B., Alpert, A., & Longoria, N. (1997, April). *Adolescent peer relations and depressive symptomatology*. Paper presented at the meeting of the Society for Research in Child Development, Washington, DC.

Horner, M. (1972). Toward an understanding of achievement-related conflicts in women. *Journal of Social Issues, 28,* 157–175.

Huang, L. N. (1989). Southeast Asian refugee children and adolescents. In J. T. Gibbs & L. N. Huang (Eds.), *Children of color.* San Francisco: Jossey-Bass.

Huang, L. N., and Ying, Y. (1989). Chinese American children and adolescents. In J. T. Gibbs and L. N. Huang, (Eds.), *Children of color.* San Francisco: Jossey-Bass.

Huebner, A. M., & Garrod, A. C. (1993). Moral reasoning among Tibetan monks: A study of Buddhist adolescents and young adults in Nepal. *Journal of Cross-Cultural Psychology, 24,* 167–185.

Huesmann, L. R. (1986). Psychological processes promoting the relation between exposure to media violence and aggressive behavior by the viewer. *Journal of Social Issues, 42,* 125–139.

Hughes, D. L. (1997, April). *Racial socialization in urban African-American and Hispanic families.* Paper presented at the meeting of the Society for Research in Child Development, Washington, DC.

Hurtado, M. T. (1997, April). *Acculturation and planning among adolescents.* Paper presented at the meeting of the Society for Research in Child Development, Washington, DC.

Huston, A. (1995, August). *Children in poverty and public policy.* Paper presented at the meeting of the American Psychological Association, New York City.

Huston, A. C. (1983). Sex-typing. In P. H. Mussen (Ed.), *Handbook of child psychology* (4th ed., Vol. 4). New York: Wiley.

Huston, A. C., & Alvarez, M. (1990). The socialization context of gender-role development in early adolescence. In R. Montemayor, G. R. Adams, & T. P. Gulotta (Eds.), *From childhood to adolescence: A transitional period?* Newbury Park, CA: Sage.

Huston, A. C., McLoyd, V. C., & Coll, C. G. (1994). Children and poverty: Issues in contemporary research. *Child Development, 65,* 275–282.

Huston, A. C., Siegle, J., & Bremer, M. (1983, April). *Family environment television use by preschool children.* Paper presented at the biennial meeting of the Society for Research in Child Development, Detroit.

Huston, A. C., & Wright, J. C. (1997). Mass media and children's development. In I.E. Siegel, & K. A. Renninger (Eds.), *Handbook of child psychology* (5th Ed., Vol. 4). New York: Wiley.

Huston, L., Hoberman, H., & Nugent, S. (1994, February). *Alcohol use and abuse in Native American adolescents.* Paper presented at the meeting of the Society for Research on Adolescence, San Diego.

Huston-Stein, A., & Higgens-Trenk, A. (1978). Development of females from childhood through adulthood. Career and feminine role orientations. In P. Baltes (Ed.), *Lifespan development and behavior* (Vol. 1). New York: Academic Press.

Hyde, J. S. (1985). *Half the human experience* (3rd ed.). Lexington, MA: D. C. Heath.

Hyde, J. S. (1993). Meta-analysis and the psychology of women. In F. L. Denmark & M. A. Paludi (Eds.), *Handbook on the psychology of women.* Westport, CT: Greenwood.

Hyde, J. S., & Plant, E. A. (1995). Magnitude of psychological gender differences: Another side of the story. *American Psychologist, 50,* 159–161.

Ianni, F. A. J., & Orr, M. T. (1996). Dropping out. In J. A. Graber, J. Brooks-Gunn, & A. C. Petersen (Eds.), *Transitions in adolescence.* Mahwah, NJ: Erlbaum.

Inoff-Germain, G., Arnold, G. S., Nottelmann, E. D., Susman, E. J., Cutler, G. B., & Chrousos, G. P. (1988). Relations between hormone levels and observational measures of aggressive behavior of young adolescents in family interactions. *Developmental Psychology, 24,* 124–139.

Intercultural Development Research Association. (1996). *More at-risk students to tutor others.* Unpublished manuscript, Intercultural Development Research Association, San Antonio, TX.

Irwin, C. E. (1993). The adolescent, health, and society: From the perspective of the physician. In S. G. Millstein, A. C. Petersen, & E. O. Nightingale (Eds.), *Promoting the health of adolescents.* New York: Oxford University Press.

Jacobs, J. (1994, February). *Adolescents' perception of risk and contraceptive decision making.* Paper presented at the meeting of the Society for Research on Adolescence, San Diego.

Jacobs, J. E., & Potenza, M. (1990, March). *The use of decision-making strategies in late adolescence.* Paper presented at the meeting of the Society for Research in Adolescence, Atlanta.

Jacobs, J. K., Garnier, H. E., & Weisner, T. (1996, March). *The impact of family life on the process of dropping out of high school.* Paper presented at the meeting of the Society for Research on Adolescence, Boston.

Jadack, R. A., Hyde, J. S., Moore, C. F., & Keller, M. L. (1995). Moral reasoning about sexually transmitted diseases. *Child Development, 66,* 167–177.

Jahnke, H. C., & Blanchard-Fields, F. (1993). A test of two models of adolescent egocentrism. *Journal of Youth and Adolescence, 22,* 313–321.

Janos, P. M., & Robinson, N. N. (1985). Psychosocial development in intellectually gifted children. In F. D. Horowitz & M. O'Brien (Eds.), *The gifted and the talented.* Washington, DC: American Psychological Association.

Janz, N. K., Zimmerman, M. A., Wren, P. A., Israel, B. A., Freudenberg, N., & Carter, R. J. (1996). Evaluation of 37 AIDS prevention projects: Successful approaches and barriers to program effectiveness. *Health Education Quarterly, 23,* 80–97.

Jarrett, R. L. (1995). Growing up poor: The family experiences of socially mobile youth in low-income African-American neighborhoods. *Journal of Adolescent Research, 10,* 111–135.

Jencks, C. S., Smith, M., Acland, H., Bane, M. J., Cohen, D., Gintis, H., Heyns, B., & Michelson, S. (1972). *Inequality: A reassessment of the effects of family and schooling in America.* New York: Basic Books.

Jensen, A. R. (1969). How much can we boost IQ and scholastic achievement? *Harvard Educational Review, 39,* 1–123.

Jensen, L. A. (1995, March). *The moral reasoning of orthodox and progressivist Indians and Americans.* Paper presented at the meeting of the Society for Research in Child Development, Indianapolis.

Jessor, L., & Jessor, R. (1975). Transition from virginity to nonvirginity among youth: A social-psychological study over time. *Developmental Psychology, 11,* 473–484.

Jessor, R. (1993). Successful adolescent development among youth in high-risk settings. *American Psychologist, 48,* 117–126.

Jessor, R., Costa, F., Jessor, L., & Donovan, J. E. (1983). Time of first intercourse: A prospective study. *Journal of Personality and Social Psychology, 44,* 608–620.

Jhally, S. (1990). *Dreamworlds: Desire/sex/power in rock video* (Video). Amherst: University of Massachusetts at Amherst, Department of Communications.

Jodl, K. M., & Dalton, R. (1996, March). *Longitudinal predictors of competence-at-a-cost in adolescents growing up in stepfamilies.* Paper presented at the meeting of the Society for Research on Adolescence, Boston.

Johnson, M. J., Swartz, J. L., & Martin, W. E. (1995). Applications of psychological theories for career development with Native Americans. In F. T. L. Leong (Ed.), *Career development and vocational behavior of racial and ethnic minorities.* Hillsdale, NJ: Erlbaum.

Johnson, S. A., & Green, V. (1993). Female adolescent contraceptive decision making and risk taking. *Adolescence, 28,* 81–96.

Johnston, J., Etteman, J., & Davidson, T. (1980). *An evaluation of "Freestyle": A television series to reduce sex-role stereotypes.* Ann Arbor: University of Michigan, Institute for Social Research.

Johnston, L., Bachman, J., & O'Malley, P. (1990). *Monitoring the future.* Ann Arbor: University of Michigan, Institute of Social Research.

Johnston, L., Bachman, J., & O'Malley, P. (1994, January 31). Drug use rises among American teenagers. News release, Institute of Social Research, University of Michigan, Ann Arbor.

Johnston, L. D., O'Malley, P. M., & Bachman, J. G. (1992, January 25). *The 1991 survey of drug use by American high school and college students.* Ann Arbor: University of Michigan, Institute of Social Research.

Johnston, L. D., O'Malley, P. M., & Bachman, J. G. (1995). *National survey results on drug use from the Monitoring the Future Study, Vol. 1: Secondary school students.* Ann Arbor, MI: Institute of Social Research.

Jones, B. F., Rasmussen, C. M., & Moffit, M. C. (1997). *Real-life problem solving.* Washington, DC: American Psychological Association.

Jones, D. C., Costin, S. E., & Ricard, R. J. (1994, February). *Ethnic and sex differences in best friendship characteristics among African-American, Mexican-American, and White adolescents.* Paper presented at the meeting of the Society for Research on Adolescence, San Diego.

Jones, D. C., & Costin, S. E. (1997, April). *The friendships of African-American and European-American adolescents.* Paper presented at the meeting of the Society for Research in Child Development, Washington, DC.

Jones, E. R., Forrest, J. D., Goldman, N., Henshaw, S. K., Lincoln, R., Rosoff, J. I., Westoff, C. G., & Wulf, D. (1985). Teenage pregnancy in developed countries: Determinants and policy implications. *Family Planning Perspectives, 17,* 53–63.

Jones, J. M. (1994). The African American: A duality dilemma? In W. J. Lonner & R. Malpass (Eds.), *Psychology and culture.* Needham Heights, MA: Allyn & Bacon.

Jones, M. C. (1965). Psychological correlates of somatic development. *Child Development, 36,* 899–911.

Jordan, J. V. (1997). *Women's growth in diversity.* New York: Guilford.

Jorgenson, S. R. (1993). Adolescent pregnancy and parenting. In T. P. Gullotta, G. R. Adams, and R. Montemayor (Eds.), *Adolescent sexuality.* Newbury Park, CA: Sage.

Josselson, R. (1973). Psychodynamic aspects of identity formation in college women. *Journal of Youth and Adolescence, 2,* 3–52.

Josselson, R. (1994). Identity and relatedness in the life cycle. In H. A. Bosma, T. L. G. Graafsma, H. D. Grotevant, & D. J. De Levita (Eds.), *Identity and development.* Newbury Park, CA: Sage.

Jozefowicz, D. M., Barber, B. L., & Mollasis, C. (1994, February). *Relations between maternal and adolescent values and beliefs: Sex differences and implications for occupational choice.* Paper presented at the meeting of the Society for Research on Adolescence, San Diego.

Juang, L. P., & Nguyen, H. H. (1997, April). *Autonomy and connectedness: Predictors of adjustment in Vietnamese adolescents.* Paper presented at the meeting of the Society for Research in Child Development, Washington, DC.

Jussim, L., & Eccles, J. S. (1993). Teacher expectations II: Construction and reflection of student achievement. *Journal of Personality and Social Psychology, 63,* 947–961.

Juster, S. M., & Vinovskis, M. A. (1991). Nineteenth-century America, adolescence in. In R. M. Lerner, A. C. Petersen, & J. Brooks-Gunn (Eds.), *Encyclopedia of adolescence* (Vol. 1). New York: Garland.

Kagan, J. (1984). *The nature of the child.* New York: Basic Books.

Kagan, J. (1992). Yesterday's premises, tomorrow's promises. *Developmental Psychology, 28,* 990–997.

Kagan, J., Snidman, N., & Arcus, D. (1995, August). *Antecedents of shyness.* Paper presented at the meeting of the American Psychological Association, New York City.

Kagan, S., & Madsen, M. C. (1972). Experimental analysis of cooperation and competition of Anglo-American and Mexican children. *Developmental Psychology, 6,* 49–59.

Kagitcibasi, C. (1995). Is psychology relevant to global human development issues? Experience from Turkey. *American Psychologist, 50,* 203–300.

Kahn, S. E., & Richardson, A. (1983). Evaluation of a course in sex roles for secondary school students. *Sex Roles, 9,* 431–440.

Kail, R., & Pellegrino, J. W. (1985). *Human intelligence.* New York: W. H. Freeman.

Kaiser Family Foundation. (1996). *Kaiser Family Foundation survey of 1,500 teenagers ages 12–18.* San Francisco: Kaiser Foundation.

Kalil, A. (1994, February). *Parent-adolescent relationships, parenting behaviors, and maternal well-being in mother-only vs. two-parent Black families.* Paper presented at the meeting of the Society for Research on Adolescence, San Diego.

Kamler, J., Irwin, C. E., Stone, G. C., & Millstein, S. G. (1987). *Optimistic bias in adolescent hemophiliacs.* Paper presented at the meeting of the Society for Research in Pediatrics, Anaheim, CA.

Kandel, D. B. (1974). The role of parents and peers in marijuana use. *Journal of Social Issues, 30,* 107–135.

Kandel, D., & Lesser, G. S. (1969). Parent-adolescent relationships and adolescence independence in the United States and Denmark. *Journal of Marriage and the Family, 31,* 348–358.

Kandel, D., & Wu, P. (1995). The contributions of mothers and fathers to the intergenerational transmission of cigarette smoking. *Journal of Research on Adolescence, 5,* 225–252.

Kane, M. J. (1988). The female athletic role as a status determinant within the social systems of high school adolescents. *Adolescence, 23,* 253–264.

Karplus, R. (1981). Education and formal thought—a modest proposal. In I. Siegel, D. Brodzinsky, & R. Golinkoff (Eds.), *Piagetian theory and research: New directions and applications.* Hillsdale, NJ: Erlbaum.

Kazdin, A. E. (1995). *Conduct disorders in childhood and adolescence.* (2nd ed.). Newbury Park, CA: Sage.

Keating, D. P. (1988). Byrnes' reformulation of Piaget's formal operations. Is what's left what's right? *Developmental Review, 8,* 376–384.

Keating, D. P. (1990). Adolescent thinking. In S. S. Feldman & G. R. Elliott (Eds.), *At the threshold: The developing adolescent.* Cambridge, MA: Harvard University Press.

Keating, D. P. (1996). Unpublished review of *Adolescence* (7th ed.) by J. W. Santrock. Dubuque, IA: Brown & Benchmark.

Keating, D. P. (in press-a). Understanding human intelligence: Toward a developmental synthesis. In C. Benbow & D. Lubinski (Eds.), *From psychometrics to giftedness: Essays in honor of Julian Stanley.* Baltimore: Johns Hopkins University Press.

Keating, D. P. (in press-b). Habits of mind: Developmental diversity in competence and coping. In D. K. Detterman (Ed.), *Current topics in human intelligence.* Norwood, NJ: Ablex.

Keating, D. P. (1997, April). Discussant, symposium on intelligence. Society for Research in Child Development, Washington, DC.

Keener, D. C., & Boykin, K. A. (1996, March). *Parental control, autonomy, and ego development.* Paper presented at the meeting of the Society for Research on Adolescence, Boston.

Keltikangas-Järvinen, L., & Raikkonen, K. (1990). Healthy and maladjusted Type-A behavior in adolescents. *Journal of Youth and Adolescence, 19,* 1–18.

Kennedy, J. H. (1990). Determinants of peer social status: Contributions of physical appearance, reputation, and behavior. *Journal of Youth and Adolescence, 19,* 233–244.

Kenney, A. M. (1987, June). Teen pregnancy: An issue for schools. *Phi Delta Kappan,* pp. 728–736.

Kenniston, K. (1970). Youth: A "new" stage of life. *American Scholar, 39,* 631–654.

Kerr, B. A. (1983). Raising the career aspirations of gifted girls. *Vocational Guidance Quarterly, 32,* 37–43.

Kett, J. F. (1977). *Rites of passage.* New York: Basic Books.

King, P. (1988). Heavy metal music and drug use in adolescents. *Postgraduate Medicine, 83,* 295–304.

Kinsey, A. C., Pomeroy, W. B., & Martin, C. E. (1948). *Sexual behavior in the human male.* Philadelphia: Saunders.

Kirby, D., Resnick, M. D., Downes, B., Kocher, T., Gunderson, P., Pothoff, S., Zelterman, D., & Blum, R. W. (1993). The effects of school-based health clinics in S. Paul on school-wide birthrates. *Family Planning Perspectives, 25,* 12–16.

Klaus, T. (1997, July). *Seven scary sexuality subjects for males... and how to address them.* Paper presented at the conference on Working with America's Youth, Pittsburgh, PA.

Klaw, E., & Saunders, N. (1994). *An ecological model of career planning in pregnant African American teens.* Paper presented at the biennial meeting of the Society for Research on Adolescence, San Diego.

Klein, H. A. (1993). Temperament and self-esteem in late adolescence. *Adolescence, 27,* 689–694.

Klein, K. (1985, April). The research on class size. *Phi Delta Kappan,* pp. 578–580.

Klerman, L. V. (1993). The influence of economic factors on health-related behaviors in adolescents. In S. G. Millstein, A. C. Petersen, & E. O. Nightingale (Eds.), *Promoting the health of adolescents.* New York: Oxford University Press.

Knox, D., & Wilson, K. (1981). Dating behaviors of university students. *Family Relations, 30,* 255–258.

Kobak, R., Cole, C., Fleming, W., Ferenz-Gilles, R., & Bamble, W. (1993). Attachment and emotional regulation during mother-teen problem-solving: A control theory analysis. *Child Development, 64,* 231–245.

Koenig, L. J., & Faigeles, R. (1995, March). *Gender differences in adolescent loneliness and maladjustment.* Paper presented at the meeting of the Society for Research in Child Development, Indianapolis.

Kohlberg, L. (1958). *The development of modes of moral thinking and choice in the years 10 to 16.* Unpublished doctoral dissertation, University of Chicago.

Kohlberg, L. (1966). A cognitive-developmental analysis of children's sex-role concepts and attitudes. In E. E. Maccoby (Ed.), *The development of sex differences.* Palo Alto, CA: Stanford University Press.

Kohlberg, L. (1969). Stage and sequence: The cognitive-developmental approach to socialization. In D. A. Goslin (Ed.), *Handbook of socialization theory and research.* Chicago: Rand McNally.

Kohlberg, L. (1976). Moral stages and moralization: The cognitive-developmental approach. In T. Lickona (Ed.), *Moral development and behavior.* New York: Holt, Rinehart & Winston.

Kohlberg, L. (1981). *The philosophy of moral development.* New York: Harper & Row.

Kohlberg, L. (1986). A current statement on some theoretical issues. In S. Modgil & C. Modgil (Eds.), *Lawrence Kohlberg.* Philadelphia: Falmer.

Kohlberg, L., & Candee, D. (1979). *Relationships between moral judgment and moral action.* Unpublished manuscript, Harvard University.

Kohn, M. L. (1977). *Class and conformity: A study in values* (2nd ed.). Chicago: University of Chicago Press.

Kolbe, L. J., Collins, J., & Cortese, P. (1997). Building the capacity of schools to improve the health of the nation. *American Psychologist, 52,* 256–265.

Koss, M. P. (1993). Rape: Scope, impact, interventions, and public policy responses. *American Psychologist, 48,* 1062–1069.

Kostelecky, K. L. (1997, April). *Stressful life events, relationships, and distress during late adolescence.* Paper presented at the meeting of the Society for Research in Child Development, Washington, DC.

Kramer, L., & Lin, L. (1997, April). *Mothers' and fathers's responses to sibling conflict.* Paper presented at the meeting of the Society for Research in Child Development, Washington, DC.

Krupnik, C. G. (1985). Women and men in the classroom: Inequality and its remedies. *On Teaching and Learning: The Journal of the Harvard University Derek Bok Center, 10,* 18–25.

Kuhn, D., & Brannock, J. (1977). Development of the isolation of variables scheme in experimental and "natural experiment" contexts. *Developmental Psychology, 13,* 9–14.

Kulick, J. A., Bangert-Drowns, R. L., & Kulik, C. C. (1984). The effectiveness of coaching for aptitude tests. *Psychological Bulletin, 95,* 179–188.

Kupersmidt, J. B., Burchinal, M. R., Leff, S. S., & Patterson, C. J. (1992, March). *A longitudinal study of perceived support and conflict with parents from middle childhood through early adolescence.* Paper presented at the meeting of the Society for Research on Adolescence, Washington, DC.

Kupersmidt, J. B., & Coie, J. D. (1990). Preadolescent peer status, aggression, and school adjustment as predictors of externalizing problems in adolescence. *Child Development, 61,* 1350–1363.

Kupersmidt, J. B., & Patterson, C. (1993, March). *Developmental patterns of peer relations and aggression in the prediction of externalizing behavior problems.* Paper presented at the biennial meeting of the Society for Research in Child Development, New Orleans.

Kurdek, L. A., & Krile, D. (1982). A developmental analysis of the relation between peer acceptance and both interpersonal understanding and perceived social self-competence. *Child Development, 53,* 1485–1491.

Kurtines, W. M., & Gewirtz, J. (Eds.). (1991). *Moral behavior and development: Advances in theory, research, and application.* Hillsdale, NJ: Erlbaum.

Kurtz, D. A., Cantu, C. L., & Phinney, J. S. (1996, March). *Group identities as predictors of self-esteem among African American, Latino, and White adolescents.* Paper presented at the meeting of the Society for Research on Adolescence, Boston.

Labouvie-Vief, G. (1982). Dynamic development and mature autonomy: A theoretical prologue. *Human Development, 25,* 161–191.

Ladd, G. W., & Le Sieur, K. D. (1995). Parents and children's peer relationships. In M. H. Bornstein (Ed.), *Children and parenting* (Vol. 4). Hillsdale, NJ: Erlbaum.

LaFromboise, T., Coleman, H. L. K., & Gerton, J. (1993). Psychological impact of biculturalism: Evidence and theory. *Psychological Bulletin, 114,* 393–412.

LaFromboise, T., & Low, K. G. (1989). American Indian children and adolescents. In J. T. Gibbs & L. N. Huang (Eds.), *Children of color.* San Francisco: Jossey-Bass.

Laganá, L., & Hayes, D. M. (1993). Contraceptive health programs for adolescents: A critical review. *Adolescence, 28,* 347–359.

Lamb, M. E. (1997). Fatherhood then and now. In A. Booth & A. C. Crouter (Eds.), *Men in families.* Mahwah, NJ: Erlbaum.

Lampl, M., & Emde, R. N. (1983). Episodic growth in infancy: A preliminary report on length, head circumference, and behavior. In *New directions for child development.* San Francisco: Jossey-Bass.

Landale, N. S. (1997). Immigration and the family: An overview. In A. Booth, A. C.

Lapsley, D. K. (1990). Continuity and discontinuity in adolescent social cognitive development. In R. Montemayor, G. Adams, & T. Gulotta (Eds.), *From childhood to adolescence: A transitional period?* Newbury Park, CA: Sage.

Lapsley, D. K. (1993). *Moral psychology after Kohlberg.* Unpublished manuscript, Department of Psychology, Brandon University, Manitoba.

Lapsley, D. K. (1993). *Towards an integrated theory of adolescent ego development: The "new look" at adolescent egocentrism.* Unpublished manuscript, Brandon University, Brandon, Manitoba, Canada.

Lapsley, D. K., Enright, R. D., & Serlin, R. C. (1985). Toward a theoretical perspective on the legislation of adolescence. *Journal of Early Adolescence, 5,* 441–466.

Lapsley, D. K., Enright, R. D., Serlin, R. C. (1986). Moral and social education. In J. Worrell & F. Danner (Eds.), *Adolescent development: Issues in education.* New York: Academic Press.

Lapsley, D. K., & Murphy, M. N. (1985). Another look at the theoretical assumptions of adolescent egocentrism. *Developmental Review, 5,* 201–217.

Lapsley, D. K., & Power, F. C. (Eds.). (1988). *Self, ego, and identity.* New York: Springer-Verlag.

Lapsley, D. K., Rice, K. G., & Shadid, G. E. (1989). Psychological separation and adjustment to college. *Journal of Counseling Psychology, 36,* 286–294.

Larson, R., & Kleiber, D. (1990). Free-time activities as factors in adolescent adjustment. In P. Tolan & B. Cohler (Eds.), *Handbook of clinical research and practice with adolescents.* New York: Oxford University Press.

Larson, R., & Richards, M. H. (1989). Introduction: The changing life space of early adolescence. *Journal of Youth and Adolescence, 18,* 501–509.

Larson, R., Kubey, R., & Colletti, J. (1989). Changing channels: Early adolescent media choices and shifting investments. *Journal of Youth and Adolescence, 18,* 583–599.

Larson, R. W., Richards, M. H., Moneta, G., Holmbeck, G., & Duckett, E. (1996). Changes in adolescents' daily interactions with their families from 10 to 18: Disengagement and transformation. *Developmental Psychology, 32,* 744–754.

Laursen, B. (1995). Conflict and social interaction in adolescent relationships. *Journal of Research on Adolescence, 5,* 55–70.

Laursen, B., & Ferreira, M. (1994, February). *Does parent-child conflict peak at mid-adolescence?* Paper presented at the meeting of the Society for Research on Adolescence, San Diego.

LaVoie, J. (1976). Ego identity formation in middle adolescence. *Journal of Youth and Adolescence, 5,* 371–385.

Law, T. C. (1992, March). *The relationship between mothers' employment status and perception of child behavior.* Paper presented at the meeting of the Society for Research on Adolescence, Washington, DC.

Lazarus, R. S. (1991). *Emotion and adaptation.* New York: Oxford University Press.

Lazarus, R. S. (1993). From psychological stress to the emotions: A history of a changing outlook. *Annual Review of Psychology, 44,* 1–21.

Leadbeater, B. J., Blatt, S. J., & Quinlan, D. M. (1995). Gender-linked vulnerabilities to depressive symptoms, stress, and problem behaviors in adolescents. *Journal of Research on Adolescence, 5,* 1–30.

Leadbetter, B. J. (1994, February). *Re-conceptualizing social supports for adolescent mothers: Grandmothers, babies, fathers, and beyond.* Paper presented at the meeting of the Society for Research on Adolescence, San Diego.

Leadbetter, B. J., Way, N., & Raden, A. (1994, February). *Barriers to involvement of fathers of the children of adolescent mothers.* Paper presented at the meeting of the Society for Research on Adolescence, San Diego.

Lee, C. C. (1985). Successful rural black adolescents: A psychological profile. *Adolescence, 20,* 129–142.

Lee, E. (1988). Cultural factors in working with Southeast Asian refugee adolescents. *Journal of Adolescence, 2,* 167–179.

Lee, L. C. (1992, August). *In search of universals: Whatever happened to race?* Paper presented at the meeting of the American Psychological Association, Washington, DC.

Lee, V. (1994). Sexism in single-sex and coeducational independent secondary schools. *Sociology of Education, 67,* 92–120.

Lee, V., & Bryk, A. (1986). Effects of single-sex secondary schools on achievement and attitudes. *Journal of Educational Psychology, 78,* 381–395.

Lee, V. E., Burkam, D. T., Zimilies, H., & Ladewski, B. (1994). Family structure and its effect on behavioral and emotional problems in young adolescents. *Journal of Research on Adolescence, 4,* 405–437.

Lee, V. E., Croninger, R. G., Linn, E., & Chen, X. (1995, March). *The culture of sexual harassment in secondary schools.* Paper presented at the meeting of the Society for Research in Child Development, Indianapolis.

Lee, V., & Marks, H. (1990). Sustained efforts of the single-sex secondary school experience on attitudes, behaviors, and values in college. *Journal of Educational Psychology, 82,* 578–592.

Leffert, N., & Blyth, D. A. (1996, March). *The effects of community contexts on early adolescents.* Paper presented at the meeting of the Society for Research on Adolescence, Boston.

Lefkowitz, E. S., Kahlbaugh, P. E., & Sigman, M. D. (1994, February). *Adolescent risk-taking and thrill-seeking: Relationship to gender, AIDS beliefs, and family interactions.* Paper presented at the meeting of the Society for Research in Adolescence, San Diego.

Leitenberg, H., Detzer, M. J., & Srebnik, D. (1993). Gender differences in masturbation and the relation of masturbation experience in preadolescence and/or early adolescence to sexual behavior and adjustment in young adulthood. *Archives of Sexual Behavior, 22,* 87–98.

Leon, G. R. (1991). Bulimia nervosa. In R. M. Lerner, A. C. Petersen, & J. Brooks-Gunn (Eds.), *Encyclopedia of adolescence* (Vol. 1). New York: Garland.

Leong, F. T. L. (1995). Introduction and overview. In F. T. L. Leong (Ed.), *Career development and vocational behavior in racial and ethnic minorities.* Hillsdale, NJ: Erlbaum.

Lepper, M., Greene, D., & Nisbett, R. R. (1973). Undermining children's intrinsic interest with extrinsic rewards. *Journal of Personality and Social Psychology, 28,* 129–137.

Lepper, M. R. (1985). Microcomputers in education: Motivational and social issues. *American Psychologist, 40,* 1–18.

Lepper, M. R., & Gurtner, J. (1989). Children and computers: Approaching the twenty-first century. *American Psychologist, 44,* 170–178.

Lerner, H. G. (1989). *The dance of intimacy.* New York: Harper & Row.

Lerner, J. V., Jacobson, L., & del Gaudio, A. (1992, March). *Maternal role satisfaction and family variables as predictors of adolescent adjustment.* Paper presented at the meeting of the Society for Research on Adolescence, Washington, DC.

Lerner, R. M. (1987). A life-span perspective for early adolescence. In R. M. Lerner & T. T. Foch (Eds.), *Biological-psychosocial interactions in early adolescence.* Hillsdale, NJ: Erlbaum.

Lerner, R. M. (1993). Early adolescence: Toward an agenda for the integration of research, policy, and intervention. In R. M. Lerner (Ed.), *Early adolescence.* Hillsdale, NJ: Erlbaum.

Lerner, R. M. (1996). Relative plasticity, integration, temporality, and diversity in human development: A developmental contextual perspective about theory, process, and method. *Developmental Psychology, 4,* 781–786.

Lerner, R. M. (1997). Introduction—theories of human developemnt. In R. M. Lerner (Ed.), *Handbook of child psychology* (5th Ed., Vol. 1). New York: Wiley.

Lerner, R. M., Entwisle, D. R., & Hauser, S. T. (1994). The crisis among contemporary American adolescents: A call for the integration of research, policies, and programs. *Journal of Research on Adolescence, 4,* 1–4.

Lerner, R. M., Lerner, J. V., von Eye, A., Ostrum, C. W., Nitz, K., Talwar-Soni, R., & Tubman, J. (1996). Continuity and discontinuity across the transition of early adolescence: A developmental contextual perspective. In J. A. Graber, J. Brooks-Gunn, & A. C. Petersen (Eds.), *Transitions through adolescence: Interpersonal domains and contexts.* Mahwah, NJ: Erlbaum.

Levant, R. F. (1995). Toward the reconstruction of masculinity. In R. F. Levant & W. S. Pollack (Eds.), *A new psychology of men.* New York: Basic.

Levant, R. F., & Pollack, W. S. (Eds.). (1995). *A new psychology of men.* New York: Basic.

LeVay, S. (1991). A difference in hypothalamic structure between heterosexual and homosexual men. *Science, 253,* 1034–1037.

Leventhal, A. (1994, February). *Peer conformity during adolescence: An integration of developmental, situational, and individual characteristics.* Paper presented at the meeting of the Society for Research on Adolescence, San Diego.

LeVine, R. A., & Shweder, R. A. (1995, March). *Culture, pluralism, and the nature-nurture problem.* Paper presented at the meeting of the Society for Research in Child Development, Indianapolis.

Levine, S. V. (1984, August). Radical departures. *Psychology Today,* pp. 18–27.

Lewinsohn, P. M., Clarke, G. N., Hops, H., & Andrews, J. (1990). Cognitive-behavioral treatment for depressed adolescents. *Behavior Therapy, 21,* 385–401.

Lewinsohn, P. M., Gotlib, I. H., & Seeley, J. R. (1994, February). *Psychosocial risk factors for depression and substance abuse in older adolescents.* Paper presented at the meeting of the Society for Research on Adolescence, San Diego.

Lewis, C. G. (1981). How adolescents approach decisions: Changes over grades seven to twelve and policy implications. *Child Development, 52,* 538–554.

Lewis, V. G., Money, J., & Bobrow, N. A. (1977). Idiopathic pubertal delay beyond the age of 15: Psychological study of 12 boys. *Adolescence, 12,* 1–11.

Lickona, T. (1993). *Educating for character.* New York: Bantam.

Lightfoot, C. (1997). *The culture of adolescent risk-taking.* Mahwah, NJ: Erlbaum.

Linn, M. C. (1991). Scientific reasoning, adolescent. In R. M. Lerner, A. C. Petersen, & J. Brooks-Gunn (Eds.), *Encyclopedia of adolescence* (Vol. 2). New York: Garland.

Liprie, M. L. (1993). Adolescents' contributions to family decision making. In B. H. Settles, R. S. Hanks, & M. B. Sussman (Eds.), *American families and the future: Analyses of possible destinies.* New York: Haworth Press.

Lipsitz, J. (1980, March). *Sexual development in young adolescents.* Invited speech given at the American Association of Sex Educators, Counselors, and Therapists, New York City.

Lipsitz, J. (1983, October). *Making it the hard way: Adolescents in the 1980s.* Testimony presented at the Crisis Intervention Task Force, House Select Committee on Children, Youth, and Families, Washington, DC.

Lipsitz, J. (1984). *Successful schools for young adolescents.* New Brunswick, NJ: Transaction Books.

Livesley, W. J., & Bromley, D. B. (1973). *Person perception in childhood and adolescence.* New York: Wiley.

Loehlin, J. (1995, August). *Genes and environment in The Bell Curve.* Paper presented at the meeting of the American Psychological Association, New York City.

Loehlin, J. (1995, August). *Heritability of intelligence.* Paper presented at the meeting of the American Psychological Association, New York City.

Loehr, J. (1989, May). Personal communication, U.S. Tennis Association Training Camp, Saddlebrook, FL.

Loewen, I. R., & Leigh, G. K. (1986). *Timing of transition to sexual intercourse: A multivariate analysis of white adolescent females ages 15–17.* Paper presented at the meeting of the Society for the Scientific Study of Sex, St. Louis.

Lomnitz, L. (1997). Family, networks, and survival on the threshold of the 21st century in urban Mexico. In S. Dreman (Ed.), *The family on the threshold of the 21st century.* Mahwah, NJ: Erlbaum.

Long, T., & Long, L. (1983). *Latchkey children.* New York: Penguin.

Lonner, W. J. (1990). An overview of cross-cultural testing and assessment. In R. W. Brislin (Ed.), *Applied cross-cultural psychology.* Newbury Park, CA: Sage.

Lord, S. (1995, March). *Parent psychological experiences as mediators of the influence of economic conditions on parenting in low income urban contexts.* Paper presented at the meeting of the Society for Research in Child Development, Indianapolis.

Lord, S. E., & Eccles, J. S. (1994, February). *James revisited: The relationship of domain self-concepts and values to Black and White adolescents' self-esteem.* Paper presented at the meeting of the Society for Research on Adolescence, San Diego.

Louv, R. (1990). *Childhood's future.* Boston, MA: Houghton Mifflin.

Luo, Q., Fang, X., & Aro, P. (1995, March). *Selection of best friends by Chinese adolescents.* Paper presented at the meeting of the Society for Research in Child Development, Indianapolis.

Luria, A., & Herzog, E. (1985, April). *Gender segregation across and within settings.* Paper presented at the biennial meeting of the Society for Research in Child Development, Toronto.

Luster, T. J., Perlstadt, J., McKinney, M. H., & Sims, K. E. (1995, March). *Factors related to the quality of the home environment adolescents provide for their infants.* Paper presented at the meeting of the Society for Research in Child Development, Indianapolis.

Lynch, M. E. (1991). Gender intensification. In R. M. Lerner, A. C. Petersen, & J. Brooks-Gunn (Eds.), *Encyclopedia of adolescence* (Vol. 1). New York: Garland.

Lyons, N. P. (1990). Listening to voices we have not heard. In C. Gilligan, N. P. Lyons, & T. J. Hanmer (Eds.), *Making connections.* Cambridge, MA: Harvard University Press.

Lytton, H. (1995, March). *Child and family predictors of conduct disorders and criminality.* Paper presented at the meeting of the Society for Research in Child Development, Indianapolis.

Maas, H. S. (1954). The role of members in clubs of lower-class and middle-class adolescents. *Child Development, 25,* 241–251.

Maccoby, E. E. (1984). Middle childhood in the context of the family. In W. A. Collins (Ed.), *Development during middle childhood.* Washington, DC: National Academy Press.

Maccoby, E. E. (1987, November). Interview with Elizabeth Hall: All in the family. *Psychology Today,* pp. 54–60.

Maccoby, E. E. (1992). Trends in the study of socialization: Is there a Lewinian heritage? *Journal of Social Issues, 48,* 171–185.

Maccoby, E. E. (1995). The two sexes and their social systems. In P. Moen, G. H. Elder, & K. Luscher (Eds.), *Examining lives in context.* Washington, DC: American Psychological Association.

Maccoby, E. E. (1996). Peer conflict and intrafamily conflict: Are there conceptual bridges? *Merrill-Palmer Quarterly, 42,* 165–176.

Maccoby, E. E., & Jacklin, C. N. (1974). *The psychology of sex differences.* Palo Alto, CA: Stanford University Press.

Maccoby, E. E., & Martin, J. A. (1983). Socialization in the context of the family: Parent-child interaction. In P. H. Mussen (Ed.), *Handbook of child psychology* (4th ed., Vol. 4). New York: Wiley.

MacDermid, S., & Crouter, A. C. (1995). Midlife, adolescence, and parental employment in family systems. *Journal of Youth and Adolescence, 24,* 29–54.

MacDonald, K. (1987). Parent-child physical play with rejected, neglected, and popular boys. *Developmental Psychology, 23,* 705–711.

MacLean, D. J., Keating, D. P., Miller, F., & Shuart, V. (1994, February). *Adolescents' decisions to pursue mathematics and science: Social and psychological factors.* Paper presented at the meeting of the Society for Research on Adolescence, San Diego.

MacLean, M. G., & Paradise, M. J. (1997, April). *Substance use and psychological health in homeless adolescents.* Paper presented at the meeting of the Society for Research in Child Development, Washington, DC.

Madison, B. E., & Foster-Clark, F. S. (1996, March). *Pathways to identity and intimacy: Effects of gender and personality.* Paper presented at the meeting of the Society for Research on Adolescence, Boston.

Magnusson, D. (1988). *Individual development from an interactional perspective: A longitudinal study.* Hillsdale, NJ: Erlbaum.

Maguin, E., Zucker, R. A., & Fitzgerald, H. E. (1995). The path to alcohol problems through conduct problems: A family-based approach to very early intervention with risk. In G. M. Boyd, J. Howard, & R. A. Zucker (Eds.), *Alcohol problems among adolescents.* Hillsdale, NJ: Erlbaum.

Malik, N. M., & Furman, W. (1993). Practitioner review: Problems in children's peer relations: What can the clinician do? *Journal of Child Psychology and Psychiatry, 34,* 1303–1326.

Manis, F. R., Keating, D. P., & Morrison, F. J. (1980). Developmental differences in the allocation of processing capacity. *Journal of Experimental Child Psychology, 29,* 156–169.

Manke, B., & Pike, A. (1997, April). *The search for new domains of nonshared environmental experience: looking outside the family.* Paper presented at the meeting of the Society for Research in Child Development, Washington, DC.

Maracek, J. (1995). Gender, politics, and psychology's ways of knowing. *American Psychologist, 50,* 162–163.

Marcia, J. (1980). Ego identity development. In J. Adelson (Ed.), *Handbook of adolescent psychology.* New York: Wiley.

Marcia, J. (1987). The identity status approach to the study of ego identity development. In T. Honess & K. Yardley (Eds.), *Self and identity: Perspectives across the lifespan.* London: Routledge & Kegan Paul.

Marcia, J. (1989). Identity and intervention. *Journal of Adolescence, 12,* 401–410.

Marcia, J. (1991). Identity and self-development. In R. M. Lerner, A. C. Petersen, & J. Brooks-Gunn (Eds.), *Encyclopedia of adolescence* (Vol. 1). New York: Garland.

Marcia, J. (1994). The empirical study of ego identity. In H. A. Bosma, T. L. G. Graafsma, H. D. Grotevant, & D. J. De Levita (Eds.), *Identity and development*. Newbury Park, CA: Sage.

Marcia, J. (1996). Unpublished review of *Adolescence* (7th ed.) by J. W. Santrock. Dubuque, IA: Brown & Benchmark.

Maris, R. W., Silverman, M., & Canetto, S. S. (1997). *Review of suicidology, 1997*. New York: Guilford.

Markstrom, C. A., & Tryon, R. J. (1997, April). *Resiliency, social support, and coping among poor African-American and European-American Appalachian adolescents*. Paper presented at the meeting of the Society for Research in Child Development, Washington, DC.

Markus, H., & Nurius, P. (1986). Possible selves. *American Psychologist, 41*, 954–969.

Marmorstein, N. R., & Shiner, R. L. (1996, March). *The family environments of depressed adolescents*. Paper presented at the meeting of the Society for Research on Adolescence, Boston.

Marshall, S., Adams, G. R., Ryan, B. A., & Keating, L. J. (1994, February). *Parental influences on adolescent empathy*. Paper presented at the meeting of the Society for Research on Adolescence, San Diego.

Martin, J. (1976). *The education of adolescents*. Washington, DC: U.S. Office of Education.

Martin, N. C. (1997, April). *Adolescents' possible selves and the transition to adulthood*. Paper presented at the meeting of the Society for Research in Child Development, Washington, DC.

Mason, C. A., Cauce, A. R., Gonzales, N., Hiraga, Y., & Grove, K. (1994). An ecological model of externalizing behaviors in African-American adolescents: No family is an island. *Journal of Research on Adolescence, 4*, 639–655.

Masten, A. M., Gest, S. D., & Reed, M. (1994, February). *Process models of resilience in adolescence*. Paper presented at the meeting of the Society for Research on Adolescence, San Diego.

Masten, A. S., & Hubbard, J. J. (1995, March). *Resilient adolescents: Do they differ from competent peers unchallenged by adversity?* Paper presented at the meeting of the Society for Research in Child Development, Indianapolis.

Masten, A. S., Neeman, J., & Andenas, S. (1994). Life events and adjustment in adolescents: The significance of event independence, desirability, and chronicity. *Journal of Research on Adolescence, 4*, 71–97.

Matlin, M. W. (1993). *The psychology of women* (2nd ed.). San Diego: Harcourt Brace Jovanovich.

Matsumoto, D. (1997). *Culture and modern life*. Pacific Grove, CA: Belmont.

Mayer, R. (1987). *Educational psychology: A cognitive approach*. Boston: Little, Brown.

McAdoo, H. P. (Ed.). (1993). *Family ethnicity*. Newbury Park, CA: Sage.

McAdoo, H. P. (1996). *Black families* (3rd Ed.). Newbury Park, CA: Sage.

McAlister, A., Perry, C., Killen, J., Slinkard, L. A., & Maccoby, N. (1980). Pilot study of smoking, alcohol, and drug abuse prevention. *American Journal of Public Health, 70*, 719–721.

McCall, R. B., Meyers, E. D., Hartman, J., & Roche, A. F. (1983). Developmental changes in head circumference and mental performance growth rates: A test of Epstein's phrenoblysis hypothesis. *Developmental Psychobiology, 16*, 457–468.

McClelland, D. C. (1955). Some social consequences of achievement motivation. In M. R. Jones (Ed.), *Nebraska Symposium on Motivation*. Lincoln: University of Nebraska Press.

McCord, J. (1990). Problem behaviors. In S. S. Feldman & G. R. Elliott (Eds.), *At the threshold: The developing adolescent*. Cambridge, MA: Harvard University Press.

McCord, W., McCord, J., & Gudeman, J. (1960). *Origins of alcoholism*. Palo Alto, CA: Stanford University Press.

McDougall, P., Schonert-Reichl, K., & Hymel, S. (1996, March). *Adolescents at risk for high school dropout: The role of social factors*. Paper presented at the meeting of the Society for Research on Adolescence, Boston.

McHale, S. M. (1995). Lessons about adolescent development from the study of African-American youth. In L. J. Crockett & A. C. Crouter (Eds.), *Pathways through adolescence*. Hillsdale, NJ: Erlbaum.

McKnight, C. C., Crosswhite, F. J., Dossey, J. A., Kifer, E., Swafford, J. O., Travers, K. J., & Cooney, T. J. (1987). *The underachieving curriculum: Assessing U.S. school mathematics from an international perspective*. Champaign, IL: Stipes.

McLaughlin, C. S., Chen, C., Greenberger, E., & Biermeier, C. (1997). Family, peer, and individual correlates of sexual experience among Caucasian and Asian American late adolescents. *Journal of Research on Adolescence, 7*, 33–54.

McLoyd, V. (1990). Minority children: An introduction to the special issue. *Child Development, 61*, 263–266.

McLoyd, V. (1990). The impact of economic hardship on Black families and children: Psychological distress, parenting, and socioemotional development. *Child Development, 61*, 311–346.

McLoyd, V. (1993, March). *Sizing up the future: Economic stress, expectations, and adolescents' achievement motivation*. Paper presented at the biennial meeting of the Society for Research in Child Development, New Orleans.

McLoyd, V. (in press). The declining fortunes of black children: Psychological distress, parenting, and socioeconomic development in the context of economic hardship. *Child Development*.

McLoyd, V. C. (1997 a). Children in poverty. In I. E. Siegel & K. A. Renninger (Eds.), *Handbook of child psychology* (5th Ed., Vol. 4). New York: Wiley.

McLoyd, V. (1997, April, b). *Reducing stressors, increasing supports in the lives of ethnic minority children in America: Social policy issues*. Paper presented at the meeting of the Society for Research in Child Development, Washington, DC.

McLoyd, V. C., & Ceballo, R. (1995, March). *Conceptualizing economic context*. Paper presented at the meeting of the Society for Research in Child Development, Indianapolis.

McLoyd, V. C., Jayaratne, T. E., Ceballo, R., & Borquez, J. (1994). Unemployment and work interruption among African American single mothers: Effects on parenting and adolescent socioemotional functioning. *Child Development, 65*, 562–589.

McMaster, L. E., & Wintre, M. G. (1994, February). *The link between parental reciprocity, parental approval, and adolescent substance abuse*. Paper presented at the meeting of the Society for Research on Adolescence, San Diego.

McPartland, J. M., & McDill, E. L. (1976). *The unique role of schools in the causes of youthful crime*. Baltimore: Johns Hopkins University Press.

McQuire, W. J. (1986). The myth of massive media impact: Savagings and salvagings. In G. Comstock (Ed.), *Public communication and behavior* (Vol. 1). Orlando: Academic Press.

McWhirter, D. P., Reinisch, J. M., & Sanders, S. A. (Eds.). (1990). *Homosexuality/heterosexuality*. New York: Oxford University Press.

Mead, M. (1928). *Coming of age in Samoa*. New York: Morrow.

Mead, M. (1978, Dec 30–Jan. 5). The American family: An endangered species. *TV Guide*.

Medrich, E. A., Rosen, J., Rubin, V., & Buckley, S. (1982). *The serious business of growing up*. Berkeley: University of California Press.

Melby, J. N. (1995, March). *Early family and peer predictors of later adolescent tobacco use*. Paper presented at the meeting of the Society for Research in Child Development, Indianapolis.

Melby, J. N., & Vargas, D. (1996, March). *Predicting patterns of adolescent tobacco use*. Paper presented at the meeting of the Society for Research on Adolescence, Boston.

Merrell, K. W., & Gimpel, G. A. (1997). *Social skills of children and adolescents*. Mahwah, NJ: Erlbaum.

Messinger, J. C. (1971). Sex and repression in an Irish folk community. In D. S. Marshal & R. C. Suggs (Eds.), *Human sexual behavior: Variations in the ethnographic spectrum* (pp. 3–37). New York: Basic Books.

Meyer-Bahlburg, H. F., Ehrhart, A. A., Rosen, L. R., Gruen, R. S., Veridiano, N. P., Vann, F. H., & Neuwalder, H. F. (1995). Prenatal estrogens and the development of homosexual orientation. *Developmental Psychology, 31*, 12–21.

Michael, R. T., Gagnon, J. H., Laumann, E. O., & Kolata, G. (1994). *Sex in America*. Boston: Little, Brown.

Miller, B. C., Christopherson, C. R., & King, P. K. (1993). Sexual behavior in adolescence. In T. P. Gullotta, G. R. Adams, & R. Montemayor (Eds.), *Adolescent sexuality*. Newbury Park, CA: Sage.

Miller, J. B. (1986). *Toward a new psychology of women* (2nd ed.). Boston: Beacon.

Miller, J. G. (1995, March). *Culture, context, and personal agency: The cultural grounding of self and morality*. Paper presented at the meeting of the Society for Research in Child Development, Indianapolis.

Miller, J. G., & Bersoff, D. M. (1993, March). *Culture and affective closeness in the morality of caring*. Paper presented at the biennial meeting of the Society for Research in Child Development, New Orleans.

Miller, J. G., & Bersoff, D. M. (in press). Culture and moral judgment: How are conflicts between justice and interpersonal responsibilities resolved? *Journal of Personality and Social Psychology*.

Miller, P. Y., & Simon, W. (1974). Adolescent sexual behavior: Context and change. *Social Problems, 22*, 58–76.

Miller, S. K., & Slap, G. G. (1989). Adolescent smoking: A review of prevalence and prevention. *Journal of Adolescent Health Care, 10*, 129–135.

Miller-Jones, D. (1989). Culture and testing. *American Psychologist, 44*, 360–366.

Millstein, G. B. (1988). *The potential of school-linked centers to promote adolescent health and development*. Washington, DC: Carnegie Council on Adolescent Development.

Millstein, S. G. (1991). Health beliefs. In R. M. Lerner, A. C. Petersen, & J. Brooks-Gunn (Eds.), *Encyclopedia of adolescence* (Vol. 1). New York: Garland.

Millstein, S. G. (1993). A view of health from the adolescent's perspective. In S. G. Millstein, A. C. Petersen, & E. O. Nightingale (Eds.), *Promoting the health of adolescents*. New York: Oxford University Press.

Millstein, S. G., Petersen, A. C., & Nightingale, E. O. (1993). (Eds.). *Promoting the health of adolescents*. New York: Oxford University Press.

Minkler, M. (1989) Health education, health promotion, and the open society: An historical perspective. *Health Education Quarterly, 16*, 17–30.

Mintz, S. (1997). From patriarchy to androgyny and other myths: Placing men's roles in historical perspective. In A. Booth & A. C. Crouter (Eds.), *Men in families*. Mahwah, NJ: Erlbaum.

Minuchin, P. P., & Shapiro, E. K. (1983). The school as a context for social development. In P. H. Mussen (Ed.), *Handbook of child psychology* (4th ed., Vol. 4). New York: Wiley.

Mischel, W. (1973). Toward a cognitive social learning reconceptualization of personality. *Psychological Review, 80*, 252–283.

Mischel, W. (1995, August). *Cognitive-affective theory of person-environment psychology*. Paper presented at the meeting of the American Psychological Association, New York City.

Mischel, W., & Gilligan, C. (1964). Delay of gratification, motivation for the prohibited gratification, and responses to temptation. *Journal of Abnormal and Social Psychology, 69*, 411–417.

Mischel, W., & Mischel, H. (1975, April). *A cognitive social-learning analysis of moral development*. Paper presented at the meeting of the Society for Research in Child Development, Denver.

Mitchell, C. M., O'Nell, T. D., Beals, J., Dick, R. W., Keane, E., & Manson, S. M. (1996). Dimensionality of alcohol use among American Indian adolescents: Latent structure, construct validity, and implications for developmental research. *Journal of Research on Adolescence, 6*, 151–180.

Montemayor, R. (1982). The relationship between parent-adolescent conflict and the amount of time adolescents spend with parents, peers, and alone. *Child Development, 53*, 1512–1519.

Montemayor, R., & Flannery, D. J. (1990). Making the transition from childhood to early adolescence. In R. Montemayor, G. R. Adams, & T. P. Gulotta (Eds.), *From childhood to adolescence: A transitional period?* Newbury Park, CA: Sage.

Montemayor, R., & Flannery, D. J. (1991). Parent-adolescent relations in middle and late adolescence. In R. M. Lerner, A. C. Petersen, & J. Brooks-Gunn (Eds.), *Encyclopedia of adolescence* (Vol. 2). New York: Garland.

Montemayor, R., Adams, G. R., & Gulotta, T. P. (Eds.). (1990). *From childhood to adolescence: A transitional period?* Newbury Park, CA: Sage.

Moore, K. A., Myers, D. E., Morrison, D. R., Nord, C. W., Brown, B., & Edmonston, B. (1993). Age at first childbirth and later poverty. *Journal of Research on Adolescence, 3*, 393–422.

Moorhead, M., & Hayward, E. (1997, July). *Utilizing peers: The important link*. Paper presented at the conference on Working with America's Youth, Pittsburgh, PA.

Moos, R. H., Finney, J. W., & Cronkite, R. C. (1990). *Alcoholism treatment: Context, process, and outcome*. New York: Oxford University Press.

Moran, P., Chang, J., & Pettit, R. (1994, February). *Gender differences in delinquency behavior among adolescents from divorced and intact families*. Paper presented at the meeting of the Society for Research on Adolescence, San Diego.

Morgan, M. (1982). Television and adolescents' sex-role stereotypes. A longitudinal study. *Journal of Personality and Social Psychology, 43*, 947–955.

Morgan, M. (1987). Television, sex-role attitudes, and sex-role behavior. *Journal of Early Adolescence, 7*, 269–282.

Morris, L., Warren, C. W., & Aral, S. O. (1993, September). Measuring adolescent sexual behaviors and related health outcomes. *Public Health Reports, 108,* 31–36.

Morrow, L. (1988, August 8). Through the eyes of children. *Time,* pp. 32–33.

Mortimer, J., & Lorence, J. (1979). Work experience and occupational value socialization: A longitudinal study. *American Journal of Sociology, 84,* 1361–1385.

Mortimer, J. T. (1991). Employment. In R. M. Lerner, A. C. Petersen, & J. Brooks-Gunn (Eds.), *Encyclopedia of adolescence* (Vol. 1). New York: Garland.

Mortimer, J. T., Finch, M., Shanahan, M., & Ryu, S. (1992). Work experience, mental health, and behavioral adjustment in adolescence. *Journal of Research on Adolescence, 2,* 24–57.

Mott, F. L., & Marsiglio, W. (1985, September/October). Early childbearing and completion of high school. *Family Planning Perspectives,* p. 234.

Mounts, N. S. (1997, April). *Parental management of adolescent friendships.* Paper presented at the meeting of the Society for Research in Child Development, Washington, DC.

Munroe, R. H., Himmin, H. S., & Munroe, R. L. (1984). Gender understanding and sex-role preference in four cultures. *Developmental Psychology, 20,* 673–682.

Munroe, R. H., Koel, A., Munroe, R. L., Bolton, R., Michelson, C., & Bolton, C. (1983). Time allocation in our societies. *Ethnology, 22,* 355–370.

Munroe, R. L., & Munroe, R. H. (1975). *Cross-cultural human development.* Monterey, CA: Brooks/Cole.

Murdock, T. B., & Davis, J. E. (1994, February). *The economic and school context of anti-academic peer norms and alienation in African-American students.* Paper presented at the meeting of the Society for Research on Adolescence, San Diego.

Murphy, K., & Schneider, B. (1994). Coaching socially rejected early adolescents regarding behaviors used by peers to infer liking: A dyad-specific intervention. *Journal of Early Adolescence, 14,* 83–95.

Murray, D. M., Matthews, K. A., Blake, S. M., Prineas, R. J., & Gillum, R. F. (1988). Type-A behavior in children: Demographic, behavioral, and physiological correlates. In B. G. Melamed & others (Eds.), *Child health psychology.* Hillsdale, NJ: Erlbaum.

Murray, H. A. (1938). *Explorations in personality.* New York: Oxford University Press.

Myers, M. G., Wagner, E. E., & Brown, S. A. (1997). Substance abuse. In V. B. Van Hasselt & M. Hersen (Eds.), *Handbook of psychological treatment protocols for children and adolescents.* Mahwah, NJ: Erlbaum.

Nagata, D. K. (1989). Japanese American children and adolescents. In J. T. Gibbs & L. N. Huang (Eds.), *Children of color.* San Francisco: Jossey-Bass.

National and Community Service Coalition. (1995). *Youth volunteerism: Here's what the surveys say.* Washington, DC: Author.

National Assessment of Educational Progress. (1976). *Adult work skills and knowledge* (Report No. 35-COD-01). Denver: National Assessment of Educational Progress.

National Health Interview Study. (1991). *Current estimates from the National Health Interview Survey.* Hyattsville, MD: National Center for Health Statistics.

National Research Council. (1987). *Risking the future: Adolescent sexuality, pregnancy, and childbearing.* Washington, DC: National Academy Press.

Neimark, E. D. (1982). Adolescent thought: Transition to formal operations. In B. B. Wolman (Ed.), *Handbook of developmental psychology.* Englewood Cliffs, NJ: Prentice Hall.

Neisser, U., Boodoo, G., Bouchard, T. J., Boykin, A. W., Brody, N., Ceci, S. J., Halpern, D. F., Loehlin, J. C., Perloff, R., Sternberg, R. J., & Urbina, S. (1996). Intelligence: Knowns and unknowns. *American Psychologist, 51,* 77–101.

Neugarten, B. L. (1988, August). *Policy issues for an aging society.* Paper presented at the meeting of the American Psychological Association, Atlanta.

Newacheck, P. W. (1989). Improving access to health services for adolescents from economically disadvantaged families. *Pediatrics, 84,* 1056–1063.

Newcomb, M. D., & Bentler, P. M. (1988). Impact of adolescent drug use and social support on problems of young adults: A longitudinal study. *Journal of Abnormal Psychology, 97,* 64–75.

Newcomb, M. D., & Bentler, P. M. (1989). Substance use and abuse among children and teenagers. *American Psychologist, 44,* 242–248.

Newcomer, S. F., & Udry, J. R. (1985). Oral sex in an adolescent population. *Archives of Sexual Behavior, 14,* 41–46.

Newman, B. S., & Muzzonigro, P. G. (1993). The effects of traditional family values on the coming out process of gay male adolescents. *Adolescence, 28,* 213–226.

Newman, D. L., & Caspi, A. (1996, March). *Temperament styles observed at age 3 predict interpersonal functioning in the transition to adulthood.* Paper presented at the meeting of the Society for Research on Adolescence, Boston.

Newman, D. L., Caspi, A., Moffitt, T. E., & Silva, P. A. (1997). Antecedents of adult interpersonal functioning: Effects of individual differences in age 3 temperament. *Developmental Psychology, 33,* 206–217.

Newman, K. S. (1996). Working poor: Low-wage employment in the lives of Harlem youth. In J. A. Graber, J. Brooks-Gunn, & A. C. Petersen (Eds.), *Transitions in adolescence.* Mahway, NJ: Erlbaum.

Nicholls, J. G. (1984). Conceptions of ability and achievement motivation. In R. E. Ames & C. Ames (Eds.), *Motivation in education.* New York: Academic Press.

Noam, G. G. (1997). Clinical developmental psychology. In I. E. Sigel & K. A. Renniger (Eds.), *Handbook of child psychology* (5th Ed., Vol. 4). New York: Wiley.

Nolen-Hoeksema, S., & Girgus, J. S. (1994). The emergence of gender differences in depression during adolescence. *Psychological Bulletin, 115,* 424–443.

Norem, J. K., & Cantor, N. (1986). Anticipatory and post-hoc cushioning strategies: Optimism and defensive pessimism in "risky" situations. *Cognitive Therapy Research, 10,* 347–362.

Nottelmann, E. D., Susman, E. J., Blue, J. H., Inoff-Germain, G., Dorn, L. D., Loriaux, D. L., Cutler, G. B., & Chrousos, G. P. (1987). Gonadal and adrenal hormone correlates of adjustment in early adolescence. In R. M. Lerner & T. T. Foch (Eds.), *Biological-psychological interactions in early adolescence.* Hillsdale, NJ: Erlbaum.

Nydegger, C. N., & Mitteness, L. S. (1991). Fathers and their adult sons and daughters. *Marriage and Family Review, 16,* 249–266.

O'Brien, R. W. (1990, March). *The use of family members and peers as resources during adolescence.* Paper presented at the meeting of the Society for Research in Adolescence, Atlanta.

O'Conner, B. P., & Nikolic, J. (1990). Identity development and formal operations as sources of adolescent egocentrism. *Journal of Youth and Adolescence, 19*, 149–158.

O'Connor, T. G. (1994, February). *Patterns of differential parental treatment.* Paper presented at the meeting of the Society for Research on Adolescence, San Diego.

O'Connor, T. G., Hetherington, E. M., Reiss, D., & Plomin, R. (1995). A twin-sibling study of observed parent-adolescent interactions. *Child Development, 66*, 812–829.

O'Donnell, J., Hawkins, J. D., & Abbott, R. D. (1995). Predicting serious delinquency and substance use among aggressive boys. *Journal of Consulting and Clinical Psychology, 63*, 529–537.

Oden, S. L., & Asher, S. R. (1975, April). *Coaching children in social skills for friendship making.* Paper presented at the meeting of the Society for Research in Child Development, Denver.

Offer, D., Ostrov, E., Howard, K. I., & Atkinson, R. (1988). *The teenage world: Adolescents' self-image in ten countries.* New York: Plenum.

Ogbu, J. U. (1989, April). *Academic socialization of black children: An inoculation against future failure?* Paper presented at the meeting of the Society for Research in Child Development, Kansas City.

Olweus, D., Matteson, A., Schalling, D., & Low, H. (1988). Circulating testosterone levels and aggression in adolescent males: A causal analysis. *Psychosomatic Medicine, 50*, 261–272.

Orlofsky, J. (1976). Intimacy status: Relationship to interpersonal perception. *Journal of Youth and Adolescence, 5*, 73–88.

Orlofsky, J., Marcia, J., & Lesser, I. (1973). Ego identity status and the intimacy vs. isolation crisis of young adulthood. *Journal of Personality and Social Psychology, 27*, 211–219.

Orthner, D. K., Giddings, M., & Quinn, W. (1987). *Youth in transition: A study of adolescents from Air Force and civilian families.* Washington, DC: U.S. Air Force.

Oser, F. (1986). Moral education and values education: The discourse perspective. In M. C. Wittrock (Ed.), *Handbook of research on teaching.* New York: Macmillan.

Oser, F., & Gmunder, P. (1991). *Religious judgment: A developmental perspective.* Birmingham, AL: Religious Education Press.

Osipow, S. H., & Littlejohn, E. M. (1995). Toward a multicultural theory of career development: Prospects and dilemmas. In F. T. L. Leong (Ed.), *Career development and vocational behavior of racial and ethnic minorities.* Hillsdale, NJ: Erlbaum.

Osofsky, J. D. (1990, Winter). Risk and protective factors for teenage mothers and their infants. *SRCD Newsletter,* pp. 1–2.

Ostrov, E., Offer, D., Howard, K. I., Kaufman, B., & Meyer, H. (1985). Adolescent sexual behavior. *Medical Aspects of Human Sexuality, 19*, 28, 30–31, 34–36.

Overton, W. F., & Byrnes, J. P. (1991). Cognitive development. In R. M. Lerner, A. C. Petersen, & J. Brooks-Gunn (Eds.), *Encyclopedia of adolescence* (Vol. 1). New York: Garland.

Overton, W. F., & Montangero, J. (1991). Piaget, Jean. In R. M. Lerner, A. C. Petersen, & J. Brooks-Gunn (Eds.), *Encyclopedia of adolescence* (Vol. 2). New York: Garland.

Paige, K. E., & Paige, J. M. (1985). *Politics and reproductive rituals.* Berkeley: University of California Press.

Paikoff, R. L., & Brooks-Gunn, J. (1990). Physiological processes: What role do they play during the transition to adolescence? In R. Montemayor, G. R. Adams, & T. P. Gulotta (Eds.), *From childhood to adolescence: A transitional period?* Newbury Park, CA: Sage.

Paikoff, R. L., Brooks-Gunn, J., & Warren, M. P. (1991). Effects of girls' hormonal status on depressive and aggressive symptoms over the course of one year. *Journal of Youth and Adolescence, 20*, 191–215.

Paikoff, R. L., Buchanan, C. M., & Brooks-Gunn, J. (1991). Hormone-behavior links at puberty, methodological links in the study of. In R. M. Lerner, A. C. Petersen, & J. Brooks-Gunn (Eds.), *Encyclopedia of adolescence.* New York: Garland.

Paloutzian, R. F. (1996). *Invitation to the psychology of religion* (2nd ed.). Needham Heights, MA: Allyn & Bacon.

Paloutzian, R. F., & Santrock, J. W. (1997). The psychology of religion. In J. W. Santrock, *Psychology* (5th ed.). Madison, WI: Brown & Benchmark.

Paludi, M. A. (1995). *The psychology of women* (2nd ed.). Dubuque, IA: Brown & Benchmark.

Papini, D. R., Roggman, L. A., & Anderson, J. (1990). *Early adolescent perceptions of attachment to mother and father: A test of the emotional distancing hypothesis.* Paper presented at the meeting of the Society for Research in Adolescence, Atlanta.

Papini, D., & Sebby, R. (1988). Variations in conflictual family issues by adolescent pubertal status, gender, and family member. *Journal of Early Adolescence, 8*, 1–15.

Parcel, G. S., Simons-Morton, G. G., O'Hara, N. M., Baranowski, T., Kolbe, L. J., & Bee, D. E. (1987). School promotion of healthful diet and exercise behavior: An integration of organizational change and social learning theory interventions. *Journal of School Health, 57*, 150–156.

Parfenoff, S. H., & McCormick, A. (1997, April). *Parenting preadolescents at risk: Knowledge, attitudes, and communication about HIV/AIDS.* Paper presented at the meeting of the Society for Research in Child Development, Washington, DC.

Parke, R. D. (1993, March). *Family processes.* Paper presented at the biennial meeting of the Society for Research in Child Development, New Orleans.

Parke, R. D. (1995). Fathers and families. In M. H. Bornstein (Ed.), *Children and parenting* (Vol. 3). Hillsdale, NJ: Erlbaum.

Parke, R. D., & Buriel, R. (1997). Socialization in the family. In N. Eisenberg (Ed.), *Handbook of child psychology* (5th Ed., Vol. 3). New York: Wiley.

Patterson, C. J. (1995). Sexual orientation and human development: An overview. *Developmental Psychology, 31*, 3–11.

Patterson, G. R., DeBaryshe, B. D., & Ramsey, E. (1989). A developmental perspective on antisocial behavior. *American Psychologist, 44*, 329–335.

Patterson, S. J., Sochting, I., & Marcia, J. E. (1992). The inner space and beyond: Women and identity. In G. R. Adams, T. P. Gullotta, & R. Montemayor (Eds.), *Adolescent identity formation.* Newbury Park, CA: Sage.

Patterson, G. R., & Stouthamer-Loeber, M. (1984). The correlation of family management practices and delinquency. *Child Development, 55*, 1299–1307.

Paul, E. L., & White, K. M. (1990). The development of intimate relationships in late adolescence. *Adolescence, 25*, 375–400.

Paulson, S. E. (1994, February). *Parenting style or parental involvement: Which is more important for adolescent achievement?* Paper presented at the meeting of the Society for Research on Adolescence, San Diego.

Paulson, S. E., Marchant, G. J., & Rothlisberg, B. (1995, March). *Relations among parent, teacher, and school factors: Implications for achievement outcome in middle-grade students.* Paper presented at the meeting of the Society for Research in Child Development, Indianapolis.

Pentz, M. A. (1993). Comparative effects of community-based drug abuse prevention. In J. S. Baer, G. A. Marlatt, & R. J. McMahon (Eds.), *Addictive behaviors across the life span.* Newbury Park, CA: Sage.

Peplau, L. A., & Perlman, D. (Eds.). (1982). *Loneliness: A sourcebook of current theory, research, and therapy.* New York: Wiley.

Perry, C., Hearn, M., Murray, D., & Klepp, K. (1988). *The etiology and prevention of adolescent alcohol and drug abuse.* Unpublished manuscript, University of Minnesota.

Perry, C. L., Kelder, S. H., & Komro, K. A. (1993). The social world of adolescents: Families, peers, schools, and the community. In S. G. Millstein, A. C. Petersen, & E. O. Nightingale (Eds.), *Promoting the health of adolescents.* New York: Oxford University Press.

Perry, I. (1988). A black student's reflection on public and private schools. *Harvard Educational Review, 58,* 332–336.

Perry, W. G. (1981). Cognitive and ethical growth. The making of meaning. In A. W. Chickering (Ed.), *The modern American college: Responding to the new realities of diverse students and a changing society.* San Francisco: Jossey-Bass.

Peskin, H. (1967). Pubertal onset and ego functioning. *Journal of Abnormal Psychology, 72,* 1–15.

Petersen, A. C. (1979, January). Can puberty come any faster? *Psychology Today,* pp. 45–56.

Petersen, A. C. (1987, September). Those gangly years. *Psychology Today,* pp. 28–34.

Petersen, A. C. (1993). Creating adolescents: The role of context and process in developmental trajectories. *Journal of Research on Adolescence, 3,* 1–18.

Petersen, A. C., & Crockett, L. (1985). Pubertal timing and grade effects on adjustment. *Journal of Youth and Adolescence, 14,* 191–206.

Petersen, A. C., Compas, B. E., Brooks-Gunn, J., Stemmler, M., Ey, S., & Grant, K. E. (1993). Depression in adolescence. *American Psychologist, 48,* 155–168.

Petersen, A. C., & Ding, S. (1995, March). *Improving coping behaviors during adolescence.* Paper presented at the meeting of the Society for Research in Child Development, Indianapolis.

Petersen, A. C., Sarigiani, P. A., & Kennedy, R. E (1991). Adolescent depression: Why more girls? *Journal of Youth and Adolescence, 20,* 247–271.

Petersen, A. C., Sarigiani, P. A., & Kennedy, R. E. (1991). Coping with adolescence. In M. E. Colte & S. Gore (Eds.), *Adolescent stress: Causes and consequences.* New York: Aldine de Gruyter.

Peterson, P. L., Hawkins, J. D., Abbott, R. D., & Catalano, R. F. (1994). Disentangling the effects of parent drinking, family management, and parental alcohol norms on current drinking by Black and White adolescents. *Journal of Research on Adolescence, 4,* 203–228.

Petraitis, J., Flay, B. R., & Miller, T. Q. (1995). Reviewing theories of adolescent substance use: Organizing pieces of the puzzle. *Psychological Bulletin, 17,* 67–86.

Pfeffer, C. R. (1986). *The suicidal child.* New York: Guilford Press.

Phillips, R. (1997, July). *Strengthening school and community partnerships: Prevention that works!* Paper presented at the conference on Working with America's Youth, Pittsburgh, PA.

Phinney, J. S. (1989). Stages of ethnic identity development in minority group adolescents. *Journal of Early Adolescence, 9,* 34–49.

Phinney, J. S., & Alipuria, L. L. (1990). Ethnic identity in college students from four ethnic groups. *Journal of Adolescence, 13,* 171–183.

Phinney, J. S., & Chavira, V. (1995). Parental ethnic socialization and adolescent coping with problems related to ethnicity. *Journal of Research on Adolescence, 5,* 31–54.

Phinney, J. S., & Devich-Navarro, M. (1997, April). *Variations in bicultural identification among African American and Mexican American adolescents.* Journal of Research on Adolescence. 7, 3–32.

Phinney, J. S., Dupont, S., Landin, J., & Onwughalu, M. (1994, February). *Social identity orientation, bicultural conflict, and coping strategies among minority adolescents.* Paper presented at the meeting of the Society for Research on Adolescence, San Diego.

Piaget, J. (1932). *The moral judgment of the child.* New York: Harcourt Brace Jovanovich.

Piaget, J. (1952). *The origins of intelligence in children.* New York: International Universities Press.

Piaget, J. (1952). Jean Piaget. In C. A. Murchison (Ed.), *A history of psychology in autobiography* (Vol. 4). Worcester, MA: Clark University Press.

Piaget, J. (1954). *The construction of reality in the child.* New York: Basic Books.

Piaget, J. (1962). *Play, dreams, and imitation.* New York: W. W. Norton.

Piaget, J. (1967). The mental development of the child. In D. Elkind (Ed.), *Six psychological studies by Piaget.* New York: Random House.

Piaget, J. (1970). Piaget's theory. In P. H. Mussen (Ed.), *Carmichael's manual of child psychology.* (3rd ed., Vol. 1). New York: Wiley.

Piaget, J. (1972). Intellectual evolution from adolescence to adulthood. *Human Development, 15,* 1–12.

Piotrowski, C. C. (1997, April). *Mother and sibling triads in conflict: Linking conflict style and the quality of sibling relationships.* Paper presented at the meeting of the Society for Research in Child Development, Washington, DC.

Place, D. M. (1975). The dating experience for adolescent girls. *Adolescence, 38,* 157–173.

Pleck, J. H. (1983). The theory of male sex role identity: Its rise and fall, 1936–present. In M. Lewin (Ed.), *In the shadow of the past: Psychology portrays the sexes.* New York: Columbia University Press.

Pleck, J. H. (1995). The gender-role strain paradigm: An update: In R. F. Levant & W. S. Pollack (Eds.), *A new psychology of men.* New York: Basic.

Pleck, J. H., Sonenstein, F., & Ku, L. (1991). Adolescent males' condom use: Relationships between perceived cost benefits and consistency. *Journal of Marriage and the Family, 53,* 733–745.

Pleck, J. H., Sonnenstein, F., & Ku, L. (in press). Problem behaviors and masculine ideology in adolescent males. In R. Ketterlinus & M. E. Lamb (Eds.), *Adolescent problem behaviors.* Hillsdale, NJ: Erlbaum.

Pleck, J. H., Sonenstein, F., Ku, L., Burbridge, L., & Mincy, R. (1994, February). *Risk and protective influences on early adolescent risk markers in males.* Paper presented at the meeting of the Society for Research on Adolescence, San Diego.

Plomin, R. (1993, March). *Human behavioral genetics and development: An overview and update*. Paper presented at the biennial meeting of the Society for Research in Child Development, New Orleans.

Plomin, R., DeFries, J. C., McClearn, G. E., & Rutter, M. (1997). *Behavioral genetics* (3rd Ed.). New York,: W. H. Freeman.

Polina, L. K., & Overby, G. (1996, March). *Perceptions of relations with fathers across three generations of adolescent females*. Paper presented at the meeting of the Society for Research on Adolescence, Boston.

Pollack, W. S. (1995). No man is an island: Toward a new psychoanalytic psychology of men. In R. F. Levant & W. S. Pollack (Eds.), *A new psychology of men*. New York: Basic.

Potthof, S. J. (1992, March). *Modeling family planning expertise to predict oral contraceptive discontinuance in teenagers*. Paper presented at the meeting of the Society for Research on Adolescence, Washington, DC.

Potvin, L., Champagne, F., & Laberge-Nadeau, C. (1988). Mandatory driver training and road safety: The Quebec experience. *American Journal of Public Health, 78*, 1206–1212.

Pressley, M., & Schneider, W. (1997). *Introduction to memory development during childhood and adolescence*. Mahwah, NJ: Erlbaum.

Price, R. H., Cioci, M., Penner, W., & Trautlein, B. (1990). *School and community support programs that enhance adolescent health and education*. Washington, DC: Carnegie Council on Adolescent Development.

Prinsky, L. E., & Rosenbaum, J. L. (1987). Leerics or lyrics? *Youth and Society, 18*, 384–394.

Prinstein, M. J., Fetter, M. D., & La Greca, A. M. (1996, March). *Can you judge adolescents by the company they keep? Peer group membership, substance use, and risk-taking behaviors*. Paper presented at the meeting of the Society for Research on Adolescence, Boston.

Prunell, M., Boada, J., Feria, M., & Benitez, M. A. (1987). Antagonism of the stimulant and depressant effects of ethanol in rats by naloxone. *Psychopharmacology, 92*, 215–218.

Psathas, G. (1957). Ethnicity, social class, and adolescent independence. *Sociological Review, 22*, 415–523.

Q

Quadrel, M. J., Fischoff, B., & Davis, W. (1993). Adolescent (in)vulnerability. *American Psychologist, 48*, 102–116.

R

Rabkin, J. (1987). *Epidemiology of adolescent violence: Risk factors, career patterns, and intervention programs*. Paper presented at the conference on adolescent violence, Stanford University, Stanford, CA.

Ramirez, O. (1989). Mexican American children and adolescents. In J. T. Gibbs & L. N. Huang (Eds.), *Children of color*. San Francisco: Jossey-Bass.

Rapport, M. D. (1997). Attention-deficit hyperactivity disorder. In V. B. Van Hasselt & M. Hersen (Eds.), *Handbook of psychological treatment protocols for children and adolescents*. Mahwah, NJ: Erlbaum.

Raskin, P. M. (1985). Identity in vocational development. In A. S. Waterman (Ed.), *Identity in adolescence*. San Francisco: Jossey-Bass.

Reinherz, H. Z., Giaconia, R. M., Silverman, A. B., & Friedman, A. C. (1994, February). *Early psychosocial risks for adolescent suicidal ideation and attempts*. Paper presented at the meeting of the Society for Research on Adolescence, San Diego.

Reinisch, J. M. (1990). *The Kinsey Institute new report on sex: What you must know to be sexually literate*. New York: St. Martin's Press.

Remafedi, G., Resnick, M., Blum, R., & Harris, L. (in press). The demography of sexual orientation in adolescents. *Pediatrics*.

Repinski, D. J., & Leffert, N. (1994, February). *Adolescents' relationships with friends: The effects of a psychoeducational intervention*. Paper presented at the biennial meeting of the Society for Research on Adolescence, San Diego.

Resnick, L. B. (1987). *Education and learning to think*. Washington, DC: National Academy Press.

Resnick, M. D., Wattenberg, E., & Brewer, R. (1992, March). *Paternity avowal/disavowal among partners of low income mothers*. Paper presented at the meeting of the Society for Research on Adolescence, Washington, DC.

Rest, J. (1995). *Concerns for the social-psychological development of youth and educational strategies: Report for the Kaufmann Foundation*. Minneapolis: University of Minnesota, Department of Educational Psychology.

Rest, J. (1996, January). Unpublished review of *Adolescence* (7th ed.) by J. W. Santrock. Dubuque, IA: Brown & Benchmark.

Rest, J. R. (1986). *Moral development: Advances in theory and research*. New York: Praeger.

Rice, K. G. (1993). Separation-individuation and adjustment to college: A longitudinal study. *Journal of Counseling Psychology, 39*, 203–213.

Richards, M., Suleiman, L., Sims, B., & Sedeno, A. (1994, February). *Experiences of ethnically diverse young adolescents growing up in poverty*. Paper presented at the meeting of the Society for Research on Adolescence, San Diego.

Richards, M. H., Boxer, A. M., Petersen, A. C., & Albrecht, R. (1990). The relationship of weight to body image in pubertal girls and boys from two communities. *Developmental Psychology, 26*, 313–321.

Richardson, J. L., Dwyer, K., McGrugan, K., Hansen, W. B., Dent, C., Johnson, C. A., Sussman, S. Y., Brannon, B., & Glay, B. (1989). Substance use among eighth-grade students who take care of themselves after school. *Pediatrics, 84*, 556–566.

Rimberg, H. M., & Lewis, R. J. (1994). Older adolescents and AIDS: Correlates of self-reported safer sex practices. *Journal of Research on Adolescence, 4*, 453–464.

Ritter, P. L., Mont-Reynaud, R., & Dornbusch, S. M. (1993). Minority parents and their youth: Concern, encouragement, and support for school achievement. In N. F. Chavkin (Ed.), *Families and schools in a pluralistic society*. Albany: State University of New York Press.

Roberts, D., Jacobson, L., & Taylor, R. D. (1996, March). *Neighborhood characteristics, stressful life events, and African-American adolescents' adjustment*. Paper presented at the meeting of the Society for Research on Adolescence, Boston.

Roberts, D. F. (1993). Adolescents and the mass media: From "Leave It to Beaver" to "Beverly Hills 90210." In R. Takanishi, (Ed.), *Adolescence in the 1990s*. New York: Teachers College Press.

Robinson, D. P., & Greene, J. W. (1988). The adolescent alcohol and drug problem: A practical approach. *Pediatric Nursing, 14*, 305–310.

Robinson, N. S. (1995). Evaluating the nature of perceived support and its relation to perceived self-worth in adolescents. *Journal of Research on Adolescence, 5*, 253–280.

Rodin, J. (1984, December). Interview: A sense of control. *Psychology Today*, pp. 38–45.

Roe, A. (1956). *The psychology of occupations*. New York: Wiley.

Roff, M., Sells, S. B., & Golden, M. W. (1972). *Social adjustment and personality development in children.* Minneapolis: University of Minnesota Press.

Rogers, A. (1987). *Questions of gender differences: Ego development and moral voice in adolescence.* Unpublished manuscript, Department of Education, Harvard University.

Rogers, C. R. (1950). The significance of the self regarding attitudes and perceptions. In M. L. Reymart (Ed.), *Feelings and emotions.* New York: McGraw-Hill.

Rogoff, B. (1993). Children's guided participation and participatory appropriation in sociocultural activity. In R. Wozniak & K. Fischer (Eds.), *Development in context: Acting and thinking in specific environments.* Hillsdale, NJ: Erlbaum.

Rogoff, B. (1997, April). *Development as transformation of participation in sociocultural activities.* Paper presented at the meeting of the Society for Research in Child Development, Washington, DC.

Rogoff, B. (1997). Cognition as a collaborative process. In D. Kuhn & R. S. Siegler (Eds.), *Handbook of child psychology* (5th Ed., Vol. 2). New York: Wiley.

Rohner, R. P., & Rohner, E. C. (1981). Parental acceptance-rejection and parental control: Cross-cultural codes. *Ethnology, 20,* 245–260.

Rohrbach, L. A., Hodgson, C. S., Broder, B. I., Montgomery, S. B., Flay, B. F., Hansen, W. B., & Pentz, M. A. (1995). Parental participation in drug abuse prevention: Results from the Midwestern Prevention Project. In G. M. Boyd, J. Howard, & R. A. Zucker (Eds.), *Alcohol problems among adolescents.* Hillsdale, NJ: Erlbaum.

Romo, H. D., & Falbo, T. (1995). *Against the odds: Latino youth and high school graduation.* Austin: University of Texas Press.

Roscoe, B., Dian, M. S., & Brooks, R. H. (1987). Early, middle, and late adolescents' views on dating and factors influencing partner's selection. *Adolescence, 22,* 59–68.

Rose, H. A., & Martin, C. L. (1993, March). *Children's gender-based inferences about others' activities, emotions, and occupations.* Paper presented at the biennial meeting of the Society for Research in Child Development, New Orleans.

Rose, S., & Frieze, I. R. (1993). Young singles' contemporary dating scripts. *Sex Roles, 28,* 499–509.

Rose, S. A., Feldman, J. F., McCarton, C. M., & Wolfson, J. (1988). Information processing in seven-month-old infants as a function of risk status. *Child Development, 59,* 489–603.

Rosenbaum, E., & Kandel, D. B. (1990). Early onset of adolescent sexual behavior and drug involvement. *Journal of Marriage and the Family, 52,* 783–798.

Rosenberg, M. (1979). *Conceiving the self.* New York: Basic Books.

Rosenberg, M. (1986). Self-concept from middle childhood through adolescence. In J. Suls & A. G. Greenwald (Eds.), *Psychological perspective on the self* (Vol. 3). Hillsdale, NJ: Erlbaum.

Rosenthal, R., & Jacobsen, L. (1968). *Pygmalian in the classroom.* New York: Holt, Rinehart & Winston.

Rosner, B. A., & Rierdan, J. (1994, February). *Adolescent girls' self-esteem: Variations in developmental trajectories.* Paper presented at the meeting of the Society for Research on Adolescence, San Diego.

Rosnow, R. L., & Rosenthal, R. (1997). *People studying people: Artifacts and ethics in behavioral research.* New York: W. H. Freeman.

Rossi, A. S. (1988). A life-course approach to gender, aging, and intergenerational relations. In K. W. Schaie & C. Schooler (Eds.), *Social structure and aging.* Hillsdale, NJ: Erlbaum.

Rotenberg, K. J. (1993, March). *Development of restrictive disclosure to friends.* Paper presented at the biennial meeting of the Society for Research in Child Development, New Orleans.

Rousseau, J. J. (1962). *The Emile of Jean-Jacques Rousseau* (W. Boyd, Ed. and Trans.). New York: Teachers College Press, Columbia University. (Original work published 1762).

Rubenstein, J., Heeren, T., Houseman, D., Rubin, C., & Stechler, G. (1989). Suicidal behavior "normal" adolescents: Risk and protective factors. *American Journal of Orthopsychiatry, 59,* 59–71.

Rubert, M. L., & Rubovits, D. S. (1997, April). *A history of adolescent pregnancy programs in the 20th century.* Paper presented at the meeting of the Society for Research in Child Development, Washington, DC.

Rubin, K. H., Bukowski, W., & Parker, J. G. (1997). Peer interactions, relationships, and groups. In N. Eisenberg (Ed.), *Handbook of child psychology* (5th Ed., Vol. 3). New York: Wiley.

Rubin, Z., & Mitchell, C. (1976). Couples research as couples counseling. *American Psychologist, 31,* 17–25.

Rubin, Z., & Sloman, J. (1984). How parents influence their children's friendships. In M. Lewis (Ed.), *Beyond the dyad.* New York: Plenum.

Ruble, D. N., Boggiano, A. K., Feldman, N. S., & Loebl, J. H. (1980). Developmental analysis of the role of social comparison in self evaluation. *Developmental Psychology, 16,* 105–115.

Ruble, D. N., & Martin, C. L. (1997). Gender development. In N. Eisenberg (Ed.), *Handbook of child psychology* (5th Ed., Vol. 3). New York: Wiley.

Rueter, M. A., & Conger, R. D. (1995). Interaction style, problem-solving behavior, and family problem-solving effectiveness. *Child Development, 66,* 98–115.

Rumberger, R. W. (1983). Dropping out of high school: The influence of race, sex, and family background. *American Educational Research Journal, 20,* 199–220.

Rumberger, R. W. (1995). Dropping out of middle school: A multilevel analysis of students and schools. *American Educational Research Journal, 3,* 583–625.

Rutter, M. (1971). Parent-child separation: Psychological effects on the children. *Journal of Child Psychology and Psychiatry, 12,* 233–256.

Rutter, M. (1979). Protective factors in children's response to stress and disadvantage. In M. W. Kent & J. E. Rolf (Eds.), *Primary prevention in psychopathology* (Vol. 3). Hanover, NH: University of New Hamphire Press.

Rutter, M., & Garmezy, N. (1983). Developmental psychopathology. In P. H. Mussen (Ed.), *Handbook of child psychology* (4th ed., Vol. 4). New York: Wiley.

Rutter, M., Maughan, B., Mortimore, P., & Ouston, J. (1979). *Fifteen thousand hours: Secondary schools and their effects on children.* Cambridge, MA: Harvard University Press.

Ryan, A. M., & Patrick, H. (1996, March). *Positive peer relationships and psychosocial adjustment during adolescence.* Paper presented at the meeting of the Society for Research on Adolescence, Boston.

Ryan, B. A., Adams, G. R., Gullotta, T. P., Weissberg, R. P., & Hampton, R. L. (Eds.) (1995). *The family-school connection.* Newbury Park, CA: Sage.

Ryan, R. M., & Lynch, J. H. (1989). Emotional autonomy versus detachment: Revisiting the vicissitudes of adolescence and young adulthood. *Child Development, 60,* 340–356.

Rybash, J., Roodin, P., & Hoyer, E. (1995). *Adult development and aging* (3rd ed.). Dubuque, IA: Brown & Benchmark.

Saarni, C. (1988). Children's understanding of the interpersonal consequences of dissemblance of nonverbal emotional-expressive behavior. *Journal of Nonverbal Behavior, 12,* 275–294.

Sadker, M., & Sadker, D. (1986, March). Sexism in the classroom: From grade school to graduate school. *Phi Delta Kappan.* pp. 512–515.

Sadker, M., & Sadker, D. (1994). *Failing at fairness.* New York: Touchstone.

Sampson, R. J., & Earls, F. (1995, April). *Community social organization in the urban mosaic: Project on human development in Chicago neighborhoods.* Paper presented at the meeting of the Society for Research in Child Development, Indianapolis.

Sampson, R. J., & Laub, J. H. (1994). Urban poverty and the family context of delinquency: A new look at structure and process in a classic study. *Child Development, 65,* 523–540.

Santrock, J. W. (1996). *Child development* (7th ed.). Dubuque, IA: Brown & Benchmark.

Santrock, J. W. (1997). *Life-span development* (6th ed.). Dubuque, IA: Brown & Benchmark.

Santrock, J. W., Sitterle, K. A., & Warshak, R. A. (1988). Parent-child relationships in stepfather families. In P. Bronstein & C. P. Cowan (Eds.), *Fatherhood today.* New York: Wiley.

Santrock, J. W., & Warshak, R. A. (1986). Development, relationships, and legal/clinical considerations in father-custody families. In M. E. Lamb (Ed.), *The father's role: Applied perspectives.* New York: Wiley.

Saraswathi, T., & Dutta, R. (1988). *Invisible boundaries: Grooming for adult roles.* New Delhi, India: Northern Book Center.

Sarrel, P., & Masters, W. (1982). Sexual molestation of men by women. *Archives of Human Sexuality, 11,* 117–131.

Savin-Williams, R. C. (1995). An exploratory study of pubertal maturation timing and self-esteem among gay and bisexual male youths. *Developmental Psychology, 31,* 56–64.

Savin-Williams, R. C., & Demo, D. H. (1983). Conceiving or misconceiving the self: Issues in adolescent self-esteem. *Journal of Early Adolescence, 3,* 121–140.

Savin-Williams, R. C., & Rodriguez, R. G. (1993). A developmental, clinical perspective on lesbian, gay male, and bisexual youths. In T. P. Gullotta, G. R. Adams, & R. Montemayor (Eds.), *Adolescent sexuality.* Newbury Park, CA: Sage.

Scales, P. (1987). How we can prevent teen pregnancy (and why it's not the real problem). *Journal of Sex Education and Therapy, 13,* 12–15.

Scales, P. (1990). Developing capable young people: An alternative strategy for prevention programs. *Journal of Early Adolescence, 10,* 420–438.

Scardamalia, M., Bereiter, C., & Goelman, H. (1982). The role of production factors in writing ability. In M. Nystrand (Ed.), *What writers know: The language, process, and structure of written discourse.* New York: Academic Press.

Scardamalia, M., Bereiter, C., McLean, R. S., Swallow, J., & Woodruff, E. (1989). Computer-supported intentional learning environments. *Journal of Educational Computing Research, 5,* 51–68.

Scardamalia, M., Bereiter, C., & Steinbach, R. (1984). Teachability of reflective processes in written composition. *Cognitive Science, 8,* 173–190.

Scarr, S. (1984, May). [Interview.] *Psychology Today,* pp. 59–63.

Scarr, S. (1989, April). *Transracial adoption.* Discussion at the biennial meeting of the Society for Research in Child Development, Kansas City.

Scarr, S. (1992). Developmental theories for the 1990s: Development and individual differences. *Child Development, 63,* 1–19.

Scarr, S., & Weinberg, R. A. (1976). IQ test performance of black children adopted by white families. *American Psychologist, 31,* 726–739.

Scarr, S., & Weinberg, R. A. (1980). Calling all camps! The war is over. *American Sociological Review, 45,* 859–865.

Scarr, S., & Weinberg, R. A. (1983). The Minnesota adoption studies: Genetic differences and malleability. *Child Development, 54,* 253–259.

Schaie, K. W. (1994). Developmental designs revisited. In S. H. Cohen & H. W. Reese (Eds.), *Life-span developmental psychology: Methodological contributions.* Hillsdale, NJ: Erlbaum.

Scheer, S. D. (1996, March). *Adolescent to adult transitions: Social status and cognitive factors.* Paper presented at the meeting of the Society for Research on Adolescence, Boston.

Scheer, S. D., & Unger, D. G. (1994, February). *Adolescents becoming adults: Attributes for adulthood.* Paper presented at the meeting of the Society for Research on Adolescence, San Diego.

Schiff, J. L., & Truglio, R. T. (1995, March). *In search of the ideal family: The use of television family portrayals during early adolescence.* Paper presented at the meeting of the Society for Research in Child Development, Indianapolis.

Schoenfeld, A. H. (1985). *Mathematical problem solving.* Orlando, FL: Academic Press.

Schorr, L. B. (1989, April). *Within our reach: Breaking the cycle of disadvantage.* Paper presented at the biennial meeting of the Society for Research in Child Development, Kansas City.

Schunk, D. H. (1983). Developing children's self-efficacy and skills: The roles of social comparative information and goal setting. *Contemporary Educational Psychology, 8,* 76–86.

Scott-Jones, D. (1993). Families as educators in a pluralistic society. In N. F. Chavkin (Ed.), *Families and schools in a pluralistic society.* Albany: State University of New York Press.

Scott-Jones, D. (1995, March). *Incorporating ethnicity and socioeconomic status in research with children.* Paper presented at the meeting of the Society for Research in Child Development, Indianapolis.

Scott-Jones, D. (1997). Editorial. *Journal of Research on Adolescence, 7,* 1–2.

Scott-Jones, D., & Clark, M. L. (1986, March). The school experiences of black girls: The interaction of gender, race, and socioeconomic status. *Phi Delta Kappan,* pp. 520–526.

Scott-Jones, D., & White, A. B. (1990). Correlates of sexual activity in early adolescence. *Journal of Early Adolescence, 10,* 221–238.

Scribner, S. (1977). Modes of thinking and ways of speaking: Culture and logic reconsidered. In P. N. Johnson-Laird & P. C. Wason (Eds.), *Thinking: Readings in cognitive science.* New York: Cambridge University Press.

Sears, D. O., Peplau, L. A., Freedman, J. L., & Taylor, S. E. (1994). *Social psychology* (8th ed.). Englewood Cliffs, NJ: Prentice Hall.

Seiffge-Krenke, I. (1995). *Stress, coping, and relationships in adolescence.* Hillsdale, NJ: Erlbaum.

Seligman, M. E. P. (1989). Why is there so much depression today? In the G. Stanley Hall Lecture Series. Washington, DC: American Psychological Association.

Selman, R., & Byrne, D. (1974). A structural developmental analysis of levels of role-taking in middle childhood. *Child Development, 45,* 803–806.

Selman, R. (1976). Social-cognitive understanding. In T. Lickona (Ed.), *Moral development and behavior.* New York: Holt, Rinehart & Winston.

Selman, R. (1980). *The growth of interpersonal understanding.* New York: Academic Press.

Selye, H. (1974). *Stress without distress.* Philadelphia: W. B. Saunders.

Selye, H. (1983). The stress concept: Past, present, and future. In C. L. Cooper (Ed.), *Stress research.* New York: Wiley.

Semaj, L. T. (1985). Afrikanity, cognition, and extended self-identity. In M. B. Spencer, G. K. Brookins, & W. R. Allen (Eds.), *Beginnings: The social and affective development of Black children.* Hillsdale, NJ: Erlbaum.

Serow, R. C., Ciechalski, J., & Daye, C. (1990). Students as volunteers: Personal competence, social diversity, and participation in community service. *Urban Education, 25,* 157–168.

Shade, B. J., Kelly, C., & Oberg, M. (1997). *Creating culturally-responsive schools.* Washington, DC: American Psychological Association.

Shagle, S. C., & Barber, B. K. (1994, February). *Effects of parenting variables, self-derogation, and depression on adolescent suicide ideation.* Paper presented at the meeting of the Society for Research on Adolescence, San Diego.

Sharma, A. R., McGue, M. K., & Benson, P. L. (1996, March). *The emotional and behavioral adjustment of United States adopted adolescents.* Paper presented at the meeting of the Society for Research on Adolescence, Boston.

Sheeber, L., Hops, H., Andrews, J. A., & Davis, B. (1997, April). *Family support and conflict: Prospective relation to adolescent depression.* Paper presented at the meeting of the Society for Research in Child Development, Washington, DC.

Sherif, M., & Sherif, C. W. (1964). *Reference groups: Exploration into conformity and deviation of adolescents.* New York: Harper.

Sherif, M., Harvey, O. J., White, B. J., Hood, W. R., & Sherif, C. W. (1961). *Intergroup conflict and cooperation: The Robber's Cave experiment.* Norman: University of Oklahoma, Institute of Group Relations.

Sherman, B. L., & Dominick, J. R. (1986). Violence and sex in music videos: TV and rock 'n' roll. *Journal of Communication, 36,* 79–93.

Sherwood, A., Light, K. C., & Blumenthal, J. A. (1989). Effects of aerobic exercise training on hemodynamic responses during psychosocial stress in normotensive and borderline hypertensive Type-A men: A preliminary report. *Psychosomatic Medicine, 51,* 123–136.

Shields, S. A. (1991). Gender in the psychology of emotion: A selective research review. In K. T. Strongman (Ed.), *International review of studies on emotion* (Vol. I). New York: Wiley.

Shneidman, E. S. (1971). Suicide among the gifted. *Suicide and life-threatening behavior, 1,* 23–45.

Short, R. J., & Talley, R. C. (1997). Rethinking psychology and the schools. *American Psychologist, 52,* 234–240.

Shweder, R., Mahapatra, M., & Miller, J. (1987). Culture and moral development. In J. Kagan & S. Lamb (Eds.), *The emergence of morality in young children.* Chicago: University of Chicago Press.

Shweder, R. A., Goodnow, J., Hatano, G., LeVine, R. A., Markus, H., & Miller, P. (1997). The cultural psychology of development. In R. M. Lerner (Ed.), *Handbook of Psychology* (5th Ed., Vol. 1).

Siegel, L. S., & Wiener, J. (1993, Spring). Canadian special education policies: Children with learning disabilities in a bilingual and multicultural society. *Social Policy Report, Society for Research in Child Development, 7,* 1–16.

Siegler, R. (1995, March). *Nothing is; everything becomes.* Paper presented at the meeting of the Society for Research in Child Development, Indianapolis.

Siegler, R. (1996). Information processing. In J. W. Santrock, *Child development* (7th ed.). Dubuque, IA: Brown & Benchmark.

Sigel, B. (1997, April). *Developmental and social policy issues and the practice of educational mainstreaming and full inclusion.* Paper presented at the meeting of the Society for Research in Child Development, Washington, DC.

Silbereisen, R. K. (1995). How parenting styles and crowd contexts interact in actualizing potentials for development: Commentary. In L. J. Crockett & A. C. Crouter (Eds.), *Pathways through adolescence.* Hillsdale, NJ: Erlbaum.

Silberg, J. L., & Rutter, M. L. (1997, April). *Pubertal status, life stress, and depression in juvenile twins: A genetic investigation.* Paper presented at the meeting of the Society for Research in Child Development, Washington, DC.

Silver, M. E. (1995, March). *Late adolescent-parent relations and the high school to college transition.* Paper presented at the meeting of the Society for Research in Child Development, Indianapolis.

Silver, S. (1988, August). *Behavior problems of children born into early-childbearing families.* Paper presented at the meeting of the American Psychological Association, Atlanta.

Silverberg, S. B., & Steinberg, L. (1990). Psychological well-being of parents with early adolescent children. *Developmental Psychology, 26,* 658–666.

Simmons, R. G., & Blyth, D. A. (1987). *Moving into adolescence.* Hawthorne, NY: Aldine.

Simons, J. M., Finlay, B., & Yang, A. (1991). *The adolescent and young adult fact book.* Washington, DC: Children's Defense Fund.

Simpson, J. A., Campbell, B., & Berscheid, E. (1986). The association between love and marriage: Kephart (1967) twice revisited. *Personality and Social Psychology Bulletin, 12,* 363–372.

Simpson, R. L. (1962). Parental influence, anticipatory socialization, and social mobility. *American Sociological Review, 27,* 517–522.

Skinner, E. A., Wellborn, J. G., & Connell, J. P. (1990). What it takes to do well in school and whether I've got it: A process model of perceived control and children's engagement and achievement in school. *Journal of Educational Psychology, 82,* 22–32.

Skoe, E. E., & Gooden, A. (1993). Ethic of care and real-life moral dilemma content in male and female early adolescents. *Journal of Early Adolescence, 13,* 154–167.

Skoe, E. E., & Marcia, J. E. (1988). *Ego identity and care-based moral reasoning in college women.* Unpublished manuscript, Acadia University.

Slavin, R. (1989). Cooperative learning and student achievement. In R. Slavin (Ed.), *School and classroom organization.* Hillsdale, NJ: Erlbaum.

Small, S. A. (1990). *Preventive programs that support families with adolescents.* Washington, DC: Carnegie Council on Adolescent Development.

Smetana, J. (1988). Concepts of self and social convention: Adolescents' and parents' reasoning about hypothetical and actual family conflicts. In M. Gunnar (Ed.), *21st Minnesota symposium on child psychology.* Hillsdale, NJ: Erlbaum.

Smetana, J. (1993, March). *Parenting styles during adolescence: Global or domain-specific?* Paper presented at the biennial meeting of the Society for Research in Child Development, New Orleans.

Smetana, J. (1997, April). *Parenting reconceptualized: A social domain analysis.* Paper presented at the meeting of the Society for Research in Child Development, Washington, DC.

Smith, E., & Udry, J. (1985). Coital and noncoital sexual behaviors of White and Black adolescents. *American Journal of Public Health, 75,* 1200–1203.

Smith, E. P. (1994, February). *The salience of ethnic identity and its role in the self-construct of African American youth.* Paper presented at the meeting of the Society for Research on Adolescence, San Diego.

Smith, J., & Baltes, P. B. (1990). Wisdom-related knowledge: Age/cohort differences in response to life-planning problems. *Developmental Psychology, 26,* 494–505.

Smith, R. C., & Crockett, L. J. (1997, April). *Positive adolescent peer relations: A potential buffer against family adversity.* Paper presented at the meeting of the Society for Research in Child Development, Washington, DC.

Snarey, J. (1987, June). A question of morality. *Psychology Today,* pp. 6–8.

Snider, B. A., & Miller, J. P. (1993). The land-grant university system and 4-H: A mutually beneficial relationship of scholars and practitioners in youth development. In R. M. Lerner (Ed.), *Early adolescence.* Hillsdale, NJ: Erlbaum.

Snowden, L. R., & Cheung, F. K. (1990). Use of inpatient mental health services by members of ethnic minority groups. *American Psychologist, 45,* 347–355.

Snyder, C. R. (1988, August). *Reality negotiation: From excuses to hope.* Paper presented at the meeting of the American Psychological Association, Atlanta.

Sommer, B. B. (1978). *Puberty and adolescence.* New York: Oxford University Press.

Sonenstein, F. L., & Pittman, K. J. (1984, January/February). The availability of sex education in large city school districts. *Family Planning Perspectives,* p. 19.

Sonenstein, F. L., Pleck, J. H., & Ku, L. C. (1989). Sexual activity, condom use, and AIDS awareness among adolescent males. *Family Planning Perspectives, 21* (4), 152–158.

Sorensen, R. C. (1973). *Adolescent sexuality in contemporary America.* New York: World.

Spade, J. Z., & Reese, C. A. (1991). We've come a long way, maybe: College students' plans for work and family. *Sex Roles, 24,* 309–321.

Spear-Swerling, L., & Sternberg, R. J. (1994). The road not taken: An integrative theoretical model of reading disability. *Journal of Learning Disabilities, 27,* 91–103.

Spearman, C. E. (1927). *The abilities of man.* New York: Macmillan.

Spence, J. T., & Helmreich, R. (1972). The Attitudes Toward Women Scale: An objective instrument to measure the rights and roles of women in contemporary society. *JSAS Catalog of Selected Documents in Psychology, 2,* 66.

Spence, J. T., & Helmreich, R. (1978). *Masculinity and femininity: Their psychological dimensions.* Austin: University of Texas Press.

Spencer, M. B., & Dornbusch, S. M. (1990). Challenges in studying minority youth. In S. S. Feldman & G. R. Elliott (Eds.), *At the threshold: The developing adolescent.* Cambridge, MA: Harvard University Press.

Spilka, B. (1991). Cults and adolescence. In R. M. Lerner, A. C. Petersen, & J. Brooks-Gunn (Eds.), *Encyclopedia of adolescence* (Vol. 1). New York: Garland.

Sputa, C. L., & Paulson, S. E. (1995, March). *A longitudinal study of changes in parenting across adolescence.* Paper presented at the meeting of the Society for Research in Child Development, Indianapolis.

Sroufe, L. A. (1996). *Emotional development.* New York: Cambridge University Press.

Stanton-Salazar, R. D., & Dornbusch, S. M. (in press). Social capital and the social reproduction of inequality: Information networks among Mexican-origin high school students. *Sociology of Education.*

Stattin, H., & Magnusson, D. (1990). *Pubertal maturation in female development: Paths through life* (Vol. 2). Hillsdale, NJ: Erlbaum.

Staub, E. (1996). Cultural-societal roots of violence. *American Psychologist, 51,* 117–132.

Staub, E. (in press). Altruism and aggression in children and youth: Origins and cures. In R. Feldman (Ed.), *The psychology of adversity.* Amherst: University of Massachusetts Press.

Staub, E., & Rosenthal, L. (1994). Mob violence: Social-cultural influences, group processes and participants. In L. Eron, J. H. Gentry, & P. Schlegel (Eds.), *Reason to hope.* Washington, DC: American Psychological Association.

Stedman, L., & Smith, M. (1983). Recent reform proposals for American education. *Contemporary Education Review, 2,* 85–104.

Steinberg, L., & Levine, A. (1990). *You and your adolescent.* New York: Harper Perennial.

Steinberg, L., Fegley, S., & Dornbusch, S. M. (1993). Negative impact of part-time work on adolescent adjustment: Evidence from a longitudinal study. *Developmental Psychology, 29,* 171–180.

Steinberg, L. D. (1981). Transformations in family relations at puberty. *Developmental Psychology, 17,* 833–840.

Steinberg, L. D. (1986). Latchkey children and susceptibility to peer pressure: An ecological analysis. *Developmental Psychology, 22,* 433–439.

Steinberg, L. D. (1988). Reciprocal relation between parent-child distance and pubertal maturation. *Developmental Psychology, 24,* 122–128.

Stengel, R. (1985, December 9). The missing-father myth. *Time,* p. 90.

Sternberg, R. J. (1977). *Intelligence, information processing, and analogical reasoning: The componential analysis of human abilities.* Hillsdale, NJ: Erlbaum.

Sternberg, R. J. (1985, December). Teaching critical thinking, Part 2: Possible solutions. *Phi Delta Kappan,* 277–280.

Sternberg, R. J. (1986). *Intelligence applied.* San Diego: Harcourt Brace Jovanovich.

Sternberg, R. J. (1997, April). *Practial intelligence differs from academic intelligence.* Paper presented at the meeting of the Society for Research in Child Development, Washington, DC.

Sternberg, R. J., Conway, B. E., Ketron, J. L., & Berstein, M. (1981). People's conceptions of intelligence. *Journal of Personality and Social Psychology, 41,* 37–55.

Sternberg, R. J., & Lubat, T. I. (1995). *Defying the crowd*. New York: Free Press.

Sternberg, R. J., & Nigro, C. (1980). Developmental patterns in the solution of verbal analogies. *Child Development, 51,* 27–38.

Sternberg, R. J., & Rifkin, B. (1979). The development of analogical reasoning processes. *Journal of Experimental Child Psychology, 27,* 195–232.

Steur, F. B., Applefield, J. M., & Smith, R. (1971). Televised aggression and the interpersonal aggression of preschool children. *Journal of Experimental Child Psychology, 11,* 442–447.

Stevens, J. H. (1984). Black grandmothers' and black adolescent mothers' knowledge about parenting. *Developmental Psychology, 20,* 1017–1025.

Stevens, R. J., & Slavin, R. E. (1995). The cooperative elementary school: Effects on students' achievement, attitudes, and social relations. *American Educational Research Journal, 32,* 321–351.

Stevenson, H. G. (1995, March). *Missing data: On the forgotten substance of race, ethnicity, and socioeconomic classifications.* Paper presented at the meeting of the Society for Research in Child Development, Indianapolis.

Stevenson, H. W. (1992, December). Learning from Asian schools. *Scientific American,* pp. 6, 70–76.

Stevenson, H. W. (1995). Mathematics achievement of American students: First in the world by the year 2000? In C. A. Nelson (Ed.), *Basic and applied perspectives on learning, cognition, and development.* Minneapolis: University of Minnesota Press.

Stevenson, H. W., Lee, S., Chen, C., Stigler, J. W., Hsu, C., & Kitamura, S. (1990). Contexts of achievement. Monograph of the *Society for Research in Child Development, 55* (Serial No. 221).

Stigler, J. W., Nusbaum, H. C., & Chalip, O. (1988). Developmental changes in speed of processing: Central limiting mechanism or skill transfer. *Child Development, 59,* 1144–1153.

Stipek, D. J., & Hoffman, J. M. (1980). Children's achievement-related expectancies as a function of academic performance histories and sex. *Journal of Educational Psychology, 72,* 861–865.

Strachen, A., & Jones, D. (1982). Changes in identification during adolescence: A personal construct theory approach. *Journal of Personality Assessment, 46,* 139–148.

Strahan, D. B. (1983). The emergence of formal operations in adolescence. *Transcendence, 11,* 7–14.

Strasburger, V. C. (1995). *Adolescents and the media.* Newbury Park, CA: Sage.

Streissguth, A. P., Martin, D. C., Barr, H. M., Sandman, B. M., Kirshner, G. L., & Darby, B. L. (1984). Intrauterine alcohol and nicotine exposure: Attention and reaction time in 4-year-old children. *Developmental Psychology, 20,* 533–541.

Streitmatter, J. (1993). Gender differences in identity development: An examination of longitudinal data. *Adolescence, 28,* 55–66.

Strickland, B. R. (1995). Research on sexual orientation and human development: A commentary. *Developmental Psychology, 31,* 137–140.

Stunkard, A. J. (1987). The regulation of body weight and the treatment of obesity. In H. Weiner & A. Baum (Eds.), *Eating regulation and discontrol.* Hillsdale, NJ: Erlbaum.

Sue, D. W., & Sue, S. (1972). Counseling Chinese-Americans. *Personnel and Guidance Journal, 50,* 637–644.

Sue, S. (1990, August). *Ethnicity and culture in psychological research and practice.* Paper presented at the meeting of the American Psychological Association, Boston.

Sullivan, H. S. (1953). *The interpersonal theory of psychiatry.* New York: W. W. Norton.

Sullivan, K., & Sullivan, A. (1980). Adolescent-parent separation. *Developmental Psychology, 16,* 93–99.

Sullivan, L. (1991, May 25). US secretary urges TV to restrict "irresponsible sex and reckless violence." *Boston Globe,* p. A1.

Suomi, S. J., Harlow, H. F., & Domek, C. J. (1970). Effect of repetitive infant-infant separations of young monkeys. *Journal of Abnormal Psychology, 76,* 161–172.

Super, D. E. (1967). *The psychology of careers.* New York: Harper & Row.

Super, D. E. (1976). *Career education and the meanings of work.* Washington, DC: U.S. Office of Education.

Susman, A. R., & Adam, E. K. (1995, March). *Poverty and educational outcomes: Context, diversity, and change.* Paper presented at the meeting of the Society for Research in Child Development, Indianapolis.

Susman, E. (1995). Unpublished review of *Adolescence* (6th ed.), by J. W. Santrock. Dubuque, IA: Brown & Benchmark.

Susman, E. J., Inoff-Germain, G. E., Nottelmann, E. D., Cutler, G. B., Loriaux, D. L., & Chrousos, G. P. (1987). Hormones, emotional dispositions, and aggressive attributes in early adolescents. *Child Development, 58,* 1114–1134.

Susman, E. J., Murowchick, E., & Worrall, B. K., & Murray, D. A. (1995, March). *Emotionality, adrenal hormones, and context interactions during puberty and pregnancy.* Paper presented at the meeting of the Society for Research in Child Development, Indianapolis.

Sutton-Smith, B. (1982). Birth order and sibling status effects. In M. E. Lamb & B. Sutton-Smith (Eds.), *Sibling relationships: Their nature and significance across the life span.* Hillsdale, NJ: Erlbaum.

Swanson, D. P. (1995, March). *The effects of racial identity and socioeconomic status on academic outcomes for adolescents.* Paper presented at the meeting of the Society for Research in Child Development, Indianapolis.

Swarr, A. E., & Richards, M. H. (1996). Longitudinal effects of adolescent girls' pubertal development, perceptions of pubertal timing, and parental relations. *Developmental Psychology, 32,* 636–646.

Swim, J. K., Aikin, K. J., Hall, W. S., & Hunter, B. A. (1995). Sexism and racism: Old-fashioned and modern prejudices. *Journal of Personality and Social Psychology, 67,* 199–214.

Switzer, G. E., & Dew, M. A. (1995, March). *Political socialization as a function of volunteerism.* Paper presented at the meeting of the Society for Research in Child Development, Indianapolis.

Swope, G. W. (1980). Kids and cults: Who joins and why? *Media and Methods, 16,* 18–21.

Szasz, T. (1977). *Psychiatric slavery: When confinement and coercion masquerade as cure.* New York: Free Press.

Takahashi, K., & Majima, N. (1992, March). *The functions of pre-established social relationships during a life transition among college freshmen.* Paper presented at the meeting of the Society for Research on Adolescence, Washington, DC.

Takahashi, K., & Majima, N. (1994). Transition from home to college dormitory: The role of preestablished affective relationships in adjustment to a new life. *Journal of Research on Adolescence, 4,* 367–384.

Takanishi, R. (1993). The opportunities of adolescence: Research, interventions, and policy. *American Psychologist, 48,* 85–87.

Takanishi, R., & DeLeon, P. H. (1994). A Head Start for the 21st century. *American Psychologist, 49,* 120–122.

Tanner, J. M. (1991). Growth spurt, adolescent. I. In R. M. Lerner, A. C. Petersen, & J. Brooks-Gunn (Eds.), *Encyclopedia of adolescence*. New York: Garland.

Tapper, J. (1996, March). *Values, lifestyles, and crowd identification in adolescence.* Paper presented at the meeting of the Society for Research on Adolescence, Boston.

Tavris, C. (1992). *The mismeasure of women.* New York: Simon & Schuster.

Tavris, C., & Wade, C. (1984). *The longest war: Sex differences in perspective* (2nd ed.). San Diego: Harcourt Brace Jovanovich.

Taylor, D. (1985). *Women: A world report.* New York: Oxford University Press.

Taylor, L. C. (1994, February). *Winning combinations: The effects of different parenting style combinations on adolescent adjustment.* Paper presented at the biennial meeting of the Society for Research in Child Development, San Diego.

Taylor, R. D. (1994, February). *Kinship support and family management in African-American families.* Paper presented at the meeting of the Society for Research on Adolescence, San Diego.

Taylor, R. D. (1996). Adolescents' perceptions of kinship support and family management practices: Association with adolescent adjustment in African American families. *Developmental Psychology, 32,* 687–695.

Taylor, R. D. (1997). The effects of economic and social stressors on parenting and adolescent adjustment in African-American families. In R. D. Taylor & M. C. Wang (Eds.), *Social and emotional adjustment and family relations in ethnic minority families.* Mahwah, NJ: Erlbaum.

Terman, L. (1925). *Genetic studies of genius: Vol. 1. Mental and physical traits of a thousand gifted children.* Stanford, CA: Stanford.

Terman, L. H., & Oden, M. H. (1959). *Genetic studies of genius: Vol. 5. The gifted group at mid-life.* Stanford, CA: Stanford University Press.

Tharp, R. G. (1989). Psychocultural variables and constants: Effects on teaching and learning in schools. *American Psychologist, 44,* 349–359.

The Carnegie Foundation. (1994). *Starting points: Meeting the needs of our youngest children.* New York: Author.

The Research Bulletin. (1991, Spring). *Disadvantaged urban eighth graders.* Washington, DC: Hispanic Policy Development Project.

Thomas, C. W., Coffman, J. K., & Kipp, K. L. (1993, March). *Are only children different from children with siblings? A longitudinal study of behavioral and social functioning.* Paper presented at the biennial meeting of the Society for Research in Child Development, New Orleans.

Thomas, G. (Ed.). (1988). *World education encyclopedia.* New York: Facts on File.

Thompson, L., & Walker, A. J. (1989). Gender in families: Women and men in marriage, work, and parenthood. *Journal of Marriage and the Family, 51,* 845–871.

Thornburg, H. D. (1981). Sources of sex education among early adolescents. *Journal of Early Adolescence, 1,* 171–184.

Thorton, A., & Camburn, D. (1989). Religious participation and sexual behavior and attitudes. *Journal of Marriage and the Family, 49,* 117–128.

Thurstone, L. L. (1938). *Primary mental abilities.* Chicago: University of Chicago Press.

Tirozzi, G. N., & Uro, G. (1997). Education reform in the United States. *American Psychologist, 52,* 241–249.

Toepfer, C. F. (1979). Brain growth periodization: A new dogma for education. *Middle School Journal, 10,* 20.

Tolan, P., Miller, L., & Thomas, P. (1988). Perception and experience of types of social stress and self-image among adolescents. *Journal of Youth and Adolescence, 17,* 147–163.

Tolan, P. H., Guerra, N. G., & Kendall, P. C. (1995). A developmental-ecological perspective on antisocial behavior in children and adolescents: Toward a unified risk and intervention framework. *Journal of Consulting and Clinical Psychology, 63,* 579–584.

Tomlinson-Keasey, C. (1972). Formal operations in females from 11 to 54 years of age. *Developmental Psychology, 6,* 364.

Tomlinson-Keasey, C. (1990). The working lives of Terman's gifted women. In H. W. Grossman & N. L. Chester (Eds.), *The experience and meaning of work in women's lives.* Hillsdale, NJ: Erlbaum.

Tomlinson-Keasey, C. (1993, August). *Tracing the lives of gifted women.* Paper presented at the meeting of the American Psychological Association, Toronto.

Tomlinson-Keasey, C., & Little, T. D. (1990). Predicting educational attainment, occupational achievement, intellectual skill, and personal adjustment among gifted men and women. *Journal of Educational Psychology, 82,* 442–455.

Tomlinson-Keasey, C., Warren, L. W., & Elliott, J. E. (1986). Suicide among gifted women: A prospective study. *Journal of Abnormal Psychology, 95,* 123–130.

Torney-Purta, J. (1993, August). *Cross-cultural examination of stages of faith development.* Paper presented at the meeting of the American Psychological Association, Toronto.

Torquati, J. C., & Vazsonyi, A. T. (1994, February). *Attachment models and emotionality: Predicting differential coping strategies in late adolescence.* Paper presented at the biennial meeting of the Society for Research on Adolescence, San Diego.

Triandis, H. C. (1990). Theoretical concepts that are applicable to the analysis of ethnocentrism. In R. W. Brislin (Ed.), *Applied cross-cultural psychology.* Newbury Park, CA: Sage.

Triandis, H. C. (1994). *Culture and social behavior.* New York: McGraw-Hill.

Trimble, J. E. (1989, August). *The enculturation of contemporary psychology.* Paper presented at the meeting of the American Psychological Association, New Orleans.

Truglio, R. T. (1990, April). *What is television teaching adolescents about sexuality?* Paper presented at the meeting of the Society for Research in Adolescence, Atlanta.

Tubman, J. G., & Windle, M. (1995). Continuity of difficult temperament in adolescence: Relations with depression, life events, family support, and substance abuse across a one-year period. *Journal of Youth and Adolescence, 24,* 133–152.

Tucker, L. A. (1987). Television, teenagers, and health. *Journal of Youth and Adolescence, 16,* 415–425.

Tuckman, B. W., & Hinkle, J. S. (1988). An experimental study of the physical and psychological effects of aerobic exercise on schoolchildren. In B. G. Melamed & others (Eds.), *Child health psychology.* Hillsdale, NJ: Erlbaum.

Tudge, J., & Winterhoff, P. (1993, March). *The cognitive consequences of collaboration: Why ask how?* Paper presented at the biennial meeting of the Society for Research in Child Development, New Orleans.

Turiel, E. (1978). Social regulations and domains of social concepts. In W. Damon (Ed.), *New directions for child development: Social cognition* (Vol. 1). San Francisco: Jossey-Bass.

Turiel, E. (1997). The development of morality. In N. Eisenberg. (Ed.), *Handbook of child psychology* (5th Ed., Vol. 3). New York: Wiley.

U.S. Bureau of the Census. (1994). Poverty in the United States, 1991. *Current Population Reports*, Series P-60, No. 181. Washington, DC: Government Printing Office.

U.S. Department of Education. (1993). *Violence in schools*. Washington, DC: Author.

U.S. Department of Health and Human Services. (1991). *Healthy people 2000*. Washington, DC: U.S. Government Printing Office.

Udry, J. R. (1990). Hormonal and social determinants of adolescent sexual initiation. In J. Brooks-Gunn & E. O. Reiter (1990). The role of pubertal processes. In S. S. Feldman & G. R. Elliott (Eds.), *At the threshold: The developing adolescent*. Cambridge, MA: Harvard University Press.

Underwood, M. K., Kupersmidt, J. B., & Coie, J. D. (1996). Childhood peer sociometric status and aggression as predictors of adolescent childbearing. *Journal of Research on Adolescence, 6,* 201–223.

Unger, R., & Crawford, M. (1992). *Women and gender* (2nd ed.). New York: McGraw-Hill.

Unger, R., & Crawford, M. (1996). *Women and gender: A feminist psychology* (2nd ed.). New York: McGraw-Hill.

Urberg, K. A., Degirmencioglu, S. M., Tolson, J. M., & Halliday-Scher, K. (1995). The structure of adolescent peer networks. *Developmental Psychology, 31,* 540–547.

Urberg, K. A., & Wolowicz, L. S. (1996, March). *Antecedents and consequents of changes in parental monitoring.* Paper presented at the meeting of the Society for Research on Adolescence, Boston.

Valois, R. F., McKeown, R. E., Garrison, C. Z., & Vincent, M. L. (1995). Correlates of aggressive and violent behaviors among high school adolescents. *Journal of Adolescent Health, 16,* 26–34.

van der Veer, R. (1996). Structure and development. In A. Tryphon & J. Voneche (Eds.), *Piaget-Vygotsky*. Mahwah, NJ: Erlbaum.

van Dijk, T. A. (1987). *Communicating racism*. Newbury Park, CA: Sage.

Vandell, D. L., Minnett, A., & Santrock, J. W. (1987). Age differences in sibling relationships during middle childhood. *Applied Developmental Psychology, 8,* 247–257.

Vernberg, E. M. (1990). Psychological adjustment and experience with peers during early adolescence: Reciprocal, incidental, or unidirectional relationships? *Journal of Abnormal Child Psychology, 18,* 187–198.

Vernberg, E. M., Ewell, K. K., Beery, S. H., & Abwender, D. A. (1994). Sophistication of adolescents' interpersonal negotiation strategies and friendship formation after relocation: A naturally occurring experiment. *Journal of Research on Adolescence, 4,* 5–19.

Vicary, J. R., Klingaman, L. R., & Harkness, W. L. (1995). Risk factors associated with date rape and sexual assault of adolescent girls. *Journal of Adolescence, 18,* 289–306.

Villani, S. L. (1997). *Motherhood at the crossroads*. New York: Plenum.

Vinton, D. (1992). Helping students find time for the job search. *Journal of Career Planning and Employment, 27,* 71–74.

Vondracek, F. W. (1991). Vocational development and choice in adolescence. In R. M. Lerner, A. C. Petersen, & J. Brooks-Gunn (Eds.), *Encyclopedia of adolescence* (Vol. 2). New York: Garland.

Voyer, D., Voyer, S., & Bryden, M. P. (1995). Magnitude of sex differences in spatial abilities: A meta-analysis and consideration of critical variables. *Psychological Bulletin, 117,* 250–270.

Waddington, C. H. (1957). *The strategy of the genes*. London: Allen & Son.

Wagennar, A. C. (1983). *Alcohol, young drivers, and traffic accidents*. Lexington, MA: D. C. Heath.

Wagennar, A. C., & Perry, C. L. (1994). Community strategies for the reduction of youth drinking: Theory and application. *Journal of Research on Adolescence, 4,* 319–346.

Wagner, B. M., Cohen, P., & Brook, J. S. (1991, March). *Parent-adolescent relationships as moderators of the effects of stressful live events during adolescence.* Paper presented at the meeting of the Society for Research in Adolescence, Atlanta.

Wakschlag, L. S., Chase-Lansdale, P. L., & Brooks-Gunn, J. (1996, March). *Not just "ghosts in the nursery": Contemporaneous intergenerational relationships and parenting in young African American families.* Paper presented at the meeting of the Society for Research on Adolescent Development, Boston.

Walker, L. J. (1984). Sex differences in the development of moral reasoning. A critical review. *Child Development, 51,* 131–139.

Walker, L. J. (1991). Sex differences in moral development. In W. M. Kurtines & J. Gewirtz (Eds.), *Moral behavior and development* (Vol. 2). Hillsdale, NJ: Erlbaum.

Walker, L. J. (1993, March). *Is the family a sphere of moral growth for children?* Paper presented at the biennial meeting of the Society for Research in Child Development, New Orleans.

Walker, L. J. (1996). Unpublished review of *Child Development* (8th ed.) by J. W. Santrock. Dubuque, IA: Brown & Benchmark.

Walker, L. J., deVries, B., & Bichard, S. L. (1984). The hierarchical nature of stages of moral development. *Developmental Psychology, 20,* 960–966.

Walker, L. J., de Vries, B., & Trevethan, S. D. (1987). Moral stages and moral orientation in real-life and hypothetical dilemmas. *Child Development, 58,* 842–858.

Walker, L. J., & Hennig, K. H. (in press). Moral functioning in the context of cognition and personality. In S. Hala (Ed.), *The development of social cognition*. London: University College of London Press.

Walker, L. J., & Taylor, J. H. (1991). Family interaction and the development of moral reasoning. *Child Development, 62,* 264–283.

Wallace-Broscious, A., Serafica, F. C., & Osipow, S. H. (1994). Adolescent career development: Relationships to self-concept and identity status. *Journal of Research on Adolescence, 4,* 127–150.

Wallerstein, J. S., Corbin, S. B., & Lewis, J. M. (1988). Children of divorce: A 10-year study. In E. M. Hetherington & J. D. Arasteh (Eds.), *Impact of divorce, single parenting, and stepparenting on children*. Hillsdale, NJ: Erlbaum.

Wallis, C. (1985, December 9). Children having children. *Time*, pp. 78–88.

Walster, E., Aronson, E., Abrahams, D., & Rottman, L. (1966). Importance of physical attractiveness in dating behavior. *Journal of Personality and Social Psychology, 4,* 508–516.

Ward, L. M. (1994, February). *The nature and prevalence of sexual messages in the television programs adolescents view most*. Paper presented at the meeting of the Society for Research on Adolescence, San Diego.

Ward, S. L. (1991). Moral development in adolescence. In R. M. Lerner, A. C. Petersen, & J. Brooks-Gunn (Eds.), *Encyclopedia of adolescence* (Vol. 2). New York: Garland.

Wartella, E., Heintz, K., Aidman, A., & Mazzarella, S. (1990). Television and beyond: Children's video media in one community. *Communications Research, 17*, 45–64.

Wass, H., Miller, M. D., & Redditt, C. A. (1991). Adolescents and destructive themes in rock music: A follow-up. *Omega, 23*, 199–206.

Waterman, A. S. (1985). Identity in the context of adolescent psychology. In A. S. Waterman (Ed.), *Identity in adolescence: Processes and contents*. San Francisco: Jossey-Bass.

Waterman, A. S. (1989). Curricula interventions for identity change: Substantive and ethical considerations. *Journal of Adolescence, 12*, 389–400.

Waterman, A. S. (1992). Identity as an aspect of optimal psychological functioning. In G. R. Adams, T. P. Gullotta, & R. Montemayor (Eds.), *Adolescent identity formation*. Newbury Park, CA: Sage.

Waters, E., Merrick, S. K., Albersheim, L. J., & Treboux, D. (1995, March). *Attachment security from infancy to early adulthood: A 20-year longitudinal study*. Paper presented at the meeting of the Society for Research in Child Development, Indianapolis.

Waters, E. (1997, April). *The secure base concept in Bowlby's theory and current research*. Paper presented at the meeting of the Society for Research in Child Development, Washington, DC.

Waters, M. C. (1997). Immigrant families at risk. In A. Booth, A. C. Crouter, & N. Landale (Eds.), *Immigration and the family*. Mahwah, NJ: Erlbaum.

Watson, F. I., & Kelly, M. J. (1989). Targeting the at-risk male: A strategy for adolescent pregnancy prevention. *Journal of the National Medical Association, 81*, 453–456.

Way, N. (1997, April). *Father-daughter relationships in urban families*. Paper presented at the meeting of the Society for Research in Child Development, Washington, DC.

Weidner, G., Sexton, G., Matarazzo, J. D., Pereira, C., & Friend, R. (1988). Type-A behavior in children, adolescents, and their parents. *Developmental Psychology, 24*, 118–121.

Weinberg, R. A. (1989). Intelligence and IQ: Landmark issues and great debates. *American Psychologist, 44*, 98–104.

Weiss, R. S. (1973). *Loneliness: The experience of emotional and social isolation*. Cambridge, MA: MIT Press.

Weissberg, R., & Caplan, M. (1989, April). *A follow-up study of a school-based social competence program for young adolescents*. Paper presented at the meeting of the Society for Research in Child Development, Kansas City.

Weissberg, R. P., & Greenberg, M. T. (1997). School and community competence—enhancement and prevention interventions. In I. E. Siegel & K. A. Renninger (Eds.), *Handbook of Child Psychology* (5th Ed., Vol. 4). New York: Wiley.

Wender, P. H., Kety, S. S., Rosenthal, D., Schulsinger, F., Ortmann, J., & Lunde, I. (1986). Psychiatric disorders in the biological and adoptive families of adopted individuals with affective disorders. *Archives of General Psychiatry, 43*, 923–929.

Weng, A., & Montemayor, R. (1997, April). *Conflict between mothers and adolescents*. Paper presented at the meeting of the Society for Research in Child Development, Washington, DC.

Wentzel, K. R., & Asher, S. R. (1995). The academic lives of neglected, rejected, popular, and controversial children. *Child Development, 66*, 754–763.

Wentzel, K. R., & Erdley, C. A. (1993). Strategies for making friends: Relations to social behavior and peer acceptance in early adolescence. *Developmental Psychology, 29*, 819–826.

Werner, E. E. (1989). High risk children in young adulthood: A longitudinal study from birth to 32 years. *American Journal of Orthopsychiatry, 59*, 72–81.

Werner, E. E., & Smith, R. S. (1992). *Overcoming the odds: High risk children from birth to adulthood*. Ithaca, NY: Cornell University Press.

Whitam, F. L., Diamond, M., & Martin, J. (1993). Homosexual orientation in twins: A report on 61 pairs and three triplet sets. *Archives of Sexual Behavior, 22*, 187–206.

White, K. M., Speisman, J. C., Costos, D., & Smith, A. (1987). Relationship maturity: A conceptual and empirical approach. In J. Meacham (Ed.), *Interpersonal relations: Family, peers, friends*. Basel, Switzerland: Karger.

Whiting, B. B. (1989, April). *Culture and interpersonal behavior*. Paper presented at the biennial meeting of the Society for Research in Child Development, Kansas City.

Whiting, B. B., & Edwards, C. P. (1988). *Children of different worlds*. Cambridge, MA: Harvard University Press.

Wilder, D. (1991, March 28). To save the Black family, the young must abstain. *Wall Street Journal*, p. A14.

William T. Grant Foundation Commission on Work, Family, and Citizenship. (1988, February). *The forgotten half: Noncollege-bound youth in America*. New York: William T. Grant Foundation.

Williams, C., & Bybee, J. (1994). What do children feel guilty about? Developmental and gender differences? *Developmental Psychology, 30*, 617–623.

Williams, J. (1987). *Psychology of women: Behavior in a biosocial context* (3rd ed.). New York: W. W. Norton.

Williams, J. E., & Best, D. I. (1989). *Sex and psyche: Self-concept viewed cross-culturally*. Newbury Park, CA: Sage.

Williams, J. E., & Best, D. L. (1982). *Measuring sex stereotypes: A thirty-nation study*. Newbury Park, CA: Sage.

Williams, M. F., & Condry, J. C. (1989, April). *Living color: Minority portrayals and cross-racial interactions on television*. Paper presented at the biennial meeting of the Society for Research in Child Development, Kansas City.

Williams, R. B. (1989). Biological mechanisms mediating the relationship between behavior and coronary-prone behavior. In A. W. Siegman & T. Dembrowski (Eds.), *In search of coronary-prone behavior: Beyond Type-A*. Hillsdale, NJ: Erlbaum.

Williams, T. M., Baron, D., Phillips, S., David, L., & Jackson, D. (1986, August). *The portrayal of sex roles on Canadian and U.S. television*. Paper presented at the conference of the International Association for Mass Media Research, New Delhi, India.

Williams, T. M., & Cox, R. (1995, March). *Informative versus other children's TV programs: Portrayals of ethnic diversity, gender, and aggression.* Paper presented at the meeting of the Society for Research in Child Development, Indianapolis.

Wilson, B. J., & Gottman, J. M. (1995). Marital interaction and parenting. In M. H. Bornstein (Ed.), *Children and parenting* (Vol. 4). Hillsdale, NJ: Erlbaum.

Wilson, J. W. (1987). *The truly disadvantaged: The inner city, the underclass, and public policy.* Chicago: University of Chicago Press.

Wilson, M., Cook, D. Y., & Arrington, E. G. (1997). African-American adolescents and academic achievement: Family and peer influences. In R. D. Taylor & M. C. Wang (Eds.), *Social and emotional adjustment and relations in ethnic minority families.* Mahwah, NJ: Erlbaum.

Wilson, M. N. (1989). Child development in the context of the black extended family. *American Psychologist, 44,* 380–383.

Wilson, W. J. (1997, April). *When work disappears: The new challenges facing families and children in America's inner cities.* Invited address, Society for Research in Child Development, Washington, DC.

Windle, M. (1989). Substance use and abuse among adolescent runaways: A four-year follow-up study. *Journal of Youth and Adolescence, 18,* 331–341.

Winstead, B. A., Derlega, V. J., & Rose, S. (1997). *Gender and close relationships.* Thousand Oaks, CA: Sage.

Wodarski, J. S., & Hoffman, S. D. (1984). Alcohol education for adolescents. *Social Work in Education, 6,* 69–92.

Wolchick, S., & Sandler, I. N. (Eds.) (1997). *Handbook of children's coping.* New York: Plenum.

Wong, C. A. (1997, April). *What does it mean to be an African-American or European-Amercian growing up in a multi-ethnic community?* Paper presented at the meeting of the Society for Research in Child Development, Washington, DC.

Wright, M. R. (1989). Body image satisfaction in adolescent girls and boys. *Journal of Youth and Adolescence, 18,* 71–84.

Wylie, R. (1979). *The self concept. Vol. 2.: Theory and research on selected topics.* Lincoln: University of Nebraska Press.

Wynne, E., & Ryan, K. (1993). *Reclaiming our schools.* New York: Macmillan.

Xiaohe, X., & Whyte, M. K. (1990). Love matches and arranged marriages. *Journal of Marriage and the Family, 52,* 709–722.

Yang, E., Satsky, M. A., Tietz, J. A., Garrison, S., Debus, J., Bell, K. L., & Allen, J. P. (1996, March). *Adolescent-father trust and communication: Reflections of marital relations between parents.* Paper presented at the meeting of the Society for Research on Adolescence, Boston.

Yankelovich, D. (1974). *The new morality: A profile of American youth in the 1970s.* New York: McGraw-Hill.

Yates, M. (1996, March). *Community service and political-moral discussions among Black urban adolescents.* Paper presented at the meeting of the Society for Research on Adolescence, Boston.

Yates, M. (1995, March). *Political socialization as a function of volunteerism.* Paper presented at the meeting of the Society for Research in Child Development, Indianapolis.

Yates, M., & Youniss, J. (1997, April). *Social capital through community service.* Paper presented at the meeting of the Society for Research in Child Development, Washington, DC.

Yin, Y., Buhrmester, D., & Hibbard, D. (1996, March). *Are there developmental changes in the influence of relationships with parents and friends on adjustment during early adolescence?* Paper presented at the meeting of the Society for Research on Adolescence, Boston.

Yoon, K. S., Eccles, J. S., Wigfield, A., & Barber, B. L. (1996, March). *Developmental trajectories of early to middle adolescents' academic achievement and motivation.* Paper presented at the meeting of the Society for Research on Adolescence, Boston.

Young, R. A. (1994). Helping adolescents with career development: The active role of parents. *Career Development Quarterly, 42,* 195–203.

Youniss, J. (1980). *Parents and peers in the social environment: A Sullivan Piaget perspective.* Chicago: University of Chicago Press.

Youniss, J., McLellan, J. A., & Strouse, D. (1994). "We're popular but we're not snobs": Adolescents describe their crowds. In R. Montemayor, G. R. Adams, & T. P. Gullotta (Eds.), *Advances in adolescent development: Vol. 6. Personal relationships during adolescence.* Newbury Park, CA: Sage.

Youniss, J., & Smollar, J. (1985). *Adolescent relations with mothers, fathers, and friends.* Chicago: University of Chicago Press.

Yussen, S. R. (1977). Characteristics of moral dilemmas written by adolescents. *Developmental Psychology, 13,* 162–163.

Zabin, L. S. (1986, May/June). Evaluation of a pregnancy prevention program for urban teenagers. *Family Planning Perspectives,* p. 119.

Zahn-Waxler, C. (1996). Environment, biology, and culture: Implications for adolescent development. *Developmental Psychology, 32,* 571–573.

Zahn-Waxler, C., Schmitz, S., Fulker, D., Robinson, J., & Emde, R. (1996). Behavior problems in 5-year-old monozygotic and dizygotic twins: Genetic and environmental influences, patterns of regulation, and internalization of control. *Development and Pathology, 8,* 103–122.

Zambrana, R. E. (Ed.). (1995). *Understanding Latino families.* Newbury Park, CA: Sage.

Zarit, S. H., & Eggebeen, D. J. (1995). Parent-child relationships in adulthood and old age. In M. H. Bornstein (Ed.), *Children and parenting* (Vol. 1). Hillsdale, NJ: Erlbaum.

Zelnik, M., & Kantner, J. F. (1977). Sexual and contraceptive experiences of young unmarried women in the United States, 1976 and 1971. *Family Planning Perspectives, 9,* 55–71.

Zimmerman, M. A., Copeland, L. A., & Shope, J. T. (1997, April). *A longitudinal study of self-esteem: Implications for adolescent development.* Paper presented at the meeting of the Society for Research in Child Development, Washington, DC.

CREDITS

Photograph

Prologue
Opener: © Tretyakov Gallery, Moscow/ Bridgeman Art Library, London/ Superstock

Section Openers
1: © Lanpher Productions; **2:** © Marc Rominelli/Image Bank, Chicago; **3:** © Tony Freeman/Photo Edit; **4:** © David Burnett/ Contact Press; **5:** © Richard Hutchings/Photo Edit

Chapter 1
Opener: © Superstock; **p. 6 (both):** AP/Wide World Photos; **p. 7:** © Owen Franken/Stock Boston; **p. 10:** © Archives of the History of American Psychology, University of Akron, OH.; **p. 11:** Courtesy of the Institute for Intercultural Studies, Inc. New York; **1.1:** © Archives of the History of American Psychology, University of Akron; **p. 14a:** © Stock Montage; **p. 14b:** © Topham/The Image Works; **p. 14c:** © Joe Monroe/Photo Reseachers, Inc.; **p. 14d:** © Jean Claude Lejeune; **p. 14e:** © Dallarhide/ Monkmeyer; **p. 15 (inset):** © Carl Purcell/Words and Pictures; **p. 15 (background):** © Alan Oddie/Photo Edit; **1.2:** © Sybil Shackman/ Monkmeyer Press; **p. 19 (top):** © Diane Carter; **p. 19 (bottom):** © Bob Daemmrich/Image Works; **1.3:** © Alan Carey/The Image Works; **p. 20:** Courtesy of Rhoda Unger/Photograph by Will Cofnuk; **1.5 (top to bottom):** © Elyse Lewin/Image Bank-Chicago, © Rhoda Sidney/ Leo de Wys, © Dan Esgro/Image Bank-Chicago, © James Shaffer, © Michael Salas/Image Bank-Chicago, © Joe Sohm/Image Works, Courtesy of John Santrock, © Landrum Shettles; **1.7:** © Tony Freeman/Photo Edit; **p. 33:** © Superstock; **p. 37:** Courtesy of Ruby Takanishi, photo by Benjamin Tice Smith

Chapter 2
Opener: © Metropolitan Museum of Art; **p. 43 (top left):** © Shooting Star; **p. 43 (top right):** © Stock Montage; **p. 43 (bottom):** © Bettmann Newsphotos; **p. 44:** © Barton Silverman/NYT Pictures; **2.2 (left):** Courtesy of Karen Horney; **2.2 (right):**
Courtesy of Nancy Chodorow, photo by Jean Margolis; **p. 46:** © Sarah Putnam/ Picture Cube; **2.3 (top to bottom):** © William Hopkins, © Suzanne Szasz/ Photo Researchers, Inc., © Suzanne Szasz/Photo Researchers, Inc., © Melchior DiGiacomo/The Image Bank, Chicago, © Sam Zarember/The Image Bank-Tx, © Brett Froomer/The Image Bank - Tx, © Alan Carey/The Image Works, © Harold Sund/The Image Bank-Tx; **p. 49:** © Yves DeBraine/ Black Star; **p. 51:** Courtesy of Albert Bandura; **2.6:** © David Austen/Stock Boston; **p. 53 (left):** Courtesy of Urie Bronfenbrenner; **p. 54:** © Fujifotos/ Image Works; **p. 53 (right):** Courtesy of Glen Elder; **p. 55 (left):** © Mark Lewis/Tony Stone Images; **2.7a:** © Jerry Alexander/Tony Stone Worldwide; **2.7b:** © James Rowan/Tony Stone Worldwide; **2.7c:** © Jacques Jangoux/ Tony Stone Worldwide; **p. 60a:** © Anthony Bannister/Earth Scenes; **p. 60b:** © Chagnon/Anthro Photo; **2.8:** © Myrleen Cate/Photo Edit; **2.9:** © Rob Nelson/Stock Boston; **p. 65:** Courtesy of Dr. Florence L. Denmark/Photo by Robert Wesner; **p. 70:** © Metropolitan Museum of Art

Chapter 3
Opener: © Superstock; **p. 80:** © Tony Freeman/Photo Edit; **p. 82:** Courtesy of Sandra Scarr; **3.2 (background):** © Butch Powell/Image Bank, Chicago; **3.2 (child):** cW/ Sally and Richard Greenhill; **3.2 (dancers):** © N. DeSciose/Photo Researchers, Inc.; **p. 86:** © Paul Conklin/Monkmeyer Press; **3.6:** © Alan Carey/The Image Works; **p. 92:** © Guiseppe Molteni/The Image Bank-Texas; **p. 96:** Courtesy of Jeanne Brooks-Gunn/Photograph by Mark Sherman; **p. 99:** © Superstock

Chapter 4
Opener: © Superstock; **4.1:** © Paul Fusco/Magnum Photos, Inc; **4.3:** © Richard Hutchings/Photo Researchers, Inc.; **4.5:** © Paul Conklin; **p. 114:** © R. Heinzen/Superstock; **p. 115 (background):** © Ellis Herwig/ Stock Boston; **p. 115 (left):** © Stacy Pick/Stock Boston; **p. 115 (right):** © Elizabeth Crews; **p. 116:** © Yves DeBraine/Black Star; **p. 117:** © M & E Bernheim/Woodfin Camp and Assoc.;
4.6: © Barros & Barros/Image Bank; **p. 122:** © Gabe Palmer/Kane Inc./ Stock Market; **4.7:** © Mary Kate Denny/Photo Edit

Chapter 5
Opener: © Superstock; **p. 134:** © David Young-Wolff/Photo Edit; **p. 135:** Courtesy of Texas Instruments; **p. 138:** © Susan Lapides; **p. 139:** © Jeff Persons/Stock Boston; **p. 140:** © Susan Lapides; **p. 142:** © James Wilson, 1990/Woodfin Camp and Assoc.; **p. 145a:** © Mark Antman/Image Works; **p. 145b:** © Dr. Rose Gantner/ Comstock; **p. 145c:** © Benn Mitchell/ Image Bank, Chicago; **p. 149:** © Rick Friedman/Black Star; **p. 158:** © Jan Doyle; **5.6A:** © David Austen/Stock Boston; **5.6B:** © Ben Simmons/The Stock Market; **p. 160:** © Mike Penney/ David Frazier Photolibrary; **p. 161:** © Richard Hutchings/Photo Edit; **p. 163:** © Superstock; **167(top left):** © Dennis MacDonald/Photo Edit; **p. 167 (top right):** © A. Ramey/Photo Edit; **p. 167 (bottom left):** © Phil McCarten/Photo Edit; **p. 167 (bottom right):** © Robert Brenner/Photo Edit

Chapter 6
Opener: Courtesy of Romare Beardon Estate; **6.1:** © Richard Hutchings/ Photo Researchers, Inc; **6.3 (top to bottom):** © Tony Freeman/Photo Edit, © Alan Oddie/Photo Edit, © John Carter/Photo Researchers, Inc., © Llewellyn/Superstock, © K. Kasmauski/Woodfin Camp; **p. 182 (left):** Courtesy of Diana Baumrind; **p.182 (right):** © Jeffry W. Myers/Stock Boston **6.4:** © Erik Leigh Simmons/ Image Bank, Chicago; **p. 186:** © Nancy Brown/Image Bank-Texas; **p. 187:** © David Wells/The Image Works; **6.5:** © Michael Melford/Image Bank, Chicago; **p. 191:** © James G. White; **p. 193:** Courtesy of Mavis Hetherington; **p. 198 (top):** © Erika Stone/Peter Arnold, Inc; **p. 198 (bottom):** © Bob Daemmrich/The Image Works; **p. 199:** © Stockphotos/ The Image Bank; **p. 202:** Courtesy of Romare Beardon Estate

Chapter 7
Opener: © Bridgeman Art Library; **p. 210:** © Dana White/Photo Edit;

Line Art and Text

Chapter 1

Cycle, 2d ed. Copyright © 1989 by Allyn and Bacon. Reprinted by permission.

Figure 6.4 (text): From E. E. Maccoby and J. A. Martin, "Socialization in the Context of the Family: Parent-Child Interaction" in P. H. Mussen (ed.), *Handbook of Child Psychology*, 4th ed., Vol. 4. Copyright © 1083 John Wiley & Sons, Inc. Reprinted by permission of John Wiley & Sons, Inc.

Ta 6.12: Reprinted by permission of The Putnam Berkley Group from *How to Deal with Your Parents When They Still Treat You Like a Child* by Lynn Osterkamp, Ph.D. Copyright © 1992 by Lynn Osterkamp, Ph.D.

Ta 6.13: Cover of *Between Parent and Teenager* by Dr. Haim Ginott. By permission of Avon Books.

Ta 6.14: From *Growing Up With Divorce* by Neil Kalter. Copyright © 1990 by Random House, Inc. Reprinted by permission of Ballantine Books, a Division of Random House, Inc.

Ta 6.15: From Richard Gardner, *The Boys and Girls Book About Divorce.* Copyright © 1983 Jason Aronson, Inc., Northvale, NJ. Reprinted by permission.

Ta 6.16: From *Raising Black Children* by James P. Comer and Alvin F. Poussaint. Copyright © 1975, 1992 by James P. Comer and Alvin F. Poussaint. Used by permission of Dutton Signet, a division of Penguin Books USA Inc.

Chapter 7

Figure 7.2: From J. R. Asarnow and J. W. Callan, "Boys with Peer Adjustment Problems: Social Cognitive Processes" in *Journal of Consulting and Clinical Psychology*, 53:80-87. Copyright 1985 by the American Psychological Association. Reprinted with permission.

Figure 7.4: Source: Data from Dexter C. Dunphy, "The Social Structure of Urban Adolescent Peer Groups" in *Sociometry*, Vol. 26. Copyright © 1963 American Sociological Association, Washington, DC.

Ta 7.9: P Zimbardo, Inc., *Shyness*, © 1977 by Phillip Zimbardo. Reprinted by permission of Addison-Wesley Longman Publishing Company, Inc. Cover illustration © 1989 by Bart Goldman.

Ta 7.10: From Lillian Rubin, *Just Friends.* Copyright © 1985 HarperCollins Publishers. Reprinted by permission.

Chapter 8

Box 364 excerpt: Reprinted by permission of Transaction Publishers. *Successful Schools for Young Adolescents* by Joan Lipsitz. Copyright © 1984 by Transaction Publishers; all rights reserved.

Figure 8.1 (graph): Alexander, W. M. and C. McEwin, C. K. (1989) *Schools in the Middle: Status & Progress.* Copyright © 1989 National Middle School Association, Columbus, OH. Reprinted by permission.

Figure 8.2: Copyright © The Carnegie Foundation for the Advancement of Teaching. Reprinted by permission.

Figure 8.3: Source: National Center for Education Statistics, *Dropout Rates in the United States: 1993*, U.S. Department of Education, 1994.

Excerpt 378: *Turning Points: Preparing American Youth for the 21st Century*, Carnegie Council on Adolescent Development, Carnegie Corporation of New York, June 1989.

Ta 8.14: Reprinted with the permission of Simon & Schuster from *Smart Kids, Smart Schools* by Edward B. Fiske.

Ta 8.17: From Joseph Fernandez, *Tales Out of School.* Copyright © 1993 Little, Brown and Company, Boston, MA. Reprinted by permission.

Ta 8.15: Reprinted by permission of Transaction Publishers. *Successful Schools for Young Adolescents* by Joan Lipsitz. Copyright © 1984 by Transaction Publishers, Rutgers University; all rights reserved.

Ta 8.16: From Ruby Takanishi (ed.), *Adolescence in the 1990s.* Copyright © 1993 Teachers College Press, New York, NY. Reprinted by permission.

Chapter 9

Figure 9.1: Where Adolescents Spend Their Time from *Being Adolescent: Conflict and Growth in the Teenage Years* by Mihaly Csikszentmihalyi and Reed Larson. Copyright © 1984 by Basic Books, Inc. Reprinted by permission of Basic Books, a division of HarperCollins Publishers, Inc.

Figure 9.2: What Adolescents Spend Their Time Doing from *Being Adolescent: Conflict and Growth in the Teenage Years* by Mihaly Csikszentmihalyi and Reed Larson. Copyright © 1984 by Basic Books, Inc. Reprinted by permission of Basic Books, a division of HarperCollins Publishers, Inc.

Figure 9.3: People With Whom Adolescents Spend Time from *Being Adolescent: Conflict and Growth in the Teenage Years* by Mihaly Csikszentmihalyi and Reed Larson. Copyright © 1984 by Basic Books, Inc. Reprinted by permission of Basic Books, a division of HarperCollins Publishers, Inc.

Figure 9.4: Source: Data from A. C.

Erlick and A. R. Starry, "Sources of Information for Career Decisions" in *Report of Poll No. 98*, Purdue Opinion Panel, © June 1973, by Purdue Research Foundation, West Lafayette, IN.

Figure 9.5: Source: Data from *Kids Count Data Book 1994: State Profiles of Child Well-Being*, Annie E. Casey Foundation, 1994.

Figure 9.6: Source: National Center for Education Statistics, *A Profile of the American Eighth Grader: NELS:88 Student Descriptive Summary*, U.S. Department of Education, 1980.

Ta 9.15: From Janet Simons, Belva Finlay, and Alice Yang, *The Adolescent and Young Adult Fact Book.* Copyright © 1991 Children's Defense Fund, Washington, DC. Reprinted by permission.

Ta 9.17: Book cover from *Understanding Culture's Influence on Behavior* by Richard Brislin, copyright © 1993 by Harcourt Brace & Company, reproduced by permission of the publisher.

Ta 9.16: From Jewelle Taylor Gibbs and Lake Nahme Huang, et al., *Children of Color.* Copyright © 1989 Jossey-Bass, Inc., Publishers. Reprinted by permission of Willi Baum.

Chapter 10

Box 476 excerpt: From Susan Harter, "Self and Identity Development" in S. Shirley Feldman and Glen R. Elliott (eds.), *At the Threshold: The Developing Adolescent* by S. Harter, Harvard University Press, 1990. Reprinted by permission.

Ta 10.8: Reprinted with the permission of Simon & Schuster from *The Road Less Traveled* by M. Scott Peck. Cover copyright © 1978 by Simon & Schuster, Inc.

Ta 10.9: Cover from *Intimate Connections* by David M. Burns. Copyright © 1985 by David M. Burns. Used by permission of Dutton Signet, a division of Penguin Books USA Inc.

Chapter 11

Figure 11.1: From Janet S. Hyde, et al., "Gender Differences in Mathematics Performance" in *Psychological Bulletin*, 107:139-155. Copyright 1990 by the American Psychological Association. Reprinted with permission.

Ta 11.10: Reprinted with the permission of Simon & Schuster from *The Mismeasure of Woman* Copyright © 1992 by Jackie Seow.

Ta 11.11: From *You Just Don't Understand* by Deborah Tannen, PhD. Copyright © 1990 by Deborah Tannen, PhD. Reprinted by permission of

Ballantine Books, a Division of Random House, Inc.
Ta 11.12: From *The New Male* by Herb Goldberg. Copyright © 1980 by Herb Goldberg. Used by permission of Dutton Signet, a division of Penguin Books USA Inc.

Chapter 12

Figure 12.1: From C. A. Darling, D. J. Kallen, and J. E. van Deusen, "Sex In Transition: 1900-1984" in *Journal of Youth and Adolescence*, 13:385-399. Copyright © 1984 Human Sciences Press, Inc., New York, NY. Reprinted by permission.
Figure 12.2: Adapted from Alfred C. Kinsey, et al., *Sexual Behavior in the Human Female*. Copyright © 1953 The Kinsey Institute for Research in Sex, Gender, and Reproduction, Inc., Bloomington, IN. Reprinted by permission of The Kinsey Institute for Research in Sex, Gender, and Reproduction, Inc.
Excerpt 577: STUDENT SECH ADVISOR PROGRAM, Princeton University Health Services, Princeton, NJ. Permission granted by Karen A. Gordon, Director of Health Education, 1987.
Figure 12.3: Source: Data from National Survey of Family Growth, 1982.
Figure 12.4: Source: Data from *Child Trends*, Child Trends, Washington, DC, 1996.
Figure 12.5: Reproduced with the permission of The Alan Guttmacher Institute from Frank L. Mott and William Marsiglio, "Early Childbearing and Completion of High School," *Family Planning Perspectives*, Volume 17, Number 5, September/October 1985.
Ta 12.7: From Wardell Pomeroy, *Girls and Sex*. Copyright © 1991 Delacorte Press, a division of Bantam, Doubleday, Dell Publishing Group, Inc. Reprinted by permission.
Ta 12.8: From Wardell Pomeroy, *Boys and Sex*. Copyright © 1991 Delacorte Press, a division of Bantam, Doubleday, Dell Publishing Group, Inc. Reprinted by permission.
Ta 12.9: From Bernie Zilbergeld, *The New Male Sexuality*. Copyright © 1992 Bantam Books, a division of Bantam Doubleday Dell Publishing Group, Inc., New York, NY. Reprinted by permission.

Chapter 13

Figure 13.1: From Steven R. Yussen, "Characteristics of Moral Dilemmas Written by Adolescents" in *Developmental Psychology*, 13:162-163.

Copyright 1977 by the American Psychological Association. Reprinted with permission.
Figure 13.A: Source: After Damon, 1988.
Figure 13.3: Source: Data from E. L. Dey, et al., *The American Freshman: Twenty-Five-Year Trends*, 1991; A. W. Astin, et al., *The American Freshman: National Norms for Fall*, 1991, 1993, 1994; and E. L. Dey, et al., *The American Freshman: National Norms for Fall*, 1992; Higher Education Research Institute, UCLA.
Ta 13.10: From *Meeting at the Crossroads* by Lyn Mikel Brown and Carol Gilligan. Copyright © 1992 by the President and Fellows of Harvard College. Reprinted by permission of Harvard University Press.
Ta 13.11: Reprinted with the permission of Simon & Schuster from *How to Save the Children* by Amy Hatkoff and Karen Klopp.
Ta 13.12: Cover from *Cults* by Marc Galanter. Copyright © 1989 Marc Galanter. Reprinted by permission of Oxford University Press, Inc.

Chapter 14

Figure 14.2: From Mark Lepper, et al., "Undermining Children's Intrinsic Interest With Extrinsic Rewards" in *Journal of Personality and Social Psychology*, 28:129-136. Copyright 1973 by the American Psychological Association. Reprinted with permission.
Figure 14.3: Source: Bureau of Labor Statistics. Chart from *Occupational Outlook Handbook*.
Figure 14.4: Reproduced by special permission of the Publisher, Psychological Assessment Resources, Inc., from *Making Vocational Choices*, Copyright 1973, 1985 by Psychological Assessment Resources, Inc. All rights reserved.
Ta 14.10: D Elkind, *All Grown Up and No Place to Go*, © 1984 David Elkind. Reprinted by permission of Addison-Wesley Longman Publishing Company, Inc.
Ta 14.12: Copyright © 1997 by Richard Nelson Bolles with permission from Ten Speed Press, PO Box 7123, Berkeley, CA 94707.
Ta 14.11: From Marian Salzman and Teresa Reisgies, *Greetings from High School*. Copyright © 1991 Peterson's Guides, Princeton, NJ. Reprinted by permission.
Ta 14.13: From Thomas Evans, *Mentors*. Copyright © 1992 Peterson's Guides, Princeton, NJ. Reprinted by permission.

Chapter 15

Poem 721: From *The Poetry of Robert Frost*, edited by Edward Connery Lathem. Copyright 1936 by Robert Frost. © 1964 by Leslie Ballantine Frost. © 1969 by Henry Holt & Co., Inc. Reprinted by permission of Henry Holt & Co., Inc.
Figure 15.1: From T. M. Achenbach and C. S. Edelbrock, "Behavioral Problems and Competencies Reported by Parents of Normal and Disturbed Children Aged Four Through Sixteen" in *Monographs of the Society for Research in Child Development*, Vol. 46, No. 1, Serial No. 188. Copyright © 1981 The Society for Research in Child Development, Inc., Chicago, IL. Reprinted by permission.
Figure 15.2: Source: Data from L. D. Johnston, J. G. Bachman, and P. M. O'Malley, Institute for Social Research, University of Michigan, 1993.
Figure 15.3: From Lloyd D. Johnston, Institute of Social Research News Release, January 31, 1994. Copyright © 1994 Institute for Social Research, Ann Arbor, MI. Reprinted by permission.
Figure 15.5: From *Adolescents at Risk: Prevalence and Prevention* by Joy G. Dryfoos. Copyright © 1991 by Joy G. Dryfoos. Used by permission of Oxford University Press, Inc.
Figure 15.6: Source: "Suicide Among Children, Adolescents, and Young Adults—United States 1980-1992" in *Morbidity and Mortality Weekly Report*, 44(15), April 21, 1995.
Ta 15.9: Times Books © Random House, Inc. Reprinted by permission.
Ta 15.8: From *Adolescents at Risk: Prevalence and Prevention* by Joy G. Dryfoos. Copyright © 1990 by Joy G. Dryfoos. Reprinted by permission of Oxford University Press, Inc.

Chapter 16

Figure 16.1: From Lee L. Langley, *Physiology of Man*. Copyright © 1971 Van Nostrand Reinhold, New York, NY. Reprinted by permission of the author.
Figure 16.2: From Virginia DeMoss, "Good, the Bad and the Edible" in *Runner's World*, June 1980. Copyright © 1980 Virginia DeMoss. Reprinted by permission.
Ta 16.10: Cover of *The New Fit or Fat*. Copyright © 1977, 1978, 1991 by Covert Bailey. Reprinted by permission of Houghton Mifflin Co. All rights reserved.
Ta 16.9: From Kenneth Cooper, *Kid Fitness*. Copyright © 1992 Bantam Books, a division of Bantam Doubleday Dell Publishing Group, Inc., New York, NY. Reprinted by permission.

NAME INDEX

Duncan, G. J., 288
Dunphy, D. C., 223, 233
Durant, D., 473
Durbin, D., 186
Durbin, D. L., 182
Durdek, L. A., 123
Durkin, K., 347
Durrett, M. E., 449
Dusenbury, L., 474
Dutta, R., 284
Dweck, C. S., 439, 442
Dweyer, K., 196

E

Eagleston, J. R., 516
Eagly, A. H., 351, 352
Earls, F., 285, 504
East, P. L., 374
Ebata, A. T., 519, 520
Eberly, M. B., 188, 417
Eccles, J., 18, 248, 256, 257, 258,
    260, 344, 345, 439, 451–52
Eccles, J. S., 196, 256, 320,
    439, 452
Edelbrock, C. S., 267, 469, 470
Edelman, M. W., 18, 20, 286,
    434, 506
Edmonston, B., 400
Educational Testing Service, 443
Edwards, C. P., 197
Ehrhart, A. A., 376
Eifter, C. W., 505
Eisenberg, N., 409, 416, 417
Ekstrom, R. B., 252
Elder, G.. H., 287
Elder, G. H., 11, 53–55, 61, 175,
    177, 196
Elias, M. J., 217
Elkind, D., 112, 113, 121, 122, 131,
    279, 439, 449
Elliot, T., 454
Elliott, D. S., 506
Elliott, G. R., 16, 19, 28
Elliott, J. E., 490
Ellis, L., 376
El-Taliawy, T., 356
Emde, R., 25
Emde, R. N., 86
Emery, R. E., 173
Enright, R. D., 11, 12, 326,
    412, 417
Entwistle, D. R., 260, 263
Epstein, H. T., 86
Epstein, J. L., 73, 258, 260
Erdley, C. A., 216
Erickson, E. H., 40, 45, 46, 92, 226,
    228, 256, 322, 323, 327, 331,
    343, 415, 424, 480
Erickson, J. B., 227
Erlick, A. C., 285
Escobedo, L. G., 506

Ethier, K., 345
Etteman, J., 347
Evans, B. J., 292
Evans, D., 373, 374
Ewell, K. K., 123
Ey, S., 41, 488
Eyler, J., 423

F

Fabes, R. A., 351
Faigel, H. C., 267
Faigeles, R., 332
Falbo, T., 252
Fang, Z., 220
Farar, E., 243
Farmer, M. C., 412
Farrell, M. P., 473, 474
Fasick, F. A., 11, 281
Fay, A. L., 131
Feeney, S., 256
Fegley, S., 435, 454
Fehr, L. A., 326
Fei, J., 232
Feiring, C., 228, 229, 230
Feist, J., 511
Feldman, D. H., 160
Feldman, J. F., 80
Feldman, N. S., 316
Feldman, S. S., 16, 19, 28, 185, 484
Felner, R. D., 320
Fenzel, L. M., 247, 260, 320
Ferreira, M., 182
Ferron, J., 288
Fetter, M. D., 227
Field, L. D., 296
Finch, M., 453
Fine, G. A., 299
Finlay, B., 73, 207, 239, 260, 273,
    295, 296, 309, 503
Finney, J. W., 473
Firpo-Triplett, R., 393
Fischer, K. W., 121
Fischer, M., 267
Fischoff, B., 140, 166
Fish, K. D., 199
Fisher, C. B., 18
Fisher, D., 188, 212
Fisher, M., 509
Fisher, T. D., 388
Fiske, S. T., 349
Fitzgerald, H. E., 475
Fitzgerald, L. F., 453
Flanagan, A. S., 393
Flanagan, C., 421
Flanagan, C. A., 196
Flannery, D. J., 26, 96
Flavell, J. H., 116, 117, 121, 125
Flay, B. F., 480
Flay, B. R., 477
Fletcher, A., 442
Follansbee, D. J., 327

Foon, A., 259
Ford Foundation, 262
Forehand, G., 262
Forrest, J. D., 372, 378, 379, 380
Foster-Clark, F. S., 351
Fouad, N. A., 453
Fowler, J. W., 426, 427
Fowler, M., 401
Fox, L. H., 452
Fraleigh, M. J., 262
Francis, J., 326
Fraser, G., 326
Fraser, S., 152
Freedman, J. L., 517
Freeman, D., 11
Freeman, H. S., 194
Freud, A., 43, 92, 211
Freud, S., 42
Freudenberg, N., 387
Frevert, R. L., 388
Friedman, A. C., 490
Friedman, H. S., 159
Friend, R., 516
Frieze, I. H., 66
Frieze, I. R., 230
Frisch, R. E., 86
Fulker, D., 25
Furman, W., 175, 189, 191, 219,
    228, 233, 374, 417
Furstenberg, F. F., 261, 394
Furstenberg, F. F. Jr., 199
Furth, H. G., 108

G

Gagnon, J. H., 372, 373, 374, 375
Galambos, N. L., 16, 82, 195,
    196, 358
Galanter, M., 427
Galloti, K. M., 139
Gallup, G. W., 424
Galotti, K. M., 412
Galperyn, K., 409
Ganong, L. J., 194
Garbarino, J., 286
Garber, J., 489
Garcia, J. C., 19
Garcia, L., 315
Gardner, H., 113, 149
Gardner, L. I., 505
Gardon, R. D., 382
Garfinkel, P. E., 510
Garmezy, N., 484, 516, 519
Garmon, L., 412
Garner, D. M., 510
Garnier, H. E., 253
Garrett, P., 288
Garrison, C. Z., 485
Garrod, A. C., 409
Gaskill, S. P., 505
Gauze, C. M., 212
Ge, X., 83, 287

George, C. M., 83
George, R., 245
Gerton, J., 280, 281
Gewirtz, J., 409
Gfellner, B. M., 473
Giaconia, R. M., 255, 490
Gibbs, J., 407
Gibbs, J. C., 412
Gibbs, J. T., 286, 442
Gibbs, N., 342
Giddings, M., 195
Giles, D., 423
Gilgun, J. F., 374
Gilligan, C., 331, 358, 360, 410, 412, 420, 483
Gillum, R. F., 516
Gimpel, G. A., 217
Gintis, H., 244
Ginzberg, E., 447
Ginzberg, S. W., 447
Giordano, R., 409
Giovino, G. A., 506
Girgus, J. S., 488
Gitleson, I. B., 358
Gjerde, P. F., 173, 178, 489
Glass, G. V., 255
Glassman, M. J., 409
Glay, B., 196
Glick, J., 118, 153
Glover, R. W., 455, 457
Glueck, E., 288, 484, 485
Glueck, S., 288, 484, 485
Gmunder, P., 425
Goelman, H., 113
Goertz, M. E., 252
Gold, M., 487
Goldberg, H., 360
Goldberg, R., 424
Golden, M. W., 211
Golden, N. H., 509
Goldman, N., 380
Goldscheider, F. C., 177
Goldsmith, H. H., 81
Goldstein, A. P., 487
Gomel, J. N., 197
Gonzales, N., 206
Gonzalez, L. S., 174
Goodchilds, J. D., 374
Gooden, A., 412
Goodlad, J. A., 463
Goodman, R. A., 472
Goodnow, J., 17
Goodnow, J. J., 17
Gordon, A. S., 183, 477
Gordon, K. A., 377
Gordon, S., 374
Gore, S., 250
Gore, T., 302
Gotlib, I. H., 41
Gottesman, I. I., 81
Gottfried, A., 441

Gottlieb, D., 260
Gottlieb, G., 83, 84
Gottman, J. M., 173, 218
Graber, J. A., 24, 93, 96, 97, 489
Grady, K., 526
Graham, S., 442
Grant, K. E., 41, 488, 489
Green, K. C., 421
Green, T. M., 175, 176
Green, V., 378
Greenberg, B. S., 300, 301
Greenberg, M. T., 16, 188, 212
Greenberger, E., 425, 454
Greene, B., 79
Greene, D., 441
Greene, J. W., 471
Greenfield, P. M., 277
Grimes, B., 512
Grober, J. S., 526
Gross, R. T., 92, 262
Grotevant, H. D., 83, 176, 327, 449, 450
Grove, K., 206
Gruen, R. S., 376
Gruskin, E., 376
Gudeman, J., 484
Guerra, N. G., 484
Guilford, J. P., 161
Gulley, B. L., 96
Gullotta, T. P., 96, 258, 471
Gunderson, P., 391
Gunn, J., 41, 488
Gunter, B., 301
Guo, G., 261, 394
Gur, R. C., 350
Gur, R. E., 350
Gurin, J., 509
Gurtner, J., 141, 142
Guttentag, M., 355

Hardy, J. B., 373
Hare, B. R., 290
Hare-Muston, R., 357
Harkenss, W. L., 393
Harkness, S., 197
Harlow, H. F., 211
Harmon, D. S., 87
Harold, R., 256, 257, 258, 260, 451–52
Harold, R. D., 452
Harris, D., 12
Harris, K. T., 199
Harris, L., 375
Hart, D., 315, 318, 435
Harter, S., 309, 314, 315, 316, 317, 319, 320, 326, 327, 339, 359
Hartman, J., 86
Hartshorne, H., 413
Hartup, W. W., 211, 214, 215
Harvard Medical Newsletter, 385
Hascall, S. A., 188
Hastorf, A. H., 262
Hatano, G., 17
Hatfield, E., 352
Hatkoff, A., 435
Hauser, S. T., 188, 327
Havighurst, R. J., 295
Hawkins, J. A., 246, 247
Hawkins, J. D., 473, 498
Hayes, C., 372
Hayes, D. M., 401
Haynie, D., 373
Hayward, E., 227
Haywood, C., 488
Hazen, C., 188
Hazuda, H. P., 505
Hearn, M., 507
Heath, S. B., 285, 329
Hechinger, J., 388
Hedges, L. V., 255
Heeren, T., 490
Heeter, C., 301
Heider, F., 440
Heilman, M. E., 349
Heintz, K., 299
Helft, L., 516
Helmreich, R., 354
Helms, J. E., 329, 330
Helson, R., 454
Henderson, K. A., 92
Henderson, V. L., 439, 442
Hennig, K. H., 405
Henry, B., 82
Henshaw, S. K., 380
Herman, J. L., 447
Hernandez, D. J., 192
Hernstein, R. J., 152
Herzog, E., 344
Hess, L., 413
Hetherington, E. M., 36, 53, 83, 192, 193, 194, 195, 233

Klaw, E., 382
Klebanov, P. K., 288
Kleiber, D., 284
Klein, K., 255
Klepp, K., 507
Klerman, L. V., 505
Kliewer, W., 229
Klingaman, L. R., 393
Klopp, K., 435
Knight, G. P., 351
Knox, D., 233
Koch, M., 489
Kocher, T., 391
Koel, A., 282
Koenig, L. J., 332
Koeppl, G. K., 215
Kohlberg, L., 121, 125, 347, 406, 407, 413, 419
Kolaric, G. C., 195
Kolata, G., 372, 373, 374, 375
Kolbe, L. J., 511, 527
Kolts, R., 472
Korbin, J. E., 298
Kormro, K. A., 507
Korn, W. S., 257, 421
Koss, M. P., 393
Kostelecky, K. L., 515
Kozberg, S. F., 139, 412
Kramer, L., 173
Krile, D., 123
Kriss, M. R., 489
Krupnik, C. G., 345
Ku, L., 357, 379
Ku, L. C., 372, 378, 386
Kubey, R., 299
Kuhn, D., 130
Kulick, J. A., 148
Kulik, C. C., 148
Kung, E., 186
Kuperminc, G. P., 188
Kupersmidt, J. B., 211, 215
Kurtines, W. M., 409
Kurtz, D. A., 327

L

Laberge-Nadeau, C., 140, 504
Labouvie-Vief, G., 114
Ladd, G. W., 212
Ladewski, B., 193
LaFromboise, T., 280, 281, 298, 328, 487
Lagana, L., 401
LaGreca, A. M., 227
Lamb, M. E., 199
Lampl, M., 86
Land, R., 83
Landale, N., 17
Landale, N. S., 177
Lander, W. S., 465
Lapsley, D., 12, 326, 412

Lapsley, D. K., 11, 111, 122, 123, 125, 131, 186, 325, 409, 412
Larson, R., 283, 284, 285, 299
Larson, R. W., 188
Laub, J. H., 288
Laumann, E. O., 372, 373, 374, 375
Laursen, B., 182
Lavalii, M., 118
Lavery, B., 487
LaVoie, J., 331
Law, T. C., 195
Lazarus, R. S., 321, 517, 519
Le Sieur, K. D., 212
Leadbetter, B. J., 382, 488
Leaper, C., 352
Lee, C. C., 296
Lee, E., 223
Lee, L., 316
Lee, L. C., 60
Lee, S., 443
Lee, V., 259
Lee, V. E., 193, 393
Leech, S., 473
LeFevre, P., 113
Leffert, N., 217, 285
Lefkowitz, E. S., 131
Leidman, P. H., 262
Leigh, G. K., 388
Leigh, J., 454
Leitenberg, H., 377
Leong, F. T. L., 453
Lepper, M., 441
Lepper, M. R., 141, 142
Lerner, H. G., 360
Lerner, J. V., 24, 195
Lerner, R. M., 24, 82, 96
Lesser, G. S., 185
Lesser, I., 331, 332
Levant, R. F., 360, 361
LeVay, S., 376
Leventhal, A., 214, 226
Levine, A., 499
Levine, C., 325
LeVine, R. A., 17
Levine, S. V., 427
Levy, V. M., 12
Lewinsohn, P. M., 41
Lewis, C. G., 139
Lewis, J. M., 193
Lewis, R. J., 379
Lewis, V. G., 103
Lickona, T., 418
Lieberman, M., 407
Light, K. C., 510
Lightfoot, C., 167
Lin, L., 173
Lincoln, R., 380
Lindenberger, U., 24
Lindholm, L., 489
Linn, E., 393
Linn, M. C., 114, 504

Linsangan, R., 301
Liprie, M. L., 140
Lipsitz, J., 196, 242, 248, 249, 381
Little, T. D., 160
Littlejohn, E. M., 452
Livesley, W. J., 124–25
Loebl, J. H., 316
Loehlin, J., 28, 83
Loehlin, J. C., 152, 155, 156
Loehr, J., 520
Loewen, I. R., 388
Lohr, M. J., 226
Lomnitz, L., 198
Long, L., 196
Long, T., 196
Longoria, N., 211
Lonky, E., 413
Lonner, W. J., 144
Lord, S., 197
Lord, S. E., 320
Lorence, J., 448
Lorenz, F. O., 287
Loriaux, D. L., 89, 97
Louv, R., 64
Low, K. G., 298, 328
Loya, F., 472
Lubat, T. I., 161
Lucas, F. L., 89
Lunde, I., 490
Luo, Q., 220
Luria, A., 344
Luster, T. J., 381
Lynch, J. H., 188
Lynch, M. E., 175, 176, 358
Lyons, N. P., 412
Lytton, H., 484

M

Maas, H. S., 223
Maccoby, E. E., 83, 176, 193, 219, 344, 350, 351
Maccoby, N., 507
MacCorquodale, P., 371
MacDermid, S., 176, 177
MacDonald, K., 177
MacLean, D. J., 452
MacLean, M. G., 187
MacLeod, M., 345
Madison, B. E., 331
Madsen, M. C., 279
Maehr, M. L., 442
Magaletta, P. R., 260
Magana, D., 505
Magnusson, D., 95, 221
Maguin, E., 475
Mahapatra, M., 411
Majima, N., 257, 503
Malik, N. M., 217
Mammersmith, S. K., 376
Manis, F. R., 137, 138

Manke, B., 83
Manke, B. A., 358
Manson, S. M., 473
Maracek, J., 352
Marchant, G. J., 440
Marcia, J., 318, 324, 325, 326,
    331, 332
Marcia, J. E., 325, 326, 331
Marcus, S. E., 506
Marecek, J., 357
Maris, R. W., 490
Markstrom, C. A., 519
Markus, H., 17, 316
Marlow, L., 175, 176
Marmorstein, N. R., 489
Marold, D. B., 316, 320
Marshall, P. M., 188
Marshall, R., 455, 457
Marshall, S., 416
Marsiglio, W., 380
Martin, C. E., 375
Martin, C. L., 348
Martin, D. C., 266
Martin, J., 243, 376
Martin, L. R., 159
Martin, N. C., 316
Martin, W. E., 474
Mason, C., 328
Mason, C. A., 206
Masten, A. S., 519
Masters, W., 393
Matarazzo, J. D., 516
Matlin, M. W., 197, 345, 349
Matsumoto, D., 277
Matthews, K. A., 516
Mattimore, K., 512
Maughan, B., 244, 255
May, M. S., 413
Mayer, R., 139
Mayes, S., 301
Mays, V. M., 387
Mazzarella, S., 299
McAdoo, H. P., 198, 202, 296,
    300, 509
McAleer, J. L., 301
McAlister, A., 507
McCall, R. B., 86
McCarton, C. M., 80
McClearn, G. E., 79
McClelland, D. C., 440
McCord, J., 484
McCord, W., 484
McCormich, A., 388
McDill, E. L., 255
McDougall, P., 252
McGee, R. O., 82
McGoldrick, M., 178
McGrugan, K., 196
McGuie, M. K., 83
McHale, S. M., 295, 358
McKeown, R. E., 485

McKinney, M. H., 381
McKnight, C. C., 443
McLaughlin, C. S., 425
McLaughlin, M. W., 329
McLean, M., 245
McLean, R. S., 141
McLellan, J. A., 226
McLoyd, V., 17, 201, 290, 292,
    294–95
McLoyd, V. C., 17, 201, 290, 291,
    292, 299
McPartland, J., 243, 244
McPartland, J. M., 255
McQuire, W. J., 301
McRoy, R. G., 83
Mead, M., 10, 20, 177
Medrich, E. A., 211
Melby, J. N., 506
Mercy, J. A., 472
Merrell, K. W., 217
Messinger, J. C., 280
Metz, K. E., 119
Meyer, C., 113
Meyer, H., 373
Meyer-Bahlburg, H. F., 376
Meyers, E. D., 86
Michael, R. T., 372, 373, 374, 375
Michelson, C., 282
Michelson, S., 244
Midgley, C., 442
Milberg, S., 417
Miller, B. C., 372
Miller, F., 452
Miller, J., 411
Miller, J. B., 360
Miller, J. G., 409, 411
Miller, J. P., 227
Miller, L., 516
Miller, M. D., 302
Miller, P., 17
Miller, P. A., 116, 117, 121
Miller, P. H., 121
Miller, P. Y., 374
Miller, S. A., 116, 117, 121
Miller, S. K., 507
Miller, T. Q., 477
Miller-Jones, D., 154
Millstein, G. B., 506
Millstein, S. G., 37, 131, 503, 504,
    506, 527
Mincy, R., 357, 379
Minkler, M., 512
Minnett, A., 191
Mintz, S., 199
Minuchin, P. P., 246, 262
Mischel, H., 413
Mischel, W., 50, 121, 413, 483
Mitchell, C., 65
Mitchell, C. M., 473
Mitteness, L. S., 180
Modell, J., 53–55

Moffit, M. C., 140
Moffitt, T. E., 82
Mollasis, C., 451
Moneta, G., 188
Money, J., 103
Monsour, A., 316
Montangero, J., 111
Montemayor, R., 26, 96, 182, 183,
    417, 471
Montgomery, S. B., 480
Mont-Reynaud, R., 73
Mood, A. M., 243, 244
Moore, C. F., 434
Moore, K. A., 400
Moorhead, M., 227
Moos, R. H., 473, 519, 520
Moosbrugger, L., 473
Moran, P., 484
Morgan, M., 346, 347
Morris, L., 384
Morris, P. A., 51
Morrison, D. R., 400
Morrison, F. J., 137, 138
Morrow, L., 7
Mortimer, A. M., 527
Mortimer, J., 448
Mortimer, J. T., 299, 453
Mortimore, P., 244, 255
Mory, M., 226
Mott, F. L., 380
Mounts, N., 225
Mounts, N. S., 212
Mozley, L. H., 471
Munroe, R. H., 54, 282, 356
Munroe, R. L., 54, 282, 356
Murdock, T. B., 225
Murphy, B., 409, 417
Murphy, K., 215
Murphy, M. N., 122
Murray, C., 152
Murray, D., 507
Murray, D. M., 516
Murray, H. A., 440
Muzzonigro, P. G., 375
Myers, D. E., 400
Myers, M. G., 480

N

Nagata, D. K., 276
National Academy of Science, 372
National and Community Service
    Coalition, 435
National Assessment of
    Educational Progress, 449
National Health Interview
    Study, 504
National Longtitudinal Study, 373
National Research Council, 373
Neiderhiser, M. M., 83
Neimark, E. D., 112
Neisser, U., 152, 155, 156

Nelson, W. M., 489
Neugarten, B. L., 21
Neuwalder, H. F., 376
Newacheck, P. W., 505
Newcomb, A. F., 219
Newcomb, M. D., 477, 480
Newcomer, S. F., 371
Newman, B. S., 375
Newman, D. L., 82
Ng'andu, N., 288
Ngini, L., 118
Nguyen, H. H., 188
Nicholls, J. G., 442
Nightingale, E. O., 37, 503, 504, 527
Nigro, C., 138
Nisbett, R. R., 441
Nitz, K., 24
Noam, G. G., 16, 327
Noir, S., 356
Nolen-Hoeksema, S., 488
Nord, C. W., 400
Norem, J. K., 520
Nottelmann, E. D., 61, 89, 90, 97
Nugent, S., 473
Nurius, P., 316
Nusbaum, H. C., 136
Nydegger, C. N., 180

O

Oberg, M., 260
O'Brien, R. W., 233, 521
Occupational Outlook Handbook, 445, 450
O'Connor, T. G., 83
Oden, M. H., 159
Oden, S. L., 217
O'Donnell, J., 498
Offer, D., 14, 15, 373
Ogbu, J. U., 263
O'Hara, N. M., 511
Olson, L., 412
O'Malley, P., 422, 476
O'Malley, P. M., 471, 472, 473, 474, 475, 476, 477, 506
Omoto, A. M., 232
O'Nell, T. D., 473
Ordonez, N., 328
Orlofsky, J., 331, 332
Orr, M. T., 252
Orthner, D. K., 195, 196
Ortmann, J., 490
Oser, F., 419, 425
Osipow, S. H., 449
Osofsky, J. D., 381
Ospiow, S. H., 452
Ostrov, E., 14, 15, 373
Ostrum, C. W., 24
Ouston, J., 244, 255
Ovellette, R., 417
Overby, G., 199
Overton, W. F., 87, 111, 112

P

Paige, J. M., 393
Paige, K. E., 393
Paik, H., 301
Paikoff, R., 92, 95, 96, 393, 394
Paikoff, R. L., 61, 89, 97, 175
Palincsar, A. M., 139
Paloutzian, R. F., 424
Paludi, M. A., 18, 65, 345, 348, 349, 357, 360, 393
Papini, D., 394
Papini, D. R., 188
Parcel, G. S., 511
Parfenoff, S. H., 388
Parke, R. D., 53–55, 177, 199
Parker, J. G., 211, 218
Parrott, S. A., 257, 421
Patrick, H., 211
Patterson, C. J., 376
Patterson, G. R., 484
Patterson, S. J., 331
Paul, E. L., 228
Paulson, S. E., 197, 440
Pedro-Carroll, J. L., 193
Pellegrino, J. W., 144, 150
Penner, W., 227
Pentz, M. A., 480
Peplau, L. A., 333, 517
Pereira, C., 516
Perlman, D., 333
Perloff, R., 152, 155, 156
Perlstadt, J., 381
Perry, C., 507
Perry, C. L., 507
Perry, I., 262
Perry, T. B., 219
Perry, W. G., 115
Peskin, H., 94, 95
Petersen, A. C., 24, 36, 37, 41, 96, 131, 358, 488, 489, 503, 504, 519, 527
Peterson, L., 504
Peterson, P. L., 473
Peterson, S. R., 320
Petraitis, J., 477
Petronio, R. J., 487
Pettit, R., 484
Phelps, E., 113
Philipp, M., 225
Phillips, R., 491
Phillips, S., 346
Phinney, J. S., 281, 327, 328–29
Piaget, J., 40, 47, 107, 111, 114, 115, 121, 125, 131, 175, 211, 405
Piirto, J., 160
Pike, A., 83
Pinus, U., 267
Piotrowski, C. C., 173
Pittman, K. J., 389
Place, D. M., 233

Plant, E. A., 349
Pleck, J. H., 357, 361, 372, 378, 379, 386
Plomin, R., 79, 81, 83, 88, 151
Polina, L. K., 199
Pollack, W. S., 360, 361
Pomeroy, W. B., 375
Potenza, M., 140
Pothoff, S., 391
Potvin, L., 140, 504
Powell, A., 243
Powell, M. C., 147
Power, F. C., 325
Powers, S. I., 327
Pressley, M., 138
Price, R. H., 227
Prineas, R. J., 516
Prinsky, L. E., 303
Prinstein, M. J., 227
Psathas, G., 185

Q

Quadrel, M. J., 140, 166
Quay, H. C., 488
Quinlan, D. M., 488
Quinn, W., 195

R

Rabkin, J., 487
Raden, A., 382
Ragosta, J., 262
Raikkonen, K., 516, 517
Ramey, C. T., 151
Ramirez, O., 292
Ramsey, E., 484
Rapkin, B. D., 247
Rapport, M. D., 266
Raskin, P. M., 449
Rasmusssen, C. M., 140
Raynor, I. O., 440
Redditt, C. A., 302
Rees, J., 509
Reese, C. A., 342
Reinherz, H. Z., 490
Reinisch, J. M., 388
Reiss, D., 83
Relethford, J. H., 505
Remafedi, G., 375
Renninger, K. A., 117
Repinski, D. J., 217
Research Bulletin, The, 286
Resnick, L. B., 119, 141
Resnick, M., 375
Resnick, M. D., 382, 391
Resnick, S. M., 350
Rest, J., 420
Rest, J. R., 404–9
Ricard, R. J., 220
Rice, K. G., 186
Richards, M., 286, 358

Simons, J. M., 73, 207, 239, 260, 273, 295, 296, 309, 503
Simons, R. L., 287
Simons-Morton, G. G., 511
Simpson, J. A., 231
Simpson, R. L., 450
Sims, B., 286
Sims, K. E., 381
Singer, L. M., 83
Singh, S., 372, 378
Sippola, L. K., 219
Sivo, P. J., 526
Skinner, B. F., 50
Skinner, E. A., 441
Skoe, E. E., 331, 412
Slap, G. G., 507
Slavin, R. E., 272
Slinkard, L. A., 507
Sloman, J., 212
Small, S. A., 200, 207
Smallish, L., 267
Smetana, J., 184
Smiley, S. S., 113
Smith, A., 332
Smith, D. W., 83
Smith, E., 371
Smith, J., 116
Smith, J. C., 472
Smith, M., 11, 244
Smith, M. L., 255
Smith, P. H., 326
Smith, R., 301
Smith, R. C., 211
Smith, R. S., 73
Smollar, J., 521
Snarey, J., 407, 409
Snider, B. A., 227
Snidman, N., 28
Snow, R. E., 256
Snowden, L. R., 505
Snyder, A. R., 199
Snyder, C. R., 520
Snyder, M., 232
Sochting, I., 331
Soderman, A., 301
Sommer, B. B., 94, 281
Sonenstein, F., 357, 379
Sonenstein, F. L., 372, 378, 386, 389
Sorensen, R. C., 229, 377
Soriano, F. I., 487
Spade, J. Z., 342
Spearman, C. E., 148
Spear-Swerling, L., 266
Speisman, J. C., 332
Spence, J. T., 354
Spencer, M. B., 223, 289, 292, 293, 295, 296, 308, 327
Spilka, B., 428
Spracklen, K. M., 215
Sputa, C. L., 197

Srebnik, D., 377
Sroufe, L. A., 27, 174
Stanley, C., 301
Stanley-Hagen, M. M., 192, 194
Stanton-Salazar, R. D., 329
Starry, A. R., 285
Stattin, H., 95
Staub, E., 485, 487
Staudinger, U. M., 24
Stechler, G., 490
Stedman, L., 11
Stein, L. J., 509
Steinbach, R., 139
Steinberg, L., 176, 182, 454, 499
Steinberg, L. D., 175, 185, 196
Steininger, P., 490
Stemmler, M., 41, 488
Stengel, R., 382
Stern, M. P., 505
Sternberg, L., 225
Sternberg, R. J., 138, 140, 148, 152, 155, 156, 160, 161, 266
Steur, F. B., 301
Stevens, J. H., 198, 296
Stevens, R. J., 272
Stevenson, D., 506
Stevenson, H. G., 17, 292
Stevenson, H. W., 279, 443, 445, 462
Stewart, M. A., 83
Stewart, R., 376
Stigler, J. W., 136, 443
Stipek, D. J., 452
Stock, W., 255
Stone, G. C., 504
Stoneman, Z., 192
Stouthamer-Loeber, M., 484
Strachen, A., 316
Strahan, D. B., 112
Strasburger, V. C., 301
Streissguth, A. P., 266
Streitmatter, J., 331
Strickland, B. R., 377
Strouse, D., 226
Stunkard, A. J., 510
Sue, D. W., 329
Sue, S., 290, 292, 293, 294
Suleiman, L., 286
Sullivan, A., 251, 357
Sullivan, H. S., 175, 211, 218, 219, 233
Sullivan, K., 251
Suomi, S. J., 211
Super, C. M., 197
Super, D. E., 447
Susman, A. R., 288
Susman, E., 91
Susman, E. J., 61, 89, 97
Sussman, S. Y., 196
Sutton-Smith, B., 191
Suzuki, L. K., 277

Swafford, J. O., 443
Swallow, J., 141
Swanson, D. P., 442
Swarr, A. E., 508
Swartz, J. L., 474
Swim, J. K., 349, 350
Switzer, G. E., 435
Swope, G. W., 427, 428
Szasz, T., 469
Sznajderman, S., 267

T

Takahashi, K., 257, 503
Takanishi, R., 20, 37
Talley, R. C., 244
Talwar-Soni, R., 24
Tapper, J., 226
Tardif, T., 285
Tavris, C., 347, 351–52, 367
Taylor, C. B., 488
Taylor, D., 94
Taylor, J. H., 408–9
Taylor, L. C., 264
Taylor, R. D., 198, 285
Taylor, S. E., 517
Terman, L., 158, 159
Thomas, A., 81
Thomas, C. W., 191
Thomas, G., 245
Thomas, P., 516
Thompson, L., 197
Thoresen, C. E., 516
Thornburg, H. D., 388, 389
Thorton, A., 425
Thurstone, L. L., 148
Tilton-Weaver, L., 16
Tinsley, B. J., 197
Tirozzi, G. N., 244
Tishy, O., 267
Tobin, D., 452
Toepfer, C. F., 86
Tolan, P., 516
Tolan, P. H., 484
Tolson, J. M., 220
Tom, D., 262
Tomlinson-Keasey, C., 112, 159, 160, 490
Torney-Purta, J., 426
Tousignant, M., 517
Trautlein, B., 227
Travers, K. J., 443
Trevethan, S. D., 409
Triandis, H. C., 54, 278
Trimble, J. E., 60
Troughton, E., 83
Truglio, R. T., 300, 301
Tryon, R. J., 519
Tubman, J., 24
Tubman, J. G., 81
Tucker, J. S., 159
Tucker, L. A., 300, 511

SUBJECT INDEX

Attachment, 187–88
  insecure attachment, 187
  and later depression, 489
  and later social/emotional
    development, 188
  secure attachment, 187, 188
Attention
  aspects of, 137
  defined, 137
  selectivity/shiftability of, 137
Attention-deficit hyperactivity
    disorder, 266–67
  signs of, 266
  treatment of, 266–67
Attribution theory, achievement,
    440–41
Authoritarian parenting, meaning
    of, 181
Authoritative parenting, meaning
    of, 181
Autonomous morality, meaning
    of, 405
Autonomy, 184–87
  complexity of, 185
  developmental views of, 185–86
  and parental attitudes, 185
  and parental conflict, 184–85
  and second individuation crisis, 186
  and transformations, 188
Autonomy versus shame and
    doubt, 45
Avoidance/avoidance conflict, 515
Avoidance strategies, coping, 520

Back-to-basics movement, 243
Barbiturates, 477
  uses/effects/addictive characteristics,
    478–79
Basal metabolism rate (BMR),
    defined, 507
Behavioral medicine, defined, 503
Behavioral theory, 49–50
  elements of, 50
Behavior genetics, 79–80
  adoption studies, 80
  twin studies, 80
Behaviorism, defined, 50
Bell curve issue, intelligence, 152
Bem Sex-Role Inventory, 354, 355
Binet intelligence tests, 144–46
  mental age (MA), 144–45
  Stanford-Binet test, 145–46
Biological processes, nature of, 22
Birth order, 191–92
  and sibling relationships, 191
  and sibling roles, 191
Bisexual
  meaning of, 375
  and sexual maturation, 376
Body image
  gender differences, 92
  and puberty, 92, 95

Boundary ambiguity, in
    stepfamilies, 194
Brain growth, 86–87
Bulimia, 510
  defined, 510
  incidence of, 510
Burnout, and college students, 515

Canada, culture of, 298
Canalization, meaning of, 79
Career development
  career self-concept theory, 447–48
  cognitive factors, 449
  critique of theories of, 448
  developmental career choice
    theory, 447
  and ethnic minorities, 452–53
  and gender, 451–52
  and identity development, 449
  occupations, growth of, 445, 447
  parental influences, 449–50,
    451–52
  peer influences, 450
  personality type theory, 448
  school influences, 450–51
  and social class, 449
  See also Work
Career self-concept theory,
    447–48
Care perspective, moral
    development, 410, 412
Case studies, 58–59
Character education, 417–18
Chicano, meaning of, 296
Childhood, period of, 23–24
Children's Aid Society, 207
Chlamydia, 384–85
Chronosystem, 53
Cigarette smoking, 475–76, 477,
    506–7
  increase among adolescents, 506
  prevention of, 507
Classification, concrete operational
    stage, 108
Class size, effects of, 255
Cliques, 226–27
  defined, 226
  influences of, 226–27
  and self-esteem, 226
Cocaine, 476
  uses/effects/addictive characteristics,
    478–79
Cognitive appraisal
  primary/secondary appraisal, 517
  and stress, 517
Cognitive development
  adolescents compared to young
    adults, 115–16
  and brain growth, 86–87
  cognitive socialization, 119–20
  and culture, 117–18
  information processing
    theory, 48–49

and risk taking, 131
and schooling, 118
and social cognition, 121
Cognitive developmental theory
  comparison of theories, 156–57
  gender development, 345
  Piaget's theory, 47–48
  religious development, 424–25
Cognitive disequilibrium theory,
    moral development, 406
Cognitive monitoring, 139
  defined, 139
  and instructional programs, 139
  social cognitive monitoring, 125
Cognitive moral education, moral
    education, 419
Cognitive processes, nature of, 22
Cognitive schema, and
    depression, 489
Cognitive socialization, 119–20
  zone of proximal development
    (ZPD), 119
Cognitive social learning theory,
    moral development, 413
Cohort effects, 64–65
Collectivistic society, and
    development, 54
College, 250–51
  burnout of students, 515
  stress/depression of students, 251
  transition from high school, 186,
    250–51
Commitment, and identity
    development, 325
Common Cents, 435
Community, and juvenile
    delinquency, 484–85
Community service, of adolescent,
    421–22
Community-wide programs,
    elements of, 491–92
Computers
  for collaborative learning, 141
  computer-assisted instruction, 141
  negative aspects of, 141–42
  positive aspects of, 141
Concrete operational stage, 107–8
  classification in, 108
  conservation in, 108
  elements of, 47–48
  horizontal décalage in, 108
Conduct disorders, 482
Conflict
  approach/approach conflict, 515
  approach/avoidance conflict, 515
  avoidance/avoidance conflict, 515
  and divorce, 193
  ethnic-related conflicts, 289
  parent-adolescent conflict, 182–85
Conformity
  defined, 213
  nonconformity/anticonformity, 214
  and peers, 212–14

Easy child, 81
Eating disorders, 508–10
   anorexia nervosa, 509–10
   bulimia, 510
   obesity, 508–9
Eclectic theoretical orientation,
   meaning of, 56
Ecological theory, 51–53
   chronosystem, 53
   exosystem, 52
   macrosystem, 52
   mesosystem, 52
   microsystem, 51–52
Education
   and cognitive development, 118
   of disabled students, 264–67
   moral education, 417–20
   and Piaget's theory, 113–14
   and social class, 286
   and social policy, 264
   See also Schools
Ego, defined, 42
Egocentrism, adolescent, 122, 131
Ego ideal, defined, 415
El Puente, 309
Emic approach, 59–60
Emile (Rousseau), 8
Emotional isolation, meaning
   of, 333
Emotion-focused coping, 519
Emotions
   gender differences, 351
   and moral development, 416
Empathy
   defined, 416
   and moral development, 416
Enlightenment, view of
   adolescents, 8–9
Equilibration, in Piaget's
   theory, 107
Erikson, Erik, youth of, 40
Erikson's theory, 45–46
   autonomy versus shame and
     doubt, 45
   generativity versus stagnation, 46
   identity, 321–24
   identity versus identity confusion,
     46, 322
   industry versus inferiority, 46
   initiative versus guilt, 45–46
   integrity versus despair, 46
   intimacy versus isolation, 46
   moral feelings, 415
   trust versus mistrust, 45
Estradiol, and puberty, 89
Estrogens, and puberty, 89
Ethical principles, and research, 65
Ethnic gloss, and cross-cultural
   research, 60
Ethnic identity, defined, 17
Ethnicity, defined, 17, 277
Ethnic minorities, 289–98
   and achievement, 442–43
   adolescents, special concerns, 292

African Americans, 295–96
and AIDS, 386
and alcohol use, 473–74
Asian Americans, 297
assimilation of, 294
and career development, 452–53
and death among adolescents, 503
diversity of groups, 292
and education/schools, 260–64
families, 197
and health behavior, 504–6
identity development, 327–31
Latinos, 296–97
and mental health, 286
Native Americans, 298
peer relationships, 223–24
and poverty, 287, 289, 290–91
and prejudice, 293
and sexual behavior, 372, 373
and social class, 289–92
and standardized tests, 59
strengths of, 291–92
television portrayal of, 300
use of term, 18
and value conflicts, 294–95
See also specific ethnic minority
   groups
Ethnocentrism, meaning of, 277
Etic approach, 59–60
Eustress, defined, 514
Evocative genotype-environment
   interactions, 82
Exercise, 510–12
   aerobic exercise, 510
   influencing factors, 511
   and overweight, 509
   for stress reduction, 511–12
Exosystem, 52
Experience sampling
   method, process of, 283
Experimental research, 61–62
   random assignment, 62
   variables in, 62–63
Extrinsic motivation, defined, 441

F

Family
   and adolescent alcohol use, 473, 474
   and adolescent changes, 175–76
   and adolescent suicide, 490
   and attachment, 187–88
   and autonomy, 184–87
   and career development, 449–50,
     451–52
   and construction of relationships,
     174–75
   and dating relationships, 233
   and depressed adolescents, 489
   divorce, 192–94
   ethnic minority families, 197, 198
   extended-family systems, 198
   family life cycle, 178, 180
   family-peer connections, 212
   father's role, 199

and gender development, 344,
   366–67
and health behavior, 506
historical changes related to,
   177–78
and identity formation, 326–27
influences on self-esteem, 320
and juvenile delinquency, 484
and moral development, 408,
   415–16
mother's role, 197, 199
parent-adolescent conflict, 182–85
and parental changes, 176–77
parental involvement in schools,
   258, 260
parenting techniques, 180–82
parent/school connection, 73
relocation, effects of, 196
siblings, 188–92
and social class, 285–86
and socialization, 173–74
and social policy, 200, 207
stepfamilies, 194–95
synchrony in, 173
unemployment, effects of, 196–97
working mothers, 195–96
Family structure model,
   divorce, 192
Family Support Act, 207
Fast-food, fat/calories from, 508
Fathers
   adolescent fathers, 382
   role in family, 199
   See also Family
Fear of success, meaning of, 440
Feminization of poverty, meaning
   of, 288
Forgiveness, adolescent views
   of, 417
Formal operational stage, 109–12
   early/late formal operational
     thought, 111–12
   elements of, 48, 109–11
   hypothetical-deductive
     reasoning, 110–11
   individual differences, 112–13
   and language development, 113
   post-operational thought, 114–16
   research study on, 130–31
Fraternal twins, 80
Freud's theory, 42–45
   anatomy is destiny concept, 343
   defense mechanisms, 42–44
   feminist-based criticism of, 45
   id/ego/superego, 42
   moral feelings, 413, 415
   psychosexual stages, 44
   revisions of, 44–45
   unconscious in, 42, 43
Friendship, 218–21
   importance of, 218
   intimacy in, 219–20
   mixed-age friendships, 220–21
   similarity in, 220
     Sullivan's theory of, 218–19

Frustration
    defined, 515
    and stress, 515
Fusion model, cultural change, 281

G

Gangs. *See* Youth gangs
Gender, defined, 18, 343
Gender development
    anatomy in destiny view, 343
    biological influences, 343
    cognitive developmental theory, 345
    gender schema theory, 348
    and media, 346–47
    parental influences, 344, 366–67
    peer influences, 344
    school/teacher influences, 344–46
    social learning theory, 344
Gender differences, 349–52
    achievement, 351, 440
    biological differences, 349–50
    body image, 92
    context, importance of, 352
    controversy related to, 351–52
    depression, 488
    emotions, 351
    hyperactivity, 266
    identity development, 331
    intergenerational relationships, 180
    and maternal employment, 195
    math ability, 350
    moral development, 410, 412
    social connectedness, 351
    spatial ability, 350
    suicide, 490
Gender inequality, in schools,
        344–46
Gender issues
    men's issues, 360–61
    women's issues, 360
Gender roles
    androgyny, 354–55
    defined, 343
    and early adolescence, 358–59
    gender intensification
        hypothesis, 358
    gender-role transcendence, 357
    Gilligan's research, 358–59
    masculinity, negative aspects of,
        356–57
    of past, 353–54
    sociocultural view, 356
Gender schema, defined, 348
Gender schema theory, gender
        development, 348
Gender stereotyping, 348–49
    defined, 348
    scope of, 348
    sexism, 349
    and television, 346–47
General adaptation syndrome
        (GAS), 514
    stages of, 514

Generational inequity, meaning
        of, 21
Generativity versus stagnation, 46
Genes, genotype/phenotype, 79
Genital herpes, 385–86
    signs of, 385
    treatment of, 385
Genital stage, meaning of, 44
Genotype, meaning of, 79
Genotype-environment
        interactions, 82–83
    and development, 83
    types of, 82
Giftedness, 157–61
    defined, 158
    factors related to, 159–60
    gifted disadvantaged children,
        160–61
    longitudinal study of, 158–59
Gilligan's theory, moral
        development, 410, 412
Gonads, 89
Gonorrhea, 384
Goodness-of-fit model,
        temperament, 82
Graduate Record Exam, 148
Group intelligence tests, 146–48
Groups, 222–23
    formation of, 222–23
    norms, 222
    Robbers Cave experiment, 222–23
    roles, 222
    same-sex/opposite-sex groups, 223
Growth spurt, during puberty, 90

H

Hallucinogens, LSD, 475
Health
    and cigarette smoking, 506–7
    and eating disorders, 508–10
    and exercise, 510–12
    and nutrition, 507–8
Health behavior
    concept of, 504
    and decision making, 504
    and ethnic minorities, 504–6
    and family, 506
    and health beliefs, 504
    health services, use of, 506
    and peers, 506
    and socioeconomic status, 504–6
Health promotion
    health goals for adolescents, 512
    life-science curriculum for, 527
    presenting to adolescents, 131
Health psychology, defined, 503
Height, and puberty, 90
Helpless orientation, and
        achievement, 442
Heredity
    behavior genetics, 79–80
    genes, 79
    reaction range, 79

Heredity/environment interaction
    and adopted children, 83
    genotype-environment interactions,
        82–83
    intelligence, 80, 150–52
    shared/nonshared environmental
        influences, 83
    temperament, 81–82
Heteronomous morality, meaning
        of, 405
High-risk youth, defined, 490–91
High schools, 243–46
    back-to-basics movement, 243
    dropouts, 252–54
    functions for adolescents, 243–44
    influence on adolescence, 244
    shopping mall high school, 243–44
    sociocultural view, 245
    transition to college, 250–51
Historical influences, importance
        of, 53, 55
History and adolescents
    adolescent stereotypes in, 13–15
    current view, 15–17
    early America, 9
    G. Stanley Hall, 9–10
    Greek era, 8
    interventionist view, 11–12
    later twentieth century America,
        12–13
    Margaret Mead, 10–11
    Middle Ages/Enlightenment, 8–9
    storm-and-stress view, 9–10
Homicide, death among
        adolescents, 503
Homophobia, 375
Homosexuality, 375–77
    adolescent self-concept, 375
    causation theories, 376
    self-recognition of, 376
    twin studies, 376–77
Horizontal décalage, concrete
        operational stage, 108
Hormones, and puberty, 89–90,
        96–97, 343
Hypothalamus, functions of, 89
Hypothetical-deductive reasoning,
        formal operational stage,
        110–11

I

Id, defined, 42
Idealism, of adolescents, 110, 131,
        315, 428
Identical twins, 80
Identity development
    and career development, 449
    and connectedness, 327
    crisis in, 325
    developmental changes, 325–26
    Erikson's theory, 321–24
    and ethnic minorities, 327–31
    family influences, 326–27
    gender differences, 331

Mastery orientation, and achievement, 442
Masturbation, 377
Matching hypothesis, and interpersonal attraction, 231–32
Math achievement
    Asian versus American students, 443–45
    gender differences, 350
    sociocultural view, 462–63
Maturation, defined, 25
Media
    functions for adolescents, 299
    and gender development, 346–47
    music, 302–3
    presentation of research information, 66–68
    and social policy, 303
    stereotyping of adolescents, 13
    television, 300–302
    uses by adolescents, 299–300
Medical model, abnormal behavior, 469
Memory, 137–38
    defined, 137
    long-term memory, 138
    short-term memory, 138
Menarche, 92–94
    antecedents of, 102–3
    defined, 88
Men's movement, 360–61
    recommendations for men, 361
Mental age (MA), 144–45
    definition of, 144
Mental health, and ethnic minorities, 286
Mental retardation
    cultural-familial retardation, 157
    defined, 157
    organic retardation, 157
Mesosystem, 52, 73
Microsystem, 51–52
Middle adulthood, time span, 25
Middle Ages, view of adolescents, 8–9
Middle/late childhood, time span, 24
Middle school
    Carnegie report recommendations, 249–50
    successful schools, characteristics of, 248–49
    top-dog phenomenon, 246–47
    transition to middle/junior high school, 246–48
Midwestern Prevention Program, 480
Minnesota Multiphasic Personality Inventory (MMPI), 59
Modeling. See Observational learning

Moral behavior, 412–13
    altruism, 416–17
    environmental determinants, 412–13
    situation-specific, 413
    social learning theory, 412–13
Moral character, elements of, 421
Moral development
    care perspective, 410, 412
    cognitive disequilibrium theory, 406
    cognitive social learning theory, 413
    defined, 405
    developmentalists study of, 405
    and emotions, 416
    and empathy, 416
    four-component model, 420–21
    gender differences, 410, 412
    Gilligan's theory, 410, 412
    justice perspective, 410
    Kohlberg's theory, 406–10
    and parental discipline, 415–16
    Piaget's theory, 405–6
    sociocultural view, 409–10, 411
Moral education, 417–20
    character education, 417–18
    cognitive moral education, 419
    comprehensive approach to, 419–20
    direct and indirect, 417
    and four-component model, 421
    values clarification, 418–19
Moral feelings
    Erikson's theory, 415
    Freud's theory, 413, 415
Moral judgment, elements of, 420–21
Moral motivation, elements of, 421
Moral reasoning, versus social conventional reasoning, 412
Moral sensitivity, elements of, 420
Mothers
    adolescent mothers, 381–82
    gender of child and career development, 451–52
    role in family, 197, 199
    working mothers, 195–96
    See also Family
Motivation
    and achievement, 439–42
    extrinsic motivation, 441
    intrinsic motivation, 441
    meaning of, 439
Multicultural model, cultural change, 280–81
Multiple-factor model, divorce, 192
Multiple-factor theory, intelligence, 148
Music, 299, 302–3
    and antisocial behavior, 302
    functions for adolescents, 302
    interpretation of lyrics, 303
    MTV and gender stereotyping, 346

National Association of Service and Conservation Corps, 435
National Service-Learning Cooperative/ Clearinghouse, 435
National Youth Service, 457
Native Americans, 298
    adolescents, characteristics of, 298
    and alcohol use, 473–74
    as ethnic minority group, 19
    health status of, 505
    identity development, 328
    problems of, 298
Naturalistic observation, 58
Nature-nurture controversy
    defined, 26
    See also Heredity/environment interaction
Neglected children, status among peers, 215
Neglectful parenting, meaning of, 181
Neo-Piagetians, 117
New Image Teen Theater, 401
Nomothetic research, 67
Nonconformity, meaning of, 214
Nonshared environmental influences, 83
Normal distribution, meaning of, 145
Norms, groups, 222
Nutrition, 507–8
    and dietary fat, 508
    and fast-food, 508

Obesity, 508–9
    factors related to, 508–9
    treatment of, 509
Observation, 57–58
    laboratory observation, 58
    naturalistic observation, 58
Observational learning, elements of, 50
Occupational Outlook Handbook, 445, 450
Occupations
    growth, future view, 445, 447
    information sources on, 445, 450
Oedipus complex, 413
    meaning of, 44
Open classrooms, 255
Operations
    Piagetian, 47
    in Piaget's theory, 107–8
Opiates, 477
    uses/effects/addictive characteristics, 478–79
Oral stage, meaning of, 44
Organic retardation, 157

Relocation, effects of, 196
Repression, meaning of, 42
Republic, The (Plato), 8
Resatellization, meaning of, 186
Research
   applied research, 36
   basic research, 36
   ethical principles, 65
   idiographic needs, 67
   journal publication of, 72–73
   media reports on, 66–68
   nomothetic research, 67
   overgeneralization in, 67
   sexist research, 65–66
Research measures
   case studies, 58–59
   cross-cultural research, 59–60
   interviews, 58
   life-history records, 60–61
   multimeasure/multisource/
     multicontext approach, 61
   observation, 57–58
   physiological research, 61
   questionnaires, 58
   standardized tests, 59
Research strategies
   cohort effects, 64–65
   correlational research, 61
   cross-sectional research, 63
   experimental research, 61–62
   longitudinal research, 64
Resilience, factors related to, 519
Risk/opportunity, and support of
   adolescents, 37
Risk taking
   and cognitive development, 131
   contextual influences, 167
Ritalin, for attention-deficit
   hyperactivity disorder,
   266–67
Rites of passage, 281–82
   sociocultural view, 281–82
Robbers Cave experiment, 222–23
Role-focused level, in
   relationship, 332
Roles, groups, 222
Romantic love, characteristics of,
   232–34
Runaways, and family, 186–87

S

Safe Schools Act, 487
Satellization, meaning of, 185
Schema, defined, 348
Scholastic Aptitude Test (SAT),
   147–48
   coaching issue, 148
Schools
   aptitude-treatment interaction
     (ATI), 256
   and career development, 450–51
   class size, 255
   college, 250–51

cooperative learning, 262–63, 272
drug use prevention, 480
and ethnic minorities, 260–64
and gender development, 344–46
high schools, 243–46
and intervention programs, 492–93
open classrooms, 255
parental involvement, 258, 260
peer interactions, 257–58
single-sex schools, 259
size, effects of, 255
and social class, 260
social contexts of, 244, 246
teachers, 256–57
Scientific method
   defined, 41
   steps in, 41
Scientific thinking, of adolescents,
   110, 130–31
Scripts
   dating scripts, 229–30
   sexual scripts, 373–74
Secondary appraisal, of stressful
   events, 517
Second individuation crisis, 186
Secure attachment, 187, 188
   meaning of, 187
Self
   possible self, 316
   real/ideal self, 316
   true/false self, 316
Self-concept
   and career development, 447–48
   defined, 318
Self-control, and juvenile
   delinquency, 483–84
Self-efficacy
   and coping, 520
   meaning of, 321
Self-esteem
   behavioral indicators of, 319
   and cliques, 226
   defined, 318
   improvement for adolescents,
     320–21
   low, consequences of, 320
   measurement of, 319
   and parents, 320
   and peers, 320
   and physical attractiveness, 319–20
   self-worth and perceived
     support, 338
Self-focused level, in
   relationship, 332
Self-Perception Profile for
   Adolescents, 319, 338
Self-understanding
   defined, 315
   elements of, 315–18
Sensorimotor stage, elements of,
   47, 107
Separation, cultural, 281
Set point, defined, 509
Seven intelligences theory, 149

Sex education, 388–92
   effectiveness of, 391–92
   sociocultural view, 392
   types of programs, 389–91
Sexism
   defined, 349
   examples of, 349
   old-fashioned/modern, 349, 350
Sexist research, 65–66
   guidelines for reduction of, 66
Sexual content, television, 301–2
Sexual harassment, forms of, 393
Sexuality
   adolescent pregnancy, 379–83
   bisexual, 375
   contraceptive use, 377–79
   developmental transitions, 393–94
   and ethnic minorities, 372, 373
   homosexuality, 375–77
   masturbation, 377
   progression of behaviors, 371
   and religious involvement, 425
   and self-concept, 374–75
   sexual activity by age/sex/
     ethnicity, 373
   sexual activity of adolescents,
     trends/incidence, 371–73
   sexual scripts, 373–74
   and social policy, 394–95
   sociocultural view, 279–80
   and vulnerable adolescents,
     374–75
Sexual knowledge, sources of,
   388, 89
Sexually transmitted disease
   AIDS, 386–88
   chlamydia, 384–85
   genital herpes, 385–86
   gonorrhea, 384
   moral reasoning about, 434
   syphillis, 384
Sexual maturation, signs of, 91
Sexual scripts, 373–74
   defined, 373
   male and female scripts, 373–74
Shared environmental
   influences, 83
Shelters, for runaways, 187
Short-term memory, 138
Siblings, 188–92
   birth order, 191–92
   differential treatment by
     parents, 192
   relationships and developmental
     changes, 189, 191
   as socialization influence, 189
Single-parent families, and
   poverty, 518
Single-sex schools, 259
Slow-to-warm-up child, 81
Social class
   and abnormal behavior, 470
   African Americans, 295
   and career development, 449
   defined, 277